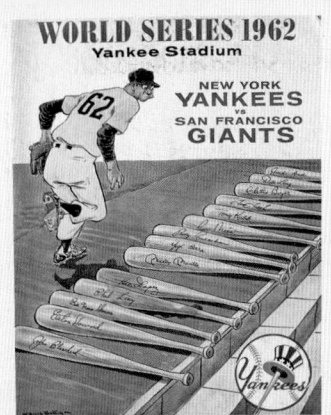
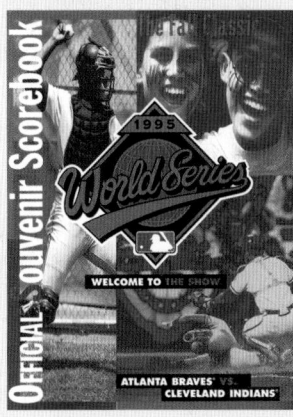
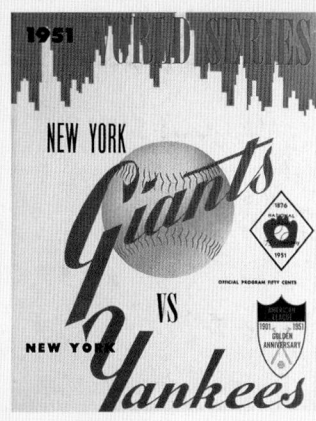

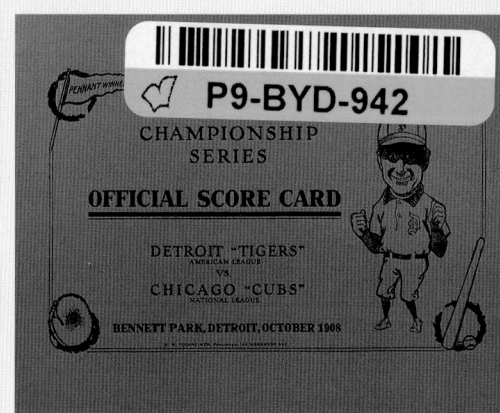

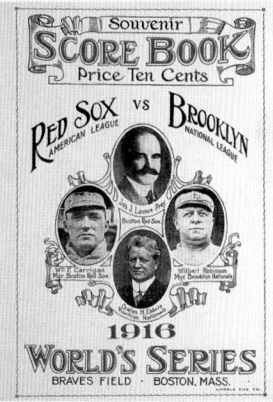

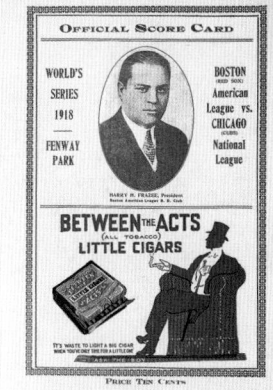
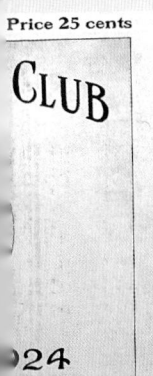

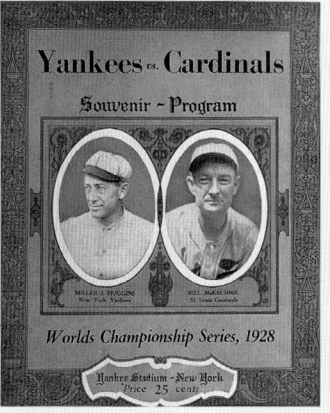
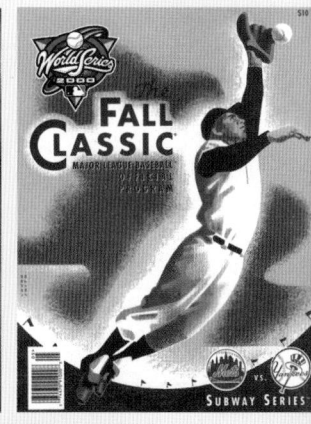

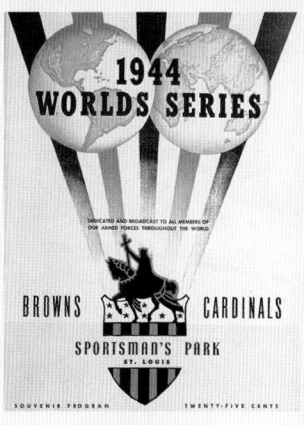
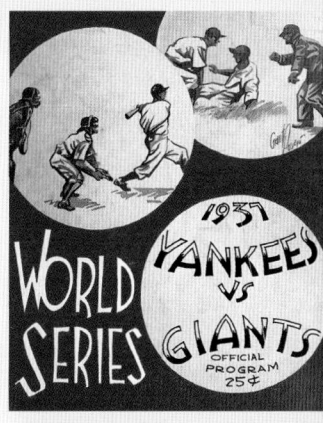

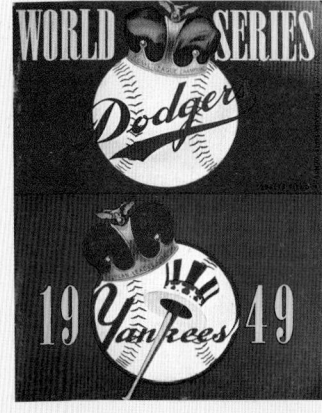

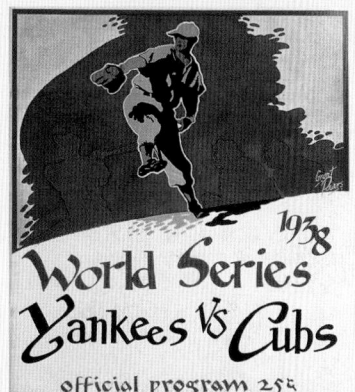
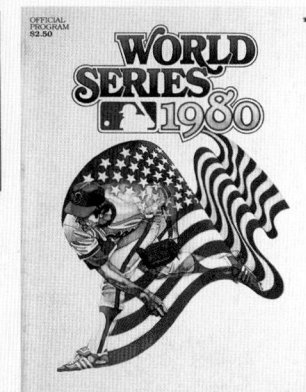
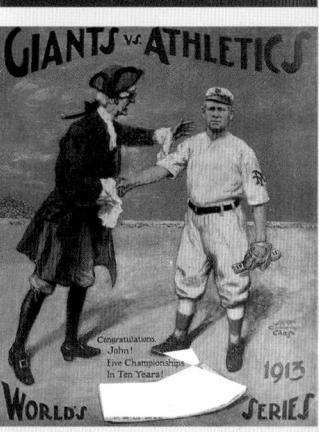

The World Series

Published by Black Dog & Leventhal Publishers, Inc.
151 West 19th Street, New York, NY 10011

Distributed by Workman Publishing Company
708 Broadway, New York, NY 10003

Art direction and design by Liz Trovato

Additional design by Brad Walrod and Tony Meisel

ISBN: 1-57912-206-x

h-g-f-e-d-c-b-a

Library of Congress Cataloging-in-Publication Data

Leventhal, Josh (Joshua), 1971- The World Series: an illustrated encyclopedia of the fall classic / by Josh Leventhal.
p. cm.
Includes indexes.
ISBN 1-57912-206-x
1. World Series (Baseball)--History--Chronology. 2. World Series   (Baseball)--History--Pictorial works.
3. Baseball--Records--United States. I. Title.

GV878.4 .L48 2001   796.357'646'03--dc21
                                                     2001037907

p. 319 constitutes a continuation of this copyright page

The World Series

An Illustrated Encyclopedia of the Fall Classic

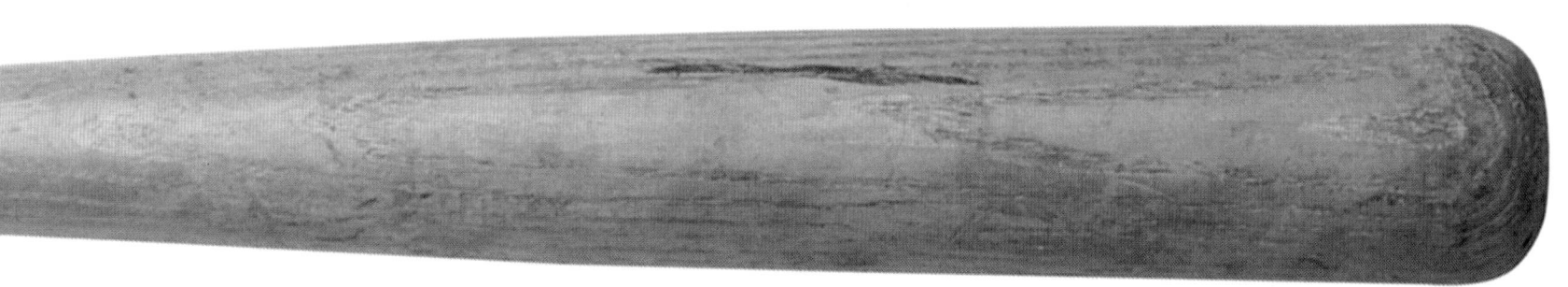

JOSH LEVENTHAL

BLACK DOG
& LEVENTHAL
PUBLISHERS
NEW YORK

Contents

Introduction

Every October, at the end of a long summer of baseball, one team is left standing as the champion of the sport. The pennant winners from the National and American Leagues compete in a series of games to decide which one shall lay claim to the title of world's best. In the course of its first century, this annual competition has emerged as an American institution, the pinnacle of the sport's year—the World Series.

While the World Series has become a regular part of our lives as the weather cools and the leaves fall from the trees with the coming of autumn, the drama and excitement of the games keeps us coming back with eager anticipation for each Fall Classic, no matter which teams or which players take the field. Sometimes the club that dominated from April through September predictably comes out on top; other times, an unexpected champion is left holding the trophy after the last pitch is thrown. The pivotal moment may be provided by a slugger knocking a ball out of the ballpark—the names Mazeroski, Fisk, Jackson and, of course, Ruth are etched in history for such deeds—or it might be a fielder depriving a slugger of the hero's mantle with spectacular glove work— we remember Mays making a sensational over-the-shoulder catch in 1954, and Robinson turning dazzling play after dazzling play at the "hot corner" in 1970. The drama might come from a pitcher standing on the mound and overpowering his foes—the unassuming Larsen producing perfection, the intimidating Gibson striking out 17, the aged Alexander fanning Lazzeri with the bases full. The World Series is a chance for the lesser-known and obscure to rise to heroic heights—the Ehmkes, the Lavagettos, the Tenaces who seized the day and left their mark on the game. Other enduring, if less endearing, marks are left by those whose foibles meant the difference between victory and defeat—Mickey Owen dropping the third strike, Bill Buckner losing the ball between his legs.

This book is a celebration of the men and the moments that have made each World Series since 1903 something to remember and cherish. Every game is de scribed to convey the experience and flavor of the contest; expanded line scores and composite box scores p rovide the statistics that baseball fans love to consume, dissect and analyze. We highlight the moments and performances that stand out among the greatest in this or any sport—the historic home runs, the dominating pitching, the shocking upsets and the dramatic clutch plays. It is baseball's biggest stage, and a great many of the game's top achievements have been produced under the bright lights of the Fall Classic.

The World Series is a time for celebration . . . and a time for heartbreak.

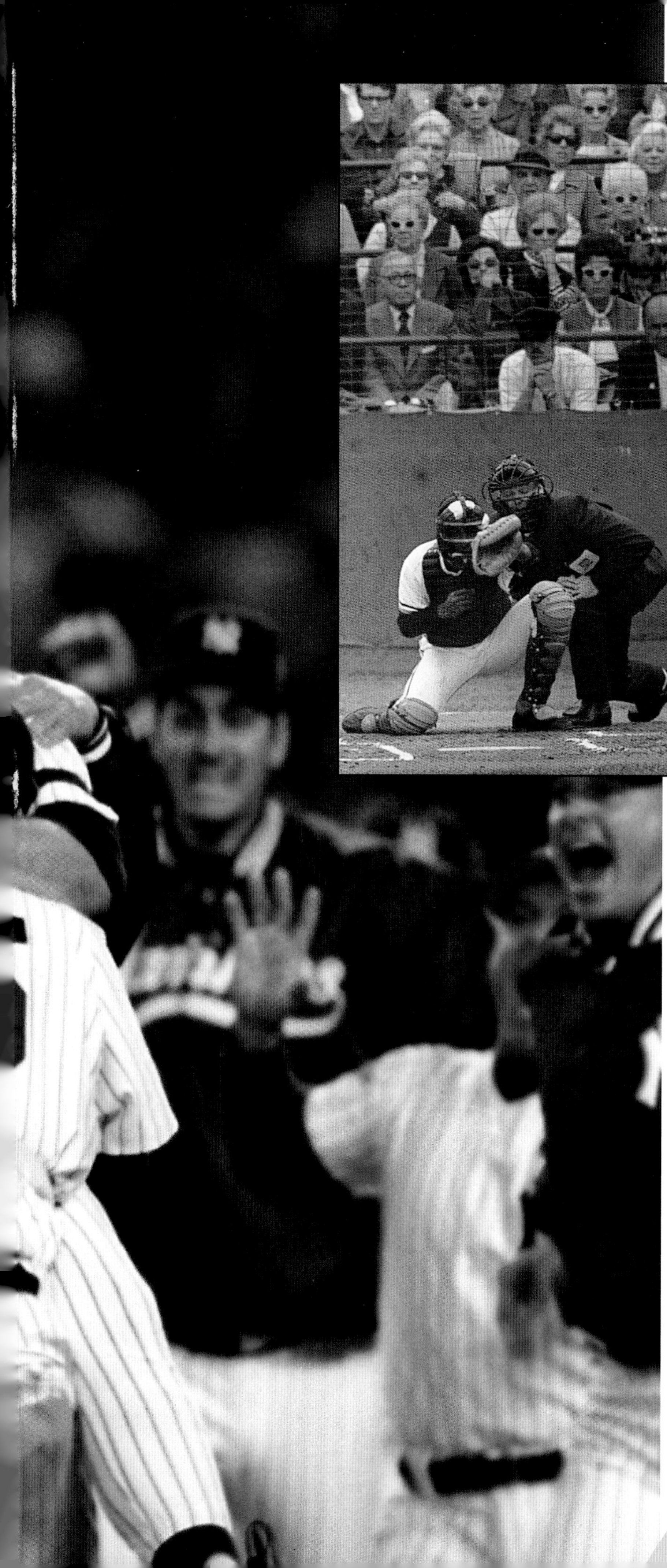

It is a time for "Great Ones" to shine . . .

. . . and for unknown heroes to emerge.

Year-By-Year Results

* Italic indicates selection made specifically for The World Series: An Illustrated Encyclopedia of the Fall Classic.

Year	Winner	Loser	Series Outstanding Player/MVP*	Series Outstanding Pitcher*
1903	Boston Red Sox, 5	Pittsburgh Pirates, 3	*Bill Dinneen, Red Sox*	*Bill Dinneen, Red Sox*
1904	No World Series Held			
1905	New York Giants, 4	Philadelphia A's, 1	*Christy Mathewson, Giants*	*Christy Mathewson, Giants*
1906	Chicago White Sox, 4	Chicago Cubs, 2	*George Rohe, White Sox*	*Ed Walsh, White Sox*
1907	Chicago Cubs, 4	Detroit Tigers, 0 (1 tie)	*Harry Steinfeldt, Cubs*	*Three Finger Brown, Cubs*
1908	Chicago Cubs, 4	Detroit Tigers, 1	*Frank Chance, Cubs*	*Three Finger Brown, Cubs*
1909	Pittsburgh Pirates, 4	Detroit Tigers, 3	*Tommy Leach, Pirates*	*Babe Adams, Pirates*
1910	Philadelphia A's, 4	Chicago Cubs, 1	*Danny Murphy, A's*	*Jack Coombs, A's*
1911	Philadelphia A's, 4	New York Giants, 2	*Frank "Home Run" Baker, A's*	*Charles "Chief" Bender, A's*
1912	Boston Red Sox, 4	New York Giants, 3 (1 tie)	*Tris Speaker, Red Sox*	*Rube Marquard, Giants*
1913	Philadelphia A's, 4	New York Giants, 1	*Frank "Home Run" Baker, A's*	*Eddie Plank, A's*
1914	Boston Braves, 4	Philadelphia A's, 0	*Hank Gowdy, Braves*	*Bill James, Braves*
1915	Boston Red Sox, 4	Philadelphia Phillies, 1	*Duffy Lewis, Red Sox*	*Rube Foster, Red Sox*
1916	Boston Red Sox, 4	Brooklyn Dodgers, 1	*Harry Hooper, Red Sox*	*Babe Ruth, Red Sox*
1917	Chicago White Sox, 4	New York Giants, 2	*Eddie Collins, White Sox*	*Red Faber, White Sox*
1918	Boston Red Sox, 4	Chicago Cubs, 2	*Carl Mays, Red Sox*	*Carl Mays, Red Sox*
1919	Cincinnati Reds, 5	Chicago White Sox, 3	*Greasy Neale, Reds*	*Hod Eller, Reds*
1920	Cleveland Indians, 5	Brooklyn Dodgers, 2	*Stan Coveleski, Indians*	*Stan Coveleski, Indians*
1921	New York Giants, 5	New York Yankees, 3	*Irish Meusel, Giants*	*Waite Hoyt, Yankees*
1922	New York Giants, 4	New York Yankees, 0 (1 tie)	*Heinie Groh, Giants*	*Art Nehf, Giants*
1923	New York Yankees, 4	New York Giants, 2	*Babe Ruth, Yankees*	*Joe Bush, Yankees*
1924	Washington Senators, 4	New York Giants, 3	*Goose Goslin, Senators*	*Tom Zachary, Senators*
1925	Pittsburgh Pirates, 4	Washington Senators, 3	*Max Carey, Pirates*	*Walter Johnson, Senators*
1926	St. Louis Cardinals, 4	New York Yankees, 3	*Tommy Thevenow, Cardinals*	*Grover Alexander, Cardinals*
1927	New York Yankees, 4	Pittsburgh Pirates, 0	*Babe Ruth, Yankees*	*Herb Pennock, Yankees*
1928	New York Yankees, 4	St. Louis Cardinals, 0	*Lou Gehrig and Babe Ruth, Yankees*	*Waite Hoyt, Yankees*
1929	Philadelphia A's, 4	Chicago Cubs, 1	*Jimmie Foxx, A's*	*Howard Ehmke, A's*
1930	Philadelphia A's, 4	St. Louis Cardinals, 2	*Al Simmons, A's*	*George Earnshaw, A's*
1931	St. Louis Cardinals, 4	Philadelphia A's, 3	*Pepper Martin, Cardinals*	*Wild Bill Hallahan, Cardinals*
1932	New York Yankees, 4	Chicago Cubs, 0	*Lou Gehrig, Yankees*	*Lefty Gomez, Yankees*
1933	New York Giants, 4	Washington Senators, 1	*Mel Ott, Giants*	*Carl Hubbell, Giants*
1934	St. Louis Cardinals, 4	Detroit Tigers, 3	*Pepper Martin, Cardinals*	*Dizzy Dean and Paul Dean, Cardinals*
1935	Detroit Tigers, 4	Chicago Cubs, 2	*Charlie Gehringer, Tigers*	*Lon Warneke, Cubs*
1936	New York Yankees, 4	New York Giants, 2	*Jake Powell, Yankees*	*Carl Hubbell, Giants*
1937	New York Yankees, 4	New York Giants, 1	*Lefty Gomez, Yankees*	*Lefty Gomez, Yankees*
1938	New York Yankees, 4	Chicago Cubs, 0	*Joe Gordon, Yankees*	*Red Ruffing, Yankees*
1939	New York Yankees, 4	Cincinnati Reds, 0	*Charlie Keller, Yankees*	*Monte Pearson, Yankees*
1940	Cincinnati Reds, 4	Detroit Tigers, 3	*Jimmy Ripple, Reds*	*Bucky Walters, Reds*
1941	New York Yankees, 4	Brooklyn Dodgers, 1	*Joe Gordon, Yankees*	*Johnny Murphy, Yankees*
1942	St. Louis Cardinals, 4	New York Yankees, 1	*Whitey Kurowski, Cardinals*	*Johnny Beazley, Cardinals*
1943	New York Yankees, 4	St. Louis Cardinals, 1	*Billy Johnson, Yankees*	*Spud Chandler, Yankees*
1944	St. Louis Cardinals, 4	St. Louis Browns, 2	*Walker Cooper, Cardinals*	*Mort Cooper, Cardinals*
1945	Detroit Tigers, 4	Chicago Cubs, 3	*Hank Greenberg, Tigers*	*Dizzy Trout, Tigers*
1946	St. Louis Cardinals, 4	Boston Red Sox, 3	*Harry Walker, Cardinals*	*Harry Brecheen, Cardinals*
1947	New York Yankees, 4	Brooklyn Dodgers, 3	*Johnny Lindell, Yankees*	*Spec Shea, Yankees*
1948	Cleveland Indians, 4	Boston Braves, 2	*Bob Elliott, Braves*	*Gene Bearden, Indians*
1949	New York Yankees, 4	Brooklyn Dodgers, 1	*Bobby Brown, Yankees*	*Allie Reynolds, Yankees*
1950	New York Yankees, 4	Philadelphia Phillies, 0	*Bobby Brown, Yankees*	*Vic Raschi, Whitey Ford and Allie Reynolds, Yankees*
1951	New York Yankees, 4	New York Giants, 2	*Phil Rizzuto, Yankees*	*Ed Lopat, Yankees*
1952	New York Yankees, 4	Brooklyn Dodgers, 3	*Duke Snider, Dodgers*	*Vic Raschi, Yankees*
1953	New York Yankees, 4	Brooklyn Dodgers, 2	*Billy Martin, Yankees*	*Ed Lopat, Yankees*
1954	New York Giants, 4	Cleveland Indians, 0	*Dusty Rhodes, Giants*	*Johnny Antonelli, Giants*
1955	Brooklyn Dodgers, 4	New York Yankees, 3	Johnny Podres, Dodgers	*Johnny Podres, Dodgers*
1956	New York Yankees, 4	Brooklyn Dodgers, 3	Don Larsen, Yankees	*Don Larsen, Yankees*
1957	Milwaukee Braves, 4	New York Yankees, 3	Lew Burdette, Braves	*Lew Burdette, Braves*
1958	New York Yankees, 4	Milwaukee Braves, 3	Bob Turley, Yankees	*Bob Turley, Yankees*
1959	Los Angeles Dodgers, 4	Chicago White Sox, 2	Larry Sherry, Dodgers	*Larry Sherry, Dodgers*
1960	Pittsburgh Pirates, 4	New York Yankees, 3	Bobby Richardson, Yankees	*Whitey Ford, Yankees*
1961	New York Yankees, 4	Cincinnati Reds, 1	Whitey Ford, Yankees	*Whitey Ford, Yankees*
1962	New York Yankees, 4	San Francisco Giants, 3	Ralph Terry, Yankees	*Ralph Terry, Yankees*
1963	Los Angeles Dodgers, 4	New York Yankees, 0	Sandy Koufax, Dodgers	*Sandy Koufax, Dodgers*
1964	St. Louis Cardinals, 4	New York Yankees, 3	Bob Gibson, Cardinals	*Bob Gibson, Cardinals*
1965	Los Angeles Dodgers, 4	Minnesota Twins, 3	Sandy Koufax, Dodgers	*Sandy Koufax, Dodgers*
1966	Baltimore Orioles, 4	Los Angeles Dodgers, 0	Frank Robinson, Orioles	*Wally Bunker, Moe Drabowsky, Dave McNally and Jim Palmer, Orioles*
1967	St. Louis Cardinals, 4	Boston Red Sox, 3	Bob Gibson, Cardinals	*Bob Gibson, Cardinals*
1968	Detroit Tigers, 4	St. Louis Cardinals, 3	Mickey Lolich, Tigers	*Mickey Lolich, Tigers*
1969	New York Mets, 4	Baltimore Orioles, 1	Donn Clendenon, Mets	*Jerry Koosman, Mets*
1970	Baltimore Orioles, 4	Cincinnati Reds, 1	Brooks Robinson, Orioles	*Clay Carroll, Reds*
1971	Pittsburgh Pirates, 4	Baltimore Orioles, 3	Roberto Clemente, Pirates	*Steve Blass, Pirates*
1972	Oakland A's, 4	Cincinnati Reds, 3	Gene Tenace, A's	*Rollie Fingers, A's*
1973	Oakland A's, 4	New York Mets, 3	Reggie Jackson, A's	*Rollie Fingers and Darold Knowles, A's*
1974	Oakland A's, 4	Los Angeles Dodgers, 1	Rollie Fingers, A's	*Rollie Fingers, A's*
1975	Cincinnati Reds, 4	Boston Red Sox, 3	Pete Rose, Reds	*Rawly Eastwick, Reds*
1976	Cincinnati Reds, 4	New York Yankees, 0	Johnny Bench, Reds	*Will McEnaney, Reds*
1977	New York Yankees, 4	Los Angeles Dodgers, 2	Reggie Jackson, Yankees	*Mike Torrez, Yankees*
1978	New York Yankees, 4	Los Angeles Dodgers, 2	Bucky Dent, Yankees	*Rich "Goose" Gossage, Yankees*
1979	Pittsburgh Pirates, 4	Baltimore Orioles, 3	Willie Stargell, Pirates	*Kent Tekulve, Pirates*
1980	Philadelphia Phillies, 4	Kansas City Royals, 2	Mike Schmidt, Phillies	*Steve Carlton, Phillies*
1981	Los Angeles Dodgers, 4	New York Yankees, 2	Pedro Guerrero, Ron Cey, Steve Yeager, Dodgers	*Tommy John, Yankees*
1982	St. Louis Cardinals, 4	Milwaukee Brewers, 3	Darrell Porter, Cardinals	*Joaquin Andujar, Cardinals*
1983	Baltimore Orioles, 4	Philadelphia Phillies, 1	Rick Dempsey, Orioles	*Mike Boddicker, Orioles*
1984	Detroit Tigers, 4	San Diego Padres, 1	Alan Trammell, Tigers	*Jack Morris, Tigers*
1985	Kansas City Royals, 4	St. Louis Cardinals, 3	Bret Saberhagen, Royals	*Bret Saberhagen, Royals*
1986	New York Mets, 4	Boston Red Sox, 3	Ray Knight, Mets	*Jesse Orosco, Mets*
1987	Minnesota Twins, 4	St. Louis Cardinals, 3	Frank Viola, Twins	*Frank Viola, Twins*
1988	Los Angeles Dodgers, 4	Oakland A's, 1	Orel Hershiser, Dodgers	*Orel Hershiser, Dodgers*
1989	Oakland A's, 4,	San Francisco Giants, 0	Dave Stewart, A's	*Dave Stewart, A's*
1990	Cincinnati Reds, 4	Oakland A's, 0	Jose Rijo, Reds	*Jose Rijo, Reds*
1991	Minnesota Twins, 4	Atlanta Braves, 3	Jack Morris, Twins	*Jack Morris, Twins*
1992	Toronto Blue Jays, 4	Atlanta Braves, 2	Pat Borders, Blue Jays	*Jimmy Key, Blue Jays*
1993	Toronto Blue Jays, 4	Philadelphia Phillies, 2	Paul Molitor, Blue Jays	*Duane Ward, Blue Jays*
1994	No World Series Held			
1995	Atlanta Braves, 4	Cleveland Indians, 2	Tom Glavine, Braves	*Tom Glavine, Braves*
1996	New York Yankees, 4	Atlanta Braves, 2	John Wetteland, Yankees	*John Wetteland, Yankees*
1997	Florida Marlins, 4	Cleveland Indians, 3	Livan Hernandez, Marlins	*Livan Hernandez, Marlins*
1998	New York Yankees, 4	San Diego Padres, 0	Scott Brosius, Yankees	*Mariano Rivera, Yankees*
1999	New York Yankees, 4	Atlanta Braves, 0	Mariano Rivera, Yankees	*Mariano Rivera, Yankees*
2000	New York Yankees, 4	New York Mets, 1	Derek Jeter, Yankees	*Roger Clemens, Yankees*

The Greatest World Series

Any discussion about the World Series—or about baseball in general—inevitably leads to one question: What is the greatest World Series of all time? Experts and casual fans alike have their opinions. There are those who insist that the great Yankee-Dodger battles in the middle of the century epitomized better than any the drama and excitement of the Fall Classic: the closely fought 1947 Series; or 1955, the year Brooklyn finally won. Others point to 1960, when a light-hitting second baseman made history by winning it all with a dramatic ninth-inning home run in Game 7. There's the Miracle Mets of 1969, and the Mets' 1986 miracle when they snatched victory from the jaws of defeat. The year Walter "Big Train" Johnson and the Senators won their only Series title (1924); the year the Yankees won their 20th (1962). All these make the short list of World Series Classics, and they receive extra treatment in these pages. Two World Series in particular, however, stand out at the top in most people's minds. The epic 1975 struggle between the Cincinnati Reds and the Boston Red Sox featured Carlton Fisk willing a ball fair in Game 6, and Joe Morgan clinching a one-run victory in the final inning of the final game—the fifth one-run contest of the Series. The "Worst-to-First" Series of 1991 also saw two teams battle through five one-run games, three in extra innings, before the Minnesota Twins topped the Atlanta Braves in a 10-inning, 1-0 masterpiece in Game 7. The sixth game of 1975 and the seventh game of 1991 qualify as perhaps the two best single games in postseason history. Both Series featured clutch home runs, heated controversy and stellar pitching. Let the debate begin.

***A Brief Note About MVP's** At the conclusion of every World Series since 1955, the nation's sportswriters select one player (or, in 1981, three players) as the Series Most Valuable Player. Although no official award was given before 1955, I have gone back and examined every World Series from 1903 to 1954 and picked a retroactive Series Outstanding Player for each year, based on the performances during that Series. In addition, I have chosen an Outstanding Pitcher for every Series, going to the person that most stood out for his actions on the mound; in some cases the Series Outstanding Pitcher is also the Outstanding Player or MVP.

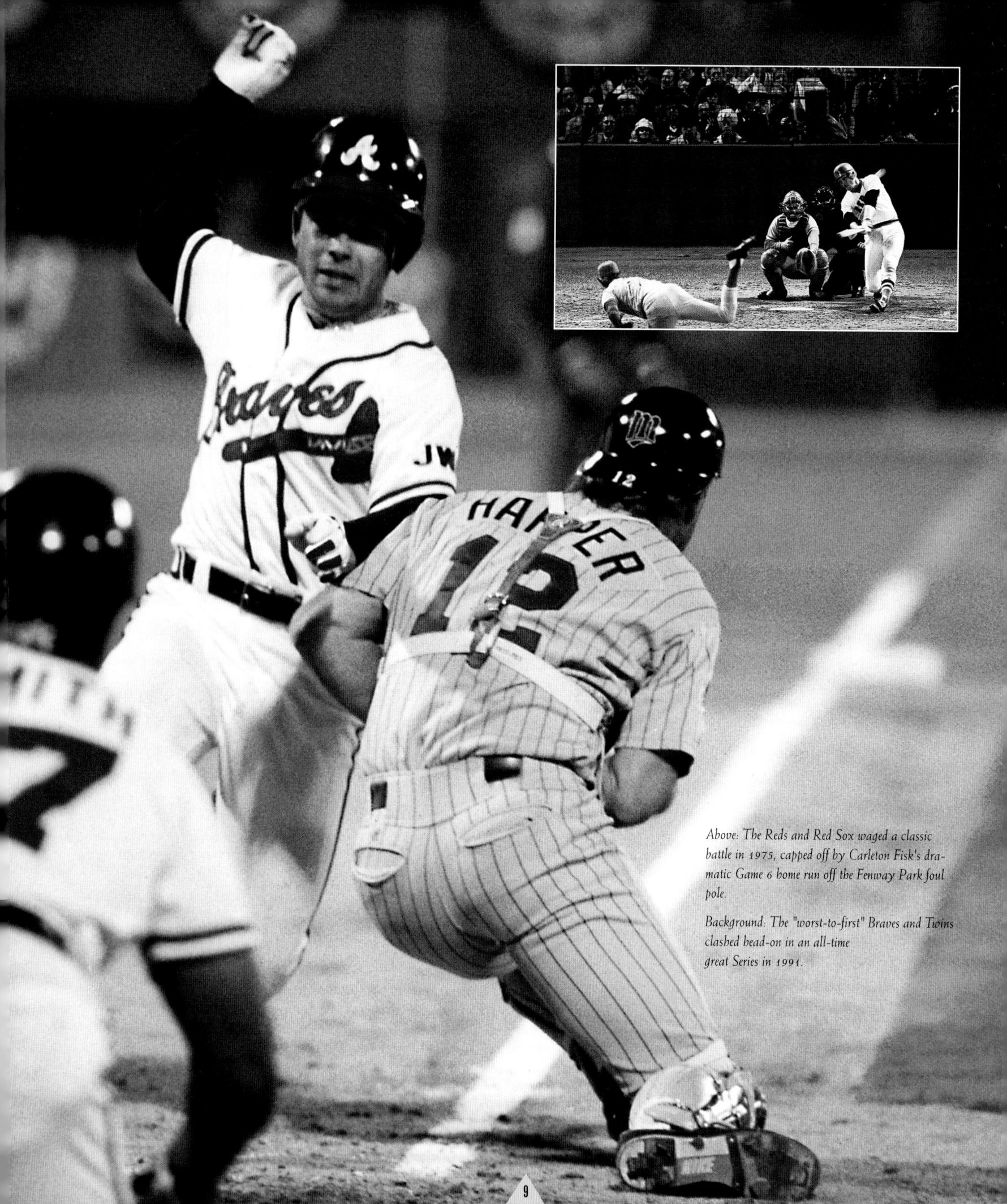

Above: The Reds and Red Sox waged a classic battle in 1975, capped off by Carleton Fisk's dramatic Game 6 home run off the Fenway Park foul pole.

Background: The "worst-to-first" Braves and Twins clashed head-on in an all-time great Series in 1991.

The Early Years: Nineteenth-Century Championships

Major League baseball as we know it today came about in 1901 when Ban Johnson's American League established itself as a major player in professional baseball. The teams organized in the National League had been the leading force in baseball since 1876, and they agreed to play the winner of the American League in an annual World Series beginning in 1903. Before that historic agreement, however, other leagues, major and minor, pitted their top teams against each other in postseason series as far back as the 1860s, when the champion clubs from various cities and towns challenged one another to stake claim as the world's best.

After the National League of Professional Base Ball Clubs emerged as the first organized "major league" in the 1870s, the first serious challenge to its supremacy was from the American Association, founded in 1882. Although the two leagues fought bitterly over players and franchises, the NL-champion Chicago White Stockings agreed to play two exhibition games against the AA-champion Cincinnati Reds at the end of the 1882 season. Each team won one shutout contest, and the first unofficial interleague championship ended in a tie. Two years later, the tensions between the leagues had cooled somewhat, and a sanctioned three-game series between the league winners was arranged to decide the "Championship of the World." The NL's Providence Grays topped the New York Metropolitans in three straight. In 1885 the Chicago White Stockings and St. Louis Browns battled in a chaotic and controversial series that spanned ten days and four cities (Pittsburgh and Cincinnati in addition to the teams' home towns), but even after seven games, the title of champion was still in dispute.

The championship series between the National League and the American Association continued for five more years, with the NL coming out on top in four of them. The 1887 series was the longest in history—15 games played over 11 days in 10 different cities—and the Detroit Wolverines were victorious in 10 of the games. In 1889, nearly 48,000 fans showed up for nine games between the New York Giants and the Brooklyn Bridegrooms in baseball's first Subway Series, which the Giants won. The 1890 Louisville Cyclones claimed the distinction of being the first "worst-to-first" champions, having finished at the bottom of the Association in '89.

Squabbling between the leagues led to cancellation of the 1891 World Series, and the American Association folded before the start of the 1892 season. Left as the only active major league, the National League started a tradition of an intraleague championship in 1892. The NL expanded to 12 teams and divided the season into two halves; the winner of the first half would play the second-half winner in a nine-game series. The split season was abandoned in 1893, but then revived again in 1894, with the winner of a best-of-seven championship series receiving the silver Temple Cup. Though the split season was discarded by 1900, that year's second-place Pittsburgh Pirate club challenged the pennant-winning team from Brooklyn, known at the time as the Superbas, to a best-of-five series. Despite a 10-0 shellacking in Game 3, the Superbas took home the coveted Pittsburgh Chronicle-Telegraph cup in baseball's final pre-World Series championship.

1884	Providence Grays NL (3) vs. New York Metropolitans AA (0)
1885	Chicago White Stockings NL (3) vs. St. Louis Browns AA (3) (one tie)
1886	St. Louis Browns AA (4) vs. Chicago White Stockings NL (2)
1887	Detroit Wolverines NL (10) vs. St. Louis Browns AA (5)
1888	New York Giants NL (6) vs. St. Louis Browns AA (4)
1889	New York Giants NL (6) vs. Brooklyn Bridegrooms AA (3)
1890	Brooklyn Bridegrooms NL (3) vs. Louisville Cyclones AA (3) (one tie)
1892	Boston Beaneaters NL (5) vs. Cleveland Spiders NL (0) (one tie)

Temple Cup
1894	New York Giants (4) vs. Baltimore Orioles (0)
1895	Cleveland Spiders (4) vs. Baltimore Orioles (1)
1896	Baltimore Orioles (4) vs. Cleveland Spiders (0)
1897	Baltimore Orioles (4) vs. Boston Beaneaters (1)

Chronicle-Telegraph Cup
| 1900 | Brooklyn Superbas (3) vs. Pittsburgh Pirates (1) |

World Series Firsts

First Pitch: Cy Young, Boston Pilgrims, to Ginger Beaumont, Game 1, 1903.
First Batter: Ginger Beaumont, Pittsburgh Pirates, Game 1, 1903. (Flied out to center field)
First Hit: Tommy Leach, Pittsburgh Pirates, 1st inning, Game 1, 1903. (Triple)
First Run: Tommy Leach, Pittsburgh Pirates, 1st inning, Game 1, 1903.
First Single: Honus Wagner, Pittsburgh Pirates, 1st inning, Game 1, 1903.
First Double: Chick Stahl, Boston Pilgrims, 1st inning, Game 2, 1903.
First Triple: Tommy Leach, Pittsburgh Pirates, 1st inning, Game 1, 1903.
First Home Run: Jimmy Sebring, Pittsburgh Pirates, 7th inning, Game 1, 1903.
First Two-Home-Run Game: Patsy Dougherty, Boston Pilgrims, 1st and 6th innings, Game 2, 1903.
First Grand Slam: Elmer Smith, Cleveland Indians, 1st inning, Game 5, 1920.

First Base on Balls: Claude Ritchey, Pittsburgh Pirates, by Cy Young, 1st inning, Game 1, 1903.
First Hit Batsman: Hobe Ferris, Boston Pilgrims, by Deacon Phillippe, 7th inning, Game 1, 1903.
First Strikeout: Ed Phelps, Pittsburgh Pirates, by Cy Young, 1st inning, Game 1, 1903.
First Pinch Hitter: Jack O'Brien, Boston Pilgrims, 9th inning, Game 1, 1903. (Struck out)
First Pinch Hit: Ira Thomas, Detroit Tigers, 9th inning, Game 1, 1908. (Single)
First Pinch-Hit Home Run: Yogi Berra, New York Yankees, 7th inning, Game 3, 1947. (Solo shot)
First Pinch Runner: Bill O'Neill, Chicago White Sox, 6th inning, Game 3, 1906.

First Stolen Base: Honus Wagner, Pittsburgh Pirates, 1st inning, Game 1, 1903.
First Steal of Home: Bill Dahlen, New York Giants, 5th inning, Game 3, 1905
First Runner Caught Stealing: Tommy Leach, Pittsburgh Pirates, by Lou Criger, 8th inning, Game 1, 1903.
First Shutout: Bill Dinneen, Boston Pilgrims, Game 2, 1903.
First (and Only) No-Hitter: Don Larsen, perfect game, New York Yankees, Game 5, 1959.
First Error: Hobe Ferris, Boston Pilgrims, 1st inning, Game 1, 1903. (E-4)
First Double Play: Hobe Ferris, unassisted, Boston Pilgrims, 4th inning, Game 2, 1903.
First (and Only) Triple Play: Bill Wambsganss, Cleveland Indians, 5th inning, Game 5, 1920.

The Birth of the Modern World Series

Three years after Ban Johnson founded the American League—and after three years of fighting over players and territory with the long-established National League—the two leagues got together and decided to revive the tradition of the top teams from each side facing off in a championship. It all started when Barney Dreyfuss, owner of the Pittsburgh Pirates, wrote to Henry Killea, owner of the Boston Pilgrims (the team that would later become the Red Sox), in August 1903. Both teams had all but clinched the pennants in their respective leagues, and Dreyfuss wrote to Killea: "The time has come for the National League and American League to organize a World Series. It is my belief that if our clubs played a series on a best-out-of-nine basis, we would create great interest in baseball, in our leagues, and in our players. I also believe it would be a financial success." The story goes that when Killea went to Ban Johnson to get his approval, Johnson's question was whether Boston could win the Series. When Killea assured the league president that his manager, Jimmy Collins, was confident that Boston pitchers Cy Young and Bill Dinneen could stop "Honus Wagner, Fred Clarke, and those other batters," Johnson proclaimed, "Then play them!" And play them they did.

Dreyfuss and Killea laid out some of the ground rules: It would be a best-of-nine series; the first team to win five games would be the champs; the two sides would split the box-office receipts. They decided on dates and umpires, and it was stipulated that no player who joined the team after September 1 could play in the World Series—a restriction that remains today to prevent owners from stacking their team with stars late in the season. Although the Boston players threatened to strike before the games began because they wanted a larger portion of their team's gate receipts, the first World Series opened as planned on October 1, 1903, with more than 16,000 fans packed into Boston's Huntington Avenue Baseball Grounds.

Opening Game Starting Pitchers

◆ Five pitchers have started World Series Game 1's on more than one team: Rube Marquard (1913 Giants, 1916 and 1920 Dodgers), Paul Derringer (1931 Cardinals, 1939–40 Reds), Sal Maglie (1954 Giants, 1956 Dodgers), Don Gullett (1976 Reds, 1977 Yankees) and Jack Morris (1984 Tigers, 1991 Twins, 1992 Blue Jays). Gullett is the only pitcher to start consecutive openers with different teams.

◆ Four pitchers who finished the regular season with losing records have gone on to start the opening game of the Series. Alvin "General" Crowder was 9-11 for Detroit in 1934 before getting the Game 1 start; Denny Galehouse finished 9-10 with the Browns in 1944; Los Angeles's Don Drysdale posted a 13-16 mark in 1966; and Jon Matlack won 13 and lost 15 for the 1973 Mets. Galehouse is the only one to get a win in the opener.

◆ Nobody has pitched a one-hitter in a Series opener, but Whitey Ford allowed only two hits in 1961's Game 1, and Orlando Hernandez and three Yankee relievers held Atlanta to two hits in the 1999 opener. The Cardinals' Mort Cooper and Blix Donnelly threw a combined two-hitter in an opening-game loss to the Browns in 1944.

Most Opening-Day Starts

Whitey Ford 8 (4-3)	Ken Holtzman 3 (2-0)
Red Ruffing 6 (5-1)	Waite Hoyt 3 (2-0)*
Charles "Chief" Bender 4 (2-2)	Carl Hubbell 3 (2-1)
Allie Reynolds 4 (1-2)	Rube Marquard 3 (0-3)
Paul Derringer 3 (0-3)	Jack Morris 3 (2-1)
Don Gullett 3 (1-1)	Dave Stewart 3 (1-1)*

Both Hoyt and Stewart also made a relief appearance in a Series opener.

Most Opening-Game Wins: Red Ruffing (5)
Most Opening-Game Losses: Paul Derringer (3), Whitey Ford (3), Rube Marquard (3)
Most Opening-Game Saves: Mariano Rivera (2)

Facts About the Opening Game

Getting off on the right foot in a World Series can be essential. In 58 of the 96 Fall Classics since 1903 (60 percent of the time), the team that took the opening game went on to win it all.

◆ Eleven teams have won the Series after losing the first two games. The New York Yankees did it four times (1956, 1958, 1978, 1996), but they've been on the losing side on three occasions (1921, 1955, 1981). The 1978 and 1996 Yankees and the 1981 Los Angeles Dodgers are the only teams to lose the first two and then take the Series in six games by winning four in a row.

◆ On only four occasions has a team lost the opener of a World Series and come back to win the next four straight games (1915, 1942, 1969, 1983).

◆ There have been 16 opening-game shutouts, including five 1-0 contests.

◆ The 1959 Chicago White Sox and 1996 Atlanta Braves hold title to the largest victories in an opener—Chicago defeated Los Angeles 11-0 and the Braves trounced the Yankees 12-1—but both teams went on to lose the Series.

◆ The 1907 Series is the only one to start with a tie game. The Cubs and Tigers were knotted at 3-3 after 12 innings when the game was called on account of darkness.

◆ Eight openers have gone into extra innings; 12 innings marks the longest Game 1, and it has happened five times (1907, 1924, 1977, 1986, 2000).

◆ Five players have connected for two home runs in a Series opener: Ted Kluszewski, 1959 White Sox; Gene Tenace, 1972 A's; Willie Aikens, 1980 Royals; Andruw Jones, 1996 Braves; and Greg Vaughn, 1998 Padres.

Boston Pilgrims (5) vs. Pittsburgh Pirates (3)

The National League champion Pittsburgh Pirates were tops in most statistical categories in 1903, having won 91 games on the year, and the lineup featured perhaps the era's greatest hitter in Honus Wagner. The Pirates also boasted one of the best pitching staffs, but two of their star hurlers were out with injuries. Sam Leever, a 25-game winner and the league ERA champ, injured his shoulder in a trap-shooting tournament just before the Series, and 16-game winner Ed Doheny was committed to a mental hospital. But Pittsburgh was not without resources, as Deacon Phillippe came through in spades, starting and completing five games in the Series (records that still stand today) and winning three. The Boston Pilgrims ran away with the American League pennant by 14½ games in the regular season. The pitching staff had three hurlers with at least 20 wins, including 28-game winner Cy Young. Young and 21-game winner Bill Dinneen started seven of the eight games for Boston and were on the mound for all but two innings of the entire Series. The 36-year-old Young faced off against Phillippe in the opener in Boston, and Phillippe came out on top, striking out 10 and walking none in the 7-3 win. Pittsburgh's Tommy Leach started a two-out rally in the top of the first inning with a triple (the teams would set a record for triples in the Series because balls hit into the overflow crowd, which spilled into the outfield,

were considered ground-rule triples), and 4 runs came across the plate in the first inning of World Series play. The ailing Leever got the start in Game 2 but lasted only an inning, while Dinneen pitched brilliantly for Boston, allowing just 3 hits and striking out 11. Boston's Patsy Dougherty supplied the first World Series home run with an inside-the-park shot in the top of the first, then he added an over-the-fence shot in the sixth. Phillippe took the hill for Pittsburgh in the next two games and walked away with two victories, putting the Pirates ahead three games to one. Young and Dinneen alternated starts in Games 5 through 8, and Boston won all four to clinch the Series. The Sox offense exploded for 11 runs on 14 hits in Game 5, including a record 5 triples—a feat they would duplicate three days later in Game 7—and they roughed up Leever for 6 runs in Game 6. Phillippe took the loss in the final two games, with the help of 6 errors by the Pittsburgh fielders. Dinneen and Young had been dominant in the Series, posting a combined ERA of 1.96 in the eight games. Perhaps their biggest accomplishment was silencing the bat of the great Wagner, who was held to only 6 hits after having led the regular season with a .355 average.

Above: Boston's legendary pitcher Cy Young notched two victories in the Series.

1903 WORLD SERIES COMPOSITE STATISTICS

BOSTON PILGRIMS/Jimmy Collins, Manager

Player	pos	G	AB	R	H	2B	3B	HR	RBI	BB	SO	SB	BA	SA	E	FPct
Jimmy Collins	3b	8	36	5	9	1	2	0	1	1	1	3	.250	.389	1	.964
Lou Criger	c	8	26	1	6	0	0	0	4	2	3	0	.231	.231	3	.952
Bill Dinneen	p	4	12	1	3	0	0	0	2	2	2	0	.250	.250	0	1.000
Patsy Dougherty	lf-rf	8	34	3	8	0	2	2	5	2	6	0	.235	.529	1	.938
Duke Farrell	ph	2	2	0	0	0	0	0	1	0	0	0	.000	.000	—	—
Hobe Ferris	2b	8	31	3	9	0	1	0	5	0	6	0	.290	.355	2	.953
Buck Freeman	rf-lf	8	32	6	9	0	3	0	4	2	2	0	.281	.469	0	1.000
Tom Hughes	p	1	0	0	0	0	0	0	0	0	0	0	—	—	0	—
Candy LaChance	1b	8	27	5	6	2	1	0	4	3	2	0	.222	.370	3	.964
Jack O'Brien	ph	2	2	0	0	0	0	0	0	0	1	0	.000	.000	—	—
Freddy Parent	ss	8	32	8	9	0	3	0	4	1	1	0	.281	.469	3	.936
Chick Stahl	cf	8	33	6	10	1	3	0	3	1	2	2	.303	.515	0	1.000
Cy Young	p	4	15	1	2	0	1	0	3	0	3	0	.133	.267	1	.889
Totals		8	282	39	71	4	16	2	34	14	29	5	.252	.401	14	.957

Pitcher	G	GS	CG	IP	H	R	ER	BB	SO	W-L	Sv	ERA
Bill Dinneen	4	4	4	35	29	8	8	8	28	3-1	0	2.06
Tom Hughes	1	1	0	2	4	3	2	2	0	0-1	0	9.00
Cy Young	4	3	3	34	31	13	7	4	17	2-1	0	1.85
Totals	8	8	7	71	64	24	17	14	45	5-3	0	2.15

PITTSBURGH PIRATES/Fred Clarke, Manager

Player	pos	G	AB	R	H	2B	3B	HR	RBI	BB	SO	SB	BA	SA	E	FPct
Ginger Beaumont	cf	8	34	6	9	0	1	0	1	2	4	2	.265	.324	0	1.000
Kitty Bransfield	1b	8	29	3	6	0	2	0	1	1	6	1	.207	.345	3	.967
Fred Clarke	lf	8	34	3	9	2	1	0	2	1	5	1	.265	.382	1	.947
Brickyard Kennedy	p	1	2	0	1	1	0	0	0	0	0	0	.500	1.000	0	1.000
Tommy Leach	3b	8	33	3	9	0	4	0	7	1	4	1	.273	.515	4	.840
Sam Leever	p	2	4	0	0	0	0	0	0	0	0	0	.000	.000	0	1.000
Eddie Phelps	c-ph	8	26	1	6	2	0	0	1	1	6	0	.231	.308	2	.953
Deacon Phillippe	p	5	18	1	4	0	0	0	1	0	3	0	.222	.222	1	.917
Claude Ritchey	2b	8	27	2	3	1	0	0	2	4	7	1	.111	.148	0	1.000
Jimmy Sebring	rf	8	30	3	11	0	1	1	3	1	4	0	.367	.533	0	1.000
Harry Smith	c	1	3	0	0	0	0	0	0	0	0	0	.000	.000	1	.750
Gus Thompson	p	1	1	0	0	0	0	0	0	0	0	0	.000	.000	0	1.000
Bucky Veil	p	1	2	0	0	0	0	0	0	0	2	0	.000	.000	0	1.000
Honus Wagner	ss	8	27	2	6	1	0	0	3	3	4	3	.222	.259	6	.875
Totals		8	270	24	64	7	9	1	21	14	45	9	.237	.341	19	.942

Pitcher	G	GS	CG	IP	H	R	ER	BB	SO	W-L	Sv	ERA
Brickyard Kennedy	1	1	0	7	11	10	4	3	0	0-1	0	5.14
Sam Leever	2	2	1	10	13	8	6	3	2	0-2	0	5.40
Deacon Phillippe	5	5	5	44	38	19	14	3	22	3-2	0	2.86
Gus Thompson	1	0	0	2	3	1	1	0	1	0-0	0	4.50
Bucky Veil	1	0	0	7	6	1	1	5	1	0-0	0	1.29
Totals	8	8	6	70	71	39	26	14	29	3-5	0	3.34

Series Outstanding Player: Bill Dinneen, Boston Pilgrims. **Series Outstanding Pitcher:** Bill Dinneen, Boston Pilgrims. **Average Length of Game:** 1 hour, 48 minutes. **Total Attendance:** 100,429. **Average Attendance:** 12,554 (12,978 at Huntington Avenue Grounds; 12,129 at Exposition Park). **Umpires:** Tommy Connolly (AL), Hank O'Day (NL). **Winning Player's Share:** $1,182. **Losing Player's Share:** $1,316.

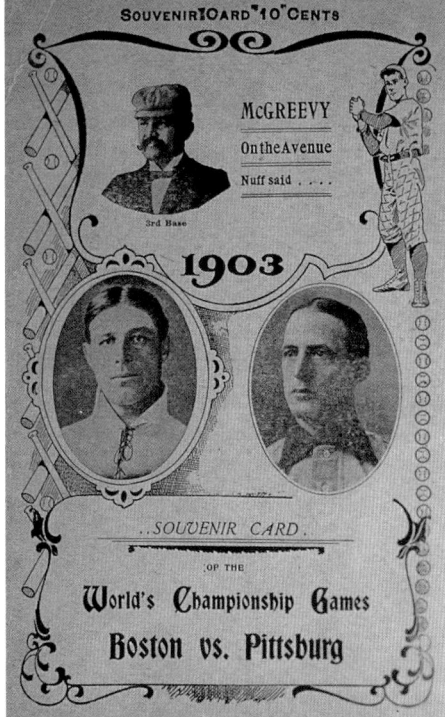

McGREEVY
On the Avenue
Nuff said . . . .

3rd Base

1903

..SOUVENIR CARD..

OF THE

World's Championship Games

Boston vs. Pittsburg

Left: 1903 program for the inaugural World Series

Though the team lost, the Pirates players' share of the World Series earnings was greater than the Pilgrims' because Pittsburgh owner Barney Dreyfuss contributed his share of the receipts to the players.

Above: Fans crowd into Huntington Avenue Grounds for the World Series of 1903.

Right: Boston's Bill Dinneen struck out 28 batters in 35 innings en route to his 3 wins in the 1903 Series.

Patsy Dougherty's two home runs in one World Series game was a feat that would not be repeated for another 12 years—in 1915 by another Boston outfielder, Harry Hooper.

Game 1 Thursday, October 1 at Huntington Avenue Grounds, Boston

	1	2	3	4	5	6	7	8	9	R	H	E
Pittsburgh Pirates	4	0	1	1	0	0	1	0	0	7	12	2
Boston Pilgrims	0	0	0	0	0	0	2	0	1	3	6	4

Pitchers Pit Deacon Phillippe (W, 1-0), 9 IP, 6 H, 3 R, 2 ER, 0 BB, 10 SO
Bos Cy Young (L, 0-1), 9 IP, 12 H, 7 R, 3 ER, 3 BB, 5 SO

Top Performers at the Plate
Pit Tommy Leach, 4 for 5, 1 R, 1 RBI, 2 3B; Jimmy Sebring 3 for 5, 1 R, 4 RBI
Bos Buck Freeman, 2 for 4, 2 R; Freddy Parent, 2 for 4, 1 R, 1 RBI

3B-Pit/Bransfield, Leach 2; Bos/Freeman, Parent. **HR**-Pit/Sebring. **SB**-Pit/Bransfield, Ritchey, Wagner. **Time** 1:55. **Attendance** 16,242.

Game 2 Friday, October 2 at Huntington Avenue Grounds, Boston

	1	2	3	4	5	6	7	8	9	R	H	E
Pittsburgh Pirates	0	0	0	0	0	0	0	0	0	0	3	2
Boston Pilgrims	2	0	0	0	0	1	0	0	x	3	9	0

Pitchers Pit Sam Leever (L, 0-1), IP 1, H 3, R 2, ER 2, BB 1, SO 0; Bucky Veil, IP 7, H 6, R 1, ER 1, BB 5, SO 1
Bos Bill Dinneen (W, 1-0), IP 9, H 3, R 0, ER 0, BB 2, SO 11

Top Performers at the Plate
Bos Patsy Dougherty, 3 for 4, 2 R, 2 RBI, 2 HR; Buck Freeman, 2 for 4, 1 RBI

2B-Bos/Stahl. **HR**-Bos/Dougherty 2. **SB**-Bos/Collins 2. **Time** 1:47. **Attendance** 9,415.

Game 3 Saturday, October 3 at Huntington Avenue Grounds, Boston

	1	2	3	4	5	6	7	8	9	R	H	E
Pittsburgh Pirates	0	1	2	0	0	0	0	1	0	4	7	1
Boston Pilgrims	0	0	0	1	0	0	0	1	0	2	4	2

Pitchers Pit Deacon Phillippe (W, 2-0), IP 9, H 4, R 2, ER 2, BB 3, SO 6
Bos Tom Hughes (L, 0-1), IP 2, H 4, R 3, ER 2, BB 2, SO 0; Cy Young, IP 7, H 3, R 1, ER 1, BB 0, SO 2

Top Performers at the Plate
Pit Eddie Phelps, 2 for 4, 1 RBI, 2 2B; Claude Ritchey, 1 for 4, 1 R, 1 RBI
Bos Jimmy Collins, 2 for 4, 2 R

2B-Pit/Clarke, Phelps 2, Ritchey, Wagner; Bos/Collins, LaChance. **Time** 1:50. **Attendance** 18,801.

Game 4 Tuesday, October 6 at Exposition Park, Pittsburgh

	1	2	3	4	5	6	7	8	9	R	H	E
Boston Pilgrims	0	0	0	0	1	0	0	0	3	4	9	1
Pittsburgh Pirates	1	0	0	0	1	0	3	0	x	5	12	1

Pitchers Pit Deacon Phillippe (W, 3-0), IP 9, H 9, R 4, ER 4, BB 0, SO 2
Bos Bill Dinneen (L, 1-1), IP 8, H 12, R 5, ER 5, BB 1, SO 7

Top Performers at the Plate
Pit Ginger Beaumont, 3 for 4, 2 R; Tommy Leach, 2 for 4, 1 R, 3 RBI
Bos Candy LaChance, 2 for 4, 1 R; Chick Stahl, 2 for 4, 1 R

3B-Pit/Beaumont, Leach. **SB**-Pit/Wagner. **Time** 1:30. **Attendance** 7,600.

Game 5 Wednesday, October 7 at Exposition Park, Pittsburgh

	1	2	3	4	5	6	7	8	9	R	H	E
Boston Pilgrims	0	0	0	0	0	6	4	1	0	11	14	2
Pittsburgh Pirates	0	0	0	0	0	0	0	2	0	2	6	4

Pitchers Bos Cy Young (W, 1-1), IP 9, H 6, R 2, ER 0, BB 0, SO 4
Pit Brickyard Kennedy (L, 0-1), IP 7, H 11, R 10, ER 4, BB 3, SO 3; Gus Thompson, IP 2, H 3, R 1, ER 1, BB 0, SO 1

Top Performers at the Plate
Bos Patsy Dougherty, 3 for 6, 3 RBI, 2 3B; Buck Freeman, 2 for 4, 2 R, 1 RBI
Pit Tommy Leach, 2 for 4, 2 RBI

2B-Pit/Kennedy. **3B**-Bos/Dougherty 2, Collins, Stahl, Young; Pit/Leach. **SB**-Bos/Collins, Stahl. **Time** 2:00. **Attendance** 12,322.

Game 6 Thursday, October 8 at Exposition Park, Pittsburgh

	1	2	3	4	5	6	7	8	9	R	H	E
Boston Pilgrims	0	0	3	0	2	0	1	0	0	6	10	1
Pittsburgh Pirates	0	0	0	0	0	0	3	0	0	3	10	3

Pitchers Bos Bill Dinneen (W, 2-1), IP 9, H 10, R 3, ER 3, BB 3, SO 3
Pit Sam Leever (L, 0-2), IP 9, H 10, R 6, ER 4, BB 2, SO 2

Top Performers at the Plate
Bos Chick Stahl, 2 for 5, 1 R, 1 RBI; Patsy Dougherty, 1 for 3, 1 R, 2 BB
Pit Ginger Beaumont, 4 for 5, 1 R, 1 RBI, 2 SB; Fred Clarke, 2 for 5, 2 RBI

2B-Bos/LaChance; Pit/Clarke. **3B**-Bos/Parent, Stahl. **SB**-Bos/Stahl; Pit/Beaumont 2, Clarke, Leach. **Time** 2:02. **Attendance** 11,556.

Game 7 Saturday, October 10 at Exposition Park, Pittsburgh

	1	2	3	4	5	6	7	8	9	R	H	E
Boston Pilgrims	2	0	0	2	0	2	0	1	0	7	11	4
Pittsburgh Pirates	0	0	0	1	0	1	0	0	1	3	10	3

Pitchers Bos Cy Young (W, 2-1), IP 9, H 10, R 3, ER 3, BB 1, SO 6
Pit Deacon Phillippe (L, 3-1), IP 9, H 11, R 7, ER 4, BB 0, SO 2

Top Performers at the Plate
Bos Lou Criger, 2 for 4, 3 RBI; Freddy Parent, 2 for 4, 2 R, 1 RBI
Pit Kitty Bransfield, 3 for 4, 1 R; Deacon Phillippe, 2 for 4, 1 RBI

3B-Bos/Collins, Ferris, Freeman, Parent, Stahl; Pit/Bransfield, Clarke. **Time** 1:45. **Attendance** 17,038.

Game 8 Tuesday, October 13 at Huntington Avenue Grounds, Boston

	1	2	3	4	5	6	7	8	9	R	H	E
Pittsburgh Pirates	0	0	0	0	0	0	0	0	0	0	4	3
Boston Pilgrims	0	0	0	2	0	1	0	0	x	3	8	0

Pitchers Pit Deacon Phillippe (L, 3-2), IP 8, H 8, R 3, ER 2, BB 0, SO 2
Bos Bill Dinneen (W, 3-1), IP 9, H 4, R 0, ER 0, BB 2, SO 7

Top Performers at the Plate
Bos Hobe Ferris, 2 for 4, 3 RBI

3B-Pit/Sebring; Bos/Freeman, LaChance. **SB**-Pit/Wagner. **Time** 1:35. **Attendance** 7,455.

New York Giants (4) vs. Philadelphia Athletics (1)

1905

The Boston Pilgrims repeated as American League champs in 1904, but they did not get a chance to defend their World Series title. The New York Giants, who won the National League pennant easily with 106 wins in 1904, were led by a pair who harbored deep resentment against the rival league. Giants owner John Brush was bitter over the placement of an American League team in New York (the Highlanders, who later became the Yankees), and manager John McGraw had had many run-ins with AL president Ban Johnson during his years as a manager in Baltimore. As a result, the Giants refused to participate in a championship series with Johnson's league in 1904. McGraw proclaimed that winning the National League, "the only real major league," was sufficient to claim the title of champions of the baseball world. The Giants players were not too pleased with the decision, as it deprived them of the additional cash that comes with a Series appearance, but Brush held firm. A year later, the Giants owner proposed a new set of rules, the so-called John T. Brush Rules, which changed the Series to a best-of-seven format and established rules for the distribution of receipts, among other regulations.

up a pairing of two legendary managers: New York's John McGraw and Philadelphia's Connie Mack. All-star pitching staffs were at the forefront on both sides, with New York presenting the imposing duo of Christy Mathewson and Joe "Iron Man" McGinnity and Philadelphia offering three future Hall of Famers in Charles "Chief" Bender, Eddie Plank and Rube Waddell (though Waddell had to sit out the Series with an injury). Mathewson followed up on his awesome regular season campaign (32-8, 1.27 ERA) by pitching three complete-game shutouts in a six-day span, allowing just 14 hits and 1 walk while striking out 18. In fact, all five games between the A's and Giants were shutouts—the only all-shutout Series in history. In addition to Mathewson's record three shutouts, McGinnity held the A's scoreless on 5 hits in Game 4, and Bender gave Philadelphia its lone win behind a 4-hit shutout in Game 2. The 3 runs scored off McGinnity in Game 2—Philadelphia's only 3 runs in the Series—were all unearned, giving the Giants an unparalleled 0.00 ERA. The A's staff fared almost as well, compiling an impressive 1.47 ERA and holding New York to a .203 team average in the five games.

The Giants participated in the first Series under Brush's rules after capturing a second straight pennant in 1905. The team was a willing participant against the AL-champion Philadelphia Athletics, setting The hitting heroes of the Series (such as they were) were New York's Roger Bresnahan, who collected 5 hits and 4 bases-on-balls, and Dan McGann, who drove in 4 runs in Game 3's 9-0 blowout.

1905 WORLD SERIES COMPOSITE STATISTICS

NEW YORK GIANTS/John McGraw, Manager

Player	pos	G	AB	R	H	2B	3B	HR	RBI	BB	SO	SB	BA	SA	E	FPct
Red Ames	p	1	0	0	0	0	0	0	0	0	0	0	—	—	0	1.000
Roger Bresnahan	c	5	16	3	5	2	0	0	1	4	0	1	.313	.438	0	1.000
George Browne	rf	5	22	2	4	0	0	0	1	0	2	2	.182	.182	1	.972
Bill Dahlen	ss	5	15	1	0	0	0	0	1	3	2	3	.000	.000	0	1.000
Art Devlin	3b	5	16	0	4	1	0	0	1	1	3	3	.250	.313	0	1.000
Mike Donlin	cf	5	19	4	5	1	0	0	1	2	1	2	.263	.316	1	.957
Billy Gilbert	2b	5	17	1	4	0	0	0	2	0	2	1	.235	.235	2	.941
Christy Mathewson	p	3	8	1	2	0	0	0	0	1	1	0	.250	.250	0	1.000
Dan McGann	1b	5	17	1	4	2	0	0	4	2	7	0	.235	.353	1	.909
Joe McGinnity	p	2	5	0	0	0	0	0	0	0	2	0	.000	.000	1	.984
Sam Mertes	lf	5	17	2	3	1	0	0	2	2	5	0	.176	.235	0	1.000
Sammy Strang	ph	1	1	0	0	0	0	0	0	0	1	0	.000	.000	—	—
Totals		**5**	**153**	**15**	**31**	**7**	**0**	**0**	**13**	**15**	**26**	**12**	**.203**	**.248**	**6**	**.977**

Pitcher	G	GS	CG	IP	H	R	ER	BB	SO	W-L	Sv	ERA
Red Ames	1	0	0	1	1	0	0	1	1	0-0	0	0.00
Christy Mathewson	3	3	3	27	14	0	0	1	18	3-0	0	0.00
Joe McGinnity	2	2	1	17	10	3	0	3	6	1-1	0	0.00
Totals	**5**	**5**	**4**	**45**	**25**	**3**	**0**	**5**	**25**	**4-1**	**0**	**0.00**

PHILADELPHIA ATHLETICS/Connie Mack, Manager

Player	pos	G	AB	R	H	2B	3B	HR	RBI	BB	SO	SB	BA	SA	E	FPct
Chief Bender	p	2	5	0	0	0	0	0	0	0	1	0	.000	.000	0	1.000
Andy Coakley	p	1	2	0	0	0	0	0	0	0	1	0	.000	.000	0	1.000
Lave Cross	3b	5	19	0	2	0	0	0	0	1	1	0	.105	.105	2	.917
Monte Cross	ss	5	17	0	3	0	0	0	0	0	7	0	.176	.176	2	.926
Harry Davis	1b	5	20	0	4	1	0	0	0	1	0	0	.200	.250	0	1.000
Topsy Hartsel	lf	5	17	1	5	1	0	0	0	2	1	2	.294	.353	1	.909
Danny Hoffman	ph	1	1	0	0	0	0	0	0	0	1	0	.000	.000	—	—
Bris Lord	cf	5	20	0	2	0	0	0	0	2	5	0	.100	.100	0	1.000
Danny Murphy	2b	5	16	0	3	1	0	0	0	0	2	0	.188	.250	4	.789
Eddie Plank	p	2	6	0	1	0	0	0	0	0	2	0	.167	.167	0	1.000
Mike Powers	c	3	7	0	1	1	0	0	0	0	0	0	.143	.286	0	1.000
Ossee Schreckengost	c	3	9	2	2	1	0	0	0	0	0	0	.222	.333	0	1.000
Socks Seybold	rf	5	16	0	2	0	0	0	0	2	3	0	.125	.125	0	1.000
Totals		**5**	**155**	**3**	**25**	**5**	**0**	**0**	**2**	**5**	**25**	**2**	**.161**	**.194**	**9**	**.958**

Pitcher	G	GS	CG	IP	H	R	ER	BB	SO	W-L	Sv	ERA
Chief Bender	2	2	2	17	9	2	2	2	17	1-1	0	1.06
Andy Coakley	1	1	1	9	8	9	2	5	2	0-1	0	2.00
Eddie Plank	2	2	2	17	14	4	3	4	11	0-2	0	1.59
Totals	**5**	**5**	**5**	**43**	**31**	**15**	**7**	**15**	**26**	**1-4**	**0**	**1.47**

Series Outstanding Player: Christy Mathewson, New York Giants. **Series Outstanding Pitcher:** Christy Mathewson, New York Giants. **Average Length of Game:** 1 hour, 49 minutes. **Total Attendance:** 91,723. **Average Attendance:** 18,345 (20,926 at the Polo Grounds; 14,473 at Baker Bowl). **Umpires:** Hank O'Day (NL), Jack Sheridan (AL). **Winning Player's Share:** $1,142. **Losing Player's Share:** $832.

Right: Manager John McGraw is surrounded by his aces, Christy Mathewson (left) and Joe McGinnity (right).

The first steal of home in World Series history was pulled off by New York's Bill Dahlen in the fifth inning of Game 3.

Above: Charles "Chief" Bender was the lone bright spot for Philadelphia, pitching a 4-hit shutout in Game 2.

Right: Christy Mathewson put on an awesome display in 1905, pitching three shutout victories.

Game 1 Monday, October 9 at Baker Bowl, Philadelphia

	1	2	3	4	5	6	7	8	9	R	H	E
New York Giants	0	0	0	0	2	0	0	0	1	3	10	1
Philadelphia Athletics	0	0	0	0	0	0	0	0	0	0	4	0

Pitchers NY Christy Mathewson (W, 1-0), IP 9, H 4, R 0, ER 0, BB 0, SO 6
Phi Eddie Plank (L, 0-1), IP 9, H 10, R 3, ER 3, BB 2, SO 5

Top Performers at the Plate
NY Roger Bresnahan, 1 for 3, 1 R, 1 RBI, 1 BB, 1 HBP; Mike Donlin, 2 for 5, 1 R, 1 RBI

2B-NY/McGann, Mertes; Phi/Davis, Murphy, Schreckengost. **SB**-NY/Bresnahan, Devlin, Donlin, Gilbert. **Time** 1:46. **Attendance** 17,955.

Game 2 Tuesday, October 10 at the Polo Grounds, New York

	1	2	3	4	5	6	7	8	9	R	H	E
Philadelphia Athletics	0	0	1	0	0	0	0	2	0	3	6	2
New York Giants	0	0	0	0	0	0	0	0	0	0	4	2

Pitchers Phi Chief Bender (W, 1-0), IP 9, H 4, R 0, ER 0, BB 3, SO 9
NY Joe McGinnity (L, 0-1), IP 8, H 5, R 3, ER 0, BB 0, SO 2; Red Ames, IP 1, H 1, R 0, ER 0, BB 1, SO 1

Top Performers at the Plate
Phi Topsy Hartsel, 2 for 4, 1 R; Bris Lord, 2 for 4, 2 RBI
NY Mike Donlin, 2 for 4

2B-Phi/Hartsel; NY/Bresnahan, Donlin. **SB**-NY/Dahlen, Devlin. **Time** 1:55. **Attendance** 24,992.

Game 3 Thursday, October 12 at Baker Bowl, Philadelphia

	1	2	3	4	5	6	7	8	9	R	H	E
New York Giants	2	0	0	0	5	0	0	0	2	9	8	1
Philadelphia Athletics	0	0	0	0	0	0	0	0	0	0	4	5

Pitchers NY Christy Mathewson (W, 2-0), IP 9, H 4, R 0, ER 0, BB 1, SO 8
Phi Andy Coakley (L, 0-1), IP 9, H 8, R 9, ER 2, BB 5, SO 2

Top Performers at the Plate
NY Mike Donlin, 1 for 3, 3 R, 2 BB; Dan McGann, 3 for 5, 1 R, 4 RBI

2B-NY/McGann. **SB**-NY/Browne 2, Dahlen, Devlin, Donlin; Phi/Hartsel. **Time** 1:55. **Attendance** 10,991.

Game 4 Friday, October 13 at the Polo Grounds, New York

	1	2	3	4	5	6	7	8	9	R	H	E
Philadelphia Athletics	0	0	0	0	0	0	0	0	0	0	5	2
New York Giants	0	0	0	1	0	0	0	0	x	1	4	1

Pitchers Phi Eddie Plank (L, 0-2), IP 8, H 4, R 1, ER 0, BB 2, SO 6
NY Joe McGinnity (W, 1-1), IP 9, H 5, R 0, ER 0, BB 3, SO 4

2B-NY/Devlin. **SB**-Phi/Hartsel. **Time** 1:55. **Attendance** 13,598.

Game 5 Saturday, October 14 at the Polo Grounds, New York

	1	2	3	4	5	6	7	8	9	R	H	E
Philadelphia Athletics	0	0	0	0	0	0	0	0	0	0	6	0
New York Giants	0	0	0	0	1	0	0	1	x	2	5	1

Pitchers Phi Chief Bender (L, 1-1), IP 8, H 5, R 2, ER 2, BB 3, SO 4
NY Christy Mathewson (W, 3-0), IP 9, H 6, R 0, ER 0, BB 0, SO 4

2B-Phi/Powers; NY/Bresnahan. **Time** 1:35. **Attendance** 24,187.

Christy Mathewson's individual record of three shutouts in one Series is a mark that has been matched by a team only twice in history (the Dodgers in 1965 and the Orioles in 1966).

Huge crowds turned out at the Polo Grounds to watch the Giants bring home the franchise's first championship.

Chicago White Sox (4) vs. Chicago Cubs (2)

1906

Heading into baseball's first intracity Series, the Cubs from Chicago's West Side were heavy favorites against their South Side foes. The powerful Cubs stormed through the regular season with 116 wins, the most in baseball history, and finished 20 games ahead of the second-place Giants. Across town, meanwhile, the "Hitless Wonders," as the White Sox were known, fairly stumbled to the pennant, batting .230 during the season, worst in the league. As snow flurries and cold temperatures gripped the city in the opening games, the teams battled through matching 4-hitters in Game 1, before the Sox squeaked out a 2-1 victory. Reserve infielder George Rohe, who was thrust into starting duty because of an injury to regular shortstop George Davis, delivered a key fifth-inning triple and then came home with the game's first run. With no travel day necessary for this all-Chicago Series, the teams met again the next day, and Ed Reulbach held the White Sox hitless for six innings before allowing a single to Jiggs Donahue in the bottom of the seventh. Reulbach held on to preserve the first 1-hitter in World Series history, and to tie the Series for the Cubs. (The White Sox's lone run in the second game came on a walk, a wild pitch and an error in the fifth.) George Rohe came through again for the Sox in Game 3, hitting a bases-loaded triple in the fifth to send in the game's only runs. Ed Walsh shut down the Cubs with 12 strikeouts while allowing only 2 hits, both in the first inning. The Game 1 starters faced off again in Game 4, and Mordecai "Three Finger" Brown pitched masterfully to lead the Cubs to a 1-0 victory. Through the first four games of the Series, the White Sox managed to collect only 11 hits, yet they had secured the same number of wins as their opponents. The Sox's bats finally came alive in Game 5, exploding for 8 runs on 12 hits. Four of those hits were doubles off the bat of Frank Isbell, establishing the single-game record for two-baggers. The White Sox lineup continued to defy its nickname the following afternoon, as the "Hitless Wonders" knocked Brown for 6 runs in just an inning and a third and walked away with an 8-3 win—the only victory by a home team in the Series. Despite batting a meager .196 for the Series and committing 15 errors in the field, the White Sox used timely hitting and nearly untouchable pitching to shock the Cubs and the baseball world.

M. BROWN. J. PFEISTER. A. HOFMAN. C.G. WILLIAMS. O. OVERALL. E. REULBACH. J. KLING.
H. GESSLER. J. TAYLOR. H. STEINFELDT. J. McCORMICK. F. CHANCE. J. SHECKARD. P. MORAN. F. SCHULTE.
C. LUNDGREN. T. WALSH. J. EVERS. J. SLAGLE. J. TINKER.

CHICAGO NATIONAL LEAGUE BALL CLUB 1906

Above: The 1906 Chicago Cubs won more games than any team in history, but they lost the Series to their cross-town foes, the White Sox.

1906 WORLD SERIES COMPOSITE STATISTICS

CHICAGO WHITE SOX/Fielder Jones, Manager

Player	pos	G	AB	R	H	2B	3B	HR	RBI	BB	SO	SB	BA	SA	E	FPct
Nick Altrock	p	2	4	0	1	0	0	0	0	1	1	0	.250	.250	0	1.000
George Davis	ss	3	13	4	4	3	0	0	6	0	1	1	.308	.538	2	.917
Jiggs Donahue	1b	6	18	0	6	2	1	0	4	3	3	0	.333	.556	1	.989
Patsy Dougherty	lf	6	20	1	2	0	0	0	1	3	4	2	.100	.100	1	.800
Ed Hahn	rf	6	22	4	6	0	0	0	0	1	1	0	.273	.273	0	1.000
Frank Isbell	2b	6	26	4	8	4	0	0	4	0	6	1	.308	.462	5	.844
Fielder Jones	cf	6	21	4	2	0	0	0	3	3	3	0	.095	.095	1	1.000
Ed McFarland	ph	1	1	0	0	0	0	0	0	0	0	0	.000	.000	–	–
Bill O'Neill	rf	1	1	1	0	0	0	0	0	0	0	0	.000	.000	0	1.000
Frank Owen	p	1	2	0	0	0	0	0	0	0	1	0	.000	.000	0	1.000
George Rohe	3b	6	21	2	7	1	2	0	4	3	1	2	.333	.571	3	.875
Billy Sullivan	c	6	21	0	0	0	0	0	0	0	9	0	.000	.000	2	.957
Lee Tannehill	ss	3	9	1	1	0	0	0	0	0	2	0	.111	.111	0	1.000
Babe Towne	ph	1	1	0	0	0	0	0	0	0	0	0	.000	.000	–	–
Ed Walsh	p	2	4	1	0	0	0	0	0	3	3	0	.000	.000	1	.800
Doc White	p	3	3	0	0	0	0	0	0	0	1	0	.000	.000	0	1.000
Totals		**6**	**187**	**22**	**37**	**10**	**3**	**0**	**19**	**18**	**35**	**6**	**.198**	**.283**	**15**	**.945**

Pitcher	G	GS	CG	IP	H	R	ER	BB	SO	W-L	Sv	ERA
Nick Altrock	2	2	2	18	11	2	2	2	5	1-1	0	1.00
Frank Owen	1	0	0	6	6	3	2	3	2	0-0	0	3.00
Ed Walsh	2	2	1	15	7	6	2	6	17	2-0	0	1.20
Doc White	3	2	1	15	12	7	3	7	4	1-1	1	1.80
Totals	**6**	**6**	**4**	**54**	**36**	**18**	**9**	**18**	**28**	**4-2**	**1**	**1.50**

CHICAGO CUBS/Frank Chance, Manager

Player	pos	G	AB	R	H	2B	3B	HR	RBI	BB	SO	SB	BA	SA	E	FPct
Three Finger Brown	p	3	6	0	2	0	0	0	0	0	4	0	.333	.333	1	.923
Frank Chance	1b	6	21	3	5	1	0	0	0	2	1	2	.238	.286	0	1.000
Johnny Evers	2b	6	20	2	3	1	0	0	1	1	3	2	.150	.200	1	.971
Doc Gessler	ph	2	1	0	0	0	0	0	0	0	1	0	.000	.000	–	–
Solly Hofman	cf	6	23	3	7	1	0	0	2	3	5	1	.304	.348	0	1.000
Johnny Kling	c	6	17	2	3	1	0	0	4	3	0	0	.176	.235	1	.982
Pat Moran	ph	2	2	0	0	0	0	0	0	0	0	0	.000	.000	–	–
Orval Overall	p	2	4	1	1	0	0	0	0	1	1	0	.250	.500	0	1.000
Jack Pfiester	p	2	2	0	0	0	0	0	0	0	1	0	.000	.000	1	.667
Ed Reulbach	p	2	3	0	0	0	0	0	0	1	0	1	.000	.000	0	1.000
Frank Schulte	rf	6	26	1	7	3	0	0	3	1	3	0	.269	.385	0	1.000
Jimmy Sheckard	lf	6	21	0	0	0	0	0	1	2	4	1	.000	.000	0	1.000
Harry Steinfeldt	3b	6	20	2	5	1	0	0	2	1	0	0	.250	.300	1	.923
Joe Tinker	ss	6	18	4	3	0	0	0	1	2	2	3	.167	.167	2	.938
Totals		**6**	**184**	**18**	**36**	**9**	**0**	**0**	**11**	**18**	**28**	**9**	**.196**	**.245**	**7**	**.972**

Pitcher	G	GS	CG	IP	H	R	ER	BB	SO	W-L	Sv	ERA
Three Finger Brown	3	3	2	19⅔	14	9	7	4	12	1-2	0	3.20
Orval Overall	2	0	0	12	10	2	3	3	8	0-0	0	2.25
Jack Pfiester	2	1	1	10⅓	7	7	7	3	11	0-2	0	6.10
Ed Reulbach	2	2	1	11	6	4	3	8	4	1-0	0	2.45
Totals	**6**	**6**	**4**	**53**	**37**	**22**	**20**	**18**	**35**	**2-4**	**0**	**3.40**

Series Outstanding Player: George Rohe, Chicago White Sox. **Series Outstanding Pitcher:** Ed Walsh, Chicago White Sox. **Average Length of Game:** 2 hours, 1 minute. **Total Attendance:** 99,845. **Average Attendance:** 16,641 (16,743 at South Side Park; 16,539 at West Side Grounds). **Umpires:** Jim Johnstone (NL), Francis O'Loughlin (AL). **Winning Player's Share:** $1,874. **Losing Player's Share:** $440.

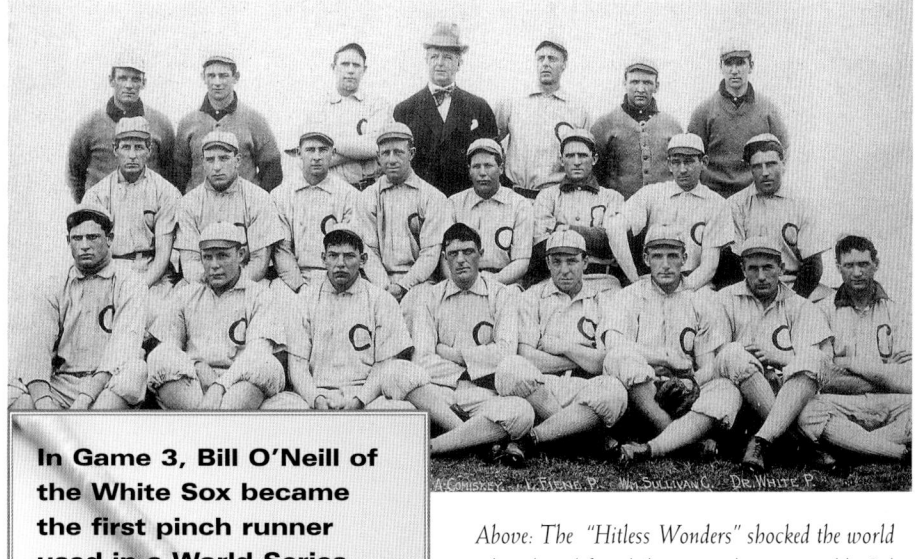

Above: The "Hitless Wonders" shocked the world when they defeated the seemingly unstoppable Cubs in 1906.

In Game 3, Bill O'Neill of the White Sox became the first pinch runner used in a World Series game. He came in to run for Eddie Hahn in the sixth inning and eventually scored on George Rohe's triple.

Right: Ed Walsh fanned a record 12 Cubs in Game 3 en route to a 3-0 win.

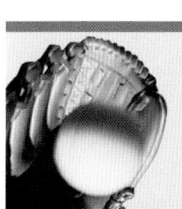

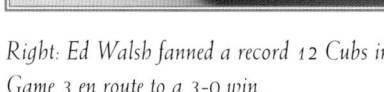
In his 12-strikeout performance in Game 3, Ed Walsh struck out at least one batter in every inning.

Below: Action during Game 5 at West Side Grounds. The White Sox won the game to take a 3-2 lead in the Series.

Game 1 Tuesday, October 9 at West Side Grounds, Chicago

	1	2	3	4	5	6	7	8	9	R	H	E
Chicago White Sox	0	0	0	0	1	1	0	0	0	2	4	1
Chicago Cubs	0	0	0	0	0	1	0	0	0	1	4	2

Pitchers ChiW Nick Altrock (W, 1-0), IP 9, H 4, R 1, ER 1, BB 1, SO 3
ChiC Three Finger Brown (L, 0-1), IP 9, H 4, R 2, ER 1, BB 1, SO 7

Top Performers at the Plate
ChiW Frank Isbell, 1 for 4, 1 RBI; Fielder Jones, 1 for 4, 1 R
ChiC Johnny Kling, 1 for 2, 1 R, 1 BB

3B-ChiW/Rohe. **SB**-ChiW/Dougherty, Isbell. **Time** 1:45. **Attendance** 12,693.

Game 2 Wednesday, October 10 at South Side Park, Chicago

	1	2	3	4	5	6	7	8	9	R	H	E
Chicago Cubs	0	3	1	0	0	1	0	2	0	7	10	2
Chicago White Sox	0	0	0	0	1	0	0	0	0	1	1	3

Pitchers ChiC Ed Reulbach (W, 1-0), IP 9, H 1, R 1, ER 0, BB 6, SO 3
ChiW Doc White (L, 0-1), IP 3, H 4, R 4, ER 0, BB 2, SO 1; Frank Owen, IP 6, H 6, R 3, ER 2, BB 3, SO 2

Top Performers at the Plate
ChiC Harry Steinfeldt, 3 for 3, 1 R, 1 RBI; Joe Tinker, 2 for 3, 3 R, 1 RBI, 1 BB, 2 SB

2B-ChiC/Kling. **SB**-ChiC/Chance 2, Evers, Hofman, Tinker 2. **Time** 1:58. **Attendance** 12,595.

Game 3 Thursday, October 11 at West Side Grounds, Chicago

	1	2	3	4	5	6	7	8	9	R	H	E
Chicago White Sox	0	0	0	0	0	3	0	0	0	3	4	1
Chicago Cubs	0	0	0	0	0	0	0	0	0	0	2	2

Pitchers ChiW Ed Walsh (W, 1-0), IP 9, H 2, R 0, ER 0, BB 1, SO 12
ChiC Jack Pfiester (L, 0-1), IP 9, H 4, R 3, ER 3, BB 2, SO 9

Top Performers at the Plate
ChiW George Rohe, 1 for 3, 3 RBI

2B-ChiC/Schulte. **3B**-ChiW/Donahue, Rohe. **SB**-ChiW/Rohe. **Time** 2:10. **Attendance** 13,667.

Game 4 Friday, October 12 at South Side Park, Chicago

	1	2	3	4	5	6	7	8	9	R	H	E
Chicago Cubs	0	0	0	0	0	0	1	0	0	1	7	1
Chicago White Sox	0	0	0	0	0	0	0	0	0	0	2	1

Pitchers ChiC Three Finger Brown (W,1-1), IP 9, H 2, R 0, ER 0, BB 2, SO 5
ChiW Nick Altrock (L, 1-1), IP 9, H 7, R 1, ER 1, BB 1, SO 2

Top Performers at the Plate
ChiC Frank Chance, 2 for 4, 1 R; Johnny Evers, 1 for 3, 1 RBI

2B-ChiC/Hofman. **SB**-ChiC/Sheckard. **Time** 1:36. **Attendance** 18,385.

Game 5 Saturday, October 13 at West Side Grounds, Chicago

	1	2	3	4	5	6	7	8	9	R	H	E
Chicago White Sox	1	0	2	4	0	1	0	0	0	8	12	6
Chicago Cubs	3	0	0	1	0	2	0	0	0	6	6	0

Pitchers ChiW Ed Walsh (W, 2-0), IP 6, H 5, R 6, ER 2, BB 5, SO 5; Doc White (Sv, 1), IP 3, H 1, R 0, ER 0, BB 1, SO 1
ChiC Ed Reulbach, IP 2, H 5, R 3, ER 3, BB 2, SO 1; Jack Pfiester (L, 0-2), IP 1⅓, H 3, R 4, ER 4, BB 1, SO 2; Orval Overall, IP 5⅔, H 4, R 1, ER 1, BB 1, SO 5

Top Performers at the Plate
ChiW George Davis, 2 for 5, 2 R, 3 RBI, 2 2B; Frank Isbell, 4 for 5, 3 R, 2 RBI, 4 2B
ChiC Solly Hofman, 1 for 3, 2 R, 2 BB; Frank Schulte, 3 for 5, 1 R, 2 RBI

2B-ChiW/Davis 2, Donahue, Isbell 4, Rohe; ChiC/Chance, Schulte, Steinfeldt. **SB**-ChiW/Davis, Dougherty; ChiC/Evers, Tinker. **Time** 2:40. **Attendance** 23,257.

Game 6 Sunday, October 14 at South Side Park, Chicago

	1	2	3	4	5	6	7	8	9	R	H	E
Chicago Cubs	1	0	0	0	1	0	0	0	1	3	7	0
Chicago White Sox	3	4	0	0	0	0	1	x		8	14	3

Pitchers ChiC Three Finger Brown (L, 1-2), IP 1⅔, H 8, R 7, ER 7, BB 1, SO 0; Orval Overall, IP 6⅓, H 6, R 1, ER 1, BB 2, SO 3
ChiW Doc White (W, 1-1), IP 9, H 7, R 3, ER 3, BB 4, SO 2

Top Performers at the Plate
ChiC Solly Hofman, 2 for 5, 1 R, 1 RBI
ChiW George Davis, 2 for 5, 2 R, 3 RBI; Ed Hahn, 4 for 5, 2 R

2B-ChiC/Evers, Overall, Schulte; ChiW/Davis, Donahue. **SB**-ChiW/Rohe. **Time** 1:55. **Attendance** 19,249.

Chicago Cubs (4) vs. Detroit Tigers (0), 1 tie

1907

Rebounding from their disappointing loss the year before, the Chicago Cubs again found themselves far atop the National League and headed for baseball's Fall Classic in 1907. This time they were matched up against the Detroit Tigers, with their dangerous outfield of Davy Jones, Sam Crawford, and 20-year-old Ty Cobb. In the opening game, the Tigers were on the verge of stealing a win in Chicago, as they carried a 3-1 lead into the bottom of the ninth. The Cubs loaded the bases with a single, a hit batsman and an error, and Frank "Wildfire" Schulte drove in a run on a groundout to first. Tiger starter Wild Bill Donovan was now one out away from a victory. He worked two strikes on pinch hitter Del Howard and then threw strike three by the batter, but the ball also got by catcher Charlie "Boss" Schmidt, allowing Howard to reach first base safely as the tying run came in from third. Detroit's lead slipped away, and after the teams fought for three scoreless extra innings, the game was called after 12 innings on account of darkness—bringing about the first tie game, as well as the first extra-inning game, in World Series play. The 3 runs that Detroit notched in the opening game proved to be half their total run production for the Series. They scattered 1 run in each of the next three games before being shut out by Three Finger Brown in the fifth game. Chicago's pitchers also helped their own cause at the plate. Ed Reulbach contributed to a three-run inning in Game 3 with an RBI single, and Orval Overall's 2-run single in the fifth inning of Game 4 put the Cubs ahead to stay. On the mound, Chicago staff held Detroit to a .209 average for the five games. Ty Cobb, who led the American League in runs batted in, stolen bases and batting average in the regular season, was limited to 4 hits in 20 at-bats, for a Series average 150 points below his regular-season mark, and he stole no bases and drove in no runs. The Chicago hitters, meanwhile, made the most of their opportunities. In the final four games, the Cubs outhit the Tigers by a margin of only 33 to 27, but they outscored them by 10 runs, utilizing sacrifices, stolen bases, walks and Detroit's fielding misplays to their advantage. The Cubs stole 16 bases in the Series, including a record 7 in Game 1. Infielders Harry Steinfeldt and Johnny Evers were particularly effective with the bat. Evers collected 7 hits in 12 at-bats in the first three games, and Steinfeldt batted an impressive .471 for the Series. Timely hitting, aggressive baserunning, solid pitching—and a fortunate passed ball in Game 1—helped the Cubs redeem themselves from the previous year and bring home their first World Series title.

Left: Detroit catcher Charlie Schmidt's passed ball denied the Tigers a win in Game 1.

1907 WORLD SERIES COMPOSITE STATISTICS

CHICAGO CUBS/Frank Chance, Manager

Player	pos	G	AB	R	H	2B	3B	HR	RBI	BB	SO	SB	BA	SA	E	FPct
Three Finger Brown	p	1	3	0	0	0	0	0	0	1	0	0	.000	.000	0	1.000
Frank Chance	1b	4	14	3	3	1	0	0	0	3	2	3	.214	.286	0	1.000
Johnny Evers	2b-ss	5	20	2	7	2	0	0	1	0	1	3	.350	.450	3	.885
Del Howard	1b	2	5	0	1	0	0	0	0	0	2	1	.200	.200	0	1.000
Johnny Kling	c	5	19	2	4	0	0	0	1	1	4	0	.211	.211	1	.972
Pat Moran	ph	1	0	0	0	0	0	0	0	0	0	0	—	—	—	—
Orval Overall	p	2	5	0	1	0	0	0	2	0	1	0	.200	.200	0	1.000
Jack Pfiester	p	1	2	0	0	0	0	0	0	0	1	0	.000	.000	0	—
Ed Reulbach	p	2	5	0	1	0	0	0	1	0	0	0	.200	.200	0	1.000
Frank Schulte	rf	5	20	3	5	0	0	0	2	1	2	0	.250	.250	1	.857
Jimmy Sheckard	lf	5	21	0	5	2	0	0	2	0	4	1	.238	.333	0	1.000
Jimmy Slagle	cf	5	22	3	6	0	0	0	4	2	3	6	.273	.273	1	.929
Harry Steinfeldt	3b	5	17	2	8	1	1	0	2	1	2	1	.471	.647	3	.938
Joe Tinker	ss	5	13	4	2	0	0	0	1	3	3	1	.154	.154	3	.929
Heinie Zimmerman	2b	1	1	0	0	0	0	0	0	0	0	0	.000	.000	0	1.000
Totals		5	167	19	43	6	1	0	16	12	26	16	.257	.305	10	.955

Pitcher	G	GS	CG	IP	H	R	ER	BB	SO	W-L	Sv	ERA
Three Finger Brown	1	1	1	9	7	0	0	1	4	1-0	0	0.00
Orval Overall	2	2	1	18	14	4	2	4	11	1-0	0	1.00
Jack Pfiester	1	1	1	9	9	1	1	3		1-0	0	1.00
Ed Reulbach	2	1	1	12	6	1	1	3	4	1-0	0	0.75
Totals	5	5	4	48	36	6	4	9	22	4-0	0	0.75

DETROIT TIGERS/Hughie Jennings, Manager

Player	pos	G	AB	R	H	2B	3B	HR	RBI	BB	SO	SB	BA	SA	E	FPct
Jimmy Archer	c	1	3	0	0	0	0	0	0	0	1	0	.000	.000	0	1.000
Ty Cobb	rf	5	20	1	4	0	1	0	0	0	3	0	.200	.300	0	1.000
Bill Coughlin	3b	5	20	0	5	0	0	0	0	1	4	1	.250	.250	2	.889
Sam Crawford	cf	5	21	1	5	1	0	0	0	3	0	0	.238	.286	0	1.000
Bill Donovan	p	2	8	0	0	0	0	0	0	0	3	0	.000	.000	0	1.000
Davy Jones	lf	5	17	1	6	0	0	0	0	4	0	3	.353	.353	1	.923
Ed Killian	p	1	2	1	1	0	0	0	0	0	0	0	.500	.500	0	—
George Mullin	p	2	6	0	0	0	0	0	0	0	1	0	.000	.000	0	1.000
Charley O'Leary	ss	5	17	0	1	0	0	0	0	0	1	3	.059	.059	2	.931
Fred Payne	c	2	4	0	1	0	0	0	1	0	0	1	.250	.250	1	.875
Claude Rossman	1b	5	20	1	8	0	1	0	2	1	0	1	.400	.500	1	.981
Germany Schaefer	2b	5	21	1	3	0	0	0	0	0	3	0	.143	.143	1	1.000
Boss Schmidt	c	4	12	0	2	0	0	0	0	2	1	0	.167	.167	2	.929
Ed Siever	p	1	1	0	0	0	0	0	0	0	0	0	.000	.000	0	—
Totals		5	172	6	36	1	2	0	6	9	22	6	.209	.238	9	.957

Pitcher	G	GS	CG	IP	H	R	ER	BB	SO	W-L	Sv	ERA
Bill Donovan	2	2	2	21	17	9	4	5	16	0-1	0	1.71
Ed Killian	1	0	0	4	3	1	1	1	1	0-0	0	2.25
George Mullin	2	2	2	17	16	5	4	6	8	0-2	0	2.12
Ed Siever	1	1	0	4	7	4	2	0	1	0-1	0	4.50
Totals	5	5	4	46	43	19	11	12	26	0-4	0	2.15

Series Outstanding Player: Harry Steinfeldt, Chicago Cubs. **Series Outstanding Pitcher:** Three Finger Brown, Chicago Cubs. **Average Length of Game:** 1 hour, 59 minutes. **Total Attendance:** 78,068. **Average Attendance:** 15,614 (19,797 at West Side Grounds; 9,338 at Bennett Park). **Umpires:** Hank O'Day (NL), Jack Sheridan (AL). **Winning Player's Share:** $2,143. **Losing Player's Share:** $1,946.

Left: Detroit manager Hugh Jennings and his players confer with Cubs skipper Frank Chace.

Below left: Sam Crawford was part of Detroit's all-star outfield in 1907, but his .238 average in the Series was less than impressive.

Below: Three Finger Brown's shutout win in Game 5 gave the Cubs their first Series title.

Below: The Chicago papers were no more merciful than the Cubs in their treatment of the Tigers.

The Chicago Cubs stole 7 bases in Game 3 with Boss Schmidt behind the plate for Detroit, the most thefts against one catcher in a Series game.

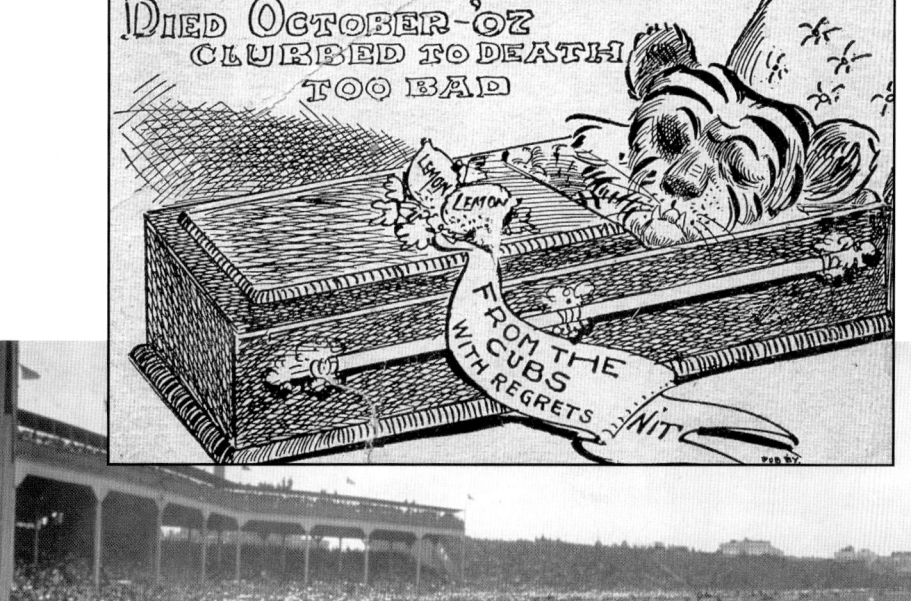

DIED OCTOBER—'07
CLUBBED TO DEATH
TOO BAD

FROM THE CUBS WITH REGRETS

After a Game 1 tie, the Cubs took the Series lead with a 3-1 victory in Game 2 at West Side Grounds, Chicago.

Game 1   Tuesday, October 8 at West Side Grounds, Chicago

	1	2	3	4	5	6	7	8	9	10	11	12	R	H	E
Detroit Tigers	0	0	0	0	0	0	0	3	0	0	0	0	3	9	3
Chicago Cubs	0	0	0	1	0	0	0	2	0	0	0	0	3	10	5

Pitchers   Det   Bill Donovan, IP 12, H 10, R 3, ER 1, BB 3, SO 12
Chi   Orval Overall, IP 9, H 9, R 3, ER 1, BB 2, SO 5; Ed Reulbach, IP 3, H 0, R 0, ER 0, BB 0, SO 2

Top Performers at the Plate
Det   Sam Crawford, 3 for 5, 1 R, 2 RBI; Davy Jones, 3 for 5, 1 R, 1 BB, 2 SB
Chi   Frank Chance, 1 for 4, 2 R, 2 BB; Johnny Kling, 2 for 4, 1 RBI, 1 BB

SB-Det/Jones 2; Chi/Chance, Evers, Howard, Sheckard, Slagle 2, Steinfeldt. **Time** 2:40.
Attendance 24,377.

Game 2   Wednesday, October 9 at West Side Grounds, Chicago

	1	2	3	4	5	6	7	8	9	R	H	E
Detroit Tigers	0	1	0	0	0	0	0	0	0	1	9	1
Chicago Cubs	0	1	0	2	0	0	0	0	x	3	9	1

Pitchers   Det   George Mullin (L, 0-1), IP 8, H 9, R 3, ER 3, BB 3, SO 6
Chi   Jack Pfiester (W, 1-0), IP 9, H 9, R 1, ER 1, BB 1, SO 3

Top Performers at the Plate
Det   Claude Rossman, 3 for 4, 1 R
Chi   Jimmy Slagle, 2 for 3, 1 R, 1 RBI, 2 SB; Joe Tinker, 1 for 2, 1 R, 1 RBI, 1 BB

2B-Chi/Sheckard. **3B**-Det/Rossman. **SB**-Det/Payne; Chi/Chance, Evers, Slagle 2. **Time** 2:13.
Attendance 21,901.

Game 3   Thursday, October 10 at West Side Grounds, Chicago

	1	2	3	4	5	6	7	8	9	R	H	E
Detroit Tigers	0	0	0	0	0	1	0	0	0	1	6	1
Chicago Cubs	0	1	0	3	1	0	0	0	x	5	10	1

Pitchers   Det   Ed Siever (L, 0-1), IP 4, H 7, R 4, ER 2, BB 0, SO 1; Ed Killian, IP 4, H 3, R 1, ER 1, BB 1, SO 1
Chi   Ed Reulbach (W, 1-0), IP 9, H 6, R 1, ER 1, BB 3, SO 2

Top Performers at the Plate
Chi   Johnny Evers, 3 for 4, 1 RBI, 2 2B; Harry Steinfeldt, 2 for 3, 1 R, 1 RBI

2B-Chi/Chance, Evers 2, Sheckard, Steinfeldt. **Time** 1:35. **Attendance** 13,114.

Game 4   Friday, October 11 at Bennett Park, Detroit

	1	2	3	4	5	6	7	8	9	R	H	E
Chicago Cubs	0	0	0	0	2	0	3	0	1	6	7	2
Detroit Tigers	0	0	0	1	0	0	0	0	0	1	5	2

Pitchers   Chi   Orval Overall (W, 1-0), IP 9, H 5, R 1, ER 1, BB 2, SO 6
Det   Bill Donovan (L, 0-1), IP 9, H 7, R 6, ER 3, BB 2, SO 4

Top Performers at the Plate
Chi   Orval Overall, 1 for 2, 2 RBI, 2 SH; Frank Schulte, 1 for 3, 2 R, 1 BB
Det   Bill Coughlin, 3 for 4

3B-Det/Cobb. **SB**-Chi/Chance, Slagle. **Time** 1:45. **Attendance** 11,306.

Game 5   Saturday, October 12 at Bennett Park, Detroit

	1	2	3	4	5	6	7	8	9	R	H	E
Chicago Cubs	1	1	0	0	0	0	0	0	0	2	7	1
Detroit Tigers	0	0	0	0	0	0	0	0	0	0	7	2

Pitchers   Chi   Three Finger Brown (W,1-0), IP 9, H 7, R 0, ER 0, BB 1, SO 4
Det   George Mullin (L, 0-2), IP 9, H 7, R 2, ER 1, BB 3, SO 2

Top Performers at the Plate
Chi   Jimmy Slagle, 1 for 4, 1 R, 1 RBI, 1 BB; Harry Steinfeldt, 3 for 4, 1 RBI

2B-Det/Crawford. **3B**-Chi/Steinfeldt. **SB**-Chi/Evers, Slagle, Tinker; Det/Coughlin, Jones, Rossman.
Time 1:42. **Attendance** 7,370.

Detroit's George Mullin is the only pitcher to lose 20 games during the regular season and appear in a World Series that same year. He was 20-20 in 1907; he went 0-2 in the postseason.

19

Hall of Fame No-Shows

Many of baseball's all-time greats have come onto the World Series stage and offered awesome displays of their talent, competitive will and mastery of the game. The Fall Classic hasn't been classic for everyone, however, and even some of the game's top players have struggled in the postseason.

Underachieving Superstars

Ty Cobb's subpar performance in the 1907 World Series does not stand alone among stars who shone dimly during the postseason. The following players rose to all-star heights from April through September before crashing down in October.

◆ In 1914, Philadelphia's Eddie Collins led the league with 122 runs scored, exactly 122 more than he scored in the World Series that year. His .214 Series average was 130 points lower than his regular-season mark.

◆ Bob Meusel was part of New York's formidable Murderer's Row in 1927, but his 7 strikeouts in the four-game Series set a new record. He collected just 2 hits in 17 at-bats.

◆ A career .358 hitter, Rogers Hornsby stormed to a .380 average in 1929 for the St. Louis Cardinals. His .238 average in that year's Series was well below his standard, as were his eight strikeouts.

Home Run Champs Who Went Homerless in the World Series

A total of 49 regular-season home-run champions have gone on to play in the World Series. 19 of those sluggers were unable to get even one homer in the Fall Classic.

	Season HR Total
Buck Freeman, Boston Red Sox, 1903	13
Harry Davis, Philadelphia Athletics, 1905	8
Sam Crawford, Detroit Tigers, 1908	7
Ty Cobb, Detroit Tigers, 1909	9
Frank "Wildfire" Schulte, Chicago Cubs, 1910	10
Tris Speaker, Boston Red Sox, 1912	10
Frank "Home Run" Baker, Philadelphia Athletics, 1914	9
Gavvy Cravath, Philadelphia Phillies, 1915	24
Dave Robertson, New York Giants, 1917	12
Babe Ruth, Boston Red Sox, 1918	11
George Kelly, New York Giants, 1921	23
Ripper Collins, St. Louis Cardinals, 1934	35
Dolph Camilli, Brooklyn Dodgers, 1941	34
Larry Doby, Cleveland Indians, 1954	32
Willie Mays, San Francisco Giants, 1962	49
Willie Stargell, Pittsburgh Pirates, 1971	48
Graig Nettles, New York Yankees, 1976	32
Gorman Thomas, Milwaukee Brewers, 1982	39
Mike Schmidt, Philadelphia Phillies, 1983	40

Although they didn't lead their league, three other players had 40 or more homers in the regular season but didn't go yard once during the World Series: Lou Gehrig had 47 homers for the 1927 Yankees, Willie Mays had 41 for the 1951 Giants, and Mickey Mantle hit 54 with the 1961 Yankees. In fact, Mays did not hit a single home run in 71 World Series at-bats during his career.

◆ Brooklyn's Dolph Camilli was voted the National League's most valuable player in 1941 after knocking 34 homers and driving in 120 runs, but his postseason stats read 0 home runs, 1 RBI, 6 strikeouts and a .167 average.

◆ Joe Gordon's well-rounded season earned him MVP honors in 1942, but his 7 strikeouts and 2 hits in 21 at-bat's earned him a .095 average in the Series. Gordon also played the goat in the Yankees' final out, getting picked off second base in the ninth inning of Game 7.

◆ Boston great Ted Williams struggled through his only World Series, batting just .200 with no extra-base hits and 1 RBI while striking out five times in 25 at-bats.

◆ 1952 was one of eight All-Star seasons for Dodger Gil Hodges, but in the 1952 World Series he went hitless in 21 times at bat, striking out 6 times.

◆ Brooklyn's Don Newcombe brought home both MVP and Cy Young hardware in 1956, but the Yanks shelled him for 11 runs in less than five innings for a 21.21 Series ERA.

◆ Eddie Mathews's 31 home runs for Milwaukee in 1958 came in a string of nine straight 30-homer seasons. He not only went homerless in the 1958 Series, he also struck out a record 11 times.

◆ Orlando Cepeda struggled mightily through the 1967 Series for St. Louis, connecting for only 3 hits and 1 RBI in 29 at-bats. And he didn't fare much better in his other two appearances; the Hall of Famer batted .171 and hit just 2 homers in 19 career postseason games.

◆ Kansas City's Willie Wilson was tops in the league in runs, hits and triples in 1980, finished second in stolen bases, and batted .326 on the year. In the World Series, he struck out a record 12 times and batted .154.

◆ Baltimore Oriole Cal Ripken's only Series appearance came after an MVP campaign in the 1983 regular season, but after leading the league with 211 hits, he managed just two against the Phillies for a .167 average.

◆ The Oakland A's Jose Canseco took home the MVP award in 1988 with a league-best 42 home runs and 124 RBI, but he had a miserable Series, getting just 1 base hit in 19 at-bats. (The one hit was a grand slam, though.)

◆ Following his record-breaking 61-homer outing in 1961, Yankee Roger Maris batted only .105 and hit just 1 long ball in the postseason. He also led all others with 6 strikeouts.

◆ Maris's teammate, Mickey Mantle, won MVP honors in 1962, but he, too, tanked in October, hitting a measly .120 and driving in no runs.

Top left: Brooklyn's Don Newcombe makes an early exit after yielding 6 runs in the opening game of the 1955 Series. Newcombe finished his career with four losses and no wins in Series play.

Above: Ty Cobb won three batting titles from 1907 to 1909, but he hit only .262 in the World Series over those years, including a rough 4-for-20 in 1907.

Winless Pitchers

Only four men have earned 4 decisions in the World Series without any in the win column. Don Newcombe won 64 games for the Brooklyn Dodgers in the pennant years of 1949, 1955 and 1956, but he was winless with 4 losses in five postseason starts. Charlie Leibrandt went 0-1 with the 1985 Kansas City Royals before losing 3 for the Atlanta Braves in 1991–92. Bill Sherdel lost 2 games for the St. Louis Cardinals in 1926 and in 1928, and Ed Summers had back-to-back 0-2 Series with the Detroit Tigers in 1908–09.

Right: Phil Niekro won 348 games in his 24-year career, but he never played in the Series. It took his brother 21 seasons to see his first Series action.

Below: The great Ernie Banks never once made it to the Fall Classic.

Close But No Cigar: Hall of Famers Who Never Appeared in a World Series

A few of baseball's all-time greats never even got a chance to show their stuff in the Fall Classic. The following is a list of members of the Hall of Fame who never appeared in the World Series, with information on their former teams and Major League tenure:

Luke Appling, Chicago White Sox, 20 seasons, 2,422 games

Ernie Banks, Chicago Cubs, 19 seasons, 2,528 games

Rod Carew, Minnesota Twins / California Angels, 19 seasons, 2,469 games

Rick Ferrell, St. Louis Browns / Boston Red Sox / Washington Senators, 18 seasons, 1,884 games

Elmer Flick, Philadelphia Phillies / Cleveland Indians, 13 seasons, 1,483 games

Harry Heilmann, Detroit Tigers / Cincinnati Reds, 17 seasons, 2,148 games

Ferguson "Fergie" Jenkins, Philadelphia Phillies / Chicago Cubs / Texas Rangers / Boston Red Sox, 19 seasons, 664 games

Addie Joss, Cleveland Indians, 9 seasons, 286 games

George Kell, Philadelphia A's / Detroit Tigers / Boston Red Sox / Chicago White Sox / Baltimore Orioles, 15 seasons, 1,795 games

Ralph Kiner, Pittsburgh Pirates / Chicago Cubs / Cleveland Indians, 10 seasons, 1,472 games

Nap Lajoie, Philadelphia Phillies / Philadelphia A's / Cleveland Indians, 21 seasons, 2,480 games

Ted Lyons, Chicago White Sox, 21 seasons, 594 games

Phil Niekro, Milwaukee/Atlanta Braves, New York Yankees / Cleveland Indians / Toronto Blue Jays, 24 seasons, 864 games

Gaylord Perry, San Francisco Giants / Cleveland Indians / Texas Rangers / San Diego Padres / New York Yankees / Atlanta Braves / Seattle Mariners / Kansas City Royals, 22 seasons, 777 games

George Sisler, St. Louis Browns / Washington Senators / Boston Braves, 15 seasons, 2,055 games

Rube Waddell, Pittsburgh Pirates / Philadelphia Athletics / St. Louis Browns, 13 seasons, 407 games (Waddell was eligible to play in the 1905 Series with Philadelphia but was out with an injury.)

Billy Williams, Chicago Cubs / Oakland A's, 18 seasons, 2,488 games

Though not in the Hall of Fame, Gene Mauch holds the dubious distinction of having the longest managerial stint without a World Series appearance. He managed four different clubs in 3,942 regular-season games during his 26-year career, but did not hand in the lineup card for a single Series game.

Chicago Cubs (4) vs. Detroit Tigers (1)

1908

Thanks to New York's Fred Merkle and the famous "Merkle's Boner" in a late-September Cubs-Giants game (when Merkle's failure to tag second base led to a force-out on what should have been the game-winning hit), the Chicago Cubs wrapped up their third straight pennant by a slim one-game lead in the National League. The Detroit Tigers also repeated as league champs, squeaking by the second-place Indians by a mere half-game. A rematch of the 1907 Series was on. The teams came in with nearly identical squads as the year before, and things started off equally tough for Detroit. Down 5-1 in Game 1, the Tigers scored 3 runs in the seventh inning and 2 in the eighth to take the lead entering the ninth. But the Cubs burst out with six consecutive singles off Ed Summers (a 24-game winner in the regular season) to score 5 runs and win the opener 10-6. The next day in Chicago, Wild Bill Donovan and Orval Overall battled through seven scoreless innings before the Cubs again came through with a big inning. Three singles, a double by Johnny Kling, a triple by Frank Schulte, a homer by Joe Tinker, three stolen bases and a wild pitch brought in 6 runs in the bottom of the eighth. In Game 3, a strong outing on the mound by George Mullin and a stellar performance by Ty Cobb at the plate finally gave Detroit a win. Cobb broke out with 4 hits and 2 runs batted in, and in the ninth inning he stole second and then third base before being caught stealing home. The Tiger lineup was all

but silenced in the next game back in Detroit. Three Finger Brown scattered four hits—two by Cobb and two by Sam Crawford—before retiring the last ten batters of the game to give the Cubs a three-games-to-one lead. A record-low 6,210 fans came out to Bennett Park on October 15 to watch Game 5, and those who did show up didn't have to stay long, as the 1-hour, 25-minute contest was the quickest in Series history. Chicago got on the board right away, scoring once in the first inning on back-to-back-to-back singles. They scored again in the fifth, but one run was all that starter Overall would need. The 27-year-old righty struck out 10 and gave up only 3 hits in the 2-0 shutout. Donovan suffered his second complete-game loss, giving him three losses and no wins to that point in his postseason career. Just as in the previous Fall Classic, Chicago put together a well-rounded hitting attack, speed on the base paths, dominating pitching and nearly flawless fielding against the Tigers, giving them their second title in as many years. The Cubs' luck would soon run out, however. Although they would win the National League pennant twice in the next decade, and seven more times overall, 1908 was the last World Series victory for the team from Wrigley Field.

OVERALL, CHICAGO NAT'L

Left: Orval Overall had pitched two of Chicago's four wins in the series.

1908 WORLD SERIES COMPOSITE STATISTICS

CHICAGO CUBS/Frank Chance, Manager

Player	pos	G	AB	R	H	2B	3B	HR	RBI	BB	SO	SB	BA	SA	E	FPct
Three Finger Brown	p	2	4	0	0	0	0	0	0	0	2	0	.000	.000	0	1.000
Frank Chance	1b	5	19	4	8	0	0	0	2	3	1	5	.421	.421	1	.985
Johnny Evers	2b	5	20	5	7	1	0	0	2	1	2	2	.350	.400	1	.962
Solly Hofman	cf	5	19	2	6	0	1	0	4	1	4	0	.316	.421	0	1.000
Del Howard	ph	1	1	0	0	0	0	0	0	0	0	0	.000	.000	—	—
Johnny Kling	c	5	16	2	4	1	0	0	2	2	2	0	.250	.313	0	1.000
Orval Overall	p	3	6	0	2	0	0	0	0	0	1	0	.333	.333	0	1.000
Jack Pfiester	p	1	2	0	0	0	0	0	0	0	2	0	.000	.000	0	—
Ed Reulbach	p	2	3	0	0	0	0	0	0	0	1	0	.000	.000	0	1.000
Frank Schulte	rf	5	18	4	7	0	1	0	2	2	1	2	.389	.500	0	1.000
Jimmy Sheckard	lf	5	21	2	5	2	0	0	1	2	3	1	.238	.333	0	1.000
Harry Steinfeldt	3b	5	16	3	4	0	0	0	3	2	5	1	.250	.250	1	.938
Joe Tinker	ss	5	19	2	5	0	0	1	4	0	2	2	.263	.421	0	1.000
Totals		**5**	**164**	**24**	**48**	**4**	**2**	**1**	**20**	**13**	**26**	**15**	**.293**	**.360**	**3**	**.986**

Pitcher	G	GS	CG	IP	H	R	ER	BB	SO	W-L	Sv	ERA
Three Finger Brown	2	1	1	11	6	1	0	1	5	2-0	0	0.00
Orval Overall	3	2	2	18⅓	7	2	2	7	15	2-0	0	0.98
Jack Pfiester	1	1	0	8	10	8	7	3	1	0-1	0	7.87
Ed Reulbach	2	1	0	7⅔	9	4	4	1	5	0-0	0	4.70
Totals	**5**	**5**	**3**	**45**	**32**	**15**	**13**	**12**	**26**	**4-1**	**0**	**2.60**

DETROIT TIGERS/Hughie Jennings, Manager

Player	pos	G	AB	R	H	2B	3B	HR	RBI	BB	SO	SB	BA	SA	E	FPct
Ty Cobb	rf	5	19	3	7	1	0	0	4	1	2	2	.368	.421	1	.750
Bill Coughlin	3b	3	8	0	1	0	0	0	1	0	1	0	.125	.125	1	.900
Sam Crawford	cf	5	21	2	5	1	0	0	1	1	2	0	.238	.286	0	1.000
Bill Donovan	p	2	4	0	0	0	0	0	0	1	1	1	.000	.000	1	.750
Red Downs	2b	2	6	1	1	1	0	0	1	1	2	0	.167	.333	1	.909
Davy Jones	ph	3	2	1	0	0	0	0	0	1	1	0	.000	.000	—	—
Ed Killian	p	1	0	0	0	0	0	0	0	0	0	0	—	—	0	1.000
Matty McIntyre	lf	5	18	2	4	1	0	0	0	3	2	1	.222	.278	1	.909
George Mullin	p	1	3	1	1	0	0	0	1	0	0	0	.333	.333	0	1.000
Charley O'Leary	ss	5	19	2	3	0	0	0	0	0	3	0	.158	.158	1	.950
Claude Rossman	1b	5	19	3	4	0	0	0	3	1	4	1	.211	.211	2	.964
Germany Schaefer	2b-3b	5	16	0	2	0	0	0	1	0	4	1	.125	.125	1	.955
Boss Schmidt	c	4	14	0	1	0	0	0	1	0	2	0	.071	.071	0	1.000
Ed Summers	p	2	5	0	1	0	0	0	1	0	2	0	.200	.200	0	1.000
Ira Thomas	ph-c	2	4	0	2	1	0	0	1	1	0	0	.500	.750	0	1.000
George Winter	pr-p	2	0	0	0	0	0	0	0	0	0	0	—	—	0	—
Totals		**5**	**158**	**15**	**32**	**5**	**0**	**0**	**14**	**12**	**26**	**6**	**.203**	**.234**	**9**	**.955**

Pitcher	G	GS	CG	IP	H	R	ER	BB	SO	W-L	Sv	ERA
Bill Donovan	2	2	2	17	17	8	8	4	10	0-2	0	4.24
Ed Killian	1	1	0	2⅓	5	4	3	3	1	0-0	0	11.57
George Mullin	1	1	1	9	7	3	0	1	8	1-0	0	0.00
Ed Summers	2	1	0	14⅔	18	8	7	4	7	0-2	0	4.30
George Winter	1	0	0	1	1	1	0	1	0	0-0	0	0.00
Totals	**5**	**5**	**3**	**44**	**48**	**24**	**18**	**13**	**26**	**1-4**	**0**	**3.68**

Series Outstanding Player: Frank Chance, Chicago Cubs. **Series Outstanding Pitcher:** Three Finger Brown, Chicago Cubs. **Average Length of Game:** 1 hour, 46 minutes. **Total Attendance:** 62,232. **Average Attendance:** 12,446 (16,152 at West Side Grounds; 9,976 at Bennett Park). **Umpires:** Tommy Connolly (AL), Bill Klem (NL), Hank O'Day (NL), Jack Sheridan (AL). **Winning Player's Share:** $1,318. **Losing Player's Share:** $870.

The legendary Ty Cobb rebounded from his 1907 slump by batting .368 in the 1908 Series, but his Tigers again fell to the Cubs.

Batting for Charley O'Leary in the ninth inning of Game 1, Ira Thomas of the Tigers became the first pinch hitter to get a base hit in Series play. He singled off Three Finger Brown and was replaced by a pinch runner.

Detroit's Boss Schmidt grounded out to the catcher for the final out of the Series in Game 5. One year and two days earlier, Schmidt had flied out to end the Tigers' chances in the 1907 Series.

JENNINGS, DETROIT

Above: Hughie Jennings didn't have much to smile about after three consecutive World Series losses from 1907 to 1909.

Game 1 Saturday, October 10 at Bennett Park, Detroit

	1	2	3	4	5	6	7	8	9	R	H	E
Chicago Cubs	0	0	4	0	0	0	1	0	5	10	14	2
Detroit Tigers	1	0	0	0	0	0	3	2	0	6	10	3

Pitchers Chi Ed Reulbach, IP 6⅔, H 8, R 4, ER 4, BB 0, SO 5; Orval Overall, IP ⅓, H 0, R 1, ER 1, BB 1, SO 0; Three Finger Brown (W, 1-0), IP 2, H 2, R 1, ER 0, BB 1, SO 1
Det Ed Killian, IP 2⅓, H 5, R 4, ER 3, BB 3, SO 1; Ed Summers (L, 0-1), IP 6⅔, H 9, R 6, ER 5, BB 1, SO 2

Top Performers at the Plate
Chi Frank Schulte, 2 for 4, 2 R, 1 RBI, 1 SH; Harry Steinfeldt, 2 for 3, 2 R, 2 RBI, 1 BB, 1 SH
Det Ty Cobb, 2 for 4, 2 R, 1 RBI, 1 SH; Claude Rossman, 2 for 4, 1 R, 1 RBI

2B-Chi/Sheckard 2; Det/Downs. **SB**-Chi/Chance 2, Hofman, Tinker 2; Det/McIntyre. **Time** 2:10. **Attendance** 10,812.

Game 2 Sunday, October 11 at West Side Grounds, Chicago

	1	2	3	4	5	6	7	8	9	R	H	E
Detroit Tigers	0	0	0	0	0	0	0	0	1	1	4	1
Chicago Cubs	0	0	0	0	0	0	0	6	x	6	7	0

Pitchers Det Bill Donovan (L, 0-1), IP 8, H 7, R 6, ER 6, BB 1, SO 7
Chi Orval Overall (W, 1-0), IP 9, H 4, R 1, ER 1, BB 2, SO 5

Top Performers at the Plate
Chi Jimmy Sheckard, 1 for 4, 1 R, 1 RBI; Joe Tinker, 1 for 3, 1 R, 2 RBI

2B-Chi/Kling. **3B**-Chi/Schulte. **HR**-Chi/Tinker. **SB**-Det/Schaefer; Chi/Chance, Evers, Sheckard. **Time** 1:30. **Attendance** 17,760.

Game 3 Monday, October 12 at West Side Grounds, Chicago

	1	2	3	4	5	6	7	8	9	R	H	E
Detroit Tigers	1	0	0	0	0	5	0	2	0	8	11	4
Chicago Cubs	0	0	0	3	0	0	0	0	0	3	7	1

Pitchers Det George Mullin (W, 1-0), IP 9, H 7, R 3, ER 0, BB 1, SO 8
Chi Jack Pfiester (L, 0-1), IP 8, H 10, R 8, ER 7, BB 3, SO 1; Ed Reulbach, IP 1, H 1, R 0, ER 0, BB 1, SO 0

Top Performers at the Plate
Det Ty Cobb, 4 for 5, 1 R, 2 RBI, 2 SB; Claude Rossman, 2 for 4, 2 R, 2 RBI, 1 BB
Chi Frank Chance, 2 for 4, 1 R, 1 RBI, 2 SB

2B-Det/Cobb, Thomas. **3B**-Det/Hofman. **SB**-Det/Cobb 2, Rossman; Chi/Chance 2, Steinfeldt. **Time** 2:10. **Attendance** 14,543.

Game 4 Tuesday, October 13 at Bennett Park, Detroit

	1	2	3	4	5	6	7	8	9	R	H	E
Chicago Cubs	0	0	2	0	0	0	0	0	1	3	10	0
Detroit Tigers	0	0	0	0	0	0	0	0	0	0	4	1

Pitchers Chi Three Finger Brown (W, 2-0), IP 9, H 4, R 0, ER 0, BB 0, SO 4
Det Ed Summers (L, 0-2), IP 8, H 9, R 2, ER 2, BB 3, SO 5; George Winter, IP 1, H 1, R 1, ER 0, BB 1, SO 0

Top Performers at the Plate
Chi Frank Chance, 2 for 4, 1 R; Frank Schulte, 2 for 3, 1 R, 2 BB, 2 SB
Det Sam Crawford, 2 for 4; Charley O'Leary, 2 for 4

2B-Det/Crawford. **SB**-Chi/Evers, Hofman, Schulte 2. **Time** 1:35. **Attendance** 12,907.

Game 5 Wednesday, October 14 at Bennett Park, Detroit

	1	2	3	4	5	6	7	8	9	R	H	E
Chicago Cubs	1	0	0	0	1	0	0	0	0	2	10	0
Detroit Tigers	0	0	0	0	0	0	0	0	0	0	3	0

Pitchers Chi Orval Overall (W, 2-0), IP 9, H 3, R 0, ER 0, BB 4, SO 10
Det Bill Donovan (L, 0-2), IP 9, H 10, R 2, ER 2, BB 3, SO 3

Top Performers at the Plate
Chi Frank Chance, 3 for 4, 1 RBI; Johnny Evers, 3 for 4, 1 R, 1 RBI

2B-Chi/Evers; Det/McIntyre. **SB**-Det/Donovan. **Time** 1:25. **Attendance** 6,210.

The 6 consecutive hits given up by Detroit's Ed Summers in the ninth inning of Game 1 are the most in a row allowed by one pitcher in a Series game.

Pittsburgh Pirates (4) vs. Detroit Tigers (3)

When the Pirates dethroned the Cubs from atop the National League and earned a trip to the 1909 World Series, it set up a battle between baseball's foremost hitters. Pittsburgh's Honus Wagner was coming off his 11th straight season batting over .300 and his fourth straight batting title. The Detroit Tigers captured their 3rd pennant in a row, and Ty Cobb's league-leading .377 average, 107 RBI, 216 hits and 76 stolen bases had a lot to do with them getting there. Though these two legendary hitters were the marquee names, other players shone as well. Both pitching staffs featured three starters with at least 19 wins, including Detroit's league-leading 29-game winner George Mullin. But it was a 27-year-old rookie named Charles "Babe" Adams who stole the show. After winning only 12 games for Pittsburgh in the regular season, Adams was responsible for three wins in the postseason, all in complete-game outings; Adams would become the only rookie ever to win three games in a World Series. The Series opened in Pittsburgh, and Adams looked shaky at the outset, walking two of the first three batters he faced. Detroit capitalized and scored one run in the first inning, but that was all they could muster against the rookie. The Pirates managed only five hits off Mullin, but it was enough to secure a 4-1 victory. The Tigers bounced back in Game 2 with seven runs, including a steal of home by Cobb in the third inning. The teams continued to alternate wins over the next five games. Pittsburgh jumped out of the gate with five runs in the first inning of Game 3. Mullin responded in Game 4 with 10 strikeouts and a 5-hit shutout. Babe Adams was dominant again in the fifth game, aided by Fred Clarke's 3-run homer. Another complete-game win by Mullin in Game 6 set the stage for baseball's first winner-take-all Game 7. Adams was back on the hill for Pittsburgh on two days' rest, and Detroit countered with Bill Donovan. Wild Bill didn't last long, however, walking six batters— including two with the bases loaded. George Mullin, making his fourth appearance of the Series, did not fare much better in relief. Pittsburgh scrapped together 6 more runs while Adams held Cobb and the rest of the Tigers in check. Though Detroit outhit Pittsburgh in the Series, the heroic performance by Babe Adams, along with Pittsburgh's timely hitting and aggressive baserunning (a record 18 stolen bases), sent the Tigers to yet another World Series defeat. It would be the great Cobb's last appearance in the Fall Classic, and it was a disappointing one for baseball's all-time leading hitter. It was also Honus Wagner's last Series, though he fared better, batting a solid .333 while stealing 6 bases and driving in 6 runs.

Above: The Bennett Park crowd met yet another disappointment when the home town Tigers dropped Game 3 of the 1909 Series to the Pirates.

1909 WORLD SERIES COMPOSITE STATISTICS

PITTSBURGH PIRATES/Fred Clarke, Manager

Player	pos	G	AB	R	H	2B	3B	HR	RBI	BB	SO	SB	BA	SA	E	FPct
Ed Abbaticchio	ph	1	1	0	0	0	0	0	0	0	0	0	.000	.000	–	–
Bill Abstein	1b	7	26	3	6	2	0	0	2	3	10	1	.231	.308	5	.938
Babe Adams	p	3	9	0	0	0	0	0	0	1	1	0	.000	.000	0	1.000
Bobby Byrne	3b	7	24	5	6	1	0	0	0	1	4	1	.250	.292	0	1.000
Howie Camnitz	p	2	1	0	0	0	0	0	0	0	0	0	.000	.000	0	1.000
Fred Clarke	lf	7	19	7	4	0	0	2	7	5	3	3	.211	.526	1	.950
George Gibson	c	7	25	2	6	2	0	0	2	1	1	2	.240	.320	0	1.000
Ham Hyatt	cf	2	4	1	0	0	0	0	1	1	0	0	.000	.000	0	–
Tommy Leach	cf-3b	7	25	8	9	4	0	0	2	2	1	1	.360	.520	0	1.000
Lefty Leifield	p	1	1	0	0	0	0	0	0	0	1	0	.000	.000	0	1.000
Nick Maddox	p	1	4	0	0	0	0	0	0	0	1	0	.000	.000	0	1.000
Dots Miller	2b	7	28	2	7	1	0	0	4	2	5	3	.250	.286	2	.938
Paddy O'Connor	ph	1	0	0	0	0	0	0	0	0	1	0	.000	.000	–	–
Deacon Phillippe	p	2	1	0	0	0	0	0	0	0	1	0	.000	.000	2	.600
Honus Wagner	ss	7	24	4	8	2	1	0	6	4	2	6	.333	.500	3	.923
Vic Willis	p	2	4	0	0	0	0	0	0	0	1	0	.000	.000	0	1.000
Chief Wilson	rf	7	26	2	4	1	0	0	1	0	2	1	.154	.192	1	.800
Totals		**7**	**223**	**34**	**50**	**13**	**1**	**2**	**25**	**20**	**34**	**18**	**.224**	**.318**	**14**	**.951**

Pitcher	G	GS	CG	IP	H	R	ER	BB	SO	W-L	Sv	ERA
Babe Adams	3	3	3	27	18	5	4	6	11	3-0	0	1.33
Howie Camnitz	2	1	0	3⅔	8	6	4	2	2	0-1	0	9.82
Lefty Leifield	1	1	0	4	7	5	5	1	0	0-1	0	11.25
Nick Maddox	1	1	1	9	10	6	1	2	4	1-0	0	1.00
Deacon Phillippe	2	0	0	6	2	0	0	1	2	0-0	0	0.00
Vic Willis	2	1	0	11⅓	10	6	5	8	3	0-1	0	3.97
Totals	**7**	**7**	**4**	**61**	**55**	**28**	**19**	**20**	**22**	**4-3**	**0**	**2.80**

DETROIT TIGERS/Hughie Jennings, Manager

Player	pos	G	AB	R	H	2B	3B	HR	RBI	BB	SO	SB	BA	SA	E	FPct
Donie Bush	ss	7	23	5	6	1	0	0	3	5	3	1	.261	.304	5	.844
Ty Cobb	rf	7	26	3	6	3	0	0	5	2	2	2	.231	.346	1	.889
Sam Crawford	cf-1b	7	28	4	7	3	0	1	4	1	1	1	.250	.464	2	.900
Jim Delahanty	2b	7	26	2	9	4	0	0	4	2	5	0	.346	.500	2	.931
Bill Donovan	p	2	4	0	0	0	0	0	0	1	0	0	.000	.000	1	.833
Davy Jones	lf-cf	7	30	6	7	0	0	1	1	2	1	1	.233	.333	1	.933
Tom Jones	1b	7	24	3	6	1	0	0	2	2	0	1	.250	.292	1	.987
Matty McIntyre	lf	4	3	0	0	0	0	0	0	0	1	0	.000	.000	0	–
George Moriarty	3b	7	22	4	6	1	0	0	1	3	1	0	.273	.318	0	1.000
George Mullin	p	6	16	1	3	1	0	0	0	1	3	0	.188	.250	0	1.000
Charley O'Leary	3b	1	3	0	0	0	0	0	0	0	0	0	.000	.000	0	1.000
Boss Schmidt	c	6	18	0	4	2	0	0	4	2	0	0	.222	.333	4	.913
Oscar Stanage	c	2	5	0	1	0	0	0	2	0	2	0	.200	.200	0	1.000
Ed Summers	p	2	3	0	0	0	0	0	0	0	2	0	.000	.000	0	1.000
Ed Willett	p	2	2	0	0	0	0	0	0	0	0	0	.000	.000	1	.800
Ralph Works	p	1	0	0	0	0	0	0	0	0	0	0	–	–	0	1.000
Totals		**7**	**233**	**28**	**55**	**16**	**0**	**2**	**26**	**20**	**22**	**6**	**.236**	**.330**	**18**	**.938**

Pitcher	G	GS	CG	IP	H	R	ER	BB	SO	W-L	Sv	ERA
Bill Donovan	2	2	1	12	7	4	4	8	7	1-1	0	3.00
George Mullin	4	3	3	32	23	14	8	8	20	2-1	0	2.25
Ed Summers	2	2	0	7⅓	13	13	7	4	4	0-2	0	8.59
Ed Willett	2	0	0	7⅔	3	1	0	0	1	0-0	0	0.00
Ralph Works	1	0	0	2	4	2	2	0	2	0-0	0	9.00
Totals	**7**	**7**	**4**	**61**	**50**	**34**	**21**	**20**	**34**	**3-4**	**0**	**3.10**

Series Outstanding Player: Tommy Leach, Pittsburgh Pirates. **Series Outstanding Pitcher:** Babe Adams, Pittsburgh Pirates. **Average Length of Game:** 1 hour, 56 minutes. **Total Attendance:** 145,295. **Average Attendance:** 20,756 (27,295 at Forbes Field; 15,853 at Bennett Park). **Umpires:** Billy Evans (AL), Jim Johnstone (NL), Bill Klem (NL), Francis O'Loughlin (AL). **Winning Player's Share:** $1,825. **Losing Player's Share:** $1,275.

Left: Honus Wagner connected for 8 hits and drove in 6 runs in 1909, his final postseason appearance.

Fred Clarke was walked 4 times in 4 plate appearances in Game 7. The 4 bases on balls set a record for a Series game that has been tied but never broken.

Left: Pirates (from left) Fred Clarke, Tommy Leach and Honus Wagner.

By earning the loss in Game 7, Detroit's Wild Bill Donovan became the first pitcher to lose the deciding game in consecutive World Series. (Christy Mathewson matched the dubious achievement in 1912-13.)

Right: Tommy Leach outclassed hitting legends Ty Cobb and Honus Wagner with his 8 runs and .360 average in the 1909 Series.

Game 1   Friday, October 8 at Forbes Field, Pittsburgh

	1	2	3	4	5	6	7	8	9	R	H	E
Detroit Tigers	1	0	0	0	0	0	0	0	0	1	6	4
Pittsburgh Pirates	0	0	0	1	2	1	0	0	x	4	5	0

Pitchers   Det   George Mullin (L, 0-1), IP 8, H 5, R 4, ER 1, BB 1, SO 4
Pit   Babe Adams (W, 1-0), IP 9, H 6, R 1, ER 1, BB 4, SO 2

Top Performers at the Plate
Det   Davy Jones, 2 for 3, 1 BB
Pit   George Gibson, 1 for 3, 1 R, 1 RBI; Honus Wagner, 1 for 3, 1 R, 1 HBP

2B-Pit/Gibson, Wagner. **HR**-Pit/Clarke. **SB**-Det/Cobb; Pit/Miller, Wilson. **Time** 1:55.
Attendance 29,264.

Game 2   Saturday, October 9 at Forbes Field, Pittsburgh

	1	2	3	4	5	6	7	8	9	R	H	E
Detroit Tigers	0	2	3	0	2	0	0	0	0	7	9	3
Pittsburgh Pirates	2	0	0	0	0	0	0	0	0	2	5	1

Pitchers   Det   Bill Donovan (W, 1-0), IP 9, H 5, R 2, ER 2, BB 2, SO 7
Pit   Howie Camnitz (L, 0-1), IP 2⅓, H 6, R 5, ER 4, BB 1, SO 2; Vic Willis, IP 6⅔,
H 3, R 2, ER 2, BB 4, SO 2

Top Performers at the Plate
Det   Jim Delahanty, 1 for 3, 1 R, 2 RBI, 1 BB; Boss Schmidt, 2 for 4, 4 RBI
Pit   Tommy Leach, 2 for 4, 1 R, 1 RBI, 2 2B

2B-Det/Crawford, Schmidt; Pit/Leach 2, Miller. **SB**-Det/Cobb; Det/Gibson, Wagner. **Time** 1:45.
Attendance 30,915.

Game 3   Monday, October 11 at Bennett Park, Detroit

	1	2	3	4	5	6	7	8	9	R	H	E
Pittsburgh Pirates	5	1	0	0	0	0	0	0	2	8	10	2
Detroit Tigers	0	0	0	0	0	0	4	0	2	6	10	5

Pitchers   Pit   Nick Maddox (W, 1-0), IP 9, H 10, R 6, ER 1, BB 2, SO 4
Det   Ed Summers (L, 0-1), IP ⅓, H 3, R 5, ER 0, BB 1, SO 0; Ed Willett, IP 6⅔, H 3,
R 1, ER 0, BB 0, SO 0; Ralph Works, IP 2, H 4, R 2, ER 2, BB 0, SO 2

Top Performers at the Plate
Pit   Tommy Leach, 2 for 4, 3 R, 1 HBP; Honus Wagner, 3 for 5, 1 R, 2 RBI, 3 SB
Det   Donie Bush, 3 for 5, 1 R, 2 RBI; Ty Cobb, 2 for 5, 2 RBI

2B-Pit/Abstein, Leach; Det/Cobb, Delahanty 2. **SB**-Pit/Wagner 3. **Time** 1:56. **Attendance** 18,277.

Game 4   Tuesday, October 12 at Bennett Park, Detroit

	1	2	3	4	5	6	7	8	9	R	H	E
Pittsburgh Pirates	0	0	0	0	0	0	0	0	0	0	5	6
Detroit Tigers	0	2	0	3	0	0	0	0	x	5	8	0

Pitchers   Pit   Lefty Leifield (L, 0-1), IP 4, H 7, R 5, ER 5, BB 1, SO 0; Deacon Phillippe, IP 4,
H 1, R 0, ER 0, BB 1, SO 1
Det   George Mullin (W, 1-1), IP 9, H 5, R 0, ER 0, BB 2, SO 10

Top Performers at the Plate
Det   Ty Cobb, 1 for 3, 2 RBI, 1 HBP; George Moriarty, 2 for 4, 1 R

2B-Pit/Byrne; Det/Bush, Cobb. **SB**-Pit/Byrne, Leach. **Time** 1:57. **Attendance** 17,036.

Game 5   Wednesday, October 13 at Forbes Field, Pittsburgh

	1	2	3	4	5	6	7	8	9	R	H	E
Detroit Tigers	1	0	0	0	0	2	0	1	0	4	6	1
Pittsburgh Pirates	1	1	1	0	0	0	4	1	x	8	10	2

Pitchers   Det   Ed Summers (L, 0-2), IP 7, H 10, R 8, ER 7, BB 3, SO 4; Ed Willett, IP 1, H 0,
R 0, ER 0, BB 0, SO 1
Pit   Babe Adams (W, 2-0), IP 9, H 6, R 4, ER 3, BB 1, SO 8

Top Performers at the Plate
Det   Sam Crawford, 3 for 4, 2 R, 2 RBI; Davy Jones, 1 for 4, 1 R, 1 RBI
Pit   Fred Clarke, 2 for 2, 2 R, 3 RBI, 1 BB, 1 SH; George Gibson, 2 for 4, 1 R, 1 RBI

2B-Det/Crawford, T. Jones; Pit/Wilson. **HR**-Det/Crawford, D. Jones; Pit/Clarke. **SB**-Det/Crawford,
T. Jones; Pit/Clarke, Gibson, Wagner 2. **Time** 1:46. **Attendance** 21,706.

Game 6   Thursday, October 14 at Bennett Park, Detroit

	1	2	3	4	5	6	7	8	9	R	H	E
Pittsburgh Pirates	3	0	0	0	0	0	0	0	1	4	8	3
Detroit Tigers	1	0	0	2	1	1	0	0	x	5	10	2

Pitchers   Pit   Vic Willis (L, 0-1), IP 5, H 7, R 4, ER 2, BB 4, SO 1; Howie Camnitz, IP 1, H 2,
R 1, ER 1, BB 1, SO 0; Deacon Phillippe, IP 2, H 1, R 0, ER 0, BB 0, SO 1
Det   George Mullin (W, 2-1), IP 9, H 8, R 4, ER 3, BB 1, SO 5

Top Performers at the Plate
Pit   Dots Miller, 2 for 3, 1 R, 1 BB; Honus Wagner, 1 for 4, 2 RBI
Det   Donie Bush, 1 for 2, 2 R, 2 BB, 1 HBP; Jim Delahanty, 2 for 4, 1 RBI

2B-Pit/Wagner; Det/Cobb, Crawford, Delahanty, Mullin. **SB**-Pit/Miller; Det/Bush, D. Jones.
Time 2:00. **Attendance** 10,535.

Game 7   Saturday, October 16 at Bennett Park, Detroit

	1	2	3	4	5	6	7	8	9	R	H	E
Pittsburgh Pirates	0	2	0	2	0	3	0	1	0	8	7	0
Detroit Tigers	0	0	0	0	0	0	0	0	0	0	6	3

Pitchers   Pit   Babe Adams (W, 3-0), IP 9, H 6, R 0, ER 0, BB 1, SO 1
Det   Bill Donovan (L, 1-1), IP 3, H 2, R 2, ER 2, BB 6, SO 0; George Mullin, IP 6,
H 5, R 6, ER 4, BB 4, SO 1

Top Performers at the Plate
Pit   Tommy Leach, 2 for 3, 2 R, 1 BB, 1 SH; Honus Wagner, 1 for 3, 1 R, 2 RBI, 2 BB
Det   Jim Delahanty, 2 for 3, 1 BB

2B-Pit/Abstein, Gibson, Leach; Det/Delahanty, Moriarty, Schmidt. **3B**-Pit/Wagner. **SB**-Pit/Abstein,
Clarke 2, Miller. **Time** 2:10. **Attendance** 17,562.

Philadelphia Athletics (4) vs. Chicago Cubs (1)

For the fourth time in five years, the Chicago Cubs charged into baseball's championship as heavy favorites. On the other side of the diamond sat Connie Mack's Athletics. The Philadelphia club had won its first pennant in five years, but this was a team on the verge of a minor dynasty of its own. The A's came into the Series with four pitchers who won more than 15 games that season, but Mack needed only two to dispose of the Cubs in five games. Thirty-one-game-winner Jack Coombs and Charles "Chief" Bender pitched all 45²/₃ innings for Philadelphia, striking out 31 and allowing only 14 earned runs. (The two also went 7 for 19 at the plate, for a .368 batting average.) Bender started the Series opener at Shibe Park and coasted to a 4-1 victory while pitching no-hit ball for seven innings. The next day, Coombs outmatched Chicago's Three Finger Brown. Brown was knocked for 13 hits and 9 runs, including 6 runs and 3 doubles in the seventh, before being pulled from the game. With only one day's rest, Coombs returned to the mound for Game 3 and walked away with another easy win. Philadelphia scored 8 runs in the first three innings, bouncing out starter Ed Reulbach and reliever Harry McIntire in the process. Danny Murphy's 3-run homer in the third became a source of controversy when Chicago's player-manager Frank Chance insisted that it should have been declared a ground-rule double. His vociferous objections resulted only in his ejection—making him the first player ejected in the World Series. Coombs helped his own cause in the game by getting 3 hits and driving in 3 runs. The Cubs avoided a clean sweep by pulling out a tight win in Game 4. Trailing 3-2 going into the bottom of the ninth, they knotted the score on a triple by Chance before putting the game away in the tenth with a two-out RBI single by Jimmy Sheckard. Brown and Coombs matched up again in the fifth game, and both pitchers went the distance, but once again Coombs came out the victor. Brown allowed only 4 hits through seven innings and kept the game close at 2-1, but the floodgates opened in the eighth when Philadelphia connected for 5 runs. It was Coombs's third win in six days, and Philadelphia's first of three World Series titles in four years. Hall of Fame second baseman Eddie Collins led the way with a .429 average and four stolen bases, and Frank Baker, another future Cooperstown inductee, chipped in with a .409 average and 6 runs scored. As a team, the A's batted a commanding .316, establishing a record that would stand for half a century. On the losing side, Chicago's Frank Chance provided leadership on the field as well as in the dugout, batting a stellar .353 and playing flawless second base in addition to his managerial duties.

Above: The A's ace Jack Coombs tossed three complete-game wins in the 1910 series.

1910 WORLD SERIES COMPOSITE STATISTICS

PHILADELPHIA ATHLETICS/Connie Mack, Manager

Player	pos	G	AB	R	H	2B	3B	HR	RBI	BB	SO	SB	BA	SA	E	FPct
Frank Baker	3b	5	22	6	9	3	0	0	4	2	1	0	.409	.545	3	.864
Jack Barry	ss	5	17	3	4	2	0	0	3	1	3	0	.235	.353	0	1.000
Chief Bender	p	2	6	1	2	0	0	0	1	1	1	0	.333	.333	0	1.000
Eddie Collins	2b	5	21	5	9	4	0	0	3	2	0	4	.429	.619	1	.972
Jack Coombs	p	3	13	0	5	1	0	0	3	0	3	0	.385	.462	2	.667
Harry Davis	1b	5	17	5	6	3	0	0	2	3	4	0	.353	.529	3	.939
Topsy Hartsel	lf	1	5	2	1	0	0	0	0	0	1	2	.200	.200	0	1.000
Jack Lapp	c	1	4	0	1	0	0	0	1	0	2	0	.250	.250	0	1.000
Bris Lord	lf-cf	5	22	3	4	2	0	0	1	1	3	0	.182	.273	0	1.000
Danny Murphy	rf	5	20	6	7	3	0	1	9	1	0	1	.350	.650	0	1.000
Amos Strunk	cf	4	18	2	5	1	1	0	2	2	5	0	.278	.444	1	.875
Ira Thomas	c	4	12	2	3	0	0	0	1	4	1	0	.250	.250	1	.972
Totals		5	177	35	56	19	1	1	30	17	24	7	.316	.452	11	.947

Pitcher	G	GS	CG	IP	H	R	ER	BB	SO	W-L	Sv	ERA
Chief Bender	2	2	2	18²/₃	12	5	4	4	14	1-1	0	1.93
Jack Coombs	3	3	3	27	23	10	10	14	17	3-0	0	3.33
Totals	5	5	5	45²/₃	35	15	14	18	31	4-1	0	2.76

CHICAGO CUBS/Frank Chance, Manager

Player	pos	G	AB	R	H	2B	3B	HR	RBI	BB	SO	SB	BA	SA	E	FPct
Jimmy Archer	1b-c	3	11	1	2	1	0	0	0	0	3	0	.182	.273	0	1.000
Ginger Beaumont	ph	3	2	1	0	0	0	0	0	1	1	0	.000	.000	–	–
Three Finger Brown	p	3	7	0	0	0	0	0	0	0	1	0	.000	.000	1	.909
Frank Chance	1b	5	17	1	6	1	1	0	4	0	3	0	.353	.529	0	1.000
King Cole	p	1	2	0	0	0	0	0	0	0	2	0	.000	.000	0	1.000
Solly Hofman	cf	5	15	2	4	0	0	0	2	4	3	0	.267	.267	1	.875
John Kane	pr	1	0	0	0	0	0	0	0	0	0	0	–	–	–	–
Johnny Kling	c	5	13	0	1	0	0	0	1	1	2	0	.077	.077	0	1.000
Harry McIntire	p	2	1	0	0	0	0	0	0	0	1	0	.000	.000	1	.500
Tom Needham	ph	1	1	0	0	0	0	0	0	0	0	0	.000	.000	–	–
Orval Overall	p	1	1	0	0	0	0	0	0	0	0	0	.000	.000	0	–
Jack Pfiester	p	1	2	0	0	0	0	0	0	0	1	0	.000	.000	0	1.000
Ed Reulbach	p	1	0	0	0	0	0	0	0	0	0	0	–	–	0	1.000
Lew Richie	p	1	0	0	0	0	0	0	0	0	0	0	–	–	0	–
Frank Schulte	rf	5	17	3	6	3	0	0	2	2	3	0	.353	.529	1	.800
Jimmy Sheckard	lf	5	14	5	4	2	0	0	1	7	2	1	.286	.429	1	.900
Harry Steinfeldt	3b	5	20	0	2	1	0	0	1	0	4	0	.100	.150	4	.778
Joe Tinker	ss	5	18	2	6	2	0	0	2	2	2	1	.333	.444	2	.923
Heinie Zimmerman	2b	5	17	0	4	1	0	0	2	1	3	1	.235	.294	1	.967
Totals		5	158	15	35	11	1	0	13	18	31	3	.222	.304	12	.945

Pitcher	G	GS	CG	IP	H	R	ER	BB	SO	W-L	Sv	ERA
Three Finger Brown	3	2	1	18	23	16	11	7	14	1-2	0	5.50
King Cole	1	1	0	8	10	3	3	3	5	0-0	0	3.38
Harry McIntire	2	0	0	5¹/₃	4	5	4	3	3	0-1	0	6.75
Orval Overall	1	1	0	3	6	3	3	1	1	0-1	0	9.00
Jack Pfiester	1	0	0	6²/₃	9	5	0	1	1	0-0	0	0.00
Ed Reulbach	1	1	0	2	3	3	2	2	0	0-0	0	9.00
Lew Richie	1	0	0	1	1	0	0	0	0	0-0	0	0.00
Totals	5	5	1	44	56	35	23	17	24	1-4	0	4.70

Series Outstanding Player: Danny Murphy, Philadelphia Athletics. **Series Outstanding Pitcher:** Jack Coombs, Philadelphia Athletics. **Average Length of Game:** 2 hours, 9 minutes. **Total Attendance:** 124,222. **Average Attendance:** 24,844 (25,744 at Shibe Park; 24,245 at West Side Grounds). **Umpires:** Tommy Connolly (AL), Hank O'Day (NL), Cy Rigler (NL), Jack Sheridan (AL). **Winning Player's Share:** $2,068. **Losing Player's Share:** $1,375.

Action during Game 2 at Shibe Park in Philadelphia. The Athletics cruised to a 9-3 win while banging out 14 hits.

Left: Connie Mack returned to the World Series in 1910 and claimed his first of three titles over the next four years.

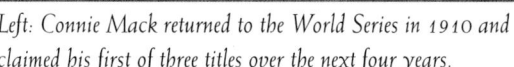

In Game 2, all nine players in the Philadelphia lineup got at least one base hit, the first time a team accomplished such a feat in the World Series.

Left: Danny Murphy knocked in 9 of the A's 30 series runs.

Above: Right fielder Frank Schulte batted a strong .353 for Chicago in the 1910 Series.

When Jimmy Archer took first base for Chicago in Game 3, he became the first player to appear in the World Series for both leagues. In 1907, Archer played in one game for the Detroit Tigers, against the Cubs.

Game 1   Monday, October 17 at Shibe Park, Philadelphia

	1	2	3	4	5	6	7	8	9	R	H	E
Chicago Cubs	0	0	0	0	0	0	0	0	1	1	3	1
Philadelphia Athletics	0	2	1	0	0	0	0	1	x	4	7	2

Pitchers   Chi   Orval Overall (L, 0-1), IP 3, H 6, R 3, ER 3, BB 1, SO 1; Harry McIntire, IP 5, H 1, R 1, ER 0, BB 3, SO 3
Phi   Chief Bender (W, 1-0), IP 9, H 3, R 1, ER 0, BB 2, SO 8

Top Performers at the Plate
Phi   Frank Baker, 3 for 4, 1 R, 2 RBI, 2 2B; Danny Murphy, 1 for 3, 1 R, 1 RBI

2B-Phi/Baker 2, Lord. **SB**-Phi/Murphy. **Time** 1:54. **Attendance** 26,891.

Game 2   Tuesday, October 18 at Shibe Park, Philadelphia

	1	2	3	4	5	6	7	8	9	R	H	E
Chicago Cubs	1	0	0	0	0	0	1	0	1	3	8	3
Philadelphia Athletics	0	0	2	0	1	0	6	0	x	9	14	4

Pitchers   Chi   Three Finger Brown (L, 0-1), IP 7, H 13, R 9, ER 7, BB 4, SO 6; Lew Richie, IP 1, H 1, R 0, ER 0, BB 0, SO 0
Phi   Jack Coombs (W, 1-0), IP 9, H 8, R 3, ER 3, BB 9, SO 5

Top Performers at the Plate
Chi   Frank Chance, 2 for 5, 1 RBI; Heinie Zimmerman, 1 for 3, 2 RBI, 1 SH, 1 BB
Phi   Eddie Collins, 3 for 4, 2 R, 1 RBI, 2 2B, 2 SB; Harry Davis, 2 for 5, 1 R, 2 RBI

2B-Chi/Sheckard, Steinfeldt, Tinker, Zimmerman; Phi/Collins 2, Davis, Murphy, Strunk. **SB**-Phi/Collins 2. **Time** 2:25. **Attendance** 24,597.

Game 3   Thursday, October 20 at West Side Grounds, Chicago

	1	2	3	4	5	6	7	8	9	R	H	E
Philadelphia Athletics	1	2	5	0	0	0	4	0	0	12	15	1
Chicago Cubs	1	2	0	0	0	0	2	0		5	6	5

Pitchers   Phi   Jack Coombs (W, 2-0), IP 9, H 6, R 5, ER 5, BB 4, SO 8
Chi   Ed Reulbach, IP 2, H 3, R 3, ER 2, BB 2, SO 0; Harry McIntire (L, 0-1), IP ⅓, H 3, R 4, ER 4, BB 0, SO 0; Jack Pfiester, IP 6⅔, H 9, R 5, ER 0, BB 1, SO 1

Top Performers at the Plate
Phi   Jack Barry, 3 for 5, 3 R, 3 RBI, 2 2B; Harry Davis, 3 for 3, 3 R, 1 BB, 1 HBP
Chi   Frank Schulte, 2 for 4, 2 RBI, 2 2B; Joe Tinker, 3 for 4, 1 R

2B-Phi/Barry 2, Coombs, Davis; Chi/Schulte 2, Tinker. **HR**-Phi/Murphy. **SB**-Chi/Tinker. **Time** 2:07. **Attendance** 26,210.

Game 4   Saturday, October 22 at West Side Grounds, Chicago

	1	2	3	4	5	6	7	8	9	10	R	H	E
Philadelphia Athletics	0	0	1	2	0	0	0	0	0	0	3	11	3
Chicago Cubs	1	0	0	1	0	0	0	0	1	1	4	9	1

Pitchers   Phi   Chief Bender (L, 1-1), IP 9⅔, H 9, R 4, ER 4, BB 2, SO 6
Chi   King Cole, IP 8, H 10, R 3, ER 3, BB 3, SO 5; Three Finger Brown (W,1-1), IP 2, H 1, R 0, ER 0, BB 0, SO 1

Top Performers at the Plate
Phi   Frank Baker, 3 for 4, 1 R, 1 BB; Danny Murphy, 2 for 4, 2 RBI, 1 SH
Chi   Frank Chance, 2 for 4, 2 RBI; Solly Hofman, 2 for 3, 1 RBI, 1 SH

2B-Phi/Baker, Davis, Murphy; Chi/Archer, Schulte. **3B**-Phi/Strunk; Chi/Chance. **SB**-Chi/Sheckard. **Time** 2:14. **Attendance** 19,150.

Game 5   Sunday, October 23 at West Side Grounds, Chicago

	1	2	3	4	5	6	7	8	9	R	H	E
Philadelphia Athletics	1	0	0	0	1	0	0	5	0	7	9	1
Chicago Cubs	0	1	0	0	0	0	0	1	0	2	9	2

Pitchers   Phi   Jack Coombs (W, 3-0), IP 9, H 9, R 2, ER 2, BB 1, SO 4
Chi   Three Finger Brown (L, 1-2), IP 9, H 9, R 7, ER 4, BB 3, SO 7

Top Performers at the Plate
Phi   Eddie Collins, 3 for 5, 2 RBI, 2 2B, 1 SB; Danny Murphy, 2 for 4, 2 R, 1 RBI
Chi   Frank Chance, 2 for 4, 1 R, 1 RBI; Jimmy Sheckard, 2 for 4, 1 R

2B-Phi/Collins 2, Lord, Murphy; Chi/Chance, Sheckard. **SB**-Phi/Collins 2, Hartsel 2; Chi/Zimmerman. **Time** 2:06. **Attendance** 27,374.

Philadelphia Athletics (4) vs. New York Giants (2)

Connie Mack and his "$100,000 Infield" of Stuffy McInnis, Eddie Collins, Jack Barry and Frank Baker were once again atop the American League in 1911, set to square off against John McGraw's Giants in a rematch of the 1905 Series. Chief Bender and Christy Mathewson faced off in Game 1 with more than 38,000 in attendance at New York's newly rebuilt Polo Grounds. The two aces pitched exquisitely, each allowing only a single earned run, but Matty's Giants prevailed 2-1, scoring their first run in the 4th inning without a base hit. The 36-year-old Eddie Plank, back at full strength after missing the 1910 Series with a shoulder injury, went up against Rube Marquard for another pitcher's duel in the second game. This time Philadelphia squeaked out a narrow victory, with Frank Baker's 2-run homer in the sixth providing the difference. New York's Josh Devore was a Plank strikeout victim four times in the game, and Devore opened up the bottom half of the first inning of Game 3 with another strikeout, for his fifth consecutive K, this one against Jack Coombs. Coombs would strike out six more in 11 innings while giving up only 3 hits in that third game. Mathewson also went the distance, shutting Philly out for eight innings until Frank "Home Run" Baker tied the game at 1-1 with his second homer of the Series—earning him the nickname that would stick for the rest of his career. Errors by Buck Herzog (his third of the game) and Art Fletcher in

the top of the 11th led to a pair of runs for the A's and a 2-games-to-1 lead. Rain delayed the start of the next game for six days, allowing McGraw to go with Mathewson for a third start. But Mathewson did not fare so well, while Bender held the Giants to 2 first-inning runs. The second extra-inning affair of the Series took place the following afternoon, and the Giants stayed alive for another day. Philadelphia held a 3-0 lead through six innings, but New York rallied for 1 in the seventh and two in the ninth to tie the game. A double by Larry Doyle was followed by a sacrifice bunt and a sacrifice fly to bring Doyle around to score. Umpire Bill Klem later said that Doyle never touched home plate, but since the A's failed to notice, the play went unprotested. Philadelphia just about doubled its run production of the previous five games with a 13-run explosion in Game 6. A 4-run fourth and a 7-run seventh helped seal the deal for Mack's crew. Continuing on Philadelphia's dominance of the Giant lineup, Bender held New York to just four hits in the final game, giving New York a .175 average for the Series. Worse still from McGraw's perspective, the team that stole a record 347 bases in the regular season was held to just 4 in the six games.

Above: New York manager John McGraw and Philadelphia captain Harry Davis confer with the umpires before the start of the 1911 Series.

1911 WORLD SERIES COMPOSITE STATISTICS

PHILADELPHIA ATHLETICS/Connie Mack, Manager

Player	pos	G	AB	R	H	2B	3B	HR	RBI	BB	SO	SB	BA	SA	E	FPct
Frank Baker	3b	6	24	7	9	2	0	2	5	1	5	0	.375	.708	2	.913
Jack Barry	ss	6	19	2	7	4	0	0	2	0	2	2	.368	.579	3	.870
Chief Bender	p	3	11	0	1	0	0	0	0	0	1	0	.091	.091	0	1.000
Eddie Collins	2b	6	21	4	6	1	0	0	1	2	2	2	.286	.333	4	.897
Jack Coombs	p	2	8	1	2	0	0	0	0	0	0	0	.250	.250	0	1.000
Harry Davis	1b	6	24	3	5	1	0	0	5	0	3	0	.208	.250	0	1.000
Jack Lapp	c	2	8	1	2	0	0	0	0	0	1	0	.250	.250	0	1.000
Bris Lord	lf	6	27	2	5	2	0	0	1	0	5	0	.185	.259	0	1.000
Stuffy McInnis	1b	1	0	0	0	0	0	0	0	0	0	0	—	—	0	1.000
Danny Murphy	rf	6	23	4	7	3	0	0	3	0	3	0	.304	.435	1	.889
Rube Oldring	cf	6	25	2	5	2	0	1	3	0	5	0	.200	.400	1	.889
Eddie Plank	p	2	3	0	0	0	0	0	0	0	2	0	.000	.000	0	1.000
Amos Strunk	pr	1	0	0	0	0	0	0	0	0	0	0	—	—	—	—
Ira Thomas	c	4	12	1	1	0	0	0	1	1	2	0	.083	.083	0	1.000
Totals		**6**	**205**	**27**	**50**	**15**	**0**	**3**	**21**	**4**	**31**	**4**	**.244**	**.361**	**11**	**.956**

Pitcher	G	GS	CG	IP	H	R	ER	BB	SO	W-L	Sv	ERA
Chief Bender	3	3	3	26	16	6	3	8	20	2-1	0	1.04
Jack Coombs	2	2	1	20	11	5	3	6	16	1-0	0	1.35
Eddie Plank	2	1	1	9⅔	6	2	2	0	8	1-1	0	1.86
Totals	**6**	**6**	**5**	**55⅔**	**33**	**13**	**8**	**14**	**44**	**4-2**	**0**	**1.29**

NEW YORK GIANTS/John McGraw, Manager

Player	pos	G	AB	R	H	2B	3B	HR	RBI	BB	SO	SB	BA	SA	E	FPct
Red Ames	p	2	2	0	1	0	0	0	0	0	1	0	.500	.500	1	.500
Beals Becker	ph	3	3	0	0	0	0	0	0	0	0	0	.000	.000	—	—
Doc Crandall	p	3	2	1	1	1	0	0	1	2	0	0	.500	1.000	0	1.000
Josh Devore	lf	6	24	1	4	1	0	0	3	1	8	0	.167	.208	1	.938
Larry Doyle	2b	6	23	3	7	3	1	0	1	2	1	2	.304	.522	1	.966
Art Fletcher	ss	6	23	1	3	1	0	0	1	0	4	0	.130	.174	4	.879
Buck Herzog	3b	6	21	3	4	2	0	0	2	3	2	2	.190	.266	3	.870
Rube Marquard	p	3	2	0	0	0	0	0	0	0	2	0	.000	.000	0	1.000
Christy Mathewson	p	3	7	0	2	0	0	0	1	1	3	0	.286	.286	1	.917
Fred Merkle	1b	6	20	1	3	1	0	0	1	2	6	0	.150	.200	2	.971
Chief Meyers	c	6	20	2	6	2	0	0	2	0	3	0	.300	.400	0	1.000
Red Murray	rf	6	21	0	0	0	0	0	0	2	5	0	.000	.000	3	.625
Fred Snodgrass	cf	6	19	1	2	0	0	0	1	2	7	0	.105	.105	0	1.000
Art Wilson	c	1	1	0	0	0	0	0	0	0	0	0	.000	.000	0	1.000
Hooks Wiltse	p	2	1	0	0	0	0	0	0	0	1	0	.000	.000	0	1.000
Totals		**6**	**189**	**13**	**33**	**11**	**1**	**0**	**10**	**14**	**44**	**4**	**.175**	**.243**	**16**	**.938**

Pitcher	G	GS	CG	IP	H	R	ER	BB	SO	W-L	Sv	ERA
Red Ames	2	1	0	8	6	5	2	1	6	0-1	0	2.25
Doc Crandall	2	0	0	4	2	0	0	0	2	1-0	0	0.00
Rube Marquard	3	2	1	11⅔	9	6	2	1	8	0-1	0	1.54
Christy Mathewson	3	3	2	27	25	8	6	2	13	1-2	0	2.00
Hooks Wiltse	2	0	0	3⅓	8	8	7	0	2	0-0	0	18.90
Totals	**6**	**6**	**2**	**54**	**50**	**27**	**17**	**4**	**31**	**2-4**	**0**	**2.83**

Series Outstanding Player: Frank "Home Run" Baker, Philadelphia Athletics. **Series Outstanding Pitcher:** Charles "Chief" Bender, Philadelphia Athletics. **Average Length of Game:** 2 hours, 11 minutes. **Total Attendance:** 179,851. **Average Attendance:** 29,975 (23,709 at Shibe Park; 36,242 at the Polo Grounds). **Umpires:** Bill Brennan (NL), Tommy Connolly (AL), Bill Dinneen (AL), Bill Klem (NL). **Winning Player's Share:** $3,655. **Losing Player's Share:** $2,436.

Left: Chief Bender's 20 strikeouts in 1911 is a record for a six-game series.

Christy Mathewson's streak of 28 2/3 consecutive scoreless innings in the World Series ended in Game 1 when Harry Davis knocked Frank Baker home with a second-inning single.

Below: Philadelphia's "$100,000 Infield" was the cornerstone of Connie Mack's dynasty in the early 1910s.

Game 1   Saturday, October 14 at the Polo Grounds, New York

	1	2	3	4	5	6	7	8	9	R	H	E
Philadelphia Athletics	0	1	0	0	0	0	0	0	0	1	6	2
New York Giants	0	0	0	1	0	0	1	0	x	2	5	0

Pitchers   Phi   Chief Bender (L, 0-1), IP 8, H 5, R 2, ER 1, BB 4, SO 11
NY   Christy Mathewson (W, 1-0), IP 9, H 6, R 1, ER 1, BB 1, SO 5

Top Performers at the Plate
Phi   Frank Baker, 2 for 4, 1 R; Rube Oldring, 2 for 4, 2 2B
NY   Josh Devore, 1 for 3, 1 RBI, 1 BB

2B-Phi/Oldring 2; NY/Devore, Meyers. **SB**-NY/Doyle. **Time** 2:12. **Attendance** 38,281.

Game 2   Monday, October 16 at Shibe Park, Phildelphia

	1	2	3	4	5	6	7	8	9	R	H	E
New York Giants	0	1	0	0	0	0	0	0	0	1	5	3
Philadelphia Athletics	1	0	0	0	0	2	0	0	x	3	4	0

Pitchers   NY   Rube Marquard (L, 0-1), IP 7, H 4, R 3, ER 2, BB 0, SO 4; Doc Crandall, IP 1, H 0, R 0, ER 0, BB 0, SO 2
Phi   Eddie Plank (W, 1-0), IP 9, H 5, R 1, ER 1, BB 0, SO 8

Top Performers at the Plate
NY   Fred Snodgrass, 2 for 3, 1 HBP
Phi   Frank Baker, 1 for 3, 1 R, 2 RBI; Eddie Collins, 2 for 3, 1 R

2B-NY/Herzog; Phi/Collins. **HR**-Phi/Baker. **Time** 1:52. **Attendance** 26,286.

Game 3   Tuesday, October 17 at the Polo Grounds, New York

	1	2	3	4	5	6	7	8	9	10	11	R	H	E
Philadelphia Athletics	0	0	0	0	0	0	0	0	1	0	2	3	9	2
New York Giants	0	0	1	0	0	0	0	0	0	0	1	2	3	5

Pitchers   Phi   Jack Coombs (W, 1-0), IP 11, H 3, R 2, ER 1, BB 4, SO 7
NY   Christy Mathewson (L,1-1), IP 11, H 9, R 3, ER 1, BB 0, SO 3

Top Performers at the Plate
Phi   Frank Baker, 2 for 5, 2 R, 1 RBI; Eddie Collins, 2 for 5, 1 R
NY   Buck Herzog, 1 for 3, 1 R, 1 BB

2B-Phi/Barry; NY/Herzog. **HR**-Phi/Baker. **SB**-Phi/Barry, Collins. **Time** 2:25. **Attendance** 37,216.

Game 4   Tuesday, October 24 at Shibe Park, Philadelphia

	1	2	3	4	5	6	7	8	9	R	H	E
New York Giants	2	0	0	0	0	0	0	0	0	2	7	3
Philadelphia Athletics	0	0	0	3	1	0	0	0	x	4	11	1

Pitchers   NY   Christy Mathewson (L, 1-2), IP 7, H 10, R 4, ER 4, BB 1, SO 5; Hooks Wiltse, IP 1, H 1, R 0, ER 0, BB 0, SO 1
Phi   Chief Bender (W, 1-1), IP 9, H 7, R 2, ER 2, BB 2, SO 4

Top Performers at the Plate
NY   Josh Devore, 2 for 4, 1 R; Larry Doyle, 1 for 3, 1 R, 1 RBI
Phi   Frank Baker, 2 for 3, 1 R, 1 RBI, 2, 2B, 1 BB; Jack Barry, 3 for 4, 2 2B

2B-NY/Merkle, Meyers; Phi/Baker 2, Barry 2, Davis, Murphy 2. **3B**-NY/Doyle. **Time** 1:49. **Attendance** 24,355.

Game 5   Wednesday, October 25 at the Polo Grounds, New York

	1	2	3	4	5	6	7	8	9	10	R	H	E
Philadelphia Athletics	0	0	3	0	0	0	0	0	0	3	7	1
New York Giants	0	0	0	0	0	1	0	2	1	4	9	2

Pitchers   Phi   Jack Coombs, IP 9, H 8, R 3, ER 2, BB 2, SO 9; Eddie Plank (L, 1-1), IP ⅔, H 1, R 1, ER 1, BB 0, SO 0
NY   Rube Marquard, IP 3, H 3, R 3, ER 0, BB 1, SO 2; Red Ames, IP 4, H 2, R 0, ER 0, BB 0, SO 2; Doc Crandall (W, 1-0), IP 3, H 2, R 0, ER 0, BB 0, SO 0

Top Performers at the Plate
Phi   Jack Coombs, 2 for 4, 1 R; Rube Oldring, 2 for 5, 1 R, 3 RBI
NY   Larry Doyle, 4 for 5, 1 R, 2 2B; Fred Merkle, 0 for 2, 1 R, 1 RBI, 1 SH, 1 HBP

2B-NY/Crandall, Doyle 2, Fletcher. **HR**-Phi/Oldring. **SB**-Phi/Barry, Collins; NY/Doyle, Herzog. **Time** 2:33. **Attendance** 33,228.

Game 6   Thursday, October 26 at Shibe Park, Philadelphia

	1	2	3	4	5	6	7	8	9	R	H	E
New York Giants	1	0	0	0	0	0	0	0	1	2	4	3
Philadelphia Athletics	0	0	1	4	0	1	7	0	x	13	13	5

Pitchers   NY   Red Ames (L, 0-1), IP 4, H 4, R 5, ER 2, BB 1, SO 4; Hooks Wiltse, IP 2⅓, H 7, R 8, ER 7, BB 0, SO 1; Rube Marquard, IP 1⅔, H 2, R 0, ER 0, BB 0, SO 2
Phi   Chief Bender (W, 2-1), IP 9, H 4, R 2, ER 0, BB 2, SO 5

Top Performers at the Plate
Phi   Bris Lord, 3 for 5, 1 R, 1 RBI, 2 2B; Danny Murphy, 4 for 4, 3 R, 1 RBI

2B-NY/Doyle; Phi/Barry, Lord 2, Murphy. **SB**-NY/Herzog. **Time** 2:12. **Attendance** 20,485.

Bill Dinneen, the Boston pitching star from the inaugural 1903 Series, was on the field again in 1911, this time as an umpire.

Boston Red Sox (4) vs. New York Giants (3), 1 tie

In 1912, John McGraw and his Giants returned to the Series to face the Boston Red Sox, who had unseated Philadelphia for the American League pennant. The Red Sox boasted one of the best defensive outfields in history with Duffy Lewis in left, Tris Speaker in center and Harry Hooper in right; Speaker posted a .383 average, hit 52 doubles and had a league-high 10 homers in 1912. "Smokey" Joe Wood put together a phenomenal season on the mound, going 35-4 with 10 shutouts and a 1.91 ERA. Christy Mathewson continued to shine for New York, and he got major help from 26-game winner Rube Marquard, who won his first 19 decisions in 1912, and

Above: The Giants take the field prior to the start of Game 1.

from rookie Jeff Tesreau, who led the league with a 1.96 ERA. Tesreau was given the start against Wood in Game 1 of the Series—and Smokey Joe was smokin'. He struck out 11 Giants, including the last 2 batters of the game with runners on second and third. The teams met at Boston's new Fenway Park the next day, and they battled to a 6-6 tie before the game was called on account of darkness after 11 innings. A strong performance from Marquard in Game 3 brought New York even in the Series. Wood was back on the hill for Boston in the fourth game, and he struck out 8 while walking none to pace Boston to a 3-1 win. Rookie Hugh Bedient matched up against Mathewson in Game 5, and the youngster got the better of his legendary counterpart by allowing only 3 base hits. A 5-run rally by the Giants in the first inning of Game 6 helped secure Marquard's second win, and another first-inning explosion the next day tied the Series at three games for each side. New York's 16 hits and 11 runs in the game gave starter Tesreau plenty of breathing room, and the young pitcher contributed 2 base hits and drove in 2 runs. Only 17,000 fans showed up to Fenway to watch

Tris Speaker is the only outfielder to turn an unassisted double play in the World Series. In the ninth inning of Game 7, he raced in to grab a short fly ball and then stepped on second to double up baserunner Art Wilson.

Mathewson and Bedient face off in the decisive eighth game. In the third inning, Red Murray doubled in the game's first run for New York, and Boston pinch hitter Olaf Henriksen evened things with a 2-out, run-scoring double in the seventh. Wood entered the game in relief in the eighth, and he and Mathewson held the teams scoreless until the tenth. In the top of the inning, Murray doubled and then scored the go-ahead run on Fred Merkle's single. Boston's first batter in the bottom half of the tenth, pinchhitter Clyde Engle, looped a ball to center fielder Fred Snodgrass. The usually sure-handed Snodgrass dropped the routine fly, and Engle was safe at second. Snodgrass redeemed himself somewhat by robbing Harry Hooper of a sure hit in the next at-bat, but with Engle now 90 feet from the plate, the pressure was on. After walking Steve Yerkes, Mathewson was set to go against Tris Speaker. Matty got Speaker to pop up a short foul ball between first and home. First baseman Merkle, who seemed to have a play on the ball, stood there watching as catcher Chief Meyers lunged for the ball in vain. This muff of another seemingly routine play gave Boston one more chance, and Speaker responded by scoring Engle on

Above: Larry Gardner's sacrifice fly in the final game clinched it for Boston.

Opposite: Christy Mathewson walked away from the Series with an impressive 1.26 ERA—but also with a disappointing two losses and no wins.

a single to right. With still just 1 out, Larry Gardner hit a long fly ball to right field, deep enough to allow Yerkes to score from third. The season in which the Giants won 103 games, and the Series in which they bounced back from a three-games-to-one deficit to come 3 outs from a title, came to a disappointing end thanks to Snodgrass's "$30,000 muff" (so called for the additional money the Giant players would have received had they won the Series) and the muffed foul pop-up by Merkle and Meyers.

Above: Shown here with teammates Josh Devore, Red Murray and Beals Becker, the usually sure-handed Fred Snodgrass (far left) committed a costly error in the final game of the Series.

1912 WORLD SERIES COMPOSITE STATISTICS

BOSTON RED SOX/Jake Stahl, Manager

Player	pos	G	AB	R	H	2B	3B	HR	RBI	BB	SO	SB	BA	SA	E	FPct
Neal Ball	ph	1	1	0	0	0	0	0	0	0	0	1	0	.000	.000	–	–
Hugh Bedient	p	4	6	0	0	0	0	0	0	0	0	0	.000	.000	0	1.00
Hick Cady	c	7	22	1	3	0	0	0	1	0	3	0	.136	.136	0	.977
Bill Carrigan	c	2	7	0	0	0	0	0	0	0	0	0	.000	.000	0	1.00
Ray Collins	p	2	5	0	0	0	0	0	0	0	2	0	.000	.000	0	1.00
Clyde Engle	ph	3	3	1	1	1	0	0	2	0	0	0	.333	.667	–	–
Larry Gardner	3b	8	28	4	5	2	1	1	5	2	5	0	.179	.429	4	.846
Charley Hall	p	2	4	0	3	1	0	0	0	1	0	0	.750	1.000	1	.833
Olaf Henriksen	ph	2	1	0	1	1	0	0	0	1	0	0	1.000	2.000	–	–
Harry Hooper	rf	8	31	3	9	2	1	0	1	4	4	2	.290	.419	0	1.00
Duffy Lewis	lf	8	32	4	5	3	0	0	2	2	2	0	.156	.281	0	.933
Buck O'Brien	p	2	2	0	0	0	0	0	0	0	2	0	.000	.000	0	1.00
Tris Speaker	cf	8	30	4	9	1	2	0	2	4	2	1	.300	.467	2	.920
Jake Stahl	1b	8	32	3	9	2	0	0	2	0	6	2	.281	.313	1	.988
Heinie Wagner	ss	8	30	1	5	1	0	0	0	3	6	1	.167	.200	3	.942
Joe Wood	p	4	7	1	2	0	0	0	1	1	0	0	.286	.286	0	1.00
Steve Yerkes	2b	8	32	3	8	0	2	0	4	2	3	0	.250	.375	1	.973
Totals		8	273	25	60	14	6	1	21	19	36	6	.220	.326	14	.958

Pitcher	G	GS	CG	IP	H	R	ER	BB	SO	W-L	Sv	ERA
Hugh Bedient	4	2	1	18	10	2	1	7	7	1-0	0	0.50
Ray Collins	2	1	0	14⅓	14	5	2	0	6	0-0	0	1.26
Charley Hall	2	0	0	10⅔	11	6	4	9	1	0-0	0	3.38
Buck O'Brien	2	2	0	9	12	7	5	3	4	0-2	0	5.00
Joe Wood	4	3	2	22	27	11	9	3	21	3-1	0	3.68
Totals	8	8	3	74	74	31	21	22	39	4-3	0	2.55

NEW YORK GIANTS/John McGraw, Manager

Player	pos	G	AB	R	H	2B	3B	HR	RBI	BB	SO	SB	BA	SA	E	FPct
Red Ames	p	1	0	0	0	0	0	0	0	0	0	0	–	–	0	1.000
Beals Becker	pr-cf	2	4	1	0	0	0	0	0	2	0	0	.000	.000	0	–
Doc Crandall	p	1	1	0	0	0	0	0	0	0	1	0	.000	.000	0	1.000
Josh Devore	lf-rf	7	24	4	6	0	0	0	7	5	4	.250	.250	1	.933	
Larry Doyle	2b	8	33	5	8	1	0	1	2	3	2	2	.242	.364	5	.891
Art Fletcher	ss	8	28	1	5	1	0	0	3	1	4	1	.179	.214	4	.909
Buck Herzog	3b	8	30	6	12	4	1	0	5	1	3	2	.400	.600	0	1.000
Rube Marquard	p	2	4	0	0	0	0	0	0	1	0	0	.000	.000	1	.800
Christy Mathewson	p	3	12	0	2	0	0	0	0	0	4	0	.167	.167	0	1.000
Moose McCormick	ph	5	4	0	1	0	0	0	1	0	0	0	.250	.250	–	–
Fred Merkle	1b	8	33	5	9	2	1	0	3	0	7	1	.273	.394	2	.976
Chief Meyers	c	8	28	2	10	0	1	0	3	2	3	1	.357	.429	1	.979
Red Murray	rf-lf	8	31	5	10	4	1	0	4	2	2	0	.323	.516	0	1.000
Tillie Shafer	ss	3	0	0	0	0	0	0	0	0	0	0	–	–	0	1.000
Fred Snodgrass	cf-lf-rf	8	33	2	7	2	0	0	2	2	5	1	.212	.273	1	.947
Jeff Tesreau	p	3	8	0	3	0	0	0	2	1	3	0	.375	.375	0	1.000
Art Wilson	c	2	1	0	1	0	0	0	0	0	0	0	1.000	1.000	–	.750
Totals		8	274	31	74	14	4	1	25	22	39	12	.270	.361	16	.953

Pitcher	G	GS	CG	IP	H	R	ER	BB	SO	W-L	Sv	ERA
Red Ames	1	0	0	2	3	1	1	1	0	0-0	0	4.50
Doc Crandall	1	0	0	2	1	0	0	0	2	0-0	0	0.00
Rube Marquard	2	2	2	18	14	3	1	2	9	2-0	0	0.50
Christy Mathewson	3	3	3	28⅔	23	11	4	5	10	0-2	0	1.26
Jeff Tesreau	3	3	1	23	19	10	8	11	15	1-2	0	3.13
Totals	8	8	6	73⅔	60	25	14	19	36	3-4	0	1.71

Series Outstanding Player: Tris Speaker, Boston Red Sox. **Series Outstanding Pitcher:** Rube Marquard, New York Giants. **Average Length of Game:** 2 hours, 14 minutes. **Total Attendance:** 252,037. **Average Attendance:** 31,505 (29,837 at Fenway Park; 34,285 at the Polo Grounds). **Umpires:** Billy Evans (AL); Bill Klem (NL); Francis O'Loughlin (AL); Cy Rigler (NL). **Winning Player's Share:** $4,025. **Losing Player's Share:** $2,566.

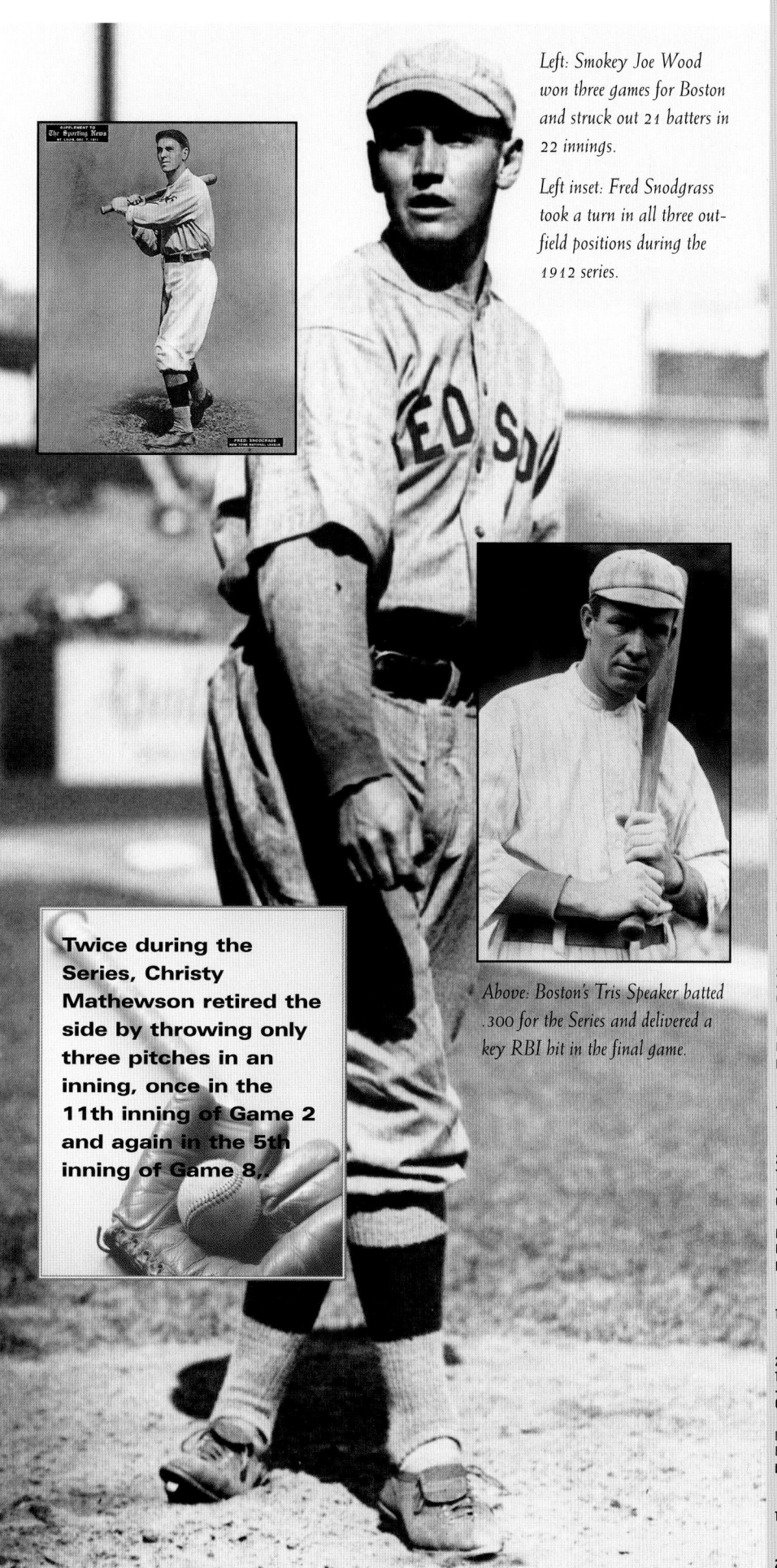

Left: Smokey Joe Wood won three games for Boston and struck out 21 batters in 22 innings.

Left inset: Fred Snodgrass took a turn in all three out-field positions during the 1912 series.

Twice during the Series, Christy Mathewson retired the side by throwing only three pitches in an inning, once in the 11th inning of Game 2 and again in the 5th inning of Game 8,

Above: Boston's Tris Speaker batted .300 for the Series and delivered a key RBI hit in the final game.

Game 1 Tuesday, October 8 at the Polo Grounds, New York

	1	2	3	4	5	6	7	8	9		R	H	E
Boston Red Sox	0	0	0	0	0	1	3	0	0		4	6	1
New York Giants	0	0	2	0	0	0	0	0	1		3	8	1

Pitchers Bos Joe Wood (W, 1-0), IP 9, H 8, R 3, ER 3, BB 2, SO 11
NY Jeff Tesreau (L, 0-1), IP 7, H 5, R 4, ER 4, BB 4, SO 4; Doc Crandall, IP 2, H 1, R 0, ER 0, BB 0, SO 2

Top Performers at the Plate
Bos Harry Hooper, 1 for 3, 1 R, 1 RBI, 1 SH; Heinie Wagner, 2 for 3, 1 R, 1 BB
NY Larry Doyle, 2 for 4, 1 R; Red Murray, 1 for 3, 2 RBI
2B-Bos/Hooper, Wagner; NY/Doyle. 3B-Bos/Speaker. **Time** 2:10. **Attendance** 35,730.

Game 2 Wednesday, October 9 at Fenway Park, Boston

	1	2	3	4	5	6	7	8	9	10	11	R	H	E
New York Giants	0	1	0	1	0	0	3	0	1	0	0	6	11	5
Boston Red Sox	3	0	0	0	1	0	0	1	0	1	0	6	10	1

Pitchers NY Christy Mathewson, IP 11, H 10, R 6, ER 2, BB 0, SO 4
Bos Ray Collins, IP 7⅓, H 9, R 5, ER 3, BB 0, SO 5; Charley Hall, IP 2⅔, H 2, R 1, ER 1, BB 4, SO 0; Hugh Bedient, IP 1, H 0, R 0, ER 0, BB 1, SO 1

Top Performers at the Plate
NY Buck Herzog, 3 for 4, 1 R, 3 RBI, 1 SH; Red Murray, 3 for 5, 2 R, 2 RBI
Bos Harry Hooper, 3 for 5, 1 R, 2 SB; Duffy Lewis, 3 for 5, 2 R, 2 2B
2B-NY/Herzog, Murray, Snodgrass; Bos/Hooper, Lewis 2. 3B-NY/Herzog, Merkle, Murray; Bos/Speaker, Yerkes. **SB**-NY/Herzog, Snodgrass; Bos/Hooper 2, Stahl. **Time** 2:38.
Attendance 30,148.

Game 3 Thursday, October 10 at Fenway Park, Boston

	1	2	3	4	5	6	7	8	9		R	H	E
New York Giants	0	1	0	0	1	0	0	0	0		2	7	1
Boston Red Sox	0	0	0	0	0	0	0	0	1		1	7	0

Pitchers NY Rube Marquard (W, 1-0), IP 9, H 7, R 1, ER 1, BB 1, SO 6
Bos Buck O'Brien (L, 0-1), IP 8, H 6, R 2, ER 2, BB 3, SO 3; Hugh Bedient, IP 1, H 1, R 0, ER 0, BB 0, SO 0

Top Performers at the Plate
NY Josh Devore, 2 for 4; Buck Herzog, 1 for 2, 1 R, 1 RBI, 1 HBP, 1 SH
Bos Duffy Lewis, 2 for 4, 1 R
2B-NY/Herzog, Murray; Bos/Gardner, Stahl. **SB**-NY/Devore, Fletcher; Bos/Wagner. **Time** 2:15.
Attendance 34,624.

Game 4 Friday, October 11 at the Polo Grounds, New York

	1	2	3	4	5	6	7	8	9		R	H	E
Boston Red Sox	0	1	0	1	0	0	0	0	1		3	8	1
New York Giants	0	0	0	0	0	0	1	0	0		1	9	1

Pitchers Bos Joe Wood (W, 2-0), IP 9, H 9, R 1, ER 1, BB 0, SO 8
NY Jeff Tesreau (L, 0-2), IP 7, H 5, R 2, ER 2, BB 2, SO 5; Red Ames, IP 2, H 3, R 1, ER 1, BB 1, SO 0

Top Performers at the Plate
Bos Larry Gardner, 2 for 3, 2 R, 1 BB; Joe Wood, 2 for 4, 1 RBI
NY Buck Herzog, 2 for 4, 1 R
2B-Bos/Speaker; NY/Fletcher. 3B-Bos/Gardner. **SB**-Bos/Stahl; NY/Merkle. **Time** 2:06.
Attendance 36,502.

Game 5 Saturday, October 12 at Fenway Park, Boston

	1	2	3	4	5	6	7	8	9		R	H	E
New York Giants	0	0	0	0	0	0	1	0	0		1	3	1
Boston Red Sox	0	0	2	0	0	0	0	0	x		2	5	1

Pitchers NY Christy Mathewson (L, 0-1), IP 8, H 5, R 2, ER 0, BB 0, SO 2
Bos Hugh Bedient (W, 1-0), IP 9, H 3, R 1, ER 1, BB 3, SO 4

Top Performers at the Plate
Bos Harry Hooper, 2 for 4, 1 R
2B-NY/Merkle. 3B-Bos/Hooper, Yerkes. **Time** 1:43. **Attendance** 34,683.

Game 6 Monday, October 14 at the Polo Grounds, New York

	1	2	3	4	5	6	7	8	9		R	H	E
Boston Red Sox	0	2	0	0	0	0	0	0	0		2	7	2
New York Giants	5	0	0	0	0	0	0	0	x		5	11	1

Pitchers Bos Buck O'Brien (L, 0-2), IP 1, H 6, R 5, ER 3, BB 0, SO 1; Ray Collins, IP 7, H 5, R 0, ER 0, BB 0, SO 1
NY Rube Marquard (W, 2-0), IP 9, H 7, R 2, ER 0, BB 1, SO 3

Top Performers at the Plate
Bos Jake Stahl, 2 for 4, 1 R
NY Fred Merkle, 2 for 3, 1 R, 1 RBI; Chief Meyers, 2 for 3, 1 R
2B-NY/Herzog, Merkle; Bos/Engle. 3B-NY/Meyers. **SB**-Bos/Speaker; NY/Doyle, Herzog, Meyers.
Time 1:58. **Attendance** 30,622.

Game 7 Tuesday, October 15 at Fenway Park, Boston

	1	2	3	4	5	6	7	8	9		R	H	E
New York Giants	6	1	0	0	0	2	1	0	1		11	16	4
Boston Red Sox	0	1	0	0	0	0	2	1	0		4	9	3

Pitchers NY Jeff Tesreau (W, 1-2), IP 9, H 9, R 4, ER 2, BB 5, SO 6
Bos Joe Wood (L, 2-1), IP 1, H 7, R 6, ER 4, BB 0, SO 0; Charley Hall, IP 8, H 9, R 5, ER 3, BB 5, SO 1

Top Performers at the Plate
NY Larry Doyle, 3 for 4, 3 R, 2 RBI, 1 BB; Chief Meyers, 3 for 4, 1 R, 1 RBI
Bos Larry Gardner, 1 for 4, 1 R, 1 RBI, 1 HBP; Charley Hall, 3 for 3, 1 BB
2B-NY/Snodgrass; Bos/Hall, Lewis. **HR**-NY/Doyle; Bos/Gardner. **SB**-NY/Devore 2, Doyle.
Time 2:21. **Attendance** 32,694.

Game 8 Wednesday, October 16 at Fenway Park, Boston

	1	2	3	4	5	6	7	8	9	10	R	H	E
New York Giants	0	0	1	0	0	0	0	0	0	1	2	9	2
Boston Red Sox	0	0	0	0	0	1	0	0	1	2	3	8	5

Pitchers NY Christy Mathewson (L, 0-2), IP 9⅔, H 8, R 3, ER 2, BB 5, SO 4
Bos Hugh Bedient, IP 7, H 6, R 1, ER 1, BB 3, SO 2; Joe Wood (W, 3-1), IP 3, H 3, R 1, ER 1, BB 1, SO 2

Top Performers at the Plate
NY Josh Devore, 1 for 3, 1 R, 2 BB; Red Murray, 2 for 5, 1 R, 1 RBI, 2 2B
Bos Tris Speaker, 2 for 4, 1 RBI; Jake Stahl, 2 for 4, 1 R
2B-NY/Herzog, Murray 2; Bos/Gardner, Henriksen, Stahl. **SB**-NY/Devore. **Time** 2:37.
Attendance 17,034.

Philadelphia Athletics (4) vs. New York Giants (1)

1913

Hoping to overcome the heartbreaking loss of the previous year, the New York Giants came into the 1913 Series with physical injuries on top of their emotional scars. Starters Fred Merkle, Fred Snodgrass and Chief Meyers—the three names at the forefront of the 1912 collapse—were all hobbled with injuries. New York's three 20-game winners were healthy, but so were Philadelphia's collection of all-stars, who were matched up against the Giants for the second time in three years. A perfect 3 for 3 day at the plate by Eddie Collins and a two-run blast by Frank "Home Run" Baker helped the A's grab the opening game by a score of 6-4. In Game 2, Christy Mathewson battled his former college rival (and future Cooperstown compatriot) Eddie Plank for nine shutout innings until the Giants rallied for three runs in the top of the tenth. Mathewson drove in the first run with an RBI single, and Art Fletcher brought two more home with a bases-loaded single. Manager John McGraw, short on healthy bodies, was forced to use pitcher Hooks Wiltse at first base for eight innings, and the risk paid off. Wiltse threw out two runners at the plate in the bottom of the ninth when the A's rallied to put two men in scoring position with nobody out. Twenty-year-old Bullet Joe Bush allowed only five hits in Game 3 to bring Philadelphia ahead in the Series two games to one. The A's pulled out a tight win in Game 4 behind Charles "Chief" Bender, but only after New York made it interesting by coming back from down 6-0 to score five runs in the seventh and eighth. Merkle came through with a three-run homer in the seventh, but it wasn't enough. Game 5 saw the fifth straight complete-game performance by a Philadelphia pitcher, as Plank got the better of Mathewson in their second head-to-head encounter in the Series. The A's came up with three runs in the first three innings while holding the Giants to just one unearned run in the fifth. For Connie Mack's Athletics, it was the franchise's third World Series championship in four years. Frank Baker hit an impressive .450 for the Series and racked up the third postseason home run of his career. For John McGraw's Giants, it was a disappointing third straight World Series defeat, a dubious achievement equaled only one other time before (the 1907–09 Tigers) and never again since. And although Christy Mathewson lost the final game of a Series for the second year in a row, he walked away from his final World Series appearance with career records in complete games (ten) and shutouts (four)—records that stand nearly nine decades later—and with an impressive career ERA of 1.06 in the Fall Classic.

Above: Joe Bush pitched a five-hitter in Game 3 to give his team a two-games-to-one lead in the Series.

1913 WORLD SERIES COMPOSITE STATISTICS																	

PHILADELPHIA ATHLETICS/Connie Mack, Manager

Player	pos	G	AB	R	H	2B	3B	HR	RBI	BB	SO	SB	BA	SA	E	FPct
Frank Baker	3b	5	20	2	9	0	0	1	7	0	2	1	.450	.600	1	.917
Jack Barry	ss	5	20	3	6	3	0	0	1	0	0	0	.300	.450	1	.958
Chief Bender	p	2	8	0	0	0	0	0	1	0	1	0	.000	.000	0	1.000
Joe Bush	p	1	4	0	1	0	0	0	0	0	1	0	.250	.250	0	1.000
Eddie Collins	2b	5	19	5	8	0	2	0	3	1	2	3	.421	.632	1	.972
Jack Lapp	c	1	4	0	1	0	0	0	0	0	1	0	.250	.250	0	1.000
Stuffy McInnis	1b	5	17	1	2	1	0	0	2	0	2	0	.118	.176	0	1.000
Eddie Murphy	rf	5	22	2	5	0	0	0	2	0	0	0	.227	.227	0	1.000
Rube Oldring	lf	5	22	5	6	0	1	0	0	0	1	1	.273	.364	0	1.000
Eddie Plank	p	2	7	0	1	0	0	0	0	0	0	0	.143	.143	1	.800
Wally Schang	c	4	14	2	5	0	1	1	7	2	4	0	.357	.714	1	.952
Amos Strunk	cf	5	17	3	2	0	0	0	2	2	2	0	.118	.118	0	1.000
Totals		5	174	23	46	4	4	2	21	7	16	5	.264	.368	5	.974

Pitcher	G	GS	CG	IP	H	R	ER	BB	SO	W-L	Sv	ERA
Chief Bender	2	2	2	18	19	9	8	1	9	2-0	0	4.00
Joe Bush	1	1	1	9	5	2	1	4	3	1-0	0	1.00
Eddie Plank	2	2	2	19	9	4	2	3	7	1-1	0	0.95
Totals	5	5	5	46	33	15	11	8	19	4-1	0	2.15

NEW YORK GIANTS/John McGraw, Manager

Player	pos	G	AB	R	H	2B	3B	HR	RBI	BB	SO	SB	BA	SA	E	FPct
George Burns	lf	5	19	2	3	2	0	0	2	1	5	1	.158	.263	1	.933
Claude Cooper	pr	2	0	0	0	0	0	0	0	0	0	1	—	—	—	—
Doc Crandall	p	4	4	0	0	0	0	0	0	0	0	0	.000	.000	0	1.000
Al Demaree	p	1	1	0	0	0	0	0	0	0	0	0	.000	.000,	0	1.000
Larry Doyle	2b	5	20	1	3	0	0	0	2	0	1	0	.150	.150	3	.914
Art Fletcher	ss	5	18	1	5	0	0	0	3	1	1	1	.278	.278	1	.947
Eddie Grant	pr-ph	2	1	1	0	0	0	0	0	0	0	0	.000	.000	—	—
Buck Herzog	3b	5	19	1	1	0	0	0	0	0	1	0	.053	.053	0	1.000
Rube Marquard	p	2	1	0	0	0	0	0	0	0	0	0	.000	.000	0	1.000
Christy Mathewson	p	2	5	1	3	0	0	0	1	1	0	0	.600	.600	0	1.000
Moose McCormick	ph	2	2	1	1	0	0	0	0	0	0	0	.500	.500	—	—
Larry McLean	c	5	12	0	6	0	0	0	2	0	0	0	.500	.500	0	1.000
Fred Merkle	1b	4	13	3	3	0	0	1	3	1	2	0	.231	.462	2	.950
Chief Meyers	c	1	4	0	0	0	0	0	0	0	0	0	.000	.000	0	1.000
Red Murray	rf	5	16	2	4	0	0	0	1	2	2	2	.250	.250	0	1.000
Tillie Shafer	cf-3b	5	19	2	3	1	1	0	1	2	3	0	.158	.316	0	1.000
Fred Snodgrass	1b-cf	2	3	0	1	0	0	0	0	0	0	0	.333	.333	0	1.000
Jeff Tesreau	p	2	2	0	0	0	0	0	0	0	1	0	.000	.000	0	1.000
Art Wilson	c	3	3	0	0	0	0	0	0	0	0	2	.000	.000	0	1.000
Hooks Wiltse	1b	2	2	0	0	0	0	0	0	0	0	1	.000	.000	0	1.000
Totals		5	164	15	33	3	1	1	15	8	19	5	.201	.250	7	.968

Pitcher	G	GS	CG	IP	H	R	ER	BB	SO	W-L	Sv	ERA
Doc Crandall	2	0	0	4⅔	4	2	2	0	2	0-0	0	3.86
Al Demaree	1	1	0	4	7	4	2	1	0	0-1	0	4.50
Rube Marquard	2	1	0	9	10	7	7	3	3	0-1	0	7.00
Christy Mathewson	2	2	2	19	14	3	2	2	7	1-1	0	0.95
Jeff Tesreau	2	1	0	8⅓	11	7	6	1	4	0-1	0	6.48
Totals	5	5	2	45	46	23	19	7	16	1-4	0	3.80

Series Outstanding Player: Frank "Home Run" Baker, Philadelphia Athletics. **Series Outstanding Pitcher:** Eddie Plank, Philadelphia Athletics. **Average Length of Game:** 2 hours, 5 minutes. **Total Attendance:** 150,950. **Average Attendance:** 30,190 (20,566 at Shibe Park; 36,606 at the Polo Grounds). **Umpires:** Tommy Connolly (AL), John Egan (AL), Bill Klem (NL), Cy Rigler (NL). **Winning Player's Share:** $3,246. **Losing Player's Share:** $2,164.

Above: The Giants and Athletics face off at the Polo Grounds for the opener of the 1913 Series.

Above: Frank Baker was the hot hitter for Philadelphia, batting .450 and driving in seven runs in the Series. Here he's out trying to advance to third in the opening game.

Above: Eddie Plank faced his former college rival Christy Mathewson twice in the Series. Plank won the deciding fifth game with a two-hitter.

Game 1   Tuesday, October 7 at the Polo Grounds, New York

	1	2	3	4	5	6	7	8	9	R	H	E
Philadelphia Athletics	0	0	0	3	2	0	0	1	0	6	11	1
New York Giants	0	0	1	0	3	0	0	0	0	4	11	0

Pitchers   Phi   Chief Bender (W, 1-0), IP 9, H 11, R 4, ER 3, BB 0, SO 4
NY   Rube Marquard (L, 0-1), IP 5, H 8, R 5, ER 5, BB 1, SO 1; Doc Crandall, IP 2, H 3, R 1, ER 1, BB 0, SO 1; Jeff Tesreau, IP 2, H 0, R 0, ER 0, BB 1, SO 1

Top Performers at the Plate
Phi   Frank Baker, 3 for 4, 1 R, 3 RBI; Eddie Collins, 3 for 3, 3 R, 1 BB
NY   Larry Doyle, 2 for 4, 1 R, 1 RBI; Fred Merkle, 2 for 4, 2 R

2B-Phi/Barry, McInnis; NY/Burns. **3B**-Phi/Collins, Schang. **HR**-Phi/Baker. **SB**-Phi/Collins.
Time 2:06. **Attendance** 36,291.

Game 2   Wednesday, October 8 at Shibe Park, Philadelphia

	1	2	3	4	5	6	7	8	9	10	R	H	E
New York Giants	0	0	0	0	0	0	0	0	0	3	3	7	2
Philadelphia Athletics	0	0	0	0	0	0	0	0	0	0	0	8	2

Pitchers   NY   Christy Mathewson (W, 1-0), IP 10, H 8, R 0, ER 0, BB 1, SO 5
Phi   Eddie Plank (L, 0-1), IP 10, H 7, R 3, ER 2, BB 2, SO 6

Top Performers at the Plate
NY   Art Fletcher, 2 for 5, 2 RBI; Christy Mathewson, 2 for 3, 1 R, 1 RBI, 1 BB
Phi   Frank Baker, 2 for 5

Time 2:22. **Attendance** 20,563.

Game 3   Thursday, October 9 at the Polo Grounds, New York

	1	2	3	4	5	6	7	8	9	R	H	E
Philadelphia Athletics	3	2	0	0	0	0	2	1	0	8	12	1
New York Giants	0	0	0	0	1	0	1	0	0	2	5	1

Pitchers   Phi   Joe Bush (W, 1-0), IP 9, H 5, R 2, ER 1, BB 4, SO 3
NY   Jeff Tesreau (L, 0-1), IP 6⅓, H 11, R 7, ER 6, BB 0, SO 3; Doc Crandall, IP 2⅔, H 1, R 1, ER 1, BB 0, SO 1

Top Performers at the Plate
Phi   Frank Baker, 2 for 4, 1 R, 2 RBI; Eddie Collins, 3 for 5, 2 R, 3 RBI
NY   Red Murray, 1 for 3, 1 R, 1 RBI, 1 BB; Tillie Shafer, 1 for 3, 1 R, 1 BB

2B-NY/Shafer. **3B**-Phi/Collins. **HR**-Phi/Schang. **SB**-Phi/Baker, Collins, Oldring; NY/Cooper, Fletcher, Murray. **Time** 2:11. **Attendance** 36,896.

Game 4   Friday, October 10 at Shibe Park, Philadelphia

	1	2	3	4	5	6	7	8	9	R	H	E
New York Giants	0	0	0	0	0	0	3	2	0	5	8	2
Philadelphia Athletics	0	1	0	3	2	0	0	0	x	6	9	0

Pitchers   NY   Al Demaree (L, 0-1), IP 4, H 7, R 4, ER 2, BB 1, SO 0; Rube Marquard, IP 4, H 2, R 2, ER 2, BB 2, SO 2
Phi   Chief Bender (W, 2-0), IP 9, H 8, R 5, ER 5, BB 1, SO 5

Top Performers at the Plate
NY   George Burns, 2 for 4, 2 R, 1 RBI; Fred Merkle, 1 for 4, 1 R, 3 RBI
Phi   Jack Barry, 3 for 4, 2 R, 2 RBI, 2 2B; Wally Schang, 2 for 2, 1 R, 3 RBI, 2 BB

2B-NY/Burns; Phi/Barry 2. **3B**-NY/Shafer; Phi/Oldring. **HR**-NY/Merkle. **SB**-NY/Burns, Murray; Phi/Collins. **Time** 2:09. **Attendance** 20,568.

Game 5   Saturday, October 11 at the Polo Grounds, New York

	1	2	3	4	5	6	7	8	9	R	H	E
Philadelphia Athletics	1	0	2	0	0	0	0	0	0	3	6	1
New York Giants	0	0	0	0	1	0	0	0	0	1	2	2

Pitchers   Phi   Eddie Plank (W, 1-1), IP 9, H 2, R 1, ER 0, BB 1, SO 1
NY   Christy Mathewson (L, 1-1), IP 9, H 6, R 3, ER 2, BB 1, SO 2

Top Performers at the Plate
Phi   Frank Baker, 2 for 3, 2 RBI, 1 SH; Eddie Murphy, 2 for 3, 1 R, 1 BB
NY   Larry McLean, 1 for 3, 1 RBI

Time 1:39. **Attendance** 36,632.

Above: Fred Merkle drove in three runs with his Game 4 homer, but New York still fell short in the game, 6-5.

Boston Braves (4) vs. Philadelphia Athletics (0)

In mid-July 1914, the Boston Braves were wallowing at the bottom of the National League. Then the team stormed ahead, winning 34 of their last 44 games, and not only were they sitting atop the standings when the season ended, but they had a 10 1/2-game margin on the second-place Giants. On October 9, the "Miracle Braves" opened the World Series in Philadelphia, with the Athletics making their fourth appearance in five years and figuring to be heavy favorites. In the opening contest, 27-game winner Dick Rudolph went the distance for Boston, allowing just one unearned run in 9 innings, while the Braves thumped Chief Bender for six runs in less than 6 innings. The teams fought through 8 innings of scoreless ball in Game 2. Boston's Bill James allowed just two hits in the game, and the Braves hitters came through in the 9th when a double by Charlie Deal and a single by Les Mann brought in the game's only run. The teams traveled to Boston for Game 3, where the Braves played temporary host at the Red Sox home field of Fenway Park, which was larger than the Braves' regular home, South End Grounds. Philadelphia got on the board early with a run in the top of the first, but the Braves responded with a run of their own in the second. Each team scored one more run, carrying a 2-2 tie through 9. The Athletics rallied together three singles and a base-on-

balls for two runs in the top of the 10th. Once again, the Braves responded, scoring two of their own in the bottom half of the inning, including a leadoff homer by Hank Gowdy. Bill James entered the game in relief in the 11th and held the A's at bay for 2 innings. Gowdy got the team going again in the 12th, leading things off with a double to left. After an intentional walk to pinch hitter Larry Gilbert, Herbie Moran bunted back to the pitcher Joe Bush. Bush made a wild throw to third base, allowing the winning run to come around to score—and ending the first three-hour game in a postseason contest. The Miracle Braves closed out their miraculous season the next day with a Game 4 win and the first four-game sweep in World Series history. Another complete game by Rudolph and a tie-breaking two-run single by veteran Johnny Evers in the 5th inning secured the game for Boston. While Rudolph and James gave up just one earned run in 29 innings and held Philadelphia to a .172 average for the Series (100 points lower than their regular-season mark), the key performer for the new world champions was catcher Hank Gowdy. A .243 hitter in the regular season, Gowdy burst out with three doubles, a triple and a home run in the four games, giving him a .545 average and a 1.273 slugging percentage.

World's Series — Braves 5 Athletics 4. 12 Innings, Fenway Park, American League Grounds, Oct. 12, 1914.

1914 WORLD SERIES COMPOSITE STATISTICS

BOSTON BRAVES/George Stallings, Manager

Player	pos	G	AB	R	H	2B	3B	HR	RBI	BB	SO	SB	BA	SA	E	FPct
Ted Cather	lf	1	5	0	0	0	0	0	0	0	1	0	.000	.000	0	1.000
Joe Connolly	lf	3	9	1	1	0	0	0	1	1	1	0	.111	.111	1	.750
Charlie Deal	3b	4	16	1	2	2	0	0	0	0	2	0	.125	.250	0	1.000
Josh Devore	ph	1	1	0	0	0	0	0	0	0	1	0	.000	.000	—	—
Johnny Evers	2b	4	16	2	7	0	0	0	2	2	2	1	.438	.438	1	.960
Larry Gilbert	ph	2	0	0	0	0	0	0	0	1	0	0	—	—	—	—
Hank Gowdy	c	4	11	3	6	3	1	1	3	5	1	1	.545	1.273	0	1.000
Bill James	p	2	4	0	0	0	0	0	0	0	4	0	.000	.000	0	1.000
Les Mann	rf-lf	3	7	1	2	0	0	0	1	0	1	0	.286	.286	0	1.000
Rabbit Maranville	ss	4	13	1	4	0	0	0	3	1	1	2	.308	.308	1	.952
Herbie Moran	rf	3	13	2	1	1	0	0	0	1	1	1	.077	.154	1	.667
Dick Rudolph	p	2	6	1	2	0	0	0	1	1	0	0	.333	.333	0	1.000
Butch Schmidt	1b	4	17	2	5	0	0	0	2	0	2	1	.294	.294	0	1.000
Lefty Tyler	p	1	3	0	0	0	0	0	0	0	1	0	.000	.000	0	1.000
Possum Whitted	cf	4	14	2	3	0	1	0	2	3	1	1	.214	.357	0	1.000
Totals		**4**	**135**	**16**	**33**	**6**	**2**	**1**	**14**	**15**	**18**	**9**	**.244**	**.341**	**4**	**.978**

Pitcher	G	GS	CG	IP	H	R	ER	BB	SO	W-L	Sv	ERA
Bill James	2	1	1	11	2	0	0	6	9	2-0	0	0.00
Dick Rudolph	2	2	2	18	12	2	1	4	15	2-0	0	0.50
Lefty Tyler	1	1	0	10	8	4	4	3	4	0-0	0	3.60
Totals	**4**	**4**	**3**	**39**	**22**	**6**	**5**	**13**	**28**	**4-0**	**0**	**1.15**

PHILADELPHIA ATHLETICS/Connie Mack, Manager

Player	pos	G	AB	R	H	2B	3B	HR	RBI	BB	SO	SB	BA	SA	E	FPct
Frank Baker	3b	4	16	0	4	2	0	0	2	1	3	0	.250	.375	0	1.000
Jack Barry	ss	4	14	1	1	0	0	0	0	1	3	1	.071	.071	1	.962
Chief Bender	p	1	2	0	0	0	0	0	0	0	0	0	.000	.000	0	1.000
Joe Bush	p	1	5	0	0	0	0	0	0	0	2	0	.000	.000	1	.833
Eddie Collins	2b	4	14	0	3	0	0	0	1	2	1	1	.214	.214	0	1.000
Jack Lapp	c	1	1	0	0	0	0	0	0	0	0	0	.000	.000	0	1.000
Stuffy McInnis	1b	4	14	2	2	1	0	0	3	3	0	0	.143	.214	0	1.000
Eddie Murphy	rf	4	16	2	3	2	0	0	0	2	2	0	.188	.313	0	1.000
Rube Oldring	lf	4	15	0	1	0	0	0	0	0	5	0	.067	.067	0	1.000
Herb Pennock	p	1	1	0	0	0	0	0	0	0	0	0	.000	.000	0	—
Eddie Plank	p	1	2	0	0	0	0	0	0	0	1	0	.000	.000	0	1.000
Wally Schang	c	4	12	1	2	1	0	0	1	0	4	0	.167	.250	1	.955
Bob Shawkey	p	1	2	0	1	1	0	0	1	0	1	0	.500	1.000	0	1.000
Amos Strunk	cf	2	7	2	2	0	0	0	0	2	0	0	.286	.286	0	1.000
Jimmy Walsh	ph-cf	3	6	0	2	1	0	0	1	3	1	0	.333	.500	0	1.000
Weldon Wyckoff	p	1	1	0	1	1	0	0	0	0	0	0	1.000	2.000	0	1.000
Totals		**4**	**128**	**6**	**22**	**9**	**0**	**0**	**5**	**13**	**28**	**2**	**.172**	**.242**	**3**	**.983**

Pitcher	G	GS	CG	IP	H	R	ER	BB	SO	W-L	Sv	ERA
Chief Bender	1	1	0	5⅓	8	6	6	2	3	0-1	0	10.13
Joe Bush	1	1	1	11	9	5	4	4	4	0-1	0	3.27
Herb Pennock	1	0	0	3	2	0	0	2	3	0-0	0	0.00
Eddie Plank	1	1	1	9	7	1	1	4	6	0-1	0	1.00
Bob Shawkey	1	1	0	5	4	3	2	2	0	0-0	0	3.60
Weldon Wyckoff	1	0	0	3⅔	3	1	1	1	2	0-0	0	2.45
Totals	**4**	**4**	**2**	**37**	**33**	**16**	**14**	**15**	**18**	**0-4**	**0**	**3.41**

Series Outstanding Player: Hank Gowdy, Boston Braves. **Series Outstanding Pitcher:** Bill James, Boston Braves. **Average Length of Game:** 2 hours, 12 minutes. **Total Attendance:** 111,009. **Average Attendance:** 27,752 (34,943 at Fenway Park; 20,562 at Shibe Park).
Umpires: Bill Byron (NL), Bill Dinneen (AL), George Hildebrand (AL), Bill Klem (NL). **Winning Player's Share:** $2,812. **Losing Player's Share:** $2,032.

Below: Hank Gowdy was phenomenal during the 1914 Series, batting .545 with a 1.273 slugging average.

Right: Charlie Deal stole third after doubling in the top of the ninth inning of Game 2 at Shibe Park; he went on to score the game-winning run.

The Braves topped the Athletics in 12 innings in Game 3 at Fenway Park, putting themselves one win away from a startling Series victory.

Right: After the heavily favored A's were swept in 1914, Connie Mack sold away his stars, sending the team straight to the bottom of the standings in the next eight seasons.

Left: Bill James and Dick Rudolph won all four games for manager George Stallings (center) in 1914.

Game 1 Friday, October 9 at Shibe Park, Philadelphia

	1	2	3	4	5	6	7	8	9	R	H	E
Boston Braves	0	2	0	0	1	3	0	1	0	7	11	2
Philadelphia Athletics	0	1	0	0	0	0	0	0	0	1	5	0

Pitchers Bos Dick Rudolph (W, 1-0), IP 9, H 5, R 1, ER 0, BB 3, SO 8
Phi Chief Bender (L, 0-1), IP 5⅓, H 8, R 6, ER 6, BB 2, SO 3; Weldon Wyckoff, IP 3⅔, H 3, R 1, ER 1, BB 1, SO 2

Top Performers at the Plate
Bos Hank Gowdy, 3 for 3, 2 R, 1 RBI, 1 BB; Possum Whitted, 1 for 3, 2 R, 2 RBI, 1 BB

2B-Bos/Gowdy; Phi/Baker, Wyckoff. **3B**-Bos/Gowdy, Whitted. **SB**-Bos/Gowdy, Moran, Schmidt. **Time** 1:58. **Attendance** 20,562.

Game 2 Saturday, October 10 at Shibe Park, Philadelphia

	1	2	3	4	5	6	7	8	9	R	H	E
Boston Braves	0	0	0	0	0	0	0	0	1	1	7	1
Philadelphia Athletics	0	0	0	0	0	0	0	0	0	0	2	1

Pitchers Bos Bill James (W, 1-0), IP 9, H 2, R 0, ER 0, BB 3, SO 8
Phi Eddie Plank (L, 0-1), IP 9, H 7, R 1, ER 1, BB 4, SO 6

Top Performers at the Plate
Bos Johnny Evers, 2 for 4, 1 BB; Les Mann, 2 for 5, 1 RBI

2B-Bos/Deal; Phi/Schang. **SB**-Bos/Deal 2; Phi/Barry. **Time** 1:56. **Attendance** 20,562.

Game 3 Monday, October 12 at Fenway Park, Boston

	1	2	3	4	5	6	7	8	9	10	11	12	R	H	E
Philadelphia Athletics	1	0	0	1	0	0	0	0	0	2	0	0	4	8	2
Boston Braves	0	1	0	1	0	0	0	0	0	2	0	1	5	9	1

Pitchers Phi Joe Bush (L, 0-1), IP 11, H 9, R 5, ER 4, BB 4, SO 4
Bos Lefty Tyler, IP 10, H 8, R 4, ER 4, BB 3, SO 4; Bill James (W, 2-0), IP 2, H 0, R 0, ER 0, BB 3, SO 1

Top Performers at the Plate
Phi Frank Baker, 2 for 5, 2 R, 1 BB; Eddie Murphy, 2 for 5, 2 R, 2 2B, 1 BB
Bos Johnny Evers, 3 for 5; Hank Gowdy 3 for 4, 1 R, 2 RBI, 1 BB

2B-Phi/Baker, McInnis, Murphy 2; Bos/Deal, Gowdy 2. **HR**-Bos/Gowdy. **SB**-Phi/Collins; Bos/Evers, Maranville 2. **Time** 3:06. **Attendance** 35,520.

Game 4 Tuesday, October 13 at Fenway Park, Boston

	1	2	3	4	5	6	7	8	9	R	H	E
Philadelphia Athletics	0	0	0	0	1	0	0	0	0	1	7	0
Boston Braves	0	0	0	1	2	0	0	0	x	3	6	0

Pitchers Phi Bob Shawkey (L, 0-1), IP 5, H 4, R 3, ER 2, BB 2, SO 0; Herb Pennock, IP 3, H 2, R 0, ER 0, BB 2, SO 3
Bos Dick Rudolph (W, 2-0), IP 8, H 7, R 1, ER 1, BB 1, SO 7

Top Performers at the Plate
Phi Jack Barry, 1 for 3, 1 R
Bos Johnny Evers, 1 for 3, 1 R, 2 RBI, 1 BB; Possum Whitted, 2 for 3, 1 BB

2B-Phi/Shawkey, Walsh; Bos/Moran. **SB**-Bos/Whitted. **Time** 1:49. **Attendance** 34,365.

Cinderella Stories
Great World Series Upsets

Anything can happen in a seven-game series. That saying has never been more true than in these ten October surprises. Sometimes a team that is considered a sure thing for a World Series victory comes up against a wily David who slays the Goliath. The contests listed here defied all pre-series predictions and saw the underdog rise to the top.

3 Pirates Stun Yanks in Dramatic Game 7 Win — 1960

The 1960 New York Yankees may not be the best team ever to lose a World Series, and the 1960 Pittsburgh Pirates were far from the worst team ever to win one. But never before or since has a team so outplayed its competition through the first 62 innings of a Fall Classic, only to lose in the final at-bat. The Yanks shat-

> The two teams that have the highest regular-season winning percentages in baseball history both went down in defeat in the Fall Classic: the 1906 Cubs and the 1954 Indians.

Below: Shea Stadium erupted in mayhem on October 16, 1969, after the Amazin' Mets secured the final out against the favored Baltimore Orioles. Above: The New York Giants of 1954 did something nobody thought possible: they defeated an awesome Cleveland team…in four straight games.

1 Mays and Rhodes Spark Giants to Sweep of Cleveland — 1954

The Cleveland Indians posted a 111-43 record in 1954, best ever in the American League. Their legendary pitching staff boasted the top three ERA leaders, and their lineup led the league in home runs. The New York Giants were definitely a good team that season—just nowhere near as good as the Indians. But the year doesn't end in September. In October, Willie Mays and Dusty Rhodes pulled the rug out from under Cleveland with dramatic plays in the opening game of the Series, and three days later, the Indians were down and out, four games to none.

2 Miracle Mets Shock the World — 1969

Before the start of the 1969 season, the New York Mets were baseball's laughingstocks. Although they catapulted from dead last to next to last in 1968, the "Amazin' Mets" lost over 100 games in six of their first eight seasons. The Baltimore Orioles, by contrast, were in the midst of a run of six pennants in eight years, and in 1969 they finished with 109 victories, fourth most of all time. It was simply no competition. But after winning 100 games in 1969 and sweeping the Braves in the playoffs, the Mets found themselves in the Fall Classic. They lost the first game to Baltimore, as everybody expected, and then swept the next four—as no one did.

tered records for runs scored, hits and batting average; they outscored the Pirates by a record 28 runs in the seven games; they clobbered them by scores of 16-3, 10-0 and 12-0 in their three wins. But the Pirates won the Series. Bill Mazeroski's home run in the bottom of the ninth inning of Game 7 stands as perhaps the greatest moment in postseason history.

4 "Hitless Wonders" Upend Baseball's Winningest Team — 1906

The 1906 Chicago Cubs won more games (116) than any team in history, and they claimed the pennant by a 20-game lead. The Chicago White Sox, meanwhile, needed a late-season 19-game winning streak to eke out a three-game edge in the American League. Both teams offered excellent pitching, but while the Cubs led their league in batting, runs and slugging, the White Sox hit a league-worst .230 and were known as the "Hitless Wonders." All signs pointed to a Cub victory—all signs, that is, but the final score in games: Chicago White Sox 4, Chicago Cubs, 2.

Above: The Miracle Braves from Boston toppled a dynasty in 1914.

5 Miracle Braves Sweep Mack's Athletics — 1914

The Philadelphia Athletics assumed the label of "dynasty" by winning four pennants in five years, culminating in a 99-win season in 1914. While the A's cruised to the top of the AL, the Boston Braves were at the bottom of the National League as late as mid-July. Then they went on a fantastic run to claim first place by Labor Day. It was a miracle that the Braves were even in the World Series in 1914, and it would take an even greater one to defeat Connie Mack's Philadelphia powerhouse. And that they did, in shocking fashion, taking the first four-game sweep in Series play.

6 Gibson Inspires Dodgers to Surprising Win — 1988 and
7 Oakland Powerhouse Overwhelmed by Reds in Four-Game Sweep — 1990

On three different occasions, the Athletics franchise put together three consecutive pennants (once in Philadelphia, twice in Oakland). The 1988–90 Oakland A's won 306 games during their three-year run, but they had only one World Series trophy to show for it. The 1988 club, winners of 104 games in the regular season, were undermined by the heroics of LA's Kirk Gibson in the Series opener and by Orel Hershiser's dominating performance on the mound. The A's rebounded from the disappointing 1988 loss with an easy victory over San Francisco in 1989 and were back in 1990 for a chance at back-to-back titles.

Oakland came into the Series against the Cincinnati Reds with a 10-game winning streak in postseason play, dating back to the 1989 ALCS. The Reds held the A's to eight runs in the 4 games, and Oakland's fortunes turned 180 degrees from the previous year. After sweeping the Giants in 4 straight in 1989, the A's were the victims in only the 13th sweep in World Series history in 1990.

8 "Dem Bums" Win! — 1955

The Brooklyn Dodger team of 1955 almost doesn't belong in a list of surprise champions. The talent-filled club earned its fifth pennant in nine years, and they led the league in most pitching and hitting categories in 1955. But in each of the Dodgers' five previous World Series appearances, they faced the same outcome: defeat at the hands of the New York Yankees. Finally in 1955, they exorcised the demons of the past and came out victorious against their old crosstown nemesis.

9 Pepper Martin Leads Cards Over A's — 1931

The old sage Connie Mack established another dynasty in Philadelphia when his Athletics won three straight pennants from 1929 to 1931. The last year in that run was the pinnacle, as the A's won a franchise-best 107 games. In the Series they were to face a St. Louis ball club that they had dispatched in 6 games a year earlier. In 1931, however, St. Louis's young outfielder Pepper Martin put together one of the all-time-best Series performances, collecting 12 hits in 24 at-bats to lead the Cardinals to a 7-game triumph.

10 Expansion Marlins Take Series As Wild Cards — 1997

In 1993, the Florida Marlins joined the National League Eastern Division as part of baseball's first expansion in 17 years. The following season Major League Baseball realigned the 28 teams into six divisions and expanded the postseason to include a wild card entrant from each league. In 1997, the Marlins became the first wild card to make it through both the divisional series and league championship to reach the final stage. They battled the Cleveland Indians in a tough seven-game contest before clinching the title as the youngest team ever to win the World Series.

The 1987 Minnesota Twins had the lowest regular-season winning percentage of any team to win the World Series; they went 85-77 (.535) during the year. The 1973 Mets had the lowest winning percentage (.509) of any team to reach the Fall Classic, but they lost to Oakland in the Series.

Left: Craig Counsell is mobbed by teammates after scoring the winning run on Edgar Renteria's hit in the bottom of the 11th inning in Game 7 of the 1997 World Series.

Boston Red Sox (4) vs. Philadelphia Phillies (1)

1915

Beantown squared off against the City of Brotherly Love for the second year in a row, but rather than the Braves and the A's, the 1915 contest featured the American League's Red Sox and the National League's Phillies, who were making their first Series appearance. Further complicating things, the Red Sox played their Series home games at newly constructed Braves Field, a "superstadium" seating some 40,000 spectators. The Sox secured their second pennant of the decade with their all-star outfield of Tris Speaker, Duffy Lewis and Harry Hooper and a strong pitching staff. Coming off a 31-win season, Grover Cleveland "Pete" Alexander brought his stuff to the mound for Philly in Game 1. Alexander allowed just one run in the game, and Philadelphia's two runs in the eighth inning (scored on two walks and two infield singles) were enough for the 3-1 win. The game also saw the World Series debut of a young pitcher who won 18 games in the regular season but whose only appearance in the 1915 Series was as a pinch hitter. The young Babe Ruth, batting for the pitcher, grounded out to first base in the ninth inning. With President Woodrow Wilson in attendance for Game 2—the first presidential appearance at a World Series—Boston's Rube Foster came through with a commanding three-hit, eight-strikeout performance. The Red Sox broke a 1-1 tie in the top of the ninth on Foster's RBI single. A record crowd of 42,300 showed up to Braves Field for the third game, with Alexander getting the start for the Phillies with only two days' rest. His arm seemed up to the task, as he scattered six hits and two runs, but Boston lefty Dutch Leonard was even better, retiring the last 20 Phillies he faced. Lewis's single in the ninth scored Hooper and gave the Sox the one-run win. Game 4 was the third straight Boston win by a 2-1 score, with starters Ernie Shore and George Chalmers both going the distance. Returning to Philadelphia for Game 5, the teams brought a little more offense to the plate. Fred Luderus gave Philadelphia the lead in the fourth inning on a solo home run, and three of Boston's first four runs came on homers: a solo blast by Hooper in the third and a two-run shot by Lewis in the eighth. With the score tied 4-4 in the ninth, the Bosox took the lead and the Series on another home run, Hooper's second of the game. The game's four round-trippers were the most hit in a Series game up till then. Though unbeknownst to them at the time, this would be the last opportunity Phillie fans would have to see their team in a World Series for more than three decades—and they would not see the Phillies win a game in the Fall Classic for another 65 years.

Above: Harry Hooper, Tris Speaker and Duffy Lewis made up an all-star outfield for Boston's 1915 world champion club.

1915 WORLD SERIES COMPOSITE STATISTICS

BOSTON RED SOX/Bill Carrigan, Manager

Player	pos	G	AB	R	H	2B	3B	HR	RBI	BB	SO	SB	BA	SA	E	FPct
Jack Barry	2b	5	17	1	3	0	0	0	1	1	2	0	.176	.176	1	.947
Hick Cady	c	4	6	0	2	0	0	0	0	1	2	0	.333	.333	0	1.000
Bill Carrigan	c	1	2	0	0	0	0	0	0	1	1	0	.000	.000	0	1.000
Rube Foster	p	2	8	0	4	1	0	0	1	0	2	0	.500	.625	0	1.000
Del Gainer	1b	1	3	1	1	0	0	0	0	0	0	0	.333	.333	0	1.000
Larry Gardner	3b	5	17	2	4	0	1	0	1	0	0	0	.235	.353	0	1.000
Olaf Henriksen	ph	2	2	0	0	0	0	0	0	0	0	0	.000	.000	–	–
Dick Hoblitzell	1b	5	16	1	5	0	0	0	1	0	1	1	.313	.313	0	.976
Harry Hooper	rf	5	20	4	7	0	0	2	2	4	0	1	.350	.650	1	.889
Hal Janvrin	ss	1	1	0	0	0	0	0	0	0	0	0	.000	.000	0	1.000
Dutch Leonard	p	1	3	0	0	0	0	0	0	0	2	0	.000	.000	0	1.000
Duffy Lewis	lf	5	18	1	8	1	0	1	5	1	4	0	.444	.667	0	1.000
Babe Ruth	ph	1	1	0	0	0	0	0	0	0	0	0	.000	.000	–	–
Everett Scott	ss	5	18	0	1	0	0	0	0	0	3	0	.056	.056	0	1.000
Ernie Shore	p	2	5	0	1	0	0	0	0	0	3	0	.200	.200	1	.833
Tris Speaker	cf	5	17	2	5	0	1	0	0	4	1	0	.294	.412	0	1.000
Pinch Thomas	c	2	5	0	1	0	0	0	0	0	2	0	.200	.200	0	1.000
Totals		5	159	12	42	2	2	3	11	11	25	1	.264	.358	4	.979

Pitcher	G	GS	CG	IP	H	R	ER	BB	SO	W-L	Sv	ERA
Rube Foster	2	2	2	18	12	5	4	2	13	2-0	0	2.00
Dutch Leonard	1	1	1	9	3	1	1	0	6	1-0	0	1.00
Ernie Shore	2	2	2	17	12	4	4	8	6	1-1	0	2.12
Totals	5	5	5	44	27	10	9	10	25	4-1	0	1.84

PHILADELPHIA PHILLIES/Pat Moran, Manager

Player	pos	G	AB	R	H	2B	3B	HR	RBI	BB	SO	SB	BA	SA	E	FPct
Pete Alexander	p	2	5	0	1	0	0	0	0	0	1	0	.200	.200	0	1.000
Dave Bancroft	ss	5	17	2	5	0	0	0	1	2	2	0	.294	.294	1	.958
Beals Becker	lf-rf	2	0	0	0	0	0	0	0	0	0	0	–	–	0	–
Ed Burns	c	5	16	1	3	0	0	0	1	1	2	0	.188	.188	1	.973
Bobby Byrne	ph	1	1	0	0	0	0	0	0	0	0	0	.000	.000	–	–
George Chalmers	p	1	3	0	1	0	0	0	0	0	1	0	.333	.333	0	1.000
Gavvy Cravath	rf	5	16	2	2	1	1	0	1	2	6	0	.125	.313	0	1.000
Oscar Dugey	pr	2	0	0	0	0	0	0	0	0	0	1	–	–	–	–
Bill Killefer	ph	1	1	0	0	0	0	0	0	0	0	0	.000	.000	–	–
Fred Luderus	1b	5	16	1	7	2	0	1	6	1	4	0	.438	.750	1	.977
Erskine Mayer	p	2	4	0	0	0	0	0	0	0	2	0	.000	.000	0	1.000
Bert Niehoff	2b	5	16	1	1	0	0	0	0	1	5	0	.063	.063	0	1.000
Dode Paskert	cf	5	19	2	3	0	0	0	0	1	2	0	.158	.158	0	1.000
Eppa Rixey	p	1	2	0	1	0	0	0	0	0	0	0	.500	.500	0	1.000
Milt Stock	3b	5	17	1	2	1	0	0	0	1	0	0	.118	.176	0	1.000
Possum Whitted	lf-1b	5	15	0	1	0	0	0	1	1	0	1	.067	.067	0	1.000
Totals		5	148	10	27	4	1	1	9	10	25	2	.182	.243	3	.984

Pitcher	G	GS	CG	IP	H	R	ER	BB	SO	W-L	Sv	ERA
Pete Alexander	2	2	2	17⅓	14	3	3	4	10	1-1	0	1.53
George Chalmers	1	1	1	8	8	2	2	3	6	0-1	0	2.25
Erskine Mayer	2	2	1	11⅓	16	4	3	2	7	0-1	0	2.38
Eppa Rixey	1	0	0	6⅔	4	3	2	2	0	0-1	0	4.05
Totals	5	5	4	43⅔	42	12	11	11	25	1-4	0	2.27

Series Outstanding Player: Duffy Lewis, Boston Red Sox. **Series Outstanding Pitcher:** Rube Foster, Boston Red Sox. **Average Length of Game:** 2 hours, 2 minutes. **Total Attendance:** 143,351. **Average Attendance:** 28,670 (41,698 at Braves Field; 19,985 at Baker Bowl).
Umpires: Billy Evans (AL), Bill Klem (NL), Francis O'Loughlin (AL), Cy Rigler (NL). **Winning Player's Share:** $3,780. **Losing Player's Share:** $2,520.

Right: In 1915, Woodrow Wilson became the first U.S. president to throw out the ceremonial first pitch at a World Series game.

Below: The Boston infield consisted of (from left to right) Larry Gardner at third, Everett Scott at short, Jack Barry at second, and Dick Hoblitzell at first.

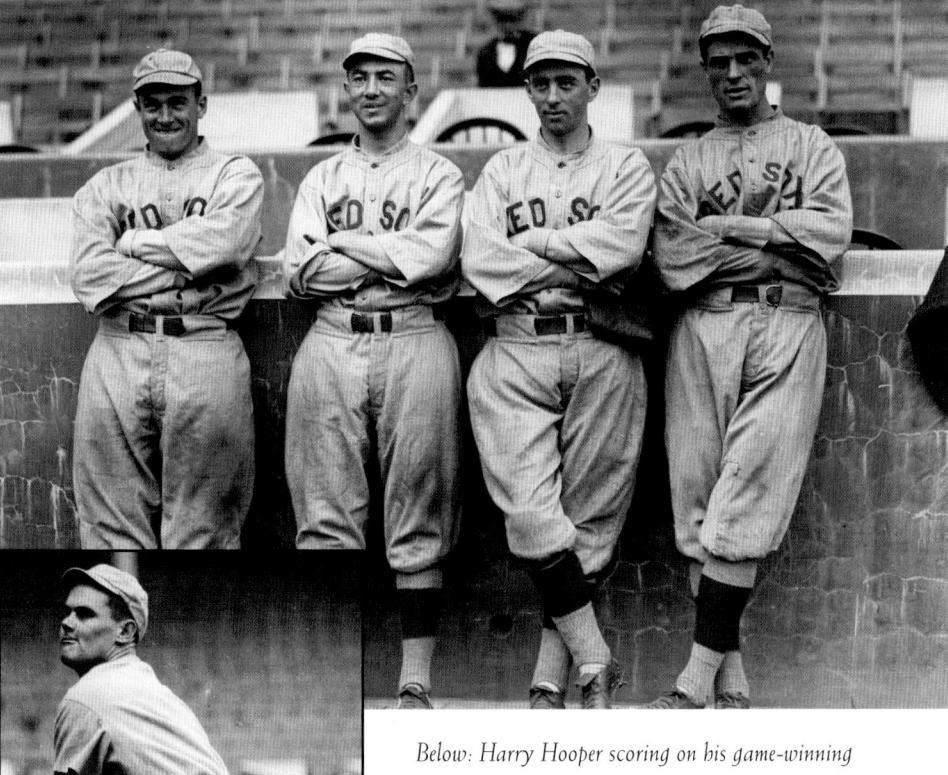

Below: Harry Hooper scoring on his game-winning homer in the final contest of 1915.

Above: Lefty Dutch Leonard three-hit the Phillies to defeat Grover Cleveland Alexander in Game 3.

Game 1   Friday, October 8 at Baker Bowl, Philadelphia

	1	2	3	4	5	6	7	8	9	R	H	E
Boston Red Sox	0	0	0	0	0	0	0	1	0	1	8	1
Philadelphia Phillies	0	0	1	0	0	0	2	x		3	5	1

Pitchers   Bos   Ernie Shore (L, 0-1), IP 8, H 5, R 3, ER 3, BB 4, SO 2
Phi   Pete Alexander (W, 1-0), IP 9, H 8, R 1, ER 1, BB 2, SO 6

Top Performers at the Plate
Bos   Duffy Lewis, 2 for 4, 1 RBI
Phi   Dode Paskert, 1 for 3, 1 R, 1 BB; Possum Whitted, 1 for 2, 1 RBI, 1 BB

SB-Bos/Hoblitzell; Phi/Whitted. **Time** 1:58. **Attendance** 19,343.

Game 2   Saturday, October 9 at Baker Bowl, Philadelphia

	1	2	3	4	5	6	7	8	9	R	H	E
Boston Red Sox	1	0	0	0	0	0	0	0	1	2	10	0
Philadelphia Phillies	0	0	0	1	0	0	0	0		1	3	1

Pitchers   Bos   Rube Foster (W, 1-0), IP 9, H 3, R 1, ER 1, BB 2, SO 8
Phi   Erskine Mayer (L, 0-1), IP 9, H 10, R 2, ER 1, BB 2, SO 7

Top Performers at the Plate
Bos   Rube Foster, 3 for 4, 1 RBI; Harry Hooper, 1 for 3, 1 R, 2 BB
Phi   Gavvy Cravath, 1 for 3, 1 R; Fred Luderus, 1 for 3, 1 RBI

2B-Bos/Foster; Phi/Cravath, Luderus. **Time** 2:05. **Attendance** 20,306.

Game 3   Monday, October 11 at Braves Field, Boston

	1	2	3	4	5	6	7	8	9	R	H	E
Philadelphia Phillies	0	0	1	0	0	0	0	0	0	1	3	0
Boston Red Sox	0	0	0	1	0	0	0	0	1	2	6	1

Pitchers   Phi   Pete Alexander (L, 1-1), IP 8⅔, H 6, R 2, ER 2, BB 2, SO 4
Bos   Dutch Leonard (W, 1-0), IP 9, H 3, R 1, ER 1, BB 0, SO 6

Top Performers at the Plate
Phi   Dave Bancroft, 1 for 3, 1 RBI, 1 SH
Bos   Duffy Lewis, 3 for 4, 1 RBI; Tris Speaker, 2 for 3, 1 R, 1 BB

2B-Phi/Stock. 3B-Bos/Speaker. **Time** 1:48. **Attendance** 42,300.

Game 4   Tuesday, October 12 at Braves Field, Boston

	1	2	3	4	5	6	7	8	9	R	H	E
Philadelphia Phillies	0	0	0	0	0	0	1	0		1	7	0
Boston Red Sox	0	0	1	0	0	1	0	0	x	2	8	1

Pitchers   Phi   George Chalmers (L, 0-1), IP 8, H 8, R 2, ER 2, BB 3, SO 6
Bos   Ernie Shore (W, 1-1), IP 9, H 7, R 1, ER 1, BB 4, SO 4

Top Performers at the Plate
Phi   Fred Luderus, 3 for 4, 1 RBI
Bos   Hick Cady, 2 for 3; Dick Hoblitzell, 3 for 4, 1 R

2B-Bos/Lewis. 3B-Phi/Cravath. SB-Phi/Dugey. **Time** 2:05. **Attendance** 41,096.

Game 5   Wednesday, October 13 at Baker Bowl, Philadelphia

	1	2	3	4	5	6	7	8	9	R	H	E
Boston Red Sox	0	1	1	0	0	0	0	2	1	5	10	1
Philadelphia Phillies	2	0	0	2	0	0	0	0	0	4	9	1

Pitchers   Bos   Rube Foster (W, 2-0), IP 9, H 9, R 4, ER 3, BB 2, SO 5
Phi   Erskine Mayer, IP 2⅓, H 6, R 2, ER 2, BB 0, SO 0; Eppa Rixey (L, 0-1), IP 6⅔, H 4, R 3, ER 3, BB 2, SO 2

Top Performers at the Plate
Bos   Harry Hooper, 3 for 4, 2 R, 2 RBI, 1 HBP, 2 HR; Duffy Lewis, 1 for 4, 1 R, 2 RBI
Phi   Dave Bancroft, 2 for 4, 1 R; Fred Luderus, 2 for 2, 1 R, 3 RBI, 1 BB, 1 HBP

2B-Phi/Luderus. 3B-Bos/Gardner. **HR**-Bos/Hooper 2, Lewis; Phi/Luderus. **Time** 2:15.
Attendance 20,306.

Boston Red Sox (4) vs. Brooklyn Robins (1)

1916

Though the Red Sox had lost their Hall of Fame outfielder Tris Speaker to Cleveland in the off-season, they still coasted to a second straight pennant, mostly on the work of a pitching staff that featured five hurlers with 13 or more wins. The leader of the staff was second-year lefty Babe Ruth and his 23 wins and 1.75 ERA. The National League sent a first-timer to the World Series for the third year in a row, as the team from Brooklyn (known then as the Robins, later the Dodgers), made their first appearance in a Fall Classic. Brooklyn manager Wilbert Robinson thought that his best chance against Boston was to send in his southpaws to start the first two games, and he went with former Giant standout Rube Marquard in the opener. The Red Sox countered with Ernie Shore. After scoring one run through the first 8, the Robins hit Shore hard for four runs in the 9th, but it was not enough, and Boston squeaked out a 6-5 win. The second game, with 47,373 in attendance, saw one of the best World Series pitching duels ever. Brooklyn opened the game with a two-out, inside-the-park home run by Hy Myers in the 1st. Boston got on the board two innings later when Everett Scott's triple was followed by an RBI grounder by the pitcher, Babe Ruth. Then starters Ruth for Boston and Sherry Smith for Brooklyn buckled down, scattering three and four hits, respectively, over ten straight shutout innings. Finally, in the 14th, with both starters still in the game, the Red Sox scored a run in the bottom half of the inning on a walk to Dick Hoblitzell (his fourth of the game) and a single by pinch hitter Del Gainer, ending the longest game by innings in Series history. The teams met at Ebbets Field the following day, and Brooklyn salvaged their first World Series win behind another Series old-timer, Jack Coombs. Ivy Olson's two-run triple in the 5th gave Brooklyn the insurance it needed, and 25-game-winner Jack Pfeffer came on in relief to retire the last eight Boston batters for a 4-3 win. Though Brooklyn scored a pair of runs in the opening stanza of Game 4 off Dutch Leonard, Larry Gardner's three-run, inside-the-park homer in the 2nd gave the Sox a 3-2 lead that they would extend by another three runs. Ernie Shore notched his second win in Game 5, holding Brooklyn to just three hits and one unearned run. While Duffy Lewis's .353 average and Harry Hooper's .333 paced Boston to its second world championship in a row, the hitting leader of the Series was Brooklyn's young right fielder, an eccentric loudmouth by the name of Casey Stengel. Thirty-three years before managing his first World Series team, Stengel hit a blistering .364 as a Dodger in 1916.

Above: Boston's formidable staff of Foster, Mays, Shore, Ruth and Leonard posted a 1.47 team ERA in the 1916 Series.

1916 WORLD SERIES COMPOSITE STATISTICS

BOSTON RED SOX/Bill Carrigan, Manager

Player	pos	G	AB	R	H	2B	3B	HR	RBI	BB	SO	SB	BA	SA	E	FPct
Hick Cady	c	2	4	1	1	0	0	0	0	3	0	0	.250	.250	0	1.000
Bill Carrigan	c	1	3	0	2	0	0	0	1	0	1	0	.667	.667	0	1.000
Rube Foster	p	1	1	0	0	0	0	0	0	0	1	0	.000	.000	0	1.000
Del Gainer	ph	1	1	0	1	0	0	0	1	0	0	0	1.000	1.000	–	–
Larry Gardner	3b	5	17	2	3	0	0	2	6	0	2	0	.176	.529	2	.929
Olaf Henriksen	ph	1	0	1	0	0	0	0	0	1	0	0	–	–	–	–
Dick Hoblitzell	1b	5	17	3	4	1	1	0	2	6	0	0	.235	.412	0	1.000
Harry Hooper	rf	5	21	6	7	1	1	0	1	3	1	1	.333	.476	0	1.000
Hal Janvrin	2b	5	23	2	5	3	0	0	1	0	6	0	.217	.348	2	.920
Dutch Leonard	p	1	3	0	0	0	0	0	0	1	3	0	.000	.000	0	1.000
Duffy Lewis	lf	5	17	3	6	2	1	0	1	2	1	0	.353	.588	0	1.000
Carl Mays	p	2	1	0	0	0	0	0	0	0	1	0	.000	.000	0	1.000
Mike McNally	pr	1	0	1	0	0	0	0	0	0	0	0	–	–	–	–
Babe Ruth	p	1	5	0	0	0	0	0	1	0	2	0	.000	.000	0	1.000
Everett Scott	ss	5	16	1	2	0	1	0	1	1	1	0	.125	.250	2	.943
Ernie Shore	p	2	7	0	0	0	0	0	0	0	2	0	.000	.000	0	1.000
Chick Shorten	cf	2	7	0	4	0	0	0	2	0	1	0	.571	.571	0	1.000
Pinch Thomas	c	3	7	0	1	0	1	0	0	0	1	0	.143	.429	0	1.000
Tilly Walker	cf	3	11	1	3	0	1	0	1	1	2	0	.273	.455	0	1.000
Jimmy Walsh	cf	1	3	0	0	0	0	0	0	0	0	0	.000	.000	0	1.000
Totals		**5**	**164**	**21**	**39**	**7**	**6**	**2**	**18**	**18**	**25**	**1**	**.238**	**.390**	**6**	**.975**

Pitcher	G	GS	CG	IP	H	R	ER	BB	SO	W-L	Sv	ERA
Rube Foster	1	0	0	3	3	0	0	0	1	0-0	0	0.00
Dutch Leonard	1	1	1	9	5	2	1	4	3	1-0	0	1.00
Carl Mays	2	1	0	5⅓	8	4	3	3	2	0-1	1	5.06
Babe Ruth	1	1	1	14	6	1	1	3	4	1-0	0	0.64
Ernie Shore	2	2	1	17⅔	12	6	3	4	9	2-0	0	1.53
Totals	**5**	**5**	**3**	**49**	**34**	**13**	**8**	**14**	**19**	**4-1**	**1**	**1.47**

BROOKLYN ROBINS/Wilbert Robinson, Manager

Player	pos	G	AB	R	H	2B	3B	HR	RBI	BB	SO	SB	BA	SA	E	FPct
Larry Cheney	p	1	0	0	0	0	0	0	0	0	0	0	–	–	1	.000
Jack Coombs	p	1	3	0	1	0	0	0	1	0	0	0	.333	.333	0	1.000
George Cutshaw	2b	5	19	2	2	1	0	0	2	1	1	0	.105	.158	2	.938
Jake Daubert	1b	4	17	1	3	0	1	0	0	2	3	0	.176	.294	0	1.000
Wheezer Dell	p	1	0	0	0	0	0	0	0	0	0	0	–	–	0	–
Gus Getz	ph	1	1	0	0	0	0	0	0	0	0	0	.000	.000	–	–
Jimmy Johnston	rf	3	10	1	3	0	1	0	0	1	0	0	.300	.500	1	.500
Rube Marquard	p	2	3	0	0	0	0	0	0	0	1	0	.000	.000	0	1.000
Fred Merkle	1b	3	4	0	1	0	0	0	1	2	0	0	.250	.250	1	.909
Chief Meyers	c	3	10	0	2	0	1	0	0	1	0	0	.200	.400	0	1.000
Otto Miller	c	2	8	0	1	0	0	0	0	0	1	0	.125	.125	0	1.000
Mike Mowrey	3b	5	17	2	3	0	0	0	1	3	2	0	.176	.176	2	.920
Hy Myers	cf	5	22	2	4	0	0	1	3	0	3	0	.182	.318	0	1.000
Ivy Olson	ss	5	16	1	4	0	1	0	2	2	2	0	.250	.375	–	–
Ollie O'Mara	ph	1	1	0	0	0	0	0	0	0	1	0	.000	.000	4	.840
Jeff Pfeffer	p	4	4	0	1	0	0	0	0	0	2	0	.250	.250	0	1.000
Nap Rucker	p	1	0	0	0	0	0	0	0	0	0	0	–	–	0	–
Sherry Smith	p	1	5	0	1	1	0	0	0	0	0	0	.200	.400	0	1.000
Casey Stengel	rf	4	11	2	4	0	0	0	0	0	1	0	.364	.364	1	.800
Zack Wheat	lf	5	19	2	4	0	1	0	1	2	2	1	.211	.316	1	.933
Totals		**5**	**170**	**13**	**34**	**2**	**5**	**1**	**11**	**14**	**19**	**1**	**.200**	**.288**	**13**	**.942**

Pitcher	G	GS	CG	IP	H	R	ER	BB	SO	W-L	Sv	ERA
Larry Cheney	1	0	0	3	4	2	1	1	5	0-0	0	3.00
Jack Coombs	1	1	0	6⅓	7	3	3	1	1	1-0	0	4.26
Wheezer Dell	1	0	0	1	1	0	0	0	0	0-0	0	0.00
Rube Marquard	2	2	0	11	12	9	8	6	9	0-2	0	6.55
Jeff Pfeffer	3	1	0	10⅔	7	5	2	4	5	0-1	1	1.69
Nap Rucker	1	0	0	2	1	0	0	0	3	0-0	0	0.00
Sherry Smith	1	1	1	13⅓	7	2	2	6	2	0-1	0	1.35
Totals	**5**	**5**	**1**	**47⅓**	**39**	**21**	**16**	**18**	**25**	**1-4**	**1**	**3.04**

Series Outstanding Player: Harry Hooper, Boston Red Sox. **Series Outstanding Pitcher:** Babe Ruth, Boston Red Sox. **Average Length of Game:** 2 hours, 32 minutes. **Total Attendance:** 163,859. **Average Attendance:** 32,772 (40,370 at Braves Field; 21,375 at Ebbets Field). **Umpires:** Tommy Connolly (AL), Bill Dinneen (AL), Hank O'Day (NL), Ernie Quigley (NL). **Winning Player's Share:** $3,910. **Losing Player's Share:** $2,835.

Babe Ruth's 14-inning performance in Game 2 was the longest complete game in World Series history. His 13 shutout innings started a streak that would continue for another 16 2/3 innings in the 1918 Series.

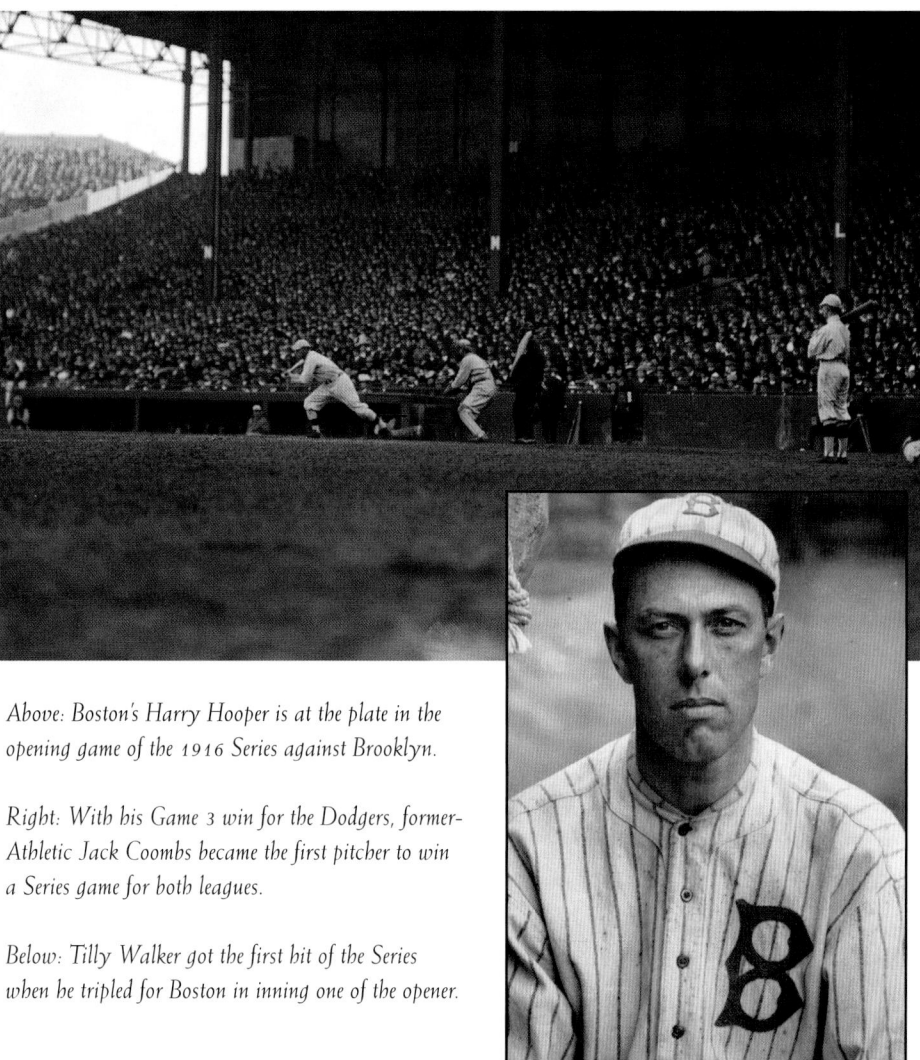

Above: Boston's Harry Hooper is at the plate in the opening game of the 1916 Series against Brooklyn.

Right: With his Game 3 win for the Dodgers, former-Athletic Jack Coombs became the first pitcher to win a Series game for both leagues.

Below: Tilly Walker got the first hit of the Series when he tripled for Boston in inning one of the opener.

Game 1 Saturday, October 7 at Braves Field, Boston

	1	2	3	4	5	6	7	8	9	R	H	E
Brooklyn Robins	0	0	0	1	0	0	0	0	4	5	10	4
Boston Red Sox	0	0	1	0	1	0	3	1	x	6	8	1

Pitchers Bro Rube Marquard (L, 0-1), IP 7, H 7, R 5, ER 4, BB 4, SO 6; Jeff Pfeffer, IP 1, H 1, R 1, ER 0, BB 2, SO 0
  Bos Ernie Shore (W, 1-0), IP 8⅔, H 9, R 5, ER 3, BB 3, SO 5; Carl Mays (Sv, 1), IP ⅓, H 1, R 0, ER 0, BB 0, SO 0

Top Performers at the Plate
  Bro Casey Stengel, 2 for 4, 2 R; Zack Wheat, 2 for 4, 1 R, 1 RBI
  Bos Hal Janvrin, 2 for 4, 1 R, 1 SH; Tilly Walker, 2 for 4, 1 R, 1 RBI, 1 BB

2B-Bos/Hooper, Janvrin, Lewis. **3B**-Bro/Meyers, Wheat; Bos/Hoblitzell, Walker. **Time** 2:16. **Attendance** 36,117.

Game 2 Monday, October 9 at Braves Field, Boston

	1	2	3	4	5	6	7	8	9	10	11	12	13	14	R	H	E
Brooklyn Robins	1	0	0	0	0	0	0	0	0	0	0	0	0	0	1	6	2
Boston Red Sox	0	0	1	0	0	0	0	0	0	0	0	0	0	1	2	7	1

Pitchers Bro Sherry Smith (L, 0-1), IP 13⅓, H 7, R 2, ER 2, BB 6, SO 2
  Bos Babe Ruth (W, 1-0), IP 14, H 6, R 1, ER 1, BB 3, SO 4

Top Performers at the Plate
  Bos Everett Scott, 2 for 4, 1 R, 1 BB

2B-Bro/Smith; Bos/Janvrin. **3B**-Bos/Scott, Thomas. **HR**-Bro/Myers. **Time** 2:32. **Attendance** 41,373.

Game 3 Tuesday, October 10 at Ebbets Field, Brooklyn

	1	2	3	4	5	6	7	8	9	R	H	E
Boston Red Sox	0	0	0	0	0	2	1	0	0	3	7	1
Brooklyn Robins	0	0	1	1	2	0	0	0	x	4	10	0

Pitchers Bos Carl Mays (L, 0-1), IP 5, H 7, R 4, ER 3, BB 3, SO 2; Rube Foster, IP 3, H 3, R 0, ER 0, BB 0, SO 1
  Bro Jack Coombs (W, 1-0), IP 6⅓, H 7, R 3, ER 3, BB 1, SO 1; Jeff Pfeffer (Sv, 1), IP 2⅔, H 0, R 0, ER 0, BB 0, SO 3

Top Performers at the Plate
  Bos Harry Hooper, 2 for 4, 1 R, 1 RBI; Chick Shorten, 3 for 4, 1 RBI
  Bro Jake Daubert, 3 for 4, 1 R; Ivy Olson, 2 for 4, 1 R, 2 RBI

3B-Bos/Hooper; Bro/Daubert, Olson. **HR**-Bos/Gardner. **SB**-Bro/Wheat. **Time** 2:01. **Attendance** 21,087.

Game 4 Wednesday, October 11 at Ebbets Field, Brooklyn

	1	2	3	4	5	6	7	8	9	R	H	E
Boston Red Sox	0	3	0	1	1	0	1	0	0	6	10	1
Brooklyn Robins	2	0	0	0	0	0	0	0	0	2	5	4

Pitchers Bos Dutch Leonard (W, 1-0), IP 9, H 5, R 2, ER 1, BB 4, SO 3
  Bro Rube Marquard (L, 0-2), IP 4, H 5, R 4, ER 4, BB 2, SO 3; Larry Cheney, IP 3, H 4, R 2, ER 1, BB 1, SO 1; Nap Rucker, IP 2, H 1, R 0, ER 0, BB 0, SO 3

Top Performers at the Plate
  Bos Dick Hoblitzell, 2 for 3, 1 R, 1 RBI, 1 BB; Duffy Lewis, 2 for 4, 2 R

2B-Bos/Hoblitzell, Lewis; Bro/Cutshaw. **3B**-Bro/Johnston. **HR**-Bos/Gardner. **SB**-Bos/Hooper. **Time** 2:30. **Attendance** 21,662.

Game 5 Thursday, October 12 at Braves Field, Boston

	1	2	3	4	5	6	7	8	9	R	H	E
Brooklyn Robins	0	1	0	0	0	0	0	0	0	1	3	3
Boston Red Sox	0	1	2	0	1	0	0	0	x	4	7	2

Pitchers Bro Jeff Pfeffer (L, 0-1), IP 7, H 6, R 4, ER 2, BB 2, SO 2; Wheezer Dell, IP 1, H 1, R 0, ER 0, BB 0, SO 0
  Bos Ernie Shore (W, 2-0), IP 9, H 3, R 1, ER 0, BB 1, SO 4

Top Performers at the Plate
  Bos Harry Hooper, 1 for 3, 2 R, 1 BB; Duffy Lewis, 2 for 3, 1 R, 1 SH

2B-Bos/Janvrin. **3B**-Bos/Lewis. **Time** 1:43. **Attendance** 43,620.

Chicago White Sox (4) vs. New York Giants (2)

Three years of rebuilding since their last World Series appearance and John McGraw's New York Giants were back in 1917. The Chicago White Sox, a team featuring all-time great hitters in "Shoeless" Joe Jackson and Eddie Collins, were representing the American League for the first time since the "Hitless Wonders" won it all in 1906. Slim Sallee and Eddie Cicotte opened the Series with matching seven-hitters, and a Happy Felsch home run in the fourth gave the ChiSox a 2-1 victory. New York's 21-game winner Ferdie Schupp was bounced out early in Game 2, and Chicago's six singles in the fourth inning led to a five-run rally and a 7-2 lead. Red Faber pitched a strong

1917

game for the Sox, though a somewhat less glorious moment met Faber in the fifth inning when he attempted to steal third base—only to find another Chicago player, Buck Weaver, already occupying the bag. Back home at the Polo Grounds for Games 3 and 4, the Giants got back-to-back shutouts by Rube Benton and Schupp to tie the Series. Giants center fielder Benny Kauff contributed two home runs in Game 4, his first two hits of the Series. New York took a 5-2 lead into the bottom of the seventh in Game 5, but two three-run innings gave the White Sox the upper hand in the game and the Series. Two days after earning the Game 5 win in relief, Faber got

Above: The World Champion Chicago White Sox of 1917.

1917 WORLD SERIES COMPOSITE STATISTICS

CHICAGO WHITE SOX/Pants Rowland, Manager

Player	pos	G	AB	R	H	2B	3B	HR	RBI	BB	SO	SB	BA	SA	E	FPct
Eddie Cicotte	p	3	7	0	1	0	0	0	0	0	1	2	0	.143	.143	1	.875
Eddie Collins	2b	6	22	4	9	1	0	0	2	2	3	3	.409	.455	0	1.000
Shano Collins	rf	6	21	2	6	1	0	0	0	0	2	0	.286	.333	3	.625
Dave Danforth	p	1	0	0	0	0	0	0	0	0	0	0	—	—	0	1.000
Red Faber	p	4	7	0	1	0	0	0	0	0	0	0	.143	.143	0	1.000
Happy Felsch	cf	6	22	4	6	1	0	1	3	1	5	0	.273	.455	0	1.000
Chick Gandil	1b	6	23	1	6	1	0	0	5	0	2	1	.261	.304	1	.986
Joe Jackson	lf	6	23	4	7	0	0	0	2	1	0	1	.304	.304	0	1.000
Nemo Leibold	rf	2	5	1	2	0	0	0	1	1	1	0	.400	.400	0	1.000
Byrd Lynn	ph	1	1	0	0	0	0	0	0	0	1	0	.000	.000	—	—
Fred McMullin	3b	6	24	1	3	1	0	0	2	1	6	0	.125	.167	1	1.000
Swede Risberg	ph	2	2	0	1	0	0	0	1	0	0	0	.500	.500	—	—
Reb Russell	p	1	0	0	0	0	0	0	0	0	0	0	—	—	0	—
Ray Schalk	c	6	19	1	5	0	0	0	2	1	1	1	.263	.263	2	.950
Buck Weaver	ss	6	21	3	7	1	0	0	1	0	2	0	.333	.381	4	.871
Lefty Williams	p	1	0	0	0	0	0	0	0	0	0	0	—	—	1	.000
Totals		**6**	**197**	**21**	**54**	**6**	**0**	**1**	**17**	**11**	**28**	**6**	**.274**	**.320**	**12**	**.952**

Pitcher	G	GS	CG	IP	H	R	ER	BB	SO	W-L	Sv	ERA
Eddie Cicotte	3	2	2	23	23	5	5	2	13	1-1	0	1.57
Dave Danforth	1	0	0	1	3	2	2	0	2	0-0	0	18.00
Red Faber	4	3	2	27	21	7	7	3	9	3-1	0	2.33
Reb Russell	1	1	0	0	2	2	1	1	0	0-0	0	—
Lefty Williams	1	0	0	1	2	1	1	0	3	0-0	0	9.00
Totals	**6**	**6**	**4**	**52**	**51**	**17**	**16**	**6**	**27**	**4-2**	**0**	**2.77**

NEW YORK GIANTS/John McGraw, Manager

Player	pos	G	AB	R	H	2B	3B	HR	RBI	BB	SO	SB	BA	SA	E	FPct
Fred Anderson	p	1	0	0	0	0	0	0	0	0	0	0	—	—	0	1.000
Rube Benton	p	2	4	0	0	0	0	0	0	0	3	0	.000	.000	0	1.000
George Burns	lf	6	22	3	5	0	0	0	2	3	6	1	.227	.227	0	1.000
Art Fletcher	ss	6	25	2	5	1	0	0	0	0	2	0	.200	.240	3	.897
Buck Herzog	2b	6	24	1	6	0	1	0	2	0	4	0	.250	.333	2	.917
Walter Holke	1b	6	21	2	6	2	0	0	1	0	6	0	.286	.381	1	.985
Benny Kauff	cf	6	25	2	4	1	0	2	5	0	2	1	.160	.440	0	1.000
Lew McCarty	c	3	5	1	2	0	1	0	1	0	0	0	.400	.800	1	.889
Pol Perritt	p	3	2	0	2	0	0	0	0	0	0	0	1.000	1.000	0	1.000
Bill Rariden	c	5	13	2	5	0	0	0	2	2	1	0	.385	.385	0	1.000
Dave Robertson	rf	6	22	3	11	1	1	0	1	0	1	0	.500	.636	1	.900
Slim Sallee	p	2	6	0	1	0	0	0	0	1	2	0	.167	.167	0	1.000
Ferdie Schupp	p	2	4	0	1	0	0	0	0	1	0	0	.250	.250	0	1.000
Jeff Tesreau	p	1	0	0	0	0	0	0	0	0	0	0	—	—	0	—
Jim Thorpe	rf	1	0	0	0	0	0	0	0	0	0	0	—	—	0	1.000
Joe Wilhoit	ph	2	1	0	0	0	0	0	0	1	0	0	.000	.000	—	—
Heinie Zimmerman	3b	6	25	1	3	0	1	0	0	1	0	0	.120	.200	3	.889
Totals		**6**	**199**	**17**	**51**	**5**	**4**	**2**	**16**	**6**	**27**	**4**	**.256**	**.352**	**11**	**.954**

Pitcher	G	GS	CG	IP	H	R	ER	BB	SO	W-L	Sv	ERA
Fred Anderson	1	0	0	2	5	4	4	0	3	0-1	0	18.00
Rube Benton	2	2	1	14	9	3	0	1	8	1-1	0	0.00
Pol Perritt	3	0	0	8⅓	9	2	1	3	3	0-0	0	1.08
Slim Sallee	2	2	1	15⅓	20	10	9	4	4	0-2	0	5.28
Ferdie Schupp	2	2	1	10⅓	11	2	2	2	9	1-0	0	1.74
Jeff Tesreau	1	0	0	1	0	0	0	1	1	0-0	0	0.00
Totals	**6**	**6**	**3**	**51**	**54**	**21**	**16**	**11**	**28**	**2-4**	**0**	**2.82**

Series Outstanding Player: Eddie Collins, Chicago White Sox. **Series Outstanding Pitcher:** Red Faber, Chicago White Sox. **Average Length of Game:** 2 hours, 10 minutes. **Total Attendance:** 186,654. **Average Attendance:** 31,109 (30,441 at Comiskey Park; 31,777 at the Polo Grounds). **Umpires:** Billy Evans (AL), Bill Klem (NL), Francis O'Loughlin (AL), Cy Rigler (NL). **Winning Player's Share:** $3,669. **Losing Player's Share:** $2,442.

the start for Chicago in Game 6 and gave up just two runs, both coming on a triple by Buck Herzog in the fifth. It took more than Faber's pitching, however, to deprive New York of a World Series title—it was another mental error that doomed McGraw's Giants. The fourth inning started off badly enough for the Giants when Chicago got two runners on base by virtue of back-to-back errors. A two-base error on a bad throw by third baseman Heinie Zimmerman and a dropped fly ball by right fielder Dave Robertson put Eddie Collins at third base and Joe Jackson at first. Felsch came to the plate next and grounded back to pitcher Rube Benton. Benton, seeing Collins break for home, threw to Zimmerman at third. Zimmerman ran toward Collins and the plate, but Collins darted past catcher Bill Rariden before Zimmerman could throw the ball. With nobody backing up Rariden, home plate was left unguarded and Collins ran home, with Zimmerman following a few paces behind. Felsch and Jackson advanced to second and third during the Collins rundown, and a single by Chick Gandil sent both runners in for Chicago. And Heinie Zimmerman's name was thus firmly set in dubious distinction alongside those of Giants Fred Merkle and Fred Snodgrass, the goats of the 1912 Series. (In all fairness to Zimmerman, the failure of first baseman Walter Holke and pitcher Benton to cover the plate allowed for the somewhat comic scene of Zimmerman chasing Collins across home plate.)

Above: Red Faber was 3–1 in the 1917 Series, including a win in relief in Game 5 and a complete-game triumph in the sixth game.

Above: Chicago's Shano Collins slides into third in the first inning of the Series.

Boston Red Sox (4) vs. Chicago Cubs (2)

With the Great War raging in Europe and ballplayers and non-ballplayers alike on the front lines, the U.S. provost marshal issued a "Work or Fight" order that stipulated all nonwar-related industry come to a halt on Labor Day. Baseball's regular season was ended with about 130 games played and the Red Sox and the Cubs holding leads in their respective leagues. A two-week grace period from the government allowed the teams to meet in a "Late-Summer Classic." The premature start didn't seem to bother Game 1 starters Babe Ruth and James "Hippo" Vaughn. A Boston run in the 4th was the only one to cross the plate that afternoon, and Ruth coasted to a 6-hit shutout win. All 11 hits in the game were singles. Opting to start only left-handed pitchers against the Boston lineup, Chicago manager Fred Mitchell went with Lefty Tyler in Game 2. Tyler limited the Red Sox to 6 hits, and a three-run 2nd inning for the Cubs was sufficient to even the Series. Due to wartime travel restrictions, the first three games were scheduled for Chicago, held at the White Sox's Comiskey Park because it was larger than the Cubs' home of Weeghman Park (later Wrigley Field). Vaughn came through with another solid outing for Chicago in Game 3, only to earn his second loss of the Series, as Carl Mays did him one better in allowing only one Cub run. Ruth kept his shutout streak alive in Game 4, holding Chicago scoreless through 7 innings—while contributing a pair of runs for himself on an RBI triple in the 4th. The Cubs finally managed to score off Ruth, collecting two runs in the 8th and tying the game. Boston brought home the game winner on an error in the bottom of the

8th, and "Bullet" Joe Bush got the save as Ruth moved to left field for the final three outs. Frustrated by the poor attendance and by the league's decision to split World Series receipts among other first-division teams, the players threatened to strike before Game 5 due to the significant reduction in their share. Nevertheless, the game went on, and Hippo Vaughn finally earned a win for all his hard work, pulling out a five-hit shutout against "Sad" Sam Jones. The fourth-lowest-scoring World Series in history ended the following day with a 2-1 win for the Red Sox. After Lefty Tyler walked two Red Sox in the 3rd inning, Chicago right fielder Max Flack dropped George Whiteman's liner, allowing both runners to come home. It's somewhat fitting that this pitcher's duel of a Series was decided by a couple of unearned runs, which Boston produced without benefit of a base hit. Though managing to bat only .186 as a team (the lowest ever by a Series victor) against a Chicago staff that allowed just six earned runs in 52 innings, the Boston Red Sox claimed their fifth World Series in five trips. Babe Ruth's two wins were a key to Boston's 1918 title; his departure following the 1919 season would be key to the Red Sox drought of 82 years (and counting) without another World Series victory—at least in the eyes of Boston fans and believers in the "Curse of the Bambino." (Of course, the Cubs haven't won one since 1908, the longest drought in all professional team sports.)

Above: Boston's pitchers were again dominant in 1918.

1918 WORLD SERIES COMPOSITE STATISTICS

BOSTON RED SOX/Ed Barrow, Manager

Player	pos	G	AB	R	H	2B	3B	HR	RBI	BB	SO	SB	BA	SA	E	FPct
Sam Agnew	c	4	9	0	0	0	0	0	0	0	0	0	.000	.000	0	1.000
Joe Bush	p	2	2	0	0	0	0	0	1	0	0	0	.000	.000	0	1.000
Jean Dubuc	ph	1	1	0	0	0	0	0	0	0	1	0	.000	.000	—	—
Harry Hooper	rf	6	20	0	4	0	0	0	2	2	0	0	.200	.200	0	1.000
Sam Jones	p	1	1	0	0	0	0	0	0	1	0	0	.000	.000	0	1.000
Carl Mays	p	2	5	1	1	0	0	0	0	1	0	0	.200	.200	0	1.000
Stuffy McInnis	1b	6	20	2	5	0	0	0	1	1	1	0	.250	.250	0	1.000
Hack Miller	ph	1	1	0	0	0	0	0	0	0	0	0	.000	.000	—	—
Babe Ruth	p-lf	3	5	0	1	0	1	0	2	0	2	0	.200	.600	0	1.000
Wally Schang	ph-c	5	9	1	4	0	0	0	1	2	3	1	.444	.444	0	1.000
Everett Scott	ss	6	20	0	2	0	0	0	1	1	1	0	.100	.100	0	1.000
Dave Shean	2b	6	19	2	4	1	0	0	0	4	3	1	.211	.263	0	1.000
Amos Strunk	cf	6	23	1	4	1	1	0	0	0	5	0	.174	.304	0	1.000
Fred Thomas	3b	6	17	0	2	0	0	0	1	2	0	0	.118	.118	0	1.000
George Whiteman	lf	6	20	2	5	0	1	0	1	2	1	1	.250	.350	1	.944
Totals		6	172	9	32	2	3	0	6	16	21	3	.186	.233	1	.996

Pitcher	G	GS	CG	IP	H	R	ER	BB	SO	W-L	Sv	ERA
Joe Bush	2	1	1	9	7	3	3	0	1	0-1	1	3.00
Sam Jones	1	1	1	9	7	3	3	5	5	0-1	0	3.00
Carl Mays	2	2	2	18	10	2	2	3	5	2-0	0	1.00
Babe Ruth	2	2	1	17	13	2	2	7	4	2-0	0	1.06
Totals	6	6	5	53	37	10	10	18	14	4-2	1	1.70

CHICAGO CUBS/Fred Mitchell, Manager

Player	pos	G	AB	R	H	2B	3B	HR	RBI	BB	SO	SB	BA	SA	E	FPct
Turner Barber	ph	3	2	0	0	0	0	0	0	0	0	0	.000	.000	—	—
Charlie Deal	3b	6	17	0	3	0	0	0	0	0	1	0	.176	.176	1	.941
Phil Douglas	p	1	0	0	0	0	0	0	0	0	0	0	—	—	1	.000
Max Flack	rf	6	19	2	5	0	0	0	0	4	1	1	.263	.263	1	.941
Claude Hendrix	p-ph	2	1	0	1	0	0	0	0	0	0	0	1.000	1.000	0	—
Charlie Hollocher	ss	6	21	2	4	0	1	0	1	1	1	1	.190	.286	1	.966
Bill Killefer	c	6	17	2	2	1	0	0	2	2	0	0	.118	.176	0	1.000
Les Mann	lf	6	22	0	5	2	0	0	2	0	0	0	.227	.318	0	1.000
Bill McCabe	pr-ph	3	1	1	0	0	0	0	0	0	0	0	.000	.000	—	—
Fred Merkle	1b	6	18	1	5	0	0	0	1	4	3	0	.278	.278	0	1.000
Bob O'Farrell	ph-c	3	3	0	0	0	0	0	0	0	0	0	.000	.000	0	—
Dode Paskert	cf	6	21	0	4	1	0	0	2	2	2	0	.190	.238	0	1.000
Charlie Pick	2b	6	18	2	7	1	0	0	0	1	1	1	.389	.444	0	1.000
Lefty Tyler	p	3	5	0	1	0	0	0	2	2	0	0	.200	.200	1	.917
Hippo Vaughn	p	3	10	0	0	0	0	0	0	0	5	0	.000	.000	0	1.000
Chuck Wortman	2b	1	0	0	0	0	0	0	0	0	0	0	.000	.000	0	1.000
Rollie Zeider	ph-3b	2	0	0	0	0	0	0	0	0	2	0	—	—	0	1.000
Totals		6	176	10	37	5	1	0	10	18	14	3	.210	.250	5	.979

Pitcher	G	GS	CG	IP	H	R	ER	BB	SO	W-L	Sv	ERA
Phil Douglas	1	0	0	1	1	1	0	0	0	0-1	0	0.00
Claude Hendrix	1	0	0	1	0	0	0	0	0	0-0	0	0.00
Lefty Tyler	3	3	1	23	14	5	3	11	4	1-1	0	1.17
Hippo Vaughn	3	3	3	27	17	3	3	5	17	1-2	0	1.00
Totals	6	6	4	52	32	9	6	16	21	2-4	0	1.04

Series Outstanding Player: Carl Mays, Boston Red Sox. **Series Outstanding Pitcher:** Carl Mays, Boston Red Sox. **Average Length of Game:** 1 hour, 51 minutes. **Total Attendance:** 128,483. **Average Attendance:** 21,414 (20,705 at Fenway Park; 22,123 at Comiskey Park).
Umpires: George Hildebrand (AL), Bill Klem (NL), Hank O'Day (NL), Clarence Owens (AL). **Winning Player's Share:** $1,103. **Losing Player's Share:** $671.

Right: Players take the field before the start of a 1918 series game.

Below: Babe Ruth won two games in 1918 and extended his scoreless streak to 29 $^2/_3$ innings.

The 1918 Series was the last in which no home runs were hit by either side.

Below: Carl Mays matched Ruth with two victories for Boston.

Left: Hippo Vaughan's strong perfomances on the mound earned him only one victory in the 1918 series defeat to the Red Sox—the last Boston championship of the century.

Game 1 Thursday, September 5 at Comiskey Park, Chicago

	1	2	3	4	5	6	7	8	9	R	H	E
Boston Red Sox	0	0	0	1	0	0	0	0	0	1	5	0
Chicago Cubs	0	0	0	0	0	0	0	0	0	0	6	0

Pitchers Bos Babe Ruth (W, 1-0), IP 9, H 6, R 0, ER 0, BB 1, SO 4
Chi Hippo Vaughn (L, 0-1), IP 9, H 5, R 1, ER 1, BB 3, SO 6

Top Performers at the Plate
Bos Dave Shean, 1 for 2, 1 R, 2 BB; George Whiteman, 2 for 4
Chi Dode Paskert, 2 for 4

Time 1:50. **Attendance** 19,274.

Game 2 Friday, September 6 at Comiskey Park, Chicago

	1	2	3	4	5	6	7	8	9	R	H	E
Boston Red Sox	0	0	0	0	0	0	0	0	1	1	6	1
Chicago Cubs	0	3	0	0	0	0	0	0	x	3	7	1

Pitchers Bos Joe Bush (L, 0-1), IP 8, H 7, R 3, ER 3, BB 3, SO 0
Chi Lefty Tyler (W, 1-0), IP 9, H 6, R 1, ER 1, BB 4, SO 2

Top Performers at the Plate
Bos George Whiteman, 1 for 3, 1 RBI, 1 BB
Chi Max Flack, 2 for 4; Lefty Tyler, 1 for 3, 2 RBI

2B-Chi/Killefer. **3B**-Bos/Strunk, Whiteman; Chi/Hollocher. **Time** 1:58. **Attendance** 20,040.

Game 3 Saturday, September 7 at Comiskey Park, Chicago

	1	2	3	4	5	6	7	8	9	R	H	E
Boston Red Sox	0	0	0	2	0	0	0	0	0	2	7	0
Chicago Cubs	0	0	0	0	1	0	0	0	0	1	7	1

Pitchers Bos Carl Mays (W, 1-0), IP 9, H 7, R 1, ER 1, BB 1, SO 4
Chi Hippo Vaughn (L, 0-2), IP 9, H 7, R 2, ER 2, BB 1, SO 7

Top Performers at the Plate
Bos Wally Schang, 2 for 4, 1 RBI
Chi Les Mann, 2 for 4; Charlie Pick, 2 for 4, 1 R

2B-Chi/Mann, Pick. **SB**-Bos/Schang, Whiteman; Chi/Pick. **Time** 1:57. **Attendance** 27,054.

Game 4 Monday, September 9 at Fenway Park, Boston

	1	2	3	4	5	6	7	8	9	R	H	E
Chicago Cubs	0	0	0	0	0	0	0	2	0	2	7	1
Boston Red Sox	0	0	0	2	0	0	0	1	x	3	4	0

Pitchers Chi Lefty Tyler, IP 7, H 3, R 2, ER 2, BB 2, SO 1; Phil Douglas (L, 0-1), IP 1, H 1, R 1, ER 0, BB 0, SO 0
Bos Babe Ruth (W, 2-0), IP 8, H 7, R 2, ER 2, BB 6, SO 0; Joe Bush (Sv, 1), IP 1, H 0, R 0, ER 0, BB 0, SO 0

Top Performers at the Plate
Chi Charlie Pick, 2 for 2
Bos Babe Ruth, 1 for 2, 2 RBI, 1 SH

2B-Bos/Shean. **3B**-Bos/Ruth. **SB**-Bos/Shean. **Time** 1:50. **Attendance** 22,183.

Game 5 Tuesday, September 10 at Fenway Park, Boston

	1	2	3	4	5	6	7	8	9	R	H	E
Chicago Cubs	0	0	1	0	0	0	0	2	0	3	7	0
Boston Red Sox	0	0	0	0	0	0	0	0	0	0	5	0

Pitchers Chi Hippo Vaughn (W, 1-2), IP 9, H 5, R 0, ER 0, BB 1, SO 4
Bos Sam Jones (L, 0-1), IP 9, H 7, R 3, ER 3, BB 5, SO 5

Top Performers at the Plate
Chi Charlie Hollocher, 3 for 3, 2 R, 1 BB; Dode Paskert, 1 for 3, 2 RBI, 1 BB

2B-Chi/Mann, Paskert; Bos/Strunk. **SB**-Chi/Hollocher. **Time** 1:42. **Attendance** 24,694.

Game 6 Wednesday, September 11 at Fenway Park, Boston

	1	2	3	4	5	6	7	8	9	R	H	E
Chicago Cubs	0	0	0	1	0	0	0	0	0	1	3	2
Boston Red Sox	0	0	2	0	0	0	0	0	x	2	5	0

Pitchers Chi Lefty Tyler (L, 1-1), IP 7, H 5, R 2, ER 0, BB 5, SO 1; Claude Hendrix, IP 1, H 0, R 0, ER 0, BB 0, SO 0
Bos Carl Mays (W, 2-0), IP 9, H 3, R 1, ER 1, BB 2, SO 1

Top Performers at the Plate
Bos Amos Strunk, 2 for 4

SB-Chi/Flack. **Time** 1:46. **Attendance** 15,238.

Take Me Out to the Ballgame
Fans and the World Series

Although wartime hardships put a damper on fan turnout in 1918, the World Series continued to grow in popularity in its second decade. Total attendance surpassed 200,000 (by a long shot) first in 1912, and average attendance broke the 30,000 mark four times in the decade. To accommodate baseball's emergence as the American pastime, newer and bigger ballparks were being built around the country, including Boston's Fenway Park. Opened in 1912, the park's 35,000-seat capacity was well more than twice the size of the Red Sox's previous home, Huntington Avenue Grounds, where the first World Series was played. Rising attendence only fueled the electricity in the air at baseball's annual championship. Since the team's earliest days, the Boston Red Sox had a dedicated and rambunctious group of supporters who called themselves the Royal Rooters. The Rooters were there backing their team in the inaugural 1903 Series, traveling back and forth between Boston and Pittsburgh to catch every game—much to the frustration of the harassed Pirate players—and they were there again in full force in 1912. Before the seventh game of the 1912 Series, the Royal Rooters held their customary parade to the ballpark, but they arrived at Fenway late, and their regular seats had been sold away to other customers. The Rooters were furious, and they barged onto the field demanding their seats. It took mounted police more than 30 minutes to clear the field and allow the game to get underway. Still fuming over their treatment the day before, the Royal Rooters staged a boycott of the final game, and only 17,034 spectators turned up at Fenway to see the Red Sox clinch the Series.

Above: Twins fans broke sound records at the Metrodome supporting their team during the 1987 and 1991 World Series.

Attendance Milestones

First game to top **20,000** attendance: **Polo Grounds**, New York, October 10, 1905, Game 2 (24,992)*
First game to top **30,000** attendance: **Forbes Field**, Pittsburgh, October 9, 1909, Game 2 (30,915)
First game to top **40,000** attendance: **Braves Field**, Boston, October 11, 1915, Game 3 (42,300)*
First game to top **50,000** attendance: **Yankee Stadium**, New York, October 10, 1923, Game 1 (55,307)*
First game to top **60,000** attendance: **Yankee Stadium**, New York, October 12, 1923, Game 3 (62,430)
First game to top **70,000** attendance: **Yankee Stadium**, New York, September 30, 1947, Game 1 (73,365)
First game to top **80,000** attendance: **Cleveland Stadium**, Cleveland, October 9, 1948, Game 4 (81,897)
First game to top **90,000** attendance: **Memorial Coliseum**, Los Angeles, October 4, 1959, Game 3 (92,394)*

* indicates the first Series game held at the ballpark.

Tiger fans at Detroit's Navin Field (later Tiger Stadium) also created a stir at the 1934 World Series against the Cardinals. The Tiger faithful were not too pleased with the hard slide that St. Louis's Joe Medwick put into third baseman Marv Owen in the seventh game, and they showed their displeasure by hurling garbage and debris at Medwick when he took the field the following inning. The baseball commissioner, watching from his seat along third base, finally intervened and told Medwick to leave the field so that play could resume.

Fortunately, the instances of fans taking out their frustrations in disruptive ways are few and far between, and more often than not baseball's dedicated devotees are more peaceful, if no less effusive, in expressing their passions. From cheering to nail-biting to sobbing, attend a few

The largest crowd at a World Series game was in 1959, when the Los Angeles Dodgers hosted the Chicago White Sox. Los Angeles's Memorial Coliseum held 92,706 fans for the fifth game of the Series. A record-total of 420,784 attended the six games, for an average of 70,131. That average was more than the total attendance at the 1908 Series. Some 62,232 fans (less than 12,450 per game) attended the five games between the Chicago Cubs and Detroit Tigers. A record-low 6,210 people turned out to Detroit's Bennett Park for the final game.

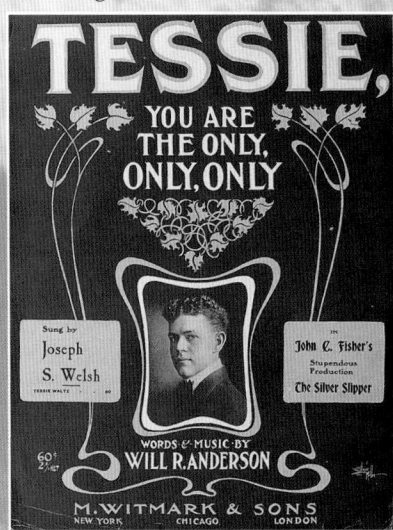

Right: Boston's "Royal Rooters" razzed New York pitcher Jeff Tesreau with their send-up version of the contemporary hit, "Tessie, You Are the Only, Only, Only."

Since the first Series in 1903, it has been common practice for teams to install temporary seating or standing-room sections in an effort to pack in as many fans as possible. In the days of the dead ball era, overflow spectators were often roped off in the outfield—thus shrinking the size of the playing field. As a result, the number of ground-rule doubles and home runs was higher than normal. In 1915, Boston's Harry Hooper hit two home runs into the temporary stands at Philadelphia's Baker Bowl in Game 5; Hooper had only two homers all season long. Game 3 in 1903 featured seven ground-rule doubles hit into the overflow crowd.

World Series games and you'll witness the full range of human emotion. Every baseball city will claim their citizens as the "greatest fans in the world," but the award for loudest crowd goes to the 55,000-plus Minnesotans who attended Games 1, 2, 6 and 7 of the 1987 Series. Hosting the first Fall Classic played under a dome, the Twins found a clear advantage as the hometown supporters frantically waved their "Homer Hankies" and broke sound records with their boisterous cheering. The Twins were 8-0 at the Metrodome in their World Series appearances in '87 and '91, giving them two world championships.

Below: Yankees and Mets fans root for their teams during the 2000 subway series.

Above: The St. Louis Cardinals and New York Yankees played to a packed Yankee Stadium during the 1926 World Series.

WORLD SERIES CLASSIC
1919
Cincinnati Reds (5) vs. Chicago White Sox (3)

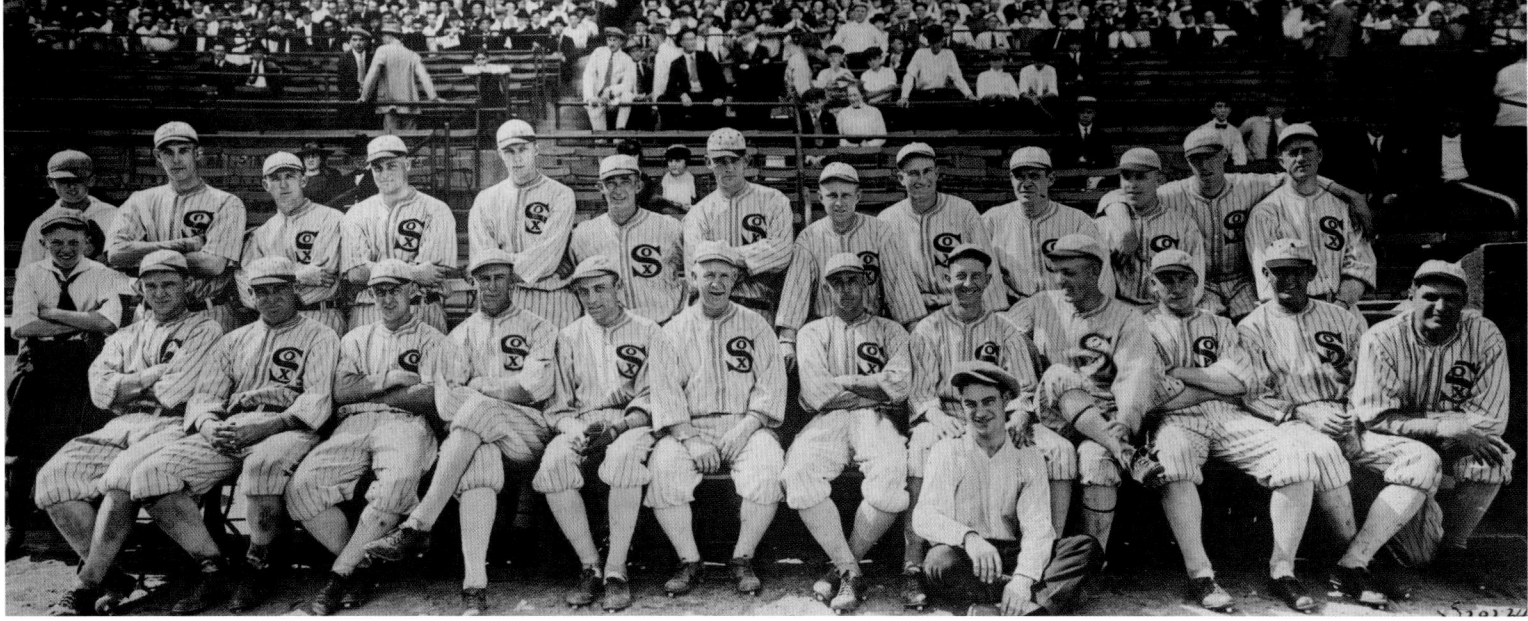

Above: The 1919 Chicago White Sox: The best team money can buy.

Anyone who was watching the betting odds as the 1919 World Series approached must have guessed that something was up. The Chicago White Sox, world champions just two years earlier and widely considered one of the best teams baseball had ever seen, were listed as 3-to-1 favorites a few days before the Series. As rumors of a "fix" were being spread and denied on the streets and in the papers, more and more money was being placed on the Cincinnati Reds, most notably by New York gambler Arnold Rothstein and his cronies. Suddenly, by the eve of the first game, the odds were in Cincinnati's favor at 8-to-5. The Reds had won 96 games that year and boasted batting-champ Edd Roush and two 20-game-winners in Hod Eller and Slim Sallee, but most baseball experts agreed that the Sox were the more talented club.

Because of excitement surrounding baseball in the nation's postwar euphoria, the 1919 Fall Classic was set up as a best-of-nine competition for the first time since 1903. The Series opened in Cincinnati on October 1. In the White Sox half of the first inning, nothing particularly suspicious seemed afoot. When the first Red batter came to the plate, however, pitcher Eddie Cicotte did something that he did only twice during the entire regular season: he hit a batter with a pitch. It was the signal that the gamblers and players had agreed upon to indicate that the fix was on. So, with his second pitch, Cicotte hit Morrie Rath in the back, sending Rath to first and a whole new flood of money in on

Cincinnati. Any doubts as to Cicotte's resolve to go through with throwing the World Series were put to rest in the fourth inning, when he gave up four singles, a double and a triple, the latter by opposing pitcher Dutch Ruether, for five Cincinnati runs. Chicago manager Kid Gleason pulled Cicotte from the game at that point, but the damage was done. The Reds walked away with a 9-1 romp in the opener. Jake Daubert, Greasy Neale and Ruether each had three hits for Cincinnati, and the only run allowed by Ruether came by benefit of an error. Lefty Williams took the hill for the Sox in Game 2, and it quickly became apparent that the 23-game-winner was another willing participant. Though he allowed only four hits that afternoon, the normally well-controlled Williams gave up six walks, including three in Cincinnati's three-run fourth inning. Chicago's rookie southpaw Dickie Kerr had not been involved in the "arrangements" surrounding the Series, and he came out with a strong three-hit shutout in the third game. Cicotte returned as the starter in Game 4, and although his control was much better than it had been in the opener, his two fielding errors in the fifth inning led to two runs and a 2-0 loss for the White Sox. Hod Eller gave up only three hits in Game 5—two by Buck Weaver and one by Ray Schalk, two non-conspirators— while Williams was shelled for four runs in the sixth inning, giving the Reds a 4-1 lead in games. A three-hit day at the plate by Weaver and a second complete-game performance by Kerr in Game 6 helped keep

Chicago alive for another day. Cicotte seemingly had a change of heart in Game 7, as his seven-hit, one-run outing secured another win for Chicago. (More likely he was sending a message to the gamblers that the players wanted their cash, which was late in arriving.) The eighth game was a different story, however, as Lefty Williams gave up four consecutive base hits in the top of the first, allowing the Reds to jump out to a four-run lead before the Sox even came to bat. Though Chicago rallied for four runs in the eighth, Cincinnati won the clinching game by a comfortable 10-5 score behind Eller's second victory.

Despite all the rumors of tainted players and thrown games, the 1919 Series was eagerly followed by the public, and denials of any wrong-doing continued for many months afterwards. It was simply a surprising upset by the Cincinnati Reds—that's all. But as the League pursued its investigation, eight players were implicated in accepting $100,000 (most of which was never delivered) from gamblers in

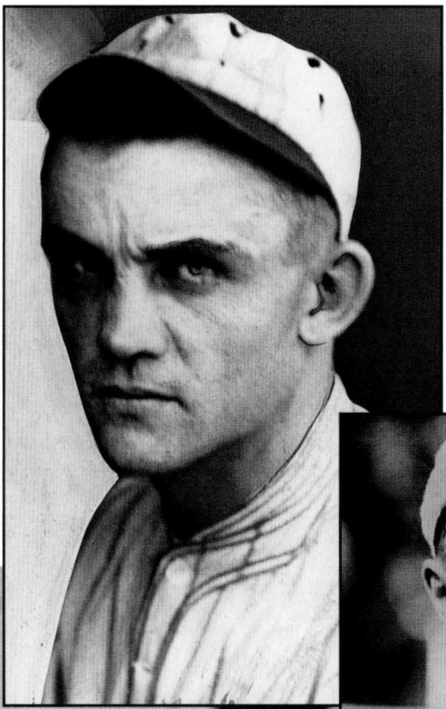

Chick Gandil (left) and Swede Risberg (below) were the ringleaders behind the 1919 scandal.

Chicago catcher Ray Schalk threw out a record 10 runners trying to steal during the 1919 Series.

Above: Third baseman Buck Weaver, shown here in Game 3 action, knew about the bribes, but didn't take any money for himself. He batted .324 for the Series.

exchange for losing the Series. The fixers were pitchers Cicotte and Williams, infielders Chick Gandil, Swede Risberg and Buck Weaver, outfielders Joe Jackson and Happy Felsch, and utility player Fred McMullin. Although Weaver did not accept any of the dirty money and put up solid numbers in the Series, he knew of the fix but kept quiet about it, and thus was forever linked with the rest of the "Black Sox." The eight were banned for life from organized baseball by the newly installed commissioner, Kenesaw Mountain Landis. To this day, "Shoeless" Joe Jackson—who is the third all-time leader in batting average in Major League baseball history, and who batted .375 and drove in six runs in the 1919 Series—is still not honored in baseball's Hall of Fame.

Above: Eddie Collins (left) and Dickie Kerr (right) were two non-conspirators in the 1919 fix.

Above: Cincinnati's Hod Eller took full advantage of the tanking Sox, winning two games and striking out 15 batters in 18 innings.

Inset: When Eddie Cicotte hit the first Cincinnati batter with a pitch in Game 1, the gamblers knew the fix was on.

One of the few standouts for the White Sox in the infamous Black Sox Series was pitcher Dickie Kerr, who went 2-0 with a 1.42 ERA in 19 innings.

1919 WORLD SERIES COMPOSITE STATISTICS

CINCINNATI REDS/Pat Moran, Manager

Player	pos	G	AB	R	H	2B	3B	HR	RBI	BB	SO	SB	BA	SA	E	FPct
Jake Daubert	1b	8	29	4	7	0	1	0	1	1	2	1	.241	.310	2	.977
Pat Duncan	lf	8	26	3	7	2	0	0	8	2	2	0	.269	.346	0	1.000
Hod Eller	p	2	7	2	2	1	0	0	0	0	2	0	.286	.429	0	1.000
Ray Fisher	p	2	2	0	1	0	0	0	0	0	0	0	.500	.500	1	.857
Heine Groh	3b	8	29	6	5	2	0	0	2	6	4	0	.172	.241	2	.929
Larry Kopf	ss	8	27	3	6	0	2	0	2	3	2	0	.222	.370	1	.975
Dolf Luque	p	2	1	0	0	0	0	0	0	0	1	0	.000	.000	0	1.000
Sherry Magee	ph	2	2	0	1	0	0	0	0	0	0	0	.500	.500	–	–
Greasy Neale	rf	8	28	3	10	1	1	0	4	2	5	1	.357	.464	1	.950
Bill Rariden	c	5	19	0	4	0	0	0	2	0	0	1	.211	.211	0	.966
Morrie Rath	2b	8	31	5	7	1	0	0	2	4	1	2	.226	.258	2	.949
Jimmy Ring	p	2	5	0	0	0	0	0	0	0	2	0	.000	.000	0	1.000
Edd Roush	cf	8	28	6	6	2	1	0	7	3	0	2	.214	.357	2	.944
Dutch Ruether	p	3	6	2	4	1	2	0	4	1	0	0	.667	1.500	0	1.000
Slim Sallee	p	2	4	0	0	0	0	0	0	0	0	0	.000	.000	0	1.000
Jimmy Smith	pr	1	0	0	0	0	0	0	0	0	0	0	–	–	–	–
Ivy Wingo	c	3	7	1	4	0	0	0	1	3	1	0	.571	.571	0	1.000
Totals		**8**	**251**	**35**	**64**	**10**	**7**	**0**	**33**	**25**	**22**	**7**	**.255**	**.351**	**12**	**.963**

Pitcher	G	GS	CG	IP	H	R	ER	BB	SO	W-L	Sv	ERA
Hod Eller	2	2	2	18	13	5	4	2	15	2-0	0	2.00
Ray Fisher	2	1	0	7⅔	7	3	2	2	2	0-1	0	2.35
Dolf Luque	2	0	0	5	1	0	0	0	6	0-0	0	0.00
Jimmy Ring	2	1	1	14	7	1	1	6	4	1-1	0	0.64
Dutch Ruether	2	2	1	14	12	5	4	4	1	1-0	0	2.57
Slim Sallee	2	2	1	13⅓	19	6	2	1	2	1-1	0	1.35
Totals	**8**	**8**	**5**	**72**	**59**	**20**	**13**	**15**	**30**	**5-3**	**0**	**1.63**

CHICAGO WHITE SOX/Kid Gleason, Manager

Player	pos	G	AB	R	H	2B	3B	HR	RBI	BB	SO	SB	BA	SA	E	FPct
Eddie Cicotte	p	3	8	0	0	0	0	0	0	0	3	0	.000	.000	2	.750
Eddie Collins	2b	8	31	2	7	1	0	0	1	1	2	1	.226	.258	2	.962
Shano Collins	rf-cf	4	16	2	4	1	0	0	0	0	1	0	.250	.313	0	1.000
Happy Felsch	cf-rf	8	26	2	5	0	1	0	3	1	4	0	.192	.231	2	.923
Chick Gandil	1b	8	30	1	7	0	1	0	5	1	3	1	.233	.300	1	.988
Joe Jackson	lf	8	32	5	12	3	0	1	6	1	2	0	.375	.563	0	1.000
Bill James	p	1	2	0	0	0	0	0	0	0	1	0	.000	.000	0	–
Dickie Kerr	p	2	6	0	1	0	0	0	0	0	0	0	.167	.167	0	1.000
Nemo Leibold	rf-ph-cf	5	18	0	1	0	0	0	0	2	3	1	.056	.056	0	1.000
Grover Lowdermilk	p	1	0	0	0	0	0	0	0	0	0	0	–	–	0	1.000
Byrd Lynn	c	1	1	0	0	0	0	0	0	0	0	0	.000	.000	0	1.000
Erskine Mayer	p	1	0	0	0	0	0	0	0	0	0	0	–	–	0	–
Fred McMullin	ph	2	2	0	1	0	0	0	0	0	1	0	.500	.500	–	–
Eddie Murphy	ph	3	2	0	0	0	0	0	0	0	1	0	.000	.000	–	–
Swede Risberg	ss	8	25	3	2	0	1	0	0	5	3	1	.080	.160	4	.930
Ray Schalk	c	8	23	1	7	0	0	0	2	4	2	1	.304	.304	1	.978
Buck Weaver	3b	8	34	4	11	4	1	0	0	0	2	0	.324	.500	0	1.000
Roy Wilkinson	p	2	2	0	0	0	0	0	0	0	1	0	.000	.000	0	1.000
Lefty Williams	p	3	5	0	1	0	0	0	0	0	3	0	.200	.200	0	1.000
Totals		**8**	**263**	**20**	**59**	**10**	**3**	**1**	**17**	**15**	**30**	**5**	**.224**	**.297**	**12**	**.965**

Pitcher	G	GS	CG	IP	H	R	ER	BB	SO	W-L	Sv	ERA
Eddie Cicotte	3	3	2	21⅔	19	9	7	5	7	1-2	0	2.91
Bill James	1	0	0	4⅔	8	4	3	3	2	0-0	0	5.79
Dickie Kerr	2	2	2	19	14	4	3	3	6	2-0	0	1.42
Grover Lowdermilk	1	0	0	1	2	1	1	1	0	0-0	0	9.00
Erskine Mayer	1	0	0	1	0	1	0	1	0	0-0	0	0.00
Roy Wilkinson	2	0	0	7⅓	9	4	1	4	3	0-0	0	1.23
Lefty Williams	3	3	1	16⅓	12	12	12	8	4	0-3	0	6.61
Totals	**8**	**8**	**5**	**71**	**64**	**35**	**27**	**25**	**22**	**3-5**	**0**	**3.42**

Series Outstanding Player: Greasy Neale, Cincinnati Reds. **Series Outstanding Pitcher:** Hod Eller, Cincinnati Reds. **Average Length of Game:** 1 hour, 50 minutes. **Total Attendance:** 236,928. **Average Attendance:** 29,616 (26,533 at Redland Field; 32,700 at Comiskey Park).
Umpires: Billy Evans (AL), Dick Nallin (AL), Ernie Quigley (NL), Cy Rigler (NL). **Winning Player's Share:** $5,207. **Losing Player's Share:** $3,254.

Above: Joe Jackson, seen here caught as he is stealing second base, put up good numbers in the 1919 Series, but his hits were scattered, keeping the damage to a minimum.

Right: Judge Landis vowed to clean up baseball after the "Black Sox Scandal." As commissioner, he ruled the game with an iron fist for 35 years.

The start by Dutch Ruether in Game 2 for Cincinnati was the 14th consecutive Series game started by a left-handed pitcher for the National League.

Below: Eight Chicago players were banned for life following Judge Kenesaw Landis's investigation of the 1919 Series.

Game 1 Wednesday, October 1 at Redland Field (Crosley Field), Cincinnati

	1	2	3	4	5	6	7	8	9	R	H	E
Chicago White Sox	0	1	0	0	0	0	0	0	0	1	6	1
Cincinnati Reds	1	0	0	5	0	0	2	1	x	9	14	1

Pitchers Chi Eddie Cicotte (L, 0-1), IP 3⅔, H 7, R 6, ER 6, BB 2, SO 1; Roy Wilkinson, IP 3⅓, H 5, R 2, ER 1, BB 0, SO 1; Grover Lowdermilk, IP 1, R 2, R 1, ER 1, BB 1, SO 0
Cin Dutch Ruether (W, 1-0), IP 9, H 6, R 1, ER 0, BB 1, SO 1

Top Performers at the Plate
Chi Chick Gandil, 2 for 4, 1 RBI
Cin Jake Daubert, 3 for 4, 1 R, 1 RBI, 1 HBP; Dutch Ruether, 3 for 3, 1 R, 3 RBI, 2 3B, 1 BB

2B-Cin/Rath. **3B**-Cin/Daubert, Ruether 2. **SB**-Cin/Roush. **Time** 1:42. **Attendance** 30,511.

Game 2 Thursday, October 2 at Redland Field (Crosley Field), Cincinnati

	1	2	3	4	5	6	7	8	9	R	H	E
Chicago White Sox	0	0	0	0	0	0	2	0	0	2	10	1
Cincinnati Reds	0	0	0	3	0	1	0	0	x	4	4	2

Pitchers Chi Lefty Williams (L, 0-1), IP 8, H 4, R 4, ER 4, BB 6, SO 1
Cin Slim Sallee (W, 1-0), IP 9, H 10, R 2, ER 0, BB 1, SO 2

Top Performers at the Plate
Chi Joe Jackson, 3 for 4; Ray Schalk, 2 for 4, 1 R
Cin Larry Kopf, 1 for 3, 2 RBI; Edd Roush, 1 for 2, 1 R, 1 RBI, 2 BB

2B-Chi/Jackson, Weaver. **3B**-Cin/Kopf. **SB**-Chi/Gandil. **Time** 1:42. **Attendance** 29,690.

Game 3 Friday, October 3 at Comiskey Park, Chicago

	1	2	3	4	5	6	7	8	9	R	H	E
Cincinnati Reds	0	0	0	0	0	0	0	0	0	0	3	1
Chicago White Sox	0	2	0	1	0	0	0	0	x	3	7	0

Pitchers Cin Ray Fisher (L, 0-1), IP 7, H 7, R 3, ER 2, BB 2, SO 1; Dolf Luque, IP 1, H 0, R 0, ER 0, BB 0, SO 1
Chi Dickie Kerr (W, 1-0), IP 9, H 3, R 0, ER 0, BB 1, SO 4

Top Performers at the Plate
Chi Chick Gandil, 1 for 3, 2 RBI; Joe Jackson, 2 for 3, 1 R

3B-Chi/Risberg. **Time** 1:30. **Attendance** 29,126.

Game 4 Saturday, October 4 at Comiskey Park, Chicago

	1	2	3	4	5	6	7	8	9	R	H	E
Cincinnati Reds	0	0	0	0	2	0	0	0	0	2	5	2
Chicago White Sox	0	0	0	0	0	0	0	0	0	0	3	2

Pitchers Cin Jimmy Ring (W, 1-0), IP 9, H 3, R 0, ER 0, BB 3, SO 2
Chi Eddie Cicotte (L, 0-2), IP 9, H 5, R 2, ER 0, BB 0, SO 2

Top Performers at the Plate
Cin Larry Kopf, 1 for 3, 1 R, 1 RBI; Ivy Wingo, 2 for 3

2B-Cin/Neale; Chi/Jackson. **SB**-Chi/Risberg. **Time** 1:37. **Attendance** 34,363.

Game 5 Monday, October 6 at Comiskey Park, Chicago

	1	2	3	4	5	6	7	8	9	R	H	E
Cincinnati Reds	0	0	0	0	0	4	0	0	1	5	4	0
Chicago White Sox	0	0	0	0	0	0	0	0	0	0	3	3

Pitchers Cin Hod Eller (W, 1-0), IP 9, H 3, R 0, ER 0, BB 1, SO 9
Chi Lefty Williams (L, 0-2), IP 8, H 4, R 4, ER 4, BB 2, SO 3; Erskine Mayer, IP 1, H 0, R 1, ER 0, BB 1, SO 0

Top Performers at the Plate
Cin Morrie Rath, 1 for 3, 1 R, 1 RBI, 1 BB; Edd Roush, 1 for 4, 2 R, 2 RBI
Chi Buck Weaver, 2 for 4

2B-Cin/Eller. **3B**-Cin/Roush; Chi/Weaver. **SB**-Cin/Roush. **Time** 1:45. **Attendance** 34,379.

Game 6 Tuesday, October 7 at Redland Field (Crosley Field), Cincinnati

	1	2	3	4	5	6	7	8	9	10	R	H	E
Chicago White Sox	0	0	0	0	1	0	3	0	0	1	5	10	3
Cincinnati Reds	0	0	2	2	0	0	0	0	0	0	4	11	0

Pitchers Chi Dickie Kerr (W, 2-0), IP 10, H 11, R 4, ER 3, BB 2, SO 2
Cin Dutch Ruether, IP 5, H 6, R 4, ER 4, BB 3, SO 0; Jimmy Ring (L, 1-1), IP 5, H 4, R 1, ER 1, BB 3, SO 2

Top Performers at the Plate
Chi Joe Jackson, 2 for 4, 1 R, 1 RBI, 1 BB; Buck Weaver, 3 for 5, 2 R
Cin Jake Daubert, 2 for 4, 1 R, 1 SH; Greasy Neale, 3 for 4, 1 R

2B-Chi/Felsch, Weaver 2; Cin/Duncan, Groh, Ruether. **3B**-Cin/Neale. **SB**-Chi/Leibold, Schalk; Cin/Daubert, Rath. **Time** 2:06. **Attendance** 32,006.

Game 7 Wednesday, October 8 at Redland Field (Crosley Field), Cincinnati

	1	2	3	4	5	6	7	8	9	R	H	E
Chicago White Sox	1	0	1	0	2	0	0	0	0	4	10	1
Cincinnati Reds	0	0	0	0	0	1	0	0	0	1	7	4

Pitchers Chi Eddie Cicotte (W, 1-2), IP 9, H 7, R 1, ER 1, BB 3, SO 4
Cin Slim Sallee (L, 1-1), IP 4⅓, H 9, R 4, ER 2, BB 0, SO 0; Ray Fisher, IP ⅔, H 0, R 0, ER 0, BB 0, SO 1; Dolf Luque, IP 4, H 1, R 0, ER 0, BB 0, SO 5

Top Performers at the Plate
Chi Shano Collins, 3 for 5, 2 R; Joe Jackson, 2 for 4, 2 RBI

2B-Chi/S. Collins; Cin/Groh. **Time** 1:47. **Attendance** 13,923.

Game 8 Thursday, October 9 at Comiskey Park, Chicago

	1	2	3	4	5	6	7	8	9	R	H	E
Cincinnati Reds	4	1	0	0	1	3	0	1	0	10	16	2
Chicago White Sox	0	0	1	0	0	0	0	4	0	5	10	1

Pitchers Cin Hod Eller (W, 2-0), IP 9, H 10, R 5, ER 4, BB 1, SO 6
Chi Lefty Williams (L, 0-3), IP ⅓, H 4, R 4, ER 4, BB 0, SO 0; Bill James, IP 4⅔, H 8, R 4, ER 3, BB 3, SO 2; Roy Wilkinson, IP 4, H 4, R 2, ER 0, BB 4, SO 2

Top Performers at the Plate
Cin Pat Duncan, 2 for 4, 1 R, 3 RBI, 1 SH; Edd Roush, 3 for 5, 2 R, 4 RBI, 2, 2B, 1 HBP
Chi Eddie Collins, 3 for 5, 1 R; Joe Jackson, 2 for 5, 2 R, 3 RBI

2B-Cin/Duncan, Roush 2; Chi/E. Collins, Jackson, Weaver. **3B**-Cin/Kopf; Chi/Gandil. **HR**-Chi/Jackson. **SB**-Cin/Neale, Rariden, Rath; Chi/E. Collins. **Time** 2:27. **Attendance** 32,930.

Cleveland Indians (5) vs. Brooklyn Robins (2)

The year 1920 was a tumultuous one for Tris Speaker's Cleveland Indians. Speaker himself batted .388 while also serving as the club's manager, and his ace pitcher, Jim Bagby, led the Majors with 31 wins. But tragedy struck the team on August 16 when their 29-year-old shortstop Ray Chapman was hit in the head with a pitched ball; Chapman died the next day. Despite the tragedy, the Indians claimed their first pennant by finishing with a two-game edge over the second-place White Sox, who lost eight players to suspension in September in the wake of the Black Sox Scandal. The Brooklyn Robins earned their second trip to the Series with the oldest team ever to reach the

1920 WORLD SERIES COMPOSITE STATISTICS

CLEVELAND INDIANS/Tris Speaker, Manager

Player	pos	G	AB	R	H	2B	3B	HR	RBI	BB	SO	SB	BA	SA	E	FPct
Jim Bagby	p	2	6	1	2	0	0	1	3	0	0	0	.333	.833	1	.833
George Burns	1b	5	10	1	3	1	0	0	3	3	3	0	.300	.400	1	.975
Ray Caldwell	p	1	0	0	0	0	0	0	0	0	0	0	–	–	0	–
Stan Coveleski	p	3	10	2	1	0	0	0	0	0	4	0	.100	.100	1	.875
Joe Evans	lf	4	13	0	4	0	0	0	0	1	0	0	.308	.308	0	1.000
Larry Gardner	3b	7	24	1	5	1	0	0	2	1	1	0	.208	.250	2	.917
Jack Graney	rf-lf	3	3	0	0	0	0	0	0	2	0	0	.000	.000	0	–
Charlie Jamieson	lf	6	15	2	5	1	0	0	1	1	0	1	.333	.400	0	1.000
Doc Johnston	1b	5	11	1	3	0	0	0	2	1	1	0	.273	.273	0	1.000
Harry Lunte	2b	1	0	0	0	0	0	0	0	0	0	0	–	–	0	–
Duster Mails	p	2	5	0	0	0	0	0	0	0	1	0	.000	.000	0	1.000
Les Nunamaker	c	2	2	0	1	0	0	0	0	0	0	0	.500	.500	0	–
Steve O'Neill	c	7	21	1	7	3	0	0	2	4	3	0	.333	.476	1	.967
Joe Sewell	ss	7	23	0	4	0	0	0	0	2	1	0	.174	.174	5	.889
Elmer Smith	rf	5	13	1	4	0	1	1	5	1	1	0	.308	.692	0	1.000
Tris Speaker	cf	7	25	6	8	2	1	0	1	3	1	0	.320	.480	0	1.000
Pinch Thomas	c	1	0	0	0	0	0	0	0	0	0	0	–	–	0	1.000
George Uhle	p	2	0	0	0	0	0	0	0	0	0	0	–	–	0	1.000
Bill Wambsganss	2b	7	26	3	4	0	0	0	1	2	1	0	.154	.154	0	1.000
Joe Wood	rf	4	10	2	2	1	0	0	1	1	2	0	.200	.300	0	1.000
Totals		**7**	**217**	**21**	**53**	**9**	**2**	**2**	**18**	**21**	**21**	**2**	**.244**	**.332**	**11**	**.961**

Pitcher	G	GS	CG	IP	H	R	ER	BB	SO	W-L	Sv	ERA
Jim Bagby	2	2	1	15	20	4	3	1	3	1-1	0	1.80
Ray Caldwell	1	1	0	1/3	2	2	1	1	0	0-1	0	27.00
Stan Coveleski	3	3	3	27	15	2	2	2	8	3-0	0	0.67
Duster Mails	2	1	1	15 2/3	6	0	0	6	6	1-0	0	0.00
George Uhle	2	0	0	3	1	0	0	0	3	0-0	0	0.00
Totals	**7**	**7**	**5**	**61**	**44**	**8**	**6**	**10**	**20**	**5-2**	**0**	**0.89**

BROOKLYN ROBINS/Wilbert Robinson, Manager

Player	pos	G	AB	R	H	2B	3B	HR	RBI	BB	SO	SB	BA	SA	E	FPct
Leon Cadore	p	2	0	0	0	0	0	0	0	0	0	0	–	–	0	1.000
Tommy Griffith	rf	7	21	1	4	2	0	0	3	0	2	0	.190	.286	0	1.000
Burleigh Grimes	p	3	6	1	2	0	0	0	0	0	0	0	.333	.333	1	.889
Jimmy Johnston	3b	4	14	2	3	0	0	0	0	0	2	1	.214	.214	0	1.000
Pete Kilduff	2b	7	21	0	2	0	0	0	0	1	4	0	.095	.095	0	1.000
Ed Konetchy	1b	7	23	0	4	0	1	0	2	3	2	0	.174	.261	1	.987
Ernie Krueger	c	4	6	0	1	0	0	0	0	0	0	0	.167	.167	0	1.000
Bill Lamar	ph	3	3	0	0	0	0	0	0	0	0	0	.000	.000	–	–
Al Mamaux	p	3	1	0	0	0	0	0	0	1	0	0	.000	.000	0	1.000
Rube Marquard	p	2	1	0	0	0	0	0	0	0	0	0	.000	.000	0	1.000
Bill McCabe	pr	1	0	0	0	0	0	0	0	0	0	0	–	–	–	–
Otto Miller	c	6	14	0	2	0	0	0	1	2	0	.143	.143	0	1.000
Clarence Mitchell	p	6	3	0	1	0	0	0	0	0	0	0	.333	.333	0	1.000
Hy Myers	cf	7	26	0	6	0	0	1	0	1	0	1	.231	.231	0	1.000
Bernie Neis	rf	4	5	0	0	0	0	0	0	1	0	0	.000	.000	0	1.000
Ivy Olson	ss	7	25	2	8	1	0	0	3	1	0	0	.320	.360	0	1.000
Jeff Pfeffer	p	1	1	0	0	0	0	0	0	0	0	0	.000	.000	0	–
Ray Schmandt	ph	1	1	0	0	0	0	0	0	0	0	0	.000	.000	0	–
Jack Sheehan	3b	3	11	0	2	0	0	0	0	0	1	0	.182	.182	2	.800
Sherry Smith	p	2	6	0	0	0	0	0	0	0	0	0	.000	.000	1	1.000
Zack Wheat	lf	7	27	2	9	2	0	0	2	1	2	0	.333	.407	2	.882
Totals		**7**	**215**	**8**	**44**	**5**	**1**	**0**	**8**	**10**	**20**	**1**	**.205**	**.237**	**6**	**.978**

Pitcher	G	GS	CG	IP	H	R	ER	BB	SO	W-L	Sv	ERA
Leon Cadore	2	1	0	2	4	2	2	1	1	0-1	0	9.00
Burleigh Grimes	3	3	1	19 1/3	23	10	9	4	4	1-2	0	4.19
Al Mamaux	3	0	0	4	2	2	2	0	5	0-0	0	4.50
Rube Marquard	2	1	0	9	7	3	3	3	6	0-1	0	3.00
Clarence Mitchell	1	0	0	4 1/3	3	1	0	3	1	0-0	0	0.00
Jeff Pfeffer	1	0	0	3	4	1	1	2	1	0-0	0	3.00
Sherry Smith	2	2	2	17	10	2	1	3	3	1-1	0	0.53
Totals	**7**	**7**	**3**	**59**	**53**	**21**	**18**	**21**	**21**	**2-5**	**0**	**2.75**

Series Outstanding Player: Stan Coveleski, Cleveland Indians. **Series Outstanding Pitcher:** Stan Coveleski, Cleveland Indians. **Average Length of Game:** 1 hour, 48 minutes. **Total Attendance:** 178,557. **Average Attendance:** 25,508 (26,834 at League Park; 23,740 at Ebbets Field). **Umpires:** Tommy Connolly (AL), Bill Dinneen (AL), Bill Klem (NL), Hank O'Day (NL). **Winning Player's Share:** $4,168. **Losing Player's Share:** $2,419.

Fall Classic. Former Giant Rube Marquard and spitball specialist Burleigh Grimes headed a talented pitching staff in Brooklyn. Despite the cloud created by the 1919 scandal, the best-of-nine 1920 World Series was well attended in both cities. Pitching was the name of the game in the first three contests, with neither side scoring more than three times in any one game. The Indians got two unearned runs off Marquard in the second inning of the opener, and Cleveland's Stan Coveleski threw a five-hitter to give Cleveland a 3-1 win. Brooklyn took the next two games behind Grimes's shutout victory in Game 2 and a three-hitter by Sherry Smith in the third game. Coveleski got the start in Game 4, and

the right-handed spitballer pitched to another five-hit win. After four games, the Series was Coveleski 2, Brooklyn 2. The next game was one for the record books—several times over. The excitement started in the bottom of the first when Cleveland loaded the bases with three consecutive singles. Up to the plate stepped rightfielder Elmer Smith, who was coming off a career season batting .316 with 103 RBIs. Smith proceeded to clear the bases by sending a Grimes pitch into the right-field seats for the first grand-slam home run in World Series history. The next few innings passed quietly enough, with neither team getting on the board. In the bottom of the fourth, Cleveland rallied again, putting two runners on base with Jim Bagby coming up. Earning the distinction of being the first pitcher to homer in a Series game, Bagby extended his team's lead to 7-0 with a three-run shot. The Robins started things off well in the top of the fifth when Pete Kilduff and Otto Miller opened the inning with back-to-back singles. Brooklyn's pitcher Clarence Mitchell, a good hitter who played some games at first base during the season, came up and smoked a line drive to the right side for an apparent base hit. The base runners were off with the hit, but Cleveland second baseman Bill Wambsganss ran a few paces to his right and made a leaping grab of Mitchell's liner. He then stepped on second base, doubling up Kilduff. Wambsganss then looked to his left to see Miller standing frozen just a few feet from the bag. Wamby tagged Miller to complete the first and only World Series triple play—unassisted. Brooklyn never recovered from the events of that fifth game, dropping the next two without scoring a run. Duster Mails, who had pitched 6 2/3 innings of scoreless relief in Game 3, started Game 6 and held Brooklyn to three hits in nine innings. The Indians eked out one run against Smith on George Burns's RBI double in the sixth. Game 7 was a match-up of spitball masters Coveleski and Grimes. Coveleski came out on top with his third five-hit shutout, giving Cleveland a championship in its first Series appearance. Coveleski finished the Series with three wins and a 0.67 ERA, and Speaker batted .320 and scored six runs—but it was the unprecedented triple play by Bill Wambsganss that stands out most from the 1920 Series.

Above: Tris Speaker was Cleveland's manager and leading hitter in 1920.

Left: Bill Wambsganss (left) and Elmer Smith (right) both accomplished notable feats in Game 5 of the 1920 World series.

Right: Zack Wheat scores Brooklyn's only run in the Series opener on Ed Konetchy's seventh-inning grounder.

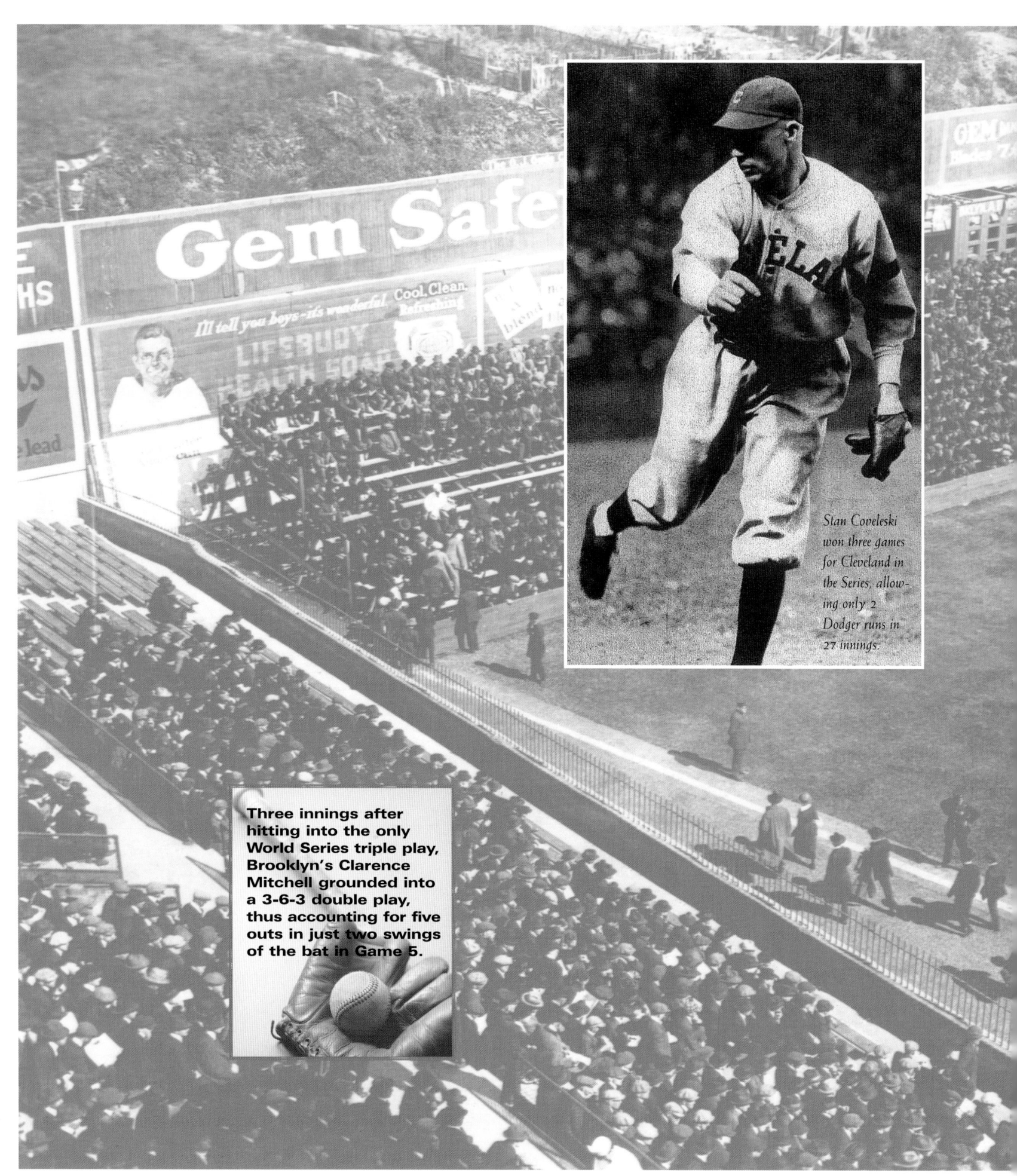

Stan Coveleski won three games for Cleveland in the Series, allowing only 2 Dodger runs in 27 innings.

Three innings after hitting into the only World Series triple play, Brooklyn's Clarence Mitchell grounded into a 3-6-3 double play, thus accounting for five outs in just two swings of the bat in Game 5.

Above: Bill Wambsganss tags Otto Miller to complete an unprecedented World Series triple play—unassisted.

Background: Ebbets Field attracted a big crowd for the opening game of the 1920 World Series.

Game 1
Tuesday, October 5 at Ebbets Field, Brooklyn

	1	2	3	4	5	6	7	8	9	R	H	E
Cleveland Indians	0	2	0	1	0	0	0	0	0	3	5	0
Brooklyn Robins	0	0	0	0	0	0	1	0	0	1	5	1

Pitchers Cle Stan Coveleski (W, 1-0), IP 9, H 5, R 1, ER 1, BB 1, SO 3
Bro Rube Marquard (L, 0-1), IP 6, H 5, R 3, ER 1, BB 2, SO 4; Al Mamaux, IP 2, H 0, R 0, ER 0, BB 0, SO 3; Leon Cadore, IP 1, H 0, R 0, ER 0, BB 0, SO 0

Top Performers at the Plate
Cle Steve O'Neill, 2 for 3, 2 RBI, 2 2B; Joe Wood, 1 for 2, 2 R, 1 BB
Bro Ivy Olson, 2 for 3

2B-Cle/O'Neill 2, Wood; Bro/Wheat. **Time** 1:41. **Attendance** 23,573.

Game 2
Wednesday, October 6 at Ebbets Field, Brooklyn

	1	2	3	4	5	6	7	8	9	R	H	E
Cleveland Indians	0	0	0	0	0	0	0	0	0	0	7	1
Brooklyn Robins	1	0	1	0	1	0	0	0	x	3	7	0

Pitchers Cle Jim Bagby (L, 0-1), IP 6, H 7, R 3, ER 2, BB 1, SO 0; George Uhle, IP 2, H 0, R 0, ER 0, BB 0, SO 3
Bro Burleigh Grimes (W, 1-0), IP 9, H 7, R 0, ER 0, BB 4, SO 2

Top Performers at the Plate
Cle Larry Gardner, 2 for 3; Tris Speaker, 2 for 3
Bro Tommy Griffith, 2 for 4, 2 RBI

2B-Cle/Gardner, Speaker; Bro/Griffith, Wheat. **SB**-Bro/J. Johnston. **Time** 1:55. **Attendance** 22,559.

Game 3
Thursday, October 7 at Ebbets Field, Brooklyn

	1	2	3	4	5	6	7	8	9	R	H	E
Cleveland Indians	0	0	0	1	0	0	0	0	0	1	3	1
Brooklyn Robins	2	0	0	0	0	0	0	0	x	2	6	1

Pitchers Cle Ray Caldwell (L, 0-1), IP ⅓, H 2, R 2, ER 1, BB 1, SO 0; Duster Mails, IP 6⅔, H 3, R 0, ER 0, BB 4, SO 2; George Uhle, IP 1, H 1, R 0, ER 0, BB 0, SO 0
Bro Sherry Smith (W, 1-0), IP 9, H 3, R 1, ER 0, BB 2, SO 2

Top Performers at the Plate
Cle Steve O'Neill, 2 for 3
Bro Hy Myers, 2 for 4, 1 RBI; Zack Wheat, 3 for 4, 1 RBI

2B-Cle/Speaker. **Time** 1:47. **Attendance** 25,088.

Game 4
Saturday, October 9 at Dunn Field (League Park), Cleveland

	1	2	3	4	5	6	7	8	9	R	H	E
Brooklyn Robins	0	0	0	1	0	0	0	0	0	1	5	1
Cleveland Indians	2	0	2	0	0	1	0	0	x	5	12	1

Pitchers Bro Leon Cadore (L, 0-1), IP 1, H 4, R 2, ER 2, BB 1, SO 1; Al Mamaux, IP 1, H 2, R 2, ER 2, BB 0, SO 1; Rube Marquard, IP 3, H 2, R 0, ER 0, BB 1, SO 2; Jeff Pfeffer, IP 3, H 4, R 1, ER 1, BB 2, SO 1
Cle Stan Coveleski (W, 2-0), IP 9, H 5, R 1, ER 1, BB 1, SO 4

Top Performers at the Plate
Bro Jimmy Johnston, 2 for 4, 1 R
Cle Tris Speaker, 2 for 5, 2 R; Bill Wambsganss, 2 for 4, 2 R, 1 RBI, 1 BB

2B-Bro/Griffith. **Time** 1:54. **Attendance** 25,734.

Game 5
Sunday, October 10 at Dunn Field (League Park), Cleveland

	1	2	3	4	5	6	7	8	9	R	H	E
Brooklyn Robins	0	0	0	0	0	0	0	1	0	1	13	1
Cleveland Indians	4	0	0	3	1	0	0	0	x	8	12	2

Pitchers Bro Burleigh Grimes (L, 1-1), IP 3⅓, H 9, R 7, ER 7, BB 1, SO 0; Clarence Mitchell, IP 4⅔, H 3, R 1, ER 0, BB 3, SO 1
Cle Jim Bagby (W, 1-1), IP 9, H 13, R 1, ER 1, BB 0, SO 3

Top Performers at the Plate
Bro Ed Konetchy, 2 for 4, 1 RBI; Zack Wheat, 2 for 4, 1 R
Cle Jim Bagby, 2 for 4, 1 R, 3 RBI; Elmer Smith, 3 for 4, 1 R, 4 RBI

3B-Bro/Konetchy; Cle/E. Smith. **HR**-Cle/Bagby, E. Smith. **Time** 1:49. **Attendance** 26,884.

Game 6
Monday, October 11 at Dunn Field (League Park), Cleveland

	1	2	3	4	5	6	7	8	9	R	H	E
Brooklyn Robins	0	0	0	0	0	0	0	0	0	0	3	0
Cleveland Indians	0	0	0	0	0	1	0	0	x	1	7	3

Pitchers Bro Sherry Smith (L, 1-1), IP 8, H 7, R 1, ER 1, BB 1, SO 1
Cle Duster Mails (W, 1-0), IP 9, H 3, R 0, ER 0, BB 2, SO 4

Top Performers at the Plate
Bro Ed Konetchy, 1 for 3, 1 BB
Cle George Burns, 1 for 2, 1 RBI, 1 BB; Joe Evans, 3 for 4

2B-Bro/Olson; Cle/Burns. **Time** 1:34. **Attendance** 27,194.

Game 7
Tuesday, October 12 at Dunn Field (League Park), Cleveland

	1	2	3	4	5	6	7	8	9	R	H	E
Brooklyn Robins	0	0	0	0	0	0	0	0	0	0	5	2
Cleveland Indians	0	0	0	1	1	0	1	0	x	3	7	3

Pitchers Bro Burleigh Grimes (L, 1-2), IP 7, H 7, R 3, ER 2, BB 4, SO 2; Al Mamaux, IP 1, H 0, R 0, ER 0, BB 0, SO 1
Cle Stan Coveleski (W, 3-0), IP 9, H 5, R 0, ER 0, BB 1, SO 1

Top Performers at the Plate
Bro Zack Wheat, 2 for 4
Cle Charlie Jamieson, 2 for 4, 1 R, 1 RBI; Tris Speaker, 1 for 3, 1 RBI, 1 BB

2B-Cle/Jamieson, O'Neill. **3B**-Cle/Speaker. **SB**-Cle/Jamieson, D. Johnston. **Time** 1:55. **Attendance** 27,525.

New York Giants (5) vs. New York Yankees (3)

New York baseball fans were treated to their first Subway Series in 1921, although no subway was needed to travel between stadiums because the two clubs shared the Polo Grounds as their home park. John McGraw's Giants were making their record sixth trip to the Series, while Miller Huggins's Yankees were coming in as first-timers in 1921. The arrival of Babe Ruth in 1920 helped catapult the Yanks to the top of the American League, and the Babe was coming off his second consecutive season with 50-plus home runs. Though Ruth's emergence signaled the end of the "dead ball" era, the first two games of the best-of-nine 1921 Series saw back-to-back shutouts by Yankee pitchers Carl Mays and Waite Hoyt. Hoyt threw a two-hitter in the second game while Art Nehf, his opponent, allowed only 3 hits, but 2 errors and a steal of home by Bob Meusel led to 3 Yankee runs. The offense came alive in Game 3, especially for the Giants. Both teams scored 4 runs in the third inning, but an 8-run explosion by the Giants in the seventh broke the 4-4 tie. The inning featured 4 hits and 1 walk before the first out was recorded. After Johnny Rawlings was caught trying to steal second base, 3 more singles, a sacrifice fly, a walk and a triple rounded out the barrage. Ross Youngs

Right: Brother against brother: Irish and Bob Meusel squared off in the 1921 Series, and again in 1922 and '23.

stroked a double as the second batter in the inning and later came up again to hit a bases-loaded triple, becoming the first player to get 2 base hits in one inning in a World Series. The Giants' 20 hits on the day set a record that still stands. Pitchers regained control in Game 4, and despite Ruth's first World Series homer, Phil Douglas and the Giants grabbed a 4-2 win. The Yanks regained the lead in the Series the next day when Hoyt earned his second victory by allowing just one unearned run in the first. Unfortunately for Huggins and the Yankees, injuries forced Ruth to sit out the rest of the Series—and the Giants took advantage, sweeping the next three games and claiming the title. Home runs by Irish Meusel and Frank Snyder helped take Game 6, while Douglas and Nehf outdueled Mays and Hoyt in tight 1-run contests in Games 7 and 8. In the final game, the Giants scored 1 run in the first on an error by shortstop Roger Peckinpaugh, and then both starters plowed through eight scoreless innings. In dramatic fashion, the Giants' second baseman Rawlings made a spectacular lunging play to rob Frank Baker of a hit in the bottom of the ninth and start a game- and Series-ending double play. After 16 years and three difficult October losses, John McGraw and his Giants finally won their second world championship, and with extra satisfaction they did it against the team that was beginning to challenge their primacy in the Big Apple.

1921 WORLD SERIES COMPOSITE STATISTICS

NEW YORK GIANTS/John McGraw, Manager

Player	pos	G	AB	R	H	2B	3B	HR	RBI	BB	SO	SB	BA	SA	E	FPct
Dave Bancroft	ss	8	33	3	5	1	0	0	3	1	5	0	.152	.182	1	.971
Jesse Barnes	p	3	9	3	4	0	0	0	0	0	0	0	.444	.444	0	1.000
George Burns	cf	8	33	2	11	4	1	0	2	3	5	1	.333	.515	0	1.000
Phil Douglas	p	3	7	0	0	0	0	0	0	0	2	0	.000	.000	0	1.000
Frankie Frisch	3b	8	30	5	9	0	1	0	1	4	3	3	.300	.367	2	.946
George Kelly	1b	8	30	3	7	1	0	0	4	3	10	0	.233	.267	0	1.000
Irish Meusel	lf	8	29	4	10	2	1	1	7	2	3	1	.345	.586	0	1.000
Art Nehf	p	3	9	0	0	0	0	0	0	1	3	0	.000	.000	1	.833
Johnny Rawlings	2b	8	30	2	10	3	0	0	4	0	3	0	.333	.433	0	1.000
Earl Smith	c	3	7	0	0	0	0	0	0	1	0	0	.000	.000	1	.900
Frank Snyder	c	7	22	4	8	1	0	1	3	0	2	0	.364	.545	0	1.000
Fred Toney	p	2	0	0	0	0	0	0	0	0	0	0	—	—	0	1.000
Ross Youngs	rf	8	25	3	7	1	1	0	4	7	2	2	.280	.400	0	1.000
Totals		**8**	**264**	**29**	**71**	**13**	**4**	**2**	**28**	**22**	**38**	**7**	**.269**	**.371**	**5**	**.984**

Pitcher	G	GS	CG	IP	H	R	ER	BB	SO	W-L	Sv	ERA
Jesse Barnes	3	0	0	16⅓	10	3	3	6	18	2-0	0	1.65
Phil Douglas	3	3	2	26	20	6	6	5	17	2-1	0	2.08
Art Nehf	3	3	3	26	13	6	4	13	8	1-2	0	1.38
Fred Toney	2	2	0	2⅔	7	7	7	3	1	0-0	0	23.63
Totals	**8**	**8**	**5**	**71**	**50**	**22**	**20**	**27**	**44**	**5-3**	**0**	**2.54**

NEW YORK YANKEES/Miller Huggins, Manager

Player	pos	G	AB	R	H	2B	3B	HR	RBI	BB	SO	SB	BA	SA	E	FPct
Frank Baker	3b	4	8	0	2	0	0	0	0	1	0	0	.250	.250	0	1.000
Rip Collins	p	1	0	0	0	0	0	0	0	0	0	0	—	—	0	—
Al DeVormer	c	2	1	0	0	0	0	0	0	0	0	0	.000	.000	0	1.000
Chick Fewster	lf	4	10	3	2	0	0	1	2	3	3	0	.200	.500	1	1.000
Harry Harper	p	1	0	0	0	0	0	0	0	0	0	0	—	—	0	—
Waite Hoyt	p	3	9	0	2	0	0	0	1	0	1	0	.222	.222	0	1.000
Carl Mays	p	3	9	0	1	0	0	0	0	1	0	0	.111	.111	0	1.000
Mike McNally	3b	7	20	3	4	1	0	0	1	1	3	2	.200	.250	3	.842
Bob Meusel	rf	8	30	3	6	2	0	0	3	2	5	1	.200	.267	0	1.000
Elmer Miller	cf	8	31	3	5	1	0	0	2	2	5	0	.161	.194	0	1.000
Roger Peckinpaugh	ss	8	28	2	5	1	0	0	4	3	0	0	.179	.214	1	.979
Bill Piercy	p	1	0	0	0	0	0	0	0	0	0	0	—	—	0	—
Wally Pipp	1b	8	26	1	4	1	0	0	2	2	3	1	.154	.192	0	1.000
Jack Quinn	p	1	2	0	0	0	0	0	0	0	1	0	.000	.000	0	1.000
Tom Rogers	p	1	0	0	0	0	0	0	0	0	0	0	—	—	0	1.000
Babe Ruth	lf	6	16	3	5	0	0	1	4	5	8	2	.313	.500	0	1.000
Wally Schang	c	8	21	1	6	1	1	0	1	5	4	0	.286	.429	0	1.000
Bob Shawkey	p	2	4	2	2	0	0	0	0	0	1	0	.500	.500	0	—
Aaron Ward	2b	8	26	1	6	0	0	0	4	2	6	0	.231	.231	2	.962
Totals		**8**	**241**	**22**	**50**	**7**	**1**	**2**	**20**	**27**	**44**	**6**	**.207**	**.270**	**6**	**.981**

Pitcher	G	GS	CG	IP	H	R	ER	BB	SO	W-L	Sv	ERA
Rip Collins	1	0	0	⅔	4	4	4	1	0	0-0	0	54.00
Harry Harper	1	1	0	1⅓	3	3	3	2	1	0-0	0	20.25
Waite Hoyt	3	3	3	27	18	2	0	11	18	2-1	0	0.00
Carl Mays	3	3	3	26	20	6	5	0	9	1-2	0	1.73
Bill Piercy	1	0	0	1	2	0	0	0	2	0-0	0	0.00
Jack Quinn	1	0	0	3⅔	8	4	4	2	2	0-1	0	9.82
Tom Rogers	1	0	0	1⅓	3	1	1	0	0	0-0	0	6.75
Bob Shawkey	2	1	0	9	13	9	7	6	5	0-1	0	7.00
Totals	**8**	**8**	**6**	**70**	**71**	**29**	**24**	**22**	**38**	**3-5**	**0**	**3.09**

Series Outstanding Player: Irish Meusel, New York Giants. **Series Outstanding Pitcher:** Waite Hoyt, New York Yankees. **Average Length of Game:** 1 hour, 59 minutes. **Total Attendance:** 269,976. **Average Attendance:** 33,747. **Umpires:** Ollie Chill (AL), George Moriarty (AL), Ernie Quigley (NL), Cy Rigler (NL). **Winning Player's Share:** $5,265. **Losing Player's Share:** $3,510.

Two of the Giants' 20 hits in Game 3 were hit by Ross Youngs—in the same inning.

Along with Christy Mathewson, Waite Hoyt is one of two men to pitch three complete games in a Series without allowing an earned run. (He did give up two unearned runs in the Series.)

Game 1 of the 1921 Series was the first Series game broadcast on the radio.

Right: Having made the switch from pitcher to full-time position player two years earlier, Babe Ruth came through with a .313 average, and one home run, in the 1921 Series.

The Yankees' Carl Mays pitched a record 26 innings without walking a batter.

59

New York Giants (4) vs. New York Yankees (0), 1 tie

1922

The Giants and Yankees were back at it in 1922, this time with the best-of-seven format reinstated. The Giants had reached baseball's ultimate goal on the backs of a lineup boasting seven players with averages over .300 and a pitching staff that finished with a league-leading 3.45 ERA. By contrast, the Yankees had struggled a bit along their road to the pennant, edging out the second-place St. Louis Browns by only a single game. Babe Ruth, their star player, was forced to sit out the first six weeks of the season (along with Bob Meusel) after Commissioner Kenesaw Landis suspended them for participating in a barnstorming tour in the off-season. That suspension, along with several other smaller ones over the course of the season, led to an off year for Ruth—by Ruthian standards. The Giants pitchers succeeded in keeping Ruth quiet during the Series as well, limiting him to just two hits in 17 times at bat, and giving Ruth his only homer-less Series in a Yankee uniform. In fact, the Giants held the entire Yankee lineup to 11 runs and a .203 average in the five games. The Yanks got a pair of those runs in Game 1, but the Giants came back to score 3 runs in the bottom of the eighth off "Bullet" Joe Bush to win the opener. A 3-run home run by Irish Meusel in the first inning gave the Giants a quick lead in Game 2 until the Yanks chipped away to send the game into extra innings. After the tenth inning, and with close to 45 minutes of daylight still to come, the umpires surprisingly decided to call the game "on account of darkness." The fans at the Polo Grounds were enraged, and they sent a barrage of debris onto the field in protest. In an effort to placate the angry New Yorkers, Landis decreed that all the receipts from the game would be donated to charities honoring military veterans. The teams met again the next afternoon in front of 37,000-plus spectators, and Jack Scott shut out the Yankees on four hits. Hugh McQuillan got the Giants' third win with the help of a 2-run single by Dave Bancroft in New York's 4-run fifth inning. Desperately clinging on for survival, the Yanks carried a slim 3-2 lead into the bottom of the eighth of Game 5, but a bases-loaded single by George Kelly and a bloop single by Lee King put the Giants ahead to stay. The two hits each by Heine Groh and Frankie Frisch in the final game capped off steller offensive performances by the two Giant infielders, and John McGraw had secured a second straight win against his New York nemeses.

1922 WORLD SERIES COMPOSITE STATISTICS

NEW YORK GIANTS/John McGraw, Manager

Player	pos	G	AB	R	H	2B	3B	HR	RBI	BB	SO	SB	BA	SA	E	FPct
Dave Bancroft	ss	5	19	4	4	0	0	0	2	2	1	0	.211	.211	1	.962
Jesse Barnes	p	1	4	0	0	0	0	0	0	0	1	0	.000	.000	0	1.000
Bill Cunningham	cf	4	10	0	2	0	0	0	2	2	1	0	.200	.200	0	1.000
Frankie Frisch	2b	5	17	3	8	1	0	0	2	1	0	1	.471	.529	1	.967
Heine Groh	3b	5	19	4	9	0	1	0	0	2	1	0	.474	.579	0	1.000
George Kelly	1b	5	18	0	5	0	0	0	2	0	3	0	.278	.278	0	1.000
Lee King	cf	2	1	0	1	0	0	0	1	0	0	0	1.000	1.000	0	—
Hugh McQuillan	p	1	4	1	1	1	0	0	0	0	1	0	.250	.500	0	—
Irish Meusel	lf	5	20	3	5	0	0	1	7	0	1	0	.250	.400	0	1.000
Art Nehf	p	2	3	0	0	0	0	0	2	0	0	0	.000	.000	1	.750
Rosy Ryan	p	1	0	0	0	0	0	0	0	0	0	0	—	—	0	—
Jack Scott	p	1	4	0	1	0	0	0	0	0	1	0	.250	.250	0	1.000
Earl Smith	c	4	7	0	1	0	0	0	0	0	2	0	.143	.143	1	1.000
Frank Snyder	c	4	15	1	5	0	0	0	0	2	1	0	.333	.333	1	.963
Casey Stengel	cf	2	5	0	2	0	0	0	0	0	1	0	.400	.400	0	1.000
Ross Youngs	rf	5	16	2	6	0	0	0	2	3	1	0	.375	.375	1	.917
Totals		5	162	18	50	2	1	1	18	12	15	1	**.309**	**.352**	5	**.976**

Pitcher	G	GS	CG	IP	H	R	ER	BB	SO	W-L	Sv	ERA
Jesse Barnes	1	1	1	10	8	3	2	2	6	0-0	0	1.80
Hugh McQuillan	1	1	1	9	8	3	3	2	4	1-0	0	3.00
Art Nehf	2	2	1	16	11	5	4	3	6	1-0	0	2.25
Rosy Ryan	1	0	0	2	1	0	0	0	2	0-0	0	0.00
Jack Scott	1	1	1	9	4	0	0	1	2	1-0	0	0.00
Totals	5	5	4	46	32	11	9	8	20	**4-0**	0	**1.76**

NEW YORK YANKEES/Miller Huggins, Manager

Player	pos	G	AB	R	H	2B	3B	HR	RBI	BB	SO	SB	BA	SA	E	FPct
Frank Baker	ph	1	1	0	0	0	0	0	0	0	0	0	.000	.000	—	1.000
Joe Bush	p	2	6	0	1	0	0	0	0	1	0	0	.167	.167	0	1.000
Joe Dugan	3b	5	20	4	5	1	0	0	0	0	1	0	.250	.300	0	1.000
Waite Hoyt	p	2	2	0	1	0	0	0	0	0	0	0	.500	.500	0	1.000
Sam Jones	p	2	0	0	0	0	0	0	0	0	0	0	—	—	0	1.000
Carl Mays	p	1	2	0	0	0	0	0	0	0	0	0	.000	.000	0	1.000
Norm McMillan	cf	1	2	0	0	0	0	0	0	0	0	0	.000	.000	0	1.000
Mike McNally	2b	1	0	0	0	0	0	0	0	0	0	0	—	—	0	1.000
Bob Meusel	lf	5	20	2	6	1	0	0	2	1	3	1	.300	.350	0	1.000
Wally Pipp	1b	5	21	0	6	1	0	0	3	0	2	1	.286	.333	0	1.000
Babe Ruth	rf	5	17	1	2	1	0	0	1	2	3	0	.118	.176	0	1.000
Wally Schang	c	5	16	0	3	1	0	0	0	3	0	0	.188	.250	0	1.000
Everett Scott	ss	5	14	0	2	0	0	0	1	1	0	0	.143	.143	0	1.000
Bob Shawkey	p	1	4	0	0	0	0	0	0	0	1	0	.000	.000	0	1.000
Elmer Smith	ph	2	2	0	0	0	0	0	0	0	2	0	.000	.000	0	1.000
Aaron Ward	2b	5	13	3	2	0	0	2	3	3	3	0	.154	.615	1	.967
Whitey Witt	cf	5	18	1	4	1	0	0	1	1	2	0	.222	.389	0	1.000
Totals		5	158	11	32	6	1	2	11	8	20	2	**.203**	**.291**	1	**.995**

Pitcher	G	GS	CG	IP	H	R	ER	BB	SO	W-L	Sv	ERA
Joe Bush	2	2	1	15	21	8	8	5	6	0-2	0	4.80
Waite Hoyt	2	1	0	8	11	3	1	2	4	0-1	0	1.13
Sam Jones	2	0	0	2	1	0	0	1	0	0-0	0	0.00
Carl Mays	1	1	0	8	9	4	4	2	1	0-1	0	4.50
Bob Shawkey	1	1	1	10	8	3	3	2	4	0-0	0	2.70
Totals	5	5	2	43	50	18	16	12	15	**0-4**	0	**3.35**

Series Outstanding Player: Heine Groh, New York Giants. **Series Outstanding Pitcher:** Art Nehf, New York Giants. **Average Length of Game:** 2 hours, 3 minutes. **Total Attendance:** 185,947. **Average Attendance:** 37,189. **Umpires:** George Hildebrand (AL), Bill Klem (NL), Barry McCormick (NL), Clarence Owens (AL). **Winning Player's Share:** $4,470. **Losing Player's Share:** $3,225.

Background: George Kelly delivered the game-winning hit in Game 5 to give the Giants their second straight victory over the Yankees.

Left: Art Nehf's complete-game win in Game 5 secured the Giants' second consecutive title over the Yanks.

Game 1   Wednesday, October 4 at the Polo Grounds, New York

	1	2	3	4	5	6	7	8	9	R	H	E
New York Yankees	0	0	0	0	0	1	1	0	0	2	7	0
New York Giants	0	0	0	0	0	0	0	3	x	3	11	2

Pitchers   NYY Joe Bush (L, 0-1), IP 7, H 11, R 3, ER 3, BB 1, SO 3; Waite Hoyt, IP 1, H 0, R 0, ER 0, BB 0, SO 2
NYG Art Nehf, IP 7, H 6, R 2, ER 1, BB 1, SO 3; Rosy Ryan (W, 1-0), IP 2, H 1, R 0, ER 0, BB 0, SO 2

Top Performers at the Plate
NYY Bob Meusel, 2 for 4, 1 R
NYG Frankie Frisch, 2 for 4, 1 R; Heine Groh, 3 for 3, 1 R, 1 BB

3B-NYY/Witt; NYG/Groh. **Time** 2:08. **Attendance** 36,514.

Game 2   Thursday, October 5 at the Polo Grounds, New York

	1	2	3	4	5	6	7	8	9	10	R	H	E
New York Giants	3	0	0	0	0	0	0	0	0	0	3	8	1
New York Yankees	1	0	0	1	0	0	0	1	0	0	3	8	0

Pitchers   NYG Jesse Barnes (nd), IP 10, H 8, R 3, ER 2, BB 2, SO 6
NYY Bob Shawkey (nd), IP 10, H 8, R 3, ER 3, BB 2, SO 4

Top Performers at the Plate
NYG Frankie Frisch, 2 for 4, 1 R; Irish Meusel, 1 for 4, 1 R, 3 RBI
NYY Joe Dugan, 2 for 5, 1 R

2B-NYY/Dugan, B.Meusel, Ruth. **HR**-NYG/I.Meusel; NYY/Ward. **SB**-NYG/Frisch. **Time** 2:40.
Attendance 37,020.

Game 3   Friday, October 6 at the Polo Grounds, New York

	1	2	3	4	5	6	7	8	9	R	H	E
New York Yankees	0	0	0	0	0	0	0	0	0	0	4	1
New York Giants	0	0	2	0	0	0	1	0	x	3	12	1

Pitchers   NYY Waite Hoyt (L, 0-1), IP 7, H 11, R 3, ER 1, BB 2, SO 2; Sam Jones, IP 1, H 1, R 0, ER 0, BB 1, SO 0
NYG Jack Scott (W, 1-0), IP 9, H 4, R 0, ER 0, BB 1, SO 2

Top Performers at the Plate
NYG Frankie Frisch, 2 for 2, 2 RBI, 1 BB, 1 SH; Ross Youngs, 3 for 4

2B-NYY/Schang. **SB**-NYY/Pipp. **Time** 1:48. **Attendance** 37,630.

Game 4   Saturday, October 7 at the Polo Grounds, New York

	1	2	3	4	5	6	7	8	9	R	H	E
New York Giants	0	0	0	0	4	0	0	0	0	4	9	1
New York Yankees	2	0	0	0	0	0	1	0	0	3	8	0

Pitchers   NYG Hugh McQuillan (W, 1-0), IP 9, H 8, R 3, ER 3, BB 2, SO 4
NYY Carl Mays (L, 0-1), IP 8, H 9, R 4, ER 4, BB 2, SO 1; Sam Jones, IP 1, H 0, R 0, ER 0, BB 0, SO 0

Top Performers at the Plate
NYG Dave Bancroft, 2 for 3, 1 R, 2 RBI, 1 BB; Ross Youngs, 2 for 4, 1 RBI
NYY Wally Pipp, 2 for 4, 1 RBI; Whitey Witt, 2 for 4, 1 R

2B-NYG/McQuillan; NYY/Pipp, Witt. **HR**-NYY/Ward. **SB**-NYY/B. Meusel. **Time** 1:41.
Attendance 36,242.

Game 5   Sunday, October 8 at the Polo Grounds, New York

	1	2	3	4	5	6	7	8	9	R	H	E
New York Yankees	1	0	0	0	1	0	1	0	0	3	5	0
New York Giants	0	2	0	0	0	0	0	3	x	5	10	0

Pitchers   NYY Joe Bush (L, 0-2), IP 8, H 10, R 5, ER 5, BB 4, SO 3
NYG Art Nehf (W, 1-0), IP 9, H 5, R 3, ER 3, BB 2, SO 3

Top Performers at the Plate
NYY Everett Scott, 1 for 2, 1 RBI, 1 SH
NYG Frankie Frisch, 2 for 4, 1 R; George Kelly, 2 for 3, 2 RBI, 1 SH

2B-NYG/Frisch. **Time** 2:00. **Attendance** 38,551.

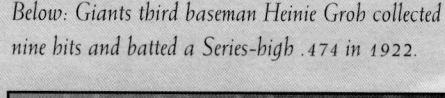

Below: Giants third baseman Heinie Groh collected nine hits and batted a Series-high .474 in 1922.

New York Yankees (4) vs. New York Giants (2)

1923

Only once in history have the same two teams faced each other in three consecutive World Series, which is what the Yankees and Giants did when they reconvened in October 1923. The setting was slightly different this time around, with the Yankees playing host in their new 62,000-seat stadium just across the Harlem River from the Giants' home park. (John McGraw and the Giants had evicted the Yankees from the Polo Grounds at the beginning of 1923.) More than 55,300 were in attendance at Yankee Stadium for the Series opener, a postseason record that would be broken two days later in Game 3, which was in turn eclipsed two days after that in the fifth game. The Yankees scored three quick runs off Mule Watson in Game 1, but the Giants came back with four runs of their own in the third. After the Yanks tied it up in the seventh inning, 34-year-old center fielder Casey Stengel came up for the Giants and ripped Joe Bush's pitch to deep left-center field. Stengel ran around the bases in a kind of gallop, with one shoe falling off, and slid into home just before the throw. The first World Series home run at Yankee Stadium was struck by the man who would later lead the Yanks to seven world championships as manager. But that was still many years off, and the Yankees were able to tie the 1923 Series the next day at the Polo Grounds behind Herb Pennock's complete-game win and Babe Ruth's home runs in back-to-back at-bats in the fourth and fifth innings.

Back at Yankee Stadium for Game 3, Art Nehf and "Sad" Sam Jones were engaged in a tight shutout duel until ol' Casey once again provided the heroics for the Giants. His line-drive homer into the right-field bleachers was the lone run of the ball game. The Yankees pounded out 13 hits to take Game 4 by an 8-4 score, and the hits kept coming in Game 5, as the Yanks coasted to an 8-1 win. Seven of the runs came in the first two innings, and "Bullet" Joe Bush had little trouble preserving that lead, holding the Giants to just one run on a trio of hits in the Yankees' first Series win in their new ballpark. Ruth's third home run of the Series came in the first inning of Game 6, but the Giants scattered four runs over six innings to take a 4-1 lead. Then the ceiling fell in on the Giants when three singles and three walks

Above: Giant outfielder Casey Stengel slides in safely with an inside-the-park home run—the first Series homer at Yankee Stadium—to give the Giants the opening-game victory.

1923 WORLD SERIES COMPOSITE STATISTICS

NEW YORK YANKEES/Miller Huggins, Manager

Player	pos	G	AB	R	H	2B	3B	HR	RBI	BB	SO	SB	BA	SA	E	FPct
Joe Bush	p	4	7	2	3	1	0	0	1	1	1	0	.429	.571	0	1.000
Joe Dugan	3b	6	25	5	7	2	1	1	5	3	0	0	.280	.560	0	1.000
Hinkey Haines	rf-cf	2	1	1	0	0	0	0	0	0	0	0	.000	.000	0	–
Harvey Hendrick	ph	1	1	0	0	0	0	0	0	0	0	0	.000	.000	–	–
Fred Hofmann	ph	2	1	0	0	0	0	0	0	1	0	0	.000	.000	–	–
Waite Hoyt	p	1	1	0	0	0	0	0	0	0	1	0	.000	.000	0	–
Ernie Johnson	ss	2	0	1	0	0	0	0	0	0	0	0	–	–	0	1.000
Sam Jones	p	2	2	0	0	0	0	0	0	0	1	0	.000	.000	0	1.000
Bob Meusel	lf	6	26	1	7	1	2	0	8	0	3	0	.269	.462	0	1.000
Herb Pennock	p	3	6	0	0	0	0	0	0	0	2	0	.000	.000	0	1.000
Wally Pipp	1b	6	20	2	5	0	0	0	2	4	1	0	.250	.250	0	1.000
Babe Ruth	rf-1b	6	19	8	7	1	1	3	3	8	6	0	.368	1.000	1	.944
Wally Schang	c	6	22	3	7	1	0	0	0	1	2	0	.318	.364	1	.958
Everett Scott	ss	6	22	2	7	0	0	0	3	0	1	0	.318	.318	1	.966
Bob Shawkey	p	1	3	0	1	0	0	0	1	0	0	0	.333	.333	0	1.000
Aaron Ward	2b	6	24	4	10	0	0	1	2	1	3	1	.417	.542	0	1.000
Whitey Witt	cf	6	25	1	6	2	0	0	4	1	1	0	.240	.320	0	1.000
Totals		**6**	**205**	**30**	**60**	**8**	**4**	**5**	**29**	**20**	**22**	**1**	**.293**	**.444**	**3**	**.988**

Pitcher	G	GS	CG	IP	H	R	ER	BB	SO	W-L	Sv	ERA
Joe Bush	3	1	1	16⅔	7	2	2	4	5	1-1	0	1.08
Waite Hoyt	1	1	0	2⅓	4	4	4	1	0	0-0	0	15.43
Sam Jones	2	1	0	10	5	1	1	2	3	0-1	1	0.90
Herb Pennock	3	2	1	17⅓	19	7	7	1	8	2-0	1	3.63
Bob Shawkey	1	1	0	7⅔	12	3	3	4	2	1-0	0	3.52
Totals	**6**	**6**	**2**	**54**	**47**	**17**	**17**	**12**	**18**	**4-2**	**2**	**2.83**

NEW YORK GIANTS/John McGraw, Manager

Player	pos	G	AB	R	H	2B	3B	HR	RBI	BB	SO	SB	BA	SA	E	FPct
Dave Bancroft	ss	6	24	1	2	0	0	0	1	1	2	1	.083	.083	0	1.000
Virgil Barnes	p	2	1	0	0	0	0	0	0	0	1	0	.000	.000	0	1.000
Jack Bentley	p	5	5	0	3	1	0	0	0	0	0	0	.600	.800	0	1.000
Bill Cunningham	cf	4	7	0	1	0	0	0	1	0	1	0	.143	.143	1	.667
Frankie Frisch	2b	6	25	2	10	0	1	0	1	0	0	0	.400	.480	1	.971
Dinty Gearin	pr	1	0	0	0	0	0	0	0	0	0	0	–	–	–	–
Hank Gowdy	c	3	4	0	0	0	0	0	0	1	0	0	.000	.000	0	1.000
Heine Groh	3b	6	22	3	4	0	1	0	2	3	1	0	.182	.273	0	1.000
Travis Jackson	ph	1	1	0	0	0	0	0	0	0	0	0	.000	.000	–	–
Claude Jonnard	p	2	0	0	0	0	0	0	0	0	0	0	–	–	0	1.000
George Kelly	1b	6	22	1	4	0	0	0	1	1	2	0	.182	.182	1	.985
Freddie Maguire	pr	2	0	1	0	0	0	0	0	0	0	0	–	–	–	–
Hugh McQuillan	p	2	3	0	0	0	0	0	0	0	1	0	.000	.000	0	1.000
Irish Meusel	lf	6	25	3	7	1	1	1	2	0	2	0	.280	.520	0	1.000
Art Nehf	p	2	6	0	1	0	0	0	0	0	4	0	.167	.167	0	1.000
Jimmy O'Connell	ph	2	1	0	0	0	0	0	0	0	1	0	.000	.000	–	–
Rosy Ryan	p	3	2	0	0	0	0	0	0	0	1	0	.000	.000	0	1.000
Jack Scott	p	2	1	0	0	0	0	0	0	0	0	0	.000	.000	1	.000
Frank Snyder	c	5	17	1	2	0	0	1	2	0	2	0	.118	.294	0	1.000
Casey Stengel	cf	6	12	3	5	0	0	2	4	4	0	0	.417	.917	0	1.000
Mule Watson	p	1	0	0	0	0	0	0	0	0	0	0	–	–	0	1.000
Ross Youngs	rf	6	23	2	8	0	0	1	3	2	0	0	.348	.478	2	.750
Totals		**6**	**201**	**17**	**47**	**2**	**3**	**5**	**17**	**12**	**18**	**1**	**.234**	**.348**	**6**	**.975**

Pitcher	G	GS	CG	IP	H	R	ER	BB	SO	W-L	Sv	ERA
Virgil Barnes	2	0	0	4⅔	4	0	0	0	4	0-0	0	0.00
Jack Bentley	2	1	0	6⅔	10	8	7	4	1	0-1	0	9.45
Claude Jonnard	2	0	0	2	1	0	0	1	1	0-0	0	0.00
Hugh McQuillan	2	1	0	9	11	5	5	4	3	0-1	0	5.00
Art Nehf	2	2	1	16⅓	10	5	5	6	7	1-1	0	2.76
Rosy Ryan	3	0	0	9⅓	11	4	1	3	3	1-0	0	0.96
Jack Scott	2	1	0	3	9	5	4	1	2	0-1	0	12.00
Mule Watson	1	1	0	2	4	3	3	1	1	0-0	0	13.50
Totals	**6**	**6**	**1**	**53**	**60**	**30**	**25**	**20**	**22**	**2-4**	**0**	**4.25**

Series Outstanding Player: Babe Ruth, New York Yankees. **Series Outstanding Pitcher:** Joe Bush, New York Yankees. **Average Length of Game:** 2 hours, 8 minutes. **Total Attendance:** 301,430. **Average Attendance:** 50,238 (60,185 at Yankee Stadium; 40,292 at the Polo Grounds). **Umpires:** Billy Evans (AL), Bob Hart (NL), Dick Nallin (AL), Hank O'Day (NL). **Winning Player's Share:** $6,143. **Losing Player's Share:** $4,113.

(including two with the bases loaded) led to five Yankee runs in the eighth inning. That was all Miller Huggins's crew would need, as Jones shut the Giants down in two innings of relief. With Ruth's three home runs and .368 batting average leading the way, the New York Yankees secured the franchise's first World Series championship—the first of many more to come.

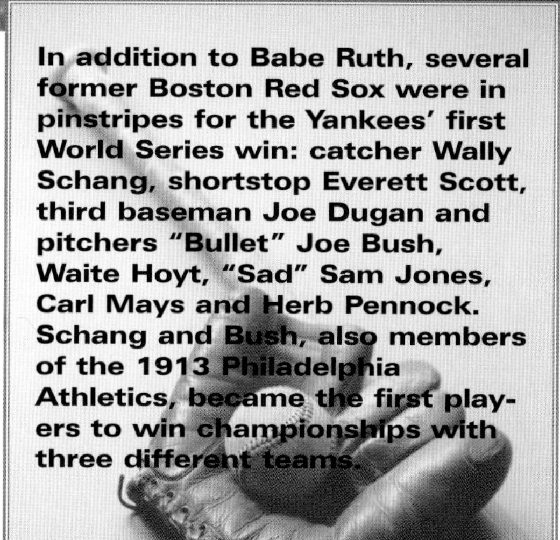

In addition to Babe Ruth, several former Boston Red Sox were in pinstripes for the Yankees' first World Series win: catcher Wally Schang, shortstop Everett Scott, third baseman Joe Dugan and pitchers "Bullet" Joe Bush, Waite Hoyt, "Sad" Sam Jones, Carl Mays and Herb Pennock. Schang and Bush, also members of the 1913 Philadelphia Athletics, became the first players to win championships with three different teams.

Above: Babe Ruth could do more than just hit the ball over the fence. Here his aggressive base running lands him at third base during the Series.

Inset: The Polo Grounds played host to a third straight World Series in 1923, but this time Giants fans saw their team go down in defeat.

Game 1   Wednesday, October 10 at Yankee Stadium, New York

	1	2	3	4	5	6	7	8	9	R	H	E
New York Giants	0	0	4	0	0	0	0	0	1	5	8	0
New York Yankees	1	2	0	0	0	0	1	0	0	4	12	1

Pitchers   NYG Mule Watson, IP 2, H 4, R 3, ER 3, BB 1, SO 1; Rosy Ryan (W, 1-0), IP 7, H 8, R 1, ER 1, BB 1, SO 2
NYY Waite Hoyt, IP 2⅓, H 4, R 4, ER 4, BB 1, SO 0; Joe Bush (L, 0-1), IP 6⅔, H 4, R 1, ER 1, BB 2, SO 2

Top Performers at the Plate
NYG Heine Groh, 2 for 4, 1 R, 2 RBI; Casey Stengel, 2 for 3, 1 R, 1 RBI, 1 BB
NYY Joe Bush, 2 for 3, 1 R; Wally Schang, 2 for 3, 1 R, 1 BB

2B-NYY/Bush, B. Meusel, Schang. **3B**-NYG/Groh; NYY/Dugan, Ruth. **HR**-NYG/Stengel. **SB**-NYG/Bancroft. **Time** 2:05. **Attendance** 55,307.

Game 2   Thursday, October 11 at the Polo Grounds, New York

	1	2	3	4	5	6	7	8	9	R	H	E
New York Yankees	0	1	0	2	1	0	0	0		4	10	0
New York Giants	0	1	0	0	0	1	0	0	0	2	9	2

Pitchers   NYY Herb Pennock (W, 1-0), IP 9, H 9, R 2, ER 2, BB 1, SO 1
NYG Hugh McQuillan (L, 0-1), IP 3⅔, H 5, R 3, ER 3, BB 2, SO 1; Jack Bentley, IP 5⅓, H 5, R 1, ER 1, BB 2, SO 0

Top Performers at the Plate
NYY Babe Ruth, 2 for 5, 2 R, 2 RBI, 2 BB, 2 HR; Aaron Ward, 2 for 4, 1 R, 1 RBI
NYG Irish Meusel, 2 for 4, 1 R, 1 RBI; Ross Youngs, 2 for 4, 1 R

2B-NYY/Dugan; NYG/Bentley. **HR**-NYY/Ruth 2, Ward; NYG/I. Meusel. **Time** 2:08. **Attendance** 40,402.

Game 3   Friday, October 12 at Yankee Stadium, New York

	1	2	3	4	5	6	7	8	9	R	H	E
New York Giants	0	0	0	0	0	0	1	0	0	1	4	0
New York Yankees	0	0	0	0	0	0	0	0	0	0	6	1

Pitchers   NYG Art Nehf (W, 1-0), IP 9, H 6, R 0, ER 0, BB 3, SO 4
NYY Sam Jones (L, 0-1), IP 8, H 4, R 1, ER 1, BB 2, SO 3; Joe Bush, IP 1, H 0, R 0, ER 0, BB 0, SO 0

Top Performers at the Plate
NYG Frankie Frisch, 2 for 4; Casey Stengel, 1 for 3, 1 R, 1 RBI, 1 BB
NYY Babe Ruth, 1 for 2, 2 BB

2B-NYY/Dugan. **HR**-NYY/Stengel. **Time** 2:05. **Attendance** 62,430.

Game 4   Saturday, October 13 at the Polo Grounds, New York

	1	2	3	4	5	6	7	8	9	R	H	E
New York Yankees	0	6	1	1	0	0	0	0		8	13	1
New York Giants	0	0	0	0	0	0	0	3	1	4	13	1

Pitchers   NYY Bob Shawkey (W, 1-0), IP 7⅔, H 12, R 3, ER 3, BB 4, SO 2; Herb Pennock (Sv, 1), IP 1⅓, H 1, R 1, ER 1, BB 0, SO 1
NYG Jack Scott (L, 0-1), IP 1, H 4, R 4, ER 3, BB 0, SO 1; Rosy Ryan, IP ⅔, H 2, R 2, ER 0, BB 1, SO 0; Hugh McQuillan, IP 5⅓, H 6, R 2, ER 2, BB 2, SO 2; Claude Jonnard, IP 1, H 1, R 0, ER 0, BB 1, SO 0; Jesse Barnes, IP 1, H 0, R 0, ER 0, BB 0, SO 0

Top Performers at the Plate
NYY Aaron Ward, 2 for 4, 2 R, 1 RBI, 1 BB; Whitey Witt, 3 for 4, 2 RBI, 1 SH, 2 2B
NYG Casey Stengel, 2 for 2, 1 R, 1 RBI, 2 BB; Ross Youngs, 4 for 5, 2 R, 1 RBI

2B-NYY/Ruth, Witt 2. **3B**-NYY/B. Meusel. **HR**-NYG/Youngs. **Time** 2:32. **Attendance** 46,302.

Game 5   Sunday, October 14 at Yankee Stadium, New York

	1	2	3	4	5	6	7	8	9	R	H	E
New York Giants	0	1	0	0	0	0	0	0	0	1	3	2
New York Yankees	3	4	0	1	0	0	0	0	x	8	14	0

Pitchers   NYG Jack Bentley (L, 0-1), IP 1⅓, H 5, R 7, ER 6, BB 2, SO 1; Jack Scott, IP 2, H 5, R 1, ER 1, BB 1, SO 1; Jesse Barnes, IP 3⅔, H 4, R 0, ER 0, BB 0, SO 2; Claude Jonnard, IP 1, H 0, R 0, ER 0, BB 0, SO 1
NYY Joe Bush (W, 1-1), IP 9, H 3, R 1, ER 1, BB 2, SO 3

Top Performers at the Plate
NYG Irish Meusel, 3 for 4, 1 R
NYY Joe Dugan, 4 for 5, 3 R, 3 RBI; Bob Meusel, 3 for 5 1 R, 3 RBI

2B-NYG/I. Meusel. **3B**-NYG/I. Meusel; NYY/B.Meusel. **HR**-NYY/Dugan. **SB**-NYY/Ward. **Time** 1:55. **Attendance** 62,817.

Game 6   Monday, October 15 at the Polo Grounds, New York

	1	2	3	4	5	6	7	8	9	R	H	E
New York Yankees	1	0	0	0	0	0	0	5	0	6	5	0
New York Giants	1	0	0	1	1	1	0	0	0	4	10	1

Pitchers   NYY Herb Pennock (W, 2-0), IP 7, H 9, R 4, ER 4, BB 0, SO 6; Sam Jones (Sv, 1), IP 2, H 1, R 0, ER 0, BB 0, SO 0
NYG Art Nehf (L, 1-1), IP 7⅓, H 4, R 5, ER 5, BB 3, SO 3; Rosy Ryan, IP 1⅔, H 1, R 1, ER 0, BB 1, SO 1

Top Performers at the Plate
NYY Babe Ruth, 1 for 3, 1 R, 1 RBI, 1 BB
NYG Frankie Frisch, 3 for 4, 2 R; Frank Snyder, 2 for 4, 1 R, 1 RBI

3B-NYG/Frisch. **HR**-NYY/Ruth; NYG/Snyder. **Time** 2:05. **Attendance** 34,172.

All in the Family
Father-Son and Brother Combos

Brothers in the World Series

Brothers Bob and Emil "Irish" Meusel were on opposite sides of the diamond in three consecutive Octobers from 1921 to 1923, with elder brother Emil coming out on top in the first two and Bob claiming victory in the third. Two other sets of brothers have gone head to head in the Series, and the older sibling prevailed in those as well. All in all, 22 pairs and one trio of brothers have appeared in the Fall Classic.

◆ Doc and Jimmy Johnston were the first brothers to face each other in the World Series. Doc's Indians beat out Jimmy's Dodgers in 1920.

◆ The Alou family is the only one to send three brothers to the World Series. Felipe and Matty both played for the 1962 Giants, and Matty was back in the Fall Classic with the 1972 A's. Youngest brother Jesus was on the A's in 1973 and 1974.

◆ In addition to San Francisco's Felipe and Matty Alou, the only brother-teammate combos are Mort and Walker Cooper of the 1942–44 Cardinals, Dizzy and Paul Dean of the 1934 Cardinals, and Paul and Lloyd Waner of the 1927 Pirates. The Deans and the Coopers paired up on winning teams.

◆ The Coopers are the only pitcher-catcher brother battery in a World Series. Walker was behind the plate in all six of Mort's starts. Mort was 2-3 in those games, while Walker batted 5 for 21.

◆ Ken and Clete Boyer are the only brothers to hit home runs in the same Series. The Boyer boys both went long in Game 7 in 1964, with Ken's Cardinals topping Clete's Yankees 7-5.

◆ The DiMaggio family has combined for the most World Series hits with 61—though Dom contributed only 7 while playing for the 1946 Red Sox, whereas Joe chipped in 54 in 10 years with the Yankees. The Meusels are second with 53; Bob was responsible for 29 against Irish's 24.

◆ The Deans and the Hernandezes lead all pitcher-brother duos in wins. Dizzy and Paul Dean won four games for St. Louis in the 1934 Series. Livan Hernandez gave Florida two wins in their 1997 championship, while younger brother Orlando "El Duque" Hernandez won one game for the Yanks in 1998 and 1999.

Above: Felipe Alou is one of three brothers to play in the World Series in the 1960s and 1970s. His son, Moises, was there as well, in 1997.

Below: The Deans—Dizzy (left) and Paul.

◆ Other notable Series siblings include: Sandy (1995, 1997 Indians) and Roberto Alomar (1992–93 Blue Jays); Jesse (1921–23 Giants) and Virgil Barnes (1924 Giants); Ken (1967 Red Sox) and George Brett (1980, 1985 Royals); Gus (1930–31 Cardinals, 1933, '36, '37 Giants) and Frank Mancuso (1944 Browns); Joe (1920 Indians, 1932 Yankees) and Luke Sewell (1933 Senators); and Dixie (1941, 1947 Dodgers) and Harry Walker (1942, 1943, 1946 Cardinals).

Father-Son Duos

Eleven men have played in the World Series and fathered sons who also played in the Series.

◆ The Billy Sullivans were the first father-son pair to both reach the Fall Classic. Billy Senior played on the 1906 White Sox, and Billy Junior went to the Series 34 years later with the Tigers. The two did not fare so well in October, however. Billy Senoir went a horrendous 0 for 21 at the plate in his one appearance, and though the son collected two hits for Detroit in 1940, his 2 for 13 performance gives the Sullivans a .059 family average.

◆ The Boones are the first three-generation family in the Major Leagues, and all three made it to the Series. While granddaddy Ray struck out in his only at-bat for the 1948 Indians, Bob and Bret both put up solid numbers. Bob batted .412 with the Phillies in 1980, and Bret stroked seven hits in 13 at-bats (.538) for Atlanta in 1999.

◆ Aside from Bob and Bret Boone, four other father-son combos collected hits in both generations: Felipe and Moises Alou (1962 Giants and 1997 Marlins), Jim and Mike Hegan (1948 and 1954 Indians, and 1972 A's), Julian and Stan Javier (1967–68 Cardinals and 1988 A's), and Bob and Terry Kennedy (1948 Indians and 1984 Padres/1989 Giants).

◆ Mike Hegan made it to the Series with the Yankees just ten years after father Jim was there with the Giants.

◆ Bob and Terry Kennedy have the longest gap between father and son in the World Series: 36 years.

◆ Three families put two generations on the mound in October: the Bagbys, Jim Senior on the 1920 Indians and Jim Junior on the 1946 Red Sox; the Borbons, Pedro Senior on the 1972, 1975 and 1976 Reds and Pedro Junior on the 1995 Braves; and the Stottlemyres, Mel on the 1964 Yankees and Todd on the 1992–93 Blue Jays.

◆ Sandy Alomar Sr., father of Major Leaguers Sandy Junior and Roberto, was on the roster for the 1976 Yankees but failed to make an appearance in the Series.

WORLD SERIES CLASSIC

1924

Washington Senators (4) vs. New York Giants (3)

After years as a regular finisher at the bottom of the standings, Washington had been pegged with the line, "First in war, first in peace and last in the American League." In 1924 (and again in 1925), it was, "First in war, first in peace and first in the American League," as 27-year-old player-manager Bucky Harris brought the Washington Senators to the franchise's first World Series. Although the Senators hit only 22 home runs as a team in 1924—less than half of Babe Ruth's total for the year—a pitching staff led by the legendary Walter "Big Train" Johnson paced the club to a two-game spread in front of the Yankees for the pennant.

President Calvin Coolidge was on hand to throw out the ceremonial first ball at the opening game in Washington, and then President Coolidge and 35,000 others watched Johnson and New York's Art Nehf battle for 12 innings. Solo homers by George Kelly and Bill Terry gave the Giants a 2-1 lead going into the 9th, when Washington tied it up on Roger Peckinpaugh's RBI double. New York rallied for 2 runs in the 12th, and although Washington scored one in the bottom half of the inning, a great bare-handed play by Kelly at second base prevented any more Senators from crossing the plate. "The Big Train" went the distance and

President Calvin Coolidge prepares to throw out the ceremonial first pitch to open the 1924 World Series.

struck out a record-tying 12 batters, but he was hit with the loss in his first World Series appearance. The Senators evened the Series the next day with a 4-3 win of their own. Goose Goslin and Bucky Harris each contributed a home run to the cause, and another clutch double by Peckinpaugh brought in the winning run with one out in the bottom of the 9th. Game 3 in New York was taken by the Giants by a 6-4 score, but Washington's 13 hits in Game 4 and Goslin's 4 for 4 day at the plate and 3-run homer brought the teams even again. Johnson was back on the hill in Game 5, and he didn't fare much better than he had in the opener, giving up 13 hits and 6 runs. With their backs against the wall, the Senators returned to Washington for Game 6, with Tom Zachary getting the start. Zachary allowed one Giant to score in the first but shut them out the rest of the day. A 2-run single by Harris in the 5th inning put the Senators ahead to stay in the third 1-run game of the Series.

The stage was set for a winner-take-all Game 7, and the result was one of the most dramatic and memorable October games ever played. Harris's second home run of the Series accounted for the first run of the game in the fourth inning. The Giants responded with 3 runs in the 6th, with the help of a couple of Washington errors, to go up 3-1. With New York just six outs away from claiming their third title in four years, fate stepped in on the side of the Senators in the bottom of the 8th. Washington strung together a double, a single and a walk to load the bases with just one man out. A short fly ball by Earl McNeely accounted for out number two, with none of the runners advancing. Manager/second baseman Harris came to the plate and hit a grounder to third. The ball took a hard bounce and skipped over the head of rookie third baseman Fred Lindstrom, bringing in two runners to tie the game. Johnson came in for the Senators to pitch the 9th, and he lasted for three more innings as the two teams stayed knotted at 3-3. In the top of the 12th, New York got the leadoff batter on base for the third straight inning but failed to score off Johnson. With one down in the Senators' half of the inning, Muddy Ruel popped a short foul behind home plate, but Hank Gowdy, the Giants' catcher, tripped over his own mask going after the ball and could not make the catch. Given a second chance, Ruel sent a

Background: Goose Goslin went 4-for-4 in Game 4, including a three-run homer in the third inning to put his team ahead 3-1.

Inset below left: Young Freddie Lindstrom batted a solid .333 at the plate, but bad hops in the field left him and his Giants losers in the deciding game.

Right: Senators manager Stanley "Bucky" Harris was the youngest manager ever to lead a team to World Series victory. He also batted .333 while playing second base.

The youth movement was alive and well in 1924. At 27 years and 11 months, Bucky Harris became the youngest manager ever to win a World Series. New York's 18-year 10-month-old third baseman Fred Lindstrom was the youngest Series participant in history.

Game 1 Saturday, October 4 at Griffith Stadium, Washington

	1	2	3	4	5	6	7	8	9	10	11	12	R	H	E
New York Giants	0	1	0	1	0	0	0	0	0	0	0	2	4	14	1
Washington Senators	0	0	0	0	0	1	0	0	1	0	0	1	3	10	1

Pitchers NY **Art Nehf** (W, 1-0), IP 12, H 10, R 3, ER 2, BB 5, SO 3
Was **Walter Johnson** (L, 0-1), IP 12, H 14, R 4, ER 3, BB 6, SO 12

Top Performers at the Plate
NY **Art Nehf**, 3 for 5, 1 R; **Bill Terry**, 3 for 5,1 R, 1 RBI, 1 BB
Was **Roger Peckinpaugh**, 2 for 5, 1 RBI; **Sam Rice**, 2 for 5, 1 RBI, 1 BB

2B-NY/Frisch, Youngs; Was/McNeely, Peckinpaugh. **HR**-NY/Kelly, Terry. **SB**-NY/Frisch; Was/Peckinpaugh, Rice. **Time** 3:07. **Attendance** 35,760.

Game 2 Sunday, October 5 at Griffith Stadium, Washington

	1	2	3	4	5	6	7	8	9	R	H	E
New York Giants	0	0	0	0	0	0	1	0	2	3	6	0
Washington Senators	2	0	0	0	1	0	0	0	1	4	6	1

Pitchers NY **Jack Bentley** (L, 0-1), IP 8⅓, H 6, R 4, ER 4, BB 4, SO 6
Was **Tom Zachary**, IP 8⅔, H 6, R 3, ER 3, BB 3, SO 0; **Firpo Marberry** (W, 1-0), IP ⅓, H 0, R 0, ER 0, BB 0, SO 1

Top Performers at the Plate
NY **Frankie Frisch**, 1 for 3, 1 R, 1 BB; **George Kelly**, 1 for 3, 2 R, 1 RBI, 1 BB
Was **Joe Judge**, 1 for 2, 1 R, 2 BB; **Sam Rice**, 2 for 3, 1 R, 1 SH

2B-Was/Peckinpaugh. **HR**-Was/Goslin, Harris. **SB**-Was/Rice. **Time** 1:58. **Attendance** 35,922.

Game 3 Monday, October 6 at the Polo Grounds, New York

	1	2	3	4	5	6	7	8	9	R	H	E
Washington Senators	0	0	0	2	0	0	0	1	1	4	9	2
New York Giants	0	2	1	1	0	1	0	1	x	6	12	0

Pitchers Was **Firpo Marberry** (L, 1-1), IP 3, H 5, R 3, ER 1, BB 2, SO 4; **Allan Russell**, IP 3, H 4, R 2, ER 1, BB 0, SO 0; **Joe Martina**, IP 1, H 0, R 0, ER 0, BB 0, SO 1; **By Speece**, IP 1, H 3, R 1, ER 1, BB 0, SO 0
NY **Hugh McQuillan** (W, 1-0), IP 3⅔, H 2, R 2, ER 2, BB 5, SO 0; **Rosy Ryan**, IP 4⅔, H 7, R 2, ER 2, BB 3, SO 2; **Claude Jonnard**, IP 0, H 0, R 0, ER 0, BB 1, SO 0; **Mule Watson** (Sv, 1), IP ⅔, H 0, R 0, ER 0, BB 0, SO 0

Top Performers at the Plate
Was **Ossie Bluege**, 1 for 3, 1 R, 2 BB; **Joe Judge**, 3 for 5, 1 R
NY **Hank Gowdy**, 2 for 4, 1 R, 2 RBI; **Bill Terry**, 2 for 4, 1 R

2B-Was/Judge; NY/Lindstrom. **HR**-NY/Ryan. **SB**-NY/Jackson. **Time** 2:25. **Attendance** 47,608.

Game 4 Tuesday, October 7 at the Polo Grounds, New York

	1	2	3	4	5	6	7	8	9	R	H	E
Washington Senators	0	0	3	0	2	0	0	2	0	7	13	3
New York Giants	1	0	0	0	0	1	0	1	1	4	6	1

Pitchers Was **George Mogridge** (W, 1-0), IP 7⅓, H 3, R 3, ER 2, BB 5, SO 2; **Firpo Marberry** (Sv, 1), IP 1⅔, H 3, R 1, ER 0, BB 1, SO 2
NY **Virgil Barnes** (L, 0-1), IP 5, H 9, R 5, ER 5, BB 0, SO 3; **Harry Baldwin**, IP 2, H 1, R 0, ER 0, BB 0, SO 1; **Wayland Dean**, IP 2, H 3, R 2, ER 1, BB 0, SO 2

Top Performers at the Plate
Was **Goose Goslin**, 4 for 4, 2 R, 4 RBI; **Earl McNeely**, 3 for 5, 2 R
NY **Fred Lindstrom**, 3 for 4, 1 R, 1 RBI, 1 BB

2B-Was/McNeely; NY/Kelly, Wilson. **HR**-Was/Goslin.. **Time** 2:10. **Attendance** 49,243.

Game 5 Wednesday, October 8 at the Polo Grounds, New York

	1	2	3	4	5	6	7	8	9	R	H	E
Washington Senators	0	0	0	1	0	0	0	1	0	2	9	1
New York Giants	0	0	1	0	2	0	0	3	x	6	13	0

Pitchers Was **Walter Johnson** (L, 0-2), IP 8, H 13, R 6, ER 3, BB 2, SO 3
NY **Jack Bentley** (W, 1-1), IP 7⅓, H 9, R 2, ER 2, BB 3, SO 4; **Hugh McQuillan** (Sv, 1), IP 1⅔, H 0, R 0, ER 0, BB 1, SO 1

Top Performers at the Plate
Was **Goose Goslin**, 2 for 4, 1 R, 1 RBI; **Joe Judge**, 3 for 4, 1 R
NY **Jack Bentley**, 2 for 3, 1 R, 2 RBI; **Fred Lindstrom**, 4 for 5, 2 RBI

2B-NY/Frisch. **3B**-NY/Terry. **HR**-Was/Goslin; NY/Bentley. **Time** 2:30. **Attendance** 49,211.

Game 6 Thursday, October 9 at Griffith Stadium, Washington

	1	2	3	4	5	6	7	8	9	R	H	E
New York Giants	1	0	0	0	0	0	0	0	0	1	7	1
Washington Senators	0	0	0	0	2	0	0	0	x	2	4	0

Pitchers NY **Art Nehf** (L, 1-1), IP 7, H 4, R 2, ER 2, BB 4, SO 4; **Rosy Ryan**, IP 1, H 0, R 0, ER 0, BB 1, SO 1
Was **Tom Zachary** (W, 1-0), IP 9, H 7, R 1, ER 1, BB 0, SO 3

Top Performers at the Plate
NY **Frankie Frisch**, 2 for 4, 2 2B; **George Kelly**, 2 for 4, 1 RBI
Was **Roger Peckinpaugh**, 2 for 2, 1 R, 1 BB

2B-NY/Frisch 2. **SB**-Was/Bluege, McNeely. **Time** 1:57. **Attendance** 34,254.

Game 7 Friday, October 10 at Griffith Stadium, Washington

	1	2	3	4	5	6	7	8	9	10	11	12	R	H	E
New York Giants	0	0	0	0	0	3	0	0	0	0	0	0	3	8	3
Washington Senators	0	0	0	1	0	0	0	2	0	0	0	1	4	10	4

Pitchers NY **Virgil Barnes**, IP 7⅔, H 6, R 3, ER 3, BB 1, SO 6; **Art Nehf**, IP ⅔, H 1, R 0, ER 0, BB 0, SO 0; **Hugh McQuillan**, IP 1⅔, H 0, R 0, ER 0, BB 0, SO 1; **Jack Bentley** (L, 1-2), IP 1⅓, H 3, R 1, ER 1, BB 1, SO 0
Was **Curly Ogden**, IP ⅓, H 0, R 0, ER 0, BB 1, SO 1; **George Mogridge**, IP 4⅔, H 4, R 2, ER 1, BB 1, SO 3; **Firpo Marberry**, IP 3, H 1, R 1, ER 0, BB 1, SO 3; **Walter Johnson** (W, 1-2), IP 4, H 3, R 0, ER 0, BB 3, SO 5

Top Performers at the Plate
NY **Frankie Frisch**, 2 for 5, 1 BB; **Ross Youngs**, 0 for 2, 1 R, 4 BB
Was **Bucky Harris**, 3 for 5, 1 R, 3 RBI; **Muddy Ruel**, 2 for 5, 2 R

2B-Was/Goslin, Leibold, McNeely, Ruel; NY/Lindstrom. **3B**-NY/Frisch. **HR**-Was/Harris. **SB**-NY/Youngs. **Time** 3:00. **Attendance** 31,667.

double down the third-base line. The next batter, Johnson, reached first safely when shortstop Travis Jackson misplayed his grounder. Washington base runners stood at first and second. McNeely stepped up and hit a grounder toward third. In a near replay of the events four innings earlier, the ball took a sudden hop on the infield dirt and leaped over the head of Lindstrom at third, and Ruel raced home to score the Series-winning run. It was the first time a World Series ended with a base hit, and it was the Senators' first championship.

For Washington, Goose Goslin and Bucky Harris provided the offensive firepower in the Series, driving in 14 of the team's 24 runs and hitting all 5 of their homers (Harris's 2 home runs were twice his regular-season total). But for baseball fans everywhere, 1924 was the year that sympathetic favorite Walter Johnson finally reached baseball's ultimate goal. Capping a 23-win season, the 36-year-old Johnson threw for 24 innings in the 1924 Fall Classic, and despite earning two hard losses in his Game 1 and 5 starts, Johnson earned a win in relief in the Series-clinching game.

Above: George Kelly rounds second in the sixth inning of Game 7. He would eventually score in New York's three-run inning, but the Senators won the game, 4-3.

1924 WORLD SERIES COMPOSITE STATISTICS

WASHINGTON SENATORS/Bucky Harris, Manager

Player	pos	G	AB	R	H	2B	3B	HR	RBI	BB	SO	SB	BA	SA	E	FPct
Ossie Bluege	3b-ss	7	26	2	5	0	0	0	3	3	4	1	.192	.192	3	.912
Goose Goslin	lf	7	32	4	11	1	0	3	7	0	7	0	.344	.688	0	1.000
Bucky Harris	2b	7	33	5	11	0	0	2	7	1	4	0	.333	.576	2	.964
Walter Johnson	p	3	9	0	1	0	0	0	0	0	0	0	.111	.111	1	.833
Joe Judge	1b	7	26	4	10	1	0	0	5	2	0	0	.385	.462	1	.985
Nemo Leibold	cf	3	6	1	1	1	0	0	0	1	0	0	.167	.333	0	1.000
Firpo Marberry	p	4	2	0	0	0	0	0	0	0	0	0	.000	.000	0	1.000
Joe Martina	p	1	0	0	0	0	0	0	0	0	0	0	—	—	0	—
Earl McNeely	cf	7	27	4	6	3	0	0	1	4	4	1	.222	.333	1	.889
Ralph Miller	3b	4	11	0	2	0	0	0	2	1	0	0	.182	.182	2	.833
George Mogridge	p	2	5	0	0	0	0	0	0	0	5	0	.000	.000	0	—
Curly Ogden	p	1	0	0	0	0	0	0	0	0	0	0	—	—	0	—
Roger Peckinpaugh	ss	4	12	1	5	2	0	0	2	1	0	1	.417	.583	0	1.000
Sam Rice	rf	7	29	2	6	0	0	0	1	3	2	2	.207	.207	1	.944
Muddy Ruel	c	7	21	2	2	1	0	0	0	6	1	0	.095	.190	0	1.000
Allan Russell	p	1	0	0	0	0	0	0	0	0	0	0	—	—	0	1.000
Mule Shirley	ph	3	2	1	1	0	0	0	1	0	0	0	.500	.500		
By Speece	p	2	0	0	0	0	0	0	0	0	0	0	—	—	0	1.000
Bennie Tate	ph	3	0	0	0	0	0	0	1	3	0	0	—	—	0	—
Tommy Taylor	3b	3	2	0	0	0	0	0	0	0	2	0	.000	.000	1	.750
Tom Zachary	p	2	5	0	0	0	0	0	0	0	0	0	.000	.000	0	1.000
Totals		7	248	26	61	9	0	5	24	29	34	5	.246	.363	12	.961

Pitcher	G	GS	CG	IP	H	R	ER	BB	SO	W-L	Sv	ERA
Walter Johnson	3	2	2	24	30	10	6	11	20	1-2	0	2.25
Firpo Marberry	4	1	0	8	9	5	1	4	10	0-1	2	1.13
Joe Martina	1	0	0	1	0	0	0	1	0	0-0	0	0.00
George Mogridge	2	1	0	12	7	5	3	6	5	1-0	0	2.25
Curly Ogden	1	1	0	⅓	0	0	0	1	1	0-0	0	0.00
Allan Russell	1	0	0	3	4	2	1	0	0	0-0	0	3.00
By Speece	1	0	0	1	3	1	1	0	0	0-0	0	9.00
Tom Zachary	2	2	1	17⅔	13	4	4	3	3	1-0	0	2.04
Totals	7	7	3	67	66	27	16	25	40	4-3	2	2.15

NEW YORK GIANTS/John McGraw, Manager

Player	pos	G	AB	R	H	2B	3B	HR	RBI	BB	SO	SB	BA	SA	E	FPct
Harry Baldwin	p	1	0	0	0	0	0	0	0	0	0	0	—	—	0	—
Virgil Barnes	p	2	4	0	0	0	0	0	0	1	2	0	.000	.000	0	1.000
Jack Bentley	p	5	7	1	2	0	0	1	2	1	1	0	.286	.714	0	1.000
Wayland Dean	p	1	0	0	0	0	0	0	0	0	0	0	—	—	0	—
Frankie Frisch	2b-3b	7	30	1	10	4	1	0	0	4	1	1	.333	.533	0	1.000
Hank Gowdy	c	7	27	4	7	0	0	0	1	2	2	0	.259	.259	1	.977
Heine Groh	ph	1	1	0	1	0	0	0	0	0	0	0	1.000	1.000	—	—
Travis Jackson	ss	7	27	3	2	0	0	0	1	1	4	1	.074	.074	3	.903
Claude Jonnard	p	1	0	0	0	0	0	0	0	0	0	0	—	—	0	—
George Kelly	cf-2b-1b	7	31	7	9	1	0	1	4	1	8	0	.290	.419	1	.983
Fred Lindstrom	3b	7	30	1	10	2	0	0	4	3	6	0	.333	.400	0	1.000
Hugh McQuillan	p	3	1	0	1	0	0	0	1	1	0	0	1.000	1.000	0	1.000
Irish Meusel	lf-rf	4	13	0	2	0	0	0	1	2	0	0	.154	.154	1	.833
Art Nehf	p	3	7	1	3	0	0	0	0	0	0	0	.429	.429	0	1.000
Rosy Ryan	p	2	2	1	1	0	0	1	2	0	0	0	.500	2.000	0	1.000
Frank Snyder	ph	1	1	0	0	0	0	0	0	0	0	0	.000	.000	—	—
Billy Southworth	cf	5	1	1	0	0	0	0	0	0	0	0	.000	.000	0	1.000
Bill Terry	1b	5	14	3	6	0	1	1	1	3	1	0	.429	.786	0	1.000
Mule Watson	p	1	0	0	0	0	0	0	0	0	0	0	—	—	0	—
Hack Wilson	lf-cf	7	30	1	7	1	0	0	3	1	9	0	.233	.267	0	1.000
Ross Youngs	rf-lf	7	27	3	5	1	0	0	1	5	6	1	.185	.222	0	1.000
Totals		7	253	27	66	9	2	4	21	25	40	3	.261	.360	6	.980

Pitcher	G	GS	CG	IP	H	R	ER	BB	SO	W-L	Sv	ERA
Harry Baldwin	1	0	0	2	1	0	0	0	1	0-0	0	0.00
Virgil Barnes	2	2	0	12⅔	15	8	8	1	9	0-1	0	5.68
Jack Bentley	3	2	1	17	18	7	6	8	10	1-2	0	3.18
Wayland Dean	1	0	0	2	3	2	1	0	2	0-0	0	4.50
Claude Jonnard	1	0	0	0	0	0	0	0	0	0-0	0	—
Hugh McQuillan	3	1	0	7	2	2	2	6	2	0-0	1	2.57
Art Nehf	3	2	1	19⅔	15	5	4	9	7	1-0	0	1.83
Rosy Ryan	2	0	0	5⅓	7	2	2	4	3	0-0	0	3.18
Mule Watson	1	0	0	⅔	0	0	0	0	0	0-0	0	0.00
Totals	7	7	2	66⅔	61	26	23	29	34	3-4	2	3.10

Series Outstanding Player: Goose Goslin, Washington Senators. **Series Outstanding Pitcher:** Tom Zachary, Washington Senators. **Average Length of Game:** 2 hours, 27 minutes. **Total Attendance:** 283,665. **Average Attendance:** 40,524 (34,401 at Griffith Stadium; 48,707 at the Polo Grounds). **Umpires:** Tommy Connolly (AL), Bill Dinneen (AL), Bill Klem (NL), Ernie Quigley (NL). **Winning Player's Share:** $5,970. **Losing Player's Share:** $3,820.

Background: The great Walter Johnson finally got a World Series ring in his 18th Major League season.

Right: Roger Peckinpaugh was having a great Series when a leg injury in the last inning of Game 6 forced him to miss the final game.

Frankie Frisch's .333 average in 1924 marked the fourth year in a row that the Hall of Famer batted over .300 in the postseason.

Pittsburgh Pirates (4) vs. Washington Senators (3)

Walter Johnson and the Senators were back in the World Series for the second year in a row, this time against the Pittsburgh Pirates. It was Pittsburgh's first appearance in 16 years, thanks in large part to an incredible .324 batting average by the starting lineup. Johnson served up a ten-strikeout performance in Game 1, and Joe Harris gave Washington an early lead with a home run in his first World Series at-bat. The Pirates got homers from Kiki Cuyler and Glenn Wright in Game 2 to help Vic Aldridge earn a slim 3-2 win over Stan Coveleski. A highly controversial play proved key in the third game. With the Senators leading 4-3 with two outs in the top of the eighth, Pittsburgh's Earl Smith sent a long fly ball to right-center. Washington's right fielder Sam Rice made a running leap for the ball and appeared to make the grab, but momentum took him over the fence and into the bleachers. After a long few seconds, Rice emerged from the crowd, ball in hand. Although the Pirates claimed that a Senator fan had handed the ball to Rice after he lunged into the crowd, Smith was called out. The play remained a subject of debate until 1974, when a sealed envelope given by Rice to the Hall of Fame was opened after Rice's death. The letter inside from Rice stated, "At no time did I lose possession of the ball." The Senators won Game 4 behind Johnson's 6-hit shutout, putting the Pirates down three games to one, a deficit that no team had overcome in World Series history. But the Pirates fought on, and

in Game 5 they broke out with 13 hits for Aldridge's second win. A Pirate comeback in Game 6, secured by Eddie Moore's solo blast in the fifth, set up a deciding Game 7. The 37-year-old Johnson went the distance in the final game, but he was hit with the loss in his last World Series appearance. Four of Pittsburgh's nine runs were unearned, however, as Washington shortstop Roger Peckinpaugh went from goat to hero to goat with two costly errors. Peckinpaugh muffed a seventh-inning pop-up, leading to two Pirate runs and tying the game at 6, but he regained the lead with a home run an inning later. In the bottom of the eighth, the shortstop committed his record eighth error of the Series and put the game back in Pittsburgh's hands. After Johnson retired the first two batters of the inning, the Pirates retied the score and had two runners on base when a Peckinpaugh throwing error kept the rally alive. Cuyler then brought two runners—and the championship—home with a ground-rule double; reliever Red Oldham, in the only postseason inning of his career, retired Washington in order in the ninth. For Peckinpaugh, the American League's regular-season MVP, the costly error established a mark for fielding futility that has never been equaled.

Above Goose Goslin homered three times in Washington's seven-game loss to the Pirates in the 1925 World Series.

Pittsburgh's Stuffy McInnis—a member of the 1911 and 1913 Athletics and the 1918 Red Sox—became the first player to win a World Series in both leagues.

Right: Sam Rice made a spectacular, if controversial, catch in Game 3 to help Washington take the lead in the Series.

Above: Pittsburgh's Max Carey hit a Series-high .458 and scored six runs in 1925.

Background: Roger Peckinpaugh was the league MVP in 1925, but his error-prone glove work in October was disastrous for the Senators.

Game 1 Wednesday, October 7 at Forbes Field, Pittsburgh

	1	2	3	4	5	6	7	8	9	R	H	E
Washington Senators	0	1	0	0	2	0	0	0	1	4	8	1
Pittsburgh Pirates	0	0	0	1	0	0	0	0	0	1	5	0

Pitchers Was Walter Johnson (W, 1-0), IP 9, H 5, R 1, ER 1, BB 1, SO 10
Pit Lee Meadows (L, 0-1), IP 8, H 6, R 3, ER 3, BB 0, SO 4; Johnny Morrison, IP 1, H 2, R 1, ER 1, BB 0, SO 1

Top Performers at the Plate
Was Ossie Bluege, 2 for 4, 1 R, 1 RBI; Joe Harris, 2 for 4, 2 R, 1 RBI
Pit Pie Traynor, 2 for 4, 1 R, 1 RBI

HR-Was/J. Harris; Pit/Traynor. **SB**-Was/Bigbee, Grantham. **Time** 1:57. **Attendance** 41,723.

Game 2 Thursday, October 8 at Forbes Field, Pittsburgh

	1	2	3	4	5	6	7	8	9	R	H	E
Washington Senators	0	1	0	0	0	0	0	0	1	2	8	2
Pittsburgh Pirates	0	0	0	1	0	0	0	2	x	3	7	0

Pitchers Was Stan Coveleski (L, 0-1), IP 8, H 7, R 3, ER 2, BB 1, SO 3
Pit Vic Aldridge (W, 1-0), IP 9, H 8, R 2, ER 2, BB 2, SO 4

Top Performers at the Plate
Was Joe Harris, 2 for 3, 1 BB; Sam Rice, 2 for 5
Pit Max Carey, 2 for 4; Glenn Wright, 2 for 4, 1 R, 1 RBI

HR-Was/Judge; Pit/Cuyler, Wright. **Time** 2:04. **Attendance** 43,364.

Game 3 Saturday, October 10 at Griffith Stadium, Washington

	1	2	3	4	5	6	7	8	9	R	H	E
Pittsburgh Pirates	0	1	0	1	0	1	0	0	0	3	8	3
Washington Senators	0	0	1	0	0	1	2	0	x	4	10	1

Pitchers Pit Ray Kremer (L, 0-1), IP 8, H 10, R 4, ER 4, BB 3, SO 5
Was Alex Ferguson (W, 1-0), IP 7, H 6, R 3, ER 2, BB 4, SO 5; Firpo Marberry (Sv, 1), IP 2, H 2, R 0, ER 0, BB 0, SO 2

Top Performers at the Plate
Pit Max Carey, 2 for 4, 1 HBP; Eddie Moore, 1 for 3, 2 BB
Was Goose Goslin, 2 for 4, 1 R, 1 RBI; Joe Harris, 2 for 4, 1 RBI

2B-Pit/Carey, Cuyler; Was/Judge. **3B**-Pit/Traynor. **HR**-Was/Goslin. **Time** 2:10. **Attendance** 36,495.

Game 4 Sunday, October 11 at Griffith Stadium, Washington

	1	2	3	4	5	6	7	8	9	R	H	E
Pittsburgh Pirates	0	0	0	0	0	0	0	0	0	0	6	1
Washington Senators	0	0	4	0	0	0	0	0	x	4	12	0

Pitchers Pit Emil Yde (L, 0-1), IP 2⅓, H 5, R 4, ER 3, BB 3, SO 1; Johnny Morrison, IP 4⅔, H 5, R 0, ER 0, BB 1, SO 4; Babe Adams, IP 1, H 2, R 0, ER 0, BB 0, SO 0
Was Walter Johnson (W, 2-0), IP 9, H 6, R 0, ER 0, BB 2, SO 2

Top Performers at the Plate
Pit George Grantham, 2 for 3; Pie Traynor, 2 for 4
Was Goose Goslin, 2 for 3, 1 R, 3 RBI, 1 BB; Muddy Ruel, 3 for 3, 1 BB

2B-Was/Ruel. **HR**-Was/Goslin, J. Harris. **SB**-Pit/Carey; Was/Peckinpaugh. **Time** 2:00. **Attendance** 38,701.

Game 5 Monday, October 12 at Griffith Stadium, Washington

	1	2	3	4	5	6	7	8	9	R	H	E
Pittsburgh Pirates	0	0	2	0	0	0	2	1	1	6	13	0
Washington Senators	1	0	0	1	0	0	1	0	0	3	8	1

Pitchers Pit Vic Aldridge (W, 2-0), IP 9, H 8, R 3, ER 3, BB 4, SO 5
Was Stan Coveleski (L, 0-2), IP 6½, H 9, R 4, ER 4, BB 4, SO 0; Win Ballou, IP ⅔, H 0, R 0, ER 0, BB 0, SO 1; Tom Zachary, IP 1⅓, H 3, R 2, ER 2, BB 1, SO 0; Firpo Marberry, IP ⅓, H 1, R 0, ER 0, BB 0, SO 0

Top Performers at the Plate
Pit Clyde Barnhart, 2 for 4, 1 R, 2 RBI, 1 BB; Max Carey, 2 for 4, 2 R, 1 BB
Was Joe Harris, 2 for 3, 1 R, 1 RBI, 1 BB; Sam Rice, 2 for 5, 1 R, 1 RBI

2B-Pit/Wright; Was/Bluege, Goslin, Leibold. **HR**-Was/J. Harris. **SB**-Pit/Barnhart, Carey. **Time** 2:26. **Attendance** 35,899.

Game 6 Tuesday, October 13 at Forbes Field, Pittsburgh

	1	2	3	4	5	6	7	8	9	R	H	E
Washington Senators	1	1	0	0	0	0	0	0	0	2	6	2
Pittsburgh Pirates	0	0	2	0	1	0	0	0	x	3	7	1

Pitchers Was Alex Ferguson (L, 1-1), IP 7, H 7, R 3, ER 3, BB 2, SO 6; Win Ballou, IP 1, H 0, R 0, ER 0, BB 1, SO 0
Pit Ray Kremer (W, 1-1), IP 9, H 6, R 2, ER 2, BB 1, SO 3

Top Performers at the Plate
Was Goose Goslin, 1 for 3, 1 R, 1 RBI, 1 BB
Pit Eddie Moore, 2 for 3, 2 R, 1 RBI, 1 BB; Pie Traynor, 2 for 4, 1 RBI

2B-Was/J. Harris, Peckinpaugh; Pit/Barnhart. **HR**-Was/Goslin; Pit/Moore. **SB**-Was/McNeely; Pit/Traynor. **Time** 1:57. **Attendance** 43,810.

Game 7 Thursday, October 15 at Forbes Field, Pittsburgh

	1	2	3	4	5	6	7	8	9	R	H	E
Washington Senators	4	0	0	2	0	0	1	0	0	7	7	2
Pittsburgh Pirates	0	0	3	0	1	0	2	3	x	9	15	3

Pitchers Was Walter Johnson (L, 2-1), IP 8, H 15, R 9, ER 5, BB 1, SO 3
Pit Vic Aldridge, IP ⅓, H 2, R 4, ER 4, BB 3, SO 0; Johnny Morrison, IP 3⅔, H 4, R 2, ER 2, BB 0, SO 2; Ray Kremer (W, 2-1), IP 4, H 1, R 1, ER 1, BB 0, SO 1; Red Oldham (Sv, 1), IP 1, H 0, R 0, ER 0, BB 0, SO 2

Top Performers at the Plate
Was Joe Harris, 1 for 3, 1 R, 2 RBI, 1 BB; Sam Rice, 2 for 5, 2 R
Pit Max Carey, 4 for 5, 3 R, 2 RBI, 3 2B; Kiki Cuyler, 2 for 4, 3 RBI, 1 SH, 2 2B

2B-Was/J. Harris; Pit/Bigbee, Carey 3, Cuyler 2, Moore, Smith. **3B**-Pit/Traynor.
HR-Was/Peckinpaugh. **SB**-Pit/Carey. **Time** 2:31. **Attendance** 42,856.

71

St. Louis Cardinals (4) vs. New York Yankees (3)

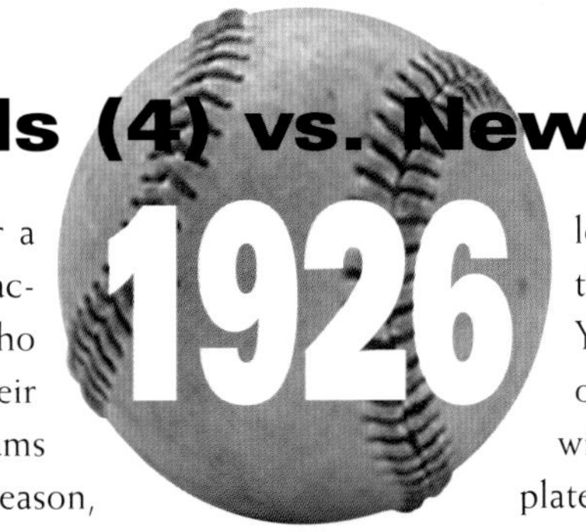

The New York Yankees were back in the Series after a two-year absence, and for the first time they were not facing the Giants. It was Rogers Hornsby's Cardinals who finished atop the National League that year, winning their first pennant in franchise history. Although the two teams led their respective leagues in home runs during the season, Game 1 of the Series was a homer-less affair, and a three-hitter by Herb Pennock brought the Yanks a 2-1 victory. A three-run home run by Billy Southworth in the seventh inning put St. Louis ahead 5-2 in Game 2, a lead that Tommy Thevenow extended with an inside-the-park homer in the ninth. Pitcher Jesse Haines helped his own cause in Game 3 with a two-run blast for the Cards, enough to protect his shutout performance on the mound. New York managed only 15 hits in the first three games combined, but in Game 4 they came alive with a vengeance, knocking 14 hits in a 10-5 win. Babe Ruth led the way with an awesome three-homer performance. His first- and third-inning home runs, solo shots off pitcher Flint Rhem, went over the bleacher roof at Sportsman's Park. Hi Bell yielded a two-run blast in the sixth for Ruth's third homer of the game. In Game 5, an RBI sacrifice fly by Tony Lazzeri in the tenth inning put New York ahead 3-2 in the game and 3-2 in the Series. The Cardinals amassed ten runs in Game 6 in New York, while Pete Alexander contributed his second strong start, allowing just two runs. St. Louis took the

lead in the decisive seventh game with a three-run rally in the fourth, aided by two Yankee errors. Ruth got New York on the board in the third with his fourth home run of the Series, and after that St. Louis took no chances with the Babe; he was walked in each of his next three plate appearances, giving him 11 bases-on-balls for the Series. The Cards held their 3-2 lead in the seventh inning when a single by Earl Combs and walks to Ruth and Lou Gehrig loaded the bases. Coming off a complete-game performance just one day earlier—and, according to rumors, coming off a long night of celebrating the night before—the 39-year-old Alexander was called in from the bull pen to relieve starter Jesse Haines with two outs and the bases jammed. Tony Lazzeri, New York's hard-hitting second baseman, stepped up for a classic October showdown. The veteran pitcher got the better of the young hitter, striking him out on four pitches. Alexander then sent the Yankees down one-two-three in the eighth, and after inducing the first two batters to ground out in the ninth, he walked Ruth on a full count. Somewhat inexplicably, Ruth tried to steal second base, but was thrown out by catcher Bob O'Farrell, and the Series came to an end.

Above: Pete Alexander's pitching performance in 1926 was simply heroic. One day after his nine-inning win in Game 6, Alexander struck out Tony Lazzeri with the bases loaded and then pitched two perfect innings to clinch the Series for St. Louis.

1926 WORLD SERIES COMPOSITE STATISTICS

ST. LOUIS CARDINALS/Rogers Hornsby, Manager

Player	pos	G	AB	R	H	2B	3B	HR	RBI	BB	SO	SB	BA	SA	E	FPct
Pete Alexander	p	3	7	1	0	0	0	0	0	0	2	0	.000	.000	1	.857
Hi Bell	p	1	0	0	0	0	0	0	0	0	0	0	–	–	0	–
Les Bell	3b	7	27	4	7	1	0	1	6	2	5	0	.259	.407	2	.920
Jim Bottomley	1b	7	29	4	10	3	0	0	5	1	2	0	.345	.448	0	1.000
Taylor Douthit	cf	4	15	3	4	2	0	0	1	3	2	0	.267	.400	0	1.000
Jake Flowers	ph	3	3	0	0	0	0	0	0	0	1	0	.000	.000	–	–
Chick Hafey	lf	7	27	2	5	2	0	0	0	0	7	0	.185	.259	0	1.000
Jesse Haines	p	3	5	1	3	0	0	1	2	0	1	0	.600	1.200	0	1.000
Bill Hallahan	p	1	0	0	0	0	0	0	0	0	0	0	–	–	0	1.000
Wattie Holm	rf-cf	5	16	1	2	0	0	0	1	1	2	0	.125	.125	0	1.000
Rogers Hornsby	2b	7	28	2	7	1	0	0	4	2	2	1	.250	.286	0	1.000
Vic Keen	p	1	0	0	0	0	0	0	0	0	0	0	–	–	0	1.000
Bob O'Farrell	c	7	23	2	7	1	0	0	2	2	2	0	.304	.348	0	1.000
Art Reinhart	p	1	0	0	0	0	0	0	0	0	0	0	–	–	0	–
Flint Rhem	p	1	1	0	0	0	0	0	0	0	1	0	.000	.000	0	1.000
Bill Sherdel	p	2	5	0	0	0	0	0	0	0	2	0	.000	.000	0	1.000
Billy Southworth	rf	7	29	6	10	1	1	1	4	0	0	1	.345	.552	0	1.000
Tommy Thevenow	ss	7	24	5	10	1	0	1	4	0	1	0	.417	.583	2	.946
Specs Toporcer	ph	1	0	0	0	0	0	0	0	1	0	0	–	–	–	–
Totals		**7**	**239**	**31**	**65**	**12**	**1**	**4**	**30**	**11**	**30**	**2**	**.272**	**.381**	**5**	**.983**

Pitcher	G	GS	CG	IP	H	R	ER	BB	SO	W-L	Sv	ERA
Pete Alexander	3	2	2	20⅓	12	4	3	4	17	2-0	1	1.33
Hi Bell	1	0	0	2	4	2	2	1	0	0-0	0	9.00
Jesse Haines	3	2	1	16⅔	13	2	2	9	5	2-0	0	1.08
Bill Hallahan	1	0	0	2	2	1	1	3	1	0-0	0	4.50
Vic Keen	1	0	0	1	0	0	0	0	0	0-0	0	0.00
Art Reinhart	1	0	0	0	1	4	4	4	0	0-1	0	–
Flint Rhem	1	1	0	4	7	3	3	2	4	0-0	0	6.75
Bill Sherdel	2	2	1	17	15	5	4	8	3	0-2	0	2.12
Totals	**7**	**7**	**4**	**63**	**54**	**21**	**19**	**31**	**31**	**4-3**	**1**	**2.71**

NEW YORK YANKEES/Miller Huggins, Manager

Player	pos	G	AB	R	H	2B	3B	HR	RBI	BB	SO	SB	BA	SA	E	FPct
Spencer Adams	ph	2	0	0	0	0	0	0	0	0	0	0	–	–	–	–
Pat Collins	c	3	2	0	0	0	0	0	0	0	1	0	.000	.000	0	1.000
Earle Combs	cf	7	28	3	10	2	0	0	2	5	2	0	.357	.429	0	1.000
Joe Dugan	3b	7	24	2	8	1	0	0	2	1	1	0	.333	.375	1	.955
Mike Gazella	3b	1	0	0	0	0	0	0	0	0	0	0	–	–	0	1.000
Lou Gehrig	1b	7	23	1	8	2	0	0	4	5	4	0	.348	.435	0	1.000
Waite Hoyt	p	2	6	0	0	0	0	0	0	0	1	0	.000	.000	0	1.000
Sam Jones	p	1	0	0	0	0	0	0	0	0	0	0	–	–	0	–
Mark Koenig	ss	7	32	2	4	1	0	0	2	0	6	0	.125	.156	4	.900
Tony Lazzeri	2b	7	26	2	5	1	0	0	3	1	6	0	.192	.231	1	.971
Bob Meusel	lf-rf	7	21	3	5	1	1	0	0	6	1	0	.238	.381	1	.929
Ben Paschal	ph	5	4	0	1	0	0	0	0	1	1	2	0	.250	.250	0	1.000
Herb Pennock	p	3	7	1	1	1	0	0	0	0	0	0	.143	.286	0	1.000
Dutch Ruether	p	3	4	0	0	0	0	0	0	0	0	0	.000	.000	0	1.000
Babe Ruth	rf-lf	7	20	6	6	0	0	4	5	11	2	1	.300	.900	0	1.000
Hank Severeid	c	7	22	1	6	1	0	0	1	1	2	0	.273	.318	0	1.000
Bob Shawkey	p	3	2	0	0	0	0	0	0	0	1	0	.000	.000	0	1.000
Urban Shocker	p	2	2	0	0	0	0	0	0	0	2	0	.000	.000	0	1.000
Myles Thomas	p	2	0	0	0	0	0	0	0	0	0	0	–	–	0	1.000
Totals		**7**	**223**	**21**	**54**	**10**	**1**	**4**	**20**	**31**	**31**	**1**	**.242**	**.350**	**7**	**.975**

Pitcher	G	GS	CG	IP	H	R	ER	BB	SO	W-L	Sv	ERA
Waite Hoyt	2	2	1	15	19	8	2	1	10	1-1	0	1.20
Sam Jones	1	0	0	2	2	1	1	2	1	0-0	0	9.00
Herb Pennock	3	2	2	22	13	3	3	4	8	2-0	0	1.23
Dutch Ruether	1	1	0	4⅓	7	4	4	2	1	0-1	0	8.31
Bob Shawkey	3	1	0	10	8	7	6	2	7	0-1	0	5.40
Urban Shocker	2	1	0	7⅔	13	7	5	0	3	0-1	0	5.87
Myles Thomas	2	0	0	3	3	1	1	0	0	0-0	0	3.00
Totals	**7**	**7**	**3**	**63**	**65**	**31**	**22**	**11**	**30**	**3-4**	**0**	**3.14**

Series Outstanding Player: Tommy Thevenow, St. Louis Cardinals. **Series Outstanding Pitcher:** Pete Alexander, St. Louis Cardinals. **Average Length of Game:** 2 hours, 7 minutes. **Total Attendance:** 328,051. **Average Attendance:** 46,864 (38,695 at Sportsman's Park; 52,992 at Yankee Stadium). **Umpires:** Bill Dinneen (AL), George Hildebrand (AL), Bill Klem (NL), Hank O'Day (NL). **Winning Player's Share:** $5,585. **Losing Player's Share:** $3,418.

Tommy Thevenow, the leading hitter of the Series with a .417 average, contributed a key home run for St. Louis in Game 2. The young shortstop would spend 12 more seasons in the Major Leagues and not hit another home run in 1,000 games.

Left: Light-hitting Tommy Thevenow batted a robust .417 to lead all hitters in the Series.

Of the eight National League teams in existence when Series play began in 1903, the St. Louis Cardinals were the last club to make it into the Fall Classic.

Right: Billy Southworth's home run in Game 2 for St. Louis tied the Series.

Above: Babe Ruth smashed three homers in the fourth game of the 1926 Series—a record he would match two years later.

On two occasions during the 1926 Series, Babe Ruth reached base safely five times in one game. In Game 4 he got three hits and walked twice, and in Game 7 homered once and received four bases on balls.

Game 1 Saturday, October 2 at Yankee Stadium, New York

	1	2	3	4	5	6	7	8	9	R	H	E
St. Louis Cardinals	1	0	0	0	0	0	0	0	0	1	3	1
New York Yankees	1	0	0	0	0	1	0	0	x	2	6	0

Pitchers StL Bill Sherdel (L, 0-1), IP 7, H 6, R 2, ER 2, BB 3, SO 1; Jesse Haines, IP 1, H 0, R 0, ER 0, BB 1, SO 0
NY Herb Pennock (W, 1-0), IP 9, H 3, R 1, ER 1, BB 3, SO 4

Top Performers at the Plate
StL Jim Bottomley, 2 for 4, 1 RBI
NY Earle Combs, 1 for 3, 1 R, 1 BB; Lou Gehrig, 1 for 4, 2 RBI

2B-StL/Douthit. **Time** 1:48. **Attendance** 61,658.

Game 2 Sunday, October 3 at Yankee Stadium, New York

	1	2	3	4	5	6	7	8	9	R	H	E
St. Louis Cardinals	0	0	2	0	0	0	3	0	1	6	12	1
New York Yankees	0	2	0	0	0	0	0	0	0	2	4	0

Pitchers StL Pete Alexander (W, 1-0), IP 9, H 4, R 2, ER 1, BB 1, SO 10
NY Urban Shocker (L,0-1), IP 7, H 10, R 5, ER 5, BB 0, SO 2; Bob Shawkey, IP 1, H 0, R 0, ER 0, BB 0, SO 2; Sam Jones, IP 1, H 2, R 1, ER 1, BB 2, SO 1

Top Performers at the Plate
StL Billy Southworth, 3 for 5, 2 R, 3 RBI; Tommy Thevenow, 3 for 4, 2 R, 1 RBI
NY Tony Lazzeri, 1 for 3, 1 R, 1 RBI

2B-StL/Hornsby, O'Farrell. **HR**-StL/Southworth, Thevenow. **Time** 1:57. **Attendance** 63,600.

Game 3 Tuesday, October 5 at Sportsman's Park, St. Louis

	1	2	3	4	5	6	7	8	9	R	H	E
New York Yankees	0	0	0	0	0	0	0	0	0	0	5	1
St. Louis Cardinals	0	0	0	3	1	0	0	0	x	4	8	0

Pitchers NY Dutch Ruether (L, 0-1), IP 4⅓, H 7, R 4, ER 2, BB 2, SO 1; Bob Shawkey, IP 2⅔, H 0, R 0, ER 0, BB 0, SO 1; Myles Thomas, IP 1, H 1, R 0, ER 0, BB 0, SO 0
StL Jesse Haines (W, 1-0), IP 9, H 5, R 0, ER 0, BB 3, SO 3

Top Performers at the Plate
NY Lou Gehrig, 2 for 4
StL Jesse Haines, 2 for 3, 1 R, 2 RBI; Billy Southworth, 2 for 3, 1 R, 1 SH

2B-StL/Hafey. **HR**-StL/Haines. **Time** 1:41. **Attendance** 37,708.

Game 4 Wednesday, October 6 at Sportsman's Park, St. Louis

	1	2	3	4	5	6	7	8	9	R	H	E
New York Yankees	1	0	1	1	3	4	2	1	0	10	14	1
St. Louis Cardinals	1	0	0	3	0	0	0	0	1	5	14	0

Pitchers NY Waite Hoyt (W, 1-0), IP 9, H 14, R 5, ER 2, BB 1, SO 8
StL Flint Rhem, IP 4, H 7, R 3, ER 3, BB 2, SO 4; Art Reinhart (L, 0-1), IP 0, H 1, R 4, ER 4, BB 4, SO 0; Hi Bell, IP 2, H 4, R 2, ER 2, BB 1, SO 1; Bill Hallahan, IP 2, H 2, R 1, ER 1, BB 3, SO 1; Vic Keen, IP 1, H 0, R 0, ER 0, BB 0, SO 0

Top Performers at the Plate
NY Babe Ruth, 3 for 3, 4 R, 4 RBI, 2 BB, 3 HR; Hank Severeid, 3 for 4, 1 R, 1 BB
StL Billy Southworth, 3 for 5; Tommy Thevenow, 2 for 4, 1 R, 1 RBI

2B-NY/Combs, Dugan, Gehrig, Koenig, Lazzeri; StL/Douthit, Thevenow. **HR**-NY/Ruth 3. **SB**-StL/Hornsby. **Time** 2:38. **Attendance** 38,825.

Game 5 Thursday, October 7 at Sportsman's Park, St. Louis

	1	2	3	4	5	6	7	8	9	10	R	H	E
New York Yankees	0	0	0	0	0	1	0	0	1	1	3	9	1
St. Louis Cardinals	0	0	0	1	0	0	1	0	0	0	2	7	1

Pitchers NY Herb Pennock (W, 2-0), IP 10, H 7, R 2, ER 2, BB 1, SO 4
StL Bill Sherdel (L, 0-2), IP 10, H 9, R 3, ER 2, BB 5, SO 2

Top Performers at the Plate
NY Lou Gehrig, 2 for 3, 1 R, 2 BB; Tony Lazzeri, 2 for 4, 1 RBI, 1 SH
StL Les Bell, 2 for 4, 1 R, 1 RBI; Bob O'Farrell, 3 for 4, 1 RBI

2B-NY/Gehrig, Pennock; StL/L. Bell, Bottomley. **SB**-StL/Southworth. **Time** 2:28. **Attendance** 39,552.

Game 6 Saturday, October 9 at Yankee Stadium, New York

	1	2	3	4	5	6	7	8	9	R	H	E
St. Louis Cardinals	3	0	0	0	1	0	5	0	1	10	13	2
New York Yankees	0	0	0	1	0	0	1	0	0	2	8	1

Pitchers StL Pete Alexander (W, 2-0), IP 9, H 8, R 2, ER 2, BB 2, SO 6
NY Bob Shawkey (L, 0-1), IP 6⅓, H 8, R 7, ER 6, BB 2, SO 4; Urban Shocker, IP ⅔, H 3, R 2, ER 2, BB 0, SO 1; Myles Thomas, IP 2, H 2, R 1, ER 1, BB 0, SO 0

Top Performers at the Plate
StL Les Bell, 3 for 3, 1 R, 4 RBI, 1 BB; Billy Southworth, 2 for 5, 3 R, 1 RBI
NY Joe Dugan, 2 for 4, 1 R; Bob Meusel, 2 for 3, 1 R, 1 BB

2B-StL/Bottomley 2, Hafey, Southworth; NY/Combs, Meusel. **3B**-StL/Southworth; NY/Meusel. **HR**-StL/L. Bell. **SB**-NY/Ruth. **Time** 2:05. **Attendance** 48,615.

Game 7 Sunday, October 10 at Yankee Stadium, New York

	1	2	3	4	5	6	7	8	9	R	H	E
St. Louis Cardinals	0	0	0	3	0	0	0	0	0	3	8	0
New York Yankees	0	0	1	0	0	1	0	0	0	2	8	3

Pitchers StL Jesse Haines (W, 2-0), IP 6⅔, H 8, R 2, ER 2, BB 5, SO 2; Grover Alexander (Sv, 1), IP 2⅓, H 0, R 0, ER 0, BB 1, SO 1
NY Waite Hoyt (L, 1-1), IP 6, H 5, R 3, ER 0, BB 0, SO 2; Herb Pennock, IP 3, H 3, R 0, ER 0, BB 0, SO 0

Top Performers at the Plate
StL Chick Hafey, 2 for 4, 1 R; Tommy Thevenow, 2 for 4, 2 RBI
NY Babe Ruth, 1 for 1, 1 R, 1 RBI, 4 BB; Hank Severeid, 2 for 3, 1 RBI

2B-NY/Severeid. **HR**-NY/Ruth. **Time** 2:15. **Attendance** 38,093.

New York Yankees (4) vs. Pittsburgh Pirates (0)

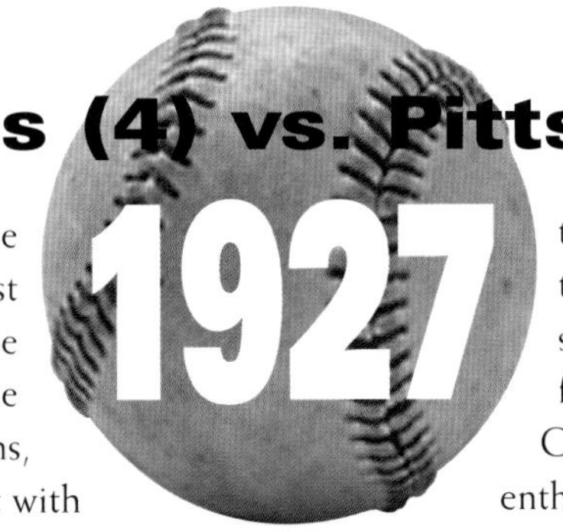

Most baseball experts and casual fans alike would put the 1927 New York Yankees on the short list of the greatest teams of all time. Led by a "Murderer's Row" of Babe Ruth, Lou Gehrig, Tony Lazzeri and Bob Meusel, the Yanks stormed over the rest of the league with 110 wins, 19 games ahead of their closest competitor. They did it with more than just their bats, too, leading the league in ERA and shutouts. The team that had the dubious honor of facing the Yanks in the Series that year was the Pittsburgh Pirates. The Pirates won 94 games in 1927 and boasted six players with averages over .300, including Paul "Big Poison" Waner's league-best .380 and Lloyd "Little Poison" Waner's .355. Even so, the Pirates were no match for the Bronx Bombers. According to baseball lore, the Pirates showed up to Forbes Field before Game 1 to watch the Yankees take batting practice, and—seeing pitch after pitch sent into the outfield seats by the Yankee juggernaut—the National League champs were psychologically defeated before the game even got under way. Whether or not the Pirates had been completely psyched out by New York's batting practice display remains the stuff of legend, but what is undeniable is that the Yankees made quick work of their foes. They outscored Pittsburgh 23 to 10 in a 4-game sweep. Waite Hoyt got the win in Game 1 thanks to three unearned runs by the Yankees in the third inning. More convincing wins followed in Games 2 and 3. The team knocked Vic Aldridge for six runs on ten hits to take the second game by a 6-2 score. Pittsburgh's Game 3 starter, Lee Meadows, didn't fare much better, giving up five runs before being pulled for a reliever. Mike Cvengros came in to pitch, with two men on, in the seventh inning and proceeded to give up a three-run homer to Ruth. Herb Pennock, meanwhile, retired the first 22 Pirates in the game before giving up a single to Pie Traynor and an RBI double to Clyde Barnhart in the eighth. Pittsburgh had Game 4 tied 3-3 going into the bottom of the ninth, but all the breaks seemed to go New York's way. After giving up a walk and an infield hit to start off the ninth, Pirate reliever Johnny Miljus threw a wild pitch to allow the runners to advance to second and third. He walked Ruth intentionally to load the bases, and then struck out Gehrig and Meusel in succession. Miljus blew the first pitch past the next batter, Tony Lazzeri, and then threw the second pitch past his own catcher. Miljus's second wild pitch of the inning allowed Earle Combs to score the winning run from third— the only time a World Series has ended with a wild pitch. The Yanks dominant season came to a close with a dominating October.

Above: "Big Poison" and "Little Poison": brothers Paul and Lloyd Waner had some success against the Yanks in 1927, but not nearly enough.

1927 WORLD SERIES COMPOSITE STATISTICS

NEW YORK YANKEES/Miller Huggins, Manager

Player	pos	G	AB	R	H	2B	3B	HR	RBI	BB	SO	SB	BA	SA	E	FPct
Benny Bengough	c	2	4	1	0	0	0	0	0	1	0	0	.000	.000	0	1.000
Pat Collins	c	2	5	0	3	1	0	0	0	3	0	0	.600	.800	0	1.000
Earle Combs	cf	4	16	6	5	0	0	0	2	1	2	0	.313	.313	0	1.000
Joe Dugan	3b	4	15	2	3	0	0	0	0	0	0	0	.200	.200	0	1.000
Cedric Durst	ph	1	1	0	0	0	0	0	0	0	0	0	.000	.000	—	—
Lou Gehrig	1b	4	13	2	4	2	2	0	4	3	3	0	.308	.769	0	1.000
Johnny Grabowski	c	1	2	0	0	0	0	0	0	0	0	0	.000	.000	0	1.000
Waite Hoyt	p	1	3	0	0	0	0	0	0	0	0	0	.000	.000	0	—
Mark Koenig	ss	4	18	5	9	2	0	0	2	0	2	0	.500	.611	0	1.000
Tony Lazzeri	2b	4	15	1	4	1	0	0	2	1	4	0	.267	.333	1	.966
Bob Meusel	lf	4	17	1	2	0	0	0	1	1	7	1	.118	.118	1	.889
Wilcy Moore	p	2	5	0	1	0	0	0	0	0	3	0	.200	.200	1	.833
Herb Pennock	p	1	4	1	0	0	0	0	1	0	1	0	.000	.000	0	1.000
George Pipgras	p	1	3	0	1	0	0	0	0	1	1	0	.333	.333	0	1.000
Babe Ruth	rf	4	15	4	6	0	0	2	7	2	2	1	.400	.800	0	1.000
Totals		**4**	**136**	**23**	**38**	**6**	**2**	**2**	**19**	**13**	**25**	**2**	**.279**	**.397**	**3**	**.981**

Pitcher	G	GS	CG	IP	H	R	ER	BB	SO	W-L	Sv	ERA
Waite Hoyt	1	1	0	7⅓	8	4	4	1	2	1-0	0	4.91
Wilcy Moore	2	1	1	10⅔	11	3	1	2	2	1-0	1	0.84
Herb Pennock	1	1	1	9	3	1	1	0	1	1-0	0	1.00
George Pipgras	1	1	1	9	7	2	2	1	2	1-0	0	2.00
Totals	**4**	**4**	**3**	**36**	**29**	**10**	**8**	**4**	**7**	**4-0**	**1**	**2.00**

PITTSBURGH PIRATES/Donie Bush, Manager

Player	pos	G	AB	R	H	2B	3B	HR	RBI	BB	SO	SB	BA	SA	E	FPct
Vic Aldridge	p	1	2	0	0	0	0	0	0	0	0	0	.000	.000	0	1.000
Clyde Barnhart	lf	4	16	0	5	1	0	0	4	0	0	0	.313	.375	0	1.000
George Brickell	ph	2	2	1	0	0	0	0	0	0	0	0	.000	.000	—	—
Mike Cvengros	p	2	0	0	0	0	0	0	0	0	0	0	—	—	0	—
Joe Dawson	p	1	0	0	0	0	0	0	0	0	0	0	—	—	0	—
Johnny Gooch	c	3	5	0	0	0	0	0	0	1	1	0	.000	.000	0	1.000
George Grantham	2b	3	11	0	4	1	0	0	0	1	1	0	.364	.455	1	.933
Heine Groh	ph	1	1	0	0	0	0	0	0	0	0	0	.000	.000	—	—
Joe Harris	1b	4	15	0	3	0	0	1	0	0	0	0	.200	.200	0	1.000
Carmen Hill	p	1	1	0	0	0	0	0	1	0	0	0	.000	.000	0	—
Ray Kremer	p	1	2	1	1	1	0	0	0	0	1	0	.500	1.000	0	—
Lee Meadows	p	1	2	0	0	0	0	0	0	0	0	0	.000	.000	0	1.000
Johnny Miljus	p	2	2	0	0	0	0	0	0	0	2	0	.000	.000	0	1.000
Hal Rhyne	2b	1	4	0	0	0	0	0	0	0	0	0	.000	.000	0	1.000
Earl Smith	c	3	8	0	0	0	0	0	0	0	0	0	.000	.000	1	.917
Roy Spencer	c	1	1	0	0	0	0	0	0	0	0	0	.000	.000	0	—
Pie Traynor	3b	4	15	1	3	1	0	0	0	0	1	0	.200	.267	1	.933
Lloyd Waner	cf	4	15	5	6	1	1	0	1	0	0	2	.400	.600	2	.818
Paul Waner	rf	4	15	0	5	1	0	0	3	0	1	0	.333	.400	0	1.000
Glenn Wright	ss	4	13	1	2	0	0	0	2	0	0	0	.154	.154	1	.947
Emil Yde	pr	1	0	1	0	0	0	0	0	0	0	0	—	—	—	—
Totals		**4**	**130**	**10**	**29**	**6**	**1**	**0**	**10**	**4**	**7**	**0**	**.223**	**.285**	**6**	**.961**

Pitcher	G	GS	CG	IP	H	R	ER	BB	SO	W-L	Sv	ERA
Vic Aldridge	1	1	0	7⅓	10	6	6	4	4	0-1	0	7.36
Mike Cvengros	2	0	0	2⅓	3	1	1	0	2	0-0	0	3.86
Joe Dawson	1	0	0	1	0	0	0	0	0	0-0	0	0.00
Carmen Hill	1	1	0	6	9	3	3	1	6	0-0	0	4.50
Ray Kremer	1	1	0	5	5	3	2	1	0	0-1	0	3.60
Lee Meadows	1	1	0	6⅓	7	7	7	1	6	0-1	0	9.95
Johnny Miljus	2	0	0	6⅔	4	1	1	4	6	0-1	0	1.35
Totals	**4**	**4**	**0**	**34⅔**	**38**	**23**	**20**	**13**	**25**	**0-4**	**0**	**5.19**

Series Outstanding Player: Babe Ruth, New York Yankees. **Series Outstanding Pitcher:** Herb Pennock, New York Yankees. **Average Length of Game:** 2 hours, 11 minutes. **Total Attendance:** 201,705. **Average Attendance:** 50,426 (59,302 at Yankee Stadium; 41,551 at Forbes Field). **Umpires:** Charlie Moran (NL), Dick Nallin (AL), Red Ormsby (AL), Ernie Quigley (NL). **Winning Player's Share:** $5,592. **Losing Player's Share:** $3,728.

Above: The 1927 World Champion New York Yankees, considered by many the greatest team of all time.

Above: Often lost in the shadow of his Hall of Fame teammates, shortstop Mark Koenig batted .500 in the 1927 Series.

Herb Pennock's win in Game 3 gave him five victories with no losses for his World Series career.

Left: Herb Pennock threw a 3-hit shutout in Game 3.

Game 1   Wednesday, October 5 at Forbes Field, Pittsburgh

	1	2	3	4	5	6	7	8	9	R	H	E
New York Yankees	1	0	3	0	1	0	0	0	0	5	6	1
Pittsburgh Pirates	1	0	1	0	1	0	0	1	0	4	9	2

Pitchers NY Waite Hoyt (W, 1-0), IP 7⅓, H 8, R 4, ER 4, BB 1, SO 2; Wilcy Moore (Sv, 1), IP 1⅔, H 1, R 0, ER 0, BB 0, SO 0
Pit Ray Kremer (L, 0-1), IP 5, H 5, R 5, ER 2, BB 3, SO 1; Johnny Miljus, IP 4, H 1, R 0, ER 0, BB 1, SO 3

Top Performers at the Plate
NY Lou Gehrig, 1 for 2, 1 R, 2 RBI, 1 BB, 1 SH; Babe Ruth, 3 for 4, 2 R
Pit Paul Waner, 3 for 4, 1 RBI; Glenn Wright, 1 for 2, 1 R, 1 RBI, 2 SH

2B-NY/Koenig, Lazzeri; Pit/Kremer, L. Waner, P. Waner. **3B**-NY/Gehrig. **Time** 2:04. **Attendance** 41,467.

Game 2   Thursday, October 6 at Forbes Field, Pittsburgh

	1	2	3	4	5	6	7	8	9	R	H	E
New York Yankees	0	0	3	0	0	0	0	3	0	6	11	0
Pittsburgh Pirates	1	0	0	0	0	0	1	0		2	7	2

Pitchers NY George Pipgras (W, 1-0), IP 9, H 7, R 2, ER 2, BB 1, SO 2
Pit Vic Aldridge (L, 0-1), IP 7⅓, H 10, R 6, ER 6, BB 4, SO 4; Mike Cvengros, IP ⅔, H 1, R 0, ER 0, BB 0, SO 0; Joe Dawson, IP 1, H 0, R 0, ER 0, BB 0, SO 0

Top Performers at the Plate
NY Mark Koenig, 3 for 5, 1 R, 1 RBI; Tony Lazzeri, 2 for 4, 1 RBI, 1 SH
Pit Clyde Barnhart, 2 for 3, 1 RBI, 1 SH; Lloyd Waner, 1 for 3, 2 R, 1 BB

2B-NY/Gehrig; Pit/Grantham, Traynor. **3B**-Pit/L. Waner. **SB**-NY/Meusel. **Time** 2:20. **Attendance** 41,634.

Game 3   Friday, October 7 at Yankee Stadium, New York

	1	2	3	4	5	6	7	8	9	R	H	E
Pittsburgh Pirates	0	0	0	0	0	0	1	0		1	3	1
New York Yankees	2	0	0	0	0	6	0	x		8	9	0

Pitchers Pit Lee Meadows (L, 0-1), IP 6⅓, H 7, R 7, ER 7, BB 1, SO 6; Mike Cvengros, IP 1⅔, H 2, R 1, ER 1, BB 0, SO 2
NY Herb Pennock (W, 1-0), IP 9, H 3, R 1, ER 1, BB 0, SO 1

Top Performers at the Plate
NY Earle Combs, 2 for 4, 2 R, 1 RBI; Lou Gehrig, 2 for 3, 2 RBI, 1 BB

2B-Pit/Barnhart; NY/Gehrig, Koenig. **3B**-NY/Gehrig. **HR**-NY/Ruth. **Time** 2:04. **Attendance** 60,695.

Game 4   Saturday, October 8 at Yankee Stadium New York

	1	2	3	4	5	6	7	8	9	R	H	E
Pittsburgh Pirates	1	0	0	0	0	2	0	0		3	10	1
New York Yankees	1	0	0	0	2	0	0	1		4	12	2

Pitchers Pit Carmen Hill, IP 6, H 9, R 3, ER 3, BB 1, SO 6; Johnny Miljus (L, 0-1), IP 2⅔, H 3, R 1, ER 1, BB 3, SO 3
NY Wilcy Moore (W,1-0), IP 9, H 10, R 3, ER 1, BB 2, SO 2

Top Performers at the Plate
Pit Joe Harris, 2 for 4; Lloyd Waner, 3 for 4, 1 R, 1 SH
NY Earle Combs, 2 for 4, 3 R, 1 BB; Babe Ruth, 2 for 4, 1 R, 3 RBI, 1 BB

2B-NY/Collins. **HR**-NY/Ruth. **SB**-NY/Ruth. **Time** 2:15. **Attendance** 57,909.

New York Yankees (4) vs. St. Louis Cardinals (0)

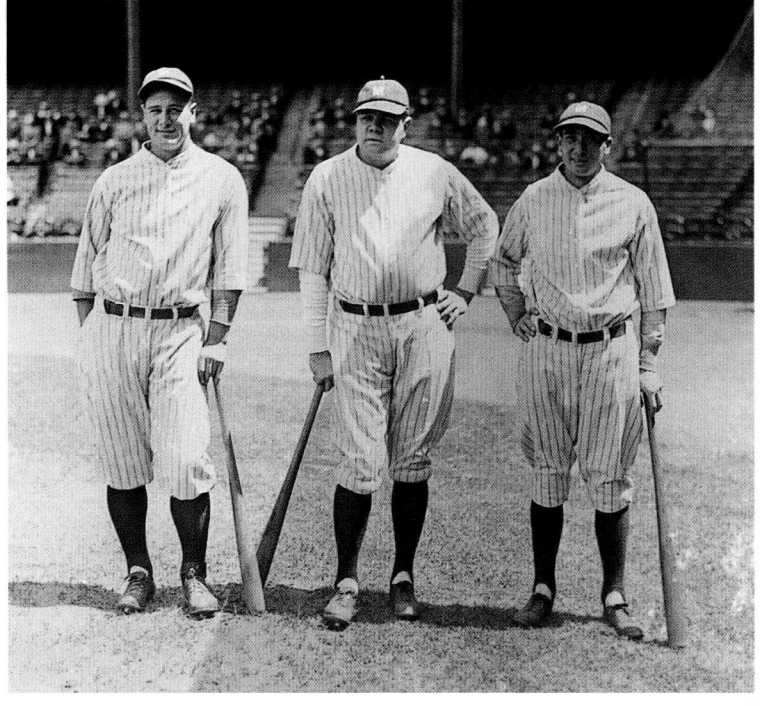

Above: Lou Gehrig, Babe Ruth and Tony Lazzeri were the heart of New York's "Murderer's Row" in 1927 and '28.

The Yankees' 2 1/2-game edge over Philadelphia for the pennant in 1928 was not as impressive as their outing the previous year, but for the second year in a row they swept their National League foes in four straight games in the World Series. This time they got their revenge against the St. Louis Cardinals, who had defeated them in the Series two years earlier. With Herb Pennock out with an injury, Miller Huggins used just three pitchers to dispose of the Cardinals. He went with Waite Hoyt in the opener, and Hoyt came through with a 3-hitter. Back-to-back doubles by Babe Ruth and Lou Gehrig brought in a first-inning run for New York, and Ruth's double in inning four was followed by a Bob Meusel home run. The Yanks amassed 9 runs on only 8 hits in Game 2. Gehrig's 3-run homer in the first inning got things going, and New York scored 5 more to send 41-year-old Grover Alexander to the showers before the third inning was through. Gehrig came back with two more home runs off Jesse Haines in Game 3. Although the Cards took their first lead of the Series on Jim Bottomley's 2-run triple in the first, Gehrig's solo homer in the second and a 2-run, inside-the-parker in the fourth keyed Tom Zachary's 7-3 triumph. St. Louis again scored first in Game 4, but they barely had time to savor it before the Ruth and Gehrig barrage took off again. After walking Gehrig in his last two plate appearances of Game 3, the Cardinal pitchers again effectively took the bat out of Gehrig's hands by walking him in his first three appearances in Game 4. Ruth received no such treatment, and he took full advantage, tying his record-setting performance of two years earlier with 3 home runs in the game. Pitcher Bill Sherdel was the victim in Ruth's solo blasts in the fourth and seventh, while Alexander had the pleasure of giving up home run number three in the eighth. The hit was Ruth's 10th of the Series, a record for a four-game series, and it was his record 9th run scored. Gehrig also put his name in the record book with his seventh-inning homer: No one has ever matched his 4 home runs in four games, nor his 9 RBIs. Even reserve outfielder Cedric Durst got into the act with a leadoff home run in the eighth. New York's accomplishment of 5 home runs in one World Series game has been

1928 WORLD SERIES COMPOSITE STATISTICS

NEW YORK YANKEES/Miller Huggins, Manager

Player	pos	G	AB	R	H	2B	3B	HR	RBI	BB	SO	SB	BA	SA	E	FPct
Benny Bengough	c	4	13	1	3	0	0	0	1	1	1	0	.231	.231	0	1.000
Pat Collins	c	1	1	0	1	1	0	0	0	0	0	0	1.000	2.000	0	1.000
Earle Combs	ph	1	0	0	0	0	0	0	1	0	0	0	—	—	—	—
Joe Dugan	3b	3	6	0	1	0	0	0	1	0	0	0	.167	.143	0	1.000
Leo Durocher	2b	4	2	0	0	0	0	0	0	0	1	0	.000	.000	0	1.000
Cedric Durst	cf	4	8	3	3	0	0	1	2	0	1	0	.375	.750	0	1.000
Lou Gehrig	1b	4	11	5	6	1	0	4	9	6	0	0	.545	1.727	0	1.000
Waite Hoyt	p	2	7	0	1	0	0	0	0	0	0	0	.143	.143	1	.750
Mark Koenig	ss	4	19	1	3	0	0	0	0	0	1	0	.158	.158	2	.905
Tony Lazzeri	2b	4	12	2	3	1	0	0	0	1	0	0	.250	.333	2	.818
Bob Meusel	lf-rf	4	15	5	3	1	0	1	3	2	5	2	.200	.467	0	1.000
Ben Paschal	cf	3	10	0	2	0	0	0	1	1	0	0	.200	.200	0	1.000
George Pipgras	p	1	2	0	0	0	0	0	1	0	1	0	.000	.000	0	1.000
Gene Robertson	3b	3	8	1	1	0	0	0	2	1	0	0	.125	.143	1	.750
Babe Ruth	rf-lf	4	16	9	10	3	0	3	4	1	2	0	.625	1.375	0	1.000
Tom Zachary	p	1	4	0	0	0	0	0	0	0	1	0	.000	.000	0	1.000
Totals		4	134	27	37	7	0	9	25	13	13	4	.276	.530	6	.958

Pitcher	G	GS	CG	IP	H	R	ER	BB	SO	W-L	Sv	ERA
Waite Hoyt	2	2	2	18	14	4	3	6	14	2-0	0	1.50
George Pipgras	1	1	1	9	4	3	2	4	8	1-0	0	2.00
Tom Zachary	1	1	1	9	9	3	3	1	7	1-0	0	3.00
Totals	4	4	4	36	27	10	8	11	29	4-0	0	2.00

ST. LOUIS CARDINALS/Bill McKechnie, Manager

Player	pos	G	AB	R	H	2B	3B	HR	RBI	BB	SO	SB	BA	SA	E	FPct
Pete Alexander	p	2	1	0	0	0	0	0	1	0	0	0	.000	.000	0	1.000
Ray Blades	ph	1	1	0	0	0	0	0	0	0	1	0	.000	.000		
Jim Bottomley	1b	4	14	1	3	0	1	1	3	2	6	0	.214	.571	0	1.000
Taylor Douthit	cf	3	11	1	1	0	0	0	1	1	1	0	.091	.091	0	1.000
Frankie Frisch	2b	4	13	1	3	0	0	0	1	2	2	2	.231	.231	0	1.000
Chick Hafey	lf	4	15	0	3	0	0	0	0	1	4	0	.200	.200	1	.889
Jesse Haines	p	1	2	0	0	0	0	0	0	0	0	0	.000	.000	0	1.000
George Harper	rf	3	9	1	1	0	0	0	0	2	2	0	.111	.111	0	1.000
Andy High	3b	4	17	1	5	2	0	0	1	1	3	0	.294	.412	0	1.000
Wattie Holm	rf	3	6	0	1	0	0	0	1	0	1	0	.167	.167	0	1.000
Syl Johnson	p	2	0	0	0	0	0	0	0	0	0	0	—	—	0	—
Rabbit Maranville	ss	4	13	2	4	1	0	0	0	1	1	1	.308	.385	1	.933
Pepper Martin	pr	1	0	1	0	0	0	0	0	0	0	0	—	—		
Clarence Mitchell	p	1	2	0	0	0	0	0	0	0	0	0	.000	.000	1	.500
Ernie Orsatti	cf	4	7	1	2	1	0	0	0	1	3	0	.286	.429	0	1.000
Flint Rhem	p	1	0	0	0	0	0	0	0	0	0	0	—	—	0	—
Bill Sherdel	p	2	5	0	0	0	0	0	0	0	2	0	.000	.000	0	1.000
Earl Smith	c	1	4	0	3	0	0	0	0	0	0	0	.750	.750	0	1.000
Tommy Thevenow	ss	1	0	0	0	0	0	0	0	0	0	0	—	—	0	1.000
Jimmie Wilson	c	3	11	1	1	1	0	0	1	0	3	0	.091	.182	2	.889
Totals		4	131	10	27	5	1	1	9	11	29	3	.206	.282	5	.965

Pitcher	G	GS	CG	IP	H	R	ER	BB	SO	W-L	Sv	ERA
Pete Alexander	2	1	0	5	10	11	11	4	2	0-1	0	19.80
Jesse Haines	1	1	0	6	6	6	3	3	3	0-1	0	4.50
Syl Johnson	2	0	0	2	4	2	1	1	1	0-0	0	4.50
Clarence Mitchell	1	0	0	5⅔	2	1	1	2	3	0-0	0	1.59
Flint Rhem	1	0	0	2	0	0	0	0	1	0-0	0	0.00
Bill Sherdel	2	2	0	13⅓	15	7	7	3	3	0-2	0	4.72
Totals	4	4	0	34	37	27	23	13	13	0-4	0	6.09

Series Outstanding Player: Lou Gehrig and Babe Ruth, New York Yankees. **Series Outstanding Pitcher:** Waite Hoyt, New York Yankees. **Average Length of Game:** 2 hours, 7 minutes. **Total Attendance:** 199,072. **Average Attendance:** 49,768 (61,070 at Yankee Stadium; 38,467 at Sportsman's Park). **Umpires:** Bill McGowan (AL), Clarence Owens (AL), Cy Pfirman (NL), Cy Rigler (NL). **Winning Player's Share:** $5,532. **Losing Player's Share:** $4,197.

matched only one other time (by the 1989 Oakland A's), and their 9 home runs is another record for a four-game contest. When all was said and done, Gehrig and Ruth walked away from the 1928 Series with a combined batting average of .593 and a slugging average of 1.519. They also contributed 14 runs and 13 RBIs. Oh, and did we mention that Ruth was playing on a bad ankle?

Bob Meusel stole home in the sixth inning of Game 3, making him the only player to steal home twice in his World Series career; he also did it in the second game in 1921. Only 11 other players have stolen home in the history of the World Series.

Below: Babe Ruth and Lou Gehrig cross home plate after Gehrig's three-run blast in the first inning of Game 2. It was the first of "Larrupin' Lou's" four homers in the Series.

Right: It was 41-year-old Pete Alexander against 27-year-old George Pipgras in Game 2, but Alexander faced only 17 batters in his final World Series appearance.

Right: Babe Ruth connects on one of his three homers in the Series' fourth and final game.

Above: Managers Bill McKechnie (left) and Miller Huggins (right) exchange pleasantries before the start of the 1928 Series.

Game 1 Thursday, October 4 at Yankee Stadium, New York

	1	2	3	4	5	6	7	8	9	R	H	E
St. Louis Cardinals	0	0	0	0	0	0	1	0	0	1	3	1
New York Yankees	1	0	0	2	0	0	0	1	x	4	7	0

Pitchers StL Bill Sherdel (L, 0-1), IP 7, H 4, R 3, ER 3, BB 0, SO 2; Syl Johnson, IP 1, H 3, R 1, ER 1, BB 0, SO 0
NY Waite Hoyt (W, 1-0), IP 9, H 3, R 1, ER 1, BB 3, SO 6

Top Performers at the Plate
StL Jim Bottomley, 2 for 3, 1 R, 1 RBI, 1 BB
NY Lou Gehrig, 2 for 4, 2 RBI; Babe Ruth, 3 for 4, 2 R, 2 2B

2B-NY/Gehrig, Ruth 2. **HR**-StL/Bottomley; NY/Meusel. **Time** 1:49. **Attendance** 61,425.

Game 2 Friday, October 5 at Yankee Stadium, New York

	1	2	3	4	5	6	7	8	9	R	H	E
St. Louis Cardinals	0	3	0	0	0	0	0	0	0	3	4	1
New York Yankees	3	1	4	0	0	0	1	0	x	9	8	2

Pitchers StL Pete Alexander (L, 0-1), IP 2⅓, H 6, R 8, ER 8, BB 4, SO 1; Clarence Mitchell, IP 5⅔, H 2, R 1, ER 1, BB 2, SO 2
NY George Pipgras (W, 1-0), IP 9, H 4, R 3, ER 2, BB 4, SO 8

Top Performers at the Plate
StL Frankie Frisch, 2 for 3
NY Cedric Durst, 2 for 2, 1 R, 1 RBI; Lou Gehrig, 1 for 3, 2 R, 3 RBI, 1 BB

2B-StL/Wilson; NY/Meusel, Ruth. **HR**-NY/Gehrig. **SB**-StL/Frisch 2; NY/Meusel. **Time** 2:04. **Attendance** 60,714.

Game 3 Sunday, October 7 at Sportsman's Park, St. Louis

	1	2	3	4	5	6	7	8	9	R	H	E
New York Yankees	0	1	0	2	0	3	1	0	0	7	7	2
St. Louis Cardinals	2	0	0	0	1	0	0	0	0	3	9	3

Pitchers NY Tom Zachary (W, 1-0), IP 9, H 9, R 3, ER 3, BB 1, SO 7
StL Jesse Haines (L, 0-1), IP 6, H 6, R 6, ER 3, BB 3, SO 3; Syl Johnson, IP 1, H 1, R 1, ER 0, BB 1, SO 1; Flint Rhem, IP 2, H 0, R 0, ER 0, BB 0, SO 1

Top Performers at the Plate
NY Lou Gehrig, 2 for 2, 2 R, 3 RBI, 2 2B, 2 HR; Babe Ruth, 2 for 4, 2 R, 1 RBI
StL Chick Hafey, 2 for 4; Andy High, 2 for 5, 1 R, 1 RBI

2B-StL/High. **3B**-StL/Bottomley. **HR**-NY/Gehrig 2. **SB**-NY/Lazzeri, Meusel. **Time** 2:09. **Attendance** 39,602.

Game 4 Tuesday, October 9 at Sportsman's Park, St. Louis

	1	2	3	4	5	6	7	8	9	R	H	E
New York Yankees	0	0	0	1	0	0	4	2	0	7	15	2
St. Louis Cardinals	0	0	1	1	0	0	0	0	1	3	11	0

Pitchers NY Waite Hoyt (W, 2-0), IP 9, H 11, R 3, ER 2, BB 3, SO 8
StL Bill Sherdel (L, 0-2), IP 6⅓, H 11, R 4, ER 4, BB 3, SO 1; Pete Alexander, IP 2⅔, H 4, R 3, ER 3, BB 0, SO 1

Top Performers at the Plate
NY Tony Lazzeri, 3 for 4, 1 R; Babe Ruth, 3 for 5, 3 R, 3 RBI, 3 HR
StL Andy High, 3 for 5; Earl Smith, 3 for 4

2B-NY/Collins, Lazzeri; StL/High, Maranville, Orsatti. **HR**-NY/Durst, Gehrig, Ruth 3. **SB**-NY/Lazzeri; StL/Maranville. **Time** 2:25. **Attendance** 37,331.

Philadelphia Athletics (4) vs. Chicago Cubs (1)

Nineteen years after the Philadelphia Athletics and Chicago Cubs first met in the Fall Classic, Connie Mack was still at the helm in Philadelphia and had put together another dynasty. The A's outpaced the formidable Yankees by 18 games to take the pennant in 1929, while Chicago reached its first Series in a decade with a 98-win campaign.

Mack had two 20-game winners to choose from to start the opener at Wrigley Field, but he made a surprise choice with Howard Ehmke. The 35-year-old Ehmke had appeared in only 11 games in the regular season, but he made Mack look like a genius. He struck out 13 Cubs—then a World Series record—and allowed only eight hits for a 3-1 victory. The aces of the Philadelphia staff, George Earnshaw and Lefty Grove, combined to strike out 13 Chicago batters in Game 2. Jimmie Foxx's three-run homer and Al Simmons's four RBIs led Philly in the 9-3 rout. Earnshaw returned to start the third game, and although he struck out 10 and allowed just six hits, the Cubs brought in three runs, and Guy Bush's strong outing on the mound helped Chicago to its first win. It appeared as if the Cubs might tie the Series in Game 4 when they jumped out to an 8-0 lead, but Philadelphia's Simmons led off the seventh inning with a homer to end the shutout, and five singles cut the lead to 8-4 against starter Charlie Root. Mule Haas, the first batter to face new pitcher Art Nehf, stroked a long fly ball that center fielder Hack Wilson lost in the sun; the

result was a three-run inside-the-park homer. Nehf walked the next batter and was promptly removed from the game. His replacement, John "Sherriff" Blake, gave up back-to-back singles to Simmons and Foxx (each one's second hit of the inning), driving in the tying run. Manager Joe McCarthy had seen enough of Blake, so he sent in Pat Malone to try to end the misery. Malone hit the first batter he faced, loading the bases, and then gave up a two-run double to Jimmy Dykes. Malone managed to strike out the last two batters of the inning, but by that point Philadelphia had compiled the single-greatest offensive inning in World Series history with a ten-run explosion. Pitching in his only inning of the Series, Eddie Rommel earned the win for the A's despite giving up two hits, a walk and a run. The fifth game saw Chicago take a 2-0 lead into the bottom of the ninth, but a two-run homer by Haas tied the score. After Mickey Cochrane grounded into the second out of the inning, Simmons hit a long double and Foxx was walked intentionally. Bing Miller then drove Simmons in with the Series-winning run on a double to the wall in right. In leading his team to their first title in 15 years, Connie Mack became the first manager to win four World Series.

Above: Hall of Famers Jimmie Foxx, Mickey Cochrane and Al Simmons fronted a powerful Philadelphia offense in 1929.

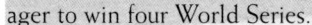

1929 WORLD SERIES COMPOSITE STATISTICS

PHILADELPHIA ATHLETICS/Connie Mack, Manager

Player	pos	G	AB	R	H	2B	3B	HR	RBI	BB	SO	SB	BA	SA	E	FPct
Max Bishop	2b	5	21	2	4	0	0	0	1	2	3	0	.190	.190	0	1.000
Joe Boley	ss	5	17	1	4	0	0	0	1	0	3	0	.235	.235	0	1.000
George Burns	ph	1	2	0	0	0	0	0	0	0	1	0	.000	.000	–	–
Mickey Cochrane	c	5	15	5	6	1	0	0	0	7	0	0	.400	.467	0	1.000
Jimmy Dykes	3b	5	19	2	8	1	0	0	4	1	1	0	.421	.474	2	.778
George Earnshaw	p	2	5	1	0	0	0	0	0	0	4	0	.000	.000	0	1.000
Howard Ehmke	p	2	5	0	1	0	0	0	0	0	1	0	.200	.200	0	1.000
Jimmie Foxx	1b	5	20	5	7	1	0	2	5	1	1	0	.350	.700	0	1.000
Walter French	ph	1	1	0	0	0	0	0	0	0	1	0	.000	.000	–	–
Lefty Grove	p	2	2	0	0	0	0	0	0	0	1	0	.000	.000	0	1.000
Mule Haas	cf	5	21	3	5	0	0	2	6	1	3	0	.238	.524	0	1.000
Bing Miller	rf	5	19	1	7	1	0	0	4	0	2	0	.368	.421	1	.929
Jack Quinn	p	1	2	0	0	0	0	0	0	0	2	0	.000	.000	0	–
Eddie Rommel	p	1	0	0	0	0	0	0	0	0	0	0	–	–	0	–
Al Simmons	lf	5	20	6	6	1	0	2	5	1	4	0	.300	.650	0	1.000
Homer Summa	ph	1	1	0	0	0	0	0	0	0	1	0	.000	.000	–	–
Rube Walberg	p	2	1	0	0	0	0	0	0	0	0	0	.000	.000	1	.500
Totals		**5**	**171**	**26**	**48**	**5**	**0**	**6**	**26**	**13**	**27**	**0**	**.281**	**.415**	**4**	**.978**

Pitcher	G	GS	CG	IP	H	R	ER	BB	SO	W-L	Sv	ERA
George Earnshaw	2	2	1	13⅔	14	6	4	6	17	1-1	0	2.63
Howard Ehmke	2	2	1	12⅔	14	3	2	3	13	1-0	0	1.42
Lefty Grove	2	0	0	6⅓	3	0	0	1	10	0-0	2	0.00
Jack Quinn	1	1	0	5	7	6	5	2	2	0-0	0	9.00
Eddie Rommel	1	0	0	1	2	1	1	1	0	1-0	0	9.00
Rube Walberg	2	0	0	6⅓	3	1	0	0	8	1-0	0	0.00
Totals	**5**	**5**	**2**	**45**	**43**	**17**	**12**	**13**	**50**	**4-1**	**2**	**2.40**

CHICAGO CUBS/Joe McCarthy, Manager

Player	pos	G	AB	R	H	2B	3B	HR	RBI	BB	SO	SB	BA	SA	E	FPct
Footsie Blair	ph	1	1	0	0	0	0	0	0	0	0	0	.000	.000	–	–
Sheriff Blake	p	2	1	0	1	0	0	0	0	0	0	0	1.000	1.000	0	–
Guy Bush	p	2	3	1	0	0	0	0	0	1	3	0	.000	.000	0	1.000
Hal Carlson	p	2	0	0	0	0	0	0	0	0	0	0	–	–	0	1.000
Kiki Cuyler	rf	5	20	4	6	1	0	0	4	1	7	0	.300	.350	1	.889
Woody English	ss	5	21	1	4	2	0	0	1	6	6	0	.190	.286	4	.833
Mike Gonzalez	c	2	1	0	0	0	0	0	0	0	1	0	.000	.000	0	1.000
Charlie Grimm	1b	5	18	2	7	0	0	1	4	1	2	0	.389	.556	0	1.000
Gabby Hartnett	ph	3	3	0	0	0	0	0	0	0	3	0	.000	.000	–	–
Cliff Heathcote	ph	2	1	0	0	0	0	0	0	0	0	0	.000	.000	–	–
Rogers Hornsby	2b	5	21	4	5	1	1	0	1	1	8	0	.238	.381	1	.950
Pat Malone	p	3	4	0	1	1	0	0	0	0	2	0	.250	.500	0	1.000
Norm McMillan	3b	5	20	0	2	0	0	0	2	6	1	0	.100	.100	0	1.000
Art Nehf	p	2	0	0	0	0	0	0	0	0	0	0	–	–	0	–
Charlie Root	p	2	5	0	0	0	0	0	0	0	3	0	.000	.000	0	–
Riggs Stephenson	lf	5	19	3	6	1	0	0	3	2	2	0	.316	.368	0	1.000
Zack Taylor	c	5	17	0	3	0	0	0	0	3	0	0	.176	.176	0	1.000
Chuck Tolson	ph	1	1	0	0	0	0	0	0	0	1	0	.000	.000	–	–
Hack Wilson	cf	5	17	2	8	0	1	0	4	3	0	0	.471	.588	1	.933
Totals		**5**	**173**	**17**	**43**	**6**	**2**	**1**	**15**	**13**	**50**	**1**	**.249**	**.324**	**7**	**.961**

Pitcher	G	GS	CG	IP	H	R	ER	BB	SO	W-L	Sv	ERA
Sheriff Blake	2	0	0	1⅓	4	2	2	0	1	0-1	0	13.50
Guy Bush	2	1	1	11	12	3	1	2	4	1-0	0	0.82
Hal Carlson	2	0	0	4	7	3	3	1	3	0-0	0	6.75
Pat Malone	3	2	1	13	12	9	6	7	11	0-2	0	4.15
Art Nehf	2	0	0	1	1	2	2	1	0	0-0	0	18.00
Charlie Root	2	2	0	13⅓	12	7	7	2	8	0-1	0	4.72
Totals	**5**	**5**	**2**	**43⅔**	**48**	**26**	**21**	**13**	**27**	**1-4**	**0**	**4.33**

Series Outstanding Player: Jimmie Foxx, Philadelphia Athletics. **Series Outstanding Pitcher:** Howard Ehmke, Philadelphia Athletics. **Average Length of Game:** 2 hours, 7 minutes. **Total Attendance:** 190,490. **Average Attendance:** 38,098 (29,921 at Shibe Park; 50,364 at Wrigley Field). **Umpires:** Bill Dinneen (AL), Bill Klem (NL), Charlie Moran (NL), Roy Van Graflan (AL). **Winning Player's Share:** $5,621. **Losing Player's Share:** $3,782.

Howard Ehmke's victory in Game 1 was the last of his Major League career; he threw for no decision in Game 5 and retired after the season.

Left: Max Bishop and Mule Haas score on Haas's ninth-inning home run in Game 5, tying the score in the Series finale.

Below: Jimmie Foxx trots across the plate after his second home run of the Series, which came with two men on base in the third inning of Game 2.

In Philadelphia's mammoth ten-run inning in Game 4, George Burns came in to pinch-hit for the pitcher with nobody out. Burns popped out to short for the first out, and when his turn came up again later in the inning, he struck out—giving Burns credit for two outs in one inning as a pinch hitter.

Background: Jimmy Dykes slides into home to give Philadelphia one of its nine runs in the second game of the 1929 Series.

Game 1 Monday, October 7 at Wrigley Field, Chicago

	1	2	3	4	5	6	7	8	9	R	H	E
Philadelphia Athletics	0	0	0	0	0	0	1	0	2	3	6	1
Chicago Cubs	0	0	0	0	0	0	0	0	1	1	8	2

Pitchers Phi Howard Ehmke (W, 1-0), IP 9, H 8, R 1, ER 0, BB 1, SO 13
Chi Charlie Root (L, 0-1), IP 7, H 3, R 1, ER 1, BB 2, SO 5; Guy Bush, IP 2, H 3, R 2, ER 0, BB 0, SO 0

Top Performers at the Plate
Phi Mickey Cochrane, 1 for 3, 1 R, 1 BB; Jimmie Foxx, 2 for 4, 1 R, 1 RBI
Chi Charlie Grimm, 2 for 2, 1 BB, 1 SH; Riggs Stephenson, 2 for 4, 1 RBI

2B-Chi/English. **HR**-Phi/Foxx. **Time** 2:03. **Attendance** 50,740.

Game 2 Wednesday, October 9 at Wrigley Field, Chicago

	1	2	3	4	5	6	7	8	9	R	H	E
Philadelphia Athletics	0	3	3	0	0	1	2	0		9	12	0
Chicago Cubs	0	0	0	3	0	0	0	0		3	11	1

Pitchers Phi George Earnshaw, IP 4⅔, H 8, R 3, ER 3, BB 4, SO 7; Lefty Grove (W, 1-0), IP 4⅓, H 3, R 0, ER 0, BB 1, SO 6
Chi Pat Malone (L, 0-1), IP 3⅔, H 5, R 6, ER 3, BB 5, SO 5; Sheriff Blake, IP 1⅓, H 2, R 0, ER 0, BB 0, SO 1; Hal Carlson, IP 3, H 5, R 3, ER 3, BB 1, SO 2; Art Nehf, IP 1, H 0, R 0, ER 0, BB 0, SO 0

Top Performers at the Plate
Phi Jimmie Foxx, 3 for 5, 2 R, 3 RBI; Al Simmons, 2 for 4, 2 R, 4 RBI, 1 BB
Chi Hack Wilson, 3 for 3, 1 R, 2 BB; Charlie Grimm, 2 for 4, 1 RBI

2B-Phi/Foxx; Chi/English. **HR**-Phi/Foxx, Simmons. **Time** 2:29. **Attendance** 49,987.

Game 3 Friday, October 11 at Shibe Park, Philadelphia

	1	2	3	4	5	6	7	8	9	R	H	E
Chicago Cubs	0	0	0	0	3	0	0	0		3	6	1
Philadelphia Athletics	0	0	0	1	0	0	0	0		1	9	1

Pitchers Chi Guy Bush (W, 1-0), IP 9, H 9, R 1, ER 1, BB 2, SO 4
Phi George Earnshaw (L, 0-1), IP 9, H 6, R 3, ER 1, BB 2, SO 10

Top Performers at the Plate
Chi Rogers Hornsby, 2 for 4, 1 R, 1 RBI; Hack Wilson, 2 for 3, 1 BB
Phi Joe Boley, 2 for 4; Mickey Cochrane, 2 for 3, 1 R, 1 BB

2B-Chi/Hornsby, Stephenson. **3B**-Chi/Wilson. **Time** 2:09. **Attendance** 29,921.

Game 4 Saturday, October 12 at Shibe Park, Philadelphia

	1	2	3	4	5	6	7	8	9	R	H	E
Chicago Cubs	0	0	0	2	0	5	1	0	0	8	10	2
Philadelphia Athletics	0	0	0	0	0	0	10	0	x	10	15	2

Pitchers Chi Charlie Root, IP 6⅓, H 9, R 6, ER 6, BB 0, SO 3; Art Nehf, IP 0, H 1, R 2, ER 2, BB 1, SO 0; Sheriff Blake (L, 0-1), IP 0, H 2, R 2, ER 2, BB 0, SO 0; Pat Malone, IP ⅔, H 1, R 0, ER 0, BB 0, SO 2; Hal Carlson, IP 1, H 2, R 0, ER 0, BB 0, SO 1
Phi Jack Quinn, IP 5, H 7, R 6, ER 5, BB 2, SO 2; Rube Walberg, IP 1, H 1, R 1, ER 0, BB 0, SO 2; Eddie Rommel (W, 1-0), IP 1, H 2, R 1, ER 1, BB 1, SO 0; Lefty Grove (Sv, 1), IP 2, H 0, R 0, ER 0, BB 0, SO 4

Top Performers at the Plate
Chi Kiki Cuyler, 3 for 4, 2 R, 2 RBI; Charlie Grimm, 2 for 4, 2 R, 2 RBI
Phi Jimmy Dykes, 3 for 4, 1 R, 3 RBI; Jimmie Foxx, 2 for 4, 2 R, 1 RBI

2B-Phi/Cochrane, Dykes. **3B**-Chi/Hornsby. **HR**-Chi/Grimm; Phi/Haas, Simmons. **Time** 2:12. **Attendance** 29,921.

Game 5 Monday, October 14 at Shibe Park, Philadelphia

	1	2	3	4	5	6	7	8	9	R	H	E
Chicago Cubs	0	0	0	2	0	0	0	0	0	2	8	1
Philadelphia Athletics	0	0	0	0	0	0	0	0	3	3	6	0

Pitchers Chi Pat Malone (L, 0-2), IP 8⅔, H 6, R 3, ER 3, BB 2, SO 4
Phi Howard Ehmke, IP 3⅔, H 6, R 2, ER 2, BB 2, SO 0; Rube Walberg (W, 1-0), IP 5⅓, H 2, R 0, ER 0, BB 0, SO 6

Top Performers at the Plate
Chi Riggs Stephenson, 1 for 2, 1 R, 2 BB
Phi Bing Miller, 2 for 4, 1 RBI; Al Simmons, 2 for 4, 1 R

2B-Chi/Cuyler, Malone; Phi/Miller, Simmons. **HR**-Phi/Haas. **SB**-Chi/McMillan. **Time** 1:42. **Attendance** 29,921.

Philadelphia Athletics (4) vs. St. Louis Cardinals (2)

Fans remember 1930 as the "Year of the Hitter," when 9 of the 16 Major League teams posted batting averages above .300 for the year. The National League-champion St. Louis Cardinals had an entire starting lineup of .300 hitters, yet their team average of .314 was only good enough for third best in the league. The Philadelphia Athletics batted "only" .294 as a team, but their 125 home runs were second only to the Yankees in the AL. The loud bats produced an awkward silence, however, when the Cardinals and A's met in October. The clubs combined to hit just .198 in the 6-game Series, and Philadelphia posted a 1.73 team ERA, more than 2 1/2 runs below their regular-season mark. George Earnshaw and Lefty Grove, both 20-game-winners, were the main purveyors of this strong pitching. Grove got the start in Game 1 against spitballer Burleigh Grimes. The A's managed only 5 hits off Grimes, each in a different inning, but all were for extra bases, enough to take the game by a 5-2 count. In Game 2, Philadelphia scored 2 runs in 3 different innings, beginning with Mickey Cochrane's 2nd home run of the Series in the bottom of the first. "Wild Bill" Hallahan shut out the powerful A's in Game 3, while Philadelphia's Rube Walberg had a perfect game going until Taylor Douthit ruined it with a leadoff homer in the fourth inning. The Cards tied the Series the next day behind Jesse Haines's 4-hitter. Starter Grove did his part for Philadelphia, but a fourth-inning error by Jimmy Dykes led to 2 runs and a 3-1 edge for St. Louis. Earnshaw and Grimes were back in Game 5, and the two kept both sides scoreless into the ninth. After allowing only 2 Cardinal hits, Earnshaw was removed for a pinchhitter in the eighth, and Grove held up the shutout in two innings of relief. Grimes worked his way out of a bases-loaded jam in the top of the eighth, but lost his shutout and the game when Jimmie Foxx crushed a 2-run homer in the ninth. A travel day between Games 5 and 6 allowed Mack to go with Earnshaw for a 3rd start. St. Louis's Hallahan lasted only 2 innings, and the A's hit reliever Syl Johnson even harder. Al Simmons welcomed Johnson with a solo homer in the third, and Dykes's 2-run shot in the fourth inning was the team's 6th of the Series. The 2 home runs were part of 7 extra-base hits for Philadelphia, once again accounting for all their hits in the game. Earnshaw kept St. Louis off the board until the ninth, when Chick Hafey hit his 5th double of the Series, scoring Andy High from second. The run ended a streak of 21 scoreless innings for St. Louis, but Philadelphia's 7-1 win in the game gave Connie Mack his 5th World Series victory.

Above: Jimmie Dykes is congratulated by the batboy after stroking a two-run homer in the fourth inning of Game 6.

1930 WORLD SERIES COMPOSITE STATISTICS

PHILADELPHIA ATHLETICS/Connie Mack, Manager

Player	pos	G	AB	R	H	2B	3B	HR	RBI	BB	SO	SB	BA	SA	E	FPct
Max Bishop	2b	6	18	5	4	0	0	0	0	7	3	0	.222	.222	0	1.000
Joe Boley	ss	6	21	1	2	0	0	0	1	0	1	0	.095	.095	1	.957
Mickey Cochrane	c	6	18	5	4	1	0	2	4	5	2	0	.222	.611	1	.976
Jimmy Dykes	3b	6	18	2	4	3	0	1	5	5	3	0	.222	.556	1	.933
George Earnshaw	p	3	9	0	0	0	0	0	0	0	5	0	.000	.000	0	1.000
Jimmie Foxx	1b	6	21	3	7	2	1	1	3	2	4	0	.333	.667	0	1.000
Lefty Grove	p	3	6	0	0	0	0	0	0	0	3	0	.000	.000	0	1.000
Mule Haas	cf	6	18	1	2	0	1	0	1	1	3	0	.111	.222	0	1.000
Eric McNair	ph	1	1	0	0	0	0	0	0	0	0	0	.000	.000	–	–
Bing Miller	rf	6	21	0	3	2	0	0	3	0	4	0	.143	.238	0	1.000
Jimmy Moore	ph-lf	3	3	0	1	0	0	0	0	1	1	0	.333	.333	0	–
Jack Quinn	p	1	0	0	0	0	0	0	0	0	0	0	–	–	0	1.000
Bill Shores	p	1	0	0	0	0	0	0	0	1	0	0	–	–	0	–
Al Simmons	lf-cf	6	22	4	8	2	0	2	4	2	2	0	.364	.727	0	1.000
Rube Walberg	p	1	2	0	0	0	0	0	0	0	1	0	.000	.000	0	–
Totals		**6**	**178**	**21**	**35**	**10**	**2**	**6**	**21**	**24**	**32**	**0**	**.197**	**.376**	**3**	**.985**

Pitcher	G	GS	CG	IP	H	R	ER	BB	SO	W-L	Sv	ERA
George Earnshaw	3	3	2	25	13	2	2	7	19	2-0	0	0.72
Lefty Grove	3	2	2	19	15	5	3	3	10	2-1	0	1.42
Jack Quinn	1	0	0	2	3	1	1	0	1	0-0	0	4.50
Bill Shores	1	0	0	1⅓	3	2	2	0	0	0-0	0	13.50
Rube Walberg	1	1	0	4⅔	4	2	2	1	3	0-1	0	3.86
Totals	**6**	**6**	**4**	**52**	**38**	**12**	**10**	**11**	**33**	**4-2**	**0**	**1.73**

ST. LOUIS CARDINALS/Gabby Street, Manager

Player	pos	G	AB	R	H	2B	3B	HR	RBI	BB	SO	SB	BA	SA	E	FPct
Sparky Adams	3b	6	21	0	3	0	0	0	1	0	4	0	.143	.143	0	1.000
Hi Bell	p	1	0	0	0	0	0	0	0	0	0	0	–	–	0	1.000
Ray Blades	rf-ph	5	9	2	1	0	0	0	0	2	2	0	.111	.111	0	1.000
Jim Bottomley	1b	6	22	1	1	1	0	0	0	2	9	0	.045	.091	0	1.000
Taylor Douthit	cf	6	24	1	2	0	0	1	2	0	2	0	.083	.208	0	1.000
Showboat Fisher	ph	2	2	0	1	0	0	0	0	0	1	0	.500	.500	–	–
Frankie Frisch	2b	6	24	0	5	2	0	0	0	0	1	1	.208	.292	3	.900
Charlie Gelbert	ss	6	17	2	6	0	1	0	2	3	3	0	.353	.471	0	1.000
Burleigh Grimes	p	2	5	0	2	0	0	0	0	0	1	0	.400	.400	0	1.000
Chick Hafey	lf	6	22	2	6	5	0	0	2	1	3	0	.273	.500	0	1.000
Jesse Haines	p	1	2	0	1	0	0	0	1	0	1	0	.500	.500	0	1.000
Bill Hallahan	p	2	2	0	0	0	0	0	0	1	1	0	.000	.000	0	1.000
Andy High	ph-3b	1	2	1	1	0	0	0	0	0	0	0	.500	.500	–	–
Syl Johnson	p	2	2	0	0	0	0	0	0	0	0	0	.000	.000	0	–
Jim Lindsey	p	2	1	1	1	0	0	0	0	0	0	0	1.000	1.000	0	1.000
Gus Mancuso	c	2	7	1	2	0	0	0	1	2	0	0	.286	.286	0	1.000
Ernie Orsatti	ph	1	1	0	0	0	0	0	0	0	0	0	.000	.000	–	–
George Puccinelli	ph	1	1	0	0	0	0	0	0	0	0	0	.000	.000	–	–
Flint Rhem	p	1	1	0	0	0	0	0	0	0	1	0	.000	.000	1	.000
George Watkins	rf	4	12	2	2	0	0	1	1	1	3	0	.167	.417	1	.833
Jimmie Wilson	c	4	15	0	4	1	0	0	2	0	1	0	.267	.333	0	1.000
Totals		**6**	**190**	**12**	**38**	**10**	**1**	**2**	**11**	**11**	**33**	**1**	**.200**	**.295**	**5**	**.977**

Pitcher	G	GS	CG	IP	H	R	ER	BB	SO	W-L	Sv	ERA
Hi Bell	1	0	0	1	0	0	0	0	0	0-0	0	0.00
Burleigh Grimes	2	2	2	17	10	7	7	6	13	0-2	0	3.71
Jesse Haines	1	1	1	9	4	1	1	4	2	1-0	0	1.00
Bill Hallahan	2	2	1	11	9	2	2	8	8	1-1	0	1.64
Syl Johnson	2	0	0	5	4	4	4	3	4	0-0	0	7.20
Jim Lindsey	2	0	0	4⅔	1	1	1	1	2	0-0	0	1.93
Flint Rhem	1	1	0	3⅓	7	6	4	2	3	0-1	0	10.80
Totals	**6**	**6**	**4**	**51**	**35**	**21**	**19**	**24**	**32**	**2-4**	**0**	**3.35**

Series Outstanding Player: Al Simmons, Philadelphia Athletics. **Series Outstanding Pitcher:** George Earnshaw, Philadelphia Athletics. **Average Length of Game:** 1 hour, 49 minutes. **Total Attendance:** 212,619. **Average Attendance:** 35,437 (32,295 at Shibe Park; 38,578 at Sportsman's Park). **Umpires:** Harry Geisel (AL), George Moriarty (AL), John Reardon (NL), Cy Rigler (NL). **Winning Player's Share:** $5,038. **Losing Player's Share:** $3,537.

Lefty Grove (above) and George Earnshaw (below) were the stars of the Philadelphia staff in 1930. They each won two games in the Series.

Right: Frankie Frisch moved into first place on the all-time World Series hit list in 1930. He currently ranks third.

Top inset: Philadelphia slugger Al Simmons belted two homers and batted .364 against St. Louis.

For the second year in a row, pitcher George Earnshaw started consecutive games in a Series. He took the hill for Philadelphia in Games 2 and 3 in 1929, and got the starts in the final two games of 1930. Nobody since Earnshaw has made back-to-back starts in a World Series.

Game 1 Wednesday, October 1 at Shibe Park, Philadelphia

	1	2	3	4	5	6	7	8	9	R	H	E
St. Louis Cardinals	0	0	2	0	0	0	0	0	0	2	9	0
Philadelphia Athletics	0	1	0	1	0	1	1	1	x	5	5	0

Pitchers StL Burleigh Grimes (L, 0-1), IP 8, H 5, R 5, ER 5, BB 3, SO 6
Phi Lefty Grove (W, 1-0), IP 9, H 9, R 2, ER 2, BB 1, SO 5

Top Performers at the Plate
StL Frankie Frisch, 2 for 4; Charlie Gelbert, 2 for 4, 1 R
Phi Mickey Cochrane, 1 for 3, 1 R, 1 RBI, 1 BB; Al Simmons, 1 for 3, 1 R, 1 RBI, 1 BB

2B-StL/Frisch, Hafey; Phi/Dykes. 3B-Phi/Foxx, Haas. HR-Phi/Cochrane, Simmons. **Time** 1:48.
Attendance 32,295.

Game 2 Thursday, October 2 at Shibe Park, Philadelphia

	1	2	3	4	5	6	7	8	9	R	H	E
St. Louis Cardinals	0	1	0	0	0	0	0	0	0	1	6	2
Philadelphia Athletics	2	0	2	2	0	0	0	0	x	6	7	2

Pitchers StL Flint Rhem (L, 0-1), IP 3⅓, H 7, R 6, ER 4, BB 2, SO 3; Jim Lindsey, IP 2⅔, H 0, R 0, ER 0, BB 0, SO 2; Syl Johnson, IP 2, H 0, R 0, ER 0, BB 2, SO 2
Phi George Earnshaw (W, 1-0), IP 9, H 6, R 1, ER 1, BB 1, SO 8

Top Performers at the Plate
StL Gus Mancuso, 1 for 3, 1 BB
Phi Mickey Cochrane, 1 for 3, 2 R, 1 RBI, 1 BB; Al Simmons, 2 for 4, 2 R, 1 RBI

2B-StL/Frisch; Phi/Dykes, Foxx, Simmons. HR-StL/Watkins; Phi/Cochrane. SB-Frisch. **Time** 1:47.
Attendance 32,295.

Game 3 Saturday, October 4 at Sportsman's Park, St. Louis

	1	2	3	4	5	6	7	8	9	R	H	E
Philadelphia Athletics	0	0	0	0	0	0	0	0	0	0	7	0
St. Louis Cardinals	0	0	0	1	1	0	2	1	x	5	10	0

Pitchers Phi Rube Walberg (L, 0-1), IP 4⅔, H 4, R 2, ER 2, BB 1, SO 3; Bill Shores, IP 1⅓, H 3, R 2, ER 2, BB 0, SO 0; Jack Quinn, IP 2, H 3, R 1, ER 1, BB 0, SO 1
StL Bill Hallahan (W, 1-0), IP 9, H 7, R 0, ER 0, BB 5, SO 6

Top Performers at the Plate
Phi Max Bishop, 3 for 4, 1 BB; Al Simmons, 2 for 4
StL Chick Hafey, 2 for 4, 1 R, 1 RBI; Jimmie Wilson, 2 for 4, 2 RBI

2B-Phi/Simmons; StL/Bottomley, Hafey. HR-StL/Douthit. **Time** 1:55. **Attendance** 36,944.

Game 4 Sunday, October 5 at Sportsman's Park, St. Louis

	1	2	3	4	5	6	7	8	9	R	H	E
Philadelphia Athletics	1	0	0	0	0	0	0	0	0	1	4	1
St. Louis Cardinals	0	0	1	2	0	0	0	0	x	3	5	1

Pitchers Phi Lefty Grove (L, 1-1), IP 8, H 5, R 3, ER 1, BB 1, SO 3
StL Jesse Haines (W, 1-0), IP 9, H 4, R 1, ER 1, BB 4, SO 2

Top Performers at the Plate
Phi Max Bishop, 1 for 3, 1 R, 1 BB; Al Simmons, 2 for 3, 1 RBI
StL Charlie Gelbert, 2 for 2, 1 R, 1 RBI, 1 BB; Jesse Haines, 1 for 2, 1 RBI, 1 SH

2B-StL/Hafey. 3B-StL/Gelbert. **Time** 1:41. **Attendance** 39,946.

Game 5 Monday, October 6 at Sportsman's Park, St. Louis

	1	2	3	4	5	6	7	8	9	R	H	E
Philadelphia Athletics	0	0	0	0	0	0	0	0	2	2	5	0
St. Louis Cardinals	0	0	0	0	0	0	0	0	0	0	3	1

Pitchers Phi George Earnshaw, IP 7, H 2, R 0, ER 0, BB 3, SO 5; Lefty Grove (W, 2-1), IP 2, H 1, R 0, ER 0, BB 1, SO 2
StL Burleigh Grimes (L, 0-2), IP 9, H 5, R 2, ER 2, BB 3, SO 7

Top Performers at the Plate
Phi Mickey Cochrane, 1 for 3, 1 R, 1 BB; Jimmie Foxx, 2 for 4, 1 R, 2 RBI

2B-StL/Wilson. HR-Phi/Foxx. **Time** 1:58. **Attendance** 38,844.

Game 6 Wednesday, October 8 at Shibe Park, Philadelphia

	1	2	3	4	5	6	7	8	9	R	H	E
St. Louis Cardinals	0	0	0	0	0	0	0	0	1	1	5	1
Philadelphia Athletics	2	0	1	2	1	1	0	0	x	7	7	0

Pitchers StL Bill Hallahan (L, 1-1), IP 2, H 2, R 2, ER 2, BB 3, SO 2; Syl Johnson, IP 3, H 4, R 4, ER 4, BB 1, SO 2; Jim Lindsey, IP 2, H 1, R 1, ER 1, BB 1, SO 0; Hi Bell, IP 1, H 0, R 0, ER 0, BB 0, SO 0
Phi George Earnshaw (W, 2-0), IP 9, H 5, R 1, ER 1, BB 3, SO 6

Top Performers at the Plate
StL Chick Hafey, 2 for 4, 1 RBI, 2 2B
Phi Mickey Cochrane, 1 for 3, 1 R, 2 RBI, 1 SH; Jimmy Dykes, 2 for 2, 2 R, 2 RBI, 2 BB

2B-StL/Fisher, Hafey 2; Phi/Cochrane, Dykes, Foxx, Miller 2. HR-Phi/Dykes, Simmons. **Time** 1:46.
Attendance 32,295.

Frankie Frisch passed Eddie Collins on the all-time World Series hit list with number 43 in Game 2. He finished his career with 58, third best of all-time.

St. Louis Cardinals (4) vs. Philadelphia Athletics (3)

The Philadelphia Athletics and St. Louis Cardinals ended the 1931 season in the same place they had the year before: with the best records in their respective leagues. Connie Mack's A's claimed another pennant with their third straight 100-win season. Lefty Grove was one of three Philadelphia pitchers with 20 or more wins; his 31 victories and 2.06 ERA were tops in the league. The Cardinals earned their trip back to the Series with a speedy lineup and deep pitching staff that helped produce 101 wins in 1931, but there was little reason to suspect that the outcome of the 1931 World Series would be any different from the previous year's. The difference turned out to be a hustling young outfielder named George "Pepper" Martin.

Lefty Grove led the A's to a 6-2 win in the opener, but the 27-year-old rookie Martin got Philadelphia's attention with his 3 hits in 4 times at bat. Martin got 2 more base hits in Game 2, stole 2 bases and scored both of St. Louis's runs in the game, the only runs for either side. In the second inning, he stretched a double and then stole third before coming home on Jimmie Wilson's sacrifice fly. Later he singled to lead off the seventh inning, stole second, advanced to third on an infield grounder and then hustled home on Charlie Gelbert's squeeze bunt. "Wild Bill" Hallahan kept the Athletics hitters at bay, giving up just 3 hits in the shutout. Martin was at it again in Game 3, knocking Grove for 2 more hits and scoring 2 of St. Louis's 5 runs. Al Simmons connected for his second 2-run homer of the Series in the bottom of the ninth, but that was all the A's could muster against 38-year-old Burleigh Grimes. Grimes retired the first nine batters of the game and didn't allow a hit until the eighth inning. George Earnshaw held St. Louis to 2 base hits in a Game 4 shutout—with Martin accounting for both Cardinal hits. Hallahan yielded just 1 run in St. Louis's Game 5 triumph. The hero on the offensive end? Once again, Pepper Martin. Manager Gabby Street moved his "secret weapon" up from the sixth spot to cleanup in the batting order for the game, and Martin responded by knocking in the game's first run with a sacrifice fly in the first inning. He accounted for his team's next 2 scores with a homer in the sixth, and used his 12th hit of the Series, an eighth-inning single, to drive in his 4th run of the game. Martin came back down to earth in Game 6, and Philadelphia trounced the Cards 8-1 behind Grove's 5-hitter. St. Louis got on the board early in Game 7 as Andy High scored on a wild pitch in the first and George Watkins came home on a passed ball two batters later. Two more scored on Watkins's third-inning homer, but Earnshaw didn't allow any more Cardinals to reach base for as long as he was on the mound. Watkins and High accounted for all 5 St. Louis hits on the day and all 4 runs. Grimes, meanwhile, carried a shutout into the ninth inning. The A's scored two on a Doc Cramer 2-out pinch-single in the last inning, but Hallahan came on with two men on base

Above: Wild Bill Hallahan won two games and saved one for the Cards, allowing only one run in 18 1/3 innings of work.

Left: The 1931 Series was the eighth and final one of Connie Mack's illustrious career. Here he meets Cardinal skipper Gabby Street before the start of Game 1.

and induced Max Bishop to line out to center field. Fittingly, Pepper Martin snared the Series' final out with a lunging grab.

Connie Mack was denied a third straight World Series win, and 1931 proved to be the legendary manager's last Fall Classic. But while one October star was fading, a new one was emerging. Despite going 0 for 6 in the final 2 games, Pepper Martin finished with a .500 average in one of the best Series performances ever. He also scored 5 runs, batted in 5 more and stole 5 bases against Hall of Fame catcher Mickey Cochrane.

In their three Series appearances from 1929 to 1931, the Philadelphia Athletics failed to steal a single base. They were caught stealing twice in 1929 and 1930, and (as a result, perhaps) they made no attempts in 1931.

Above: Chick Hafey, George Watkins, John "Pepper" Martin and Walter Roettger roamed the outfield for St. Louis in 1931. The one with the dirty, ripped pants is Martin.

Pepper Martin matched Buck Herzog (1912), Joe Jackson (1919) and Sam Rice (1924) for most hits in one World Series (12), a record that stood for more than 30 years.

Pepper Martin was the sparkplug behind St. Louis' surprise victory over the A's in 1931.

1931 WORLD SERIES COMPOSITE STATISTICS

ST. LOUIS CARDINALS/Gabby Street, Manager

Player	pos	G	AB	R	H	2B	3B	HR	RBI	BB	SO	SB	BA	SA	E	FPct
Sparky Adams	3b	2	4	0	1	0	0	0	0	0	1	0	.250	.250	0	1.000
Ray Blades	ph	2	2	0	0	0	0	0	0	0	2	0	.000	.000	—	—
Jim Bottomley	1b	7	25	2	4	1	0	0	2	2	5	0	.160	.200	1	.984
Ripper Collins	ph	2	2	0	0	0	0	0	0	0	1	0	.000	.000	—	—
Paul Derringer	p	3	2	0	0	0	0	0	0	0	1	0	.000	.000	0	1.000
Jake Flowers	ph-3b	5	11	1	1	1	0	0	0	1	0	0	.091	.182	1	.875
Frankie Frisch	2b	7	27	2	7	2	0	0	1	1	2	1	.259	.333	0	1.000
Charlie Gelbert	ss	7	23	0	6	1	0	0	3	0	4	0	.261	.304	0	1.000
Burleigh Grimes	p	2	7	0	2	0	0	0	2	0	2	0	.286	.286	0	1.000
Chick Hafey	lf	6	24	1	4	0	0	0	0	0	5	1	.167	.167	1	.889
Bill Hallahan	p	3	6	0	0	0	0	0	0	0	3	0	.000	.000	0	—
Andy High	3b-pr	4	15	3	4	0	0	0	0	0	2	0	.267	.267	0	1.000
Syl Johnson	p	3	2	0	0	0	0	0	0	0	2	0	.000	.000	0	1.000
Jim Lindsey	p	2	0	0	0	0	0	0	0	0	0	0	—	—	0	—
Gus Mancuso	ph-c	2	1	0	0	0	0	0	0	0	0	0	.000	.000	0	1.000
Pepper Martin	cf	7	24	5	12	4	0	1	5	2	3	5	.500	.792	0	1.000
Ernie Orsatti	lf	1	3	0	0	0	0	0	0	0	3	0	.000	.000	—	—
Flint Rhem	p	1	0	0	0	0	0	0	0	0	0	0	—	—	0	—
Wally Roettger	rf	3	14	1	4	1	0	0	0	0	3	0	.286	.357	0	1.000
George Watkins	rf-pr	5	14	4	4	1	0	1	2	2	1	1	.286	.571	0	1.000
Jimmie Wilson	c	7	23	0	5	0	0	0	2	1	1	0	.217	.217	1	.981
Totals		7	229	19	54	11	0	2	17	9	41	8	.236	.310	4	.985

Pitcher	G	GS	CG	IP	H	R	ER	BB	SO	W-L	Sv	ERA
Paul Derringer	3	2	0	12⅔	14	10	6	7	14	0-2	0	4.26
Burleigh Grimes	2	2	1	17⅔	9	4	4	9	11	2-0	0	2.04
Bill Hallahan	3	2	2	18⅓	12	1	1	8	12	2-0	1	0.49
Syl Johnson	3	1	0	9	10	3	3	1	6	0-1	0	3.00
Jim Lindsey	2	0	0	3⅓	4	4	2	3	2	0-0	0	5.40
Flint Rhem	1	0	0	1	1	0	0	0	1	0-0	0	0.00
Totals	7	7	3	62	50	22	16	28	46	43	1	2.32

PHILADELPHIA ATHLETICS/Connie Mack, Manager

Player	pos	G	AB	R	H	2B	3B	HR	RBI	BB	SO	SB	BA	SA	E	FPct
Max Bishop	2b	7	27	4	4	0	0	0	0	3	5	0	.148	.148	0	1.000
Joe Boley	ph	1	1	0	0	0	0	0	0	0	1	0	.000	.000	—	—
Mickey Cochrane	c	7	25	2	4	0	0	0	1	5	2	0	.160	.160	1	.978
Doc Cramer	ph	2	2	0	1	0	0	0	2	0	0	0	.500	.500	—	—
Jimmy Dykes	3b	7	22	2	5	0	0	0	2	5	1	0	.227	.227	0	1.000
George Earnshaw	p	3	8	0	0	0	0	0	0	0	2	0	.000	.000	0	1.000
Jimmie Foxx	1b	7	23	3	8	0	0	1	3	6	5	0	.348	.478	1	.986
Lefty Grove	p	3	10	0	0	0	0	0	0	0	7	0	.000	.000	0	—
Mule Haas	cf	7	23	1	3	1	0	0	2	3	5	0	.130	.174	0	1.000
Johnny Heving	ph	1	1	0	0	0	0	0	0	0	0	0	.000	.000	—	—
Waite Hoyt	p	1	2	0	0	0	0	0	0	0	0	0	.000	.000	0	—
Roy Mahaffey	p	1	0	0	0	0	0	0	0	0	0	0	—	—	0	1.000
Eric McNair	pr-ph-2b	2	2	1	0	0	0	0	0	0	1	0	.000	.000	0	1.000
Bing Miller	rf	7	26	3	7	1	0	0	1	0	4	0	.269	.308	0	1.000
Jimmy Moore	ph-lf	2	3	0	1	0	0	0	0	0	1	0	.333	.333	0	1.000
Eddie Rommel	p	1	0	0	0	0	0	0	0	0	0	0	—	—	0	—
Al Simmons	lf-cf	7	27	4	9	2	0	2	8	3	3	0	.333	.630	0	1.000
Phil Todt	ph	1	0	0	0	0	0	0	0	1	0	0	—	—	—	—
Rube Walberg	p	2	0	0	0	0	0	0	0	0	0	0	—	—	0	—
Dib Williams	ss	7	25	2	8	1	0	0	1	2	9	0	.320	.360	0	1.000
Totals		7	227	22	50	5	0	3	20	28	46	0	.220	.282	2	.992

Pitcher	G	GS	CG	IP	H	R	ER	BB	SO	W-L	Sv	ERA
George Earnshaw	3	3	2	24	12	6	5	4	20	1-2	0	1.88
Lefty Grove	3	3	2	26	28	7	7	2	16	2-1	0	2.42
Waite Hoyt	1	1	0	6	7	3	3	0	1	0-1	0	4.50
Roy Mahaffey	1	0	0	1	1	1	1	1	0	0-0	0	9.00
Eddie Rommel	1	0	0	1	3	1	1	0	0	0-0	0	9.00
Rube Walberg	2	0	0	3	3	1	1	2	4	0-0	0	3.00
Totals	7	7	4	61	54	19	18	9	41	3-4	0	2.66

Series Outstanding Player: Pepper Martin, St. Louis Cardinals. **Series Outstanding Pitcher:** Wild Bill Hallahan, St. Louis Cardinals. **Average Length of Game:** 1 hour, 57 minutes. **Total Attendance:** 231,567. **Average Attendance:** 33,081 (33,671 at Sportsman's Park; 32,295 at Shibe Park). **Umpires:** Bill Klem (NL), Bill McGowan (AL), Dick Nallin (AL), Albert Stark (NL). **Winning Player's Share:** $4,468. **Losing Player's Share:** $3,023.

Above: Manager Gabby Street (left) prepares a strategy with his Game 3 battery, pitcher Burleigh Grimes and catcher Jimmie Wilson.

Philadelphia's Lefty Grove fielded no batted balls during his 26 innings of work in 1931.

Above: Jimmie Foxx belted one over the second tier at Shibe Park in Game 4. Philadelphia won the game 3-0 and tied the series.

Game 1 Thursday, October 1 at Sportsman's Park, St. Louis

	1	2	3	4	5	6	7	8	9	R	H	E
Philadelphia Athletics	0	0	4	0	0	0	2	0	0	6	11	0
St. Louis Cardinals	2	0	0	0	0	0	0	0	0	2	12	0

Pitchers Phi Lefty Grove (W, 1-0), IP 9, H 12, R 2, ER 2, BB 0, SO 7
StL Paul Derringer (L, 0-1), IP 7, H 11, R 6, ER 6, BB 3, SO 9; Syl Johnson, IP 2, H 0, R 0, ER 0, BB 0, SO 2

Top Performers at the Plate
Phi Mickey Cochrane, 2 for 4, 2 R, 1 BB; Jimmie Foxx, 2 for 4, 2 RBI
StL Frankie Frisch, 2 for 4, 1 R; Pepper Martin, 3 for 4, 1 RBI

2B-Phi-Haas; StL/Gelbert, Martin. **HR**-Phi/Simmons. **SB**-StL/Hafey, Martin. **Time** 1:55. **Attendance** 38,529.

Game 2 Friday, October 2 at Sportsman's Park, St. Louis

	1	2	3	4	5	6	7	8	9	R	H	E
Philadelphia Athletics	0	0	0	0	0	0	0	0	0	0	3	0
St. Louis Cardinals	0	1	0	0	0	1	0	x	2	6	1	

Pitchers Phi George Earnshaw (L, 0-1), IP 8, H 6, R 2, ER 2, BB 1, SO 5
StL Bill Hallahan (W, 1-0), IP 9, H 3, R 0, ER 0, BB 7, SO 8

Top Performers at the Plate
Phi Jimmie Foxx, 1 for 2, 2 BB
StL Pepper Martin, 2 for 3, 2 R, 2 SB; George Watkins, 2 for 4

2B-StL/Frisch, Martin, Watkins. **SB**-Martin 2. **Time** 1:49. **Attendance** 35,947.

Game 3 Monday, October 5 at Shibe Park, Philadelphia

	1	2	3	4	5	6	7	8	9	R	H	E
St. Louis Cardinals	0	2	0	0	0	0	0	0	1	5	12	0
Philadelphia Athletics	0	0	0	0	0	0	0	2		2	2	0

Pitchers StL Burleigh Grimes (W, 1-0), IP 9, H 2, R 2, ER 2, BB 4, SO 5
Phi Lefty Grove (L, 1-1), IP 8, H 11, R 4, ER 4, BB 1, SO 2; Roy Mahaffey, IP 1, H 1, R 1, ER 1, BB 1, SO 0

Top Performers at the Plate
StL Pepper Martin, 2 for 4, 2 R; Jimmie Wilson, 3 for 4, 1 RBI
Phi Al Simmons, 1 for 4, 1 R, 2 RBI

2B-StL/Bottomley, Martin, Roettger. **HR**-Phi/Simmons. **Time** 2:10. **Attendance** 32,295.

Game 4 Tuesday, October 6 at Shibe Park, Philadelphia

	1	2	3	4	5	6	7	8	9	R	H	E
St. Louis Cardinals	0	0	0	0	0	0	0	0	0	0	2	1
Philadelphia Athletics	1	0	0	0	0	2	0	0	x	3	10	0

Pitchers StL Syl Johnson (L, 0-1), IP 5⅔, H 9, R 3, ER 3, BB 1, SO 2; Jim Lindsey, IP 1⅓, H 1, R 0, ER 0, BB 1, SO 2; Paul Derringer, IP 1 H 0, R 0, ER 0, BB 0, SO 1
Phi George Earnshaw (W, 1-1), IP 9, H 2, R 0, ER 0, BB 1, SO 8

Top Performers at the Plate
StL Pepper Martin, 2 for 3
Phi Max Bishop, 2 for 4, 1 R; Al Simmons, 2 for 4, 1 RBI

2B-StL/Martin; Phi/Miller, Simmons. **HR**-Phi/Foxx. **SB**-StL/Frisch, Martin. **Time** 1:58. **Attendance** 32,295.

Game 5 Wednesday, October 7 at Shibe Park, Philadelphia

	1	2	3	4	5	6	7	8	9	R	H	E
St. Louis Cardinals	1	0	0	0	0	2	0	1	1	5	12	0
Philadelphia Athletics	0	0	0	0	0	0	1	0	0	1	9	0

Pitchers StL Bill Hallahan (W, 1-0), IP 9, H 9, R 1, ER 1, BB 1, SO 4
Phi Waite Hoyt (L, 0-1), IP 6, H 7, R 3, ER 3, BB 0, SO 1; Rube Walberg, IP 2, H 2, R 1, ER 1, BB 1, SO 2; Eddie Rommel, IP 1, H 3, R 1, ER 1, BB 0, SO 0

Top Performers at the Plate
StL Frankie Frisch, 2 for 4, 1 R; Pepper Martin, 3 for 4, 1 R, 4 RBI
Phi Jimmie Foxx, 2 for 3, 1 BB; Al Simmons, 3 for 4, 1 R

2B-StL/Frisch; Phi/Simmons. **HR**-StL/Martin. **SB**-StL/Watkins. **Time** 1:56. **Attendance** 32,295.

Game 6 Friday, October 9 at Sportsman's Park, St. Louis

	1	2	3	4	5	6	7	8	9	R	H	E
Philadelphia Athletics	0	0	0	0	4	0	4	0	0	8	8	1
St. Louis Cardinals	0	0	0	0	0	1	0	0	0	1	5	2

Pitchers Phi Lefty Grove (W, 2-1), IP 9, H 5, R 1, ER 1, BB 1, SO 7
StL Paul Derringer (L, 0-2), IP 4⅓, H 3, R 4, ER 0, BB 4, SO 4; Syl Johnson, IP 1⅓, H 1, R 0, ER 0, BB 0, SO 2; Jim Lindsey, IP 2, H 3, R 4, ER 2, BB 2, SO 0; Flint Rhem, IP 1, H 1, R 0, ER 0, BB 0, SO 1

Top Performers at the Plate
Phi Jimmie Foxx, 2 for 5, 2 R; Dib Williams, 2 for 4, 1 R, 1 RBI

2B-Phi/Williams; StL/Flowers. **Time** 1:57. **Attendance** 39,401.

Game 7 Saturday, October 10 at Sportsman's Park, St. Louis

	1	2	3	4	5	6	7	8	9	R	H	E
Philadelphia Athletics	0	0	0	0	0	0	0	2		2	7	1
St. Louis Cardinals	2	0	2	0	0	0	0	0	x	4	5	0

Pitchers Phi George Earnshaw (L, 1-2), IP 7, H 4, R 4, ER 3, BB 2, SO 7; Rube Walberg, IP 1, H 1, R 0, ER 0, BB 1, SO 2
StL Burleigh Grimes (W, 2-0), IP 8⅔, H 7, R 2, ER 2, BB 5, SO 6; Bill Hallahan (Sv, 1), IP ⅓, H 0, R 0, ER 0, BB 0, SO 0

Top Performers at the Plate
Phi Bing Miller, 3 for 4, 1 R; Dib Williams, 2 for 4
StL Andy High, 3 for 4, 2 R; George Watkins, 2 for 3, 2 R, 2 RBI, 1 BB

HR-StL/Watkins. **SB**-StL/Martin. **Time** 1:57. **Attendance** 20,805.

New York Yankees (4) vs. Chicago Cubs (0)

Was he really pointing to the fence to let the world know where he was planning to send the next pitch? The question is a matter of continuing debate, but the legend of Babe Ruth's "called shot" in the 1932 World Series remains one of baseball's most celebrated moments. Whatever the true meaning behind Ruth's gesture, it clearly represented the high emotions running through the Series that year. The New York Yankees were led to their first pennant in four years under the tutelage of Joe McCarthy, who had been unceremoniously fired by Chicago two years earlier. Additional ill will was generated by the Cubs' decision to offer late-season acquisition Mark Koenig only a half share of the Series money. The Yankee players took exception to this slap in the face to a former teammate, and harsh words were exchanged across dugouts throughout the four games. Red Ruffing and Lefty Gomez, making their first postseason appearances, started the first two games for New York and brought the team a 2-

0 lead. Lou Gehrig's 2-run homer in Game 1 put the Yankees ahead 3-2 in the third inning and launched what would be a tremendous Series for the first baseman. New York collected 10 singles and 4 walks in the second game to defeat Lon Warneke 5-2. The scene shifted to Chicago for Game 3, where angry Cub fans hurled insults and the occasional piece of rotted fruit at the Yankees, particularly Ruth. "The Bambino" started things off for New York with a 3-run homer in the first, and Gehrig followed with a solo shot two innings later. The Cubs tied the game at 4 heading into the fifth inning. Starter Charlie Root was still on the mound for Chicago, and with one out, the mighty Ruth stepped to the plate. Root got 2 strikes by him, and after each one the Babe raised a finger to count them off. As the invectives from the fans and opposing players turned up a notch, Ruth made another gesture in the direction of

Left: The nearly 50,000 fans who packed into Wrigley Field for the third game of the 1932 Series witnessed a classic October moment: Babe Ruth's "called shot."

1932 WORLD SERIES COMPOSITE STATISTICS

NEW YORK YANKEES/Joe McCarthy, Manager

Player	pos	G	AB	R	H	2B	3B	HR	RBI	BB	SO	SB	BA	SA	E	FPct
Johnny Allen	p	1	0	0	0	0	0	0	0	0	0	0	–	–	0	–
Sammy Byrd	lf	1	0	0	0	0	0	0	0	0	0	0	–	–	0	–
Ben Chapman	lf-rf	4	17	1	5	2	0	0	6	2	4	0	.294	.412	0	1.000
Earle Combs	cf	4	16	8	6	1	0	1	4	4	3	0	.375	.625	0	1.000
Frankie Crosetti	ss	4	15	2	2	1	0	0	0	2	3	0	.133	.200	4	.846
Bill Dickey	c	4	16	2	7	0	0	0	4	2	1	0	.438	.438	0	1.000
Lou Gehrig	1b	4	17	9	9	1	0	3	8	2	1	0	.529	1.118	1	.975
Lefty Gomez	p	1	3	0	0	0	0	0	0	0	2	0	.000	.000	0	1.000
Myril Hoag	pr	1	0	1	0	0	0	0	0	0	0	0	–	–	–	–
Tony Lazzeri	2b	4	17	4	5	0	0	2	5	2	1	0	.294	.647	1	.950
Wilcy Moore	p	1	3	0	1	0	0	0	0	0	2	0	.333	.333	0	1.000
Herb Pennock	p	2	1	0	0	0	0	0	0	0	0	0	.000	.000	0	1.000
George Pipgras	p	1	5	0	0	0	0	0	0	0	5	0	.000	.000	0	–
Red Ruffing	p-ph	2	4	0	0	0	0	0	0	1	1	0	.000	.000	0	1.000
Babe Ruth	rf-lf	4	15	6	5	0	0	2	6	4	3	0	.333	.733	1	.857
Joe Sewell	3b	4	15	4	5	1	0	0	3	4	0	0	.333	.400	1	.909
Totals		4	144	37	45	6	0	8	36	23	26	0	.313	.521	8	.949

Pitcher	G	GS	CG	IP	H	R	ER	BB	SO	W-L	Sv	ERA
Johnny Allen	1	1	0	⅔	5	4	3	0	0	0-0	0	40.50
Lefty Gomez	1	1	1	9	9	2	1	1	8	1-0	0	1.00
Wilcy Moore	1	0	0	5⅓	2	1	0	0	1	1-0	0	0.00
Herb Pennock	2	0	0	4	2	1	1	1	4	0-0	2	2.25
George Pipgras	1	1	0	8	9	5	4	3	1	1-0	0	4.50
Red Ruffing	1	1	1	9	10	6	4	6	10	1-0	0	4.00
Totals	4	4	2	36	37	19	13	11	24	4-0	2	3.25

CHICAGO CUBS/Charlie Grimm, Manager

Player	pos	G	AB	R	H	2B	3B	HR	RBI	BB	SO	SB	BA	SA	E	FPct
Guy Bush	p	2	1	0	0	0	0	0	0	1	0	0	.000	.000	0	1.000
Kiki Cuyler	rf	4	18	2	5	1	1	1	2	0	3	1	.278	.611	0	1.000
Frank Demaree	cf	2	7	1	2	0	0	1	4	1	0	0	.286	.714	1	.800
Woody English	3b	4	17	2	3	0	0	0	1	2	2	0	.176	.176	1	.875
Burleigh Grimes	p	2	1	0	0	0	0	0	0	0	1	0	.000	.000	0	–
Charlie Grimm	1b	4	15	2	5	2	0	0	1	2	2	0	.333	.467	0	1.000
Marv Gudat	ph	2	2	0	0	0	0	0	0	1	0	0	.000	.000	–	–
Stan Hack	pr	1	0	0	0	0	0	0	0	0	0	0	–	–	–	–
Gabby Hartnett	c	4	16	2	5	2	0	1	1	1	3	0	.313	.625	1	.974
Rollie Hemsley	ph-c	3	3	0	0	0	0	0	0	0	3	0	.000	.000	0	–
Billy Herman	2b	4	18	5	4	1	0	0	1	1	3	0	.222	.278	1	.944
Billy Jurges	ss	3	11	1	4	1	0	0	1	0	1	2	.364	.455	2	.905
Mark Koenig	ss-ph	2	4	1	1	0	1	0	1	1	0	0	.250	.750	0	1.000
Pat Malone	p	1	0	0	0	0	0	0	0	0	0	0	–	–	0	–
Jakie May	p	2	2	0	0	0	0	0	0	0	0	0	.000	.000	0	1.000
Johnny Moore	cf	2	7	1	0	0	0	0	0	2	1	0	.000	.000	0	1.000
Charlie Root	p	1	2	0	0	0	0	0	0	0	1	0	.000	.000	0	–
Bob Smith	p	1	0	0	0	0	0	0	0	0	0	0	–	–	0	–
Riggs Stephenson	lf	4	18	2	8	1	0	0	4	0	0	0	.444	.500	0	1.000
Bud Tinning	p	2	0	0	0	0	0	0	0	0	0	0	–	–	0	1.000
Lon Warneke	p	2	4	0	0	0	0	0	0	0	3	0	.000	.000	0	1.000
Totals		4	146	19	37	8	2	3	16	11	24	3	.253	.397	6	.959

Pitcher	G	GS	CG	IP	H	R	ER	BB	SO	W-L	Sv	ERA
Guy Bush	2	2	0	5⅔	5	9	9	6	2	0-1	0	14.29
Burleigh Grimes	2	0	0	2⅔	7	7	7	2	0	0-0	0	23.63
Pat Malone	1	0	0	2⅔	1	0	0	4	4	0-0	0	0.00
Jakie May	2	0	0	4⅔	9	7	6	3	4	0-1	0	11.57
Charlie Root	1	1	0	4⅓	6	6	5	3	4	0-1	0	10.38
Bob Smith	1	0	0	1	2	1	1	0	1	0-0	0	9.00
Bud Tinning	2	0	0	2⅓	0	0	0	3	3	0-0	0	0.00
Lon Warneke	2	1	1	10⅔	15	7	7	5	8	0-1	0	5.91
Totals	4	4	1	34	45	37	35	23	26	0-4	0	9.26

Series Outstanding Player: Lou Gehrig, New York Yankees. **Series Outstanding Pitcher:** Lefty Gomez, New York Yankees. **Average Length of Game:** 2 hours, 14 minutes. **Total Attendance:** 191,998. **Average Attendance:** 48,000 (46,084 at Yankee Stadium; 49,915 at Wrigley Field). **Umpires:** Bill Dinneen (AL), Bill Klem (NL), George Magerkurth (NL), Roy Van Graflan (AL). **Winning Player's Share:** $5,232. **Losing Player's Share:** $4,245.

center field. He swung at the next pitch and deposited the ball in the center-field bleachers. Many observers insisted that Ruth had called his home run, but others offered alternate explanations. Some said he was simply pointing at Root to let him know he still had one strike to go; others claim the gesture was aimed at the loudmouths in the Chicago dugout. Whatever his intentions, history records the moment as "Ruth's called shot." What is generally overlooked is the fact that Gehrig followed Ruth's famous blast with a home run of his own—his second of the day—and that Tony Lazzeri had a 2-homer display in the clinching game the following afternoon. The Yanks knocked Chicago for a total of 13 runs in Game 4 to complete the sweep. In grand fashion, Ruth had helped his team to victory in the last World Series of his career.

Right: Tony Lazzeri's two-run homer in the ninth inning of Game 4 was the capper in New York's four-game rout of the Cubs.

Babe Ruth's most famous Series home run, the "Called Shot" in Game 3, was the last of his career. His 15 World Series home runs stood as a record until Mickey Mantle hit his 16th in 1964.

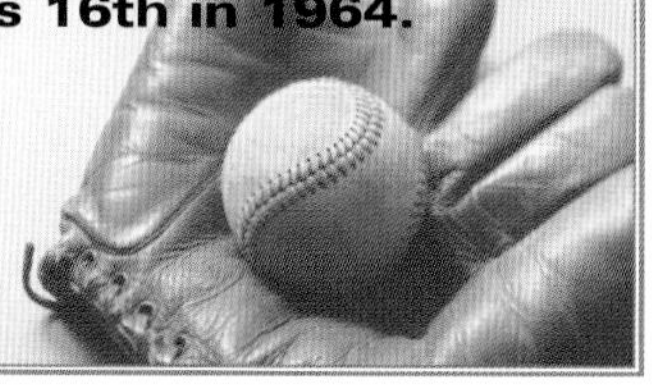

Above: One of Lou Gehrig's nine runs during the '32 Series came on Ben Chapman's third-inning single in Game 2.

Right: Lou Gehrig greets Babe Ruth with a smirk after Ruth hit his famous Game 3 homer.

Game 1	Wednesday, September 28 at Yankee Stadium, New York												
		1	2	3	4	5	6	7	8	9	R	H	E
Chicago Cubs		2	0	0	0	0	0	2	2	0	6	10	1
New York Yankees		0	0	0	3	0	5	3	1	x	12	8	2

Pitchers Chi Guy Bush (L, 0-1), IP 5⅓, H 3, R 8, BB 5, SO 2; Burleigh Grimes, IP 1⅔, H 3, R 3, ER 3, BB 1, SO 0; Bob Smith, IP 1, H 2, R 1, ER 1, BB 0, SO 1
NY Red Ruffing (W, 1-0), IP 9, H 10, R 6, ER 4, BB 6, SO 10

Top Performers at the Plate
Chi Billy Herman, 2 for 5, 2 R, 1 RBI; Riggs Stephenson, 3 for 5, 3 RBI
NY Earle Combs, 2 for 4, 2 R, 2 RBI, 1 BB; Lou Gehrig, 2 for 4, 3 R, 2 RBI, 1 BB

2B-Chi/Hartnett 2; NY/Combs. **3B**-NY/Koenig. **HR**-NY/Gehrig. **SB**-Chi/Cuyler. **Time** 2:31. **Attendance** 41,459.

Game 2	Thursday, September 29 at Yankee Stadium, New York												
		1	2	3	4	5	6	7	8	9	R	H	E
Chicago Cubs		1	0	1	0	0	0	0	0	0	2	9	0
New York Yankees		2	0	2	0	1	0	0	0	x	5	10	1

Pitchers Chi Lon Warneke (L, 0-1), IP 8, H 10, R 5, ER 5, BB 4, SO 7
NY Lefty Gomez (W, 1-0), IP 9, H 9, R 2, ER 1, BB 1, SO 8

Top Performers at the Plate
Chi Charlie Grimm, 2 for 4; Riggs Stephenson, 2 for 4, 1 R, 1 RBI
NY Bill Dickey, 2 for 3, 2 RBI, 1 BB; Lou Gehrig, 3 for 4, 2 R, 1 RBI

2B-Chi/Herman, Stephenson. **3B**-Chi/Cuyler. **Time** 1:46. **Attendance** 50,709.

Game 3	Saturday, October 1 at Wrigley Field, Chicago												
		1	2	3	4	5	6	7	8	9	R	H	E
New York Yankees		3	0	1	0	2	0	0	0	1	7	8	1
Chicago Cubs		1	0	2	1	0	0	0	0	1	5	9	4

Pitchers NY George Pipgras (W, 1-0), IP 8, H 9, R 5, ER 4, BB 3, SO 1; Herb Pennock (Sv, 1), IP 1, H 0, R 0, ER 0, BB 0, SO 1
Chi Charlie Root (L, 0-1), IP 4⅓, H 6, R 6, ER 5, BB 3, SO 4; Pat Malone, IP 2⅔, H 1, R 0, ER 0, BB 4, SO 4; Jakie May, IP 1⅓, H 1, R 1, ER 0, BB 0, SO 1; Bud Tinning, IP ⅔, H 0, R 0, ER 0, BB 0, SO 1

Top Performers at the Plate
NY Lou Gehrig, 2 for 5, 2 R, 2 RBI, 2 HR; Babe Ruth, 2 for 4, 2 R, 4 RBI, 1 BB, 2 HR
Chi Kiki Cuyler, 3 for 4, 1 R, 2 RBI; Billy Jurges, 3 for 4, 1 R, 2 SB

2B-NY/Chapman; Chi/Cuyler, Grimm, Jurges. **HR**-NY/Gehrig 2, Ruth 2; Chi/Cuyler, Hartnett. **SB**-Chi/Jurges 2. **Time** 2:11. **Attendance** 49,986.

Game 4	Sunday, October 2 at Wrigley Field, Chicago												
		1	2	3	4	5	6	7	8	9	R	H	E
New York Yankees		1	0	2	0	0	2	4	0	4	13	19	4
Chicago Cubs		4	0	0	0	0	1	0	0	1	6	9	1

Pitchers NY Johnny Allen, IP ⅔, H 5, R 4, ER 3, BB 0, SO 0; Wilcy Moore (W, 1-0), IP 5⅓, H 2, R 1, ER 0, BB 0, SO 1; Herb Pennock (Sv, 2), IP 3, H 2, R 1, ER 1, BB 1, SO 3
Chi Guy Bush, IP ⅓, H 2, R 1, ER 1, BB 1, SO 0; Lon Warneke, IP 2⅔, H 5, R 2, ER 2, BB 1, SO 0; Jakie May (L, 0-1), IP 3⅓, H 8, R 6, ER 6, BB 3, SO 3; Bud Tinning, IP 1⅔, H 0, R 0, ER 0, BB 0, SO 2; Burleigh Grimes, IP 1, H 4, R 4, ER 4, BB 1, SO 0

Top Performers at the Plate
NY Earle Combs, 3 for 4, 4 R, 2 RBI, 2 BB; Tony Lazzeri, 3 for 5, 2 R, 4 RBI, 1 BB, 2 HR
Chi Charlie Grimm, 2 for 4, 2 R; Riggs Stephenson, 2 for 5, 1 R

2B-NY/Chapman, Crosetti, Gehrig, Sewell; Chi/Grimm. **HR**-NY/Combs, Lazzeri 2; Chi/Demaree. **Time** 2:27. **Attendance** 49,844.

New York Giants (4) vs. Washington Senators (1)

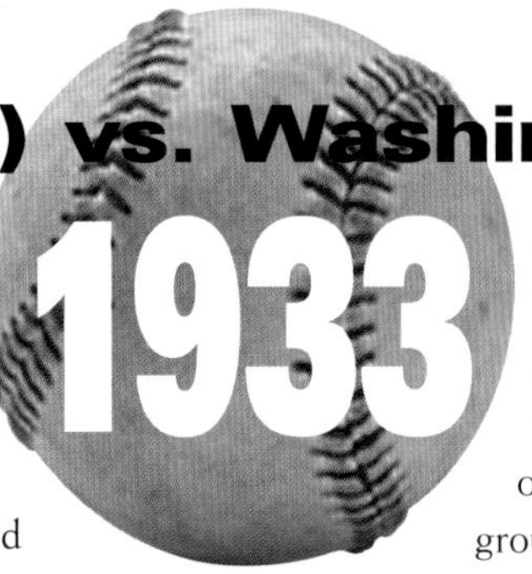

The 1933 season brought the New York Giants their ninth pennant in franchise history, but it was the first one with someone other than John McGraw at the helm. McGraw had retired for health reasons a year earlier and was replaced by Bill Terry, his 34-year-old first baseman. Lefty Carl Hubbell, the league leader in wins, ERA and shutouts, formed the heart of a tough pitching staff in New York. Washington's player-manager Joe Cronin, just a few weeks shy of his 27th birthday, was the youngest man ever to lead a team to the World Series, and he posted a .309 average and 118 RBI as the club's starting shortstop. The Senators were projected to duplicate their 1924 victory over New York, but Hubbell and outfielder Mel Ott had other ideas. Hubbell struck out ten Senators in Game 1, allowing two unearned runs, while Ott went 4 for 4 and hit a two-run home run in the 1st inning. Hal Schumacher kept the Senators quiet again in Game 2, giving up just a solo homer to Goose Goslin for Washington's only run. Buddy Myer drove in two runs in the third game, and Earl Whitehill shut the Giants out on six hits to give the Senators their first win. Hubbell took control from the mound again in Game 4, his only major lapse being a fielding error in the 7th. Monty Weaver was equally effective for Cronin's crew, limiting New York's run production to a Bill Terry solo shot in the 4th. With the game tied at one, neither team scored in the 8th, 9th or 10th innings, but in

the top of the 11th a couple of singles and a sacrifice hit brought Travis Jackson home for the Giants. Washington appeared to have Hubbell up against the wall in the bottom half of the inning with the bases full and just one out, but Hubbell induced pinchhitter Cliff Bolton to ground into a game-ending double play. The teams battled to a second straight extra-inning contest the next day, with each team scoring three in regulation. The Senators bunched their runs in the 6th inning on a game-tying homer by Fred Schulte. Jack Russell (who led the American League in saves in 1933) was in the game for Washington with the Senators down two in the 10th when Ott knocked a deep fly ball to center field. Center fielder Fred Schulte leaped for it, but the ball deflected off his mitt and sailed over the fence. The 43-year-old Cuban-born Dolf Luque continued his strong relief work by retiring the Senators in the bottom of the 10th, and New York won the Series with a 4-3 triumph in Game 5. Though John McGraw was no longer in the dugout, he still considered the Giants his team, and the victory was a fond farewell to the "Little Napoleon," who passed away before the start of the 1934 season.

Above: Managers Bill Terry and Joe Cronin join President Franklin Roosevelt as he prepares to throw out the ceremonial first pitch before Game 3 of the 1933 Series.

1933 WORLD SERIES COMPOSITE STATISTICS

NEW YORK GIANTS/Bill Terry, Manager

Player	pos	G	AB	R	H	2B	3B	HR	RBI	BB	SO	SB	BA	SA	E	FPct
Hi Bell	p	1	0	0	0	0	0	0	0	0	0	0	—	—	0	—
Hughie Critz	2b	5	22	2	3	0	0	0	0	1	0	0	.136	.136	1	.971
Kiddo Davis	cf	5	19	1	7	1	0	0	0	0	3	0	.368	.421	0	1.000
Freddie Fitzsimmons	p	1	2	0	1	0	0	0	0	0	0	0	.500	.500	0	1.000
Carl Hubbell	p	2	7	0	2	0	0	0	0	0	0	0	.286	.286	1	.833
Travis Jackson	3b	5	18	3	4	1	0	0	2	1	3	0	.222	.278	1	.950
Dolf Luque	p	1	1	0	1	0	0	0	0	0	0	0	1.000	1.000	0	1.000
Gus Mancuso	c	5	17	2	2	1	0	0	2	3	0	0	.118	.176	0	1.000
Jo-Jo Moore	lf	5	22	1	5	1	0	0	1	1	3	0	.227	.273	0	1.000
Lefty O'Doul	ph	1	1	1	1	0	0	0	2	0	0	0	1.000	1.000	—	—
Mel Ott	rf	5	18	3	7	0	0	2	4	4	4	0	.389	.722	0	1.000
Homer Peel	cf-ph	2	2	0	1	0	0	0	0	0	0	0	.500	.500	0	—
Blondy Ryan	ss	5	18	0	5	0	0	0	1	1	5	0	.278	.278	1	.966
Hal Schumacher	p	2	7	0	2	0	0	0	3	0	3	0	.286	.286	0	1.000
Bill Terry	1b	5	22	3	6	1	0	1	1	0	0	0	.273	.455	0	1.000
Totals		**5**	**176**	**16**	**47**	**5**	**0**	**3**	**16**	**11**	**21**	**0**	**.267**	**.347**	**4**	**.981**

Pitcher	G	GS	CG	IP	H	R	ER	BB	SO	W-L	Sv	ERA
Hi Bell	1	0	0	1	0	0	0	0	0	0-0	0	0.00
Freddie Fitzsimmons	1	1	0	7	9	4	4	0	2	0-1	0	5.14
Carl Hubbell	2	2	2	20	13	3	0	6	15	2-0	0	0.00
Dolf Luque	1	0	0	4⅓	2	0	0	2	5	1-0	0	0.00
Hal Schumacher	2	2	1	14⅔	13	4	4	5	3	1-0	0	2.45
Totals	**5**	**5**	**3**	**47**	**37**	**11**	**8**	**13**	**25**	**4-1**	**0**	**1.53**

WASHINGTON SENATORS/Joe Cronin, Manager

Player	pos	G	AB	R	H	2B	3B	HR	RBI	BB	SO	SB	BA	SA	E	FPct
Ossie Bluege	3b	5	16	1	2	1	0	0	1	1	6	0	.125	.188	0	1.000
Cliff Bolton	ph	2	2	0	0	0	0	0	0	0	0	0	.000	.000	—	—
Joe Cronin	ss	5	22	1	7	0	0	0	2	0	2	0	.318	.318	1	.957
General Crowder	p	2	4	0	1	0	0	0	0	0	0	0	.250	.250	0	1.000
Goose Goslin	rf-lf	5	20	2	5	1	0	1	1	1	3	0	.250	.450	0	1.000
Dave Harris	ph-rf	3	2	0	0	0	0	0	0	2	0	0	.000	.000	—	—
John Kerr	pr	1	0	0	0	0	0	0	0	0	0	0	—	—	—	—
Joe Kuhel	1b	5	20	1	3	0	0	0	1	1	4	0	.150	.150	0	1.000
Heinie Manush	lf	5	18	2	2	0	0	0	0	2	1	0	.111	.111	0	1.000
Alex McColl	p	1	0	0	0	0	0	0	0	0	0	0	—	—	0	1.000
Buddy Myer	2b	5	20	2	6	1	0	0	2	2	3	0	.300	.350	0	.900
Sam Rice	ph	1	1	0	1	0	0	0	0	0	0	0	1.000	1.000	—	—
Jack Russell	p	3	2	0	0	0	0	0	0	0	1	0	.000	.000	0	1.000
Fred Schulte	cf	5	21	1	7	1	0	1	4	1	1	0	.333	.524	0	1.000
Luke Sewell	c	5	17	1	3	0	0	0	1	2	0	1	.176	.176	0	1.000
Lefty Stewart	p	1	1	0	0	0	0	0	0	0	1	0	.000	.000	—	—
Tommy Thomas	p	2	0	0	0	0	0	0	0	0	0	0	—	—	0	—
Monte Weaver	p	1	4	0	0	0	0	0	0	0	2	0	.000	.000	0	1.000
Earl Whitehill	p	1	3	0	0	0	0	0	0	0	0	0	.000	.000	0	1.000
Totals		**5**	**173**	**11**	**37**	**4**	**0**	**2**	**11**	**13**	**25**	**1**	**.214**	**.272**	**4**	**.981**

Pitcher	G	GS	CG	IP	H	R	ER	BB	SO	W-L	Sv	ERA
General Crowder	2	2	0	11	16	9	9	5	7	0-1	0	7.36
Alex McColl	1	0	0	2	0	0	0	0	0	0-0	0	0.00
Jack Russell	3	0	0	10⅓	8	1	1	0	7	0-1	0	0.87
Lefty Stewart	1	1	0	2	6	4	2	0	0	0-1	0	9.00
Tommy Thomas	2	0	0	1⅓	1	0	0	2	0	0-0	0	0.00
Monte Weaver	1	1	0	10⅓	11	2	2	4	3	0-1	0	1.74
Earl Whitehill	1	1	1	9	5	0	0	2	2	1-0	0	0.00
Totals	**5**	**5**	**1**	**46**	**47**	**16**	**14**	**11**	**21**	**1-4**	**0**	**2.74**

Series Outstanding Player: Mel Ott, New York Giants. **Series Outstanding Pitcher:** Carl Hubbell, New York Giants. **Average Length of Game:** 2 hours, 22 minutes. **Total Attendance:** 163,076. **Average Attendance:** 32,615 (41,067 at the Polo Grounds; 26,981 at Griffith Stadium). **Umpires:** Charlie Moran (NL), George Moriarty (AL), Red Ormsby (AL), Cy Pfirman (NL). **Winning Player's Share:** $4,257. **Losing Player's Share:** $3,010.

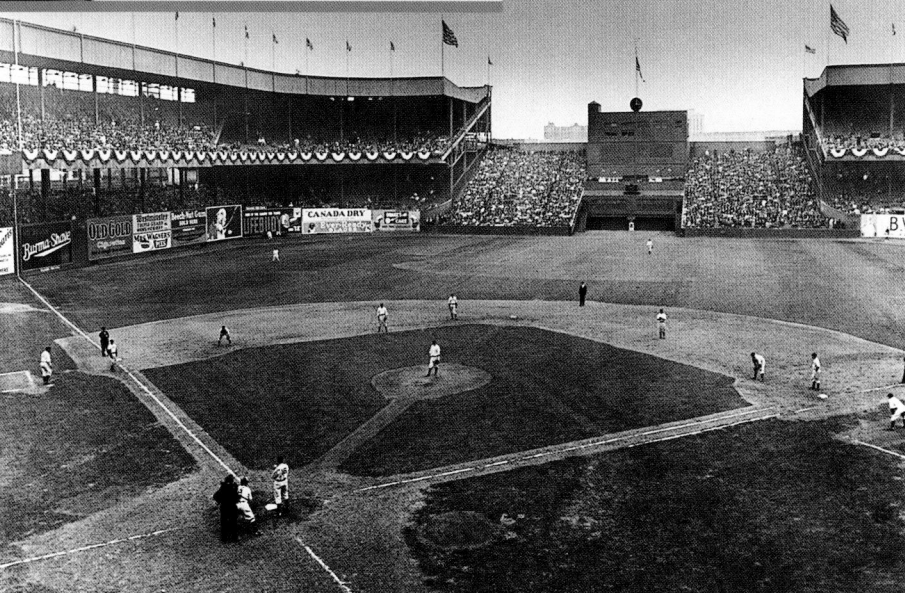

Dolf Luque holds the distinction of being the oldest player to win a World Series game. He turned 43 on August 4, 1933.

Above: The World Series returned to the Polo Grounds for the first time in a decade when the Giants hosted the Senators in the opening game of the 1933 Series.

Above: With the bases jammed in the eighth, Lefty O'Doul broke Game 2 open with a two-run single. New York scored six in the inning against Alvin "General" Crowder.

Game 1 Tuesday, October 3 at the Polo Grounds, New York

	1	2	3	4	5	6	7	8	9	R	H	E
Washington Senators	0	0	0	1	0	0	0	0	1	2	5	3
New York Giants	2	0	2	0	0	0	0	0	x	4	10	2

Pitchers Was Lefty Stewart (L, 0-1), IP 2, H 6, R 4, ER 2, BB 0, SO 0; Jack Russell, IP 5, H 4, R 0, ER 0, BB 0, SO 3; Tommy Thomas, IP 1, H 0, R 0, ER 0, BB 0, SO 2
NY Carl Hubbell (W, 1-0), IP 9, H 5, R 2, ER 0, BB 2, SO 10

Top Performers at the Plate
Was Joe Cronin, 2 for 4, 1 RBI; Fred Schulte, 2 for 4
NY Kiddo Davis, 2 for 4; Mel Ott, 4 for 4, 1 R, 3 RBI

HR-NY/Ott. **Time** 2:07. **Attendance** 46,672.

Game 2 Wednesday, October 4 at the Polo Grounds, New York

	1	2	3	4	5	6	7	8	9	R	H	E
Washington Senators	0	0	1	0	0	0	0	0	0	1	5	0
New York Giants	0	0	0	0	0	6	0	0	x	6	10	0

Pitchers Was General Crowder (L, 0-1), IP 5⅔, H 9, R 6, ER 6, BB 3, SO 3; Tommy Thomas, IP ⅓, H 1, R 0, ER 0, BB 0, SO 0; Alex McColl, IP 2, H 0, R 0, ER 0, BB 0, SO 0
NY Hal Schumacher (W, 1-0), IP 9, H 5, R 1, ER 1, BB 4, SO 2

Top Performers at the Plate
Was Goose Goslin, 2 for 4, 1 R, 1 RBI
NY Travis Jackson, 1 for 3, 1 R, 1 RBI, 1 SH; Jo-Jo Moore, 2 for 4, 1 RBI

2B-NY/Terry. **HR**-Was/Goslin. **Time** 2:09. **Attendance** 35,461.

Game 3 Thursday, October 5 at Griffith Stadium, Washington

	1	2	3	4	5	6	7	8	9	R	H	E
New York Giants	0	0	0	0	0	0	0	0	0	0	5	0
Washington Senators	2	1	0	0	0	0	1	0	x	4	9	1

Pitchers NY Freddie Fitzsimmons (L, 0-1), IP 7, H 9, R 4, ER 4, BB 0, SO 2; Hi Bell, IP 1, H 0, R 0, ER 0, BB 0, SO 0
Was Earl Whitehill (W, 1-0), IP 9, H 5, R 0, ER 0, BB 2, SO 2

Top Performers at the Plate
NY Travis Jackson, 1 for 3, 1 BB
Was Buddy Myer, 3 for 4, 1 R, 2 RBI; Fred Schulte, 2 for 4, 1 RBI

2B-NY/Jackson; Was/Bluege, Goslin, Myer, Schulte. **SB**-Was/Sewell. **Time** 1:55. **Attendance** 25,727.

Game 4 Friday, October 6 at Griffith Stadium, Washington

	1	2	3	4	5	6	7	8	9	10	11	R	H	E
New York Giants	0	0	0	1	0	0	0	0	0	0	1	2	11	1
Washington Senators	0	0	0	0	0	0	1	0	0	0	0	1	8	0

Pitchers NY Carl Hubbell (W, 2-0), IP 11, H 8, R 1, ER 0, BB 4, SO 5
Was Monte Weaver (L, 0-1), IP 10⅓, H 11, R 2, ER 2, BB 4, SO 3; Jack Russell, IP ⅔, H 0, R 0, ER 0, BB 0, SO 1

Top Performers at the Plate
NY Blondy Ryan, 2 for 5, 1 RBI; Bill Terry, 2 for 5, 1 R, 1 RBI
Was Buddy Myer, 2 for 4, 1 BB; Luke Sewell, 2 for 4, 1 RBI, 1 BB

2B-NY/Moore. **HR**-NY/Terry. **Time** 2:59. **Attendance** 26,762.

Game 5 Saturday, October 7 at Griffith Stadium, Washington

	1	2	3	4	5	6	7	8	9	10	R	H	E
New York Giants	0	2	0	0	0	1	0	0	0	1	4	11	1
Washington Senators	0	0	0	0	3	0	0	0	0	0	3	10	0

Pitchers NY Hal Schumacher, IP 5⅔, H 8, R 3, ER 3, BB 1, SO 1; Dolf Luque (W, 1-0), IP 4⅓, H 2, R 0, ER 0, BB 2, SO 5
Was General Crowder, IP 5⅓, H 7, R 3, ER 3, BB 2, SO 4; Jack Russell (L, 0-1), IP 4⅔, H 4, R 1, ER 1, BB 0, SO 3

Top Performers at the Plate
NY Kiddo Davis, 2 for 5, 1 R; Gus Mancuso, 1 for 3, 1 R, 1 RBI, 1 BB
Was Joe Cronin, 3 for 5, 1 R; Fred Schulte, 2 for 4, 1 R, 3 RBI, 1 BB

2B-NY/Davis, Mancuso. **HR**-NY/Ott; Was/Schulte. **Time** 2:38. **Attendance** 28,454.

Above: Carl Hubbell didn't allow an earned run in 20 innings, helping him to two victories in the Series.

St. Louis Cardinals (4) vs. Detroit Tigers (3)

1934

Frankie Frisch's Cardinal team of the mid-1930s was a colorful, bombastic bunch, highlighted by Leo "The Lip" Durocher at short, John "Pepper" Martin at third, Joe "Ducky" Medwick in left and brothers Joe "Dizzy" Dean and Paul "Daffy" Dean on the mound. With less talk but an impressive 101 victories, the Detroit Tigers claimed the American League pennant in 1934 behind future Hall of Famers Hank Greenberg, Charlie Gehringer, Goose Goslin and player-manager Mickey Cochrane.

Dizzy Dean, winner of 30 games in 1934, bested Cochrane's surprise starter, Alvin "General" Crowder, in the Series opener, though Crowder can't take all the blame for the 8-3 loss. Five Detroit errors in the first 3 innings allowed St. Louis to jump out to a 3-0 lead, and reliever Firpo Marberry gave up 4 runs in the 6th. Medwick got a base hit in his first four times up to bat, including a 5th-inning home run. Detroit came back in Game 2 behind 12 innings of strong pitching by Schoolboy Rowe. After falling behind 2-0 after 3 innings, Rowe retired 22 Cardinals in a row and allowed only 1 hit in the game's final 9 innings; he also didn't walk a batter during the entire game. The Tigers tied the score in the bottom of the 9th when Gee Walker's pinch-hit single scored Pete Fox. Goslin knocked home the game winner with a 12th-inning single after Gehringer and Greenberg walked. Dean won Game 3 for St. Louis, but this time it was younger brother Paul getting the W. A 2-for-3 day from 1931's "Mr. October," Pepper Martin, helped secure the 4-1 victory. The Tigers got the upper hand against the Cardinal pitching in Game 4, breaking out for 13 hits and 10 runs. Greenberg doubled twice and singled twice to drive in 3 runs, and Billy Rogell knocked in 2 runs in each of Detroit's big innings. Aside from the 10-4 final, St. Louis got a big scare in the 4th inning when Dizzy Dean,

Above: Babe Ruth was on hand for the classic battle between the Cardinals and Tigers in 1934. With Ruth are (left to right) Dizzy Dean, Frankie Frisch, Mickey Cochrane and Schoolboy Rowe.

Left: Pepper Martin continued his October magic in 1934. Here he slides headfirst into home to score his team's sixth run in the opening game, courtesy of Joe Medwick's fourth hit of the day.

Insets: The Dean boys, Dizzy and Paul, won four games between them to bring St. Louis the title in 1934. They are the only brother duo to win in the same World Series.

1934 WORLD SERIES COMPOSITE STATISTICS

ST. LOUIS CARDINALS/Frankie Frisch, Manager

Player	pos	G	AB	R	H	2B	3B	HR	RBI	BB	SO	SB	BA	SA	E	FPct
Tex Carleton	p	2	1	0	0	0	0	0	0	0	0	0	.000	.000	0	–
Ripper Collins	1b	7	30	4	11	1	0	0	3	1	2	0	.367	.400	1	.984
Pat Crawford	ph	2	2	0	0	0	0	0	0	0	0	0	.000	.000	–	–
Spud Davis	ph	2	2	0	2	0	0	0	1	0	0	0	1.000	1.000	–	–
Dizzy Dean	p-pr	4	12	3	3	2	0	1	0	3	0	.250	.417	0	1.000
Paul Dean	p	2	6	0	1	0	0	0	2	0	1	0	.167	.167	1	1.000
Bill DeLancey	c	7	29	3	5	3	0	1	4	2	8	0	.172	.379	2	.966
Leo Durocher	ss	7	27	4	7	1	1	0	0	0	6	0	.259	.370	0	1.000
Frankie Frisch	2b	7	31	2	6	1	0	0	4	0	1	0	.194	.226	2	.956
Chick Fullis	cf-lf	3	5	0	2	0	0	0	0	0	0	0	.400	.400	1	.857
Jesse Haines	p	1	0	0	0	0	0	0	0	0	0	0	–	–	0	–
Bill Hallahan	p	1	3	0	0	0	0	0	0	0	1	0	.000	.000	1	.800
Pepper Martin	3b	7	31	8	11	3	1	0	4	3	2	2	.355	.516	4	.789
Joe Medwick	lf	7	29	4	11	0	1	1	5	1	7	0	.379	.552	0	1.000
Jim Mooney	p	1	0	0	0	0	0	0	0	0	0	0	–	–	0	1.000
Ernie Orsatti	cf-ph	7	22	3	7	0	1	0	2	3	1	0	.318	.409	2	.895
Jack Rothrock	rf	7	30	3	7	3	1	0	6	1	2	0	.233	.400	1	.950
Dazzy Vance	p	1	0	0	0	0	0	0	0	0	0	0	–	–	0	–
Bill Walker	p	2	2	0	0	0	0	0	0	0	2	0	.000	.000	1	.500
Burgess Whitehead	pr-ss	1	0	0	0	0	0	0	0	0	0	0	–	–	0	1.000
Totals		**7**	**262**	**34**	**73**	**14**	**5**	**2**	**32**	**11**	**31**	**2**	**.279**	**.393**	**16**	**.944**

Pitcher	G	GS	CG	IP	H	R	ER	BB	SO	W-L	Sv	ERA
Tex Carleton	2	1	0	3⅔	5	3	3	2	2	0-0	0	7.36
Dizzy Dean	3	3	2	26	20	6	5	5	17	2-1	0	1.73
Paul Dean	2	2	2	18	15	4	2	7	11	2-0	0	1.00
Jesse Haines	1	0	0	⅔	1	0	0	0	2	0-0	0	0.00
Bill Hallahan	1	1	0	8⅓	6	2	2	4	6	0-0	0	2.16
Jim Mooney	1	0	0	1	1	0	0	0	0	0-0	0	0.00
Dazzy Vance	1	0	0	1⅓	2	1	0	1	3	0-0	0	0.00
Bill Walker	2	0	0	6⅓	6	7	5	6	2	0-2	0	7.11
Totals	**7**	**7**	**4**	**65⅓**	**56**	**23**	**15**	**25**	**43**	**4-3**	**0**	**2.34**

DETROIT TIGERS/Mickey Cochrane, Manager

Player	pos	G	AB	R	H	2B	3B	HR	RBI	BB	SO	SB	BA	SA	E	FPct
Eldon Auker	p	2	4	0	0	0	0	0	0	0	2	0	.000	.000	0	1.000
Tommy Bridges	p	3	7	1	1	0	0	0	0	1	4	0	.143	.143	0	1.000
Mickey Cochrane	c	7	28	2	6	1	0	0	1	4	3	0	.214	.250	0	1.000
General Crowder	p	2	1	0	0	0	0	0	0	0	0	0	.000	.000	0	–
Frank Doljack	ph-cf	2	2	0	0	0	0	0	0	0	0	0	.000	.000	0	1.000
Pete Fox	rf	7	28	1	8	6	0	0	2	1	4	0	.286	.500	0	1.000
Charlie Gehringer	2b	7	29	5	11	1	0	1	2	3	0	1	.379	.517	3	.936
Goose Goslin	lf	7	29	2	7	1	0	0	2	3	1	0	.241	.276	2	.913
Hank Greenberg	1b	7	28	4	9	2	1	1	7	4	9	1	.321	.571	1	.985
Ray Hayworth	c	1	0	0	0	0	0	0	0	0	0	0	–	–	0	1.000
Chief Hogsett	p	3	3	0	0	0	0	0	0	0	0	0	.000	.000	0	1.000
Firpo Marberry	p	2	0	0	0	0	0	0	0	0	0	0	–	–	0	1.000
Marv Owen	3b	7	29	0	2	0	0	0	1	0	5	1	.069	.069	2	.900
Billy Rogell	ss	7	29	3	8	1	0	0	4	1	4	1	.276	.310	3	.903
Schoolboy Rowe	p	3	7	0	0	0	0	0	0	0	5	0	.000	.000	1	1.000
Gee Walker	ph	3	3	0	1	0	0	0	0	1	0	0	.333	.333	–	–
Jo-Jo White	cf	7	23	6	3	0	0	0	0	8	4	1	.130	.130	1	.955
Totals		**7**	**250**	**23**	**56**	**12**	**1**	**2**	**20**	**25**	**43**	**5**	**.224**	**.304**	**12**	**.957**

Pitcher	G	GS	CG	IP	H	R	ER	BB	SO	W-L	Sv	ERA
Eldon Auker	2	2	1	11½	16	8	7	5	2	1-1	0	5.56
Tommy Bridges	3	2	1	17⅓	21	9	7	1	12	1-1	0	3.63
General Crowder	2	1	0	6	6	4	1	1	2	0-1	0	1.50
Chief Hogsett	3	0	0	7⅓	6	1	1	3	3	0-0	0	1.23
Firpo Marberry	2	0	0	1⅔	5	4	4	1	0	0-0	0	21.60
Schoolboy Rowe	3	2	2	21⅓	19	8	7	0	12	1-1	0	2.95
Totals	**7**	**7**	**4**	**65**	**73**	**34**	**27**	**11**	**31**	**3-4**	**0**	**3.74**

Series Outstanding Player: Pepper Martin, St. Louis Cardinals. **Series Outstanding Pitchers:** Dizzy Dean and Paul Dean, St. Louis Cardinals. **Average Length of Game:** 2 hours, 18 minutes. **Total Attendance:** 281,510. **Average Attendance:** 40,216 (36,700 at Sportsman's Park; 42,852 at Navin Field). **Umpires:** Harry Geisel (AL), Bill Klem (NL), Clarence Owens (AL), John Reardon (NL). **Winning Player's Share:** $5,390. **Losing Player's Share:** $3,355.

in as a pinch runner, was struck in the head by a ball thrown from short-stop Rogell to first base on an attempted double play. Fortunately, as Dean later remarked, "they X-rayed my head and found nothing," and he was back on the mound the next day. Diz pitched well, but Detroit's Tommy Bridges pitched better, and the Tigers grabbed a 3-games-to-2 lead, with the teams headed back to Detroit for Games 6 and 7. Another great performance by Paul Dean edged out Rowe 4-3 in Game 6, with Dean providing the game-winning hit on a 7th-inning single. The elder Dean got the start for the crucial Game 7, while Cochrane went with his Game 4 winner, Eldon Auker. St. Louis crushed Auker and three relievers for 7 runs in the 3rd inning, beginning with Dean's stretch double. Detroit found itself deep in the hole, and things took an even darker turn in the 6th. Medwick smashed a two-out RBI triple to right field and slid

hard into third baseman Marv Owen. Owen allegedly spiked him in retaliation, and a brief altercation ensued. After the smoke cleared, Ripper Collins scored Medwick with his fourth successive hit of the afternoon, and the Cards were up 9-0. When Medwick took the field the next inning, irate Tiger fans pelted him with bottles, fruit and all manner of trash. Medwick retreated to the dugout three different times, and each time he tried to retake his place in left field, the bombardment began anew. From his box seat, Commissioner Kenesaw Landis ordered Medwick to leave the game. With a comfortable lead in hand, St. Louis was unaffected by Medwick's departure, and they extended the final score to an 11-0 rout. The Dean brothers earned all four wins for the Cards, and the "Gas House Gang," as the team later became known, claimed the franchise's third world championship.

Above left: The Detroit crowd showered Medwick with trash when he took the field following his controversial slide into third the previous half inning. Above right: Commissioner Landis ordered Medwick to leave the game so that play could resume. The Cardinals were up by nine at the time (they added two more runs), so his departure hardly threatened St. Louis's lead.

Below: Dizzy Dean, feeling dizzier than usual, is carried off the field after being beaned by a throw from Billy Rogell while running to second base in Game 4. Dean returned to pitch eight innings the following day.

The Series played in 1934 would be the last involving two player-managers. Mickey Cochrane also played catcher for Detroit, while Frankie Frisch was the Cardinals' starting second baseman.

Background: Joe Medwick's hard slide into third baseman Marv Owen led to flared tempers in the final game. The action occurred on Medwick's sixth-inning triple.

Above: Dizzy and Paul Dean celebrate with manager Frisch and catcher Bill DeLancey following the younger Dean's triumph over the Tigers in Game 6.

Below: Shown here sliding into third in Game 7, St. Louis's Frankie Frisch ended his illustrious World Series career with four rings and 58 hits in 50 career games.

The last game of 1934 was the 50th and final World Series game of Frankie Frisch's career. It was also his 50th postseason game without a home run, the most homerless Series games by any player.

Game 1 Wednesday, October 3 at Navin Field (Tiger Stadium), Detroit

	1	2	3	4	5	6	7	8	9	R	H	E
St. Louis Cardinals	0	2	1	0	1	4	0	0	0	8	13	2
Detroit Tigers	0	0	1	0	0	1	0	1	0	3	8	5

Pitchers StL Dizzy Dean (W, 1-0), IP 9, H 8, R 3, ER 3, BB 2, SO 6
Det General Crowder (L, 0-1), IP 5, H 6, R 4, ER 1, BB 1, SO 1; Firpo Marberry, IP ⅔, H 4, R 4, ER 4, BB 0, SO 0; Chief Hogsett, IP 3⅓, H 3, R 0, ER 0, BB 0, SO 1

Top Performers at the Plate
StL Joe Medwick, 4 for 5, 2 R, 2 RBI; Jack Rothrock, 2 for 4, 2 RBI, 1 SH
Det Charlie Gehringer, 2 for 4, 1 RBI; Hank Greenberg, 2 for 4, 2 R, 1 RBI

2B-StL/D. Dean, DeLancey. **HR**-StL/Medwick; Det/Greenberg. **Time** 2:13. **Attendance** 42,505.

Game 2 Thursday, October 4 at Navin Field (Tiger Stadium), Detroit

	1	2	3	4	5	6	7	8	9	10	11	12	R	H	E
St. Louis Cardinals	0	1	1	0	0	0	0	0	0	0	0	0	2	7	3
Detroit Tigers	0	0	0	1	0	0	0	0	1	0	0	1	3	7	0

Pitchers StL Bill Hallahan, IP 8⅓, H 6, R 2, ER 2, BB 4, SO 6; Bill Walker (L, 0-1), IP 3, H 1, R 1, ER 1, BB 3, SO 2
Det Schoolboy Rowe (W, 1-0), IP 12, H 7, R 2, ER 2, BB 0, SO 7

Top Performers at the Plate
StL Pepper Martin, 2 for 5, 1 R
Det Pete Fox, 2 for 5, 1 R, 1 RBI

2B-StL/Martin; Det/Fox, Rogell. **3B**-StL/Orsatti. **SB**-Det/Gehringer. **Time** 2:49. **Attendance** 43,451.

Game 3 Friday, October 5 at Sportsman's Park, St. Louis

	1	2	3	4	5	6	7	8	9	R	H	E
Detroit Tigers	0	0	0	0	0	0	0	0	1	1	8	2
St. Louis Cardinals	1	1	0	0	2	0	0	0	x	4	9	1

Pitchers Det Tommy Bridges (L, 0-1), IP 4, H 8, R 4, ER 4, BB 1, SO 3; Chief Hogsett, IP 4, H 1, R 0, ER 0, BB 1, SO 2
StL Paul Dean (W, 1-0), IP 9, H 8, R 1, ER 1, BB 5, SO 7

Top Performers at the Plate
Det Charlie Gehringer, 2 for 5,; Jo-Jo White, 2 for 5, 1 R
StL Ripper Collins, 2 for 4, 1 R; Pepper Martin, 2 for 3, 2 R, 1 BB

2B-Det/Gehringer; StL/DeLancey, Martin. **3B**-Det/Greenberg; StL/Martin, Rothrock. **Time** 2:07. **Attendance** 34,073.

Game 4 Saturday, October 6 at Sportsman's Park, St. Louis

	1	2	3	4	5	6	7	8	9	R	H	E
Detroit Tigers	0	0	3	1	0	0	1	5	0	10	13	1
St. Louis Cardinals	0	1	1	2	0	0	0	0	0	4	10	6

Pitchers Det Eldon Auker (W, 1-0), IP 9, H 10, R 4, ER 3, BB 4, SO 1
StL Tex Carleton, IP 2⅔, H 4, R 3, ER 3, BB 2, SO 2; Dazzy Vance, IP 1⅓, H 2, R 1, ER 0, BB 1, SO 3; Bill Walker (L, 0-2), IP 3⅓, H 5, R 6, ER 4, BB 3, SO 0; Jesse Haines, IP ⅔, H 1, R 0, ER 0, BB 0, SO 2; Jim Mooney, IP 1, H 1, R 0, ER 0, BB 0, SO 0

Top Performers at the Plate
Det Hank Greenberg, 4 for 5, 1 R, 3 RBI, 2 2B; Billy Rogell, 2 for 5, 1 R, 4 RBI
StL Joe Medwick, 2 for 3, 1 R, 1 BB; Ernie Orsatti, 2 for 4, 1 R, 1 RBI

2B-Det/Cochrane, Fox, Greenberg 2; StL/Collins. **SB**-Det/Greenberg, Owen, White. **Time** 2:43. **Attendance** 37,492.

Game 5 Sunday, October 7 at Sportsman's Park, St. Louis

	1	2	3	4	5	6	7	8	9	R	H	E
Detroit Tigers	0	1	0	0	0	2	0	0	0	3	7	0
St. Louis Cardinals	0	0	0	0	0	1	0	0	0	1	7	1

Pitchers Det Tommy Bridges (W, 1-1), IP 9, H 7, R 1, ER 1, BB 0, SO 7
StL Dizzy Dean (L, 1-1), IP 8, H 6, R 3, ER 2, BB 3, SO 6; Tex Carleton, IP 1, H 1, R 0, ER 0, BB 0, SO 0

Top Performers at the Plate
Det Billy Rogell, 2 for 4, 1 R
StL Pepper Martin, 2 for 4

2B-Det/Fox, Goslin; StL/Martin. **HR**-Det/Gehringer; StL/DeLancey. **SB**-Det/Rogell. **Time** 1:58. **Attendance** 38,536.

Game 6 Monday, October 8 at Navin Field (Tiger Stadium), Detroit

	1	2	3	4	5	6	7	8	9	R	H	E
St. Louis Cardinals	1	0	0	0	2	0	1	0	0	4	10	2
Detroit Tigers	0	0	1	0	0	2	0	0	0	3	7	1

Pitchers StL Paul Dean (W, 2-0), IP 9, H 7, R 3, ER 1, BB 2, SO 4
Det Schoolboy Rowe (L, 1-1), IP 9, H 10, R 4, ER 3, BB 0, SO 5

Top Performers at the Plate
StL Leo Durocher, 3 for 4, 2 R; Jack Rothrock, 2 for 4, 1 R, 1 RBI
Det Mickey Cochrane, 3 for 4, 1 RBI; Jo-Jo White, 0 for 2, 2 R, 2 BB

2B-StL/Durocher, Rothrock; Det/Fox. **Time** 1:58. **Attendance** 44,551.

Game 7 Tuesday, October 9 at Navin Field (Tiger Stadium), Detroit

	1	2	3	4	5	6	7	8	9	R	H	E
St. Louis Cardinals	0	0	7	0	0	2	2	0	0	11	17	1
Detroit Tigers	0	0	0	0	0	0	0	0	0	0	6	3

Pitchers StL Dizzy Dean (W, 2-1), IP 9, H 6, R 0, ER 0, BB 0, SO 5
Det Eldon Auker (L,1-1), IP 2⅓, H 6, R 4, ER 4, BB 1, SO 1; Schoolboy Rowe, IP ⅓, H 2, R 2, ER 2, BB 0, SO 0; Chief Hogsett, IP 0, H 2, R 1, ER 1, BB 2, SO 0; Tommy Bridges, IP 4⅓, H 6, R 4, ER 2, BB 0, SO 2; Firpo Marberry, IP 1, H 1, R 0, ER 0, BB 1, SO 0; General Crowder, IP 1, H 0, R 0, ER 0, BB 0, SO 0

Top Performers at the Plate
StL Ripper Collins, 4 for 5, 1 R, 2 RBI; Pepper Martin, 2 for 5, 3 R, 1 RBI, 1 BB, 2 SB
Det Pete Fox, 2 for 3, 2 2B; Charlie Gehringer, 2 for 4

2B-StL/D. Dean, DeLancey, Frisch, Rothrock 2; Det/Fox 2. **3B**-StL/Durocher, Medwick. **SB**-StL/Martin 2. **Time** 2:19. **Attendance** 40,902.

At the Helm
World Series Managers

Going Both Ways: Player-Managers

Leading a team to a pennant is a difficult-enough challenge for any manager standing on the sidelines. Leading your team to the World Series while also contributing on the field is something that only 17 men have accomplished (9 of them more than once). Following is a look at how these player-managers fared in their dual roles.

Jimmy Collins, 1903 Boston Red Sox
As manager: Defeated Pirates, 5-3
As third baseman: 9 for 36 (.250), 5 R, 3 SB

Fred Clarke, 1903 Pittsburgh Pirates
As manager: Lost to Red Sox, 3-5
As left fielder: 9 for 34 (.265), 3 R, 2 RBI

Fielder Jones, 1906 Chicago White Sox
As manager: Defeated Cubs, 4-2
As center fielder: 2 for 21 (.095), 4 R

Frank Chance, 1906 Chicago Cubs
As manager: Lost to White Sox, 2-4
As first baseman: 5 for 21 (.238), 3 R

Frank Chance, 1907 Chicago Cubs
As manager: Defeated Tigers, 4-0
As first baseman: 3 for 14 (.214), 3 R, 3 SB

Frank Chance, 1908 Chicago Cubs
As manager: Defeated Tigers, 4-1
As first baseman: 8 for 19 (.421), 4 R, 5 SB

Fred Clarke, 1909 Pittsburgh Pirates
As manager: Defeated Tigers, 4-3
As left fielder: 4 for 19 (.211), 7 R, 7 RBI, 2 HR

Frank Chance, 1910 Chicago Cubs
As manager: Lost to Athletics, 1-4
As first baseman: 6 for 17 (.353), 4 RBI

Jake Stahl, 1912 Boston Red Sox
As manager: Defeated Giants, 4-3
As first baseman: 8 for 32 (.250), 3 R, 2 SB

Bill Carrigan, 1915 Boston Red Sox
As manager: Defeated Athletics, 4-3
As catcher: 0 for 2 (.000)

Bill Carrigan, 1916 Boston Red Sox
As manager: Defeated Dodgers, 4-1
As catcher: 2 for 3 (.667)

Tris Speaker, 1920 Cleveland Indians
As manager: Defeated Dodgers, 5-2
As center fielder: 8 for 25 (.320), 6 R, 3 BB

Bucky Harris, 1924 Washington Senators
As manager: Defeated Giants, 4-3
As second baseman: 11 for 33 (.333), 5 R, 7 RBI

Bucky Harris, 1925 Washington Senators
As manager: Lost to Pirates, 3-4
As second baseman: 2 for 23 (.087)

Rogers Hornsby, 1926 St. Louis Cardinals
As manager: Defeated Yankees, 4-3
As second baseman: 7 for 28 (.250), 4 RBI

Bill Terry, 1933 New York Giants
As manager: Defeated Senators, 4-1
As first baseman: 6 for 22 (.273), 3 R, .455 SA

Joe Cronin, 1933 Washington Senators
As manager: Lost to Giants, 1-4
As shortstop: 7 for 22 (.318), 2 RBI

Frankie Frisch, 1934 St. Louis Cardinals
As manager: Defeated Tigers, 4-3
As second baseman: 6 for 31 (.194), 4 RBI

Mickey Cochrane, 1934 Detroit Tigers
As manager: Lost to Cardinals, 3-4
As catcher: 6 for 28 (.214), 4 BB

Mickey Cochrane, 1935 Detroit Tigers
As manager: Defeated Cubs, 4-2
As catcher: 7 for 24 (.292), 3 R, 4 BB

Bill Terry, 1936 New York Giants
As manager: Lost to Yankees, 2-4
As first baseman: 6 for 25 (.240), 5 RBI

Gabby Hartnett, 1938 Chicago Cubs
As manager: Lost to Yankees, 0-4
As catcher: 1 for 11 (.091)

Lou Boudreau, 1948 Cleveland Indians
As manager: Defeated Braves, 4-2
As shortstop: 6 for 22 (.273), 4 2B, 3 RBI

Aside from the 17 individuals who played and managed in the same World Series, 20 former participants went on to lead a team in the postseason as manager later in their careers. October regulars as players on the 1950s Yankees, Yogi Berra, Billy Martin and Hank Bauer all later returned to the Fall Classic as managers (Berra and Martin in Yankee pinstripes). Lou Piniella was on four Yankee pennant winners (1976–78 and 1981) during his playing days, and he won a World Series in his first year as manager of the Cincinnati Reds in 1990. Davey Johnson appeared in four Series as Baltimore's second baseman, and later led the Mets to a title in 1986. Pitcher Roger Craig was a three-time winner and one-time loser while playing with the Dodgers and Cardinals, but Manager Craig didn't win a game in the '89 Series with the San Francisco Giants.

Casey Stengel, who managed in more World Series than anyone, was no stranger to playing in the Fall Classic, either. He went three times as an outfielder, once with Brooklyn and twice with the Giants. By contrast, the manager tied with Stengel on the all-time Series wins list, Joe McCarthy, never played in a Major League game, let alone in a World Series. Eight other men who managed in at least one Series never played Major League ball: Ed Barrow, Jim Frey, Johnny Keane, Jim Leyland, Paul Owens, Pants Rowland, Eddie Sawyer and Earl Weaver.

Manager Charlie Grimm was on the active roster for his Chicago Cubs in the 1935 Series, but he never took himself off the bench. Leo Durocher did part-time duty at shortstop while managing the Brooklyn Dodgers during the 1941 season, but he did not make any on-field appearances in the World Series.

Teams skippered by player-managers have a 15-11 record in World Series play.

Above left: The 1934 Series was the last to feature a match-up of player-managers. Here St. Louis's Frankie Frisch and Detroit's Mickey Cochrane shake hands before Game 1.

Eighty-four different men have led their teams to the World Series, and 43 of them have been there more than once. While 57 men can claim a World Series title on their managerial resumes, only 19 are fortunate enough to qualify as multiple winners. Here are some more interesting facts about the dugout leaders.

◆ Thirteen managers have led more than one team to the World Series, but only three have won it with two different teams. Bill McKechnie led the 1925 Pirates and the 1940 Reds to the title, Bucky Harris won with the 1924 Senators and the 1947 Yankees, and Sparky Anderson, the only man to win in both leagues, skippered the 1975–76 Reds and the 1984 Tigers to championships.

◆ Pat Moran took the 1915 Phillies and the 1919 Reds to the World Series, becoming the first manager to get there with two teams. Joe McCarthy was the first manager to win a pennant in both leagues. He lost in his postseason debut with the 1932 Cubs, but more than made up for it with seven Series titles with the Yankees.

◆ Bill McKechnie and Dick Williams are the only men to manage three different teams in the World Series. McKechnie did it with the 1925 Pirates, 1928 Cardinals and 1939–40 Reds, and Williams with the 1967 Red Sox, 1972–73 A's and 1984 Padres.

◆ Connie Mack had the longest span between his first and last managerial appearances. He led the Philadelphia Athletics to the second Fall Classic in 1905, and his final Series came 26 years later, in 1931.

◆ The Washington Senators reached the postseason only three times in their history, but they did it with youngsters leading the way. In 1933, Joe Cronin became the youngest person to manage in a Series, and nine years earlier, Bucky Harris had the distinction of being the youngest to win one. Cronin was 26 years, 11 months and 21 days old when the 1933 Series began, and Harris was 27 years, 10 months and 26 days for Game 1 in 1924.

◆ Fifteen men have gone to the World Series in their first season as Major League managers, but only three were victorious in their rookie campaigns. Washington's player-manager Bucky Harris led the Senators to a championship in his first season as manager in 1924,

Above: John McGraw and Connie Mack managed in a combined 17 World Series, including three head to head. Both are among the top five managers in Series appearances, as well as losses.

the Cardinals won the title under rookie skipper Eddie Dyer in 1946, and Ralph Houk was a winner with the Yankees in his first two seasons as a manager, in 1961 and 1962.

◆ Six managers won a World Series in their first full season as manager after having taken over the reins of the team midway through the previous year: Tris Speaker, 1920 Indians; Rogers Hornsby, 1926 Cardinals; Bill Terry, 1933 Giants; Frankie Frisch, 1934 Cardinals; Dallas Green, 1980 Phillies; and Tom Kelly, 1987 Twins.

◆ Detroit's Hughie Jennings is the only man to get to the Series in his first three years as a Major League manager—but he lost all three, losing to the Cubs in 1907 and 1908 and to the Pirates in 1909.

◆ Seven teams have gone to the World Series after a midseason managerial change, but only Bob Lemon's 1978 Yankees came out victorious. He was George Steinbrenner's third manager during the club's pennant run that year. After getting fired midway through 1979, Lemon rejoined New York with 25 games left in the 1981 baseball season and managed in a Series loss to the Dodgers. The Cubs had two part-season managers go all the way to the Series: Charlie Grimm in 1932 and Gabby

Hartnett (replacing the fired Grimm) in 1938. After winning the first two games of 1947 under Clyde Sukeforth, the Brooklyn Dodgers went 92-60 under Burt Shotton to win the pennant. Harvey Kuenn and Paul Owens, of the 1982 Brewers and 1983 Phillies, respectively, are the last two to take a team to the World Series without managing a full season.

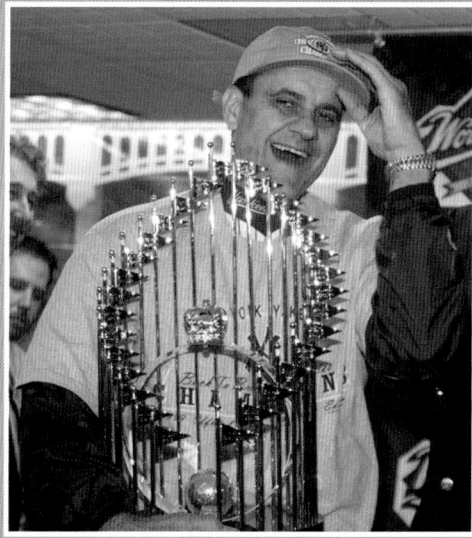

Above: After appearing in more than 2,200 games without a postseason appearance as a player, Joe Torre celebrated four Series victories in his first five seasons as Yankee manager.

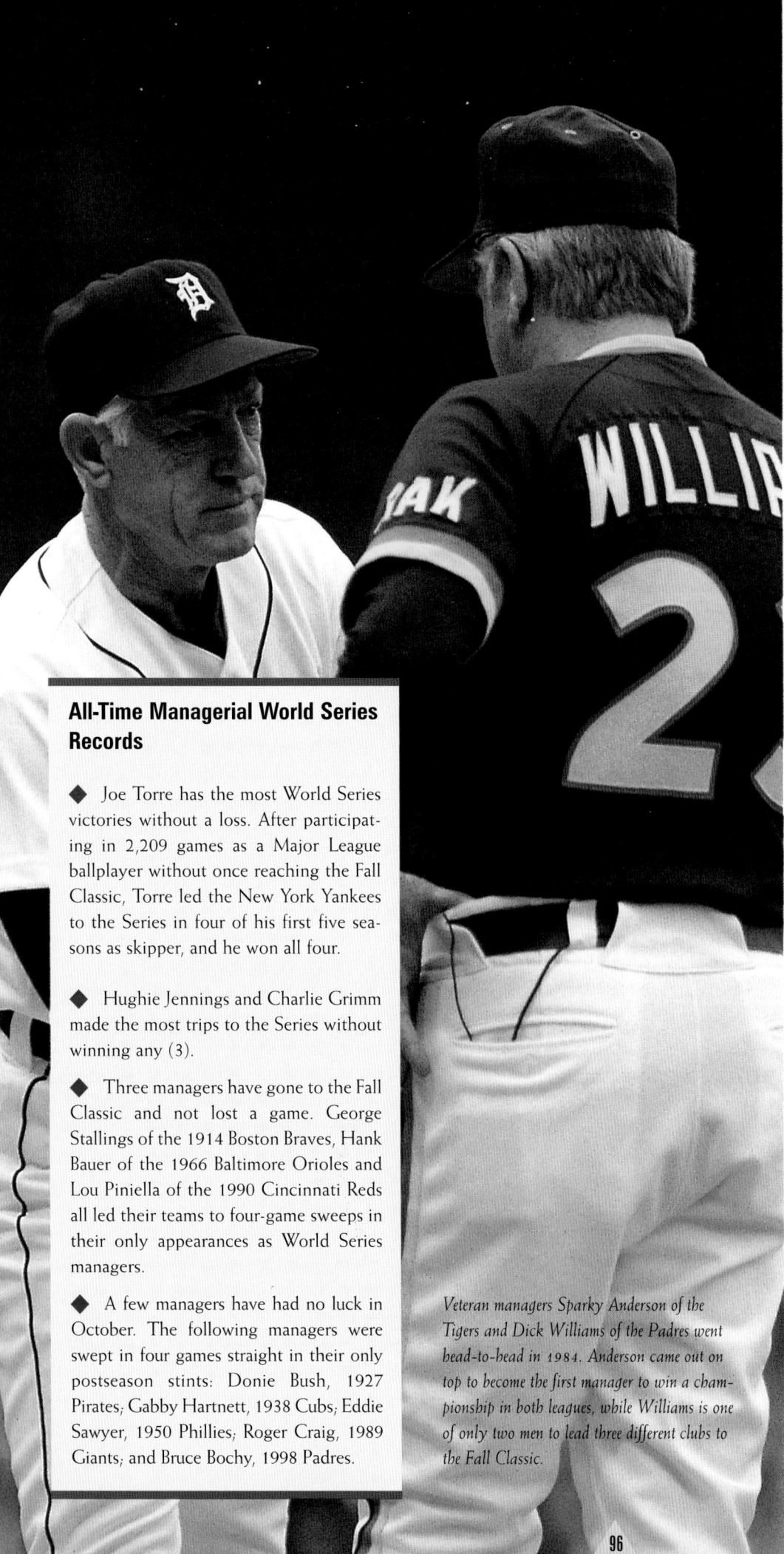

All-Time Managerial World Series Records

◆ Joe Torre has the most World Series victories without a loss. After participating in 2,209 games as a Major League ballplayer without once reaching the Fall Classic, Torre led the New York Yankees to the Series in four of his first five seasons as skipper, and he won all four.

◆ Hughie Jennings and Charlie Grimm made the most trips to the Series without winning any (3).

◆ Three managers have gone to the Fall Classic and not lost a game. George Stallings of the 1914 Boston Braves, Hank Bauer of the 1966 Baltimore Orioles and Lou Piniella of the 1990 Cincinnati Reds all led their teams to four-game sweeps in their only appearances as World Series managers.

◆ A few managers have had no luck in October. The following managers were swept in four games straight in their only postseason stints: Donie Bush, 1927 Pirates; Gabby Hartnett, 1938 Cubs; Eddie Sawyer, 1950 Phillies; Roger Craig, 1989 Giants; and Bruce Bochy, 1998 Padres.

Veteran managers Sparky Anderson of the Tigers and Dick Williams of the Padres went head-to-head in 1984. Anderson came out on top to become the first manager to win a championship in both leagues, while Williams is one of only two men to lead three different clubs to the Fall Classic.

Top Five Mangers in Series Appearances
1. Casey Stengel, 10
2. Joe McCarthy, 9
3. John McGraw, 9
4. Connie Mack, 8
5. Walter Alston, 7

Top Five Managers in Series Wins
1. Joe McCarthy, 7
2. Casey Stengel, 7
3. Connie Mack, 5
4. Walter Alston, 4
5. Joe Torre, 4

Top Five Managers in Series Losses
1. John McGraw, 6
2. Bobby Cox, 4
   Earl Weaver, 4
4. Walter Alston, 3
   Charlie Grimm, 3
   Miller Huggins, 3
   Hughie Jennings, 3
   Connie Mack, 3
   Casey Stengel, 3

Top Five Mangers in Series Games
1. Casey Stengel, 63
2. John McGraw, 54
3. Connie Mack, 43
   Joe McCarthy, 43
5. Walter Alston, 40

Top Five Managers in Series Games Won
1. Casey Stengel, 37
2. Joe McCarthy, 30
3. John McGraw, 26
4. Connie Mack, 24
5. Walter Alston, 20

Top Five Managers in Series Games Lost
1. John McGraw, 28
2. Casey Stengel, 26
3. Walter Alston, 20
4. Connie Mack, 19
5. Bobby Cox, 18

Fred Clarke, Bucky Harris and Bill Terry are the only player-managers to homer in the Series. Clarke did it twice in 1909, Harris hit two homers for Washington in 1924, and Terry went long once in the 1933 Series.

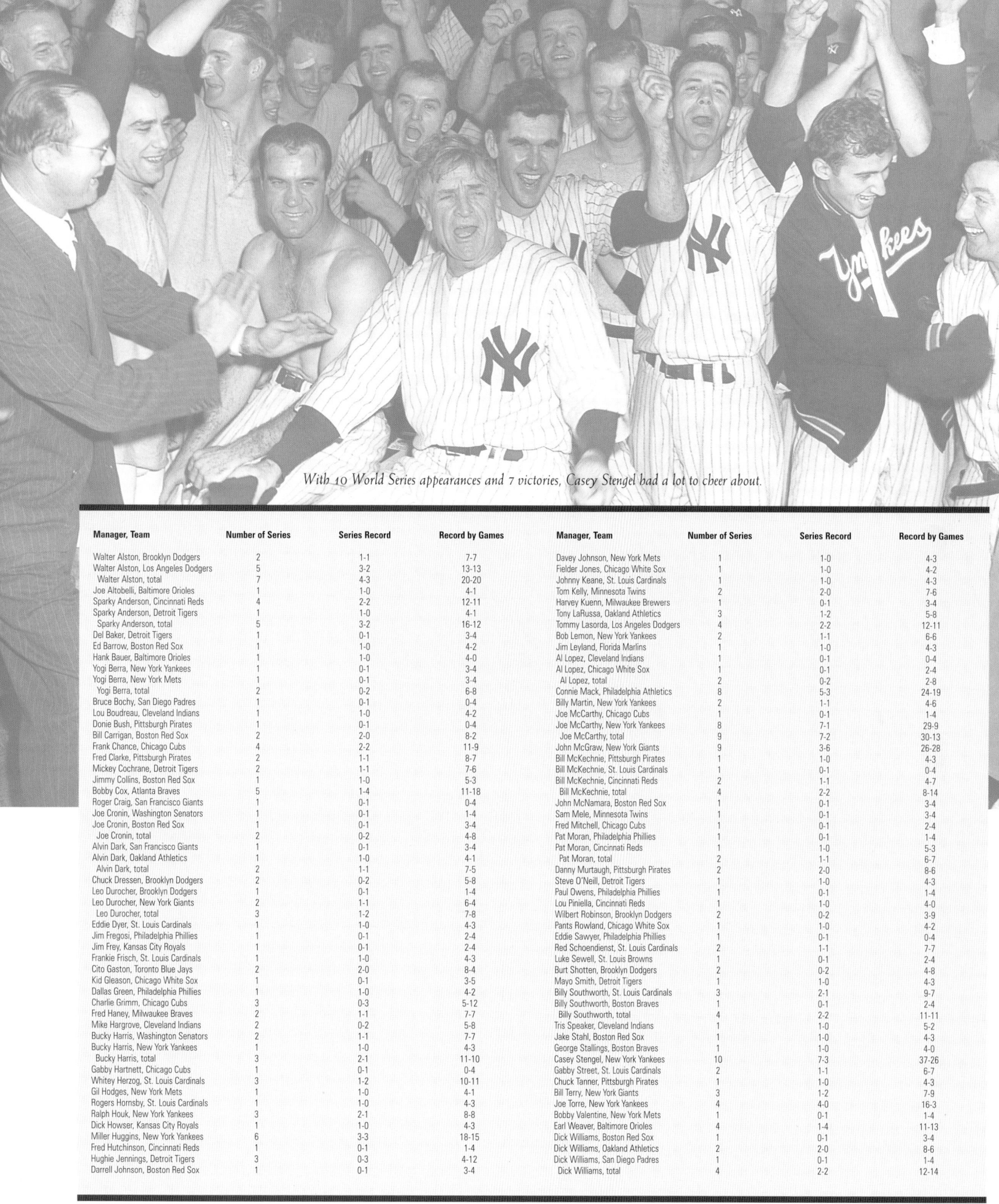

With 10 World Series appearances and 7 victories, Casey Stengel had a lot to cheer about.

Manager, Team	Number of Series	Series Record	Record by Games
Walter Alston, Brooklyn Dodgers	2	1-1	7-7
Walter Alston, Los Angeles Dodgers	5	3-2	13-13
Walter Alston, total	7	4-3	20-20
Joe Altobelli, Baltimore Orioles	1	1-0	4-1
Sparky Anderson, Cincinnati Reds	4	2-2	12-11
Sparky Anderson, Detroit Tigers	1	1-0	4-1
Sparky Anderson, total	5	3-2	16-12
Del Baker, Detroit Tigers	1	0-1	3-4
Ed Barrow, Boston Red Sox	1	1-0	4-2
Hank Bauer, Baltimore Orioles	1	1-0	4-0
Yogi Berra, New York Yankees	1	0-1	3-4
Yogi Berra, New York Mets	1	0-1	3-4
Yogi Berra, total	2	0-2	6-8
Bruce Bochy, San Diego Padres	1	0-1	0-4
Lou Boudreau, Cleveland Indians	1	1-0	4-2
Donie Bush, Pittsburgh Pirates	1	0-1	0-4
Bill Carrigan, Boston Red Sox	2	2-0	8-2
Frank Chance, Chicago Cubs	4	2-2	11-9
Fred Clarke, Pittsburgh Pirates	2	1-1	8-7
Mickey Cochrane, Detroit Tigers	2	1-1	7-6
Jimmy Collins, Boston Red Sox	1	1-0	5-3
Bobby Cox, Atlanta Braves	5	1-4	11-18
Roger Craig, San Francisco Giants	1	0-1	0-4
Joe Cronin, Washington Senators	1	0-1	1-4
Joe Cronin, Boston Red Sox	1	0-1	3-4
Joe Cronin, total	2	0-2	4-8
Alvin Dark, San Francisco Giants	1	0-1	3-4
Alvin Dark, Oakland Athletics	1	1-0	4-1
Alvin Dark, total	2	1-1	7-5
Chuck Dressen, Brooklyn Dodgers	2	0-2	5-8
Leo Durocher, Brooklyn Dodgers	1	0-1	1-4
Leo Durocher, New York Giants	2	1-1	6-4
Leo Durocher, total	3	1-2	7-8
Eddie Dyer, St. Louis Cardinals	1	1-0	4-3
Jim Fregosi, Philadelphia Phillies	1	0-1	2-4
Jim Frey, Kansas City Royals	1	0-1	2-4
Frankie Frisch, St. Louis Cardinals	1	1-0	4-3
Cito Gaston, Toronto Blue Jays	2	2-0	8-4
Kid Gleason, Chicago White Sox	1	0-1	3-5
Dallas Green, Philadelphia Phillies	1	1-0	4-2
Charlie Grimm, Chicago Cubs	3	0-3	5-12
Fred Haney, Milwaukee Braves	2	1-1	7-7
Mike Hargrove, Cleveland Indians	2	0-2	5-8
Bucky Harris, Washington Senators	2	1-1	7-7
Bucky Harris, New York Yankees	1	1-0	4-3
Bucky Harris, total	3	2-1	11-10
Gabby Hartnett, Chicago Cubs	1	0-1	0-4
Whitey Herzog, St. Louis Cardinals	3	1-2	10-11
Gil Hodges, New York Mets	1	1-0	4-1
Rogers Hornsby, St. Louis Cardinals	1	1-0	4-3
Ralph Houk, New York Yankees	3	2-1	8-8
Dick Howser, Kansas City Royals	1	1-0	4-3
Miller Huggins, New York Yankees	6	3-3	18-15
Fred Hutchinson, Cincinnati Reds	1	0-1	1-4
Hughie Jennings, Detroit Tigers	3	0-3	4-12
Darrell Johnson, Boston Red Sox	1	0-1	3-4
Davey Johnson, New York Mets	1	1-0	4-3
Fielder Jones, Chicago White Sox	1	1-0	4-2
Johnny Keane, St. Louis Cardinals	1	1-0	4-3
Tom Kelly, Minnesota Twins	2	2-0	7-6
Harvey Kuenn, Milwaukee Brewers	1	0-1	3-4
Tony LaRussa, Oakland Athletics	3	1-2	5-8
Tommy Lasorda, Los Angeles Dodgers	4	2-2	12-11
Bob Lemon, New York Yankees	2	1-1	6-6
Jim Leyland, Florida Marlins	1	1-0	4-3
Al Lopez, Cleveland Indians	1	0-1	0-4
Al Lopez, Chicago White Sox	1	0-1	2-4
Al Lopez, total	2	0-2	2-8
Connie Mack, Philadelphia Athletics	8	5-3	24-19
Billy Martin, New York Yankees	2	1-1	4-6
Joe McCarthy, Chicago Cubs	1	0-1	1-4
Joe McCarthy, New York Yankees	8	7-1	29-9
Joe McCarthy, total	9	7-2	30-13
John McGraw, New York Giants	9	3-6	26-28
Bill McKechnie, Pittsburgh Pirates	1	1-0	4-3
Bill McKechnie, St. Louis Cardinals	1	0-1	0-4
Bill McKechnie, Cincinnati Reds	2	1-1	4-7
Bill McKechnie, total	4	2-2	8-14
John McNamara, Boston Red Sox	1	0-1	3-4
Sam Mele, Minnesota Twins	1	0-1	3-4
Fred Mitchell, Chicago Cubs	1	0-1	2-4
Pat Moran, Philadelphia Phillies	1	0-1	1-4
Pat Moran, Cincinnati Reds	1	1-0	5-3
Pat Moran, total	2	1-1	6-7
Danny Murtaugh, Pittsburgh Pirates	2	2-0	8-6
Steve O'Neill, Detroit Tigers	1	1-0	4-3
Paul Owens, Philadelphia Phillies	1	0-1	1-4
Lou Piniella, Cincinnati Reds	1	1-0	4-0
Wilbert Robinson, Brooklyn Dodgers	2	0-2	3-9
Pants Rowland, Chicago White Sox	1	1-0	4-2
Eddie Sawyer, Philadelphia Phillies	1	0-1	0-4
Red Schoendienst, St. Louis Cardinals	2	1-1	7-7
Luke Sewell, St. Louis Browns	1	0-1	2-4
Burt Shotton, Brooklyn Dodgers	2	0-2	4-8
Mayo Smith, Detroit Tigers	1	1-0	4-3
Billy Southworth, St. Louis Cardinals	3	2-1	9-7
Billy Southworth, Boston Braves	1	0-1	2-4
Billy Southworth, total	4	2-2	11-11
Tris Speaker, Cleveland Indians	1	1-0	5-2
Jake Stahl, Boston Red Sox	1	1-0	4-3
George Stallings, Boston Braves	1	1-0	4-0
Casey Stengel, New York Yankees	10	7-3	37-26
Gabby Street, St. Louis Cardinals	2	1-1	6-7
Chuck Tanner, Pittsburgh Pirates	1	1-0	4-3
Bill Terry, New York Giants	3	1-2	7-9
Joe Torre, New York Yankees	4	4-0	16-3
Bobby Valentine, New York Mets	1	0-1	1-4
Earl Weaver, Baltimore Orioles	4	1-4	11-13
Dick Williams, Boston Red Sox	1	0-1	3-4
Dick Williams, Oakland Athletics	2	2-0	8-6
Dick Williams, San Diego Padres	1	0-1	1-4
Dick Williams, total	4	2-2	12-14

Detroit Tigers (4) vs. Chicago Cubs (2)

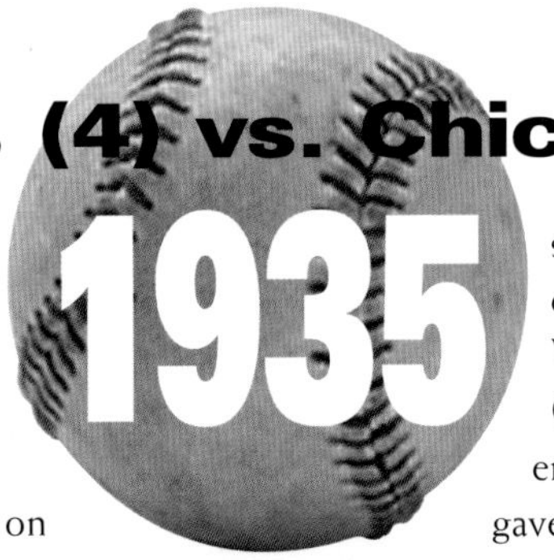

1935

With a very different cast of characters, the Chicago Cubs and Detroit Tigers revived their matchups of 1907 and 1908 with another World Series showdown in 1935. Neither team entered the Series with especially impressive October résumés: Detroit was coming off their fourth World Series loss the year before, and the Cubs had been on the short end of five Fall Classics. Somebody was going to come out the winner in this one, and Chicago took the upper hand behind Lon Warneke's 4-hit shutout in Game 1. Detroit opened Game 2 with a single, a double, another single and finally a 2-run homer, by Hank Greenberg, to account for 4 runs before the first out was recorded. They added 3 more in the 4th inning and 1 in the 7th to win 8-3. The victory was not without its costs, however, as Greenberg was hit by a pitched ball in the 7th; the righty slugger, whose 36 homers and 170 RBI were tops in all of baseball during the 1935 season, would have to sit out the remainder of the Series with a broken wrist. Goose Goslin and Billy Rogell, among others, picked up the slack left by Greenberg's absence, as the two combined for 6 hits and 4 RBI the following afternoon. A clutch 2-run single by Chicago pinch hitter Ken O'Dea sent the game into extra innings with the score tied at 5. It stayed that way until the top of the 11th, when Jo-Jo White brought in the game winner with a two-out

Left: Tommy Bridges started and won two games for Detroit in the 1935 Series.

single for Detroit. General Crowder, loser of one game in each of the previous two World Series (1933 with Washington and 1934 with Detroit), finally tasted October victory with a 5-hitter in Game 4. Consecutive errors by Chicago's Augie Galan and Billy Jurges in the 6th gave Detroit a 2-1 lead, which Crowder held. Down 3 games to 1, the Cubs stayed around for another day by victimizing Schoolboy Rowe for his second loss of the Series. Chuck Klein's 2-run homer in the 3rd secured the 3-1 Game 5 victory. Despite earning the loss in the 12-inning fourth game, Larry French got the start for Chicago in Game 6, and he lasted the entire game. French and Tommy Bridges traded 3 runs for each side through the first 8 innings. Stan Hack led off Chicago's half of the 9th with a triple to center field, but a strikeout, an infield grounder and a fly ball got Bridges out of the jam. Detroit took advantage in the bottom of the inning. Mickey Cochrane stroked a one-out single, and Charlie Gehringer advanced him into scoring position on a grounder to first. With two out, Goose Goslin came up and drove Cochrane home with a single to right, ending the Series. The city of Detroit immediately erupted into raucous celebration of its first championship, a party that lasted well into the next morning.

1935 WORLD SERIES COMPOSITE STATISTICS

DETROIT TIGERS/Mickey Cochrane, Manager

Player	pos	G	AB	R	H	2B	3B	HR	RBI	BB	SO	SB	BA	SA	E	FPct
Eldon Auker	p	1	2	0	0	0	0	0	0	0	1	0	.000	.000	0	1.000
Tommy Bridges	p	2	8	1	1	0	0	0	1	0	3	0	.125	.125	0	1.000
Flea Clifton	3b	4	16	1	0	0	0	0	2	4	0	.000	.000	1	.917
Mickey Cochrane	c	6	24	3	7	1	0	0	1	4	1	0	.292	.333	1	.973
General Crowder	p	1	3	1	1	0	0	0	1	0	0	0	.333	.333	0	1.000
Pete Fox	rf	6	26	1	10	3	1	0	4	0	1	0	.385	.577	1	.923
Charlie Gehringer	2b	6	24	4	9	3	0	0	4	2	1	1	.375	.500	0	1.000
Goose Goslin	lf	6	22	2	6	1	0	0	3	5	0	0	.273	.318	1	.923
Hank Greenberg	1b	2	6	1	1	0	0	1	2	1	0	0	.167	.667	3	.864
Chief Hogsett	p	1	0	0	0	0	0	0	0	0	0	0	—	—	0	1.000
Marv Owen	3b-1b	6	20	2	1	0	0	0	1	2	3	0	.050	.050	1	.981
Billy Rogell	ss	6	24	1	7	2	0	0	1	2	5	0	.292	.375	0	1.000
Schoolboy Rowe	p	3	8	0	2	1	0	0	0	0	1	0	.250	.375	0	.889
Gee Walker	cf	3	4	1	1	0	0	0	0	1	0	0	.250	.250	0	—
Jo-Jo White	cf	5	19	3	5	0	0	0	1	5	7	0	.263	.263	0	1.000
Totals		6	206	21	51	11	1	1	18	25	27	1	.248	.325	9	.963

Pitcher	G	GS	CG	IP	H	R	ER	BB	SO	W-L	Sv	ERA
Eldon Auker	1	1	0	6	6	3	2	2	1	0-0	0	3.00
Tommy Bridges	2	2	2	18	18	6	5	4	9	2-0	0	2.50
General Crowder	1	1	1	9	5	1	1	3	5	1-0	0	1.00
Chief Hogsett	1	0	0	1	0	0	0	0	0	0-0	0	0.00
Schoolboy Rowe	3	2	2	21	19	8	6	1	14	1-2	0	2.57
Totals	6	6	5	55	48	18	14	11	29	4-2	0	2.29

CHICAGO CUBS/Charlie Grimm, Manager

Player	pos	G	AB	R	H	2B	3B	HR	RBI	BB	SO	SB	BA	SA	E	FPct
Tex Carleton	p	1	1	0	0	0	0	0	0	1	1	0	.000	.000	0	1.000
Phil Cavarretta	1b	6	24	1	3	0	0	0	0	1	5	0	.125	.125	1	.984
Frank Demaree	rf-cf	6	24	2	6	1	0	2	2	1	4	0	.250	.542	0	1.000
Larry French	p	2	4	1	1	0	0	0	0	0	2	0	.250	.250	0	1.000
Augie Galan	lf	6	25	2	4	1	0	0	2	2	2	0	.160	.200	1	.933
Stan Hack	3b-ss	6	22	2	5	1	1	0	0	2	2	1	.227	.364	0	1.000
Gabby Hartnett	c	6	24	1	7	0	0	1	2	0	3	0	.292	.417	0	1.000
Roy Henshaw	p	1	1	0	0	0	0	0	0	0	0	0	.000	.000	0	—
Billy Herman	2b	6	24	3	8	2	1	1	6	0	2	0	.333	.625	1	.971
Billy Jurges	ss	6	16	3	4	0	0	0	1	4	4	0	.250	.250	1	.969
Chuck Klein	ph-rf-cf	5	12	2	4	0	0	1	2	0	2	0	.333	.583	0	1.000
Fabian Kowalik	p	1	2	1	1	0	0	0	0	1	0	0	.500	.500	0	.667
Bill Lee	p	2	1	0	0	0	0	0	0	1	0	0	.000	.000	0	1.000
Freddy Lindstrom	cf-3b	4	15	0	3	1	0	0	0	1	1	0	.200	.267	1	.900
Ken O'Dea	ph	1	1	0	1	0	0	0	1	0	0	0	1.000	1.000	—	—
Charlie Root	p	2	0	0	0	0	0	0	0	0	0	0	—	—	0	1.000
Walter Stephenson	ph	1	1	0	0	0	0	0	0	0	0	1	.000	.000	—	—
Lon Warneke	p	3	5	0	1	0	0	0	0	0	0	0	.200	.200	0	1.000
Totals		6	202	18	48	6	2	5	17	11	29	1	.238	.361	6	.976

Pitcher	G	GS	CG	IP	H	R	ER	BB	SO	W-L	Sv	ERA
Tex Carleton	1	1	0	7	6	2	1	7	4	0-1	0	1.29
Larry French	2	1	1	10⅔	15	5	4	2	8	0-2	0	3.38
Roy Henshaw	1	0	0	3⅔	2	3	3	5	2	0-0	0	7.36
Fabian Kowalik	1	0	0	4⅓	3	1	1	1	1	0-0	0	2.08
Bill Lee	2	1	0	10⅓	11	5	5	5	5	0-0	1	4.35
Charlie Root	2	1	0	2	5	4	4	1	2	0-1	0	18.00
Lon Warneke	3	2	1	16⅔	9	1	1	4	5	2-0	0	0.54
Totals	6	6	2	54⅔	51	21	19	25	27	2-4	1	3.13

Series Outstanding Player: Charlie Gehringer, Detroit Tigers. **Series Outstanding Pitcher:** Lon Warneke, Chicago Cubs. **Average Length of Game:** 2 hours, 5 minutes. **Total Attendance:** 286,672. **Average Attendance:** 47,779 (47,518 at Navin Field; 48,040 at Wrigley Field).
Umpires: Bill McGowan (AL), George Moriarty (AL), Ernie Quigley (NL), Albert Stark (NL). **Winning Player's Share:** $6,545. **Losing Player's Share:** $4,199.

Right: Mickey Cochrane crosses the plate on Goose Goslin's single in the ninth inning of Game 6, ending the Series with Detroit as champions.

Umpire George Moriarty played for Detroit from 1909 to 1915 and managed the team in 1927 through 1928. As a result, Chicago's manager and players rode Moriarty hard throughout the 1935 Series, leading to multiple ejections.

Above: Chicago's Freddie Lindstrom is tagged out by Charlie Gehringer trying to steal, resulting in a strike-'em-out, thrown-'em-out double play in the opening game.

Below: Catcher Gabby Hartnett prevents Hank Greenberg from scoring in Game 2. Greenberg had reached base when hit by a pitch that broke his wrist, sidelining him for the rest of the Series.

A 6th-inning single by Detroit's Marv Owen in Game 6 was his first base hit in 31 Series at-bats, a streak of futility dating back to the 4th game of 1934.

Game 1 Wednesday, October 2 at Navin Field (Tiger Stadium), Detroit

	1	2	3	4	5	6	7	8	9	R	H	E
Chicago Cubs	2	0	0	0	0	0	0	0	1	3	7	0
Detroit Tigers	0	0	0	0	0	0	0	0	0	0	4	3

Pitchers Chi Lon Warneke (W, 1-0), IP 9, H 4, R 0, ER 0, BB 4, SO 1
          Det Schoolboy Rowe (L, 0-1), IP 9, H 7, R 3, ER 2, BB 0, SO 8

Top Performers at the Plate
          Chi Frank Demaree, 2 for 4, 1 R, 1 RBI; Gabby Hartnett, 2 for 4, 1 RBI
          Det Pete Fox, 2 for 4

2B-Chi/Galan; Det/Fox, Rowe. **HR**-Chi/Demaree. **Time** 1:51. **Attendance** 47,391.

Game 2 Thursday, October 3 at Navin Field (Tiger Stadium), Detroit

	1	2	3	4	5	6	7	8	9	R	H	E
Chicago Cubs	0	0	0	0	1	0	2	0	0	3	6	1
Detroit Tigers	4	0	0	3	0	0	1	0	x	8	9	2

Pitchers Chi Charlie Root (L, 0-1), IP 0, H 4, R 4, ER 4, BB 0, SO 0; Roy Henshaw, IP 3⅔,
          H 2, R 3, ER 3, BB 5, SO 2; Fabian Kowalik, IP 4⅓, H 3, R 1, ER 1, BB 1, SO 1
          Det Tommy Bridges (W, 1-0), IP 9, H 6, R 3, ER 2, BB 4, SO 2

Top Performers at the Plate
          Chi Billy Jurges, 1 for 3, 1 R, 1 RBI, 1 BB
          Det Charlie Gehringer, 2 for 3, 2 R, 3 RBI, 1 BB; Jo-Jo White, 1 for 3, 2 R, 2 BB

2B-Chi/Demaree; Det/Cochrane, Rogell. **HR**-Det/Greenberg. **Time** 1:59. **Attendance** 46,742.

Game 3 Friday, October 4 at Wrigley Field, Chicago

	1	2	3	4	5	6	7	8	9	10	11	R	H	E
Detroit Tigers	0	0	0	0	0	1	0	4	0	0	1	6	12	2
Chicago Cubs	0	2	0	0	1	0	0	0	2	0	0	5	10	3

Pitchers Det Eldon Auker, IP 6, H 6, R 3, ER 2, BB 2, SO 1; Chief Hogsett, IP 1, H 0, R 0,
          ER 0, BB 1, SO 0; Schoolboy Rowe (W, 1-1), IP 4, H 4, R 2, ER 2, BB 0, SO 3
          Chi Bill Lee, IP 7⅓, H 7, R 4, ER 4, BB 3, SO 3; Lon Warneke, IP 1⅔, H 2, R 1,
          ER 1, BB 0, SO 2; Larry French (L, 0-1), IP 2, H 3, R 1, ER 0, BB 0, SO 1

Top Performers at the Plate
          Det Goose Goslin, 3 for 5, 2 R, 2 RBI; Jo-Jo White, 2 for 5, 1 R, 1 RBI, 1 BB
          Chi Augie Galan, 2 for 4, 2 RBI, 1 BB; Stan Hack, 2 for 5, 2 R

2B-Det/Gehringer, Goslin; Chi/Lindstrom. **3B**-Det/Fox. **HR**-Chi/Demaree. **SB**-Chi/Hack. **Time** 2:27.
Attendance 45,532.

Game 4 Saturday, October 5 at Wrigley Field, Chicago

	1	2	3	4	5	6	7	8	9	R	H	E
Detroit Tigers	0	0	1	0	0	1	0	0	0	2	7	0
Chicago Cubs	0	1	0	0	0	0	0	0	0	1	5	2

Pitchers Det General Crowder (W, 1-0), IP 9, H 5, R 1, ER 1, BB 3, SO 5
          Chi Tex Carleton (L, 0-1), IP 7, H 6, R 2, ER 1, BB 7, SO 4; Charlie Root, IP 2, H 1,
          R 0, ER 0, BB 1, SO 2

Top Performers at the Plate
          Det Charlie Gehringer, 2 for 4, 1 RBI, 1 SH; General Crowder, 1 for 3, 1 R, 1 BB
          Chi Phil Cavarretta, 2 for 4

2B-Det/Fox, Gehringer; Chi/Herman. **HR**-Chi/Hartnett. **SB**-Det/Gehringer. **Time** 2:28.
Attendance 49,350.

Game 5 Sunday, October 6 at Wrigley Field, Chicago

	1	2	3	4	5	6	7	8	9	R	H	E
Detroit Tigers	0	0	0	0	0	0	0	0	1	1	7	1
Chicago Cubs	0	0	2	0	0	0	1	0	x	3	8	0

Pitchers Det Schoolboy Rowe (L, 1-2), IP 8, H 8, R 3, ER 2, BB 1, SO 3
          Chi Lon Warneke (W, 2-0), IP 6, H 3, R 0, ER 0, BB 0, SO 2; Bill Lee (Sv, 1), IP 3,
          H 4, R 1, ER 1, BB 2, SO 2

Top Performers at the Plate
          Det Mickey Cochrane, 2 for 4; Pete Fox, 2 for 4, 1 RBI
          Chi Billy Herman, 2 for 4, 1 R, 1 RBI; Chuck Klein, 2 for 4, 1 R, 2 RBI

2B-Chi/Herman. **3B**-Chi/Herman. **HR**-Chi/Klein. **Time** 1:49. **Attendance** 49,237.

Game 6 Monday, October 7 at Navin Field (Tiger Stadium), Detroit

	1	2	3	4	5	6	7	8	9	R	H	E
Chicago Cubs	0	0	1	0	2	0	0	0	0	3	12	0
Detroit Tigers	1	0	0	1	0	1	0	0	1	4	12	1

Pitchers Chi Larry French (L, 0-2), IP 8⅔, H 12, R 4, ER 4, BB 2, SO 7
          Det Tommy Bridges (W, 2-0), IP 9, H 12, R 3, ER 3, BB 0, SO 7

Top Performers at the Plate
          Chi Stan Hack, 2 for 4; Babe Herman, 3 for 4, 1 R, 3 RBI
          Det Mickey Cochrane, 3 for 5, 2 R; Pete Fox, 2 for 4, 1 RBI

2B-Chi/Hack; Det/Fox, Gehringer, Rogell. **3B**-Chi/Hack. **HR**-Chi/Herman. **Time** 1:57.
Attendance 48,420.

New York Yankees (4) vs. New York Giants (2)

1936

After finishing in second place three years in a row, the New York Yankees launched an unprecedented run beginning in 1936. They were without Babe Ruth for the first time in a World Series, but Lou Gehrig was still going strong, and a young phenom named Joe DiMaggio had just donned Yankee pinstripes. The team finished 1936 with 102 wins and a record 19 1/2-game lead in the American League. The New York Giants did their part to bring about the first Subway Series in 13 years, with Mel Ott spearheading the offense and Carl Hubbell dominating opposing hitters from the mound. Hubbell defeated Red Ruffing in the Series opener, yielding only a solo home run among 7 scattered hits. The Giants held a slim 2-1 lead until the 8th, when Hubbell's bases-clearing single (plus 2 Yankee errors) broke the game open. Lefty Gomez had a rough day on the mound in Game 2, giving up 4 runs and 7 walks, but it was of no consequence, as the Yankees blasted five Giant pitchers for 18 runs on 17 hits. A grand slam by Tony Lazzeri—the second in Series history—was part of a 7-run 3rd inning, and Bill Dickey's homer in the 9th sent in 3 of the 6 runs scored that inning. There was no such offensive onslaught when the teams met at Yankee Stadium for Game 3. Leadoff home runs by Gehrig in the 2nd inning and by Jimmy Ripple in the top of the 5th provided all the scoring until Frankie Crosetti's single off the glove of pitcher Freddie Fitzsimmons broke the 1-1 tie in the 8th. Fitzsimmons took the loss for the Giants despite giving up only 4 hits in the game. A Series-record 66,669 fans showed up to the Stadium the next day to get another look at Hubbell. The great lefty was tagged with his first loss since midseason (ending his 17-game streak), while Yankee Monte Pearson went the distance for a 5-2 victory. The Giants jumped out to a 3-0 lead in Game 6, but the Yanks battled back to tie it at 4 in the 6th inning. Hal Schumacher kept "The Bombers" scoreless the rest of the way, and Johnny Moore doubled and scored the game-winning run in the top of the 10th. Fitzsimmons's mastery over the Yankee bats continued into the 1st inning of Game 6, and then the Yankees broke out for 9 hits and 5 runs, knocking Fitzsimmons out of the game by inning four. The Giants worked their way back to come within a run going into the last inning, when the Yanks put the game and the Series out of reach with a 7-run barrage. Although the Giants managed to win 2 games in the Series, Joe McCarthy's Yankees outscored them by 20, and their .302 team average was more than 50 points higher than the Giants'.

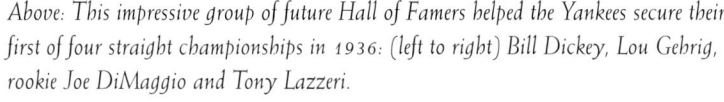

Above: This impressive group of future Hall of Famers helped the Yankees secure their first of four straight championships in 1936: (left to right) Bill Dickey, Lou Gehrig, rookie Joe DiMaggio and Tony Lazzeri.

1936 WORLD SERIES COMPOSITE STATISTICS

NEW YORK YANKEES/Joe McCarthy, Manager

Player	pos	G	AB	R	H	2B	3B	HR	RBI	BB	SO	SB	BA	SA	E	FPct
Frankie Crosetti	ss	6	26	5	7	2	0	0	3	3	5	0	.269	.346	2	.931
Bill Dickey	c	6	25	5	3	0	0	1	5	3	4	0	.120	.240	1	.977
Joe DiMaggio	cf	6	26	3	9	3	0	0	3	1	3	0	.346	.462	1	.944
Lou Gehrig	1b	6	24	5	7	1	0	2	7	3	2	0	.292	.583	0	1.000
Lefty Gomez	p	2	8	1	2	0	0	0	3	0	3	0	.250	.250	0	1.000
Bump Hadley	p	1	2	0	0	0	0	0	0	0	1	0	.000	.000	0	1.000
Roy Johnson	pr-ph	2	1	0	0	0	0	0	0	0	1	0	.000	.000	–	–
Tony Lazzeri	2b	6	20	4	5	0	0	1	7	4	4	0	.250	.400	0	1.000
Pat Malone	p	2	1	0	1	0	0	0	0	0	0	0	1.000	1.000	0	1.000
Johnny Murphy	p	1	2	1	1	0	0	0	1	0	1	0	.500	.500	0	–
Monte Pearson	p	1	4	0	2	1	0	0	0	0	0	0	.500	.750	0	1.000
Jake Powell	lf	6	22	8	10	1	0	1	5	4	4	1	.455	.636	0	1.000
Red Rolfe	3b	6	25	5	10	0	0	0	4	3	1	0	.400	.400	1	.955
Red Ruffing	p-ph	3	5	0	0	0	0	0	0	1	2	0	.000	.000	0	1.000
Bob Seeds	pr	1	0	0	0	0	0	0	0	0	0	0	–	–	–	–
George Selkirk	rf	6	24	6	8	0	1	2	3	4	4	0	.333	.667	1	.900
Totals		**6**	**215**	**43**	**65**	**8**	**1**	**7**	**41**	**26**	**35**	**1**	**.302**	**.447**	**6**	**.973**

Pitcher	G	GS	CG	IP	H	R	ER	BB	SO	W-L	Sv	ERA
Lefty Gomez	2	2	1	15⅓	14	8	8	11	9	2-0	0	4.70
Bump Hadley	1	1	0	8	10	1	1	1	2	1-0	0	1.13
Pat Malone	2	0	0	5	2	1	1	1	2	0-1	1	1.80
Johnny Murphy	1	0	0	2⅔	1	1	1	1	1	0-0	1	3.38
Monte Pearson	1	1	1	9	7	2	2	2	7	1-0	0	2.00
Red Ruffing	2	2	1	14	16	10	7	5	12	0-1	0	4.50
Totals	**6**	**6**	**3**	**54**	**50**	**23**	**20**	**21**	**33**	**4-2**	**2**	**3.33**

NEW YORK GIANTS/Bill Terry, Manager

Player	pos	G	AB	R	H	2B	3B	HR	RBI	BB	SO	SB	BA	SA	E	FPct
Dick Bartell	ss	6	21	5	8	3	0	1	3	4	4	0	.381	.667	1	.955
Slick Castleman	p	1	2	0	1	0	0	0	0	0	0	0	.500	.500	0	–
Dick Coffman	p	2	0	0	0	0	0	0	0	0	0	0	–	–	0	1.000
Harry Danning	ph-c	2	2	0	0	0	0	0	0	0	1	0	.000	.000	1	.750
Kiddo Davis	ph-pr	4	2	2	1	0	0	0	0	0	0	0	.500	.500	–	–
Freddie Fitzsimmons	p	2	4	0	2	0	0	0	0	0	1	0	.500	.500	0	1.000
Frank Gabler	p	2	0	0	0	0	0	0	0	1	0	0	–	–	0	1.000
Harry Gumbert	p	2	0	0	0	0	0	0	0	0	0	0	–	–	0	–
Carl Hubbell	p	2	6	0	2	0	0	0	1	0	0	0	.333	.333	1	.800
Travis Jackson	3b	6	21	1	4	0	0	0	1	1	3	0	.190	.190	3	.769
Mark Koenig	ph-2b	3	3	0	1	0	0	0	0	0	1	0	.333	.333	0	1.000
Hank Leiber	cf	2	6	0	0	0	0	0	0	2	2	0	.000	.000	0	1.000
Sam Leslie	ph	3	3	0	2	0	0	0	0	0	0	0	.667	.667	–	–
Gus Mancuso	c	6	19	3	5	2	0	0	1	3	3	0	.263	.368	0	1.000
Eddie Mayo	3b	1	1	0	0	0	0	0	0	0	0	0	.000	.000	0	1.000
Jo-Jo Moore	lf	6	28	4	6	2	0	1	1	1	4	0	.214	.393	0	1.000
Mel Ott	rf	6	23	4	7	2	0	1	3	3	1	0	.304	.522	1	.923
Jimmy Ripple	cf-ph	5	12	2	4	0	0	1	3	3	3	0	.333	.583	0	1.000
Hal Schumacher	p	2	4	0	0	0	0	0	0	1	3	0	.000	.000	0	1.000
Al Smith	p	1	0	0	0	0	0	0	0	0	0	0	–	–	0	–
Bill Terry	1b	6	25	1	6	0	0	0	5	1	4	0	.240	.240	0	1.000
Burgess Whitehead	2b	6	21	1	1	0	0	0	2	1	3	0	.048	.048	0	1.000
Totals		**6**	**203**	**23**	**50**	**9**	**0**	**4**	**20**	**21**	**33**	**0**	**.246**	**.350**	**7**	**.969**

Pitcher	G	GS	CG	IP	H	R	ER	BB	SO	W-L	Sv	ERA
Slick Castleman	1	0	0	4⅓	3	1	1	2	5	0-0	0	2.08
Dick Coffman	2	0	0	1⅔	5	6	6	1	1	0-0	0	32.40
Freddie Fitzsimmons	2	2	1	11⅔	13	7	7	2	6	0-2	0	5.40
Frank Gabler	2	0	0	5	7	4	4	4	0	0-0	0	7.20
Harry Gumbert	2	0	0	2	7	8	8	4	2	0-0	0	36.00
Carl Hubbell	2	2	1	16	15	5	4	2	10	1-1	0	2.25
Hal Schumacher	2	2	1	12	13	9	7	10	11	1-1	0	5.25
Al Smith	1	0	0	⅓	2	3	3	1	0	0-0	0	81.00
Totals	**6**	**6**	**3**	**53**	**65**	**43**	**40**	**26**	**35**	**2-4**	**0**	**6.79**

Series Outstanding Player: Jake Powell, New York Yankees. **Series Outstanding Pitcher:** Carl Hubbell, New York Giants. **Average Length of Game:** 2 hours, 33 minutes. **Total Attendance:** 302,924. **Average Attendance:** 50,487 (60,512 at Yankee Stadium; 40,463 at the Polo Grounds). **Umpires:** Harry Geisel (AL), George Magerkurth (NL), Cy Pfirman (NL), Bill Summers (AL). **Winning Player's Share:** $6,431. **Losing Player's Share:** $4,656.

Right: Showing his characteristic leg kick, Mel Ott flies out to center field in the eighth inning of Game 5.

Below: First baseman Bill Terry is unable to snag Travis Jackson's errant throw in the sixth inning of Game 5, allowing Jake Powell to reach base safely. Powell went on to score the tying run.

Left: Red Rolfe slides into third in the third inning of Game 6. He would score on the following play to give the Yanks a 3-2 lead, which they extended to a 13-5 rout in the Series finale.

Game 1 Wednesday, September 30 at the Polo Grounds, New York

	1	2	3	4	5	6	7	8	9	R	H	E
New York Yankees	0	0	1	0	0	0	0	0	0	1	7	2
New York Giants	0	0	0	0	1	1	0	4	x	6	9	1

Pitchers NYY Red Ruffing (L, 0-1), IP 8, H 9, R 6, ER 4, BB 4, SO 5
NYG Carl Hubbell (W, 1-0), IP 9, H 7, R 1, ER 1, BB 1, SO 8

Top Performers at the Plate
NYY Jake Powell, 3 for 4
NYG Dick Bartell, 2 for 4, 1 R, 1 RBI; Mel Ott, 2 for 2, 2 R, 2 BB

2B-NYY/Crosetti, Powell; NYG/Ott. **HR**-NYY/Selkirk; NYG/Bartell. **Time** 2:40. **Attendance** 39,419.

Game 2 Friday, October 2 at the Polo Grounds, New York

	1	2	3	4	5	6	7	8	9	R	H	E
New York Yankees	2	0	7	0	0	1	2	0	6	18	17	0
New York Giants	0	1	0	3	0	0	0	0	0	4	6	1

Pitchers NYY Lefty Gomez (W, 1-0), IP 9, H 6, R 4, ER 4, BB 7, SO 8
NYG Hal Schumacher (L, 0-1), IP 2, H 3, R 5, ER 4, BB 4, SO 1; Al Smith, IP ⅓, H 2, R 3, ER 3, BB 1, SO 0; Dick Coffman, IP 1⅔, H 2, R 1, ER 1, BB 1, SO 1; Frank Gabler, IP 4, H 5, R 3, ER 3, BB 3, SO 0; Harry Gumbert, IP 1, H 5, R 6, ER 6, BB 1, SO 1

Top Performers at the Plate
NYY Bill Dickey, 2 for 5, 3 R, 5 RBI, 1 BB; Joe DiMaggio, 3 for 5, 2 R, 2 RBI, 1 SF
NYG Gus Mancuso, 1 for 2, 2 R, 2 BB; Bill Terry, 2 for 5, 2 RBI

2B-NYY/DiMaggio; NYG/Bartell, Mancuso. **HR**-NYY/Dickey, Lazzeri. **SB**-NYY/Powell. **Time** 2:49. **Attendance** 43,543.

Game 3 Saturday, October 3 at Yankee Stadium, New York

	1	2	3	4	5	6	7	8	9	R	H	E
New York Giants	0	0	0	0	1	0	0	0	0	1	11	0
New York Yankees	0	1	0	0	0	0	0	1	x	2	4	0

Pitchers NYG Freddie Fitzsimmons (L, 0-1), IP 8, H 4, R 2, ER 2, BB 2, SO 5
NYY Bump Hadley (W, 1-0), IP 8, H 10, R 1, ER 1, BB 1, SO 2; Pat Malone (Sv, 1), IP 1, H 1, R 0, ER 0, BB 0, SO 1

Top Performers at the Plate
NYG Freddie Fitzsimmons, 2 for 3; Mel Ott, 2 for 4
NYY Lou Gehrig, 1 for 3, 1 R, 1 RBI

2B-NYY/DiMaggio. **HR**-NYG/Ripple; NYY/Gehrig. **Time** 2:01. **Attendance** 64,842.

Game 4 Sunday, October 4 at Yankee Stadium, New York

	1	2	3	4	5	6	7	8	9	R	H	E
New York Giants	0	0	0	1	0	0	0	1	0	2	7	1
New York Yankees	0	1	3	0	0	0	1	x		5	10	1

Pitchers NYG Carl Hubbell (L, 1-1), IP 7, H 8, R 4, ER 3, BB 1, SO 2; Frank Gabler, IP 1, H 2, R 1, ER 1, BB 1, SO 0
NYY Monte Pearson (W, 1-0), IP 9, H 7, R 2, ER 2, BB 2, SO 7

Top Performers at the Plate
NYG Jimmy Ripple, 2 for 4, 1 RBI
NYY Lou Gehrig, 2 for 4, 2 R, 2 RBI; Red Rolfe, 2 for 3, 1 R, 1 RBI, 1 BB

2B-NYY/Crosetti, Gehrig, Pearson. **HR**-NYY/Gehrig. **Time** 2:12. **Attendance** 66,669.

Game 5 Monday, October 5 at Yankee Stadium, New York

	1	2	3	4	5	6	7	8	9	10	R	H	E
New York Giants	3	0	0	0	0	1	0	0	0	1	5	8	3
New York Yankees	0	1	1	0	2	0	0	0	0	0	4	10	1

Pitchers NYG Hal Schumacher (W, 1-1), IP 10, H 10, R 4, ER 3, BB 6, SO 10
NYY Red Ruffing, IP 6, H 7, R 4, ER 3, BB 1, SO 7; Pat Malone (L, 0-1), IP 4, H 1, R 1, ER 1, BB 1, SO 1

Top Performers at the Plate
NYG Gus Mancuso, 2 for 3, 1 SH; Jo-Jo Moore, 2 for 5, 2 R, 2 2B
NYY Red Rolfe, 2 for 5; George Selkirk, 2 for 4, 2 R, 1 RBI, 1 BB

2B-NYG/Bartell, Mancuso, Moore 2; NYY/DiMaggio. **HR**-NYY/Selkirk. **Time** 2:45. **Attendance** 50,024.

Game 6 Tuesday, October 6 at the Polo Grounds, New York

	1	2	3	4	5	6	7	8	9	R	H	E
New York Yankees	0	2	1	2	0	0	0	1	7	13	17	2
New York Giants	2	0	0	1	0	1	1	0	0	5	9	1

Pitchers NYY Lefty Gomez (W, 2-0), IP 6⅓, H 8, R 4, ER 4, BB 4, SO 1; Johnny Murphy (Sv, 1), IP 2⅔, H 1, R 1, ER 1, BB 1, SO 1
NYG Freddie Fitzsimmons (L, 0-2), IP 3⅔, H 9, R 5, ER 5, BB 0, SO 1; Slick Castleman, IP 4⅓, H 3, R 1, ER 1, BB 2, SO 5; Dick Coffman, IP 0, H 3, R 5, ER 5, BB 1, SO 0; Harry Gumbert, IP 1, H 2, R 2, ER 2, BB 3, SO 1

Top Performers at the Plate
NYY Tony Lazzeri, 3 for 4, 2 R, 1 RBI, 1 BB; Jake Powell, 3 for 5, 3 R, 4 RBI
NYG Dick Bartell, 2 for 3, 2 R, 2 BB; Mel Ott, 2 for 4, 1 R, 3 RBI, 1 BB

2B-NYG/Bartell, Ott. **3B**-NYY/Selkirk. **HR**-NYY/Powell; NYG/Moore, Ott. **Time** 2:50. **Attendance** 38,427.

All nine Yankees had at least one base hit and scored at least one run in their 18-4 trouncing of the Giants in Game 2.

New York Yankees (4) vs. New York Giants (1)

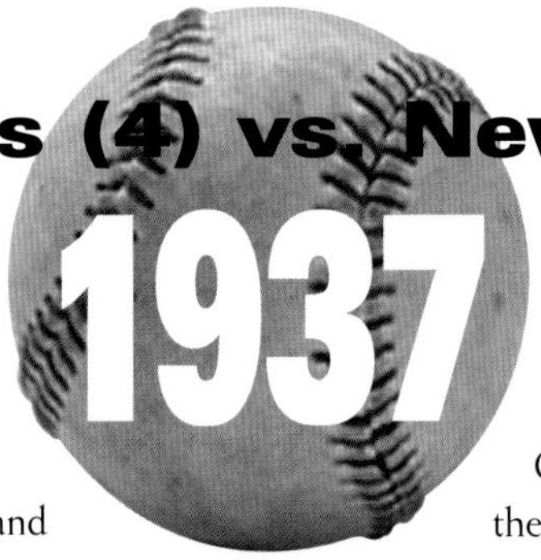

1937

The New York Giants repeated as National League champions in 1937 to set up a rematch with their crosstown foes, the Yankees. The American League pennant winners completed their second straight 102-win season to end with a 13-game margin over second-place Detroit. Once again, the powerful Yanks were led by Lou Gehrig—who hit over .350 and collected more than 150 RBI in the same season for the fifth time in his career—and Joe DiMaggio—whose .346 average, 46 home runs and 167 RBI marked him as one of baseball's best. On the pitching side, Lefty Gomez and Red Ruffing posted the only 20-win performances in the American League. Gomez continued his winning October ways with a 6-hitter in Game 1 of the Series. After being held scoreless by Carl Hubbell with only 1 base hit through five innings, the Yankee hitters scored 7 runs in the sixth, marking the third time in two years that "The Bronx Bombers" scored that many runs in a World Series inning. Tony Lazzeri's home run in the eighth made it the ninth straight Series game for the Yankees in which at least one player homered, a streak dating back to Game 3 in 1932. The Yanks coasted to another 8-1 win in the second game behind Ruffing's 8 strikeouts and 3 runs batted in at the plate. With the scene switching to the Polo Grounds for Game 3, Monte Pearson retired the first 14 Giants he faced and, with last-out help from

reliever Johnny Murphy, held them to a single run for the third game in a row. Hubbell and the Giants avoided a clean sweep at the hands of the Yankees by scoring 6 runs in the second inning of Game 4 and finishing with a 7-3 win. Center fielder Hank Leiber hit two of the Giants' 6 singles in the inning. A ninth-inning face-off between Hubbell and Gehrig saw the Iron Horse hit his 10th and last World Series home run in Hubbell's last World Series inning. Mel Ott's 2-run home run in the third inning was the only scoring that the Giants could pull off against Gomez in Game 5. Joe DiMaggio recorded his 1st World Series homer in the game, a solo shot in the third, and the light-hitting Gomez helped his own cause with an RBI single in the fifth. For the second year in a row, the Yankees outscored their opponents by a wide margin, and for the first time ever, by any team, they played the entire Series without committing a single error. Often lost in the star-packed Yankee lineup, George Selkirk, who had replaced Ruth as the regular right fielder in 1935, drove in 6 runs and scored 5, and Tony Lazzeri closed out his prestigious Yankee career with a Series-best .400 average.

Above: Lefty Gomez (left) and Red Ruffing (right) won a combined eight Series games in the Yankees' four titles from 1936 to 1939. Gomez took two games in 1937 and Ruffing one.

1937 WORLD SERIES COMPOSITE STATISTICS

NEW YORK YANKEES/Joe McCarthy, Manager

Player	pos	G	AB	R	H	2B	3B	HR	RBI	BB	SO	SB	BA	SA	E	FPct
Ivy Andrews	p	1	2	0	0	0	0	0	0	0	1	0	.000	.000	0	1.000
Frankie Crosetti	ss	5	21	2	1	0	0	0	0	3	2	0	.048	.048	0	1.000
Bill Dickey	c	5	19	3	4	0	1	0	3	2	2	0	.211	.316	0	1.000
Joe DiMaggio	cf	5	22	2	6	0	0	1	4	0	3	0	.273	.409	0	1.000
Lou Gehrig	1b	5	17	4	5	1	1	1	3	5	4	0	.294	.647	0	1.000
Lefty Gomez	p	2	6	2	1	0	0	0	1	2	1	0	.167	.167	0	1.000
Bump Hadley	p	1	0	0	0	0	0	0	0	0	0	0	–	–	0	–
Myril Hoag	lf	5	20	4	6	1	0	1	2	0	1	0	.300	.500	0	1.000
Tony Lazzeri	2b	5	15	3	6	0	1	1	2	3	3	0	.400	.733	0	1.000
Johnny Murphy	p	1	0	0	0	0	0	0	0	0	0	0	–	–	0	–
Monte Pearson	p	1	3	0	0	0	0	0	0	1	1	0	.000	.000	0	–
Jake Powell	ph	1	1	0	0	0	0	0	0	0	1	0	.000	.000	–	–
Red Rolfe	3b	5	20	3	6	2	1	0	1	3	2	0	.300	.500	0	1.000
Red Ruffing	p	1	4	0	2	1	0	0	3	0	0	0	.500	.750	0	1.000
George Selkirk	rf	5	19	5	5	1	0	0	6	2	0	0	.263	.316	0	1.000
Kemp Wicker	p	1	0	0	0	0	0	0	0	0	0	0	–	–	0	–
Totals		5	169	28	42	6	4	4	25	21	21	0	.249	.402	0	1.000

Pitcher	G	GS	CG	IP	H	R	ER	BB	SO	W-L	Sv	ERA
Ivy Andrews	1	0	0	5⅔	6	2	2	4	1	0-0	0	3.18
Lefty Gomez	2	2	2	18	16	3	3	2	8	2-0	0	1.50
Bump Hadley	1	1	0	1⅓	6	5	5	0	0	0-1	0	33.75
Johnny Murphy	1	0	0	⅓	0	0	0	0	0	0-0	1	0.00
Monte Pearson	1	1	0	8⅔	5	1	1	2	4	1-0	0	1.04
Red Ruffing	1	1	1	9	7	1	1	3	8	1-0	0	1.00
Kemp Wicker	1	0	0	1	0	0	0	0	0	0-0	0	0.00
Totals	5	5	3	44	40	12	12	11	21	4-1	1	2.45

NEW YORK GIANTS/Bill Terry, Manager

Player	pos	G	AB	R	H	2B	3B	HR	RBI	BB	SO	SB	BA	SA	E	FPct
Dick Bartell	ss	5	21	3	5	1	0	0	1	0	3	0	.238	.286	3	.889
Wally Berger	ph	3	3	0	0	0	0	0	0	0	1	0	.000	.000	–	–
Don Brennan	p	2	0	0	0	0	0	0	0	0	0	0	–	–	0	–
Lou Chiozza	cf	2	7	0	2	0	0	0	0	1	1	0	.286	.286	1	.857
Dick Coffman	p	2	1	0	0	0	0	0	0	0	1	0	.000	.000	0	1.000
Harry Danning	c	3	12	0	3	1	0	0	2	0	2	0	.250	.333	0	1.000
Harry Gumbert	p	2	0	0	0	0	0	0	0	0	0	0	–	–	0	–
Carl Hubbell	p	2	6	1	0	0	0	0	1	0	0	0	.000	.000	0	1.000
Hank Leiber	cf	3	11	2	4	0	0	0	2	1	1	0	.364	.364	0	1.000
Sam Leslie	ph	2	1	0	0	0	0	0	0	1	0	0	.000	.000	–	–
Gus Mancuso	c-ph	3	8	0	0	0	0	0	0	1	0	0	.000	.000	0	1.000
Johnny McCarthy	1b	5	19	1	4	1	0	0	1	1	2	0	.211	.263	2	.951
Cliff Melton	p	3	2	0	0	0	0	0	0	0	1	0	.000	.000	1	1.000
Jo-Jo Moore	lf	5	23	1	9	1	0	0	1	0	1	0	.391	.435	0	1.000
Mel Ott	3b	5	20	1	4	0	0	1	3	1	4	0	.200	.350	1	.933
Jimmy Ripple	rf	5	17	2	5	0	0	0	0	3	1	0	.294	.294	0	1.000
Blondy Ryan	ph	1	1	0	0	0	0	0	0	0	1	0	.000	.000	–	–
Hal Schumacher	p	1	0	0	0	0	0	0	0	0	1	0	.000	.000	0	1.000
Al Smith	p	2	0	0	0	0	0	0	0	0	0	0	–	–	0	1.000
Burgess Whitehead	2b	5	16	1	4	2	0	0	2	0	1	1	.250	.375	1	.962
Totals		5	169	12	40	6	0	1	11	11	21	1	.237	.290	9	.951

Pitcher	G	GS	CG	IP	H	R	ER	BB	SO	W-L	Sv	ERA
Don Brennan	2	0	0	3	1	0	0	1	1	0-0	0	0.00
Dick Coffman	2	0	0	4⅓	2	2	2	5	1	0-0	0	4.15
Harry Gumbert	2	0	0	1⅓	4	4	4	1	1	0-0	0	27.00
Carl Hubbell	2	2	1	14⅓	12	10	6	4	7	1-1	0	3.77
Cliff Melton	3	2	0	11	12	6	6	6	7	0-2	0	4.91
Hal Schumacher	1	1	0	6	9	5	4	4	3	0-1	0	6.00
Al Smith	2	0	0	3	2	1	1	0	1	0-0	0	3.00
Totals	5	5	1	43	42	28	23	21	21	1-4	0	4.81

Series Outstanding Player: Lefty Gomez, New York Yankees. **Series Outstanding Pitcher:** Lefty Gomez, New York Yankees. **Average Length of Game:** 2 hours, 8 minutes. **Total Attendance:** 238,142. **Average Attendance:** 47,628 (59,124 at Yankee Stadium; 39,965 at the Polo Grounds). **Umpires:** George Barr (NL), Steve Basil (AL), Red Ormsby (AL), Bill Stewart (NL). **Winning Player's Share:** $6,471. **Losing Player's Share:** $4,490.

In the Yankees' seven-run sixth inning in Game 1, pitcher Lefty Gomez received two bases-on-balls in the inning.

Right: In his final season as a Yankee, Tony Lazzeri contributed a .400 average in the 1937 Series, including this Game 1 homer.

Above: Batter Joe DiMaggio, catcher Harry Danning and umpire Red Ormsby follow the flight of DiMaggio's third-inning shot into the bleachers in Game 5. It was Joltin' Joe's first World Series homer.

Right: In Game 3, a bobbled grounder and poor throw by Giants first baseman Johnny McCarthy allows George Selkirk to reach second base. Selkirk eventually scored, for one of his five Series runs.

Game 1   Wednesday, October 6 at Yankee Stadium, New York

	1	2	3	4	5	6	7	8	9	R	H	E
New York Giants	0	0	0	0	1	0	0	0	0	1	6	2
New York Yankees	0	0	0	0	0	7	0	1	x	8	7	0

Pitchers   NYG Carl Hubbell (L, 0-1), IP 5⅓, H 6, R 7, ER 4, BB 3, SO 3; Harry Gumbert, IP 0, H 0, R 0, ER 0, BB 0, SO 0; Dick Coffman, IP 1⅔, H 0, R 0, ER 0, BB 4, SO 0; Al Smith, IP 1, H 1, R 1, ER 1, BB 0, SO 0; NYY Lefty Gomez (W, 1-0), IP 9, H 6, R 1, ER 1, BB 1, SO 2

Top Performers at the Plate
NYG Jo-Jo Moore, 2 for 4
NYY Bill Dickey, 1 for 3, 1 R, 1 RBI, 1 BB; Joe DiMaggio, 2 for 4, 2 RBI

2B-NYG/Whitehead. **HR**-NYY/Lazzeri. **Time** 2:20. **Attendance** 60,573.

Game 2   Thursday, October 7 at Yankee Stadium, New York

	1	2	3	4	5	6	7	8	9	R	H	E
New York Giants	1	0	0	0	0	0	0	0	0	1	7	0
New York Yankees	0	0	0	0	2	4	2	0	x	8	12	0

Pitchers   NYG Cliff Melton (L, 0-1), IP 4, H 6, R 2, ER 2, BB 1, SO 2; Harry Gumbert, IP 1⅓, H 4, R 4, ER 4, BB 1, SO 1; Dick Coffman, IP 2⅔, H 2, R 2, ER 2, BB 1, SO 1; NYY Red Ruffing (W, 1-0), IP 9, H 7, R 1, ER 1, BB 3, SO 8

Top Performers at the Plate
NYG Dick Bartell, 2 for 4, 1 R; Jo-Jo Moore, 2 for 5
NYY Red Ruffing, 2 for 4, 3 RBI; George Selkirk, 2 for 4, 2 R, 3 RBI

2B-NYG/Bartell, Moore; NYY/Hoag, Ruffing, Selkirk. **Time** 2:11. **Attendance** 57,675.

Game 3   Friday, October 8 at the Polo Grounds, New York

	1	2	3	4	5	6	7	8	9	R	H	E
New York Yankees	0	1	2	1	1	0	0	0	0	5	9	0
New York Giants	0	0	0	0	0	0	1	0	0	1	5	4

Pitchers   NYY Monte Pearson (W, 1-0), IP 8⅔, H 5, R 1, ER 1, BB 2, SO 4; Johnny Murphy (Sv, 1), IP ⅓, H 0, R 0, ER 0, BB 0, SO 0; NYG Hal Schumacher (L, 0-1), IP 6, H 9, R 5, ER 4, BB 4, SO 3; Cliff Melton, IP 2, H 0, R 0, ER 0, BB 2, SO 0; Don Brennan, IP 1, H 0, R 0, ER 0, BB 0, SO 0

Top Performers at the Plate
NYY Red Rolfe, 2 for 4, 1 R, 1 BB, 2 2B; George Selkirk, 1 for 4, 2 R, 1 RBI, 1 BB
NYG Johnny McCarthy, 1 for 3, 1 RBI, 1 BB

2B-NYY/Rolfe 2; NYG/McCarthy. **3B**-NYY/Dickey. **Time** 2:07. **Attendance** 37,385.

Game 4   Saturday, October 9 at the Polo Grounds, New York

	1	2	3	4	5	6	7	8	9	R	H	E
New York Yankees	1	0	1	0	0	0	0	0	1	3	6	0
New York Giants	0	6	0	0	0	1	0	x		7	12	3

Pitchers   NYY Bump Hadley (L, 0-1), IP 1⅓, H 6, R 5, ER 5, BB 0, SO 0; Ivy Andrews, IP 5⅔, H 6, R 2, ER 2, BB 4, SO 1; Kemp Wicker, IP 1, H 0, R 0, ER 0, BB 0, SO 0; NYG Carl Hubbell (W, 1-1), IP 9, H 6, R 3, ER 2, BB 1, SO 4

Top Performers at the Plate
NYY Myril Hoag, 2 for 4; Red Rolfe, 2 for 4, 1 R
NYG Harry Danning, 3 for 4, 2 RBI; Hank Leiber, 2 for 3, 2 R, 2 RBI, 1 BB

2B-NYG/Danning. **3B**-NYY/Rolfe. **HR**-NYY/Gehrig. **SB**-NYG/Whitehead. **Time** 1:57. **Attendance** 44,293.

Game 5   Sunday, October 10 at the Polo Grounds, New York

	1	2	3	4	5	6	7	8	9	R	H	E
New York Yankees	0	1	1	0	2	0	0	0	0	4	8	0
New York Giants	0	0	2	0	0	0	0	0	0	2	10	0

Pitchers   NYY Lefty Gomez (W, 2-0), IP 9, H 10, R 2, ER 2, BB 1, SO 6; NYG Cliff Melton (L, 0-2), IP 5, H 6, R 4, ER 4, BB 3, SO 5; Al Smith, IP 2, H 1, R 0, ER 0, BB 0, SO 1; Don Brennan, IP 2, H 1, R 0, ER 0, BB 1, SO 1

Top Performers at the Plate
NYY Lou Gehrig, 2 for 4, 1 RBI, 1 BB
NYG Jo-Jo Moore, 3 for 5; Mel Ott, 1 for 3, 1 R, 2 RBI, 1 BB

2B-NYY/Gehrig; NYG/Whitehead. **3B**-NYY/Gehrig, Lazzeri. **HR**-NYY/DiMaggio, Hoag; NYG/Ott. **Time** 2:06. **Attendance** 38,216.

New York Yankees (4) vs. Chicago Cubs (0)

1938

The Chicago Cubs finished 1938 with a two-game edge in the National League, having grabbed first place from the Pittsburgh Pirates in dramatic fashion during the last week of the season. The pennant earned them the right to face the New York Yankees in the World Series for the second time in the decade. The Yankees fell one game short of a third straight 100-win season, but 99 victories was more than enough to claim the pennant. They returned to their third straight Fall Classic with two new additions to the starting line-up, and newcomer Joe Gordon provided an immediate impact with his six RBI and .400 average in the World Series. Just like in 1932, Red Ruffing won the Series opener for New York with a complete-game performance. Bill Dickey went 4 for 4 on the day, scoring one run and driving in another. Chicago had acquired former Cardinal All-Star Dizzy Dean in the off-season, and Dean got the start against Lefty Gomez in Game 2. He kept the Yankees in check with his off-speed pitches, allowing only three hits through seven. A Joe Marty double in the third inning put the Cubs up 3-2, but two-run homers by the light-hitting Frankie Crosetti in the eighth and Joe DiMaggio in the ninth put New York ahead for a 6-3 final. It was Gomez's sixth win in six World Series games in his career. Johnny Murphy pitched two shutout innings to earn the save in the only noncomplete game by a Yankee starter. In Game 3, Chicago's Clay Bryant didn't give up any base hits for the first 4 2/3 innings, but then was knocked for six hits and four runs before the being yanked in the sixth. Monte Pearson, meanwhile, held the Cubs to just five hits and struck out nine. Gordon got the Yankee offense going with a solo homer in the fifth and then added a two-run single in the sixth, giving him three RBI on the day. The Yankees' other new starter, Tommy Henrich, contributed a solo home run in the sixth inning of Game 4, and Crosetti knocked home four runs in the game, including a bases-clearing triple in the second. Ruffing's eight-hitter gave New York the sweep and Ruffing his second win of the Series. The New York Yankees became the first team ever to win three World Series in a row, while the Cubs suffered their sixth straight October defeat, punctuated by another four-game sweep at the hands of New York.

Lou Gehrig went homer-less in the final World Series of his career, though he scored a run in each of the four games.

Above: Lou Gehrig scores the first run of the 1938 World Series in the second inning of the opener. It would be the Iron Horse's final Series, as illness forced him into retirement in 1939.

1938 WORLD SERIES COMPOSITE STATISTICS

NEW YORK YANKEES/Joe McCarthy, Manager

Player	pos	G	AB	R	H	2B	3B	HR	RBI	BB	SO	SB	BA	SA	E	FPct
Frankie Crosetti	ss	4	16	1	4	2	1	1	6	2	4	0	.250	.688	1	.964
Bill Dickey	c	4	15	2	6	0	0	1	2	1	0	1	.400	.600	0	1.000
Joe DiMaggio	cf	4	15	4	4	0	0	1	2	1	1	0	.267	.467	0	1.000
Lou Gehrig	1b	4	14	4	4	0	0	0	0	2	3	0	.286	.286	0	1.000
Lefty Gomez	p	1	2	0	0	0	0	0	0	0	0	0	.000	.000	0	1.000
Joe Gordon	2b	4	15	3	6	2	0	1	6	1	3	1	.400	.733	2	.920
Tommy Henrich	rf	4	16	3	4	1	0	1	1	0	1	0	.250	.500	1	.857
Myril Hoag	ph-lf	2	5	3	2	1	0	0	1	0	0	0	.400	.600	0	1.000
Johnny Murphy	p	1	0	0	0	0	0	0	0	0	0	0	—	—	0	—
Monte Pearson	p	1	3	1	1	0	0	0	1	0	1	0	.333	.333	0	1.000
Jake Powell	lf	1	0	0	0	0	0	0	0	0	0	0	—	—	0	—
Red Rolfe	3b	4	18	0	3	0	0	0	1	0	3	1	.167	.167	2	.667
Red Ruffing	p	2	6	1	1	0	0	0	1	1	0	0	.167	.167	0	1.000
George Selkirk	lf	3	10	0	2	0	0	0	1	2	1	0	.200	.200	0	1.000
Totals		4	135	22	37	6	1	5	21	11	16	3	.274	.444	6	.961

Pitcher	G	GS	CG	IP	H	R	ER	BB	SO	W-L	Sv	ERA
Lefty Gomez	1	1	0	7	9	3	3	1	5	1-0	0	3.86
Johnny Murphy	1	0	0	2	2	0	0	1	1	0-0	1	0.00
Monte Pearson	1	1	1	9	5	2	1	2	9	1-0	0	1.00
Red Ruffing	2	2	2	18	17	4	3	2	11	2-0	0	1.50
Totals	4	4	3	36	33	9	7	6	26	4-0	1	1.75

CHICAGO CUBS/Gabby Hartnett, Manager

Player	pos	G	AB	R	H	2B	3B	HR	RBI	BB	SO	SB	BA	SA	E	FPct
Clay Bryant	p	1	2	0	0	0	0	0	0	0	1	0	.000	.000	0	—
Tex Carleton	p	1	0	0	0	0	0	0	0	0	0	0	—	—	0	—
Phil Cavarretta	rf-ph	4	13	1	6	1	0	0	0	0	1	0	.462	.538	0	1.000
Ripper Collins	1b	4	15	1	2	0	0	0	0	0	3	0	.133	.133	0	1.000
Dizzy Dean	p	2	3	0	2	0	0	0	0	0	0	0	.667	.667	0	1.000
Frank Demaree	lf-rf	3	10	1	1	0	0	0	0	1	2	0	.100	.100	0	1.000
Larry French	p	3	0	0	0	0	0	0	0	0	0	0	—	—	0	1.000
Augie Galan	ph	2	2	0	0	0	0	0	0	0	1	0	.000	.000	0	—
Stan Hack	3b	4	17	3	8	1	0	0	1	1	2	0	.471	.529	0	1.000
Gabby Hartnett	c	3	11	0	1	0	1	0	0	2	0	0	.091	.273	0	1.000
Billy Herman	2b	4	16	1	3	0	0	0	1	0	4	0	.188	.188	2	.909
Billy Jurges	ss	4	13	0	3	1	0	0	1	3	0	0	.231	.308	1	.947
Tony Lazzeri	ph	2	2	0	0	0	0	0	0	1	0	0	.000	.000	0	—
Bill Lee	p	2	3	0	0	0	0	0	0	0	1	0	.000	.000	0	1.000
Joe Marty	cf	3	12	1	6	1	0	1	5	0	2	0	.500	.833	0	1.000
Ken O'Dea	ph-c	3	5	1	1	0	0	0	1	2	1	0	.200	.800	0	1.000
Vince Page	p	1	0	0	0	0	0	0	0	0	0	0	—	—	0	1.000
Carl Reynolds	cf-lf-ph	4	12	0	0	0	0	0	0	1	3	0	.000	.000	0	1.000
Charlie Root	p	1	0	0	0	0	0	0	0	0	0	0	—	—	0	—
Jack Russell	p	2	0	0	0	0	0	0	0	0	0	0	—	—	0	—
Totals		4	136	9	33	4	1	2	8	6	26	0	.243	.331	3	.979

Pitcher	G	GS	CG	IP	H	R	ER	BB	SO	W-L	Sv	ERA
Clay Bryant	1	1	0	5 1/3	6	4	4	5	3	0-1	0	6.75
Tex Carleton	1	0	0	0	1	2	2	2	0	0-0	0	—
Dizzy Dean	2	1	0	8 1/3	8	6	6	1	2	0-1	0	6.48
Larry French	3	0	0	3 1/3	1	1	1	1	2	0-0	0	2.70
Bill Lee	2	2	0	11	15	6	3	1	8	0-2	0	2.45
Vance Page	1	0	0	1 1/3	2	2	2	0	0	0-0	0	13.50
Charlie Root	1	0	0	3	3	1	1	0	1	0-0	0	3.00
Jack Russell	2	0	0	1 2/3	1	0	0	1	0	0-0	0	0.00
Totals	4	4	0	34	37	22	19	11	16	0-4	0	5.03

Series Outstanding Player: Joe Gordon, New York Yankees. **Series Outstanding Pitcher:** Red Ruffing, New York Yankees. **Average Length of Game:** 1 hour, 59 minutes. **Total Attendance:** 200,833. **Average Attendance:** 50,208 (57,542 at Yankee Stadium; 42,875 at Wrigley Field). **Umpires:** Cal Hubbard (AL), Lou Kolls (AL), Charlie Moran (NL), John Sears (NL). **Winning Player's Share:** $5,783. **Losing Player's Share:** $4,675.

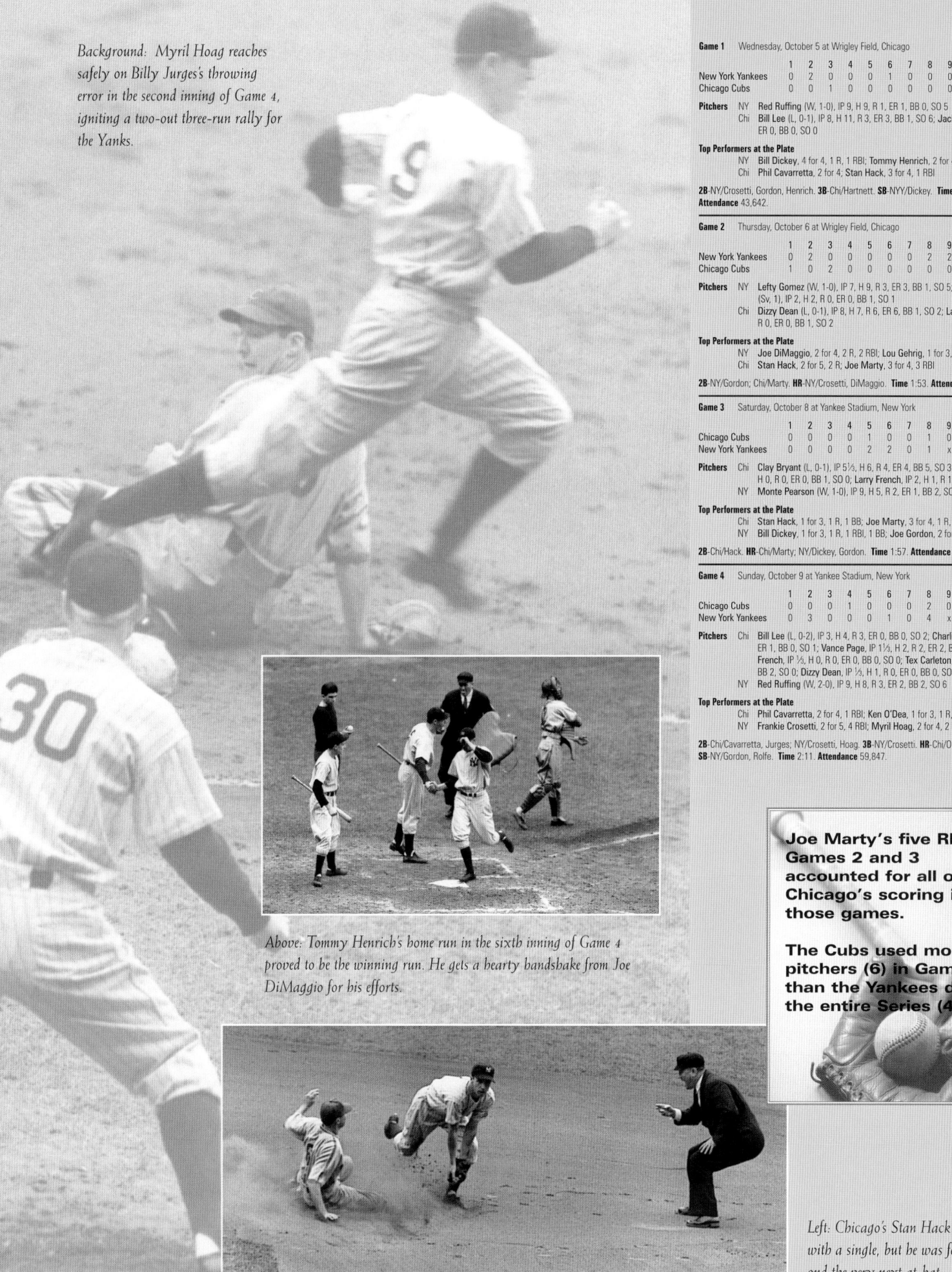

Background: Myril Hoag reaches safely on Billy Jurges's throwing error in the second inning of Game 4, igniting a two-out three-run rally for the Yanks.

Game 1 Wednesday, October 5 at Wrigley Field, Chicago

	1	2	3	4	5	6	7	8	9	R	H	E
New York Yankees	0	2	0	0	0	1	0	0	0	3	12	1
Chicago Cubs	0	0	1	0	0	0	0	0	0	1	9	1

Pitchers NY Red Ruffing (W, 1-0), IP 9, H 9, R 1, ER 1, BB 0, SO 5
Chi Bill Lee (L, 0-1), IP 8, H 11, R 3, ER 3, BB 1, SO 6; Jack Russell, IP 1, H 1, R 0, ER 0, BB 0, SO 0

Top Performers at the Plate
NY Bill Dickey, 4 for 4, 1 R, 1 RBI; Tommy Henrich, 2 for 4, 1 R
Chi Phil Cavarretta, 2 for 4; Stan Hack, 3 for 4, 1 RBI

2B-NY/Crosetti, Gordon, Henrich. **3B**-Chi/Hartnett. **SB**-NY/Dickey. **Time** 1:53. **Attendance** 43,642.

Game 2 Thursday, October 6 at Wrigley Field, Chicago

	1	2	3	4	5	6	7	8	9	R	H	E
New York Yankees	0	2	0	0	0	0	0	2	2	6	7	2
Chicago Cubs	1	0	2	0	0	0	0	0	0	3	11	0

Pitchers NY Lefty Gomez (W, 1-0), IP 7, H 9, R 3, ER 3, BB 1, SO 5; Johnny Murphy (Sv, 1), IP 2, H 2, R 0, ER 0, BB 1, SO 1
Chi Dizzy Dean (L, 0-1), IP 8, H 7, R 6, ER 6, BB 1, SO 2; Larry French, IP 1, H 0, R 0, ER 0, BB 1, SO 2

Top Performers at the Plate
NY Joe DiMaggio, 2 for 4, 2 R, 2 RBI; Lou Gehrig, 1 for 3, 1 R, 1 BB
Chi Stan Hack, 2 for 5, 2 R; Joe Marty, 3 for 4, 3 RBI

2B-NY/Gordon; Chi/Marty. **HR**-NY/Crosetti, DiMaggio. **Time** 1:53. **Attendance** 42,108.

Game 3 Saturday, October 8 at Yankee Stadium, New York

	1	2	3	4	5	6	7	8	9	R	H	E
Chicago Cubs	0	0	0	0	1	0	0	1	0	2	5	1
New York Yankees	0	0	0	0	2	2	0	1	x	5	7	2

Pitchers Chi Clay Bryant (L, 0-1), IP 5⅓, H 6, R 4, ER 4, BB 5, SO 3; Jack Russell, IP ⅔, H 0, R 0, ER 0, BB 1, SO 0; Larry French, IP 2, H 1, R 1, ER 1, BB 0, SO 0
NY Monte Pearson (W, 1-0), IP 9, H 5, R 2, ER 1, BB 2, SO 9

Top Performers at the Plate
Chi Stan Hack, 1 for 3, 1 R, 1 BB; Joe Marty, 3 for 4, 1 R, 2 RBI
NY Bill Dickey, 1 for 3, 1 R, 1 RBI, 1 BB; Joe Gordon, 2 for 4, 1 R, 3 RBI

2B-Chi/Hack. **HR**-Chi/Marty; NY/Dickey, Gordon. **Time** 1:57. **Attendance** 55,236.

Game 4 Sunday, October 9 at Yankee Stadium, New York

	1	2	3	4	5	6	7	8	9	R	H	E
Chicago Cubs	0	0	0	1	0	0	0	2	0	3	8	1
New York Yankees	3	0	0	0	1	0	4	x		8	11	1

Pitchers Chi Bill Lee (L, 0-2), IP 3, H 4, R 3, ER 0, BB 0, SO 2; Charlie Root, IP 3, H 3, R 1, ER 1, BB 0, SO 1; Vance Page, IP 1⅓, H 2, R 2, ER 2, BB 0, SO 0; Larry French, IP ⅓, H 0, R 0, ER 0, BB 0, SO 0; Tex Carleton, IP 0, H 1, R 2, ER 2, BB 2, SO 0; Dizzy Dean, IP ⅓, H 1, R 0, ER 0, BB 0, SO 0
NY Red Ruffing (W, 2-0), IP 9, H 8, R 3, ER 2, BB 2, SO 6

Top Performers at the Plate
Chi Phil Cavarretta, 2 for 4, 1 RBI; Ken O'Dea, 1 for 3, 1 R, 2 RBI, 1 BB
NY Frankie Crosetti, 2 for 5, 4 RBI; Myril Hoag, 2 for 4, 2 R, 1 RBI

2B-Chi/Cavarretta, Jurges; NY/Crosetti, Hoag. **3B**-NY/Crosetti. **HR**-Chi/O'Dea; NY/Henrich. **SB**-NY/Gordon, Rolfe. **Time** 2:11. **Attendance** 59,847.

Above: Tommy Henrich's home run in the sixth inning of Game 4 proved to be the winning run. He gets a hearty handshake from Joe DiMaggio for his efforts.

Joe Marty's five RBI in Games 2 and 3 accounted for all of Chicago's scoring in those games.

The Cubs used more pitchers (6) in Game 4 than the Yankees did in the entire Series (4).

Left: Chicago's Stan Hack led off Game 4 with a single, but he was forced out at second the very next at-bat.

New York Yankees (4) vs. Cincinnati Reds (0)

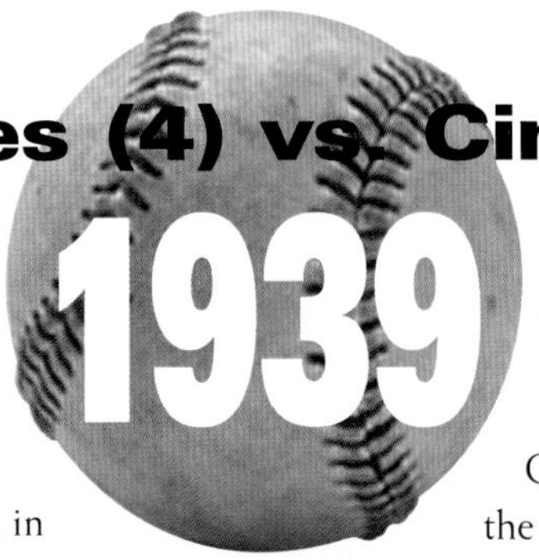

Despite losing Lou Gehrig to a debilitating muscle disorder midway through the season, Joe McCarthy's Yankees continued their incredible run of four consecutive pennants with a 106-win season and a 17-game lead over the next-best finisher. And they continued their incredible October streak with a fourth World Series win in as many years. Manager Bill McKechnie had a very good club in Cincinnati, winning 97 games and boasting the 2 winningest pitchers in baseball, but they were simply no match. Although the teams collected the same number of hits in the Series, the Yankees parlayed it into 20 runs, whereas Cincinnati brought only 8 runners across the plate. The Reds went the first 3 games without an extra-base hit, and though they outhit the Yankees in Game 3, 4 of New York's 5 hits were home runs. New York also claimed victory in quick fashion, with the games averaging 1 hour and 46 minutes—the shortest average since 1908 and the quickest ever for a 4-game series. Things started off well enough for the Reds, as Game 1 starter Paul Derringer retired the first 8 batters he faced, and Frank McCormick drove in the 1st run with a single in the 4th. But after giving up a leadoff single in the 5th inning, Red Ruffing shut down the last 14 Reds in order. A triple by rookie Charlie Keller and a single by Bill

Dickey broke a 1-1 tie in the bottom of the 9th to give New York the opener. In Game 2, Monte Pearson held the Reds hitless until the 8th inning and ended up allowing just 2 hits and 1 walk for a 4-0 win. Relieving Lefty Gomez in Game 3 after 1 inning, Bump Hadley pitched the next 8 innings, and shut the Reds out for the final 7 of those. A 2-run homer by Keller in the 1st, a 2-run blast by Joe DiMaggio in the 3rd, another 2-run shot by Keller and a solo one by Dickey, both in the 5th inning, accounted for all the Yankees' scoring. Both sides had 4 runs through 9 innings in Game 4, until New York put runners on first and third with 1 out in the top of the 10th. DiMaggio hit a single to right field, scoring Frankie Crosetti easily from third. Ival Goodman's bobble in right allowed Keller to come around from first, with Keller and the ball arriving at home plate simultaneously. Keller collided with catcher Ernie Lombardi, knocking the ball out of his glove and Lombardi to the ground. As the stunned catcher lay in a daze, DiMaggio circled all the way around the

Above: This triple by Charlie Keller came with the opening game tied 1-1 in the ninth. He scored the winning run two batters later, giving his team the Series edge and launching a superb four games by the Yankee outfielder.

1939 WORLD SERIES COMPOSITE STATISTICS

NEW YORK YANKEES/Joe McCarthy, Manager

Player	pos	G	AB	R	H	2B	3B	HR	RBI	BB	SO	SB	BA	SA	E	FPct
Frankie Crosetti	ss	4	16	2	1	0	0	0	1	2	2	0	.063	.063	0	1.000
Babe Dahlgren	1b	4	14	2	3	2	0	1	2	0	4	0	.214	.571	0	1.000
Bill Dickey	c	4	15	2	4	0	0	2	5	1	2	0	.267	.667	0	1.000
Joe DiMaggio	cf	4	16	3	5	0	0	1	3	1	1	0	.313	.500	0	1.000
Lefty Gomez	p	1	1	0	0	0	0	0	0	0	1	0	.000	.000	0	—
Joe Gordon	2b	4	14	1	2	0	0	0	1	0	2	0	.143	.143	0	1.000
Bump Hadley	p	1	3	0	0	0	0	0	0	0	0	0	.000	.000	1	.667
Oral Hildebrand	p	1	1	0	0	0	0	0	0	0	1	0	.000	.000	0	—
Charlie Keller	rf	4	16	8	7	1	1	3	6	1	2	0	.438	1.188	0	1.000
Johnny Murphy	p	1	2	0	0	0	0	0	0	1	0	0	.000	.000	0	1.000
Monte Pearson	p	1	2	0	0	0	0	0	0	0	1	0	.000	.000	0	1.000
Red Rolfe	3b	4	16	2	2	0	0	0	0	0	0	0	.125	.125	1	.923
Red Ruffing	p	1	3	0	1	0	0	0	0	0	1	0	.333	.333	0	1.000
George Selkirk	lf	4	12	0	2	1	0	0	3	2	0	0	.167	.250	0	1.000
Steve Sundra	p	1	0	0	0	0	0	0	0	1	0	0	—	—	0	—
Totals		**4**	**131**	**20**	**27**	**4**	**1**	**7**	**18**	**9**	**20**	**0**	**.206**	**.412**	**2**	**.988**

Pitcher	G	GS	CG	IP	H	R	ER	BB	SO	W-L	Sv	ERA
Lefty Gomez	1	1	0	1	3	1	1	0	1	0-0	0	9.00
Bump Hadley	1	0	0	8	7	2	2	3	2	1-0	0	2.25
Oral Hildebrand	1	1	0	4	2	0	0	0	3	0-0	0	0.00
Johnny Murphy	1	0	0	3⅓	5	1	1	0	2	1-0	0	2.70
Monte Pearson	1	1	1	9	2	0	0	1	8	1-0	0	0.00
Red Ruffing	1	1	1	9	4	1	1	1	4	1-0	0	1.00
Steve Sundra	1	0	0	2⅔	4	3	0	1	2	0-0	0	0.00
Totals	**4**	**4**	**2**	**37**	**27**	**8**	**5**	**6**	**22**	**4-0**	**0**	**1.22**

CINCINNATI REDS/Bill McKechnie, Manager

Player	pos	G	AB	R	H	2B	3B	HR	RBI	BB	SO	SB	BA	SA	E	FPct
Wally Berger	lf-cf	4	15	0	0	0	0	0	1	0	4	0	.000	.000	0	1.000
Nino Bongiovanni	ph	1	1	0	0	0	0	0	0	0	0	0	.000	.000	—	—
Frenchy Bordagaray	pr	2	0	0	0	0	0	0	0	0	0	0	—	—	—	—
Harry Craft	cf	4	11	0	1	0	0	0	0	0	6	0	.091	.091	0	1.000
Paul Derringer	p	2	5	0	1	0	0	0	1	0	0	0	.200	.200	0	1.000
Lonny Frey	2b	4	17	0	0	0	0	0	0	1	4	0	.000	.000	0	1.000
Lee Gamble	ph	1	1	0	0	0	0	0	0	0	0	1	0	.000	—	—
Ival Goodman	rf	4	15	3	5	1	0	0	1	1	2	1	.333	.400	1	.929
Lee Grissom	p	1	0	0	0	0	0	0	0	0	0	0	—	—	0	—
Willard Hershberger	c-ph	3	2	0	1	0	0	0	1	0	0	0	.500	.500	0	1.000
Ernie Lombardi	c	4	14	0	3	0	0	0	2	0	1	0	.214	.214	1	.958
Frank McCormick	1b	4	15	1	6	1	0	0	1	0	1	0	.400	.467	0	1.000
Whitey Moore	p	1	1	0	0	0	0	0	0	0	0	0	.000	.000	0	1.000
Billy Myers	ss	4	12	2	4	0	1	0	0	2	3	0	.333	.500	2	.895
Al Simmons	lf	1	4	1	1	1	0	0	0	0	0	0	.250	.500	0	1.000
Junior Thompson	p	1	1	0	1	0	0	0	0	0	0	0	1.000	1.000	0	—
Bucky Walters	p	2	3	0	0	0	0	0	0	0	0	0	.000	.000	0	1.000
Bill Werber	3b	4	16	1	4	0	0	0	2	2	0	0	.250	.250	0	1.000
Totals		**4**	**133**	**8**	**27**	**3**	**1**	**0**	**8**	**6**	**22**	**1**	**.203**	**.241**	**4**	**.972**

Pitcher	G	GS	CG	IP	H	R	ER	BB	SO	W-L	Sv	ERA
Paul Derringer	2	2	1	15⅓	9	4	4	3	9	0-1	0	2.35
Lee Grissom	1	0	0	1⅓	0	0	0	0	1	0-0	0	0.00
Whitey Moore	1	0	0	3	0	0	0	0	2	0-0	0	0.00
Junior Thompson	1	1	0	4⅔	5	7	7	4	3	0-1	0	13.50
Bucky Walters	2	1	1	11	13	9	6	1	6	0-2	0	4.91
Totals	**4**	**4**	**2**	**35⅓**	**27**	**20**	**17**	**9**	**20**	**0-4**	**0**	**4.33**

Series Outstanding Player: Charlie Keller, New York Yankees. **Series Outstanding Pitcher:** Monte Pearson, New York Yankees. **Average Length of Game:** 1 hour, 46 minutes. **Total Attendance:** 183,849. **Average Attendance:** 45,962 (59,166 at Yankee Stadium; 32,759 at Crosley Field). **Umpires:** Bill McGowan (AL), Babe Pinelli (NL), John Reardon (AL), Bill Summers (AL). **Winning Player's Share:** $5,542. **Losing Player's Share:** $4,193.

bases and slid in for another score. After the first 2 Cincinnati batters reached base in the bottom of the inning, Johnny Murphy got the next 3 out to preserve the 7-4 win. Aided by "Lombardi's Snooze" in the final inning, New York earned its second straight World Series sweep.

Above: It's the 10th inning of Game 4 and Reds catcher Ernie Lombardi is preparing to field the throw from the outfield after DiMaggio's hit. Frankie Crosetti (1) has just scored the go-ahead run, and Charlie Keller is racing in from third, about to slam into Lombardi.

Above: Keller leaps past a prostrate Lombardi as the ball trickles away.

Bill McKechnie was the first manager to lead three different teams to the World Series. He took the Pittsburgh Pirates to the Fall Classic in 1925, the St. Louis Cardinals in 1928, and the Reds in 1939 and 1940.

Joe DiMaggio slides past a dazed Ernie Lombardi in the 10th inning of Game 4 of the 1939 Series. The "Lombardi Snooze" marks a classic October moment—probably less so for Cincinnati fans.

Game 1 Wednesday, October 4 at Yankee Stadium, New York

	1	2	3	4	5	6	7	8	9	R	H	E
Cincinnati Reds	0	0	0	1	0	0	0	0	0	1	4	0
New York Yankees	0	0	0	0	1	0	0	0	1	2	6	0

Pitchers Cin Paul Derringer (L, 0-1), IP 8⅓, H 6, R 2, ER 2, BB 1, SO 7
NY Red Ruffing (W, 1-0), IP 9, H 4, R 1, ER 1, BB 1, SO 4

Top Performers at the Plate
Cin Frank McCormick, 2 for 3, 1 RBI
NY Babe Dahlgren, 1 for 3, 1 RBI; Joe Gordon, 1 for 3, 1 R

2B-NY/Dahlgren. **3B**-NY/Keller. **SB**-Cin/Goodman. **Time** 1:33. **Attendance** 58,541.

Game 2 Thursday, October 5 at Yankee Stadium, New York

	1	2	3	4	5	6	7	8	9	R	H	E
Cincinnati Reds	0	0	0	0	0	0	0	0	0	0	2	0
New York Yankees	0	0	3	1	0	0	0	0	x	4	9	0

Pitchers Cin Bucky Walters (L, 0-1), IP 8, H 9, R 4, ER 4, BB 0, SO 5
NY Monte Pearson (W, 1-0), IP 9, H 2, R 0, ER 0, BB 1, SO 8

Top Performers at the Plate
NY Babe Dahlgren, 2 for 3, 2 R, 1 RBI; Charlie Keller, 2 for 4, 1 R, 1 RBI

2B-NY/Dahlgren, Keller. **HR**-NY/Dahlgren. **Time** 1:27. **Attendance** 59,791.

Game 3 Saturday, October 7 at Crosley Field, Cincinnati

	1	2	3	4	5	6	7	8	9	R	H	E
New York Yankees	2	0	2	0	3	0	0	0		7	5	1
Cincinnati Reds	1	2	0	0	0	0	0	0		3	10	0

Pitchers NY Lefty Gomez, IP 1, H 3, R 1, ER 1, BB 0, SO 1; Bump Hadley (W, 1-0), IP 8, H 7, R 2, ER 2, BB 3, SO 2
Cin Junior Thompson (L, 0-1), IP 4⅔, H 5, R 7, ER 7, BB 4, SO 3; Lee Grissom, IP 1⅓, H 0, R 0, ER 0, BB 1, SO 0; Whitey Moore, IP 3, H 0, R 0, ER 0, BB 0, SO 2

Top Performers at the Plate
NY Bill Dickey, 1 for 3, 1 R, 1 RBI, 1 BB; Charlie Keller, 2-for3, 3 R, 4 RBI, 1 BB, 2 HR
Cin Ival Goodman, 3 for 5, 1 R, 1 RBI; Billy Myers, 2 for 3, 1 R, 1 BB

HR-NY/Dickey, DiMaggio, Keller 2. **Time** 2:01. **Attendance** 32,723.

Game 4 Sunday, October 8 at Crosley Field, Cincinnati

	1	2	3	4	5	6	7	8	9	10	R	H	E
New York Yankees	0	0	0	0	0	0	2	0	2	3	7	7	1
Cincinnati Reds	0	0	0	0	0	0	3	1	0	0	4	11	4

Pitchers NY Oral Hildebrand, IP 4, H 2, R 0, ER 0, BB 0, SO 3; Steve Sundra, IP 2⅔, H 4, R 3, ER 0, BB 1, SO 2; Johnny Murphy (W, 1-0), IP 3⅓, H 5, R 1, ER 1, BB 0, SO 2
Cin Paul Derringer, IP 7, H 3, R 2, ER 2, BB 2, SO 2; Bucky Walters (L, 0-2), IP 3, H 4, R 5, ER 2, BB 1, SO 1

Top Performers at the Plate
NY Joe DiMaggio, 2 for 5, 2 R, 1 RBI; Charlie Keller, 2 for 5, 3 R, 1 RBI
Cin Ival Goodman, 2 for 5, 1 R; Frank McCormick, 2 for 4, 1 R, 1 SH

2B-NY/Selkirk; Cin/Goodman, McCormick, Simmons. **3B**-Cin/Myers. **HR**-NY/Dickey, Keller. **Time** 2:04. **Attendance** 32,794.

107

Cincinnati Reds (4) vs. Detroit Tigers (3)

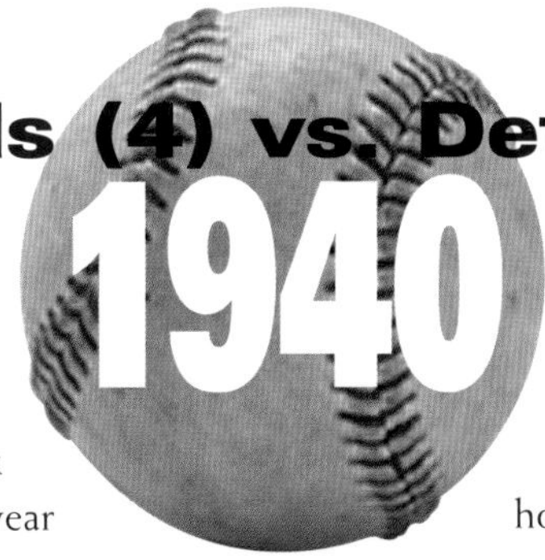

The Cincinnati Reds finished with a 100-53 record in 1940 to repeat as national League champions, but they didn't have to play in a rematch with the Yankees, as the Detroit Tigers grabbed the top spot in the American League. The Tiger offense had a lot of pop, with Hank Greenberg knocking a league-leading 41 homers on the year and Rudy York adding 33. The offense was on full display in the opening game of the Series in Cincinnati. Five singles and a couple of errors led to five runs off Paul Derringer in the second inning. Detroit's Bobo Newsom scattered eight hits in the 7-2 Game 1 win. Bucky Walters walked the first two Detroit batters he faced in Game 2 and gave up two runs in the first inning before settling down to finish the game with a three-hitter. Cincinnati scored five runs by the fifth inning, including two on a home run by Jimmy Ripple, for a 5-3 final. Jim Turner and Tommy Bridges faced off in Game 3, and the two veterans battled in a 1-1 tie for 6½ innings. In the bottom of the seventh, Detroit got two-run homers from York and Pinky Higgins to break the game open. The Series was knotted at two games apiece after Paul Derringer pitched Cincinnati to a 5-2 win in Game 4. Higgins claimed two of Detroit's five hits on the day, and he was splendid in the field as well, recording a record nine assists in the game. Newsom, whose father had died of a heart attack the morning after his Game 1 victory, was on the mound again in the fifth game. He came out with an inspired performance, allowing only three hits and keeping the Reds scoreless. The Tiger hitters did their part, bringing in three runs in the third inning and four in the fourth en route to an 8-0 final; Greenberg's monstrous homer in the third provided the first three runs. Walters got his second win of the Series and sent the teams to a winner-take-all final game when he shut the Tigers out on five hits in Game 6. Walters eighth-inning homer was the icing on the cake. With only one day's rest, Newsom started the seventh game for Detroit, matched up against his Game 1 opponent, Derringer. The Tigers scored one unearned run in the third, and Newsom held the slim lead through six. Back-to-back doubles by Frank McCormick and Jimmy Ripple tied the game in the bottom of the seventh inning, and Ripple ultimately scored on a sacrifice fly, courtesy of Billy Myers. Charlie Gehringer got a leadoff single in the eighth for Detroit, but Derringer retired the next six batters to hold Cincinnati's 2-1 victory. Derringer and Walters earned all four wins for Cincinnati, giving the franchise its first championship since the tainted 1919 Black Sox Series.

Above: Catcher Birdie Tebbetts vainly attempts to prevent Cincinnati's Bill Baker from scoring in Game 3, but his Tigers still won the game, 7-4.

1940 WORLD SERIES COMPOSITE STATISTICS

CINCINNATI REDS/Bill McKechnie, Manager

Player	pos	G	AB	R	H	2B	3B	HR	RBI	BB	SO	SB	BA	SA	E	FPct
Morrie Arnovich	ph-lf	1	1	0	0	0	0	0	0	0	0	0	.000	.000	0	1.000
Bill Baker	c	3	4	1	1	0	0	0	0	0	1	0	.250	.250	1	.875
Joe Beggs	p	1	0	0	0	0	0	0	0	0	0	0	—	—	0	—
Harry Craft	ph	1	1	0	0	0	0	0	0	0	0	0	.000	.000	—	—
Paul Derringer	p	3	7	0	0	0	0	0	0	0	1	0	.000	.000	0	1.000
Lonny Frey	ph-pr-2b	3	2	0	0	0	0	0	0	0	0	0	.000	.000	0	1.000
Ival Goodman	rf	7	29	5	8	2	0	0	5	0	3	0	.276	.345	0	1.000
Johnny Hutchings	p	1	0	0	0	0	0	0	0	0	0	0	—	—	0	1.000
Eddie Joost	2b	7	25	0	5	0	0	0	2	1	2	0	.200	.200	0	1.000
Ernie Lombardi	ph-c	2	3	0	1	1	0	0	1	0	0	0	.333	.667	0	1.000
Frank McCormick	1b	7	28	2	6	1	0	0	1	1	1	0	.214	.250	0	.984
Mike McCormick	cf	7	29	1	9	3	0	0	2	1	6	0	.310	.414	1	.960
Whitey Moore	p	3	2	0	0	0	0	0	0	0	1	0	.000	.000	0	1.000
Billy Myers	ss	7	23	0	3	0	0	0	2	2	5	0	.130	.130	3	.912
Elmer Riddle	p	1	0	0	0	0	0	0	0	0	0	0	—	—	0	—
Lew Riggs	ph	3	3	1	0	0	0	0	0	0	2	0	.000	.000	—	—
Jimmy Ripple	lf	7	21	3	7	2	0	1	6	4	2	0	.333	.524	0	1.000
Junior Thompson	p	1	1	0	0	0	0	0	0	0	1	0	.000	.000	0	1.000
Jim Turner	p	1	2	0	0	0	0	0	0	0	0	0	.000	.000	0	1.000
Johnny Vander Meer	p	1	0	0	0	0	0	0	0	0	0	0	—	—	0	—
Bucky Walters	p	2	7	2	2	1	0	1	2	0	1	0	.286	.857	0	1.000
Bill Werber	3b	7	27	5	10	4	0	0	2	4	2	0	.370	.519	2	.926
Jimmie Wilson	c	6	17	2	6	0	0	0	1	2	1	1	.353	.353	0	1.000
Totals		7	232	22	58	14	0	2	21	15	30	1	.250	.336	6	.969

Pitcher	G	GS	CG	IP	H	R	ER	BB	SO	W-L	Sv	ERA
Joe Beggs	1	0	0	1	3	2	2	0	1	0-0	0	18.00
Paul Derringer	3	3	2	19⅓	17	8	6	10	6	2-1	0	2.79
Johnny Hutchings	1	0	0	1	2	1	1	1	0	0-0	0	9.00
Whitey Moore	3	0	0	8⅓	8	3	3	6	7	0-0	0	3.24
Elmer Riddle	1	0	0	1	0	0	0	0	2	0-0	0	0.00
Junior Thompson	1	1	0	3⅓	8	6	6	4	2	0-1	0	16.20
Jim Turner	1	1	0	6	8	5	5	0	4	0-1	0	7.50
Johnny Vander Meer	1	0	0	3	2	0	0	3	2	0-0	0	0.00
Bucky Walters	2	2	2	18	8	3	3	6	6	2-0	0	1.50
Totals	7	7	4	61	56	28	26	30	30	4-3	0	3.84

DETROIT TIGERS/Del Baker, Manager

Player	pos	G	AB	R	H	2B	3B	HR	RBI	BB	SO	SB	BA	SA	E	FPct
Earl Averill	ph	3	3	0	0	0	0	0	0	0	0	0	.000	.000	—	—
Dick Bartell	ss	7	26	2	7	2	0	0	3	3	3	0	.269	.346	1	.958
Tommy Bridges	p	1	3	0	0	0	0	0	0	0	0	0	.000	.000	0	1.000
Bruce Campbell	rf	7	25	4	9	1	0	1	5	4	4	0	.360	.520	0	1.000
Frank Croucher	ss	1	0	0	0	0	0	0	0	0	0	0	—	—	0	—
Pete Fox	ph	1	1	0	0	0	0	0	0	0	0	0	.000	.000	—	—
Charlie Gehringer	2b	7	28	3	6	0	0	0	1	2	0	0	.214	.214	0	1.000
Johnny Gorsica	p	2	4	0	0	0	0	0	0	0	2	0	.000	.000	0	1.000
Hank Greenberg	lf	7	28	5	10	2	1	1	6	2	5	0	.357	.607	0	1.000
Mike Higgins	3b	7	24	2	8	3	1	1	6	3	3	0	.333	.667	2	.944
Fred Hutchinson	p	1	0	0	0	0	0	0	0	0	0	0	—	—	0	—
Barney McCosky	cf	7	23	5	7	1	0	0	1	7	0	0	.304	.348	0	1.000
Archie McKain	p	1	0	0	0	0	0	0	0	0	0	0	—	—	0	1.000
Bobo Newsom	p	3	10	1	1	0	0	0	0	0	1	0	.100	.100	0	1.000
Schoolboy Rowe	p	2	1	0	0	0	0	0	0	0	1	0	.000	.000	0	1.000
Clay Smith	p	1	1	0	0	0	0	0	0	0	1	0	.000	.000	0	1.000
Billy Sullivan	c-ph	5	13	3	2	0	0	0	0	5	2	0	.154	.154	0	1.000
Birdie Tebbetts	c-ph	4	11	0	0	0	0	0	0	1	2	0	.000	.000	1	.941
Dizzy Trout	p	1	1	0	0	0	0	0	0	0	0	0	.000	.000	0	1.000
Rudy York	1b	7	26	3	6	0	1	1	2	4	7	0	.231	.423	0	1.000
Totals		7	228	28	56	9	3	4	24	30	30	0	.246	.364	4	.985

Pitcher	G	GS	CG	IP	H	R	ER	BB	SO	W-L	Sv	ERA
Tommy Bridges	1	1	1	9	10	4	3	1	5	1-0	0	3.00
Johnny Gorsica	2	0	0	11⅓	6	1	1	4	4	0-0	0	0.79
Fred Hutchinson	1	0	0	1	1	1	1	1	1	0-0	0	9.00
Archie McKain	1	0	0	3	4	1	1	0	0	0-0	0	3.00
Bobo Newsom	3	3	3	26	18	4	4	4	17	2-1	0	1.38
Schoolboy Rowe	2	2	0	3⅔	12	7	7	1	1	0-2	0	17.18
Clay Smith	1	0	0	4	1	1	1	3	1	0-0	0	2.25
Dizzy Trout	1	1	0	2	6	3	2	1	1	0-1	0	9.00
Totals	7	7	4	60	58	22	20	15	30	3-4	0	3.00

Series Outstanding Player: Jimmy Ripple, Cincinnati Reds. **Series Outstanding Pitcher:** Bucky Walters, Cincinnati Reds. **Average Length of Game:** 2 hours, 4 minutes. **Total Attendance:** 281,927. **Average Attendance:** 40,275 (29,942 at Crosley Field; 54,053 at Tiger Stadium). **Umpires:** Lee Ballanfant (NL), Steve Basil (AL), Bill Klem (NL), Red Ormsby (AL). **Winning Player's Share:** $5,804. **Losing Player's Share:** $3,532.

Above: The Reds players swarm around pitcher Paul Derringer after he won Game 7 of the 1940 Series, giving Cincinnati its first championship since 1919.

Above: Hank Greenberg smacks a towering three-run shot at Tiger Stadium in Game 5. Left: Bobo Newsom went the distance in the opener, leading Detroit to a 7-2 win.

Above: Forty-year-old Jimmie Wilson steals second base in Game 7—the only theft of the Series.

Forty-year-old former catcher Jimmie Wilson was a coach for Cincinnati in 1940, but when the Reds' regular backstop, Ernie Lombardi, went down with an injury, Wilson took over the starting role for the final few weeks of the season and all but one game in the Series. He batted an impressive .353 in 17 Series at-bats.

Game 1 Wednesday, October 2 at Crosley Field, Cincinnati

	1	2	3	4	5	6	7	8	9	R	H	E
Detroit Tigers	0	5	0	0	2	0	0	0		7	10	1
Cincinnati Reds	0	0	0	1	0	0	0	1	0	2	8	3

Pitchers Det Bobo Newsom (W, 1-0), IP 9, H 8, R 2, ER 2, BB 1, SO 4
Cin Paul Derringer (L, 0-1), IP 1⅓, H 5, R 5, ER 4, BB 1, SO 1; Whitey Moore, IP 6⅔, H 5, R 2, ER 2, BB 4, SO 7; Elmer Riddle, IP 1, H 0, R 0, ER 0, BB 0, SO 2

Top Performers at the Plate
Det Bruce Campbell, 2 for 3, 1 R, 2 RBI, 1 BB, 1 SH; Rudy York, 2 for 4, 2 R, 1 BB
Cin Ival Goodman, 2 for 4, 1 R, 1 RBI; Eddie Joost, 2 for 4

2B-Cin/Goodman, M. McCormick, Werber. **3B**-Det/York. **HR**-Det/Campbell. **SB**-Det/Bartell.
Time 2:09. **Attendance** 31,793.

Game 2 Thursday, October 3 at Crosley Field, Cincinnati

	1	2	3	4	5	6	7	8	9	R	H	E
Detroit Tigers	2	0	0	0	0	1	0	0	0	3	3	1
Cincinnati Reds	0	2	2	1	0	0	0	0	x	5	9	0

Pitchers Det Schoolboy Rowe (L, 0-1), IP 3⅓, H 8, R 5, ER 5, BB 1, SO 1; Johnny Gorsica, IP 4⅔, H 1, R 0, ER 0, BB 0, SO 1
Cin Bucky Walters (W, 1-0), IP 9, H 3, R 3, ER 3, BB 4, SO 4

Top Performers at the Plate
Cin Bill Werber, 1 for 3, 1 RBI, 1 BB; Jimmie Wilson, 2 for 4, 1 R

2B-Det/Greenberg, Higgins; Cin/Walters, Werber. **HR**-Cin/Ripple. **Time** 1:54. **Attendance** 30,640.

Game 3 Friday, October 4 at Tiger Stadium, Detroit

	1	2	3	4	5	6	7	8	9	R	H	E
Cincinnati Reds	1	0	0	0	0	0	0	1	2	4	10	1
Detroit Tigers	0	0	0	1	0	0	4	2	x	7	13	1

Pitchers Cin Jim Turner (L, 0-1), IP 6, H 8, R 5, ER 5, BB 0, SO 4; Whitey Moore, IP 1, H 2, R 0, ER 0, BB 0, SO 0; Joe Beggs, IP 1, H 3, R 2, ER 2, BB 0, SO 1
Det Tommy Bridges (W, 1-0), IP 9, H 10, R 4, ER 3, BB 1, SO 5

Top Performers at the Plate
Cin Mike McCormick, 2 for 5, 1 RBI; Bill Werber, 3 for 4, 1 R, 1 RBI, 1 BB
Det Bruce Campbell, 3 for 4, 2 R, 1 RBI; Mike Higgins, 2 for 4, 1 R, 3 RBI

2B-Cin/Lombardi, Werber; Det/Campbell, Higgins, McCosky. **3B**-Det/Greenberg. **HR**-Det/Higgins, York. **Time** 2:08. **Attendance** 52,877.

Game 4 Saturday, October 5 at Tiger Stadium, Detroit

	1	2	3	4	5	6	7	8	9	R	H	E
Cincinnati Reds	2	0	1	1	0	0	0	1	0	5	11	1
Detroit Tigers	0	0	1	0	0	1	0	0	0	2	5	1

Pitchers Cin Paul Derringer (W, 1-1), IP 9, H 5, R 2, ER 2, BB 6, SO 4
Det Dizzy Trout (L, 0-1), IP 2, H 6, R 3, ER 2, BB 1, SO 1; Clay Smith, IP 4, H 1, R 1, ER 1, BB 3, SO 1; Archie McKain, IP 3, H 4, R 1, ER 1, BB 0, SO 0

Top Performers at the Plate
Cin Ival Goodman, 2 for 5, 2 R, 2 RBI; Bill Werber, 2 for 3, 2 R, 2 BB
Det Mike Higgins, 2 for 4, 1 RBI; Barney McCoskey, 1 for 2, 1 R, 2 BB

2B-Cin/Goodman, M. McCormick, Ripple; Det/Greenberg. **3B**-Det/Higgins. **Time** 2:06. **Attendance** 54,093.

Game 5 Sunday, October 6 at Tiger Stadium Detroit

	1	2	3	4	5	6	7	8	9	R	H	E
Cincinnati Reds	0	0	0	0	0	0	0	0	0	0	3	0
Detroit Tigers	0	0	3	4	0	0	0	1	x	8	13	0

Pitchers Cin Junior Thompson (L, 0-1), IP 3⅓, H 8, R 6, ER 6, BB 4, SO 2; Whitey Moore, IP ⅔, H 1, R 1, ER 1, BB 2, SO 0; Johnny Vander Meer, IP 3, H 2, R 0, ER 0, BB 3, SO 2; Johnny Hutchings, IP 1, H 2, R 1, ER 1, BB 1, SO 0
Det Bobo Newsom (W, 2-0), IP 9, H 3, R 0, ER 0, BB 2, SO 7

Top Performers at the Plate
Det Hank Greenberg, 3 for 5, 2 R, 4 RBI; Barney McCoskey, 2 for 3, 2 R, 2 BB

2B-Det/Bartell. **HR**-Det/Greenberg. **Time** 2:26. **Attendance** 55,189.

Game 6 Monday, October 7 at Crosley Field, Cincinnati

	1	2	3	4	5	6	7	8	9	R	H	E
Detroit Tigers	0	0	0	0	0	0	0	0	0	0	5	0
Cincinnati Reds	2	0	0	0	0	1	0	1	x	4	10	2

Pitchers Det Schoolboy Rowe (L, 0-2), IP ⅓, H 4, R 2, ER 2, BB 0, SO 0; Johnny Gorsica, IP 6⅔, H 5, R 1, ER 1, BB 4, SO 3; Fred Hutchinson, IP 1, H 1, R 1, ER 1, BB 1, SO 1
Cin Bucky Walters (W, 2-0), IP 9, H 5, R 0, ER 0, BB 2, SO 2

Top Performers at the Plate
Det Dick Bartell, 2 for 3; Rudy York, 2 for 4
Cin Ival Goodman, 2 for 4, 1 R, 1 RBI, 1 SH; Jimmy Ripple, 2 for 2, 1 RBI, 2 BB

2B-Det/Bartell; Cin/Werber. **HR**-Cin/Walters. **Time** 2:01. **Attendance** 30,481.

Game 7 Tuesday, October 8 at Crosley Field, Cincinnati

	1	2	3	4	5	6	7	8	9	R	H	E
Detroit Tigers	0	0	1	0	0	0	0	0	0	1	7	0
Cincinnati Reds	0	0	0	0	0	0	2	0	x	2	7	1

Pitchers Det Bobo Newsom (L, 2-1), IP 8, H 7, R 2, ER 2, BB 1, SO 6
Cin Paul Derringer (W, 2-1), IP 9, H 7, R 1, ER 0, BB 3, SO 1

Top Performers at the Plate
Det Charlie Gehringer, 2 for 4; Hank Greenberg, 2 for 4
Cin Jimmy Ripple, 1 for 3, 1 R, 1 RBI; Jimmie Wilson, 2 for 4, 1 SH

2B-Det/Higgins; Cin/F. McCormick, M. McCormick, Ripple. **SB** – Wilson. **Time** 1:47. **Attendance** 26,854.

New York Yankees (4) vs. Brooklyn Dodgers (1)

1941

The borough of Brooklyn hadn't seen a pennant in more than two decades when the Dodgers won 100 games in 1941 to earn a World Series showdown with their crosstown rivals from the Bronx. It was the 1st of 7 matchups between the Yankees and Dodgers over the next 15 years—and as much as any other, the 1941 Fall Classic would come to represent the frustrations of Brooklynites. A record 68,500 fans came out to Yankee Stadium for Game 1 to watch the Yankees eke out a 3-2 victory. Red Ruffing got the win in the 5th opening-game start of his career by holding Brooklyn to six hits. Whit Wyatt shut the Yankees out for the last six innings in Game 2 to preserve a 3-2 edge for his Dodgers. With the Series tied, the scene shifted to Ebbets Field, where strong outings by starters Marius Russo and Freddie Fitzsimmons kept Game 3 scoreless through seven innings. With two out in the seventh, Russo hit a line drive that hit Fitzsimmons in the knee. Although Pee Wee Reese caught the ball on the ricochet for the out, Fitzsimmons was gone from the game with a broken kneecap. The Yankees got the better of reliever Hugh Casey the next inning and scored two runs on four straight singles. Russo, meanwhile, held Brooklyn to one run for a 2-1 win. Things looked promising for Brooklyn in Game 4 when a two-run double by pinch hitter Jimmy Wasdell and a two-run homer by Pete Reiser gave them a 4-3 lead. The score held into the ninth, and Casey got the first two Yankees out to put the Dodgers one out away from tying the Series. Casey worked Tommy Henrich to a full count, and then threw strike three past Henrich. But as the Dodgers jubilantly headed in for the celebration, they quickly realized that the ball had gotten away from catcher Mickey Owen, and Henrich adeptly raced safely to first. The Yanks were still alive, and they took advantage. Up to the plate stepped Joe DiMaggio—coming off a season in which he hit safely in 56 consecutive games—and he ripped a single to left. Then Charlie Keller drove in Henrich and DiMaggio with a double, Bill Dickey reached first on a walk, and Joe Gordon sent in two more runs with a double. Brooklyn went from the game's apparent final out to a four-run deficit in a matter of minutes. The demoralized Dodgers went down one-two-three in the bottom of the ninth. Ernie "Tiny" Bonham held Brooklyn to just four hits the next day, leading New York to a 3-1 win in Game 5 and a 4-1 win in the Series. It was the Yanks' 32nd win in 36 Series games since 1927 and their 8th straight Series without a loss. And Mickey Owen would be forever vilified by the Brooklyn faithful.

Above: Although umpire Larry Goetz is signaling strike three, Tommy Henrich races to first as the ball gets by catcher Mickey Owen. The misplay led to a four-run rally for New York and a Game 4 defeat for Brooklyn.

1941 WORLD SERIES COMPOSITE STATISTICS

NEW YORK YANKEES/Joe McCarthy, Manager

Player	pos	G	AB	R	H	2B	3B	HR	RBI	BB	SO	SB	BA	SA	E	FPct
Tiny Bonham	p	1	4	0	0	0	0	0	0	0	4	0	.000	.000	0	1.000
Frenchy Bordagaray	pr	1	0	0	0	0	0	0	0	0	0	0	—	—	0	—
Marv Breuer	p	1	1	0	0	0	0	0	0	0	0	0	.000	.000	0	1.000
Spud Chandler	p	1	2	0	1	0	0	0	1	0	0	0	.500	.500	0	—
Bill Dickey	c	5	18	3	3	1	0	0	1	3	1	0	.167	.222	0	1.000
Joe DiMaggio	cf	5	19	1	5	0	0	0	1	2	2	0	.263	.263	0	1.000
Atley Donald	p	1	2	0	0	0	0	0	0	0	1	0	.000	.000	0	1.000
Joe Gordon	2b	5	14	2	7	1	1	1	5	7	0	0	.500	.929	1	.963
Tommy Henrich	rf	5	18	4	3	1	0	1	1	3	3	0	.167	.389	0	1.000
Charlie Keller	lf	5	18	5	7	2	0	0	5	3	1	0	.389	.500	0	1.000
Johnny Murphy	p	2	2	0	0	0	0	0	0	0	1	0	.000	.000	0	1.000
Phil Rizzuto	ss	5	18	0	2	0	0	0	0	3	1	1	.111	.111	1	.968
Red Rolfe	3b	5	20	2	6	0	0	0	0	2	1	0	.300	.300	1	1.000
Buddy Rosar	c	1	0	0	0	0	0	0	0	0	0	0	—	—	0	—
Red Ruffing	p	1	3	0	0	0	0	0	0	0	0	0	.000	.000	0	—
Marius Russo	p	1	4	0	0	0	0	0	0	0	1	0	.000	.000	0	1.000
George Selkirk	ph	2	2	0	1	0	0	0	0	0	0	0	.500	.500	0	—
Johnny Sturm	1b	5	21	0	6	0	0	0	0	2	1	0	.286	.286	0	1.000
Totals		**5**	**166**	**17**	**41**	**5**	**1**	**2**	**16**	**23**	**18**	**2**	**.247**	**.325**	**2**	**.990**

Pitcher	G	GS	CG	IP	H	R	ER	BB	SO	W-L	Sv	ERA
Tiny Bonham	1	1	1	9	4	1	1	2	2	1-0	0	1.00
Marv Breuer	1	0	0	3	3	0	0	1	2	0-0	0	0.00
Spud Chandler	1	1	0	5	4	3	2	2	2	0-1	0	3.60
Atley Donald	1	1	0	4	6	4	4	3	2	0-0	0	9.00
Johnny Murphy	2	0	0	6	2	0	0	1	3	1-0	0	0.00
Red Ruffing	1	1	1	9	6	2	1	3	5	1-0	0	1.00
Marius Russo	1	1	1	9	4	1	1	2	5	1-0	0	1.00
Totals	**5**	**5**	**3**	**45**	**29**	**11**	**9**	**14**	**21**	**4-1**	**0**	**1.80**

BROOKLYN DODGERS/Leo Durocher, Manager

Player	pos	G	AB	R	H	2B	3B	HR	RBI	BB	SO	SB	BA	SA	E	FPct
Johnny Allen	p	3	0	0	0	0	0	0	0	0	0	0	—	—	0	—
Dolph Camilli	1b	5	18	1	3	1	0	0	1	1	6	0	.167	.222	0	1.000
Hugh Casey	p	3	2	0	1	0	0	0	0	0	1	0	.500	.500	0	1.000
Pete Coscarart	2b	3	7	1	0	0	0	0	0	1	2	0	.000	.000	0	1.000
Curt Davis	p	1	2	0	0	0	0	0	0	0	0	0	.000	.000	0	1.000
Freddie Fitzsimmons	p	1	2	0	0	0	0	0	0	0	1	0	.000	.000	0	1.000
Herman Franks	c	1	1	0	0	0	0	0	0	0	0	0	.000	.000	0	1.000
Larry French	p	2	0	0	0	0	0	0	0	0	0	0	—	—	0	—
Augie Galan	ph	2	2	0	0	0	0	0	0	0	1	0	.000	.000	—	—
Billy Herman	2b	4	8	0	1	0	0	0	0	2	0	0	.125	.125	0	1.000
Kirby Higbe	p	1	1	0	1	0	0	0	0	0	0	0	1.000	1.000	0	1.000
Cookie Lavagetto	3b	5	10	1	1	0	0	0	0	2	0	0	.100	.100	0	1.000
Joe Medwick	lf	5	17	1	4	1	0	0	0	1	2	0	.235	.294	1	1.000
Mickey Owen	c	5	12	1	2	0	1	0	2	3	0	0	.167	.333	1	.960
Pee Wee Reese	ss	5	20	1	4	0	0	0	2	0	0	0	.200	.200	3	.900
Pete Reiser	cf	5	20	1	4	1	1	1	3	1	6	0	.200	.500	0	1.000
Lew Riggs	ph-3b	3	8	0	2	0	0	0	0	1	1	0	.250	.250	0	1.000
Dixie Walker	rf	5	18	3	4	2	0	0	0	2	1	0	.222	.333	0	1.000
Jimmy Wasdell	ph-lf	3	5	0	1	1	0	0	2	0	0	0	.200	.400	0	1.000
Whit Wyatt	p	2	6	1	1	1	0	0	0	0	1	0	.167	.333	0	1.000
Totals		**5**	**159**	**11**	**29**	**7**	**2**	**1**	**11**	**14**	**21**	**0**	**.182**	**.270**	**4**	**.979**

Pitcher	G	GS	CG	IP	H	R	ER	BB	SO	W-L	Sv	ERA
Johnny Allen	3	0	0	3⅔	1	0	0	3	0	0-0	0	0.00
Hugh Casey	3	0	0	5⅓	9	6	2	1	0	0-2	0	3.38
Curt Davis	1	1	0	5⅓	6	3	3	3	1	0-1	0	5.06
Freddie Fitzsimmons	1	1	0	7	4	0	0	3	1	0-0	0	0.00
Larry French	2	0	0	1	0	0	0	0	0	0-0	0	0.00
Kirby Higbe	1	1	0	3⅔	6	3	3	2	1	0-0	0	7.36
Whit Wyatt	2	2	2	18	15	5	5	10	11	1-1	0	2.50
Totals	**5**	**5**	**2**	**44**	**41**	**17**	**13**	**23**	**18**	**1-4**	**0**	**2.66**

Series Outstanding Player: Joe Gordon, New York Yankees. **Series Outstanding Pitcher:** Johnny Murphy, New York Yankees. **Average Length of Game:** 2 hours, 26 minutes. **Total Attendance:** 235,773. **Average Attendance:** 47,155 (67,394 at Yankee Stadium; 33,662 at Ebbets Field). **Umpires:** Larry Goetz (NL), Bill Grieve (AL), Bill McGowan (AL), Babe Pinelli (NL). **Winning Player's Share:** $5,493. **Losing Player's Share:** $4,829.

Background: Brooklyn's first World Series in more than two decades pitted the Dodgers in a Subway Series with the Yanks.

Left: Phil Rizzuto makes an acrobatic play to turn a double play and end Game 1 at Yankee Stadium.

Game 1 Wednesday, October 1 at Yankee Stadium, New York

	1	2	3	4	5	8	7	8	9	R	H	E
Brooklyn Dodgers	0	0	0	0	1	0	1	0	0	2	6	0
New York Yankees	0	1	0	1	0	1	0	0	x	3	6	1

Pitchers Bro Curt Davis (L, 0-1), IP 5⅓, H 6, R 3, ER 3, BB 3, SO 1; Hugh Casey, IP ⅔, H 0, R 0, ER 0, BB 0, SO 0; Johnny Allen, IP 2, H 0, R 0, ER 0, BB 2, SO 0
NY Red Ruffing (W, 1-0), IP 9, H 6, R 2, ER 1, BB 3, SO 5

Top Performers at the Plate
Bro Pee Wee Reese, 3 for 4, 1 R
NY Bill Dickey, 2 for 4, 1 RBI; Joe Gordon, 2 for 2, 1 R, 2 RBI, 2 BB

2B-NY/Dickey. 3B-Bro/Owen. HR-NY/Gordon. Time 2:08. Attendance 68,540.

Game 2 Thursday, October 2 at Yankee Stadium, New York

	1	2	3	4	5	5	7	8	9	R	H	E
Brooklyn Dodgers	0	0	0	0	2	1	0	0	0	3	6	2
New York Yankees	0	1	1	0	0	0	0	0	0	2	9	1

Pitchers Bro Whit Wyatt (W, 1-0), IP 9, H 9, R 2, ER 2, BB 5, SO 5
NY Spud Chandler (L, 0-1), IP 5, H 4, R 3, ER 2, BB 2, SO 2; Johnny Murphy, IP 4, H 2, R 0, ER 0, BB 1, SO 2

Top Performers at the Plate
Bro Dolph Camilli, 1 for 3, 1 R, 1 RBI, 1 BB; Joe Medwick, 2 for 4, 1 R
NY Charlie Keller, 2 for 4, 1 R, 1 RBI

2B-Bro/Medwick; NY/Henrich. Time 2:31. Attendance 66,248.

Game 3 Friday, October 3 at Ebbets Field, Brooklyn

	1	2	3	4	5	6	7	8	9	R	H	E
New York Yankees	0	0	0	0	0	0	2	0		2	8	0
Brooklyn Dodgers	0	0	0	0	0	0	1	0		1	4	0

Pitchers NY Marius Russo (W, 1-0), IP 9, H 4, R 1, ER 1, BB 2, SO 5
Bro Freddie Fitzsimmons, IP 7, H 4, R 0, ER 0, BB 3, SO 1; Hugh Casey (L, 0-1), IP ⅓, H 4, R 2, ER 2, BB 0, SO 0; Larry French, IP ⅔, H 0, R 0, ER 0, BB 0, SO 0; Johnny Allen, IP 1, H 0, R 0, ER 0, BB 0, SO 0

Top Performers at the Plate
NY Joe DiMaggio, 2 for 4, 1 RBI; Red Rolfe, 2 for 4, 1 R
Bro Dixie Walker, 1 for 3, 1 R

2B – Bro/Reiser, Walker. 3B-NY/Gordon. SB-NY/Rizzuto, Sturm. Time 2:22. Attendance 33,100.

Game 4 Sunday, October 5 at Ebbets Field, Brooklyn

	1	2	3	4	5	6	7	8	9	R	H	E
New York Yankees	1	0	0	2	0	0	0	0	4	7	12	0
Brooklyn Dodgers	0	0	0	2	2	0	0	0	0	4	9	1

Pitchers NY Atley Donald, IP 4, H 6, R 4, ER 4, BB 3, SO 2; Marv Breuer, IP 3, H 3, R 0, ER 0, BB 1, SO 2; Johnny Murphy (W, 1-0), IP 2, H 0, R 0, ER 0, BB 0, SO 1
Bro Kirby Higbe, IP 3⅔, H 6, R 3, ER 3, BB 2, SO 1; Larry French, IP ⅓, H 0, R 0, ER 0, BB 0, SO 0; Johnny Allen, IP ⅔, H 1, R 0, ER 0, BB 1, SO 0; Hugh Casey (L, 0-2), IP 4⅓, H 5, R 4, ER 0, BB 2, SO 1

Top Performers at the Plate
NY Joe Gordon, 2 for 5, 1 R, 2 RBI; Charlie Keller, 4 for 5, 1 R, 3 RBI, 2 2B
Bro Pete Reiser, 2 for 5, 1 R, 2 RBI; Dixie Walker, 2 for 5, 1 R

2B-NY/Gordon, Keller 2; Bro/Camilli, Walker, Wasdell. HR-Bro/Reiser. Time 2:54. Attendance 33,813.

Game 5 Monday, October 6 at Ebbets Field, Brooklyn

	1	2	3	4	5	6	7	8	9	R	H	E
New York Yankees	0	2	0	0	1	0	0	0	0	3	6	0
Brooklyn Dodgers	0	0	1	0	0	0	0	0	0	1	4	1

Pitchers NY Tiny Bonham (W, 1-0), IP 9, H 4, R 1, ER 1, BB 2, SO 2
Bro Whit Wyatt (L, 1-1), IP 9, H 6, R 3, ER 3, BB 5, SO 9

Top Performers at the Plate
NY Joe Gordon, 1 for 3, 1 RBI, 1 BB; Tommy Henrich, 1 for 3, 1 R, 1 RBI, 1 BB

2B-Bro/Wyatt. 3B-Bro/Reiser. HR-NY/Henrich. Time 2:13. Attendance 34,072.

Above inset: Joe Gordon slides into third with a fifth-inning triple in Game 3. Gordon batted .500 for the Series.

Right: Two batters after dropping the infamous third strike in the ninth inning of Game 4, Mickey Owen is helpless as Joe DiMaggio slides in with the winning run.

All-Time World Series Goats

At its essence, the World Series is a time of glory and success, when baseball's best display their greatness. Oftentimes, however, it's a misplay, a muff, a boner that means do or die for a team in October. These names are remembered more for the mistakes than their heroics.

◆ Snodgrass's "$30,000 Muff" — Fred Snodgrass
Merkle and Meyers Blunder Allows Red Sox to Rally to Victory — Chief Meyers and Fred Merkle, New York Giants, October 16, 1912
The New York Giants suffered a most frustrating defeat in the 1912 World Series when two seemingly routine plays were botched by fielders. Center fielder Fred Snodgrass dropped a fly ball in the bottom of the 10th inning of Game 8, allowing Boston to get the first batter of the inning on base. Three batters later, catcher Chief Meyers and first baseman Fred Merkle let a foul ball fall between them, giving Hall of Fame hitter Tris Speaker a second chance at the plate. Speaker responded with an RBI single, and the Giants went on to lose the game and the Series.

Above: Fred Merkle has the rare distinction of playing the role of goat in important games during the regular season and World Series.

◆ Zimmerman Chases Collins Across Home Plate — Heinie Zimmerman, New York Giants, October 15, 1917
Another New York Giant joined the all-time goat list when Heinie Zimmerman chased Chicago's Eddie Collins across home plate in Game 6 of 1917, failing to catch him in a rundown. In fairness, Zimmerman alone shouldn't shoulder the blame, since neither the Giants' first baseman nor their pitcher backed up the plate on the run-down. But Zimmerman started the mess when his throwing error put Collins on base in the first place. The White Sox scored three unearned runs in the inning and won the Series finale by a 4-2 score.

◆ Peckinpaugh's Eight Errors Doom Senators — Roger Peckinpaugh, Washington Senators, October 7–15, 1925
By the sixth game of the 1925 Series, Washington shortstop Roger Peckinpaugh had tied the record for most errors in a World Series. In the seventh inning of Game 7, his dropped pop fly set a new record and sparked a two-run Pittsburgh rally. After the Pirates scored the game-tying run in the eighth, Peckinpaugh's two-out error loaded the bases and allowed them to score the two runs they needed to win the decisive game and the championship. Peckinpaugh's eight errors still stand as a record for a Series of any length.

◆ Yankees Win on Miljus's Pair of Wild Pitches — Johnny Miljus, Pittsburgh Pirates, October 8, 1927
The Pittsburgh Pirates likely had little chance of defeating the 1927 New York Yankees even before the Series began, but Johnny Miljus made it that much easier for the "Bronx Bombers" when he threw two wild pitches in the ninth inning of Game 4. With the score tied 3-3, Miljus advanced runners to second and third base with his first wild pitch, and after loading the bases, uncorked another wild one to bring home the game- and Series-ending run. It's the only time a Series has ended with a wild pitch.

◆ Passed Ball by Owen Opens Door for Yankees — Mickey Owen, Brooklyn Dodgers, October 5, 1941
The Brooklyn Dodgers held a 4-3 lead with two outs in the ninth inning of Game 4 in 1941, one out away from tying the Series. Reliever Hugh Casey threw a curveball by New York's Tommy Henrich for strike three, but the ball got by catcher Mickey Owen, and Henrich reached first base safely. The Yankees then scored four runs in the inning, securing the Game 4 win, and then clinched the Series in Game 5 the following day. The All-Star catcher had committed only two passed balls in 128 games during the season, but Owen's muff in Game 4 of the World Series cost Brooklyn a chance at the title.

◆ Davis Makes Record Three Errors in Inning — Willie Davis, Los Angeles Dodgers, October 6, 1966
With the Dodgers and Orioles battling through a scoreless tie in the fifth inning of Game 2, Los Angeles center fielder Willie Davis committed three errors on two plays to allow Baltimore to score three runs. He lost two fly balls in the sun and then, trying to hold the runners, made a poor throw after the second error. On that day, sunny Southern California was not kind to the three-time Gold Glove winner.

Below: Despite his 2,715 career hits, Bill Buckner will always be remembered for the one that got away...between his legs.

◆ Ball Goes Through Buckner's Legs; Mets Stay Alive for Game 7 — Bill Buckner, Boston Red Sox, October 25, 1986

Although Bill Buckner's through-the-legs error in the sixth game of the Series is the blunder most closely associated with Boston's historic 1986 collapse, others must at least share the goat label. Manager John McNamara decided against putting in a late-inning defensive replacement for Buckner, as was his usual strategy; Calvin Schiraldi gave up three straight hits after bringing his team one strike away from victory; Bob Stanley's wild pitch at Mookie Wilson's feet brought home the game-tying run even before Buckner had a chance to field the ground ball.

◆ "Wild Thing" Gives Up Series-Winning Homer — Mitch Williams, Philadelphia Phillies, October 23, 1993

Mitch "Wild Thing" Williams was the Phillies' ace reliever all through the 1993 season, but when he came in to face Toronto's Joe Carter in the sixth game of the World Series, fortune would not be on his side. His 2-2 fastball was crushed by Carter for a Series-ending homer. Three days earlier, Williams got the loss in Game 4 when he gave up three runs to allow the Blue Jays to come back and win a 15-14 slugfest.

◆ Andrews "Fired" by Owner After His Two Errors — Mike Andrews, Oakland Athletics, October 14, 1973

It's not so much the two errors that Oakland second baseman Mike Andrews committed in the 12th inning of Game 2—though the errors cost the A's the game, the team ended up winning the 1973 Series—but more the humiliation that accompanied owner Charles O. Finley's attempt to cut Andrews from the team after the game, on claims the ballplayer was injured. It took intervention by the baseball commissioner to keep Andrews on the World Series roster.

Above: Los Angeles' Willie Davis set a dubious record with three errors in one inning during the 1966 World Series. Here he drops Paul Blair's fly after losing it in the sun.

St. Louis Cardinals (4) vs. New York Yankees (1)

The year 1942 saw the Yankees' sixth trip to the World Series in seven outings. The key names from the previous year's title team were back in the lineup—DiMaggio, Gordon, Dickey, Keller, Rizzuto—as was the pitching staff that had dominated the Dodgers in 1941. Going up against the veteran defending-champions was a talented but young Cardinal team that needed 43 wins in its last 51 games to edge out Brooklyn for the pennant. The Yanks were heavy favorites going into the Series, and after the first eight innings of Game 1, it seemed as if they would do it in quick fashion. Red Ruffing had a no-hitter for 8 2/3 innings until Terry Moore broke it up with a single to right. The Yanks were up 7-0 heading into the last of the ninth, with more than a little help from four errors by St. Louis's typically solid defense. Although there was no dramatic eight-run rally, the Cardinals did score four off Ruffing and had the tying run on and the bases loaded when the final out was recorded. The young Cards had sent a message that they would not go down easy, and the momentum carried over into Game 2. A two-run double by Walker Cooper in the first gave St. Louis an early lead, and pitcher Johnny Beazley kept New York off the board through seven. The Yanks tied the game in the eighth, but a double by Enos "Country" Slaughter and a single by the 21-year-old Stan Musial put St. Louis up 4-3 in the bottom of the inning. New York rallied in the ninth, but a great throw by Slaughter from right field cut down pinch runner Tuck Stainback at third base and helped forestall a Yankee comeback. Ernie White shut the Yankees out on six hits in Game 3 at Yankee Stadium, while the Cards scored one in the first (without hitting a ball out of the infield) and added an insurance run in the ninth. Sensational fielding helped preserve White's shutout, as Musial and Slaughter robbed Joe Gordon and Charlie Keller of home runs with back-to-back leaping catches at the wall in the seventh. A big fourth inning gave St. Louis a 6-1 lead in Game 4, until the Yankees came back with five runs of their own, thanks in part to Keller's three-run homer. Max Lanier held New York scoreless for the last three innings while the Cardinal bats collected three more runs for a 9-6 victory. After losing the opener to a heavily favored Yankee team, the Cardinals took three straight and were on the verge of winning their first championship since 1934. In Game 5, another good outing on the mound by Beazley and a tie-breaking two-run home run by Whitey Kurowski in the top of the ninth sealed the deal. The 1942 Cardinals became the first team since the 1926 Cardinals to defeat the New York Yankees in the World Series.

Above: Whitey Kurowski, Enos Slaughter and Johnny Beazley celebrate St. Louis's victory over New York in the 1942 Series.

1942 WORLD SERIES COMPOSITE STATISTICS

ST. LOUIS CARDINALS/Billy Southworth, Manager

Player	pos	G	AB	R	H	2B	3B	HR	RBI	BB	SO	SB	BA	SA	E	FPct
Johnny Beazley	p	2	7	0	1	0	0	0	0	0	5	0	.143	.143	1	.667
Jimmy Brown	2b	5	20	2	6	0	0	0	1	3	0	0	.300	.300	3	.880
Mort Cooper	p	2	5	1	1	0	0	0	2	0	1	0	.200	.200	0	1.000
Walker Cooper	c	5	21	3	6	1	0	0	4	0	1	0	.286	.333	1	.963
Creepy Crespi	pr	4	0	1	0	0	0	0	0	0	0	0	—	—	—	—
Harry Gumbert	p	2	0	0	0	0	0	0	0	0	0	0	—	—	0	1.000
Johnny Hopp	1b	5	17	3	3	0	0	0	0	1	1	0	.176	.176	1	.980
Whitey Kurowski	3b	5	15	3	4	0	1	1	5	2	3	0	.267	.600	1	.917
Max Lanier	p	2	1	0	1	0	0	0	1	0	0	0	1.000	1.000	2	.333
Marty Marion	ss	5	18	2	2	0	1	0	3	1	2	0	.111	.222	0	1.000
Terry Moore	cf	5	17	2	5	1	0	0	2	2	3	0	.294	.353	0	1.000
Stan Musial	lf	5	18	2	4	1	0	0	2	4	0	0	.222	.278	0	1.000
Ken O'Dea	ph	3	1	0	1	0	0	0	1	0	0	0	1.000	1.000	—	—
Howie Pollet	p	1	0	0	0	0	0	0	0	0	0	0	—	—	0	—
Ray Sanders	ph	2	1	1	0	0	0	0	0	1	0	0	.000	.000	—	—
Enos Slaughter	rf	5	19	3	5	1	0	1	2	3	2	0	.263	.474	1	.909
Harry Walker	ph	1	1	0	0	0	0	0	0	0	1	0	.000	.000	—	—
Ernie White	p	1	2	0	0	0	0	0	0	0	0	0	.000	.000	0	—
Totals		5	163	23	39	4	2	2	23	17	19	0	.239	.325	10	.947

Pitcher	G	GS	CG	IP	H	R	ER	BB	SO	W-L	Sv	ERA
Johnny Beazley	2	2	2	18	17	5	5	3	6	2-0	0	2.50
Mort Cooper	2	2	0	13	17	10	8	4	9	0-1	0	5.54
Harry Gumbert	2	0	0	⅔	1	1	0	0	0	0-0	0	0.00
Max Lanier	2	0	0	4	3	2	0	1	1	1-0	1	0.00
Howie Pollet	1	0	0	⅓	0	0	0	0	0	0-0	0	0.00
Ernie White	1	1	1	9	6	0	0	0	6	1-0	0	0.00
Totals	5	5	3	45	44	18	13	8	22	4-1	0	2.60

NEW YORK YANKEES/Joe McCarthy, Manager

Player	pos	G	AB	R	H	2B	3B	HR	RBI	BB	SO	SB	BA	SA	E	FPct
Tiny Bonham	p	2	2	0	0	0	0	0	0	1	0	0	.000	.000	0	1.000
Hank Borowy	p	1	1	0	0	0	0	0	0	0	1	0	.000	.000	0	1.000
Marv Breuer	p	1	0	0	0	0	0	0	0	0	0	0	—	—	1	.000
Spud Chandler	p	2	2	0	0	0	0	0	0	0	1	0	.000	.000	0	1.000
Frankie Crosetti	3b	1	3	0	0	0	0	0	0	0	1	0	.000	.000	0	1.000
Roy Cullenbine	rf	5	19	3	5	1	0	0	2	1	2	1	.263	.316	0	1.000
Bill Dickey	c	5	19	1	5	0	0	0	1	0	0	0	.263	.263	1	.963
Joe DiMaggio	cf	5	21	3	7	0	0	0	3	0	1	0	.333	.333	0	1.000
Atley Donald	p	1	2	0	0	0	0	0	0	0	0	0	.000	.000	0	—
Joe Gordon	2b	5	21	1	2	1	0	0	0	0	7	0	.095	.143	0	1.000
Buddy Hassett	1b	3	9	3	3	1	0	0	2	0	1	0	.333	.444	1	.941
Charlie Keller	lf	5	20	4	4	0	0	2	5	1	3	0	.200	.500	0	1.000
Jerry Priddy	3b-1b	3	10	0	1	1	0	0	1	1	0	0	.100	.100	0	.963
Phil Rizzuto	ss	5	21	2	8	0	0	1	1	2	1	2	.381	.524	1	.968
Red Rolfe	3b	4	17	5	6	2	0	0	1	2	0	0	.353	.471	0	1.000
Buddy Rosar	ph	1	1	0	1	0	0	0	0	0	0	0	1.000	1.000	—	—
Red Ruffing	p-ph	4	9	0	2	0	0	0	0	0	2	0	.222	.222	0	1.000
George Selkirk	ph	1	1	0	0	0	0	0	0	0	0	0	.000	.000	—	—
Tuck Stainback	pr	2	0	0	0	0	0	0	0	0	0	0	—	—	—	—
Jim Turner	p	1	0	0	0	0	0	0	0	0	0	0	—	—	0	—
Totals		5	178	18	44	6	0	3	14	8	22	3	.247	.331	5	.973

Pitcher	G	GS	CG	IP	H	R	ER	BB	SO	W-L	Sv	ERA
Tiny Bonham	2	1	1	11	9	5	5	3	3	0-1	0	4.09
Hank Borowy	1	1	0	3	6	6	6	3	1	0-0	0	18.00
Marv Breuer	1	0	0	2	1	0	0	0	0	0-0	0	—
Spud Chandler	2	1	0	8⅓	5	1	1	1	3	0-1	1	1.08
Atley Donald	1	0	0	3	3	2	2	1	1	0-1	0	6.00
Red Ruffing	2	2	1	17⅔	14	8	8	7	11	1-1	0	4.08
Jim Turner	1	0	0	1	0	0	0	1	0	0-0	0	0.00
Totals	5	5	2	44	39	23	22	17	19	1-4	1	4.50

Series Outstanding Player: Whitey Kurowski, St. Louis Cardinals. **Series Outstanding Pitcher:** Johnny Beazley, St. Louis Cardinals. **Average Length of Game:** 2 hours, 18 minutes. **Total Attendance:** 277,101. **Average Attendance:** 55,420 (34,512 at Sportsman's Park; 69,359 at Yankee Stadium). **Umpires:** George Barr (NL), Cal Hubbard (AL), George Magerkurth (NL), Bill Summers (AL). **Winning Player's Share:** $6,193. **Losing Player's Share:** $3,352.

In Game 2, Ernie White became the first pitcher since 1926 to shutout the Yankees in a Series game.

The victory in Game 1 gave Red Ruffing five wins in World Series openers, a record for any pitcher.

Above inset: Lacking a certain grace that would characterize his later years, rookie Stan Musial stumbles into home.

Right: Pitcher Mort Cooper (left) and catcher Walker Cooper (right) were the first brother battery to appear in a World Series.

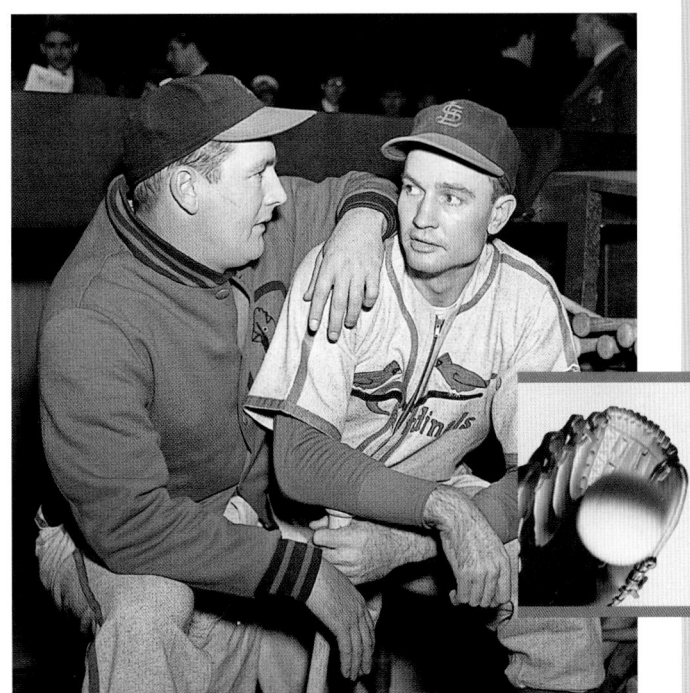

In Game 1, Mort and Walker Cooper became the first and only brother/pitcher-catcher battery in a World Series. They would pair up a total of six times in the 1942, 1943 and 1944 Series.

Game 1 Wednesday, September 30 at Sportsman's Park, St. Louis

	1	2	3	4	5	6	7	8	9	R	H	E
New York Yankees	0	0	0	1	1	0	0	3	2	7	11	0
St. Louis Cardinals	0	0	0	0	0	0	0	0	4	4	7	4

Pitchers NY Red Ruffing (W, 1-0), IP 8⅔, H 5, R 4, ER 4, BB 1, SO 8; Spud Chandler (Sv, 1), IP ⅓, H 2, R 0, ER 0, BB 0, SO 0
StL Mort Cooper (L, 0-1), IP 7⅔, H 10, R 5, ER 3, BB 3, SO 7; Harry Gumbert, IP ⅓, H 0, R 0, ER 0, BB 0, SO 0; Max Lanier, IP 1, H 1, R 2, ER 2, BB 1, SO 1

Top Performers at the Plate
NY Joe DiMaggio, 3 for 5, 2 R, 1 RBI; Buddy Hassett, 2 for 4, 1 R, 2 RBI
StL Terry Moore, 2 for 4, 1 RBI, 1 BB

2B-NY/Cullenbine, Hassett. **3B**-StL/Marion. **Time** 2:35. **Attendance** 34,769.

Game 2 Thursday, October 1 at Sportsman's Park, St. Louis

	1	2	3	4	5	6	7	8	9	R	H	E
New York Yankees	0	0	0	0	0	0	3	0		3	10	2
St. Louis Cardinals	2	0	0	0	0	0	1	1	x	4	6	0

Pitchers NY Tiny Bonham (L, 0-1), IP 8, H 6, R 4, ER 4, BB 1, SO 3
StL Johnny Beazley (W, 1-0), IP 9, H 10, R 3, ER 3, BB 2, SO 4

Top Performers at the Plate
NY Bill Dickey, 2 for 4; Charlie Keller, 2 for 4, 1 R, 2 RBI
StL Johnny Hopp, 2 for 3, 1 R; Whitey Kurowski, 1 for 3, 1 RBI

2B-NY/Gordon, Rolfe; StL/W. Cooper, Slaughter. **3B**-StL/Kurowski. **HR**-NY/Keller. **SB**-NY/Cullenbine, Rizzuto. **Time** 1:57. **Attendance** 34,255.

Game 3 Saturday, October 3 at Yankee Stadium, New York

	1	2	3	4	5	6	7	8	9	R	H	E
St. Louis Cardinals	0	0	1	0	0	0	0	0	1	2	5	1
New York Yankees	0	0	0	0	0	0	0	0	0	0	6	1

Pitchers StL Ernie White (W, 1-0), IP 9, H 6, R 0, ER 0, BB 0, SO 6
NY Spud Chandler (L, 0-1), IP 8, H 3, R 1, ER 1, BB 1, SO 3; Marv Breuer, IP 0, H 2, R 1, ER 0, BB 0, SO 0; Jim Turner, IP 1, H 0, R 0, ER 0, BB 1, SO 0

Top Performers at the Plate
StL Whitey Kurowski, 1 for 2, 1 R, 1 BB
NY Joe DiMaggio, 2 for 4; Phil Rizzuto, 2 for 4

SB-NY/Rizzuto. **Time** 2:30. **Attendance** 69,123.

Game 4 Sunday, October 4 at Yankee Stadium, New York

	1	2	3	4	5	6	7	8	9	R	H	E
St. Louis Cardinals	0	0	0	6	0	0	2	0	1	9	12	1
New York Yankees	1	0	0	0	0	5	0	0	0	6	10	1

Pitchers StL Mort Cooper, IP 5⅓, H 7, R 5, ER 5, BB 1, SO 2; Harry Gumbert, IP ⅓, H 1, R 1, ER 0, BB 0, SO 0; Howie Pollet, IP ⅓, H 0, R 0, ER 0, BB 0, SO 0; Max Lanier (W, 1-0), IP 3, H 2, R 0, ER 0, BB 0, SO 0
NY Hank Borowy, IP 3, H 6, R 6, ER 6, BB 3, SO 1; Atley Donald (L, 0-1), IP 3, H 3, R 2, ER 2, BB 2, SO 1; Tiny Bonham, IP 3, H 3, R 1, ER 1, BB 2, SO 0

Top Performers at the Plate
StL Whitey Kurowski, 1 for 3, 1 R, 2 RBI, 1 BB, 1 SH; Stan Musial, 2 for 3, 2 R, 1 RBI, 2 BB
NY Roy Cullenbine, 2 for 4, 1 R, 2 RBI; Phil Rizzuto, 3 for 5, 1 R

2B-StL/Moore, Musial; NY/Priddy, Rolfe. **HR**-NY/Keller. **Time** 2:28. **Attendance** 69,902.

Game 5 Monday, October 5 at Yankee Stadium, New York

	1	2	3	4	5	6	7	8	9	R	H	E
St. Louis Cardinals	0	0	1	0	1	0	0	2		4	9	4
New York Yankees	1	0	0	1	0	0	0	0	0	2	7	1

Pitchers StL Johnny Beazley (W, 2-0), IP 9, H 7, R 2, ER 2, BB 1, SO 2
NY Red Ruffing (L, 1-1), IP 9, H 9, R 4, ER 4, BB 1, SO 3

Top Performers at the Plate
StL Walker Cooper, 2 for 4, 1 R, 1 RBI; Enos Slaughter, 2 for 4, 1 R, 1 RBI
NY Phil Rizzuto, 2 for 4, 1 R, 1 RBI

HR-StL/Kurowski, Slaughter; NY/Rizzuto. **Time** 1:58. **Attendance** 69,052.

New York Yankees (4) vs. St. Louis Cardinals (1)

The New York Yankees only had to wait one year to get the chance to redeem their previous year's loss in a rematch with the St. Louis Cardinals. Both teams lost several players to military service in 1943—most notably, Joe DiMaggio, Phil Rizzuto and Red Ruffing for New York and Enos Slaughter, Terry Moore and Johnny Beazley for St. Louis—but both clubs took their pennants with double-digit leads over the second-place teams. St. Louis stormed through the season with 105 wins and an 18-game lead on Cincinnati. In only his second full season in the Majors, Cardinal right fielder Stan Musial led the National League in batting (.354) as well as hits, doubles, triples and slugging. But Musial and his teammates managed just two runs and seven hits off New York's Game 1 starter Spud Chandler. Joe Gordon's 450-foot home run in the fourth, three singles and a wild pitch in the sixth accounted for all the scoring for the Yankees. Mort Cooper led St. Louis to a 4-3 win in Game 2, with help from Ray Sanders's two-run blast in the fourth inning, which put his team up 4-1. A double and a triple by the Yanks in the bottom of the ninth gave St. Louis a scare, but New York could manage no more than two runs in the inning. Cardinal fans were envisioning another four straight wins to the title, as in 1942. Hank Borowy cut those dreams short by holding St. Louis to two runs on six hits in

Game 3; meanwhile, New York got a five-run inning in the eighth to put the game away. Billy Johnson's bases-loaded triple keyed the attack. Returning home to St. Louis for Game 4, the Cards didn't fare much better. Marius Russo pitched a masterful game and prevented any Cardinals from reaching second base until the seventh inning, when errors by Frankie Crosetti and Billy Johnson led to St. Louis's only run on the day. Max Lanier and Harry Brecheen put in good performances for St. Louis, but a single by Bill Dickey and a sacrifice fly by Crosetti drove in two runs for the Yankees for a 2-1 win. Russo scored the game-winning run after hitting a leadoff double in the eighth inning. The next day, the New York Yankees claimed their 10th World Series Championship behind Chandler's complete-game shutout. Mort Cooper started off well for St. Louis, striking out the first five Yankee batters of the game— a World Series record—but Dickey tagged Cooper in the sixth with a home run onto the Sportman's Park roof to bring in the game's only runs. It was Joe McCarthy's seventh World Series victory, a record that has been tied but never broken.

Left: New York's Spud Chandler and St. Louis's Max Lanier faced off in the first game of the 1943 Series. Chandler won the opener and then closed the Series out six days later in Game 5.

1943 WORLD SERIES COMPOSITE STATISTICS

NEW YORK YANKEES/Joe McCarthy, Manager

Player	pos	G	AB	R	H	2B	3B	HR	RBI	BB	SO	SB	BA	SA	E	FPct
Tiny Bonham	p	1	2	0	0	0	0	0	0	0	0	0	.000	.000	0	–
Hank Borowy	p	1	2	1	1	1	0	0	0	0	1	0	.500	1.000	0	1.000
Spud Chandler	p	2	6	0	1	0	0	0	0	0	2	0	.167	.167	0	1.000
Frankie Crosetti	ss	5	18	4	5	0	0	1	4	2	3	1	.278	.278	3	.893
Bill Dickey	c	5	18	1	5	0	0	1	4	2	2	0	.278	.444	0	1.000
Nick Etten	1b	5	19	0	2	0	0	0	2	1	2	0	.105	.105	1	.980
Joe Gordon	2b	5	17	2	4	1	0	1	2	3	3	0	.235	.471	0	1.000
Billy Johnson	3b	5	20	3	6	1	1	0	3	0	3	0	.300	.450	1	.917
Charlie Keller	lf	5	18	3	4	0	1	0	2	2	5	1	.222	.333	0	1.000
Johnny Lindell	cf-rf	4	9	1	1	0	0	0	1	0	4	0	.111	.111	0	1.000
Bud Metheny	rf	2	8	0	1	0	0	0	0	0	2	0	.125	.125	0	1.000
Johnny Murphy	p	2	0	0	0	0	0	0	0	0	0	0	–	–	0	1.000
Marius Russo	p	1	3	1	2	2	0	0	1	1	0	0	.667	1.333	0	1.000
Tuck Stainback	rf-cf	5	17	0	3	0	0	0	0	0	2	0	.176	.176	0	1.000
Snuffy Stirnweiss	ph	1	1	0	0	0	0	0	0	0	0	0	.000	.000	–	–
Roy Weatherly	ph	1	1	0	0	0	0	0	0	0	0	0	.000	.000	–	–
Totals		5	159	17	35	5	2	2	14	12	30	2	.220	.314	5	.975

Pitcher	G	GS	CG	IP	H	R	ER	BB	SO	W-L	Sv	ERA
Tiny Bonham	1	1	0	8	6	4	4	3	9	0-1	0	4.50
Hank Borowy	1	1	0	8	6	2	2	3	4	1-0	0	2.25
Spud Chandler	2	2	2	18	17	2	1	3	10	2-0	0	0.50
Johnny Murphy	2	0	0	2	1	0	0	1	1	0-0	1	0.00
Marius Russo	1	1	1	9	7	1	0	1	2	1-0	0	0.00
Totals	5	5	3	45	37	9	7	11	25	4-1	1	1.40

ST. LOUIS CARDINALS/Billy Southworth, Manager

Player	pos	G	AB	R	H	2B	3B	HR	RBI	BB	SO	SB	BA	SA	E	FPct
Al Brazle	p	1	3	0	0	0	0	0	0	0	1	0	.000	.000	0	1.000
Harry Brecheen	p	3	0	0	0	0	0	0	0	0	0	0	–	–	0	1.000
Mort Cooper	p	2	5	0	0	0	0	0	0	0	3	0	.000	.000	0	1.000
Walker Cooper	c	5	17	1	5	0	0	0	0	0	1	0	.294	.294	2	.939
Frank Demaree	ph	1	1	0	0	0	0	0	0	0	0	0	.000	.000	–	–
Murry Dickson	p	1	0	0	0	0	0	0	0	0	0	0	–	–	0	1.000
Debs Garms	ph-lf	2	5	0	0	0	0	0	0	0	2	0	.000	.000	0	1.000
Johnny Hopp	cf	1	4	0	0	0	0	0	0	0	1	0	.000	.000	0	1.000
Lou Klein	2b	5	22	0	3	0	0	0	0	1	2	0	.136	.136	2	.920
Howie Krist	p	1	0	0	0	0	0	0	0	0	0	0	–	–	0	1.000
Whitey Kurowski	3b	5	18	2	4	1	0	0	1	0	3	0	.222	.278	2	.889
Max Lanier	p	3	4	0	1	0	0	0	1	0	0	0	.250	.250	1	.750
Danny Litwhiler	lf-ph	5	15	0	4	1	0	0	2	2	4	0	.267	.333	0	1.000
Marty Marion	ss	5	14	1	5	2	0	1	2	3	1	1	.357	.714	1	.957
Stan Musial	rf	5	18	2	5	0	0	0	2	2	0	0	.278	.278	0	1.000
Sam Narron	ph	1	1	0	0	0	0	0	0	0	0	0	.000	.000	–	–
Ken O'Dea	ph-c	2	3	0	2	0	0	0	0	0	0	0	.667	.667	0	1.000
Ray Sanders	1b	5	17	3	5	0	0	1	2	3	4	0	.294	.471	0	1.000
Harry Walker	cf-ph	5	18	0	3	1	0	0	0	2	0	0	.167	.222	2	.833
Ernie White	pr	1	0	0	0	0	0	0	0	0	0	0	–	–	–	–
Totals		5	185	9	37	5	0	2	8	11	26	1	.224	.291	10	.948

Pitcher	G	GS	CG	IP	H	R	ER	BB	SO	W-L	Sv	ERA
Al Brazle	1	1	0	7⅓	6	5	3	2	4	0-1	0	3.68
Harry Brecheen	3	0	0	3⅔	5	1	1	3	3	0-1	0	2.45
Mort Cooper	2	2	1	16	11	5	5	3	10	1-1	0	2.81
Murry Dickson	1	0	0	⅔	0	0	0	1	0	0-0	0	0.00
Howie Krist	1	0	0	0	1	0	0	0	0	0-0	0	–
Max Lanier	3	2	0	15⅓	13	5	3	3	13	0-1	0	1.76
Totals	5	5	1	43	35	17	12	12	30	1-4	0	2.51

Series Outstanding Player: Billy Johnson, New York Yankees. **Series Outstanding Pitcher:** Spud Chandler, New York Yankees. **Average Length of Game:** 2 hours, 11 minutes. **Total Attendance:** 277,312. **Average Attendance:** 55,462 (69,081 at Yankee Stadium; 35,034 at Sportsman's Park). **Umpires:** John Reardon (NL), Eddie Rommel (AL), Joe Rue (AL), Bill Stewart (NL). **Winning Player's Share:** $6,139. **Losing Player's Share:** $4,322.

Right: Johnny Lindell dislodges the ball from Whitey Kurowski's grasp to advance to third on a bunt in Game 3. The play preceded a five-run rally for New York.

Below: Marius Russo allowed only one unearned run in a close fourth game contest.

The Cardinals collected 10 hits in Game 5 without scoring a run, the most hits by a team shut out in a Series game.

Above: Billy Johnson was a rookie in 1943, but his six hits in the Series topped even the savviest veterans.

Right: An error by Johnson allowed Cardinal Ray Sanders to score from third and tie Game 4 in the seventh inning.

Game 1 Tuesday, October 5 at Yankee Stadium, New York

	1	2	3	4	5	6	7	8	9	R	H	E
St. Louis Cardinals	0	1	0	0	1	0	0	0	0	2	7	2
New York Yankees	0	0	0	2	0	2	0	0	x	4	8	2

Pitchers StL Max Lanier (L, 0-1), IP 7, H 7, R 4, ER 2, BB 0, SO 7; Harry Brecheen, IP 1, H 1, R 0, ER 0, BB 1, SO 1
NY Spud Chandler (W, 1-0), IP 9, H 7, R 2, ER 1, BB 1, SO 3

Top Performers at the Plate
StL Ray Sanders, 2 for 4, 1 R
NY Joe Gordon, 1 for 3, 1 R, 1 RBI, 1 BB; Billy Johnson, 2 for 4, 1 R

2B-StL/Marion. **HR**-NY/Gordon. **SB**-NY/Crosetti. **Time** 2:07. **Attendance** 68,676.

Game 2 Wednesday, October 6 at Yankee Stadium, New York

	1	2	3	4	5	6	7	8	9	R	H	E
St. Louis Cardinals	0	0	1	3	0	0	0	0	0	4	7	2
New York Yankees	0	0	0	1	0	0	0	0	2	3	6	0

Pitchers StL Mort Cooper (W, 1-0), IP 9, H 6, R 3, ER 3, BB 1, SO 4
NY Tiny Bonham (L, 0-1), IP 8, H 6, R 4, ER 4, BB 3, SO 9; Johnny Murphy, IP 1, H 1, R 0, ER 0, BB 1, SO 0

Top Performers at the Plate
StL Marty Marion, 1 for 3, 1 R, 1 RBI, 1 BB; Ray Sanders, 1 for 3, 1 R, 2 RBI, 1 BB
NY Frankie Crosetti, 2 for 4, 1 R; Billy Johnson, 2 for 4, 1 R

2B-NY/Johnson. **3B**-NY/Keller. **HR**-StL/Marion, Sanders. **SB**-Marion. **Time** 2:08. **Attendance** 68,578.

Game 3 Thursday, October 7 at Yankee Stadium, New York

	1	2	3	4	5	6	7	8	9	R	H	E
St. Louis Cardinals	0	0	0	2	0	0	0	0	0	2	6	4
New York Yankees	0	0	0	0	1	0	5	x		6	8	0

Pitchers StL Al Brazle (L, 0-1), IP 7⅓, H 5, R 6, ER 3, BB 2, SO 4; Howie Krist, IP 0, H 1, R 0, ER 0, BB 0, SO 0; Harry Brecheen, IP ⅔, H 2, R 0, ER 0, BB 0, SO 0
NY Hank Borowy (W, 1-0), IP 8, H 6, R 2, ER 2, BB 3, SO 4; Johnny Murphy (Sv, 1), IP 1, H 0, R 0, ER 0, BB 0, SO 1

Top Performers at the Plate
StL Danny Litwhiler, 2 for 4, 2 RBI
NY Bill Dickey, 2 for 4; Billy Johnson, 1 for 4, 1 R, 3 RBI

2B-StL/Kurowski, Walker; NY/Borowy. **3B**-NY/Johnson. **Time** 2:10. **Attendance** 69,990.

Game 4 Sunday, October 10 at Sportsman's Park, St. Louis

	1	2	3	4	5	6	7	8	9	R	H	E
New York Yankees	0	0	0	1	0	0	0	1	0	2	6	2
St. Louis Cardinals	0	0	0	0	0	1	0	0		1	7	1

Pitchers NY Marius Russo (W, 1-0), IP 9, H 7, R 1, ER 0, BB 1, SO 2
StL Max Lanier, IP 7, H 4, R 1, ER 1, BB 1, SO 5; Harry Brecheen (L, 0-1), IP 2, H 2, R 1, ER 1, BB 2, SO 2

Top Performers at the Plate
NY Bill Dickey, 1 for 3, 1 RBI, 1 BB; Marius Russo, 2 for 3, 1 R, 1 BB, 2 2B
StL Marty Marion, 2 for 3, 1 BB; Stan Musial, 2 for 4

2B-NY/Gordon, Russo 2; StL/Litwhiler, Marion. **SB**-NY/Keller. **Time** 2:06. **Attendance** 36,196.

Game 5 Monday, October 11 at Sportsman's Park, St. Louis

	1	2	3	4	5	6	7	8	9	R	H	E
New York Yankees	0	0	0	0	0	2	0	0	0	2	7	1
St. Louis Cardinals	0	0	0	0	0	0	0	0	0	0	10	1

Pitchers NY Spud Chandler (W, 2-0), IP 9, H 10, R 0, ER 0, BB 2, SO 7
StL Mort Cooper (L, 1-1), IP 7, H 5, R 2, ER 2, BB 2, SO 6; Max Lanier, IP 1⅓, H 2, R 0, ER 0, BB 2, SO 1; Murry Dickson, IP ⅔, H 0, R 0, ER 0, BB 1, SO 0

Top Performers at the Plate
NY Charlie Keller, 1 for 3, 1 R, 1 BB
StL Whitey Kurowski, 2 for 4; Ken O'Dea, 2 for 2

HR-NY/Dickey. **Time** 2:24. **Attendance** 33,872.

117

St. Louis Cardinals (4) vs. St. Louis Browns (2)

By 1944—in fact, by 1926—every one of the original 16 Major League teams had reached baseball's ultimate goal, the World Series, except one. The St. Louis Browns had never finished higher than second in the American League, and in the 14 seasons preceding 1944, they managed only 1 winning season. Finally, in a war-depleted league, Luke Sewell's ragtag bunch grabbed the franchise's first pennant with a last-day victory. The Browns would get the chance to play the Cardinals for city bragging rights in the Fall Classic. The Cards enjoyed their 3rd straight 100-win season and were heavy favorites over their landlords. (The Browns owned Sportman's Park, which the Cardinals had been calling home since 1920.) Denny Galehouse won only 9 games for the Browns in 1944, but he got the Game 1 start against Mort Cooper. The Cardinal hurlers appeared to be in control, with Cooper allowing two hits in 7 innings and Blix Donnelly pitching 2 perfect innings in relief. The only trouble was that the two hits came consecutively in the 4th inning: a single by Gene Moore and a two-run homer by George McQuinn—the Browns' only World Series home run. Galehouse kept the Cardinals from scoring until the 9th inning, and the Browns had a 2-1 victory in their first World Series game. Another low-scoring affair took place in Game 2, with the teams locked in a 2-2 tie through 10 innings until Cardinal pinch hitter Ken O'Dea drove in the game-winner in the bottom of the 11th. The Browns

regained the Series lead the next day, behind a 10-strikeout performance by Jack Kramer. The Browns strung five consecutive singles together with a walk and a wild pitch to score four runs with two outs in the 3rd inning en route to a 6-2 win. Through the first 3 games, the Browns had given up only six runs, three of them unearned. The Cardinals got consecutive complete-game outings from Harry Brecheen and Mort Cooper to win Games 4 and 5 and take a 3-games-to-2 lead in the Series. A 3-for-4 day by Stan Musial, including a two-run blast in the 1st, paced the Cards to a 5-1 win in the 4th game, and solo homers by Ray Sanders and Danny Litwhiler accounted for all the scoring in Game 5. The Browns scored first in Game 6 on Chet Laabs's triple and McQuinn's single, but a throwing error by shortstop Vern Stephens in the 4th led to a three-run inning for the Cardinals. The Cards' Ted Wilks then pitched perfect ball in the final 3 2/3 innings, giving the club its 5th championship banner in franchise history. The Browns, meanwhile, went down to disappointing defeat in their one and only Series appearance. Despite their strong pitching, the Browns' 10 errors in the Series, compared to the Cardinals' 1 were their downfall.

Above: St. Louians had the World Series all to themselves in 1944 when the Browns and Cardinals met in the Fall Classic.

1944 WORLD SERIES COMPOSITE STATISTICS

ST. LOUIS CARDINALS/Billy Southworth, Manager

Player	pos	G	AB	R	H	2B	3B	HR	RBI	BB	SO	SB	BA	SA	E	FPct
Augie Bergamo	ph-lf	3	6	0	0	0	0	0	1	2	3	0	.000	.000	0	1.000
Harry Brecheen	p	1	4	0	0	0	0	0	0	0	1	0	.000	.000	0	1.000
Bud Byerly	p	1	0	0	0	0	0	0	0	0	0	0	—	—	0	—
Mort Cooper	p	2	4	0	0	0	0	0	0	0	2	0	.000	.000	0	1.000
Walker Cooper	c	6	22	1	7	2	1	0	2	3	2	0	.318	.500	0	1.000
Blix Donnelly	p	2	1	0	0	0	0	0	0	1	0	0	.000	.000	0	1.000
George Fallon	2b	2	2	0	0	0	0	0	0	1	0	0	.000	.000	0	—
Debs Garms	ph	2	2	0	0	0	0	0	0	0	0	0	.000	.000	—	—
Johnny Hopp	cf	6	27	2	5	0	0	0	0	8	0	0	.185	.185	0	1.000
Al Jurisich	p	1	0	0	0	0	0	0	0	0	0	0	—	—	0	—
Whitey Kurowski	3b	6	23	2	5	1	0	0	1	1	4	0	.217	.261	0	1.000
Max Lanier	p	2	4	0	2	0	0	0	1	0	0	0	.500	.500	0	1.000
Danny Litwhiler	lf	5	20	2	4	1	0	1	1	2	7	0	.200	.400	0	1.000
Marty Marion	ss	6	22	1	5	3	0	0	2	2	3	0	.227	.364	0	1.000
Stan Musial	rf	6	23	2	7	2	0	1	2	2	0	0	.304	.522	1	.917
Ken O'Dea	ph	3	3	0	1	0	0	0	2	0	0	0	.333	.333	—	—
Ray Sanders	1b	6	21	5	6	0	0	1	1	5	8	0	.286	.429	0	1.000
Freddy Schmidt	p	1	1	0	0	0	0	0	0	0	1	0	.000	.000	0	—
Emil Verban	2b	6	17	1	7	0	0	0	2	2	0	0	.412	.412	0	1.000
Ted Wilks	p	2	2	0	0	0	0	0	0	0	0	0	.000	.000	0	1.000
Totals		**6**	**204**	**16**	**49**	**9**	**1**	**3**	**15**	**19**	**43**	**0**	**.240**	**.338**	**1**	**.996**

Pitcher	G	GS	CG	IP	H	R	ER	BB	SO	W-L	Sv	ERA
Harry Brecheen	1	1	1	9	9	1	1	4	4	1-0	0	1.00
Bud Byerly	1	0	0	1⅓	0	0	0	0	1	0-0	0	0.00
Mort Cooper	2	2	1	16	9	2	2	5	16	1-1	0	1.13
Blix Donnelly	2	0	0	6	2	0	0	1	9	1-0	0	0.00
Al Jurisich	1	0	0	⅔	2	2	2	1	0	0-0	0	27.00
Max Lanier	2	2	0	12⅓	8	3	3	8	11	1-0	0	2.19
Freddy Schmidt	1	0	0	3⅓	1	0	0	1	1	0-0	0	0.00
Ted Wilks	2	1	0	6⅓	5	4	4	3	7	0-1	1	5.68
Totals	**6**	**6**	**2**	**55**	**36**	**12**	**12**	**23**	**49**	**4-2**	**1**	**1.96**

ST. LOUIS BROWNS/Luke Sewell, Manager

Player	pos	G	AB	R	H	2B	3B	HR	RBI	BB	SO	SB	BA	SA	E	FPct
Floyd Baker	ph-2b	2	2	0	0	0	0	0	0	0	2	0	.000	.000	0	1.000
Milt Byrnes	ph	3	2	0	0	0	0	0	0	1	2	0	.000	.000	—	—
Mike Chartak	ph	2	2	0	0	0	0	0	0	0	0	0	.000	.000	—	—
Mark Christman	3b	6	22	0	2	0	0	0	1	0	6	0	.091	.091	1	.923
Ellis Clary	ph	1	1	0	0	0	0	0	0	0	0	0	.000	.000	—	—
Denny Galehouse	p	2	5	0	1	0	0	0	0	1	1	0	.200	.200	0	1.000
Don Gutteridge	2b	6	21	1	3	1	0	0	0	3	5	0	.143	.190	3	.897
Red Hayworth	c	6	17	1	2	1	0	0	1	3	1	0	.118	.176	1	.979
Al Hollingsworth	p	1	1	0	0	0	0	0	0	0	0	0	.000	.000	0	1.000
Sig Jakucki	p	1	0	0	0	0	0	0	0	0	0	0	—	—	0	1.000
Jack Kramer	p	2	4	0	0	0	0	0	0	0	2	0	.000	.000	0	1.000
Mike Kreevich	cf	6	26	0	6	3	0	0	0	0	5	0	.231	.346	0	1.000
Chet Laabs	lf-ph	5	15	1	3	1	1	0	0	2	6	0	.200	.400	0	1.000
Frank Mancuso	ph-c	2	3	0	2	0	0	0	1	0	0	0	.667	.667	0	1.000
George McQuinn	1b	6	16	2	7	2	0	1	5	7	2	0	.438	.750	0	1.000
Gene Moore	rf	6	22	4	4	0	0	0	3	6	0	0	.182	.182	0	1.000
Bob Muncrief	p	2	1	0	0	0	0	0	0	0	1	0	.000	.000	0	1.000
Nels Potter	p	2	4	0	0	0	0	0	0	1	0	0	.000	.000	2	.500
Tex Shirley	pr-p	2	0	0	0	0	0	0	0	0	0	0	—	—	0	1.000
Vern Stephens	ss	6	22	2	5	1	0	0	3	3	3	0	.227	.273	3	.903
Tom Turner	ph	1	1	0	0	0	0	0	0	0	0	0	.000	.000	—	—
Al Zarilla	ph-lf	4	10	1	1	0	0	0	1	0	4	0	.100	.100	0	1.000
Totals		**6**	**197**	**12**	**36**	**9**	**1**	**1**	**9**	**23**	**49**	**0**	**.183**	**.254**	**10**	**.957**

Pitcher	G	GS	CG	IP	H	R	ER	BB	SO	W-L	Sv	ERA
Denny Galehouse	2	2	2	18	13	3	3	5	15	1-1	0	1.50
Al Hollingsworth	1	0	0	4	5	1	1	2	1	0-0	0	2.25
Sig Jakucki	1	1	0	3	5	4	3	0	4	0-1	0	9.00
Jack Kramer	2	1	1	11	9	2	0	4	12	1-0	0	0.00
Bob Muncrief	2	0	0	6⅔	5	1	1	4	4	0-1	0	1.35
Nels Potter	2	2	0	9⅔	10	5	1	3	6	0-1	0	0.93
Tex Shirley	1	0	0	2	2	0	0	1	1	0-0	0	0.00
Totals	**6**	**6**	**3**	**54⅓**	**49**	**16**	**9**	**19**	**43**	**2-4**	**0**	**1.49**

Series Outstanding Player: Walker Cooper, St. Louis Cardinals. **Series Outstanding Pitcher:** Mort Cooper, St. Louis Cardinals. **Average Length of Game:** 2 horus, 15 minutes. **Total Attendance:** 206,708. **Average Attendance:** 34,451. **Umpires:** Tom Dunn (NL), Bill McGowan (AL), George Pipgras (AL), John Sears (NL). **Winning Player's Share:** $4,626. **Losing Player's Share:** $2,744.

Left: George McQuinn comes home with the only World Series home run in Browns history.

Below: Whitey Kurowski is caught in a pickle between first and second in the sixth inning of the final game. He didn't survive the rundown, but the Cardinals won the game.

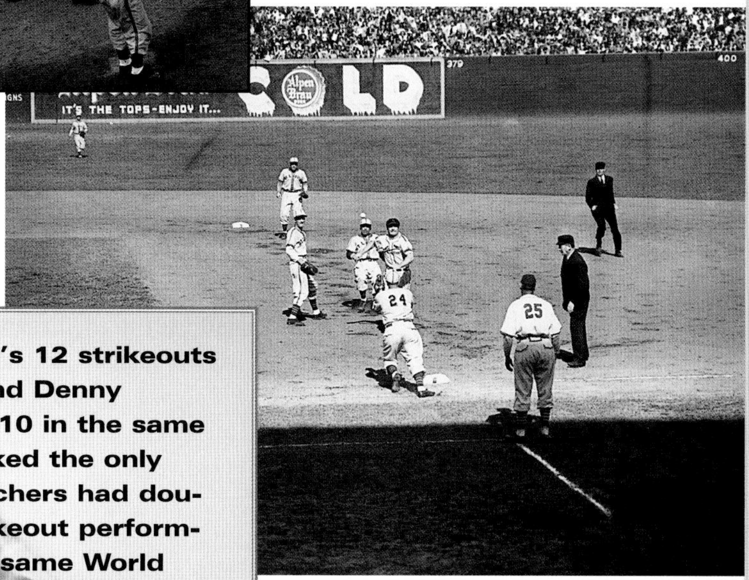

Mort Cooper's 12 strikeouts in Game 5 and Denny Galehouse's 10 in the same contest marked the only time two pitchers had double-digit strikeout performances in the same World Series game. The 22 strikeouts on the day were part of a combined 92 for the Series, a record for a six-game Series.

Below: Ray Sanders scores on Emil Verban's sacrifice fly for the Cardinals' second run of Game 2.

Below: Pitcher Ted Wilks gets a handshake from catcher Walker Cooper after Wilks nailed down the save, and the Series, in Game 6.

The Browns sent up three pinch hitters in the final inning of Game 5, and Mort Cooper struck them all out. In fact, the Browns used eight pinch hitters in the last two games, and each one went down on strikes.

Game 1 Wednesday, October 4 at Sportsman's Park, St. Louis

	1	2	3	4	5	6	7	8	9	R	H	E
St. Louis Browns	0	0	0	2	0	0	0	0	0	2	2	0
St. Louis Cardinals	0	0	0	0	0	0	0	0	1	1	7	0

Pitchers StLB Denny Galehouse (W, 1-0), IP 9, H 7, R 1, ER 1, BB 4, SO 5
StLC Mort Cooper (L, 0-1), IP 7, H 2, R 2, ER 2, BB 3, SO 4; Blix Donnelly, IP 2, H 0, R 0, ER 0, BB 0, SO 2

Top Performers at the Plate
StLB George McQuinn, 1 for 3, 1 R, 2 RBI; Gene Moore, 1 for 3, 1 R, 1 BB
StLC Marty Marion, 2 for 4, 1 R, 2 2B

2B-StLC/Marion 2. **HR**-StLB/McQuinn. **Time** 2:05. **Attendance** 33,242.

Game 2 Thursday, October 5 at Sportsman's Park, St. Louis

	1	2	3	4	5	6	7	8	9	10	11	R	H	E
St. Louis Browns	0	0	0	0	0	0	2	0	0	0	0	2	7	4
St. Louis Cardinals	0	0	1	1	0	0	0	0	0	0	1	3	7	0

Pitchers StLB Nels Potter, IP 6, H 4, R 2, ER 0, BB 2, SO 3; Bob Muncrief (L, 0-1), IP 4⅓, H 3, R 1, ER 1, BB 3, SO 4
StLC Max Lanier, IP 7, H 5, R 2, ER 2, BB 3, SO 6; Blix Donnelly (W, 1-0), IP 4, H 2, R 0, ER 0, BB 1, SO 7

Top Performers at the Plate
StLB George McQuinn, 1 for 2, 3 BB; Gene Moore, 2 for 5, 1 R
StLC Whitey Kurowski, 2 for 4, 1 SH; Ray Sanders, 1 for 3, 2 R, 2 BB

2B-StLB/Hayworth, Kreevich, McQuinn; StLC/W. Cooper, Kurowski. **Time** 2:32. **Attendance** 35,076.

Game 3 Friday, October 6 at Sportsman's Park, St. Louis

	1	2	3	4	5	6	7	8	9	R	H	E
St. Louis Cardinals	1	0	0	0	0	1	0	0		2	7	0
St. Louis Browns	0	0	4	0	0	2	0	x		6	8	2

Pitchers StLC Ted Wilks (L, 0-1), IP 2⅔, H 5, R 4, ER 4, BB 3, SO 3; Freddy Schmidt, IP 3⅓, H 1, R 0, ER 0, BB 1, SO 1; Al Jurisich, IP ⅔, H 2, R 2, ER 2, BB 1, SO 0; Bud Byerly, IP 1⅓, H 0, R 0, ER 0, BB 0, SO 1
StLB Jack Kramer (W, 1-0), IP 9, H 7, R 2, ER 0, BB 2, SO 10

Top Performers at the Plate
StLC Walker Cooper, 2 for 4, 1 RBI; Marty Marion, 2 for 4, 1 RBI
StLB George McQuinn, 3 for 3, 1 R, 2 RBI, 1 BB; Vern Stephens, 1 for 2, 2 R, 2 BB

2B-StLC/W. Cooper; StLB/Gutteridge, McQuinn. **Time** 2:19. **Attendance** 34,737.

Game 4 Saturday, October 7 at Sportsman's Park, St. Louis

	1	2	3	4	5	6	7	8	9	R	H	E
St. Louis Cardinals	2	0	2	0	0	1	0	0		5	12	0
St. Louis Browns	0	0	0	0	0	0	1	0		1	9	1

Pitchers StLC Harry Brecheen (W, 1-0), IP 9, H 9, R 1, ER 1, BB 4, SO 4
StLB Sig Jakucki (L, 0-1), IP 3, H 5, R 4, ER 3, BB 0, SO 4; Al Hollingsworth, IP 4, H 5, R 1, ER 1, BB 2, SO 1; Tex Shirley, IP 2, H 2, R 0, ER 0, BB 1, SO 1

Top Performers at the Plate
StLC Stan Musial, 3 for 4, 2 R, 2 RBI, 1 BB; Walker Cooper, 2 for 4, 1 RBI, 1 BB
StLB Don Gutteridge, 2 for 4, 1 BB; Chet Laabs, 2 for 4

2B-StLC/Marion, Musial; StLB/Laabs. **3B**-StLC/W. Cooper. **HR**-StLC/Musial. **Time** 2:22. **Attendance** 35,455.

Game 5 Sunday, October 8 at Sportsman's Park, St. Louis

	1	2	3	4	5	6	7	8	9	R	H	E
St. Louis Cardinals	0	0	0	0	1	0	1	0		2	6	1
St. Louis Browns	0	0	0	0	0	0	0	0		0	7	1

Pitchers StLC Mort Cooper (W, 1-1), IP 9, H 7, R 0, ER 0, BB 2, SO 12
StLB Denny Galehouse (L, 1-1), IP 9, H 6, R 2, ER 2, BB 1, SO 10

Top Performers at the Plate
StLC Danny Litwhiler, 2 for 4, 1 R, 1 RBI
StLB Mike Kreevich, 2 for 4; Vern Stephens, 3 for 4

2B-StLC/Litwhiler, Musial; StLB/Kreevich, Stephens. **HR**-StLC/Litwhiler, Sanders. **Time** 2:04. **Attendance** 36,568.

Game 6 Monday, October 9 at Sportsman's Park, St. Louis

	1	2	3	4	5	6	7	8	9	R	H	E
St. Louis Browns	0	1	0	0	0	0	0	0	0	1	3	2
St. Louis Cardinals	0	0	0	3	0	0	0	0	x	3	10	0

Pitchers StLB Nels Potter (L, 0-1), IP 3⅔, H 6, R 3, ER 1, BB 1, SO 3; Bob Muncrief, IP 2⅓, H 2, R 0, ER 0, BB 1, SO 0; Jack Kramer, IP 2, H 2, R 0, ER 0, BB 2, SO 2
StLC Max Lanier (W, 1-0), IP 5⅓, H 3, R 1, ER 1, BB 5, SO 5; Ted Wilks (S, 1), IP 3⅔, H 0, R 0, ER 0, BB 0, SO 4

Top Performers at the Plate
StLB Chet Laabs, 1 for 2, 1 R, 2 BB; George McQuinn, 1 for 2, 1 RBI, 1 BB, 1 SH
StLC Walker Cooper, 2 for 3, 1 R, 1 BB; Emil Verban, 3 for 3, 1 RBI, 1 BB

2B-StLB/Kreevich. **3B**-StLB/Laabs. **Time** 2:06. **Attendance** 31,630.

Detroit Tigers (4) vs. Chicago Cubs (3)

After missing three full seasons while serving in the U.S. Army Air Corps, Hank Greenberg rejoined the Detroit Tigers in the middle of the 1945 season and helped the franchise win its first pennant in five years. Virgil Trucks also returned following the end of the war. Trucks pitched in the pennant-clinching final game, his only appearance of the regular season, with Greenberg delivering a pinch-hit grand slam in the 9th inning of that game. The Chicago Cubs had a well-rounded team that led the National League in batting average and ERA. Hank Borowy, a midseason acquisition from the Yankees, got the start for Chicago against 25-game winner Hal Newhouser in the Series opener. The Cubs shelled Newhouser for seven runs in the first 3 innings, while Borowy kept Detroit off the board with a six-hitter to win in a 9-0 blowout. Trucks pitched his second game of 1945 in Game 2 of the Series, and another key home run by Hank Greenberg, a three-run blast in the 5th inning, gave "Fire" Trucks the victory. A 2nd-inning single by Rudy York and a walk to Bob Swift in the 6th provided the only baserunners for Detroit in Game 3, as Chicago's Claude Passeau hurled only the second one-hitter in World Series history. Dizzy Trout tied the Series at 2-2 with a five-hitter in Game 4. The only Cub run came on a throwing error by York in the 6th, but Detroit had plenty of breathing room, thanks to a four-run 4th inning. In Game 5, Borowy didn't have the stuff he had in Game 1. The Tigers knocked him for four straight base hits to start off the 6th inning, and with the help of a couple walks, turned them into four runs. Newhouser went the distance for Detroit to earn his first win of the Series. The teams battled for nearly $3\frac{1}{2}$ hours in Game 6 the following day. Chicago rallied for four runs in the 5th and tacked on three more in the next 2 innings, but Detroit got its fifth four-run inning of the Series to bring the teams even at 7-7 in the 8th. Trout and Borowy each pitched 4 innings of scoreless ball in relief, until a pinch-hit single by Frank Secory and an RBI double by Stan Hack—Hack's fourth hit of the game—gave Chicago an 8-7 win in the 12th. After a day of rain, Cubs manager Charlie Grimm gave Borowy the start in the deciding Game 7, where he was matched up with Newhouser. Borowy was hit hard again, as Detroit's first three batters singled before Borowy was yanked from the game. All three of Borowy's runners eventually scored in a five-run 1st inning. Newhouser effectively protected that lead with a 10-strikeout performance. The Tigers finished with a 9-3 win in the final game, and Detroit had its second World Series championship.

Above: After spending most of the year in the Navy, Virgil Trucks won in his second appearance of 1945 in Game 2 of the World Series.

1945 WORLD SERIES COMPOSITE STATISTICS

DETROIT TIGERS/Steve O'Neill, Manager

Player	pos	G	AB	R	H	2B	3B	HR	RBI	BB	SO	SB	BA	SA	E	FPct
Al Benton	p	3	0	0	0	0	0	0	0	0	0	0	–	–	0	1.000
Red Borom	ph	2	1	0	0	0	0	0	0	0	0	0	.000	.000	–	–
Tommy Bridges	p	1	0	0	0	0	0	0	0	0	0	0	–	–	0	–
George Caster	p	1	0	0	0	0	0	0	0	0	0	0	–	–	0	–
Doc Cramer	cf	7	29	7	11	0	0	0	4	1	0	1	.379	.379	0	1.000
Roy Cullenbine	rf	7	22	5	5	2	0	0	4	8	2	1	.227	.318	0	1.000
Zeb Eaton	ph	1	1	0	0	0	0	0	0	0	1	0	.000	.000		
Hank Greenberg	lf	7	23	7	7	3	0	2	7	6	5	0	.304	.696	0	1.000
Joe Hoover	ss	1	3	1	1	0	0	0	1	0	0	0	.333	.333	0	1.000
Chuck Hostetler	ph	3	3	0	0	0	0	0	0	0	0	0	.000	.000	–	–
Bob Maier	ph	1	1	0	1	0	0	0	0	0	0	0	1.000	1.000	–	–
Eddie Mayo	2b	7	28	4	7	1	0	0	2	3	2	0	.250	.286	2	.939
John McHale	ph	3	3	0	0	0	0	0	0	0	1	0	.000	.000	–	–
Ed Mierkowicz	lf	1	0	0	0	0	0	0	0	0	0	0	–	–	0	–
Les Mueller	p	1	0	0	0	0	0	0	0	0	0	0	–	–	0	–
Hal Newhouser	p	3	8	0	0	0	0	0	1	1	1	0	.000	000	1	.889
Jimmy Outlaw	3b	7	28	1	5	0	0	0	3	2	1	1	.179	.179	0	1.000
Stubby Overmire	p	1	1	0	0	0	0	0	0	0	0	0	.000	.000	0	1.000
Paul Richards	c	7	19	0	4	2	0	0	6	4	3	0	.211	.316	1	.981
Bob Swift	c	3	4	1	1	0	0	0	0	2	0	0	.250	.250	0	1.000
Jim Tobin	p	1	1	0	0	0	0	0	0	0	0	0	.000	.000	0	1.000
Dizzy Trout	p	2	6	0	1	0	0	0	0	0	0	0	.167	.167	0	1.000
Virgil Trucks	p	2	4	0	0	0	0	0	0	1	1	0	.000	.000	0	1.000
Hub Walker	ph	2	2	1	1	1	0	0	0	0	0	0	.500	1.000	–	–
Skeeter Webb	ss	7	27	4	5	0	0	0	1	2	1	0	.185	.185	0	1.000
Rudy York	1b	7	28	1	5	1	0	0	3	3	4	0	.179	.214	1	.987
Totals		**7**	**242**	**32**	**54**	**10**	**0**	**2**	**32**	**33**	**22**	**3**	**.223**	**.289**	**5**	**.983**

Pitcher	G	GS	CG	IP	H	R	ER	BB	SO	W-L	Sv	ERA
Al Benton	3	0	0	$4\frac{2}{3}$	6	1	1	0	5	0-0	0	1.93
Tommy Bridges	1	0	0	$1\frac{2}{3}$	3	3	3	3	1	0-0	0	16.20
George Caster	1	0	0	$\frac{2}{3}$	0	0	0	0	1	0-0	0	0.00
Les Mueller	1	0	0	2	0	0	0	1	1	0-0	0	0.00
Hal Newhouser	3	3	2	$20\frac{2}{3}$	25	14	14	4	22	2-1	0	6.10
Stubby Overmire	1	1	0	6	4	2	2	2	2	0-1	0	3.00
Jim Tobin	1	0	0	3	4	2	2	1	0	0-0	0	6.00
Dizzy Trout	2	1	1	$13\frac{2}{3}$	9	2	1	3	9	1-1	0	0.66
Virgil Trucks	2	2	1	$13\frac{1}{3}$	14	5	5	5	7	1-0	0	3.38
Totals	**7**	**7**	**4**	$\mathbf{65\frac{2}{3}}$	**65**	**29**	**28**	**19**	**48**	**4-3**	**0**	**3.84**

CHICAGO CUBS/Charlie Grimm, Manager

Player	pos	G	AB	R	H	2B	3B	HR	RBI	BB	SO	SB	BA	SA	E	FPct
Heinz Becker	ph	3	2	0	1	0	0	0	0	1	1	0	.500	.500	–	–
Cy Block	pr	1	0	0	0	0	0	0	0	0	0	0	–	–	–	–
Hank Borowy	p	4	6	1	1	1	0	0	0	0	3	0	.167	.333	0	1.000
Phil Cavarretta	1b	7	26	7	11	2	0	1	5	4	3	0	.423	.615	0	1.000
Bob Chipman	p	1	0	0	0	0	0	0	0	0	0	0	–	–	0	–
Paul Derringer	p	3	0	0	0	0	0	0	0	0	0	0	–	–	0	–
Paul Erickson	p	4	0	0	0	0	0	0	0	0	0	0	–	–	0	1.000
Paul Gillespie	ph-c	3	6	0	0	0	0	0	0	0	0	0	.000	.000	0	1.000
Stan Hack	3b	7	30	1	11	3	0	0	4	4	2	0	.367	.467	3	.893
Roy Hughes	ss	6	17	1	5	1	0	0	3	4	5	0	.294	.353	0	1.000
Don Johnson	2b	7	29	4	5	2	1	0	0	0	8	1	.172	.310	1	.971
Mickey Livingston	c	6	22	3	8	3	0	0	4	1	1	0	.364	.500	0	1.000
Peanuts Lowrey	lf	7	29	4	9	1	0	0	0	1	2	0	.310	.345	0	1.000
Clyde McCullough	ph	1	1	0	0	0	0	0	0	0	1	0	.000	.000		
Lennie Merullo	pr-ss	3	2	0	0	0	0	0	0	0	1	0	.000	.000	0	1.000
Bill Nicholson	rf	7	28	1	6	1	1	0	8	2	5	0	.214	.321	1	.900
Andy Pafko	cf	7	28	5	6	2	1	0	2	2	5	1	.214	.357	1	.960
Claude Passeau	p	3	7	1	0	0	0	0	1	0	4	0	.000	.000	0	1.000
Ray Prim	p	2	0	0	0	0	0	0	0	0	0	0	–	–	0	1.000
Eddie Sauer	ph	2	2	0	0	0	0	0	0	0	2	0	.000	.000	–	–
Bill Schuster	ss-pr	2	1	1	0	0	0	0	0	0	0	0	.000	.000	0	1.000
Frank Secory	ph	5	5	0	2	0	0	0	0	0	2	0	.400	.400	–	–
Hy Vandenberg	p	3	1	0	0	0	0	0	0	0	0	0	.000	.000	0	1.000
Dewey Williams	ph-c	2	2	0	0	0	0	0	0	0	1	0	.000	.000	0	1.000
Hank Wyse	p	3	3	0	0	0	0	0	0	0	2	0	.000	.000	0	1.000
Totals		**7**	**247**	**29**	**65**	**16**	**3**	**1**	**27**	**19**	**48**	**2**	**.263**	**.384**	**6**	**.978**

Pitcher	G	GS	CG	IP	H	R	ER	BB	SO	W-L	Sv	ERA
Hank Borowy	4	3	1	18	21	8	8	6	8	2-2	0	4.00
Bob Chipman	1	0	0	$\frac{1}{3}$	0	0	0	1	0	0-0	0	0.00
Paul Derringer	3	0	0	$5\frac{1}{3}$	5	4	4	7	1	0-0	0	6.75
Paul Erickson	4	0	0	7	8	3	3	3	5	0-0	0	3.86
Claude Passeau	3	2	1	$16\frac{2}{3}$	7	5	5	8	3	1-0	0	2.70
Ray Prim	2	1	0	4	4	5	4	1	1	0-1	0	9.00
Hy Vandenberg	3	0	0	6	1	0	0	3	3	0-0	0	0.00
Hank Wyse	3	1	0	$7\frac{2}{3}$	8	7	6	4	1	0-1	0	7.04
Totals	**7**	**7**	**2**	**65**	**54**	**32**	**30**	**33**	**22**	**3-4**	**0**	**4.15**

Series Outstanding Player: Hank Greenberg, Detroit Tigers. **Series Outstanding Pitcher:** Dizzy Trout, Detroit Tigers. **Average Length of Game:** 2 hours, 18 minutes. **Total Attendance:** 333,457. **Average Attendance:** 47,637 (54,591 at Tiger Stadium; 42,421 at Wrigley Field). **Umpires:** Jocko Conlan (NL), Lou Jorda (NL), Art Passarella (AL), Bill Summers (AL). **Winning Player's Share:** $6,443. **Losing Player's Share:** $3,930.

When Clyde McCullough came in to pinch-hit for Chicago in the last of the ninth in Game 7, he became the first man to appear in the postseason without playing a game in the regular season. McCullough was in military service for the entire 1945 season. Virgil Trucks's Game 2 victory made him the first to win a World Series game after winning none all year.

Right: Phil Cavaretta congratulates Claude Passeau after Passeau tossed the second one-hitter in Series history, on October 5, 1945.

Below: Hank Greenberg's three-run homer in Game 2 gave Detroit a comfortable 4-1 lead in the game.

Right: The ball gets by Chicago catcher Mickey Livingston as Eddie Mayo scores in the eighth inning of Detroit's Game 7 victory.

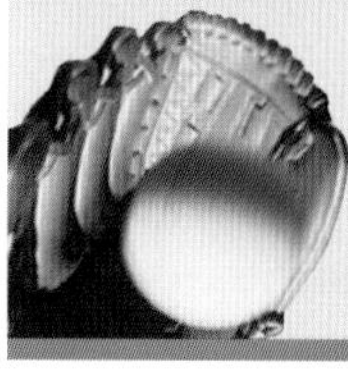

Lingering wartime travel restrictions meant that the first three games of the Series were held in Detroit, with the teams moving to Chicago for the final four games.

Game 1 Wednesday, October 3 at Tiger Stadium, Detroit

	1	2	3	4	5	6	7	8	9	R	H	E
Chicago Cubs	4	0	3	0	0	0	2	0	0	9	13	0
Detroit Tigers	0	0	0	0	0	0	0	0	0	0	6	0

Pitchers Chi **Hank Borowy** (W, 1-0), IP 9, H 6, R 0, ER 0, BB 5, SO 4
Det **Hal Newhouser** (L, 0-1), IP 2⅔, H 8, R 7, ER 7, BB 1, SO 3; **Al Benton**, IP 1⅓, H 1, R 0, ER 0, BB 0, SO 1; **Jim Tobin**, IP 3, H 4, R 2, ER 2, BB 1, SO 0; **Les Mueller**, IP 2, H 0, R 0, ER 0, BB 1, SO 1

Top Performers at the Plate
Chi **Phil Cavarretta**, 3 for 4, 3 R, 2 RBI, 1 BB; **Andy Pafko**, 3 for 4, 3 R, 1 RBI, 1 BB
Det **Hank Greenberg**, 1 for 2, 1, BB, 1 HBP; **Eddie Mayo**, 2 for 4

2B-Chi/Johnson, Pafko. **3B**-Chi/Nicholson. **HR**-Chi/Cavarretta. **SB**-Chi/Johnson, Pafko. **Time** 2:10. **Attendance** 54,637.

Game 2 Thursday, October 4 at Tiger Stadium, Detroit

	1	2	3	4	5	6	7	8	9	R	H	E
Chicago Cubs	0	0	0	1	0	0	0	0	0	1	7	0
Detroit Tigers	0	0	0	0	4	0	0	0	x	4	7	0

Pitchers Chi **Hank Wyse** (L, 0-1), IP 6, H 5, R 4, ER 4, BB 3, SO 1; **Paul Erickson**, IP 2, H 2, R 0, ER 0, BB 1, SO 1
Det **Virgil Trucks** (W, 1-0), IP 9, H 7, R 1, ER 1, BB 3, SO 4

Top Performers at the Plate
Chi **Stan Hack**, 3 for 3, 1 BB; **Peanuts Lowrey**, 2 for 4
Det **Doc Cramer**, 3 for 4, 1 R, 1 RBI; **Hank Greenberg**, 1 for 3, 1 R, 3 RBI, 1BB

2B-Chi/Cavarretta, Hack. **HR**-Det/Greenberg. **Time** 1:47. **Attendance** 53,636.

Game 3 Friday, October 5 at Tiger Stadium, Detroit

	1	2	3	4	5	6	7	8	9	R	H	E
Chicago Cubs	0	0	0	2	0	0	1	0	0	3	8	0
Detroit Tigers	0	0	0	0	0	0	0	0	0	0	1	2

Pitchers Chi **Claude Passeau** (W, 1-0), IP 9, H 1, R 0, ER 0, BB 1, SO 1
Det **Stubby Overmire** (L, 0-1), IP 6, H 4, R 2, ER 2, BB 2, SO 2; **Al Benton**, IP 3, H 4, R 1, ER 1, BB 0, SO 3

Top Performers at the Plate
Chi **Roy Hughes**, 1 for 3, 1 RBI, 1 SH; **Peanuts Lowrey**, 2 for 4, 1 R

2B-Chi/Hack, Livingston, Lowrey. **Time** 1:55. **Attendance** 55,500.

Game 4 Saturday, October 6 at Wrigley Field, Chicago

	1	2	3	4	5	6	7	8	9	R	H	E
Detroit Tigers	0	0	0	4	0	0	0	0	0	4	7	1
Chicago Cubs	0	0	0	0	0	1	0	0	0	1	5	1

Pitchers Det **Dizzy Trout** (W, 1-0), IP 9, H 5, R 1, ER 0, BB 1, SO 6
Chi **Ray Prim** (L, 0-1), IP 3⅓, H 3, R 4, ER 4, BB 1, SO 1; **Paul Derringer**, IP 1⅔, H 2, R 0, ER 0, BB 2, SO 1; **Hy Vandenberg**, IP 2, H 0, R 0, ER 0, BB 0, SO 0; **Paul Erickson**, IP 2, H 2, R 0, ER 0, BB 1, SO 2

Top Performers at the Plate
Det **Doc Cramer**, 2 for 4, 1 R; **Roy Cullenbine**, 1 for 3, 1 R, 1 RBI, 1 BB
Chi **Don Johnson**, 2 for 4, 1 R

2B-Det/Cullenbine. **3B**-Chi/Johnson. **Time** 2:00. **Attendance** 42,923.

Game 5 Sunday, October 7 at Wrigley Field, Chicago

	1	2	3	4	5	6	7	8	9	R	H	E
Detroit Tigers	0	0	1	0	0	4	1	0	2	8	11	0
Chicago Cubs	0	0	1	0	0	0	2	0	1	4	7	2

Pitchers Det **Hal Newhouser**(W, 1-1), IP 9, H 7, R 4, ER 4, BB 2, SO 9
Chi **Hank Borowy** (L, 1-1), IP 5, H 8, R 5, ER 5, BB 1, SO 4; **Hy Vandenberg**, IP ⅔, H 0, R 0, ER 0, BB 2, SO 0; **Bob Chipman**, IP ⅓, H 0, R 0, ER 0, BB 1, SO 0; **Paul Derringer**, IP 2, H 1, R 1, ER 1, BB 0, SO 0; **Paul Erickson**, IP 1, H 2, R 2, ER 2, BB 0, SO 0

Top Performers at the Plate
Det **Roy Cullenbine**, 2 for 4, 1 R, 2 RBI, 1 SH; **Hank Greenberg**, 3 for 5, 3 R, 1 RBI, 3 2B
Chi **Stan Hack**, 1 for 3, 1 RBI, 1 BB

2B-Det/Cullenbine, Greenberg 3; Chi/Borowy, Cavarretta, Livingston. **Time** 2:18. **Attendance** 43,463.

Game 6 Monday, October 8 at Wrigley Field, Chicago

	1	2	3	4	5	6	7	8	9	10	11	12	R	H	E
Detroit Tigers	0	1	0	0	0	0	2	4	0	0	0	0	7	13	1
Chicago Cubs	0	0	0	0	4	1	2	0	0	0	0	1	8	15	3

Pitchers Det **Virgil Trucks**, IP 4⅓, H 7, R 4, ER 4, BB 2, SO 3; **George Caster**, IP ⅔, H 0, R 0, ER 0, BB 0, SO 1; **Tommy Bridges**, IP 1⅔, H 3, R 3, ER 3, BB 3, SO 1; **Al Benton**, IP ⅓, H 1, R 0, ER 0, BB 0, SO 1; **Dizzy Trout** (L, 1-1), IP 4⅔, H 4, R 1, ER 1, BB 2, SO 3
Chi **Claude Passeau**, IP 6⅔, H 5, R 3, ER 3, BB 6, SO 2; **Hank Wyse**, IP ⅔, H 3, R 3, ER 2, BB 1, SO 0; **Ray Prim**, IP ⅔, H 1, R 1, ER 0, BB 0, SO 0; **Hank Borowy** (W, 2-1), IP 4, H 4, R 0, ER 0, BB 0, SO 0

Top Performers at the Plate
Det **Doc Cramer**, 2 for 6, 1 R, 1 RBI; **Roy Cullenbine**, 2 for 5, 1 R, 1 RBI, 1 BB
Chi **Stan Hack**, 4 for 5, 1 R, 3 RBI, 1 BB; **Roy Hughes**, 3 for 4, 1 R, 2 RBI

2B-Det/Walker, York; Chi/Hack, Hughes, Livingston, Pafko. **HR**-Det/Greenberg. **SB**-Det/Cullenbine. **Time** 3:28. **Attendance** 41,708.

Game 7 Wednesday, October 10 at Wrigley Field, Chicago

	1	2	3	4	5	6	7	8	9	R	H	E
Detroit Tigers	5	1	0	0	0	0	1	2	0	9	9	1
Chicago Cubs	1	0	0	1	0	0	0	1	0	3	10	0

Pitchers Det **Hal Newhouser** (W, 2-1), IP 9, H 10, R 3, ER 3, BB 1, SO 10
Chi **Hank Borowy** (L, 2-2), IP 0, H 3, R 3, ER 3, BB 0, SO 0; **Paul Derringer**, IP 1⅔, H 2, R 3, ER 3, BB 5, SO 0; **Hy Vandenberg**, IP 3⅓, H 1, R 0, ER 0, BB 1, SO 3; **Paul Erickson**, IP 2, H 2, R 1, ER 1, BB 1, SO 2; **Claude Passeau**, IP 1, H 1, R 2, ER 2, BB 1, SO 0; **Hank Wyse**, IP 1, H 0, R 0, ER 0, BB 0, SO 0

Top Performers at the Plate
Det **Doc Cramer**, 3 for 5, 2 R, 1 RBI; **Paul Richards**, 2 for 4, 4 RBI, 2 2B
Chi **Phil Cavarretta**, 3 for 4, 1 R, 1 RBI; **Peanuts Lowrey**, 2 for 4, 1 R

2B-Det/Mayo, Richards 2; Chi/Johnson, Nicholson. **3B**-Chi/Pafko. **SB**-Det/Cramer, Outlaw. **Time** 2:31. **Attendance** 41,590.

St. Louis Cardinals (4) vs. Boston Red Sox (3)

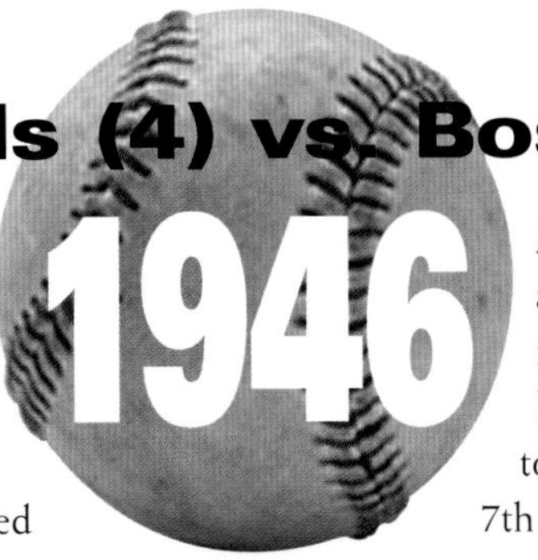

1946

In 1946, for the first time in Major League history, two teams in the same league ended the season with the same record. The St. Louis Cardinals and Brooklyn Dodgers played a best-of-3 playoff series to decide who would go on to that year's World Series. St. Louis took the playoff in 2 games, and then welcomed the AL-champion Boston Red Sox, who won their first pennant in the post-Ruth era by a 12-game margin. Boston's Ted Williams and St. Louis's Stan Musial both returned from military service with MVP seasons in 1946, though neither had MVP-caliber Octobers. Game 1 was an extra-inning affair. Howie Pollet went the distance for St. Louis, but lost the game on Rudy York's 10th-inning homer. Harry Brecheen got a shutout win for the Cards in Game 2, allowing only 4 base hits. Brecheen also drove in the team's first run with a single in the 3rd, and he scored a run after reaching base on an error in the 5th. York knocked a 3-run homer for Boston in the 1st inning of Game 3, and Dave "Boo" Ferriss shut St. Louis out to get the 4-0 win. The Cardinal offense exploded for 20 hits in Game 4, tying the single-game record. Three Cardinals—Joe Garagiola, Whitey Kurowski and Enos Slaughter—had 4 hits in the game, and even Boston's Wally Moses got in on the action with a 4-for-5 day. The Red Sox used a pair of doubles, 2 intentional walks and an error by Marty Marion in the 7th inning of Game 5 to score 3 runs and grab a 3-2 lead in the Series. Joe Dobson got the win for Boston, yielding 3 unearned runs on 4 hits. Back in St. Louis for Game 6, the Cards rallied for 3 runs in the 3rd to take the lead to stay and send the Series to a deciding 7th game. After allowing a run in the top of the 1st inning of Game 7, Murry Dickson held the Red Sox to just 1 hit in the next 6 innings, and his RBI double in the 5th helped put St. Louis up 3-1. Boston came back to tie the game on Dom DiMaggio's 2-run double in the top of the 8th. St. Louis's Enos Slaughter led off the bottom of the inning with a single, but 2 quick outs left him stranded at first base. Finally, Harry Walker came through with a single to left-center field. Slaughter was running full-speed all the way, and when shortstop Johnny Pesky hesitated for a split second in relaying the throw to the plate, Slaughter was able to slide in just ahead of the tag. Brecheen, pitching in relief, got out of a jam in the 9th to preserve the 1-run lead and earn his third win of the Series. Slaughter's daring "Mad Dash" gave St. Louis its third championship in five years.

Left: That's not a game of leapfrog—that's second baseman Red Schoendienst completing a double play after forcing Johnny Pesky out at second.

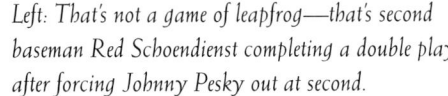

1946 WORLD SERIES COMPOSITE STATISTICS

ST. LOUIS CARDINALS/Eddie Dyer, Manager

Player	pos	G	AB	R	H	2B	3B	HR	RBI	BB	SO	SB	BA	SA	E	FPct
Johnny Beazley	p	1	0	0	0	0	0	0	0	0	0	0	—	—	0	1.000
Al Brazle	p	1	2	0	0	0	0	0	0	0	0	0	.000	.000	0	1.000
Harry Brecheen	p	3	8	2	1	0	0	0	1	0	1	0	.125	.125	0	1.000
Murry Dickson	p	2	5	1	2	2	0	0	1	0	1	0	.400	.800	0	1.000
Erv Dusak	ph-lf	4	4	0	1	1	0	0	0	2	2	0	.250	.500	0	1.000
Joe Garagiola	c	5	19	2	6	2	0	0	4	0	3	0	.316	.421	0	1.000
Nippy Jones	ph	1	1	0	0	0	0	0	0	0	1	0	.000	.000	—	—
Whitey Kurowski	3b	7	27	5	8	3	0	0	2	0	3	0	.296	.407	1	.957
Marty Marion	ss	7	24	1	6	2	0	0	4	1	1	0	.250	.333	2	.944
Terry Moore	cf	7	27	1	4	0	0	0	2	2	6	0	.148	.148	0	1.000
George Munger	p	1	4	0	1	0	0	0	0	0	2	0	.250	1.250	0	1.000
Stan Musial	1b	7	27	3	6	4	1	0	4	4	2	1	.222	.444	0	1.000
Howie Pollet	p	2	4	0	0	0	0	0	0	0	1	0	.000	.000	0	—
Del Rice	c	3	6	2	3	1	0	0	0	2	0	0	.500	.667	0	1.000
Red Schoendienst	2b	7	30	3	7	1	0	0	1	0	2	1	.233	.267	1	.974
Dick Sisler	ph	2	2	0	0	0	0	0	0	0	0	0	.000	.000	—	—
Enos Slaughter	rf	7	25	5	8	1	1	1	2	4	3	1	.320	.560	0	1.000
Harry Walker	lf-rf-ph	7	17	3	7	2	0	0	6	4	2	0	.412	.529	0	1.000
Ted Wilks	p	1	0	0	0	0	0	0	0	0	0	0	—	—	0	1.000
Totals		7	232	28	60	19	2	1	27	19	30	3	.259	.371	4	.985

Pitcher	G	GS	CG	IP	H	R	ER	BB	SO	W-L	Sv	ERA
Johnny Beazley	1	0	0	1	1	0	0	1	0	0-0	0	0.00
Al Brazle	1	0	0	6⅔	7	5	4	6	4	0-1	0	5.40
Harry Brecheen	3	2	2	20	14	1	1	5	11	3-0	0	0.45
Murry Dickson	2	2	0	14	11	6	6	4	7	0-1	0	3.86
George Munger	1	1	1	9	9	3	1	3	2	1-0	0	1.00
Howie Pollet	2	2	1	10⅓	12	4	4	4	3	0-1	0	3.48
Ted Wilks	1	0	0	1	2	1	0	0	0	0-0	0	0.00
Totals	7	7	4	62	56	20	16	22	28	4-3	0	2.32

BOSTON RED SOX/Joe Cronin, Manager

Player	pos	G	AB	R	H	2B	3B	HR	RBI	BB	SO	SB	BA	SA	E	FPct
Jim Bagby Jr.	p	1	1	0	0	0	0	0	0	0	0	0	.000	.000	0	1.000
Mace Brown	p	1	0	0	0	0	0	0	0	0	0	0	—	—	0	—
Paul Campbell	pr	1	0	0	0	0	0	0	0	0	0	0	—	—	—	—
Leon Culberson	rf-cf	5	9	1	2	0	0	1	1	1	2	1	.222	.556	0	1.000
Dom DiMaggio	cf	7	27	2	7	3	0	0	3	2	2	0	.259	.370	0	1.000
Joe Dobson	p	3	3	0	0	0	0	0	0	2	0	0	.000	.000	0	1.000
Bobby Doerr	2b	6	22	1	9	1	0	1	3	2	2	0	.409	.591	0	1.000
Clem Dreisewerd	p	1	0	0	0	0	0	0	0	0	0	0	—	—	—	1.000
Boo Ferriss	p	2	6	0	0	0	0	0	0	0	0	0	.000	.000	0	1.000
Don Gutteridge	pr-2b	3	5	1	2	0	0	0	1	0	0	0	.400	.400	0	1.000
Mickey Harris	p	2	3	0	1	0	0	0	0	0	1	0	.333	.333	0	1.000
Mike Higgins	3b	7	24	1	5	1	0	0	2	2	0	0	.208	.250	2	.857
Tex Hughson	p	3	3	0	1	0	0	0	0	1	0	0	.333	.333	1	.500
Earl Johnson	p	3	1	0	0	0	0	0	0	0	0	0	.000	.000	0	1.000
Bob Klinger	p	1	0	0	0	0	0	0	0	0	0	0	—	—	0	1.000
Tom McBride	rf-ph	5	12	0	2	0	0	0	1	0	1	0	.167	.167	1	.800
Catfish Metkovich	ph	2	2	1	1	1	0	0	0	0	0	0	.500	1.000	—	—
Wally Moses	rf	4	12	1	5	0	0	0	1	2	0	0	.417	.417	0	1.000
Roy Partee	ph-c	5	10	1	1	0	0	0	1	1	2	0	.100	.100	0	1.000
Johnny Pesky	ss	7	30	2	7	0	0	0	0	0	3	1	.233	.233	4	.882
Rip Russell	ph-3b	2	2	1	2	0	0	0	0	0	0	0	1.000	1.000	0	—
Mike Ryba	p	1	0	0	0	0	0	0	0	0	0	0	—	—	1	.000
Hal Wagner	c	5	13	0	0	0	0	0	0	0	1	0	.000	.000	0	1.000
Ted Williams	lf	7	25	2	5	0	0	0	1	5	5	0	.200	.200	0	1.000
Rudy York	1b	7	23	6	6	1	1	2	5	6	4	0	.261	.652	1	.984
Bill Zuber	p	1	0	0	0	0	0	0	0	0	0	0	—	—	0	—
Totals		7	233	20	56	7	1	4	18	22	28	2	.240	.330	10	.963

Pitcher	G	GS	CG	IP	H	R	ER	BB	SO	W-L	Sv	ERA
Jim Bagby Jr.	1	0	0	3	6	1	1	1	1	0-0	0	3.00
Mace Brown	1	0	0	1	4	3	3	1	0	0-0	0	27.00
Joe Dobson	3	1	1	12⅔	4	3	0	3	10	1-0	0	0.00
Clem Dreisewerd	1	0	0	⅓	0	0	0	0	0	0-0	0	0.00
Boo Ferriss	2	2	1	13⅓	13	3	3	2	4	1-0	0	2.03
Mickey Harris	2	2	0	9⅔	11	6	5	4	5	0-2	0	4.66
Tex Hughson	3	2	0	14⅓	14	8	5	3	8	0-1	0	3.14
Earl Johnson	3	0	0	3⅓	1	1	1	2	1	1-0	0	2.70
Bob Klinger	1	0	0	⅔	2	1	1	1	0	0-1	0	13.50
Mike Ryba	1	0	0	⅔	2	1	0	1	0	0-0	0	0.00
Bill Zuber	1	0	0	2	3	1	1	0	1	0-0	0	4.50
Totals	7	7	2	61	60	28	20	19	30	3-4	0	2.95

Series Outstanding Player: Harry Walker, St. Louis Cardinals. **Series Outstanding Pitcher:** Harry Brecheen, St. Louis Cardinals. **Average Length of Game:** 2 hours, 14 minutes. **Total Attendance:** 250,071. **Average Attendance:** 35,724 (35,986 at Sportsman's Park; 35,376 at Fenway Park). **Umpires:** Lee Ballanfant (NL), Al Barlick (NL), Charlie Berry (AL), Cal Hubbard (AL). **Winning Player's Share:** $3,742. **Losing Player's Share:** $2,141.

The Boston Red Sox sent 11 different pitchers to the mound over the seven games, the most by one team in a Series.

Above: The Cardinals employed a radical fielding shift in an effort to limit the success of pull-hitting Ted Williams, putting three infielders to the right of second base. Williams hit just .200 in the six games.

Right: Enos Slaughter's "Mad Dash" to home in the eighth inning of Game 7 was the key play of the Series.

St. Louis's Harry Brecheen was the first left-handed pitcher, and the ninth overall, to win three games in one World Series.

Above: Harry "The Cat" Brecheen is hoisted up by Cardinal teammates after closing out the clinching seventh game of 1946.

Game 1   Sunday, October 6 at Sportsman's Park, St. Louis

	1	2	3	4	5	6	7	8	9	10	R	H	E
Boston Red Sox	0	1	0	0	0	0	0	0	1	1	3	9	2
St. Louis Cardinals	0	0	0	0	0	1	0	1	0	0	2	7	0

Pitchers Bos Tex Hughson, IP 8, H 7, R 2, ER 2, BB 2, SO 5; Earl Johnson (W, 1-0), IP 2, H 0, R 0, ER 0, BB 0, SO 1
StL Howie Pollet (L, 0-1), IP 10, H 9, R 3, ER 3, BB 4, SO 3

Top Performers at the Plate
Bos Mike Higgins, 2 for 4, 1 RBI; Rudy York, 1 for 4, 2 R, 1 RBI, 1 HBP
StL Whitey Kurowski, 1 for 3, 1 R, 1 HBP; Red Schoendienst, 2 for 5, 1 R

2B-StL/Garagiola, Musial. **3B**-StL/Slaughter. **HR**-Bos/York. **SB**-StL/Schoendienst. **Time** 2:39.
Attendance 36,218.

Game 2   Monday, October 7 at Sportsman's Park, St. Louis

	1	2	3	4	5	6	7	8	9	R	H	E
Boston Red Sox	0	0	0	0	0	0	0	0	0	0	4	1
St. Louis Cardinals	0	0	1	0	2	0	0	0	x	3	6	0

Pitchers Bos Mickey Harris (L, 0-1), IP 7, H 6, R 3, ER 2, BB 3, SO 3; Joe Dobson, IP 1, H 0, R 0, ER 0, BB 0, SO 0
StL Harry Brecheen (W, 1-0), IP 9, H 4, R 0, ER 0, BB 3, SO 4

Top Performers at the Plate
StL Terry Moore, 1 for 3, 1 RBI, 1 BB; Del Rice, 2 for 2, 2 R, 1 BB

2B-StL/Dusak, Rice. **Time** 1:56. **Attendance** 35,815.

Game 3   Wednesday, October 9 at Fenway Park, Boston

	1	2	3	4	5	6	7	8	9	R	H	E
St. Louis Cardinals	0	0	0	0	0	0	0	0	0	0	6	1
Boston Red Sox	3	0	0	0	0	0	0	1	x	4	8	0

Pitchers StL Murry Dickson (L, 0-1), IP 7, H 6, R 3, ER 3, BB 3, SO 4; Ted Wilks, IP 1, H 2, R 1, ER 0, BB 0, SO 0
Bos Boo Ferriss (W, 1-0), IP 9, H 6, R 0, ER 0, BB 1, SO 2

Top Performers at the Plate
StL Stan Musial, 1 for 3, 1 BB
Bos Johnny Pesky, 2 for 4, 1 R; Rudy York, 2 for 4, 2 R, 3 RBI

2B-StL/Dickson; Bos/DiMaggio, Doerr. **3B**-StL/Musial. **HR**-Bos/York. **SB**-StL/Musial. **Time** 1:54.
Attendance 34,500.

Game 4   Thursday, October 10 at Fenway Park, Boston

	1	2	3	4	5	6	7	8	9	R	H	E
St. Louis Cardinals	0	3	3	0	1	0	1	0	4	12	20	1
Boston Red Sox	0	0	0	1	0	0	2	0		3	9	4

Pitchers StL George Munger (W, 1-0), IP 9, H 9, R 3, ER 3, BB 3, SO 2
Bos Tex Hughson (L, 0-1), IP 2, H 5, R 6, ER 3, BB 0, SO 1; Jim Bagby Jr., IP 3,
H 6, R 1, ER 1, BB 1, SO 1; Bill Zuber, IP 2, H 3, R 1, ER 1, BB 1, SO 1; Mace
Brown, IP 1, H 4, R 3, ER 3, BB 1, SO 0; Mike Ryba, IP ⅔, H 2, R 1, ER 0, BB 1,
SO 0; Clem Dreisewerd, IP ⅓, H 0, R 0, ER 0, BB 0, SO 0

Top Performers at the Plate
StL Joe Garagiola, 4 for 5, 1 R, 3 RBI; Enos Slaughter, 4 for 6, 4 R, 1 RBI
Bos Bobby Doerr, 2 for 3, 1 R, 2 RBI, 1 BB; Wally Moses, 4 for 5

2B-StL/Garagiola, Kurowski 2, Marion, Musial, Slaughter; Bos/York. **HR**-StL/Slaughter; Bos/Doerr.
Time 2:31. **Attendance** 35,645.

Game 5   Friday, October 11 at Fenway Park, Boston

	1	2	3	4	5	6	7	8	9	R	H	E
St. Louis Cardinals	0	1	0	0	0	0	0	2		3	4	1
Boston Red Sox	1	1	0	0	0	1	3	0	x	6	11	3

Pitchers StL Howie Pollet, IP ⅓, H 3, R 1, ER 1, BB 0, SO 0; Al Brazle (L, 0-1), IP 6⅔, H 7,
R 5, ER 4, BB 6, SO 4; Johnny Beazley, IP 1, H 1, R 0, ER 0, BB 0, SO 1
Bos Joe Dobson (W, 1-0), IP 9, H 4, R 3, ER 0, BB 1, SO 8

Top Performers at the Plate
StL Harry Walker, 2 for 4, 3 RBI
Bos Leon Culberson, 2 for 3, 1 R, 1 RBI, 1 BB; Johnny Pesky, 3 for 5, 1 R

2B-StL/Musial, Walker; Bos/DiMaggio, Higgins. **HR**-Bos/Culberson. **SB**-StL/Slaughter;
Bos/Culberson, Pesky. **Time** 2:23. **Attendance** 35,982.

Game 6   Sunday, October 13 at Sportsman's Park, St. Louis

	1	2	3	4	5	6	7	8	9	R	H	E
Boston Red Sox	0	0	0	0	0	0	1	0	0	1	7	0
St. Louis Cardinals	0	0	3	0	0	0	0	1	x	4	8	0

Pitchers Bos Mickey Harris (L, 0-2), IP 2⅔, H 5, R 3, ER 3, BB 1, SO 2; Tex Hughson, IP 4⅓,
H 2, R 0, ER 0, BB 1, SO 2; Earl Johnson, IP 1, H 1, R 1, ER 1, BB 2, SO 0
StL Harry Brecheen (W, 2-0), IP 9, H 7, R 1, ER 1, BB 2, SO 6

Top Performers at the Plate
Bos Bobby Doerr, 1 for 3, 1 RBI
StL Marty Marion, 2 for 4, 1 RBI; Enos Slaughter, 1 for 2, 1 RBI, 2 BB

2B-StL/Marion, Schoendienst. **3B**-Bos/York. **Time** 1:56. **Attendance** 35,768.

Game 7   Tuesday, October 15 at Sportsman's Park, St. Louis

	1	2	3	4	5	6	7	8	9	R	H	E
Boston Red Sox	1	0	0	0	0	0	2	0		3	8	0
St. Louis Cardinals	0	1	0	0	2	0	0	1	x	4	9	1

Pitchers Bos Boo Ferriss, IP 4⅓, H 7, R 3, ER 3, BB 1, SO 2; Joe Dobson, IP 2⅔, H 0, R 0,
ER 0, BB 2, SO 2; Bob Klinger (L, 0-1), IP ⅔, H 2, R 1, ER 1, BB 1, SO 0; Earl
Johnson, IP ⅓, H 0, R 0, ER 0, BB 0, SO 0
StL Murry Dickson, IP 7, H 5, R 3, ER 3, BB 1, SO 3; Harry Brecheen (W, 3-0),
IP 2, H 3, R 0, ER 0, BB 0, SO 1

Top Performers at the Plate
Bos Dom DiMaggio, 1 for 3, 3 RBI, 1 BB; Bobby Doerr, 2 for 4
StL Red Schoendienst, 2 for 4, 1 RBI; Harry Walker, 2 for 3, 1 R, 2 RBI, 1 BB

2B-Bos/DiMaggio, Metkovich; StL/Dickson, Kurowski, Musial, Walker. **Time** 2:17.
Attendance 36,143.

Big Day for the Little Guy
Unlikely October Heroes

Enos Slaughter got all the attention in 1946 for his famous "Mad Dash," but it was Harry Walker's 2-out double that sent him running. After batting a meager .237 with 27 RBI in the regular season, Walker was a clutch performer in October, posting a .417 average and 6 RBI in the seven games. Here are some other players who had relatively minor roles in a team's pennant-winning campaign during the season, but stepped up big when it mattered most.

◆ An injury to the starting shortstop thrust utilityman George Rohe into starting duty for the White Sox in the 1906 Series, and Rohe came through big. He led all players with a .333 average and drove in several key runs.

◆ Pittsburgh's Babe Adams, a 27-year-old rookie in 1909, won 12 games during the year—fifth best on the Pirate staff—but he posted complete-game victories in Games 1, 5 and 7 of the Series to become the only rookie to win 3 games.

◆ Hank Gowdy was a .243 hitter for the Miracle Braves in 1914, but his .545 Series average against the Athletics ranks as the fifth best of all time. He also drove in three runs, scored three and walked five times in the four games.

◆ Rogers Hornsby, Jim Bottomley and Billy Southworth were the cornerstones of a fearsome Cardinal lineup in 1926, but light-hitting rookie shortstop Tommy Thevenow topped them all by batting .417 in the Series.

◆ Howard Ehmke won only one game for the Athletics in 1929, but he produced a dominating 13-strikeout victory over the Cubs in the Series opener. The 35-year-old Ehmke never won another game in the Majors.

◆ The St. Louis Cardinals used John "Pepper" Martin in left field for 123 games during the 1931 season, but few expected him to put on the display that he did during the World Series. The first man to bat .500 in a 7-game series, he collected 12 hits and 5 stolen bases against the formidable Philadelphia Athletics.

◆ Cincinnati's Jimmy Ripple played in only 39 games in 1940. He must have been saving it for October. In the 7 games of the World Series, he batted .300, drove in game-winning runs in Games 2 and 4, and scored the go-ahead run in Game 7.

Above: John "Pepper" Martin surprised everyone with his tremendous performance in 1931.

Below: In a Yankee-Dodger duel replete with future Hall of Famers, Cookie Lavagetto was one of the unlikely heroes to come through with a clutch performance in the 1947 Series.

◆ On a team featuring names like DiMaggio, Berra and Rizzuto, Johnny Lindell was the surprise hero of the 1947 Yankees. He batted .500, hit in all six games he played in and drove in a team-best seven runs.

◆ Brooklyn produced a pair of unlikely heroes in the 1947 Series. Cookie Lavagetto broke up Bill Bevens's Game 4 no-hitter with a game-winning, pinch-hit double in the bottom of the ninth, while Al Gionfriddo's phenomenal catch of Joe DiMaggio's deep fly ball saved Game 6 for the Dodgers. In the regular season, the two appeared in only 37 and 41 games, respectively; neither one played in another Major League game after that year's Fall Classic.

◆ Johnny Podres had a losing record (9-10) for the Dodgers in 1955, but he was the MVP performer in Brooklyn's long-awaited Series victory by winning two games and posting a 1.00 ERA against the Yankees.

◆ Al Weis, a .215 hitter during the year, batted .455 for the New York Mets in the 1969 Series. He drove in three runs, including the go-ahead run in Game 2 and a game-tying homer in Game 5.

◆ Gene Tenace was a platoon catcher for Oakland in 1972, batting .225 in 82 games. Against Cincinnati in the Series, he stroked four homers (one shy of his season total), drove in nine runs and hit .348.

◆ Infielders Brian Doyle and Bucky Dent were wearing Major League uniforms in 1978 because of their defense—they hit a combined .237 on the year. But in October they batted .438 and .417, respectively, for the Yankees, and Dent took home the MVP for his efforts.

◆ Rick Dempsey was in his 15th season in the Majors when he made his first trip to the World Series with Baltimore in 1983. Dempsey batted ninth all year for the Orioles, and did so in the postseason as well, but he bumped his batting average up more than 150 points by going .385 in the Series, earning him MVP honors.

◆ When the Blue Jays brought the World Series trophy north of the border in 1992, a little-known player by the name of Borders was a key to their success. Pat Borders' .450 average was more than 200 points above his regular-season mark.

◆ Ricky Ledee was hardly the first name off people's lips when discussing the Yankees' incredible 114-win season in 1998, but his .600 average and four RBI in the four-game Series made everyone take notice.

New York Yankees (4) vs. Brooklyn Dodgers (3)

In a World Series that featured legendary names like Berra and DiMaggio, Robinson and Reese, it was guys named Bevens, Gionfriddo and Lavagetto who stood out as the pivotal players. Still, while those ball players had brief moments in the sun in October, Dodgers owner Branch Rickey and infielder Jackie Robinson eclipsed all other baseball news that year when Robinson became the first African American to play for a Major League team in the 20th century. Robinson would win baseball's first Rookie of the Year honor, and Brooklyn captured the pennant with 94 wins. The Dodgers' Series opponent was the Yankees, who used a 19-game winning streak in late June to propel themselves to the top of the American League.

In the Series opener, throngs packed Yankee Stadium to watch rookie Frank "Spec" Shea pitch two-hit ball for five innings for New York. Ralph Branca kept the Yankees off the base paths for four innings by retiring the first 12 batters he faced, until Joe DiMaggio led off the fifth with a single. DiMaggio's hit was followed by a walk, an RBI double by Johnny Lindell, two more walks, and a two-run single by Tommy Henrich. The Yanks were up 5-0, and Joe Page got the save despite allowing two runs in four innings of relief. New York's Allie Reynolds claimed his first postseason victory (the first of many) in Game 2. Lindell drove in two runs for the second day in a row in the 10-3 win. Back home at Ebbets Field, the Dodgers jumped out with six runs in the

Above: The focal points of 1947's drama meet a day later. Cookie Lavagetto (left) broke up Bill Bevens' Game 4 no-hitter with a ninth-inning pinch-hit double.

Above: Jackie Robinson is trapped by pitcher Spec Shea and shortstop Phil Rizzuto as he tries to advance to third in the first inning of Game 1. Rizzuto eventually tags Robinson out. Right: Pete Reiser is caught stealing in the first inning of Game 3—making matters worse, Reiser injured his ankle on the play and had to leave the game.

second inning, capped by a two-run, pinch-hit double by Carl Furillo. New York chipped away with two runs in each of the next three innings, with DiMaggio contributing a two-run clout in the fifth. Brooklyn scored three more off Yankee relievers, and despite Yogi Berra's pinch-hit homer in the sixth—the first pinch-homer ever in a World Series—the Dodgers held on for a 9-8 victory. A day later, one man fell just short of unprecedented October magic. Bill Bevens finished 1947 with an unremarkable 7-13 record, but he got the start in Game 4 of the Series. Bevens's control was surely less than spectacular; the young righty gave up ten walks on the day, including two in the fifth inning that led to a Brooklyn run. What was spectacular, however, was that Bevens did not allow a single base hit in the first eight innings of the game. The Yankees, meanwhile, scattered a pair of runs to go up 2-1. Heading into the bottom of the ninth, Bevens found himself just three outs away from the first World Series no-hitter. He got the first batter to fly out, walked Furillo, and then popped Spider Jorgensen out at first base. Bevens was now one out away. The speedy Al Gionfriddo went in to run for Furillo and promptly stole second base. The Yanks walked pinch hitter Pete Reiser intentionally, and after Eddie Miksis came in to run for Reiser, Brooklyn sent backup infielder Cookie Lavagetto to bat for Eddie Stanky. Lavagetto ripped Bevens's second pitch off the right-field wall, and both Gionfriddo and Miksis came around to score. Lavagetto's double—the only hit off Bill Bevens all game—gave Brooklyn a 3-2 victory, tying the Series. Another one-run game followed in Game 5, though in slightly less dramatic fashion. Shea got his second win of the Series behind a four-hitter, and DiMaggio's solo homer in the fifth delivered the eventual game-winning run.

A record 74,065 fans turned up at Yankee Stadium for Game 6. New York overcame an early 4-0 deficit to take the lead with a four-run third inning and a single run in the fourth. Brooklyn responded with a four-run inning of its own, as Reese's two-run single gave the Dodgers their seventh and eighth runs of the game. Down three runs going into the bottom of the sixth, the Yankees put two runners on base with Joe DiMaggio coming to the plate and two men out. DiMaggio took Joe Hatten's pitch deep to left-center field, and it looked as if the Yanks might tie the game with one swing of the bat. But left fielder Al Gionfriddo, who entered the game at the start of the inning as a defensive replacement, raced to the wall and made a reaching, one-handed catch over the bull-pen fence, 415 feet from home plate, to rob "Joltin' Joe" of a homer and preserve Brooklyn's lead. The normally staid DiMaggio kicked the dirt in frustration, and the Dodgers sent the Series to a climactic seventh game.

Game 7 was held the next day at the Stadium. Spec Shea took the mound for New York with hopes of a third victory, but the Dodgers bounced him out before the end of the second inning. The 2-0 score after 1 1/2 innings marked the last time the Dodgers would have the lead. New York put together five runs on the day, and Joe Page allowed only one Dodger to reach base in the final five innings to give the Yankees a 5-2 win in the deciding game. For the Yankees, it was World Series win number 11—and for Bevens, Gionfriddo and Lavagetto, it was the last Major League contest in which any of them would ever participate.

The opening game of the 1947 Series was the first televised World Series game.

Johnny Lindell was the surprise hero for New York, batting .500 and driving in seven runs.

Left: Joe DiMaggio's two-run homer in Game 3 came in a losing effort.

Game 1   Tuesday, September 30 at Yankee Stadium, New York

	1	2	3	4	5	6	7	8	9	R	H	E
Brooklyn Dodgers	1	0	0	0	0	1	1	0	0	3	6	0
New York Yankees	0	0	0	0	5	0	0	0	x	5	4	0

Pitchers Bro Ralph Branca (L, 0-1), IP 4, H 2, R 5, ER 5, BB 3, SO 5; Hank Behrman, IP 2, H 1, R 0, ER 0, BB 0, SO 0; Hugh Casey, IP 2, H 1, R 0, ER 0, BB 0, SO 1
NY Spec Shea (W, 1-0), IP 5, H 2, R 1, ER 1, BB 2, SO 3; Joe Page (Sv, 1), IP 4, H 4, R 2, ER 2, BB 1, SO 2

Top Performers at the Plate
Bro Dixie Walker, 2 for 4, 1 RBI
NY Johnny Lindell, 1 for 3, 2 RBI; Phil Rizzuto, 1 for 2, 1 R, 1 BB
2B-NY/Lindell. **SB**-Bro/Reese, Robinson. **Time** 2:20. **Attendance** 73,365.

Game 2   Wednesday, October 1 at Yankee Stadium, New York

	1	2	3	4	5	6	7	8	9	R	H	E
Brooklyn Dodgers	0	0	1	0	0	0	0	0	1	3	9	2
New York Yankees	1	0	1	1	2	1	4	0	x	10	15	1

Pitchers Bro Vic Lombardi (L, 0-1), IP 4, H 9, R 5, ER 5, BB 1, SO 3; Hal Gregg, IP 2, H 2, R 1, ER 1, BB 1, SO 2; Hank Behrman, IP ⅓, H 3, R 4, ER 4, BB 1, SO 0; Rex Barney, IP 1⅔, H 1, R 0, ER 0, BB 1, SO 0
NY Allie Reynolds (W, 1-0), IP 9, H 9, R 3, ER 3, BB 2, SO 6

Top Performers at the Plate
Bro Pee Wee Reese, 2 for 3, 1 R, 1 BB; Jackie Robinson, 2 for 4, 1 RBI
NY Johnny Lindell, 2 for 4, 1 R, 2 RBI, 1 BB; Snuffy Stirnweiss, 3 for 4, 2 R, 1 RBI, 1 BB
2B-Bro/Robinson; NY/Lindell, Rizzuto. **3B**-NY/Johnson, Lindell, Stirnweiss. **HR**-Bro/Walker; NY/Henrich. **SB**-Bro/Reese. **Time** 2:36. **Attendance** 69,865.

Game 3   Thursday, October 2 at Ebbets Field, Brooklyn

	1	2	3	4	5	6	7	8	9	R	H	E
New York Yankees	0	0	2	2	2	1	1	0	0	8	13	0
Brooklyn Dodgers	0	6	1	2	0	0	0	0	x	9	13	1

Pitchers NY Bobo Newsom (L, 0-1), IP 1⅔, H 5, R 5, ER 5, BB 2, SO 0; Vic Raschi, IP ⅓, H 2, R 1, ER 1, BB 0, SO 0; Karl Drews, IP 1, H 1, R 1, ER 1, BB 0, SO 0; Spud Chandler, IP 2, H 2, R 2, ER 2, BB 3, SO 1; Joe Page, IP 3, H 3, R 0, ER 0, BB 1, SO 3
Bro Joe Hatten, IP 4⅓, H 8, R 6, ER 6, BB 3, SO 3; Ralph Branca, IP 2, H 4, R 2, ER 2, BB 2, SO 1; Hugh Casey (W, 1-0), IP 2⅔, H 1, R 0, ER 0, BB 1, SO 1

Top Performers at the Plate
NY Joe DiMaggio, 2 for 4, 1 R, 3 RBI, 1 BB; Sherm Lollar, 2 for 3, 2 R, 1 RBI
Bro Carl Furillo, 2 for 3, 1 R, 2 RBI, 1 BB; Gene Hermanski, 1 for 3, 2 R, 1 RBI, 1 BB, 1 HBP
2B-NY/Brown, Henrich, Lollar; Bro/Edwards, Furillo, Jorgensen, Stanky. **HR**-NY/Berra, DiMaggio. **SB**-Bro/Robinson, Walker. **Time** 3:05. **Attendance** 33,098.

Game 4   Friday, October 3 at Ebbets Field, Brooklyn

	1	2	3	4	5	6	7	8	9	R	H	E
New York Yankees	1	0	0	1	0	0	0	0	0	2	8	1
Brooklyn Dodgers	0	0	0	0	1	0	0	0	2	3	1	3

Pitchers NY Bill Bevens (L, 0-1), IP 8⅔, H 1, R 3, ER 3, BB 10, SO 5
Bro Harry Taylor, IP 0, H 2, R 1, ER 0, BB 1, SO 0; Hal Gregg, IP 7, H 4, R 1, ER 1, BB 3, SO 5; Hank Behrman, IP 1⅓, H 2, R 0, ER 0, BB 0, SO 0; Hugh Casey (W, 2-0), IP ⅔, H 0, R 0, ER 0, BB 0, SO 0

Top Performers at the Plate
NY Johnny Lindell, 2 for 3, 1 RBI, 1 BB; Snuffy Stirnweiss, 2 for 4, 1 R, 1 BB
Bro Cookie Lavagetto, 1 for 1, 2 RBI
2B-NY/Lindell; Bro/Lavagetto. **3B**-NY/Johnson. **SB**-NY/Rizzuto; Bro/Gionfriddo, Reese. **Time** 2:20. **Attendance** 33,443.

Game 5   Saturday, October 4 at Ebbets Field, Brooklyn

	1	2	3	4	5	6	7	8	9	R	H	E
New York Yankees	0	0	0	1	1	0	0	0	0	2	5	0
Brooklyn Dodgers	0	0	0	0	0	1	0	0	0	1	4	1

Pitchers NY Spec Shea (W, 2-0), IP 9, H 4, R 1, ER 1, BB 5, SO 7
Bro Rex Barney (L, 0-1), IP 4⅔, H 3, R 2, ER 2, BB 9, SO 3; Joe Hatten, IP 1⅓, H 0, R 0, ER 0, BB 0, SO 1; Hank Behrman, IP 1, H 1, R 0, ER 0, BB 1, SO 2; Hugh Casey, IP 2, H 1, R 0, ER 0, BB 0, SO 1

Top Performers at the Plate
NY Tommy Henrich, 2 for 4, 1 BB; Spec Shea, 2 for 4, 1 RBI
2B-NY/Henrich, Shea, Bro/Vaughan. **HR**-NY/DiMaggio. **Time** 2:46. **Attendance** 34,379.

Game 6   Sunday, October 5 at Yankee Stadium, New York

	1	2	3	4	5	6	7	8	9	R	H	E
Brooklyn Dodgers	2	0	2	0	0	4	0	0	0	8	12	1
New York Yankees	0	0	4	1	0	0	0	0	1	6	15	2

Pitchers Bro Vic Lombardi, IP 2⅔, H 5, R 4, ER 4, BB 0, SO 2; Ralph Branca (W, 1-1), IP 2⅓, H 6, R 1, ER 1, BB 0, SO 2; Joe Hatten, IP 3, H 3, R 1, ER 1, BB 4, SO 0; Hugh Casey (Sv, 1), IP 1, H 1, R 0, ER 0, BB 0, SO 0
NY Allie Reynolds, IP 2⅓, H 6, R 4, ER 3, BB 1, SO 0; Karl Drews, IP 2, H 1, R 0, ER 0, BB 1, SO 0; Joe Page (L, 0-1), IP 1, H 4, R 4, ER 4, BB 0, SO 1; Bobo Newsom, IP ⅔, H 1, R 0, ER 0, BB 0, SO 0; Vic Raschi, IP 1, H 0, R 0, ER 0, BB 0, SO 1; Butch Wensloff, IP 2, H 0, R 0, ER 0, BB 0, SO 0

Top Performers at the Plate
Bro Pee Wee Reese, 3 for 4, 2 R, 2 RBI; Eddie Stanky, 2 for 5, 2 R
NY Yogi Berra, 2 for 3, 1 RBI; Johnny Lindell, 2 for 2, 1 R, 1 RBI
2B-Bro/Bragan, Furillo, Reese, J. Robinson, Walker; NY/Lollar. **Time** 3:19. **Attendance** 74,065.

Game 7   Monday, October 6 at Yankee Stadium, New York

	1	2	3	4	5	6	7	8	9	R	H	E
Brooklyn Dodgers	0	2	0	0	0	0	0	0	0	2	7	0
New York Yankees	0	1	0	2	0	1	1	0	x	5	7	0

Pitchers Bro Hal Gregg (L, 0-1), IP 3⅔, H 3, R 3, ER 3, BB 4, SO 3; Hank Behrman, IP 1⅔, H 2, R 1, ER 1, BB 3, SO 1; Joe Hatten, IP ⅓, H 1, R 0, ER 0, BB 0, SO 1; Rex Barney, IP ⅓, H 0, R 0, ER 0, BB 0, SO 0; Hugh Casey, IP 2, H 1, R 1, ER 1, BB 0, SO 0
NY Spec Shea, IP 1⅓, H 4, R 2, ER 2, BB 1, SO 0; Bill Bevens, IP 2⅔, H 2, R 0, ER 0, BB 1, SO 2; Joe Page (W, 1-1), IP 5, H 1, R 0, ER 0, BB 0, SO 1

Top Performers at the Plate
Bro Bruce Edwards, 2 for 4, 1 R, 1 RBI
NY Phil Rizzuto, 3 for 4, 2 R, 1 RBI
2B-Bro/Jorgensen; NY/Brown. **3B**-Bro/Hermanski; NY/Johnson. **SB**-NY/Rizzuto. **Time** 2:19. **Attendance** 71,548.

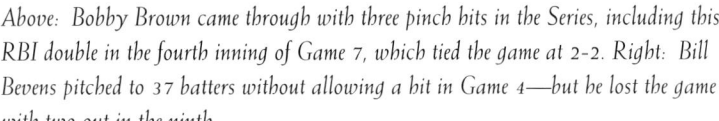

Above: Bobby Brown came through with three pinch hits in the Series, including this RBI double in the fourth inning of Game 7, which tied the game at 2-2. Right: Bill Bevens pitched to 37 batters without allowing a hit in Game 4—but he lost the game with two out in the ninth.

1947 WORLD SERIES COMPOSITE STATISTICS

NEW YORK YANKEES/Bucky Harris, Manager

Player	pos	G	AB	R	H	2B	3B	HR	RBI	BB	SO	SB	BA	SA	E	FPct
Yogi Berra	c-ph-rf	6	19	2	3	0	0	1	2	1	2	0	.158	.316	2	.923
Bill Bevens	p	2	4	0	0	0	0	0	0	0	2	0	.000	.000	0	1.000
Bobby Brown	ph	4	3	2	3	2	0	0	3	1	0	0	1.000	1.667	0	—
Spud Chandler	p	1	0	0	0	0	0	0	0	0	0	0	—	—	0	—
Allie Clark	ph-rf	3	2	1	1	0	0	0	1	1	0	0	.500	.500	0	1.000
Joe DiMaggio	cf	7	26	4	6	0	0	2	5	6	2	0	.231	.462	0	1.000
Karl Drews	p	2	2	0	0	0	0	0	0	0	2	0	.000	.000	0	1.000
Lonny Frey	ph	1	1	0	0	0	0	0	1	0	0	0	.000	.000	—	—
Tommy Henrich	rf-lf	7	31	2	10	2	0	1	5	2	3	0	.323	.484	0	1.000
Ralph Houk	ph	1	1	0	1	0	0	0	0	0	0	0	1.000	1.000	—	—
Bill Johnson	3b	7	26	8	7	0	3	0	2	3	4	0	.269	.500	0	1.000
Johnny Lindell	lf	6	18	3	9	3	1	0	7	5	2	0	.500	1.000	0	1.000
Sherm Lollar	c	2	4	3	3	2	0	0	1	0	0	0	.750	1.250	0	1.000
George McQuinn	1b	7	23	3	3	0	0	0	1	5	8	0	.130	.130	1	.981
Bobo Newsom	p	2	0	0	0	0	0	0	0	0	0	0	—	—	0	1.000
Joe Page	p	4	4	0	0	0	0	0	0	0	1	0	.000	.000	0	1.000
Jack Phillips	ph-1b	2	2	0	0	0	0	0	0	0	0	0	.000	.000	0	1.000
Vic Raschi	p	2	0	0	0	0	0	0	0	0	0	0	—	—	0	—
Allie Reynolds	p	2	4	2	2	0	0	0	1	0	0	0	.500	.500	0	1.000
Phil Rizzuto	ss	7	26	3	8	1	0	0	2	4	0	2	.308	.346	0	1.000
Aaron Robinson	c	3	10	2	2	0	0	0	1	2	1	0	.200	.200	1	.938
Spec Shea	p	3	5	0	2	1	0	0	1	0	2	0	.400	.600	0	1.000
Snuffy Stirnweiss	2b	7	27	3	7	0	1	0	3	8	8	0	.259	.333	0	1.000
Butch Wensloff	p	1	0	0	0	0	0	0	0	0	0	0	—	—	0	1.000
Totals		7	238	38	67	11	5	4	36	38	37	2	.282	.420	4	.985

Pitcher	G	GS	CG	IP	H	R	ER	BB	SO	W-L	Sv	ERA
Bill Bevens	2	1	1	11⅓	3	3	3	11	7	0-1	0	2.38
Spud Chandler	1	0	0	2	2	2	2	3	1	0-0	0	9.00
Karl Drews	2	0	0	3	2	1	1	1	0	0-0	0	3.00
Bobo Newsom	2	1	0	2⅓	6	5	5	2	0	0-1	0	19.29
Joe Page	4	0	0	13	12	6	6	2	7	1-1	0	4.15
Vic Raschi	2	0	0	1⅓	2	1	1	0	1	0-0	0	6.75
Allie Reynolds	2	2	1	11⅓	15	7	6	3	6	1-0	0	4.76
Spec Shea	3	3	1	15⅓	10	4	4	8	10	2-0	0	2.35
Butch Wensloff	1	0	0	2	0	0	0	0	0	0-0	0	0.00
Totals	7	7	3	61⅔	52	29	28	30	32	4-3	1	4.09

BROOKLYN DODGERS/Burt Shotten, Manager

Player	pos	G	AB	R	H	2B	3B	HR	RBI	BB	SO	SB	BA	SA	E	FPct
Dan Bankhead	pr	1	0	1	0	0	0	0	0	0	0	0	—	—	—	—
Rex Barney	p	3	1	0	0	0	0	0	0	0	0	0	.000	.000	0	1.000
Hank Behrman	p	5	0	0	0	0	0	0	0	0	0	0	—	—	0	1.000
Bobby Bragan	ph	1	1	0	1	1	0	0	1	0	0	0	1.000	2.000	—	—
Ralph Branca	p	3	4	0	0	0	0	0	0	0	1	0	.000	.000	0	1.000
Hugh Casey	p	6	1	0	0	0	0	0	0	0	1	0	.000	.000	0	1.000
Bruce Edwards	c	7	27	3	6	1	0	0	2	2	7	0	.222	.259	1	.980
Carl Furillo	ph-cf	6	17	2	6	2	0	0	3	3	0	0	.353	.471	0	.938
Al Gionfriddo	ph-pr-lf	4	3	2	0	0	0	0	0	1	0	1	.000	.000	0	1.000
Hal Gregg	p	3	3	0	0	0	0	0	0	1	1	0	.000	.000	0	1.000
Joe Hatten	p	4	3	1	1	0	0	0	0	0	0	0	.333	.333	0	—
Gene Hermanski	lf	7	19	4	3	0	1	0	1	3	3	0	.158	.263	0	1.000
Gil Hodges	ph	1	1	0	0	0	0	0	0	0	0	0	.000	.000	—	—
Spider Jorgensen	3b	7	20	1	4	2	0	0	3	2	4	0	.200	.300	2	.905
Cookie Lavagetto	ph-3b	5	7	0	1	1	0	0	3	0	2	0	.143	.286	0	1.000
Vic Lombardi	p-pr	3	3	0	0	0	0	0	0	0	0	0	.000	.000	0	—
Eddie Miksis	ph-pr-2b-lf	5	4	1	1	0	0	0	0	0	1	0	.250	.250	0	.800
Pee Wee Reese	ss	7	23	5	7	1	0	0	4	6	3	3	.304	.348	1	.960
Pete Reiser	cf-lf-ph	5	8	1	2	0	0	0	3	1	0	0	.250	.250	1	.875
Jackie Robinson	1b	7	27	3	7	2	0	0	3	2	4	2	.259	.333	0	1.000
Eddie Stanky	2b	7	25	4	6	1	0	0	2	3	2	0	.240	.280	1	.973
Harry Taylor	p	1	0	0	0	0	0	0	0	0	0	0	—	—	0	—
Arky Vaughan	ph	3	2	0	1	1	0	0	0	1	0	0	.500	1.000	—	—
Dixie Walker	rf	7	27	1	6	0	0	1	4	3	1	1	.222	.370	0	1.000
Totals		7	226	29	52	13	1	1	26	30	32	7	.230	.310	8	.889

Pitcher	G	GS	CG	IP	H	R	ER	BB	SO	W-L	Sv	ERA
Rex Barney	3	1	0	6⅔	4	2	2	10	3	0-1	0	2.70
Hank Behrman	5	0	0	6⅓	9	5	5	5	3	0-0	0	7.11
Ralph Branca	3	1	0	8⅓	12	8	8	5	8	1-1	0	8.64
Hugh Casey	6	0	0	10⅓	5	1	1	3	2-0		1	0.87
Hal Gregg	3	1	0	12⅔	9	5	5	8	10	0-1	0	3.55
Joe Hatten	4	1	0	9	12	7	7	5	0-0		0	7.00
Vic Lombardi	2	2	0	6⅔	14	9	9	1	5	0-1	0	12.15
Harry Taylor	1	1	0	0	2	1	0	1	0	0-0	0	—
Totals	7	7	0	60	87	38	37	38	37	3-4	1	5.55

Series Outstanding Player: Johnny Lindell, New York Yankees. **Series Outstanding Pitcher:** Spec Shea, New York Yankees. **Average Length of Game:** 2 hours, 41 minutes. **Total Attendance:** 389,763. **Average Attendance:** 55,680 (72,211 at Yankee Stadium; 33,640 at Ebbets Field). **Umpires:** Jim Boyer (AL), Larry Goetz (NL), George Magerkurth (NL), Bill McGowan (AL), Babe Pinelli (NL), Eddie Rommel (AL). **Winning Player's Share:** $5,830. **Losing Player's Share:** $4,081.

Left: A dejected Bevens heads to the locker room after losing both a no-hitter and the game.

Below: Al Gionfriddo earns a kiss from Pee Wee Reese after Gionfriddo's superb catch of Joe DiMaggio's drive preserved the Game 6 victory for Brooklyn.

Right: Spec Shea won twice for the Yanks, including a pivotal complete-game four-hitter in Game 5.

Cleveland Indians (4) vs. Boston Braves (2)

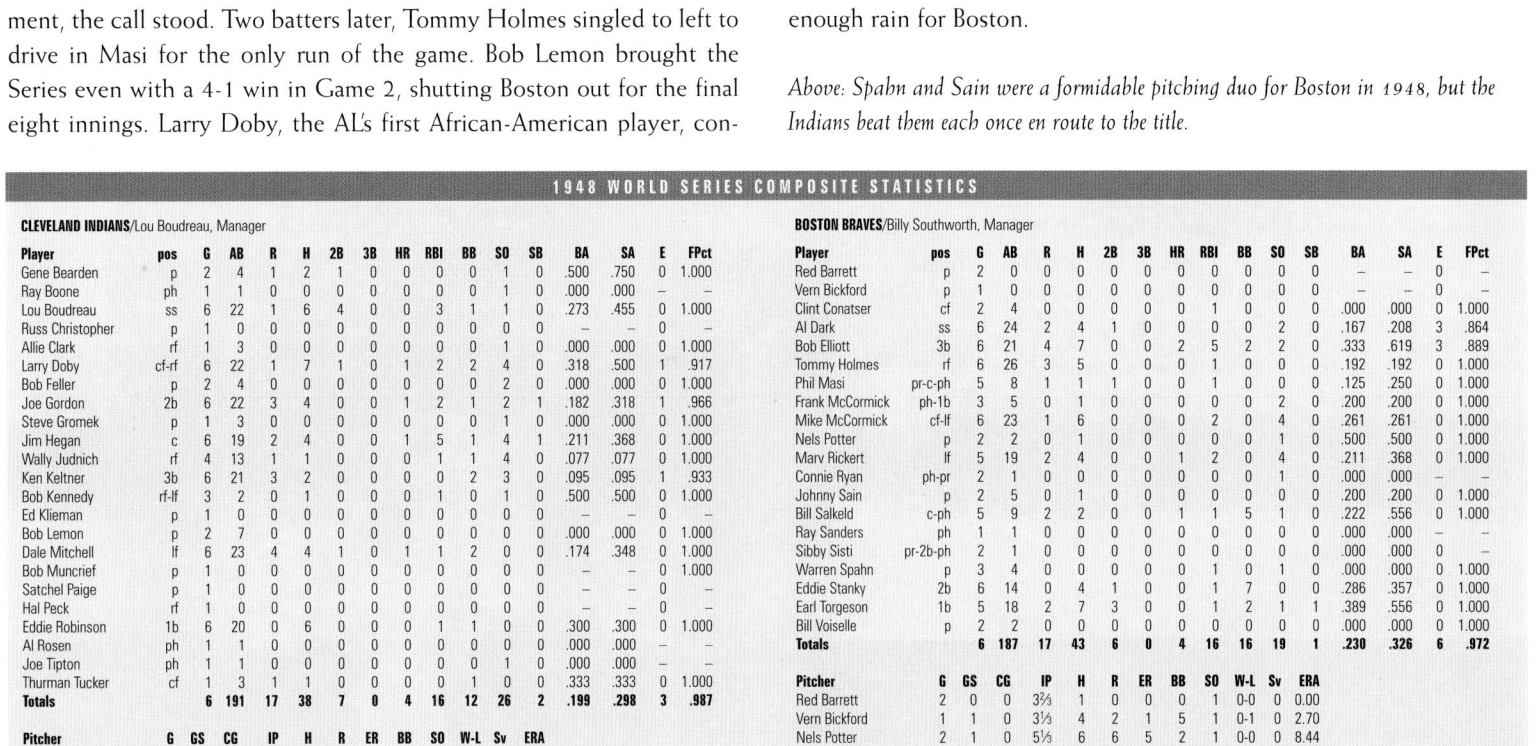

For the second time in three years, 154 games was not sufficient to determine baseball's pennant winners, and the Boston Red Sox and Cleveland Indians met in a one-game playoff for the 1948 pennant. Cleveland manager/shortstop Lou Boudreau hit two home runs in the game to send his team to their first Series in 28 years—and thus deprive Bostonians of an all-city World Series, as the Boston Braves had grabbed the National League flag. The Braves boasted the mighty arms of Warren Spahn and Johnny Sain, and "Spahn and Sain and two days of rain" was the mantra for Boston's hopes. In a Series featuring the team-ERA leaders from both leagues, it's no surprise that Game 1 was a classic pitcher's duel. The Braves didn't get a man on base against Bob Feller until Earl Torgeson's two-out, fourth-inning walk; a leadoff single in the fifth accounted for their only other baserunner until inning eight. With the game still scoreless, two walks (one intentional) put Braves on first and second when a controversy erupted on a pickoff play. Feller wheeled around and threw to Boudreau to seemingly nab pinch runner Phil Masi at second base, but umpire Bill Stewart called him safe. Despite Boudreau's spirited argument, the call stood. Two batters later, Tommy Holmes singled to left to drive in Masi for the only run of the game. Bob Lemon brought the Series even with a 4-1 win in Game 2, shutting Boston out for the final eight innings. Larry Doby, the AL's first African-American player, contributed an RBI single in the fourth. Rookie Gene Bearden pitched a masterful five-hit shutout for the Indians back in Cleveland, good enough for a 2-0 win in Game 3. Bearden also doubled and scored the game's first run. In Game 4, the Indians got only five hits for the second day in a row, and for the second day in a row they ended up with a victory. Boudreau's RBI double in the first and Doby's solo homer in the third were all they needed. Bob Elliott's two home runs, including a three-run shot in the first, headed a Boston barrage in Game 5. Although Cleveland briefly took the lead in the fourth inning, the Braves rallied together six more runs in the seventh, and Spahn pitched one-hit ball in relief for the W. Although the Indians lost the game, they made history by bringing in Negro Leagues legend Satchel Paige with one out in the seventh. Becoming the first African American to pitch in a World Series game, Paige retired both batters he faced. In Game 6, Cleveland edged out a one-run win, holding off a late Boston rally. Despite a disappointing Series for the great Bob Feller, and despite batting under .200 as a team, the Cleveland Indians were baseball's champions in 1948. There simply had not been enough rain for Boston.

Above: Spahn and Sain were a formidable pitching duo for Boston in 1948, but the Indians beat them each once en route to the title.

1948 WORLD SERIES COMPOSITE STATISTICS

CLEVELAND INDIANS/Lou Boudreau, Manager

Player	pos	G	AB	R	H	2B	3B	HR	RBI	BB	SO	SB	BA	SA	E	FPct
Gene Bearden	p	2	4	1	2	1	0	0	0	0	1	0	.500	.750	0	1.000
Ray Boone	ph	1	1	0	0	0	0	0	0	0	1	0	.000	.000	–	–
Lou Boudreau	ss	6	22	1	6	4	0	0	3	1	1	0	.273	.455	0	1.000
Russ Christopher	p	1	0	0	0	0	0	0	0	0	0	0	–	–	0	–
Allie Clark	rf	1	3	0	0	0	0	0	0	0	1	0	.000	.000	0	1.000
Larry Doby	cf-rf	6	22	1	7	1	0	1	2	2	4	0	.318	.500	1	.917
Bob Feller	p	2	4	0	0	0	0	0	0	0	2	0	.000	.000	0	1.000
Joe Gordon	2b	6	22	3	4	0	0	1	2	1	2	1	.182	.318	1	.966
Steve Gromek	p	1	3	0	0	0	0	0	0	0	0	0	.000	.000	0	1.000
Jim Hegan	c	6	19	2	4	0	0	1	5	1	4	1	.211	.368	0	1.000
Wally Judnich	rf	4	13	1	1	0	0	0	1	1	4	0	.077	.077	0	1.000
Ken Keltner	3b	6	21	3	2	0	0	0	2	3	0	1	.095	.095	1	.933
Bob Kennedy	rf-lf	3	2	0	1	0	0	0	1	0	1	0	.500	.500	0	1.000
Ed Klieman	p	1	0	0	0	0	0	0	0	0	0	0	–	–	0	–
Bob Lemon	p	2	7	0	0	0	0	0	0	0	0	0	.000	.000	0	1.000
Dale Mitchell	lf	6	23	4	4	1	0	1	1	2	0	0	.174	.348	0	1.000
Bob Muncrief	p	1	0	0	0	0	0	0	0	0	0	0	–	–	0	1.000
Satchel Paige	p	1	0	0	0	0	0	0	0	0	0	0	–	–	0	–
Hal Peck	rf	1	0	0	0	0	0	0	0	0	0	0	–	–	0	–
Eddie Robinson	1b	6	20	0	6	0	0	0	1	1	0	0	.300	.300	0	1.000
Al Rosen	ph	1	1	0	0	0	0	0	0	0	0	0	.000	.000	–	–
Joe Tipton	ph	1	1	0	0	0	0	0	0	0	1	0	.000	.000	–	–
Thurman Tucker	cf	1	3	1	1	0	0	0	0	1	0	0	.333	.333	0	1.000
Totals		6	191	17	38	7	0	4	16	12	26	2	.199	.298	3	.987

Pitcher	G	GS	CG	IP	H	R	ER	BB	SO	W-L	Sv	ERA
Gene Bearden	2	1	1	10⅔	6	0	0	1	4	1-0	1	0.00
Russ Christopher	1	0	0	0	2	1	1	0	0	0-0	0	–
Bob Feller	2	2	1	14⅓	10	8	8	5	7	0-2	0	5.02
Steve Gromek	1	1	1	9	7	1	1	1	2	1-0	0	1.00
Ed Klieman	1	0	0	0	1	3	3	2	0	0-0	0	–
Bob Lemon	2	2	1	16⅓	16	4	3	7	6	2-0	0	1.65
Bob Muncrief	1	0	0	2	1	0	0	0	0	0-0	0	0.00
Satchel Paige	1	0	0	⅔	0	0	0	0	0	0-0	0	0.00
Totals	6	6	4	53	43	17	16	16	19	4-2	1	2.72

BOSTON BRAVES/Billy Southworth, Manager

Player	pos	G	AB	R	H	2B	3B	HR	RBI	BB	SO	SB	BA	SA	E	FPct
Red Barrett	p	2	0	0	0	0	0	0	0	0	0	0	–	–	0	–
Vern Bickford	p	1	0	0	0	0	0	0	0	0	0	0	–	–	0	–
Clint Conatser	cf	2	4	0	0	0	0	0	1	0	0	0	.000	.000	0	1.000
Al Dark	ss	6	24	2	4	1	0	0	0	0	2	0	.167	.208	3	.864
Bob Elliott	3b	6	21	4	7	0	0	2	5	2	2	0	.333	.619	3	.889
Tommy Holmes	rf	6	26	3	5	0	0	0	1	0	0	0	.192	.192	0	1.000
Phil Masi	pr-c-ph	5	8	1	1	1	0	0	1	0	0	0	.125	.250	0	1.000
Frank McCormick	ph-1b	3	5	0	1	0	0	0	0	0	2	0	.200	.200	0	1.000
Mike McCormick	cf-lf	6	23	1	6	0	0	0	2	0	4	0	.261	.261	0	1.000
Nels Potter	p	2	2	0	1	0	0	0	0	0	1	0	.500	.500	0	1.000
Marv Rickert	lf	5	19	2	4	0	0	1	2	0	4	0	.211	.368	0	1.000
Connie Ryan	ph-pr	2	1	0	0	0	0	0	0	0	1	0	.000	.000	–	–
Johnny Sain	p	2	5	0	1	0	0	0	0	0	0	0	.200	.200	0	1.000
Bill Salkeld	c-ph	5	9	2	2	0	0	1	1	5	1	0	.222	.556	0	1.000
Ray Sanders	ph	1	1	0	0	0	0	0	0	0	0	0	.000	.000	–	–
Sibby Sisti	pr-2b-ph	2	1	0	0	0	0	0	0	0	0	0	.000	.000	–	–
Warren Spahn	p	3	4	0	0	0	0	0	1	0	1	0	.000	.000	0	1.000
Eddie Stanky	2b	6	14	0	4	1	0	0	1	7	0	0	.286	.357	0	1.000
Earl Torgeson	1b	5	18	2	7	3	0	0	1	2	1	1	.389	.556	0	1.000
Bill Voiselle	p	2	2	0	0	0	0	0	0	0	0	0	.000	.000	0	1.000
Totals		6	187	17	43	6	0	4	16	16	19	1	.230	.326	6	.972

Pitcher	G	GS	CG	IP	H	R	ER	BB	SO	W-L	Sv	ERA
Red Barrett	2	0	0	3⅔	1	0	0	1	1	0-0	0	0.00
Vern Bickford	1	1	0	3⅓	4	2	1	5	2	0-1	0	2.70
Nels Potter	2	1	0	5⅓	6	6	5	2	1	0-0	0	8.44
Johnny Sain	2	2	2	17	9	2	2	0	9	1-1	0	1.06
Warren Spahn	3	1	0	12	10	4	4	3	12	1-1	0	3.00
Bill Voiselle	2	1	0	10⅔	8	3	3	2	2	0-1	0	2.53
Totals	6	6	2	52	38	17	15	12	26	2-4	0	2.60

Series Outstanding Player: Bob Elliott, Boston Braves. **Series Outstanding Pitcher:** Gene Bearden, Cleveland Indians. **Average Length of Game:** 2 hours. **Total Attendance:** 358,362. **Average Attendance:** 59,727 (79,497 at Cleveland Stadium; 39,957 at Braves Field).
Umpires: George Barr (NL), Bill Grieve (AL), Joe Paparella (AL), Babe Pinelli (NL), Bill Stewart (NL), Bill Summers (AL). **Winning Player's Share:** $6,772. **Losing Player's Share:** $4,571.

Left: Boston's all-star lefty Warren Spahn opens the second game of the Series with a hard throw to Dale Mitchell.

Below: This photo captures the controversial pick-off play in Game 1. Boston runner Phil Masi is clearly tagged before getting back to second base, but umpire Bill Stewart saw it differently.

Right: Satchel Paige made history by becoming the first African American to pitch in a World Series.

Cleveland shattered the single-game attendance record when 86,288 showed up for Game 5. They first broke the 80,000 barrier in Game 4, with just under 82,000 in attendance.

Above: Pitcher Gene Bearden is practically dragged off the field by jubilant teammates after closing out the sixth game of the 1948 Series for a Cleveland championship.

Game 1 Wednesday, October 6 at Braves Field, Boston

	1	2	3	4	5	6	7	8	9	R	H	E
Cleveland Indians	0	0	0	0	0	0	0	0	0	0	4	0
Boston Braves	0	0	0	0	0	0	1	x		1	2	2

Pitchers Cle Bob Feller (L, 0-1), IP 8, H 2, R 1, ER 1, BB 3, SO 2
Bos Johnny Sain (W, 1-0), IP 9, H 4, R 0, ER 0, BB 0, SO 6

SB-Cle/Gordon, Hegan; Bos/Torgeson. **Time** 1:42. **Attendance** 40,135.

Game 2 Thursday, October 7 at Braves Field, Boston

	1	2	3	4	5	6	7	8	9	R	H	E
Cleveland Indians	0	0	0	2	1	0	0	0	1	4	8	1
Boston Braves	1	0	0	0	0	0	0	0	0	1	8	3

Pitchers Cle Bob Lemon (W, 1-0), IP 9, H 8, R 1, ER 0, BB 3, SO 5
Bos Warren Spahn (L, 0-1), IP 4⅓, H 6, R 3, ER 3, BB 2, SO 1; Red Barrett, IP 2⅔, H 1, R 0, ER 0, BB 0, SO 1; Nels Potter, IP 2, H 1, R 1, ER 0, BB 0, SO 1

Top Performers at the Plate
Cle Lou Boudreau, 2 for 5, 1 R, 1 RBI; Larry Doby, 2 for 4, 1 RBI
Bos Mike McCormick, 2 for 4; Earl Torgeson, 2 for 4

2B-Cle/Boudreau, Doby; Bos/Stanky. **Time** 2:14. **Attendance** 39,633.

Game 3 Friday, October 8 at Cleveland Stadium, Cleveland

	1	2	3	4	5	6	7	8	9	R	H	E
Boston Braves	0	0	0	0	0	0	0	0		0	5	1
Cleveland Indians	0	0	1	1	0	0	0	0	x	2	5	0

Pitchers Bos Vern Bickford (L, 0-1), IP 3⅓, H 4, R 2, ER 1, BB 5, SO 1; Bill Voiselle, IP 3⅔, H 1, R 0, ER 0, BB 0, SO 0; Red Barrett, IP 1, H 0, R 0, ER 0, BB 0, SO 0
Cle Gene Bearden (W, 1-0), IP 9, H 5, R 0, ER 0, BB 0, SO 4

Top Performers at the Plate
Cle Gene Bearden, 2 for 3, 1 R; Jim Hegan, 1 for 3, 1 RBI

2B-Bos/Dark; Cle/Bearden. **Time** 1:36. **Attendance** 70,306.

Game 4 Saturday, October 9 at Cleveland Stadium, Cleveland

	1	2	3	4	5	6	7	8	9	R	H	E
Boston Braves	0	0	0	0	0	0	1	0		1	7	0
Cleveland Indians	1	0	1	0	0	0	0	0	x	2	5	0

Pitchers Bos Johnny Sain (L, 1-1), IP 8, H 5, R 2, ER 2, BB 0, SO 3
Cle Steve Gromek (W, 1-0), IP 9, H 7, R 1, ER 1, BB 1, SO 2

Top Performers at the Plate
Bos Marv Rickert, 2 for 4, 1 R, 1 RBI; Earl Torgeson, 2 for 3, 2 2B
Cle Larry Doby, 1 for 3, 1 R, 1 RBI; Eddie Robinson, 2 for 3

2B-Bos/Torgeson 2; Cle/Boudreau. **HR**-Bos/Rickert; Cle/Doby. **Time** 1:31. **Attendance** 81,897.

Game 5 Sunday, October 10 at Cleveland Stadium, Cleveland

	1	2	3	4	5	6	7	8	9	R	H	E
Boston Braves	3	0	1	0	0	1	6	0	0	11	12	0
Cleveland Indians	1	0	0	4	0	0	0	0	0	5	6	2

Pitchers Bos Nels Potter, IP 3⅓, H 5, R 5, ER 5, BB 2, SO 0; Warren Spahn (W, 1-1), IP 5⅔, H 1, R 0, ER 0, BB 1, SO 7
Cle Bob Feller (L, 0-2), IP 6⅓, H 8, R 7, ER 7, BB 2, SO 5; Ed Klieman, IP 0, H 1, R 3, ER 3, BB 2, SO 0; Russ Christopher, IP 0, H 2, R 1, ER 1, BB 0, SO 0; Satchel Paige, IP ⅔, H 0, R 0, ER 0, BB 0, SO 0; Bob Muncrief, IP 2, H 1, R 0, ER 0, BB 0, SO 0

Top Performers at the Plate
Bos Bob Elliott, 2 for 4, 3 R, 4 RBI, 1 BB, 2 HR; Tommy Holmes, 2 for 5, 2 R
Cle Lou Bourdeau, 2 for 4; Jim Hegan, 1 for 4, 1 R, 3 RBI

2B-Cle/Boudreau. **HR**-Bos/Elliott 2, Salkeld; Cle/Hegan, Mitchell. **Time** 2:39. **Attendance** 86,288.

Game 6 Monday, October 11 at Braves Field, Boston

	1	2	3	4	5	6	7	8	9	R	H	E
Cleveland Indians	0	0	1	0	0	2	0	1	0	4	10	0
Boston Braves	0	0	0	1	0	0	0	2	0	3	9	0

Pitchers Cle Bob Lemon (W, 2-0), IP 7⅓, H 8, R 3, ER 3, BB 4, SO 1; Gene Bearden (S, 1), IP 1⅔, H 1, R 0, ER 0, BB 1, SO 0
Bos Bill Voiselle (L, 0-1), IP 7, H 7, R 3, ER 3, BB 2, SO 2; Warren Spahn, IP 2, H 3, R 1, ER 0, BB 0, SO 4

Top Performers at the Plate
Cle Lou Boudreau, 1 for 3, 1 RBI, 1 HBP; Eddie Robinson, 2 for 4, 1 RBI
Bos Bob Elliott, 3 for 3, 1 R, 1 BB; Tommy Holmes, 2 for 5, 1 R

2B-Cle/Boudreau, Mitchell; Bos/Masi, Torgeson. **HR**-Cle/Gordon. **Time** 2:16. **Attendance** 40,103.

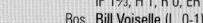

Three members of the 1948 Indians—Ray Boone, Jim Hegan and Bob Kennedy—had sons who later played in the World Series.

New York Yankees (4) vs. Brooklyn Dodgers (1)

The New York Yankees were making their 16th Series appearance in 1949, but this time they had a new leader at the helm. The man who had hit the first World Series home run at Yankee Stadium, and who had batted over .400 in two contests against the Yanks as a player, was named the club's new manager at the start of the 1949 season. Charles Dillon "Casey" Stengel led New York to a pennant in his rookie managerial outing, edging out the Red Sox by one game on the final day of the season. The Brooklyn Dodgers also eked out a last-day pennant win, setting up the second Brooklyn-New York pairing in three years. The Series opened at the Stadium with the starting pitchers offering up stingy performances from the mound. Allie Reynolds and Don Newcombe—the latter a former Negro Leagues standout and the first African-American pitcher to start a World Series game—battled for 8¹/₂ scoreless innings, with the Yankees scattering four base hits and the Dodgers managing only two. Leading off the bottom of the ninth, New York's Tommy Henrich stroked Newcombe's third pitch for a line-drive home run to right to claim the opener. The 1-0 final score was repeated the next day, only this time with Brooklyn on top. Gil Hodges's single in the second inning scored Jackie Robinson for the game's lone run; Preacher Roe hurled the six-hit shutout for the Dodgers. The teams were locked at one run apiece until the ninth inning in Game 3 at Ebbets Field. A two-run single by pinch hitter (and former New York Giant) Johnny Mize and an RBI single by Jerry Coleman put the Yanks up 4-1 going into the last of the ninth. The Dodgers got close with a solo home run by Luis Olmo (who had only one homer all year) and another by Roy Campanella, but they fell short, 4-3. Game 4 saw more runs cross the plate than in the three previous games combined, with New York pulling out a 6-4 victory. Three doubles in the fourth inning and a bases-loaded triple by Bobby Brown in the fifth provided the scoring for the Yanks. The Dodgers rallied together seven singles for four runs in the sixth, but Reynolds came on in relief for New York and retired the last ten Brooklyn batters in the game, including five on strikeouts. The Yankees staked a big lead quickly in Game 5 and held it, despite Hodges's seventh-inning, three-run blast. Joe Page came in to relieve Vic Raschi in the seventh and got the save. Although New York got miserable performances from legends Yogi Berra and Joe DiMaggio (a combined 3 for 34 in the Series), lesser known Yankees like Tommy Henrich, Bobby Brown and Gene Woodling picked up the slack with some key production in the Series. And Ol' Casey had his first taste of October glory as a manager.

Above: Pinch-hitter Johnny Mize slams a clutch single to give New York a ninth-inning lead in Game 3.

1949 WORLD SERIES COMPOSITE STATISTICS

NEW YORK YANKEES/Casey Stengel, Manager

Player	pos	G	AB	R	H	2B	3B	HR	RBI	BB	SO	SB	BA	SA	E	FPct
Hank Bauer	rf-pr-ph	3	6	0	1	0	0	0	0	0	0	0	.167	.167	0	1.000
Yogi Berra	c	4	16	2	1	0	0	0	1	1	0	0	.063	.063	0	1.000
Bobby Brown	ph-3b	4	12	4	6	1	2	0	5	2	2	0	.500	.917	0	1.000
Tommy Byrne	p	1	1	0	1	0	0	0	0	0	0	0	1.000	1.000	0	—
Jerry Coleman	2b	5	20	1	5	3	0	0	4	0	4	0	.250	.400	1	.950
Joe DiMaggio	cf	5	18	2	2	0	0	1	2	3	5	0	.111	.278	1	1.000
Tommy Henrich	1b	5	19	4	5	0	0	1	1	3	0	0	.263	.421	0	1.000
Bill Johnson	3b	2	7	0	1	0	0	0	0	0	2	1	.143	.143	0	1.000
Johnny Lindell	lf	2	7	0	1	0	0	0	0	0	2	0	.143	.143	1	.750
Ed Lopat	p	1	3	0	1	1	0	0	1	0	0	0	.333	.667	0	1.000
Cliff Mapes	rf	4	10	3	1	1	0	0	2	2	4	0	.100	.200	1	.889
Johnny Mize	ph	2	2	0	2	0	0	0	2	0	0	0	1.000	1.000	—	—
Gus Niarhos	c	1	0	0	0	0	0	0	0	0	0	0	—	—	0	—
Joe Page	p	3	4	0	0	0	0	0	0	0	2	0	.000	.000	0	1.000
Vic Raschi	p	2	5	0	1	0	0	0	1	1	1	0	.200	.200	0	—
Allie Reynolds	p	2	4	0	2	1	0	0	0	0	1	0	.500	.750	0	1.000
Phil Rizzuto	ss	5	18	2	3	0	0	0	1	3	1	1	.167	.167	0	1.000
Charlie Silvera	c	1	2	0	0	0	0	0	0	0	0	0	.000	.000	0	1.000
Snuffy Stirnweiss	pr	1	0	0	0	0	0	0	0	0	0	0	—	—	0	—
Gene Woodling	lf	3	10	4	4	3	0	0	0	3	0	0	.400	.700	0	1.000
Totals		**5**	**164**	**21**	**37**	**10**	**2**	**2**	**20**	**18**	**27**	**2**	**.228**	**.348**	**3**	**.984**

Pitcher	G	GS	CG	IP	H	R	ER	BB	SO	W-L	Sv	ERA
Tommy Byrne	1	1	0	3¹/₃	2	1	1	2	1	0-0	0	2.70
Ed Lopat	1	1	0	5²/₃	9	4	4	1	4	1-0	0	6.35
Joe Page	3	0	0	9	6	2	2	3	8	1-0	1	2.00
Vic Raschi	2	2	0	14²/₃	15	7	7	5	11	1-1	0	4.30
Allie Reynolds	2	1	1	12¹/₃	2	0	0	4	14	1-0	1	0.00
Totals	**5**	**5**	**1**	**45**	**34**	**14**	**14**	**15**	**38**	**4-1**	**2**	**2.80**

BROOKLYN DODGERS/Burt Shotten, Manager

Player	pos	G	AB	R	H	2B	3B	HR	RBI	BB	SO	SB	BA	SA	E	FPct
Jack Banta	p	3	1	0	0	0	0	0	0	0	0	0	.000	.000	0	1.000
Rex Barney	p	1	0	0	0	0	0	0	0	0	0	0	—	—	1	.667
Ralph Branca	p	1	3	0	0	0	0	0	0	0	3	0	.000	.000	0	1.000
Tommy Brown	ph	2	2	0	0	0	0	0	0	0	1	0	.000	.000	—	—
Roy Campanella	c	5	15	2	4	1	0	1	2	3	1	0	.267	.533	0	1.000
Billy Cox	ph-3b	2	3	0	1	0	0	0	0	0	1	0	.333	.333	0	1.000
Bruce Edwards	ph	2	2	0	1	0	0	0	0	0	1	0	.500	.500	—	—
Carl Erskine	p	2	0	0	0	0	0	0	0	0	0	0	—	—	0	—
Carl Furillo	rf-ph	3	8	0	1	0	0	0	0	1	0	0	.125	.125	0	1.000
Joe Hatten	p	2	0	0	0	0	0	0	0	0	0	0	—	—	0	—
Gene Hermanski	rf-lf	4	13	1	4	0	1	0	2	3	3	0	.308	.462	0	1.000
Gil Hodges	1b	5	17	2	4	0	0	1	4	1	4	0	.235	.412	0	1.000
Spider Jorgensen	3b-ph	4	11	1	2	2	0	0	0	2	2	0	.182	.364	0	1.000
Mike McCormick	rf	1	0	0	0	0	0	0	0	0	0	0	—	—	0	1.000
Eddie Miksis	3b-ph	3	7	0	2	1	0	0	0	0	1	0	.286	.429	1	.857
Paul Minner	p	1	0	0	0	0	0	0	0	0	0	0	—	—	0	1.000
Don Newcombe	p	2	4	0	0	0	0	0	0	0	3	0	.000	.000	0	1.000
Luis Olmo	lf	4	11	3	3	0	0	1	2	0	2	0	.273	.545	0	1.000
Erv Palica	p	1	0	0	0	0	0	0	0	0	0	0	—	—	0	1.000
Marv Rackley	lf	2	5	0	0	0	0	0	0	0	2	0	.000	.000	0	1.000
Pee Wee Reese	ss	5	19	2	6	1	0	1	2	1	0	1	.316	.526	1	.933
Jackie Robinson	2b	5	16	2	3	1	0	0	2	4	2	0	.188	.250	1	.955
Preacher Roe	p	1	3	0	0	0	0	0	0	0	3	0	.000	.000	1	.667
Duke Snider	cf	5	21	2	3	1	0	0	0	0	8	0	.143	.190	0	1.000
Dick Whitman	ph	1	1	0	0	0	0	0	0	0	1	0	.000	.000	—	—
Totals		**5**	**162**	**14**	**34**	**7**	**1**	**4**	**14**	**15**	**38**	**1**	**.210**	**.340**	**5**	**.972**

Pitcher	G	GS	CG	IP	H	R	ER	BB	SO	W-L	Sv	ERA
Jack Banta	3	0	0	5²/₃	5	2	2	1	4	0-0	0	3.18
Rex Barney	1	1	0	2²/₃	3	5	5	6	2	0-1	0	16.88
Ralph Branca	1	1	0	8¹/₃	4	4	4	4	6	0-1	0	4.15
Carl Erskine	2	0	0	1²/₃	3	3	3	1	0	0-0	0	16.20
Joe Hatten	2	0	0	1²/₃	4	3	3	2	0	0-0	0	16.20
Paul Minner	1	0	0	1	1	0	0	0	0	0-0	0	0.00
Don Newcombe	2	2	1	11²/₃	10	4	4	3	11	0-2	0	3.09
Erv Palica	1	0	0	2	1	0	0	1	1	0-0	0	0.00
Preacher Roe	1	1	1	9	6	0	0	0	3	1-0	0	0.00
Totals	**5**	**5**	**2**	**44**	**37**	**21**	**21**	**18**	**27**	**1-4**	**0**	**4.30**

Series Outstanding Player: Bobby Brown, New York Yankees. **Series Outstanding Pitcher:** Allie Reynolds, New York Yankees. **Average Length of Game:** 2 hours, 38 minutes. **Total Attendance:** 236,710. **Average Attendance:** 47,342 (68,139 at Yankee Stadium; 34,478 at Ebbets Field). **Umpires:** George Barr (NL), Cal Hubbard (AL), Eddie Hurley (AL), Lou Jorda (NL), Art Passarella (AL), John Reardon (NL). **Winning Player's Share:** $5,627. **Losing Player's Share:** $4,273.

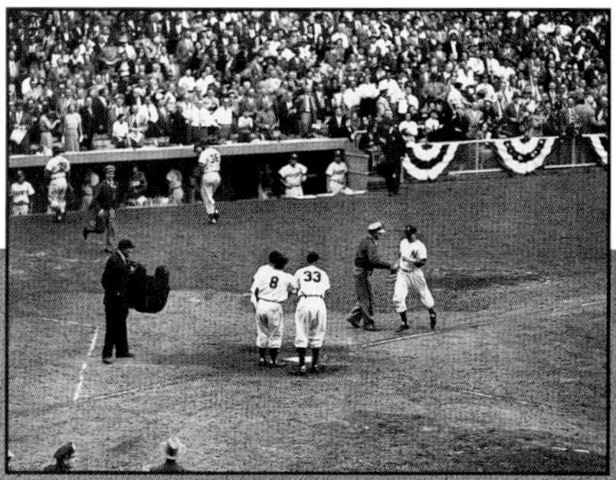

Left: Tommy Henrich's dramatic homer in the ninth inning of the 1949 Series opener set the Yankees on their way to a five-game triumph over Brooklyn.

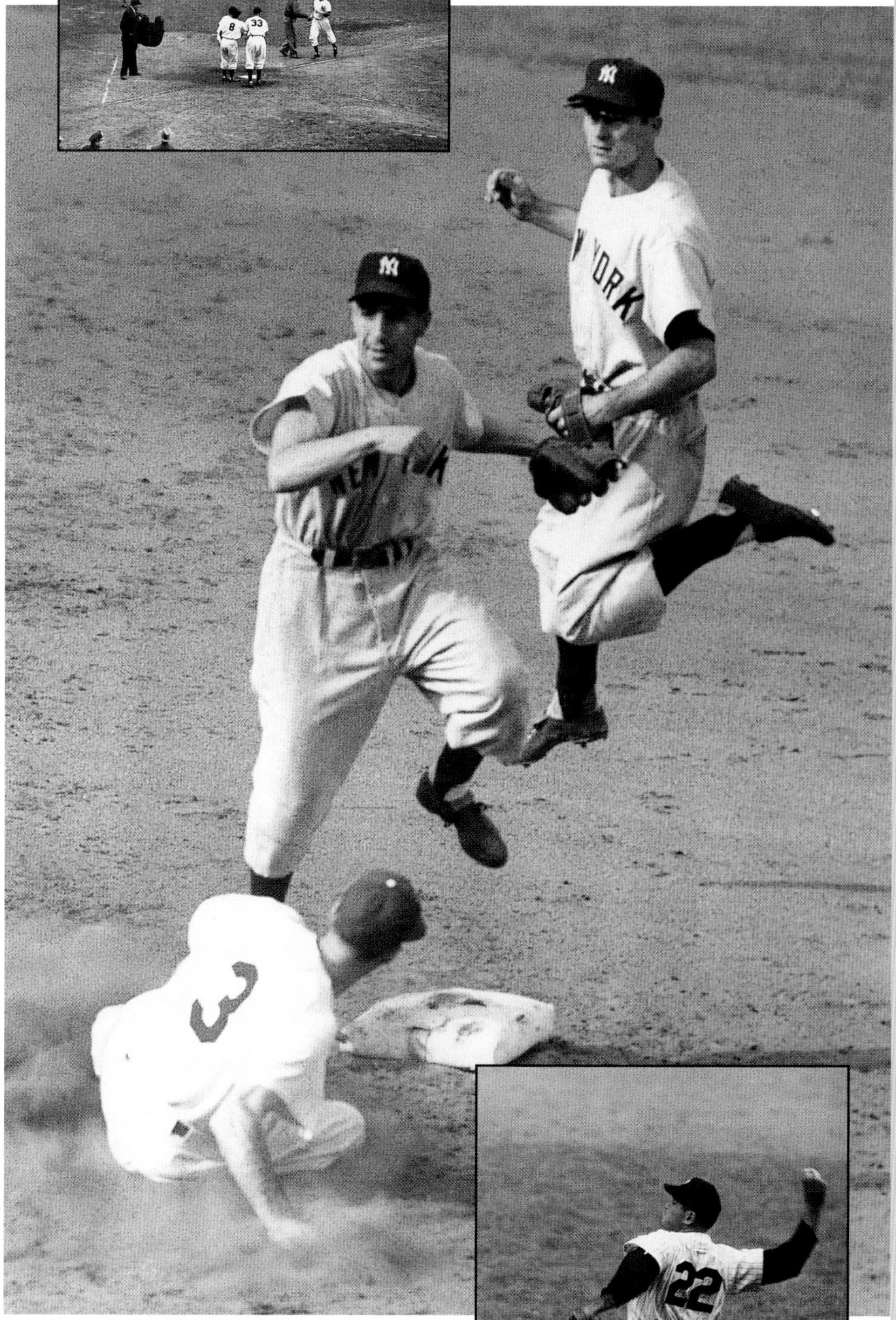

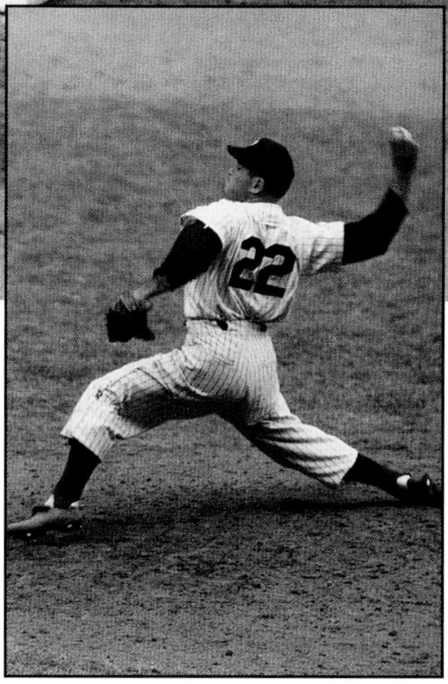

Above: Yankee shortstop Phil Rizzuto leaps over Billy Cox and whips the ball to first to turn a double play in Game 4. Second baseman Jerry Coleman is behind Rizzuto

Right: Allie Reynolds two-hit the Dodgers in Game 1 to top Don Newcombe in a 1-0 duel.

Far right: Joe DiMaggio struggled mightily in the Series, but he did contribute a solo homer in Game 5.

Game 1 Wednesday, October 5 at Yankee Stadium, New York

	1	2	3	4	5	6	7	8	9	R	H	E
Brooklyn Dodgers	0	0	0	0	0	0	0	0	0	0	2	0
New York Yankees	0	0	0	0	0	0	0	0	1	1	5	1

Pitchers Bro **Don Newcombe** (L, 0-1), IP 8, H 5, R 1, ER 1, BB 0, SO 11
NY **Allie Reynolds** (W, 1-0), IP 9, H 2, R 0, ER 0, BB 4, SO 9

Top Performers at the Plate
NY **Tommy Henrich**, 1 for 4, 1 R, 1 RBI; **Allie Reynolds**, 2 for 3

2B-Bro/Jorgensen; NY/Coleman, Reynolds. **HR**-NY/Henrich. **SB**-Bro/Reese. **Time** 2:24. **Attendance** 66,224.

Game 2 Thursday, October 6 at Yankee Stadium, New York

	1	2	3	4	5	6	7	8	9	R	H	E
Brooklyn Dodgers	0	1	0	0	0	0	0	0	0	1	7	2
New York Yankees	0	0	0	0	0	0	0	0	0	0	6	1

Pitchers Bro **Preacher Roe** (W, 1-0), IP 9, H 6, R 0, ER 0, BB 0, SO 3
NY **Vic Raschi** (L, 0-1), IP 8, H 6, R 1, ER 1, BB 1, SO 4; **Joe Page**, IP 1, H 1, R 0, ER 0, BB 0, SO 0

Top Performers at the Plate
Bro **Gil Hodges**, 1 for 3, 1 RBI; **Jackie Robinson**, 1 for 3, 1 R, 1 SH

2B-Bro/Jorgensen, Robinson; NY/Coleman. **3B**-Bro/Hermanski. **SB**-NY/Johnson, Rizzuto. **Time** 2:30. **Attendance** 70,053.

Game 3 Friday, October 7 at Ebbets Field, Brooklyn

	1	2	3	4	5	6	7	8	9	R	H	E
New York Yankees	0	0	1	0	0	0	0	0	3	4	5	0
Brooklyn Dodgers	0	0	0	1	0	0	0	0	2	3	5	0

Pitchers NY **Tommy Byrne**, IP 3⅓, H 2, R 1, ER 1, BB 2, SO 1; **Joe Page** (W, 1-0), IP 5⅔, H 3, R 2, ER 2, BB 2, SO 4
Bro **Ralph Branca** (L, 0-1), IP 8⅔, H 4, R 4, ER 4, BB 4, SO 6; **Jack Banta**, IP ⅓, H 1, R 0, ER 0, BB 0, SO 1

Top Performers at the Plate
NY **Gene Woodling**, 1 for 3, 1 R, 1 BB
Bro **Pee Wee Reese**, 1 for 2, 1 R, 1 RBI, 1 BB, 1 HBP

2B-NY/Woodling. **HR**-Bro/Campanella, Olmo, Reese. **Time** 2:30. **Attendance** 32,788.

Game 4 Saturday, October 8 at Ebbets Field, Brooklyn

	1	2	3	4	5	6	7	8	9	R	H	E
New York Yankees	0	0	0	3	3	0	0	0	0	6	10	0
Brooklyn Dodgers	0	0	0	0	0	4	0	0	0	4	9	1

Pitchers NY **Ed Lopat** (W, 1-0), IP 5⅔, H 9, R 4, ER 4, BB 1, SO 4; **Allie Reynolds** (Sv, 1), IP 3⅓, H 0, R 0, ER 0, BB 0, SO 5
Bro **Don Newcombe** (L, 0-2), IP 3⅔, H 5, R 3, ER 3, BB 3, SO 0; **Joe Hatten**, IP 1⅓, H 3, R 3, ER 3, BB 2, SO 0; **Carl Erskine**, IP 1, H 1, R 0, ER 0, BB 0, SO 0; **Jack Banta**, IP 3, H 1, R 0, ER 0, BB 1, SO 1

Top Performers at the Plate
NY **Bobby Brown**, 2 for 3, 1 R, 3 RBI, 1 BB; **Tommy Henrich**, 3 for 4, 1 R, 1 BB
Bro **Pee Wee Reese**, 2 for 4, 1 R; **Jackie Robinson**, 1 for 3, 1 R, 1 RBI, 1 BB

2B-NY/B. Brown, Lopat, Mapes; Bro/Reese. **3B**-NY/B. Brown. **Time** 2:42. **Attendance** 33,934.

Game 5 Sunday, October 9 at Ebbets Field, Brooklyn

	1	2	3	4	5	6	7	8	9	R	H	E
New York Yankees	2	0	3	1	1	3	0	0	0	10	11	1
Brooklyn Dodgers	0	0	1	0	0	1	4	0	0	6	11	2

Pitchers NY **Vic Raschi** (W, 1-1), IP 6⅔, H 9, R 6, ER 6, BB 4, SO 7; **Joe Page** (Sv, 1), IP 2⅓, H 2, R 0, ER 0, BB 1, SO 4
Bro **Rex Barney** (L, 0-1), IP 2⅔, H 3, R 5, ER 5, BB 6, SO 2; **Jack Banta**, IP 2⅓, H 3, R 2, ER 2, BB 0, SO 2; **Carl Erskine**, IP ⅔, H 2, R 3, ER 3, BB 1, SO 0; **Joe Hatten**, IP ⅓, H 1, R 0, ER 0, BB 0, SO 0; **Erv Palica**, IP 2, H 1, R 0, ER 0, BB 1, SO 1; **Paul Minner**, IP 1, H 1, R 0, ER 0, BB 0, SO 0

Top Performers at the Plate
NY **Bobby Brown**, 3 for 4, 2 R, 2 RBI, 1 BB; **Gene Woodling**, 3 for 4, 2 R, 1 BB, 2 2B
Bro **Gil Hodges**, 2 for 5, 1 R, 3 RBI; **Duke Snider**, 2 for 5, 2 R

2B-NY/Coleman, Woodling 2; Bro/Campanella, Miksis, Snider. **3B**-NY/B. Brown. **HR**-NY/DiMaggio; Bro/Hodges. **Time** 3:04. **Attendance** 33,711.

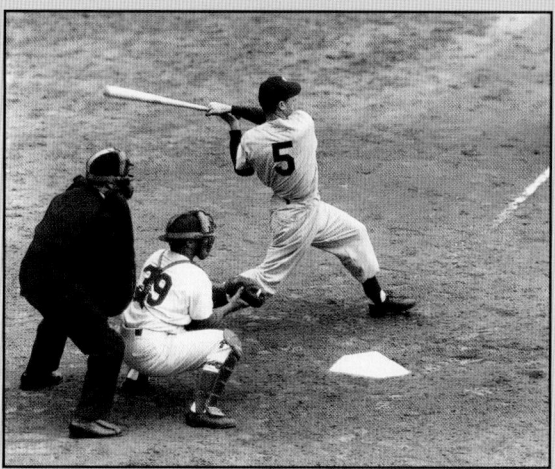

New York Yankees (4) vs. Philadelphia Phillies (0)

1950

On the final day of the 1950 season, a young, upstart Philadelphia Phillie team known familiarly as the "Whiz Kids" defeated the defending league-champion Dodgers in 10 innings to win the pennant. Unfortunately for the "City of Brotherly Love," the joy that came with the Phillies' first trip to the World Series since 1915 was soon followed by a quick exit from baseball's pinnacle event. They went up against Casey Stengel's New York Yankees and went down in four straight losses. Jim Konstanty was given the start for Philadelphia in Game 1 of the Series. Konstanty had earned league MVP honors for his outstanding work on the mound in 1950, but all 74 of his appearances during the season had been in relief. Tired arms and untimely injuries had forced manager Eddie Sawyer to give Konstanty his first start of the year in the crucial Series opener. Konstanty fared well, allowing just four hits and one run before being lifted for a pinch hitter in the 8th. The lone run that he let up—resulting from a Bobby Brown double and two fly balls—proved to be a costly one, however; New York's 21-game winner, Vic Raschi, shut down the Phillie lineup with a two-hitter. The dueling pitchers theme continued in Game 2, with Allie Reynolds and Robin Roberts matching one-run ball through 9 innings. Philadelphia was handed another tough defeat when Joe DiMaggio hit a leadoff home run in the 10th to win the game. The Phillies took a 2-1 lead into the 8th inning of Game 3 in New York, but then Ken

Heintzelman walked three straight Yankees with two outs to load the bases. Konstanty came in to bail out Heintzelman, but an error by Granny Hamner on Brown's routine grounder allowed the tying run to score. Yankee reliever Tom Ferrick worked around a leadoff double by Hamner to keep Philadelphia from scoring in the top of the 9th, and consecutive singles by Gene Woodling, Phil Rizzuto and Coleman—the first two not leaving the infield—brought in the game winner with two men out in the bottom of the 9th. The Whiz Kids had been outscored by a mere three runs in the first three games, and they had three losses to show for it. Whether they were deflated by the near-misses or simply outmatched by a better team, the Phillies fell behind quickly in the fourth game. Two runs came in for New York in the 1st inning, thanks to an error by Mike Goliat and base hits by Yogi Berra and Joe DiMaggio. The Yanks scored three more in the 6th on Berra's leadoff homer and Brown's two-run triple. Down five with two outs in the 9th, the Phillies put two runs on the board when Woodling dropped a fly ball to ruin rookie Whitey Ford's shutout attempt. Allie Reynolds came in to strike out the final batter of the game and close out the sweep.

Above: Philadelphia pitcher and NL MVP Jim Konstanty delivers the first pitch of the 1950 World Series to New York's Gene Woodling.

1950 WORLD SERIES COMPOSITE STATISTICS

NEW YORK YANKEES/Casey Stengel, Manager

Player	pos	G	AB	R	H	2B	3B	HR	RBI	BB	SO	SB	BA	SA	E	FPct
Hank Bauer	rf-lf	4	15	0	2	0	0	0	1	0	0	0	.133	.133	0	1.000
Yogi Berra	c	4	15	2	3	0	0	1	2	2	1	0	.200	.400	0	1.000
Bobby Brown	3b-ph	4	12	2	4	1	1	0	1	0	0	0	.333	.583	1	.500
Jerry Coleman	2b	4	14	2	4	1	0	0	3	2	0	0	.286	.357	0	1.000
Joe Collins	1b	1	0	0	0	0	0	0	0	0	0	0	—	—	0	1.000
Joe DiMaggio	cf	4	13	2	4	1	0	1	2	3	1	0	.308	.615	0	1.000
Tom Ferrick	p	1	0	0	0	0	0	0	0	0	0	0	—	—	0	—
Whitey Ford	p	1	3	0	0	0	0	0	0	0	2	0	.000	.000	0	1.000
Johnny Hopp	1b-pr	3	2	0	0	0	0	0	0	0	0	0	.000	.000	0	1.000
Jackie Jensen	pr	1	0	0	0	0	0	0	0	0	0	0	—	—	0	—
Bill Johnson	3b	4	6	0	0	0	0	0	0	0	3	0	.000	.000	0	1.000
Ed Lopat	p	1	2	0	1	0	0	0	0	0	1	0	.500	.500	0	1.000
Cliff Mapes	rf	1	4	0	0	0	0	0	0	0	1	0	.000	.000	0	1.000
Johnny Mize	1b	4	15	0	2	0	0	0	0	1	0	0	.133	.133	0	1.000
Vic Raschi	p	1	3	0	1	0	0	0	0	0	0	0	.333	.333	0	1.000
Allie Reynolds	p	2	3	0	1	0	0	0	0	1	2	0	.333	.333	0	1.000
Phil Rizzuto	ss	4	14	1	2	0	0	0	0	3	0	1	.143	.143	0	1.000
Gene Woodling	lf-ph	4	14	2	6	0	0	0	1	2	0	0	.429	.429	1	.875
Totals		4	135	11	30	3	1	2	10	13	12	1	.222	.304	2	.987

Pitcher	G	GS	CG	IP	H	R	ER	BB	SO	W-L	Sv	ERA
Tom Ferrick	1	0	0	1	1	0	0	1	0	1-0	0	0.00
Whitey Ford	1	1	0	8⅔	7	2	0	1	7	1-0	0	0.00
Ed Lopat	1	1	0	8	9	2	2	0	5	0-0	0	2.25
Vic Raschi	1	1	1	9	2	0	0	1	5	1-0	0	0.00
Allie Reynolds	2	1	1	10⅓	7	1	1	4	7	1-0	1	0.87
Totals	4	4	2	37	26	5	3	7	24	4-0	1	0.73

PHILADELPHIA PHILLIES/Eddie Sawyer, Manager

Player	pos	G	AB	R	H	2B	3B	HR	RBI	BB	SO	SB	BA	SA	E	FPct
Richie Ashburn	cf	4	17	0	3	1	0	0	1	0	4	0	.176	.235	0	1.000
Jimmy Bloodworth	2b	1	0	0	0	0	0	0	0	0	0	0	—	—	0	—
Putsy Caballero	pr-ph	3	1	0	0	0	0	0	0	1	0	0	.000	.000	0	—
Del Ennis	rf	4	14	1	2	1	0	0	0	1	0	0	.143	.214	0	1.000
Mike Goliat	2b	4	14	1	3	0	0	0	1	2	0	0	.214	.214	1	.957
Granny Hamner	ss	4	14	1	6	2	1	0	1	2	1	0	.429	.714	1	.929
Ken Heintzelman	p	1	2	0	0	0	0	0	0	0	0	0	.000	.000	0	1.000
Ken Johnson	pr	1	0	1	0	0	0	0	0	0	0	0	—	—	0	—
Willie Jones	3b	4	14	1	4	1	0	0	0	0	3	0	.286	.357	1	.944
Jim Konstanty	p	3	4	0	1	0	0	0	0	0	1	0	.250	.250	0	1.000
Stan Lopata	c-ph	2	1	0	0	0	0	0	0	0	1	0	.000	.000	0	1.000
Jackie Mayo	ph-lf-pr	3	0	0	0	0	0	0	0	0	1	0	—	—	0	1.000
Russ Meyer	p	2	0	0	0	0	0	0	0	0	0	0	—	—	0	1.000
Bob Miller	p	1	0	0	0	0	0	0	0	0	0	0	—	—	0	—
Robin Roberts	p	2	2	0	0	0	0	0	0	0	1	0	.000	.000	0	—
Andy Seminick	c	4	11	0	2	0	0	0	0	1	3	0	.182	.182	1	.941
Ken Silvestri	c	1	0	0	0	0	0	0	0	0	0	0	—	—	0	1.000
Dick Sisler	lf	4	17	0	1	0	0	0	1	0	5	0	.059	.059	0	1.000
Eddie Waitkus	1b	4	15	0	4	1	0	0	0	2	0	0	.267	.333	0	1.000
Dick Whitman	ph	3	2	0	0	0	0	0	0	0	0	0	.000	.000	0	—
Totals		4	128	5	26	6	1	0	3	7	24	1	.203	.266	4	.972

Pitcher	G	GS	CG	IP	H	R	ER	BB	SO	W-L	Sv	ERA
Ken Heintzelman	1	1	0	7⅔	4	2	1	6	3	0-0	0	1.17
Jim Konstanty	3	1	0	15	9	4	4	4	3	0-1	0	2.40
Russ Meyer	2	0	0	1⅔	4	1	1	0	1	0-1	0	5.40
Bob Miller	1	1	0	⅓	2	2	1	0	0	0-1	0	27.00
Robin Roberts	2	1	1	11	11	2	2	3	5	0-1	0	1.64
Totals	4	4	1	35⅔	30	11	9	13	12	0-4	0	2.27

Series Outstanding Player: Bobby Brown, New York Yankees. **Series Outstanding Pitchers:** Vic Raschi, Whitey Ford and Allie Reynolds, New York Yankees. **Average Length of Game:** 2 hours, 31 minutes. **Total Attendance:** 196,009. **Average Attendance:** 49,002 (66,302 at Yankee Stadium; 31,703 at Shibe Park). **Umpires:** Al Barlick (NL), Charlie Berry (AL), Dusty Boggess (NL), Jocko Conlan (NL), Bill McGowan (AL), Bill McKinley (AL). **Winning Player's Share:** $5,738. **Losing Player's Share:** $4,081.

(Cubs), Tigers - 1907 - 1 tie   1

(Boston Braves) Philadelphia Athletics - 1914   2

(NY GIANTS) NY YANKEES - 1922 - 1 tie   3

(NY YANKEES) PIRATES - 1927 -   4

(NY YANKEES) Cardinals - 1928   5

(NY YANKEES) - Cubs - 1932   6

(NY YANKEES) - Cubs - 1938   7

(NY YANKEES) - REDS - 1939   8

(NY YANKEES) - Phillies · 1950   9

(NY GIANTS) - Indians - 1954   10

(LA DODGERS) NY YANKEES - 1963   11

(Orioles) Dodgers - 1966   12

(REDS) NY YANKEES - 1976   13

(A's) vs. S.F. GIANTS - 1989   14

(Reds) vs. A's - 1990   15

(NY YANKEES) S.D. Padres 1998   16

(NY YANKEES) 1999   17

YANKEES - WON 26 - LOST 12

REDSOX - 1903, 1912, 1915, 1916, 1918
            1942, 1967, 1972,

~~Filters 16×25×1~~	—
Sugar ~~Steel~~ 99¢	B1/G1
~~Kleenex Cottonelle~~ #5	Twinelip
H.N. Cheerios $2	Chuck Breast
Tropicana OJ 2⁹⁹	Roasters
grapes	Cocktail Shrimp
red pepper	Strawberries
Oscar Mayer Bacon	
~~Cracker Barrel~~	
Cashew Halves	
Snickers 2/$4	
~~Fig Newtons~~	
Butter	

Left: Gene Woodling puts New York on the board early in Game 4, scoring on Yogi Berra's first-inning single.

Below: Berra tags out Granny Hamner to complete a double play in the fourth inning of the final game.

Left: Righty Vic Raschi held the Phillies to just two hits in the Series opener.

Below: In Game 3, Phil Rizzuto steals second with two out in the third and then advances to third base when the ball gets by second baseman Mike Goliat.

The 1950 Series marked the seventh four-game sweep in history; the New York Yankees were on the upside of six of them (1927, 1928, 1932, 1938, 1939 and 1950).

Game 1 Wednesday, October 4 at Shibe Park, Philadelphia

	1	2	3	4	5	6	7	8	9		R	H	E
New York Yankees	0	0	0	1	0	0	0	0	0		1	5	0
Philadelphia Phillies	0	0	0	0	0	0	0	0	0		0	2	1

Pitchers NY Vic Raschi (W, 1-0), IP 9, H 2, R 0, ER 0, BB 1, SO 5
Phi Jim Konstanty (L, 0-1), IP 8, H 4, R 1, ER 1, BB 4, SO 0; Russ Meyer, IP 1, H 1, R 0, ER 0, BB 0, SO 0

Top Performers at the Plate
NY Gene Woodling, 1 for 3, 2 BB

2B-NY/Brown. **Time** 2:17. **Attendance** 30,746.

Game 2 Thursday, October 5 at Shibe Park, Philadelphia

	1	2	3	4	5	6	7	8	9	10	R	H	E
New York Yankees	0	1	0	0	0	0	0	0	0	1	2	10	0
Philadelphia Phillies	0	0	0	0	1	0	0	0	0	0	1	7	0

Pitchers NY Allie Reynolds (W, 1-0), IP 10, H 7, R 1, ER 1, BB 4, SO 6
Phi Robin Roberts (L, 0-1), IP 10, H 10, R 2, ER 2, BB 3, SO 5

Top Performers at the Plate
NY Jerry Coleman, 1 for 3, 1 R, 1 BB; Gene Woodling, 2 for 5, 1 RBI
Phi Richie Ashburn, 2 for 5, 1 RBI; Granny Hamner, 2 for 3, 1 BB

2B-NY/Coleman; Phi/Ashburn, Hamner, Waitkus. **3B**-Phi/Hamner. **HR**-NY/DiMaggio.
SB-Phi/Hamner. **Time** 3:06. **Attendance** 32,660.

Game 3 Friday, October 6 at Yankee Stadium, New York

	1	2	3	4	5	6	7	8	9		R	H	E
Philadelphia Phillies	0	0	0	0	0	1	1	0	0		2	10	2
New York Yankees	0	0	1	0	0	0	0	1	1		3	7	0

Pitchers Phi Ken Heintzelman, IP 7⅔, H 4, R 2, ER 1, BB 6, SO 3; Jim Konstanty, IP ⅓, H 0, R 0, ER 0, BB 0, SO 0; Russ Meyer (L, 0-1), IP ⅔, H 3, R 1, ER 1, BB 0, SO 1
NY Ed Lopat, IP 8, H 9, R 2, ER 2, BB 0, SO 5; Tom Ferrick (W, 1-0), IP 1, H 1, R 0, ER 0, BB 1, SO 0

Top Performers at the Plate
Phi Mike Goliat, 1 for 3, 1 RBI, 1 BB; Granny Hamner, 3 for 4, 1 R
NY Jerry Coleman, 3 for 4, 1 R, 2 RBI, 1 BB; Phil Rizzuto, 1 for 3, 1 R, 2 BB

2B-Phi/Ennis, Hamner. **SB**-NY/Rizzuto. **Time** 2:35. **Attendance** 64,505.

Game 4 Saturday, October 7 at Yankee Stadium, New York

	1	2	3	4	5	6	7	8	9		R	H	E
Philadelphia Phillies	0	0	0	0	0	0	0	2			2	7	1
New York Yankees	2	0	0	0	3	0	0	x			5	8	2

Pitchers Phi Bob Miller (L, 0-1), IP ⅓, H 2, R 2, ER 1, BB 0, SO 0; Jim Konstanty, IP 6⅔, H 5, R 3, ER 3, BB 0, SO 3; Robin Roberts, IP 1, H 1, R 0, ER 0, BB 0, SO 0
NY Whitey Ford (W, 1-0), IP 8⅔, H 7, R 2, ER 0, BB 1, SO 7; Allie Reynolds (Sv, 1), IP ⅓, H 0, R 0, ER 0, BB 0, SO 1

Top Performers at the Plate
Phi Willie Jones, 2 for 4, 1 R
NY Yogi Berra, 2 for 4, 2 R, 2 RBI; Joe DiMaggio, 2 for 3, 1 R, 1 RBI, 1 HBP

2B-Phi/Jones; NY/DiMaggio. **3B**-NY/Brown. **HR**-NY/Berra. **Time** 2:05. **Attendance** 68,098.

New York Yankees (4) vs. New York Giants (2)

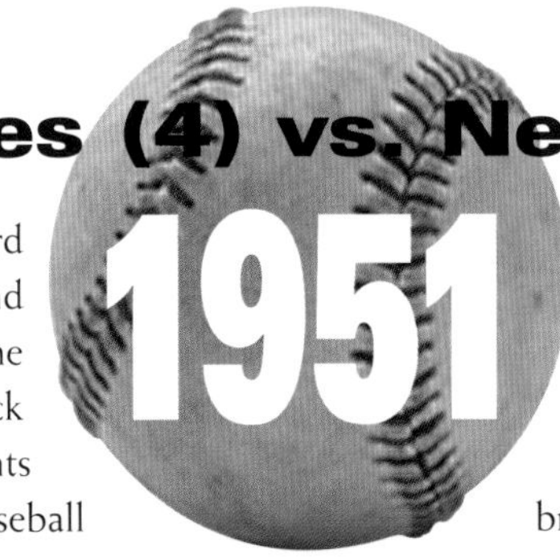

While the New York Yankees quietly captured a third straight pennant in 1951, the New York Giants and Brooklyn Dodgers were engaged in an epic struggle for the National League title. Capping a remarkable comeback from a 13½-game deficit in the standings, the Giants defeated the Dodgers in one of the greatest games in baseball history. Bobby Thomson's "Shot Heard 'Round the World" in the deciding game of the three-game playoff sent the Giants to their sixth and final Subway Series against the Yankees, and the momentum from that great finish carried the Giants to a win in the Series opener. They put runs on the board in the first inning, when Whitey Lockman's ground-rule double scored Hank Thompson and moved Monte Irvin to third base. Irvin, who ended up with four hits on the day, stole home for another run. A three-run homer by Alvin Dark put the Giants up 5-1 in the sixth, and starter Dave Koslo kept the Yanks from scoring any more. Ed Lopat scattered five hits to lead the Yanks to victory in the following game, but the team lost a crucial player in the process. In the fifth inning of Game 2, rookie right fielder Mickey Mantle was chasing a fly ball off the bat of rookie Willie Mays when he caught his foot in a drainage hole in the Yankee Stadium outfield. The knee injury suffered on the play forced Mantle out for the remainder of the Series. The Giants recaptured the Series lead behind a five-run fifth inning in Game 3. Eddie Stanky started the rally

by reaching first on a walk and then working his way to third by kicking the ball out of Phil Rizzuto's glove on a steal attempt at second base. Dark then scored Stanky with a single, and Whitey Lockman followed Hank Thompson's single with a three-run homer. Allie Reynolds brought the Yankees back even in Game 4, and they took a 3-games-to-2 lead the next day with a convincing 13-1 victory. Gil McDougald, the AL Rookie of the Year in 1951, hit the third grand slam in Series history in the third inning of Game 5, and Rizzuto contributed a two-run blast in the fourth. Yankee starter Lopat gave up two singles and an unearned run in the first inning, then allowed just three hits the rest of the afternoon. The Giants' miracle season came to an end on October 10, when a sixth-inning bases-loaded triple by Hank Bauer (Mantle's replacement in the Series) put the Yanks up 4-1 in Game 6. The Giants scored two in the top of the ninth, but with the tying run in scoring position, Bauer made a diving catch on a Sal Yvars liner to right to end the Series. The game was the final one in Joe DiMaggio's illustrious career, but 1951 marked a bright beginning for two future legends: Mickey Mantle and Willie Mays.

Above: The Yankee hero of Game 6, Hank Bauer, receives a wet one from Phil Rizzuto (left) and Yogi Berra (right).

1951 WORLD SERIES COMPOSITE STATISTICS

NEW YORK YANKEES/Casey Stengel, Manager

Player	pos	G	AB	R	H	2B	3B	HR	RBI	BB	SO	SB	BA	SA	E	FPct
Hank Bauer	lf-rf	6	18	0	3	0	1	0	3	1	1	0	.167	.278	0	1.000
Yogi Berra	c	6	23	4	6	1	0	0	0	2	1	0	.261	.304	2	.968
Bobby Brown	ph-3b	5	14	1	5	1	0	0	2	1	0	0	.357	.429	0	1.000
Jerry Coleman	2b-pr	5	8	2	2	0	0	0	1	2	0	0	.250	.250	0	1.000
Joe Collins	1b-rf	6	18	2	4	0	0	1	3	2	1	0	.222	.389	0	1.000
Joe DiMaggio	cf	6	23	3	6	2	0	1	5	2	4	0	.261	.478	0	1.000
Bobby Hogue	p	2	0	0	0	0	0	0	0	0	0	0	—	—	0	1.000
Johnny Hopp	ph	1	0	0	0	0	0	0	0	1	0	0	—	—	—	—
Bob Kuzava	p	1	0	0	0	0	0	0	0	0	0	0	—	—	0	—
Ed Lopat	p	2	8	0	1	0	0	0	1	0	2	0	.125	.125	0	1.000
Mickey Mantle	rf	2	5	1	1	0	0	0	0	2	1	0	.200	.200	0	1.000
Billy Martin	pr	1	0	1	0	0	0	0	0	0	0	0	—	—	—	—
Gil McDougald	3b-2b	6	23	2	6	1	0	1	7	2	2	0	.261	.435	1	.960
Johnny Mize	ph-1b	4	7	2	2	1	0	0	1	2	0	0	.286	.429	0	1.000
Tom Morgan	p	1	0	0	0	0	0	0	0	0	0	0	—	—	0	1.000
Joe Ostrowski	p	1	0	0	0	0	0	0	0	0	0	0	—	—	0	—
Vic Raschi	p	2	2	0	0	0	0	0	0	2	1	0	.000	.000	0	—
Allie Reynolds	p	2	6	0	2	0	0	0	1	0	1	0	.333	.333	0	1.000
Phil Rizzuto	ss	6	25	5	8	0	0	1	3	2	3	0	.320	.440	1	.974
Johnny Sain	p	1	1	0	0	0	0	0	0	0	0	0	.000	.000	0	—
Gene Woodling	ph-lf	6	18	6	3	1	1	1	1	5	3	0	.167	.500	1	.947
Totals		**6**	**199**	**29**	**49**	**7**	**2**	**5**	**25**	**26**	**23**	**0**	**.246**	**.377**	**4**	**.983**

Pitcher	G	GS	CG	IP	H	R	ER	BB	SO	W-L	Sv	ERA
Bobby Hogue	2	0	0	2⅔	2	0	0	0	0	0-0	0	0.00
Bob Kuzava	1	0	0	1	0	0	0	0	0	0-0	1	0.00
Ed Lopat	2	2	2	18	10	2	1	3	4	2-0	0	0.50
Tom Morgan	1	0	0	2	2	0	0	1	3	0-0	0	0.00
Joe Ostrowski	1	0	0	2	1	0	0	0	0	0-0	0	0.00
Vic Raschi	2	2	0	10⅓	12	7	1	8	4	1-1	0	0.87
Allie Reynolds	2	2	1	15	16	7	7	11	8	1-1	0	4.20
Johnny Sain	1	0	0	2	4	2	2	2	2	0-0	0	9.00
Totals	**6**	**6**	**3**	**53**	**46**	**18**	**11**	**25**	**22**	**4-2**	**1**	**1.87**

NEW YORK GIANTS/Leo Durocher, Manager

Player	pos	G	AB	R	H	2B	3B	HR	RBI	BB	SO	SB	BA	SA	E	FPct
Al Corwin	p	1	0	0	0	0	0	0	0	0	0	0	—	—	0	1.000
Alvin Dark	ss	6	24	5	10	3	0	1	4	2	3	0	.417	.667	0	1.000
Clint Hartung	rf	2	4	0	0	0	0	0	0	0	0	0	.000	.000	0	.667
Jim Hearn	p	2	3	0	0	0	0	0	0	0	1	0	.000	.000	0	1.000
Monte Irvin	lf	6	24	3	11	0	1	0	2	2	1	2	.458	.542	1	.944
Larry Jansen	p	3	2	0	0	0	0	0	0	0	0	0	.000	.000	0	1.000
Sheldon Jones	p	2	0	0	0	0	0	0	0	0	0	0	—	—	0	1.000
Monte Kennedy	p	2	0	0	0	0	0	0	0	0	0	0	—	—	0	1.000
Alex Konikowski	p	1	0	0	0	0	0	0	0	0	0	0	—	—	0	—
Dave Koslo	p	2	5	0	0	0	0	0	0	2	0	0	.000	.000	0	1.000
Whitey Lockman	1b	6	25	1	6	2	0	1	4	1	2	0	.240	.440	2	.964
Jack Lohrke	ph	2	2	0	0	0	0	0	0	0	1	0	.000	.000	—	—
Sal Maglie	p	1	1	0	0	0	0	0	0	0	1	0	.000	.000	0	—
Willie Mays	cf	6	22	1	4	0	0	0	1	2	2	0	.182	.182	0	1.000
Ray Noble	ph-c	2	2	0	0	0	0	0	0	0	1	0	.000	.000	0	1.000
Bill Rigney	ph	4	4	0	1	0	0	0	0	1	1	0	.250	.250	—	—
Hank Schenz	pr	1	0	0	0	0	0	0	0	0	0	0	—	—	0	1.000
George Spencer	p	2	0	0	0	0	0	0	0	0	0	0	—	—	0	—
Eddie Stanky	2b	6	22	3	3	0	0	0	1	3	2	0	.136	.136	1	.967
Hank Thompson	rf	5	14	3	2	0	0	0	0	1	1	0	.143	.143	2	.667
Bobby Thomson	3b	6	21	1	5	1	0	0	2	5	0	0	.238	.286	2	.933
Wes Westrum	c	6	17	1	4	1	0	0	0	5	3	0	.235	.294	1	.969
Davey Williams	ph-pr	2	1	0	0	0	0	0	0	0	0	0	.000	.000	—	—
Sal Yvars	ph	1	1	0	0	0	0	0	0	0	0	0	.000	.000	—	—
Totals		**6**	**194**	**18**	**46**	**7**	**1**	**2**	**15**	**25**	**22**	**2**	**.237**	**.314**	**10**	**.957**

Pitcher	G	GS	CG	IP	H	R	ER	BB	SO	W-L	Sv	ERA
Al Corwin	1	0	0	1⅔	1	0	0	0	1	0-0	0	0.00
Jim Hearn	2	1	0	8⅔	5	1	1	8	1	1-0	0	1.04
Larry Jansen	3	2	0	10	8	7	7	4	6	0-2	0	6.30
Sheldon Jones	2	0	0	4⅓	5	3	1	1	2	0-0	1	2.08
Monte Kennedy	2	0	0	3	3	2	2	1	4	0-0	0	6.00
Alex Konikowski	1	0	0	1	1	0	0	0	0	0-0	0	0.00
Dave Koslo	2	2	1	15	12	5	5	7	6	1-1	0	3.00
Sal Maglie	1	1	0	5	8	4	4	3	3	0-1	0	7.20
George Spencer	2	0	0	3⅓	6	7	7	3	0	0-0	0	18.90
Totals	**6**	**6**	**1**	**52**	**49**	**29**	**27**	**26**	**23**	**2-4**	**1**	**4.67**

Series Outstanding Player: Phil Rizzuto, New York Yankees. **Series Outstanding Pitcher:** Ed Lopat, New York Yankees. **Average Length of Game:** 2 hours, 42 minutes. **Total Attendance:** 341,977. **Average Attendance:** 56,996 (64,467 at Yankee Stadium; 49,525 at the Polo Grounds). **Umpires:** Lee Ballanfant (NL), Al Barlick (NL), Artie Gore (NL), Joe Paparella (AL), Johnny Stevens (AL), Bill Summers (AL). **Winning Player's Share:** $6,446. **Losing Player's Share:** $4,951.

Left: Gil McDougald's grand slam home run in Game 5 scored Johnny Mize, Joe DiMaggio and Yogi Berra, and it contributed to the Yanks' 13-1 romp in the game.

Right: Monte Irvin steals home for the Giants in the first inning of the Series as batter Bobby Thomson falls out of the way of the play.

Left: Hank Bauer blasts a triple over the head of left fielder Monte Irvin with the bases loaded, giving New York a 4-1 lead in the sixth game.

Monte Irvin's steal of home in Game 1 was the first in a World Series since Hank Greenberg did it in 1934; it was the first steal of home since 1921 that was not part of a double steal.

Below: On his steal of second in the fifth inning of Game 3, Eddie Stanky kicks the ball out of Phil Rizzuto's glove, allowing him to advance to third. The play sparked a five-run rally for the Giants.

Game 1 Thursday, October 4 at Yankee Stadium, New York

	1	2	3	4	5	6	7	8	9	R	H	E
New York Giants	2	0	0	0	0	3	0	0	0	5	10	1
New York Yankees	0	1	0	0	0	0	0	0	0	1	7	1

Pitchers NYG Dave Koslo (W, 1-0), IP 9, H 7, R 1, ER 1, BB 3, SO 3
NYY Allie Reynolds (L, 0-1), IP 6, H 8, R 5, ER 5, BB 7, SO 1; Bobby Hogue, IP 1, H 0, R 0, ER 0, BB 0, SO 0; Tom Morgan, IP 2, H 2, R 0, ER 0, BB 1, SO 3

Top Performers at the Plate
NYG Alvin Dark, 2 for 5, 1 R, 3 RBI; Monte Irvin, 4 for 5, 1 R
NYY Phil Rizzuto, 2 for 4

2B-NYG/Lockman; NYY/McDougald. **3B**-NYG/Irvin. **HR**-NYG/Dark. **SB**-NYG/Irvin. **Time** 2:58.
Attendance 65,673.

Game 2 Friday, October 5 at Yankee Stadium, New York

	1	2	3	4	5	6	7	8	9	R	H	E
New York Giants	0	0	0	0	0	0	1	0	0	1	5	1
New York Yankees	1	1	0	0	0	0	0	1	x	3	6	0

Pitchers NYG Larry Jansen (L, 0-1), IP 6, H 4, R 2, ER 2, BB 0, SO 5; George Spencer, IP 2, H 2, R 1, ER 1, BB 0, SO 0
NYY Ed Lopat (W, 1-0), IP 9, H 5, R 1, ER 1, BB 2, SO 1

Top Performers at the Plate
NYG Monte Irvin, 3 for 4, 1 R
NYY Joe Collins, 1 for 3, 1 R, 1 RBI

HR-NYY/Collins. **SB**-NYG/Irvin. **Time** 2:05. **Attendance** 66,018.

Game 3 Saturday, October 6 at the Polo Grounds, New York

	1	2	3	4	5	6	7	8	9	R	H	E
New York Yankees	0	0	0	0	0	0	0	1	1	2	5	2
New York Giants	0	1	0	0	5	0	0	0	x	6	7	2

Pitchers NYY Vic Raschi (L, 0-1), IP 4⅓, H 5, R 6, ER 1, BB 3, SO 3; Bobby Hogue, IP 1⅔, H 1, R 0, ER 0, BB 0, SO 0; Joe Ostrowski, IP 2, H 1, R 0, ER 0, BB 0, SO 1
NYG Jim Hearn (W, 1-0), IP 7⅔, H 4, R 1, ER 1, BB 8, SO 1; Sheldon Jones (Sv, 1), IP 1⅓, H 1, R 1, ER 1, BB 0, SO 0

Top Performers at the Plate
NYY Gil McDougald, 2 for 3, 2 BB; Gene Woodling, 1 for 4, 1 R, 1 RBI, 1 BB
NYG Willie Mays, 2 for 4, 1 RBI; Whitey Lockman, 1 for 4, 1 R, 3 RBI

2B-NYG/Thomson. **HR**-NYY/Woodling; NYG/Lockman. **Time** 2:42. **Attendance** 52,035.

Game 4 Monday, October 8 at the Polo Grounds, New York

	1	2	3	4	5	6	7	8	9	R	H	E
New York Yankees	0	1	0	1	2	0	2	0	0	6	12	0
New York Giants	1	0	0	0	0	0	0	0	1	2	8	2

Pitchers NYY Allie Reynolds (W, 1-1), IP 9, H 8, R 2, ER 2, BB 4, SO 7
NYG Sal Maglie (L, 0-1), IP 5, H 8, R 4, ER 4, BB 2, SO 3; Sheldon Jones, IP 3, H 4, R 2, ER 0, BB 1, SO 2; Monte Kennedy, IP 1, H 0, R 0, ER 0, BB 0, SO 2

Top Performers at the Plate
NYY Bobby Brown, 2 for 4, 1 R; Joe DiMaggio, 2 for 5, 1 R, 2 RBI
NYG Alvin Dark, 3 for 4, 1 R, 3 2B; Bobby Thomson, 2 for 2, 1 RBI, 2 BB

2B-NYY/Brown, Woodling; NYG/Dark 3. **HR**-NYY/DiMaggio. **Time** 2:57. **Attendance** 49,010.

Game 5 Tuesday, October 9 at the Polo Grounds, New York

	1	2	3	4	5	6	7	8	9	R	H	E
New York Yankees	0	0	5	2	0	2	4	0	0	13	12	1
New York Giants	1	0	0	0	0	0	0	0	0	1	5	3

Pitchers NYY Ed Lopat (W, 2-0), IP 9, H 5, R 1, ER 0, BB 1, SO 3
NYG Larry Jansen (L, 0-2), IP 3, H 3, R 5, ER 5, BB 4, SO 1; Monte Kennedy, IP 2, H 3, R 2, ER 2, BB 1, SO 2; George Spencer, IP 1⅓, H 4, R 6, ER 6, BB 3, SO 0; Al Corwin, IP 1⅔, H 1, R 0, ER 0, BB 0, SO 1; Alex Konikowski, IP 1, H 1, R 0, ER 0, BB 0, SO 0

Top Performers at the Plate
NYY Joe DiMaggio, 3 for 5, 1 R, 3 RBI; Phil Rizzuto, 2 for 4, 3 R, 3 RBI, 2 BB
NYG Alvin Dark, 2 for 4, 1 R; Monte Irvin, 2 for 4

2B-NYY/DiMaggio, Mize; NYG/Westrum. **3B**-NYY/Woodling. **HR**-NYY/McDougald, Rizzuto.
Time 2:31. **Attendance** 47,530.

Game 6 Wednesday, October 10 at Yankee Stadium, New York

	1	2	3	4	5	6	7	8	9	R	H	E
New York Giants	0	0	0	1	0	0	0	2		3	11	1
New York Yankees	1	0	0	0	3	0	0	x		4	7	0

Pitchers NYG Dave Koslo (L, 1-1), IP 6, H 5, R 4, ER 4, BB 4, SO 3; Jim Hearn, IP 1, H 1, R 0, ER 0, BB 0, SO 0; Larry Jansen, IP 1, H 1, R 0, ER 0, BB 0, SO 0
NYY Vic Raschi (W, 1-1), IP 6, H 7, R 1, ER 0, BB 5, SO 1; Johnny Sain, IP 2, H 4, R 2, ER 2, BB 2, SO 2; Bob Kuzava (Sv, 1), IP 1, H 0, R 0, ER 0, BB 0, SO 0

Top Performers at the Plate
NYG Whitey Lockman, 3 for 5; Willie Mays, 2 for 3, 1 R, 1 BB
NYY Hank Bauer, 1 for 3, 3 RBI; Yogi Berra, 2 for 4, 1 R

2B-NYG/Lockman; NYY/Berra, DiMaggio. **3B**-NYY/Bauer. **Time** 2:59. **Attendance** 61,711.

New York Yankees (4) vs. Brooklyn Dodgers (3)

Casey Stengel led the New York Yankees to three straight World Series victories from 1949 to 1951, and in 1952, he was looking to join Joe McCarthy as the only managers to win four in a row. The Yankees would have to do it without the retired Joe DiMaggio, but they had a young scrapper at second base, Billy Martin, joining a star-studded lineup. Over in the National League, the Brooklyn Dodgers reclaimed the top spot after near-misses in 1950 and 1951. They still had the key pieces from the 1949 pennant team, and although they lost

pitcher Don Newcombe to military service, a hard-throwing righty named Joe Black took Rookie of the Year honors with a 15-4 record and 15 saves in 1952. Black had started only two games all season long, but Brooklyn manager Chuck Dressen gave him the start in Game 1 of the Series. Black came through with a six-hitter to outmatch Allie Reynolds, the AL leader in wins and ERA. Solo home runs by Jackie Robinson and Pee Wee Reese and a two-runner by Duke Snider brought in all four Brooklyn runs. Three Dodger singles scored a run in

Above: The Yankees' 1952 lineup: Johnny Mize, Joe Collins, Gene Woodling, Gil McDougald, Hank Bauer, Phil Rizzuto, Billy Martin, Irv Noren, Yogi Berra and Mickey Mantle.

1952 WORLD SERIES COMPOSITE STATISTICS

NEW YORK YANKEES/Casey Stengel, Manager

Player	pos	G	AB	R	H	2B	3B	HR	RBI	BB	SO	SB	BA	SA	E	FPct
Hank Bauer	rf	7	18	2	1	0	0	0	1	4	3	0	.056	.056	0	1.000
Yogi Berra	c	7	28	2	6	1	0	2	3	2	4	0	.214	.464	1	.985
Ewell Blackwell	p	1	1	0	0	0	0	0	0	0	0	0	.000	.000	0	1.000
Joe Collins	1b	6	12	1	0	0	0	0	0	1	3	0	.000	.000	0	1.000
Tom Gorman	p	1	0	0	0	0	0	0	0	0	0	0	–	–	0	–
Ralph Houk	ph	1	1	0	0	0	0	0	0	0	0	0	.000	.000	–	–
Bob Kuzava	p	1	1	0	0	0	0	0	0	0	0	0	.000	.000	0	1.000
Ed Lopat	p	2	3	0	1	0	0	0	1	1	1	0	.333	.333	0	1.000
Mickey Mantle	cf	7	29	5	10	1	1	2	3	3	4	0	.345	.655	0	1.000
Billy Martin	2b	7	23	2	5	0	0	1	4	2	2	0	.217	.348	1	.969
Gil McDougald	3b	7	25	5	5	0	0	1	3	5	2	1	.200	.320	4	.826
Johnny Mize	1b	5	15	3	6	1	0	3	6	3	1	0	.400	1.067	0	1.000
Irv Noren	lf-ph-rf	4	10	0	3	0	0	0	1	1	3	0	.300	.300	0	1.000
Vic Raschi	p	3	6	0	1	0	0	0	1	1	2	0	.167	.167	0	1.000
Allie Reynolds	p	4	7	0	0	0	0	0	0	0	2	0	.000	.000	2	.600
Phil Rizzuto	ss	7	27	2	4	1	0	0	0	5	2	0	.148	.185	1	.968
Johnny Sain	p	2	3	0	0	0	0	0	0	0	0	0	.000	.000	0	1.000
Ray Scarborough	p	1	0	0	0	0	0	0	0	0	0	0	–	–	0	1.000
Gene Woodling	lf	7	23	4	8	1	1	1	3	3	0	1	.348	.609	1	.947
Totals		**7**	**232**	**26**	**50**	**5**	**2**	**10**	**24**	**31**	**32**	**1**	**.216**	**.384**	**10**	**.963**

Pitcher	G	GS	CG	IP	H	R	ER	BB	SO	W-L	Sv	ERA
Ewell Blackwell	1	1	0	5	4	4	4	3	4	0-0	0	7.20
Tom Gorman	1	0	0	⅔	1	0	0	0	0	0-0	0	0.00
Bob Kuzava	1	0	0	2⅔	0	0	0	2	0	0-0	1	0.00
Ed Lopat	2	2	0	11⅓	14	6	6	4	3	0-1	0	4.76
Vic Raschi	3	2	1	17	12	3	3	8	18	2-0	0	1.59
Allie Reynolds	4	2	1	20⅓	12	4	4	6	18	2-1	1	1.77
Johnny Sain	1	0	0	6	6	2	2	3	3	0-1	0	3.00
Ray Scarborough	1	0	0	1	1	1	1	0	1	0-0	0	9.00
Totals	**7**	**7**	**2**	**64**	**50**	**20**	**20**	**24**	**49**	**4-3**	**2**	**2.81**

BROOKLYN DODGERS/Chuck Dressen, Manager

Player	pos	G	AB	R	H	2B	3B	HR	RBI	BB	SO	SB	BA	SA	E	FPct
Sandy Amoros	pr	1	0	0	0	0	0	0	0	0	0	0	–	–	–	–
Joe Black	p	3	6	0	0	0	0	0	0	1	6	0	.000	.000	0	1.000
Roy Campanella	c	7	28	0	6	0	0	0	1	1	6	0	.214	.214	0	1.000
Billy Cox	3b	7	27	4	8	2	0	0	3	4	0	0	.296	.370	1	.958
Carl Erskine	p	3	6	1	0	0	0	0	0	1	0	0	.000	.000	0	1.000
Carl Furillo	rf	7	23	1	4	2	0	0	3	3	0	0	.174	.261	0	1.000
Gil Hodges	1b	7	21	1	0	0	0	0	1	5	6	0	.000	.000	1	.985
Tommy Holmes	lf	3	1	0	0	0	0	0	0	0	0	0	.000	.000	0	1.000
Ken Lehman	p	1	0	0	0	0	0	0	0	0	0	0	–	–	0	1.000
Billy Loes	p	2	3	0	1	0	0	0	0	1	1	1	.333	.333	1	1.000
Bobby Morgan	3b	2	1	0	0	0	0	0	0	0	0	0	.000	.000	0	1.000
Rocky Nelson	ph	4	3	0	0	0	0	0	0	1	2	0	.000	.000	–	–
Andy Pafko	lf-rf-ph	7	21	0	4	0	0	0	2	0	4	0	.190	.190	0	1.000
Pee Wee Reese	ss	7	29	4	10	0	0	1	4	2	1	1	.345	.448	2	.943
Jackie Robinson	2b	7	23	4	4	0	0	1	2	7	5	2	.174	.304	0	1.000
Preacher Roe	p	3	2	0	0	0	0	0	0	0	0	0	.000	.000	0	1.000
Johnny Rutherford	p	1	0	0	0	0	0	0	0	0	0	0	–	–	0	–
George Shuba	lf	4	10	0	3	1	0	0	0	0	4	0	.300	.400	0	1.000
Duke Snider	cf	7	29	5	10	2	0	4	8	1	5	0	.345	.828	0	1.000
Totals		**7**	**233**	**20**	**50**	**7**	**0**	**6**	**18**	**24**	**49**	**5**	**.215**	**.322**	**4**	**.985**

Pitcher	G	GS	CG	IP	H	R	ER	BB	SO	W-L	Sv	ERA
Joe Black	3	3	1	21⅓	15	6	6	8	9	1-2	0	2.53
Carl Erskine	3	2	1	18	12	9	9	10	10	1-1	0	4.50
Ken Lehman	1	0	0	2	2	0	0	1	0	0-0	0	0.00
Billy Loes	2	1	0	10⅓	11	6	5	5	5	0-1	0	4.35
Preacher Roe	3	1	1	11⅓	9	4	4	6	7	1-0	0	3.18
Johnny Rutherford	1	0	0	1	1	1	1	1	1	0-0	0	9.00
Totals	**7**	**7**	**3**	**64**	**50**	**26**	**25**	**31**	**32**	**3-4**	**0**	**3.52**

Series Outstanding Player: Duke Snider, Brooklyn Dodgers. **Series Outstanding Pitcher:** Vic Raschi, New York Yankees. **Average Length of Game:** 2 hours, 47 minutes. **Total Attendance:** 340,906. **Average Attendance:** 48,701 (69,674 at Yankee Stadium; 32,971 at Ebbets Field). **Umpires:** Dusty Boggess (NL), Larry Goetz (NL), Jim Honochick (AL), Bill McKinley (AL), Art Passarella (AL), Babe Pinelli (NL). **Winning Player's Share:** $5,983. **Losing Player's Share:** $4,201.

Background: Billy Martin's running catch of Jackie Robinson's infield pop-up in Game 7 was the pivotal moment of the 1952 World Series.

Right: Brooklyn's Joe Black was the first African-American pitcher to win a World Series game.

Left: Duke Snider smacked four home runs in the Series for the Dodgers.

Right: Mickey Mantle's solo homer in Game 7 gave the Yanks the lead to stay in the clinching game. It was the second World Series home run of Mantle's career; he would go on to hit a record 14 more.

Duke Snider's four home runs in 1952 tied the record at the time for most home runs in a Series.

the 3rd inning of Game 2, but those were the only hits given up by Vic Raschi all afternoon, as the Yanks coasted to a 7-1 victory. Martin contributed four RBI in the game, including a three-run homer. Preacher Roe threw a complete-game six-hitter in Game 3 to regain the Series lead for Brooklyn. Yogi Berra brought New York within a run with his 8th-inning homer, but his costly passed ball in the bottom of the inning allowed two Dodgers to cross the plate, providing the final 5-3 margin. For the second year in a row, Reynolds brought his team even in the Series by winning the crucial fourth game. He struck out 10 while giving up four hits in the shutout. Joe Black surpassed his Game 1 performance by allowing just three hits, but one was a costly home run by Johnny Mize. Mize, who had taken over the starting role at first base for a struggling Joe Collins, was at it again in Game 5, knocking his third homer of the Series to cap a five-run 5th inning. Those five runs were all the Yankees produced, however, while the Dodgers got a sixth run on Snider's RBI double in the top of the 11th. Brooklyn's Carl Erskine secured the win by retiring the last 19 batters of the game, but center fielder Carl Furillo deserved a save for robbing Mize of a homer in the last of the 11th. Up

three games to two, the Dodgers were headed back to Ebbets Field to host the remaining games. Snider collected his third and fourth home runs with a pair of solo shots in Game 6, but Mantle's first World Series homer put New York ahead to stay. Joe Black started the deciding seventh game for Brooklyn but didn't get past the 5th inning. The Yankees scored one run in 4 straight innings to go up 4-2, heading into the bottom of the 7th. Raschi came on in relief and promptly loaded the bases on a single and two walks. Bob Kuzava, making his only appearance of the Series, entered the game for New York and quickly secured the inning's second out against the dangerous Snider. The next batter, Jackie Robinson, popped Kuzava's 3-2 pitch to the right side of the infield. First baseman Joe Collins lost the ball in the sun; Kuzava didn't budge from the mound. It looked like the harmless pop-up might drop safely as two Dodgers crossed the plate. Suddenly, second baseman Martin made a last-second dash and caught the ball at the knees, negating the runs and ending the inning. Kuzava went on to keep Brooklyn scoreless in the final 2 innings, and Stengel's Yanks were October winners for the fourth year in a row.

Left: Filling in at first base, veteran Johnny Mize knocked 3 home runs in 15 at-bats during the Series.

Left: Though the expressions on their faces seem to belie the outcome, a smiling Chuck Dressen congratulates a dour Casey Stengel after Stengel's Yanks topped Dressen's Dodgers in the 1952 Series.

Right: Yogi Berra expresses his displeasure with home plate umpire Art Passarella over balls and strikes in Game 6.

By earning the victory in Game 1, Joe Black became the first African-American pitcher to get a World Series win.

Left: Carl Erskine retired the last 19 Yankee batters in Game 5 en route to securing an 11-inning complete-game win for Brooklyn.

Game 1 Wednesday, October 1 at Ebbets Field, Brooklyn

	1	2	3	4	5	6	7	8	9	R	H	E
New York Yankees	0	0	1	0	0	0	0	1	0	2	6	2
Brooklyn Dodgers	0	1	0	0	0	2	0	1	x	4	6	0

Pitchers NY **Allie Reynolds** (L, 0-1), IP 7, H 5, R 3, ER 3, BB 2, SO 4; **Ray Scarborough**, IP 1, H 1, R 1, ER 1, BB 0, SO 1
Bro **Joe Black** (W, 1-0), IP 9, H 6, R 2, ER 2, BB 2, SO 6

Top Performers at the Plate
NY **Mickey Mantle**, 2 for 4; **Gil McDougald**, 1 for 2, 1 R, 1 RBI, 1 BB
Bro **Pee Wee Reese**, 2 for 4, 2 R, 1 RBI; **Duke Snider**, 2 for 4, 1 R, 2 RBI

2B-Bro/Snider. **3B**-NY/Woodling. **HR**-NY/McDougald; Bro/Reese, Robinson, Snider. **Time** 2:21. **Attendance** 34,861.

Game 2 Thursday, October 2 at Ebbets Field, Brooklyn

	1	2	3	4	5	6	7	8	9	R	H	E
New York Yankees	0	0	0	1	1	5	0	0	0	7	10	0
Brooklyn Dodgers	0	0	1	0	0	0	0	0	0	1	3	1

Pitchers NY **Vic Raschi** (W, 1-0), IP 9, H 3, R 1, ER 1, BB 5, SO 9
Bro **Carl Erskine** (L, 0-1), IP 5, H 6, R 4, ER 4, BB 6, SO 4; **Billy Loes**, IP 2, H 2, R 3, ER 2, BB 0, SO 2; **Ken Lehman**, IP 2, H 2, R 0, ER 0, BB 1, SO 0

Top Performers at the Plate
NY **Mickey Mantle**, 3 for 5, 2 R; **Billy Martin**, 2 for 4, 1 R, 4 RBI
Bro **Pee Wee Reese**, 1 for 3, 1 R, 1 BB

2B-NY/Mantle. **HR**-NY/Martin. **SB**-NY/McDougald. **Time** 2:47. **Attendance** 33,792.

Game 3 Friday, October 3 at Yankee Stadium, New York

	1	2	3	4	5	6	7	8	9	R	H	E
Brooklyn Dodgers	0	0	1	0	1	0	0	1	2	5	11	0
New York Yankees	0	1	0	0	0	0	0	1	1	3	6	2

Pitchers Bro **Preacher Roe** (W, 1-0), IP 9, H 6, R 3, ER 3, BB 5, SO 5
NY **Ed Lopat** (L, 0-1), IP 8⅓, H 10, R 5, ER 5, BB 4, SO 0; **Tom Gorman**, IP ⅔, H 1, R 0, ER 0, BB 0, SO 0

Top Performers at the Plate
Bro **Pee Wee Reese**, 3 for 5, 1 R, 1 RBI; **Jackie Robinson**, 2 for 4, 2 R, 1 RBI, 1 BB
NY **Yogi Berra**, 3 for 4, 1 R, 1 RBI

2B-Bro/Furillo; NY/Berra. **HR**-NY/Berra, Mize. **SB**-Bro/Reese, Robinson, Snider. **Time** 2:56. **Attendance** 66,698.

Game 4 Saturday, October 4 at Yankee Stadium, New York

	1	2	3	4	5	6	7	8	9	R	H	E
Brooklyn Dodgers	0	0	0	0	0	0	0	0	0	0	4	1
New York Yankees	0	0	0	1	0	0	0	1	x	2	4	1

Pitchers Bro **Joe Black** (L, 1-1), IP 7, H 3, R 1, ER 1, BB 5, SO 2; **Johnny Rutherford**, IP 1, H 1, R 1, ER 1, BB 1, SO 1
NY **Allie Reynolds** (W, 1-1), IP 9, H 4, R 0, ER 0, BB 3, SO 10

Top Performers at the Plate
Bro **Pee Wee Reese**, 2 for 4
NY **Mickey Mantle**, 1 for 3, 1 R, 1 BB; **Johnny Mize**, 2 for 3, 1 R, 1 RBI, 1 BB

2B-NY/Mize, Woodling. **3B**-NY/Mantle. **HR**-NY/Mize. **Time** 2:33. **Attendance** 71,787.

Game 5 Sunday, October 5 at Yankee Stadium, New York

	1	2	3	4	5	6	7	8	9	10	11	R	H	E
Brooklyn Dodgers	0	1	0	0	3	0	1	0	0	0	1	6	10	0
New York Yankees	0	0	0	0	5	0	0	0	0	0	0	5	5	1

Pitchers Bro **Carl Erskine** (W, 1-1), IP 11, H 5, R 5, ER 5, BB 3, SO 6
NY **Ewell Blackwell**, IP 5, H 4, R 4, ER 4, BB 3, SO 4; **Johnny Sain** (L, 0-1), IP 6, H 6, R 2, ER 2, BB 3, SO 3

Top Performers at the Plate
Bro **Billy Cox**, 3 for 5, 2 R, 1 SH; **Duke Snider**, 3 for 5, 1 R, 4 RBI, 1 HBP
NY **Johnny Mize**, 1 for 5, 1 R, 3 RBI

2B-Bro/Furillo, Snider. **HR**-Bro/Snider; NY/Mize. **SB**-Bro/Robinson. **Time** 3:00. **Attendance** 70,536.

Game 6 Monday, October 6 at Ebbets Field, Brooklyn

	1	2	3	4	5	6	7	8	9	R	H	E
New York Yankees	0	0	0	0	0	0	2	1	0	3	9	0
Brooklyn Dodgers	0	0	0	0	0	1	0	1	0	2	8	1

Pitchers NY **Vic Raschi** (W, 2-0), IP 7⅔, H 8, R 2, ER 2, BB 1, SO 9; **Allie Reynolds** (Sv, 1), IP 1⅓, H 0, R 0, ER 0, BB 1, SO 2
Bro **Billy Loes** (L, 0-1), IP 8⅓, H 9, R 3, ER 3, BB 5, SO 3; **Preacher Roe**, IP ⅔, H 0, R 0, ER 0, BB 1, SO 1

Top Performers at the Plate
NY **Mickey Mantle**, 1 for 3, 1 R, 1 RBI, 2 BB; **Gene Woodling**, 2 for 3, 1 R, 1 BB
Bro **Billy Cox**, 2 for 5; **Duke Snider**, 2 for 3, 2 R, 2 RBI, 1 BB, 2 HR

2B-Bro/Cox, Shuba. **HR**-NY/Berra, Mantle; Bro/Snider 2. **SB**-Bro/Loes. **Time** 2:56. **Attendance** 30,037.

Game 7 Tuesday, October 7 at Ebbets Field, Brooklyn

	1	2	3	4	5	6	7	8	9	R	H	E
New York Yankees	0	0	0	1	1	1	1	0	0	4	10	4
Brooklyn Dodgers	0	0	0	1	1	0	0	0	0	2	8	1

Pitchers NY **Ed Lopat**, IP 3, H 4, R 1, ER 1, BB 0, SO 3; **Allie Reynolds** (W, 2-1), IP 3, H 3, R 1, ER 1, BB 0, SO 2; **Vic Raschi**, IP ⅓, H 1, R 0, ER 0, BB 2, SO 0; **Bob Kuzava** (Sv, 1), IP 2⅔, H 0, R 0, ER 0, BB 0, SO 2
Bro **Joe Black** (L, 1-2), IP 5⅓, H 6, R 3, ER 3, BB 1, SO 1; **Preacher Roe**, IP 1⅔, H 3, R 1, ER 1, BB 0, SO 1; **Carl Erskine**, IP 2, H 1, R 0, ER 0, BB 1, SO 0

Top Performers at the Plate
NY **Mickey Mantle**, 2 for 5, 1 R, 2 RBI; **Johnny Mize**, 2 for 3, 1 RBI, 1 BB
Bro **Roy Campanella**, 2 for 4; **Billy Cox**, 2 for 5, 1 R

2B-NY/Rizzuto; Bro/Cox. **HR**-NY/Mantle, Woodling. **Time** 2:54. **Attendance** 33,195.

New York Yankees (4) vs. Brooklyn Dodgers (2)

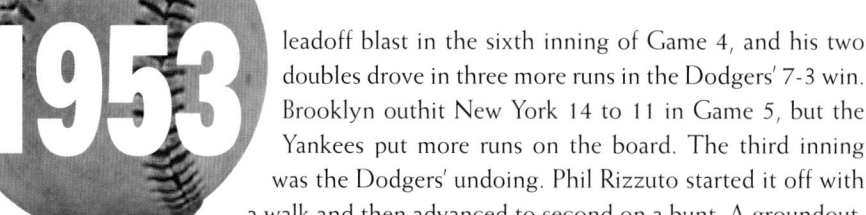

The New York Yankees won an unprecedented fifth consecutive pennant in 1953, and their 99 wins that year were topped by only one other club: the National League-champion Brooklyn Dodgers. Behind a 105-win season, the Dodgers won their third pennant in five years with a powerful lineup that included a pair of 40-homer sluggers in Duke Snider and MVP Roy Campanella and the league batting leader in Carl Furillo. Brooklyn was still smarting from the back-to-back home losses in Games 6 and 7 of the 1952 Series, and the "Boys of Summer" seemed poised to win the big one. Things, however, did not start off well for the Dodgers and Game 1 starter Carl Erskine. A bases-clearing triple by Billy Martin was part of a 4-run first inning in the opener, and although the Dodgers came back to tie the score in the top of the seventh, New York went on to win by a 9-5 count. Preacher Roe held the Yanks to 5 hits in Game 2, but 3 walks in the first inning and home runs by Billy Martin and Mickey Mantle in the seventh and eighth cost him the game. Brooklyn evened the Series with home wins in Games 3 and 4. Campanella's eighth-inning homer provided the difference in the third game, while Erskine redeemed his earlier struggles with a record-breaking 14 strikeouts; Mantle and Joe Collins each fanned four times. Duke Snider added to his career postseason home run total with a

leadoff blast in the sixth inning of Game 4, and his two doubles drove in three more runs in the Dodgers' 7-3 win. Brooklyn outhit New York 14 to 11 in Game 5, but the Yankees put more runs on the board. The third inning was the Dodgers' undoing. Phil Rizzuto started it off with a walk and then advanced to second on a bunt. A groundout, an error, a hit batsman and another walk brought Rizzuto around to score and left the bases loaded. Russ Meyer came into the game in relief of starter Johnny Podres and proceeded to give up a bases-clearing home run to Mantle. In Game 6, the Dodgers fell behind 3-0 after two innings, but they scored one in the sixth and tied the game in the top of the ninth on a 2-run homer by Furillo. Hank Bauer led off the Yankee half of the ninth with a walk, and after Yogi Berra lined out to right, Mantle hit an infield single. Billy Martin, who had already driven in 7 runs in the Series, stepped to the plate in this clutch situation and came through once again, stroking a single to center field to bring Bauer home for the Series-winning run. It was a record-tying 12th hit for Martin, and a historic fifth World Series triumph for the Yankees in five years.

Above: Carl Erskine receives kudos after completing a record-setting performance with 14 strikeouts in Game 3.

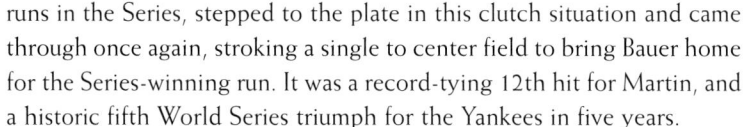

1953 WORLD SERIES COMPOSITE STATISTICS

NEW YORK YANKEES/Casey Stengel, Manager

Player	pos	G	AB	R	H	2B	3B	HR	RBI	BB	SO	SB	BA	SA	E	FPct
Hank Bauer	rf	6	23	6	6	0	1	0	1	2	4	0	.261	.348	0	1.000
Yogi Berra	c	6	21	3	9	1	0	1	4	3	3	0	.429	.619	0	1.000
Don Bollweg	1b	3	2	0	0	0	0	0	0	0	2	0	.000	.000	0	—
Joe Collins	1b	6	24	4	4	1	0	1	2	3	8	0	.167	.333	0	1.000
Whitey Ford	p	2	3	0	1	0	0	0	0	0	0	0	.333	.333	0	1.000
Tom Gorman	p	1	1	0	0	0	0	0	0	0	1	0	.000	.000	0	1.000
Bob Kuzava	p	1	1	0	0	0	0	0	0	0	1	0	.000	.000	0	—
Ed Lopat	p	1	3	0	0	0	0	0	0	0	2	0	.000	.000	0	1.000
Mickey Mantle	cf	6	24	3	5	0	0	2	7	3	8	0	.208	.458	0	1.000
Billy Martin	2b	6	24	5	12	1	2	2	8	1	2	1	.500	.958	0	1.000
Jim McDonald	p	1	2	0	1	1	0	0	1	1	1	0	.500	1.000	0	1.000
Gil McDougald	3b	6	24	2	4	0	1	2	4	1	3	0	.167	.500	0	1.000
Johnny Mize	ph	3	3	0	0	0	0	0	0	0	1	0	.000	.000	—	—
Irv Noren	ph	2	1	0	0	0	0	0	0	1	0	0	.000	.000	—	—
Vic Raschi	p	1	2	0	0	0	0	0	0	0	1	0	.000	.000	0	1.000
Allie Reynolds	p	3	2	0	1	0	0	0	0	1	1	0	.500	.500	0	—
Phil Rizzuto	ss	6	19	4	6	1	0	0	0	3	2	1	.316	.368	1	.968
Johnny Sain	p	2	2	1	1	1	0	0	2	0	1	0	.500	1.000	0	—
Art Schallock	p	1	0	0	0	0	0	0	0	0	0	0	—	—	0	1.000
Gene Woodling	lf	6	20	5	6	0	0	1	3	6	2	0	.300	.450	0	1.000
Totals		6	201	33	56	6	4	9	32	25	43	2	.279	.483	1	.995

Pitcher	G	GS	CG	IP	H	R	ER	BB	SO	W-L	Sv	ERA
Whitey Ford	2	2	0	8	9	4	4	2	7	0-1	0	4.50
Tom Gorman	1	0	0	3	4	1	1	0	1	0-0	0	3.00
Bob Kuzava	1	0	0	⅔	1	1	1	0	1	0-0	0	13.50
Ed Lopat	1	1	1	9	9	2	2	4	3	1-0	0	2.00
Jim McDonald	1	1	0	7⅔	12	6	5	0	3	1-0	0	5.87
Vic Raschi	1	1	1	8	9	3	3	4	9	0-1	0	3.38
Allie Reynolds	3	1	0	8	9	6	6	4	9	1-0	1	6.75
Johnny Sain	2	0	0	5⅔	8	3	3	1	1	1-0	0	4.76
Art Schallock	1	0	0	2	2	1	1	1	1	0-0	0	4.50
Totals	6	6	2	52	64	27	26	15	30	4-2	1	4.50

BROOKLYN DODGERS/Chuck Dressen, Manager

Player	pos	G	AB	R	H	2B	3B	HR	RBI	BB	SO	SB	BA	SA	E	FPct
Wayne Belardi	ph	2	2	0	0	0	0	0	0	0	1	0	.000	.000	—	—
Joe Black	p	1	0	0	0	0	0	0	0	0	0	0	—	—	0	—
Roy Campanella	c	6	22	6	6	0	0	1	2	2	3	0	.273	.409	0	1.000
Billy Cox	3b	6	23	3	7	3	0	1	6	1	4	0	.304	.565	1	.917
Carl Erskine	p	3	4	1	1	0	0	0	0	0	1	0	.250	.250	1	.750
Carl Furillo	rf	6	24	4	8	2	0	1	4	1	3	0	.333	.542	2	.833
Jim Gilliam	2b	6	27	4	8	3	0	2	4	0	2	0	.296	.630	1	.969
Gil Hodges	1b	6	22	3	8	0	0	1	1	3	3	1	.364	.500	1	.981
Jim Hughes	p	1	1	0	0	0	0	0	0	0	1	0	.000	.000	1	.000
Clem Labine	p	3	2	0	0	0	0	0	0	0	1	0	.000	.000	0	1.000
Billy Loes	p	1	3	0	2	0	0	0	0	0	1	0	.667	.667	0	—
Russ Meyer	p	1	1	0	0	0	0	0	0	0	1	0	.000	.000	0	1.000
Bob Milliken	p	1	0	0	0	0	0	0	0	0	0	0	—	—	0	—
Bobby Morgan	ph	1	1	0	0	0	0	0	0	0	0	0	.000	.000	—	—
Johnny Podres	p	1	1	0	1	0	0	0	0	0	0	0	1.000	1.000	0	1.000
Pee Wee Reese	ss	6	24	0	5	1	0	0	4	1	0	1	.208	.292	0	1.000
Jackie Robinson	lf	6	25	3	8	2	0	0	2	1	1	0	.320	.400	0	1.000
Preacher Roe	p	1	3	0	0	0	0	0	0	0	2	0	.000	.000	0	1.000
George Shuba	ph	2	1	1	1	0	0	1	2	0	0	0	1.000	4.000	—	—
Duke Snider	cf	6	25	3	8	3	0	1	5	2	6	0	.320	.560	0	1.000
Don Thompson	lf	2	0	0	0	0	0	0	0	0	0	0	—	—	0	1.000
Ben Wade	p	2	0	0	0	0	0	0	0	0	0	0	—	—	—	—
Dick Williams	ph	3	2	0	1	0	0	0	0	1	1	0	.500	.500	—	—
Totals		6	213	27	64	13	1	8	26	15	30	2	.300	.484	7	.969

Pitcher	G	GS	CG	IP	H	R	ER	BB	SO	W-L	Sv	ERA
Joe Black	1	0	0	1	1	1	1	0	2	0-0	0	9.00
Carl Erskine	3	3	1	14	14	9	9	9	16	1-0	0	5.79
Jim Hughes	1	0	0	4	3	1	1	1	3	0-0	0	2.25
Clem Labine	3	0	0	5	10	2	2	1	3	0-2	1	3.60
Billy Loes	1	1	0	8	8	3	3	2	8	1-0	0	3.38
Russ Meyer	1	0	0	4⅓	8	4	3	4	5	0-0	0	6.23
Bob Milliken	1	0	0	2	2	0	0	1	0	0-0	0	0.00
Johnny Podres	1	1	0	2⅔	9	5	1	2	0	0-0	0	3.38
Preacher Roe	1	1	1	8	5	4	4	4	4	0-1	0	4.50
Ben Wade	2	0	0	2⅓	4	4	4	1	2	0-0	0	15.43
Totals	6	6	2	51⅓	56	33	28	25	43	2-4	1	4.91

Series Outstanding Player: Billy Martin, New York Yankees. **Series Outstanding Pitcher:** Ed Lopat, New York Yankees. **Average Length of Game:** 2 hours, 56 minutes. **Total Attendance:** 307,350. **Average Attendance:** 51,225 (66,177 at Yankee Stadium; 36,273 at Ebbets Field). **Umpires:** Frank Dascoli (NL), Artie Gore (NL), Bill Grieve (AL), Eddie Hurley (AL), Hank Soar (AL), Bill Stewart (NL). **Winning Player's Share:** $8,281. **Losing Player's Share:** $6,178.

Below: Mickey Mantle sends Russ Meyer's first pitch over the left-center field wall for a grand slam in Game 5.

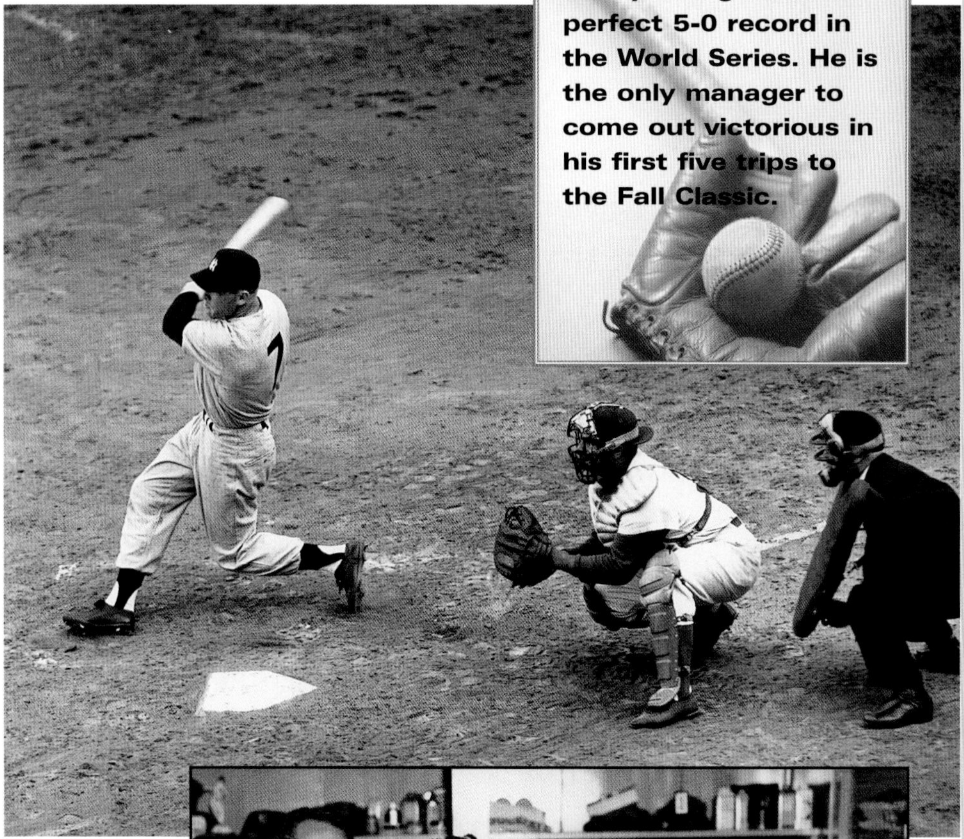

With the 1953 win, Casey Stengel had a perfect 5-0 record in the World Series. He is the only manager to come out victorious in his first five trips to the Fall Classic.

Right: Billy Martin collected 12 hits, including the Series-winner in Game 6, in the 1953 Series.

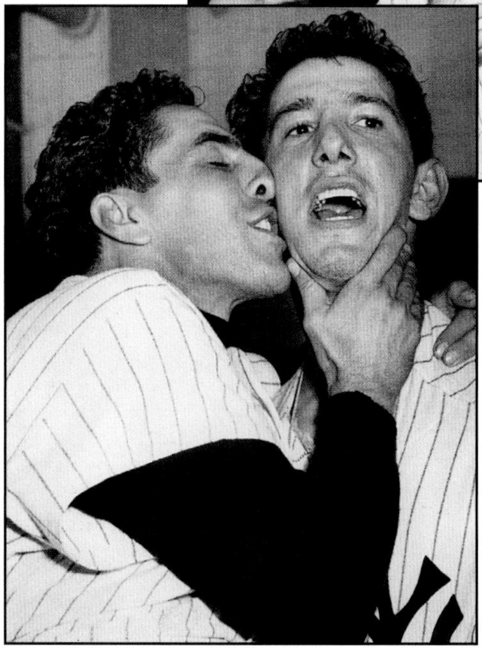

Left: Phil Rizzuto gives Billy Martin a congratulatory peck after Martin helped lead the Yanks to their fifth straight World Series title.

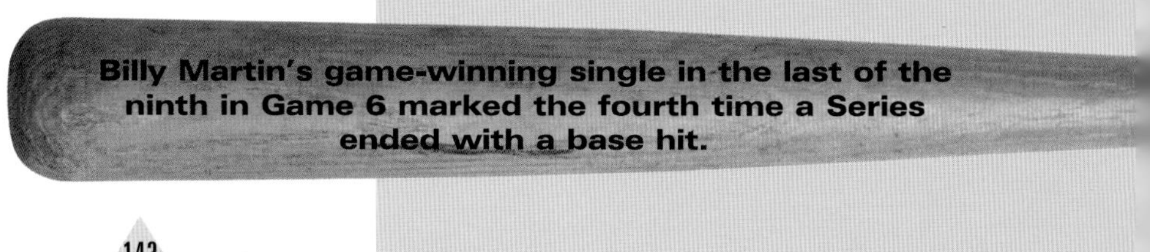

Billy Martin's game-winning single in the last of the ninth in Game 6 marked the fourth time a Series ended with a base hit.

Game 1 Wednesday, September 30 at Yankee Stadium, New York

	1	2	3	4	5	6	7	8	9	R	H	E
Brooklyn Dodgers	0	0	0	1	3	1	0	0		5	12	2
New York Yankees	4	0	0	0	1	0	1	3	x	9	12	0

Pitchers Bro Carl Erskine, IP 1, H 2, R 4, ER 4, BB 3, SO 1; Jim Hughes, IP 4, H 3, R 1, ER 1, BB 1, SO 3; Clem Labine (L, 0-1), IP 1⅔, H 4, R 1, ER 1, BB 0, SO 1; Ben Wade, IP 1⅓, H 3, R 3, ER 3, BB 1, SO 2
NY Allie Reynolds, IP 5⅓, H 7, R 4, ER 4, BB 3, SO 6; Johnny Sain (W, 1-0), IP 3⅔, H 5, R 1, ER 1, BB 1, SO 0

Top Performers at the Plate
Bro Jim Gilliam, 2 for 5, 1 R, 1 RBI; Gil Hodges, 3 for 5, 1 R, 1 RBI
NY Joe Collins, 2 for 4, 2 R, 2 RBI, 1 BB; Billy Martin, 3 for 4, 1 R, 3 RBI

2B-Bro/Cox, Snider; NY/Sain. **3B**-NY/Bauer, Martin. **HR**-Bro/Gilliam, Hodges, Shuba; NY/Berra, Collins. **SB**-NY/Martin. **Time** 3:10. **Attendance** 69,374.

Game 2 Thursday, October 1 at Yankee Stadium, New York

	1	2	3	4	5	6	7	8	9	R	H	E
Brooklyn Dodgers	0	0	0	2	0	0	0	0	0	2	9	1
New York Yankees	1	0	0	0	0	1	2	x		4	5	0

Pitchers Bro Preacher Roe (L, 0-1), IP 8, H 5, R 4, ER 4, BB 4, SO 4
NY Ed Lopat (W, 1-0), IP 9, H 9, R 2, ER 2, BB 4, SO 3

Top Performers at the Plate
Bro Billy Cox, 1 for 3, 2 RBI, 1 BB; Gil Hodges, 2 for 3, 1 R, 1 BB
NY Mickey Mantle, 1 for 3, 1 R, 2 RBI, 1 BB; Billy Martin, 2 for 3, 1 R, 1 RBI

2B-Bro/Cox, Furillo; NY/Rizzuto. **3B**-Bro/Reese. **HR**-NY/Mantle, Martin. **SB**-Bro/Hodges. **Time** 2:42. **Attendance** 66,786.

Game 3 Friday, October 2 at Ebbets Field, Brooklyn

	1	2	3	4	5	6	7	8	9	R	H	E
New York Yankees	0	0	0	1	0	0	1	0	0	2	6	0
Brooklyn Dodgers	0	0	0	0	1	1	0	1	x	3	9	0

Pitchers NY Vic Raschi (L, 0-1), IP 8, H 9, R 3, ER 3, BB 3, SO 4
Bro Carl Erskine (W, 1-0), IP 9, H 6, R 2, ER 2, BB 3, SO 14

Top Performers at the Plate
NY Yogi Berra, 1 for 1, 1 BB, 2 HBP; Billy Martin, 1 for 3, 1 R, 1 BB
Bro Jackie Robinson, 3 for 4, 1 R, 1 RBI; Duke Snider, 1 for 3, 1 R, 1 BB

2B-Bro/Robinson. **HR**-Bro/Campanella. **Time** 3:00. **Attendance** 35,270.

Game 4 Saturday, October 3 at Ebbets Field, Brooklyn

	1	2	3	4	5	6	7	8	9	R	H	E
New York Yankees	0	0	0	0	2	0	0	0	1	3	9	0
Brooklyn Dodgers	3	0	0	1	0	2	1	0	x	7	12	0

Pitchers NY Whitey Ford (L, 0-1), IP 1, H 3, R 3, ER 3, BB 1, SO 0; Tom Gorman, IP 3, H 4, R 1, ER 1, BB 0, SO 1; Johnny Sain, IP 2, H 3, R 2, ER 2, BB 0, SO 1; Art Schallock, IP 2, H 2, R 1, ER 1, BB 1, SO 1
Bro Billy Loes (W, 1-0), IP 8, H 8, R 3, ER 3, BB 2, SO 8; Clem Labine (Sv, 1), IP 1, H 1, R 0, ER 0, BB 0, SO 1

Top Performers at the Plate
NY Billy Martin, 2 for 4, 1 R; Gil McDougald, 1 for 3, 1 R, 2 RBI, 1 BB
Bro Jim Gilliam, 3 for 5, 1 R, 2 RBI, 3 2B; Duke Snider, 3 for 4, 1 R, 4 RBI, 2 2B

2B-NY/Cox, Gilliam 3, Snider 2. **3B**-NY/Martin. **HR**-NY/McDougald; Bro/Snider. **Time** 2:46. **Attendance** 36,775.

Game 5 Sunday, October 4 at Ebbets Field, Brooklyn

	1	2	3	4	5	6	7	8	9	R	H	E
New York Yankees	1	0	5	0	0	0	3	1	1	11	11	1
Brooklyn Dodgers	0	1	0	0	1	0	0	4	1	7	14	1

Pitchers NY Jim McDonald (W, 1-0), IP 7⅔, H 12, R 6, ER 5, BB 0, SO 3; Bob Kuzava, IP ⅔, H 2, R 1, ER 1, BB 0, SO 1; Allie Reynolds (Sv, 1), IP ⅔, H 0, R 0, ER 0, BB 0, SO 0
Bro Johnny Podres (L, 0-1), IP 2⅔, H 1, R 5, ER 1, BB 2, SO 0; Russ Meyer, IP 4⅓, H 8, R 4, ER 3, BB 4, SO 5; Ben Wade, IP 1, H 1, R 1, ER 1, BB 0, SO 0; Joe Black, IP 1, H 1, R 1, ER 1, BB 0, SO 2

Top Performers at the Plate
NY Yogi Berra, 2 for 4, 2 R, 1 RBI, 1 BB; Gil McDougald, 2 for 5, 1 R, 1 RBI
Bro Roy Campanella, 3 for 4, 2 R; Jim Gilliam, 2 for 4, 2 R, 1 RBI

2B-NY/Collins, McDonald. **3B**-NY/McDougald. **HR**-NY/Mantle, Martin, McDougald, Woodling; Bro/Cox, Gilliam. **SB**-NY/Rizzuto. **Time** 3:02. **Attendance** 36,775.

Game 6 Monday, October 5 at Yankee Stadium, New York

	1	2	3	4	5	6	7	8	9	R	H	E
Brooklyn Dodgers	0	0	0	0	1	0	0	2		3	8	3
New York Yankees	2	1	0	0	0	0	0	1		4	13	0

Pitchers Bro Carl Erskine, IP 4, H 6, R 3, ER 3, BB 3, SO 1; Bob Milliken, IP 2, H 2, R 0, ER 0, BB 1, SO 0; Clem Labine (L, 0-2), IP 2⅓, H 5, R 1, ER 1, BB 1, SO 1
NY Whitey Ford, IP 7, H 6, R 1, ER 1, BB 1, SO 7; Allie Reynolds (W, 1-0), IP 2, H 2, R 2, ER 2, BB 1, SO 3

Top Performers at the Plate
Bro Carl Furillo, 3 for 4, 1 R, 2 RBI; Jackie Robinson, 2 for 4, 1 R
NY Billy Martin, 2 for 5, 2 RBI; Gene Woodling, 2 for 4, 1 R, 1 RBI, 1 BB

2B-Bro/Furillo, Robinson; NY/Berra, Martin. **HR**-Bro/Furillo. **SB**-Bro/Robinson. **Time** 2:55. **Attendance** 62,370.

New York Giants (4) vs. Cleveland Indians (0)

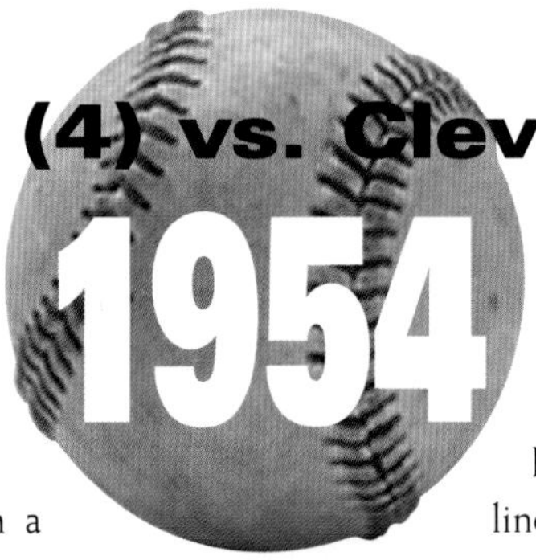

Usurping the New York Yankees from atop the American League, the Cleveland Indians put together a remarkable season in 1954, winning a league-record 111 games with one of the best pitching staffs ever assembled. The New York Giants took the National League pennant as center fielder Willie Mays mounted an MVP performance with a league-leading .345 average to go with his 41 homers and 110 RBI. But it was Mays's glove that was the story in the 1954 Series. The Indians and Giants were knotted in a 2-2 tie in the 8th inning of Game 1 when Vic Wertz came up to bat with two runners on base. Wertz's 1st-inning triple had been responsible for Cleveland's 2 runs in the game, and he got base hits in his next two times at bat as well. All 3 of Wertz's hits were against starter Sal Maglie, so New York manager Leo Durocher brought in Don Liddle in relief. Liddle threw one pitch, and Wertz drove it 450 feet to dead center field. The speedy Mays took off with his back to the plate as soon as the ball left the bat. He ran it down and, about 10 feet from the wall, made a spectacular over-the-shoulder catch. Mays then wheeled around and made an equally amazing throw to the infield to prevent the runners from scoring. "The Catch" killed the Cleveland rally, and the teams went into extra innings. Despite a leadoff double by Wertz in the 10th—which Mays adeptly cut off to prevent what might well have been an inside-the-park home run—the

Indians failed to break the tie. When the Giants took their turn in the bottom of the inning, they put two men on with one out. Durocher sent in pinch hitter Dusty Rhodes to face Cleveland starter and 23-game winner Bob Lemon. Rhodes lined Lemon's first pitch down the short right-field line, and the ball dropped into the seats for a home run. In the last World Series held in the Polo Grounds, the ballpark's unique dimensions played a pivotal role: Wertz's 8th-inning fly ball had traveled some 450 feet for an out; Rhodes's game-winning homer went barely 260 feet. The Indians were crushed by the opening game's turn of events, and they proceeded to drop the next 3. Rhodes was the hero again in Game 2. He came in to pinch-hit in the 5th inning and singled in the tying run; remaining in the game, he then delivered a 2-run homer in the 7th for the win. New York held Cleveland to 4 hits in Game 3 to claim a 6-2 victory, with Rhodes driving in 2 with a bases-loaded pinch single. In Game 4, the Giants jumped out to a 7-0 lead and held on to win 7-4, grabbing their first championship in 21 years. Although many had predicted that the 1954 Series might end in a 4-game sweep, few thought that New York would be holding the broom.

Above: The greatest World Series catch of all-time? Willie Mays's over-the-shoulder snag of Vic Wertz's drive was pure greatness.

1954 WORLD SERIES COMPOSITE STATISTICS

NEW YORK GIANTS/Leo Durocher, Manager

Player	pos	G	AB	R	H	2B	3B	HR	RBI	BB	SO	SB	BA	SA	E	FPct
Johnny Antonelli	p	2	3	0	0	0	0	0	1	0	0	0	.000	.000	0	1.000
Alvin Dark	ss	4	17	2	7	0	0	0	1	1	1	0	.412	.412	1	.947
Ruben Gomez	p	1	4	0	0	0	0	0	0	0	2	0	.000	.000	0	1.000
Marv Grissom	p	1	1	0	0	0	0	0	0	0	1	0	.000	.000	0	—
Monte Irvin	lf	4	9	1	2	1	0	0	2	0	3	0	.222	.333	1	.889
Don Liddle	p	2	3	0	0	0	0	0	0	0	2	0	.000	.000	1	.500
Whitey Lockman	1b	4	18	2	2	0	0	0	0	1	2	0	.111	.111	0	1.000
Sal Maglie	p	1	3	0	0	0	0	0	0	0	2	0	.000	.000	0	1.000
Willie Mays	cf	4	14	4	4	1	0	0	3	4	1	1	.286	.357	0	1.000
Don Mueller	rf	4	18	4	7	0	0	0	1	0	1	0	.389	.389	2	.600
Dusty Rhodes	ph-lf	3	6	2	4	0	0	2	7	1	2	0	.667	1.667	0	1.000
Hank Thompson	3b	4	11	6	4	1	0	0	2	7	1	0	.364	.455	1	1.000
Wes Westrum	c	4	11	0	3	0	0	0	3	1	3	0	.273	.273	0	1.000
Hoyt Wilhelm	p	2	1	0	0	0	0	0	0	0	1	0	.000	.000	1	.500
Davey Williams	2b	4	11	0	0	0	0	0	1	2	2	0	.000	.000	1	.950
Totals		**4**	**130**	**21**	**33**	**3**	**0**	**2**	**20**	**17**	**24**	**1**	**.254**	**.323**	**7**	**.956**

Pitcher	G	GS	CG	IP	H	R	ER	BB	SO	W-L	Sv	ERA
Johnny Antonelli	2	1	1	10⅔	8	1	1	7	12	1-0	1	0.84
Ruben Gomez	1	1	0	7⅓	4	2	2	3	2	1-0	0	2.45
Marv Grissom	1	0	0	2⅔	1	0	0	3	2	1-0	0	0.00
Don Liddle	2	1	0	7	5	4	1	1	2	1-0	0	1.29
Sal Maglie	1	1	0	7	7	2	2	2	2	0-0	0	2.57
Hoyt Wilhelm	2	0	0	2⅓	1	0	0	0	3	0-0	1	0.00
Totals	**4**	**4**	**1**	**37**	**26**	**9**	**6**	**16**	**23**	**4-0**	**2**	**1.46**

CLEVELAND INDIANS/Al Lopez, Manager

Player	pos	G	AB	R	H	2B	3B	HR	RBI	BB	SO	SB	BA	SA	E	FPct
Bobby Avila	2b	4	15	1	2	0	0	0	0	2	1	0	.133	.133	0	1.000
Sam Dente	ss	3	3	1	0	0	0	0	0	0	1	0	.000	.000	0	1.000
Larry Doby	cf	4	16	0	2	0	0	0	0	2	4	0	.125	.125	0	1.000
Mike Garcia	p	2	0	0	0	0	0	0	0	0	0	0	—	—	1	.667
Bill Glynn	ph-1b	2	2	1	1	0	0	0	0	0	1	0	.500	1.000	0	1.000
Mickey Grasso	c	1	0	0	0	0	0	0	0	0	0	0	—	—	0	1.000
Jim Hegan	c	4	13	1	2	1	0	0	0	1	1	0	.154	.231	0	1.000
Art Houtteman	p	1	0	0	0	0	0	0	0	0	0	0	—	—	0	—
Bob Lemon	p-ph	3	6	0	0	0	0	0	0	1	1	0	.000	.000	0	1.000
Hank Majeski	ph-3b	4	6	1	1	0	0	1	3	0	1	0	.167	.667	0	1.000
Dale Mitchell	ph	3	2	0	0	0	0	0	0	1	0	0	.000	.000	—	—
Don Mossi	p	3	0	0	0	0	0	0	0	0	0	0	—	—	0	1.000
Hal Naragon	c	1	0	0	0	0	0	0	0	0	0	0	—	—	0	1.000
Ray Narleski	p	2	0	0	0	0	0	0	0	0	0	0	—	—	0	1.000
Hal Newhouser	p	1	0	0	0	0	0	0	0	0	0	0	—	—	0	—
Dave Philley	rf-ph	4	8	0	1	0	0	0	0	1	3	0	.125	.125	0	1.000
Dave Pope	ph-rf-lf	3	3	0	0	0	0	0	0	1	1	0	.000	.000	0	—
Rudy Regalado	pr-3b-ph	4	3	0	1	0	0	0	0	1	0	0	.333	.333	0	—
Al Rosen	3b	3	12	0	3	0	0	0	0	1	1	0	.250	.250	0	1.000
Al Smith	lf	4	14	2	3	0	0	1	2	2	2	0	.214	.429	0	1.000
George Strickland	ss	3	9	0	0	0	0	0	0	0	2	0	.000	.000	1	.933
Vic Wertz	1b	4	16	2	8	2	1	1	3	2	0	0	.500	.938	1	.975
Wally Westlake	rf	2	7	0	1	0	0	0	0	1	3	0	.143	.143	0	.857
Early Wynn	p	1	2	0	1	1	0	0	0	0	1	0	.500	1.000	0	1.000
Totals		**4**	**137**	**9**	**26**	**5**	**1**	**3**	**9**	**16**	**23**	**0**	**.190**	**.307**	**4**	**.973**

Pitcher	G	GS	CG	IP	H	R	ER	BB	SO	W-L	Sv	ERA
Mike Garcia	2	1	0	5	6	4	3	4	4	0-1	0	5.40
Art Houtteman	1	0	0	2	2	1	1	1	1	0-0	0	4.50
Bob Lemon	2	2	1	13⅓	16	11	10	8	11	0-2	0	6.75
Don Mossi	3	0	0	4	3	0	0	0	0	0-0	0	0.00
Ray Narleski	2	0	0	4	1	1	1	1	2	0-0	0	2.25
Hal Newhouser	1	0	0	0	1	1	1	1	0	0-0	0	—
Early Wynn	1	1	0	7	4	3	3	2	5	0-1	0	3.86
Totals	**4**	**4**	**1**	**35⅓**	**33**	**21**	**19**	**17**	**24**	**0-4**	**0**	**4.84**

Series Outstanding Player: Dusty Rhodes, New York Giants. **Series Outstanding Pitcher:** Johnny Antonelli, New York Giants. **Average Length of Game:** 2 hours, 50 minutes. **Total Attendance:** 251,507. **Average Attendance:** 62,877 (50,925 at the Polo Grounds; 74,829 at Cleveland Stadium). **Umpires:** Al Barlick (NL), Charlie Berry (AL), Jocko Conlan (NL), Larry Napp (AL), Johnny Stevens (AL), Lon Warneke (NL). **Winning Player's Share:** $11,118. **Losing Player's Share:** $6,713.

With Bobby Avila's .341 average leading the American League and Willie Mays's .345 earning him a National League batting title, 1954 was the first World Series since 1931 to feature a matchup of batting champs.

Left: Cleveland's Vic Wertz had a great Series, but his team went down in a disappointing four-game sweep.

Right: Indians outfielder Dave Pope leaps in vain for Dusty Rhodes' game-winning pinch-hit homer in the 1954 opener.

Below: Johnny Antonelli was New York's top hurler, getting the victory as a starter in Game 2 and earning the save in relief in the Series clincher.

Game 1   Wednesday, September 29 at the Polo Grounds, New York

	1	2	3	4	5	6	7	8	9	10	R	H	E
Cleveland Indians	2	0	0	0	0	0	0	0	0	0	2	8	0
New York Giants	0	0	2	0	0	0	0	0	0	3	3	5	9	3

Pitchers Cle Bob Lemon (L, 0-1), IP 9⅓, H 9, R 5, ER 5, BB 5, SO 6
NY Sal Maglie, IP 7, H 7, R 2, ER 2, BB 2, SO 2; Don Liddle, IP ⅓, H 0, R 0, ER 0, BB 0, SO 0; Marv Grissom (W, 1-0), IP 2⅔, H 1, R 0, ER 0, BB 3, SO 2

Top Performers at the Plate
Cle Vic Wertz, 4 for 5, 2 RBI
NY Don Mueller, 2 for 5, 1 R, 1 RBI; Dusty Rhodes, 1 for 1, 1 R, 3 RBI

2B-Cle/Wertz. **3B**-Cle/Wertz. **HR**-NY/Rhodes. **SB**-NY/Mays. **Time** 3:11. **Attendance** 52,751.

Game 2   Thursday, September 30 at the Polo Grounds, New York

	1	2	3	4	5	6	7	8	9		R	H	E
Cleveland Indians	1	0	0	0	0	0	0	0	0		1	8	0
New York Giants	0	0	0	2	0	1	0	x		3	4	0

Pitchers Cle Early Wynn (L, 0-1), IP 7, H 4, R 3, ER 3, BB 2, SO 5; Don Mossi, IP 1, H 0, R 0, ER 0, BB 0, SO 0
NY Johnny Antonelli (W, 1-0), IP 9, H 8, R 1, ER 1, BB 6, SO 9

Top Performers at the Plate
Cle Al Smith, 2 for 4, 1 R, 1 RBI, 1 BB; Vic Wertz, 1 for 3, 1 BB
NY Dusty Rhodes, 2 for 2, 1 R, 2 RBI; Hank Thompson, 1 for 3, 1 R

2B-Cle/Hegan, Wynn. **HR**-Cle/Smith; NY/Rhodes. **Time** 2:50. **Attendance** 49,099.

Game 3   Friday, October 1 at Cleveland Stadium, Cleveland

	1	2	3	4	5	6	7	8	9		R	H	E
New York Giants	1	0	3	0	1	1	0	0		6	10	1
Cleveland Indians	0	0	0	0	0	0	1	1	0		2	4	2

Pitchers NY Ruben Gomez (W, 1-0), IP 7⅓, H 4, R 2, ER 2, BB 3, SO 2; Hoyt Wilhelm (Sv, 1), IP 1⅔, H 0, R 0, ER 0, BB 0, SO 2
Cle Mike Garcia (L, 0-1), IP 3, H 5, R 4, ER 3, BB 3, SO 3; Art Houtteman, IP 2, H 2, R 1, ER 1, BB 1, SO 1; Ray Narleski, IP 3, H 1, R 1, ER 1, BB 1, SO 2; Don Mossi, IP 1, H 2, R 0, ER 0, BB 0, SO 1

Top Performers at the Plate
NY Willie Mays, 3 for 5, 1 R, 1 RBI; Don Mueller, 2 for 5, 2 R

2B-NY/Thompson; Cle/Glynn. **HR**-Cle/Wertz. **Time** 2:28. **Attendance** 71,555.

Game 4   Saturday, October 2 at Cleveland Stadium, Cleveland

	1	2	3	4	5	6	7	8	9		R	H	E
New York Giants	0	2	1	0	4	0	0	0		7	10	3
Cleveland Indians	0	0	0	0	3	0	1	0	0		4	6	2

Pitchers NY Don Liddle (W, 1-0), IP 6⅔, H 5, R 4, ER 1, BB 1, SO 2; Hoyt Wilhelm, IP ⅔, H 1, R 0, ER 0, BB 0, SO 1; Johnny Antonelli (Sv, 1), IP 1⅔, H 0, R 0, ER 0, BB 1, SO 3
Cle Bob Lemon (L, 0-2), IP 4, H 7, R 6, ER 5, BB 3, SO 5; Hal Newhouser, IP 0, H 1, R 1, ER 1, BB 1, SO 0; Ray Narleski, IP 1, H 0, R 0, ER 0, BB 0, SO 0; Don Mossi, IP 2, H 1, R 0, ER 0, BB 0, SO 0; Mike Garcia, IP 2, H 1, R 0, ER 0, BB 1, SO 1

Top Performers at the Plate
NY Alvin Dark, 3 for 5, 2 R; Monte Irvin, 2 for 4, 1 R, 2 R
Cle Hank Majeski, 1 for 1, 1 R, 3 RBI; Vic Wertz, 2 for 4, 1 R

2B-NY/Irvin, Mays; Cle/Wertz. **HR**-Cle/Majeski. **Time** 2:52. **Attendance** 78,102.

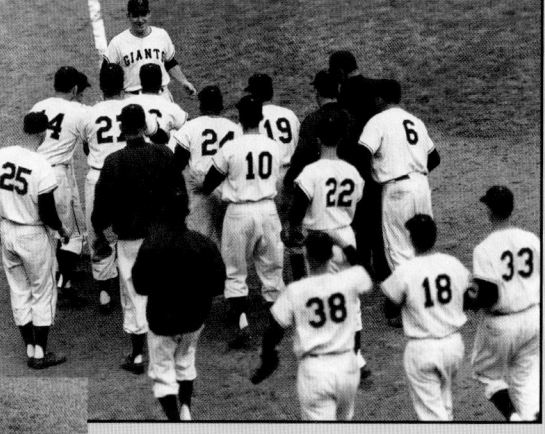

Above: The Giants await their Game 1 hero, as Dusty Rhodes approaches home plate after his clutch home run.

All You Need is Glove
Great Fielding Feats

Most fielding plays don't show up in the box scores like home runs and strikeouts. Still, exceptional glove work has saved many a World Series game. Whether a rally-killing dive at third or a leaping, home-run-robbing snare at the wall, the following list of fielding gems—starting with Willie Mays's epic save in the 1954 Series—did much to change a team's fortunes in the Fall Classic.

1 Mays's Spectacular Catch Deflates Cleveland in Opener — Willie Mays, New York Giants, September 29, 1954

Willie Mays always insisted that his over-the-shoulder catch of Vic Wertz's deep drive in the opening game of the 1954 World Series was not the greatest he ever made. Knowing the grace and mastery that Mays displayed in the outfield during his 22-year career, that's perhaps believable. But never did he, or anyone else, make as good a defensive play in as big a situation. And the catch was just half the story; his whirling, no-look throw into the infield prevented a run from scoring and did as much to take the wind out of Cleveland's sails as the catch.

2 Amoros Grab Leads "Bums" to Victory — Sandy Amoros, Brooklyn Dodgers, October 4, 1955

By 1955, the Brooklyn Dodgers and their fans had waited long and hard for a World Series victory over the Yankees—and they might have had to wait even longer had it not been for a sensational play by Sandy Amoros in the final game of the 1955 Series. New York had two runners on base and nobody out in the sixth inning when Amoros robbed Yogi Berra with a running catch in the left-field corner. Sticking the knife in deeper, Amoros then rifled the ball to Pee Wee Reese, who helped turn the would-be hit into a double play.

Above: Sandy Amoros robbed Yogi Berra of an extra-base hit with a fantastic catch in the left-field corner at Yankee Stadium in Game 7 of the 1955 Series.

3 Human Vacuum Cleans Up for Baltimore—Brooks Robinson, Baltimore Orioles, October 10–15, 1970

Series MVP Brooks Robinson batted a stellar .429 in the 1970 Series, but it was his glove that stole the show. In Game 1, the thirdbaseman made a backhanded stab and a wheeling throw to first for an out on a hard smash down the line; in Game 2, he dove to his left to turn a possible base hit into a force-out, and two innings later dove to his right to start a 5-4-3 double play; in Game 3, he made a leaping grab on a high chopper to start a double play, made a barehanded play on a slow infield roller and made a diving snag on a low liner; and in Game 5, another backhanded dive by Robinson secured the first out in the last inning. All told, Robinson pulled the rug out from under several Cincinnati rallies.

Below: Willie Mays's unbelievable play to catch Vic Wertz's 450-foot blast at the Polo Grounds, and then make a whirling throw back to the infield, is the standard against which fielding greatness is measured.

4 Agee Robs Two Orioles of Hits in Game 3 — Tommie Agee, New York Mets, October 14, 1969

In the third game of the 1969 World Series, Mets center fielder Tommie Agee used his glove and speed to twice deprive the Orioles of run-scoring hits. In the fourth inning, Agee ran down Ellie Hendricks' two-out drive at the 396-foot mark in left-center field, robbing him of an extra-base hit with two runners on. In the seventh, he made a head-first dive to snare Paul Blair's liner with the bases loaded, again taking away sure extra bases. New York won the game by a 5-0 margin; Agee's play in the outfield alone prevented at least four runs.

5 Nettles Sparkles at the Hot Corner — Graig Nettles, New York Yankees, October 13, 1978

Following in the footsteps of the great Brooks Robinson, Graig Nettles created his own personal highlight reel at third base during Game 3 of the 1978 Series. First he made a diving play on a hard grounder by Los Angeles's Reggie Smith to end the third inning. Two innings later and with two men on base, he turned Smith's potential extra-base hit into an infield single; Nettles then speared Steve Garvey's two-out grounder to strand three men on base. Finally, he got the Yanks out of a bases-loaded jam in the sixth with a diving play on the line.

Though he leads all outfielders in career chances and putouts in the World Series, Joe DiMaggio did not have a single assist in 51 games.

Miscellaneous World Series Fielding Records

Most Consecutive Games Without Committing an Error

1b	Bill Skowron, Yankees / Dodgers, October 10, 1956–October 6, 1963	31
2b	Billy Martin, Yankees, October 5, 1952–October 10, 1956	23
3b	Ron Cey, Dodgers, October 13, 1974–October 28, 1981	22
ss	Phil Rizzuto, Yankees, October 3, 1942–October 5, 1951	21
of	Joe DiMaggio, Yankees, October 6, 1937–October 10, 1951	45
c	Yogi Berra, Yankees, October 4, 1952–October 9, 1957	30
p	Whitey Ford, Yankees, October 7, 1950–October 8, 1962	18

Most Chances Without an Error, Single Series

1b	George Kelly, Giants, 1921; Wally Pipp, Yankees, 1921	93
2b	Bobby Doerr, Red Sox, 1946	49
3b	Denis Menke, Reds, 1972	29
ss	Charlie Gelbert, Cardinals, 1931	42
of	Mickey Rivers, Yankees, 1977	25
c	Jerry Grote, Mets, 1973	71
p	Nick Altrock, White Sox, 1906; James "Hippo" Vaughn, Cubs, 1918	17

Above: Graig Nettles was all over the hot corner in Game 5 of the 1978 Series, going to his left and his right to grab anything the Dodgers sent his way.

Above left: After making the running one-handed catch, Amoros threw the ball in to shortstop Pee Wee Reese, who made a perfect throw to Gil Hodges at first to double up Gil McDougald.

Career Fielding Records by Position

Position	Games Played	Total Chances	Putouts	Assists	Errors	Double Plays
1b	Gil Hodges, 38	Gil Hodges, 350	Gil Hodges, 326	Bill Skowron, 29	Fred Merkle, 8	Gil Hodges, 31
2b	Frankie Frisch, 42	Frankie Frisch, 239	Frankie Frisch, 104	Frankie Frisch, 135	Eddie Collins and Larry Doyle, 8	Frankie Frisch, 24
3b	Gil McDougald, 31	Graig Nettles, 96	Frank Baker, 37	Graig Nettles, 68	Larry Gardner, 8	Graig Nettles, 7
ss	Phil Rizzuto, 52	Phil Rizzuto, 250	Phil Rizzuto, 107	Phil Rizzuto, 143	Art Fletcher, 12	Phil Rizzuto, 32
of	Mickey Mantle, 63	Joe DiMaggio, 150	Joe DiMaggio, 150	Harry Hooper and Ross Youngs 5	Ross Youngs, 4	Held by many players, 2
c	Yogi Berra, 63	Yogi Berra, 457	Yogi Berra, 421	Yogi Berra, 36	Boss Schmidt, 7	Johnny Bench and Yogi Berra, 6
p	Whitey Ford, 22	Christy Mathewson, 40	Whitey Ford, 11	Christy Mathewson, 34	Eddie Cicotte, Max Lanier and Deacon Phillippe, 3	Chief Bender, Joe Bush and Allie Reynolds, 3

Below: Putting on a veritable fielding clinic, Brooks Robinson silenced several Cincinnati rallies during the 1970 Series. Here he dives to his left to snare Johnny Bench's liner, ending the sixth inning of Game 3.

6 Wambsganss Turns Unassisted Triple Play — Bill Wambsganss, Cleveland Indians, October 10, 1920

There have been more than 900 double plays turned in the World Series since 1903, but only one triple play—and it was unassisted. In fact, in the tens of thousands of Major League games, regular season and postseason, only 11 players have ever pulled off an unassisted triple play. Bill Wambsganss managed this rare fielding feat in the fifth game of a World Series.

7 "Joltin' Joe" Robbed by Gionfriddo — Al Gionfriddo, Brooklyn Dodgers, October 5, 1947

Reserve outfielder Al Gionfriddo entered the sixth game of the 1947 World Series in a manager's defensive switch, and the move paid off. His running catch of Joe DiMaggio's smash at the fence in deepest left field took three runs away from the Yankees and left a frustrated DiMaggio kicking the dirt. Although the Dodgers eventually lost Game 7, the unbelievable play by the scrappy 5'6" outfielder kept Brooklyn alive for another day.

8 Giants Win on Sensational Double Play — Johnny Rawlings and George Kelly, New York Giants, October 13, 1921

The first double play to end a World Series was also one of the best ever turned. It was the bottom of the ninth inning in Game 8 of the 1921 Series, with the Giants holding on to a 1-0 lead over the Yankees. Giants second baseman Johnny Rawlings made a superb stop to prevent Frank Baker's grounder from getting through to the outfield and threw Baker

out at first. First baseman George Kelly then fired the ball to third base, where base runner Aaron Ward was tagged for the final out of the inning, the game and the Series.

9 Martin Snags Game-Saving Pop-Up — Billy Martin, New York Yankees, October 7, 1952

On the scale of difficulty, Billy Martin's catch of Jackie Robinson's pop-up in the seventh game of the 1952 Series might not stack up with the Robinsons and the Mayses of the world. But as far as coming through in the clutch, Martin's fielding heroism ranks right up there. The Dodgers had the bases loaded with two out in the seventh inning when Robinson lifted the ball to the right side of the infield. Neither the Yankee pitcher nor the first baseman made a move; at the last moment, second baseman Martin zipped in and snared the ball at the knees. Two Dodgers had already crossed the plate, but Martin's grab negated the runs and preserved New York's lead in the decisive game.

10 White Nearly Starts Triple Play with Leaping Catch — Devon White, Toronto Blue Jays, October 20, 1992

An umpire's miscall in Game 3 of the 1992 Series is all that prevented the second triple play in World Series history, but Devon White's leaping, backhanded catch of David Justice's 400-foot drive stands as one of the top fielding moments in October. The second out on the play came when Terry Pendleton was ruled out for passing front-runner Deion Sanders on the base paths, and Sanders should have been called out, as Kelly Gruber retrieved the throw from White and tagged Sanders before he got back to the base. The umpire, however, didn't see the tag, and so White's play led "only" to a double play.

Above: The sensational glove work by center fielder Tommie Agee helped lead the Mets to victory in 1969. His belly-first catch of Paul Blair's seventh-inning drive left three Orioles stranded on base and helped preserve New York's 4-0 lead at that point.

WORLD SERIES CLASSIC
1955
Brooklyn Dodgers (4) vs. New York Yankees (3)

The Yankees were back in 1955. So were the Dodgers. The Yanks were hoping for their 17th championship, the Dodgers their first. Brooklyn had made it this far five times in the previous 14 years, and each time they went down in defeat at the hands of the Yankees. Adding in the losses in 1916 and 1920, the Brooklyn franchise was 0-7 in the World Series. Walter Alston took over as manager in 1955, but otherwise the cast that won the pennant that year was largely the same as the one that won it two years earlier. They had future Hall of Famers in Roy Campanella, Pee Wee Reese, Jackie Robinson and Duke Snider, a perennial All-Star in Gil Hodges, and former Rookies of the Year in Don Newcombe and Jim Gilliam. But "Dem Bums" lacked the one thing that mattered most to the Brooklyn faithful: a World Series victory.

After the first two games at Yankee Stadium, it looked like the 1955 Series would be the same old story. Brooklyn's ace Don Newcombe lost the opener to Whitey Ford, New York's star lefty. The Dodgers had three runs by the third inning, but the Yanks countered with three of their own and then added three more. Ford shut Brooklyn down for four innings before they rallied for two in the eighth. The second run of the inning came when Robinson stole home in a close play at the plate; catcher Yogi Berra argued vehemently (and continues to argue a half century later) that Robinson missed home plate, but to no avail. Still, the Dodgers fell a run short, and then they fell two games down when Tommy Byrne pitched a five-hitter for New York in Game 2. Four Yankees scored in the fourth inning, with Byrne delivering a two-run, bases-loaded single. The Dodgers would need a three-game sweep at Ebbets Field to take the Series lead before having to return to the Bronx—and they did just that. Pitching on his 23rd birthday, Johnny Podres outdueled New York's Bob Turley in Game 3 to give Brooklyn its first win. Campanella's home run put them up 2-0 in the first, but the Yanks came back in the second on a leadoff homer by Mickey Mantle and an RBI single by Phil Rizzuto. Two bases-loaded walks in the bottom of the inning regained the lead for Brooklyn, which they ultimately extended to 8-3. The Dodgers tied the Series the next day with home runs by Campanella, Hodges and Snider leading the way; Campy and Hodges bunched theirs together in a three-run fourth, and Snider added three more runs with one swing an inning later. Though starter Carl Erskine didn't last more than three innings, Don Bessent and Clem Labine combined to preserve the lead in relief. Alston gave rookie Roger Craig the start in Game 5, and his six innings plus Labine's three in relief did the trick. The long ball provided the offensive firepower, with a two-run home run by Sandy Amoros and a solo one by Snider putting Dodgers up 3-0 after three. Snider added another solo blast in the fifth.

Back at the Stadium for Game 6, Ford dominated the Dodger line-up while the Yankee hitters shelled young Brooklyn starter Karl Spooner for five runs in the first inning. Although Russ Meyer and Ed Roebuck were able to shut the Yanks out the rest of the way, the Dodgers could

Above: They finally did it! Pitcher Johnny Podres and catcher Roy Campanella celebrate the Dodgers' defeat of the Yankees in 1955.

not manage more than one run off Ford all afternoon, and New York evened the Series at three games apiece. It would all come down to a single game. Either the Dodgers would finally grab that elusive first world championship, or the Yankees would add one to their ever-growing list. Brooklyn had the young Podres going up against the 35-year-old Byrne, and both pitchers kept runs off the board through three. In the top of the fourth, Campanella hit a one-out double, and Hodges drove him in with a single to left. Berra led off the Yankee half of the inning with a double, but Podres kept him stranded on base. Reese started the sixth with a single and worked his way around to third on an error and a sacrifice. Brooklyn got their second run of the game when Hodges's deep fly ball allowed Reese to tag up and score. At the start of the bottom of the sixth,

Alston inserted Sandy Amoros as a defensive replacement in left field. Billy Martin opened the inning with a walk, and Gil McDougald's bunt single put runners on first and second with nobody out. Then Berra came up and drove one toward the left-field corner. Amoros was shaded toward center, and it looked like the ball might fall in for extra bases. Amoros raced over and made a fantastic one-handed catch near the line. He then turned and fired the ball in to Reese, who made a sparkling throw to Hodges, doubling up McDougald at first. Podres hung on to get the third out, and then worked himself out of a jam in the eighth inning before sending the Yanks down in order in the ninth.

Next year had arrived. The Brooklyn Dodgers captured their first World Series win, wiping out years of frustration and heartbreak.

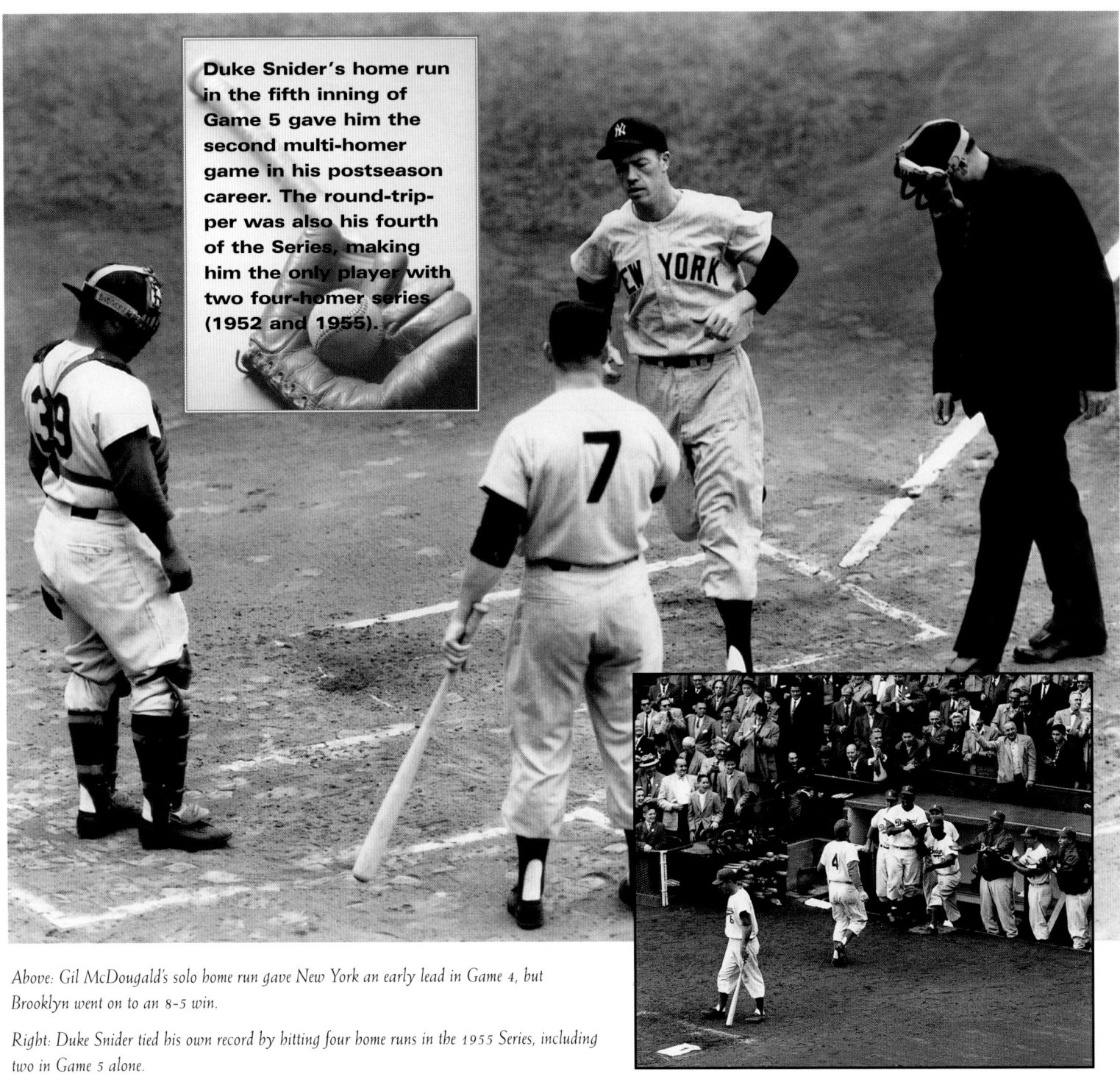

Duke Snider's home run in the fifth inning of Game 5 gave him the second multi-homer game in his postseason career. The round-tripper was also his fourth of the Series, making him the only player with two four-homer series (1952 and 1955).

Above: Gil McDougald's solo home run gave New York an early lead in Game 4, but Brooklyn went on to an 8-5 win.

Right: Duke Snider tied his own record by hitting four home runs in the 1955 Series, including two in Game 5 alone.

Above: Jackie Robinson is called safe on his steal of home in the eighth inning of Game 1.

Below: Yankee catcher Yogi Berra gets in umpire Bill Summers' face to dispute the call on Robinson's steal of home, claiming that Robinson never touched the plate.

Game 1 Wednesday, September 28 at Yankee Stadium, New York

	1	2	3	4	5	6	7	8	9	R	H	E
Brooklyn Dodgers	0	2	1	0	0	0	0	2	0	5	10	0
New York Yankees	0	2	1	1	0	2	0	0	x	6	9	1

Pitchers — Bro Don Newcombe (L, 0-1), IP 5⅔, H 8, R 6, ER 6, BB 2, SO 4; Don Bessent, IP 1⅓, H 0, R 0, ER 0, BB 0, SO 0; Clem Labine, IP 1, H 1, R 0, ER 0, BB 1, SO 0
NY Whitey Ford (W, 1-0), IP 8, H 9, R 5, ER 3, BB 4, SO 2; Bob Grim (Sv, 1), IP 1, H 1, R 0, ER 0, BB 0, SO 2

Top Performers at the Plate
Bro Carl Furillo, 3 for 4, 2 R, 1 RBI, 1 BB; Duke Snider, 2 for 5, 1 R, 1 RBI
NY Joe Collins, 2 for 3, 3 R, 3 RBI, 1 BB, 2 HR; Billy Martin, 2 for 3

3B-Bro/J. Robinson; NY/Martin. HR-Bro/Furillo, Snider; NY/Collins 2, Howard. SB-Bro/J. Robinson. Time 2:31. Attendance 63,869.

Game 2 Thursday, September 29 at Yankee Stadium, New York

	1	2	3	4	5	6	7	8	9	R	H	E
Brooklyn Dodgers	0	0	0	1	1	0	0	0		2	5	2
New York Yankees	0	0	0	4	0	0	0	0	x	4	8	0

Pitchers — Bro Billy Loes (L, 0-1), IP 3⅔, H 7, R 4, ER 4, BB 1, SO 5; Don Bessent, IP ⅓, H 0, R 0, ER 0, BB 0, SO 0; Karl Spooner, IP 3, H 1, R 0, ER 0, BB 1, SO 5; Clem Labine, IP 1, H 0, R 0, ER 0, BB 0, SO 1
NY Tommy Byrne (W, 1-0), IP 9, H 5, R 2, ER 2, BB 5, SO 6

Top Performers at the Plate
Bro Pee Wee Reese, 2 for 4, 1 R
NY Yogi Berra, 2 for 3, 1 R, 1 HBP; Billy Martin, 1 for 3, 1 R, 1 RBI

2B-Bro/Reese. Time 2:28. Attendance 64,707.

Game 3 Friday, September 30 at Ebbets Field, Brooklyn

	1	2	3	4	5	6	7	8	9	R	H	E
New York Yankees	0	2	0	0	0	0	1	0	0	3	7	0
Brooklyn Dodgers	2	2	0	2	0	0	2	0	x	8	11	1

Pitchers — NY Bob Turley (L, 0-1), IP 1⅓, H 3, R 4, ER 4, BB 2, SO 1; Tom Morgan, IP 2⅔, H 3, R 2, ER 2, BB 3, SO 1; Johnny Kucks, IP 2, H 1, R 0, ER 0, BB 1, SO 0; Tom Sturdivant, IP 2, H 4, R 2, ER 2, BB 1, SO 0
Bro Johnny Podres (W, 1-0), IP 9, H 7, R 3, ER 2, BB 2, SO 6

Top Performers at the Plate
NY Phil Rizzuto, 1 for 2, 1 R, 2 BB; Bill Skowron, 2 for 4, 1 R
Bro Roy Campanella, 3 for 5, 1 R, 3 RBI; Pee Wee Reese, 1 for 3, 1 R, 2 RBI, 2 BB

2B-NY/Skowron; Bro/Campanella, Furillo, Robinson. 3B-NY/Carey. HR-NY/Mantle; Bro/Campanella. Time 2:20. Attendance 34,209.

Game 4 Saturday, October 1 at Ebbets Field, Brooklyn

	1	2	3	4	5	6	7	8	9	R	H	E
New York Yankees	1	1	0	1	0	2	0	0	0	5	9	0
Brooklyn Dodgers	0	0	1	3	3	0	1	0	x	8	14	0

Pitchers — NY Don Larsen (L, 0-1), IP 4, H 5, R 5, ER 5, BB 2, SO 2; Johnny Kucks, IP 1, H 3, R 2, ER 2, BB 0, SO 1; Rip Coleman, IP 1, H 5, R 1, ER 1, BB 0, SO 1; Tom Morgan, IP 1, H 0, R 0, ER 0, BB 0, SO 0; Tom Sturdivant, IP 1, H 1, R 0, ER 0, BB 1, SO 0
Bro Carl Erskine, IP 3, H 3, R 3, ER 3, BB 2, SO 1; Don Bessent, IP 1⅔, H 3, R 0, ER 0, BB 1, SO 1; Clem Labine (W, 1-0), IP 4⅓, H 3, R 2, ER 2, BB 1, SO 0

Top Performers at the Plate
NY Billy Martin, 2 for 4, 1 R, 2 RBI; Phil Rizzuto, 1 for 3, 1 RBI, 1 BB
Bro Roy Campanella, 3 for 5, 2 R, 1 RBI; Gil Hodges, 3 for 4, 1 R, 3 RBI

2B-NY/Martin; Bro/Campanella, Gilliam. HR-NY/McDougald; Bro/Campanella, Hodges, Snider. SB-NY/Collins, Rizzuto; Bro/Gilliam. Time 2:57. Attendance 36,242.

Game 5 Sunday, October 2 at Ebbets Field, Brooklyn

	1	2	3	4	5	6	7	8	9	R	H	E
New York Yankees	0	0	0	1	0	0	1	1	0	3	6	0
Brooklyn Dodgers	0	2	1	0	1	0	0	1	x	5	9	2

Pitchers — NY Bob Grim (L, 0-1), IP 6, H 6, R 4, ER 4, BB 4, SO 5; Bob Turley, IP 2, H 3, R 1, ER 1, BB 1, SO 5
Bro Roger Craig (W, 1-0), IP 6, H 4, R 2, ER 2, BB 5, SO 4; Clem Labine (Sv, 1), IP 3, H 2, R 1, ER 1, BB 0, SO 1

Top Performers at the Plate
NY Yogi Berra, 2 for 4, 2 R, 1 RBI
Bro Gil Hodges, 2 for 3, 1 R, 1 SH; Duke Snider, 3 for 4, 2 R, 2 RBI, 2 HR

2B-Bro/Snider. HR-NY/Berra, Cerv; Bro/Amoros, Snider 2. Time 2:40. Attendance 36,796.

Game 6 Monday, October 3 at Yankee Stadium, New York

	1	2	3	4	5	6	7	8	9	R	H	E
Brooklyn Dodgers	0	0	0	1	0	0	0	0	0	1	4	1
New York Yankees	5	0	0	0	0	0	0	0	x	5	8	0

Pitchers — Bro Karl Spooner (L, 0-1), IP ⅓, H 3, R 5, ER 5, BB 2, SO 1; Russ Meyer, IP 5⅔, H 4, R 0, ER 0, BB 2, SO 4; Ed Roebuck, IP 2, H 1, R 0, ER 0, BB 0, SO 0
NY Whitey Ford (W, 2-0), IP 9, H 4, R 1, ER 1, BB 4, SO 8

Top Performers at the Plate
NY Hank Bauer, 3 for 4, 1 R, 1 RBI; Yogi Berra, 2 for 3, 1 R, 1 RBI, 1 BB

HR-NY/Skowron. SB-NY/Rizzuto. Time 2:34. Attendance 64,022.

Game 7 Tuesday, October 4 at Yankee Stadium, New York

	1	2	3	4	5	6	7	8	9	R	H	E
Brooklyn Dodgers	0	0	0	1	0	1	0	0	0	2	5	0
New York Yankees	0	0	0	0	0	0	0	0	0	0	8	1

Pitchers — Bro Johnny Podres (W, 2-0), IP 9, H 8, R 0, ER 0, BB 2, SO 4
NY Tommy Byrne (L, 1-1), IP 5⅓, H 3, R 2, ER 1, BB 3, SO 2; Bob Grim, IP 1⅔, H 1, R 0, ER 0, BB 1, SO 1; Bob Turley, IP 2, H 1, R 0, ER 0, BB 1, SO 1

Top Performers at the Plate
Bro Roy Campanella, 1 for 3, 1 R, 1 SH; Gil Hodges, 1 for 2, 2 RBI, 1 BB, 1 SF
NY Gil McDougald, 3 for 4

2B-Bro/Campanella; NY/Berra, Skowron. Time 2:44. Attendance 62,465.

Above: Billy Martin's attempt to steal home in the sixth inning of Game 1 comes up a bit short.

Below: Brooklyn was ecstatic after wining in its eighth Series match-up against the Yanks.

Background: Sandy Amoros's lunging catch of Yogi Berra's drive in the sixth inning of Game 7 robbed Berra of a hit and helped preserve Brooklyn's slim lead in the deciding game.

1955 WORLD SERIES COMPOSITE STATISTICS

BROOKLYN DODGERS/Walter Alston, Manager

Player	pos	G	AB	R	H	2B	3B	HR	RBI	BB	SO	SB	BA	SA	E	FPct
Sandy Amoros	lf-cf	5	12	3	4	0	0	1	3	4	4	0	.333	.583	0	1.000
Don Bessent	p	3	1	0	0	0	0	0	0	0	1	0	.000	.000	0	1.000
Roy Campanella	c	7	27	4	7	3	0	2	4	3	3	0	.259	.593	1	.978
Roger Craig	p	1	0	0	0	0	0	0	0	1	0	0	—	—	0	1.000
Carl Erskine	p	1	1	0	0	0	0	0	0	0	0	0	.000	.000	0	1.000
Carl Furillo	rf	7	27	4	8	1	0	1	3	3	5	0	.296	.462	0	1.000
Jim Gilliam	lf-2b	7	24	2	7	1	0	0	3	8	1	1	.292	.333	0	1.000
Don Hoak	pr-ph-3b	3	3	0	1	0	0	0	2	0	0	0	.333	.333	0	1.000
Gil Hodges	1b	7	24	2	7	0	0	1	5	3	2	0	.292	.417	0	1.000
Frank Kellert	ph	3	3	0	1	0	0	0	0	0	0	0	.333	.333	—	—
Clem Labine	p	4	4	0	0	0	0	0	0	0	3	0	.000	.000	0	1.000
Billy Loes	p	1	1	0	0	0	0	0	0	0	0	0	.000	.000	0	—
Russ Meyer	p	1	2	0	0	0	0	0	0	0	1	0	.000	.000	0	1.000
Don Newcombe	p	1	3	0	0	0	0	0	0	0	0	0	.000	.000	0	1.000
Johnny Podres	p	2	7	1	1	0	0	0	0	0	1	0	.143	.143	0	1.000
Pee Wee Reese	ss	7	27	5	8	1	0	0	2	3	5	0	.296	.333	1	.974
Jackie Robinson	3b	6	22	5	4	1	1	0	1	2	1	1	.182	.318	2	.917
Ed Roebuck	p	1	0	0	0	0	0	0	0	0	0	0	—	—	0	1.000
George Shuba	ph	1	1	0	0	0	0	0	0	0	0	0	.000	.000	—	—
Duke Snider	cf	7	25	5	8	1	0	4	7	2	6	0	.320	.840	0	1.000
Karl Spooner	p	2	0	0	0	0	0	0	0	0	0	0	—	—	0	1.000
Don Zimmer	2b-ph	4	9	0	2	0	0	0	2	2	5	0	.222	.222	2	.857
Totals		7	223	31	58	8	1	9	30	33	38	2	.260	.428	6	.978

Pitcher	G	GS	CG	IP	H	R	ER	BB	SO	W-L	Sv	ERA
Don Bessent	3	0	0	3⅓	3	0	0	1	1	0-0	0	0.00
Roger Craig	1	1	0	6	4	2	2	5	4	1-0	0	3.00
Carl Erskine	1	1	0	3	3	3	3	2	3	0-0	0	9.00
Clem Labine	4	0	0	9⅓	6	3	3	2	2	1-0	1	2.89
Billy Loes	1	1	0	3⅔	7	4	4	1	5	0-1	0	9.82
Russ Meyer	1	0	0	5⅔	4	0	0	2	4	0-0	0	0.00
Don Newcombe	1	1	0	5⅔	8	6	6	2	4	0-1	0	9.53
Johnny Podres	2	2	2	18	15	3	2	4	10	2-0	0	1.00
Ed Roebuck	1	0	0	2	1	0	0	0	0	0-0	0	0.00
Karl Spooner	2	1	0	3⅓	4	5	5	3	6	0-1	0	13.50
Totals	7	7	2	60	55	26	25	22	39	4-3	1	3.75

NEW YORK YANKEES/Casey Stengel, Manager

Player	pos	G	AB	R	H	2B	3B	HR	RBI	BB	SO	SB	BA	SA	E	FPct
Hank Bauer	rf-ph	6	14	1	6	0	0	0	1	0	1	0	.429	.429	0	1.000
Yogi Berra	c	7	24	5	10	1	0	1	2	3	1	0	.417	.583	0	1.000
Tommy Byrne	p-ph	3	6	0	1	0	0	0	2	0	2	0	.167	.167	0	1.000
Andy Carey	ph	2	2	0	1	0	1	0	1	0	0	0	.500	1.500	0	—
Tom Carroll	pr	2	0	0	0	0	0	0	0	0	0	0	—	—	—	—
Bob Cerv	cf-lf-ph	5	16	1	2	0	0	1	1	0	4	0	.125	.313	0	1.000
Jerry Coleman	ss-pr	3	3	0	0	0	0	0	0	0	1	0	.000	.000	0	1.000
Rip Coleman	p	1	0	0	0	0	0	0	0	0	0	0	—	—	0	—
Joe Collins	1b-rf-ph	5	12	6	2	0	0	2	3	6	4	1	.167	.667	0	1.000
Whitey Ford	p	2	6	1	0	0	0	0	0	1	1	0	.000	.000	0	1.000
Bob Grim	p	3	2	0	0	0	0	0	0	0	0	0	.000	.000	0	1.000
Elston Howard	lf-rf	7	26	3	5	0	0	1	3	1	8	0	.192	.308	0	1.000
Johnny Kucks	p	2	0	0	0	0	0	0	0	0	0	0	—	—	0	1.000
Don Larsen	p	1	2	0	0	0	0	0	0	0	1	0	.000	.000	0	1.000
Mickey Mantle	cf-rf-ph	3	10	1	2	0	0	1	1	0	2	0	.200	.500	0	1.000
Billy Martin	2b	7	25	2	8	1	1	0	4	1	5	0	.320	.440	0	1.000
Gil McDougald	3b	7	27	2	7	0	0	1	1	2	6	0	.259	.370	1	.950
Tom Morgan	p	2	0	0	0	0	0	0	0	0	0	0	—	—	0	—
Irv Noren	cf-lf	5	16	0	1	0	0	0	1	1	1	0	.063	.063	0	1.000
Phil Rizzuto	ss	7	15	2	4	0	0	0	1	5	1	2	.267	.267	0	1.000
Eddie Robinson	ph-1b	4	3	0	2	0	0	0	1	2	1	0	.667	.667	0	1.000
Bill Skowron	1b-ph	5	12	2	4	2	0	1	3	0	1	0	.333	.750	0	.962
Tom Sturdivant	p	2	0	0	0	0	0	0	0	0	0	0	—	—	0	1.000
Bob Turley	p	3	0	0	0	0	0	0	0	0	0	0	.000	.000	0	1.000
Totals		7	222	26	55	4	2	8	25	22	39	3	.248	.392	2	.992

Pitcher	G	GS	CG	IP	H	R	ER	BB	SO	W-L	Sv	ERA
Tommy Byrne	2	2	1	14⅓	8	4	3	8	8	1-1	0	1.88
Rip Coleman	1	0	0	1	5	1	1	0	0	0-0	0	9.00
Whitey Ford	2	2	1	17	13	6	4	8	10	2-0	0	2.12
Bob Grim	3	1	0	8⅔	8	4	4	5	8	0-1	1	4.15
Johnny Kucks	2	0	0	3	4	2	2	1	1	0-0	0	6.00
Don Larsen	1	1	0	4	5	5	5	2	2	0-1	0	11.25
Tom Morgan	2	0	0	3⅔	3	2	2	3	1	0-0	0	4.91
Tom Sturdivant	2	0	0	3	6	3	2	2	0	0-0	0	6.00
Bob Turley	3	1	0	5⅓	7	5	5	4	7	0-1	0	8.44
Totals	7	7	1	60	58	31	28	33	38	3-4	1	4.20

Series MVP: Johnny Podres, Brooklyn Dodgers. **Series Outstanding Pitcher:** Johnny Podres, Brooklyn Dodgers. **Average Length of Game:** 2 hours, 36 minutes. **Total Attendance:** 362,310. **Average Attendance:** 51,759 (35,749 at Ebbets Field; 63,766 at Yankee Stadium).
Umpires: Lee Ballanfant (NL), Frank Dascoli (NL), Augie Donatelli (NL), Red Flaherty (AL), Jim Honochick (AL), Bill Summers (AL). **Winning Player's Share:** $9,768. **Losing Player's Share:** $5,599.

Above: On the day of his 23rd birthday, Johnny Podres delivered a complete-game win in Game 3.

Top inset: Duke Snider and Don Newcombe bathe in some bubbly after their long-awaited championship.

Above: Dodger owner Walter O'Malley hugs his manager after the Series. Two years later O'Malley would move the Dodgers out of Brooklyn.

New York Yankees (4) vs. Brooklyn Dodgers (3)

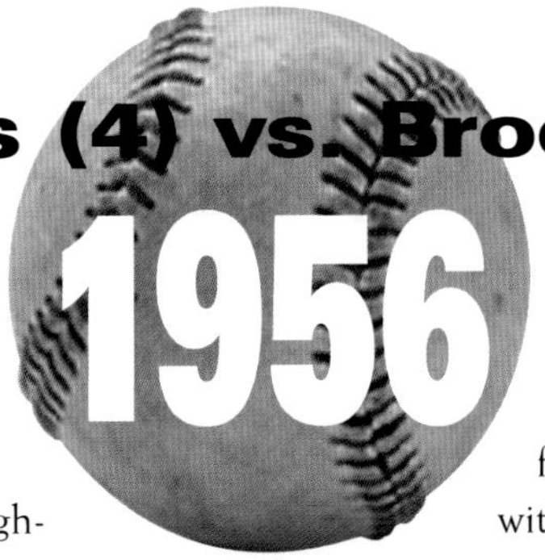

The Dodgers followed up their 1955 Series triumph with another trip to the postseason. They did it by defeating the second-place Milwaukee Braves on the final day of the season for a 1-game margin. Not surprisingly, Brooklyn's opponent in the 1956 Fall Classic was none other than Casey Stengel's Yankees. New York's 97-win season was highlighted by Mickey Mantle's Triple Crown feat of 52 homers, 130 RBI and a .353 average. Stengel sent his 19-game winner, Whitey Ford, to start the 1st game of the Series. Brooklyn manager Walter Alston went with Sal Maglie, a former Giant picked up in mid-season. The 39-year-old Maglie yielded a 2-run homer to Mantle in the 1st, but then settled down to strike out 10 and lead Brooklyn to a 6-3 win. Gil Hodges's 3-run homer broke a 2-2 tie in the 3rd. The scoring came early and often in the 2nd game. The Yankees scored 6 in less than 2 innings off Don Newcombe, the 1956 Cy Young winner, with Yogi Berra's grand slam capping a 5-run 2nd inning. The Dodgers got it all back in the bottom of the inning, however, producing 6 unearned runs. New York's starter lasted only 10 batters into the contest—but the young Don Larsen would get another chance to prove himself later in the Series. Brooklyn went on to score 7 more against the Yankee bull pen to finish with a 13-8 romp in the longest postseason game to date. Ford redeemed his earlier loss with a complete-game victory in Game 3. A 3-run shot by former National League standout Enos Slaughter helped pace the Yanks to the 5-3 win. Tom Sturdivant went the distance with a 6-hitter in Game 4, bringing New York even in the Series after dropping the first 2 games. The next day, Maglie again came through with a strong outing for Brooklyn, retiring the first 11 batters he faced before giving up a solo blast to Mantle in the 4th. New York's starter Don Larsen also retired his first 11 opponents in Game 5, and then struck out Duke Snider for number 12. Jackie Robinson flied out to right to open the 5th inning, and Mantle made a backhanded running catch of Hodges's long drive for the 2nd out. Sandy Amoros hit a deep fly to right that landed just foul before grounding out to end the inning. With 15 batters up and 15 batters down, Larsen went on to retire the next 9 in order, putting him 3 outs away from history: the first World Series no-hitter and perfect game. In a tension-filled 9th inning, Larsen got Carl Furillo to fly to right, grounded Roy Campanella out to second, and then struck out pinch hitter Dale Mitchell on 5 pitches. Don Larsen threw only 97 pitches in the historic game, and allowed 3 balls on a hitter only once (the 2nd batter of the game, Pee

Above: Don Larsen on a fateful October afternoon.

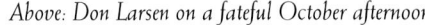

1956 WORLD SERIES COMPOSITE STATISTICS

NEW YORK YANKEES/Casey Stengel, Manager

Player	pos	G	AB	R	H	2B	3B	HR	RBI	BB	SO	SB	BA	SA	E	FPct
Hank Bauer	rf	7	32	3	9	0	0	1	3	0	5	1	.281	.375	1	.938
Yogi Berra	c	7	25	5	9	2	0	3	10	4	1	0	.360	.800	0	1.000
Tommy Byrne	ph-p	2	1	0	0	0	0	0	0	0	0	0	.000	.000	0	–
Andy Carey	3b	7	19	2	3	0	0	0	0	1	6	0	.158	.158	2	.895
Bob Cerv	ph	1	1	0	1	0	0	0	0	0	0	0	1.000	1.000	–	–
Jerry Coleman	2b	2	2	0	0	0	0	0	0	0	0	0	.000	.000	0	1.000
Joe Collins	1b-ph	6	21	2	5	2	0	0	2	2	3	0	.238	.333	2	.943
Whitey Ford	p	2	4	0	0	0	0	0	0	0	3	0	.000	.000	0	1.000
Elston Howard	lf	1	5	1	2	1	0	1	1	0	0	0	.400	1.200	0	1.000
Johnny Kucks	p	3	3	0	0	0	0	0	0	0	1	0	.000	.000	0	1.000
Don Larsen	p	2	3	1	1	0	0	0	1	0	1	0	.333	.333	0	1.000
Mickey Mantle	cf	7	24	6	6	1	0	3	4	6	5	1	.250	.667	0	1.000
Billy Martin	2b-3b	7	27	5	8	0	0	2	3	1	6	0	.296	.519	0	1.000
Mickey McDermott	p	1	1	0	1	0	0	0	0	0	0	0	1.000	1.000	0	–
Gil McDougald	ss	7	21	0	3	0	0	0	1	3	6	0	.143	.143	0	1.000
Tom Morgan	p	2	1	1	1	0	0	0	0	0	0	0	1.000	1.000	0	–
Norm Siebern	ph	1	1	0	0	0	0	0	0	0	0	0	.000	.000	–	–
Bill Skowron	1b-ph	3	10	1	1	0	0	1	4	0	3	0	.100	.400	1	.960
Enos Slaughter	lf	6	20	6	7	0	0	1	4	4	0	0	.350	.500	0	1.000
Tom Sturdivant	p	2	3	0	1	0	0	0	0	0	1	0	.333	.333	0	1.000
Bob Turley	p	3	4	0	0	0	0	0	0	0	1	0	.000	.000	0	1.000
George Wilson	ph	1	1	0	0	0	0	0	0	0	1	0	.000	.000	–	–
Totals		**7**	**229**	**33**	**58**	**6**	**0**	**12**	**33**	**21**	**43**	**2**	**.253**	**.437**	**6**	**.977**

Pitcher	G	GS	CG	IP	H	R	ER	BB	SO	W-L	Sv	ERA
Tommy Byrne	1	0	0	$\frac{1}{3}$	1	1	0	0	1	0-0	0	0.00
Whitey Ford	2	2	1	12	14	8	7	2	8	1-1	0	5.25
Johnny Kucks	3	1	1	11	6	2	1	3	2	1-0	0	0.82
Don Larsen	2	2	1	$10\frac{2}{3}$	1	4	0	4	7	1-0	0	0.00
Mickey McDermott	1	0	0	3	2	2	1	3	3	0-0	0	3.00
Tom Morgan	2	0	0	4	6	4	4	4	3	0-1	0	9.00
Tom Sturdivant	2	1	1	$9\frac{2}{3}$	8	3	3	8	9	1-0	0	2.79
Bob Turley	3	1	1	11	4	1	1	8	14	0-1	0	0.82
Totals	**7**	**7**	**5**	**$61\frac{2}{3}$**	**42**	**25**	**17**	**32**	**47**	**4-3**	**0**	**2.48**

BROOKLYN DODGERS/Walter Alston, Manager

Player	pos	G	AB	R	H	2B	3B	HR	RBI	BB	SO	SB	BA	SA	E	FPct
Sandy Amoros	lf	6	19	1	1	0	0	0	1	2	4	0	.053	.053	0	1.000
Don Bessent	p	2	2	0	1	0	0	0	1	1	1	0	.500	.500	0	–
Roy Campanella	c	7	22	2	4	1	0	0	3	3	7	0	.182	.227	0	1.000
Gino Cimoli	lf	1	0	0	0	0	0	0	0	0	0	0	–	–	0	1.000
Roger Craig	p	2	2	0	1	0	0	0	0	0	0	0	.500	.500	0	1.000
Don Drysdale	p	1	0	0	0	0	0	0	0	0	0	0	–	–	0	–
Carl Erskine	p	2	1	0	0	0	0	0	0	0	1	0	.000	.000	0	1.000
Carl Furillo	rf	7	25	2	6	2	0	0	1	2	3	0	.240	.320	0	1.000
Jim Gilliam	2b-lf	7	24	2	2	0	0	0	2	7	3	1	.083	.083	0	1.000
Gil Hodges	1b	7	23	5	7	2	0	1	8	4	4	0	.304	.522	0	1.000
Randy Jackson	ph	3	3	0	0	0	0	0	0	0	2	0	.000	.000	–	–
Clem Labine	p	2	4	0	1	1	0	0	0	0	2	0	.250	.500	0	1.000
Sal Maglie	p	2	5	0	0	0	0	0	0	0	2	0	.000	.000	0	1.000
Dale Mitchell	ph	4	4	0	0	0	0	0	0	0	1	0	.000	.000	–	–
Charlie Neal	2b	1	4	0	0	0	0	0	0	0	1	0	.000	.000	1	.800
Don Newcombe	p	2	1	0	0	0	0	0	0	0	0	0	.000	.000	0	1.000
Pee Wee Reese	ss	7	27	3	6	0	1	0	2	2	6	0	.222	.296	1	.972
Jackie Robinson	3b	7	24	5	6	1	0	1	2	5	2	0	.250	.417	0	1.000
Ed Roebuck	p	3	0	0	0	0	0	0	0	0	0	0	–	–	0	–
Duke Snider	cf	7	23	5	7	1	0	1	4	6	8	0	.304	.478	0	1.000
Rube Walker	ph	2	2	0	0	0	0	0	0	0	0	0	.000	.000	–	–
Totals		**7**	**215**	**25**	**42**	**8**	**1**	**3**	**24**	**32**	**47**	**1**	**.195**	**.284**	**2**	**.992**

Pitcher	G	GS	CG	IP	H	R	ER	BB	SO	W-L	Sv	ERA
Don Bessent	2	0	0	10	8	2	2	3	5	1-0	0	1.80
Roger Craig	2	1	0	6	10	8	8	3	4	0-1	0	12.00
Don Drysdale	1	0	0	2	2	2	2	1	1	0-0	0	9.00
Carl Erskine	2	1	0	5	4	3	3	2	2	0-1	0	5.40
Clem Labine	2	1	1	12	8	1	0	3	7	1-0	0	0.00
Sal Maglie	2	2	2	17	14	5	5	6	15	1-1	0	2.65
Don Newcombe	2	2	0	$4\frac{2}{3}$	11	11	11	3	4	0-1	0	21.21
Ed Roebuck	3	0	0	$4\frac{1}{3}$	1	1	1	0	5	0-0	0	2.08
Totals	**7**	**7**	**3**	**61**	**58**	**33**	**32**	**21**	**43**	**3-4**	**0**	**4.72**

Series MVP: Don Larsen, Yankees. **Series Outstanding Pitcher:** Don Larsen, Yankees. **Average Length of Game:** 2 hours, 34 minutes. **Total Attendance:** 345,903. **Average Attendance:** 49,415 (69,400 at Yankee Stadium; 34,426 at Ebbets Field). **Umpires:** Dusty Boggess (NL), Tom Gorman (NL), Larry Napp (AL), Babe Pinelli (NL), Ed Runge (AL), Hank Soar (AL). **Winning Player's Share:** $8,715. **Losing Player's Share:** $6,934.

Don Larsen's perfect game was his first World Series win.

Below: Don Larsen delivers a pitch in his World Series perfect game.

Background: Perfection! Yogi Berra leaps into the arms of Don Larsen after Larsen completed the only no-run, no-hit, no-walk, no-error game in World Series history.

Below: Larsen rushes to the dugout after making history in Game 5.

Left: Defense again comes through for Larsen. Shortstop Gil McDougald prevents an infield hit by fielding Jackie Robinson's grounder after it deflected off third baseman Andy Carey's glove.

Wee Reese). New York got another tremendous performance on the mound in Game 6 as Bob Turley struck out 11 and allowed only 4 hits, but Brooklyn's Clem Labine, normally a reliever, pitched a 10-inning shutout to send it to a 7th game. Jim Gilliam scored the game-winning run when Robinson drove him in with a 2-out single in the 10th. Yankee pitching continued to baffle the Dodger hitters in the finale. Johnny Kucks gave up only 3 singles in the Game 7 shutout, and New York scored all 9 of their runs on home runs—Yogi Berra's pair of 2-run shots, Elston Howard's solo blast, and Bill Skowron's grand slam (the only Game 7 slam in history). The game marked the Yankees' record-tying 5th complete game, the only time 5 different pitchers have had complete games for one team. Don Larsen's unprecedented and unmatched performance in Game 5 was the climax of championship number 17, as the Yankees came out on top in the city's last Subway Series of the century.

Yogi Berra's grand slam in Game 2 was the first World Series slam by a player in a losing effort.

Above: A smiling Duke Snider stroked a three-run homer in the second inning of Game 2 to tie the game at 6. The Dodgers went on to win in a 13-8 slugfest.

Left: Thirty-nine-year-old former Giant Sal Maglie won the opener with a 10-strikeout day, but was also the no-luck opponent in Don Larsen's Game 5 masterpiece.

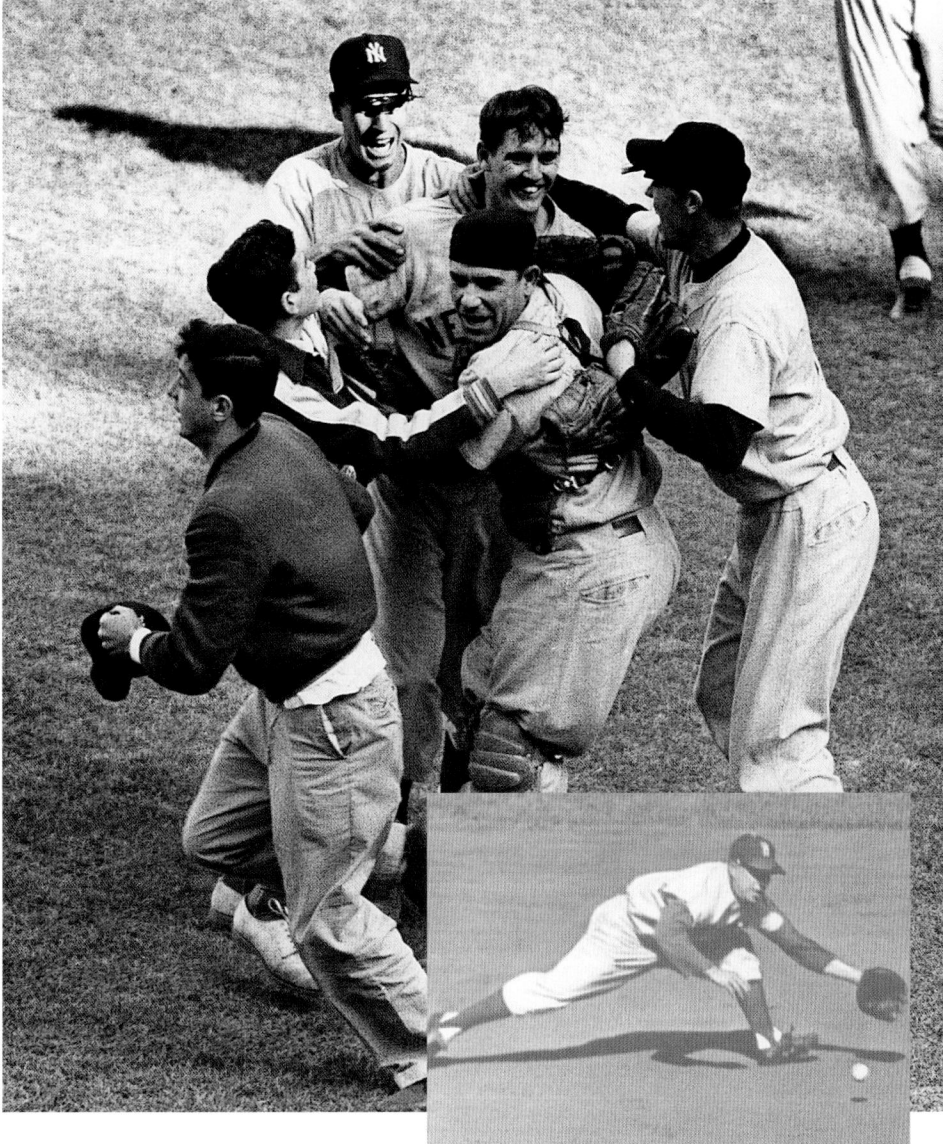

Above: A hatless Johnny Kucks is mobbed by teammates after winning the clinching game of the Series. A lucky fan is running off with Kucks's cap.

Right: Pee Wee Reese makes a diving stop of Joe Collins's grounder in the third inning of Game 6.

Pee Wee Reese was the only player to appear in all of the Subway Series matchups between the Yankees and Dodgers from 1941 to 1956—44 games in all.

Game 1 Wednesday, October 3 at Ebbets Field, Brooklyn

	1	2	3	4	5	6	7	8	9	R	H	E
New York Yankees	2	0	0	1	0	0	0	0	0	3	9	1
Brooklyn Dodgers	0	2	3	1	0	0	0	0	x	6	9	0

Pitchers NY Whitey Ford (L, 0-1), IP 3, H 6, R 5, ER 5, BB 0, SO 1; Johnny Kucks, IP 2, H 2, R 1, ER 1, BB 0, SO 1; Tom Morgan, IP 2, H 1, R 0, ER 0, BB 2, SO 0; Bob Turley, IP 1, H 0, R 0, ER 0, BB 0, SO 2
Bro Sal Maglie (W, 1-0), IP 9, H 9, R 3, ER 3, BB 4, SO 10

Top Performers at the Plate
NY Mickey Mantle, 1 for 3, 1 R, 2 RBI, 2 BB; Enos Slaughter, 3 for 5, 1 R
Bro Gil Hodges, 2 for 4, 2 R, 3 RBI; Pee Wee Reese, 2 for 4, 1 R

2B-Bro/Campanella, Furillo. **HR**-NY/Mantle, Martin; Bro/Hodges, Robinson. **SB**-Bro/Gilliam.
Time 2:32. **Attendance** 34,479.

Game 2 Friday, October 5 at Ebbets Field, Brooklyn

	1	2	3	4	5	6	7	8	9	R	H	E
New York Yankees	1	5	0	1	0	0	0	0	1	8	12	2
Brooklyn Dodgers	0	6	1	2	2	0	0	2	x	13	12	0

Pitchers NY Don Larsen, IP 1⅔, H 1, R 4, ER 0, BB 4, SO 0; Johnny Kucks, IP 0, H 1, R 1, ER 0, BB 0, SO 0; Tommy Byrne, IP ⅓, H 1, R 1, ER 0, BB 0, SO 1; Tom Sturdivant, IP ⅔, H 2, R 1, ER 1, BB 2, SO 2; Bob Turley, IP ⅓, H 0, R 0, ER 0, BB 0, SO 1; Mickey McDermott, IP 3, H 2, R 2, ER 1, BB 3, SO 3
Bro Don Newcombe, IP 1⅔, H 6, R 6, ER 6, BB 2, SO 0; Ed Roebuck, IP ⅓, H 0, R 0, ER 0, BB 0, SO 0; Don Bessent (W, 1-0), IP 7, H 6, R 2, ER 2, BB 2, SO 4

Top Performers at the Plate
NY Yogi Berra, 2 for 4, 1 R, 4 RBI, 1 BB; Enos Slaughter, 2 for 4, 3 R, 1 RBI, 1 SF
Bro Gil Hodges, 3 for 3, 2 R, 4 RBI, 2 BB, 2 2B; Duke Snider, 2 for 4, 3 R, 3 RBI, 2 BB

2B-Bro/Hodges 2. **HR**-NY/Berra; Bro/Snider. **Time** 3:26. **Attendance** 36,217.

Game 3 Saturday, October 6 at Yankee Stadium, New York

	1	2	3	4	5	6	7	8	9	R	H	E
Brooklyn Dodgers	0	1	0	0	0	1	1	0	0	3	8	1
New York Yankees	0	1	0	0	0	3	0	1	x	5	8	1

Pitchers Bro Roger Craig (L, 0-1), IP 6, H 7, R 4, ER 4, BB 1, SO 4; Clem Labine, IP 2, H 1, R 1, ER 0, BB 1, SO 2
NY Whitey Ford (W, 1-1), IP 9, H 8, R 3, ER 2, BB 2, SO 7

Top Performers at the Plate
Bro Roy Campanella, 1 for 3, 1 RBI, 1 SF; Pee Wee Reese, 2 for 4, 1 R
NY Yogi Berra, 2 for 4, 1 R, 1 RBI; Enos Slaughter, 2 for 3, 1 R, 3 RBI, 1 BB

2B-Bro/Furillo; NY/Berra. **3B**-Bro/Reese. **HR**-NY/Martin, Slaughter. **Time** 2:17. **Attendance** 73,977.

Game 4 Sunday, October 7 at Yankee Stadium, New York

	1	2	3	4	5	6	7	8	9	R	H	E
Brooklyn Dodgers	0	0	0	1	0	0	0	0	1	2	6	0
New York Yankees	1	0	0	2	0	1	2	0	x	6	7	2

Pitchers Bro Carl Erskine (L, 0-1), IP 4, H 4, R 3, ER 3, BB 2, SO 2; Ed Roebuck, IP 2, H 1, R 1, ER 1, BB 0, SO 2; Don Drysdale, IP 2, H 2, R 2, ER 2, BB 1, SO 1
NY Tom Sturdivant (W, 1-0), IP 9, H 6, R 2, ER 2, BB 6, SO 7

Top Performers at the Plate
Bro Roy Campanella, 2 for 2, 1 RBI, 2 BB; Jackie Robinson, 1 for 3, 1 R, 1 BB
NY Joe Collins, 1 for 3, 1 R, 1 BB; Mickey Mantle, 1 for 3, 2 R, 1 RBI, 1 BB

2B-Bro/Robinson, Snider; NY/Collins. **HR**-NY/Bauer, Mantle. **SB**-NY/Mantle. **Time** 2:43.
Attendance 69,705.

Game 5 Monday, October 8 at Yankee Stadium, New York

	1	2	3	4	5	6	7	8	9	R	H	E
Brooklyn Dodgers	0	0	0	0	0	0	0	0	0	0	0	0
New York Yankees	0	0	0	1	0	1	0	0	x	2	5	0

Pitchers Bro Sal Maglie (L, 1-1), IP 8, H 5, R 2, ER 2, BB 2, SO 5
NY Don Larsen (W, 1-0), IP 9, H 0, R 0, ER 0, BB 0, SO 7

Top Performers at the Plate
NY Mickey Mantle, 1 for 3, 1 R, 1 RBI

HR-NY/Mantle. **Time** 2:06. **Attendance** 64,519.

Game 6 Tuesday, October 9 at Ebbets Field, Brooklyn

	1	2	3	4	5	6	7	8	9	10	R	H	E
New York Yankees	0	0	0	0	0	0	0	0	0	0	0	7	0
Brooklyn Dodgers	0	0	0	0	0	0	0	0	0	1	1	4	0

Pitchers NY Bob Turley (L, 0-1), IP 9⅔, H 4, R 1, ER 1, BB 8, SO 11
Bro Clem Labine (W, 1-0), IP 10, H 7, R 0, ER 0, BB 2, SO 5

Top Performers at the Plate
NY Hank Bauer, 2 for 5; Yogi Berra, 2 for 4
Bro Jim Gilliam, 1 for 3, 1 R, 2 BB; Jackie Robinson, 1 for 4, 1 RBI, 1 BB

2B-NY/Berra, Collins; Bro/Labine. **Time** 2:37. **Attendance** 33,224.

Game 7 Wednesday, October 10 at Ebbets Field, Brooklyn

	1	2	3	4	5	6	7	8	9	R	H	E
New York Yankees	2	0	2	1	0	0	4	0	0	9	10	0
Brooklyn Dodgers	0	0	0	0	0	0	0	0	0	0	3	1

Pitchers NY Johnny Kucks (W, 1-0), IP 9, H 3, R 0, ER 0, BB 3, SO 1
Bro Don Newcombe (L, 0-1), IP 3, H 5, R 5, ER 5, BB 1, SO 4; Don Bessent, IP 3, H 2, R 0, ER 0, BB 1, SO 1; Roger Craig, IP 0, H 3, R 4, ER 4, BB 2, SO 0; Ed Roebuck, IP 2, H 0, R 0, ER 0, BB 0, SO 3; Carl Erskine, IP 1, H 0, R 0, ER 0, BB 0, SO 0

Top Performers at the Plate
NY Yogi Berra, 2 for 3, 3 R, 4 RBI, 2 BB, 2 HR; Bill Skowron, 1 for 5, 1 R, 4 RBI
Bro Duke Snider, 2 for 4

2B-NY/Howard, Mantle. **HR**-NY/Berra 2, Howard, Skowron. **SB**-NY/Bauer. **Time** 2:19.
Attendance 33,782.

Milwaukee Braves (4) vs. New York Yankees (3)

After relocating from Boston to Milwaukee in 1953, the Braves endured three second-place finishes before finally getting over the hump and supplanting the Dodgers as National League champs in 1957. The New York Yankees once again finished ahead of the pack in the American League. Pitching was a strength on both squads, and two of the best faced off in the opener. Lefties Whitey Ford and Warren Spahn pitched scoreless ball through 4 innings until a Hank Bauer double in the 5th put New York on the board. They added two more to Milwaukee's one to claim Game 1. Lew Burdette brought the Braves even in Game 2 with a 4-2 win. Wes Covington broke a 2-2 tie in the game with his 4th-inning single. Milwaukee fans got their first firsthand glimpse of World Series play in Game 3 but went home disappointed as the Yanks cruised in a 12-3 rout. New York's Milwaukee-born rookie Tony Kubek provided two home runs and four RBI in the game. Two home runs in the 4th inning of Game 4—including a three-run shot by a 23-year-old Hank Aaron—gave the Braves a 4-1 lead before Elston Howard tied it in the top of the 9th with a three-run drive over the left-field wall. Spahn fell behind in the 10th on Bauer's RBI triple, but the Braves came back with three in the bottom of the inning for the win. The inning was not without controversy, however. The first pitch to pinch hitter Nippy Jones was practically in the dirt, and umpire Augie Donatelli called it ball one. Jones insisted that it hit

1957

him in the foot, and he came forth with evidence by pointing out a smudge of shoe polish on the ball. Jones was awarded first base. Felix Mantilla came in to pinch-run, and Johnny Logan drove him in with a double. Eddie Mathews then ended the tie and the game with a two-run blast. Ford and Burdette orchestrated a real pitcher's duel in Game 5. The matching shutouts came to an end in Milwaukee's half of the 6th on consecutive singles by Mathews, Aaron and Joe Adcock. All five runs in Game 6 came on the long ball, and New York secured the 3-2 win on Bauer's tiebreaker in the 7th. With only two days' rest, Burdette was back on the hill for Milwaukee in the all-important seventh game. Don Larsen, the 1956 hero, was going for the Yanks. This time, Larsen didn't make it past the 3rd inning; the Braves brought four runners across the plate against Larsen and reliever Bobby Shantz. The early lead held as Burdette came through with his second shutout and third complete-game victory of the Series. Usually known for his bat, Eddie Mathews made a fantastic glove play on Bill Skowron's grounder with two out and the bases loaded to end the game—treating the city of Milwaukee to its first baseball championship.

Above: The Braves celebrate their first championship in the city of Milwaukee after downing the Yankees in seven games.

1957 WORLD SERIES COMPOSITE STATISTICS

MILWAUKEE BRAVES/Fred Haney, Manager

Player	pos	G	AB	R	H	2B	3B	HR	RBI	BB	SO	SB	BA	SA	E	FPct
Hank Aaron	cf	7	28	5	11	0	1	3	7	1	6	0	.393	.786	0	1.000
Joe Adcock	1b-ph	5	15	1	3	0	0	2	0	2	0	0	.200	.200	1	.976
Bob Buhl	p	2	1	0	0	0	0	0	0	0	1	0	.000	.000	1	.667
Lew Burdette	p	3	8	0	0	0	0	0	0	1	2	0	.000	.000	0	1.000
Gene Conley	p	1	0	0	0	0	0	0	0	0	0	0	—	—	0	1.000
Wes Covington	lf	7	24	1	5	1	0	0	1	2	6	1	.208	.250	0	1.000
Del Crandall	c	6	19	1	4	0	0	1	1	1	1	0	.211	.368	0	1.000
John DeMerit	pr	1	0	0	0	0	0	0	0	0	0	0	—	—	0	—
Bob Hazle	rf	4	13	2	2	0	0	0	0	1	2	0	.154	.154	0	1.000
Ernie Johnson	p	3	1	0	0	0	0	0	0	0	1	0	.000	.000	0	1.000
Nippy Jones	ph	3	2	0	0	0	0	0	0	0	0	0	.000	.000	—	—
Johnny Logan	ss	7	27	5	5	1	0	1	2	3	6	0	.185	.333	0	1.000
Felix Mantilla	pr-2b	4	10	1	0	0	0	0	0	0	0	0	.000	.000	0	1.000
Eddie Mathews	3b	7	22	4	5	3	0	1	4	8	5	0	.227	.500	1	.964
Don McMahon	p	3	0	0	0	0	0	0	0	0	0	0	—	—	0	1.000
Andy Pafko	rf-ph	6	14	1	3	0	0	0	0	1	0	0	.214	.214	0	1.000
Juan Pizarro	p	1	1	0	0	0	0	0	0	0	0	0	.000	.000	0	—
Del Rice	c	2	6	0	1	0	0	0	0	1	2	0	.167	.167	0	1.000
Carl Sawatski	ph	2	2	0	0	0	0	0	0	0	0	0	.000	.000	—	—
Red Schoendienst	2b	5	18	0	5	1	0	0	2	0	1	0	.278	.333	0	1.000
Warren Spahn	p	2	4	0	0	0	0	0	0	1	2	0	.000	.000	0	1.000
Frank Torre	1b-ph	7	10	2	3	0	0	2	3	2	0	0	.300	.900	0	1.000
Bob Trowbridge	p	1	0	0	0	0	0	0	0	0	0	0	—	—	0	—
Totals		**7**	**225**	**23**	**47**	**6**	**1**	**8**	**22**	**22**	**40**	**1**	**.209**	**.351**	**3**	**.989**

Pitcher	G	GS	CG	IP	H	R	ER	BB	SO	W-L	Sv	ERA
Bob Buhl	2	2	0	3⅓	6	5	4	6	4	0-1	0	10.80
Lew Burdette	3	3	3	27	21	2	2	4	13	3-0	0	0.67
Gene Conley	1	0	0	1⅔	2	2	2	1	0	0-0	0	10.80
Ernie Johnson	3	0	0	7	2	1	1	1	8	0-1	0	1.29
Don McMahon	3	0	0	5	3	0	0	3	5	0-0	0	0.00
Juan Pizarro	1	0	0	1⅔	3	2	2	2	4	0-0	0	10.80
Warren Spahn	2	2	1	15⅓	18	8	8	2	2	1-1	0	4.70
Bob Trowbridge	1	0	0	1	2	5	5	3	1	0-0	0	45.00
Totals	**7**	**7**	**4**	**62**	**57**	**25**	**24**	**22**	**34**	**4-3**	**0**	**3.48**

NEW YORK YANKEES/Casey Stengel, Manager

Player	pos	G	AB	R	H	2B	3B	HR	RBI	BB	SO	SB	BA	SA	E	FPct
Hank Bauer	rf	7	31	3	8	2	1	2	6	1	6	0	.258	.581	0	1.000
Yogi Berra	c	7	25	5	8	1	0	1	2	4	0	0	.320	.480	1	.979
Tommy Byrne	p	2	2	0	1	0	0	0	0	1	0	0	.500	.500	0	—
Andy Carey	3b	2	7	0	2	1	0	0	1	1	0	0	.286	.429	0	1.000
Jerry Coleman	2b	7	22	2	8	2	0	0	2	3	1	0	.364	.455	1	1.000
Joe Collins	1b-ph	6	5	0	0	0	0	0	0	0	3	0	.000	.000	0	1.000
Art Ditmar	p	2	1	0	0	0	0	0	0	0	0	0	.000	.000	0	—
Whitey Ford	p	2	5	0	0	0	0	0	0	0	1	0	.000	.000	0	1.000
Bob Grim	p	2	0	0	0	0	0	0	0	0	0	0	—	—	0	—
Elston Howard	1b-ph	6	11	2	3	0	0	1	3	1	3	0	.273	.545	1	.957
Tony Kubek	lf-3b-cf	7	28	4	8	0	0	2	4	0	4	0	.286	.500	2	.917
Johnny Kucks	p	1	0	0	0	0	0	0	0	0	0	0	—	—	0	—
Don Larsen	p	2	2	1	0	0	0	0	0	0	2	1	.000	.000	0	1.000
Jerry Lumpe	ph-3b	6	14	0	4	0	0	0	2	1	1	0	.286	.286	0	1.000
Mickey Mantle	cf-pr	6	19	3	5	0	0	1	2	3	1	0	.263	.421	1	.889
Gil McDougald	ss	7	24	3	6	0	0	0	2	3	3	1	.250	.250	1	.974
Bobby Richardson	pr-2b	2	0	0	0	0	0	0	0	0	0	0	—	—	0	1.000
Bobby Shantz	p	3	1	0	0	0	0	0	0	0	0	0	.000	.000	0	1.000
Harry Simpson	1b-ph	5	12	0	1	0	0	0	1	0	4	0	.083	.083	0	1.000
Bill Skowron	1b-ph	2	4	0	0	0	0	0	0	0	0	0	.000	.000	0	1.000
Enos Slaughter	lf	5	12	2	3	1	0	0	0	3	2	0	.250	.333	0	1.000
Tom Sturdivant	p	2	1	0	0	0	0	0	0	0	0	0	.000	.000	0	1.000
Bob Turley	p	3	4	0	0	0	0	0	0	0	2	0	.000	.000	0	1.000
Totals		**7**	**230**	**25**	**57**	**7**	**1**	**7**	**25**	**22**	**34**	**1**	**.248**	**.378**	**6**	**.977**

Pitcher	G	GS	CG	IP	H	R	ER	BB	SO	W-L	Sv	ERA
Tommy Byrne	2	0	0	3⅓	1	2	2	1	1	0-0	0	5.40
Art Ditmar	2	1	0	6	2	0	0	2	0	0-0	0	0.00
Whitey Ford	2	2	1	16	11	2	2	5	7	1-1	0	1.13
Bob Grim	2	0	0	2⅓	3	2	2	0	2	0-1	0	7.71
Johnny Kucks	1	0	0	⅔	1	0	0	1	1	0-0	0	0.00
Don Larsen	2	1	0	9⅔	8	5	4	5	6	1-1	0	3.72
Bobby Shantz	3	1	0	6⅔	8	5	3	2	7	0-1	0	4.05
Tom Sturdivant	2	1	0	6	6	4	4	1	2	0-0	0	6.00
Bob Turley	3	2	1	11⅔	7	3	3	6	12	1-0	0	2.31
Totals	**7**	**7**	**2**	**62⅓**	**47**	**23**	**20**	**22**	**40**	**3-4**	**0**	**2.89**

Series MVP: Lew Burdette, Milwaukee Braves. **Series Outstanding Pitcher:** Lew Burdette, Milwaukee Braves. **Average Length of Game:** 2 hours, 27 minutes. **Total Attendance:** 394,712. **Average Attendance:** 56,387 (45,806 at Milwaukee County Stadium; 64,323 at Yankee Stadium). **Umpires:** Nestor Chylak (AL), Jocko Conlan (NL), Augie Donatelli (NL), Bill McKinley (AL), Joe Paparella (AL), Frank Secory (NL). **Winning Player's Share:** $8,924. **Losing Player's Share:** $5,606.

Right: *Lew Burdette pitched three complete-game wins in 1957, allowing only 2 runs in 27 innings and striking out 14.*

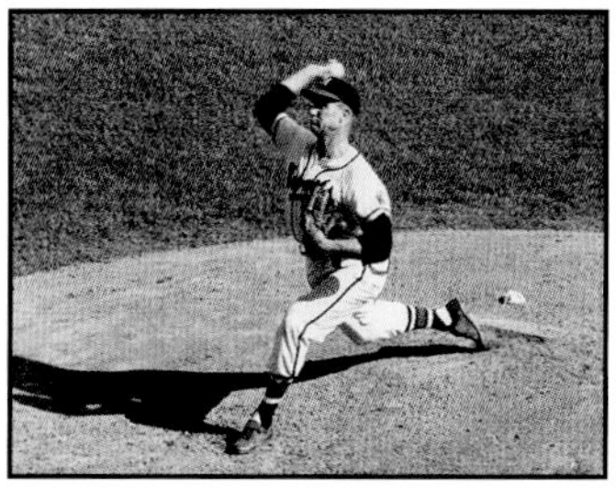

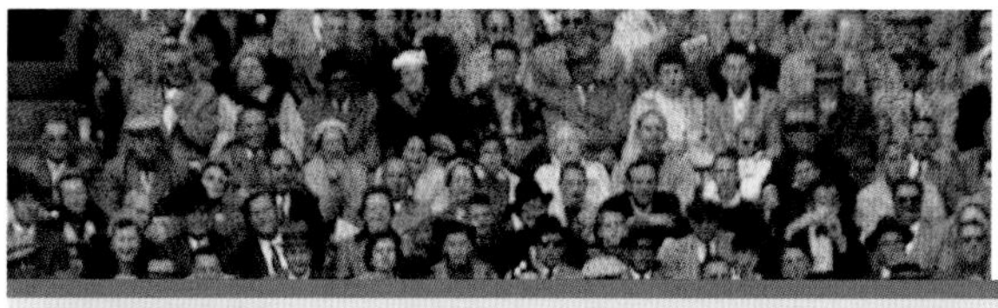

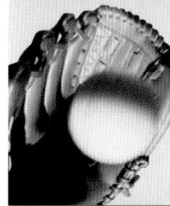

Braves pitcher Gene Conley won a World Series ring with Milwaukee in 1957, and in 1959, he won a championship with another team: the Boston Celtics of the National Basketball Association.

Left: The young Henry Aaron batted .393 and drove in 7 runs in 1957.

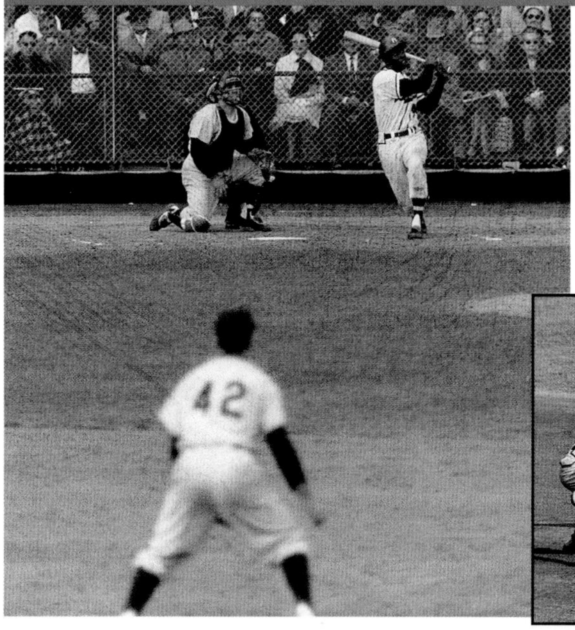

Below: New York's Hank Bauer slides safely in the first inning of Game 7. Caught in a rundown, Bauer retreated to second, where he was met by Enos Slaughter, whose double, which started all the action, was then ruled an out.

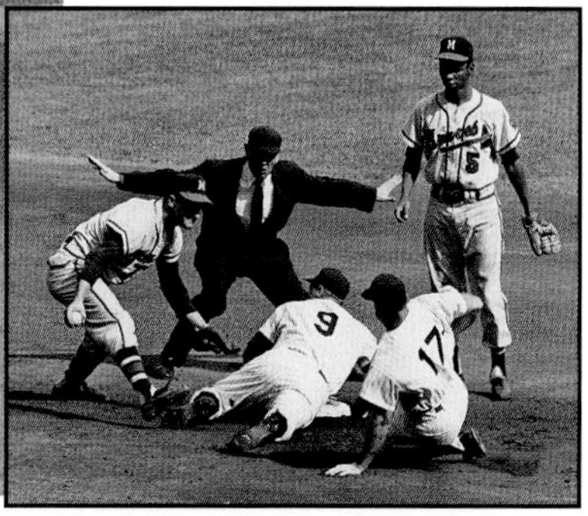

For the second consecutive year, Hank Bauer hit safely in all 7 games of the World Series, extending his postseason hitting streak to 14 games.

Right: After being shown shoe polish marks on the ball, umpire Augie Donatelli is convinced that Milwaukee's Nippy Jones was in fact hit by the pitch.

The 1957 Series was the third in a row to feature the leagues' two MVPs: Mickey Mantle claimed his second straight honor in 1957, and Hank Aaron earned his first with a 42 home run, 132 RBI, .322 batting season.

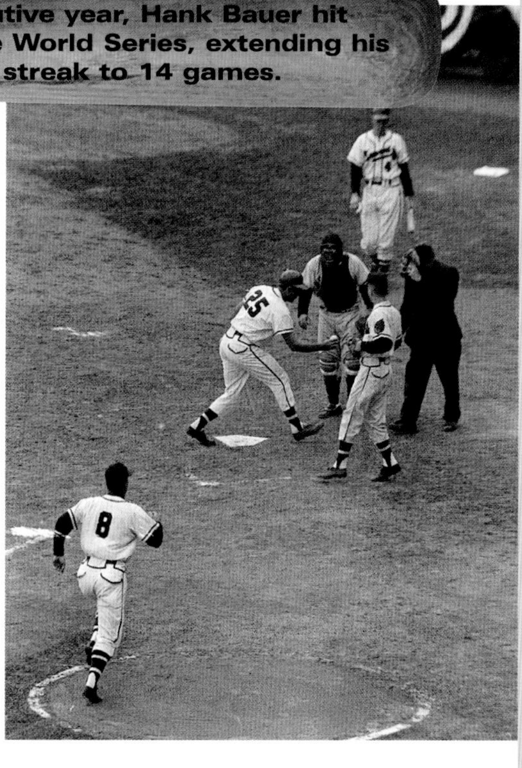

Game 1 Wednesday, October 2 at Yankee Stadium, New York

	1	2	3	4	5	6	7	8	9	R	H	E
Milwaukee Braves	0	0	0	0	0	0	1	0	0	1	5	0
New York Yankees	0	0	0	0	1	2	0	0	x	3	9	1

Pitchers Mil **Warren Spahn** (L, 0-1), IP 5⅓, H 7, R 3, ER 3, BB 1, SO 0; **Ernie Johnson**, IP ⅔, H 0, R 0, ER 0, BB 0, SO 1; **Don McMahon**, IP 2, H 2, R 0, ER 0, BB 1, SO 3
NY **Whitey Ford** (W, 1-0), IP 9, H 5, R 1, ER 1, BB 4, SO 5

Top Performers at the Plate
Mil **Wes Covington**, 2 for 4, 1 R
NY **Andy Carey**, 1 for 3, 1 RBI, 1 BB; **Jerry Coleman**, 2 for 3, 1 R, 1 RBI, 1 SH

2B-Mil/Covington; NY/Bauer, Coleman. **Time** 2:10. **Attendance** 69,476.

Game 2 Thursday, October 3 at Yankee Stadium, New York

	1	2	3	4	5	6	7	8	9	R	H	E
Milwaukee Braves	0	1	1	2	0	0	0	0	0	4	8	0
New York Yankees	0	1	1	0	0	0	0	0	0	2	7	2

Pitchers Mil **Lew Burdette** (W, 1-0), IP 9, H 7, R 2, ER 2, BB 3, SO 5
NY **Bobby Shantz** (L, 0-1), IP 3, H 6, R 4, ER 3, BB 1, SO 3; **Art Ditmar**, IP 4, H 1, R 0, ER 0, BB 0, SO 1; **Bob Grim**, IP 2, H 1, R 0, ER 0, BB 0, SO 2

Top Performers at the Plate
Mil **Joe Adcock**, 2 for 4, 1 R, 1 RBI; **Wes Covington**, 2 for 4, 1 RBI
NY **Tony Kubek**, 2 for 4; **Enos Slaughter**, 1 for 3, 1 R, 1 BB

2B-NY/Slaughter. **3B**-Mil/Aaron. **HR**-Mil/Logan; NY/Bauer. **Time** 2:26. **Attendance** 65,202.

Game 3 Saturday, October 5 at County Stadium, Milwaukee

	1	2	3	4	5	6	7	8	9	R	H	E
New York Yankees	3	0	2	2	0	0	5	0	0	12	9	0
Milwaukee Braves	0	1	0	0	2	0	0	0	0	3	8	1

Pitchers NY **Bob Turley**, IP 1⅔, H 3, R 1, ER 1, BB 4, SO 2; **Don Larsen** (W, 1-0), IP 7⅓, H 5, R 2, ER 2, BB 4, SO 4
Mil **Bob Buhl** (L, 0-1), IP ⅔, H 2, R 3, ER 2, BB 2, SO 0; **Juan Pizarro**, IP 1⅔, H 3, R 2, ER 2, BB 2, SO 1; **Gene Conley**, IP 1⅔, H 2, R 2, ER 2, BB 1, SO 0; **Ernie Johnson**, IP 2, H 0, R 0, ER 0, BB 1, SO 2; **Bob Trowbridge**, IP 1, H 2, R 5, ER 5, BB 3, SO 1; **Don McMahon**, IP 2, H 0, R 0, ER 0, BB 2, SO 2

Top Performers at the Plate
NY **Tony Kubek**, 3 for 5, 3 R, 4 RBI, 2 HR; **Mickey Mantle**, 2 for 3, 2 R, 2 RBI, 2 BB
Mil **Hank Aaron**, 2 for 5, 1 R, 2 RBI; **Red Schoendienst**, 3 for 5, 1 RBI

HR-NY/Kubek 2, Mantle; Mil/Aaron. **SB**-NY/McDougald. **Time** 3:18. **Attendance** 45,804.

Game 4 Sunday, October 6 at County Stadium, Milwaukee

	1	2	3	4	5	6	7	8	9	10	R	H	E
New York Yankees	1	0	0	0	0	0	0	0	3	1	5	11	0
Milwaukee Braves	0	0	0	4	0	0	0	0	0	3	7	7	0

Pitchers NY **Tom Sturdivant**, IP 4, H 4, R 4, ER 4, BB 1, SO 1; **Bobby Shantz**, IP 3, H 0, R 0, ER 0, BB 1, SO 4; **Johnny Kucks**, IP ⅔, H 1, R 0, ER 0, BB 1, SO 1; **Tommy Byrne**, IP 1⅓, H 0, R 1, ER 1, BB 0, SO 1; **Bob Grim** (L, 0-1), IP ⅓, H 2, R 2, ER 2, BB 0, SO 0
Mil **Warren Spahn** (W, 1-1), IP 10, H 11, R 5, ER 5, BB 1, SO 2

Top Performers at the Plate
NY **Yogi Berra**, 2 for 3, 1 R, 1 BB; **Gil McDougald**, 2 for 4, 1 R, 1 RBI
Mil **Hank Aaron**, 2 for 3, 1 R, 3 RBI, 1 BB; **Eddie Mathews**, 2 for 4, 2 R, 2 RBI, 1 BB

2B-NY/Carey; Mil/Logan, Mathews, Schoendienst. **3B**-NY/Bauer. **HR**-NY/Howard; Mil/Aaron, Mathews, Torre. **SB**-Mil/Covington. **Time** 2:31. **Attendance** 45,804.

Game 5 Monday, October 7 at County Stadium, Milwaukee

	1	2	3	4	5	6	7	8	9	R	H	E
New York Yankees	0	0	0	0	0	0	0	0	0	0	7	0
Milwaukee Braves	0	0	0	0	0	1	0	0	x	1	6	1

Pitchers NY **Whitey Ford** (L, 1-1), IP 7, H 6, R 1, ER 1, BB 1, SO 2; **Bob Turley**, IP 1, H 0, R 0, ER 0, BB 0, SO 2
Mil **Lew Burdette** (W, 2-0), IP 9, H 7, R 0, ER 0, BB 0, SO 5

Top Performers at the Plate
NY **Hank Bauer**, 2 for 4; **Enos Slaughter**, 2 for 3
Mil **Hank Aaron**, 2 for 3; **Eddie Mathews**, 1 for 3, 1 R, 1 BB

Time 22:00. **Attendance** 45,811.

Game 6 Wednesday, October 9 at Yankee Stadium, New York

	1	2	3	4	5	6	7	8	9	R	H	E
Milwaukee Braves	0	0	0	0	1	0	1	0	0	2	4	0
New York Yankees	0	0	2	0	0	0	1	0	x	3	7	0

Pitchers Mil **Bob Buhl**, IP 2⅔, H 4, R 2, ER 2, BB 4, SO 4; **Ernie Johnson** (L, 0-1), IP 4⅓, H 2, R 1, ER 1, BB 0, SO 5; **Don McMahon**, IP 1, H 1, R 0, ER 0, BB 0, SO 0
NY **Bob Turley** (W, 1-0), IP 9, H 4, R 2, ER 2, BB 2, SO 8

Top Performers at the Plate
Mil **Frank Torre**, 2 for 3, 1 R, 1 RBI
NY **Yogi Berra**, 3 for 4, 1 R, 2 RBI

2B-Mil/Mathews; NY/Berra, Coleman. **HR**-Mil/Aaron, Torre; NY/Bauer, Berra. **Time** 2:09. **Attendance** 61,408.

Game 7 Thursday, October 10 at Yankee Stadium, New York

	1	2	3	4	5	6	7	8	9	R	H	E
Milwaukee Braves	0	0	4	0	0	0	0	1	0	5	9	1
New York Yankees	0	0	0	0	0	0	0	0	0	0	7	3

Pitchers Mil **Lew Burdette** (W, 3-0), IP 9, H 7, R 0, ER 0, BB 1, SO 3
NY **Don Larsen** (L, 1-1), IP 2⅓, H 3, R 3, ER 2, BB 1, SO 2; **Bobby Shantz**, IP ⅔, H 2, R 1, ER 0, BB 0, SO 0; **Art Ditmar**, IP 2, H 1, R 0, ER 0, BB 0, SO 1; **Tom Sturdivant**, IP 2, H 2, R 0, ER 0, BB 0, SO 1; **Tommy Byrne**, IP 2, H 1, R 1, ER 1, BB 2, SO 0

Top Performers at the Plate
Mil **Hank Aaron**, 2 for 5, 1 R, 1 RBI; **Del Crandall**, 2 for 4, 1 R, 1 RBI
NY **Jerry Coleman**, 2 for 4

2B-Mil/Mathews; NY/Bauer. **HR**-Mil/Crandall. **Time** 2:34. **Attendance** 61,207.

New York Yankees (4) vs. Milwaukee Braves (3)

1958

With the 1958 American League title, the New York Yankees claimed their 9th pennant in 10 seasons under manager Casey Stengel. It also gave them the chance to avenge their 1957 Series loss in a rematch with the Milwaukee Braves. Warren Spahn and Lew Burdette gave the Braves a two-games-to-none lead to start the Series. Spahn pitched all 10 innings in the opener, a 4-3 squeaker. He retired 12 consecutive batters heading into the extra inning, and worked around New York's two-out rally in the 10th. Billy Bruton sent Joe Adcock home with a single in the bottom of the inning for the game winner. Burdette helped his own cause in Game 2 by stroking a three-run homer in the 1st. Spotted a 7-1 lead after one, he coasted to a 13-5 victory. In Game 3, Don Larsen pitched the second Series shutout of his career in a combined effort with ace reliever Ryne Duren. Hank Bauer drove in all the game's runs with a two-run single in the 5th and a two-run homer in the 7th; it was Bauer's 3rd straight game with a home run, and his 17th consecutive World Series game with a base hit. Spahn kept Bauer and 12 other Yankees hitless in Game 4, giving up only two hits on the day. The Braves scattered three runs to take a 3-games-to-1 lead. With their backs against the wall, the Yanks burst out with a six-run 6th inning in Game 5 to give Burdette his first postseason defeat. Bob Turley threw a five-hit shutout for New York while striking out 10. Spahn lasted to the 10th inning again in Game 6, but this time he was handed the loss when New York got a pair of runs from Gil McDougald's home run and Bill Skowron's RBI single. The Braves scored one off Duren in the bottom of the inning, but Turley came on in relief to secure the final out with two men on base. The last two World Series MVPs were matched up in Game 7: Larsen vs. Burdette. Larsen yielded a Milwaukee run in the first inning, and Turley came on in the 3rd to get him out of a jam. Making his 4th appearance of the Series, Turley gave up one run in 6 innings, and the teams were locked in a 2-2 tie heading into the 8th. Burdette had allowed only three hits up to this point, but he suddenly came apart. After the first two batters of the inning went down, Yogi Berra ripped a double and then scored on an Elston Howard single for the go-ahead run. Andy Carey singled and Skowron followed with a three-run homer, and suddenly Milwaukee was down 6-2. The Braves failed to score in the final 2 innings, and the Yankees became the first team since 1925 to come back from a 3-games-to-1 deficit to win the World Series.

Above: After lasting only a third of an inning in Game 2, Bob Turley earned two victories behind a 10-strikeout fifth game and a two-hitter in relief in Game 7.

1958 WORLD SERIES COMPOSITE STATISTICS

NEW YORK YANKEES/Casey Stengel, Manager

Player	pos	G	AB	R	H	2B	3B	HR	RBI	BB	SO	SB	BA	SA	E	FPct
Hank Bauer	rf	7	31	6	10	0	0	4	8	0	5	0	.323	.710	0	1.000
Yogi Berra	c	7	27	3	6	3	0	0	2	1	0	0	.222	.333	0	1.000
Andy Carey	3b	5	12	1	1	0	0	0	0	0	3	0	.083	.083	0	1.000
Murry Dickson	p	2	0	0	0	0	0	0	0	0	0	0	—	—	0	—
Art Ditmar	p	1	1	0	0	0	0	0	0	0	0	0	.000	.000	1	.500
Ryne Duren	p	3	3	0	0	0	0	0	0	0	2	0	.000	.000	0	1.000
Whitey Ford	p	3	4	1	0	0	0	0	0	2	2	0	.000	.000	0	1.000
Elston Howard	lf-ph	6	18	4	4	0	0	0	2	1	4	1	.222	.222	0	1.000
Tony Kubek	ss	7	21	0	1	0	0	0	1	1	7	0	.048	.048	2	.920
Johnny Kucks	p	2	1	0	1	0	0	0	0	0	0	0	1.000	1.000	0	—
Don Larsen	p	2	2	0	0	0	0	0	0	1	0	0	.000	.000	0	1.000
Jerry Lumpe	3b-ss-ph	6	12	0	2	0	0	0	1	2	0	0	.167	.167	0	1.000
Duke Maas	p	1	0	0	0	0	0	0	0	0	0	0	—	—	0	—
Mickey Mantle	cf	7	24	4	6	0	1	2	3	7	4	0	.250	.583	0	1.000
Gil McDougald	2b	7	28	5	9	2	0	2	4	2	4	0	.321	.607	0	1.000
Zack Monroe	p	1	0	0	0	0	0	0	0	0	0	0	—	—	0	—
Bobby Richardson	3b	4	5	0	0	0	0	0	0	0	0	0	.000	.000	0	1.000
Norm Siebern	lf	3	8	1	1	0	0	0	0	3	2	0	.125	.125	0	1.000
Bill Skowron	1b	7	27	3	7	0	0	2	7	1	4	0	.259	.481	0	1.000
Enos Slaughter	ph	4	3	1	0	0	0	0	0	1	1	0	.000	.000	—	—
Marv Throneberry	ph	1	1	0	0	0	0	0	0	0	1	0	.000	.000	—	—
Bob Turley	p	4	5	0	1	0	0	0	2	0	1	0	.200	.200	0	1.000
Totals		7	233	29	49	5	1	10	29	21	42	1	.210	.369	3	.988

Pitcher	G	GS	CG	IP	H	R	ER	BB	SO	W-L	Sv	ERA
Murry Dickson	2	0	0	4	4	2	2	0	1	0-0	0	4.50
Art Ditmar	1	0	0	3⅔	2	0	0	0	2	0-0	0	0.00
Ryne Duren	3	0	0	9⅓	7	2	2	6	14	1-1	1	1.93
Whitey Ford	3	3	0	15⅓	19	8	7	5	16	0-1	0	4.11
Johnny Kucks	2	0	0	4⅓	4	1	1	1	0	0-0	0	2.08
Don Larsen	2	2	0	9⅓	9	1	1	6	9	1-0	0	0.96
Duke Maas	1	0	0	⅓	2	3	3	1	0	0-0	0	81.00
Zack Monroe	1	0	0	1	3	3	3	1	1	0-0	0	27.00
Bob Turley	4	2	1	16⅓	10	5	5	7	13	2-1	1	2.76
Totals	7	7	1	63⅔	60	25	24	27	56	4-3	2	3.39

MILWAUKEE BRAVES/Fred Haney, Manager

Player	pos	G	AB	R	H	2B	3B	HR	RBI	BB	SO	SB	BA	SA	E	FPct
Hank Aaron	rf-cf	7	27	3	9	2	0	0	2	4	6	0	.333	.407	0	1.000
Joe Adcock	1b-ph	4	13	1	4	0	0	0	1	1	3	0	.308	.308	0	1.000
Bill Bruton	ph-cf-pr	7	17	2	7	0	0	1	2	5	5	0	.412	.588	1	.923
Lew Burdette	p	3	9	1	1	0	1	0	1	3	0	3	0	.111	.444	0	1.000
Wes Covington	lf	7	26	2	7	0	0	0	4	2	4	0	.269	.269	0	1.000
Del Crandall	c	7	25	4	6	0	0	1	3	3	10	0	.240	.360	0	1.000
Harry Hanebrink	ph	2	2	0	0	0	0	0	0	0	0	0	.000	.000	—	—
Johnny Logan	ss	7	25	3	3	2	0	0	2	2	4	0	.120	.200	2	.944
Felix Mantilla	ss-pr	4	0	1	0	0	0	0	0	0	0	0	—	—	0	1.000
Eddie Mathews	3b	7	25	3	4	2	0	0	3	6	11	1	.160	.240	1	.944
Don McMahon	p	3	0	0	0	0	0	0	0	0	0	0	—	—	0	1.000
Andy Pafko	cf-rf-lf	4	9	0	3	1	0	0	1	0	0	0	.333	.444	0	1.000
Juan Pizarro	p	1	0	0	0	0	0	0	0	0	0	0	—	—	0	1.000
Bob Rush	p	1	2	0	0	0	0	0	0	0	2	0	.000	.000	0	1.000
Red Schoendienst	2b	7	30	5	9	3	1	0	0	2	1	0	.300	.467	1	.974
Warren Spahn	p	3	12	0	4	0	0	0	3	0	6	0	.333	.333	0	1.000
Frank Torre	1b-ph	4	17	0	3	0	0	0	1	2	0	0	.176	.176	2	.953
Carl Willey	p	1	0	0	0	0	0	0	0	0	0	0	—	—	0	—
Casey Wise	ph-pr	2	1	0	0	0	0	0	0	0	1	0	.000	.000	—	—
Totals		7	240	25	60	10	1	3	24	27	56	1	.250	.338	7	.974

Pitcher	G	GS	CG	IP	H	R	ER	BB	SO	W-L	Sv	ERA
Lew Burdette	3	3	1	22⅓	22	17	14	4	12	1-2	0	5.64
Don McMahon	3	0	0	3⅓	3	2	2	3	5	0-0	0	5.40
Juan Pizarro	1	0	0	1⅔	2	1	1	3	0	0-0	0	5.40
Bob Rush	1	1	0	6	3	2	2	5	2	0-1	0	3.00
Warren Spahn	3	3	2	28⅔	19	7	7	8	18	2-1	0	2.20
Carl Willey	1	0	0	1	0	0	0	2	0	0-0	0	0.00
Totals	7	7	3	63	49	29	26	21	42	3-4	0	3.71

Series MVP: Bob Turley, New York Yankees. **Series Outstanding Pitcher:** Bob Turley, New York Yankees. **Average Length of Game:** 2 hours, 41 minutes. **Total Attendance:** 393,909. **Average Attendance:** 56,273 (69,480 at Yankee Stadium; 46,367 at Milwaukee County Stadium). **Umpires:** Al Barlick (NL), Charlie Berry (AL), Red Flaherty (AL), Tom Gorman (NL), Bill Jackowski (NL), Frank Umont (AL). **Winning Player's Share:** $8,759. **Losing Player's Share:** $5,896.

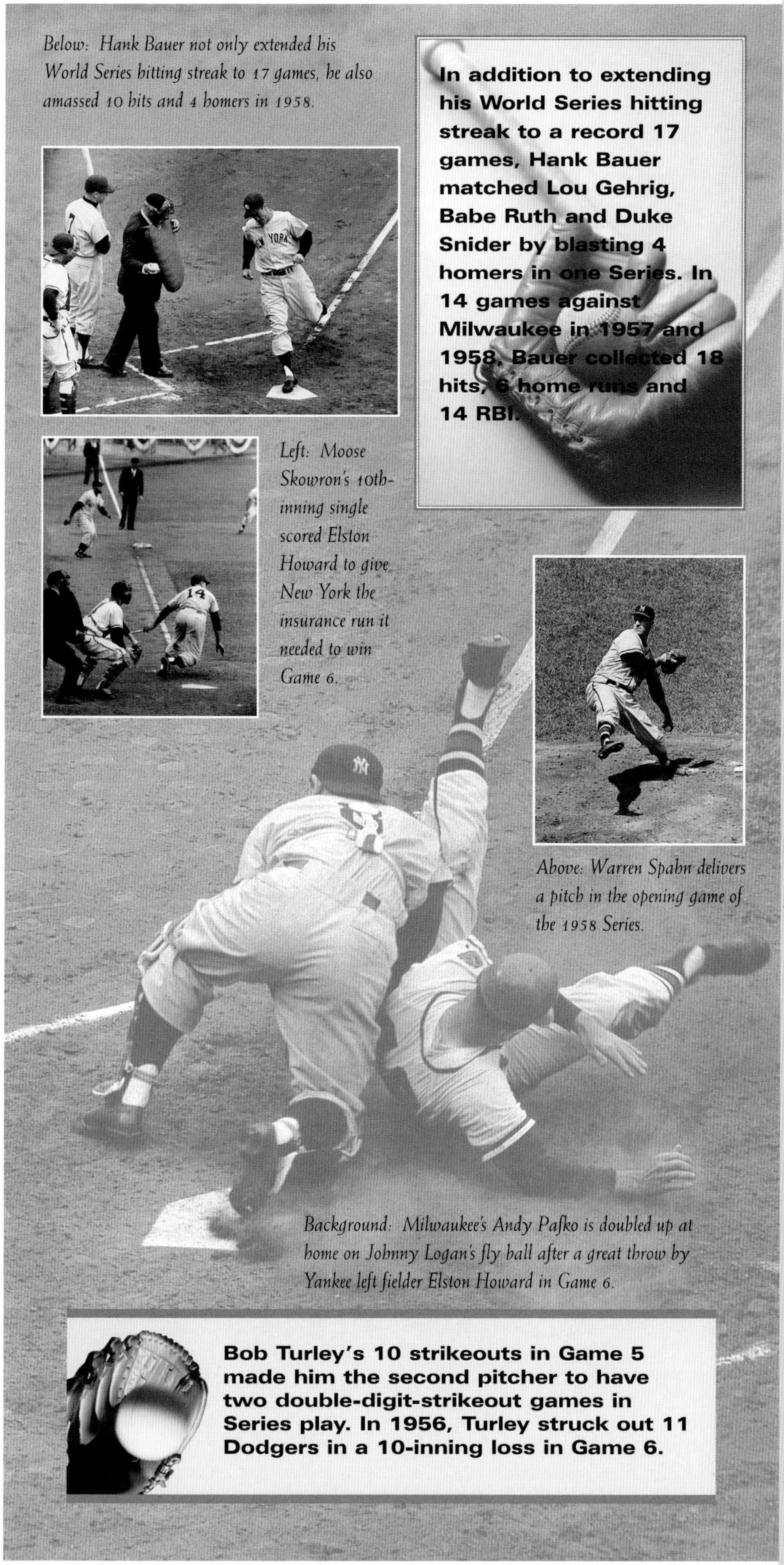

Below: Hank Bauer not only extended his World Series hitting streak to 17 games, he also amassed 10 hits and 4 homers in 1958.

In addition to extending his World Series hitting streak to a record 17 games, Hank Bauer matched Lou Gehrig, Babe Ruth and Duke Snider by blasting 4 homers in one Series. In 14 games against Milwaukee in 1957 and 1958, Bauer collected 18 hits, 6 home runs and 14 RBI.

Left: Moose Skowron's 10th-inning single scored Elston Howard to give New York the insurance run it needed to win Game 6.

Above: Warren Spahn delivers a pitch in the opening game of the 1958 Series.

Background: Milwaukee's Andy Pafko is doubled up at home on Johnny Logan's fly ball after a great throw by Yankee left fielder Elston Howard in Game 6.

Bob Turley's 10 strikeouts in Game 5 made him the second pitcher to have two double-digit-strikeout games in Series play. In 1956, Turley struck out 11 Dodgers in a 10-inning loss in Game 6.

Game 1 Wednesday, October 1 at County Stadium, Milwaukee

	1	2	3	4	5	6	7	8	9	10	R	H	E
New York Yankees	0	0	0	1	2	0	0	0	0	0	3	8	1
Milwaukee Braves	0	0	0	2	0	0	0	1	0	1	4	10	0

Pitchers NY Whitey Ford, IP 7, H 6, R 3, ER 3, BB 3, SO 8; Ryne Duren (L, 0-1), IP 2⅔, H 4, R 1, ER 1, BB 1, SO 5
Mil Warren Spahn (W, 1-0), IP 10, H 8, R 3, ER 3, BB 4, SO 6

Top Performers at the Plate
NY Hank Bauer, 2 for 5, 1 R, 2 RBI; Bill Skowron, 2 for 4, 1 R, 1 RBI
Mil Joe Adcock, 2 for 5, 1 R; Del Crandall, 2 for 5, 1 R, 1 RBI

2B-NY/Berra; Mil/Aaron, Logan. **HR**-NY/Bauer, Skowron. **Time** 3:09. **Attendance** 46,367.

Game 2 Thursday, October 2 at County Stadium, Milwaukee

	1	2	3	4	5	6	7	8	9	R	H	E
New York Yankees	1	0	0	1	0	0	0	0	3	5	7	0
Milwaukee Braves	7	1	0	0	0	0	2	3	x	13	15	1

Pitchers NY Bob Turley (L, 0-1), IP ⅓, H 3, R 4, ER 4, BB 1, SO 1; Duke Maas, IP ⅓, H 2, R 3, ER 3, BB 1, SO 0; Johnny Kucks, IP 3⅓, H 3, R 1, ER 1, BB 0, SO 0; Murry Dickson, IP 3, H 4, R 2, ER 2, BB 0, SO 1; Zack Monroe, IP 1, H 3, R 3, ER 3, BB 1, SO 1
Mil Lew Burdette (W, 1-0), IP 9, H 7, R 5, ER 4, BB 1, SO 5

Top Performers at the Plate
NY Hank Bauer, 2 for 4, 2 R, 1 RBI; Mickey Mantle, 2 for 3, 2 R, 3 RBI, 1 BB, 2 HR
Mil Bill Bruton, 3 for 4, 2 R, 1 RBI, 1 BB; Wes Covington, 3 for 4, 1 R, 2 RBI

2B-Mil/Mathews, Schoendienst 2. **HR**-NY/Bauer, Mantle 2; Mil/Bruton, Burdette. **SB**-Mil/Mathews. **Time** 2:43. **Attendance** 46,367.

Game 3 Saturday, October 4 at Yankee Stadium, New York

	1	2	3	4	5	6	7	8	9	R	H	E
Milwaukee Braves	0	0	0	0	0	0	0	0	0	0	6	0
New York Yankees	0	0	0	0	2	0	2	0	x	4	4	0

Pitchers Mil Bob Rush (L, 0-1), IP 6, H 3, R 2, ER 2, BB 5, SO 2; Don McMahon, IP 2, H 1, R 2, ER 2, BB 2, SO 2
NY Don Larsen (W, 1-0), IP 7, H 6, R 0, ER 0, BB 3, SO 8; Ryne Duren (Sv, 1), IP 2, H 0, R 0, ER 0, BB 3, SO 1

Top Performers at the Plate
Mil Red Schoendienst, 2 for 4; Frank Torre, 2 for 4
NY Hank Bauer, 3 for 4, 1 R, 4 RBI

HR-NY/Bauer. **Time** 2:42. **Attendance** 71,599.

Game 4 Sunday, October 5 at Yankee Stadium, New York

	1	2	3	4	5	6	7	8	9	R	H	E
Milwaukee Braves	0	0	0	0	1	1	1	0	0	3	9	0
New York Yankees	0	0	0	0	0	0	0	0	0	0	2	1

Pitchers Mil Warren Spahn (W, 2-0), IP 9, H 2, R 0, ER 0, BB 2, SO 7
NY Whitey Ford (L, 0-1), IP 7, H 8, R 3, ER 2, BB 1, SO 6; Johnny Kucks, IP 1, H 1, R 0, ER 0, BB 1, SO 0; Murry Dickson, IP 1, H 0, R 0, ER 0, BB 0, SO 0

Top Performers at the Plate
Mil Del Crandall, 2 for 3, 1 R, 1 BB

2B-Mil/Aaron, Logan, Mathews, Pafko. **3B**-Mil/Schoendienst; NY/Mantle. **Time** 2:17. **Attendance** 71,563.

Game 5 Monday, October 6 at Yankee Stadium, New York

	1	2	3	4	5	6	7	8	9	R	H	E
Milwaukee Braves	0	0	0	0	0	0	0	0	0	0	5	0
New York Yankees	0	0	1	0	0	6	0	0	x	7	10	0

Pitchers Mil Lew Burdette (L, 1-1), IP 5⅓, H 8, R 6, ER 6, BB 1, SO 4; Juan Pizarro, IP 1⅔, H 2, R 1, ER 1, BB 1, SO 3; Carl Willey, IP 1, H 0, R 0, ER 0, BB 0, SO 2
NY Bob Turley (W, 1-1), IP 9, H 5, R 0, ER 0, BB 3, SO 10

Top Performers at the Plate
Mil Bill Bruton, 2 for 3, 1 BB
NY Mickey Mantle, 2 for 3, 1 R, 1 BB; Gil McDougald, 2 for 4, 2 R, 3 MVP

2B-NY/Berra, McDougald. **HR**-NY/McDougald. **Time** 2:19. **Attendance** 65,279.

Game 6 Wednesday, October 8 at County Stadium, Milwaukee

	1	2	3	4	5	6	7	8	9	10	R	H	E
New York Yankees	1	0	0	0	0	1	0	0	2	4	10	1
Milwaukee Braves	1	1	0	0	0	0	0	0	1	3	10	4

Pitchers NY Whitey Ford, IP 1⅓, H 5, R 2, ER 2, BB 1, SO 2; Art Ditmar, IP 3⅔, H 2, R 0, ER 0, BB 0, SO 2; Ryne Duren (W, 1-1), IP 4⅔, H 3, R 1, ER 1, BB 2, SO 8; Bob Turley (Sv, 1), IP ⅓, H 0, R 0, ER 0, BB 0, SO 0
Mil Warren Spahn (L, 2-1), IP 9⅔, H 9, R 4, ER 4, BB 2, SO 5; Don McMahon, IP ⅓, H 1, R 0, ER 0, BB 0, SO 1

Top Performers at the Plate
NY Hank Bauer, 2 for 5, 1 R, 1 RBI; Gil McDougald, 2 for 5, 1 R, 1 RBI
Mil Hank Aaron, 3 for 5, 2 RBI; Red Schoendienst, 2 for 4, 1 R, 1 BB

2B-Mil/Schoendienst. **HR**-NY/Bauer, McDougald. **Time** 3:07. **Attendance** 46,367.

Game 7 Thursday, October 9 at County Stadium, Milwaukee

	1	2	3	4	5	6	7	8	9	R	H	E
New York Yankees	0	2	0	0	0	0	4	0		6	8	0
Milwaukee Braves	1	0	0	1	0	0	0	0		2	5	2

Pitchers NY Don Larsen, IP 2⅓, H 3, R 1, ER 1, BB 3, SO 1; Bob Turley (W, 2-1), IP 6⅔, H 2, R 1, ER 1, BB 3, SO 2
Mil Lew Burdette (L, 1-2), IP 8, H 7, R 6, ER 4, BB 2, SO 3; Don McMahon, IP 1, H 1, R 0, ER 0, BB 1, SO 2

Top Performers at the Plate
NY Elston Howard, 2 for 3, 2 R, 1 RBI, 1 SH; Bill Skowron, 2 for 4, 1 R, 4 RBI

2B-NY/Berra, McDougald. **HR**-NY/Skowron; Mil/Crandall. **SB**-NY/Howard. **Time** 2:31. **Attendance** 46,367.

Los Angeles Dodgers (4) vs. Chicago White Sox (2)

Two years after Brooklyn got its long-awaited World Series title in 1955, Dodger owner Walter O'Malley packed up and moved his team West. The citizens of Los Angeles had to wait just two years to see their first World Series, though it was a struggle getting there. After finishing seventh in their first year in California, the Dodgers ended in a dead heat for first with Milwaukee in 1959. They edged out the Braves in two one-run playoff games, setting up an October encounter with the Chicago White Sox, who were making their first appearance since the notorious 1919 Series. The "Go-Go Sox" were a team built on speed and pitching, but they got a big dose of power in Game 1. Ted Kluszewski hit a pair of two-run homers in Chicago's 11-0 trouncing of Los Angeles. Pinch hitter Chuck Essegian helped bring Johnny Podres a win in Game 2. Batting for Podres with two out in the seventh, Essegian tied the game with a solo home run. Charlie Neal then put the Dodgers in front 4-2 with a two-run shot later in the inning. Chicago scored one in the eighth, but their rally ended when Sherm Lollar was thrown out at the plate attempting to bring in the tying run. On October 4, a record 92,394 fans showed up at Memorial Coliseum to watch the first World Series game played on the West Coast. The Dodgers got a good performance from Don Drysdale, and reliever Larry Sherry earned his second save in two games. Chicago's Dick Donovan allowed only one base runner until the seventh inning, when

Carl Furillo's pinch-hit single scored two. LA went on to win 3-1. Five consecutive two-out singles (plus an error and a passed ball) led to four Dodger runs in the third inning of Game 4. The White Sox would get it all back in the seventh on Kluszewski's RBI single and Lollar's three-run clout, but a leadoff homer by Gil Hodges in the eighth put Los Angeles up three games to one. In Game 5, a 23-year-old lefty named Sandy Koufax started in front of another huge crowd—the largest ever to see a postseason contest. Koufax allowed one run and scattered five hits in seven innings but was pegged with the loss as the Dodgers failed to score. Back in Chicago for Game 6, the Dodgers broke out for nine runs. Chuck Essegian put his name in the record books by hitting his second pinch-hit home run of the Series with a solo shot in the ninth. Kluszewski earned his record-breaking tenth RBI on a three-run homer in the fourth, but Sherry secured his second win with five-plus innings of relief work. Although the White Sox outscored the Dodgers over the six games and finished with an identical batting average, the "Go-Go Sox" were taken out of their usual game plan, as Los Angeles catcher Johnny Roseboro held them to just one stolen base in four attempts. The true difference, however, was pitcher Larry Sherry, who notched two wins and two saves in relief for LA.

Above: Big Ted Kluszewski went deep twice in the opening game of the 1959 Series.

1959 WORLD SERIES COMPOSITE STATISTICS

LOS ANGELES DODGERS/Walter Alston, Manager

Player	pos	G	AB	R	H	2B	3B	HR	RBI	BB	SO	SB	BA	SA	E	FPct
Chuck Churn	p	1	0	0	0	0	0	0	0	0	0	0	—	—	0	1.000
Roger Craig	p	2	3	0	0	0	0	0	0	0	2	0	.000	.000	0	1.000
Don Demeter	cf-pr	6	12	2	3	0	0	0	1	3	0	0	.250	.250	0	1.000
Don Drysdale	p	1	2	0	0	0	0	0	0	0	2	0	.000	.000	0	1.000
Chuck Essegian	ph	4	3	2	2	0	0	2	2	1	1	0	.667	2.667	—	—
Ron Fairly	ph-rf-cf-pr	6	3	0	0	0	0	0	0	1	0	0	.000	.000	0	—
Carl Furillo	ph-rf	4	4	0	1	0	0	0	2	0	1	0	.250	.250	0	—
Jim Gilliam	3b	6	25	2	6	0	0	0	2	2	2	2	.240	.240	0	1.000
Gil Hodges	1b	6	23	2	9	0	1	1	2	1	2	0	.391	.609	0	1.000
Johnny Klippstein	p	1	0	0	0	0	0	0	0	0	0	0	—	—	0	1.000
Sandy Koufax	p	2	2	0	0	0	0	0	0	0	1	0	.000	.000	0	—
Clem Labine	p	1	0	0	0	0	0	0	0	0	0	0	—	—	0	—
Norm Larker	rf-lf	6	16	2	3	0	0	0	0	2	3	0	.188	.188	0	1.000
Wally Moon	lf-rf-cf	6	23	3	6	0	0	1	2	2	2	1	.261	.391	0	1.000
Charlie Neal	2b	6	27	4	10	2	0	2	6	0	1	1	.370	.667	1	.974
Joe Pignatano	c	1	0	0	0	0	0	0	0	0	0	0	—	—	0	1.000
Johnny Podres	p-pr	3	4	1	2	1	0	0	1	0	0	0	.500	.750	0	1.000
Rip Repulski	ph-rf	1	0	0	0	0	0	0	0	1	0	0	—	—	0	—
Johnny Roseboro	c	6	21	0	2	0	0	0	1	0	2	0	.095	.095	0	1.000
Larry Sherry	p-ph	5	4	0	2	0	0	0	0	0	1	0	.500	.500	0	1.000
Duke Snider	cf-ph-rf	4	10	1	2	0	0	1	2	2	0	0	.200	.500	2	.714
Stan Williams	p	1	0	0	0	0	0	0	0	0	0	0	—	—	0	—
Maury Wills	ss	6	20	2	5	0	0	0	1	0	3	1	.250	.250	1	.969
Don Zimmer	pr-ss	1	1	0	0	0	0	0	0	0	0	0	.000	.000	0	1.000
Totals		**6**	**203**	**21**	**53**	**3**	**1**	**7**	**19**	**12**	**27**	**5**	**.261**	**.389**	**4**	**.983**

Pitcher	G	GS	CG	IP	H	R	ER	BB	SO	W-L	Sv	ERA
Chuck Churn	1	0	0	⅔	5	6	2	0	0	0-0	0	27.00
Roger Craig	2	2	0	9⅓	15	9	9	5	8	0-1	0	8.68
Don Drysdale	1	1	0	7	11	1	1	4	5	1-0	0	1.29
Johnny Klippstein	1	0	0	2	1	0	0	0	2	0-0	0	0.00
Sandy Koufax	2	1	0	9	5	1	1	1	7	0-1	0	1.00
Clem Labine	1	0	0	1	0	0	0	0	1	0-0	0	0.00
Johnny Podres	2	2	0	9⅓	7	5	5	6	4	1-0	0	4.82
Larry Sherry	4	0	0	12⅔	8	1	1	2	5	2-0	2	0.71
Stan Williams	1	0	0	2	0	0	0	2	1	0-0	0	0.00
Totals	**6**	**6**	**0**	**53**	**52**	**23**	**19**	**20**	**33**	**4-2**	**2**	**3.23**

CHICAGO WHITE SOX/Al Lopez, Manager

Player	pos	G	AB	R	H	2B	3B	HR	RBI	BB	SO	SB	BA	SA	E	FPct
Luis Aparicio	ss	6	26	1	8	1	0	0	0	2	3	1	.308	.346	2	.929
Norm Cash	ph	4	4	0	0	0	0	0	0	0	2	0	.000	.000	—	—
Dick Donovan	p	3	3	0	1	0	0	0	0	0	1	0	.333	.333	0	1.000
Sammy Esposito	3b-pr	2	2	0	0	0	0	0	0	0	1	0	.000	.000	0	1.000
Nellie Fox	2b	6	24	4	9	3	0	0	0	4	1	0	.375	.500	1	1.000
Billy Goodman	3b-ph	5	13	1	3	0	0	0	1	5	0	0	.231	.231	0	1.000
Ted Kluszewski	1b	6	23	5	9	1	0	3	10	2	0	0	.391	.826	0	1.000
Jim Landis	cf	6	24	6	7	0	0	0	1	7	1	0	.292	.292	1	.900
Sherm Lollar	c	6	22	3	5	0	0	1	5	1	3	0	.227	.364	0	1.000
Turk Lown	p	3	0	0	0	0	0	0	0	0	0	0	—	—	0	—
Jim McAnany	rf-lf	3	5	0	0	0	0	0	0	1	0	0	.000	.000	0	1.000
Ray Moore	p	1	0	0	0	0	0	0	0	0	0	0	—	—	0	—
Bubba Phillips	3b-rf	3	10	0	3	1	0	0	0	0	0	0	.300	.400	0	1.000
Billy Pierce	p	3	0	0	0	0	0	0	0	0	0	0	—	—	1	.000
Jim Rivera	rf	5	11	1	0	0	0	0	0	3	1	0	.000	.000	0	1.000
John Romano	ph	1	1	0	0	0	0	0	0	0	0	0	.000	.000	—	—
Bob Shaw	p	2	4	0	1	0	0	0	0	0	2	0	.250	.250	0	1.000
Al Smith	lf-rf	6	20	1	5	3	0	0	1	4	4	0	.250	.400	0	1.000
Gerry Staley	p	4	1	0	0	0	0	0	0	1	1	0	.000	.000	0	1.000
Earl Torgeson	pr-1b-ph	3	1	1	0	0	0	0	0	1	0	0	.000	.000	0	—
Early Wynn	p	3	5	0	1	0	0	0	0	0	2	0	.200	.200	0	1.000
Totals		**6**	**199**	**23**	**52**	**10**	**0**	**4**	**19**	**20**	**33**	**2**	**.261**	**.372**	**4**	**.982**

Pitcher	G	GS	CG	IP	H	R	ER	BB	SO	W-L	Sv	ERA
Dick Donovan	3	1	0	8⅓	4	5	5	3	5	0-1	1	5.40
Turk Lown	3	0	0	3⅓	2	0	0	1	3	0-0	0	0.00
Ray Moore	1	0	0	1	1	1	1	0	1	0-0	0	9.00
Billy Pierce	3	0	0	4	2	0	0	2	3	0-0	0	0.00
Bob Shaw	2	2	0	14	17	4	4	2	2	1-1	0	2.57
Gerry Staley	4	0	0	8⅓	8	2	2	0	3	0-1	1	2.16
Early Wynn	3	3	0	13	19	9	8	4	10	1-1	0	5.54
Totals	**6**	**6**	**0**	**52**	**53**	**21**	**20**	**12**	**27**	**2-4**	**2**	**3.46**

Series MVP: Larry Sherry, Los Angeles Dodgers. **Series Outstanding Pitcher:** Larry Sherry, Los Angeles Dodgers. **Average Length of Game:** 2 hours, 30 minutes. **Total Attendance:** 420,784. **Average Attendance:** 70,131 (92,583 at Los Angeles Memorial Coliseum; 47,678 at Comiskey Park). **Umpires:** Frank Dascoli (NL), Hal Dixon (NL), Eddie Hurley (AL), John Rice (AL), Frank Secory (NL), Bill Summers (AL). **Winning Player's Share:** $11,231. **Losing Player's Share:** $7,275.

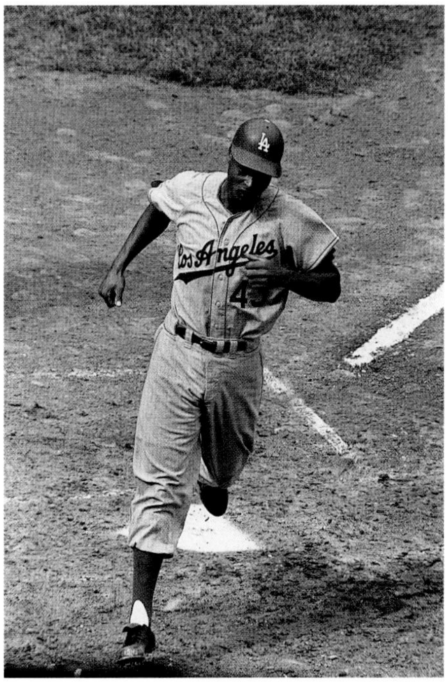

Right: Charlie Neal homered twice in Game 2 to help Los Angeles to a 4-3 win.

The two home runs by Chicago's Ted Kluszewski in Game 1 marked the first time that someone playing for a team from a city other than Boston or New York had a multi-homer game in the World Series. The previous 18 multi-homer games were accomplished by two Boston Red Sox, one Boston Brave, one New York Giant, eight New York Yankees and one Brooklyn Dodger.

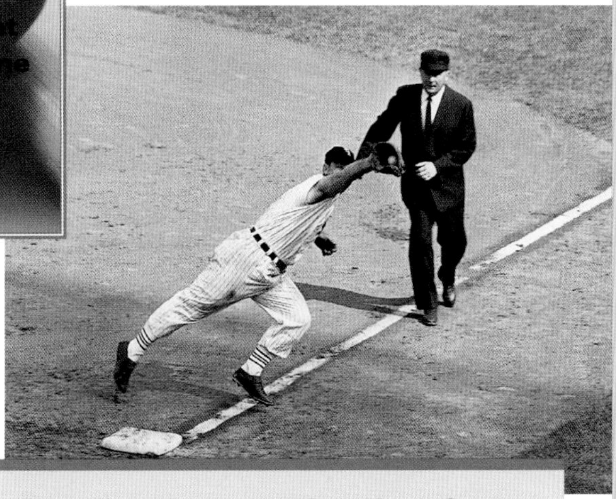

Right: Kluszewski was not all bat. He makes a nice play to stab Junior Gilliam's line drive in Game 2.

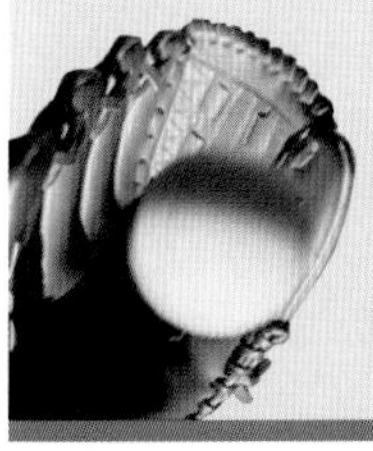

Al Lopez was the only manager other than Casey Stengel to lead an American League team to the World Series in the 1950s. In addition to his 1959 appearance with the White Sox, Lopez was the skipper on Cleveland's 1954 pennant-winning club. He finished with an 0-2 record in the Fall Classic.

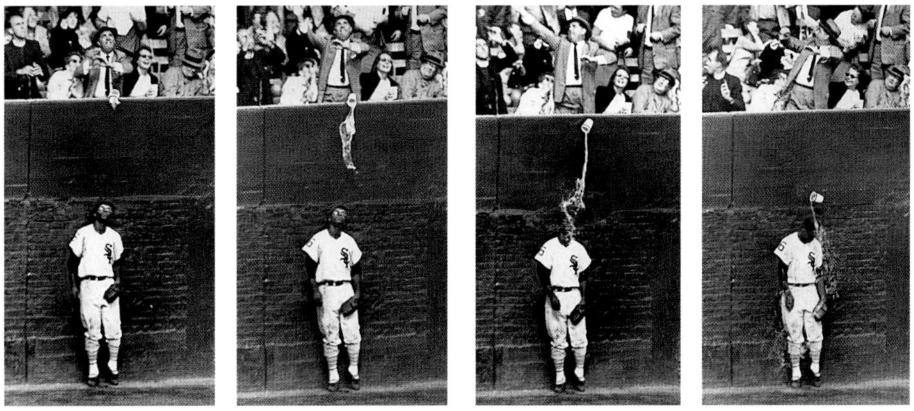

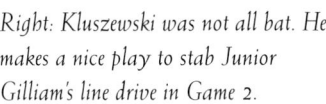

Above: Chicago outfielder Al Smith gets an unexpected shower when a distracted fan dumps his beer on Smith while going after Charlie Neal's Game 2 homer.

Game 1 Thursday, October 1 at Comiskey Park, Chicago

	1	2	3	4	5	6	7	8	9	R	H	E
Los Angeles Dodgers	0	0	0	0	0	0	0	0	0	0	8	3
Chicago White Sox	2	0	7	2	0	0	0	0	x	11	11	0

Pitchers LA **Roger Craig** (L, 0-1), IP 2⅓, H 5, R 5, ER 5, BB 1, SO 1; **Chuck Churn**, IP ⅔, H 5, R 6, ER 2, BB 0, SO 0; **Clem Labine**, IP 1, H 0, R 0, ER 0, BB 0, SO 1; **Sandy Koufax**, IP 2, H 0, R 0, ER 0, BB 0, SO 1; **Johnny Klippstein**, IP 2, H 1, R 0, ER 0, BB 0, SO 2
Chi **Early Wynn** (W, 1-0), IP 7, H 6, R 0, ER 0, BB 1, SO 6; **Gerry Staley** (Sv, 1), IP 2, H 2, R 0, ER 0, BB 0, SO 1

Top Performers at the Plate
LA **Gil Hodges**, 2 for 4; **Charlie Neal**, 2 for 4
Chi **Ted Kluszewski**, 3 for 4, 2 R, 5 RBI, 2 HR; **Jim Landis**, 3 for 4, 3 R, 1 RBI

2B-Chi/Fox, Smith 2, Wynn. **HR**-Chi/Kluszewski 2. **SB**-LA/Neal. **Time** 2:35. **Attendance** 48,013.

Game 2 Friday, October 2 at Comiskey Park, Chicago

	1	2	3	4	5	6	7	8	9	R	H	E
Los Angeles Dodgers	0	0	0	0	1	0	3	0	0	4	9	1
Chicago White Sox	2	0	0	0	-0	0	0	1	0	3	8	0

Pitchers LA **Johnny Podres** (W, 1-0), IP 6, H 5, R 2, ER 2, BB 3, SO 3; **Larry Sherry** (Sv, 1), IP 3, H 3, R 1, ER 1, BB 0, SO 1
Chi **Bob Shaw** (1, 0-1), IP 6⅔, H 8, R 4, ER 4, BB 1, SO 1; **Turk Lown**, IP 2⅓, H 1, R 0, ER 0, BB 1, SO 3

Top Performers at the Plate
LA **Chuck Essegian**, 1 for 1, 1 R, 1 RBI; **Charlie Neal**, 2 for 5, 2 R, 3 RBI, 2 HR
Chi **Luis Aparicio**, 2 for 5, 1 R; **Sherm Lollar**, 2 for 4, 1 RBI

2B-Chi/Aparicio, Phillips, Smith. **HR**-LA/Essegian, Neal 2. **SB**-LA/Gilliam, Moon. **Time** 2:21. **Attendance** 47,368.

Game 3 Sunday, October 4 at Memorial Coliseum, Los Angeles

	1	2	3	4	5	6	7	8	9	R	H	E
Chicago White Sox	0	0	0	0	0	0	0	1	0	1	12	0
Los Angeles Dodgers	0	0	0	0	0	0	2	1	x	3	5	0

Pitchers Chi **Dick Donovan** (L, 0-1), IP 6⅔, H 2, R 2, ER 2, BB 2, SO 5; **Gerry Staley**, IP 1⅓, H 3, R 1, ER 1, BB 0, SO 0
LA **Don Drysdale** (W, 1-0), IP 7, H 11, R 1, ER 1, BB 4, SO 5; **Larry Sherry** (Sv, 2), IP 2, H 1, R 0, ER 0, BB 0, SO 3

Top Performers at the Plate
Chi **Nellie Fox**, 3 for 4, 1 BB; **Ted Kluszewski**, 1 for 3, 1 RBI, 1 BB
LA **Charlie Neal**, 2 for 4, 1 R, 1 RBI

2B-LA/Neal. **SB**-Chi/Landis. **Time** 2:33. **Attendance** 92,394.

Game 4 Monday, October 5 at Memorial Coliseum, Los Angeles

	1	2	3	4	5	6	7	8	9	R	H	E
Chicago White Sox	0	0	0	0	0	0	4	0	0	4	10	3
Los Angeles Dodgers	0	0	4	0	0	0	0	1	x	5	9	0

Pitchers Chi **Early Wynn**, IP 2⅔, H 8, R 4, ER 3, BB 0, SO 2; **Turk Lown**, IP ⅓, H 0, R 0, ER 0, BB 0, SO 0; **Billy Pierce**, IP 3, H 0, R 0, ER 0, BB 1, SO 2; **Gerry Staley** (L, 0-1), IP 2, H 1, R 1, ER 1, BB 0, SO 2
LA **Roger Craig**, IP 7, H 10, R 4, ER 4, BB 4, SO 7; **Larry Sherry** (W, 1-0), IP 2, H 0, R 0, ER 0, BB 1, SO 0

Top Performers at the Plate
Chi **Nellie Fox**, 3 for 5, 1 R; **Ted Kluszewski**, 2 for 4, 1 R, 1 RBI, 1 BB
LA **Gil Hodges**, 2 for 4, 2 R, 2 RBI; **Wally Moon**, 2 for 4, 1 R

2B-Chi/Fox. **HR**-Chi/Lollar; LA/Hodges. **SB**-Chi/Aparicio; LA/Wills. **Time** 2:30. **Attendance** 92,650.

Game 5 Tuesday, October 6 at Memorial Coliseum, Los Angeles

	1	2	3	4	5	6	7	8	9	R	H	E
Chicago White Sox	0	0	0	1	0	0	0	0	0	1	5	0
Los Angeles Dodgers	0	0	0	0	0	0	0	0	0	0	9	0

Pitchers Chi **Bob Shaw** (W, 1-1), IP 7⅓, H 9, R 0, ER 0, BB 1, SO 1; **Billy Pierce**, IP 0, H 0, R 0, ER 0, BB 1, SO 0; **Dick Donovan** (Sv, 1), IP 1⅔, H 0, R 0, ER 0, BB 0, SO 0
LA **Sandy Koufax** (L, 0-1), IP 7, H 5, R 1, ER 1, BB 1, SO 6; **Stan Williams**, IP 2, H 0, R 0, ER 0, BB 2, SO 1

Top Performers at the Plate
Chi **Luis Aparicio**, 2 for 4; **Nellie Fox**, 1 for 3, 1 R, 1 BB
LA **Jim Gilliam**, 4 for 5; **Gil Hodges**, 3 for 4

3B-LA/Hodges. **SB**-LA/Gilliam. **Time** 2:28. **Attendance** 92,706.

Game 6 Thursday, October 8 at Comiskey Park, Chicago

	1	2	3	4	5	6	7	8	9	R	H	E
Los Angeles Dodgers	0	0	2	6	0	0	0	0	1	9	13	0
Chicago White Sox	0	0	0	3	0	0	0	0	0	3	6	1

Pitchers LA **Johnny Podres**, IP 3⅓, H 2, R 3, ER 3, BB 3, SO 1; **Larry Sherry** (W, 2-0), IP 5⅔, H 4, R 0, ER 0, BB 1, SO 1
Chi **Early Wynn** (L, 1-1), IP 3⅓, H 5, R 5, ER 5, BB 3, SO 2; **Dick Donovan**, IP 0, H 2, R 3, ER 3, BB 1, SO 0; **Turk Lown**, IP ⅔, H 1, R 0, ER 0, BB 0, SO 0; **Gerry Staley**, IP 3, H 2, R 0, ER 0, BB 0, SO 0; **Billy Pierce**, IP 1, H 2, R 0, ER 0, BB 0, SO 1; **Ray Moore**, IP 1, H 1, R 1, ER 1, BB 0, SO 1

Top Performers at the Plate
LA **Charlie Neal**, 3 for 5, 1 R, 2 RBI; **Duke Snider**, 1 for 3, 1 R, 2 RBI, 1 BB
Chi **Ted Kluszewski**, 2 for 4, 1 R, 3 RBI; **Jim Landis**, 1 for 3, 1 R, 1 HBP

2B-LA/Neal, Podres; Chi/Fox, Kluszewski. **HR**-LA/Essegian, Moon, Snider; Chi/Kluszewski. **Time** 2:33. **Attendance** 47,653.

Down to the Wire
Facts About Game 7s

In 1905, New York Giants owner John T. Brush laid out some ground rules for the young tradition of the World Series, among them that the two sides would play in a best-four-out-of-seven format. And that's how the Series has been organized ever since—with the exception of a three-year interlude in 1919–21, when it was expanded to a best five-out-of-nine. Since the first Series in 1903, whether set up as a seven-game or nine-game contest, the two combatants have required the full allowance of games to decide the winner on 33 occasions, just over one-third of all Series.

◆ Although the American League has won the majority of World Series since 1903 (57-39), the National League has won more Series that have gone the distance. National League teams have 19 wins and 14 losses in Game 7s.

◆ So much for home-field advantage: the visiting team has come out victorious in 17 of the 33 Game 7s ever played.

◆ The Pittsburgh Pirates and Detroit Tigers were the first to go the full distance in the World Series. The two sides alternated wins in 1909 before the Pirates earned an easy victory in Detroit in the final game.

◆ The longest streak of seven-game Series was from 1955 to 1958, all four involving the Yankees—twice against the Dodgers and twice against the Braves. In all four Series, the visiting team won the deciding game.

◆ The Yankees and Cardinals have appeared in the most seven-game Series, with 10 each. St. Louis's last seven trips to the Fall Classic have all gone seven games, dating back to 1946. The two teams faced each other in a seven-game battle twice, and the Cards came out on top in both 1926 and 1964.

◆ St. Louis has won the most Game 7s overall, holding a 7-3 record; the Yankees are 5-5.

◆ The Cardinals have been on both ends of the largest routs in Game 7 history. In 1934 they defeated the Tigers 11-0 to win the title; 51 years later the Royals trounced St. Louis by the same score in 1985.

◆ The 10-9 finale of the 1960 Series between the Pirates and Yankees was the highest scoring seventh game.

◆ The Pirates have played in the most seven-game Series without suffering a loss. They are 5-0 in those contests, defeating Detroit in 1909,

Above: Kent Hrbek (14) and Don Baylor let the champagne flow after the Twins won the 1987 Series in seven games. All three World Series trips by the Minnesota franchise went the distance: a seven-game loss to the Dodgers in 1965 and a seven-game win over Atlanta in 1991. Below: Bob Gibson and the St. Louis Cardinals played in three seven-game Series in the 1960s. Here Gibson celebrates with catcher Tim McCarver in 1967, after Gibson won the second Game 7 of his career.

Washington in 1925, the Yanks in 1960, and Baltimore in 1971 and 1979.

◆ Hard luck has met the Boston Red Sox in their Game 7 appearances. After winning the 1912 Series in eight games, the franchise has played in four Game 7s and lost them all: twice to the Cardinals (1946 and 1967) and once each to Cincinnati (1975) and the Mets (1986).

◆ Teams have gone beyond the limit on four different occasions, playing into extra innings in the winner-take-all final game. The Senators eked out a 4-3 win over the Giants in 12 innings in 1924 in the longest seventh game ever played. The Giants and Red Sox were the first to go into overtime in the deciding game when Boston won in the bottom of the 10th inning of 1912's Game 8.

◆ The Pirate-Tiger Series of 1909 was one of only three in which the two teams alternated wins. The Yankees won Games 1, 3, 5 and 7 over the Giants in 1962, as did the Marlins against the Indians in 1997.

◆ Bob Gibson is the only man to start three seventh games, and the only one to win two. He won the deciding game for St. Louis in 1964 and 1967 but lost in a complete-game battle to Detroit's Mickey Lolich in 1968. In addition to Gibson, Walter Johnson and Lew Burdette are the only pitchers to earn a decision in Game 7s in consecutive years. Johnson won the 1924 Series in relief, but lost in a complete-game start in 1925. Burdette got the start for the Braves in the final game of 1957 and 1958; he won the first but lost the second. (Don Larsen started both games for New York against Burdette, but he didn't get a decision in 1958.)

◆ The losses by Johnson in 1925 and Gibson in 1968 are two of four complete-game performances by a losing pitcher in a Game 7. Christy Mathewson lost the final game of 1912 in 10 innings, and Detroit's Bobo Newsom went down in defeat in 1940 despite allowing only two runs in nine innings.

◆ A total of 40 home runs have been hit in seventh games, 27 for the winning side and 13 for the losers. Five home runs were hit in the 1960 and 1964 Game 7s. Yogi Berra is the only player to strike two home runs in a Game 7; he did it in the Yankees' 9-0 rout over the Dodgers in the 1956 Series. Bill Skowron is the only man to hit a Game 7 home run in three different years: a grand slam in 1956, a three-run homer in 1958, and a solo shot in 1960. All three were with the Yankees.

WORLD SERIES CLASSIC 1960

Pittsburgh Pirates (4) vs. New York Yankees (3)

A look at the stats for the 1960 World Series and you might think that the New York Yankees had overpowered their foes to capture yet another World Championship. Making their 10th appearance in 12 years, they established single-series records for runs scored (55), hits (91), extra-base hits (27), and team batting average (.338). Yankee infielder Bobby Richardson collected a record 12 RBI and walked away with the Series Most Valuable Player trophy. Pitcher Whitey Ford dominated the opposition for 18 scoreless innings in Games 3 and 6. Meanwhile, the National League champion Pittsburgh Pirates managed only 27 runs in the seven games, and the pitching staff limped away with a 7.11 ERA, the highest mark by any team in a Series since 1932. But these statistics did not concern

Above: Mickey Mantle crushes a homer for one of his four hits during New York's 10-0 trouncing of the Pirates in Game 3 at Yankee Stadium.

Above: Pittsburgh reliever Elroy Face earned the save in three of the Pirates' four wins in the Series.

Right: New York got two complete-game shutouts from Whitey Ford in the 1960 Series.

Below right: At Yankee Stadium in Game 4, Bill Virdon helped Pittsburgh even the Series with his leaping catch to rob Bob Cerv of a seventh-inning homer at the wall in right-center.

Whitey Ford's 18 innings of shutout pitching in 1960 began a record streak of 33⅓ consecutive scoreless innings that would continue through the next two World Series.

Manager Danny Murtaugh or the rest of the Pirate squad, thanks to the heroics of second baseman Bill Mazeroski—providing perhaps the most dramatic moment in World Series history.

The Series opened at Forbes Field in Pittsburgh, and the Pirates withstood 13 Yankee hits to capture Game 1. A three-run first inning and a two-run homer by Bill Mazeroski in the fourth paced Pittsburgh in the 6-4 win. In the second game things took a dramatic turn for the worse for Pittsburgh, as the Bronx Bombers victimized six Pirate pitchers for 16 runs on 19 hits, including two home runs and five RBI by Mickey Mantle. The Pirates got 13 hits of their own, setting the record for the most hits by two teams in one game, but Pittsburgh brought only three around to score. The scene switched to Yankee Stadium for Game 3, and the Yankees continued to slug away while the Pirate bats went quiet. The six runs chalked up by New York in the bottom of the first gave starter Whitey Ford plenty of breathing room, and he went on to pitch a four-hit shutout. Bobby Richardson, who had only one home run all season, put the game out of reach with his fourth-inning grand slam, collecting four of his record six RBI for the game. The Pirates evened the Series the following day, again behind the strong arm of Game 1 winner Vern Law. Center fielder Bill Virdon, whose RBI single put Pittsburgh up 3-1 in the fifth, helped preserve the win with a leaping catch to rob Bob Cerv of a home run with two on in the bottom of the seventh. The unlikely became likelier when the Pirates stole another game at the Stadium to take a three-games-to-two lead. New York's Art Ditmar was hit early in Game 5, giving up three runs in the first inning and a third. Harvey Haddix pitched five-hit ball in the start for Pittsburgh, and Roy Face shut the Yanks down in the last two and two-thirds innings to collect his third save of the Series.

The action returned to Pittsburgh for Game 6, and the Yankee bats came alive again while Whitey Ford ruled from the mound. With the seemingly unstoppable southpaw on the hill, the Yankees' 17 hits and 12 runs were more than enough to tie the Series. Despite having

Right: Second baseman Bobby Richardson calls for time after Tony Kubek was hit in the throat on a bad hop off of a Bill Virdon ground ball in Game 7.

Left: The trainer attends to Kubek after the freak injury that forced him out of the game. The play also helped keep a Pirate rally going in the eighth inning of the final game.

Along with his Series-record six RBI in Game 3, Bobby Richardson became the fourth player ever to hit two triples in one World Series game, accomplished in Game 6 at Pittsburgh.

Above: Bobby Richardson drove in a record six runs in Game 3. With 12 RBI and a .367 average at Series end, he became the only player from a losing team to be named World Series MVP.

Game 1 Wednesday, October 5 at Forbes Field, Pittsburgh

	1	2	3	4	5	6	7	8	9	R	H	E
New York Yankees	1	0	0	1	0	0	0	0	2	4	13	2
Pittsburgh Pirates	3	0	0	2	0	1	0	0	x	6	8	0

Pitchers NY Art Ditmar (L, 0-1), IP ⅓, H 3, R 3, ER 3, BB 1, SO 0; Jim Coates, IP 3⅔, H 3, R 2, ER 2, BB 1, SO 2; Duke Maas, IP 2, H 2, R 1, ER 1, BB 0, SO 1; Ryne Duren, IP 2, H 0, R 0, ER 0, BB 1, SO 1
Pit Vern Law (W, 1-0), IP 7, H 10, R 2, ER 2, BB 1, SO 3; Roy Face (Sv, 1), IP 2, H 3, R 2, ER 2, BB 0, SO 2

Top Performers at the Plate
NY Roger Maris, 3 for 4, 2 R, 1 RBI; Bill Skowron, 2 for 4, 1 RBI
Pit Dick Groat, 2 for 4, 1 R, 1 RBI; Bill Mazeroski, 2 for 4, 2 R, 2 RBI

2B-Pit/Groat, Virdon. **HR**-NY/Howard, Maris; Pit/Mazeroski. **SB**-Pit/Skinner, Virdon. **Time** 2:29. **Attendance** 36,676.

Game 2 Thursday, October 6 at Forbes Field, Pittsburgh

	1	2	3	4	5	6	7	8	9	R	H	E
New York Yankees	0	0	2	1	2	7	3	0	1	16	19	1
Pittsburgh Pirates	0	0	0	1	0	0	0	0	2	3	13	1

Pitchers NY Bob Turley (W, 1-0), IP 8⅓, H 13, R 3, ER 2, BB 3, SO 0; Bobby Shantz (Sv, 1), IP ⅔, H 0, R 0, ER 0, BB 0, SO 0
Pit Bob Friend (L, 0-1), IP 4, H 6, R 3, ER 2, BB 2, SO 6; Fred Green, IP 1, H 3, R 4, ER 4, BB 1, SO 0; Clem Labine, IP ⅔, H 3, R 5, ER 0, BB 1, SO 1; George Witt, IP ⅓, H 2, R 0, ER 0, BB 0, SO 0; Joe Gibbon, IP 2, H 4, R 3, ER 3, BB 0, SO 2; Tom Cheney, IP 1, H 1, R 1, ER 1, BB 1, SO 2

Top Performers at the Plate
NY Mickey Mantle, 2 for 4, 3 R, 5 RBI, 2 BB, 2 HR; Bobby Richardson, 3 for 4, 3 R, 2 RBI, 1 BB
Pit Gino Cimoli, 2 for 4, 1 R, 1 RBI, 1 BB; Don Hoak, 2 for 5, 1 RBI, 2 2B

2B-NY/Boyer, McDougald, Richardson; Pit/Hoak 2, Mazeroski. **3B**-NY/Howard. **HR**-NY/Mantle 2. **Time** 3:14. **Attendance** 37,308.

Game 3 Saturday, October 8 at Yankee Stadium, New York

	1	2	3	4	5	6	7	8	9	R	H	E
Pittsburgh Pirates	0	0	0	0	0	0	0	0	0	0	4	0
New York Yankees	6	0	0	4	0	0	0	0	x	10	16	1

Pitchers Pit Vinegar Bend Mizell (L, 0-1), IP ⅓, H 3, R 4, ER 4, BB 1, SO 0; Clem Labine, IP ⅓, H 4, R 2, ER 2, BB 0, SO 0; Fred Green, IP 3, H 5, R 4, ER 4, BB 0, SO 3; George Witt, IP 1⅓, H 3, R 0, ER 0, BB 2, SO 1; Tom Cheney, IP 2, H 1, R 0, ER 0, BB 0, SO 3; Joe Gibbon, IP 1, H 0, R 0, ER 0, BB 1, SO 0
NY Whitey Ford (W, 1-0), IP 9, H 4, R 0, ER 0, BB 1, SO 3

Top Performers at the Plate
NY Mickey Mantle, 4 for 5, 2 R, 2 RBI; Bobby Richardson, 2 for 5, 1 R, 6 RBI

2B-Pit/Virdon; NY/Mantle. **HR**-NY/Mantle, Richardson. **Time** 2:41. **Attendance** 70,001.

Game 4 Sunday, October 9 at Yankee Stadium, New York

	1	2	3	4	5	6	7	8	9	R	H	E
Pittsburgh Pirates	0	0	0	0	3	0	0	0	0	3	7	0
New York Yankees	0	0	0	1	0	0	1	0	0	2	8	0

Pitchers Pit Vern Law (W, 2-0), IP 6⅓, H 8, R 2, ER 2, BB 1, SO 5; Roy Face (Sv, 2), IP 2⅔, H 0, R 0, ER 0, BB 0, SO 1
NY Ralph Terry (L, 0-1), IP 6⅓, H 6, R 3, ER 3, BB 1, SO 5; Bobby Shantz, IP ⅔, H 0, R 0, ER 0, BB 0, SO 1; Jim Coates, IP 2, H 1, R 0, ER 0, BB 0, SO 1

Top Performers at the Plate
Pit Vern Law, 2 for 3, 1 R, 1 RBI; Bill Virdon, 1 for 4, 2 RBI
NY Bobby Richardson, 2 for 3, 1 RBI; Bill Skowron, 2 for 4, 2 R, 1 RBI

2B-Pit/Law; NY/Kubek, Richardson, Skowron. **HR**-NY/Skowron. **Time** 2:29. **Attendance** 67,812.

Game 5 Monday, October 10 at Yankee Stadium, New York

	1	2	3	4	5	6	7	8	9	R	H	E
Pittsburgh Pirates	0	3	1	0	0	0	0	0	1	5	10	2
New York Yankees	0	1	1	0	0	0	0	0	0	2	5	2

Pitchers Pit Harvey Haddix (W, 1-0), IP 6⅓, H 5, R 2, ER 2, BB 2, SO 6; Roy Face (Sv, 3), IP 2⅔, H 0, R 0, ER 0, BB 1, SO 1
NY Art Ditmar (L, 0-2), IP 1⅓, H 3, R 3, ER 1, BB 0, SO 0; Luis Arroyo, IP ⅔, H 2, R 1, ER 1, BB 0, SO 1; Bill Stafford, IP 5, H 3, R 0, ER 0, BB 0, SO 2; Ryne Duren, IP 2, H 2, R 1, ER 0, BB 0, SO 4

Top Performers at the Plate
Pit Smoky Burgess, 2 for 4, 1 R; Don Hoak, 2 for 4, 1 R, 2 RBI
NY Elston Howard, 1 for 3, 1 R

2B-Pit/Burgess, Groat, Mazeroski, Virdon; NY/Howard. **HR**-NY/Maris. **Time** 2:32. **Attendance** 62,753.

Game 6 Wednesday, October 12 at Forbes Field, Pittsburgh

	1	2	3	4	5	6	7	8	9	R	H	E
New York Yankees	0	1	5	0	0	2	2	2	0	12	17	1
Pittsburgh Pirates	0	0	0	0	0	0	0	7	1	0	7	1

Pitchers NY Whitey Ford (W, 2-0), IP 9, H 7, R 0, ER 0, BB 1, SO 5
Pit Bob Friend (L, 0-2), IP 2, H 5, R 5, ER 5, BB 1, SO 1; Tom Cheney, IP 1, H 2, R 1, ER 1, BB 0, SO 1; Vinegar Bend Mizell, IP 2, H 1, R 0, ER 0, BB 1, SO 1; Fred Green, IP 0, H 3, R 2, ER 2, BB 0, SO 0; Clem Labine, IP 3, H 6, R 4, ER 4, BB 0, SO 1; George Witt, IP 1, H 0, R 0, ER 0, BB 0, SO 0

Top Performers at the Plate
NY Yogi Berra, 3 for 4, 3 R, 2 RBI, 1 BB; Bobby Richardson, 2 for 5, 1 R, 3 RBI, 2 3B
Pit Roberto Clemente, 2 for 4; Hal Smith, 2 for 4

2B-NY/Blanchard 2, Maris, Skowron. **3B**-NY/Boyer, Richardson 2. **Time** 2:38. **Attendance** 38,580.

Game 7 Wednesday, October 13 at Forbes Field, Pittsburgh

	1	2	3	4	5	6	7	8	9	R	H	E
New York Yankees	0	0	0	0	1	4	0	2	2	9	13	1
Pittsburgh Pirates	2	2	0	0	0	0	0	5	1	10	11	0

Pitchers NY Bob Turley, IP 1, H 2, R 3, ER 3, BB 1, SO 0; Bill Stafford, IP 1, H 2, R 1, ER 1, BB 1, SO 0; Bobby Shantz, IP 5, H 4, R 3, ER 3, BB 1, SO 0; Jim Coates, IP ⅔, H 2, R 2, ER 2, BB 0, SO 0; Ralph Terry (L, 0-2), IP ⅓, H 1, R 1, ER 1, BB 0, SO 0
Pit Vern Law, IP 5, H 4, R 3, ER 3, BB 1, SO 0; Roy Face, IP 3, H 6, R 4, ER 4, BB 1, SO 0; Bob Friend, IP 0, H 2, R 2, ER 2, BB 0, SO 0; Harvey Hadddix (W, 2-0), IP 1, H 1, R 0, ER 0, BB 0, SO 0

Top Performers at the Plate
NY Yogi Berra, 1 for 4, 2 R, 4 RBI, 1 BB; Mickey Mantle, 3 for 5, 1 R, 2 RBI
Pit Bill Mazeroski, 2 for 4, 2 R, 1 RBI; Bill Virdon, 2 for 4, 1 R, 2 RBI

2B-NY/Boyer. **HR**-NY/Berra, Skowron; Pit/Mazeroski, Nelson, Smith. **Time** 2:36. **Attendance** 36,683.

Below: The Game 7 home run in 1960 was a once-in-a-lifetime moment for Bill Mazeroski, and one of the most dramatic moments in sports history.

Left: As fans and coaches offer enthusiastic congratulations, Bill Mazeroski gallops around third base on his way home after his dramatic hit.

Below: Art Ditmar delivers the first pitch of Game 5 to Pittsburgh's Bill Virdon. The Pirates took the Series lead with a 5-2 win in the game.

1960 WORLD SERIES COMPOSITE STATISTICS

PITTSBURGH PIRATES/Danny Murtaugh, Manager

Player	pos	G	AB	R	H	2B	3B	HR	RBI	BB	SO	SB	BA	SA	E	FPct
Gene Baker	ph	3	3	0	0	0	0	0	0	0	1	0	.000	.000	—	—
Smoky Burgess	c	5	18	2	6	1	0	0	0	2	1	0	.333	.389	0	1.000
Tom Cheney	p	3	0	0	0	0	0	0	0	0	0	0	—	—	0	1.000
Joe Christopher	ph-pr	3	0	2	0	0	0	0	0	0	0	0	—	—	0	—
Gino Cimoli	lf-ph	7	20	4	5	0	0	0	1	2	4	0	.250	.250	0	1.000
Roberto Clemente	rf	7	29	1	9	0	0	0	3	0	4	0	.310	.310	0	1.000
Roy Face	p	4	3	0	0	0	0	0	0	0	2	0	.000	.000	0	1.000
Bob Friend	p	3	1	0	0	0	0	0	0	0	0	0	.000	.000	0	1.000
Joe Gibbon	p	2	0	0	0	0	0	0	0	0	0	0	—	—	0	1.000
Fred Green	p	3	1	0	0	0	0	0	0	0	0	0	.000	.000	0	—
Dick Groat	ss	7	28	3	6	2	0	0	2	0	1	0	.214	.286	2	.923
Harvey Haddix	p	2	3	0	1	0	0	0	0	0	1	0	.333	.333	0	1.000
Don Hoak	3b	7	23	3	5	2	0	0	3	4	1	0	.217	.304	1	.947
Clem Labine	p	3	0	0	0	0	0	0	0	0	0	0	—	—	0	1.000
Vern Law	p	3	6	1	2	1	0	0	1	0	1	0	.333	.500	0	1.000
Bill Mazeroski	2b	7	25	4	8	2	0	2	5	0	3	0	.320	.640	0	1.000
Vinegar Bend Mizell	p	2	0	0	0	0	0	0	0	0	0	0	—	—	0	—
Rocky Nelson	1b-ph	4	9	2	3	0	0	1	2	1	1	0	.333	.667	0	1.000
Bob Oldis	c	2	0	0	0	0	0	0	0	0	0	0	—	—	0	1.000
Dick Schofield	ph-ss	3	3	0	1	0	0	0	0	1	0	0	.333	.333	0	1.000
Bob Skinner	lf	2	5	2	1	0	0	0	1	1	0	1	.200	.200	0	1.000
Hal Smith	c	3	8	1	3	0	0	1	3	0	0	0	.375	.375	0	1.000
Dick Stuart	1b	5	20	0	3	0	0	0	0	0	3	0	.150	.150	0	1.000
Bill Virdon	cf	7	29	2	7	3	0	0	5	1	3	1	.241	.345	1	.947
George Witt	p	3	0	0	0	0	0	0	0	0	0	0	—	—	0	—
Totals		7	234	27	60	11	0	4	26	12	26	2	.256	.355	4	.984

Pitcher	G	GS	CG	IP	H	R	ER	BB	SO	W-L	Sv	ERA
Tom Cheney	3	0	0	4	4	2	2	1	6	0-0	0	4.50
Roy Face	4	0	0	10⅓	9	6	6	2	4	0-0	3	5.23
Bob Friend	3	2	0	6	13	10	9	3	7	0-2	0	13.50
Joe Gibbon	2	0	0	3	4	3	3	1	2	0-0	0	9.00
Fred Green	3	0	0	4	11	10	10	1	3	0-0	0	22.50
Harvey Haddix	2	1	0	7⅓	6	2	2	2	6	2-0	0	2.45
Clem Labine	3	0	0	4	13	11	6	1	3	0-0	0	13.50
Vern Law	3	3	0	18⅓	22	7	7	3	8	2-0	0	3.44
Vinegar Bend Mizell	2	1	0	2⅓	4	4	4	2	1	0-1	0	15.43
George Witt	3	0	0	2⅔	5	0	0	2	1	0-0	0	0.00
Totals	7	7	0	62	91	55	49	18	40	4-3	3	7.11

NEW YORK YANKEES/Casey Stengel, Manager

Player	pos	G	AB	R	H	2B	3B	HR	RBI	BB	SO	SB	BA	SA	E	FPct
Luis Arroyo	p	1	1	0	0	0	0	0	0	0	0	0	.000	.000	0	—
Yogi Berra	c-lf-rf-ph	7	22	6	7	0	0	1	8	2	0	0	.318	.455	0	1.000
Johnny Blanchard	ph-c	5	11	2	5	2	0	0	2	0	0	0	.455	.636	0	1.000
Clete Boyer	3b-ss	4	12	1	3	2	1	0	1	0	1	0	.250	.583	0	1.000
Bob Cerv	ph-lf	4	14	1	5	0	0	0	0	0	3	0	.357	.357	1	.889
Jim Coates	p	3	1	0	0	0	0	0	0	0	1	0	.000	.000	0	1.000
Joe DeMaestri	ss-pr	4	2	1	1	0	0	0	0	0	0	0	.500	.500	0	1.000
Art Ditmar	p	2	0	0	0	0	0	0	0	0	0	0	—	—	0	—
Ryne Duren	p	2	0	0	0	0	0	0	0	0	0	0	—	—	0	1.000
Whitey Ford	p	2	8	1	2	0	0	0	2	0	2	0	.250	.250	0	1.000
Eli Grba	pr	1	0	0	0	0	0	0	0	0	0	0	—	—	0	—
Elston Howard	ph-c	5	13	4	6	1	0	1	4	1	4	0	.462	.923	0	1.000
Tony Kubek	ss-lf	7	30	6	10	1	0	0	3	2	2	0	.333	.367	3	.932
Dale Long	ph	3	3	0	1	0	0	0	0	0	0	0	.333	.333	—	—
Hector Lopez	lf-ph	3	7	3	3	0	0	0	0	0	0	0	.429	.429	0	1.000
Duke Maas	p	1	0	0	0	0	0	0	0	0	0	0	—	—	0	—
Mickey Mantle	cf	7	25	8	10	1	0	3	11	8	9	0	.400	.800	0	1.000
Roger Maris	rf-pr	7	30	6	8	1	0	2	2	2	4	0	.267	.500	1	.923
Gil McDougald	3b-pr	6	18	4	5	1	0	0	2	2	3	0	.278	.333	1	.923
Bobby Richardson	2b	7	30	8	11	2	2	1	12	1	1	0	.367	.667	2	.961
Bobby Shantz	p	3	3	0	1	0	0	0	0	1	0	0	.333	.333	0	1.000
Bill Skowron	1b	7	32	7	12	2	0	2	6	0	6	0	.375	.625	0	1.000
Bill Stafford	p	2	1	0	0	0	0	0	0	0	0	0	.000	.000	0	1.000
Ralph Terry	p	2	2	0	0	0	0	0	0	0	1	0	.000	.000	0	1.000
Bob Turley	p	2	4	1	1	0	0	0	1	0	1	0	.250	.250	0	1.000
Totals		7	269	55	91	13	4	10	54	18	40	0	.338	.528	8	.972

Pitcher	G	GS	CG	IP	H	R	ER	BB	SO	W-L	Sv	ERA
Luis Arroyo	1	0	0	⅔	2	1	1	0	1	0-0	0	13.50
Jim Coates	3	0	0	6⅓	8	6	4	4	3	0-0	0	5.68
Art Ditmar	2	2	0	1⅔	6	6	4	1	0	0-2	0	21.60
Ryne Duren	2	0	0	4	2	1	1	1	5	0-0	0	2.25
Whitey Ford	2	2	2	18	11	0	0	2	8	2-0	0	0.00
Duke Maas	1	0	0	2	1	1	1	0	1	0-0	0	4.50
Bobby Shantz	3	0	0	6⅓	6	4	3	1	1	0-0	1	4.26
Bill Stafford	2	0	0	6	5	1	1	1	2	0-0	1	1.50
Ralph Terry	2	1	0	6⅔	6	5	4	1	5	0-2	0	5.40
Bob Turley	2	2	0	9⅓	15	6	5	4	0	1-0	0	4.82
Totals	7	7	2	61	60	27	24	12	26	3-4	1	3.54

Series MVP: Bobby Richardson, New York Yankees. **Series Outstanding Pitcher:** Whitey Ford, New York Yankees. **Average Length of Game:** 2 hours, 40 minutes. **Total Attendance:** 349,813. **Average Attendance:** 49,973 (37,312 at Forbes Field; 66,855 at Yankee Stadium). **Umpires:** Dusty Boggess (NL), Nestor Chylak (AL), Jim Honochick (AL), Bill Jackowski (NL), Stan Landes (NL), Johnny Stevens (AL). **Winning Player's Share:** $8,418. **Losing Player's Share:** $5,125.

Roger Maris's home run in Game 1 came in his first World Series at-bat.

Background: A dejected Ralph Terry leaves the mound as Pittsburgh fans rush onto the field after Bill Mazeroski stroked his Series-winning homer.

outscored the Pirates 46-17 in the first six games—and 38-3 in their three victories—the Yankees found themselves fighting for their lives in a win-ner-take-all Game 7 at Forbes Field. The Pirates struck early, scoring two runs in each of the first two innings. Although Law continued his mastery over the Yankees early in the game, holding them to one hit through four innings, the Yanks began chipping away and took the lead on Yogi Berra's three-run homer in the sixth. Two more runs in the eighth gave New York a 7-4 lead with six outs to go. But the game see-sawed back in Pittsburgh's favor in the bottom half of the inning, with the help of a pebble on the infield dirt. After the leadoff hitter reached first, Virdon hit a hard grounder to short for a seemingly ideal double-play ball, but the ball took a bad hop and hit shortstop Tony Kubek in the throat. Kubek was rushed to the hospital, and the Pittsburgh rally stayed alive. A single by Roberto

Clemente was followed by a three-run clout by back-up catcher Hal Smith, and five Pirates crossed the plate by the time the inning was over. Behind by two runs and down to their last at-bats, the Yankees would not quit. Richardson started it off with his 11th base hit of the Series, and clutch hitting by Dale Long and Mickey Mantle allowed New York to knot the score at 9-9. Scheduled to lead off the bottom of the ninth was the stocky infielder Bill Mazeroski. Pitcher Ralph Terry's first offering was a ball, but on the second pitch, Mazeroski connected and sent the ball over the ivy-covered brick wall in left-center field. "Maz" leaped around the bases and was mobbed by fans and teammates as he scored the game- and Series-winning run. It was the first time a World Series had ever ended on a home run, and the only time such dramatics ever occurred in a deciding seventh game.

New York Yankees (4) vs. Cincinnati Reds (1)

The New York Yankees were back for their 26th World Series in 1961, but for the first time since 1947, they were there without Casey Stengel. The 72-year-old manager had been dismissed by the Yankees after the 1960 Series and was replaced by 42-year-old rookie skipper Ralph Houk. Hoping to rebound from their shocking defeat at the hands of the Pirates the previous year, the Yankees ran away with the pennant with 109 wins. The team featured an awesome home run attack led by the duo of Roger Maris and Mickey Mantle. They also got 25 wins from Cy Young winner Whitey Ford, and Luis Arroyo led the majors with 29 saves in 1961. The Cincinnati Reds had great hitters in Frank Robinson and Vada Pinson, but no member of the Cincinnati roster had ever played in a World Series before. In the end, they would prove little match for the experienced Yankee machine. Ford started the opener for New York and silenced the Reds with a two-hitter in his third consecutive Series shutout. Cincinnati's Jim O'Toole pitched well, but a solo homer by Elston Howard in the fourth broke the scoreless tie, and Bill Skowron belted another one two innings later. Cincinnati's 21-game-winner Joey Jay took one from the Yanks in Game 2 at Yankee Stadium. He held the hard-hitting squad to just two runs, both coming on a Yogi Berra home run. The Reds came through with six runs on the day, starting with a two-run homer by Gordy Coleman in the top of the fourth. Game 3 starter Bob Purkey held the Yanks scoreless through six innings, until Berra drove in Tony Kubek with a two-out single in the seventh to tie the game 1-1. Cincinnati retook the lead in the bottom of the inning when Johnny Edwards came home after doubling, but New York came back to score one run in each of the last two innings. Johnny Blanchard's pinch-hit home run in the eighth brought the score to 2-2, and Maris got the game-winner with a leadoff blast in the ninth, his first hit of the Series. Arroyo earned the win with two shutout innings in relief. Although an ankle injury forced him out in the sixth inning of Game 4, Ford extended his scoreless streak to 32 consecutive innings, breaking Babe Ruth's record of 29 innings. Jim Coates preserved the shutout by allowing just one hit in four innings of relief work, and New York walked away with a 7-0 victory. The clincher came quickly in Game 5, with the Yankees scoring five in the first, one in the second, and five more in the fourth. Hector Lopez, playing in place of a hobbling Mantle, tripled, homered and drove in five runs on the day. Though Frank Robinson connected for his first World Series homer in the third inning, the Yankees closed the door on another title with a convincing 13-5 win.

Above: Whitey Ford delivers the first pitch of the 1961 World Series to Cincinnati's Don Blasingame. The Yankee Stadium scoreboard offers congratulations for the Yankees' 26th Series.

1961 WORLD SERIES COMPOSITE STATISTICS

NEW YORK YANKEES/Ralph Houk, Manager

Player	pos	G	AB	R	H	2B	3B	HR	RBI	BB	SO	SB	BA	SA	E	FPct
Luis Arroyo	p	2	0	0	0	0	0	0	0	0	0	0	–	–	1	.667
Yogi Berra	lf	4	11	2	3	0	0	1	3	5	1	0	.273	.545	1	.917
Johnny Blanchard	ph-rf	4	10	4	4	1	0	2	3	2	0	0	.400	1.100	0	1.000
Clete Boyer	3b	5	15	0	4	2	0	0	3	4	0	0	.267	.400	1	.947
Jim Coates	p	1	1	0	0	0	0	0	0	0	1	0	.000	.000	0	–
Bud Daley	p	2	1	0	0	0	0	0	0	1	0	0	.000	.000	1	.000
Whitey Ford	p	2	5	1	0	0	0	0	0	1	0	0	.000	.000	0	1.000
Billy Gardner	ph	1	1	0	0	0	0	0	0	0	0	0	.000	.000	–	–
Elston Howard	c	5	20	5	5	3	0	1	1	2	3	0	.250	.550	1	1.000
Tony Kubek	ss	5	22	3	5	0	0	0	1	1	4	0	.227	.227	1	1.000
Hector Lopez	rf-ph-pr-lf	4	9	3	3	0	1	1	7	2	3	0	.333	.889	1	1.000
Mickey Mantle	cf	2	6	0	1	0	0	0	0	0	2	0	.167	.167	0	1.000
Roger Maris	cf-rf	5	19	4	2	1	0	1	2	4	6	0	.105	.316	0	1.000
Jack Reed	cf	3	0	0	0	0	0	0	0	0	0	0	–	–	0	–
Bobby Richardson	2b	5	23	2	9	1	0	0	0	0	0	1	.391	.435	0	1.000
Bill Skowron	1b	5	17	3	6	0	0	1	5	3	4	0	.353	.529	0	1.000
Bill Stafford	p	1	2	0	0	0	0	0	0	0	0	0	.000	.000	0	.500
Ralph Terry	p	2	3	0	0	0	0	0	0	0	1	0	.000	.000	0	1.000
Totals		5	165	27	42	8	1	7	26	24	25	1	.255	.442	5	.974

Pitcher	G	GS	CG	IP	H	R	ER	BB	SO	W-L	Sv	ERA
Luis Arroyo	2	0	0	4	4	2	1	2	3	1-0	0	2.25
Jim Coates	1	0	0	4	1	0	0	1	2	0-0	1	0.00
Bud Daley	2	0	0	7	5	2	0	0	3	1-0	0	0.00
Whitey Ford	2	2	1	14	6	0	0	1	7	2-0	0	0.00
Bill Stafford	1	1	0	6⅔	7	2	2	2	5	0-0	0	2.70
Ralph Terry	2	2	0	9⅓	12	7	5	2	7	0-1	0	4.82
Totals	5	5	1	45	35	13	8	8	27	4-1	1	1.60

CINCINNATI REDS/Fred Hutchinson, Manager

Player	pos	G	AB	R	H	2B	3B	HR	RBI	BB	SO	SB	BA	SA	E	FPct
Gus Bell	ph	3	3	0	0	0	0	0	0	0	0	0	.000	.000	–	–
Don Blasingame	2b-pr	3	7	1	1	0	0	0	0	0	3	0	.143	.143	0	1.000
Jim Brosnan	p	3	0	0	0	0	0	0	0	0	0	0	–	–	0	–
Leo Cardenas	ph	3	3	0	1	1	0	0	0	0	1	0	.333	.667	0	–
Elio Chacon	2b-ph	4	12	2	3	0	0	0	0	1	2	0	.250	.250	0	1.000
Gordy Coleman	1b	5	20	2	5	0	0	1	2	0	1	0	.250	.400	1	.971
Johnny Edwards	c	3	11	1	4	2	0	0	2	0	0	0	.364	.545	0	1.000
Gene Freese	3b	5	16	0	1	1	0	0	0	3	4	0	.063	.125	0	1.000
Dick Gernert	ph	4	4	0	0	0	0	0	0	0	1	0	.000	.000	–	–
Bill Henry	p	2	0	0	0	0	0	0	0	0	0	0	–	–	0	1.000
Ken Hunt	p	1	0	0	0	0	0	0	0	0	0	0	–	–	0	1.000
Joey Jay	p	2	4	0	0	0	0	0	0	0	2	0	.000	.000	0	1.000
Darrell Johnson	c	2	4	0	2	0	0	0	0	0	0	0	.500	.500	0	1.000
Ken Johnson	p	1	0	0	0	0	0	0	0	0	0	0	–	–	0	–
Sherman Jones	p	1	0	0	0	0	0	0	0	0	0	0	–	–	0	–
Eddie Kasko	ss	5	22	1	7	0	0	0	1	0	2	0	.318	.318	1	.963
Jerry Lynch	ph	4	3	0	0	0	0	0	0	1	1	0	.000	.000	–	–
Jim Maloney	p	1	0	0	0	0	0	0	0	0	0	0	–	–	0	1.000
Jim O'Toole	p	2	3	0	0	0	0	0	0	0	1	0	.000	.000	0	1.000
Vada Pinson	cf	5	22	0	2	1	0	0	0	0	1	0	.091	.136	1	.950
Wally Post	lf-rf	5	18	3	6	1	0	1	2	0	1	0	.333	.556	0	1.000
Bob Purkey	p	2	3	0	0	0	0	0	0	0	3	0	.000	.000	1	.875
Frank Robinson	rf-lf	5	15	3	3	2	0	1	4	3	4	0	.200	.533	0	1.000
Jerry Zimmerman	c	2	0	0	0	0	0	0	0	0	0	0	–	–	0	1.000
Totals		5	170	13	35	8	0	3	11	8	27	0	.206	.306	4	.978

Pitcher	G	GS	CG	IP	H	R	ER	BB	SO	W-L	Sv	ERA
Jim Brosnan	3	0	0	6	9	5	5	4	5	0-0	0	7.50
Bill Henry	2	0	0	2⅓	4	5	5	2	3	0-0	0	19.29
Ken Hunt	1	0	0	1	0	0	0	1	1	0-0	0	0.00
Joey Jay	2	2	1	9⅔	8	6	6	6	6	1-1	0	5.59
Ken Johnson	1	0	0	⅔	0	0	0	0	0	0-0	0	0.00
Sherman Jones	1	0	0	⅔	0	0	0	0	0	0-0	0	0.00
Jim Maloney	1	0	0	⅔	4	2	2	1	1	0-0	0	27.00
Jim O'Toole	2	2	0	12	11	4	4	7	4	0-2	0	3.00
Bob Purkey	2	1	1	11	6	5	2	3	5	0-1	0	1.64
Totals	5	5	2	44	42	27	24	24	25	1-4	0	4.91

Series MVP: Whitey Ford, New York Yankees. **Series Outstanding Pitcher:** Whitey Ford, New York Yankees. **Average Length of Game:** 2 hours, 32 minutes. **Total Attendance:** 223,247. **Average Attendance:** 44,649 (62,740 at Yankee Stadium; 32,589 at Crosley Field).
Umpires: Jocko Conlan (NL), Henry Crawford (NL), Augie Donatelli (NL), Ed Runge (AL), Bob Stewart (AL), Frank Umont (AL). **Winning Player's Share:** $7,389. **Losing Player's Share:** $5,356.

Left: Hector Lopez did a splendid job filling in for an injured Mickey Mantle. He drove in seven runs in the Series, including five in Game 5.

Below: Roger Maris breaks an 0-for-10 slump with this game-winning, ninth-inning homer in Game 3.

Above: A young Frank Robinson played in his first Series in 1961 and got his first postseason homer in the final game.

Below: New York celebrates another championship. Pitcher Bud Daley and Elston Howard watch as Hector Lopez fields Vada Pinson's fly ball for the final out.

The Cincinnati Reds were the first pennant-winning team since 1944, and the last since 1961, to come to the World Series without any players who could boast postseason experience. After the first four contests in 1903 to 1907, the 1912 Boston Red Sox and the 1944 St. Louis Browns were the only other teams with all first-timers in the World Series.

Game 1   Wednesday, October 4 at Yankee Stadium, New York

	1	2	3	4	5	6	7	8	9		R	H	E
Cincinnati Reds	0	0	0	0	0	0	0	0	0		0	2	0
New York Yankees	0	0	0	1	0	1	0	0	x		2	6	0

Pitchers Cin   Jim O'Toole (L, 0-1), IP 7, H 6, R 2, ER 2, BB 4, SO 2; Jim Brosnan, IP 1, H 0, R 0, ER 0, BB 1, SO 1
          NY   Whitey Ford (W, 1-0), IP 9, H 2, R 0, ER 0, BB 1, SO 6

Top Performers at the Plate
          NY   Bobby Richardson, 3 for 4; Bill Skowron, 1 for 3, 1 R, 1 RBI, 1 BB

HR-NY/Howard, Skowron. **Time** 2:11. **Attendance** 62,397.

Game 2   Thursday, October 5 at Yankee Stadium, New York

	1	2	3	4	5	6	7	8	9		R	H	E
Cincinnati Reds	0	0	0	2	1	1	0	2	0		6	9	0
New York Yankees	0	0	0	2	0	0	0	0	0		2	4	3

Pitchers Cin   Joey Jay (W, 1-0), IP 9, H 4, R 2, ER 2, BB 6, SO 6
          NY   Ralph Terry (L, 0-1), IP 7, H 6, R 4, ER 2, BB 2, SO 7; Luis Arroyo, IP 2, H 3, R 2, ER 1, BB 2, SO 1

Top Performers at the Plate
          Cin   Gordy Coleman, 2 for 5, 1 R, 2 RBI; Johnny Edwards, 2 for 4, 2 RBI
          NY   Yogi Berra, 2 for 4, 1 R, 2 RBI

2B-Cin/Edwards, Pinson, Post. **HR**-Cin/Coleman; NY/Berra. **Time** 2:43. **Attendance** 63,083.

Game 3   Saturday, October 7 at Crosley Field, Cincinnati

	1	2	3	4	5	6	7	8	9		R	H	E
New York Yankees	0	0	0	0	0	0	1	1	1		3	6	1
Cincinnati Reds	0	0	1	0	0	0	1	0	0		2	8	0

Pitchers NY   Bill Stafford, IP 6⅔, H 7, R 2, ER 2, BB 2, SO 5; Bud Daley, IP ⅓, H 0, R 0, ER 0, BB 0, SO 0; Luis Arroyo (W, 1-0), IP 2, H 1, R 0, ER 0, BB 0, SO 2
          Cin   Bob Purkey (L, 0-1), IP 9, H 6, R 3, ER 2, BB 1, SO 3

Top Performers at the Plate
          NY   Yogi Berra, 1 for 3, 1 RBI, 1 BB; Johnny Blanchard, 1 for 1, 1 R, 1 RBI
          Cin   Gordy Coleman, 2 for 4; Eddie Kasko, 2 for 4, 1 RBI

2B-NY/Howard; Cin/Cardenas, Edwards, Robinson. **HR**-NY/Blanchard, Maris. **SB**-NY/Richardson. **Time** 2:15. **Attendance** 32,589.

Game 4   Sunday, October 8 at Crosley Field, Cincinnati

	1	2	3	4	5	6	7	8	9		R	H	E
New York Yankees	0	0	0	1	1	2	3	0	0		7	11	0
Cincinnati Reds	0	0	0	0	0	0	0	0	0		0	5	1

Pitchers NY   Whitey Ford (W, 2-0), IP 5, H 4, R 0, ER 0, BB 0, SO 1; Jim Coates (Sv, 1), IP 4, H 1, R 0, ER 0, BB 1, SO 2
          Cin   Jim O'Toole (L, 0-2), IP 5, H 5, R 2, ER 2, BB 3, SO 2; Jim Brosnan, IP 3, H 6, R 5, ER 5, BB 3, SO 3; Bill Henry, IP 1, H 0, R 0, ER 0, BB 0, SO 2

Top Performers at the Plate
          NY   Bobby Richardson, 3 for 5, 1 R; Bill Skowron, 3 for 3, 1 RBI, 1 BB
          Cin   Darrell Johnson, 2 for 2; Frank Robinson, 0 for 1, 1 BB, 2 HBP

2B-NY/Boyer, Howard, Richardson. **Time** 2:27. **Attendance** 32,589.

Game 5   Monday, October 9 at Crosley Field, Cincinnati

	1	2	3	4	5	6	7	8	9		R	H	E
New York Yankees	5	1	0	5	0	2	0	0	0		13	15	1
Cincinnati Reds	0	0	3	0	2	0	0	0	0		5	11	3

Pitchers NY   Ralph Terry, IP 2⅓, H 6, R 3, ER 3, BB 0, SO 0; Bud Daley (W, 1-0), IP 6⅔, H 5, R 2, ER 0, BB 0, SO 3
          Cin   Joey Jay (L, 1-1), IP ⅔, H 4, R 4, ER 4, BB 0, SO 0; Jim Maloney, IP ⅔, H 4, R 2, ER 2, BB 1, SO 1; Ken Johnson, IP ⅔, H 0, R 0, ER 0, BB 0, SO 0; Bill Henry, IP 1⅓, H 4, R 5, ER 5, BB 2, SO 1; Sherman Jones, IP ⅔, H 0, R 0, ER 0, BB 0, SO 0; Bob Purkey, IP 2, H 0, R 2, ER 0, BB 2, SO 2; Jim Brosnan, IP 2, H 3, R 0, ER 0, BB 0, SO 1; Ken Hunt, IP 1, H 0, R 0, ER 0, BB 1, SO 1

Top Performers at the Plate
          NY   Johnny Blanchard, 3 for 4, 3 R, 2 RBI, 2 BB; Hector Lopez, 2 for 4, 2 R, 5 RBI, 1 SH
          Cin   Wally Post, 2 for 3, 1 R, 2 RBI, 1 HBP; Frank Robinson, 2 for 4,1 R, 3 RBI

2B-NY/Blanchard, Boyer, Howard, Maris; Cin/Freese, Robinson. **3B**-NY/Lopez. **HR**-NY/Blanchard, Lopez; Cin/Post, Robinson. **Time** 3:05. **Attendance** 32,589.

Pinstripes in October
The Yankee Dynasty

All-Time Cumulative Records

In the process of playing in a record 206 World Series games, the Yankees have established all-time marks in practically every major category.

Most Series Played	37		Most Total Bases	2,677
Most Series Won	26		Most Runs	922
Most Series Sweeps	8		Most Runs Batted In	870
Most Consecutive Appearances	5 (1949–53 & 1960–64)		Most Bases On Balls	732
Most Consecutive Wins	5 (1949–53)		Most Times Hit By Pitch	44
Most Games Played	206		Most Times Struck-out	1,129
Most Games Won	125		Most Sacrifice Hits	115
Most Games Lost	80		Most Stolen Bases	71
Most Consecutive Games Won	14 (1996, 1998–2000)		Most Putouts	5,508
Most Consecutive Games Lost	8 (1921–23)		Most Assists	2,171
Most At-Bats	6,909		Most Double Plays	180
Most Hits	1,738		Most Errors	150
Most Singles	1,244		Most Innings Pitched	1,856
Most Doubles	246		Most Complete Games	79
Most Triples	51		Most Shutouts	18
Most Home Runs	197		Most Strikeouts	1,126
Most Grand Slam Home Runs	8		Most Hits Allowed	1,634
Most Pinch-Hit Home Runs	6		Most Runs Allowed	715
Most Extra-Base Hits	494			

Without question, the New York Yankees have been the dominant franchise in the World Series since its inception. Although it took them 17 years to reach their first Fall Classic in 1921, the Yanks have since appeared in 37 Series—far more than any other club. (The Brooklyn/Los Angeles Dodgers are second with 18.) With 26 titles, they are also far ahead of any other franchise in victories. New York has won 70 percent of the Series in which they've played and 61 percent of the total games. They have swept their opposition eight times, including three consecutive sweeps in 1927, 1928 and 1932. (There have been only 15 four-game sweeps ever in the World Series.) Put another way, from 1927 to 1932, the New York Yankees played in 12 Series games without losing a one. And that's not even the record. After losing the first two games in 1996, the Yanks won the next four; in their next two World Series, in 1998 and 1999, New York downed the Padres and Braves, respectively, in four straight, and then came back to win the first two against the Mets in 2000—14 straight games without a loss. Following the franchise's 15-year absence between 1981 and 1996, the Bronx Bombers returned as October regulars in the late 1990s and are undefeated in four trips in a five-year span. The list of feats goes on and on.

◆ The Yankees played in eight World Series from 1927 to 1941 and won them all.

◆ They won seven without a loss from 1943 to 1953.

◆ They played in 42 Series games between October 6, 1926, and October 1, 1942, without being shutout once.

◆ They missed the Fall Classic only three times between 1947 and 1964.

◆ Each time the Yankees lost a World Series between 1941 and 1958 (which was three times) they came back the next year to beat the very team that had defeated them the previous October.

◆ Between 1921 and 1964, the longest the Yankees went without a World Series appearance was four years.

◆ After 1921, the club's longest drought without a pennant was 15 years, from 1981 to 1996. The longest stretch without a Series win was 18 years (1978–96).

Above: Yankee Stadium has been the site of 100 World Series games in its history, more than any other ballpark.

Above inset: Manager Casey Stengel and catcher Yogi Berra teamed up on seven Yankee championship teams between 1949 and 1960. No manager has won more World Series than Stengel, and no player has won more than Berra.

Above left: Joe Torre brought the Bronx Bombers back to the top of the baseball world in the late '90s, claiming four titles in five years. The run included a 14-game World Series winning streak.

Year-by-Year Results

1921	Giants (5)	Yankees (3)		1953	Yankees (4)	Dodgers (2)
1922	Giants (4)	Yankees (0)		1955	Dodgers (4)	Yankees (3)
1923	Yankees (4)	Giants (2)		1956	Yankees (4)	Dodgers (3)
1926	Cardinals (4)	Yankees (3)		1957	Braves (4)	Yankees (3)
1927	Yankees (4)	Pirates (0)		1958	Yankees (4)	Braves (3)
1928	Yankees (4)	Cardinals (0)		1960	Pirates (4)	Yankees (3)
1932	Yankees (4)	Cubs (0)		1961	Yankees (4)	Reds (1)
1936	Yankees (4)	Giants (2)		1962	Yankees (4)	Giants (3)
1937	Yankees (4)	Giants (1)		1963	Dodgers (4)	Yankees (0)
1938	Yankees (4)	Cubs (0)		1964	Cardinals (4)	Yankees (3)
1939	Yankees (4)	Reds (0)		1976	Reds (4)	Yankees (0)
1941	Yankees (4)	Dodgers (1)		1977	Yankees (4)	Dodgers (2)
1942	Cardinals (4)	Yankees (1)		1978	Yankees (4)	Dodgers (2)
1943	Yankees (4)	Cardinals (1)		1981	Dodgers (4)	Yankees (2)
1947	Yankees (4)	Dodgers (3)		1996	Yankees (4)	Braves (2)
1949	Yankees (4)	Dodgers (1)		1998	Yankees (4)	Padres (0)
1950	Yankees (4)	Phillies (0)		1999	Yankees (4)	Braves (0)
1951	Yankees (4)	Giants (2)		2000	Yankees (4)	Mets (1)
1952	Yankees (4)	Dodgers (3)				

WORLD SERIES CLASSIC

1962

New York Yankees (4) vs. San Francisco Giants (3)

It was a familiar scene: the Giants and Dodgers facing off in a playoff to decide the National League pennant and the chance to battle the Yankees in the World Series. Of course, the 1962 playoff took place 3,000 miles away from the famous Brooklyn-New York contest of 1951, as both teams had relocated to California in 1958. But the outcome was the same as it had been 11 years earlier (if achieved in less dramatic fashion), with the Giants winning a tight three-game series. The Yankees did their part to bring about the first fully transcontinental Series by finishing five games atop the American League.

The World Series opened at San Francisco's Candlestick Park the very day after the Giants wrapped up the playoff against the Dodgers in LA. New York's Whitey Ford continued his October success in Game 1, posting a 6-2 complete-game triumph. Clete Boyer's leadoff homer in the seventh broke a 2-2 tie and proved to be the game-winner. Although Ford's consecutive scoreless innings streak ended at $33^{2}/_{3}$ when Willie Mays scored in the bottom of the second, the great lefty shut the Giants out for the final six innings. The two teams' winningest pitchers faced off in the second game: 23-game-winner Ralph Terry vs. 24-game-winner Jack Sanford. San Francisco's ace came out ahead, as Sanford pitched a three-hit shutout to give the California Giants their first Series win. Willie McCovey belted a monsterous homer in the eighth for the game's second and final run. Reconvening on the other side of the continent, the teams waged a scoreless battle in Game 3 until the Yanks rallied together three runs in the seventh. Bill Stafford held SF scoreless on two hits through eight before Ed Bailey's two-run homer closed the gap to a 3-2 final. The Giants scored a pair runs off Ford again in Game 4, and San Francisco's high-kicking Dominican Juan

Above: American League Rookie of the Year Tom Tresh (left) and National League home run champ Willie Mays (right) chat before the start of the 1962 Series.

Left: Here Tresh robs Mays of a hit with a running one-handed catch in the left-field corner at Candlestick Park in Game 7.

Marichal had a two-hit shutout going when he was forced to leave with an injury in the fifth. The Yanks took advantage of reliever Bobby Bolin to tie the game in a two-run sixth. That tie was broken (and then some) the next inning. With the bases loaded and two outs, up stepped light-hitting second baseman Chuck Hiller, possessor of only 21 home runs in his eight-year Major League career. But Hiller came through when it mattered most and knocked the eighth World Series grand slam in history. Don Larsen—on the hill for the Giants six years to the day after throwing his perfect game in a Yankee uniform—was the pitcher of record and earned the win despite facing only two batters. Overcoming a 10-strikeout performance by Sanford, the Yankees regained the Series lead in Game 5. A wild pitch in the fourth and a passed ball in the sixth led to two New York runs, each coming an inning after the Giants put a run on the board. Rookie Tom Tresh's three-run homer in the eighth sealed the 5-3 win. Terry went the distance for the Yankees to earn his first postseason win in five attempts. After rain delayed the start of Game 6 for several days in San Francisco, the Series swung back even behind Billy Pierce's three-hitter. Pierce was perfect until Maris hit a one-out homer in the fifth, and he yielded just one other run in the game, giving the Giants a cozy 5-2 victory over Ford.

Game 7 at Candlestick Park featured Ralph Terry and Jack Sanford in their third match-up of the Series, and it was a doozy. The teams combined for only one hit in the first four innings (a single by Tony Kubek), and Terry retired the first 17 Giants of the game. The first, and only, run of the game came on a double play in the top of the fifth. The

Yankees opened the inning with two singles and a walk to load the bases, and Kubek came up and grounded to short for a 6-4-3 double play; while nailing down the two outs, the Giants allowed Bill Skowron to race home from third. New York held the tenuous 1-0 lead into the last inning. Reliever Billy O'Dell had pulled Sanford out of a bases-loaded jam in the eighth, and the Giants entered the ninth needing just one run, with the top of the order due up. Pinch hitter Matty Alou led off with a bunt single—only the team's third hit of the day. Terry then struck out the next two batters before Willie Mays ripped a double to right. Roger Maris made a nice play to cut the ball off and keep Alou held at third. Just two years and three days after giving up the nightmarish home run to Bill Mazeroski in the 1960 Series, Terry now had to face the powerful Willie McCovey with runners on second and third in the last of the ninth. With

Above: Chuck Hiller watches the flight of the ball as he breaks a 2-2 tie in Game 4 with a bases-loaded homer into the right-field seats at Yankee Stadium. Yankee catcher Elston Howard and umpire Jim Honochick also fix their glances on the ball.

Below: Game 2 hero Willie McCovey is welcomed by his teammates after driving a deep home run to right field in the seventh inning at Candlestick Park.

San Francisco's Jack Sanford allowed only three hits in his shutout victory in Game 2.

The grand slam home run by San Francisco's Chuck Hiller in Game 4 was the first by a National Leaguer in World Series history.

Right: Several Yankees converge to trap Tom Haller in a rundown between third and home after Jack Sanford missed on a squeeze bunt attempt in Game 2. Haller was ultimately tagged out by shortstop Tony Kubek.

Above: After losing 2-0 in Game 2, Ralph Terry came back to win two games for New York, including a commanding four-hit shutout in the final game.

Left: Now donning a Giants' uniform, Don Larsen went up against his former Yankee mates in 1962 and came away with a win in Game 4 despite recording only one out.

Game 1 Thursday, October 4 at Candlestick Park, San Francisco

	1	2	3	4	5	6	7	8	9	R	H	E
New York Yankees	2	0	0	0	0	0	1	2	1	6	11	0
San Francisco Giants	0	1	1	0	0	0	0	0	0	2	10	0

Pitchers NY **Whitey Ford** (W, 1-0), IP 9, H 10, R 2, ER 2, BB 2, SO 6
SF **Billy O'Dell** (L, 0-1), IP 7⅓, H 9, R 5, ER 5, BB 3, SO 8; **Don Larsen**, IP 1, H 1, R 1, ER 1, BB 1, SO 0; **Stu Miller**, IP ⅔, H 1, R 0, ER 0, BB 1, SO 0

Top Performers at the Plate
NY **Elston Howard**, 2 for 3, 1 R, 1 RBI, 1 BB, 1 HBP; **Roger Maris**, 2 for 4, 1 R, 2 RBI, 1 BB
SF **Willia Mays**, 3 for 4, 1 R, 1 RBI; **Jose Pagan**, 3 for 4, 1 RBI

2B-NY/Maris; SF/Hiller. **HR**-NY/Boyer. **SB**-NY/Mantle, Tresh. **Time** 2:43. **Attendance** 43,852.

Game 2 Friday, October 5 at Candlestick Park, San Francisco

	1	2	3	4	5	6	7	8	9	R	H	E
New York Yankees	0	0	0	0	0	0	0	0	0	0	3	1
San Francisco Giants	1	0	0	0	0	0	1	0	x	2	6	0

Pitchers NY **Ralph Terry** (L, 0-1), IP 7, H 5, R 2, ER 2, BB 1, SO 5; **Bud Daley**, IP 1, H 1, R 0, ER 0, BB 1, SO 0
SF **Jack Sanford** (W, 1-0), IP 9, H 3, R 0, ER 0, BB 3, SO 6

Top Performers at the Plate
NY **Tom Tresh**, 1 for 3, 1 BB
SF **Chuck Hiller**, 1 for 3, 1 R, 1 BB; **Willie McCover**, 1 for 4, 1 R, 1 RBI

2B-NY/Mantle; SF/Hiller. **HR**-SF/McCovey. **SB**-NY/Tresh. **Time** 2:11. **Attendance** 43,910.

Game 3 Sunday, October 7 at Yankee Stadium, New York

	1	2	3	4	5	6	7	8	9	R	H	E
San Francisco Giants	0	0	0	0	0	0	0	0	2	2	4	3
New York Yankees	0	0	0	0	0	0	3	0	x	3	5	1

Pitchers SF **Billy Pierce** (L, 0-1), IP 6, H 5, R 3, ER 2, BB 0, SO 3; **Don Larsen**, IP 1, H 0, R 0, ER 0, BB 0, SO 0; **Bobby Bolin**, IP 1, H 0, R 0, ER 0, BB 0, SO 1
NY **Bill Stafford** (W, 1-0), IP 9, H 4, R 2, ER 2, BB 2, SO 5

Top Performers at the Plate
SF **Ed Bailey**, 1 for 4, 1 R, 2 RBI
NY **Mickey Mantle**, 1 for 3, 1 R; **Roger Maris**, 1 for 3, 1 R, 2 RBI

2B-SF/Davenport, Mays; NY/Howard, Kubek. **HR**-SF/Bailey. **Time** 2:06. **Attendance** 71,434.

Game 4 Monday, October 8 at Yankee Stadium, New York

	1	2	3	4	5	6	7	8	9	R	H	E
San Francisco Giants	0	2	0	0	0	0	4	0	1	7	9	1
New York Yankees	0	0	0	0	0	2	0	0	1	3	9	1

Pitchers SF **Juan Marichal**, IP 4, H 2, R 0, ER 0, BB 2, SO 4; **Bobby Bolin**, IP 1⅔, H 4, R 2, ER 2, BB 2, SO 1; **Don Larsen** (W, 1-0), IP ⅓, H 0, R 0, ER 0, BB 1, SO 0; **Billy O'Dell** (Sv, 1), IP 3, H 3, R 1, ER 1, BB 0, SO 0
NY **Whitey Ford**, IP 6, H 5, R 2, ER 2, BB 1, SO 3; **Jim Coates** (L, 0-1), IP ⅓, H 1, R 2, ER 2, BB 1, SO 1; **Marshall Bridges**, IP 2⅔, H 3, R 3, ER 2, BB 2, SO 3

Top Performers at the Plate
SF **Tom Haller**, 2 for 4, 1 R, 2 RBI; **Chuck Hiller**, 2 for 5, 1 R, 4 RBI
NY **Bill Skowron**, 3 for 4, 1 RBI; **Tom Tresh**, 2 for 5, 1 RBI

2B-SF/F. Alou, M. Alou. **3B**-NY/Skowron. **HR**-SF/Haller, Hiller. **Time** 2:55. **Attendance** 66,607.

Game 5 Wednesday, October 10 at Yankee Stadium, New York

	1	2	3	4	5	6	7	8	9	R	H	E
San Francisco Giants	0	0	1	0	1	0	0	0	1	3	8	2
New York Yankees	0	0	0	1	0	1	0	3	x	5	6	0

Pitchers SF **Jack Sanford** (L, 1-1), IP 7⅓, H 6, R 5, ER 4, BB 1, SO 10; **Stu Miller**, IP ⅔, H 0, R 0, ER 0, BB 1, SO 0
NY **Ralph Terry** (W, 1-1), IP 9, H 8, R 3, ER 3, BB 1, SO 7

Top Performers at the Plate
SF **Felipe Alou**, 2 for 4; **Joe Pagan**, 2 for 4, 2 R, 1 RBI
NY **Bobby Richardson**, 2 for 4, 2 R; **Tom Tresh**, 2 for 3, 2 R, 3 RBI, 1 SH

2B-SF/Haller, Hiller; NY/Tresh. **3B**-SF/F. Alou. **HR**-SF/Pagan; NY/Tresh. **SB**-NY/Mantle. **Time** 2:42. **Attendance** 63,165.

Game 6 Monday, October 15 at Candlestick Park, San Francisco

	1	2	3	4	5	6	7	8	9	R	H	E
New York Yankees	0	0	0	0	1	0	0	1	0	2	3	2
San Francisco Giants	0	0	0	3	2	0	0	0	x	5	10	1

Pitchers NY **Whitey Ford** (L, 1-1), IP 4⅔, H 9, R 5, ER 5, BB 1, SO 3; **Jim Coates**, IP 2⅓, H 0, R 0, ER 0, BB 0, SO 2; **Marshall Bridges**, IP 1, H 1, R 0, ER 0, BB 0, SO 0
SF **Billy Pierce** (W, 1-1), IP 9, H 3, R 2, ER 2, BB 2, SO 2

Top Performers at the Plate
NY **Clete Boyer**, 1 for 2, 1 R, 1 BB; **Roger Maris**, 1 for 3, 1 R, 1 RBI, 1 BB
SF **Felipe Alou**, 2 for 4, 1 R, 1 RBI; **Orlando Cepeda**, 3 for 4, 1 R, 2 RBI

2B-NY/Boyer; SF/Cepeda. **HR**-NY/Maris. **SB**-SF/Mays. **Time** 2:00. **Attendance** 43,948.

Game 7 Tuesday, October 16 at Candlestick Park, San Francisco

	1	2	3	4	5	6	7	8	9	R	H	E
New York Yankees	0	0	0	0	1	0	0	0	0	1	7	0
San Francisco Giants	0	0	0	0	0	0	0	0	0	0	4	1

Pitchers NY **Ralph Terry** (W, 2-1), IP 9, H 4, R 0, ER 0, BB 0, SO 4
SF **Jack Sanford** (L, 1-2), IP 7, H 7, R 1, ER 1, BB 4, SO 3; **Billy O'Dell**, IP 2, H 0, R 0, ER 0, BB 0, SO 1

Top Performers at the Plate
NY **Clete Boyer**, 2 for 4

2B-SF/Mays. **3B**-SF/McCovey. **Time** 2:29. **Attendance** 43,948.

one ball and one strike, McCovey hit a scorching line drive to the right side. Second baseman Bobby Richardson moved just a step to his left and reached up to nab the liner. Reversing his 1960 role, Terry walked away a hero in 1962, and the Yankees walked away champions despite a miserable 3 for 25 performance from league MVP Mickey Mantle and a .199 team average.

Above: In a cloud of dust, San Francisco's Orlando Cepeda slides, spikes up, into second base as Bobby Richardson fires to first, too late to turn a double play on Ed Bailey's ground ball.

Left: Bobby Richardson slides into first base to beat out an infield hit in the sixth inning of Game 5. He came around to score the game-tying run on two ground balls and a passed ball.

1962 WORLD SERIES COMPOSITE STATISTICS

NEW YORK YANKEES/Ralph Houk, Manager

Player	pos	G	AB	R	H	2B	3B	HR	RBI	BB	SO	SB	BA	SA	E	FPct
Yogi Berra	c-ph	2	2	0	0	0	0	0	0	2	0	0	.000	.000	0	1.000
Johnny Blanchard	ph	1	1	0	0	0	0	0	0	0	1	0	.000	.000	–	–
Clete Boyer	3b	7	22	2	7	1	0	1	4	1	3	0	.318	.500	2	.926
Marshall Bridges	p	2	0	0	0	0	0	0	0	0	0	0	–	–	0	1.000
Jim Coates	p	2	0	0	0	0	0	0	0	0	0	0	–	–	0	–
Bud Daley	p	1	0	0	0	0	0	0	0	0	0	0	–	–	0	–
Whitey Ford	p	3	7	0	0	0	0	0	0	1	3	0	.000	.000	1	.800
Elston Howard	c	6	21	1	3	1	0	0	1	1	4	0	.143	.190	0	1.000
Tony Kubek	ss	7	29	2	8	1	0	1	1	3	0	0	.276	.310	1	.967
Dale Long	1b	2	5	0	1	0	0	0	1	0	1	0	.200	.200	0	1.000
Hector Lopez	ph	2	2	0	0	0	0	0	0	0	0	0	.000	.000	–	–
Mickey Mantle	cf	7	25	2	3	1	0	0	0	4	5	2	.120	.160	0	1.000
Roger Maris	rf	7	23	4	4	1	0	1	5	5	2	0	.174	.348	0	1.000
Bobby Richardson	2b	7	27	3	4	0	0	0	0	3	1	0	.148	.148	1	.974
Bill Skowron	1b	6	18	1	4	0	1	0	1	1	5	0	.222	.333	0	1.000
Bill Stafford	p	1	3	0	0	0	0	0	0	0	1	0	.000	.000	0	1.000
Ralph Terry	p	3	8	0	1	0	0	0	0	1	6	0	.125	.125	0	1.000
Tom Tresh	lf	7	28	5	9	1	0	1	4	1	4	2	.321	.464	0	1.000
Totals		**7**	**221**	**20**	**44**	**6**	**1**	**3**	**17**	**21**	**39**	**4**	**.199**	**.276**	**5**	**.980**

Pitcher	G	GS	CG	IP	H	R	ER	BB	SO	W-L	Sv	ERA
Marshall Bridges	2	0	0	3⅔	4	3	2	2	3	0-0	0	4.91
Jim Coates	2	0	0	2⅔	1	2	2	1	3	0-1	0	6.75
Bud Daley	1	0	0	1	1	0	0	1	0	0-0	0	0.00
Whitey Ford	3	3	1	19⅔	24	9	9	4	12	1-1	0	4.12
Bill Stafford	1	1	1	9	4	2	2	2	5	1-0	0	2.00
Ralph Terry	3	3	2	25	17	5	5	2	16	2-1	0	1.80
Totals	**7**	**7**	**4**	**61**	**51**	**21**	**20**	**12**	**39**	**4-3**	**0**	**2.95**

SAN FRANCISCO GIANTS/Alvin Dark, Manager

Player	pos	G	AB	R	H	2B	3B	HR	RBI	BB	SO	SB	BA	SA	E	FPct
Felipe Alou	rf-lf	7	26	2	7	1	1	0	1	1	4	0	.269	.385	1	.900
Matty Alou	lf-ph-rf	6	12	2	4	1	0	0	1	0	1	0	.333	.417	0	1.000
Ed Bailey	c	6	14	1	1	0	0	1	2	0	3	0	.071	.286	0	1.000
Bobby Bolin	p	2	0	0	0	0	0	0	0	0	0	0	–	–	0	–
Ernie Bowman	ss-pr	2	1	1	0	0	0	0	0	0	0	0	.000	.000	0	1.000
Orlando Cepeda	1b	5	19	1	3	1	0	0	2	0	4	0	.158	.211	0	1.000
Jim Davenport	3b	7	22	1	3	1	0	0	1	4	7	0	.136	.182	3	.857
Tom Haller	c	4	14	1	4	1	0	1	3	0	2	0	.286	.571	0	1.000
Chuck Hiller	2b	7	26	4	7	3	0	1	5	3	4	0	.269	.500	1	.974
Harvey Kuenn	lf-rf	3	12	1	1	0	0	0	0	1	1	0	.083	.083	0	1.000
Don Larsen	p	3	0	0	0	0	0	0	0	0	0	0	–	–	0	1.000
Juan Marichal	p	1	2	0	0	0	0	0	0	0	1	0	.000	.000	0	1.000
Willie Mays	cf	7	28	3	7	2	0	0	1	1	5	1	.250	.321	0	1.000
Willie McCovey	1b-rf-lf	4	15	2	3	0	1	1	1	1	3	0	.200	.533	2	.931
Stu Miller	p	2	0	0	0	0	0	0	0	0	0	0	–	–	0	1.000
Bob Nieman	ph	1	0	0	0	0	0	0	0	0	0	0	–	–	0	–
Billy O'Dell	p	3	3	0	1	0	0	0	0	0	0	0	.333	.333	0	–
John Orsino	c	1	1	0	0	0	0	0	0	0	0	0	.000	.000	0	–
Jose Pagan	ss	7	19	2	7	0	0	1	2	0	1	0	.368	.526	1	.957
Billy Pierce	p	2	5	0	0	0	0	0	0	0	1	0	.000	.000	0	1.000
Jack Sanford	p	3	7	0	3	0	0	0	0	0	2	0	.429	.429	0	1.000
Totals		**7**	**226**	**21**	**51**	**10**	**2**	**5**	**19**	**12**	**39**	**1**	**.226**	**.354**	**8**	**.969**

Pitcher	G	GS	CG	IP	H	R	ER	BB	SO	W-L	Sv	ERA
Bobby Bolin	2	0	0	2⅔	4	2	2	2	2	0-0	0	6.75
Don Larsen	3	0	0	2⅓	1	1	1	2	0	1-0	0	3.86
Juan Marichal	1	1	0	4	2	0	0	2	4	0-0	0	0.00
Stu Miller	2	0	0	1⅓	1	0	0	0	2	0-0	0	0.00
Billy O'Dell	3	1	0	12⅓	12	6	6	3	9	0-1	1	4.38
Billy Pierce	2	2	1	15	8	5	4	2	5	1-1	0	2.40
Jack Sanford	3	3	1	23⅓	16	6	5	8	19	1-2	0	1.93
Totals	**7**	**7**	**2**	**61**	**44**	**20**	**18**	**21**	**39**	**3-4**	**1**	**2.66**

Series MVP: Ralph Terry, New York Yankees. **Series Outstanding Pitcher:** Ralph Terry, New York Yankees. **Average Length of Game:** 2 hours, 27 minutes. **Total Attendance:** 376,864. **Average Attendance:** 53,838 (67,069 at Yankee Stadium; 43,915 at Candlestick Park). **Umpires:** Al Barlick (NL), Charlie Berry (AL), Ken Burkhart (NL), Jim Honochick (AL), Stan Landes (NL), Hank Soar (AL). **Winning Player's Share:** $9,883. **Losing Player's Share:** $7,291

Left: Pinch-hitting for Whitey Ford in the sixth inning of Game 4, Yogi Berra takes exception to umpire Jim Honochick's strike call. Berra eventually earned a walk.

Below: Jim Honochick gives the "safe" sign as Willie Mays gets back in time to beat a pickoff play at third base in Game 1. Moments later Mays would score on Jose Pagan's bunt single, ending Whitey Ford's consecutive scoreless streak.

Background: Just two years after giving up the fateful home run to Pittsburgh's Bill Mazeroski, Yankee pitcher Ralph Terry gets a ride from his teammates in victory as the hero of 1962's Game 7.

The 1962 Series was only the second in history where the teams alternated wins in every game. The Yanks won the odd-numbered games, while San Francisco claimed Games 2, 4 and 6.

Los Angeles Dodgers (4) vs. New York Yankees (0)

In their fourth World Series of the decade, the Yankees again faced one of their former cross-town rivals, now relocated across country. The Yankee-Dodger slugfests of the 1950s were a thing of the past, however, as pitchers dominated the 1963 Series. The Dodgers had three ace starters in Sandy Koufax, Don Drysdale and Johnny Podres and a formidable stopper in Ron Perranoski; New York boasted two 20-game-winners—Whitey Ford and young fireballer Jim Bouton. Koufax put together one of the best seasons since the dead ball era (25-5, 306 strikeouts, 1.88 ERA). Ford had 24 wins in 1963 and a history of postseason success. The two legendary lefties matched up in the Series opener in New York. While Ford struggled in his five innings of work, Koufax was nothing short of sensational. He struck out the first five batters he faced and didn't allow a Yankee to reach base, or even hit a ball out of the infield, until the fifth inning. After New York loaded the bases on three singles, Koufax struck out Hector Lopez—his 11th victim—to end the threat. He struck out one in the seventh and two in the eighth to match the single-game record. With two outs in the ninth, Koufax registered record-breaking strikeout number 15. A two-run homer by Tom Tresh was Koufax's only mistake, but Johnny Roseboro put the Dodgers ahead for good with a three-run blast in the third inning. In Game 2, Podres kept the Yankee offense at bay, shutting them out for eight and a third. Willie

Davis's first-inning double put LA up 2-0 early, and a solo homer by former Yankee Bill Skowron and an RBI triple by Tommy Davis brought the final score to 4-1 in the Dodgers' favor. Pitching remained the name of the game when the two teams headed west to Los Angeles. Bouton gave up a lone run in the first inning of Game 3 and allowed just four hits all afternoon, but a 1-0 margin was sufficient for the commanding Drysdale, who shut the Yanks out on three hits. The next day, Los Angeles made it a four-game sweep behind another stunning performance by Koufax. His strikeout of the game's leadoff hitter, Tony Kubek, put Koufax in the record books once again by giving him the most strikeouts by one pitcher in a four-game Series; he then went on to fan 7 more, establishing a new mark of 23. Los Angeles managed only two hits against Ford, but one of them was a towering home run by Frank Howard. The other Dodger run was unearned, following Joe Pepitone's seventh-inning error. A Mickey Mantle home run in the top of the seventh was New York's only run, and Koufax earned his second complete-game win. The Dodgers held New York to a measly four runs and .171 team average in the four games, bringing them their second California championship in five years.

Left: Johnny Roseboro drove in three runs for Los Angeles in Game 1 with this shot into the Yankee Stadium upper deck in the second inning.

Right: In his second start of the Series, Koufax pitches another complete-game gem, this time striking out "only" eight while walking none.

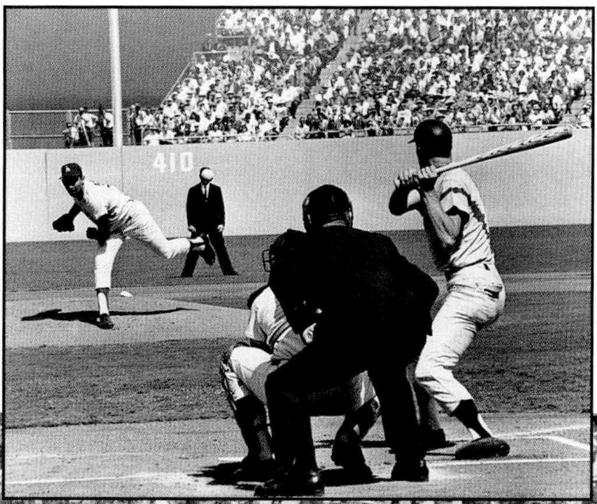

Below: Don Drysdale shut the Yankees out with a three-hitter in Game 3—the first World Series game at Los Angeles' Dodger Stadium. Here he fires the first pitch in to Tony Kubek.

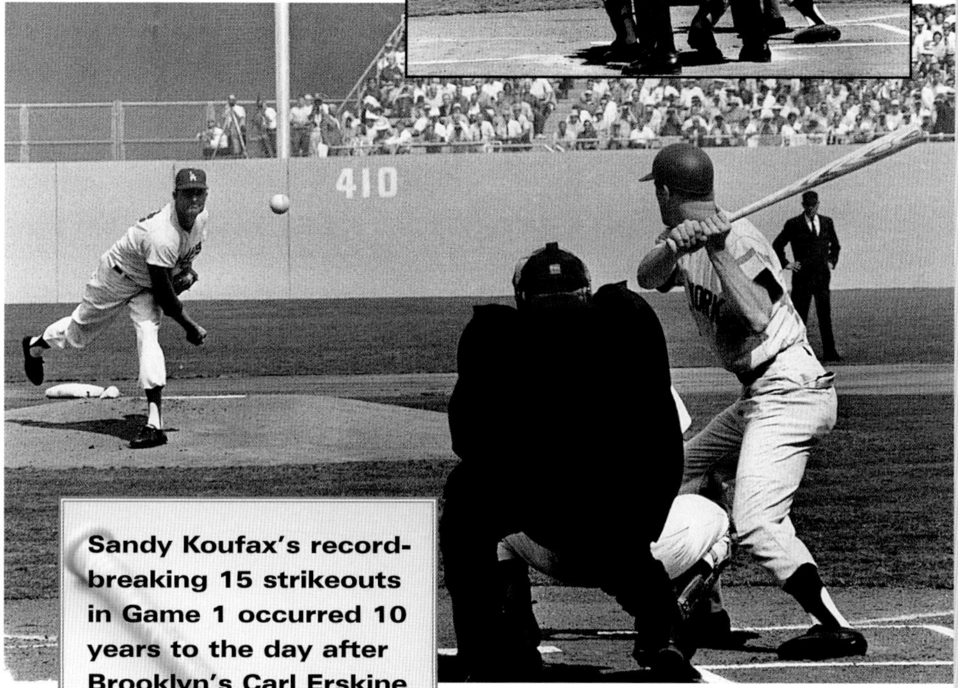

Sandy Koufax's record-breaking 15 strikeouts in Game 1 occurred 10 years to the day after Brooklyn's Carl Erskine set the previous mark at 14 on October 2, 1953. Exactly five years after Koufax's accomplishment, Bob Gibson of St. Louis would establish a new record with 17, on October 2, 1968.

Game 1 Wednesday, October 2 at Yankee Stadium, New York

	1	2	3	4	5	6	7	8	9	R	H	E
Los Angeles Dodgers	0	4	1	0	0	0	0	0	0	5	9	0
New York Yankees	0	0	0	0	0	0	0	2	0	2	6	0

Pitchers LA **Sandy Koufax** (W, 1-0), IP 9, H 6, R 2, ER 2, BB 3, SO 15
NY **Whitey Ford** (L, 0-1), IP 5, H 8, R 5, ER 5, BB 2, SO 4; **Stan Williams**, IP 3, H 1, R 0, ER 0, BB 0, SO 5; **Steve Hamilton**, IP 1, H 0, R 0, ER 0, BB 0, SO 1

Top Performers at the Plate
LA **Tommy Davis**, 3 for 4; **Bill Skowron**, 2 for 3, 1 R, 2 RBI, 1 BB
NY **Joe Pepitone**, 2 for 4; **Tom Tresh**, 1 for 3, 1 R, 2 RBI, 1 BB

2B-LA/F. Howard. **HR**-LA/Roseboro; NY/Tresh. **SB**-LA/T. Davis. **Time** 2:09. **Attendance** 69,000.

Game 2 Thursday, October 3 at Yankee Stadium, New York

	1	2	3	4	5	6	7	8	9	R	H	E
Los Angeles Dodgers	2	0	0	1	0	0	0	1	0	4	10	1
New York Yankees	0	0	0	0	0	0	0	0	1	1	7	0

Pitchers LA **Johnny Podres** (W, 1-0), IP 8⅓, H 6, R 1, ER 1, BB 1, SO 4; **Ron Perranoski** (Sv, 1), IP ⅔, H 1, R 0, ER 0, BB 0, SO 1
NY **Al Downing** (L, 0-1), IP 5, H 7, R 3, ER 3, BB 1, SO 6; **Ralph Terry**, IP 3, H 3, R 1, ER 1, BB 1, SO 0; **Hal Reniff**, IP 1, H 0, R 0, ER 0, BB 0, SO 0

Top Performers at the Plate
LA **Willie Davis**, 2 for 4, 1 R, 2 RBI, 2 2B; **Bill Skowron**, 2 for 4, 1 R, 1 RBI
NY **Elston Howard**, 2 for 4, 1 RBI; **Hector Lopez**, 2 for 3, 1 R, 2 3B

2B-LA/W. Davis 2; NY/Lopez 2. **3B**-LA/T. Davis 2. **HR**-LA/Skowron. **SB**-LA/Wills. **Time** 2:13. **Attendance** 66,455.

Game 3 Saturday, October 5 at Dodger Stadium, Los Angeles

	1	2	3	4	5	6	7	8	9	R	H	E
New York Yankees	0	0	0	0	0	0	0	0	0	0	3	0
Los Angeles Dodgers	1	0	0	0	0	0	0	0	x	1	4	1

Pitchers NY **Jim Bouton** (L, 0-1), IP 7, H 4, R 1, ER 1, BB 5, SO 4; **Hal Reniff**, IP 1, H 0, R 0, ER 0, BB 1, SO 1
LA **Don Drysdale** (W, 1-0), IP 9, H 3, R 0, ER 0, BB 1, SO 9

Top Performers at the Plate
NY **Tony Kubek**, 2 for 4
LA **Jim Gilliam**, 0 for 2, 1 R, 2 BB

Time 12:05. **Attendance** 55,912.

Game 4 Sunday, October 6 at Dodger Stadium, Los Angeles

	1	2	3	4	5	6	7	8	9	R	H	E
New York Yankees	0	0	0	0	0	0	1	0	0	1	6	1
Los Angeles Dodgers	0	0	0	0	1	0	1	0	x	2	2	1

Pitchers NY **Whitey Ford** (L, 0-2), IP 7, H 2, R 2, ER 1, BB 1, SO 4; **Hal Reniff**, IP 1, H 0, R 0, ER 0, BB 0, SO 0
LA **Sandy Koufax** (W, 2-0), IP 9, H 6, R 1, ER 1, BB 0, SO 8

Top Performers at the Plate
NY **Elston Howard**, 2 for 4; **Bobby Richardson**, 2 for 4
LA **Frank Howard**, 2 for 3, 1 R, 1 RBI

2B-NY/Richardson. **HR**-NY/Mantle; LA F. Howard. **Time** 1:50. **Attendance** 55,912.

Below: Victim #10: Mickey Mantle swings meekly at a third strike from Sandy Koufax in the fifth inning of Game 1. Koufax set a new record that afternoon with 15 strikeouts.

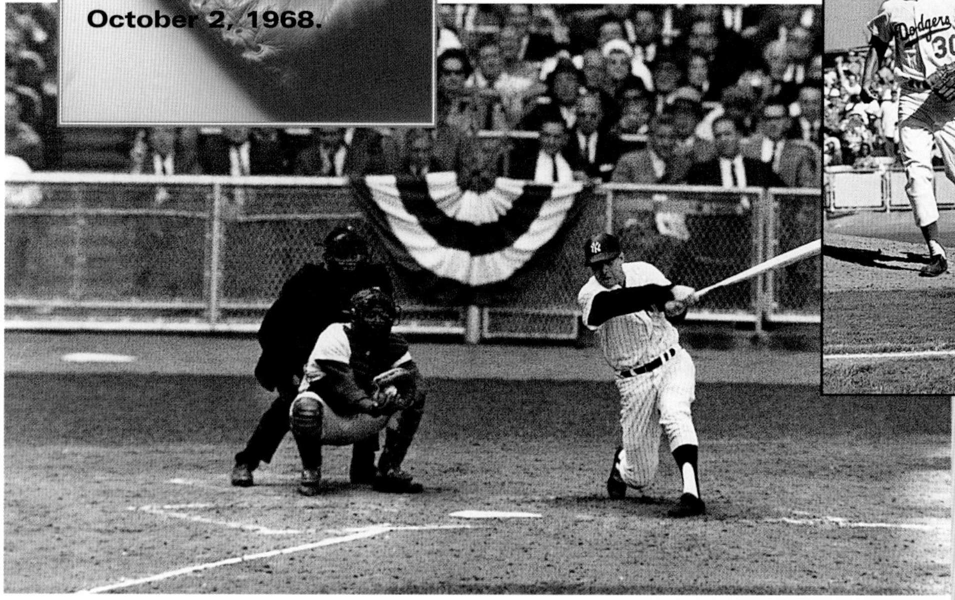

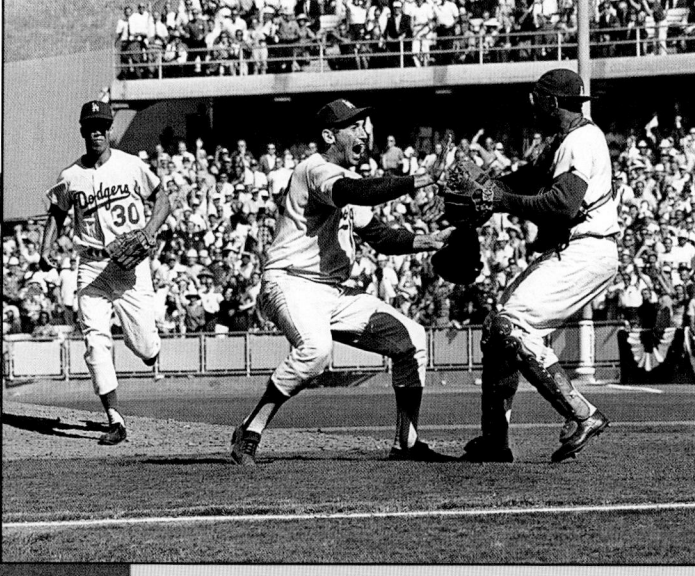

Above: An ecstatic Sandy Koufax whoops it up with catcher Johnny Roseboro after clinching a four-game sweep over the rival Yankees.

St. Louis Cardinals (4) vs. New York Yankees (3)

1964

With a fifth consecutive World Series appearance—the 15th in 18 years—the Yankee dynasty continued in Yogi Berra's first year as manager. Berra led the Yanks to 99 wins in 1964 and a one-game lead in first place. A late-season collapse by the Philadelphia Phillies helped the St. Louis Cardinals storm to their first pennant since 1946, inching out the Phillies and Reds by a single game. Manager Johnny Keane had three top starters in Ray Sadecki, Curt Simmons and Bob Gibson, with the trio combining for 57 wins on the year. Sadecki topped Yankee ace Whitey Ford in the opener. Tom Tresh helped New York to an early 4-2 lead with a two-run homer in the second and an RBI double in the fifth, but the Cardinals produced four runs in the sixth and then put the game out of reach with a three-run eighth. New York did more than fall behind in the Series with the Game 1 loss; they lost their ace pitcher when arm trouble forced Ford to make an early exit, never to return in the World Series. The Yanks got even in Game 2 by roughing up the hard-throwing Gibson for four runs, and then they added four more against two relievers in the last inning. Rookie Mel Stottlemyre went the distance for New York to earn the W. The 24-year-old Jim Bouton faced 35-year-old veteran Curt Simmons in a Game 3 pitcher's duel. Clete Boyer's RBI double in the second for New York and

Simmons's run-scoring single in the fifth provided all the scoring through eight and a half. Barney Schultz came in for Simmons to open the bottom of the ninth and threw one pitch, which Mickey Mantle smashed into the right-field seats to win the game. The Yanks scored early in Game 4, opening the bottom of the first with back-to-back doubles and three straight singles to drive in three runs. Al Downing held the 3-0 lead into the sixth inning, but Ken Boyer, the Cardinal third baseman and older brother of Yankee Clete, hit a bases-loaded home run to take the lead and even the Series. Gibson was overpowering in Game 5, striking out 13 and holding New York scoreless through eight. After Mantle reached first on an error in the bottom of the ninth, Tom Tresh hit a two-out home run to send the game to extra innings. A walk and a bunt single put two Cardinals on base in the tenth, and Tim McCarver brought them all home with a three-run shot for the victory. Back-to-back solo homers by Maris and Mantle broke a 1-1 tie in the sixth inning of Game 6, and a grand slam by Joe Pepitone turned it into an 8-3 final. Gibson and Stottlemyre took the hill for the deciding Game 7 at Busch Stadium, each pitching on two days' rest. The Cards scored first with three in the fourth, including McCarver's steal of home plate, and they added three more in the fifth. Mantle cut the

Mickey Mantle's Game 3 home run was the 16th Series round-tripper of his career, moving him ahead of Babe Ruth on the all-time list.

Left: Bob Gibson fires home at Yankee Stadium during his first World Series win. He struck out 13 and allowed no earned runs in his 10-inning performance in Game 5.

Left inset: The 24-year-old Mel Stottlemyre had only 13 Major League games under his belt going into the Series, but he bested Gibson in Game 2 in St. Louis.

Right: Third basemen Clete (left) and Ken Boyer smile together before the two brothers opposed each other in the 1964 Fall Classic. In Game 7 of the Series, the two would become the only brothers to homer in the same World Series game.

Above: Manager Yogi Berra calls for reliever Al Downing from the bullpen to replace an ailing Whitey Ford in Game 1. Ford had just given up a two-run homer and a double in the sixth inning.

Right: Ken Boyer's grand-slam homer gave St. Louis a crucial come-from-behind win in Game 4.

Game 1 Wednesday, October 7 at Busch Stadium, St. Louis

	1	2	3	4	5	6	7	8	9	R	H	E
New York Yankees	0	3	0	0	1	0	0	1	0	5	12	2
St. Louis Cardinals	1	1	0	0	0	4	0	3	x	9	12	0

Pitchers NY **Whitey Ford** (L, 0-1), IP 5⅓, H 8, R 5, ER 5, BB 1, SO 4; **Al Downing**, IP 1⅔, H 2, R 1, ER 1, BB 0, SO 1; **Rollie Sheldon**, IP ⅔, H 0, R 2, ER 0, BB 2, SO 0; **Pete Mikkelsen**, IP ⅓, H 2, R 1, ER 0, BB 1, SO 0
StL **Ray Sadecki** (W, 1-0), IP 6, H 8, R 4, ER 4, BB 5, SO 2; **Barney Schultz** (Sv, 1), IP 3, H 4, R 1, ER 1, BB 1, SO 1

Top Performers at the Plate
NY **Elston Howard**, 2 for 4, 1 R, 1 BB; **Tom Tresh**, 2 for 4, 1 R, 3 RBI, 1 BB
StL **Lou Brock**, 2 for 5, 1 R, 2 RBI; **Mike Shannon**, 2 for 4, 3 R, 2 RBI

2B-NY/Blanchard, Tresh; StL/Brock, McCarver. **3B**-StL/Flood, McCarver. **HR**-NY/Tresh; StL/Shannon. **SB**-NY/C. Boyer. **Time** 2:42. **Attendance** 30,805.

Game 2 Thursday, October 8 at Busch Stadium, St. Louis

	1	2	3	4	5	6	7	8	9	R	H	E
New York Yankees	0	0	0	1	0	1	2	0	4	8	12	0
St. Louis Cardinals	0	0	1	0	0	0	0	1	1	3	7	0

Pitchers NY **Mel Stottlemyre** (W, 1-0), IP 9, H 7, R 3, ER 3, BB 2, SO 4
StL **Bob Gibson** (L, 0-1), IP 8, H 8, R 4, ER 4, BB 3, SO 9; **Barney Schultz**, IP ⅓, H 2, R 2, ER 2, BB 0, SO 0; **Gordie Richardson**, IP ⅓, H 2, R 2, ER 2, BB 2, SO 0; **Roger Craig**, IP ⅓, H 0, R 0, ER 0, BB 0, SO 1

Top Performers at the Plate
NY **Phil Linz**, 3 for 4, 2 R, 1 RBI, 1 BB; **Mickey Mantle**, 1 for 4, 2 R, 2 RBI, 1 BB
StL **Dick Groat**, 1 for 3, 1 R, 1 BB

2B-NY/B. Richardson, Howard, Mantle, Pepitone; StL/Skinner. **3B**-StL/Groat. **HR**-NY/Linz. **Time** 2:29. **Attendance** 30,805.

Game 3 Saturday, October 10 at Yankee Stadium, New York

	1	2	3	4	5	6	7	8	9	R	H	E
St. Louis Cardinals	0	0	0	0	1	0	0	0	0	1	6	0
New York Yankees	0	1	0	0	0	0	0	0	1	2	5	2

Pitchers StL **Curt Simmons**, IP 8, H 4, R 1, ER 1, BB 3, SO 2; **Barney Schultz** (L, 0-1), IP 0, H 1, R 1, ER 1, BB 0, SO 0
NY **Jim Bouton** (W, 1-0), IP 9, H 6, R 1, ER 0, BB 3, SO 2

Top Performers at the Plate
StL **Tim McCarver**, 1 for 2, 1 R, 2 BB; **Curt Simmons**, 1 for 2, 1 RBI, 1 SH
NY **Clete Boyer**, 1 for 3, 1 RBI; **Mickey Mantle**, 2 for 3, 1 R, 1 RBI, 1 BB

2B-StL/Groat, Maxvill; NY/C. Boyer, Mantle. **HR**-NY/Mantle. **Time** 2:16. **Attendance** 67,101.

Game 4 Sunday, October 11 at Yankee Stadium, New York

	1	2	3	4	5	6	7	8	9	R	H	E
St. Louis Cardinals	0	0	0	0	0	4	0	0	0	4	6	1
New York Yankees	3	0	0	0	0	0	0	0	0	3	6	1

Pitchers StL **Ray Sadecki**, IP ⅓, H 4, R 3, ER 2, BB 0, SO 0; **Roger Craig** (W, 1-0), IP 4⅔, H 2, R 0, ER 0, BB 3, SO 8; **Ron Taylor** (Sv, 1), IP 4, H 0, R 0, ER 0, BB 1, SO 2
NY **Al Downing** (L, 0-1), IP 6, H 4, R 4, ER 3, BB 2, SO 4; **Pete Mikkelsen**, IP 1, H 0, R 0, ER 0, BB 0, SO 1; **Ralph Terry**, IP 2, H 2, R 0, ER 0, BB 0, SO 3

Top Performers at the Plate
StL **Ken Boyer**, 1 for 4, 1 R, 4 RBI; **Curt Flood**, 2 for 4, 1 R
NY **Elston Howard**, 1 for 3, 1 RBI, 1 BB; **Mickey Mantle**, 1 for 2, 1 RBI, 2 BB

2B-NY/Linz, Richardson. **HR**-StL/K. Boyer. **Time** 2:18. **Attendance** 66,312.

Game 5 Monday, October 12 at Yankee Stadium, New York

	1	2	3	4	5	6	7	8	9	10	R	H	E
St. Louis Cardinals	0	0	0	0	2	0	0	0	0	3	5	10	1
New York Yankees	0	0	0	0	0	0	0	0	2	0	2	6	2

Pitchers StL **Bob Gibson** (W, 1-1), IP 10, H 6, R 2, ER 0, BB 2, SO 13
NY **Mel Stottlemyre**, IP 7, H 6, R 2, ER 1, BB 2, SO 6; **Hal Reniff**, IP ⅓, H 2, R 0, ER 0, BB 0, SO 0; **Pete Mikkelsen** (L, 0-1), IP 2⅔, H 2, R 3, ER 3, BB 1, SO 3

Top Performers at the Plate
StL **Lou Brock**, 2 for 5, 1 RBI; **Tim McCarver**, 3 for 5, 1 R, 3 RBI
NY **Bobby Richardson**, 3 for 5; **Tom Tresh**, 1 for 3, 1 R, 2 RBI, 1 BB

HR-StL/McCarver; NY/Tresh. **SB**-StL/White. **Time** 2:37. **Attendance** 65,633.

Game 6 Wednesday, October 14 at Busch Stadium, St. Louis

	1	2	3	4	5	6	7	8	9	R	H	E
New York Yankees	0	0	0	0	1	2	0	5	0	8	10	0
St. Louis Cardinals	1	0	0	0	0	0	0	1	1	3	10	1

Pitchers NY **Jim Bouton** (W, 2-0), IP 8⅓, H 9, R 3, ER 3, BB 2, SO 5; **Steve Hamilton** (Sv, 1), IP ⅔, H 1, R 0, ER 0, BB 0, SO 0
StL **Curt Simmons** (L, 0-1), IP 6⅓, H 7, R 3, ER 3, BB 0, SO 6; **Ron Taylor**, IP ⅔, H 0, R 0, ER 0, BB 0, SO 0; **Barney Schultz**, IP ⅔, H 2, R 4, ER 4, BB 2, SO 0; **Gordie Richardson**, IP ⅓, H 1, R 1, ER 1, BB 0, SO 0; **Bob Humphreys**, IP 1, H 0, R 0, ER 0, BB 0, SO 1

Top Performers at the Plate
NY **Joe Pepitone**, 1 for 4, 1 R, 4 RBI; **Tom Tresh**, 1 for 3, 2 R, 1 BB
StL **Lou Brock**, 3 for 4; **Curt Flood**, 1 for 3, 2 R, 2 BB

2B-NY/Tresh; StL/Brock. **HR**-NY/Mantle, Maris, Pepitone. **SB**-NY/B. Richardson. **Time** 2:37. **Attendance** 30,805.

Game 7 Thursday, October 15 at Busch Stadium, St. Louis

	1	2	3	4	5	6	7	8	9	R	H	E
New York Yankees	0	0	0	0	0	3	0	0	2	5	9	2
St. Louis Cardinals	0	0	0	3	3	0	1	0	x	7	10	1

Pitchers NY **Mel Stottlemyre** (L, 1-1), IP 4, H 5, R 3, ER 3, BB 2, SO 2; **Al Downing**, IP 0, H 3, R 3, ER 3, BB 0, SO 0; **Rollie Sheldon**, IP 2, H 0, R 0, ER 0, BB 0, SO 2; **Steve Hamilton**, IP 1⅓, H 2, R 1, ER 1, BB 0, SO 2; **Pete Mikkelsen**, IP ⅔, H 0, R 0, ER 0, BB 0, SO 0
StL **Bob Gibson** (W, 2-1), IP 9, H 9, R 5, ER 5, BB 3, SO 9

Top Performers at the Plate
NY **Phil Linz**, 2 for 5, 1 R, 1 RBI; **Mickey Mantle**, 1 for 4, 1 R, 3 RBI
StL **Ken Boyer**, 3 for 4, 3 R, 1 RBI; **Lou Brock**, 2 for 4, 1 R, 1 RBI

2B-StL/K. Boyer, White. **HR**-NY/C. Boyer, Linz, Mantle; StL/K. Boyer, Brock. **SB**-StL/McCarver, Shannon. **Time** 2:40. **Attendance** 30,346.

Left: *Smiling before the Series began, lifelong Yankee Yogi Berra would be abruptly fired after it—to be replaced by Cardinal manager Johnny Keane.*

Below: *New York took a two-games-to-one lead at Yankee Stadium in Game 3, defeating Cardinal veteran Curt Simmons, shown here pitching to Roger Maris.*

The consecutive home runs by Roger Maris and Mickey Mantle in the sixth inning of Game 6 marked the only time the "M&M Boys" homered in the same World Series game.

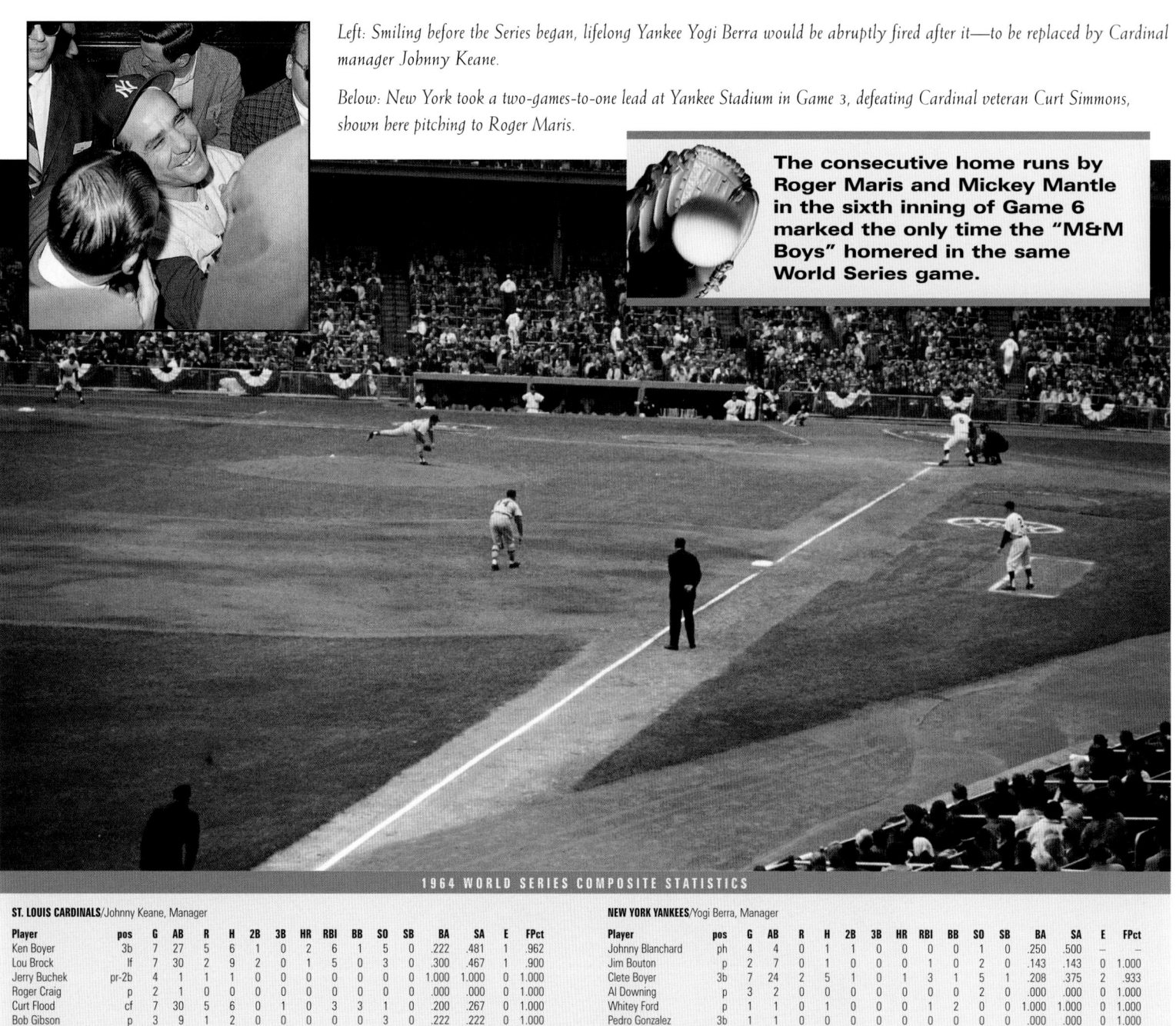

1964 WORLD SERIES COMPOSITE STATISTICS

ST. LOUIS CARDINALS/Johnny Keane, Manager

Player	pos	G	AB	R	H	2B	3B	HR	RBI	BB	SO	SB	BA	SA	E	FPct
Ken Boyer	3b	7	27	5	6	1	0	2	6	1	5	0	.222	.481	1	.962
Lou Brock	lf	7	30	2	9	2	0	1	5	0	3	0	.300	.467	1	.900
Jerry Buchek	pr-2b	4	1	1	1	0	0	0	0	0	0	0	1.000	1.000	0	1.000
Roger Craig	p	2	1	0	0	0	0	0	0	0	0	0	.000	.000	0	1.000
Curt Flood	cf	7	30	5	6	0	1	0	3	3	1	0	.200	.267	0	1.000
Bob Gibson	p	3	9	1	2	0	0	0	0	0	3	0	.222	.222	0	1.000
Dick Groat	ss	7	26	3	5	1	1	0	1	4	3	0	.192	.308	2	.931
Bob Humphreys	p	1	0	0	0	0	0	0	0	0	0	0	–	–	0	–
Charlie James	ph	3	3	0	0	0	0	0	0	0	0	1	.000	.000	–	–
Julian Javier	pr-2b	1	0	1	0	0	0	0	0	0	0	0	–	–	0	1.000
Dal Maxvill	2b	7	20	0	4	1	0	0	1	1	4	0	.200	.250	0	1.000
Tim McCarver	c	7	23	4	11	1	1	1	5	5	1	1	.478	.739	0	1.000
Gordie Richardson	p	2	0	0	0	0	0	0	0	0	0	0	–	–	0	–
Ray Sadecki	p	2	2	0	1	0	0	0	1	0	1	0	.500	.500	0	1.000
Barney Schultz	p	4	1	0	0	0	0	0	0	0	0	0	.000	.000	0	–
Mike Shannon	rf	7	28	6	6	0	0	1	2	0	9	1	.214	.321	0	1.000
Curt Simmons	p	2	4	0	2	0	0	0	1	0	1	0	.500	.500	0	1.000
Bob Skinner	ph	4	3	0	2	1	0	0	1	1	0	0	.667	1.000	–	–
Ron Taylor	p	2	1	0	0	0	0	0	0	0	1	0	.000	.000	0	1.000
Carl Warwick	ph	5	4	2	3	0	0	0	1	1	0	0	.750	.750	–	–
Bill White	1b	7	27	2	3	1	0	0	2	2	6	1	.111	.148	0	1.000
Totals		7	240	32	61	8	3	5	29	18	39	3	.254	.375	4	.984

Pitcher	G	GS	CG	IP	H	R	ER	BB	SO	W-L	Sv	ERA
Roger Craig	2	0	0	5	2	0	0	3	9	1-0	0	0.00
Bob Gibson	3	3	2	27	23	11	9	8	31	2-1	0	3.00
Bob Humphreys	1	0	0	1	0	0	0	0	1	0-0	0	0.00
Gordie Richardson	2	0	0	⅔	3	3	3	2	0	0-0	0	40.50
Ray Sadecki	2	2	0	6⅓	12	7	6	5	2	1-0	0	8.53
Barney Schultz	4	0	0	4	9	8	8	3	1	0-1	1	18.00
Curt Simmons	2	2	0	14⅓	11	4	4	3	8	0-1	0	2.51
Ron Taylor	2	0	0	4⅔	0	0	0	1	2	0-0	1	0.00
Totals	7	7	2	63	60	33	30	25	54	4-3	2	4.29

NEW YORK YANKEES/Yogi Berra, Manager

Player	pos	G	AB	R	H	2B	3B	HR	RBI	BB	SO	SB	BA	SA	E	FPct
Johnny Blanchard	ph	4	4	0	1	1	0	0	0	0	1	0	.250	.500	–	–
Jim Bouton	p	2	7	0	1	0	0	0	1	0	2	0	.143	.143	0	1.000
Clete Boyer	3b	7	24	2	5	1	0	1	3	1	5	1	.208	.375	2	.933
Al Downing	p	3	2	0	0	0	0	0	0	0	2	0	.000	.000	0	1.000
Whitey Ford	p	1	1	0	1	0	0	0	0	1	2	0	1.000	1.000	0	1.000
Pedro Gonzalez	3b	1	1	0	0	0	0	0	0	0	0	0	.000	.000	0	1.000
Steve Hamilton	p	2	0	0	0	0	0	0	0	0	0	0	–	–	0	–
Mike Hegan	pr-ph	3	1	1	0	0	0	0	0	1	1	0	.000	.000	–	–
Elston Howard	c	7	24	5	7	1	0	0	2	4	6	0	.292	.333	1	.977
Phil Linz	ss	7	31	5	7	1	0	2	2	2	5	0	.226	.452	2	.933
Hector Lopez	rf-ph	3	2	0	0	0	0	0	0	0	2	0	.000	.000	0	–
Mickey Mantle	rf	7	24	8	8	2	0	3	8	6	8	0	.333	.792	2	.857
Roger Maris	cf	7	30	4	6	0	0	1	1	1	4	0	.200	.300	0	1.000
Pete Mikkelsen	p	4	0	0	0	0	0	0	0	0	0	0	–	–	0	1.000
Joe Pepitone	1b	7	26	1	4	1	0	1	5	2	3	0	.154	.308	0	1.000
Hal Reniff	p	1	0	0	0	0	0	0	0	0	0	0	–	–	0	–
Bobby Richardson	2b	7	32	3	13	2	0	0	3	0	2	1	.406	.469	2	.950
Rollie Sheldon	p	2	0	0	0	0	0	0	0	0	0	0	–	–	0	1.000
Mel Stottlemyre	p	3	8	0	1	0	0	0	0	0	6	0	.125	.125	0	1.000
Ralph Terry	p	1	0	0	0	0	0	0	0	0	0	0	–	–	0	–
Tom Tresh	lf	7	22	4	6	2	0	2	7	6	7	0	.273	.636	0	1.000
Totals		7	239	33	60	11	0	10	33	25	54	2	.251	.423	9	.968

Pitcher	G	GS	CG	IP	H	R	ER	BB	SO	W-L	Sv	ERA
Jim Bouton	2	2	1	17⅓	15	4	3	5	7	2-0	0	1.56
Al Downing	3	1	0	7⅔	9	8	7	2	5	0-1	0	8.22
Whitey Ford	1	1	0	5⅓	8	5	5	1	4	0-1	0	8.44
Steve Hamilton	2	0	0	2	3	1	1	0	2	0-0	1	4.50
Pete Mikkelsen	4	0	0	4⅔	4	4	3	2	4	0-1	0	5.79
Hal Reniff	1	0	0	⅓	2	0	0	0	0	0-0	0	0.00
Rollie Sheldon	2	0	0	2⅔	0	2	0	2	2	0-0	0	0.00
Mel Stottlemyre	3	3	1	20	18	8	7	6	12	1-1	0	3.15
Ralph Terry	1	0	0	2	2	0	0	0	3	0-0	0	0.00
Totals	7	7	2	62	61	32	26	18	39	3-4	1	3.77

Series MVP: Bob Gibson, St. Louis Cardinals. **Series Outstanding Pitcher:** Bob Gibson, St. Louis Cardinals. **Average Length of Game:** 2 hours, 31 minutes. **Total Attendance:** 321,807. **Average Attendance:** 45,972 (30,690 at Busch Stadium; 66,349 at Yankee Stadium). **Umpires:** Ken Burkhart (NL), Bill McKinley (AL), Frank Secory (NL), Al Smith (AL), Vinnie Smith (NL), Hank Soar (AL). **Winning Player's Share:** $8,622. **Losing Player's Share:** $5,309.

deficit in half with a three-run blast, but it was not enough. Solo home runs by Ken Boyer in the seventh and Clete Boyer in the ninth not only contributed to the 7-5 final score, it also marked the first and only time that two brothers homered in the same World Series, let alone the same game. Other milestones in the dramatic seventh game included Bobby Richardson getting his 13th hit of the Series, breaking his own single-series record, and Gibson notching his record 31st strikeout. The 1964 loss marked the beginning of the Yankees' longest postseason drought since the pre-Ruth days. Berra was fired after the season and, in an odd twist, was replaced by Cardinal manager Johnny Keane for the 1965 season. For Gibson and the rest of the Cardinal players, 1964 marked the first of three Series appearances in the decade.

Left: Mickey Mantle gets a handshake from third base coach Frank Crosetti after he homered to win Game 3 in the ninth inning. It was Mantle's 16th career World Series home run, breaking Babe Ruth's mark.

Background: As part of a double steal with Mike Shannon running from first, St. Louis's Tim McCarver slides in past catcher Elston Howard on a steal of home in the fourth inning of Game 7.

Above: Pitcher Roger Craig (41) leaps to the top of the pile as the Cardinals converge on Bob Gibson near the mound after securing the final out of the 1964 World Series.

Right: The controversial pitcher Jim Bouton won two games for New York in the 1964 Series. This delivery to St. Louis's Curt Flood opened Game 3, which Bouton went on to win in a 2-1 classic.

Los Angeles Dodgers (4) vs. Minnesota Twins (3)

1965

After the fall of the mighty Yankee dynasty, a once-perennial second-division team grabbed the American League pennant in 1965. The club formerly known as the Washington Senators had relocated to Minnesota in 1961, and they rebounded from a seventh-place finish in 1964 with 102 wins in 1965. Paced by Harmon Killebrew's 25, the Twins smacked 150 home runs during the season, and they had the league's leading hitter in Tony Oliva. The Los Angeles Dodgers hit a league-worst 78 homers in 1965, but they won the National League pennant with speed and pitching. Sandy Koufax had another monumental year—26 wins, 2.04 ERA, 382 strikeouts—but he sat out the Series opener because it fell on the Jewish holiday of Yom Kippur. So the lefty's partner in crime, Don Drysdale, got the start. Drysdale had an uncharacteristically poor showing as the Twins rocked him for seven runs in less than three innings, starting with Don Mincher's solo homer in the second and Zoilo Versalles's three-run homer in the third. Minnesota's 21-game-winner, Jim "Mudcat" Grant, scattered 10 hits and two runs in nine innings. Koufax was on the mound for Game 2, but Jim Kaat gave up only one run to win it for the Twins. Minnesota capitalized on a Jim Gilliam error in the sixth to rally for two runs off Koufax, and they tacked on three more against reliever Ron Perranoski. A five-hit shutout in Game 3 by the Dodgers' number three starter, Claude Osteen, and a Johnny Roseboro two-run single in

the fourth inning, gave LA its first win of the Series. The Dodgers evened things at two games apiece the following day when Drysdale came through with an 11-strikeout, five-hit outing. He yielded bases-empty homers to Killebrew and Oliva, but LA's seven runs gave Drysdale all the support he needed. Koufax also rebounded from his previous loss with a double-digit strikeout performance, holding Minnesota to just four singles in a Game 5 shutout. The Dodgers manufactured seven runs on 12 singles, two doubles, a couple of sacrifices and four stolen bases, including three by Willie Davis. Mudcat Grant got his second complete-game win of the Series in Game 6, with his own three-run homer in the sixth providing key support. Choosing between two dominating hurlers, manager Walter Alston opted for Koufax on two days' rest over Drysdale on three days' rest to start Game 7 against Minnesota's own southpaw, Jim Kaat. Kaat was bounced from the game in the third after giving up a leadoff homer to Lou Johnson and a run-scoring single by Wes Parker, but four Minnesota relievers came in to shut LA down on just two hits in the final five innings. But it wasn't good enough, as Koufax's three-hit, 10-strikeout pitching led Los Angeles to World Series victory and earned Koufax his second Series MVP in three years.

Above: Sandy Koufax struck out 29 and allowed only 1 earned run in 24 innings in the 1965 World Series.

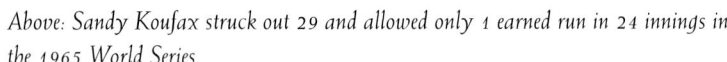

1965 WORLD SERIES COMPOSITE STATISTICS

LOS ANGELES DODGERS/Walter Alston, Manager

Player	pos	G	AB	R	H	2B	3B	HR	RBI	BB	SO	SB	BA	SA	E	FPct
Jim Brewer	p	1	0	0	0	0	0	0	0	0	0	0	—	—	0	—
Willie Crawford	ph	2	2	0	1	0	0	0	0	0	1	0	.500	.500	—	—
Willie Davis	cf	7	26	3	6	0	0	0	0	0	2	3	.231	.231	0	1.000
Don Drysdale	p-ph	3	5	0	0	0	0	0	0	0	4	0	.000	.000	0	1.000
Ron Fairly	rf	7	29	7	11	3	0	2	6	0	1	0	.379	.690	0	1.000
Jim Gilliam	3b	7	28	2	6	1	0	0	2	1	0	0	.214	.250	2	.833
Lou Johnson	lf	7	27	3	8	2	0	2	4	1	3	0	.296	.593	1	.933
John Kennedy	3b-pr	4	1	0	0	0	0	0	0	0	0	0	.000	.000	1	.667
Sandy Koufax	p	3	9	0	1	0	0	0	0	1	1	5	.111	.111	0	1.000
Jim Lefebvre	2b	3	10	2	4	0	0	0	0	0	0	0	.400	.400	1	.909
Don LeJohn	ph	1	1	0	0	0	0	0	0	0	1	0	.000	.000	—	—
Bob Miller	p	2	0	0	0	0	0	0	0	0	0	0	—	—	0	—
Wally Moon	ph	2	2	0	0	0	0	0	0	0	0	0	.000	.000	—	—
Claude Osteen	p	2	3	0	1	0	0	0	0	0	0	0	.333	.333	0	1.000
Wes Parker	1b	7	23	3	7	0	1	1	2	3	3	2	.304	.522	0	1.000
Ron Perranoski	p	2	0	0	0	0	0	0	0	0	0	0	—	—	0	1.000
Howie Reed	p	2	0	0	0	0	0	0	0	0	0	0	—	—	0	1.000
John Roseboro	c	7	21	1	6	1	0	0	3	5	3	1	.286	.333	0	1.000
Dick Tracewski	ph-2b	6	17	0	2	0	0	0	0	1	5	0	.118	.118	1	.957
Maury Wills	ss	7	30	3	11	3	0	0	3	1	3	3	.367	.467	0	1.000
Totals		**7**	**234**	**24**	**64**	**10**	**1**	**5**	**21**	**13**	**31**	**9**	**.274**	**.389**	**6**	**.977**

Pitcher	G	GS	CG	IP	H	R	ER	BB	SO	W-L	Sv	ERA
Jim Brewer	1	0	0	2	3	1	1	0	1	0-0	0	4.50
Don Drysdale	2	2	1	11⅔	12	9	5	3	15	1-1	0	3.86
Sandy Koufax	3	3	2	24	13	2	1	5	29	2-1	0	0.38
Bob Miller	2	0	0	1⅓	0	0	0	0	0	0-0	0	0.00
Claude Osteen	2	2	1	14	9	2	1	5	4	1-1	0	0.64
Ron Perranoski	2	0	0	3⅔	3	3	3	4	1	0-0	0	7.36
Howie Reed	2	0	0	3⅓	2	3	3	2	4	0-0	0	8.10
Totals	**7**	**7**	**4**	**60**	**42**	**20**	**14**	**19**	**54**	**4-3**	**0**	**2.10**

MINNESOTA TWINS/Sam Mele, Manager

Player	pos	G	AB	R	H	2B	3B	HR	RBI	BB	SO	SB	BA	SA	E	FPct
Bob Allison	lf	5	16	3	2	1	0	1	2	2	9	1	.125	.375	0	1.000
Earl Battey	c	7	25	1	3	0	1	0	2	0	5	0	.120	.200	0	1.000
Dave Boswell	p	1	0	0	0	0	0	0	0	0	0	0	—	—	0	—
Mudcat Grant	p	3	8	3	2	1	0	1	3	0	1	0	.250	.750	0	1.000
Jimmie Hall	cf	7	27	0	1	0	0	0	0	1	5	0	.143	.143	0	1.000
Jim Kaat	p	3	6	0	1	0	0	0	0	2	0	5	0	.167	.167	0	1.000
Harmon Killebrew	3b	7	21	2	6	0	0	1	2	6	4	0	.286	.429	1	.947
Johnny Klippstein	p	2	0	0	0	0	0	0	0	0	0	0	—	—	0	—
Jim Merritt	p	2	0	0	0	0	0	0	0	0	0	0	—	—	0	1.000
Don Mincher	1b	7	23	3	3	0	0	1	1	2	7	0	.130	.261	0	1.000
Joe Nossek	cf-ph	6	20	0	4	0	0	0	0	0	1	0	.200	.200	0	1.000
Tony Oliva	rf	7	26	2	5	1	0	1	2	1	6	0	.192	.346	1	.952
Camilo Pascual	p	1	1	0	0	0	0	0	0	0	0	0	.000	.000	0	1.000
Jim Perry	p	2	0	0	0	0	0	0	0	0	0	0	—	—	0	1.000
Bill Pleis	p	1	0	0	0	0	0	0	0	0	0	0	—	—	0	—
Frank Quilici	2b	7	20	2	4	2	0	0	1	4	3	0	.200	.300	2	.943
Rich Rollins	ph	3	2	0	0	0	0	0	0	1	0	0	.000	.000	—	—
Sandy Valdespino	lf-ph	5	11	1	3	1	0	0	0	0	1	0	.273	.364	0	1.000
Zoilo Versalles	ss	7	28	3	8	1	1	1	4	2	7	1	.286	.500	0	1.000
Al Worthington	p	2	0	0	0	0	0	0	0	0	0	0	—	—	1	.667
Jerry Zimmerman	c	2	1	0	0	0	0	0	0	0	0	0	.000	.000	0	1.000
Totals		**7**	**215**	**20**	**42**	**7**	**2**	**6**	**19**	**19**	**54**	**2**	**.195**	**.330**	**5**	**.979**

Pitcher	G	GS	CG	IP	H	R	ER	BB	SO	W-L	Sv	ERA
Dave Boswell	1	0	0	2⅔	3	1	1	2	3	0-0	0	3.38
Mudcat Grant	3	3	2	23	22	8	7	2	12	2-1	0	2.74
Jim Kaat	3	3	1	14⅓	18	7	6	2	6	1-2	0	3.77
Johnny Klippstein	2	0	0	2⅔	2	0	0	2	3	0-0	0	0.00
Jim Merritt	2	0	0	3⅓	2	1	1	0	1	0-0	0	2.70
Camilo Pascual	1	1	0	5	8	3	3	1	0	0-1	0	5.40
Jim Perry	2	0	0	4	5	2	2	2	4	0-0	0	4.50
Bill Pleis	1	0	0	1	2	1	1	0	0	0-0	0	9.00
Al Worthington	2	0	0	4	2	1	0	2	2	0-0	0	0.00
Totals	**7**	**7**	**3**	**60**	**64**	**24**	**21**	**13**	**31**	**3-4**	**0**	**3.15**

Series MVP: Sandy Koufax, Los Angeles Dodgers. **Series Outstanding Pitcher:** Sandy Koufax, Los Angeles Dodgers. **Average Length of Game:** 2 hours, 20 minutes. **Total Attendance:** 364,326. **Average Attendance:** 52,047 (55,885 at Dodger Stadium; 49,168 at Metropolitan Stadium). **Umpires:** Red Flaherty (AL), Eddie Hurley (AL), Bob Stewart (AL), Ed Sudol (NL), Ed Vargo (NL), Tony Venzon (NL). **Winning Player's Share:** $10,297. **Losing Player's Share:** $6,634.

Right: Jim "Mudcat" Grant gives himself some offensive support in Game 6 by connecting on this three-run homer in the sixth. He pitched a six-hitter from the hill.

Below: Tony Oliva makes a lunging catch for Lou Johnson's hit in the first inning of Game 7. He would add another great catch against Johnson four innings later.

Left: Minnesota's Jim Kaat faced Koufax three times in the 1965 Series, coming out the loser twice. Here he delivers to the plate during his Game 2 win.

In 1965, Sandy Koufax became the first pitcher to have two double-digit strikeout games in one Series.

Above: Ron Fairly's second-inning homer put LA on the board first in the Series, but the Dodgers lost the opener 8-3.

The winner-take-all Game 7 was the only contest won by a visiting team in the 1965 Fall Classic.

Game 1   Wednesday, October 6 at Metropolitan Stadium, Minnesota

	1	2	3	4	5	6	7	8	9	R	H	E
Los Angeles Dodgers	0	1	0	0	0	0	0	0	1	2	10	1
Minnesota Twins	0	1	6	0	0	1	0	0	x	8	10	0

Pitchers   LA   Don Drysdale (L, 0-1), IP 2⅔, H 7, R 7, ER 3, BB 1, SO 4; Howie Reed, IP 1⅓, H 0, R 0, ER 0, BB 0, SO 1; Jim Brewer, IP 2, H 3, R 1, ER 1, BB 0, SO 1; Ron Perranoski, IP 2, H 0, R 0, ER 0, BB 2, SO 0
Min   Mudcat Grant (W, 1-0), IP 9, H 10, R 2, ER 2, BB 1, SO 5

Top Performers at the Plate
LA   Maury Wills, 2 for 5, 1 RBI
Min   Don Mincher, 1 for 3, 2 R, 1 RBI, 1 BB; Zoilo Versalles, 2 for 5, 1 R, 4 RBI

2B-Min/Grant, Quilici, Valdespino. **HR**-LA/Fairly; Min/Mincher, Versalles. **SB**-Min/Versalles. **Time** 2:29. **Attendance** 47,797.

Game 2   Thursday, October 7 at Metropolitan Stadium, Minnesota

	1	2	3	4	5	6	7	8	9	R	H	E
Los Angeles Dodgers	0	0	0	0	0	1	0	0		1	7	3
Minnesota Twins	0	0	0	0	2	1	2	x		5	9	0

Pitchers   LA   Sandy Koufax (L, 0-1), IP 6, H 6, R 2, ER 1, BB 1, SO 9; Ron Perranoski, IP 1⅔, H 3, R 3, ER 3, BB 2, SO 1; Bob Miller, IP ⅓, H 0, R 0, ER 0, BB 0, SO 0
Min   Jim Kaat (W, 1-0), IP 9, H 7, R 1, ER 1, BB 1, SO 3

Top Performers at the Plate
LA   Ron Fairly, 2 for 4, 1 R; Jim Lefebvre, 2 for 4
Min   Harmon Killebrew, 2 for 3, 1 R, 1 BB

2B-Min/Allison, Oliva. **3B**-Min/Versalles. **Time** 2:13. **Attendance** 48,700.

Game 3   Saturday, October 9 at Dodger Stadium Los Angeles

	1	2	3	4	5	6	7	8	9	R	H	E
Minnesota Twins	0	0	0	0	0	0	0	0	0	0	5	0
Los Angeles Dodgers	0	0	0	2	1	1	0	0	x	4	10	1

Pitchers   Min   Camilo Pascual (L, 0-1), IP 5, H 8, R 3, ER 3, BB 1, SO 0; Jim Merritt, IP 2, H 2, R 1, ER 1, BB 0, SO 0; Johnny Klippstein, IP 1, H 0, R 0, ER 0, BB 1, SO 1
LA   Claude Osteen (W, 1-0), IP 9, H 5, R 0, ER 0, BB 2, SO 2

Top Performers at the Plate
Min   Zoilo Versalles, 2 for 3
LA   Lou Johnson, 2 for 2, 1 RBI, 1 BB, 1 SH, 2 2B; John Roseboro, 1 for 3, 2 RBI

2B-Min/Versalles; LA/Fairly, Gilliam, Johnson 2, Wills. **SB**-LA/Parker, Roseboro, Wills. **Time** 2:06. **Attendance** 55,934.

Game 4   Sunday, October 10 at Dodger Stadium Los Angeles

	1	2	3	4	5	6	7	8	9	R	H	E
Minnesota Twins	0	0	0	1	0	1	0	0		2	5	2
Los Angeles Dodgers	1	1	0	1	0	3	0	1	x	7	10	0

Pitchers   Min   Mudcat Grant (L, 1-1), IP 5, H 6, R 5, ER 4, BB 1, SO 2; Al Worthington, IP 2, H 2, R 1, ER 0, BB 1, SO 2; Bill Pleis, IP 1, H 2, R 1, ER 1, BB 0, SO 0
LA   Don Drysdale (W, 1-1), IP 9, H 5, R 2, ER 2, BB 2, SO 11

Top Performers at the Plate
Min   Harmon Killebrew, 1 for 2, 1 R, 1 RBI, 2 BB
LA   Ron Fairly, 1 for 4, 1 R, 3 RBI; Wes Parker, 2 for 4, 2 R, 1 RBI

HR-Min/Killebrew, Oliva; LA/Johnson, Parker. **SB**-LA/Parker, Wills. **Time** 2:15. **Attendance** 55,920.

Game 5   Monday, October 11 at Dodger Stadium Los Angeles

	1	2	3	4	5	6	7	8	9	R	H	E
Minnesota Twins	0	0	0	0	0	0	0	0	0	0	4	1
Los Angeles Dodgers	2	0	2	1	0	0	2	0	x	7	14	0

Pitchers   Min   Jim Kaat (L, 1-1), IP 2⅓, H 6, R 4, ER 3, BB 0, SO 1; Dave Boswell, IP 2⅔, H 3, R 1, ER 1, BB 2, SO 3; Jim Perry, IP 3, H 5, R 2, ER 2, BB 1, SO 3
LA   Sandy Koufax (W, 1-1), IP 9, H 4, R 0, ER 0, BB 1, SO 10

Top Performers at the Plate
LA   Ron Fairly, 3 for 5, 1 R, 1 RBI; Maury Wills, 4 for 5, 2 R, 1 RBI, 2 2B

2B-LA/Fairly, Wills 2. **SB**-LA/Davis 3, Wills. **Time** 2:34. **Attendance** 55,801.

Game 6   Wednesday, October 13 at Metropolitan Stadium, Minnesota

	1	2	3	4	5	6	7	8	9	R	H	E
Los Angeles Dodgers	0	0	0	0	0	0	1	0	0	1	6	1
Minnesota Twins	0	0	0	2	0	3	0	0	x	5	6	1

Pitchers   LA   Claude Osteen (L, 1-1), IP 5, H 4, R 2, ER 1, BB 3, SO 2; Howie Reed, IP 2, H 2, R 3, ER 3, BB 2, SO 3; Bob Miller, IP 1, H 0, R 0, ER 0, BB 0, SO 0
Min   Mudcat Grant (W, 2-1), IP 9, H 6, R 1, ER 1, BB 0, SO 5

Top Performers at the Plate
LA   Ron Fairly, 2 for 4, 1 R, 1 RBI
Min   Bob Allison, 1 for 3, 2 R, 2 RBI, 1 BB; Mudcat Grant, 1 for 3, 1 R, 3 RBI

3B-Min/Battey. **HR**-LA/Fairly; Min/Allison, Grant. **SB**-Min/Allison. **Time** 2:16. **Attendance** 49,578.

Game 7   Thursday, October 14 at Metropolitan Stadium, Minnesota

	1	2	3	4	5	6	7	8	9	R	H	E
Los Angeles Dodgers	0	0	0	2	0	0	0	0	0	2	7	0
Minnesota Twins	0	0	0	0	0	0	0	0	0	0	3	1

Pitchers   LA   Sandy Koufax (W, 2-1), IP 9, H 3, R 0, ER 0, BB 3, SO 10
Min   Jim Kaat (L, 1-2), IP 3, H 5, R 2, ER 2, BB 1, SO 2; Al Worthington, IP 2, H 0, R 0, ER 0, BB 1, SO 0; Johnny Klippstein, IP 1⅓, H 2, R 0, ER 0, BB 1, SO 2; Jim Merritt, IP 1⅓, H 0, R 0, ER 0, BB 0, SO 1; Jim Perry, IP 1, H 0, R 0, ER 0, BB 1, SO 1

Top Performers at the Plate
LA   Jim Gilliam, 2 for 5; Wes Parker, 2 for 4, 1 RBI
Min   Harmon Killebrew, 1 for 3, 1 BB

2B-LA/Fairly, Roseboro; Min/Quilici. **3B**-LA/Parker. **HR**-LA/Johnson. **Time** 2:27. **Attendance** 50,596.

Baltimore Orioles (4) vs. Los Angeles Dodgers (0)

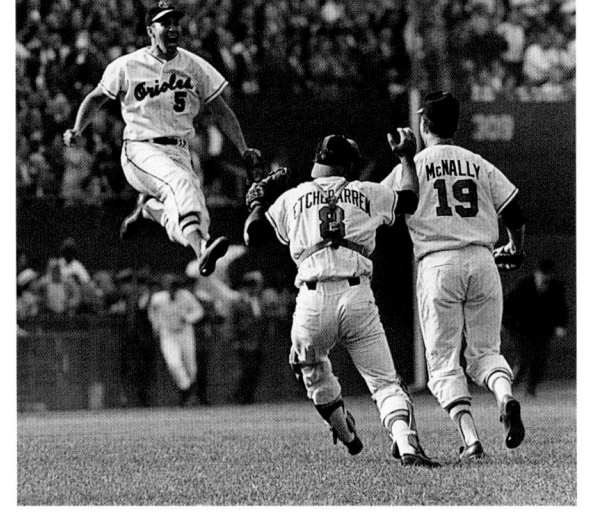

In their two previous World Series appearances, the Los Angeles Dodgers demonstrated that good pitching can beat good hitting. In 1966, the Baltimore Orioles showed that the one thing that beats good pitching is great pitching. Baltimore won 97 games in 1966 to claim the franchise's first pennant since their St. Louis Brown forebears won it in 1944. A deep pitching staff was led by Jim Palmer and Dave McNally, and Frank Robinson powered the offense with a Triple Crown campaign in his first year with Baltimore. Brooks Robinson and veteran Luis Aparicio formed a solid defense for Hank Bauer's crew. The Dodger staff was tops in the league in ERA, strikeouts and shutouts during the season, led by Sandy Koufax's second straight season winning pitching's Triple Crown (leading in wins, ERA and strikeouts). Back-to-back homers by the two Robinsons helped Baltimore jump out to a three-run lead in the first inning of Game 1 against Don Drysdale. The Orioles scored another in the second before Los Angeles cut the lead to 4-2 on a home run by Jim Lefebvre and a bases-loaded walk to Jim Gilliam an inning later, forcing in Lou Johnson from third. When Johnson crossed the plate in that inning, it was not only the Dodgers' last run of the game, it was their last run of the entire Series. After reliever Moe Drabowsky finished Game 1 with six shutout innings—including a stretch of six consecutive strikeouts—Palmer, Wally Bunker and McNally threw three complete-game shutouts

for the O's. Palmer's four-hitter blanked the Dodgers in Game 2, the 21-year-old Bunker allowed only seven to reach base in Game 3, and McNally edged out Don Drysdale in Game 4 in a battle of four-hitters. Poor fielding contributed to LA's troubles in Game 2, as center fielder Willie Davis coughed up a record three errors in one inning. Boog Powell opened the Baltimore half of the fifth with a single, and Paul Blair followed with a deep fly ball, which Davis lost in the sun for a two-base error. The next batter, Andy Etchebarren, hit another fly in Davis's direction, and again the center fielder lost sight of it. After the ball dropped out of his grasp, Davis made a wild throw to third, allowing Powell and Blair to score. Davis's disastrous inning staked Baltimore to a 3-0 lead, which they extended to 6-0. The Dodgers received noble performances from their hurlers in Games 3 and 4, giving up just seven hits and two runs in the two games, but home runs by Blair in the third game and Frank Robinson in the finale provided the difference in the two 1-0 contests. In sweeping the Dodgers for their first World Series title, the Orioles did more than hold LA to a lowly .142 team average—they also played errorless ball in the field, and limited the speedy Dodgers to one stolen base.

Above: Brooks Robinson leaps for joy after the Orioles defeated the Dodgers in a dominating four-game sweep in 1966.

1966 WORLD SERIES COMPOSITE STATISTICS

BALTIMORE ORIOLES/Hank Bauer, Manager

Player	pos	G	AB	R	H	2B	3B	HR	RBI	BB	SO	SB	BA	SA	E	FPct
Luis Aparicio	ss	4	16	0	4	1	0	0	2	0	0	0	.250	.313	0	1.000
Paul Blair	cf	4	6	2	1	0	0	1	1	1	0	0	.167	.667	0	1.000
Curt Blefary	lf	4	13	0	1	0	0	0	0	2	3	0	.077	.077	0	1.000
Wally Bunker	p	1	2	0	0	0	0	0	0	0	1	0	.000	.000	0	1.000
Moe Drabowsky	p	1	2	0	0	0	0	0	0	1	1	0	.000	.000	0	–
Andy Etchebarren	c	4	12	2	1	0	0	0	2	4	0	0	.083	.083	0	1.000
Dave Johnson	2b	4	14	1	4	1	0	0	1	0	1	0	.286	.357	0	1.000
Dave McNally	p	2	3	0	0	0	0	0	0	0	1	0	.000	.000	0	–
Jim Palmer	p	1	4	0	0	0	0	0	0	0	2	0	.000	.000	0	1.000
Boog Powell	1b	4	14	1	5	1	0	0	1	0	1	0	.357	.429	0	1.000
Brooks Robinson	3b	4	14	2	3	0	0	1	1	1	0	0	.214	.429	0	1.000
Frank Robinson	rf	4	14	4	4	0	1	2	3	2	3	0	.286	.857	0	1.000
Russ Snyder	cf-lf	3	6	1	1	0	0	0	1	2	0	0	.167	.167	0	–
Totals		**4**	**120**	**13**	**24**	**3**	**1**	**4**	**10**	**11**	**17**	**0**	**.200**	**.342**	**0**	**1.000**

Pitcher	G	GS	CG	IP	H	R	ER	BB	SO	W-L	Sv	ERA
Wally Bunker	1	1	1	9	6	0	0	1	6	1-0	0	0.00
Moe Drabowsky	1	0	0	6⅔	1	0	0	2	11	1-0	0	0.00
Dave McNally	2	2	1	11⅓	6	2	2	7	5	1-0	0	1.59
Jim Palmer	1	1	1	9	4	0	0	3	6	1-0	0	0.00
Totals	**4**	**4**	**3**	**36**	**17**	**2**	**2**	**13**	**28**	**4-0**	**0**	**0.50**

LOS ANGELES DODGERS/Walter Alston, Manager

Player	pos	G	AB	R	H	2B	3B	HR	RBI	BB	SO	SB	BA	SA	E	FPct
Jim Barbieri	ph	1	1	0	0	0	0	0	0	0	1	0	.000	.000	–	–
Jim Brewer	p	1	0	0	0	0	0	0	0	0	0	0	–	–	0	–
Wes Covington	ph	1	1	0	0	0	0	0	0	0	1	0	.000	.000	–	–
Tommy Davis	lf	4	8	0	2	0	0	0	0	1	1	0	.250	.250	0	1.000
Willie Davis	cf	4	16	0	1	0	0	0	0	0	4	0	.063	.063	3	.667
Don Drysdale	p	2	2	0	0	0	0	0	0	0	1	0	.000	.000	0	1.000
Ron Fairly	ph-rf-1b	3	7	0	1	0	0	0	0	2	4	0	.143	.143	1	.833
Al Ferrara	ph	1	1	0	1	0	0	0	0	0	0	0	1.000	1.000	–	–
Jim Gilliam	3b	2	6	0	0	0	0	0	1	2	0	0	.000	.000	1	.875
Lou Johnson	rf-lf	4	15	1	4	1	0	0	0	1	1	0	.267	.333	0	1.000
John Kennedy	3b	2	5	0	1	0	0	0	0	0	0	0	.200	.200	0	1.000
Sandy Koufax	p	1	2	0	0	0	0	0	0	0	0	0	.000	.000	0	1.000
Jim Lefebvre	2b	4	12	1	2	0	0	1	1	3	4	0	.167	.417	0	1.000
Bob Miller	p	1	0	0	0	0	0	0	0	0	0	0	–	–	0	1.000
Joe Moeller	p	1	0	0	0	0	0	0	0	0	0	0	–	–	0	–
Nate Oliver	pr	1	0	0	0	0	0	0	0	0	0	0	–	–	–	–
Claude Osteen	p	1	2	0	0	0	0	0	0	0	1	0	.000	.000	0	1.000
Wes Parker	1b	4	13	0	3	2	0	0	0	1	3	0	.231	.385	0	1.000
Ron Perranoski	p	2	0	0	0	0	0	0	0	0	0	0	–	–	1	.667
Phil Regan	p	2	0	0	0	0	0	0	0	0	0	0	–	–	0	1.000
John Roseboro	c	4	14	0	1	0	0	0	0	0	3	0	.071	.071	0	1.000
Dick Stuart	ph	2	2	0	0	0	0	0	0	0	1	0	.000	.000	–	–
Maury Wills	ss	4	13	0	1	0	0	0	0	0	3	1	.077	.077	0	1.000
Totals		**4**	**120**	**2**	**17**	**3**	**0**	**1**	**2**	**13**	**28**	**1**	**.142**	**.192**	**6**	**.961**

Pitcher	G	GS	CG	IP	H	R	ER	BB	SO	W-L	Sv	ERA
Jim Brewer	1	0	0	1	0	0	0	0	1	0-0	0	0.00
Don Drysdale	2	2	1	10	8	5	5	3	6	0-2	0	4.50
Sandy Koufax	1	1	0	6	6	4	1	2	2	0-1	0	1.50
Bob Miller	1	0	0	3	2	0	0	2	1	0-0	0	0.00
Joe Moeller	1	0	0	2	1	1	1	0	0	0-0	0	4.50
Claude Osteen	1	1	0	7	3	1	1	1	3	0-1	0	1.29
Ron Perranoski	2	0	0	3⅓	4	2	2	1	2	0-0	0	5.40
Phil Regan	2	0	0	1⅔	0	0	0	0	2	0-0	0	0.00
Totals	**4**	**4**	**1**	**34**	**24**	**13**	**10**	**11**	**17**	**0-4**	**0**	**2.65**

Series MVP: Frank Robinson, Baltimore Orioles. **Series Outstanding Pitchers:** Baltimore Orioles Pitching Staff. **Average Length of Game:** 2 hours, 16 minutes. **Total Attendance:** 220,791. **Average Attendance:** 55,198 (54,452 at Memorial Stadium; 55,944 at Dodger Stadium).
Umpires: Nestor Chylak (AL), Cal Drummond (AL), Bill Jackowski (NL), Chris Pelekoudas (NL), John Rice (AL), Mel Steiner (NL). **Winning Player's Share:** $11,683. **Losing Player's Share:** $8,189.

Back-to-Back Robinsons: After Frank Robinson (left) cranked a homer into the left-field stands in the first inning of Game 1, Brooks Robinson (below) followed with another one over the fences in left.

The 33 consecutive shutout innings pitched by the Baltimore Oriole staff is a World Series record.

Right: With one out to go in Game 2 of the '66 Series, Jim Palmer is about to become the youngest player ever to pitch a World Series shutout.

Below: Game 2 was a bad one for Willie Davis. Although this wasn't one of his three errors on the day, Davis's misplay on a fly ball in the sixth inning allowed Frank Robinson to reach with a triple.

Game 1 Wednesday, October 5 at Dodger Stadium, Los Angeles

	1	2	3	4	5	6	7	8	9	R	H	E
Baltimore Orioles	3	1	0	1	0	0	0	0	0	5	9	0
Los Angeles Dodgers	0	1	1	0	0	0	0	0	0	2	3	0

Pitchers Bal Dave McNally, IP 2⅓, H 2, R 2, ER 2, BB 5, SO 1; Moe Drabowsky (W, 1-0), IP 6⅔, H 1, R 0, ER 0, BB 2, SO 11
LA Don Drysdale (L, 0-1), IP 2, H 4, R 4, ER 4, BB 2, SO 1; Joe Moeller, IP 2, H 1, R 1, ER 1, BB 1, SO 0; Bob Miller, IP 3, H 2, R 0, ER 0, BB 2, SO 1; Ron Perranoski, IP 2, H 2, R 0, ER 0, BB 0, SO 1

Top Performers at the Plate
Bal Frank Robinson, 2 for 5, 1 R, 2 RBI; Russ Snyder, 1 for 3, 1 R, 1 RBI, 2 BB
LA Jim Gilliam, 0 for 2, 1 RBI, 2 BB; Jim Lefebvre, 1 for 3, 1 R, 1 RBI, 1 BB

2B-Bal/D. Johnson, Powell; LA/Parker. **HR**-Bal/B. Robinson, F. Robinson; LA/Lefebvre.
SB-LA/Wills. **Time** 2:56. **Attendance** 55,941.

Game 2 Thursday, October 6 at Dodger Stadium, Los Angeles

	1	2	3	4	5	6	7	8	9	R	H	E
Baltimore Orioles	0	0	0	3	1	0	2	0	0	6	8	0
Los Angeles Dodgers	0	0	0	0	0	0	0	0	0	0	4	6

Pitchers Bal Jim Palmer (W, 1-0), IP 9, H 4, R 0, ER 0, BB 3, SO 6
LA Sandy Koufax (L, 0-1), IP 6, H 6, R 4, ER 1, BB 2, SO 2; Ron Perranoski, IP 1⅓, H 2, R 2, ER 2, BB 1, SO 1; Phil Regan, IP ⅔, H 0, R 0, ER 0, BB 1, SO 1; Jim Brewer, IP 1, H 0, R 0, ER 0, BB 0, SO 1

Top Performers at the Plate
Bal Boog Powell, 2 for 3, 1 R, 1 RBI, 1 SH; Frank Robinson, 1 for 3, 2 R, 2 BB

2B-Bal/Aparicio; LA/L. Johnson. **3B**-Bal/F. Robinson. **Time** 2:26. **Attendance** 55,947.

Game 3 Saturday, October 8 at Memorial Stadium, Baltimore

	1	2	3	4	5	6	7	8	9	R	H	E
Los Angeles Dodgers	0	0	0	0	0	0	0	0	0	0	6	0
Baltimore Orioles	0	0	0	0	1	0	0	0	x	1	3	0

Pitchers LA Claude Osteen (L, 0-1), IP 7, H 3, R 1, ER 1, BB 1, SO 3; Phil Regan, IP 1, H 0, R 0, ER 0, BB 0, SO 1
Bal Wally Bunker (W, 1-0), IP 9, H 6, R 0, ER 0, BB 1, SO 6

Top Performers at the Plate
LA Lou Johnson, 2 for 4
Bal Paul Blair, 1 for 3, 1 R, 1 RBI

2B-LA/Parker. **HR**-Bal/Blair. **Time** 1:55. **Attendance** 54,445.

Game 4 Sunday, October 9 at Memorial Stadium, Baltimore

	1	2	3	4	5	6	7	8	9	R	H	E
Los Angeles Dodgers	0	0	0	0	0	0	0	0	0	0	4	0
Baltimore Orioles	0	0	0	1	0	0	0	0	x	1	4	0

Pitchers LA Don Drysdale (L, 0-2), IP 8, H 4, R 1, ER 1, BB 1, SO 5
Bal Dave McNally (W, 1-0), IP 9, H 4, R 0, ER 0, BB 2, SO 4

Top Performers at the Plate
Bal Frank Robinson, 1 for 3, 1 R, 1 RBI

HR-Bal/F. Robinson. **Time** 1:45. **Attendance** 54,458.

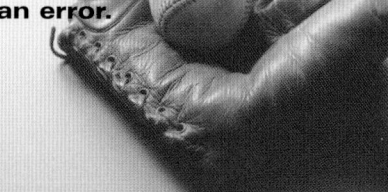

Jim Palmer was nine days shy of his 21st birthday when he shut out LA in Game 2, making him the youngest to hurl a shutout in World Series play.

The 1966 Orioles were only the second team (after the 1937 Yankees) to play a full Series without committing an error.

St. Louis Cardinals (4) vs. Boston Red Sox (3)

After finishing 26 games out of first in 1966 with a ninth-place finish, the Boston Red Sox realized their "impossible dream" in 1967 by edging out the Twins and Tigers for the pennant on the last day of the season. Carl Yastrzemski led the ride with a Triple Crown, and Jim Lonborg started 39 games for Boston and won 22 of them. The St. Louis Cardinals secured their pennant more convincingly, coasting to a 10 1/2-game lead in the NL. Although he missed two months of the season with a broken leg, Cardinal ace Bob Gibson was healthy and ready to go in Game 1 of the World Series. He struck out 10 and allowed six hits in a 2-1 triumph over Boston's Jose Santiago. Santiago provided his team's only run with a third-inning home run. Lou Brock broke a 1-1 tie in the seventh by singling, stealing second and advancing to third and then home on infield grounders. Lonborg started for Boston in Game 2, and he was spectacular. He retired the first 19 Cardinal batters of the game before yielding a one-out walk in the seventh. After Lonborg got the next four batters out, Julian Javier stroked a double to left, breaking up the no-hitter with two outs in the eighth. No serious damage was done, however, and Lonborg closed the door on his one-hitter with a 5-0 victory. "Yaz" did his part with the bat by driving in four with two

home runs. The young Nelson Briles pitched a complete-game win in Game 3 to give St. Louis a two-games-to-one advantage. Brock scored the game's first run after leading off the first inning with a triple. Mike Shannon followed Tim McCarver's second-inning single with a homer to left to produce an early 3-0 lead, which was extended to 5-2. In Game 4, Gibson put the Red Sox further in the hole with a five-hit shutout. Roger Maris's double drove in two runs for the Cards as part of a four-run first inning. Just four days after his one-hit performance, Lonborg held St. Louis to three hits in Game 5. A solo homer by Maris in the bottom of the ninth was the Cardinals' only run off Lonborg, while Boston scored an unearned run against lefty Steve Carlton in the third, and two runs came across in the ninth on a bases-loaded single by Elston Howard. The teams combined for 20 hits in Game 6, with Rico Petrocelli starting things off with a solo homer in the second. Petrocelli hit another one two innings later as part of a record three-homer inning for Boston. Yastrzemski led off the fourth with a shot to left-center, and two batters later, Reggie Smith and Petrocelli hit back-to-back blasts. Brock drove in three Cardinal runs, including two on a game-tying seventh-inning homer. Boston came back with four runs

Left: Bob Gibson struck out 10 Red Sox in his Game 1 victory at Fenway Park.

Below: A happy Bob Gibson is congratulated by catcher Tim McCarver and third baseman Mike Shannon after clinching the seventh game of the 1967 World Series. Bobby Tolan and Orlando Cepeda are running in to join the celebration.

Above: Jim Lonborg was nearly unstoppable in Game 2, pitching no-hit ball for seven and two-thirds innings.

Jim Lonborg's Game 2 one-hitter and Game 5 three-hitter accounted for the fewest hits given up by a pitcher in two consecutive complete games.

Above: Lou Brock is on his way to third in Game 7 with his sixth steal of the Series. He would get the seventh four innings later.

Left: A week after breaking up Jim Lonborg's no-hitter, Julian Javier again gets the better of the Boston pitcher, delivering a three-run homer to put St. Louis ahead 7-1 in the final game.

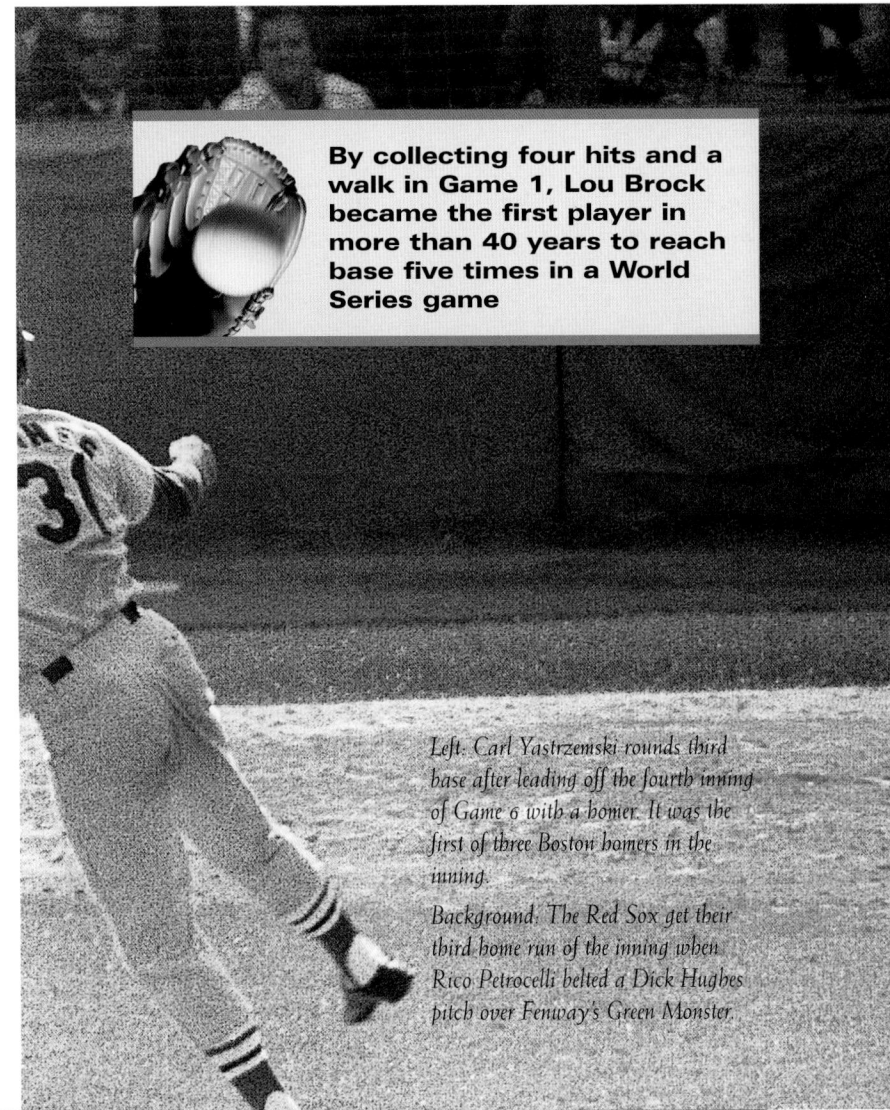

against four different Cardinal pitchers in the bottom of the inning to win 8-4. After falling behind three games to one, the Red Sox had pushed the Series to a decisive seventh game, and their ace, Jim Lonborg, was ready to go on two days' rest. Facing Lonborg was the top pitcher from the other side of the diamond, Bob Gibson. The match-up of star pitchers didn't quite turn out like the Red Sox had hoped, as Lonborg struggled through six innings. Ten Cardinal hits led to seven runs, including a solo homer by Gibson in the fifth. Gibson came through on the mound as well, striking out 10 and allowing only three hits for his third complete-game victory of the Series. Boston's impossible dream came to a rude awakening in the form of Bob Gibson. Lou Brock helped, too, batting .414 in the seven games and stealing a record seven bases without being caught.

Left: Carl Yastrzemski rounds third base after leading off the fourth inning of Game 6 with a homer. It was the first of three Boston homers in the inning.

Background: The Red Sox get their third home run of the inning when Rico Petrocelli belted a Dick Hughes pitch over Fenway's Green Monster.

1967 WORLD SERIES COMPOSITE STATISTICS

ST. LOUIS CARDINALS/Red Schoendienst, Manager

Player	pos	G	AB	R	H	2B	3B	HR	RBI	BB	SO	SB	BA	SA	E	Pct
Eddie Bressoud	ss	2	0	0	0	0	0	0	0	0	0	0	.000	–	0	1.000
Nelson Briles	p	2	3	0	0	0	0	0	0	0	0	0	.000	.000	0	–
Lou Brock	lf	7	29	8	12	2	1	1	3	2	3	7	.414	.655	0	1.000
Steve Carlton	p	1	1	0	0	0	0	0	0	0	0	0	.000	.000	0	–
Orlando Cepeda	1b	7	29	1	3	2	0	0	1	0	4	0	.103	.172	0	1.000
Curt Flood	cf	7	28	2	5	1	0	0	3	3	3	0	.179	.214	0	1.000
Phil Gagliano	ph	1	1	0	0	0	0	0	0	0	0	0	.000	.000	–	–
Bob Gibson	p	3	11	1	1	0	0	1	1	1	2	0	.091	.364	0	1.000
Joe Hoerner	p	2	0	0	0	0	0	0	0	0	0	0	–	–	0	–
Dick Hughes	p	2	3	0	0	0	0	0	0	0	3	0	.000	.000	0	1.000
Larry Jaster	p	1	0	0	0	0	0	0	0	0	0	0	–	–	0	–
Julian Javier	2b	7	25	2	9	3	0	1	4	0	6	0	.360	.600	1	.970
Jack Lamabe	p	3	0	0	0	0	0	0	0	0	0	0	–	–	0	1.000
Roger Maris	rf	7	26	3	10	1	0	1	7	3	1	0	.385	.538	1	.938
Dal Maxvill	ss	7	19	1	3	0	1	0	1	4	1	0	.158	.263	0	1.000
Tim McCarver	c	7	24	3	3	1	0	0	2	2	2	0	.125	.167	0	1.000
Dave Ricketts	ph	3	3	0	0	0	0	0	0	0	0	0	.000	.000	–	–
Mike Shannon	3b	7	24	3	5	1	0	1	2	1	4	0	.208	.375	2	.900
Ed Spiezio	ph	1	1	0	0	0	0	0	0	0	0	0	.000	.000	–	–
Bobby Tolan	ph	3	2	1	0	0	0	0	0	1	1	0	.000	.000	–	–
Ray Washburn	p	2	0	0	0	0	0	0	0	0	0	0	–	–	0	1.000
Ron Willis	p	3	0	0	0	0	0	0	0	0	0	0	–	–	0	–
Hal Woodeshick	p	1	0	0	0	0	0	0	0	0	0	0	–	–	0	1.000
Totals		7	229	25	51	11	2	5	24	17	30	7	.223	.354	4	.984

Pitcher	G	GS	CG	IP	H	R	ER	BB	SO	W-L	Sv	ERA
Nelson Briles	2	1	1	11	7	2	2	1	4	1-0	0	1.64
Steve Carlton	1	1	0	6	3	1	0	2	5	0-1	0	0.00
Bob Gibson	3	3	3	27	14	3	3	5	26	3-0	0	1.00
Joe Hoerner	2	0	0	⅔	4	3	3	1	0	0-0	0	40.50
Dick Hughes	2	2	0	9	9	6	5	3	7	0-1	0	5.00
Larry Jaster	1	0	0	⅓	2	0	0	0	0	0-0	0	0.00
Jack Lamabe	3	0	0	2⅔	5	2	2	0	4	0-1	0	6.75
Ray Washburn	2	0	0	2⅓	1	0	0	0	2	0-0	0	0.00
Ron Willis	3	0	0	1	2	4	3	4	1	0-0	0	27.00
Hat Woodeshick	1	0	0	1	1	0	0	0	0	0-0	0	0.00
Totals	7	7	4	61	48	21	18	17	49	4-3	0	2.66

BOSTON RED SOX/Dick Williams, Manager

Player	pos	G	AB	R	H	2B	3B	HR	RBI	BB	SO	SB	BA	SA	E	FPct
Jerry Adair	2b-ph	5	16	0	2	0	0	0	1	0	3	1	.125	.125	0	1.000
Mike Andrews	ph-2b	5	13	2	4	0	0	0	1	0	1	0	.308	.308	0	1.000
Gary Bell	p	3	0	0	0	0	0	0	0	0	0	0	–	–	0	1.000
Ken Brett	p	2	0	0	0	0	0	0	0	0	0	0	–	–	0	–
Joe Foy	ph-3b	6	15	2	2	1	0	0	1	5	5	0	.133	.200	1	.944
Russ Gibson	c	2	2	0	0	0	0	0	0	0	2	0	.000	.000	0	1.000
Ken Harrelson	rf	4	13	0	1	0	0	0	1	1	3	0	.077	.077	0	1.000
Elston Howard	c	7	18	0	2	0	0	0	1	1	2	0	.111	.111	0	1.000
Dalton Jones	3b-ph	6	18	2	7	0	0	0	1	1	3	0	.389	.389	0	1.000
Jim Lonborg	p	3	9	0	0	0	0	0	0	0	7	0	.000	.000	0	1.000
Dave Morehead	p	2	0	0	0	0	0	0	0	0	0	0	–	–	0	–
Dan Osinski	p	2	0	0	0	0	0	0	0	0	0	0	–	–	0	–
Rico Petrocelli	ss	7	20	3	4	1	0	2	3	3	8	0	.200	.550	2	.939
Mike Ryan	c	1	2	0	0	0	0	0	0	0	1	0	.000	.000	0	1.000
Jose Santiago	p	3	2	1	1	0	0	0	1	0	1	0	.500	2.000	0	–
George Scott	1b	7	26	3	6	1	1	0	3	6	6	0	.231	.346	0	1.000
Norm Siebern	ph-rf	3	3	0	1	0	0	0	1	0	0	0	.333	.333	0	–
Reggie Smith	cf	7	24	3	6	1	0	2	3	2	2	0	.250	.542	0	1.000
Lee Stange	p	3	0	0	0	0	0	0	0	0	0	0	–	–	1	.000
Jerry Stephenson	p	1	0	0	0	0	0	0	0	0	0	0	–	–	0	–
Jose Tartabull	pr-rf-ph	7	13	1	2	0	0	0	0	1	2	0	.154	.154	0	1.000
George Thomas	ph-rf	2	0	0	0	0	0	0	0	1	0	0	.000	.000	0	1.000
Gary Waslewski	p	2	1	0	0	0	0	0	0	0	1	0	.000	.000	0	1.000
John Wyatt	p	2	0	0	0	0	0	0	0	0	0	0	–	–	0	–
Carl Yastrzemski	lf	7	25	4	10	2	0	3	5	4	1	0	.400	.840	0	1.000
Totals		7	222	21	48	6	1	8	19	17	49	1	.216	.360	4	.984

Pitcher	G	GS	CG	IP	H	R	ER	BB	SO	W-L	Sv	ERA
Gary Bell	3	1	0	5⅓	8	3	3	1	1	0-1	1	5.06
Ken Brett	2	0	0	1⅓	0	0	0	1	1	0-0	0	0.00
Jim Lonborg	3	3	2	24	14	8	7	2	11	2-1	0	2.63
Dave Morehead	2	0	0	3⅓	0	0	0	4	3	0-0	0	0.00
Dan Osinski	2	0	0	1⅓	2	1	1	0	0	0-0	0	6.75
Jose Santiago	3	2	0	9⅔	16	6	6	3	6	0-2	0	5.59
Lee Stange	1	0	0	2	3	1	0	0	0	0-0	0	0.00
Jerry Stephenson	1	0	0	2	3	2	2	1	0	0-0	0	9.00
Gary Waslewski	2	1	0	8⅓	4	2	2	2	7	0-0	0	2.16
John Wyatt	2	0	0	3⅔	1	2	2	3	1	1-0	0	4.91
Totals	7	7	2	61	51	25	23	17	30	3-4	1	3.39

Series MVP: Bob Gibson, St. Louis Cardinals. **Series Outstanding Pitcher:** Bob Gibson, St. Louis Cardinals. **Average Length of Game:** 2 hours, 22 minutes. **Total Attendance:** 304,085. **Average Attendance:** 43,441 (54,575 at Busch Stadium; 35,090 at Fenway Park). **Umpires:** Al Barlick (NL), Augie Donatelli (NL), Paul Pryor (NL), Ed Runge (AL), Johnny Stevens (AL), Frank Umont (AL). **Winning Player's Share:** $8,315. **Losing Player's Share:** $5,115.

St. Louis used a record eight pitchers in the 8-4 loss in Game 6. Boston's three hurlers set the two-team record of 11 pitchers in one game.

Left: Lou Brock, Julian Javier and Bob Gibson—St. Louis's leading players in the 1967 championship—are triumphant in the locker room after Game 7.

Game 1	Wednesday, October 4 at Fenway Park, Boston												
	1	2	3	4	5	6	7	8	9		R	H	E
St. Louis Cardinals	0	0	1	0	0	0	1	0	0		2	10	0
Boston Red Sox	0	0	1	0	0	0	0	0	0		1	6	0

Pitchers StL Bob Gibson (W, 1-0), IP 9, H 6, R 1, ER 1, BB 1, SO 10
Bos Jose Santiago (L, 0-1), IP 7, H 10, R 2, ER 2, BB 3, SO 5; John Wyatt, IP 2, H 0, R 0, ER 0, BB 2, SO 1

Top Performers at the Plate
StL Lou Brock, 4 for 4, 2 R, 1 BB, 2 SB; Roger Maris, 1 for 4, 2 RBI, 1 BB
Bos Jose Santiago, 1 for 2, 1 R, 1 RBI; George Scott, 2 for 3, 1 BB
2B-StL/Flood; Bos/Scott. **HR**-Bos/Santiago. **SB**-StL/Brock 2. **Time** 2:22. **Attendance** 34,796.

Game 2	Thursday, October 5 at Fenway Park, Boston												
	1	2	3	4	5	6	7	8	9		R	H	E
St. Louis Cardinals	0	0	0	0	0	0	0	0	0		0	1	1
Boston Red Sox	0	0	0	1	0	1	3	0	x		5	9	0

Pitchers StL Dick Hughes (L, 0-1), IP 5⅓, H 4, R 2, ER 1, BB 3, SO 5; Ron Willis, IP ⅔, H 1, R 2, ER 2, BB 2, SO 1; Joe Hoerner, IP ⅔, H 2, R 1, ER 1, BB 1, SO 0; Jack Lamabe, IP 1⅓, H 2, R 0, ER 0, BB 0, SO 2
Bos Jim Lonborg (W, 1-0), IP 9, H 1, R 0, ER 0, BB 1, SO 4

Top Performers at the Plate
Bos Dalton Jones, 2 for 5, 1 R; Carl Yastrzemski, 3 for 4, 2 R, 4 RBI, 1 BB
2B-StL/Javier. **HR**-Bos/Yastrzemski 2. **SB**-Bos/Adair. **Time** 2:24. **Attendance** 35,188.

Game 3	Saturday, October 7 at Busch Stadium, St. Louis												
	1	2	3	4	5	6	7	8	9		R	H	E
Boston Red Sox	0	0	0	0	1	1	0	0			2	7	1
St. Louis Cardinals	1	2	0	0	0	1	0	1	x		5	10	0

Pitchers Bos Gary Bell (L, 0-1), IP 2, H 5, R 3, ER 3, BB 0, SO 1; Gary Waslewski, IP 3, H 0, R 0, ER 0, BB 0, SO 3; Lee Stange, IP 2, H 3, R 1, ER 0, BB 0, SO 0; Dan Osinski, IP 1, H 2, R 1, ER 1, BB 0, SO 0
StL Nelson Briles (W, 1-0), IP 9, H 7, R 2, ER 2, BB 0, SO 4

Top Performers at the Plate
Bos Dalton Jones, 3 for 4, 1 RBI; Reggie Smith, 2 for 4, 1 R, 1 RBI
StL Lou Brock, 2 for 4, 2 R; Mike Shannon, 2 for 3, 1 R, 2 RBI
2B-StL/Cepeda. **3B**-StL/Brock. **HR**-Bos/Smith; StL/Shannon. **Time** 2:15. **Attendance** 54,575.

Game 4	Sunday, October 8 at Busch Stadium, St. Louis												
	1	2	3	4	5	6	7	8	9		R	H	E
Boston Red Sox	0	0	0	0	0	0	0	0	0		0	5	0
St. Louis Cardinals	4	0	2	0	0	0	0	x			6	9	0

Pitchers Bos Jose Santiago (L, 0-2), IP ⅔, H 6, R 4, ER 4, BB 0, SO 0; Gary Bell, IP 1⅓, H 0, R 0, ER 0, BB 0, SO 0; Jerry Stephenson, IP 2, H 3, R 2, ER 2, BB 1, SO 0; Dave Morehead, IP 3, H 0, R 0, ER 0, BB 1, SO 2; Ken Brett, IP 1, H 0, R 0, ER 0, BB 1, SO 1
StL Bob Gibson (W, 2-0), IP 9, H 5, R 0, ER 0, BB 1, SO 6

Top Performers at the Plate
Bos Jose Tartabull, 2 for 4; Carl Yastrzemski, 2 for 4
StL Julian Javier, 2 for 4, 1 RBI; Tim McCarver, 1 for 3, 1 R, 2 RBI, 1 SF
2B-Bos/Yastrzemski; StL/Brock, Cepeda, Javier, Maris. **SB**-StL/Brock. **Time** 2:05. **Attendance** 54,575.

Game 5	Monday, October 9 at Busch Stadium, St. Louis												
	1	2	3	4	5	6	7	8	9		R	H	E
Boston Red Sox	0	0	1	0	0	0	0	2			3	6	1
St. Louis Cardinals	0	0	0	0	0	0	0	1			1	3	2

Pitchers Bos Jim Lonborg (W, 2-0), IP 9, H 3, R 1, ER 1, BB 0, SO 4
StL Steve Carlton (L, 0-1), IP 6, H 3, R 1, ER 0, BB 2, SO 5; Ray Washburn, IP 2, H 1, R 0, ER 0, BB 0, SO 2; Ron Willis, IP 0, H 1, R 2, ER 1, BB 2, SO 0; Jack Lamabe, IP 1, H 1, R 0, ER 0, BB 0, SO 2

Top Performers at the Plate
Bos Ken Harrelson, 1 for 3, 1 RBI, 1 BB; Carl Yastrzemski, 1 for 3, 1 BB
StL Roger Maris, 2 for 4, 1 R, 1 RBI
2B-Bos/Smith, Yastrzemski. **HR**-StL/Maris. **Time** 2:20. **Attendance** 54,575.

Game 6	Wednesday, October 11 at Fenway Park, Boston												
	1	2	3	4	5	6	7	8	9		R	H	E
St. Louis Cardinals	0	0	2	0	0	0	2	0	0		4	8	0
Boston Red Sox	0	1	0	3	0	0	4	0	x		8	12	1

Pitchers StL Dick Hughes, IP 3⅔, H 5, R 4, ER 4, BB 0, SO 2; Ron Willis, IP ⅓, H 0, R 0, ER 0, BB 0, SO 0; Nelson Briles, IP 2, H 0, R 0, ER 0, BB 1, SO 0; Jack Lamabe (L, 0-1), IP ⅓, H 2, R 2, ER 2, BB 0, SO 0; Joe Hoerner, IP 0, H 2, R 2, ER 2, BB 0, SO 0; Larry Jaster, IP ⅓, H 2, R 0, ER 0, BB 0, SO 0; Ray Washburn, IP ⅓, H 0, R 0, ER 0, BB 1, SO 0; Hal Woodeshick, IP 1, H 1, R 0, ER 0, BB 0, SO 0
Bos Gary Waslewski, IP 5⅓, H 4, R 2, ER 2, BB 2, SO 4; John Wyatt (W, 1-0), IP 1⅔, H 1, R 2, ER 2, BB 1, SO 0; Gary Bell (Sv, 1), IP 2, H 3, R 0, ER 0, BB 1, SO 0

Top Performers at the Plate
StL Lou Brock, 2 for 5, 2 R, 3 RBI; Roger Maris, 2 for 4
Bos Rico Petrocelli, 2 for 3, 2 R, 2 RBI, 1 BB, 2 HR; Carl Yastrzemski, 3 for 4, 2 R, 1 RBI, 1 BB
2B-StL/Javier, Shannon; Bos/Foy. **HR**-StL/Brock; Bos/Petrocelli 2, Smith, Yastrzemski. **SB**-StL/Brock. **Time** 2:48. **Attendance** 35,188.

Game 7	Thursday, October 12 at Fenway Park, Boston												
	1	2	3	4	5	6	7	8	9		R	H	E
St. Louis Cardinals	0	0	2	0	2	3	0	0	0		7	10	1
Boston Red Sox	0	0	0	0	0	1	0	0			2	3	1

Pitchers StL Bob Gibson (W, 3-0), IP 9, H 3, R 2, ER 2, BB 3, SO 10
Bos Jim Lonborg (L, 2-1), IP 6, H 10, R 7, ER 6, BB 1, SO 3; Jose Santiago, IP 2, H 0, R 0, ER 0, BB 0, SO 1; Dave Morehead, IP ⅓, H 0, R 0, ER 0, BB 3, SO 1; Dan Osinski, IP ⅓, H 0, R 0, ER 0, BB 0, SO 0; Ken Brett, IP ⅓, H 0, R 0, ER 0, BB 0, SO 0

Top Performers at the Plate
StL Lou Brock, 2 for 4, 1 R, 1 BB, 3 SB; Julian Javier, 2 for 4, 1 R, 3 RBI
Bos Rico Petrocelli, 1 for 3, 1 R
2B-StL/Brock, McCarver; Bos/Petrocelli. **3B**-StL/Maxvill; Bos/Scott. **HR**-StL/B. Gibson, Javier. **SB**-StL/Brock 3. **Time** 2:23. **Attendance** 35,188.

Detroit Tigers (4) vs. St. Louis Cardinals (3)

1968

In 1968, the "Year of the Pitcher," baseball's two top hurlers faced off in the opening game of the World Series. Detroit's Denny McLain was the Majors' first 30-game winner in 34 years with his 31-6 record, helping the Tigers reach the pennant for the first time since 1945. St. Louis's Bob Gibson compiled a staggering 1.12 ERA—the lowest baseball had seen since 1914—to go with his 22 victories. Both pitchers started out well in Game 1. Neither side crossed the plate until the Cardinals rallied for three runs against McLain in the fourth inning on two singles, two walks and an error. Gibson, meanwhile, had 10 strike-outs to his credit before the first Tiger baserunner reached scoring position. The intimidating righty got out of a sixth-inning jam with a strikeout, then fanned three of the next four batters, putting him one away from Sandy Koufax's single-game record, and one inning to go. After allowing a leadoff single in the ninth, Gibson struck out Al Kaline to tie Koufax's mark. The next batter, Norm Cash, became the record-breaking 16th casualty, and Gibson rounded out the phenomenal afternoon by getting Willie Horton looking at strike three for number 17. (Kaline and Cash were victimized three times apiece by

Gibson.) In Game 2, the Tigers managed to get their bats on the ball against Nelson Briles, scoring eight runs on 13 hits. Mickey Lolich allowed 6 hits and struck out 9 for Detroit, and he joined Cash and Horton as home-run hitters for the day—it was the first and only home run of Lolich's 16-year career. Kaline put Detroit up 2-0 in Game 3 with a third-inning homer, but Tim McCarver and Orlando Cepeda each knocked three-run blasts for St. Louis, giving the Cardinals a 7-3 win. Lou Brock scored St. Louis's first run in the fifth after he singled and stole second base, his record third steal of the day. McLain and Gibson squared off again in Game 4, and while McLain was tagged with his second loss, Gibson was in total control in a 10-1 romp. He struck out 10, gave up just 5 hits, and hit his second career World Series home run. Brock led the game off with an upper-deck homer, then added a triple in the fourth and a bases-loaded double in the eighth. His steal of third base gave him seven for the Series, tying the record he set a year earlier. After dropping two games at

Left: Tiger pitcher Mickey Lolich allowed only five runs in his three victories over the Cardinals in the 1968 Fall Classic.

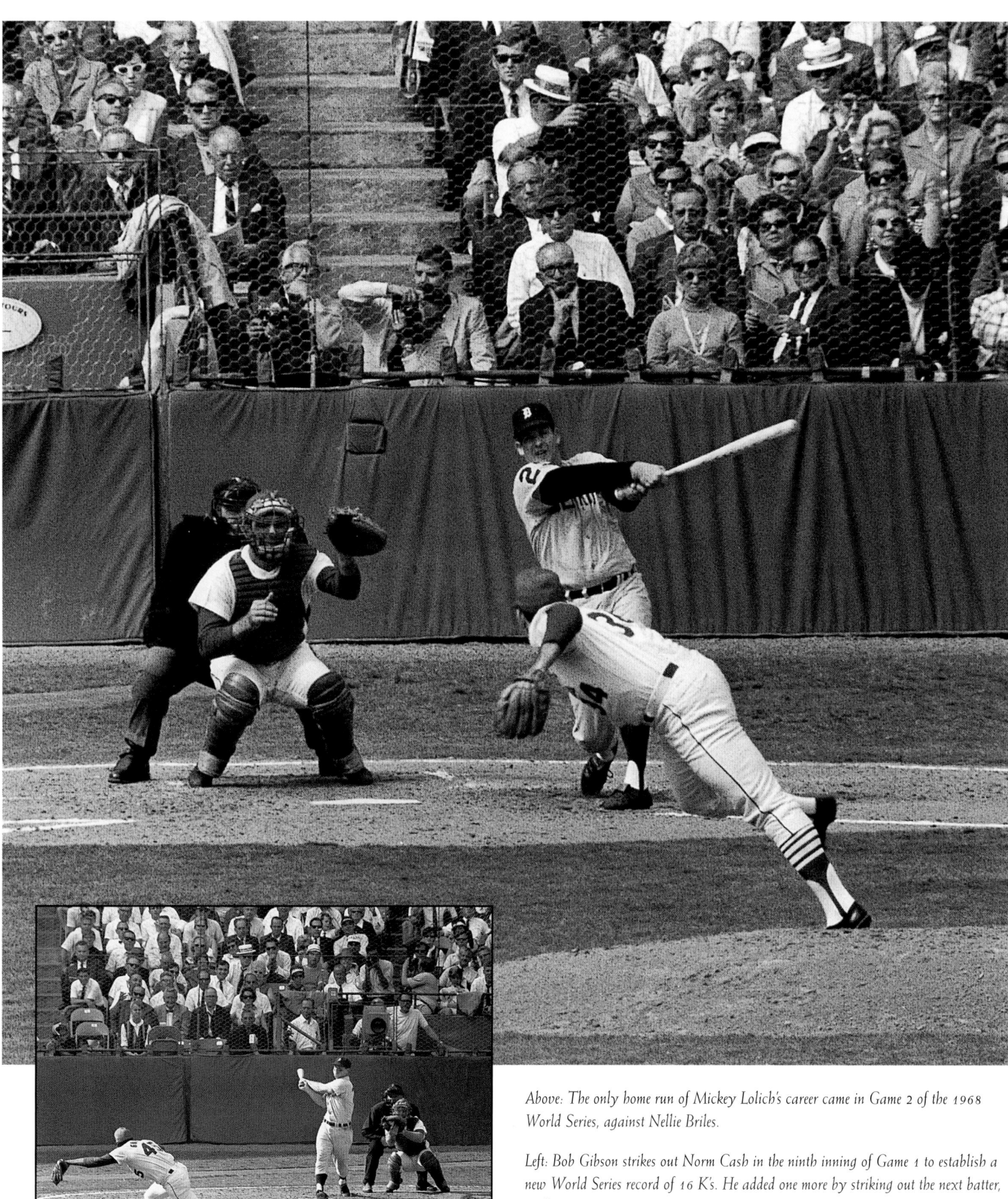

Above: The only home run of Mickey Lolich's career came in Game 2 of the 1968 World Series, against Nellie Briles.

Left: Bob Gibson strikes out Norm Cash in the ninth inning of Game 1 to establish a new World Series record of 16 K's. He added one more by striking out the next batter, Willie Horton.

home, the Tigers had their backs against the wall going into Game 5. Lolich fell behind 3-0 after one but went on to hurl another complete-game triumph. And again he chipped in with the bat, starting off a three-run seventh inning with a bloop single. McLain finally came alive in Game 6, holding St. Louis to one run and striking out seven. The Detroit lineup exploded for 10 runs in the third inning (tying a record), with Jim Northrup's grand slam leading the way. Lolich and Gibson were both going after win number three in the Game 7 finale in St. Louis. Gibson allowed only an infield single through the first six innings, but the Tigers put together three runs in the seventh. With two out and two on, Curt Flood misjudged Northrup's deep fly ball, resulting in a two-run triple. Lolich got himself out of a potential sixth-inning jam by picking off Brock and then Flood at first base after each one singled. He ended up with a five-hitter in his third complete-game victory, and Detroit had the championship. Lou Brock's superior play at the plate and on the base paths led to record-tying numbers in hits (13) and stolen bases (7) while batting .464, but it was the heroic performances by Lolich and Gibson that made the 1968 World Series a memorable one.

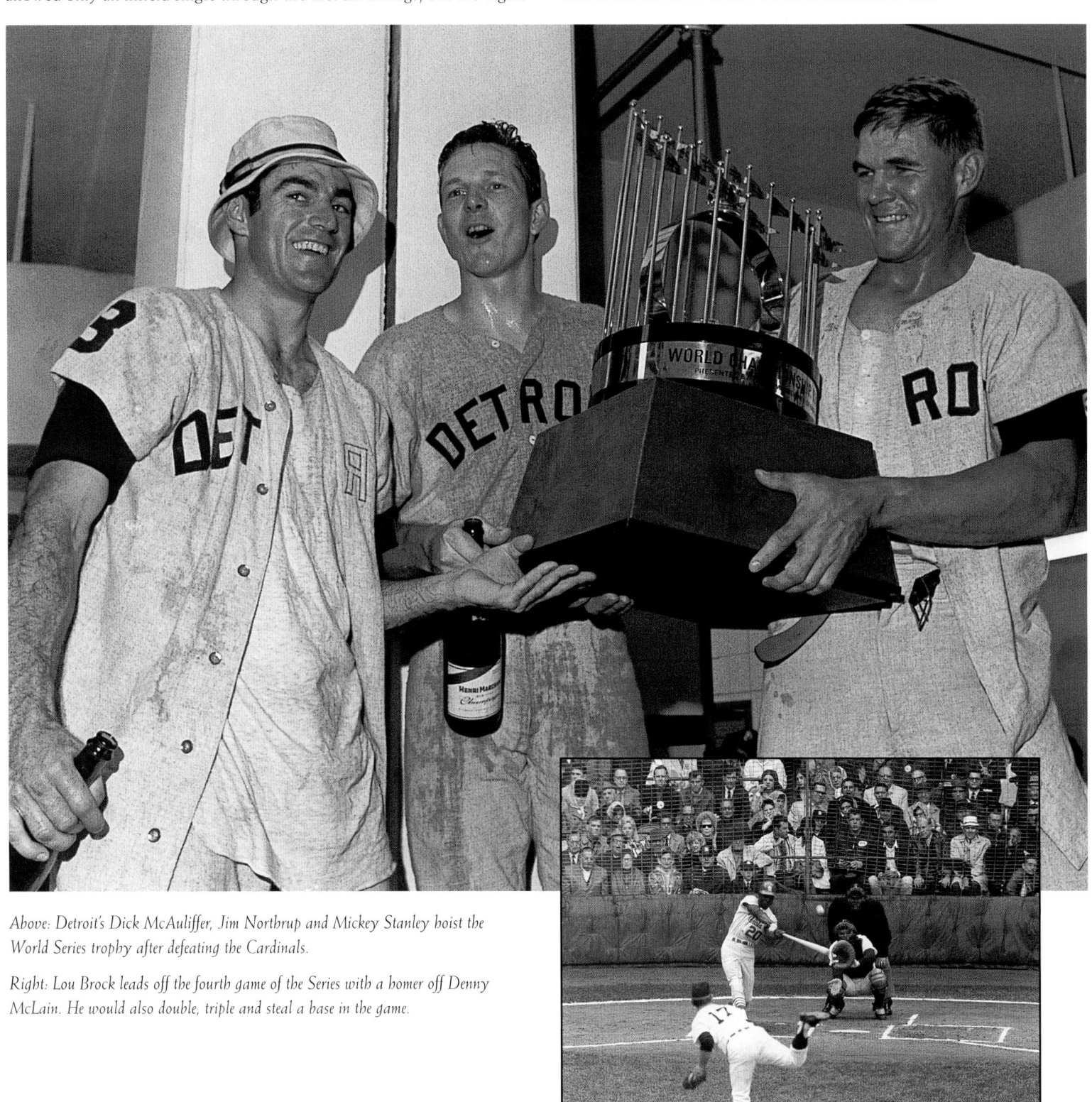

Above: Detroit's Dick McAuliffer, Jim Northrup and Mickey Stanley hoist the World Series trophy after defeating the Cardinals.

Right: Lou Brock leads off the fourth game of the Series with a homer off Denny McLain. He would also double, triple and steal a base in the game.

Right: Denny McLain won 31 games in 1968, but he lost twice to Bob Gibson in the Series, including the opener at Busch Stadium. Below: The Tigers ran up a record 10 runs in the third inning of Game 6, giving them a comfortable 12-0 edge.

Above: Detroit's Jim Northrup vaults onto home plate after clearing the bases with his third-inning grand slam in Game 6.

Game 1   Wednesday, October 2 at Busch Stadium, St. Louis

	1	2	3	4	5	6	7	8	9	R	H	E
Detroit Tigers	0	0	0	0	0	0	0	0	0	0	5	3
St. Louis Cardinals	0	0	3	0	0	1	0	x		4	6	0

Pitchers Det Denny McLain (L, 0-1), IP 5, H 3, R 3, ER 2, BB 3, SO 3; Pat Dobson, IP 2, H 2, R 1, ER 1, BB 1, SO 0; Don McMahon, IP 1, H 1, R 0, ER 0, BB 0, SO 0
StL Bob Gibson (W, 1-0), IP 9, H 5, R 0, ER 0, BB 1, SO 17

Top Performers at the Plate
Det Mickey Stanley, 2 for 4
StL Julian Javier, 1 for 3, 2 RBI, 1 BB; Mike Shannon, 2 for 4, 1 R, 1 RBI

2B-Det/Kaline. **3B**-StL/McCarver. **HR**-StL/Brock. **SB**-StL/Brock, Flood, Javier. **Time** 2:29. **Attendance** 54,692.

Game 2   Thursday, October 3 at Busch Stadium, St. Louis

	1	2	3	4	5	6	7	8	9	R	H	E
Detroit Tigers	0	1	1	0	0	3	1	0	2	8	13	1
St. Louis Cardinals	0	0	0	0	0	1	0	0	0	1	6	1

Pitchers Det Mickey Lolich (W, 1-0), IP 9, H 6, R 1, ER 1, BB 2, SO 9
StL Nelson Briles (L, 0-1), IP 5, H 7, R 4, ER 4, BB 1, SO 2; Steve Carlton, IP 1, H 4, R 2, ER 2, BB 1, SO 1; Ron Willis, IP 2, H 1, R 0, ER 0, BB 2, SO 2; Joe Hoerner, IP 1, H 1, R 2, ER 0, BB 3, SO 1

Top Performers at the Plate
Det Norm Cash, 3 for 5, 2 R, 1 RBI; Mickey Lolich, 2 for 4, 1 R, 2 RBI, 1 BB
StL Lou Brock, 1 for 3, 1 R, 1 BB, 2 SB; Orlando Cepeda, 2 for 4, 1 RBI

HR-Det/Cash, Horton, Lolich. **SB**-StL/Brock 2. **Time** 2:41. **Attendance** 54,692.

Game 3   Saturday, October 5 at Tiger Stadium, Detroit

	1	2	3	4	5	6	7	8	9	R	H	E
St. Louis Cardinals	0	0	0	0	4	0	3	0	0	7	13	0
Detroit Tigers	0	0	2	0	1	0	0	0	0	3	4	0

Pitchers StL Ray Washburn (W, 1-0), IP 5⅓, H 3, R 3, ER 3, BB 4, SO 3; Joe Hoerner (Sv, 1), IP 3⅔, H 1, R 0, ER 0, BB 1, SO 2
Det Earl Wilson (L, 0-1), IP 4⅓, H 4, R 3, ER 3, BB 6, SO 3; Pat Dobson, IP ⅔, H 2, R 1, ER 1, BB 0, SO 0; Don McMahon, IP 1, H 3, R 3, ER 3, BB 0, SO 1; Daryl Patterson, IP 1, H 0, R 0, ER 0, BB 0, SO 0; John Hiller, IP 2, H 4, R 0, ER 0, BB 1, SO 1

Top Performers at the Plate
StL Lou Brock, 3 for 4, 1 R, 1 BB, 3 SB; Tim McCarver, 2 for 5, 1 R, 3 RBI
Det Al Kaline, 1 for 4, 1 R, 2 RBI; Dick McAuliffe, 2 for 4, 2 R, 1 RBI

2B-StL/Flood, Maris. **HR**-StL/Cepeda, McCarver; Det/Kaline, McAuliffe. **SB**-StL/Brock 3. **Time** 3:17. **Attendance** 53,634.

Game 4   Sunday, October 6 at Tiger Stadium, Detroit

	1	2	3	4	5	6	7	8	9	R	H	E
St. Louis Cardinals	2	0	2	2	0	0	0	4	0	10	13	0
Detroit Tigers	0	0	0	0	0	0	0	1	0	1	5	4

Pitchers StL Bob Gibson (W, 2-0), IP 9, H 5, R 1, ER 1, BB 2, SO 10
Det Denny McLain (L, 0-2), IP 2⅔, H 6, R 4, ER 3, BB 1, SO 3; Joe Sparma, IP ⅓, H 2, R 2, ER 2, BB 0, SO 0; Daryl Patterson, IP 2, H 1, R 0, ER 0, BB 1, SO 0; Fred Lasher, IP 2, H 1, R 0, ER 0, BB 0, SO 1; John Hiller, IP 0, H 2, R 4, ER 3, BB 2, SO 0; Pat Dobson, IP 2, H 1, R 0, ER 0, BB 0, SO 0

Top Performers at the Plate
StL Lou Brock, 3 for 5, 2 R, 4 RBI; Bob Gibson, 1 for 3, 2 R, 2 RBI, 1 BB
Det Al Kaline, 2 for 4

2B-StL/Brock, Javier, Shannon; Det/Kaline. **3B**-StL/Brock, McCarver. **HR**-StL/Brock, Gibson; Det/Northrup. **SB**-StL/Brock. **Time** 2:34. **Attendance** 53,634.

Game 5   Monday, October 7 at Tiger Stadium, Detroit

	1	2	3	4	5	6	7	8	9	R	H	E
St. Louis Cardinals	3	0	0	0	0	0	0	0	0	3	9	0
Detroit Tigers	0	0	0	2	0	0	3	0	x	5	9	1

Pitchers StL Nelson Briles, IP 6⅓, H 6, R 3, ER 3, BB 3, SO 5; Joe Hoerner (L, 0-1), IP 0, H 3, R 2, ER 2, BB 1, SO 0; Ron Willis, IP 1⅔, H 0, R 0, ER 0, BB 0, SO 1
Det Mickey Lolich (W, 2-0), IP 9, H 9, R 3, ER 3, BB 1, SO 8

Top Performers at the Plate
StL Lou Brock, 3 for 5, 1 R, 2 2B; Orlando Cepeda, 1 for 4, 1 R, 2 RBI
Det Norm Cash, 2 for 2, 2 RBI, 1 BB, 1 SF; Al Kaline, 2 for 4, 2 RBI

2B-StL/Brock 2. **3B**-Det/Horton, Stanley. **HR**-StL/Cepeda. **SB**-StL/Flood. **Time** 2:43. **Attendance** 53,634.

Game 6   Wednesday, October 9 at Busch Stadium, St. Louis

	1	2	3	4	5	6	7	8	9	R	H	E
Detroit Tigers	0	2	10	0	1	0	0	0	0	13	12	1
St. Louis Cardinals	0	0	0	0	0	0	0	0	1	1	9	1

Pitchers Det Denny McLain (W, 1-2), IP 9, H 9, R 1, ER 1, BB 0, SO 7
StL Ray Washburn (L, 1-1), IP 2, H 4, R 5, ER 5, BB 3, SO 3; Larry Jaster, IP 0, H 2, R 3, BB 1, SO 0; Ron Willis, IP ⅔, H 1, R 4, ER 4, BB 2, SO 0; Dick Hughes, IP ⅓, H 2, R 0, ER 0, BB 0, SO 0; Steve Carlton, IP 3, H 3, R 1, ER 1, BB 0, SO 2; Wayne Granger, IP 2, H 0, R 0, ER 0, BB 1, SO 1; Mel Nelson, IP 1, H 0, R 0, ER 0, BB 0, SO 1

Top Performers at the Plate
Det Willie Horton, 2 for 3, 2 R, 2 RBI, 1 BB, 1 HBP; Al Kaline, 3 for 4, 3 R, 4 RBI, 1 HBP
StL Orlando Cepeda, 2 for 4; Roger Maris, 2 for 4, 1 R

2B-Det/Horton. **HR**-Det/Kaline, Northrup. **Time** 2:26. **Attendance** 54,692.

Game 7   Thursday, October 10 at Busch Stadium, St. Louis

	1	2	3	4	5	6	7	8	9	R	H	E
Detroit Tigers	0	0	0	0	0	0	3	0	1	4	8	1
St. Louis Cardinals	0	0	0	0	0	0	0	0	1	1	5	0

Pitchers Det Mickey Lolich (W, 3-0), IP 9, H 5, R 1, ER 1, BB 3, SO 4
StL Bob Gibson (L, 2-1), IP 9, H 8, R 4, ER 4, BB 1, SO 8

Top Performers at the Plate
Det Willie Horton, 2 for 4, 1 R; Jim Northrup, 2 for 4, 1 R, 2 RBI
StL Curt Flood, 2 for 4

2B-Det/Freehan. **3B**-Det/Northrup. **HR**-StL/Shannon. **SB**-StL/Flood. **Time** 2:07. **Attendance** 54,692.

Highlights from the Mound
Great Pitching Performances

If the 1968 baseball season marked the year of the pitcher, then the 1968 Fall Classic could be considered the Series of the pitcher. In the first postseason matchup of Cy Young winners, National League-winner Bob Gibson set new records for strikeouts in a game and a Series; while American League honoree Denny McLain suffered two defeats, teammate Mickey Lolich became the 12th and (to date) final pitcher to win three games in a single Series. These are just two of many historic performances on the mound in October over the years.

The 10 Greatest Pitching Performances, Game and Series

While dramatic home runs tend to create the most hoopla at all levels of baseball, spectacular pitching can be equally electrifying—and there is no shortage of such moments from the World Series. Many of the game's greatest hurlers have reached baseball's pinnacle and wowed us all with masterful performances. The following represent the best of the best.

1 Larsen Throws Perfect Game — Don Larsen, New York Yankees, October 8, 1956

What could top it? He walked nobody, gave up no hits, allowed no base runners. Don Larsen's World Series perfect game is simply unmatched; nobody has pitched so much as a no-hitter in postseason play. Larsen drew a count of three balls on only one batter, and closed the game with his seventh strikeout of the day.
IP 9, H 0, R 0, ER 0, BB 0, SO 7

Above: Don Larsen's perfect game marked the epitome of World Series pitching greatness. Teammates, batboys, reporters and cops all run to join the post-game celebration on October 8, 1956.

Above: Bob Gibson set a new record when he struck out 17 Tiger batters during the first game of the 1968 World Series. The intimidating righty struck out 10 or more batters in a Series game five different times in his career.

2 Mathewson Shuts Out Athletics Three Times — Christy Mathewson, New York Giants, October 9–14, 1905

Christy Mathewson was the first pitcher to win three games in one World Series, and he did it with three complete-game shutouts. In 27 innings, he walked just one batter, struck out 18, and gave up only 14 hits—all within the space of six days.
IP 9, H 4, R 0, ER 0, BB 0, SO 6 (Game 1)
IP 9, H 4, R 0, ER 0, BB 1, SO 8 (Game 3)
IP 9, H 6, R 0, ER 0, BB 0, SO 4 (Game 5)

3 Morris Pitches 10 Shutout Innings in Game 7 — Jack Morris, Minnesota Twins, October 27, 1991

In the all-important seventh game of the World Series, Jack Morris shut out the Atlanta Braves for 10 innings. It was the first extra-inning Series shutout in 35 years, the third ever, and the only one in a decisive Game 7.
IP 10, H 7, R 0, ER 0, BB 2, SO 8

4 Gibson Strikes Out 17 Tigers — Bob Gibson, St. Louis Cardinals, October 2, 1968

In the 1968 opener, Bob Gibson fanned at least 1 batter in every inning, K'd 7 of the first 9 batters he faced (including 5 in a row) and struck out the side in the ninth. On top of the record 17 strikeouts, Gibson gave up just 1 walk and 5 hits.
IP 9, H 5, R 0, ER 0, BB 1, SO 17

5 Ruth Pitches to 14-Inning Win — Babe Ruth, Boston Red Sox, October 9, 1916

In the longest complete-game victory in Series history, Babe Ruth shut Brooklyn out for 13 straight innings after giving up an inside-the-park home run in the 1st. He didn't allow a hit in the last 6 innings. The game started Ruth's scoreless streak of 29$\frac{2}{3}$ innings extending into the 1918 Series.
IP 14, H 6, R 1, ER 1, BB 3, SO 4

6 **Baltimore Shuts Out Opposition for 33 Consecutive Innings —
Baltimore Orioles staff, October 5–9, 1966**

The Baltimore Oriole pitchers posted a composite 0.50 ERA in 1966 by shutting out the Dodgers for 33 straight innings after the 3rd inning of the opening game. They held the Dodgers to a record-low .142 team average in the four games.
IP 36, H 17, R 2, ER 2, BB 13, SO 28

7 **Alexander Strikes Out Lazzeri With Bases Loaded —
Pete Alexander, St. Louis Cardinals, October 10, 1926**

A 39-year-old Grover Cleveland "Pete" Alexander came in to pitch with the bases full in the seventh inning of Game 7 and his team holding a one-run lead against the New York Yankees. Alexander, who had a complete-game victory a day earlier, struck out Tony Lazzeri for the final out of the seventh and then pitched no-hit ball in the last two innings.
IP 2$\frac{1}{3}$, H 0, R 0, ER 0, BB 1, SO 1

8 **Ehmke Surprises Cubs in 1929 Opener — Howard Ehmke,
Philadelphia Athletics, October 8, 1929**

Howard Ehmke appeared in only 11 games during the 1929 season but was Connie Mack's choice to start Game 1 of the World Series. He shut the Cubs out for eight innings and established a new Series record with 13 strikeouts.
IP 9, H 8, R 1, ER 0, BB 1, SO 13

9 **Koufax K's 15 Yanks — Sandy Koufax, Brooklyn Dodgers,
October 2, 1963**

Sandy Koufax struck out the first 5 batters in the opening game of the 1963 Series and retired the first 14 without letting the ball out of the infield. At the end of the day, Koufax had a new World Series record of 15 strikeouts.
IP 9, H 6, R 2, ER 2, BB 3, SO 15

10 **Coveleski Tops Brooklyn Three Times in Series — Stan Coveleski,
Cleveland Indians, October 5–12, 1920**

For 27 innings, Stan Coveleski held Brooklyn to just 2 runs and 15 hits. He didn't throw more than 90 pitches in any of his 3 appearances, and gave Cleveland 3 victories in the best-of-9 Series.
IP 9, H 5, R 1, ER 1, BB 1, SO 3 (Game 1)
IP 9, H 5, R 1, ER 1, BB 1, SO 4 (Game 4)
IP 9, H 5, R 0, ER 0, BB 0, SO 1 (Game 7)

Top 10 Single-Game Strikeout Performances

There have been a total of 46 double-digit strikeout performances in the World Series. The following are the top ten single-game strikeout totals.

1.	Bob Gibson, St. Louis Cardinals, vs. Detroit Tigers, October 2, 1968, Game 1	17
2.	Sandy Koufax, Los Angeles Dodgers, vs. New York Yankees, October 2, 1963, Game 1	15
3.	Carl Erskine, Brooklyn Dodgers, vs. New York Yankees, October 2, 1953, Game 3	14
4.	Howard Ehmke, Philadelphia Athletics, vs. Chicago Cubs, October 8, 1929, Game 1	13
	Bob Gibson, St. Louis Cardinals, vs. New York Yankees, October 12, 1964, Game 5 (10 innings)	13
6.	Ed Walsh, Chicago White Sox, vs. Chicago Cubs, October 11, 1906, Game 3	12
	Wild Bill Donovan, Detroit Tigers, vs. Chicago Cubs, October 8, 1907, Game 1 (12 innings)	12
	Walter Johnson, Washington Senators, vs. New York Giants, October 4, 1924, Game 1 (12 innings)	12
	Mort Cooper, St. Louis Cardinals, vs. St. Louis Browns, October 8, 1944, Game 5	12
	Tom Seaver, New York Mets, vs. Oakland Athletics, October 16, 1973, Game 3 (8 innings)	12

Below: With a 0.95 ERA and 61 strikeouts in 57 innings of work, Sandy Koufax was a dominating presence in October in four Series with the Dodgers.

Carl Erskine, Sandy Koufax and Bob Gibson each established new World Series strikeout records on the same date (October 2).

Below: Lefty Harry Brecheen won two games as a starter and one in relief for St. Louis in 1946.

Three Wins in a Single Series

Only 12 pitchers have won three games in one World Series, and 8 of them have done it without a loss.

	G	CG	IP	H	BB	SO	ERA	W-L
Bill Dinneen, Boston Pilgrims, 1903, Games 2, 6 & 8	4	4	35	29	8	28	2.06	3-1
Deacon Phillippe, Pittsburgh Pirates, 1903, Games 1, 3 & 4	5	5	44	38	3	22	2.86	3-2
Christy Mathewson, New York Giants, 1905, Games 1, 3 & 5	3	3	27	14	1	18	0.00	3-0
Babe Adams, Pittsburgh Pirates, 1909, Games 1, 5 & 7	3	3	27	18	6	11	1.33	3-0
Jack Coombs, Philadelphia Athletics, 1910, Games 2, 3 & 5	3	3	27	23	14	17	3.33	3-0
Joe Wood, Boston Red Sox, 1912, Games 1, 4 & 8	4	2	22	27	3	21	3.68	3-1
Red Faber, Chicago White Sox, 1917, Games 2, 5 & 6	4	2	27	21	3	9	2.33	3-1
Stan Coveleski, Cleveland Indians, 1920, Games 1, 4 & 7	3	3	27	15	2	8	0.67	3-0
Harry Brecheen, St. Louis Cardinals, 1946, Games 2, 6 & 7	3	2	20	14	5	11	0.45	3-0
Lew Burdette, Milwaukee Braves, 1957, Games 2, 5 & 7	3	3	27	21	4	13	0.67	3-0
Bob Gibson, St. Louis Cardinals, 1967, Games 1, 4 & 7	3	3	27	14	5	26	1.00	3-0
Mickey Lolich, Detroit Tigers, 1968, Games 2, 5 & 7	3	3	27	20	6	21	1.67	3-0

Top Five Pitchers in World Series History

More than dominating an opponent for a single game or even a single series, being able to continually perform at the highest level when everything is on the line in October is something only a rare few achieve. These five pitchers put up exquisite performances again and again when taking the mound in the World Series.

Mordecai "Three Finger" Brown pitched 57²/₃ innings in four World Series for the Chicago Cubs (1906, 1907, 1908 and 1910) and didn't give up a single home run.

Above: Christy Mathewson shutout the Philadelphia Athletics three times in the 1905 Series. Only two other pitchers (Whitey Ford and Three Finger Brown) have that many shutouts in their World Series careers.

Above right: From 1960 to 1966, Whitey Ford and Sandy Koufax started 16 World Series games between them. The two lefties went head-to-head twice in 1963, and Koufax came out the victor in both contests.

Above: Whitey Ford rears back and fires one in during the fourth game of the 1950 Series. The game marked the first of Ford's record 10 career World Series victories.

① **Bob Gibson, St. Louis Cardinals, 1964, 1967, 1968**

Second all-time in strikeouts; tied for second in wins; first in strikeouts per nine innings; third in complete games; tied for fourth in shutouts. Holds single-game and single-series strikeout records; struck out ten or more in a game five different times. Won seven straight games without a loss from 1964 to 1967. Pitched eight consecutive complete games. Won Series opener two years in a row (1967–68); twice won a decisive Game 7 (1964 and 1967).

② **Whitey Ford, New York Yankees, 1950, 1953, 1955–58, 1960–64**

First all-time in games pitched, starts, innings, strikeouts, wins and losses; tied for second in shutouts; fifth in complete games. Pitched a record 33²/₃ consecutive scoreless innings, 1960 through 1962. Started eight Series openers, more than any other pitcher, finishing with 4-3 record.

③ **Christy Mathewson, New York Giants, 1905, 1911–13**

First all-time in shutouts and complete games; second in innings pitched; tied for second in games started. Among the top ten in wins and strikeouts. Pitched three complete-game shutouts in 1905, 27 consecutive scoreless innings. Holds record for strikeouts in five-game series (18 in 1905). Posted a 0.20 ERA in his five career victories. Hurled four extra-inning complete games.

④ **Sandy Koufax, Los Angeles Dodgers, 1959, 1963, 1965, 1966**

Two-time World Series MVP (1963 and 1965). Fourth all-time in strikeouts; tied for fourth in shutouts; fifth in ERA. Holds the record for strikeouts in a four-game series (23). Set single-game record of 15 strikeouts in 1963 (broken by Gibson in 1968); struck out ten or more batters three different times.

⑤ **Lefty Gomez, New York Yankees, 1932, 1936–39**

Six World Series wins with no losses, the most among undefeated pitchers; fifth all-time in wins. Won final game of Series two years in a row (1936–37).

World Series Career Totals									
	Yrs	G	CG	Sho	IP	H	BB	SO	W-L	ERA
Whitey Ford	11	22	7	3	146	132	34	94	10-8	2.71
Bob Gibson	3	9	8	2	81	55	17	92	7-2	1.89
Lefty Gomez	5	7	4	0	50 ¹/₃	51	15	31	6-0	2.86
Sandy Koufax	4	8	4	2	57	36	11	61	4-3	0.95
Christy Mathewson	4	11	10	4	101 ²/₃	76	10	48	5-5	1.06

1969

New York Mets (4) vs. Baltimore Orioles (1)

Above: It was indeed a miracle season for the New York Mets, capped by a five-game win over the dangerous Baltimore Orioles.

Left: Allowing only seven hits over two games and pitching a complete-game win in Game 5, Jerry Koosman was the main man on the mound for New York.

Earl Weaver's Baltimore Orioles seemed to have it all in 1969. A powerful lineup featured Boog Powell, Frank Robinson and Brooks Robinson. The pitching staff included 20-game-winners Mike Cuellar and Dave McNally, with Jim Palmer contributing 16 wins against 4 losses. They won their division by 19 games and swept the Twins in the league championship series. (This was the first year of baseball's multi-division alignment.) Baltimore's World Series opponent, in contrast, was a team that nobody expected to see playing in October. Since entering the league as an expansion club in 1962, the New York Mets finished in tenth place five times and in ninth twice. In 1969, however, they won 100 games to overtake the Chicago Cubs for the Eastern Division title, and then bested a heavily favored Atlanta Braves team in the NLCS. They got to this point largely on the strength of their pitching, headed by Tom Seaver and his 25 wins.

Met manager Gil Hodges started his ace in the Series opener, but the young Seaver went down in defeat. His second pitch of the game was sent over the right-field fence by Don Buford, and the Orioles scored three more in the fourth. Cuellar handled New York's hitters, lim-

iting them to a lone run on six hits. As most of the baseball world had expected, Baltimore grabbed an easy win against the underdog Mets. But Jerry Koosman turned things around for New York in the second game, pitching no-hit ball for six innings before giving up two singles in the seventh—Baltimore's only two hits of the game. McNally allowed only six Met hits, but a leadoff homer to Donn Clendenon in the fourth inning and three consecutive singles in the ninth led to a 2-1 loss. Back in New York for Game 3, the Mets scored three against Palmer in the first two innings. Tommie Agee led the game off with a home run, and pitcher Gary Gentry drove in two with a double in the second. On the mound, Gentry kept Baltimore scoreless and hitless until the fourth. Singles by Frank Robinson and Powell put runners on the corners with two down and Ellie Hendricks up to bat. Hendricks smoked a liner to the gap in center. Running at full speed, Agee closed that gap and made a sno-cone grab at the wall. Three innings later, Gentry got into trouble again by walking the bases full with two out, and Hodges brought Nolan Ryan in to face Paul Blair. Blair ripped a Ryan fastball to right-center, but Agee chased this one down, too, making a spectacular diving catch to

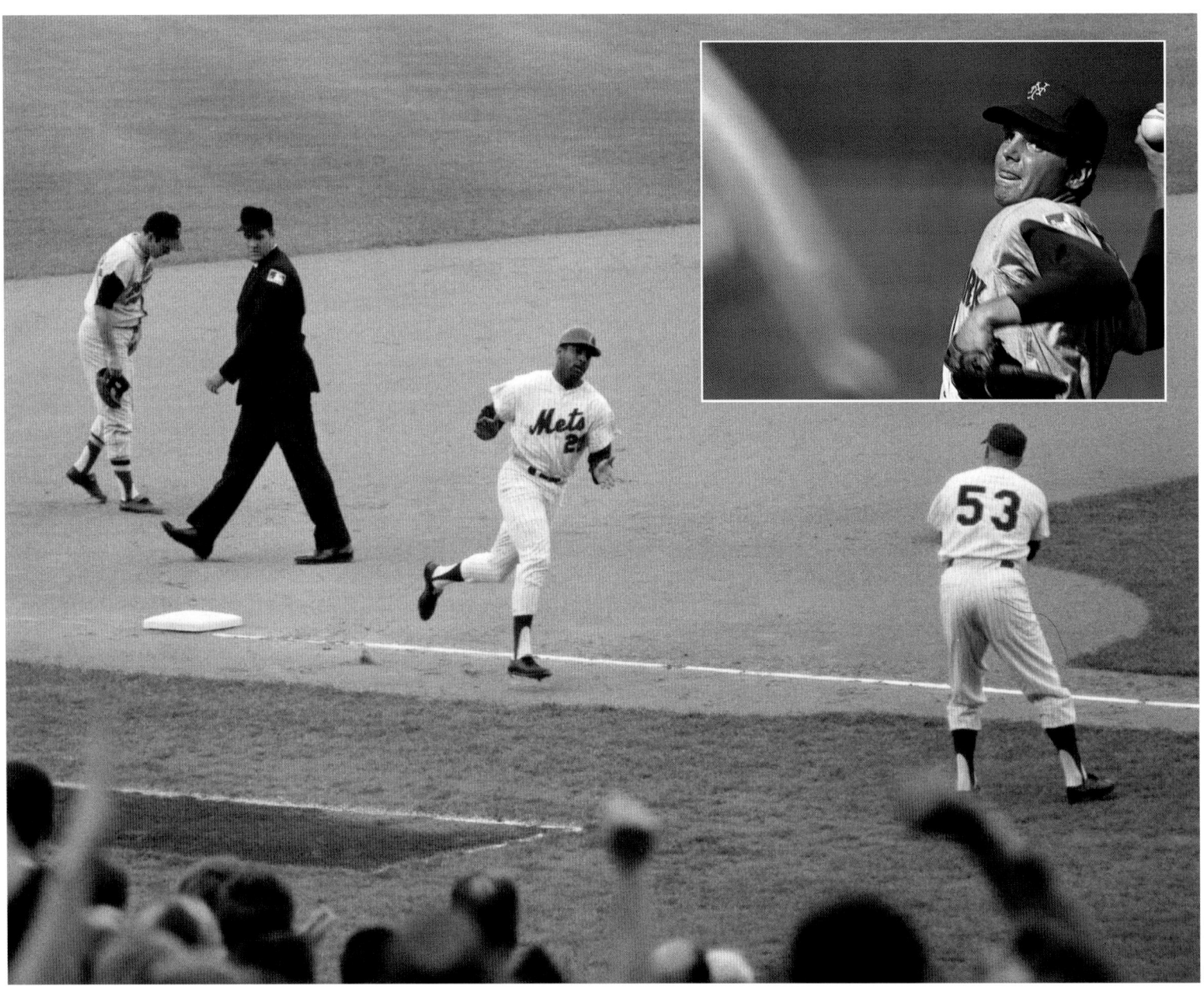

Right: Manager Gil Hodges shows umpire Lou DiMuro the tainted ball to prove that Cleon Jones had indeed been hit by Dave McNally's pitch in Game 5.

Above and right: Tommie Agee made two spectacular catches in Game 3 to save the Mets at least four runs, the first on a running catch of Ellie Hendrick's drive to the wall and the second a diving catch with the bases loaded against Paul Blair.

Left: Agee was also a threat with the bat in Game 3. Here he rounds third after his first-inning homer.

Left inset: Tom "Terrific" Seaver lost the Series opener in Baltimore, but he came back with a 10-inning triumph in Game 4 at Shea.

| **Game 1** | Saturday, October 11 at Memorial Stadium, Baltimore |

	1	2	3	4	5	6	7	8	9		R	H	E
New York Mets	0	0	0	0	0	0	1	0	0		1	6	1
Baltimore Orioles	1	0	0	3	0	0	0	0	x		4	6	0

Pitchers NY Tom Seaver (L, 0-1), IP 5, H 6, R 4, ER 4, BB 1, SO 3; Don Cardwell, IP 1, H 0, R 0, ER 0, BB 0, SO 0; Ron Taylor, IP 2, H 0, R 0, ER 0, BB 1, SO 3
Bal Mike Cuellar (W, 1-0), IP 9, H 6, R 1, ER 1, BB 4, SO 8

Top Performers at the Plate
NY Donn Clendenon, 2 for 4, 1 R
Bal Mark Belanger, 1 for 3, 1 R, 1 RBI; Don Buford, 2 for 4, 1 R, 2 RBI

2B-NY/Clendenon; Bal/Buford. **HR**-Bal/Buford. **Time** 2:13. **Attendance** 50,429.

| **Game 2** | Sunday, October 12 at Memorial Stadium, Baltimore |

	1	2	3	4	5	6	7	8	9		R	H	E
New York Mets	0	0	0	1	0	0	0	0	1		2	6	0
Baltimore Orioles	0	0	0	0	0	0	0	1	0		1	2	0

Pitchers NY Jerry Koosman (W, 1-0), IP 8⅔, H 2, R 1, ER 1, BB 3, SO 4; Ron Taylor (Sv, 1), IP ⅓, H 0, R 0, ER 0, BB 0, SO 0
Bal Dave McNally (L, 0-1), IP 9, H 6, R 2, ER 2, BB 3, SO 7

Top Performers at the Plate
NY Ed Charles, 2 for 4, 1 R; Al Weis, 2 for 3, 1 RBI, 1 BB

2B-NY/Charles. **HR**-NY/Clendenon. **SB**-Bal/Blair. **Time** 2:20. **Attendance** 50,850.

| **Game 3** | Tuesday, October 14 at Shea Stadium, New York |

	1	2	3	4	5	6	7	8	9		R	H	E
Baltimore Orioles	0	0	0	0	0	0	0	0	0		0	4	1
New York Mets	1	2	0	0	0	1	0	1	x		5	6	0

Pitchers Bal Jim Palmer (L, 0-1), IP 6, H 5, R 4, ER 4, BB 4, SO 5; Dave Leonhard, IP 2, H 1, R 1, ER 1, BB 1, SO 1
NY Gary Gentry (W, 1-0), IP 6⅔, H 3, R 0, ER 0, BB 5, SO 4; Nolan Ryan (Sv, 1), IP 2⅓, H 1, R 0, ER 0, BB 2, SO 3

Top Performers at the Plate
Bal Boog Powell, 2 for 4
NY Tommie Agee, 1 for 3, 1 R, 1 RBI, 1 BB; Gary Gentry, 1 for 3, 2 RBI

2B-NY/Gentry, Grote. **HR**-NY/Agee, Kranepool. **Time** 2:23. **Attendance** 56,335.

| **Game 4** | Wednesday, October 15 at Shea Stadium, New York |

	1	2	3	4	5	6	7	8	9	10	R	H	E
Baltimore Orioles	0	0	0	0	0	0	0	1	0	0	1	6	1
New York Mets	0	1	0	0	0	0	0	0	0	1	2	10	1

Pitchers Bal Mike Cuellar, IP 7, H 7, R 1, ER 1, BB 0, SO 5; Eddie Watt, IP 2, H 2, R 0, ER 0, BB 0, SO 2; Dick Hall (L, 0-1), IP 0, H 1, R 1, ER 0, BB 1, SO 0; Pete Richert, IP 0, H 0, R 0, ER 0, BB 0, SO 0
NY Tom Seaver (W, 1-1), IP 10, H 6, R 1, ER 1, BB 2, SO 6

Top Performers at the Plate
NY Donn Clendenon, 1 for 4, 1 R, 1 RBI; Ron Swoboda, 3 for 4

2B-NY/Grote. **HR**-NY/Clendenon. **Time** 2:33. **Attendance** 57,367.

| **Game 5** | Thursday, October 16 at Shea Stadium, New York |

	1	2	3	4	5	8	7	8	9		R	H	E
Baltimore Orioles	0	0	3	0	0	0	0	0			3	5	2
New York Mets	0	0	0	0	2	1	2	x			5	7	0

Pitchers Bal Dave McNally, IP 7, H 5, R 3, ER 3, BB 2, SO 6; Eddie Watt (L, 0-1), IP 1, H 2, R 2, ER 1, BB 0, SO 1
NY Jerry Koosman (W, 2-0), IP 9, H 5, R 3, ER 3, BB 1, SO 5

Top Performers at the Plate
Bal Dave McNally, 1 for 2, 1 R, 2 RBI; Frank Robinson, 1 for 3, 1 R, 1 RBI, 1 BB
NY Donn Clendenon, 1 for 3, 1 R, 2 RBI, 1 BB; Cleon Jones, 1 for 3, 2 R, 1 HBP

2B-NY/Jones, Koosman, Swoboda. **HR**-Bal/McNally, F. Robinson; NY/Clendenon, Weis.
SB-NY/Agee. **Time** 2:14. **Attendance** 57,397.

end the inning. Ryan finished the game for the save in New York's 5-0 win. Seaver and Cuellar battled through a tight contest in Game 4. With one out in the ninth inning, Frank Robinson singled and Powell pushed him to third with another single. Brooks Robinson then hit a sinking liner to right-center field. Perhaps inspired by his outfield mate's heroics of the previous day, right-fielder Ron Swoboda made a diving, backhanded catch to rob Brooks of a hit. Frank Robinson tagged up to tie the score at 1-1, but Swoboda helped avoid further damage with another great catch on Hendricks's drive to right for the final out. Seaver kept Baltimore from scoring in the top of the tenth, and Jerry Grote opened the Met half of

This throw to first base by Pete Richert (24) in the 10th inning of Game 4 is about to hit J. C. Martin on the wrist as Martin runs out his bunt. The ball ricocheted into the outfield, allowing New York to score the winning run. Inset left: After arguing the call from the dugout, Baltimore's fiery manager Earl Weaver is booted from Game 4 by umpire Shag Crawford.

1969 WORLD SERIES COMPOSITE STATISTICS

NEW YORK METS/Gil Hodges, Manager

Player	pos	G	AB	R	H	2B	3B	HR	RBI	BB	SO	SB	BA	SA	E	FPct
Tommie Agee	cf	5	18	1	3	0	0	1	1	2	5	1	.167	.333	0	1.000
Ken Boswell	2b	1	3	1	1	0	0	0	0	0	0	0	.333	.333	0	1.000
Don Cardwell	p	1	0	0	0	0	0	0	0	0	0	0	—	—	0	—
Ed Charles	3b	4	15	1	2	1	0	0	0	0	2	0	.133	.200	0	1.000
Donn Clendenon	1b	4	14	4	5	1	0	3	4	2	6	0	.357	1.071	0	1.000
Duffy Dyer	ph	1	1	0	0	0	0	0	0	0	0	0	.000	.000	—	—
Wayne Garrett	3b	2	1	0	0	0	0	0	0	2	1	0	.000	.000	1	.500
Rod Gaspar	ph-rf-pr	3	2	1	0	0	0	0	0	0	0	0	.000	.000	0	1.000
Gary Gentry	p	1	3	0	1	1	0	0	2	0	2	0	.333	.667	0	—
Jerry Grote	c	5	19	1	4	2	0	0	1	1	3	0	.211	.316	0	1.000
Bud Harrelson	ss	5	17	1	3	0	0	0	0	3	4	0	.176	.176	0	1.000
Cleon Jones	lf	5	19	1	3	1	0	0	0	0	1	0	.158	.211	0	1.000
Jerry Koosman	p	2	7	0	1	1	0	0	0	0	4	0	.143	.286	0	1.000
Ed Kranepool	1b	1	4	1	1	0	0	1	1	0	0	0	.250	1.000	0	1.000
J. C. Martin	ph	1	0	0	0	0	0	0	0	0	0	0	—	—	0	—
Nolan Ryan	p	1	0	0	0	0	0	0	0	0	0	0	—	—	0	—
Tom Seaver	p	2	4	0	0	0	0	0	0	0	2	0	.000	.000	0	1.000
Art Shamsky	ph-rf	3	6	0	0	0	0	0	0	0	0	0	.000	.000	0	1.000
Ron Swoboda	rf	4	15	1	6	1	0	0	1	1	3	0	.400	.467	0	1.000
Ron Taylor	p	2	0	0	0	0	0	0	0	0	0	0	—	—	0	1.000
Al Weis	2b	5	11	1	5	0	0	1	3	4	2	0	.455	.727	1	.923
Totals		5	159	15	35	8	0	6	13	15	35	1	.220	.384	2	.989

Pitcher	G	GS	CG	IP	H	R	ER	BB	SO	W-L	Sv	ERA
Don Cardwell	1	0	0	1	0	0	0	0	0	0-0	0	0.00
Gary Gentry	1	1	0	6⅔	3	0	0	5	4	1-0	0	0.00
Jerry Koosman	2	2	1	17⅔	7	4	4	4	9	2-0	0	2.04
Nolan Ryan	1	0	0	2⅓	1	0	0	2	3	0-0	1	0.00
Tom Seaver	2	2	1	15	12	5	5	3	9	1-1	0	3.00
Ron Taylor	2	0	0	2⅓	0	0	0	1	3	0-0	0	0.00
Totals	5	5	2	45	23	9	9	15	28	4-1	2	1.80

BALTIMORE ORIOLES/Earl Weaver, Manager

Player	pos	G	AB	R	H	2B	3B	HR	RBI	BB	SO	SB	BA	SA	E	FPct
Mark Belanger	ss	5	15	2	3	0	0	0	1	2	1	0	.200	.200	0	1.000
Paul Blair	cf	5	20	1	2	0	0	0	0	2	5	1	.100	.100	0	1.000
Don Buford	lf	5	20	1	2	1	0	1	2	2	4	0	.100	.300	0	1.000
Mike Cuellar	p	2	5	0	2	0	0	0	1	0	3	0	.400	.400	0	1.000
Clay Dalrymple	ph	2	2	0	2	0	0	0	0	0	0	0	1.000	1.000	—	—
Andy Etchebarren	c	2	6	0	0	0	0	0	0	0	1	0	.000	.000	0	1.000
Dick Hall	p	1	0	0	0	0	0	0	0	0	0	0	—	—	0	—
Ellie Hendricks	c	3	10	1	1	0	0	0	0	0	1	0	.100	.100	0	1.000
Dave Johnson	2b	5	16	1	1	0	0	0	0	2	1	0	.063	.063	0	1.000
Dave Leonhard	p	1	0	0	0	0	0	0	0	0	0	0	—	—	0	1.000
Dave May	ph	2	1	0	0	0	0	0	0	1	1	0	.000	.000	0	—
Dave McNally	p	2	5	1	1	0	0	1	2	0	2	0	.200	.800	0	1.000
Curt Motton	ph	1	1	0	0	0	0	0	0	0	0	0	.000	.000	—	—
Jim Palmer	p	1	2	0	0	0	0	0	0	0	0	0	.000	.000	1	.500
Boog Powell	1b	5	19	0	5	0	0	0	0	1	4	0	.263	.263	1	.980
Merv Rettenmund	pr	1	0	0	0	0	0	0	0	0	0	0	—	—	—	—
Pete Richert	p	1	0	0	0	0	0	0	0	0	0	0	—	—	1	.000
Brooks Robinson	3b	5	19	0	1	0	0	0	2	3	0	.053	.053	0	1.000
Frank Robinson	rf	5	16	2	3	0	0	1	1	4	3	0	.188	.375	0	1.000
Chico Salmon	pr	2	0	0	0	0	0	0	0	0	0	0	—	—	0	1.000
Eddie Watt	p	2	0	0	0	0	0	0	0	0	0	0	—	—	1	.000
Totals		5	157	9	23	1	0	3	9	15	28	1	.146	.210	4	.978

Pitcher	G	GS	CG	IP	H	R	ER	BB	SO	W-L	Sv	ERA
Mike Cuellar	2	2	1	16	13	2	2	4	13	1-0	0	1.13
Dick Hall	1	0	0	0	1	1	0	1	0	0-1	0	—
Dave Leonhard	1	0	0	2	1	1	1	1	1	0-0	0	4.50
Dave McNally	2	2	0	16	11	5	5	5	13	0-1	0	2.81
Jim Palmer	1	1	0	6	5	4	4	4	5	0-1	0	6.00
Pete Richert	1	0	0	0	0	0	0	0	0	0-0	0	—
Eddie Watt	2	0	0	3	4	2	1	0	3	0-1	0	3.00
Totals	5	5	2	43	35	15	13	15	35	1-4	0	2.72

Series MVP: Donn Clendenon, New York Mets. **Series Outstanding Pitcher:** Jerry Koosman, New York Mets. **Average Length of Game:** 2 hours, 21 minutes. **Total Attendance:** 272,378. **Average Attendance:** 54,476 (57,033 at Shea Stadium; 50,640 at Memorial Stadium). **Umpires:** Henry Crawford (NL), Lou DiMuro (AL), Larry Napp (AL), Frank Secory (NL), Hank Soar (AL), Lee Weyer (NL). **Winning Player's Share:** $18,338. **Losing Player's Share:** $14,904.

the inning with a double that fell in when Buford misjudged the ball. Al Weis was walked intentionally, and J. C. Martin came in to pinch hit for Seaver. Martin laid down a bunt in front of the plate, which Baltimore's Pete Richert fielded from the mound. Richert fired to first, but the throw hit Martin on the wrist, sending the ball into the outfield. Rod Gasper, pinch-running for Grote, came around from second to score. Earl Weaver argued that Martin was running out of the base line and so should be called out for interference, but the play stood as the game-winner.

Hoping to avoid elimination and an embarrassing upset, the Orioles jumped out to a 3-0 lead in the third inning of Game 5 on home runs by pitcher McNally, a two-run shot, and Frank Robinson. McNally shut the Mets out through five innings, until a bizarre play got things going for New York in the sixth. Reminiscent of a play from the 1957 Series

involving Milwaukee's Nippy Jones, Cleon Jones (no relation) jumped out of the way of a pitch in the dirt, which umpire Lou DiMuro ruled a ball. Jones insisted that the pitch hit him in the foot, and he produced the shoe-polish-smudged ball as proof. Jones was awarded first base, and the next batter, Clendenon, belted a two-run homer. Al Weis's solo shot tied the game in the seventh, and with reliever Eddie Watt in for McNally, the Mets scored two more in the eighth on doubles by Jones and Swoboda and an error by Boog Powell. Jerry Koosman closed the book on his five-hit victory, and the Miracle Mets accomplished what few thought possible, defeating a mighty Baltimore team in five games. Donn Clendenon provided key home runs for New York in Games 2, 4 and 5 to earn the Series MVP, but it was the clutch fielding of Agee and Swoboda that saved the Series.

Baltimore Orioles (4) vs. Cincinnati Reds (1)

1970

The Baltimore Orioles rebounded from their stinging upset loss to the Mets in 1969 by coasting to another pennant in 1970 with 108 wins. Rookie manager Sparky Anderson had a well-rounded group of stars in Cincinnati, led by MVP Johnny Bench, but his pitching staff was crippled by injuries heading into October. The Orioles started off their redemption campaign with an opening-game victory behind Jim Palmer's five-hitter. Cincinnati scored first and extended to a 3-0 lead on Lee May's two-run homer in the third, but Boog Powell's two-run shot in the fourth and Elrod Hendricks's leadoff homer in the fifth tied the game. After a sensational fielding play by Brooks Robinson robbed May of a sure double for the first out in the sixth, the Reds rallied to put men on the corners. Pinch hitter Ty Cline hit a short roller in front of the plate, which catcher Hendricks fielded. Hendricks turned and lunged at Bernie Carbo trying to score from third. Home plate umpire Ken Burkhart, who collided with Hendricks, called Carbo out. Photos later revealed that Carbo had indeed been tagged by the catcher, but Hendricks tagged him with his empty glove while holding the ball in his other hand. The miscall helped Baltimore out of the jam, and they came back to win on Brooks Robinson's seventh-inning homer. Despite falling behind again, the Orioles won the second game with a five-run fifth inning. Pete Rose and Bobby Tolan got back-to-back hits for the Reds in the first inning of Game 3, but Robinson turned a Tony Perez chopper into a double play. The Orioles' awesome fielding display continued in the second and sixth innings—depriving Cincinnati of a couple of base hits—and Robinson contributed to Baltimore's offensive production with a double and a run in the bottom of the sixth. Following Robinson's two-bagger, Cincinnati's Wayne Granger loaded the bases with two outs and the pitcher, Dave McNally, due up. McNally hit Granger's pitch into the left-field bleachers—the first and only World Series grand slam by a pitcher—and gave the Orioles a commanding lead in the game. Baltimore took the edge in Game 4 on Brooks Robinson's two RBI and 4 for 4 day, but Cincinnati came back on a three-run homer by Lee May in the eighth to stay alive for another day. One more day is all they would get as Cuellar pitched Baltimore to a 9-3 win in Game 5. After allowing three runs on four hits in the top of the first, Cuellar shut the Reds out the rest of the way and allowed only two more hits, clinching the Series for Baltimore. Baltimore's Paul Blair batted a blistering .474 in the five games, but Brooks Robinson did it all. He used his glove to repeatedly rob the opposition of base hits, and he used his bat to gather nine hits and drive in six runs, earning him the Series MVP.

Above: Brooks Robinson was the star of the 1970 World Series for Baltimore. Here he sends one over the fence to give the Orioles a 4-3 lead in the seventh inning of Game 1.

1970 WORLD SERIES COMPOSITE STATISTICS

BALTIMORE ORIOLES/Earl Weaver, Manager

Player	pos	G	AB	R	H	2B	3B	HR	RBI	BB	SO	SB	BA	SA	E	FPct
Mark Belanger	ss	5	19	0	2	0	0	0	1	1	2	0	.105	.105	1	.962
Paul Blair	cf	5	19	5	9	1	0	0	3	2	4	0	.474	.526	1	.947
Don Buford	lf	4	15	3	4	0	0	1	1	3	2	0	.267	.467	0	1.000
Terry Crowley	ph	1	1	0	0	0	0	0	0	0	0	0	.000	.000	–	–
Mike Cuellar	p	2	4	0	0	0	0	0	0	0	2	0	.000	.000	0	1.000
Moe Drabowsky	p	2	1	0	0	0	0	0	0	0	1	0	.000	.000	0	1.000
Andy Etchebarren	c	2	7	1	1	0	0	0	0	2	3	0	.143	.143	1	.909
Dick Hall	p	1	1	0	0	0	0	0	0	0	1	0	.000	.000	0	–
Elrod Hendricks	c	3	11	1	4	1	0	1	4	1	2	0	.364	.727	1	.950
Dave Johnson	2b	5	16	2	5	2	0	0	2	5	2	0	.313	.438	0	1.000
Marcelino Lopez	p	1	0	0	0	0	0	0	0	0	0	0	–	–	0	–
Dave McNally	p	1	4	1	1	0	0	1	4	0	2	0	.250	1.000	0	1.000
Jim Palmer	p	2	7	1	1	0	0	0	0	0	3	0	.143	.143	0	–
Tom Phoebus	p	1	0	0	0	0	0	0	0	0	0	0	–	–	0	–
Boog Powell	1b	5	17	6	5	1	0	2	5	5	2	0	.294	.706	0	1.000
Merv Rettenmund	ph-lf	2	5	2	2	0	0	1	2	1	0	0	.400	1.000	0	1.000
Pete Richert	p	1	0	0	0	0	0	0	0	0	0	0	–	–	0	–
Brooks Robinson	3b	5	21	5	9	2	0	2	6	0	2	0	.429	.810	1	.958
Frank Robinson	rf	5	22	5	6	0	0	2	4	0	5	0	.273	.545	0	1.000
Chico Salmon	ph	1	1	1	1	0	0	0	0	0	0	0	1.000	1.000	–	–
Eddie Watt	p	1	0	0	0	0	0	0	0	0	0	0	–	–	0	–
Totals		**5**	**171**	**33**	**50**	**7**	**0**	**10**	**32**	**20**	**33**	**0**	**.292**	**.509**	**5**	**.973**

Pitcher	G	GS	CG	IP	H	R	ER	BB	SO	W-L	Sv	ERA
Mike Cuellar	2	2	1	11⅓	10	7	4	2	5	1-0	0	3.18
Moe Drabowsky	2	0	0	3⅓	2	1	1	1	1	0-0	0	2.70
Dick Hall	1	0	0	2⅓	0	0	0	0	0	0-0	1	0.00
Marcelino Lopez	1	0	0	⅓	0	0	0	0	0	0-0	0	0.00
Dave McNally	1	1	1	9	9	3	3	2	5	1-0	0	3.00
Jim Palmer	2	2	0	15⅔	11	8	8	9	9	1-0	0	4.60
Tom Phoebus	1	0	0	1⅔	1	0	0	0	0	1-0	0	0.00
Pete Richert	1	0	0	⅓	0	0	0	0	0	0-0	1	0.00
Eddie Watt	1	0	0	1	2	1	1	1	3	0-1	0	9.00
Totals	**5**	**5**	**2**	**45**	**35**	**20**	**17**	**15**	**23**	**4-1**	**2**	**3.40**

CINCINNATI REDS/Sparky Anderson, Manager

Player	pos	G	AB	R	H	2B	3B	HR	RBI	BB	SO	SB	BA	SA	E	FPct
Johnny Bench	c	5	19	3	4	0	0	1	3	1	2	0	.211	.368	0	1.000
Angel Bravo	ph	4	2	0	0	0	0	0	0	1	1	0	.000	.000	–	–
Bernie Carbo	lf-ph	4	8	0	0	0	0	0	0	2	3	0	.000	.000	0	1.000
Clay Carroll	p	4	1	0	0	0	0	0	0	0	1	0	.000	.000	0	–
Darrel Chaney	ss	3	1	0	0	0	0	0	0	0	1	0	.000	.000	0	1.000
Ty Cline	ph	3	3	0	1	0	0	0	0	0	0	0	.333	.333	–	–
Tony Cloninger	p	2	2	0	0	0	0	0	0	0	1	0	.000	.000	0	1.000
Dave Concepcion	ss	3	9	0	3	0	1	0	3	0	0	0	.333	.556	0	1.000
Pat Corrales	ph	1	1	0	0	0	0	0	0	0	0	0	.000	.000	–	–
Wayne Granger	p	2	0	0	0	0	0	0	0	0	0	0	–	–	0	1.000
Don Gullett	p	3	1	0	0	0	0	0	0	0	1	0	.000	.000	0	–
Tommy Helms	2b	5	18	1	4	0	0	0	0	1	1	0	.222	.222	0	1.000
Lee May	1b	5	18	6	7	2	0	2	8	2	2	0	.389	.833	0	1.000
Jim McGlothlin	p	1	2	0	0	0	0	0	0	0	1	0	.000	.000	0	–
Hal McRae	lf	3	11	1	5	2	0	0	3	0	1	0	.455	.636	0	1.000
Jim Merritt	p	1	1	0	0	0	0	0	0	0	1	0	.000	.000	0	–
Gary Nolan	p	2	3	0	0	0	0	0	0	0	0	0	.000	.000	0	1.000
Tony Perez	3b	5	18	2	1	0	0	0	0	3	4	0	.056	.056	1	.944
Pete Rose	rf	5	20	2	5	1	0	1	2	2	0	0	.250	.450	1	.938
Jimmy Stewart	ph	2	2	0	0	0	0	0	0	0	1	0	.000	.000	–	–
Bobby Tolan	cf	5	19	5	4	1	0	1	1	3	2	1	.211	.421	1	.800
Ray Washburn	p	1	0	0	0	0	0	0	0	0	0	0	–	–	0	1.000
Milt Wilcox	p	2	0	0	0	0	0	0	0	0	0	0	–	–	0	1.000
Woody Woodward	ss-ph	4	5	0	1	0	0	0	0	0	0	0	.200	.200	0	1.000
Totals		**5**	**164**	**20**	**35**	**6**	**1**	**5**	**20**	**15**	**23**	**1**	**.213**	**.354**	**3**	**.984**

Pitcher	G	GS	CG	IP	H	R	ER	BB	SO	W-L	Sv	ERA
Clay Carroll	4	0	0	9	5	0	0	2	11	1-0	0	0.00
Tony Cloninger	2	1	0	7⅓	10	6	6	5	4	0-1	0	7.36
Wayne Granger	2	0	0	1⅓	7	5	5	1	1	0-0	0	33.75
Don Gullett	3	0	0	6⅔	5	2	1	4	4	0-0	0	1.35
Jim McGlothlin	1	1	0	4⅓	6	4	4	2	2	0-0	0	8.31
Jim Merritt	1	1	0	1⅔	3	4	4	1	0	0-1	0	21.60
Gary Nolan	2	2	0	9⅓	9	8	8	3	9	0-1	0	7.71
Ray Washburn	1	0	0	1⅓	2	2	2	2	0	0-0	0	13.50
Milt Wilcox	2	0	0	2	3	2	2	0	2	0-1	0	9.00
Totals	**5**	**5**	**0**	**43**	**50**	**33**	**32**	**20**	**33**	**1-4**	**0**	**6.70**

Series MVP: Brooks Robinson, Baltimore Orioles. **Series Outstanding Pitcher:** Clay Carroll, Cincinnati Reds. **Average Length of Game:** 2 hours, 24 minutes. **Total Attendance:** 253,183. **Average Attendance:** 50,637 (50,040 at Memorial Stadium; 51,531 at Riverfront Stadium). **Umpires:** Emmett Ashford (AL), Ken Burkhart (NL), Red Flaherty (AL), Bob Stewart (AL), Tony Venzon (NL), Bill Williams (NL). **Winning Player's Share:** $18,216. **Losing Player's Share:** $13,688.

Left: Pitcher Dave McNally is greeted by teammates Paul Blair (6), Don Buford (9) and Davey Johnson (15) after knocking them all in with a grand slam in Game 3.

Game 1 of the 1970 World Series at Riverfront Stadium was the first Series game ever played on artificial turf.

Game 1 Saturday, October 10 at Riverfront Stadium, Cincinnati

	1	2	3	4	5	6	7	8	9	R	H	E
Baltimore Orioles	0	0	0	2	1	0	1	0	0	4	7	2
Cincinnati Reds	1	0	2	0	0	0	0	0	0	3	5	0

Pitchers Bal **Jim Palmer** (W, 1-0), IP 8⅔, H 5, R 3, ER 3, BB 5, SO 2; **Pete Richert** (Sv, 1), IP ⅓, H 0, R 0, ER 0, BB 0, SO 0
Cin **Gary Nolan** (L, 0-1), IP 6⅔, H 5, R 4, ER 4, BB 1, SO 7; **Clay Carroll**, IP 2⅓, H 2, R 0, ER 0, BB 2, SO 4

Top Performers at the Plate
Bal **Boog Powell**, 1 for 3, 1 R, 2 RBI, 1 BB
Cin **Lee May**, 2 for 4, 1 R, 2 RBI

2B-Bal/Johnson; Cin/Tolan. **HR**-Bal/Hendricks, Powell, B. Robinson; Cin/May. **SB**-Cin/Tolan. **Time** 2:24. **Attendance** 51,531.

Game 2 Sunday, October 11 at Riverfront Stadium, Cincinnati

	1	2	3	4	5	6	7	8	9	R	H	E
Baltimore Orioles	0	0	0	1	5	0	0	0	0	6	10	2
Cincinnati Reds	3	0	1	0	0	1	0	0	0	5	7	0

Pitchers Bal **Mike Cuellar**, IP 2⅓, H 4, R 4, ER 1, BB 1, SO 1; **Tom Phoebus** (W, 1-0), IP 1⅔, H 1, R 0, ER 0, BB 0, SO 0; **Moe Drabowsky**, IP 2⅓, H 2, R 1, ER 1, BB 1, SO 1; **Marcelino Lopez**, IP ⅓, H 0, R 0, ER 0, BB 0, SO 0; **Dick Hall** (Sv, 1), IP 2⅓, H 0, R 0, ER 0, BB 0, SO 0
Cin **Jim McGlothlin**, IP 4⅓, H 6, R 4, ER 4, BB 2, SO 2; **Milt Wilcox** (L, 0-1), IP ⅓, H 3, R 2, ER 2, BB 0, SO 0; **Clay Carroll**, IP 2⅓, H 1, R 0, ER 0, BB 0, SO 1; **Don Gullett**, IP 2, H 0, R 0, ER 0, BB 3, SO 2

Top Performers at the Plate
Bal **Don Buford**, 2 for 4, 1 R, 1 BB; **Boog Powell**, 2 for 3, 2 R, 2 RBI, 2 BB
Cin **Johnny Bench**, 1 for 3, 1 R, 1 RBI, 1 BB; **Hal McRae**, 2 for 4, 1 RBI

2B-Bal/Hendricks; Cin/May, McRae. **HR**-Bal/Powell; Cin/Bench, Tolan. **Time** 2:26. **Attendance** 51,531.

Game 3 Tuesday, October 13 at Memorial Stadium, Baltimore

	1	2	3	4	5	6	7	8	9	R	H	E
Cincinnati Reds	0	1	0	0	0	0	2	0	0	3	9	0
Baltimore Orioles	2	0	1	0	1	4	1	0	x	9	10	1

Pitchers Cin **Tony Cloninger** (L, 0-1), IP 5⅓, H 6, R 5, ER 5, BB 3, SO 3; **Wayne Granger**, IP ⅔, H 2, R 3, ER 3, BB 1, SO 1; **Don Gullett**, IP 2, H 2, R 1, ER 1, BB 1, SO 0
Bal **Dave McNally** (W, 1-0), IP 9, H 9, R 3, ER 3, BB 2, SO 5

Top Performers at the Plate
Cin **Dave Concepcion**, 1 for 3, 2 RBI, 1 SF; **Pete Rose**, 2 for 5, 1 RBI
Bal **Paul Blair**, 3 for 3, 1 R, 1 RBI, 1 BB; **Frank Robinson**, 3 for 4, 2 R, 1 RBI

2B-Bal/Blair, B. Robinson 2. **HR**-Bal/Buford, McNally, F. Robinson. **Time** 2:09. **Attendance** 51,773.

Game 4 Wednesday, October 14 at Memorial Stadium, Baltimore

	1	2	3	4	5	6	7	8	9	R	H	E
Cincinnati Reds	0	1	1	0	1	0	0	3	0	6	8	3
Baltimore Orioles	0	1	3	0	0	1	0	0	0	5	8	0

Pitchers Cin **Gary Nolan**, IP 2⅔, H 4, R 4, ER 4, BB 2, SO 2; **Don Gullett**, IP 2⅔, H 3, R 1, ER 0, BB 0, SO 2; **Clay Carroll** (W, 1-0), IP 3⅔, H 1, R 0, ER 0, BB 0, SO 4
Bal **Jim Palmer**, IP 7, H 6, R 5, ER 5, BB 4, SO 7; **Eddie Watt** (L, 0-1), IP 1, H 2, R 1, ER 1, BB 1, SO 3; **Moe Drabowsky**, IP 1, H 0, R 0, ER 0, BB 0, SO 0

Top Performers at the Plate
Cin **Lee May**, 2 for 3, 2 R, 4 RBI, 1 BB; **Pete Rose**, 2 for 5, 1 R, 1 RBI
Bal **Elrod Hendricks**, 2 for 4, 1 RBI; **Brooks Robinson**, 4 for 4, 2 R, 2 RBI

3B-Cin/Concepcion. **HR**-Cin/May, Rose; Bal/B. Robinson. **Time** 2:26. **Attendance** 53,007.

Game 5 Thursday, October 15 at Memorial Stadium, Baltimore

	1	2	3	4	5	8	7	8	9	R	H	E
Cincinnati Reds	3	0	0	0	0	0	0	0	0	3	6	0
Baltimore Orioles	2	2	2	0	1	0	0	2	x	9	15	0

Pitchers Cin **Jim Merritt** (L, 0-1), IP 1⅔, H 3, R 4, ER 4, BB 1, SO 0; **Wayne Granger**, IP ⅔, H 5, R 2, ER 2, BB 0, SO 0; **Milt Wilcox**, IP 1⅔, H 0, R 0, ER 0, BB 0, SO 2; **Tony Cloninger**, IP 2, H 4, R 1, ER 1, BB 2, SO 1; **Ray Washburn**, IP 1⅓, H 2, R 2, ER 2, BB 2, SO 0; **Clay Carroll**, IP ⅔, H 1, R 0, ER 0, BB 0, SO 2
Bal **Mike Cuellar** (W, 1-0), IP 9, H 6, R 3, ER 3, BB 1, SO 4

Top Performers at the Plate
Cin **Hal McRae**, 1 for 3, 2 RBI
Bal **Paul Blair**, 3 for 4, 2 R, 1 RBI, 1 BB; **Dave Johnson**, 3 for 4, 1 R, 2 RBI, 1 BB

2B-Cin/May, McRae, Rose; Bal/Johnson, Powell. **HR**-Bal/Rettenmund, F. Robinson. **Time** 2:35. **Attendance** 45,341.

Above: Brooks Robinson displays his fielding prowess with a diving catch of a Johnny Bench liner in the final inning of Game 5.

Left: Lee May's three-run homer in the eighth inning of Game 4 gave Cincinnati its lone win of the Series.

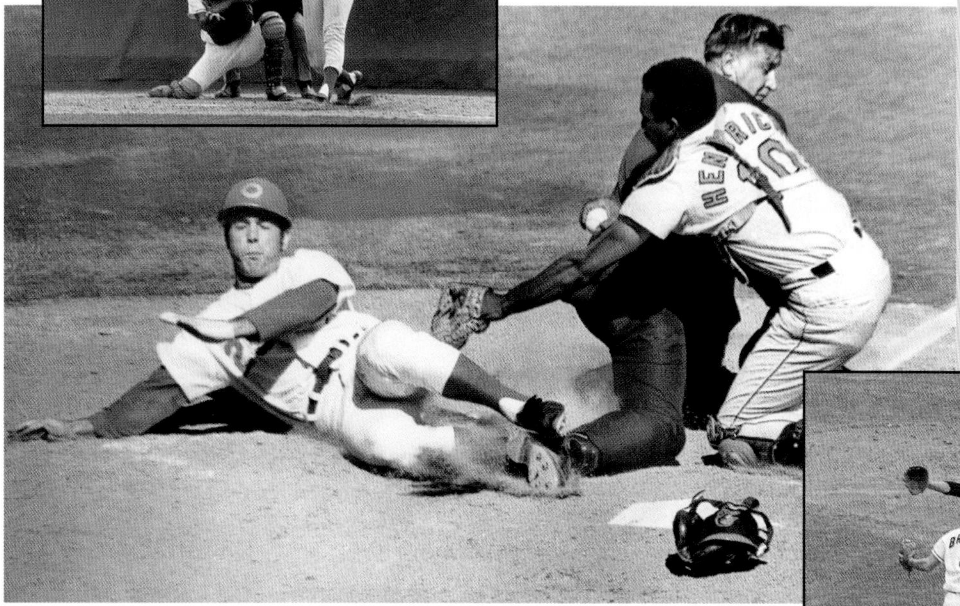

Above: With umpire Ken Burkhart caught in the middle, catcher Ellie Hendricks applies a glove tag to a sliding Bernie Carbo while holding the ball in his other hand—leading to much controversy.

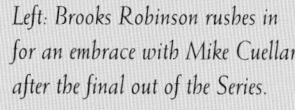

Left: Brooks Robinson rushes in for an embrace with Mike Cuellar after the final out of the Series.

Pittsburgh Pirates (4) vs. Baltimore Orioles (3)

The Baltimore Orioles made it three in a row in 1971, becoming the first non-Yankee team in 40 years to win three straight American League pennants. They came to the 1971 Series with the same crew that got them there the two previous years, only this time with a record four pitchers notching 20 or more wins on the year: Mike Cuellar, Pat Dobson, Dave McNally and Jim Palmer. Willie Stargell was the main power on a Pittsburgh Pirate team that marched to its first Series since 1960, but the leader of the club was 37-year-old Roberto Clemente. Clemente got two hits in the first game, but only one other Pirate managed a base hit against McNally, who held them to three unearned runs. The Orioles scored five, all with the long ball. In Game 2, Baltimore cruised to an 11-3 win against four pitchers named Bob (plus a Bruce and a Dave) for a two-game sweep at home. Steve Blass went the distance for Pittsburgh in Game 3, allowing only one run on three hits, to give the Bucs their first win. Clemente's infield grounder brought in a run in the first, and Bob Robertson knocked a three-run blast in the seventh for a 5-1 final. The historic fourth game of the 1971 Fall Classic—the first World Series game played at night—saw the Pirates tie the Series behind eight-plus innings of shutout relief work by Bruce Kison and Dave Giusti. Pinch hitter Milt May broke a 3-3 tie in the bottom of the seventh with a game-winning single. Nellie Briles coasted to a 4-0 win in

Game 5 on a marvelous two-hitter. With the teams heading to Baltimore for the last two games, Pittsburgh needed one win to clinch the Series. Clemente's second-inning homer put the Pirates up 2-0 in Game 6, but the Orioles came back to tie it on a Don Buford homer and an RBI single by Davey Johnson. McNally entered the game in the tenth inning and got Al Oliver to fly out with the bases loaded. Frank Robinson earned a one-out walk in the bottom of the inning, and he raced to third on Merv Rettenmund's single. Robinson hustled home with the game-winner on Brooks Robinson's sacrifice fly to short center field. It was Steve Blass vs. Mike Cuellar in the crucial seventh game. Clemente's two-out solo homer put Pittsburgh on the board in the fourth inning, and when Jose Pagan doubled home Stargell in the top of the eighth, Blass was six outs away from a championship. Elrod Hendricks and Mark Belanger singled to start Baltimore's half of the eighth, but only one of them scored, and Blass sent the O's down in order in the ninth to give the Pirates the clincher. Clemente's Game 7 homer was his 12th hit of the Series, and his .414 average was tops on both sides—a fine climax to a legendary career for "The Great One."

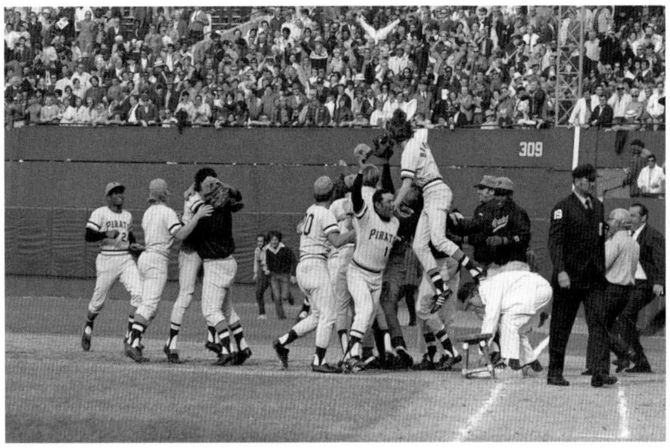

Above: The seven-game victory over the Orioles in 1971 brought Pittsburgh its first championship in 11 years.

1971 WORLD SERIES COMPOSITE STATISTICS

PITTSBURGH PIRATES/Danny Murtaugh, Manager

Player	pos	G	AB	R	H	2B	3B	HR	RBI	BB	SO	SB	BA	SA	E	FPct
Gene Alley	ss-pr	2	2	0	0	0	0	0	0	1	0	0	.000	.000	0	1.000
Steve Blass	p	2	7	0	0	0	0	0	0	0	1	0	.000	.000	0	1.000
Nelson Briles	p	1	2	0	1	0	0	0	1	0	1	0	.500	.500	0	1.000
Dave Cash	2b	7	30	2	4	1	0	0	1	3	1	1	.133	.167	0	1.000
Roberto Clemente	rf	7	29	3	12	2	1	2	4	2	2	0	.414	.759	0	1.000
Gene Clines	cf	3	11	2	1	0	1	0	0	1	1	1	.091	.273	0	1.000
Vic Davalillo	ph-lf-cf	3	3	1	1	0	0	0	0	0	0	0	.333	.333	0	1.000
Dock Ellis	p	1	1	0	0	0	0	0	0	0	1	0	.000	.000	0	—
Dave Giusti	p	3	0	0	0	0	0	0	0	0	0	0	—	—	0	—
Richie Hebner	3b	3	12	2	2	0	0	1	3	3	3	0	.167	.417	1	.800
Jackie Hernandez	ss	7	18	2	4	0	0	0	1	2	5	1	.222	.222	0	1.000
Bob Johnson	p	2	3	0	0	0	0	0	0	0	2	0	.000	.000	0	1.000
Bruce Kison	p	2	2	0	0	0	0	0	0	1	2	0	.000	.000	0	1.000
Milt May	ph	2	2	0	1	0	0	0	1	0	0	0	.500	.500	—	—
Bill Mazeroski	ph	1	1	0	0	0	0	0	0	0	0	0	.000	.000	—	—
Bob Miller	p	3	0	0	0	0	0	0	0	0	0	0	—	—	0	1.000
Bob Moose	p	3	2	0	0	0	0	0	0	0	1	0	.000	.000	0	1.000
Al Oliver	ph-cf	5	19	1	4	2	0	0	2	2	5	0	.211	.316	1	.917
Jose Pagan	3b	4	15	0	4	2	0	0	2	0	1	0	.267	.400	0	1.000
Bob Robertson	1b	7	25	4	6	0	0	2	5	4	8	0	.240	.480	1	.986
Charlie Sands	ph	1	1	0	0	0	0	0	0	0	1	0	.000	.000	—	—
Manny Sanguillen	c	7	29	3	11	1	0	0	0	0	3	2	.379	.414	0	1.000
Willie Stargell	lf	7	24	3	5	1	0	0	1	7	9	0	.208	.250	0	1.000
Bob Veale	p	1	0	0	0	0	0	0	0	0	0	0	—	—	0	1.000
Luke Walker	p	1	0	0	0	0	0	0	0	0	0	0	—	—	0	—
Totals		**7**	**238**	**23**	**56**	**9**	**2**	**5**	**21**	**26**	**47**	**5**	**.235**	**.353**	**3**	**.988**

Pitcher	G	GS	CG	IP	H	R	ER	BB	SO	W-L	Sv	ERA
Steve Blass	2	2	2	18	7	2	2	4	13	2-0	0	1.00
Nelson Briles	1	1	1	9	2	0	0	2	2	1-0	0	0.00
Dock Ellis	1	1	0	2⅓	4	4	4	1	1	0-1	0	15.43
Dave Giusti	3	0	0	5⅓	3	0	0	2	4	0-0	1	0.00
Bob Johnson	2	1	0	5	5	5	3	3	0	0-0	0	9.00
Bruce Kison	2	0	0	6⅓	1	0	0	2	3	1-0	0	0.00
Bob Miller	3	0	0	4⅔	7	2	2	1	2	0-1	0	3.86
Bob Moose	3	1	0	9⅔	12	7	7	2	7	0-0	0	6.52
Bob Veale	1	0	0	⅔	1	1	1	2	0	0-0	0	13.50
Luke Walker	1	1	0	⅔	3	3	1	0	0	0-0	0	40.50
Totals	**7**	**7**	**3**	**61⅔**	**45**	**24**	**24**	**20**	**35**	**4-3**	**1**	**3.50**

BALTIMORE ORIOLES/Earl Weaver, Manager

Player	pos	G	AB	R	H	2B	3B	HR	RBI	BB	SO	SB	BA	SA	E	FPct
Mark Belanger	ss	7	21	4	5	0	1	0	0	5	2	1	.238	.333	3	.912
Paul Blair	cf-pr	4	9	2	3	1	0	0	0	0	1	0	.333	.444	1	.889
Don Buford	lf	6	23	3	6	1	0	2	4	3	3	0	.261	.565	0	1.000
Mike Cuellar	p	2	3	0	0	0	0	0	0	1	2	0	.000	.000	1	.750
Pat Dobson	p	3	2	0	0	0	0	0	0	0	2	0	.000	.000	0	1.000
Tom Dukes	p	2	0	0	0	0	0	0	0	0	0	0	—	—	0	—
Andy Etchebarren	c	1	2	0	0	0	0	0	0	0	0	0	.000	.000	0	1.000
Dick Hall	p	1	0	0	0	0	0	0	0	0	0	0	—	—	0	1.000
Elrod Hendricks	c	6	19	3	5	1	0	0	1	3	3	0	.263	.316	1	.978
Grant Jackson	p	1	0	0	0	0	0	0	0	0	0	0	—	—	0	—
Dave Johnson	2b	7	27	1	4	0	0	0	3	0	1	0	.148	.148	0	1.000
Dave Leonhard	p	1	0	0	0	0	0	0	0	0	0	0	—	—	0	—
Dave McNally	p	4	4	0	0	0	0	0	0	0	3	0	.000	.000	0	1.000
Jim Palmer	p	2	4	0	0	0	0	0	0	2	2	0	.000	.000	0	1.000
Boog Powell	1b	7	27	1	3	0	0	0	1	1	3	0	.111	.111	1	.982
Merv Rettenmund	cf-rf-lf-ph	7	27	3	5	0	0	1	4	0	4	0	.185	.296	0	1.000
Pete Richert	p	1	0	0	0	0	0	0	0	0	0	0	—	—	0	—
Brooks Robinson	3b	7	22	2	7	0	0	0	5	3	1	0	.318	.318	2	.920
Frank Robinson	rf	7	25	5	7	0	0	2	2	2	8	0	.280	.520	0	1.000
Tom Shopay	ph	5	4	0	0	0	0	0	0	0	0	0	.000	.000	—	—
Eddie Watt	p	2	0	0	0	0	0	0	0	0	0	0	—	—	0	—
Totals		**7**	**219**	**24**	**45**	**3**	**1**	**5**	**22**	**20**	**35**	**1**	**.205**	**.297**	**9**	**.966**

Pitcher	G	GS	CG	IP	H	R	ER	BB	SO	W-L	Sv	ERA
Mike Cuellar	2	2	0	14	11	7	6	6	10	0-2	0	3.86
Pat Dobson	3	1	0	6⅔	13	3	3	4	6	0-0	0	4.05
Tom Dukes	2	0	0	4	2	0	0	0	1	0-0	0	0.00
Dick Hall	1	0	0	1	1	0	0	0	0	0-0	1	0.00
Grant Jackson	1	0	0	⅔	0	0	0	0	1	0-0	0	0.00
Dave Leonhard	1	0	0	1	0	0	0	1	0	0-0	0	0.00
Dave McNally	4	2	1	13⅔	10	7	3	5	12	2-1	0	1.98
Jim Palmer	2	2	0	17	15	5	5	9	15	1-0	0	2.65
Pete Richert	1	0	0	⅔	0	0	0	1	0	0-0	0	0.00
Eddie Watt	2	0	0	2⅓	4	1	1	0	2	0-1	0	3.86
Totals	**7**	**7**	**1**	**61**	**56**	**23**	**18**	**26**	**47**	**3-4**	**1**	**2.66**

Series MVP: Roberto Clemente, Pittsburgh Pirates. **Series Outstanding Pitcher:** Steve Blass, Pittsburgh Pirates. **Average Length of Game:** 2 hours, 31 minutes. **Total Attendance:** 351,091. **Average Attendance:** 50,156 (51,053 at Three Rivers Stadium; 49,483 at Memorial Stadium). **Umpires:** Nestor Chylak (AL), John Kibler (NL), Jim Odom (AL), John Rice (AL), Ed Sudol (NL), Ed Vargo (NL). **Winning Player's Share:** $18,165. **Losing Player's Share:** $13,906.

Pitcher Jim Palmer was walked twice with the bases loaded in Game 2, giving him two RBI on the day.

Below: Dave McNally made two starts and two relief appearances for Baltimore, finishing with two wins and a loss.

Above: Enroute to his second complete-game win, Steve Blass sticks his tongue out while delivering a pitch in Game 7.

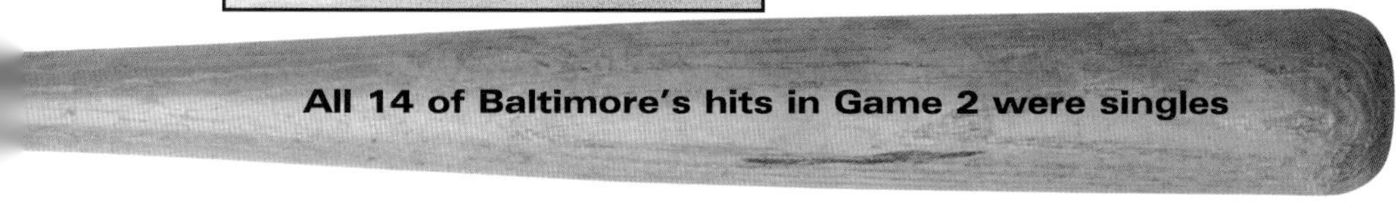
All 14 of Baltimore's hits in Game 2 were singles

Roberto Clemente knocked two homers in the Series, a solo shot in Game 6 (above) and another one to put Pittsburgh ahead 1-0 in the deciding game (right). "The Great One" hit safely in all seven games of the Series to bring home MVP honors.

Game 1 Saturday, October 9 at Memorial Stadium, Baltimore

	1	2	3	4	5	6	7	8	9	R	H	E
Pittsburgh Pirates	0	3	0	0	0	0	0	0	0	3	3	0
Baltimore Orioles	0	1	3	0	1	0	0	0	x	5	10	3

Pitchers Pit **Dock Ellis** (L, 0-1), IP 2⅓, H 4, R 4, ER 4, BB 1, SO 1; **Bob Moose**, IP 3⅔, H 3, R 1, ER 1, BB 0, SO 4; **Bob Miller**, IP 2, H 3, R 0, ER 0, BB 0, SO 1
Bal **Dave McNally** (W, 1-0), IP 9, H 3, R 3, ER 0, BB 2, SO 9

Top Performers at the Plate
Pit **Roberto Clemente**, 2 for 4; **Jackie Hernandez**, 0 for 2, 1 R, 1 RBI, 1 SH
Bal **Don Buford**, 2 for 4, 2 R, 1 RBI; **Merv Rettenmund**, 1 for 4, 1 R, 3 RBI

2B-Pit/Clemente. **3B**-Bal/Belanger. **HR**-Bal/Buford, Rettenmund, F. Robinson. **Time** 2:06. **Attendance** 53,229.

Game 2 Monday, October 11 at Memorial Stadium, Baltimore

	1	2	3	4	5	6	7	8	9	R	H	E
Pittsburgh Pirates	0	0	0	0	0	0	0	3	0	3	8	1
Baltimore Orioles	0	1	0	3	6	1	0	0	x	11	14	1

Pitchers Pit **Bob Johnson** (L, 0-1), IP 3⅓, H 4, R 4, ER 4, BB 2, SO 1; **Bruce Kison**, IP 0, H 0, R 0, ER 0, BB 2, SO 0; **Bob Moose**, IP 1, H 5, R 5, ER 5, BB 0, SO 0; **Bob Veale**, IP ⅔, H 1, R 1, ER 1, BB 2, SO 0; **Bob Miller**, IP 2, H 3, R 1, ER 1, BB 0, SO 1; **Dave Giusti**, IP 1, H 1, R 0, ER 0, BB 1, SO 0
Bal **Jim Palmer** (W, 1-0), IP 8, H 7, R 3, ER 3, BB 8, SO 10; **Dick Hall** (Sv, 1), IP 1, H 1, R 0, ER 0, BB 0, SO 0

Top Performers at the Plate
Pit **Roberto Clemente**, 2 for 5; **Richie Hebner**, 1 for 3, 1 R, 3 RBI, 2 BB
Bal **Elrod Hendricks**, 2 for 3, 2 R, 1 RBI, 1 BB, 1 HBP; **Brooks Robinson**, 3 for 3, 2 R, 3 RBI, 2 BB

2B-Pit/Clemente. **HR**-Pit/Hebner. **Time** 2:55. **Attendance** 53,239.

Game 3 Tuesday, October 12 at Three Rivers Stadium, Pittsburgh

	1	2	3	4	5	6	7	8	9	R	H	E
Baltimore Orioles	0	0	0	0	0	0	1	0	0	1	3	3
Pittsburgh Pirates	1	0	0	0	0	1	3	0	x	5	7	0

Pitchers Bal **Mike Cuellar** (L, 0-1), IP 6, H 7, R 5, ER 4, BB 6, SO 4; **Tom Dukes**, IP 1, H 0, R 0, ER 0, BB 0, SO 0; **Eddie Watt**, IP 1, H 0, R 0, ER 0, BB 0, SO 1
Pit **Steve Blass** (W, 1-0), IP 9, H 3, R 1, ER 1, BB 2, SO 8

Top Performers at the Plate
Bal **Frank Robinson**, 2 for 4, 1 R, 1 RBI
Pit **Jose Pagan**, 2 for 4, 1 RBI; **Bob Robertson**, 1 for 4, 1 R, 3 RBI

2B-Pit/Cash, Pagan, Sanguillen. **HR**-Bal/F. Robinson; Pit/Robertson. **Time** 2:20. **Attendance** 50,403.

Game 4 Wednesday, October 13 at Three Rivers Stadium, Pittsburgh

	1	2	3	4	5	6	7	8	9	R	H	E
Baltimore Orioles	3	0	0	0	0	0	0	0	0	3	4	1
Pittsburgh Pirates	2	0	1	0	0	0	1	0	x	4	14	0

Pitchers Bal **Pat Dobson**, IP 5⅓, H 10, R 3, ER 3, BB 3, SO 4; **Grant Jackson**, IP ⅔, H 0, R 0, ER 0, BB 1, SO 0; **Eddie Watt** (L, 0-1), IP 1⅓, H 4, R 1, ER 1, BB 0, SO 1; **Pete Richert**, IP ⅔, H 0, R 0, ER 0, BB 0, SO 1
Bal **Luke Walker**, IP ⅔, H 3, R 3, ER 3, BB 1, SO 0; **Bruce Kison** (W, 1-0), IP 6⅓, H 1, R 0, ER 0, BB 0, SO 3; **Dave Giusti** (Sv, 1), IP 2, H 0, R 0, ER 0, BB 0, SO 1

Top Performers at the Plate
Bal **Paul Blair**, 2 for 4, 1 R
Pit **Al Oliver**, 2 for 4, 2 RBI, 1 BB; **Willie Stargell**, 2 for 5, 1 R, 1 RBI

2B-Bal/Blair; Pit/Oliver, Stargell. **SB**-Pit/Hernandez, Sanguillen. **Time** 2:48. **Attendance** 51,378.

Game 5 Thursday, October 14 at Three Rivers Stadium, Pittsburgh

	1	2	3	4	5	6	7	8	9	R	H	E
Baltimore Orioles	0	0	0	0	0	0	0	0	0	0	2	1
Pittsburgh Pirates	0	2	1	0	1	0	0	0	x	4	9	0

Pitchers Bal **Dave McNally** (L, 1-1), IP 4, H 7, R 4, ER 3, BB 2, SO 3; **Dave Leonhard**, IP 1, H 0, R 0, ER 0, BB 1, SO 0; **Tom Dukes**, IP 3, H 2, R 0, ER 0, BB 0, SO 1
Pit **Nelson Briles** (W, 1-0), IP 9, H 2, R 0, ER 0, BB 2, SO 2

Top Performers at the Plate
Pit **Gene Clines**, 1 for 3, 2 R, 1 BB; **Bob Robertson**, 1 for 3, 1 R, 1 RBI, 1 BB

3B-Pit/Clines. **HR**-Pit/Robertson. **SB**-Pit/Clines, Sanguillen. **Time** 2:16. **Attendance** 51,377.

Game 6 Saturday, October 16 at Memorial Stadium, Baltimore

	1	2	3	4	5	6	7	8	9	10	R	H	E
Pittsburgh Pirates	0	1	1	0	0	0	0	0	0	0	2	9	1
Baltimore Orioles	0	0	0	0	0	1	1	0	0	1	3	8	0

Pitchers Pit **Bob Moose**, IP 5, H 4, R 1, ER 1, BB 2, SO 3; **Bob Johnson**, IP 1⅔, H 1, R 1, ER 1, BB 1, SO 2; **Dave Giusti**, IP 2⅓, H 2, R 0, ER 0, BB 1, SO 3; **Bob Miller** (L, 0-1), IP ⅔, H 1, R 1, ER 1, BB 1, SO 0
Bal **Jim Palmer**, IP 9, H 8, R 2, ER 2, BB 1, SO 5; **Pat Dobson**, IP ⅔, H 1, R 0, ER 0, BB 1, SO 1; **Dave McNally** (W, 2-1), IP ⅓, H 0, R 0, ER 0, BB 1, SO 0

Top Performers at the Plate
Pit **Roberto Clemente**, 2 for 4, 1 R, 1 RBI, 1 BB; **Manny Sanguillen**, 3 for 4
Bal **Mark Belanger**, 1 for 1, 1 R, 3 BB; **Don Buford**, 3 for 4, 1 R, 1 RBI, 1 BB

2B-Pit/Oliver; Bal/Buford. **3B**-Pit/Clemente. **HR**-Pit/Clemente; Bal/Buford. **SB**-Pit/Cash; Bal/Belanger. **Time** 2:59. **Attendance** 44,174.

Game 7 Sunday, October 17 at Memorial Stadium, Baltimore

	1	2	3	4	5	6	7	8	9	R	H	E
Pittsburgh Pirates	0	0	0	1	0	0	0	1	0	2	6	1
Baltimore Orioles	0	0	0	0	0	0	0	1	0	1	4	0

Pitchers Pit **Steve Blass** (W, 2-0), IP 9, H 4, R 1, ER 1, BB 2, SO 5
Bal **Mike Cuellar** (L, 0-2), IP 8, H 4, R 2, ER 2, BB 0, SO 6; **Pat Dobson**, IP ⅔, H 2, R 0, ER 0, BB 0, SO 1; **Dave McNally**, IP ⅓, H 0, R 0, ER 0, BB 0, SO 0

Top Performers at the Plate
Pit **Roberto Clemente**, 1 for 4, 1 R, 1 RBI; **Jose Pagan**, 1 for 3, 1 RBI
Bal **Don Buford**, 1 for 3, 1 RBI, 1 BB; **Elrod Hendricks**, 2 for 3, 1 R

2B-Pit/Pagan; Bal/Hendricks. **HR**-Pit/Clemente. **Time** 2:10. **Attendance** 47,291.

Oakland Athletics (4) vs. Cincinnati Reds (3)

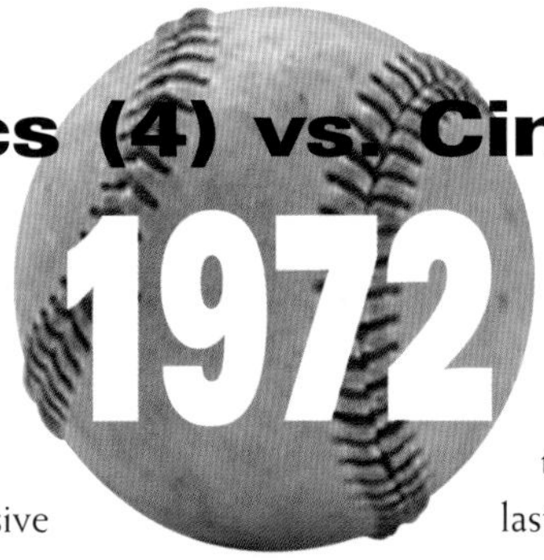

Two of baseball's premier teams of the 1970s went head-to-head in the 1972 World Series. The Oakland A's were making their first of three straight Series appearances with a star-filled squad. Although Reggie Jackson missed the 1972 Series with a hamstring injury, Sal Bando, Bert Campaneris, Joe Rudi and Mike Epstein all put up impressive numbers for manager Dick Williams. On the mound, Jim "Catfish" Hunter, Ken Holtzman and John "Blue Moon" Odom each won at least 15 games in 1972; out of the bullpen, they had the league's premier reliever in Rollie Fingers. Sparky Anderson and the Big Red Machine were back for their second of four Fall Classics, and they had added all-time-great Joe Morgan since their last trip in 1970. The 1972 Series was hotly contested, as the clubs battled through six one-run games and posted identical batting averages when it was all over.

Oakland's back-up catcher Gene Tenace celebrated his first Series by smashing a two-run homer in his first at-bat in Game 1 to put his team ahead 2-0. The Reds tied the score in the fourth, but Tenace reclaimed the lead—and made history—by stroking another home run in his very next plate appearance. The A's took the second game in Cincinnati as well, with Joe Rudi playing the hero's role. Rudi's second-inning homer proved to be the game-winner, and his leaping, backhanded catch at the wall in the ninth robbed Denis Menke of an extra-base hit and the Reds of a run. Cincinnati did score in the inning to end Hunter's shutout bid, but Rudi's fielding gem and last-out help from Fingers assured Oakland a 2-1 edge in the final score. Jack Billingham and John "Blue Moon" Odom squared off in a Game 3 pitcher's duel in Oakland. The game stayed scoreless until Cesar Geronimo drove Tony Perez home with a single in the seventh. Billingham held the A's to three hits for the win, and Clay Carroll got the save by retiring the side in the ninth. Tenace's fifth-inning homer was the only scoring in Game 4 until Cincinnati took the lead on a two-run double by Bobby Tolan in the eighth. Oakland used three pinch hitters and two pinch-runners in the last of the ninth to snatch the victory and a three-games-to-one advantage. Gonzalo Marquez started it off with a pinch-single, and after Allen Lewis replaced him on the base paths, Tenace

Above: Leading the two dominant teams of the first part of the decade, managers Sparky Anderson and Dick Williams went head-to-head in an epic battle in 1972.

1972 WORLD SERIES COMPOSITE STATISTICS

OAKLAND ATHLETICS/Dick Williams, Manager

Player	pos	G	AB	R	H	2B	3B	HR	RBI	BB	SO	SB	BA	SA	E	FPct
Matty Alou	rf	7	24	0	1	0	0	0	0	3	0	1	.042	.042	1	.923
Sal Bando	3b	7	26	2	7	1	0	0	1	2	5	0	.269	.308	1	.941
Vida Blue	p	4	1	0	0	0	0	0	0	2	1	0	.000	.000	0	1.000
Bert Campaneris	ss	7	28	1	5	0	0	0	0	1	4	0	.179	.179	1	.970
Dave Duncan	ph-c	3	5	0	1	0	0	0	0	1	3	0	.200	.200	0	1.000
Mike Epstein	1b	6	16	1	0	0	0	0	0	5	3	0	.000	.000	2	.949
Rollie Fingers	p	6	1	0	0	0	0	0	0	0	0	0	.000	.000	0	1.000
Dick Green	2b	7	18	0	6	2	0	0	1	0	4	0	.333	.444	0	1.000
Dave Hamilton	p	2	0	0	0	0	0	0	0	0	0	0	–	–	0	–
Mike Hegan	1b-ph	6	5	0	1	0	0	0	0	0	2	0	.200	.200	0	1.000
George Hendrick	cf	5	15	3	2	0	0	0	0	1	2	0	.133	.133	0	1.000
Ken Holtzman	p	3	5	0	0	0	0	0	0	0	0	0	.000	.000	1	.750
Joe Horlen	p	1	0	0	0	0	0	0	0	0	0	0	–	–	0	1.000
Jim "Catfish" Hunter	p	3	5	0	1	0	0	0	1	2	1	0	.200	.200	1	.750
Ted Kubiak	2b	4	3	0	1	0	0	0	0	0	0	0	.333	.333	0	1.000
Allan Lewis	pr	6	0	2	0	0	0	0	0	0	0	0	–	–	–	–
Bob Locker	p	1	0	0	0	0	0	0	0	0	0	0	–	–	0	–
Angel Mangual	ph-cf	4	10	1	3	0	0	0	1	0	0	0	.300	.300	1	.857
Gonzalo Marquez	ph	5	5	0	3	0	0	0	1	0	0	0	.600	.600	–	–
Don Mincher	ph	3	1	0	1	0	0	0	1	0	0	0	1.000	1.000	–	–
Blue Moon Odom	p	4	4	0	0	0	0	0	0	0	3	0	.000	.000	0	1.000
Joe Rudi	lf	7	25	1	6	0	0	1	1	2	5	0	.240	.360	0	1.000
Gene Tenace	c-1b	7	23	5	8	1	0	4	9	2	4	0	.348	.913	1	.981
Totals		**7**	**220**	**16**	**46**	**4**	**0**	**5**	**16**	**21**	**37**	**1**	**.209**	**.295**	**9**	**.966**

Pitcher	G	GS	CG	IP	H	R	ER	BB	SO	W-L	Sv	ERA
Vida Blue	4	1	0	8⅔	8	4	4	5	5	0-1	1	4.15
Rollie Fingers	6	0	0	10⅓	4	2	2	4	11	1-1	2	1.74
Dave Hamilton	2	0	0	1⅓	3	4	4	1	1	0-0	0	27.00
Ken Holtzman	3	2	0	12⅔	11	3	3	3	4	1-0	0	2.13
Joe Horlen	1	0	0	1⅓	2	1	1	2	1	0-0	0	6.75
Jim "Catfish" Hunter	3	2	0	16	12	5	5	6	11	2-0	0	2.81
Bob Locker	1	0	0	⅓	1	0	0	0	0	0-0	0	0.00
Blue Moon Odom	2	2	0	11⅓	5	2	2	6	13	0-1	0	1.59
Totals	**7**	**7**	**0**	**62**	**46**	**21**	**21**	**27**	**46**	**4-3**	**3**	**3.05**

CINCINNATI REDS/Sparky Anderson, Manager

Player	pos	G	AB	R	H	2B	3B	HR	RBI	BB	SO	SB	BA	SA	E	FPct
Johnny Bench	c	7	23	4	6	1	0	1	1	5	5	2	.261	.435	1	.980
Jack Billingham	p	3	5	0	0	0	0	0	0	0	4	0	.000	.000	0	1.000
Pedro Borbon	p	6	0	0	0	0	0	0	0	0	0	0	–	–	0	1.000
Clay Carroll	p	5	0	0	0	0	0	0	0	0	0	0	–	–	0	1.000
Darrel Chaney	ss-ph	4	7	0	0	0	0	0	0	2	2	0	.000	.000	0	1.000
Dave Concepcion	ss-pr-ph	6	13	2	4	0	1	0	2	2	2	1	.308	.462	1	.938
George Foster	ph-rf	2	0	0	0	0	0	0	0	0	0	0	–	–	0	–
Cesar Geronimo	rf-cf	7	19	1	3	0	0	0	3	1	4	1	.158	.158	0	1.000
Ross Grimsley	p	4	2	0	0	0	0	0	0	0	2	0	.000	.000	0	1.000
Don Gullett	p	1	2	0	0	0	0	0	0	0	0	0	.000	.000	0	1.000
Joe Hague	ph-rf	3	3	0	0	0	0	0	0	0	0	0	.000	.000	0	–
Tom Hall	p	4	2	0	0	0	0	0	0	0	1	0	.000	.000	0	1.000
Julian Javier	ph	4	2	0	0	0	0	0	0	0	0	0	.000	.000	–	–
Jim McGlothlin	p	1	1	0	0	0	0	0	0	0	0	0	.000	.000	0	1.000
Hal McRae	ph-rf	5	9	1	4	1	0	0	2	0	1	0	.444	.556	0	1.000
Denis Menke	3b	7	24	1	2	0	0	1	2	2	6	0	.083	.208	0	1.000
Joe Morgan	2b	7	24	4	3	2	0	0	1	6	3	2	.125	.208	1	.973
Gary Nolan	p	2	3	0	0	0	0	0	0	0	3	0	.000	.000	0	1.000
Tony Perez	1b	7	23	3	10	2	0	0	2	4	4	0	.435	.522	1	.987
Pete Rose	lf	7	28	3	6	0	0	1	2	4	4	1	.214	.321	0	1.000
Bobby Tolan	cf	7	26	2	7	1	0	0	6	1	4	5	.269	.308	1	.917
Ted Uhlaender	ph	4	4	0	1	1	0	0	0	0	1	0	.250	.500	–	–
Totals		**7**	**220**	**21**	**46**	**8**	**1**	**3**	**21**	**27**	**46**	**12**	**.209**	**.295**	**5**	**.982**

Pitcher	G	GS	CG	IP	H	R	ER	BB	SO	W-L	Sv	ERA
Jack Billingham	3	2	0	13⅔	6	1	0	4	11	1-0	1	0.00
Pedro Borbon	6	0	0	7	7	3	3	2	4	0-1	0	3.86
Clay Carroll	5	0	0	5⅔	6	1	1	4	3	0-1	1	1.59
Ross Grimsley	4	1	0	7	7	2	2	3	2	2-1	0	2.57
Don Gullett	1	1	0	7	5	1	1	2	4	0-0	0	1.29
Tom Hall	4	0	0	8⅓	6	0	0	2	7	0-0	1	0.00
Jim McGlothlin	1	1	0	3	2	4	4	2	3	0-0	0	12.00
Gary Nolan	2	2	0	10⅔	7	4	4	2	3	0-1	0	3.38
Totals	**7**	**7**	**0**	**62⅓**	**46**	**16**	**15**	**21**	**37**	**3-4**	**3**	**2.17**

Series MVP: Gene Tenace, Oakland Athletics. **Series Outstanding Pitcher:** Rollie Fingers, Oakland Athletics. **Average Length of Game:** 2 hours, 24 minutes. **Total Attendance:** 363,149. **Average Attendance:** 51,878 (49,410 at Oakland-Alameda County Stadium; 53,730 at Riverfront Stadium). **Umpires:** Bob Engel (NL), Bill Haller (AL), Jim Honochick (AL), Chris Pelekoudas (NL), Mel Steiner (NL), Frank Umont (AL). **Winning Player's Share:** $20,705. **Losing Player's Share:** $15,080.

Oakland's Allan Lewis appeared in nine Series games in 1972 and 1973—all as a pinch-runner.

Above: The Oakland A's had to do without an injured Reggie Jackson in the 1972 Series.

Left: In Game 1, Gene Tenace shakes off the nerves by driving a home run in his first World Series at-bat.

Below: Two-for-two: a smiling Gene Tenace is greeted by teammates after the catcher homered in his second plate appearance of the Series.

Gene Tenace's pair of home runs in the opening game made him the first player to homer in his first two World Series at-bats. (Atlanta's Andruw Jones matched the feat in 1996.)

Above: Sal Bando's double in the sixth inning of Game 7 proved to be the Series clincher, driving home Allan Lewis to give the A's a 3-1 edge.

Left: Sal Bando jumps on the back of Rollie Fingers after Pete Rose flied to left for the final out of the Series.

Above: In full extension, Joe Rudi leaps for Denis Menke's drive at the wall, robbing Cincinnati of a hit with a man on base in the ninth inning of Game 2

advanced Lewis to second with a single. A single by pinch hitter Don Mincher brought Lewis home, and Mincher's pinch-runner, Odom, scored on Angel Mangual's pinch-hit single past a drawn-in infield. It was Cincinnati's turn for some last-inning dramatics in Game 5. With the score tied at four and Oakland's ace reliever on the hill, Pete Rose scored Geronimo from second with the game-winner on a single against Fingers. The A's threatened to score in their half of the inning by putting men on the corners with one out, but Odom, pinch-running for Tenace, was thrown out at the plate trying to tag up on a foul pop to Joe Morgan. Back in Cincinnati for Game 6, the Reds provided the only blowout of the Series with an 8-1 rout; Tolan and Geronimo each drove in two with singles in Cincinnati's five-run seventh inning. Gene Tenace continued his clutch October performance in the all-important Game 7. He drove in the game's first run with a two-out single after Mangual reached third on Tolan's error. The Reds tied the game in the fifth, but Tenace came through again with an RBI double in the sixth. Each team added another run, and Fingers came on to seal the last six outs and give Oakland the 3-2 win. Forty-one years and two cities since their last Series appearance, the Athletics were finally world champions again. And it was only the beginning.

Left: Pinch running in the last inning of Game 5, pitcher John "Blue Moon" Odom breaks for home on a foul pop, as catcher Johnny Bench waits intently for the throw.

Below: Bench effectively blocks home plate and tags Odom to end the game. Odom argued the call, but all angles showed him clearly out.

Jack Billingham's 13-plus innings of scoreless pitching in 1972 contributed to his career-leading 0.36 ERA in the World Series.

Above: Jack Billingham appeared in three games for the Reds in the Series, not allowing an earned run in nearly 14 innings.

Game 1 Saturday, October 14 at Riverfront Stadium, Cincinnati

	1	2	3	4	5	6	7	8	9	R	H	E
Oakland Athletics	0	2	0	0	1	0	0	0	0	3	4	0
Cincinnati Reds	0	1	0	1	0	0	0	0	0	2	7	0

Pitchers Oak Ken Holtzman (W, 1-0), IP 5, H 5, R 2, ER 2, BB 3, SO 3; Rollie Fingers, IP 1⅔, H 1, R 0, ER 0, BB 1, SO 3; Vida Blue (Sv, 1), IP 2⅓, H 1, R 0, ER 0, BB 1, SO 1
Cin Gary Nolan (L, 0-1), IP 6, H 4, R 3, ER 3, BB 2, SO 0; Pedro Borbon, IP 1, H 0, R 0, ER 0, BB 0, SO 0; Clay Carroll, IP 2, H 0, R 0, ER 0, BB 2, SO 1

Top Performers at the Plate
Oak Bert Campaneris, 2 for 3, 1 SH; Gene Tenace, 2 for 3, 2 R, 3 RBI, 2 HR
Cin Johnny Bench, 2 for 3, 2 R; Dave Concepcion, 1 for 2, 1 RBI, 1 BB, 1 SH

2B-Cin/Bench. **HR**-Oak/Tenace 2. **Time** 2:18. **Attendance** 52,918.

Game 2 Sunday, October 15 at Riverfront Stadium, Cincinnati

	1	2	3	4	5	6	7	8	9	R	H	E
Oakland Athletics	0	1	1	0	0	0	0	0	0	2	9	2
Cincinnati Reds	0	0	0	0	0	0	0	0	1	1	6	0

Pitchers Oak Jim "Catfish" Hunter (W, 1-0), IP 8⅔, H 6, R 1, ER 1, BB 3, SO 6; Rollie Fingers (Sv, 1), IP ⅓, H 0, R 0, ER 0, BB 0, SO 0
Cin Ross Grimsley (L, 0-1), IP 5, H 6, R 2, ER 2, BB 0, SO 1; Pedro Borbon, IP 2, H 0, R 0, ER 0, BB 1, SO 4; Tom Hall, IP 2, H 3, R 0, ER 0, BB 2, SO 2

Top Performers at the Plate
Oak Jim "Catfish" Hunter, 1 for 3, 1 RBI, 1 BB; Joe Rudi, 2 for 3, 1 R, 1 RBI, 1 BB
Cin Tony Perez, 2 for 3, 1 R, 1 BB

2B-Cin/Uhlaender. **HR**-Oak/Rudi. **SB**-Oak/Alou; Cin/Morgan. **Time** 2:26. **Attendance** 53,224.

Game 3 Wednesday, October 18 at Oakland-Alameda County Coliseum, Oakland

	1	2	3	4	5	6	7	8	9	R	H	E
Cincinnati Reds	0	0	0	0	0	0	1	0	0	1	4	2
Oakland Athletics	0	0	0	0	0	0	0	0	0	0	3	2

Pitchers Cin Jack Billingham (W, 1-0), IP 8, H 3, R 0, ER 0, BB 3, SO 7; Clay Carroll (Sv, 1), IP 1, H 0, R 0, ER 0, BB 0, SO 0
Oak Blue Moon Odom (L, 0-1), IP 7, H 3, R 1, ER 1, BB 2, SO 11; Vida Blue, IP ⅓, H 1, R 0, ER 0, BB 1, SO 0; Rollie Fingers, IP 1⅔, H 0, R 0, ER 0, BB 1, SO 3

Top Performers at the Plate
Cin Tony Perez, 1 for 3, 1 R, 1 BB

SB-Cin/Geronimo, Rose, Tolan. **Time** 2:24. **Attendance** 49,410.

Game 4 Thursday, October 19 at Oakland-Alameda County Coliseum, Oakland

	1	2	3	4	5	6	7	8	9	R	H	E
Cincinnati Reds	0	0	0	0	0	0	2	0	0	2	7	1
Oakland Athletics	0	0	0	0	1	0	0	2		3	10	1

Pitchers Cin Don Gullett, IP 7, H 5, R 1, ER 1, BB 2, SO 4; Pedro Borbon, IP 1⅓, H 2, R 1, ER 1, BB 0, SO 0; Clay Carroll (L, 0-1), IP 0, H 3, R 1, ER 1, BB 0, SO 0
Oak Ken Holtzman, IP 7⅔, H 5, R 1, ER 1, BB 0, SO 1; Vida Blue, IP ⅓, H 2, R 1, ER 1, BB 1, SO 0; Rollie Fingers (W, 1-0), IP 1, H 0, R 0, ER 0, BB 0, SO 1

Top Performers at the Plate
Cin Johnny Bench, 2 for 4; Bobby Tolan, 1 for 4, 2 RBI
Oak Sal Bando, 2 for 3, 1 BB; Gene Tenace, 2 for 4, 2 R, 1 RBI

2B-Cin/Tolan; Oak/Green. **HR**-Oak/Tenace. **SB**-Cin/Bench. **Time** 2:06. **Attendance** 49,410.

Game 5 Friday, October 20 at Oakland-Alameda County Coliseum, Oakland

	1	2	3	4	5	6	7	8	9	R	H	E
Cincinnati Reds	1	0	0	1	0	0	1	1		5	8	0
Oakland Athletics	0	3	0	1	0	0	0	0	0	4	7	2

Pitchers Cin Jim McGlothlin, IP 3, H 2, R 4, ER 4, BB 2, SO 3; Pedro Borbon, IP 1, H 1, R 0, ER 0, BB 1, SO 0; Tom Hall, IP 2, H 0, R 0, ER 0, BB 0, SO 1; Clay Carroll, IP 1⅔, H 3, R 0, ER 0, BB 0, SO 1; Ross Grimsley (W, 1-1), IP ⅔, H 0, R 0, ER 0, BB 1, SO 0; Jack Billingham (Sv, 1), IP ⅔, H 1, R 0, ER 0, BB 0, SO 0
Oak Jim "Catfish" Hunter, IP 4⅔, H 5, R 3, ER 3, BB 2, SO 2; Rollie Fingers (L, 1-1), IP 3⅔, H 3, R 2, ER 2, BB 1, SO 4; Dave Hamilton, IP ⅔, H 0, R 0, ER 0, BB 0, SO 0

Top Performers at the Plate
Cin Pete Rose, 3 for 5, 1 R, 2 RBI; Bobby Tolan, 2 for 4, 2 RBI, 2 SB
Oak Sal Bando, 1 for 3, 1 R, 1 BB; Gene Tenace, 1 for 3, 1 R, 3 RBI, 2 BB

2B-Cin/Perez. **HR**-Cin/Menke, Rose; Oak/Tenace. **SB**-Cin/Morgan, Tolan 2. **Time** 2:26. **Attendance** 49,410.

Game 6 Saturday, October 21 at Riverfront Stadium, Cincinnati

	1	2	3	4	5	6	7	8	9	R	H	E
Oakland Athletics	0	0	0	0	0	0	1	0		1	7	1
Cincinnati Reds	0	0	0	1	1	1	5	0	x	8	10	0

Pitchers Oak Vida Blue (L, 0-1), IP 5⅔, H 4, R 3, ER 3, BB 2, SO 4; Bob Locker, IP ⅓, H 1, R 0, ER 0, BB 0, SO 0; Dave Hamilton, IP ⅔, H 3, R 4, ER 4, BB 1, SO 1; Joe Horlen, IP 1⅓, H 2, R 1, ER 1, BB 2, SO 1
Cin Gary Nolan, IP 4⅔, H 3, R 1, ER 1, BB 0, SO 3; Ross Grimsley (W, 2-1), IP 1, H 1, R 0, ER 0, BB 1, SO 0; Pedro Borbon, IP 1, H 1, R 0, ER 0, BB 0, SO 0; Tom Hall (Sv, 1), IP 2⅓, H 2, R 0, ER 0, BB 0, SO 1

Top Performers at the Plate
Oak Sal Bando, 2 for 4, 1 R; Dick Green, 1 for 2, 1 RBI
Cin Johnny Bench, 1 for 2, 2 R, 1 RBI, 1 BB, 2 2B; Bobby Tolan, 2 for 4, 2 R, 2 RBI, 2 SB

2B-Oak/Green; Cin/McRae, Morgan. **3B**-Cin/Concepcion. **HR**-Cin/Bench. **SB**-Cin/Concepcion, Tolan 2. **Time** 2:21. **Attendance** 52,737.

Game 7 Sunday, October 22 at Riverfront Stadium, Cincinnati

	1	2	3	4	5	6	7	8	9	R	H	E
Oakland Athletics	1	0	0	0	0	2	0	0	0	3	6	1
Cincinnati Reds	0	0	0	1	0	0	1	0	0	2	4	2

Pitchers Oak Blue Moon Odom, IP 4⅓, H 2, R 1, ER 1, BB 4, SO 2; Jim "Catfish" Hunter (W, 2-0), IP 2⅔, H 1, R 1, ER 1, BB 1, SO 3; Ken Holtzman, IP 0, H 1, R 0, ER 0, BB 0, SO 0; Rollie Fingers (Sv, 2), IP 2, H 0, R 0, ER 0, BB 1, SO 0
Cin Jack Billingham, IP 5, H 2, R 1, ER 0, BB 1, SO 4; Pedro Borbon (L, 0-1), IP ⅔, H 3, R 2, ER 2, BB 0, SO 0; Clay Carroll, IP 1, H 0, R 0, ER 0, BB 2, SO 1; Ross Grimsley, IP ⅓, H 0, R 0, ER 0, BB 1, SO 1; Tom Hall, IP 2, H 1, R 0, ER 0, BB 0, SO 3

Top Performers at the Plate
Oak Bert Campaneris, 2 for 4, 1 R, 1 SH; Gene Tenace, 2 for 3, 2 RBI
Cin Tony Perez, 2 for 2, 1 R, 1 RBI, 1 BB, 1 SF; Pete Rose, 2 for 5, 1 R

2B-Oak/Bando, Tenace; Cin/Morgan, Perez. **SB**-Cin/Bench. **Time** 2:50. **Attendance** 56,040.

Oakland Athletics (4) vs. New York Mets (3)

1973

Four years after their miracle 1969 season, the New York Mets were back in the Fall Classic under equally unlikely circumstances. They won their division despite finishing barely above .500 at 82-79, and then defeated a tough Cincinnati club in the league championship series. To be sure, the Mets were heavy underdogs when they arrived in Oakland for the opening game of the World Series. Oakland's eccentric owner Charles O. Finley had assembled a veritable dynasty around a powerful lineup and a pitching staff full of 20-game winners. Ken Holtzman led the A's to victory in Game 1, with Rollie Fingers and Darold Knowles chipping in four shutout innings in relief. In addition to yielding just four hits in the 2-1 win, Holtzman, who did not bat all season long because of the new designated hitter rule in the American League, came to the plate in the third inning and doubled and scored a run. The two teams battled for over four hours in Game 2 before New York claimed victory. The A's scored two runs with two out in the bottom of the ninth to tie the game at six and send it into extra innings. In the top of the 12th, 42-year-old Willie Mays

drove in a run on a two-out single, and then Cleon Jones singled to load the bases. The next batter, John Milner, hit a routine grounder to the right side of the infield. The ball went through the legs of second baseman Mike Andrews, and two runners scurried home. On the very next play, Andrews fielded Jerry Grote's grounder cleanly but made a wild throw to first, allowing Jones to score New York's fourth run of the inning. Oakland got a run in the bottom of the inning, but the damage was done, and the A's fell 10-7 in 12 innings. When the game was over, Finley announced that he was removing Andrews from the roster, ostensibly on the grounds that Andrews had a shoulder injury. Oakland's fans, players and manager alike were outraged, seeing this as a ploy simply to punish Andrews for his errors; Commissioner Bowie Kuhn fined Finley and ordered Andrews reinstated. The A's rebounded with an 11-inning victory in Game 3, overcoming 12 strikeouts by Tom Seaver. Jim "Catfish" Hunter gave up two Met runs in the bottom of the first, but he and three relievers combined to shut them out the rest of the way. An RBI single by Bert

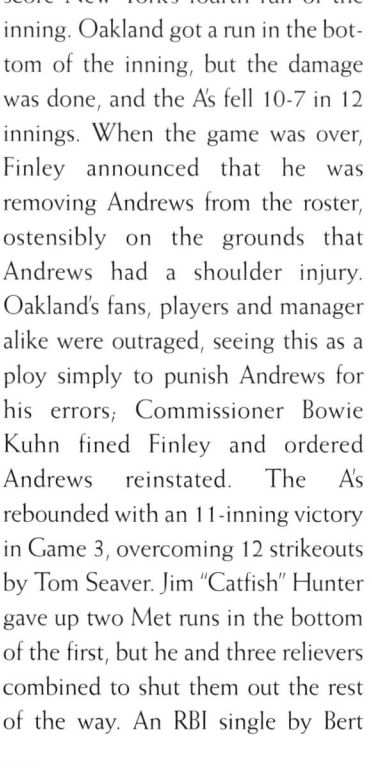

Above left: Rollie Fingers and his distinctive handlebar mustache get a champagne shower from Blue Moon Odom after Oakland claimed its second straight title in 1973.

Left: Collecting one of his 11 hits of the Series, Rusty Staub drives a pitch to right-center to send in the Mets' first run of Game 7.

Gene Tenace's third-inning walk in Game 7 gave him 11 bases on balls, tying the single-Series record set by Babe Ruth in 1926.

Above: Allowing just one earned run in 13²/₃ innings, Rollie Fingers earned two saves in the '73 Series.

Left: Mike Andrews had a rough go of it in the second game, leading to an embarrassing attempt at dismissal by Oakland owner Charlie Finley.

Game 1   Saturday, October 13 at Oakland-Alameda County Coliseum, Oakland

	1	2	3	4	5	6	7	8	9	R	H	E
New York Mets	0	0	0	1	0	0	0	0	0	1	7	2
Oakland Athletics	0	0	2	0	0	0	0	0	x	2	4	0

Pitchers   NY   Jon Matlack (L, 0-1), IP 6, H 3, R 2, ER 2, BB 2, SO 3; Tug McGraw, IP 2, H 1, R 0, ER 0, BB 1, SO 1
Oak   Ken Holtzman (W, 1-0), IP 5, H 4, R 1, ER 1, BB 3, SO 2; Rollie Fingers, IP 3⅓, H 3, R 0, ER 0, BB 1, SO 3; Darold Knowles (Sv, 1), IP ⅔, H 0, R 0, ER 0, BB 0, SO 0

Top Performers at the Plate
NY   Cleon Jones, 2 for 4, 1 R; John Milner, 2 for 4, 1 RBI
Oak   Ken Holtzman, 1 for 1, 1 R; Joe Rudi, 1 for 3, 1 RBI, 1 SH

2B-NY/Jones; Oak/Holtzman. **3B**-NY/Millan. **SB**-Oak/Campaneris. **Time** 2:26. **Attendance** 46,021.

Game 2   Sunday, October 14 at Oakland-Alameda County Coliseum, Oakland

	1	2	3	4	5	6	7	8	9	10	11	12	R	H	E
New York Mets	0	1	1	0	0	4	0	0	0	0	0	4	10	15	1
Oakland Athletics	2	1	0	0	1	0	0	1	0	2	0	0	1	7	13	5

Pitchers   NY   Jerry Koosman, IP 2⅓, H 6, R 3, ER 3, BB 3, SO 4; Ray Sadecki, IP 1⅔, H 0, R 0, ER 0, BB 0, SO 3; Harry Parker, IP 1, H 1, R 0, ER 0, BB 0, SO 0; Tug McGraw (W, 1-0), IP 6, H 5, R 4, ER 4, BB 3, SO 8; George Stone (Sv, 1), IP 1, H 1, R 0, ER 0, BB 1, SO 0
Oak   Vida Blue, IP 5⅓, H 4, R 4, ER 4, BB 2, SO 4; Horacio Pina, IP 0, H 2, R 2, ER 0, BB 0, SO 0; Darold Knowles, IP 1⅔, H 1, R 0, ER 0, BB 2, SO 2; Blue Moon Odom, IP 2, H 2, R 0, ER 0, BB 0, SO 2; Rollie Fingers (L, 0-1), IP 2⅔, H 6, R 4, ER 1, BB 0, SO 2; Paul Lindblad, IP ⅓, H 0, R 0, ER 0, BB 0, SO 0

Top Performers at the Plate
NY   Bud Harrelson, 3 for 6, 1 R, 1 RBI; Cleon Jones, 3 for 5, 3 R, 1 RBI, 1 BB, 1 HBP
Oak   Jesus Alou, 3 for 6, 2 RBI; Reggie Jackson, 4 for 6, 1 R, 2 RBI

2B-NY/Harrelson; Oak/Alou, Jackson, Johnson, Rudi. **3B**-Oak/Bando, Campaneris, Jackson. **HR**-NY/Garrett, Jones. **SB**-Oak/Campaneris. **Time** 4:13. **Attendance** 49,151.

Game 3   Tuesday, October 16 at Shea Stadium, New York

	1	2	3	4	5	6	7	8	9	10	11	R	H	E
Oakland Athletics	0	0	0	0	0	1	0	1	0	0	1	3	10	1
New York Mets	2	0	0	0	0	0	0	0	0	0	0	2	10	2

Pitchers   Oak   Jim "Catfish" Hunter, IP 6, H 7, R 2, ER 2, BB 3, SO 5; Darold Knowles, IP 2, H 0, R 0, ER 0, BB 1, SO 0; Paul Lindblad (W, 1-0), IP 2, H 3, R 0, ER 0, BB 1, SO 0; Rollie Fingers (Sv, 1), IP 1, H 0, R 0, ER 0, BB 0, SO 0
NY   Tom Seaver, IP 8, H 7, R 2, ER 2, BB 1, SO 12; Ray Sadecki, IP 0, H 1, R 0, ER 0, BB 0, SO 0; Tug McGraw, IP 2, H 1, R 0, ER 0, BB 1, SO 1; Harry Parker (L, 0-1), IP 1, H 1, R 1, ER 0, BB 1, SO 1

Top Performers at the Plate
Oak   Bert Campaneris, 3 for 6, 1 R, 1 RBI; Joe Rudi, 2 for 5, 1 RBI
NY   Wayne Garrett, 2 for 4, 1 R, 1 RBI, 2 BB; Felix Millan, 2 for 5, 1 R, 1 SH

2B-Oak/Bando, Rudi, Tenace; NY/Hahn, Staub. **HR**-NY/Garrett. **SB**-Oak/Campaneris. **Time** 3:15. **Attendance** 54,817.

Game 4   Wednesday, October 17 at Shea Stadium, New York

	1	2	3	4	5	6	7	8	9	R	H	E
Oakland Athletics	0	0	0	1	0	0	0	0	0	1	5	1
New York Mets	3	0	0	3	0	0	0	0	x	6	13	1

Pitchers   Oak   Ken Holtzman (L, 1-1), IP ⅓, H 4, R 3, ER 3, BB 1, SO 0; Blue Moon Odom, IP 2⅔, H 3, R 2, ER 2, BB 2, SO 0; Darold Knowles, IP 1, H 1, R 1, ER 0, BB 1, SO 1; Horacio Pina, IP 3, H 4, R 0, ER 0, BB 2, SO 0; Paul Lindblad, IP 1, H 1, R 0, ER 0, BB 0, SO 1
NY   Jon Matlack (W, 1-1), IP 8, H 3, R 1, ER 0, BB 2, SO 5; Ray Sadecki (Sv, 1), IP 1, H 2, R 0, ER 0, BB 1, SO 2

Top Performers at the Plate
Oak   Gene Tenace, 1 for 3, 1 RBI, 1 BB
NY   Jerry Grote, 3 for 4; Rusty Staub, 4 for 4, 1 R, 5 RBI, 1 BB

HR-NY/Staub. **Time** 2:41. **Attendance** 54,817.

Game 5   Thursday, October 18 at Shea Stadium, New York

	1	2	3	4	5	6	7	8	9	R	H	E
Oakland Athletics	0	0	0	0	0	0	0	0	0	0	3	1
New York Mets	0	1	0	0	0	1	0	0	x	2	7	1

Pitchers   Oak   Vida Blue (L, 0-1), IP 5⅔, H 6, R 2, ER 2, BB 1, SO 4; Darold Knowles, IP ⅓, H 0, R 0, ER 0, BB 1, SO 1; Rollie Fingers, IP 2, H 1, R 0, ER 0, BB 2, SO 1
NY   Jerry Koosman (W, 1-0), IP 6⅓, H 3, R 0, ER 0, BB 4, SO 4; Tug McGraw (Sv, 1), IP 2⅔, H 0, R 0, ER 0, BB 3, SO 3

Top Performers at the Plate
NY   Cleon Jones, 2 for 4, 1 R; John Milner, 2 for 4, 1 RBI

2B-Oak/Fosse; NY/Jones. **3B**-NY/Hahn. **Time** 2:39. **Attendance** 54,817.

Game 6   Saturday, October 20 at Oakland-Alameda County Coliseum, Oakland

	1	2	3	4	5	6	7	8	9	R	H	E
New York Mets	0	0	0	0	0	0	0	1	0	1	6	2
Oakland Athletics	1	0	1	0	0	0	0	1	x	3	7	0

Pitchers   NY   Tom Seaver (L, 0-1), IP 7, H 6, R 2, ER 2, BB 2, SO 6; Tug McGraw, IP 1, H 1, R 1, ER 0, BB 1, SO 1
Oak   Jim "Catfish" Hunter (W, 1-0), IP 7⅓, H 4, R 1, ER 1, BB 1, SO 1; Darold Knowles, IP ⅓, H 2, R 0, ER 0, BB 0, SO 1; Rollie Fingers (Sv, 2), IP 1⅓, H 0, R 0, ER 0, BB 0, SO 0

Top Performers at the Plate
Oak   Reggie Jackson, 3 for 4, 1 R, 2 RBI; Joe Rudi, 1 for 3, 1 R, 1 BB

2B-Oak/Jackson 2. **Time** 2:07. **Attendance** 49,333.

Game 7   Sunday, October 21 at Oakland-Alameda County Coliseum, Oakland

	1	2	3	4	5	6	7	8	9	R	H	E
New York Mets	0	0	0	0	0	1	0	0	1	2	8	1
Oakland Athletics	0	4	0	1	0	0	0	0	x	5	9	1

Pitchers   NY   Jon Matlack (L, 1-2), IP 2⅔, H 4, R 4, ER 4, BB 1, SO 3; Harry Parker, IP 1⅓, H 0, R 0, ER 0, BB 1, SO 1; Ray Sadecki, IP 2, H 2, R 1, ER 1, BB 0, SO 1; George Stone, IP 2, H 3, R 0, ER 0, BB 0, SO 3
Oak   Ken Holtzman (W, 2-1), IP 5⅓, H 5, R 1, ER 1, BB 1, SO 4; Rollie Fingers, IP 3⅓, H 3, R 1, ER 0, BB 1, SO 2; Darold Knowles (Sv, 2), IP ⅓, H 0, R 0, ER 0, BB 0, SO 0

Top Performers at the Plate
NY   Don Hahn, 3 for 4; Rusty Staub, 2 for 4, 1 RBI
Oak   Bert Campaneris, 3 for 4, 2 R, 2 RBI; Joe Rudi, 2 for 3, 1 R, 1 RBI, 1 BB

2B-NY/Millan, Staub; Oak/Holtzman. **HR**-Oak/Campaneris, Jackson. **Time** 2:37. **Attendance** 49,333.

Campaneris in the 11th gave Oakland a 3-2 final. Jon Matlack held the A's to one unearned run in eight innings in Game 4. Rusty Staub, who batted .423 for the Series, went a perfect 4 for 4 and drove in five of New York's six runs, including a three-run homer in the first. Jerry Koosman and Tug McGraw blanked Oakland on three hits in Game 5 to give the Mets a three-games-to-two Series advantage. A battle of future Hall of Famers in

Game 6 saw Hunter beat out Seaver 3-1. Hunter kept the Mets scoreless through seven, and Reggie Jackson drove in two runs on a pair of doubles. A four-run fourth inning gave the A's all they needed to claim the seventh game. Pitcher Holtzman started the rally with his second double of the Series, which Campaneris followed with a homer to right. Jackson, who sat out the 1972 Series with an injury, delivered his first World Series home

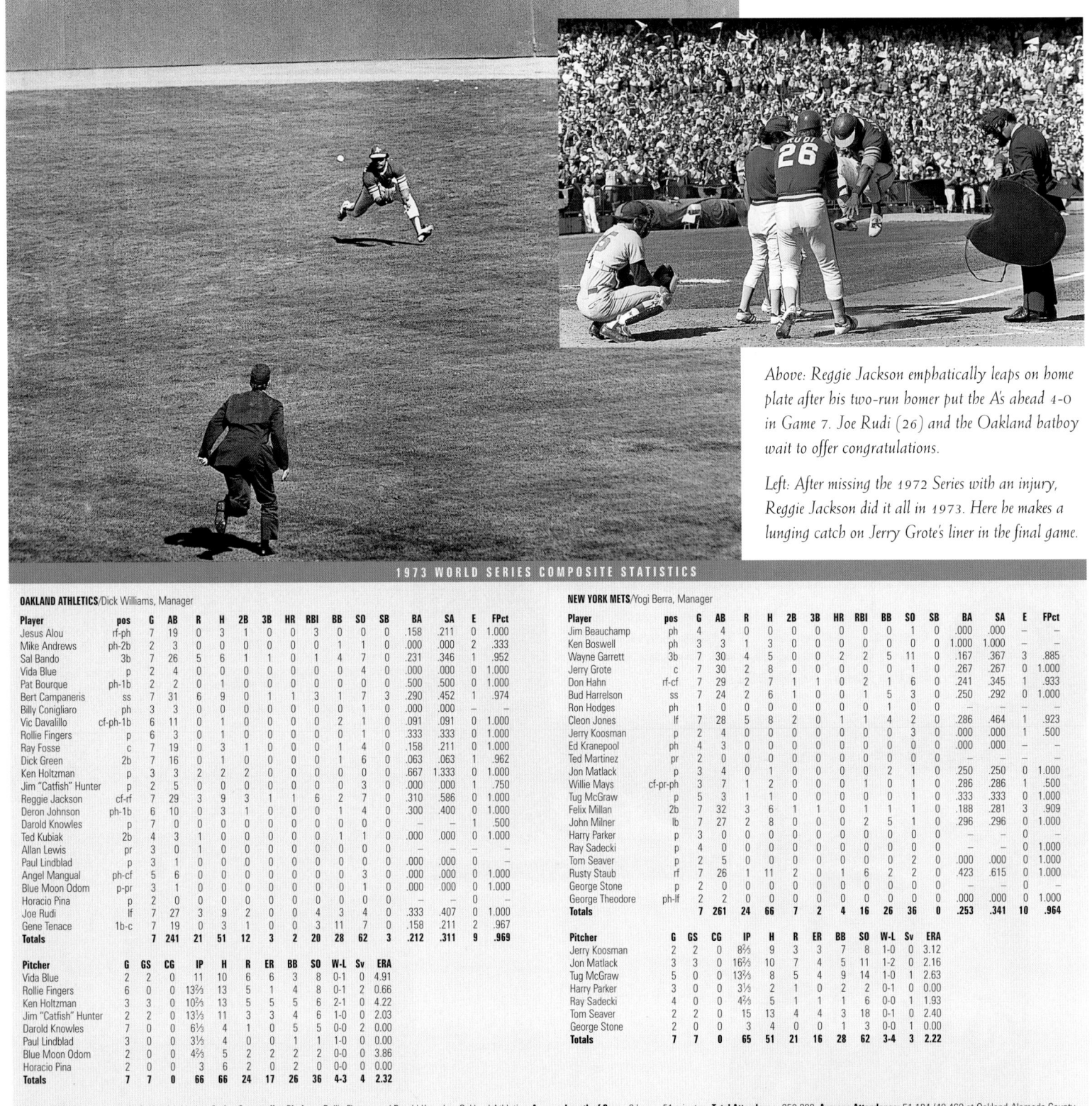

Above: Reggie Jackson emphatically leaps on home plate after his two-run homer put the A's ahead 4-0 in Game 7. Joe Rudi (26) and the Oakland batboy wait to offer congratulations.

Left: After missing the 1972 Series with an injury, Reggie Jackson did it all in 1973. Here he makes a lunging catch on Jerry Grote's liner in the final game.

1973 WORLD SERIES COMPOSITE STATISTICS

OAKLAND ATHLETICS/Dick Williams, Manager

Player	pos	G	AB	R	H	2B	3B	HR	RBI	BB	SO	SB	BA	SA	E	FPct
Jesus Alou	rf-ph	7	19	0	3	1	0	0	3	0	0	0	.158	.211	0	1.000
Mike Andrews	ph-2b	2	3	0	0	0	0	0	1	1	0	0	.000	.000	2	.333
Sal Bando	3b	7	26	5	6	1	1	0	1	4	7	0	.231	.346	1	.952
Vida Blue	p	2	4	0	0	0	0	0	0	0	4	0	.000	.000	0	1.000
Pat Bourque	ph-1b	2	2	0	1	0	0	0	0	0	0	0	.500	.500	0	1.000
Bert Campaneris	ss	7	31	6	9	0	1	1	3	1	7	3	.290	.452	1	.974
Billy Conigliaro	ph	3	3	0	0	0	0	0	0	0	1	0	.000	.000	–	–
Vic Davalillo	cf-ph-1b	6	11	0	1	0	0	0	2	1	0	0	.091	.091	0	1.000
Rollie Fingers	p	6	3	0	1	0	0	0	0	0	1	0	.333	.333	0	1.000
Ray Fosse	c	7	19	0	3	1	0	0	1	4	0	0	.158	.211	0	1.000
Dick Green	2b	7	16	0	1	0	0	0	0	1	6	0	.063	.063	1	.962
Ken Holtzman	p	3	3	2	2	2	0	0	0	0	0	0	.667	1.333	0	1.000
Jim "Catfish" Hunter	p	2	5	0	0	0	0	0	0	0	3	0	.000	.000	1	.750
Reggie Jackson	cf-rf	7	29	3	9	3	1	1	6	2	7	0	.310	.586	0	1.000
Deron Johnson	ph-1b	6	10	0	3	1	0	0	1	4	0	10	.300	.400	0	1.000
Darold Knowles	p	7	0	0	0	0	0	0	0	0	0	0	–	–	1	.500
Ted Kubiak	2b	4	3	1	0	0	0	0	0	1	1	0	.000	.000	0	1.000
Allan Lewis	pr	3	0	1	0	0	0	0	0	0	0	0	–	–	0	–
Paul Lindblad	p	3	1	0	0	0	0	0	0	0	0	0	.000	.000	0	–
Angel Mangual	ph-cf	5	6	0	0	0	0	0	0	0	3	0	.000	.000	0	1.000
Blue Moon Odom	p-pr	3	1	0	0	0	0	0	0	0	1	0	.000	.000	0	–
Horacio Pina	p	2	0	0	0	0	0	0	0	0	0	0	–	–	0	–
Joe Rudi	lf	7	27	3	9	2	0	0	4	3	4	0	.333	.407	0	1.000
Gene Tenace	1b-c	7	19	0	3	1	0	0	3	11	7	0	.158	.211	2	.967
Totals		**7**	**241**	**21**	**51**	**12**	**3**	**2**	**20**	**28**	**62**	**3**	**.212**	**.311**	**9**	**.969**

Pitcher	G	GS	CG	IP	H	R	ER	BB	SO	W-L	Sv	ERA
Vida Blue	2	2	0	11	10	6	6	3	8	0-1	0	4.91
Rollie Fingers	6	0	0	13⅔	13	5	1	4	8	0-1	2	0.66
Ken Holtzman	3	3	0	10⅔	13	5	5	5	6	2-1	0	4.22
Jim "Catfish" Hunter	2	2	0	13⅓	11	3	3	4	6	1-0	0	2.03
Darold Knowles	7	0	0	6⅓	4	1	0	5	5	0-0	2	0.00
Paul Lindblad	3	0	0	3⅓	4	0	0	1	1	1-0	0	0.00
Blue Moon Odom	2	0	0	4⅔	5	2	2	2	2	0-0	0	3.86
Horacio Pina	2	0	0	3	6	2	0	2	0	0-0	0	0.00
Totals	**7**	**7**	**0**	**66**	**66**	**24**	**17**	**26**	**36**	**4-3**	**4**	**2.32**

NEW YORK METS/Yogi Berra, Manager

Player	pos	G	AB	R	H	2B	3B	HR	RBI	BB	SO	SB	BA	SA	E	FPct
Jim Beauchamp	ph	4	4	0	0	0	0	0	0	0	1	0	.000	.000	–	–
Ken Boswell	ph	3	3	1	3	0	0	0	0	0	0	0	1.000	1.000	–	–
Wayne Garrett	3b	7	30	4	5	0	0	2	2	5	11	0	.167	.367	3	.885
Jerry Grote	c	7	30	2	8	0	0	0	1	0	1	0	.267	.267	0	1.000
Don Hahn	rf-cf	7	29	2	7	1	1	0	2	1	6	0	.241	.345	1	.933
Bud Harrelson	ss	7	24	2	6	1	0	0	1	5	3	0	.250	.292	0	1.000
Ron Hodges	ph	1	0	0	0	0	0	0	0	1	0	0	–	–	–	–
Cleon Jones	lf	7	28	5	8	2	0	1	1	4	2	0	.286	.464	1	.923
Jerry Koosman	p	2	4	0	0	0	0	0	0	0	3	0	.000	.000	1	.500
Ed Kranepool	ph	4	3	0	0	0	0	0	0	0	0	0	.000	.000	–	–
Ted Martinez	pr	2	0	0	0	0	0	0	0	0	0	0	–	–	–	–
Jon Matlack	p	3	4	0	1	0	0	0	0	0	2	1	.250	.250	0	1.000
Willie Mays	cf-pr-ph	3	7	1	2	0	0	0	1	0	1	0	.286	.286	1	.500
Tug McGraw	p	5	3	1	1	0	0	0	0	0	1	0	.333	.333	0	1.000
Felix Millan	2b	7	32	3	6	1	1	0	1	1	3	0	.188	.281	3	.909
John Milner	1b	7	27	2	8	0	0	0	2	5	1	0	.296	.296	0	1.000
Harry Parker	p	3	0	0	0	0	0	0	0	0	0	0	–	–	0	1.000
Ray Sadecki	p	4	0	0	0	0	0	0	0	0	0	0	–	–	0	1.000
Tom Seaver	p	2	5	0	0	0	0	0	0	0	2	0	.000	.000	0	1.000
Rusty Staub	rf	7	26	1	11	2	0	1	6	2	2	0	.423	.615	0	1.000
George Stone	p	2	0	0	0	0	0	0	0	0	0	0	–	–	0	–
George Theodore	ph-lf	2	2	0	0	0	0	0	0	0	0	0	.000	.000	0	1.000
Totals		**7**	**261**	**24**	**66**	**7**	**2**	**4**	**16**	**26**	**36**	**0**	**.253**	**.341**	**10**	**.964**

Pitcher	G	GS	CG	IP	H	R	ER	BB	SO	W-L	Sv	ERA
Jerry Koosman	2	2	0	8⅔	9	3	3	7	8	1-0	0	3.12
Jon Matlack	3	3	0	16⅔	10	7	4	5	11	1-2	0	2.16
Tug McGraw	5	0	0	13⅔	8	5	4	9	14	1-0	1	2.63
Harry Parker	3	0	0	3⅓	2	1	0	2	2	0-1	0	0.00
Ray Sadecki	4	0	0	4⅔	5	1	1	1	6	0-0	1	1.93
Tom Seaver	2	2	0	15	13	4	4	3	18	0-1	0	2.40
George Stone	2	0	0	3	4	0	0	1	3	0-0	1	0.00
Totals	**7**	**7**	**0**	**65**	**51**	**21**	**16**	**28**	**62**	**3-4**	**3**	**2.22**

Series MVP: Reggie Jackson, Oakland Athletics. **Series Outstanding Pitchers:** Rollie Fingers and Darold Knowles, Oakland Athletics. **Average Length of Game:** 2 hours, 51 minutes. **Total Attendance:** 358,289. **Average Attendance:** 51,184 (48,460 at Oakland-Alameda County Stadium; 54,817 at Shea Stadium). **Umpires:** Augie Donatelli (NL), Russ Goetz (AL), Jerry Neudecker (AL), Paul Pryor (NL), Marty Springstead (AL), Harry Wendelstedt (NL). **Winning Player's Share:** $24,618. **Losing Player's Share:** $14,950.

run, a two-run blast, later in the inning. The Mets scored a run in the ninth and had two runners on base when Darold Knowles, making his seventh appearance in seven games, got Wayne Garrett to pop up for the final out. Although the Mets out-hit and out-scored them in the Series, the A's squeaked out a pair of one-run wins and took the last two to grab the necessary four games for their second straight championship.

Above: Tom Seaver struck out 12 Oakland batters in Game 3, but his Mets fell in 11 innings.

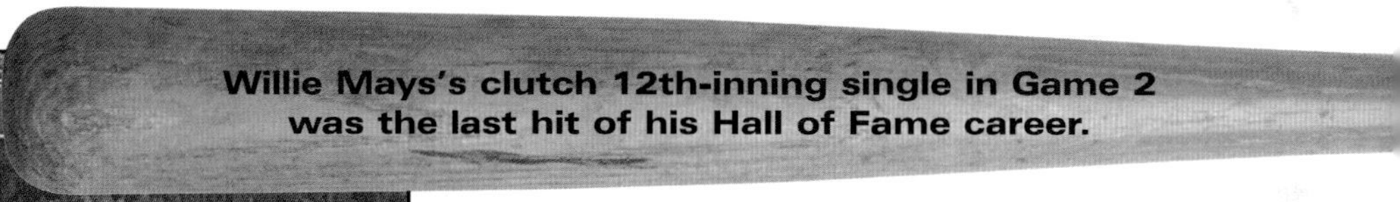

Above: All-time-legend Willie Mays comes through with a clutch hit in the second game. Oakland catcher Ray Fosse holds his hands up in despair.

Willie Mays's clutch 12th-inning single in Game 2 was the last hit of his Hall of Fame career.

In the 10th inning of a tied Game 2, Bud Harrelson tries to leap past Ray Fosse as umpire Augie Donatelli crouches in for a close look (right). The on-deck batter Willie Mays also looks on intently. Mays can't believe it when Harrelson is called out, and he pleads his case to Donatelli (above).

Oakland Athletics (4) vs. Los Angeles Dodgers (1)

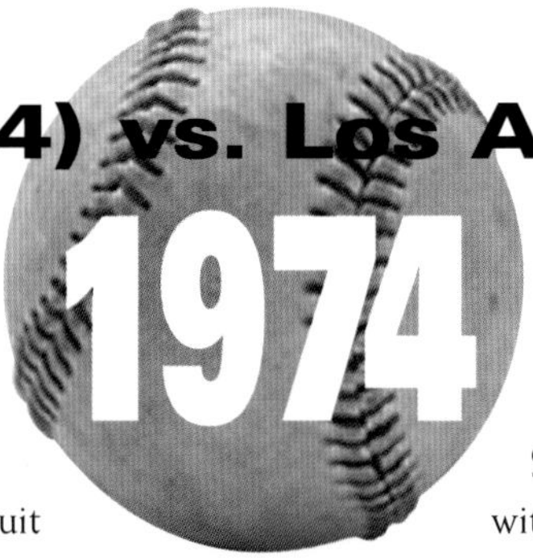

Overcoming internal turmoil, the Oakland Athletics won their third straight pennant in 1974. Manager Dick Williams quit the team at the end of 1973 because of continual clashes with meddlesome owner Charles Finley, culminating in the Mike Andrews "firing" during the 1973 Series. Andrews, who retired in the off-season, filed a libel suit against Finley. Despite these and other distractions, new manager Alvin Dark skippered the same all-star cast that made the A's October regulars. The Los Angeles Dodgers set up the first all-California contest by claiming the National League pennant with a hard-hitting, hard-throwing squad. LA's 20-game-winner Andy Messersmith pitched eight strong innings in Game 1, but Ron Cey's throwing error in the eighth gave Oakland three runs to the Dodgers' two. Making his first relief appearance of the year, Jim "Catfish" Hunter struck out the last batter of the game to earn the save, while Rollie Fingers was credited with the win. In Game 2, the Dodgers staked a 3-0 lead on Joe Ferguson's two-run homer in the sixth, but a two-run single by Joe Rudi in the ninth put the A's in striking distance. Oakland's "designated runner," Herb Washington, came in to pinch-run for Rudi with one out and LA's workhorse reliever Mike Marshall on the mound. Washington, who appeared in 92 games during the season, all as a pinch-runner, was picked off first by Marshall. Marshall went on to save Don Sutton's victory. Moving up the coast to Oakland for Game 3, Hunter won another one-run decision for the A's. An error by Ferguson led to two Oakland runs in the third, and Dick Green scored on a Bert Campaneris single in the fourth. For the second year in a row, pitcher Ken Holtzman entered the World Series with no regular-season at-bats, yet came through with major offensive contributions. After hitting a double in Game 1, Holtzman belted a solo homer in the third inning of Game 4 to put Oakland up 1-0. A four-run sixth inning assured Holtzman the W, with Jim Holt's pinch-single driving in two. Vida Blue kept the Dodgers scoreless until the sixth inning of Game 5 after the A's took a 2-0 lead. LA tied the game in the sixth, but Rudi broke the tie with a home run on the first pitch of the following inning. Bill Buckner opened the top of the eighth with a single to right-center field, and when the ball got past center fielder Bill North, Buckner tried to stretch it to a triple. Perfect throws from right fielder Reggie Jackson to second baseman Green to third baseman Sal Bando nailed Buckner at third. Rollie Fingers made his fifth appearance of the Series and kept LA from scoring. With the victory, the Oakland Athletics became the first club in 20 years to win three straight World Series—and the only non-Yankee team ever to accomplish the feat.

Above: Three in a row. First baseman Gene Tenace leaps into the arms of Rollie Fingers after the A's secured another World Series victory in 1974.

1974 WORLD SERIES COMPOSITE STATISTICS

OAKLAND ATHLETICS/Alvin Dark, Manager

Player	pos	G	AB	R	H	2B	3B	HR	RBI	BB	SO	SB	BA	SA	E	FPct
Jesus Alou	ph	1	1	0	0	0	0	0	0	0	1	0	.000	.000	–	–
Sal Bando	3b	5	16	3	1	0	0	0	2	2	5	0	.063	.063	0	1.000
Vida Blue	p	2	4	0	0	0	0	0	0	0	4	0	.000	.000	0	1.000
Bert Campaneris	ss	5	17	1	6	2	0	0	2	0	2	1	.353	.471	2	.917
Rollie Fingers	p	4	2	0	0	0	0	0	0	0	1	0	.000	.000	0	1.000
Ray Fosse	c	5	14	1	2	0	0	1	1	1	5	0	.143	.357	0	1.000
Dick Green	2b	5	13	1	0	0	0	0	1	1	4	0	.000	.000	1	.967
Larry Haney	c	2	0	0	0	0	0	0	0	0	0	0	–	–	0	1.000
Jim Holt	ph-1b	4	3	0	2	0	0	0	2	0	0	0	.667	.667	0	1.000
Ken Holtzman	p	2	4	2	2	1	0	1	1	1	1	0	.500	1.500	0	1.000
Jim "Catfish" Hunter	p	2	2	0	0	0	0	0	0	0	2	0	.000	.000	0	1.000
Reggie Jackson	rf	5	14	3	4	1	0	1	1	5	3	1	.286	.571	1	.900
Angel Mangual	ph	1	1	0	0	0	0	0	0	0	1	0	.000	.000	–	–
Dal Maxvill	2b-pr	2	0	0	0	0	0	0	0	0	0	0	–	–	0	–
Bill North	cf	5	17	3	1	0	0	0	0	2	5	1	.059	.059	1	.944
Blue Moon Odom	p	2	0	0	0	0	0	0	0	0	0	0	–	–	0	–
Joe Rudi	lf-1b	5	18	1	6	0	0	1	4	0	3	0	.333	.500	0	1.000
Gene Tenace	1b	5	9	0	2	0	0	0	0	3	4	0	.222	.222	0	1.000
Claudell Washington	rf-ph-cf-lf	5	7	1	4	0	0	0	0	1	1	0	.571	.571	0	1.000
Herb Washington	pr	3	0	0	0	0	0	0	0	0	0	0	–	–	–	–
Totals		**5**	**142**	**16**	**30**	**4**	**0**	**4**	**14**	**16**	**42**	**3**	**.211**	**.324**	**5**	**.974**

Pitcher	G	GS	CG	IP	H	R	ER	BB	SO	W-L	Sv	ERA
Vida Blue	2	2	0	13⅔	10	5	5	7	9	0-1	0	3.29
Rollie Fingers	4	0	0	9⅓	8	2	2	2	6	1-0	2	1.93
Ken Holtzman	2	2	0	12	13	3	2	4	10	1-0	0	1.50
Jim "Catfish" Hunter	2	1	0	7⅔	5	1	1	2	5	1-0	1	1.17
Blue Moon Odom	2	0	0	1⅓	0	0	0	1	2	1-0	0	0.00
Totals	**5**	**5**	**0**	**44**	**36**	**11**	**10**	**16**	**32**	**4-1**	**3**	**2.05**

LOS ANGELES DODGERS/Walter Alston, Manager

Player	pos	G	AB	R	H	2B	3B	HR	RBI	BB	SO	SB	BA	SA	E	FPct
Rick Auerbach	pr	1	0	0	0	0	0	0	0	0	0	0	–	–	–	–
Jim Brewer	p	1	0	0	0	0	0	0	0	0	0	0	–	–	0	–
Bill Buckner	lf	5	20	1	5	1	0	1	1	0	1	0	.250	.450	0	1.000
Ron Cey	3b	5	17	1	3	0	0	0	0	3	3	0	.176	.176	1	.933
Willie Crawford	ph-rf	3	6	1	2	0	0	1	1	0	0	0	.333	.833	0	1.000
Al Downing	p	1	1	0	0	0	0	0	0	0	0	0	.000	.000	0	1.000
Joe Ferguson	rf-c	5	16	2	2	0	0	1	2	4	6	1	.125	.313	2	.889
Steve Garvey	1b	5	21	2	8	0	0	0	1	0	3	0	.381	.381	0	1.000
Charlie Hough	p	1	0	0	0	0	0	0	0	0	0	0	–	–	0	–
Von Joshua	ph	4	4	0	0	0	0	0	0	0	0	0	.000	.000	–	–
Lee Lacy	ph	1	1	0	0	0	0	0	0	0	1	0	.000	.000	–	–
Davey Lopes	2b	5	18	2	2	0	0	0	0	3	4	2	.111	.111	0	1.000
Mike Marshall	p	5	0	0	0	0	0	0	0	1	0	0	–	–	0	1.000
Andy Messersmith	p	2	4	0	2	0	0	0	0	0	2	0	.500	.500	1	.833
Tom Paciorek	pr-ph	3	2	1	1	1	0	0	0	0	0	0	.500	1.000	–	–
Bill Russell	ss	5	18	0	4	0	1	0	2	0	2	0	.222	.333	1	.938
Don Sutton	p	2	3	0	0	0	0	0	0	0	2	0	.000	.000	0	1.000
Jimmy Wynn	cf	5	16	1	3	1	0	1	2	4	4	0	.188	.438	0	1.000
Steve Yeager	c	4	11	0	4	1	0	0	1	1	4	0	.364	.455	1	.973
Totals		**5**	**158**	**11**	**36**	**4**	**1**	**4**	**10**	**16**	**32**	**3**	**.228**	**.342**	**6**	**.967**

Pitcher	G	GS	CG	IP	H	R	ER	BB	SO	W-L	Sv	ERA
Jim Brewer	1	0	0	⅓	0	0	0	0	1	0-0	0	0.00
Al Downing	1	1	0	3⅔	4	3	1	4	3	0-1	0	2.45
Charlie Hough	1	0	0	2	0	0	0	1	4	0-0	0	0.00
Mike Marshall	5	0	0	9	6	1	1	1	10	0-1	1	1.00
Andy Messersmith	2	2	0	14	11	8	7	7	12	0-2	0	4.50
Don Sutton	2	2	0	13	9	4	4	3	12	1-0	0	2.77
Totals	**5**	**5**	**0**	**42**	**30**	**18**	**13**	**16**	**42**	**1-4**	**1**	**2.79**

Series MVP: Rollie Fingers, Oakland Athletics. **Series Outstanding Pitcher:** Rollie Fingers, Oakland Athletics. **Average Length of Game:** 2 hours, 32 minutes. **Total Attendance:** 260,004. **Average Attendance:** 52,001 (49,347 at Oakland-Alameda County Coliseum; 55,982 at Dodger Stadium). **Umpires:** Don Denkinger (AL), Tom Gorman (NL), Doug Harvey (NL), Bill Kunkel (AL), Ron Luciano (AL), Andy Olsen (NL). **Winning Player's Share:** $22,219. **Losing Player's Share:** $15,704.

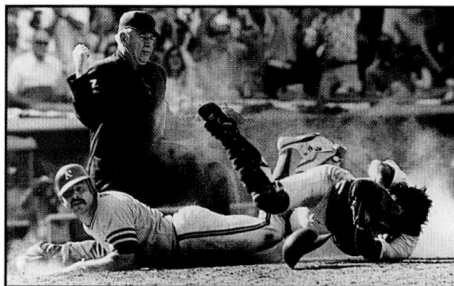

With his solo blast in Game 4, Ken Holtzman became the only player to hit a World Series home run after having no base hits all season. He is also the 14th pitcher to homer in a Series game.

Left: Sal Bando employs brute force to try to score from third on a Game 1 fly ball, but Los Angeles catcher Steve Yeager holds on for the out.

Below: In Game 2, Dodger first baseman Steve Garvey awaits the throw from Mike Marshall as they catch Oakland's "designated runner" Herb Washington off base in the ninth.

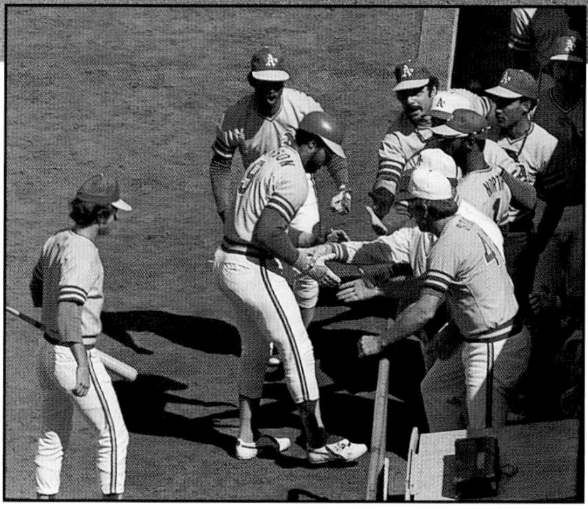

Left: Reggie Jackson provided the first run of the 1974 Series with a solo blast in the second inning of the opener.

Right: Ray Fosse's lead-off homer against Don Sutton in the second inning put Oakland up 2-0 in the fifth game.

Game 1 Saturday, October 12 at Dodger Stadium, Los Angeles

	1	2	3	4	5	6	7	8	9	R	H	E
Oakland Athletics	0	1	0	0	1	0	0	0	1	3	6	2
Los Angeles Dodgers	0	0	0	0	1	0	0	0	1	2	11	1

Pitchers Oak Ken Holtzman, IP 4⅓, H 7, R 1, ER 0, BB 2, SO 3; Rollie Fingers (W, 1-0), IP 4⅓, H 4, R 1, ER 1, BB 1, SO 3; Jim "Catfish" Hunter (Sv, 1), IP ⅓, H 0, R 0, ER 0, BB 0, SO 1
LA Andy Messersmith (L, 0-1), IP 8, H 5, R 3, ER 2, BB 3, SO 8; Mike Marshall, IP 1, H 1, R 0, ER 0, BB 1, SO 1

Top Performers at the Plate
Oak Bert Campaneris, 1 for 2, 1 R, 1 RBI, 2 SH; Reggie Jackson, 1 for 3, 1 R, 1 RBI, 1 BB
LA Bill Buckner, 2 for 5; Andy Messersmith, 2 for 3

2B-Oak/Holtzman. HR-Oak/Jackson; LA/Wynn. Time 2:43. Attendance 55,974.

Game 2 Sunday, October 13 at Dodger Stadium, Los Angeles

	1	2	3	4	5	6	7	8	9	R	H	E
Oakland Athletics	0	0	0	0	0	0	0	2		2	6	0
Los Angeles Dodgers	0	1	0	0	2	0	0	x		3	6	1

Pitchers Oak Vida Blue (L, 0-1), IP 7, H 6, R 3, ER 3, BB 2, SO 5; Blue Moon Odom, IP 1, H 0, R 0, ER 0, BB 1, SO 2
LA Don Sutton (W, 1-0), IP 8, H 5, R 2, ER 2, BB 2, SO 9; Mike Marshall (Sv, 1), IP 1, H 1, R 0, ER 0, BB 0, SO 2

Top Performers at the Plate
Oak Reggie Jackson, 2 for 3, 1 R, 1 BB; Joe Rudi, 1 for 4, 2 RBI
LA Joe Ferguson, 1 for 3, 1 R, 2 RBI, 1 BB; Steve Garvey, 2 for 4, 1 R

2B-Oak/Campaneris, Jackson. HR-LA/Ferguson. SB-LA/Ferguson. Time 2:40. Attendance 55,989.

Game 3 Tuesday, October 15 at Oakland-Alameda County Coliseum, Oakland

	1	2	3	4	5	6	7	8	9	R	H	E
Los Angeles Dodgers	0	0	0	0	0	0	0	1	7	2	7	2
Oakland Athletics	0	0	2	1	0	0	0	x		3	5	2

Pitchers LA Al Downing (L, 0-1), IP 3⅔, H 4, R 3, ER 1, BB 4, SO 3; Jim Brewer, IP ⅓, H 0, R 0, ER 0, BB 0, SO 1; Charlie Hough, IP 2, H 0, R 0, ER 0, BB 1, SO 4; Mike Marshall, IP 2, H 1, R 0, ER 0, BB 0, SO 1
Oak Jim "Catfish" Hunter (W, 1-0), IP 7⅓, H 5, R 1, ER 1, BB 2, SO 4; Rollie Fingers, IP 1⅔, H 2, R 1, ER 1, BB 0, SO 1

Top Performers at the Plate
LA Davey Lopes, 2 for 3, 1 BB, 2 SB
Oak Bert Campaneris, 2 for 4, 1 RBI

2B-Oak/Campaneris. HR-LA/Buckner, Crawford. SB-LA/Lopes 2; Oak/Jackson. Time 2:35. Attendance 49,347.

Game 4 Wednesday, October 16 at Oakland-Alameda County Coliseum, Oakland

	1	2	3	4	5	6	7	8	9	R	H	E
Los Angeles Dodgers	0	0	0	2	0	0	0	0	0	2	7	1
Oakland Athletics	0	0	1	0	0	4	0	0	x	5	7	0

Pitchers LA Andy Messersmith (L, 0-2), IP 6, H 6, R 5, ER 5, BB 4, SO 4; Mike Marshall, IP 2, H 1, R 0, ER 0, BB 0, SO 2
Oak Ken Holtzman (W, 1-0), IP 7⅔, H 6, R 2, ER 2, BB 2, SO 7; Rollie Fingers (Sv, 1), IP 1⅓, H 1, R 0, ER 0, BB 0, SO 2

Top Performers at the Plate
LA Steve Garvey, 2 for 4, 1 R; Bill Russell, 1 for 4, 2 RBI
Oak Ken Holtzman, 1 for 3, 1 R, 1 RBI; Claudell Washington, 2 for 3, 1 R, 1 BB

2B-LA/Buckner, Wynn, Yeager. 3B-LA/Russell. HR-Oak/Holtzman. Time 2:17. Attendance 49,347.

Game 5 Thursday, October 17 at Oakland-Alameda County Coliseum, Oakland

	1	2	3	4	5	6	7	8	9	R	H	E
Los Angeles Dodgers	0	0	0	0	0	2	0	0		2	5	1
Oakland Athletics	1	1	0	0	0	0	1	0	x	3	6	1

Pitchers LA Don Sutton, IP 5, H 4, R 2, ER 2, BB 1, SO 3; Mike Marshall (L, 0-1), IP 3, H 2, R 1, ER 1, BB 0, SO 4
Oak Vida Blue, IP 6⅔, H 4, R 2, ER 2, BB 5, SO 4; Blue Moon Odom (W, 1-0), IP ⅓, H 0, R 0, ER 0, BB 0, SO 0; Rollie Fingers (Sv, 2), IP 2, H 1, R 0, ER 0, BB 1, SO 0

Top Performers at the Plate
LA Davey Lopes, 0 for 2, 1 R, 2 BB; Tom Paciorek, 1 for 1, 1 R
Oak Ray Fosse, 1 for 3, 1 R, 1 RBI; Joe Rudi, 2 for 3, 1 R, 1 RBI

2B-LA/Paciorek. HR-Oak/Fosse, Rudi. SB-Oak/Campaneris, North. Time 2:23. Attendance 49,347.

WORLD SERIES CLASSIC

1975

Cincinnati Reds (4) vs. Boston Red Sox (3)

When the sixth game of the 1975 World Series ended, players on both sides, winners and losers alike, knew that they had just participated in one of the greatest baseball games ever played. And they still had one more to play to find out who would be world champions.

Cincinnati's Big Red Machine had only gotten stronger since their last Series appearance in 1972, adding up-and-coming stars George Foster and Ken Griffey Sr. to a lineup full of future Hall of Famers in Johnny Bench, Joe Morgan, Tony Perez and Pete Rose. The American League's Rookie of the Year and MVP, Fred Lynn, joined a productive offense in Boston that usurped the Oakland A's in a three-game sweep in the league championship series.

The opening game was the only blowout of the 1975 Series, with Luis Tiant leading the way on the mound and at the plate. Tiant hadn't batted in an official game in three years, but he singled to open the bottom of the seventh and eventually scored on Carl Yastrzemski's single. The Red Sox brought in six runs in the inning, and Tiant retired the last six Cincinnati batters to seal the win. The next game saw Boston take a 2-1 lead into the top of the ninth behind the pitching of "Spaceman" Bill Lee. Johnny Bench opened the ninth with a double, and Dave Concepcion drove him home with an infield single; Griffey then doubled to send Concepcion in with the go-ahead run. Game 3 was a tightly fought 10-inning affair that was not without controversy. A two-run

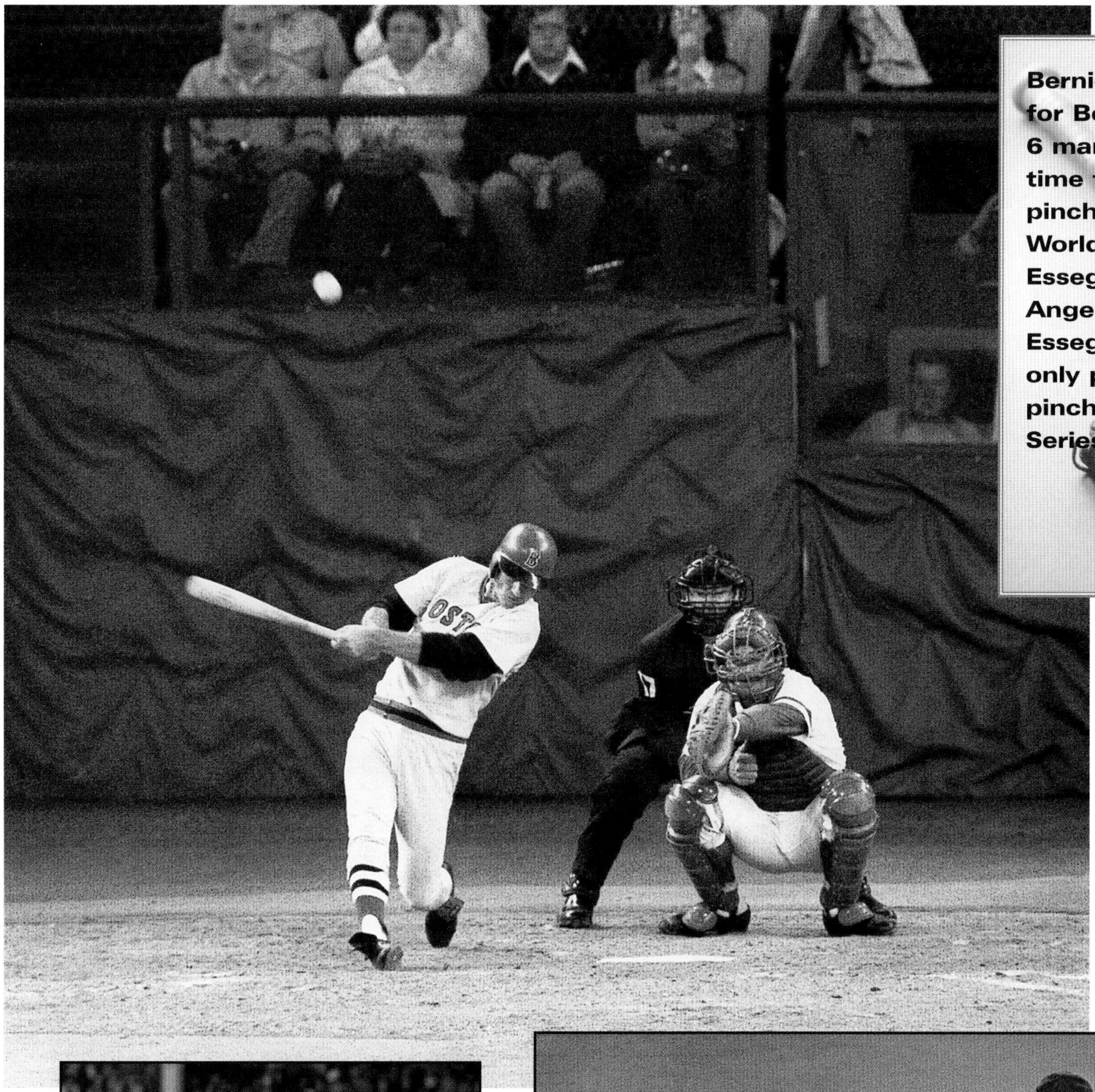

Bernie Carbo's home runs for Boston in Games 3 and 6 marked only the second time that somebody hit two pinch-hit homers in one World Series. Chuck Essegian did it for Los Angeles in 1959. In fact, Essegian and Carbo are the only players with two pinch-homers in their Series careers.

Far left: One of the most vivid images from any World Series: Carlton Fisk waves his arms to will the ball fair in Game 6 of the 1975 Fall Classic.

Left: Carl Yastrzemski singles to drive in a run in Boston's five-run fourth inning in Game 4.

Below: Joe Morgan and Johnny Bench greet Tony Perez after Perez drove them both home with his sixth-inning homer in Game 5.

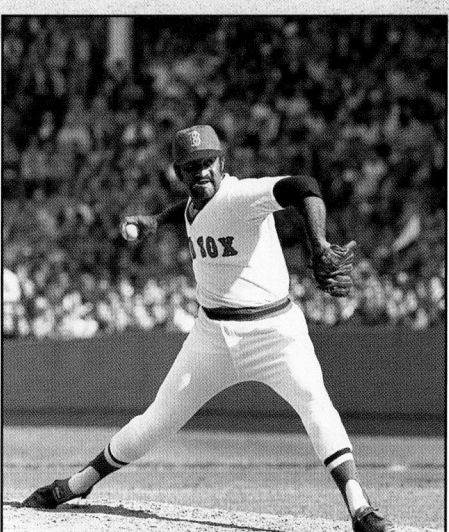

Above: Luis Tiant won two games in the Series, including a Game 1 shutout to give Boston a 1-0 lead in the Series.

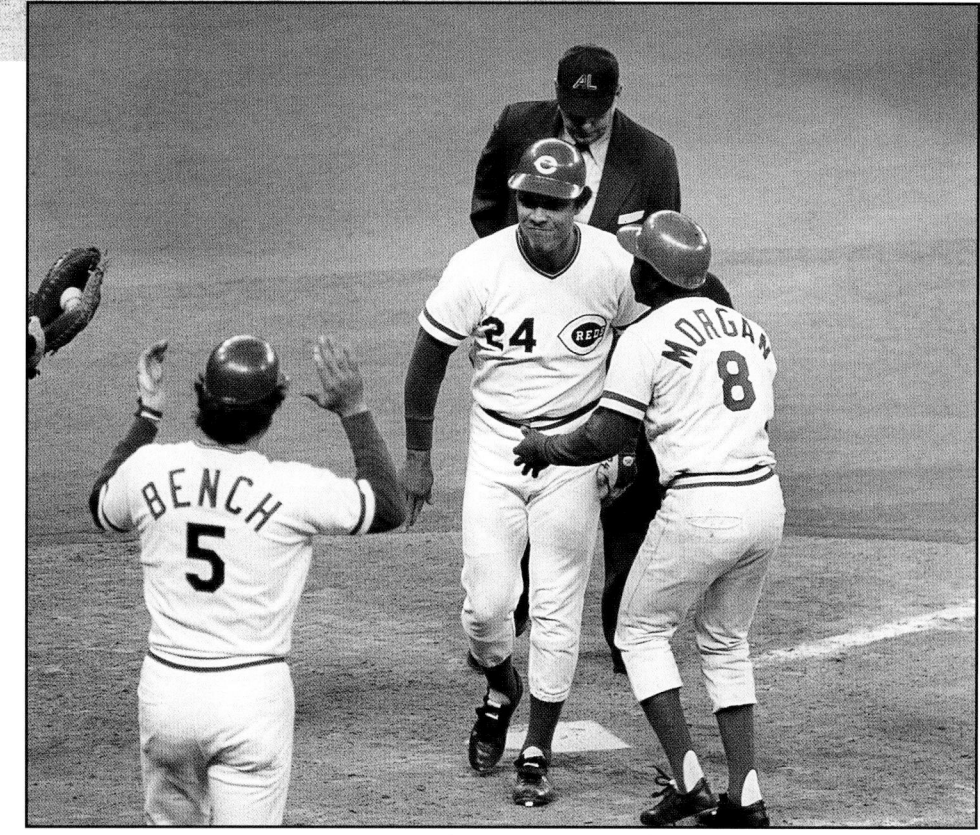

Above: Fred Lynn makes a great diving catch on Johnny Bench's fly in Game 2. Right: In a less victorious moment in Game 6, Lynn collided with Fenway Park's center-field wall chasing down a drive by Ken Griffey Sr. Lynn was shaken up on the play, and Griffey ended up with a triple.

homer by Bench and back-to-back clouts by Concepcion and Cesar Geronimo helped Cincinnati gain a 5-2 lead after six. Building on Bernie Carbo's pinch-homer in the seventh, Dwight Evans's two-run blast brought Boston even in the ninth. Geronimo led off the bottom of the tenth with a single, and pinch hitter Ed Armbrister followed by laying down a bunt in front of home plate. Catcher Carlton Fisk rushed out to field it, but Armbrister got in his way, and the catcher made a wild throw into the outfield. As Geronimo advanced to third and Armbrister to second, Fisk argued furiously that Armbrister should be called out for interference. Umpire Larry Barnett refused, and two batters later, Joe Morgan delivered the game-winning hit. A big inning in Game 4 produced another victory for Tiant and the Red Sox. With Tiant contributing his second hit of the Series and Evans knocking a two-run triple, Boston scored five in the fourth. Lynn helped preserve the one-run edge with an over-the-shoulder catch of Griffey's deep drive with two runners on in the ninth. Don Gullett's five-hitter in Game 5, along with two home runs and four RBI by Perez, gave the Reds the Series lead heading into Game 6 in Boston.

Rain delayed the start of the sixth game for three days, allowing manager Deron Johnson to go with Tiant in the crucial contest. The Cuban righty held the Reds to two base hits through four innings, and Fred Lynn put the Red Sox up 3-0 with one swing in the first. In the fifth inning, Griffey drove in two with a triple and then tied the game on Bench's RBI single. A two-run double by Foster and a solo homer by Geronimo knocked Tiant out of the game and gave Cincinnati a three-run

lead, but Boston got it all back in the bottom of the eighth when Bernie Carbo, pinch hitting with two men on base, sent a Rawly Eastwick pitch into the center-field bleachers. The Sox threatened in the last of the ninth, loading the bases with nobody out, but failed to score. The key play came when George Foster caught Lynn's fly in right and nailed Denny Doyle trying to score from third. In the 11th, Evans denied Cincinnati a chance to take the lead when he turned Joe Morgan's probable home run into a double play with a leaping catch at the wall. The stage was set for drama as the game headed into inning 12. Carlton Fisk, Boston's leadoff hitter in the bottom of the inning, drove the second pitch from Pat Darcy down the left-field line. It was deep enough and high enough to clear Fenway's imposing Green Monster; the only question was whether it would stay fair. As Fisk stood waving his arms to coax it fair, the ball hit the foul pole for a home run. Boston was victorious, 7-6. The grueling, emotion-packed sixth game was followed by another nail-biter in Game 7. Boston jumped ahead in the third inning while Bill Lee kept the Reds under control until the sixth, when Perez's two-run homer put them within a run. They got that run the following inning on Rose's RBI single. In the top of the ninth, Griffey walked and advanced to third on infield grounders. With two outs and the go-ahead run 90 feet from the plate, Joe Morgan blooped a single to center to score Griffey. Cincinnati's Will McEnaney retired the Red Sox in order in the bottom of the ninth, and the Series was over. The Reds won one more game than Boston and brought home the trophy, but the Red Sox battled valiantly to the end in perhaps the greatest World Series ever played.

Above: Carlton Fisk ends a truly memorable World Series game by knocking Pat Darcy's pitch off the foul pole in Fenway Park. The home run sent the Series to a winner-take-all seventh game.

Below: The entire Red Sox team is out to greet Fisk as he leaps on home plate.

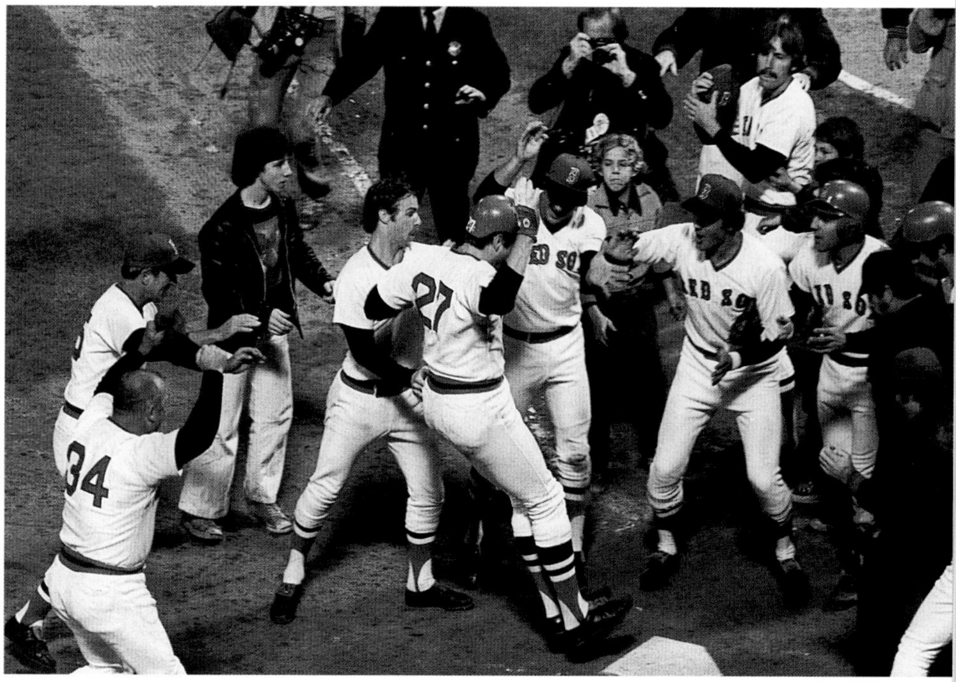

Game 1 Saturday, October 11 at Fenway Park, Boston

	1	2	3	4	5	6	7	6	9	R	H	E
Cincinnati Reds	0	0	0	0	0	0	0	0	0	0	5	0
Boston Red Sox	0	0	0	0	0	0	6	0	x	6	12	0

Pitchers Cin **Don Gullett** (L, 0-1), IP 6, H 10, R 4, ER 4, BB 4, SO 3; **Clay Carroll**, IP 0, H 0, R 1, ER 1, BB 1, SO 0; **Will McEnaney**, IP 2, H 2, R 1, ER 1, BB 1, SO 1
Bos **Luis Tiant** (W, 1-0), IP 9, H 5, R 0, ER 0, BB 2, SO 3

Top Performers at the Plate
Cin **George Foster**, 2 for 4; **Joe Morgan**, 2 for 4
Bos **Rick Burleson**, 3 for 3, 1 RBI, 1 BB; **Rico Petrocelli**, 2 for 3, 1 R, 2 RBI, 1 BB

2B-Cin/Griffey, Morgan; Bos/Petrocelli. **Time** 2:27. **Attendance** 35,205.

Game 2 Sunday, October 12 at Fenway Park, Boston

	1	2	3	4	5	6	7	8	9	R	H	E
Cincinnati Reds	0	0	0	1	0	0	0	0	2	3	7	1
Boston Red Sox	1	0	0	0	0	1	0	0	0	2	7	0

Pitchers Cin **Jack Billingham**, IP 5⅔, H 6, R 2, ER 1, BB 2, SO 5; **Pedro Borbon**, IP ⅓, H 0, R 0, ER 0, BB 0, SO 0; **Will McEnaney**, IP 1, H 0, R 0, ER 0, BB 0, SO 2; **Rawly Eastwick** (W, 1-0), IP 2, H 1, R 0, ER 0, BB 1, SO 1
Bos **Bill Lee**, IP 8, H 5, R 2, ER 2, BB 2, SO 5; **Dick Drago** (L, 0-1), IP 1, H 2, R 1, ER 1, BB 1, SO 0

Top Performers at the Plate
Cin **Johnny Bench**, 2 for 4, 1 R; **Pete Rose**, 2 for 4
Bos **Rico Petrocelli**, 2 for 4, 1 RBI; **Carl Yastrzemski**, 1 for 3, 2 R, 1 BB

2B-Cin/Bench, Griffey; Bos/Cooper. **SB**-Cin/Concepcion. **Time** 2:38. **Attendance** 35,205.

Game 3 Tuesday, October 14 at Riverfront Stadium, Cincinnati

	1	2	3	4	5	6	7	8	9	10	R	H	E
Boston Red Sox	0	1	0	0	0	1	1	0	2	0	5	10	2
Cincinnati Reds	0	0	0	2	3	0	0	0	0	1	6	7	0

Pitchers Bos **Rick Wise**, IP 4⅓, H 4, R 5, ER 5, BB 2, SO 1; **Jim Burton**, IP ⅓, H 0, R 0, ER 0, BB 1, SO 0; **Reggie Cleveland**, IP 1⅓, H 0, R 0, ER 0, BB 0, SO 2; **Jim Willoughby** (L, 0-1), IP 3, H 2, R 1, ER 0, BB 0, SO 1; **Roger Moret**, IP ⅓, H 1, R 0, ER 0, BB 1, SO 1
Cin **Gary Nolan**, IP 4, H 3, R 1, ER 1, BB 1, SO 0; **Pat Darcy**, IP 2, H 2, R 1, ER 1, BB 2, SO 0; **Clay Carroll**, IP ⅔, H 1, R 1, ER 1, BB 0, SO 0; **Will McEnaney**, IP 1⅔, H 1, R 1, ER 1, BB 0, SO 2; **Rawly Eastwick** (W, 2-0), IP 1⅔, H 3, R 1, ER 1, BB 0, SO 0

Top Performers at the Plate
Bos **Dwight Evans**, 2 for 4, 1 R, 2 RBI; **Carlton Fisk**, 1 for 3, 1 R, 1 RBI, 2 BB
Cin **Cesar Geronimo**, 2 for 4, 2 R, 1 RBI; **Joe Morgan**, 1 for 4, 2 RBI

3B-Cin/Rose. **HR**-Bos/Carbo, Evans, Fisk; Cin/Bench, Concepcion, Geronimo. **SB**-Cin/Foster, Griffey, Perez. **Time** 3:03. **Attendance** 55,392.

Game 4 Wednesday, October 15 at Riverfront Stadium, Cincinnati

	1	2	3	4	5	6	7	8	9	R	H	E
Boston Red Sox	0	0	0	5	0	0	0	0	0	5	11	1
Cincinnati Reds	2	0	0	2	0	0	0	0	0	4	9	1

Pitchers Bos **Luis Tiant** (W, 2-0), IP 9, H 9, R 4, ER 4, BB 4, SO 4
Cin **Fred Norman** (L, 0-1), IP 3⅓, H 7, R 4, ER 4, BB 1, SO 2; **Pedro Borbon**, IP ⅔, H 2, R 1, ER 0, BB 0, SO 0; **Clay Carroll**, IP 2, H 2, R 0, ER 0, BB 0, SO 2; **Rawly Eastwick**, IP 3, H 0, R 0, ER 0, BB 1, SO 0

Top Performers at the Plate
Bos **Dwight Evans**, 2 for 4, 1 R, 2 RBI; **Carl Yastrzemski**, 2 for 4, 1 R, 1 BB
Cin **George Foster**, 2 for 4, 1 R; **Cesar Geronimo**, 3 for 4, 1 RBI

2B-Bos/Burleson; Cin/Bench, Concepcion, Griffey. **3B**-Bos/Evans; Cin/Geronimo. **Time** 2:52. **Attendance** 55,667.

Game 5 Thursday, October 16 at Riverfront Stadium, Cincinnati

	1	2	3	4	5	6	7	8	9	R	H	E
Boston Red Sox	1	0	0	0	0	0	0	0	1	2	5	0
Cincinnati Reds	0	0	0	1	1	3	0	1	x	6	8	0

Pitchers Bos **Reggie Cleveland** (L, 0-1), IP 5, H 7, R 5, ER 5, BB 2, SO 3; **Jim Willoughby**, IP 2, H 1, R 0, ER 0, BB 0, SO 1; **Dick Pole**, IP 0, H 0, R 1, ER 1, BB 2, SO 0; **Diego Segui**, IP 1, H 0, R 0, ER 0, BB 0, SO 0
Cin **Don Gullett** (W, 1-1), IP 8⅔, H 5, R 2, ER 2, BB 1, SO 7; **Rawly Eastwick** (Sv, 1), IP ⅓, H 0, R 0, ER 0, BB 0, SO 1

Top Performers at the Plate
Bos **Carl Yastrzemski**, 1 for 3, 1 R, 1 RBI, 1 SF
Cin **Johnny Bench**, 1 for 3, 2 R, 1 BB; **Tony Perez**, 2 for 3, 2 R, 4 RBI, 1 BB

2B-Bos/Lynn; Cin/Rose. **3B**-Bos/Doyle. **HR**-Cin/Perez 2. **SB**-Cin/Concepcion, Morgan. **Time** 2:23. **Attendance** 56,393.

Game 6 Tuesday, October 21 at Fenway Park, Boston

	1	2	3	4	5	6	7	8	9	10	11	12	R	H	E
Cincinnati Reds	0	0	0	0	3	0	2	1	0	0	0	0	6	14	0
Boston Red Sox	3	0	0	0	0	0	0	3	0	0	0	1	7	10	1

Pitchers Cin **Gary Nolan**, IP 2, H 3, R 3, ER 3, BB 0, SO 2; **Fred Norman**, IP ⅔, H 1, R 0, ER 0, BB 2, SO 0; **Jack Billingham**, IP 1⅓, H 1, R 0, ER 0, BB 1, SO 1; **Clay Carroll**, IP 1, H 1, R 0, ER 0, BB 0, SO 0; **Pedro Borbon**, IP 2, H 1, R 2, ER 2, BB 2, SO 1; **Rawly Eastwick**, IP 1, H 2, R 1, ER 1, BB 1, SO 2; **Will McEnaney**, IP 1, H 0, R 0, ER 0, BB 1, SO 0; **Pat Darcy** (L, 0-1), IP 2, H 1, R 1, ER 1, BB 0, SO 1
Bos **Luis Tiant**, IP 7, H 11, R 6, ER 6, BB 2, SO 5; **Roger Moret**, IP 1, H 0, R 0, ER 0, BB 0, SO 0; **Dick Drago**, IP 3, H 1, R 0, ER 0, BB 0, SO 1; **Rick Wise** (W, 1-0), IP 1, H 2, R 0, ER 0, BB 0, SO 1

Top Performers at the Plate
Cin **George Foster**, 2 for 6, 2 RBI; **Ken Griffey**, 2 for 5, 2 R, 2 RBI, 1 BB
Bos **Carlton Fisk**, 2 for 4, 2 R, 1 RBI, 2 BB; **Fred Lynn**, 2 for 4, 2 R, 3 RBI, 1 BB

2B-Cin/Foster; Bos/Doyle, Evans. **3B**-Cin/Griffey. **HR**-Cin/Geronimo; Bos/Carbo, Fisk, Lynn. **SB**-Cin/Concepcion. **Time** 4:01. **Attendance** 35,205.

Game 7 Wednesday, October 22 at Fenway Park, Boston

	1	2	3	4	5	6	7	8	9	R	H	E
Cincinnati Reds	0	0	0	0	0	2	1	0	1	4	9	0
Boston Red Sox	0	0	3	0	0	0	0	0	0	3	5	2

Pitchers Cin **Don Gullett**, IP 4, H 4, R 3, ER 3, BB 5, SO 5; **Jack Billingham**, IP 2, H 1, R 0, ER 0, BB 2, SO 1; **Clay Carroll** (W, 1-0), IP 2, H 0, R 0, ER 0, BB 1, SO 1; **Will McEnaney** (Sv, 1), IP 1, H 0, R 0, ER 0, BB 0, SO 0
Bos **Bill Lee**, IP 6⅓, H 7, R 3, ER 3, BB 1, SO 2; **Roger Moret**, IP ⅓, H 1, R 0, ER 0, BB 2, SO 0; **Jim Willoughby**, IP 1⅓, H 0, R 0, ER 0, BB 0, SO 0; **Jim Burton** (L, 0-1), IP ⅔, H 1, R 1, ER 1, BB 2, SO 0; **Reggie Cleveland**, IP ⅓, H 0, R 0, ER 0, BB 1, SO 0

Top Performers at the Plate
Cin **Ken Griffey**, 1 for 2, 2 R, 2 BB; **Joe Morgan**, 2 for 4, 1 RBI, 1 BB
Bos **Bernie Carbo**, 1 for 3, 1 R, 1 BB; **Rico Petrocelli**, 1 for 3, 1 RBI, 1 BB

2B-Bos/Carbo. **HR**-Cin/Perez. **SB**-Cin/Griffey, Morgan. **Time** 2:52. **Attendance** 35,205.

Above: The ever-aggressive "Charlie Hustle," Pete Rose slides headfirst into third base on Joe Morgan's game-winning single in the ninth inning of Game 7. Right: Johnny Bench and manager Sparky Anderson soak in the thrill of winning the great 1975 World Series.

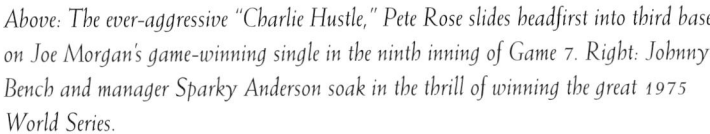

1975 WORLD SERIES COMPOSITE STATISTICS

CINCINNATI REDS/Sparky Anderson, Manager

Player	pos	G	AB	R	H	2B	3B	HR	RBI	BB	SO	SB	BA	SA	E	FPct
Ed Armbrister	ph	4	1	1	0	0	0	0	0	2	0	0	.000	.000	—	—
Johnny Bench	c	7	29	5	6	2	0	1	4	2	4	0	.207	.379	0	1.000
Jack Billingham	p	3	2	0	0	0	0	0	0	0	0	0	.000	.000	0	1.000
Pedro Borbon	p	3	1	0	0	0	0	0	0	0	0	0	.000	.000	0	—
Clay Carroll	p	5	0	0	0	0	0	0	0	0	0	0	—	—	0	1.000
Darrel Chaney	ph	2	2	0	0	0	0	0	0	1	0	0	.000	.000	—	—
Dave Concepcion	ss	7	28	3	5	1	0	1	4	0	1	3	.179	.321	1	.972
Terry Crowley	ph	2	2	0	1	0	0	0	0	0	1	0	.500	.500	—	—
Pat Darcy	p	2	1	0	0	0	0	0	0	0	1	0	.000	.000	0	1.000
Dan Driessen	ph	2	2	0	0	0	0	0	0	0	0	0	.000	.000	—	—
Rawly Eastwick	p	5	1	0	0	0	0	0	0	0	0	0	.000	.000	0	—
George Foster	lf	7	29	1	8	1	0	0	2	1	1	1	.276	.310	0	1.000
Cesar Geronimo	cf	7	25	3	7	0	1	2	3	3	5	0	.280	.600	0	1.000
Ken Griffey	rf	7	26	4	7	3	1	0	4	4	2	2	.269	.462	0	1.000
Don Gullett	p	3	7	1	2	0	0	0	0	0	2	0	.286	.286	0	—
Will McEnaney	p	5	1	0	1	0	0	0	0	0	0	0	1.000	1.000	0	—
Joe Morgan	2b	7	27	4	7	1	0	0	3	5	1	2	.259	.296	0	1.000
Gary Nolan	p	2	1	0	0	0	0	0	0	0	0	0	.000	.000	0	1.000
Fred Norman	p	2	1	0	0	0	0	0	0	0	0	0	.000	.000	0	—
Tony Perez	1b	7	28	4	5	0	0	3	7	3	9	1	.179	.500	1	.986
Merv Rettenmund	ph	3	3	0	0	0	0	0	0	0	1	0	.000	.000	—	—
Pete Rose	3b	7	27	3	10	1	1	0	2	5	1	0	.370	.481	0	1.000
Totals		**7**	**244**	**29**	**59**	**9**	**3**	**7**	**29**	**25**	**30**	**9**	**.242**	**.389**	**2**	**.993**

Pitcher	G	GS	CG	IP	H	R	ER	BB	SO	W-L	Sv	ERA
Jack Billingham	3	1	0	9	8	2	1	5	7	0-0	0	1.00
Pedro Borbon	3	0	0	3	3	2	2	1	0	0-0	0	6.00
Clay Carroll	5	0	0	5⅔	4	2	2	2	3	1-0	0	3.18
Pat Darcy	2	0	0	4	3	2	2	2	1	0-1	0	4.50
Rawly Eastwick	5	0	0	8	6	2	2	3	4	2-0	1	2.25
Don Gullett	3	3	0	18⅔	19	9	9	10	15	1-1	0	4.34
Will McEnaney	5	0	0	6⅔	3	2	2	2	5	0-0	1	2.70
Gary Nolan	2	2	0	6	6	4	4	1	2	0-0	0	6.00
Fred Norman	2	1	0	4	8	4	4	3	2	0-1	0	9.00
Totals	**7**	**7**	**0**	**65**	**60**	**30**	**28**	**30**	**40**	**4-3**	**2**	**3.88**

BOSTON RED SOX/Darrell Johnson, Manager

Player	pos	G	AB	R	H	2B	3B	HR	RBI	BB	SO	SB	BA	SA	E	FPct
Juan Beniquez	lf-ph	3	8	0	1	0	0	0	1	1	1	0	.125	.125	0	1.000
Rick Burleson	ss	7	24	1	7	1	0	0	2	4	2	0	.292	.333	1	.966
Jim Burton	p	2	0	0	0	0	0	0	0	0	0	0	—	—	0	—
Bernie Carbo	ph-lf	4	7	3	3	1	0	2	4	1	1	0	.429	1.429	0	1.000
Reggie Cleveland	p	3	2	0	0	0	0	0	0	0	2	0	.000	.000	0	—
Cecil Cooper	1b-ph	5	19	0	1	1	0	0	1	0	3	0	.053	.105	0	1.000
Denny Doyle	2b	7	30	3	8	1	1	0	0	2	1	0	.267	.367	3	.921
Dick Drago	p	2	0	0	0	0	0	0	0	0	0	0	—	—	0	—
Dwight Evans	rf	7	24	3	7	1	1	1	5	3	4	0	.292	.542	0	1.000
Carlton Fisk	c	7	25	5	6	0	0	2	4	7	7	0	.240	.480	2	.952
Doug Griffin	ph	1	1	0	0	0	0	0	0	0	0	0	.000	.000	—	—
Bill Lee	p	2	6	0	1	0	0	0	0	0	3	0	.167	.167	0	1.000
Fred Lynn	cf	7	25	3	7	1	0	1	5	3	5	0	.280	.440	0	1.000
Rick Miller	lf	3	2	0	0	0	0	0	0	0	0	0	.000	.000	0	1.000
Bob Montgomery	ph	1	1	0	0	0	0	0	0	0	0	0	.000	.000	—	—
Roger Moret	p	3	0	0	0	0	0	0	0	0	0	0	—	—	0	1.000
Rico Petrocelli	3b	7	26	3	8	1	0	0	4	3	6	0	.308	.346	1	1.000
Dick Pole	p	1	0	0	0	0	0	0	0	0	0	0	—	—	0	—
Diego Segui	p	1	0	0	0	0	0	0	0	0	0	0	—	—	0	—
Luis Tiant	p	3	8	2	2	0	0	0	0	2	4	0	.250	.250	0	1.000
Jim Willoughby	p	3	0	0	0	0	0	0	0	0	0	0	—	—	0	1.000
Rick Wise	p	2	2	0	0	0	0	0	0	0	0	0	.000	.000	0	—
Carl Yastrzemski	lf-1b	7	29	7	9	0	0	0	4	4	1	0	.310	.310	0	1.000
Totals		**7**	**239**	**30**	**60**	**7**	**2**	**6**	**30**	**30**	**40**	**0**	**.251**	**.372**	**6**	**.978**

Pitcher	G	GS	CG	IP	H	R	ER	BB	SO	W-L	Sv	ERA
Jim Burton	2	0	0	1	1	1	1	3	0	0-1	0	9.00
Reggie Cleveland	3	1	0	6⅔	5	5	5	3	5	0-1	0	6.75
Dick Drago	2	0	0	4	3	1	1	1	1	0-1	0	2.25
Bill Lee	2	2	0	14⅓	12	5	5	3	7	0-0	0	3.14
Roger Moret	3	0	0	1⅔	2	0	0	3	1	0-0	0	0.00
Dick Pole	1	0	0	0	0	0	1	1	2	0-0	0	—
Diego Segui	1	0	0	1	0	0	0	0	0	0-0	0	0.00
Luis Tiant	3	3	2	25	25	10	10	8	12	2-0	0	3.60
Jim Willoughby	3	0	0	6⅓	3	1	0	0	2	0-1	0	0.00
Rick Wise	2	1	0	5⅓	6	5	5	2	2	1-0	0	8.44
Totals	**7**	**7**	**2**	**65⅓**	**59**	**29**	**28**	**25**	**30**	**3-4**	**0**	**3.86**

Series MVP: Pete Rose, Cincinnati Reds. **Series Outstanding Pitcher:** Rawly Eastwick, Cincinnati Reds. **Average Length of Game:** 2 hours, 54 minutes. **Total Attendance:** 308,272. **Average Attendance:** 44,039 (55,817 at Riverfront Stadium; 35,205 at Fenway Park).
Umpires: Larry Barnett (AL), Nick Colosi (NL), Satch Davidson (NL), Art Frantz (AL), George Maloney (AL), Dick Stello (NL). **Winning Player's Share:** $19,060. **Losing Player's Share:** $13,326.

Left: Joe Morgan was the hero of more than just the seventh game. His bases-loaded single won Game 3 with two out in the 10th.

Below: Red Sox right fielder Dwight Evans makes a great running catch to snare Joe Morgan's long fly in the 11th inning of Game 6. Evans recovered to throw the ball into the infield and double up Ken Griffey.

Below: Johnny Bench struggled a bit at the plate in the 1975 Series, but the Hall of Fame catcher delivered a two-run homer in the fourth inning of Game 3.

Cincinnati Reds (4) vs. New York Yankees (0)

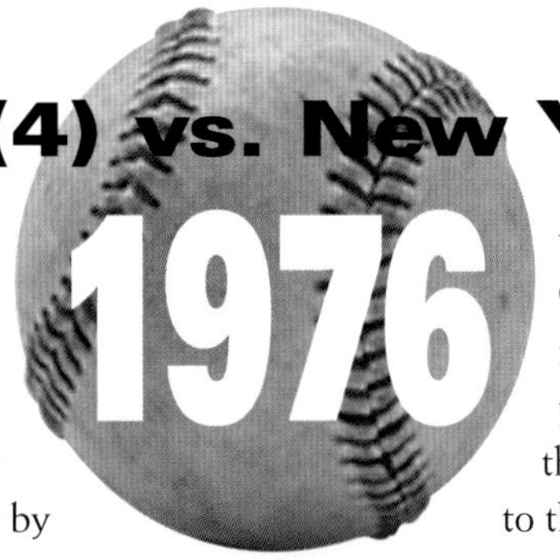

The Cincinnati Reds dominated the National League in 1976, leading all teams in hits, runs, home runs, batting average, stolen bases and just about every other category. Seven pitchers won 11 or more games, and the Big Red Machine finished atop their division by 10 games. The Reds would get a chance to defend their World Series title by facing the New York Yankees. With former Yankee second baseman Billy Martin at the reins, the Bronx Bombers were making their first appearance in 12 years, ending the longest drought the franchise had experienced since its World Series debut in 1921. MVP Joe Morgan set the tone for the Series with his first-inning homer in Game 1, part of a 10-hit day for the Reds. Don Gullett held New York to one run on five hits, and reliever Pedro Borbon closed it out by retiring all five batters he faced. In Game 2, Jim "Catfish" Hunter, a free-agent acquisition for New York, settled down after a three-run second inning by the Reds to carry a 3-3 tie into the ninth. After the first two batters flied out in the bottom of the ninth, Ken Griffey reached second base on a throwing error by shortstop Fred Stanley; he went on to score the game-winner on Tony Perez's single. In New York for Game 3, the Reds again established an early lead. The Yankees closed the gap on a seventh-inning homer by Jim Mason (in the only World Series at-bat of Mason's career), but Morgan doubled in a run in the eighth and scored to extend the lead to 6-2. Thurman Munson collected his third hit of the day with two down in the ninth, but reliever Will McEnaney got Chris Chambliss for the final out. Cincinnati's Dan Driessen, the first National League designated hitter in World Series play, went 3 for 3 in the game with a home run. Down to their last gasps, Martin sent 19-game-winner Ed Figueroa to the mound for Game 4, and Gary Nolan started for Sparky Anderson's crew. Chambliss's RBI double in the first inning gave the Yanks their first lead of the Series, but it was quickly wiped away when Johnny Bench belted a home run with a man on in the fourth. Munson's fifth-inning RBI single brought New York within one, but they failed to score any more, and Bench continued his offensive barrage with a three-run homer in the ninth. Cesar Geronimo and Dave Concepcion hit back-to-back ground-rule doubles on two fan-interference plays to bring in run number seven, and McEnaney retired the Yanks in order to end the game. The Yankees' long-awaited return to the Fall Classic ended in disappointment, as they fell victim to a sweep for just the third time in 30 appearances. The Cincinnati Reds, meanwhile, established themselves as one of the all-time great teams with their second straight championship—the first repeat by a National League team since the 1922 New York Giants.

Left: After pitching 2 1/3 innings of shutout ball in Game 4, reliever Will McEnaney holds his arms up in celebration of Cincinnati's four-game sweep over the Yankees.

1976 WORLD SERIES COMPOSITE STATISTICS

CINCINNATI REDS/Sparky Anderson, Manager

Player	pos	G	AB	R	H	2B	3B	HR	RBI	BB	SO	SB	BA	SA	E	FPct
Johnny Bench	c	4	15	4	8	1	1	2	6	0	1	0	.533	1.133	0	1.000
Jack Billingham	p	1	0	0	0	0	0	0	0	0	0	0	—	—	0	1.000
Pedro Borbon	p	1	0	0	0	0	0	0	0	0	0	0	—	—	0	1.000
Dave Concepcion	ss	4	14	1	5	1	1	0	3	1	3	1	.357	.571	1	.944
Dan Driessen	dh	4	14	4	5	2	0	1	1	2	0	1	.357	.714	—	—
George Foster	lf	4	14	3	6	1	0	0	4	2	3	0	.429	.500	0	1.000
Cesar Geronimo	cf	4	13	3	4	2	0	0	1	2	2	2	.308	.462	0	.923
Ken Griffey	rf	4	17	2	1	0	0	0	1	0	1	1	.059	.059	0	1.000
Don Gullett	p	1	0	0	0	0	0	0	0	0	0	0	—	—	0	1.000
Will McEnaney	p	2	0	0	0	0	0	0	0	0	0	0	—	—	0	1.000
Joe Morgan	2b	4	15	3	5	1	1	1	2	2	2	2	.333	.733	2	.920
Gary Nolan	p	1	0	0	0	0	0	0	0	0	0	0	—	—	0	1.000
Fred Norman	p	1	0	0	0	0	0	0	0	0	0	0	—	—	0	1.000
Tony Perez	1b	4	16	1	5	1	0	0	2	1	2	0	.313	.375	0	1.000
Pete Rose	3b	4	16	1	3	1	0	0	1	2	2	0	.188	.250	0	1.000
Pat Zachry	p	1	0	0	0	0	0	0	0	0	0	0	—	—	1	.667
Totals		**4**	**134**	**22**	**42**	**10**	**3**	**4**	**21**	**12**	**16**	**7**	**.313**	**.522**	**5**	**.966**

Pitcher	G	GS	CG	IP	H	R	ER	BB	SO	W-L	Sv	ERA
Jack Billingham	1	0	0	2⅔	0	0	0	0	1	1-0	0	0.00
Pedro Borbon	1	0	0	1⅔	0	0	0	0	0	0-0	0	0.00
Don Gullett	1	1	0	7⅓	5	1	1	3	4	1-0	0	1.23
Will McEnaney	2	0	0	4⅔	2	0	0	1	2	0-0	2	0.00
Gary Nolan	1	1	0	6⅔	8	2	2	1	1	1-0	0	2.70
Fred Norman	1	1	0	6⅓	9	3	3	2	2	0-0	0	4.26
Pat Zachry	1	1	0	6⅔	6	2	2	5	6	1-0	0	2.70
Totals	**4**	**4**	**0**	**36**	**30**	**8**	**8**	**12**	**16**	**4-0**	**2**	**2.00**

NEW YORK YANKEES/Billy Martin, Manager

Player	pos	G	AB	R	H	2B	3B	HR	RBI	BB	SO	SB	BA	SA	E	FPct
Doyle Alexander	p	1	0	0	0	0	0	0	0	0	0	0	—	—	0	1.000
Chris Chambliss	1b	4	16	1	5	1	0	0	1	0	2	0	.313	.375	1	.967
Dock Ellis	p	1	0	0	0	0	0	0	0	0	0	0	—	—	0	—
Ed Figueroa	p	1	0	0	0	0	0	0	0	0	0	0	—	—	0	1.000
Oscar Gamble	ph-rf	3	8	0	1	0	0	0	1	0	0	0	.125	.125	0	1.000
Elrod Hendricks	ph	2	2	0	0	0	0	0	0	0	0	0	.000	.000	—	—
Jim "Catfish" Hunter	p	1	0	0	0	0	0	0	0	0	0	0	—	—	0	1.000
Grant Jackson	p	1	0	0	0	0	0	0	0	0	0	0	—	—	0	1.000
Sparky Lyle	p	2	0	0	0	0	0	0	0	0	0	0	—	—	0	—
Elliott Maddox	rf-dh	2	5	0	1	0	1	0	1	0	1	2	.200	.600	0	—
Jim Mason	ss	3	1	1	1	0	0	1	1	0	0	0	1.000	4.000	0	1.000
Carlos May	ph-dh	4	9	0	0	0	0	0	0	0	1	0	.000	.000	—	—
Thurman Munson	c	4	17	2	9	0	0	0	2	0	1	0	.529	.529	0	1.000
Graig Nettles	3b	4	12	0	3	0	0	0	2	3	1	0	.250	.250	0	1.000
Lou Piniella	dh-rf-ph	4	9	1	3	1	0	0	0	0	0	0	.333	.444	0	—
Willie Randolph	2b	4	14	1	1	0	0	0	0	1	3	0	.071	.071	0	1.000
Mickey Rivers	cf	4	18	1	3	0	0	0	0	1	2	1	.167	.167	0	1.000
Fred Stanley	ss	4	6	1	1	1	0	0	1	3	1	0	.167	.333	1	.917
Dick Tidrow	p	2	0	0	0	0	0	0	0	0	0	0	—	—	0	—
Otto Velez	ph	3	3	0	0	0	0	0	0	0	3	0	.000	.000	—	—
Roy White	lf	4	15	0	2	0	0	0	0	3	2	0	.133	.133	0	1.000
Totals		**4**	**135**	**8**	**30**	**3**	**1**	**1**	**8**	**12**	**16**	**1**	**.222**	**.281**	**2**	**.986**

Pitcher	G	GS	CG	IP	H	R	ER	BB	SO	W-L	Sv	ERA
Doyle Alexander	1	1	0	6	9	5	5	2	1	0-1	0	7.50
Dock Ellis	1	1	0	3⅓	7	4	4	0	1	0-1	0	10.80
Ed Figueroa	1	1	0	8	6	5	5	5	2	0-1	0	5.63
Jim "Catfish" Hunter	1	1	1	8⅔	10	4	3	4	5	0-1	0	3.12
Grant Jackson	1	0	0	3⅔	4	2	2	0	3	0-0	0	4.91
Sparky Lyle	2	0	0	2⅔	1	0	0	0	3	0-0	0	0.00
Dick Tidrow	2	0	0	2⅓	5	2	2	1	1	0-0	0	7.71
Totals	**4**	**4**	**1**	**34⅔**	**42**	**22**	**21**	**12**	**16**	**0-4**	**0**	**5.45**

Series MVP: Johnny Bench, Cincinnati Reds. **Series Outstanding Pitcher:** Will McEnaney, Cincinnati Reds. **Average Length of Game:** 2 hours, 32 minutes. **Total Attendance:** 223,009. **Average Attendance:** 55,752 (54,821 at Riverfront Stadium; 56,684 at Yankee Stadium). **Umpires:** Bill Deegan (AL), Lou DiMuro (AL), Bruce Froemming (NL), Dave Phillips (AL), Lee Weyer (NL), Bill Williams (NL). **Winning Player's Share:** $26,367. **Losing Player's Share:** $19,935.

Left: The first National League designated hitter, Dan Driessen, swings for the seats in Game 3 at Yankee Stadium.

Above: Joe Morgan acknowledges the Riverfront Stadium crowd after giving the Reds a 1-0 lead in the opening game with a first-inning homer.

The 1976 Series was the first in which the designated hitter was used. The DH would appear in alternate years until 1986, after which it was employed in games at American League parks only.

Left: Catcher Thurman Munson lunges into press row to grab a foul pop. Teammate Graig Nettles (9) makes the out call.

Below: Johnny Bench's bat was scorching in 1976. The catcher hit .533 in the Series and had four extra-base hits.

Game 1 Saturday, October 16 at Riverfront Stadium, Cincinnati

	1	2	3	4	5	6	7	8	9	R	H	E
New York Yankees	0	1	0	0	0	0	0	0	0	1	5	1
Cincinnati Reds	1	0	1	0	0	1	2	0	x	5	10	1

Pitchers NY **Doyle Alexander** (L, 0-1), IP 6, H 9, R 5, ER 5, BB 2, SO 1; **Sparky Lyle**, IP 2, H 1, R 0, ER 0, BB 0, SO 3
Cin **Don Gullett** (W, 1-0), IP 7⅓, H 5, R 1, ER 1, BB 3, SO 4; **Pedro Borbon**, IP 1⅔, H 0, R 0, ER 0, BB 0, SO 0

Top Performers at the Plate
NY **Lou Piniella**, 1 for 3, 1 R
Cin **Johnny Bench**, 2 for 3, 1 R, 1 RBI; **Tony Perez**, 3 for 4, 1 RBI

2B-NY/Piniella; Cin/Geronimo, Perez. **3B**-NY/Maddox; Cin/Bench, Concepcion. **HR**-Cin/Morgan. **SB**-Cin/Griffey. **Time** 2:18. **Attendance** 54,826.

Game 2 Sunday, October 17 at Riverfront Stadium, Cincinnati

	1	2	3	4	5	6	7	8	9	R	H	E
New York Yankees	0	0	0	1	0	0	2	0	0	3	9	1
Cincinnati Reds	0	3	0	0	0	0	0	0	1	4	10	0

Pitchers NY **Jim "Catfish" Hunter** (L, 0-1), IP 8⅔, H 10, R 4, ER 3, BB 4, SO 5
Cin **Fred Norman**, IP 6⅓, H 9, R 3, ER 3, BB 2, SO 2; **Jack Billingham** (W, 1-0), IP 2⅔, H 0, R 0, ER 0, BB 0, SO 1

Top Performers at the Plate
NY **Chris Chambliss**, 2 for 4; **Fred Stanley**, 1 for 3, 1 R, 1 RBI, 1 BB
Cin **Dan Driessen**, 2 for 4, 1 R; **Tony Perez**, 2 for 5, 1 RBI

2B-NY/Stanley; Cin/Bench, Driessen. **3B**-Cin/Morgan. **SB**-Cin/Concepcion, Morgan. **Time** 2:33. **Attendance** 54,816.

Game 3 Tuesday, October 19 at Yankee Stadium, New York

	1	2	3	4	5	6	7	8	9	R	H	E
Cincinnati Reds	0	3	0	1	0	0	0	2	0	6	13	2
New York Yankees	0	0	0	1	0	0	1	0	0	2	8	0

Pitchers Cin **Pat Zachry** (W, 1-0), IP 6⅔, H 6, R 2, ER 2, BB 5, SO 6; **Will McEnaney** (Sv, 1), IP 2⅓, H 2, R 0, ER 0, BB 0, SO 1
NY **Dock Ellis** (L, 0-1), IP 3⅓, H 7, R 4, ER 4, BB 0, SO 1; **Grant Jackson**, IP 3⅔, H 4, R 2, ER 2, BB 0, SO 3; **Dick Tidrow**, IP 2, H 2, R 0, ER 0, BB 1, SO 1

Top Performers at the Plate
Cin **Dan Driessen**, 2 for 3, 2 R, 1 RBI, 1 BB; **George Foster**, 2 for 4, 1 R, 2 RBI
NY **Thurman Munson**, 3 for 5; **Mickey Rivers**, 2 for 4, 1 BB

2B-Cin/Driessen, Foster, Morgan. **HR**-Cin/Driessen; NY/Mason. **SB**-Cin/Driessen, Geronimo. **Time** 2:40. **Attendance** 56,667.

Game 4 Thursday, October 21 at Yankee Stadium, New York

	1	2	3	4	5	6	7	8	9	R	H	E
Cincinnati Reds	0	0	0	3	0	0	0	0	4	7	9	2
New York Yankees	1	0	0	0	1	0	0	0	0	2	8	0

Pitchers Cin **Gary Nolan** (W, 1-0), IP 6⅔, H 8, R 2, ER 2, BB 1, SO 1; **Will McEnaney** (Sv, 2), IP 2⅓, H 0, R 0, ER 0, BB 1, SO 1
NY **Ed Figueroa** (L, 0-1), IP 8, H 6, R 5, ER 5, BB 5, SO 2; **Dick Tidrow**, IP ⅓, H 3, R 2, ER 2, BB 0, SO 0; **Sparky Lyle**, IP ⅔, H 0, R 0, ER 0, BB 0, SO 0

Top Performers at the Plate
Cin **Johnny Bench**, 2 for 4, 2 R, 5 RBI, 2 HR; **Dave Concepcion**, 2 for 3, 1 RBI, 1 BB
NY **Thurman Munson**, 4 for 4, 1 R, 1 RBI; **Graig Nettles**, 2 for 3, 1 BB

2B-Cin/Concepcion, Geronimo, Rose; NY/Chambliss. **HR**-Cin/Bench 2. **SB**-Cin/Geronimo, Morgan; NY/Rivers. **Time** 2:36. **Attendance** 56,700.

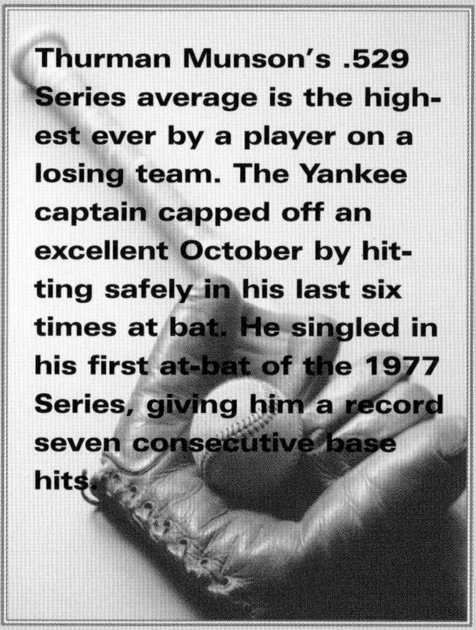

Thurman Munson's .529 Series average is the highest ever by a player on a losing team. The Yankee captain capped off an excellent October by hitting safely in his last six times at bat. He singled in his first at-bat of the 1977 Series, giving him a record seven consecutive base hits.

New York Yankees (4) vs. Los Angeles Dodgers (2)

The New York Yankees were looking to redeem their quick and unceremonious defeat in the 1976 World Series, so they made a few changes to the 1977 squad. The addition of Don Gullett and Mike Torrez to the pitching rotation brought 28 wins, and Bucky Dent came over from Chicago to assume the shortstop duties. But the Yankees' most significant acquisition was undoubtedly that of free-agent outfielder Reggie Jackson. Jackson had been a key contributor to Oakland's championships earlier in the decade, but it was in Yankee pinstripes that he emerged as "Mr. October." Reviving an old rivalry, the Yanks faced the Dodgers in the World Series. Under new manager

Tommy Lasorda, Los Angeles usurped Cincinnati as division champs and got past Philadelphia in the league championship series to capture the franchise's 16th pennant. The Dodger lineup featured a record four players with 30 or more home runs (Steve Garvey, Reggie Smith, Ron Cey and Dusty Baker), and Lasorda's deep pitching rotation boasted five players with double-digit victories in 1977. Gullett started Game 1 for the Yankees—making the former Red the only man to start consecutive Series openers in different uniforms. LA jumped out with a two-run first inning against Gullett before the postseason veteran regained control, holding the Dodgers to one run the rest

Above: Mr. October comes alive. Reggie Jackson set all sorts of records at the plate in the 1977 Series. Above inset: The often-volatile relationship between Reggie Jackson and his manager, Billy Martin, takes a decidedly more cheerful tone after the Game 6 win in 1977.

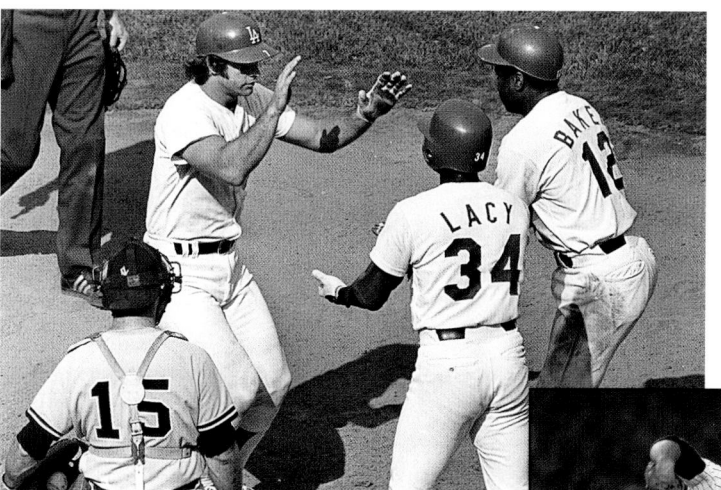

Left: Steve Yeager gave the Dodgers a comfortable lead in Game 5 when he drove Dusty Baker and Lee Lacy in with a three-run homer in the fourth.

Right: Getting the Game 1 start for New York, Don Gullet became the only pitcher to start opening games in consecutive World Series with two different teams.

Below: Three of Los Angeles's four 30-homer hitters went deep in Game 2 (counter clockwise from upper left): Ron Cey, Reggie Smith and Steve Garvey. Steve Yeager (upper right) had 16 homers in the regular season, and added one in Game 2 of the Series for good measure.

Jackson hit a home run in his last at-bat of Game 5—his last plate appearance before his historic three consecutive homers in Game 6—for an unprecedented four home runs in four straight at-bats.

Game 1 Tuesday, October 11 at Yankee Stadium, New York

	1	2	3	4	5	6	7	8	9	10	11	12	R	H	E
Los Angeles Dodgers	2	0	0	0	0	0	0	1	0	0	0	0	3	6	0
New York Yankees	1	0	0	1	0	1	0	0	0	0	0	1	4	11	0

Pitchers LA Don Sutton, IP 7, H 8, R 3, ER 3, BB 1, SO 4; Lance Rautzhan, IP ⅓, H 0, R 0, ER 0, BB 2, SO 0; Elias Sosa, IP ⅔, H 0, R 0, ER 0, BB 0, SO 1; Mike Garman, IP 3, H 1, R 0, ER 0, BB 1, SO 3; Rick Rhoden (L, 0-1), IP 0, H 2, R 1, ER 1, BB 1, SO 0
NY Don Gullett, IP 8⅓, H 5, R 3, ER 3, BB 6, SO 6; Sparky Lyle (W, 1-0), IP 3⅔, H 1, R 0, ER 0, BB 2, SO 2

Top Performers at the Plate
LA Dusty Baker, 1 for 4, 1 R, 1 HBP; Lee Lacy, 1 for 1, 1 RBI
NY Thurman Munson, 2 for 4, 1 R, 1 RBI, 2 BB; Willie Randolph, 2 for 5, 3 R, 1 RBI, 1 BB

2B-NY/Munson, Randolph. **3B**-LA/Russell. **HR**-NY/Randolph. **Time** 3:24. **Attendance** 56,668.

Game 2 Wednesday, October 12 at Yankee Stadium, New York

	1	2	3	4	5	6	7	8	9	R	H	E
Los Angeles Dodgers	2	1	2	0	0	0	0	0	1	6	9	0
New York Yankees	0	0	0	1	0	0	0	0	0	1	5	0

Pitchers LA Burt Hooton (W, 1-0), IP 9, H 5, R 1, ER 1, BB 1, SO 8
NY Jim "Catfish" Hunter (L, 0-1), IP 2⅓, H 5, R 5, ER 5, BB 0, SO 0; Dick Tidrow, IP 2⅔, H 3, R 0, ER 0, BB 0, SO 1; Ken Clay, IP 3, H 0, R 0, ER 0, BB 1, SO 0; Sparky Lyle, IP 1, H 1, R 1, ER 1, BB 0, SO 0

Top Performers at the Plate
LA Steve Garvey, 2 for 4, 1 R, 1 RBI; Reggie Smith, 2 for 3, 2 R, 2 RBI, 1 BB

2B-LA/Smith. **HR**-LA/Cey, Garvey, Smith, Yeager. **Time** 2:27. **Attendance** 56,691.

Game 3 Friday, October 14 at Dodger Stadium, Los Angeles

	1	2	3	4	5	6	7	8	9	R	H	E
New York Yankees	3	0	0	1	1	0	0	0	0	5	10	0
Los Angeles Dodgers	0	0	3	0	0	0	0	0	0	3	7	1

Pitchers NY Mike Torrez (W, 1-0), IP 9, H 7, R 3, ER 3, BB 3, SO 9
LA Tommy John (L, 0-1), IP 6, H 9, R 5, ER 4, BB 3, SO 7; Charlie Hough, IP 3, H 1, R 0, ER 0, BB 0, SO 2

Top Performers at the Plate
NY Reggie Jackson, 1 for 3, 2 R, 1 RBI, 1 BB; Mickey Rivers, 3 for 5, 1 R, 1 RBI, 2 2B
LA Dusty Baker, 2 for 4, 1 R, 3 RBI; Steve Garvey, 2 for 4, 1 R

2B-NY/Munson, Rivers 2; LA/Yeager. **HR**-LA/Baker. **SB**-NY/Rivers; LA/Lopes. **Time** 2:31. **Attendance** 55,992.

Game 4 Saturday, October 15 at Dodger Stadium, Los Angeles

	1	2	3	4	5	6	7	8	9	R	H	E
New York Yankees	0	3	0	0	0	1	0	0	0	4	7	0
Los Angeles Dodgers	0	0	2	0	0	0	0	0	0	2	4	0

Pitchers NY Ron Guidry (W, 1-0), IP 9, H 4, R 2, ER 2, BB 3, SO 7
LA Doug Rau (L, 0-1), IP 1, H 4, R 3, ER 3, BB 0, SO 0; Rick Rhoden, IP 7, H 2, R 1, ER 1, BB 0, SO 5; Mike Garman, IP 1, H 1, R 0, ER 0, BB 0, SO 0

Top Performers at the Plate
NY Chris Chambliss, 1 for 3, 1 R; Reggie Jackson, 2 for 4, 2 R, 1 RBI
LA Ron Cey, 2 for 4; Davey Lopes, 1 for 2, 1 R, 2 RBI, 2 BB

2B-NY/Chambliss, Jackson; LA/Cey, Rhoden. **HR**-NY/Jackson; LA/Lopes. **SB**-LA/Lopes. **Time** 2:07. **Attendance** 55,995.

Game 5 Sunday, October 16 at Dodger Stadium, Los Angeles

	1	2	3	4	5	6	7	8	9	R	H	E
New York Yankees	0	0	0	0	0	0	2	2	0	4	9	2
Los Angeles Dodgers	1	0	0	4	3	2	0	0	x	10	13	0

Pitchers NY Don Gullett (L, 0-1), IP 4⅓, H 8, R 7, ER 6, BB 1, SO 4; Ken Clay, IP ⅔, H 2, R 1, ER 1, BB 0, SO 0; Dick Tidrow, IP 1, H 2, R 2, ER 2, BB 0, SO 0; Jim "Catfish" Hunter, IP 2, H 1, R 0, ER 0, BB 0, SO 1
LA Don Sutton (W, 1-0), IP 9, H 9, R 4, ER 4, BB 0, SO 2

Top Performers at the Plate
NY Reggie Jackson, 2 for 4, 2 R, 1 RBI; Thurman Munson, 2 for 4, 1 R, 1 RBI
LA Dusty Baker, 3 for 4, 2 R, 2 RBI; Steve Yeager, 1 for 2, 1 R, 4 RBI, 1 SF

2B-NY/Nettles, Randolph; LA/Garvey. **3B**-LA/Lopes. **HR**-NY/Jackson, Munson; LA/Smith, Yeager. **Time** 2:29. **Attendance** 55,955.

Game 6 Tuesday, October 18 at Yankee Stadium, New York

	1	2	3	4	5	6	7	8	9	R	H	E
Los Angeles Dodgers	2	0	1	0	0	0	0	0	1	4	9	0
New York Yankees	0	2	0	3	2	0	0	1	x	8	8	1

Pitchers LA Burt Hooton (L, 1-1), IP 3, H 3, R 4, ER 4, BB 1, SO 1; Elias Sosa, IP 1⅔, H 3, R 3, ER 3, BB 1, SO 0; Doug Rau, IP 1⅓, H 0, R 0, ER 0, BB 0, SO 1; Charlie Hough, IP 2, H 2, R 1, ER 1, BB 0, SO 3
NY Mike Torrez (W, 2-0), IP 9, H 9, R 4, ER 2, BB 2, SO 6

Top Performers at the Plate
LA Steve Garvey, 2 for 4, 1 R, 2 RBI
NY Chris Chambliss, 2 for 4, 2 R, 2 RBI; Reggie Jackson, 3 for 3, 4 R, 5 RBI, 1 BB, 3 HR

2B-NY/Chambliss. **3B**-LA/Garvey. **HR**-LA/Smith; NY/Chambliss, Jackson 3. **Time** 2:18. **Attendance** 56,407.

of the way. New York scattered three runs, two scored by Willie Randolph, to take the lead until Lee Lacy's pinch-single in the ninth knotted the game at 3-3. Yankee reliever Sparky Lyle shut the Dodgers out in three extra innings heading into the 12th. Randolph opened the bottom of the inning with a double and scored the game-winner on Paul Blair's single to left. The Dodgers evened the Series in Game 2 by knocking an ailing Catfish Hunter for five runs in three innings, while Burt Hooten held the Yanks to five hits. Three of LA's four 30-homer men went yard in the game; Garvey hit a solo shot, and Cey and Smith

Left: A smiling Reggie Jackson is greeted by teammates Thurman Munson (15) and Chris Chambliss after knocking his first home run of Game 6. Above: Pitcher Elias Sosa was the victim in Jackson's second Game 6 homer, which came on the first throw of the at-bat. Right: In a familiar pose, Mr. October takes time to admire his home run, his third of the game.

1977 WORLD SERIES COMPOSITE STATISTICS

NEW YORK YANKEES/Billy Martin, Manager

Player	pos	G	AB	R	H	2B	3B	HR	RBI	BB	SO	SB	BA	SA	E	FPct
Paul Blair	rf-ph	4	4	0	1	0	0	0	1	0	0	0	.250	.250	0	1.000
Chris Chambliss	1b	6	24	4	7	2	0	1	4	0	2	0	.292	.500	0	1.000
Ken Clay	p	2	0	0	0	0	0	0	0	0	0	0	—	—	0	1.000
Bucky Dent	ss	6	19	0	5	0	0	0	2	2	1	0	.263	.263	1	.944
Ron Guidry	p	1	2	0	0	0	0	0	0	0	1	0	.000	.000	0	—
Don Gullett	p	2	2	0	0	0	0	0	0	0	2	0	.000	.000	0	1.000
Jim "Catfish" Hunter	p	2	0	0	0	0	0	0	0	0	0	0	—	—	0	1.000
Reggie Jackson	rf	6	20	10	9	1	0	5	8	3	4	0	.450	1.250	0	1.000
Cliff Johnson	ph-c	2	1	0	0	0	0	0	0	0	0	0	.000	.000	—	—
Sparky Lyle	p	2	2	0	0	0	0	0	0	0	0	0	.000	.000	0	—
Thurman Munson	c	6	25	4	8	2	0	1	3	2	8	0	.320	.520	0	1.000
Graig Nettles	3b	6	21	1	4	1	0	0	2	2	3	0	.190	.238	1	.944
Lou Piniella	lf	6	22	1	6	0	0	0	3	0	3	0	.273	.273	0	1.000
Willie Randolph	2b	6	25	5	4	2	0	1	1	2	2	0	.160	.360	0	1.000
Mickey Rivers	cf	6	27	1	6	2	0	0	1	0	2	1	.222	.296	0	1.000
Fred Stanley	ss	1	0	0	0	0	0	0	0	0	0	0	—	—	0	1.000
Dick Tidrow	p	2	1	0	0	0	0	0	0	0	1	0	.000	.000	0	1.000
Mike Torrez	p	2	6	0	0	0	0	0	0	0	4	0	.000	.000	0	1.000
Roy White	ph	2	2	0	0	0	0	0	0	0	0	0	.000	.000	—	—
George Zeber	ph	2	2	0	0	0	0	0	0	0	0	0	.000	.000	—	—
Totals		6	205	26	50	10	0	8	25	11	37	1	.244	.410	3	.987

Pitcher	G	GS	CG	IP	H	R	ER	BB	SO	W-L	Sv	ERA
Ken Clay	2	0	0	3⅓	2	1	1	1	0	0-0	0	2.45
Ron Guidry	1	1	1	9	4	2	2	3	7	1-0	0	2.00
Don Gullett	2	2	0	12⅔	13	10	9	7	10	0-1	0	6.39
Jim "Catfish" Hunter	2	1	0	4⅓	6	5	5	0	1	0-1	0	10.38
Sparky Lyle	2	0	0	4⅔	2	1	1	0	2	1-0	0	1.93
Dick Tidrow	2	0	0	3⅔	5	2	2	0	1	0-0	0	4.91
Mike Torrez	2	2	2	18	16	7	5	5	15	2-0	0	2.50
Totals	6	6	3	56	48	28	25	16	36	4-2	0	4.02

LOS ANGELES DODGERS/Tommy Lasorda, Manager

Player	pos	G	AB	R	H	2B	3B	HR	RBI	BB	SO	SB	BA	SA	E	FPct
Dusty Baker	lf	6	24	4	7	0	0	1	5	0	2	0	.292	.417	1	.923
Glenn Burke	cf	3	5	0	1	0	0	0	0	0	1	0	.200	.200	0	1.000
Ron Cey	3b	6	21	2	4	1	0	1	3	3	5	0	.190	.381	0	1.000
Vic Davalillo	ph	3	3	0	1	0	0	0	1	0	0	0	.333	.333	—	—
Mike Garman	p	2	0	0	0	0	0	0	0	0	0	0	—	—	0	—
Steve Garvey	1b	6	24	5	9	1	1	1	3	1	4	0	.375	.625	0	1.000
Ed Goodson	ph	1	1	0	0	0	0	0	0	0	1	0	.000	.000	—	—
Jerry Grote	c	1	1	0	0	0	0	0	0	0	0	0	.000	.000	0	1.000
Burt Hooten	p	2	5	0	0	0	0	0	0	0	2	0	.000	.000	0	—
Charlie Hough	p	2	0	0	0	0	0	0	0	0	0	0	—	—	0	—
Tommy John	p	1	2	0	0	0	0	0	0	0	2	0	.000	.000	0	—
Lee Lacy	ph-rf	4	7	1	3	0	0	0	0	2	1	1	.429	.429	0	1.000
Rafael Landestoy	pr	1	0	0	0	0	0	0	0	0	0	0	—	—	0	1.000
Davey Lopes	2b	6	24	3	4	0	1	1	2	4	3	2	.167	.375	0	1.000
Rick Monday	cf	4	12	0	2	0	0	0	0	3	3	0	.167	.167	0	1.000
Manny Mota	ph	3	3	0	0	0	0	0	0	0	1	0	.000	.000	—	—
Johnny Oates	ph-c	1	1	0	0	0	0	0	0	0	0	0	.000	.000	0	1.000
Doug Rau	p	2	0	0	0	0	0	0	0	0	0	0	—	—	0	—
Lance Rautzhan	p	1	0	0	0	0	0	0	0	0	0	0	—	—	0	1.000
Rick Rhoden	p	2	2	1	1	1	0	0	0	0	0	0	.500	1.000	0	1.000
Bill Russell	ss	6	26	3	4	0	1	0	2	1	3	0	.154	.231	0	1.000
Reggie Smith	rf-cf	6	22	7	6	1	0	3	5	4	3	0	.273	.727	0	1.000
Elias Sosa	p	2	0	0	0	0	0	0	0	0	0	0	—	—	0	—
Don Sutton	p	2	6	0	0	0	0	0	0	1	4	0	.000	.000	0	1.000
Steve Yeager	c	6	19	2	6	1	0	2	5	1	1	0	.316	.684	0	1.000
Totals		6	208	28	48	5	3	9	28	16	36	2	.231	.413	1	.996

Pitcher	G	GS	CG	IP	H	R	ER	BB	SO	W-L	Sv	ERA
Mike Garman	2	0	0	4	2	0	0	1	3	0-0	0	0.00
Burt Hooten	2	2	1	12	8	5	5	2	9	1-1	0	3.75
Charlie Hough	2	0	0	5	3	1	1	0	5	0-0	0	1.80
Tommy John	1	1	0	6	9	5	4	3	7	0-1	0	6.00
Doug Rau	2	1	0	2⅓	4	3	3	0	1	0-1	0	11.57
Lance Rautzhan	1	0	0	⅓	0	0	0	2	0	0-0	0	0.00
Rick Rhoden	2	0	0	7	4	2	2	1	5	1-1	0	2.57
Elias Sosa	2	0	0	2⅓	3	3	3	1	1	0-0	0	11.57
Don Sutton	2	2	1	16	17	7	7	1	6	1-0	0	3.94
Totals	6	6	2	55	50	26	25	11	37	2-4	0	4.09

Series MVP: Reggie Jackson, New York Yankees. **Series Outstanding Pitcher:** Mike Torrez, New York Yankees. **Average Length of Game:** 2 hours, 33 minutes. **Total Attendance:** 337,708. **Average Attendance:** 56,285 (56,589 at Yankee Stadium; 55,981 at Dodger Stadium).
Umpires: Nestor Chylak (AL), Jerry Dale (NL), Jim Evans (AL), Larry McCoy (AL), John McSherry (NL), Ed Sudol (NL). **Winning Player's Share:** $27,758. **Losing Player's Share:** $20,899.

delivered two-run shots. After splitting the first two games at home, the Yankees went into Dodger Stadium and took the first two to claim a three-games-to-one lead. Torrez went the distance in Game 3, besting LA's 20-game winner, Tommy John, 5-3. In Game 4, New York's young lefty Ron Guidry gave up a ground-rule double and a two-run homer in the third inning, but the Dodgers got only two more hits off "Louisiana Lightning" all night. Jackson doubled and scored in the second inning and hit a solo homer in the sixth to bring in two of New York's four runs in the game. Reggie hit another home run in Game 5, part of back-to-back jobs with Thurman Munson in the eighth, but the Dodgers and Don Sutton established a comfortable 10-4 margin to win the game and send the Series back to New York. Getting a two-run triple from Garvey and a solo homer from

Smith, LA grabbed a 3-2 lead after three innings in Game 6. Then Mr. October took center stage. After Munson led off the bottom of the fourth with a single, Jackson belted the first pitch from Hooton over the fence to put New York up 4-3. The Yanks scored another in the inning, and Jackson came up again in the fifth, again with a runner on base. And again Jackson crushed the first pitch he saw, this one from Elias Sosa, into the right-field seats for a two-run homer. The Yanks were leading 7-3 and in good position to clinch their first World Series triumph since 1962. The Dodgers may have appeared done, but Jackson wasn't. Leading off the eighth and facing knuckleballer Charlie Hough, Jackson crushed the first pitch of the inning, sending it deep into the center-field bleachers. Three pitches, three home runs. The Yankees were back on top, and Mr. October had arrived.

Right: Making a rare plate appearance because of the designated hitter rule, Mike Torrez advances two runners with a bunt in Game 3. The game's go-ahead run came in one batter later.

Below: Catcher Thurman Munson (15) and infielders Willie Randolph and Graig Nettles swarm around Mike Torrez after clinching the 1977 Series.

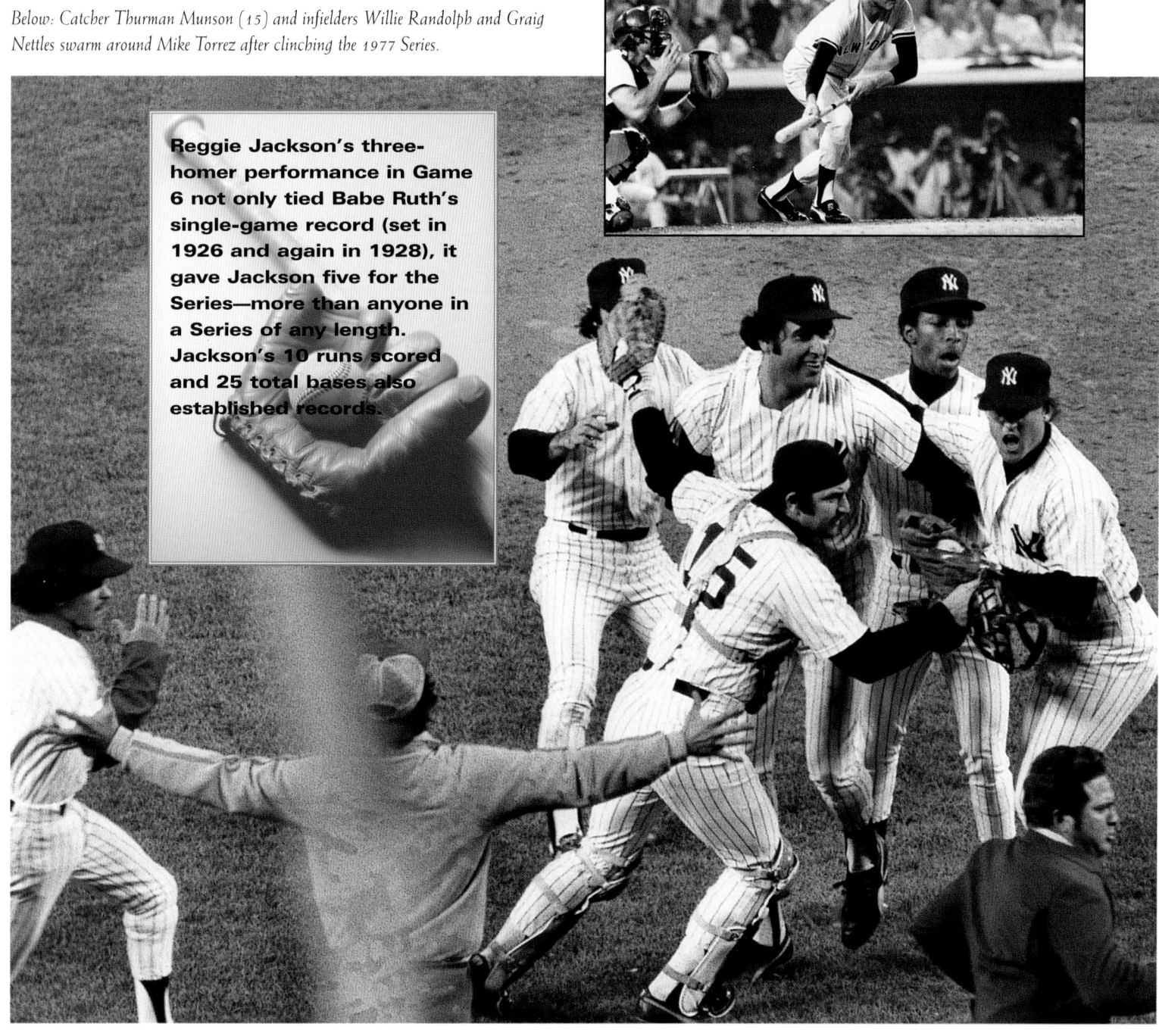

Reggie Jackson's three-homer performance in Game 6 not only tied Babe Ruth's single-game record (set in 1926 and again in 1928), it gave Jackson five for the Series—more than anyone in a Series of any length. Jackson's 10 runs scored and 25 total bases also established records.

Going, Going, Gone
The World Series and the Home Run

Above: Three pitches, three home runs. Reggie Jackson connects for three homers against the Dodgers in the sixth game of the 1977 Series.

Multi-Homer Games

Reggie Jackson's three home runs in the sixth game of 1977 matched a feat that had been accomplished only two other times in World Series history—and both of the previous three-homer performances were by Babe Ruth. Only 33 players have hit two round-trippers in one game, and five did it more than once. Willie Mays Aikens is the only player to have two multi-homer games in the same Series.

Three Home Runs

Babe Ruth, New York Yankees, 1926, Game 4
Babe Ruth, New York Yankees, 1928, Game 4
Reggie Jackson, New York Yankees, 1977, Game 6

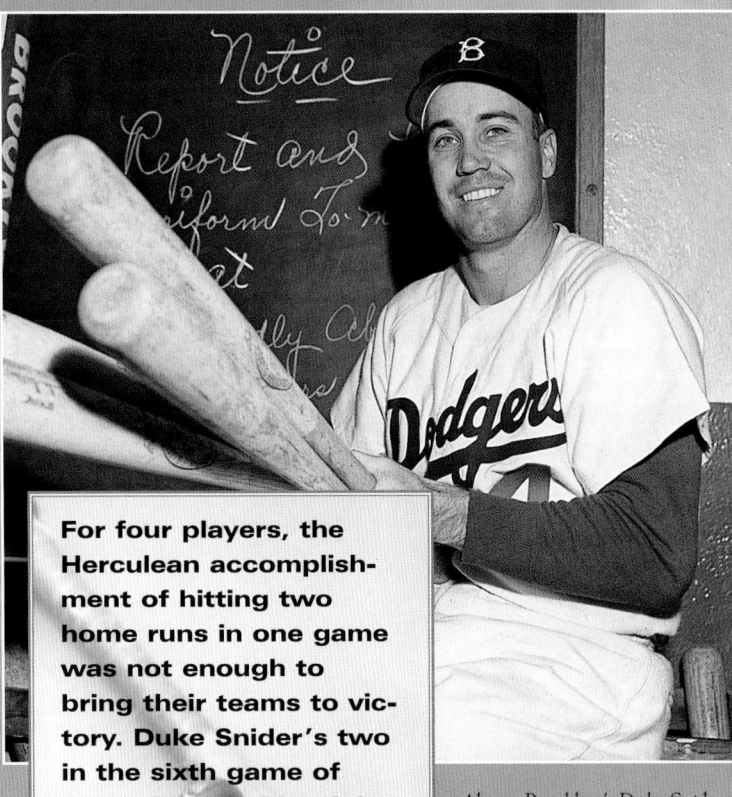

For four players, the Herculean accomplishment of hitting two home runs in one game was not enough to bring their teams to victory. Duke Snider's two in the sixth game of 1952, Mickey Mantle's in 1958, Willie Aikens's multi-homer outing in the 1980 opener, and Greg Vaughn's pair in 1998 all came in games that their teams lost.

Above: Brooklyn's Duke Snider is in elite company with Ruth, Gehrig, Mantle and ... Aikens, as the only players to twice hit two home runs in a World Series game.

Two Home Runs

Patsy Dougherty, Boston Red Sox, 1903, Game 2
Harry Hooper, Boston Red Sox, 1915, Game 5
Benny Kauff, New York Giants, 1917, Game 4
Babe Ruth, New York Yankees, 1923, Game 2
Lou Gehrig, New York Yankees, 1928, Game 3
Lou Gehrig, New York Yankees, 1932, Game 3
Babe Ruth, New York Yankees, 1932, Game 3
Tony Lazzeri, New York Yankees, 1932, Game 4
Charlie Keller, New York Yankees, 1939, Game 3
Bob Elliott, Boston Braves, 1948, Game 5
Duke Snider, Brooklyn Dodgers, 1952, Game 6
Joe Collins, New York Yankees, 1955, Game 1
Duke Snider, Brooklyn Dodgers, 1955, Game 5
Yogi Berra, New York Yankees, 1956, Game 7
Tony Kubek, New York Yankees, 1957, Game 3
Mickey Mantle, New York Yankees, 1958, Game 2
Ted Kluszewski, Chicago White Sox, 1959, Game 1
Charlie Neal, Los Angeles Dodgers, 1959, Game 2
Mickey Mantle, New York Yankees, 1960, Game 2
Carl Yastrzemski, Boston Red Sox, 1967, Game 2
Rico Petrocelli, Boston Red Sox, 1967, Game 6
Gene Tenace, Oakland Athletics, 1972, Game 1
Tony Perez, Cincinnati Reds, 1975, Game 5
Johnny Bench, Cincinnati Reds, 1976, Game 4
Davey Lopes, Los Angeles Dodgers, 1978, Game 1
Willie Aikens, Kansas City Royals, 1980, Game 1
Willie Aikens, Kansas City Royals, 1980, Game 4
Willie McGee, St. Louis Cardinals, 1982, Game 3
Eddie Murray, Baltimore Orioles, 1983, Game 5
Alan Trammell, Detroit Tigers, 1984, Game 4
Kirk Gibson, Detroit Tigers, 1984, Game 5
Gary Carter, New York Mets, 1986, Game 4
Dave Henderson, Oakland Athletics, 1989, Game 3
Chris Sabo, Cincinnati Reds, 1990, Game 3
Andruw Jones, Atlanta Braves, 1996, Game 1
Greg Vaughn, San Diego Padres, 1998, Game 1
Scott Brosius, New York Yankees, 1998, Game 3
Chad Curtis, New York Yankees, 1999, Game 3 (10 innings)

Top Ten World Series Home Runs

Only two players have ended a World Series by hitting the ball over the fence—these rank as the top two World Series home runs of all time—but many homers have proved pivotal in deciding a champion. Ten of the most memorable are ranked here. Four of the homers in this list were hit in the final game, and three took place in the opener. Only one of the ten greatest was by a player on the losing side of the Series (which is why Fisk's memorable blast doesn't rank higher in the list).

① Mazeroski Topples Yankees with Ninth-Inning Blast — Bill Mazeroski, Pittsburgh Pirates, October 13, 1960

Tie game, bottom of the ninth, Game 7 of the World Series—every player's fantasy. Bill Mazeroski secured Pittsburgh's unlikely victory over New York with the only Series-ending homer in a winner-take-all seventh game. Simply the greatest October moment.

② Carter's Three-Run Clout Wins Series for Jays — Joe Carter, Toronto Blue Jays, October 23, 1993

Only the second Series-ending home run in history, Joe Carter's blast gave Toronto a come-from-behind win in Game 6. The dramatic hit marked the only time a team came from behind to win a World Series in the final inning.

③ Hobbling Gibson Provides Game-Winning Spark — Kirk Gibson, Los Angeles Dodgers, October 15, 1988

An injured Kirk Gibson came in unexpectedly to pinch hit in the ninth inning of Game 1 and hit a two-run homer to give the Dodgers a 5-4 victory. It was Gibson's only appearance of the Series, and the Dodgers went on to defeat the heavily favored Oakland A's in five games.

④ Puckett Smash Sends Series to Seventh Game — Kirby Puckett, Minnesota Twins, October 26, 1991

Kirby Puckett's leadoff homer in the 11th inning of Game 6 kept his team alive for another day. The Twins wrapped up the Series with a 10-inning thriller the following night.

⑤ Rhodes's Pinch-Hit Homer Gives Giants Victory — Dusty Rhodes, New York Giants, September 29, 1954

Two innings after Willie Mays made his famous over-the-shoulder catch, Dusty Rhodes came in to pinch hit with two men on in the bottom of the 10th and knocked the first pitch he saw over the right-field fence. Rhodes's homer sparked the Giants to an upset sweep of the Cleveland Indians.

⑥ Fisk Ends 12-Inning Game 6 with Dramatic Homer — Carlton Fisk, Boston Red Sox, October 21, 1975

The sixth game of the 1975 Series ranks among the greatest of all time. With the score tied in the 12th, Carlton Fisk opened the bottom of the inning with a towering blast down the left-field line. As Fisk stood jumping and waving his arms to coax it fair, the ball ricocheted off the foul pole for a game-winning home run.

⑦ Jackson Crushes Three Homers on Three Pitches — Reggie Jackson, New York Yankees, October 18, 1977

In possibly the greatest single-game performance by a hitter, Reggie Jackson drilled three home runs in three consecutive plate appearances against three different pitchers—each one on the first pitch of the at-bat. The Yanks claimed the 1977 Series with the win.

⑧ Ruth Calls Shot — Babe Ruth, New York Yankees, October 1, 1932

Though it was one of four home runs hit by New York in the game, and one of two by "The Bambino," Babe Ruth's confident, if controversial, gesture toward the center-field bleachers before depositing a home run in that very location is the stuff of legends.

⑨ Henrich Ends Scoreless Battle with Leadoff Homer in Ninth — Tommy Henrich, New York Yankees, October 5, 1949

The Yankees and Dodgers combined to collect only six hits through eight and a half innings in the opener of the 1949 Series, until Tommy Henrich ended the dual-shutout with one swing of the bat, a leadoff homer to right field.

⑩ Ott's 10th-Inning Homer Brings Giants the Title — Mel Ott, New York Giants, October 7, 1933

The Giants and Senators were tied 3-3 after nine innings in Game 5 of the 1933 Series, and Mel Ott broke the tie in the top of the 10th with a two-out solo shot. The win gave the Giants their clinching fourth victory of the Series.

Left: Barely able to walk with his injured knees, Kirk Gibson brought a fairy tale ending to the 1988 opener. The game-winning homer came in Gibson's only appearance of the Series.

Players Homering in Their First Series At-Bat

Some ballplayers thrive under the pressure of their first World Series experience. The following 25 men stepped up to the plate for their first Series at-bat and chased away the jitters by hitting home runs.

Joe Harris, Washington Senators, 1925, Game 1
George Watkins, St. Louis Cardinals, 1930, Game 2
Mel Ott, New York Giants, 1933, Game 1
George Selkirk, New York Yankees, 1936, Game 1
Dusty Rhodes, New York Giants, 1954, Game 1
Elston Howard, New York Yankees, 1955, Game 1
Roger Maris, New York Yankees, 1960, Game 1
Don Mincher, Minnesota Twins, 1965, Game 1
Brooks Robinson, Baltimore Orioles, 1966, Game 1
Jose Santiago, Boston Red Sox, 1967, Game 1
Mickey Lolich, Detroit Tigers, 1968, Game 2
Don Buford, Baltimore Orioles, 1969, Game 1
Gene Tenace, Oakland A's, 1972, Game 1 *
Jim Mason, New York Yankees, 1976, Game 3
Doug DeCinces, Baltimore Orioles, 1979, Game 1
Amos Otis, Kansas City Royals, 1980, Game 1
Bob Watson, New York Yankees, 1981, Game 1
Jim Dwyer, Baltimore Orioles, 1983, Game 1
Jose Canseco, Oakland A's, 1988, Game 1 (grand slam)
Mickey Hatcher, Los Angeles Dodgers, 1988, Game 1
Bill Bathe, San Francisco Giants, 1989, Game 3
Eric Davis, Cincinnati Reds, 1990, Game 1
Ed Sprague, Toronto Blue Jays, 1992, Game 2
Fred McGriff, Atlanta Braves, 1995, Game 1
Andruw Jones, Atlanta Braves, 1996, Game 1 *

* Homered in first two at-bats.

Players with World Series Home Runs in Both Leagues

Enos Slaughter: St. Louis Cardinals, 1942, 1946 (2);
    New York Yankees, 1956 (1)
Bill Skowron: New York Yankees, 1955–56, 1958, 1960–61 (7);
    Los Angeles Dodgers, 1963 (1)
Roger Maris: New York Yankees, 1960–62, 1964 (5);
    St. Louis Cardinals, 1967 (1)
Frank Robinson: Cincinnati Reds, 1961 (1);
    Baltimore Orioles, 1966, 1969–71 (7)
Reggie Smith: Boston Red Sox, 1967 (2);
    Los Angeles Dodgers, 1977–78 (4)
Kirk Gibson: Detroit Tigers, 1984 (2 HR);
    Los Angeles Dodgers, 1988 (1 HR)
Matt Williams: San Francisco Giants, 1989 (1);
    Cleveland Indians, 1997 (1)

"Walk-Off" Home Runs

Home runs have won many a World Series game, but only 11 times has a homer ended a game then and there by driving in the winning run in the bottom half of the final inning.

Tommy Henrich, New York Yankees, 1949, Game 1, 9th inning, no outs, no men on base, 1-0 final
Dusty Rhodes, New York Giants, 1954, Game 1, 10th inning, one out, two men on base, 5-2 final
Eddie Mathews, Milwaukee Braves, 1957, Game 4, 10th inning, one out, one man on base, 7-5 final
Bill Mazeroski, Pittsburgh Pirates, 1960, Game 7, 9th inning, no outs, no men on base, 10-9 final (* Series winner)
Mickey Mantle, New York Yankees, 1964, Game 3, 9th inning, no outs, no men on base, 2-1 final
Carlton Fisk, Boston Red Sox, 1975, Game 6, 12th inning, no outs, no men on base, 7-6 final
Kirk Gibson, Los Angeles Dodgers, 1988, Game 1, 9th inning, two outs, one man on base, 5-4 final
Mark McGwire, Oakland A's, 1988, Game 3, 9th inning, one out, no men on base, 2-1 final
Kirby Puckett, Minnesota Twins, 1991, Game 6, 11th inning, no outs, no men on base, 4-3 final
Joe Carter, Toronto Blue Jays, 1993, Game 6, 9th inning, one out, two men on base, 8-6 final (* Series winner)
Chad Curtis, New York Yankees, 1999, Game 3, 10th inning, no outs, no men on base, 6-5 final

Left: Joy in Beantown. Carlton Fisk leaps for joy after his 12th-inning home run stayed fair, giving his Red Sox a dramatic Game 6 victory at Fenway in 1975.

Right: Tommy Henrich reaches home plate after winning Game 1 of the 1949 Series with a leadoff homer in the ninth. It was the first Series game to end with a home run.

World Series Grand Slams

More than 700 home runs have been hit in the 564 World Series games played through 2000; 17 were knocked with the bases full. Only Berra's and Canseco's grand slams came in losing efforts.

Elmer Smith, Cleveland Indians, 1920, Game 5, 1st inning
Tony Lazzeri, New York Yankees, 1936, Game 2, 3rd inning
Gil McDougald, New York Yankees, 1951, Game 5, 3rd inning
Mickey Mantle, New York Yankees, 1953, Game 5, 3rd inning
Yogi Berra, New York Yankees, 1956, Game 2, 2nd inning
Bill Skowron, New York Yankees, 1956, Game 7, 7th inning
Bobby Richardson, New York Yankees, 1960, Game 3, 1st inning
Chuck Hiller, San Francisco Giants, 1962, Game 4, 7th inning
Ken Boyer, St. Louis Cardinals, 1964, Game 4, 6th inning
Joe Pepitone, New York Yankees, 1964, Game 6, 8th inning
Jim Northrup, Detroit Tigers, 1968, Game 6, 3rd inning
Dave McNally, Baltimore Orioles, 1970, Game 3, 6th inning
Dan Gladden, Minnesota Twins, 1987, Game 1, 4th inning

Kent Hrbek, Minnesota Twins, 1987, Game 6, 6th inning
Jose Canseco, Oakland A's, 1988, Game 1, 2nd inning
Lonnie Smith, Atlanta Braves, 1992, Game 5, 5th inning
Tino Martinez, New York Yankees, 1998, Game 1, 7th inning

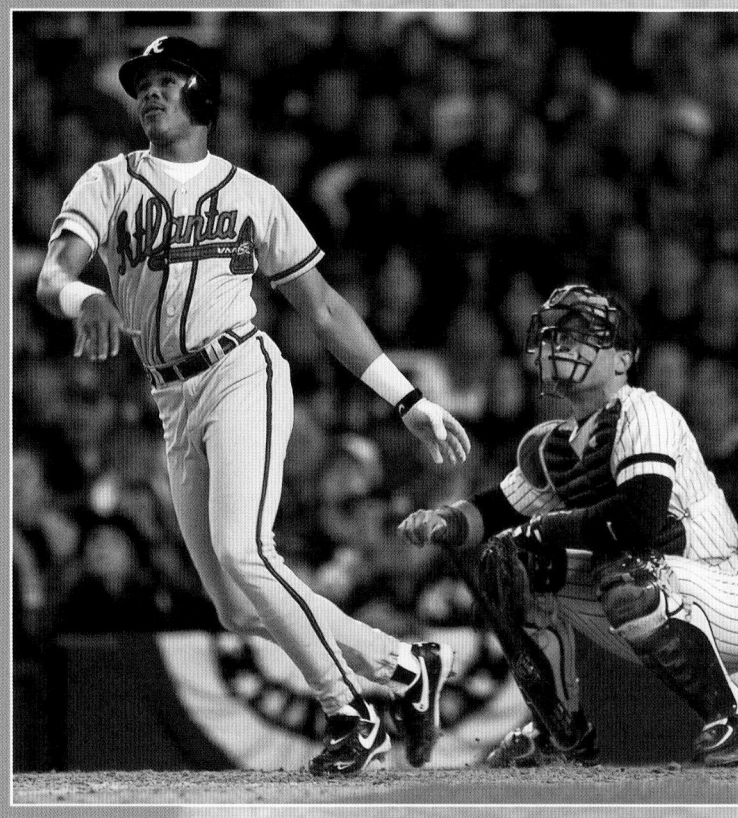

Above: Nineteen-year-old Andruw Jones admires his second homer of the opening game of the 1996 Series. Jones, the youngest player to go yard in a World Series, became only the second player to hit home runs in his first two Series at-bats.

Single-Series Home Run Records by Decade

The Yankees and Dodgers combined to hit a record 17 home runs during the 1977 Series. The most productive home run World Series from each decade are listed here.

	One Team	Two Teams
1900s	Boston Red Sox, 1903; Pittsburgh Pirates, 1909; Detroit Tigers, 1909 — 2	Pittsburgh Pirates and Detroit Tigers, 1909 — 4
1910s	Boston Red Sox, 1915 — 3	Boston Red Sox and Philadelphia Phillies, 1915 — 4
1920s	New York Yankees, 1928 — 9	Pittsburgh Pirates and Washington Senators, 1925 — 12
1930s	New York Yankees, 1932 — 8	New York Yankees and Chicago Cubs, 1932; New York Yankees and New York Giants, 1936 — 11
1940s	Detroit Tigers, 1940; Boston Red Sox, 1946; New York Yankees, 1947; Cleveland Indians, 1948; Boston Braves, 1948; Brooklyn Dodgers, 1949 — 4	Cleveland Indians and Boston Braves, 1948 — 8
1950s	New York Yankees, 1956 — 12	New York Yankees and Brooklyn Dodgers, 1953 and 1955 — 17
1960s	New York Yankees, 1960 and 1964 — 10	St. Louis Cardinals and New York Yankees, 1964; Detroit Tigers and St. Louis Cardinals, 1968 — 15
1970s	Baltimore Orioles, 1970 — 10	New York Yankees and Los Angeles Dodgers, 1977 — 17
1980s	Oakland A's, 1989 — 9	Oakland A's and San Francisco Giants, 1989 — 13
1990s	Minnesota Twins, 1991; Atlanta Braves, 1991 and 1995; Florida Marlins, 1997 — 8	Minnesota Twins and Atlanta Braves, 1991 — 16

New York Yankees (4) vs. Los Angeles Dodgers (2)

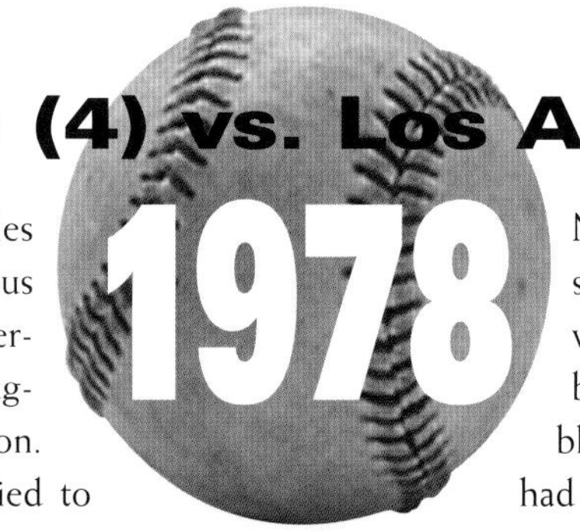

The New York Yankees had to overcome a few obstacles to repeat in 1978. Manager Billy Martin's tempestuous relationship with owner George Steinbrenner and superstar Reggie Jackson, coupled with the club's on-field struggles, led to Martin's firing midway through the season. After Bob Lemon took over as skipper, the team rallied to overcome a 14-game deficit to the Red Sox and finish in a tie for first. They topped Boston in a dramatic one-game playoff and defeated the Royals in the ALCS for the third year in a row to set up a World Series rematch with Los Angeles. The Dodgers had used a late-season run to seize their second straight pennant with the same lineup as the year before. In the opening game of the Series, LA roughed up four Yankee pitchers for 11 runs, and New York fell deeper in the hole with a 4-3 loss in Game 2. Jackson drove in three runs for New York in the second game, but Ron Cey's RBI single and three-run homer gave the Dodgers the edge. With two men on in the ninth, 21-year-old rookie pitcher Bob Welch came in for LA and struck out Jackson in an epic nine-pitch battle to end the game. The Yanks won Game 3 behind the pitching of Cy Young winner Ron Guidry, though it was Graig Nettles's fielding at third that made the difference. Several sensational plays by Nettles, including two with the bases loaded, helped save the 5-1 victory. In Game 4, Reggie Smith's three-run homer had LA ahead 3-1 when

New York put two runners on base with one out in the sixth. Lou Piniella hit a low liner to shortstop Bill Russell, who let the ball drop from his glove, stepped on second base and threw to first for a possible inning-ending double play. The throw hit Reggie Jackson in the hip (Jackson had stopped in the base paths after being forced out) and ricocheted into the outfield, allowing Piniella to reach first and Thurman Munson to come around to score. Russell and the Dodgers argued furiously that Jackson deliberately stuck his hip in the way and that Piniella should be called out due to interference. Los Angeles lost the argument, and after the Yanks tied the score, LA ultimately lost the game. Rich "Goose" Gossage retired six straight in the final two innings, and in the bottom of the 10th, Piniella singled home the winning run, tying the Series. The dramatic, if controversial, Game 4 win inspired the Yankees, as they exploded for 18 hits and 12 runs in Game 5 and then marched to another title with a 7-2 victory in Game 6. Jackson provided a two-run homer in the final game to cap another awesome October, but light-hitting infielders Bucky Dent and Brian Doyle were the Series' leading batters, with averages of .417 and .438, respectively. It was New York's tenth repeat championship in their history.

Left: A frustrated Reggie Jackson yells after going down on strikes against Bob Welch to end Game 2 of the 1978 Series.

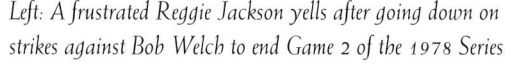

1978 WORLD SERIES COMPOSITE STATISTICS

NEW YORK YANKEES/Bob Lemon, Manager

Player	pos	G	AB	R	H	2B	3B	HR	RBI	BB	SO	SB	BA	SA	E	FPct
Jim Beattie	p	1	0	0	0	0	0	0	0	0	0	0	—	—	0	1.000
Paul Blair	cf-ph-pr	6	8	2	3	1	0	0	1	4	0	0	.375	.500	0	1.000
Chris Chambliss	1b	3	11	1	2	0	0	0	1	1	1	0	.182	.182	0	1.000
Ken Clay	p	1	0	0	0	0	0	0	0	0	0	0	—	—	0	—
Bucky Dent	ss	6	24	3	10	1	0	0	7	1	2	0	.417	.458	2	.923
Brian Doyle	2b	6	16	4	7	1	0	0	2	0	0	0	.438	.500	0	1.000
Ed Figueroa	p	2	0	0	0	0	0	0	0	0	0	0	—	—	0	—
Rich "Goose" Gossage	p	3	0	0	0	0	0	0	0	0	0	0	—	—	0	—
Ron Guidry	p	1	0	0	0	0	0	0	0	0	0	0	—	—	0	1.000
Mike Heath	c	1	0	0	0	0	0	0	0	0	0	0	—	—	0	—
Jim "Catfish" Hunter	p	2	0	0	0	0	0	0	0	0	0	0	—	—	0	1.000
Reggie Jackson	dh	6	23	2	9	1	0	2	8	3	7	0	.391	.696	—	—
Cliff Johnson	ph	2	2	0	0	0	0	0	0	0	1	0	.000	.000	—	—
Jay Johnstone	rf	2	0	0	0	0	0	0	0	0	0	0	—	—	0	1.000
Paul Lindblad	p	1	0	0	0	0	0	0	0	0	0	0	—	—	0	—
Thurman Munson	c	6	25	5	8	3	0	0	7	3	7	1	.320	.440	0	1.000
Graig Nettles	3b	6	25	2	4	0	0	0	1	0	6	0	.160	.160	0	1.000
Lou Piniella	rf	6	25	3	7	0	0	0	4	0	0	1	.280	.280	0	1.000
Mickey Rivers	cf-ph	5	18	2	6	0	0	0	1	0	2	1	.333	.333	0	1.000
Jim Spencer	1b-ph	4	12	3	2	0	0	0	2	4	0	0	.167	.167	0	1.000
Fred Stanley	2b	3	5	0	1	1	0	0	0	1	0	0	.200	.400	0	1.000
Gary Thomasson	lf-cf	3	4	0	1	0	0	0	0	0	1	0	.250	.250	0	1.000
Dick Tidrow	p	2	0	0	0	0	0	0	0	0	0	0	—	—	0	—
Roy White	lf	6	24	9	8	0	0	1	4	4	5	2	.333	.458	0	1.000
Totals		**6**	**222**	**36**	**68**	**8**	**0**	**3**	**34**	**16**	**40**	**5**	**.306**	**.383**	**2**	**.991**

Pitcher	G	GS	CG	IP	H	R	ER	BB	SO	W-L	Sv	ERA
Jim Beattie	1	1	1	9	9	2	2	4	8	1-0	0	2.00
Ken Clay	1	0	0	2⅓	4	4	3	2	2	0-0	0	11.57
Ed Figueroa	2	2	0	6⅔	9	6	6	5	2	0-1	0	8.10
Rich "Goose" Gossage	3	0	0	6	1	0	0	1	4	1-0	0	0.00
Ron Guidry	1	1	1	9	8	1	1	7	4	1-0	0	1.00
Jim "Catfish" Hunter	2	2	0	13	13	6	6	1	5	1-1	0	4.15
Paul Lindblad	1	0	0	2⅓	4	3	3	0	1	0-0	0	11.57
Dick Tidrow	2	0	0	4⅔	4	1	1	0	5	0-0	0	1.93
Totals	**6**	**6**	**2**	**53**	**52**	**23**	**22**	**20**	**31**	**4-2**	**0**	**3.74**

LOS ANGELES DODGERS/Tommy Lasorda, Manager

Player	pos	G	AB	R	H	2B	3B	HR	RBI	BB	SO	SB	BA	SA	E	FPct
Dusty Baker	lf	6	21	2	5	0	0	1	1	1	3	0	.238	.381	0	1.000
Ron Cey	3b	6	21	2	6	0	0	1	4	3	3	0	.286	.429	0	1.000
Vic Davalillo	ph-dh	2	3	0	1	0	0	0	0	0	0	0	.333	.333	—	—
Joe Ferguson	c	2	4	1	2	2	0	0	0	0	1	0	.500	1.000	1	.917
Terry Forster	p	3	0	0	0	0	0	0	0	0	0	0	—	—	0	1.000
Steve Garvey	1b	6	24	1	5	1	0	0	0	1	7	1	.208	.250	1	.984
Jerry Grote	c	2	0	0	0	0	0	0	0	0	0	0	—	—	0	1.000
Burt Hooton	p	2	0	0	0	0	0	0	0	0	0	0	—	—	0	1.000
Charlie Hough	p	2	0	0	0	0	0	0	0	0	0	0	—	—	0	1.000
Tommy John	p	2	0	0	0	0	0	0	0	0	0	0	—	—	0	1.000
Lee Lacy	dh	4	14	0	2	0	0	0	1	1	3	0	.143	.143	—	—
Davey Lopes	2b	6	26	7	8	0	0	3	7	2	1	2	.308	.654	1	.967
Rick Monday	cf-dh	5	13	2	2	1	0	0	0	4	3	0	.154	.231	0	1.000
Manny Mota	ph	1	0	0	0	0	0	0	0	1	0	0	—	—	—	—
Bill North	ph-cf	4	8	2	1	1	0	0	2	1	0	1	.125	.250	0	1.000
Johnny Oates	ph-c	1	1	0	1	0	0	0	0	1	0	0	1.000	1.000	0	1.000
Doug Rau	p	1	0	0	0	0	0	0	0	0	0	0	—	—	0	1.000
Lance Rautzhan	p	2	0	0	0	0	0	0	0	0	0	0	—	—	0	—
Bill Russell	ss	6	26	1	11	2	0	0	2	2	2	1	.423	.500	3	.912
Reggie Smith	rf	6	25	3	5	0	0	1	5	2	6	0	.200	.320	1	.923
Don Sutton	p	2	0	0	0	0	0	0	0	0	0	0	—	—	0	—
Bob Welch	p	3	0	0	0	0	0	0	0	0	0	0	—	—	0	—
Steve Yeager	c	5	13	2	3	1	0	0	1	1	2	0	.231	.308	0	1.000
Totals		**6**	**199**	**23**	**52**	**8**	**0**	**6**	**22**	**20**	**31**	**5**	**.261**	**.392**	**7**	**.969**

Pitcher	G	GS	CG	IP	H	R	ER	BB	SO	W-L	Sv	ERA
Terry Forster	3	0	0	4	5	0	0	1	6	0-0	0	0.00
Burt Hooton	2	2	0	8⅓	13	7	6	3	6	1-1	0	6.48
Charlie Hough	2	0	0	5⅓	10	5	5	2	5	0-0	0	8.44
Tommy John	2	2	0	14⅔	14	8	5	4	6	1-0	0	3.07
Doug Rau	1	0	0	2	1	0	0	3	0	0-0	0	0.00
Lance Rautzhan	2	0	0	2	4	3	3	0	0	0-0	0	13.50
Don Sutton	2	2	0	12	17	10	10	4	8	0-2	0	7.50
Bob Welch	3	0	0	4⅓	4	3	3	2	6	0-1	1	6.23
Totals	**6**	**6**	**0**	**52⅔**	**68**	**36**	**32**	**16**	**40**	**2-4**	**1**	**5.47**

Series MVP: Bucky Dent, New York Yankees. **Series Outstanding Pitcher:** Rich "Goose" Gossage, New York Yankees. **Average Length of Game:** 2 hours, 47 minutes. **Total Attendance:** 337,304. **Average Attendance:** 56,217 (56,447 at Yankee Stadium; 55,988 at Dodger Stadium). **Umpires:** Joe Brinkman (AL), Bill Haller (AL), John Kibler (NL), Frank Pulli (NL), Marty Springstead (AL), Ed Vargo (NL). **Winning Player's Share:** $31,236. **Losing Player's Share:** $25,483.

Reggie Jackson's two home runs in 1978 gave him the record for most homers in two consecutive World Series (7).

Above: Picking up where he left off a year earlier, Reggie Jackson blasts one into the right-field seats at Dodger Stadium. Los Angeles won the first game easily, 11-5.

Below: In a controversial play in Game 4, shortstop Bill Russell heads toward second base to force out Reggie Jackson running from first, while New York's Thurman Munson takes off for third. After securing the first out on the play, Russell's throw to first base hit Jackson on the hip, allowing Munson to score.

Above: Dodger catcher Steve Yeager extends a hand to Bob Welch after the rookie struck out Reggie Jackson in a tough battle in the ninth inning of Game 2.

Below: Brian Doyle's RBI double in the second inning of Game 6 was just one of many key—and surprising—contributions by the infielder.

Game 1 Tuesday, October 10 at Dodger Stadium, Los Angeles

	1	2	3	4	5	6	7	8	9	R	H	E
New York Yankees	0	0	0	0	0	0	3	2	0	5	9	1
Los Angeles Dodgers	0	3	0	3	1	0	3	1	x	11	15	2

Pitchers NY **Ed Figueroa** (L, 0-1), IP 1⅔, H 5, R 3, ER 3, BB 1, SO 0; **Ken Clay**, IP 2⅓, H 4, R 4, ER 3, BB 2, SO 2; **Paul Lindblad**, IP 2⅓, H 4, R 3, ER 3, BB 0, SO 1; **Dick Tidrow**, IP 1⅔, H 2, R 1, ER 1, BB 0, SO 1

LA **Tommy John** (W, 1-0), IP 7⅔, H 8, R 5, ER 3, BB 2, SO 4; **Terry Forster**, IP 1⅓, H 1, R 0, ER 0, BB 0, SO 3

Top Performers at the Plate

NY **Reggie Jackson**, 3 for 4, 1 R, 1 RBI

LA **Dusty Baker**, 3 for 4, 2 R, 1 RBI; **Davey Lopes**, 2 for 5, 2 R, 5 RBI, 2 HR

2B-NY/Stanley; LA/Monday, North, Russell. **HR**-NY/Jackson; LA/Baker, Lopes 2. **Time** 2:48. **Attendance** 55,997.

Game 2 Wednesday, October 11 at Dodger Stadium, Los Angeles

	1	2	3	4	5	6	7	8	9	R	H	E
New York Yankees	0	0	2	0	0	0	1	0	0	3	11	0
Los Angeles Dodgers	0	0	0	1	0	3	0	0	x	4	7	0

Pitchers NY **Jim "Catfish" Hunter** (L, 0-1), IP 6, H 7, R 4, ER 4, BB 0, SO 2; **Rich "Goose" Gossage**, IP 2, H 0, R 0, ER 0, BB 0, SO 0

LA **Burt Hooton** (W, 1-0), IP 6, H 8, R 3, ER 3, BB 1, SO 5; **Terry Forster**, IP 2⅓, H 3, R 0, ER 0, BB 1, SO 3; **Bob Welch** (Sv, 1), IP ⅔, H 0, R 0, ER 0, BB 0, SO 1

Top Performers at the Plate

NY **Reggie Jackson**, 1 for 4, 3 RBI, 1 HBP; **Roy White**, 2 for 5, 2 R

LA **Ron Cey**, 2 for 3, 1 R, 4 RBI

2B-NY/Blair, Jackson, Munson. **HR**-LA/Cey. **SB**-NY/White. **Time** 2:37. **Attendance** 55,982.

Game 3 Friday, October 13 at Yankee Stadium, New York

	1	2	3	4	5	6	7	8	9	R	H	E
Los Angeles Dodgers	0	0	1	0	0	0	0	0	0	1	8	0
New York Yankees	1	1	0	0	0	0	3	0	x	5	10	1

Pitchers LA **Don Sutton** (L, 0-1), IP 6⅓, H 9, R 5, ER 5, BB 3, SO 2; **Lance Rautzhan**, IP ⅔, H 1, R 0, ER 0, BB 0, SO 0; **Charlie Hough**, IP 1, H 0, R 0, ER 0, BB 0, SO 0

NY **Ron Guidry** (W, 1-0), IP 9, H 8, R 1, ER 1, BB 7, SO 4

Top Performers at the Plate

LA **Dusty Baker**, 2 for 3, 1 BB; **Bill Russell**, 2 for 4, 1 R, 1 BB

NY **Mickey Rivers**, 3 for 4; **Roy White**, 1 for 3, 2 R, 1 RBI, 1 BB

2B-LA/Garvey. **HR**-NY/White. **SB**-LA/North; NY/Piniella. **Time** 2:27. **Attendance** 56,447.

Game 4 Saturday, October 14 at Yankee Stadium, New York

	1	2	3	4	5	6	7	8	9	10	R	H	E
Los Angeles Dodgers	0	0	0	0	3	0	0	0	0	0	3	6	1
New York Yankees	0	0	0	0	0	2	0	1	0	1	4	9	0

Pitchers LA **Tommy John**, IP 7, H 6, R 3, ER 2, BB 2, SO 2; **Terry Forster**, IP ⅓, H 1, R 0, ER 0, BB 0, SO 0; **Bob Welch** (L, 0-1), IP 2⅓, H 2, R 1, ER 1, BB 1, SO 3

NY **Ed Figueroa**, IP 5, H 4, R 3, ER 3, BB 4, SO 2; **Dick Tidrow**, IP 3, H 2, R 0, ER 0, BB 0, SO 4; **Rich "Goose" Gossage** (W, 1-0), IP 2, H 0, R 0, ER 0, BB 1, SO 2

Top Performers at the Plate

LA **Bill Russell**, 2 for 5; **Reggie Smith**, 1 for 4, 1 R, 3 RBI, 1 BB

NY **Thurman Munson**, 2 for 3, 1 R, 1 RBI, 2 BB; **Roy White**, 1 for 3, 2 R, 1 BB, 1 SH

2B-LA/Yeager; NY/Munson. **HR**-LA/Smith. **SB**-LA/Garvey; NY/Munson. **Time** 3:17. **Attendance** 56,445.

Game 5 Sunday, October 15 at Yankee Stadium, New York

	1	2	3	4	5	6	7	8	9	R	H	E
Los Angeles Dodgers	1	0	1	0	0	0	0	0	0	2	9	3
New York Yankees	0	0	4	3	0	0	4	1	x	12	18	0

Pitchers LA **Burt Hooton** (L, 1-1), IP 2⅓, H 5, R 4, ER 3, BB 2, SO 1; **Lance Rautzhan**, IP 1⅓, H 3, R 3, ER 3, BB 0, SO 0; **Charlie Hough**, IP 4⅓, H 10, R 5, ER 5, BB 2, SO 5

NY **Jim Beattie** (W, 1-0), IP 9, H 9, R 2, ER 2, BB 4, SO 8

Top Performers at the Plate

LA **Davey Lopes**, 2 for 4, 2 R, 1 BB; **Bill Russell**, 2 for 5, 1 RBI

NY **Thurman Munson**, 3 for 5, 1 R, 5 RBI; **Roy White**, 2 for 5, 2 R, 3 RBI

2B-LA/Russell; NY/Dent, Munson. **SB**-LA/Lopes, Russell; NY/Rivers, White. **Time** 2:56. **Attendance** 56,448.

Game 6 Tuesday, October 17 at Dodger Stadium, Los Angeles

	1	2	3	4	5	6	7	8	9	R	H	E
New York Yankees	0	3	0	0	0	2	2	0	0	7	11	0
Los Angeles Dodgers	1	0	1	0	0	0	0	0	0	2	7	1

Pitchers NY **Jim "Catfish" Hunter** (W, 1-1), IP 7, H 6, R 2, ER 2, BB 1, SO 3; **Rich "Goose" Gossage**, IP 2, H 1, R 0, ER 0, BB 0, SO 2

LA **Don Sutton** (L, 0-2), IP 5⅔, H 8, R 5, ER 5, BB 1, SO 6; **Bob Welch**, IP 1⅓, H 2, R 2, ER 2, BB 1, SO 2; **Doug Rau**, IP 2, H 1, R 0, ER 0, BB 0, SO 3

Top Performers at the Plate

NY **Bucky Dent**, 3 for 4, 3 RBI; **Brian Doyle**, 3 for 4, 2 R, 2 RBI

LA **Joe Ferguson**, 2 for 3, 1 R, 2 2B; **Davey Lopes**, 2 for 4, 1 R, 2 RBI

2B-NY/Doyle; LA/Ferguson 2. **HR**-NY/Jackson; LA/Lopes. **SB**-LA/Lopes. **Time** 2:34. **Attendance** 55,985.

The 1978 New York Yankees were the first team to lose the first two games and come back to sweep the next four.

Pittsburgh Pirates (4) vs. Baltimore Orioles (3)

The 1970s came to close with a disco tune that captured the spirit of baseball's world champions. "We Are Family" was the slogan of a closely knit Pirate club led by 39-year-old Willie "Pops" Stargell. Pops belted 32 homers and brought home MVP honors in 1979, as Pittsburgh won its first pennant in eight years. In a reprise of the 1971 Fall Classic, the Bucs paired up with Earl Weaver's Baltimore Orioles in the Series. The 23 wins by Cy Young winner Mike Flanagan paced a tough pitching staff in Baltimore, and three Orioles stroked 25 or more home runs, led by Ken Singleton's 35. The Orioles wasted no time displaying their offensive prowess in the opening game, breaking out with five runs in the first inning, including a two-run clout by Doug DeCinces. Pittsburgh chipped away, and Stargell brought them within a run with a leadoff homer in the eighth, but Flanagan got Stargell to fly out in the ninth with a runner on second to escape without further damage. Starters Bert Blyleven and Jim Palmer battled in a 2-2 tie in Game 2. Bill Madlock drove in both Pirate runs with a second-inning single, and Eddie Murray brought in two for Baltimore on a solo homer and an RBI double. Pittsburgh won the game with two outs in the ninth when Manny Sanguillen hit a

pinch-single against Baltimore's ace reliever Don Stanhouse with runners on first and second. Back home at Three Rivers Stadium, the Pirates took an early lead in Game 3, but the Orioles quickly turned the tables. They scored two in the third on Benny Ayala's homer, and five more came across in the fourth inning, with Kiko Garcia chipping in a bases-loaded triple for one of his four hits in the game. Baltimore used another big inning in Game 4 to take a formidable lead in the Series. After Pittsburgh mounted a 6-3 advantage behind six doubles and Stargell's two-run homer, the Orioles stormed back in the top of the eighth. Bases-loaded doubles from pinch hitters John Lowenstein and Terry Crowley brought in two runs apiece, and a one-out RBI single by pitcher Tim Stoddard secured the 9-6 victory. Stoddard's hit was in his first Major League at-bat.

Only three teams had ever come back from a three-games-to-one deficit in the World Series, and the Pirates would have to win one at home and two on the road to do it. They took care of business in Pittsburgh in Game 5, topping Flanagan 7-1. Pittsburgh starter Jim Rooker held the Orioles to three hits before Blyleven came on in relief and shut them out for four innings. Madlock gave his team four singles in four times at bat, and Tim Foli drove in three runs in the last two innings. John Candelaria and Pittsburgh's lanky side-armer Kent

Pittsburgh's Tim Foli set a record in the 1979 Series by going to the plate 33 times and not striking out once.

Above: Willie "Pops" Stargell was the emotional leader for the 1979 Pirates—and his clutch homer in Game 7 was appreciated by his teammates as well.

Left: After collecting his fourth hit of Game 1, Dave Parker reaches second when shortstop Mark Belanger dropped the throw on Parker's stolen-base attempt.

Above: Pittsburgh shortstop Tim Foli lies on the ground after throwing out Doug DeCinces on a slow grounder in Game 2. Above inset: Phil Garner dives to stop Al Bumbry's liner from getting through to the outfield, helping to prevent Baltimore from scoring in the fifth inning of Game 3.

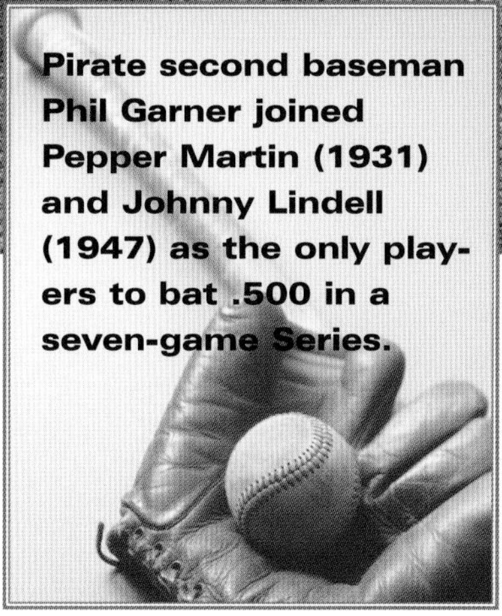

Pirate second baseman Phil Garner joined Pepper Martin (1931) and Johnny Lindell (1947) as the only players to bat .500 in a seven-game Series.

Above inset: Reserve player Manny Sanguillen wasn't used to getting much attention around the locker room, but when he won Game 2 with a pinch-single in the ninth, he was a popular attraction.

Above: Kiko Garcia went 4 for 4 in Game 3. This fourth-inning triple scored three runs for the Orioles.

Tekulve combined to shut Baltimore out in Game 6. Palmer kept the Pirates scoreless through six, but three singles and a sacrifice fly produced two runs in the seventh; two more runs in the eighth made for a 4-0 final. Rich Dauer's leadoff blast in the third inning of Game 7 put the Orioles on the board first in the final game. The Pirates failed to score off McGregor until Stargell walloped a homer with a man on in the sixth to give them the lead. While the Orioles used five pitchers in the last inning alone, three Pirate relievers combined to hold Baltimore scoreless in the final five innings, with Tekulve retiring the side in the ninth for his third save. Phil Garner went 1 for 3 in the final game to give him 12 hits in 24 at-bats, but the Series MVP went to Stargell. Like he had been all year, Pops was the leader of the Family in October, supplying three homers, seven RBI and a .400 average.

1979 WORLD SERIES COMPOSITE STATISTICS

PITTSBURGH PIRATES/Chuck Tanner, Manager

Player	pos	G	AB	R	H	2B	3B	HR	RBI	BB	SO	SB	BA	SA	E	FPct
Matt Alexander	pr-lf	1	0	0	0	0	0	0	0	0	0	0	—	—	0	—
Jim Bibby	p	2	4	0	0	0	0	0	0	0	1	0	.000	.000	0	1.000
Bert Blyleven	p	2	3	0	0	0	0	0	0	0	0	0	.000	.000	0	1.000
John Candelaria	p	2	3	0	1	0	0	0	0	0	2	0	.333	.333	0	1.000
Mike Easler	ph	2	1	0	0	0	0	0	0	1	0	0	.000	.000	—	—
Tim Foli	ss	7	30	6	10	1	1	0	3	2	0	0	.333	.433	3	.930
Phil Garner	2b	7	24	4	12	4	0	0	5	3	1	0	.500	.667	2	.956
Grant Jackson	p	4	1	0	0	0	0	0	0	0	0	0	.000	.000	0	1.000
Bruce Kison	p	1	0	0	0	0	0	0	0	0	0	0	—	—	0	1.000
Lee Lacy	ph	4	4	0	1	0	0	0	0	0	1	0	.250	.250	—	—
Bill Madlock	3b	7	24	2	9	1	0	0	3	5	1	0	.375	.417	1	.929
John Milner	lf-ph	3	9	2	3	1	0	0	1	2	0	0	.333	.444	0	1.000
Omar Moreno	cf	7	33	4	11	2	0	0	3	1	7	0	.333	.394	0	1.000
Steve Nicosia	c	4	16	1	1	0	0	0	0	0	2	0	.063	.063	0	1.000
Ed Ott	c	3	12	2	4	1	0	0	3	0	2	0	.333	.417	0	1.000
Dave Parker	rf	7	29	2	10	3	0	0	4	2	7	0	.345	.448	1	.933
Bill Robinson	lf	7	19	2	5	1	0	0	2	0	4	0	.263	.316	0	1.000
Don Robinson	p	4	0	0	0	0	0	0	0	0	0	0	—	—	0	1.000
Enrique Romo	p	2	1	0	0	0	0	0	0	0	0	0	.000	.000	0	1.000
Jim Rooker	p	2	2	0	0	0	0	0	0	0	1	0	.000	.000	0	1.000
Manny Sanguillen	ph	3	3	0	1	0	0	0	1	0	0	0	.333	.333	—	—
Willie Stargell	1b	7	30	7	12	4	0	3	7	0	6	0	.400	.833	2	.968
Rennie Stennett	ph	1	1	0	1	0	0	0	0	0	0	0	1.000	1.000	—	—
Kent Tekulve	p	5	2	0	0	0	0	0	0	0	0	0	.000	.000	0	1.000
Totals		7	251	32	81	18	1	3	32	16	35	0	.323	.438	9	.967

Pitcher	G	GS	CG	IP	H	R	ER	BB	SO	W-L	Sv	ERA
Jim Bibby	2	2	0	10⅓	10	4	3	2	10	0-0	0	2.61
Bert Blyleven	2	1	0	10	8	2	2	3	4	1-0	0	1.80
John Candelaria	2	2	0	9	14	6	5	2	4	1-1	0	5.00
Grant Jackson	4	0	0	4⅔	1	0	0	2	2	1-0	0	0.00
Bruce Kison	1	1	0	⅓	3	5	4	2	0	0-1	0	108.00
Don Robinson	4	0	0	5	4	3	3	6	3	1-0	0	5.40
Enrique Romo	2	0	0	4⅔	5	2	2	3	4	0-0	0	3.86
Jim Rooker	2	1	0	8⅔	5	1	1	3	4	0-0	0	1.04
Kent Tekulve	5	0	0	9⅓	4	3	3	10	10	0-1	3	2.89
Totals	7	7	0	62	54	26	23	26	41	4-3	3	3.34

BALTIMORE ORIOLES/Earl Weaver, Manager

Player	pos	G	AB	R	H	2B	3B	HR	RBI	BB	SO	SB	BA	SA	E	FPct
Benny Ayala	lf-ph	4	6	1	2	0	0	1	2	1	0	0	.333	.833	0	1.000
Mark Belanger	ss-pr	5	6	1	0	0	0	0	0	1	1	0	.000	.000	1	.909
Al Bumbry	cf-ph	7	21	3	3	0	0	0	1	2	1	0	.143	.143	1	.938
Terry Crowley	ph	5	4	0	1	1	0	0	2	1	0	0	.250	.500	—	—
Rich Dauer	2b-ph	6	17	2	5	1	0	1	1	1	0	1	.294	.529	0	1.000
Doug DeCinces	3b	7	25	2	5	0	0	1	3	5	5	1	.200	.320	3	.903
Rick Dempsey	c	7	21	3	6	2	0	0	0	1	3	0	.286	.381	0	1.000
Mike Flanagan	p	3	5	0	0	0	0	0	1	2	0	0	.000	.000	0	1.000
Kiko Garcia	ss	6	20	4	8	2	1	0	6	1	3	0	.400	.600	1	.964
Pat Kelly	ph	5	4	0	1	0	0	0	0	1	1	0	.250	.250	—	—
John Lowenstein	lf-ph	6	13	2	3	1	0	0	3	1	3	0	.231	.308	1	.857
Dennis Martinez	p	2	0	0	0	0	0	0	0	0	0	0	—	—	0	1.000
Tippy Martinez	p	3	0	0	0	0	0	0	0	0	0	0	—	—	0	—
Lee May	ph	2	1	0	0	0	0	0	0	0	1	0	.000	.000	—	—
Scott McGregor	p	2	4	1	0	0	0	0	0	0	2	1	.000	.000	0	1.000
Eddie Murray	1b	7	26	3	4	1	0	1	2	4	4	1	.154	.308	0	1.000
Jim Palmer	p	2	4	0	0	0	0	0	0	3	0	0	.000	.000	0	1.000
Gary Roenicke	lf-cf-ph	6	16	1	2	1	0	0	0	6	0	0	.125	.188	0	1.000
Ken Singleton	rf	7	28	1	10	1	0	0	2	2	5	0	.357	.393	0	1.000
Dave Skaggs	c	1	3	1	1	0	0	0	0	0	0	0	.333	.333	0	1.000
Billy Smith	2b-ph	4	7	1	2	0	0	0	0	2	0	0	.286	.286	0	1.000
Don Stanhouse	p	3	0	0	0	0	0	0	0	0	0	0	—	—	1	.000
Sammy Stewart	p	1	1	0	0	0	0	0	0	0	1	0	.000	.000	—	—
Tim Stoddard	p	4	1	0	1	0	0	0	1	0	0	0	1.000	1.000	1	.833
Steve Stone	p	1	0	0	0	0	0	0	0	0	0	0	—	—	0	—
Totals		7	233	26	54	10	1	4	23	26	41	2	.232	.335	9	.968

Pitcher	G	GS	CG	IP	H	R	ER	BB	SO	W-L	Sv	ERA
Mike Flanagan	3	2	1	15	18	7	5	2	13	1-1	0	3.00
Dennis Martinez	2	1	0	2	6	4	4	0	0	0-0	0	18.00
Tippy Martinez	3	0	0	1⅓	3	1	1	1	0	0-0	0	6.75
Scott McGregor	2	2	1	17	16	6	6	2	8	1-1	0	3.18
Jim Palmer	2	2	0	15	18	6	6	5	8	0-1	0	3.60
Don Stanhouse	3	0	0	2	6	3	3	3	0	0-1	0	13.50
Sammy Stewart	1	0	0	2⅔	4	0	0	1	0	0-0	0	0.00
Tim Stoddard	4	0	0	5	6	3	3	1	3	1-0	0	5.40
Steve Stone	1	0	0	2	4	2	2	2	2	0-0	0	9.00
Totals	7	7	2	62	81	32	30	16	35	3-4	0	4.35

Series MVP: Willie Stargell, Pittsburgh Pirates. **Series Outstanding Pitcher:** Kent Tekulve, Pittsburgh Pirates. **Average Length of Game:** 3 hours, 4 minutes. **Total Attendance:** 367,597. **Average Attendance:** 52,514 (50,884 at Three Rivers Stadium; 53,737 at Memorial Stadium). **Umpires:** Bob Engel (NL), Russ Goetz (AL), Jim McKean (AL), Jerry Neudecker (AL), Paul Runge (NL), Terry Tata (NL). **Winning Player's Share:** $28,264. **Losing Player's Share:** $22,114.

Left: With an appropriate statistic on the scoreboard in the background—"Willie has hit 20 or more home runs 15 times in his ML career"—Stargell circles the bases behind pitcher Scott McGregor after giving Pittsburgh the lead in Game 7 with a two-run homer.

Right: With his awkward sidearm delivery, reliever Kent Tekulve was effective against Baltimore in the Series, earning him three saves.

Below: The Family Wins! Kent Tekulve and catcher Steve Nicosia celebrate the Pirates' Game 7 win in 1979.

Game 1   Wednesday, October 10 at Memorial Stadium, Baltimore

	1	2	3	4	5	6	7	8	9	R	H	E
Pittsburgh Pirates	0	0	0	1	0	2	0	1	0	4	11	3
Baltimore Orioles	5	0	0	0	0	0	0	x		5	6	3

Pitchers   Pit   Bruce Kison (L, 0-1), IP ⅓, H 3, R 5, ER 4, BB 2, SO 0; Jim Rooker, IP 3⅔, H 2, R 0, ER 0, BB 1, SO 2; Enrique Romo, IP 1, H 0, R 0, ER 0, BB 2, SO 0; Don Robinson, IP 2, H 0, R 0, ER 0, BB 1, SO 1; Grant Jackson, IP 1, H 1, R 0, ER 0, BB 0, SO 1
Bal   Mike Flanagan (W, 1-0), IP 9, H 11, R 4, ER 2, BB 1, SO 7

Top Performers at the Plate
Pit   Phil Garner, 3 for 4, 2 RBI; Dave Parker, 4 for 5, 1 RBI
Bal   Doug DeCinces, 1 for 3, 1 R, 2 RBI, 1 BB; Eddie Murray, 1 for 2, 1 R, 2 BB

2B-Pit/Garner, Parker. **HR**-Pit/Stargell; Bal/DeCinces. **SB**-Bal/Murray. **Time** 3:18. **Attendance** 53,735.

Game 2   Thursday, October 11 at Memorial Stadium, Baltimore

	1	2	3	4	5	6	7	8	9	R	H	E
Pittsburgh Pirates	0	2	0	0	0	0	0	0	1	3	11	2
Baltimore Orioles	0	1	0	0	0	1	0	0	0	2	6	1

Pitchers   Pit   Bert Blyleven, IP 6, H 5, R 2, ER 2, BB 2, SO 1; Don Robinson (W, 1-0), IP 2, H 1, R 0, ER 0, BB 3, SO 2; Kent Tekulve (Sv, 1), IP 1, H 0, R 0, ER 0, BB 0, SO 2
Bal   Jim Palmer, IP 7, H 8, R 2, ER 2, BB 2, SO 3; Tippy Martinez, IP 1, H 1, R 0, ER 0, BB 0, SO 1; Don Stanhouse (L, 0-1), IP 1, H 2, R 1, ER 1, BB 1, SO 0

Top Performers at the Plate
Pit   Bill Madlock, 2 for 4, 1 RBI; Ed Ott, 1 for 3, 1 R, 1 RBI, 1 SF
Bal   Eddie Murray, 3 for 3, 1 R, 2 RBI, 1 BB

2B-Bal/Murray. **HR**-Bal/Murray. **Time** 3:13. **Attendance** 53,739.

Game 3   Friday, October 12 at Three Rivers Stadium, Pittsburgh

	1	2	3	4	5	6	7	8	9	R	H	E
Baltimore Orioles	0	0	2	5	0	0	1	0	0	8	13	0
Pittsburgh Pirates	1	2	0	0	0	1	0	0	0	4	9	2

Pitchers   Bal   Scott McGregor (W, 1-0), IP 9, H 9, R 4, ER 4, BB 0, SO 6
Pit   John Candelaria (L, 0-1), IP 3, H 8, R 6, ER 5, BB 2, SO 2; Enrique Romo, IP 3⅔, H 5, R 2, ER 2, BB 1, SO 4; Grant Jackson, IP ⅓, H 0, R 0, ER 0, BB 0, SO 0; Kent Tekulve, IP 2, H 0, R 0, ER 0, BB 0, SO 1

Top Performers at the Plate
Bal   Benny Ayala, 2 for 2, 1 R, 2 RBI; Kiko Garcia, 4 for 4, 2 R, 4 RBI, 1 BB
Pit   Omar Moreno, 2 for 4, 1 R; Willie Stargell, 2 for 4, 2 R

2B-Bal/Dauer, Dempsey, Garcia; Pit/Garner, Moreno 2. Stargell. **3B**-Bal/Garcia. **HR**-Bal/Ayala. **Time** 2:51. **Attendance** 50,848.

Game 4   Saturday, October 13 at Three Rivers Stadium, Pittsburgh

	1	2	3	4	5	6	7	8	9	R	H	E
Baltimore Orioles	0	0	3	0	0	0	0	6	0	9	12	0
Pittsburgh Pirates	0	4	0	0	1	1	0	0	0	6	17	1

Pitchers   Bal   Dennis Martinez, IP 1⅓, H 6, R 4, ER 4, BB 0, SO 0; Sammy Stewart, IP 2⅔, H 4, R 0, ER 0, BB 1, SO 0; Steve Stone, IP 2, H 4, R 2, ER 2, BB 2, SO 2; Tim Stoddard (W, 1-0), IP 3, H 3, R 0, ER 0, BB 1, SO 3
Pit   Jim Bibby, IP 6⅓, H 7, R 3, ER 2, BB 2, SO 7; Grant Jackson, IP ⅔, H 0, R 0, ER 0, BB 0, SO 0; Don Robinson, IP ⅓, H 2, R 3, ER 3, BB 1, SO 0; Kent Tekulve (L, 0-1), IP 1⅔, H 3, R 3, ER 3, BB 2, SO 1

Top Performers at the Plate
Bal   Kiko Garcia, 2 for 5, 2 R, 2 RBI; John Lowenstein, 1 for 2, 1 R, 2 RBI
Pit   Tim Foli, 3 for 4, 2 R, 1 BB; Willie Stargell, 3 for 5, 1 R, 1 RBI

2B-Bal/Crowley, Garcia, Lowenstein, Singleton; Pit/Madlock, Milner, Ott, Parker, Stargell. **HR**-Pit/Stargell. **SB**-Bal/DeCinces. **Time** 3:48. **Attendance** 50,883.

Game 5   Sunday, October 14 at Three Rivers Stadium, Pittsburgh

	1	2	3	4	5	6	7	8	9	R	H	E
Baltimore Orioles	0	0	0	0	1	0	0	0	0	1	6	2
Pittsburgh Pirates	0	0	0	0	0	2	2	3	x	7	13	1

Pitchers   Bal   Mike Flanagan (L, 1-1), IP 6, H 6, R 2, ER 2, BB 1, SO 6; Tim Stoddard, IP ⅔, H 2, R 2, ER 2, BB 0, SO 0; Tippy Martinez, IP ⅓, H 2, R 1, ER 1, BB 0, SO 0; Don Stanhouse, IP 1, H 3, R 2, ER 2, BB 2, SO 0
Pit   Jim Rooker, IP 5, H 3, R 1, ER 1, BB 2, SO 2; Bert Blyleven (W, 1-0), IP 4, H 3, R 0, ER 0, BB 1, SO 3

Top Performers at the Plate
Bal   Doug DeCinces, 2 for 4; Rick Dempsey, 2 for 4
Pit   Tim Foli, 2 for 4, 2 R, 3 RBI, 1 BB; Bill Madlock, 4 for 4, 1 R, 1 RBI

2B-Bal/Dempsey, Roenicke; Pit/Parker, Robinson. **3B**-Pit/Foli. **Time** 2:54. **Attendance** 50,920.

Game 6   Tuesday, October 16 at Memorial Stadium, Baltimore

	1	2	3	4	5	6	7	8	9	R	H	E
Pittsburgh Pirates	0	0	0	0	0	0	2	2	0	4	10	0
Baltimore Orioles	0	0	0	0	0	0	0	0	0	0	7	1

Pitchers   Pit   John Candelaria (W, 1-1), IP 6, H 6, R 0, ER 0, BB 0, SO 2; Kent Tekulve (Sv, 2), IP 3, H 1, R 0, ER 0, BB 0, SO 4
Bal   Jim Palmer (L, 0-1), IP 8, H 10, R 4, ER 4, BB 3, SO 5; Tim Stoddard, IP 1, H 0, R 0, ER 0, BB 0, SO 0

Top Performers at the Plate
Pit   Phil Garner, 2 for 3, 1 R, 1 HBP; Omar Moreno, 3 for 5, 1 R, 1 RBI
Bal   Ken Singleton, 3 for 4

2B-Pit/Foli, Garner. **Time** 2:30. **Attendance** 53,739.

Game 7   Wednesday, October 17 at Memorial Stadium, Baltimore

	1	2	3	4	5	6	7	8	9	R	H	E
Pittsburgh Pirates	0	0	0	0	2	0	0	2		4	10	0
Baltimore Orioles	0	0	1	0	0	0	0	0	0	1	4	2

Pitchers   Pit   Jim Bibby, IP 4, H 3, R 1, ER 1, BB 0, SO 3; Don Robinson, IP ⅔, H 1, R 0, ER 0, BB 1, SO 0; Grant Jackson (W, 1-0), IP 2⅔, H 0, R 0, ER 0, BB 2, SO 1; Kent Tekulve (Sv, 3), IP 1⅔, H 0, R 0, ER 0, BB 1, SO 2
Bal   Scott McGregor (L, 1-1), IP 8, H 7, R 2, ER 2, BB 2, SO 2; Tim Stoddard, IP ⅓, H 1, R 1, ER 1, BB 0, SO 0; Mike Flanagan, IP 0, H 1, R 1, ER 1, BB 0, SO 0; Don Stanhouse, IP 0, H 1, R 0, ER 0, BB 0, SO 0; Tippy Martinez, IP 0, H 0, R 0, ER 0, BB 0, SO 0; Dennis Martinez, IP ⅔, H 0, R 0, ER 0, BB 0, SO 0

Top Performers at the Plate
Pit   Omar Moreno, 3 for 5, 1 R, 1 RBI; Willie Stargell, 4 for 5, 1 R, 2 RBI, 2 BB
Bal   Rich Dauer, 1 for 3, 1 R, 1 RBI; Doug DeCinces, 2 for 4

2B-Pit/Garner, Stargell 2. **HR**-Pit/Stargell; Bal/Dauer. **Time** 2:54. **Attendance** 53,733.

Philadelphia Phillies (4) vs. Kansas City Royals (2)

The Philadelphia Phillies and the Kansas City Royals each won their respective division three years in a row from 1976 to 1978, but neither team had been able to win the League Championship and move on to the World Series. In 1980, both finally reached the pinnacle. The Royals did it with third baseman George Brett leading the way. Brett's .390 average was tops in all of baseball, and the highest since Ted Williams hit .406 in 1941. The Phillies got past their competition largely on the bat of their third baseman, Mike Schmidt, who belted a league-best 48 homers, and on the arm of 24-game-winner Steve Carlton. Game 1 in Philadelphia saw the Royals take an early 4-0 lead on two-run homers by Amos Otis and Willie Mays Aikens. The Phillies rallied for five runs in the bottom of the third, and then added one more in each of the next two innings. Celebrating his 26th birthday, Aikens hit his second two-run homer of the day to put the Royals within one, but reliever Tug McGraw came on for Philadelphia and shut the door with a 1-2-3 ninth inning. Carlton kept KC under control in Game 2 until Otis scored on an error in the sixth. As part of a three-run seventh, Otis hit a bases-loaded double to drive in two, giving the Royals a 4-2 edge. Kansas City's relief wiz Dan Quisenberry sent the Phillies down in order in the seventh, but in the eighth he was rocked for four runs, putting Philadelphia up 6-4 in the game and 2-0 in the Series. On the off day between Games 2 and 3, the Royals announced that their star player, Brett, was having hemorrhoid surgery. Things were looking grim for Kansas City, but Brett put his troubles behind him and bounced back for the third game. He came through with a first-inning homer and added a double in the eighth. Each team scattered a single run every third inning to enter the 10th in a 3-3 tie. The Royals scored the game-winner off McGraw when Aikens hit a two-out single to score Willie Wilson from second. Kansas City brought the Series even in Game 4 behind a first-inning onslaught. Aikens's homer to right brought in two of the Royals' four runs in the inning, and the slugging first baseman added his second round-tripper an inning later, pacing his team to a 5-3 final. Schmidt broke a scoreless tie in Game 5 with a two-run homer in the fourth, but Kansas City rallied back to take a 3-2 lead. Facing Quisenberry to start the ninth, Schmidt hit a single off Brett's glove. Pinch

Left: Second baseman Frank White throws to first to complete a double play in Game 2, as Keith Moreland tries to break up the DP.

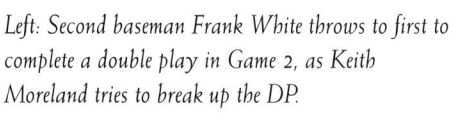

PHILADELPHIA PHILLIES/Dallas Green, Manager

Player	pos	G	AB	R	H	2B	3B	HR	RBI	BB	SO	SB	BA	SA	E	FPct
Bob Boone	c	6	17	3	7	2	0	0	4	4	0	0	.412	.529	0	1.000
Larry Bowa	ss	6	24	3	9	1	0	0	2	0	0	3	.375	.417	0	1.000
Warren Brusstar	p	1	0	0	0	0	0	0	0	0	0	0	—	—	0	—
Marty Bystrom	p	1	0	0	0	0	0	0	0	0	0	0	—	—	0	1.000
Steve Carlton	p	2	0	0	0	0	0	0	0	0	0	0	—	—	0	1.000
Larry Christenson	p	1	0	0	0	0	0	0	0	0	0	0	—	—	1	.000
Greg Gross	ph-lf	4	2	0	0	0	0	0	0	0	0	0	.000	.000	0	1.000
Greg Luzinski	dh-lf	3	9	0	0	0	0	0	1	5	0	0	.000	.000	0	1.000
Garry Maddox	cf	6	22	1	5	2	0	0	1	1	3	0	.227	.318	0	1.000
Bake McBride	rf	6	23	3	7	1	0	1	5	2	1	0	.304	.478	0	1.000
Tug McGraw	p	4	0	0	0	0	0	0	0	0	0	0	—	—	0	1.000
Keith Moreland	dh	3	12	1	4	0	0	0	1	0	1	0	.333	.333		
Dickie Noles	p	1	0	0	0	0	0	0	0	0	0	0	—	—	0	1.000
Ron Reed	p	2	0	0	0	0	0	0	0	0	0	0	—	—	0	—
Pete Rose	1b	6	23	2	6	1	0	0	1	2	2	0	.261	.304	0	1.000
Dick Ruthven	p	1	0	0	0	0	0	0	0	0	0	0	—	—	0	—
Kevin Saucier	p	1	0	0	0	0	0	0	0	0	0	0	—	—	0	—
Mike Schmidt	3b	6	21	6	8	1	0	2	7	4	3	0	.381	.714	0	1.000
Lonnie Smith	lf-dh-pr	6	19	2	5	1	0	0	1	1	1	0	.263	.316	0	1.000
Manny Trillo	2b	6	23	4	5	2	0	0	2	0	0	0	.217	.304	1	.975
Del Unser	ph-cf-lf	3	6	2	3	2	0	0	2	0	1	0	.500	.833	0	1.000
Bob Walk	p	1	0	0	0	0	0	0	0	0	0	0	—	—	0	1.000
Totals		6	201	27	59	13	0	3	26	15	17	3	.294	.403	2	.991

Pitcher	G	GS	CG	IP	H	R	ER	BB	SO	W-L	Sv	ERA
Warren Brusstar	1	0	0	2⅓	0	0	0	1	0	0-0	0	0.00
Marty Bystrom	1	1	0	5	10	3	3	1	4	0-0	0	5.40
Steve Carlton	2	2	0	15	14	5	4	9	17	2-0	0	2.40
Larry Christenson	1	1	0	⅓	5	4	4	1	0	0-1	0	108.00
Tug McGraw	4	0	0	7⅔	7	1	1	8	10	1-1	2	1.17
Dickie Noles	1	0	0	4⅔	5	1	1	2	6	0-0	0	1.93
Ron Reed	2	0	0	2	2	0	0	2		0-0	1	0.00
Dick Ruthven	1	1	0	9	9	3	3	0	7	0-0	0	3.00
Kevin Saucier	1	0	0	⅔	0	0	0	2	0	0-0	0	0.00
Bob Walk	1	1	0	7	8	6	6	3	3	1-0	0	7.71
Totals	6	6	0	53⅔	60	23	22	27	49	4-2	3	3.69

KANSAS CITY ROYALS/Jim Frey, Manager

Player	pos	G	AB	R	H	2B	3B	HR	RBI	BB	SO	SB	BA	SA	E	FPct
Willie Aikens	1b	6	20	5	8	0	1	4	8	6	8	0	.400	1.100	2	.966
George Brett	3b	6	24	3	9	2	1	1	3	2	4	1	.375	.667	1	.955
Jose Cardenal	ph-rf	4	10	0	2	0	0	0	0	0	3	0	.200	.200	0	1.000
Dave Chalk	3b	1	0	1	0	0	0	0	0	1	0	1	—	—	0	1.000
Onix Concepcion	pr	3	0	0	0	0	0	0	0	0	0	0	—	—	0	1.000
Rich Gale	p	2	0	0	0	0	0	0	0	0	0	0	—	—	0	1.000
Larry Gura	p	2	0	0	0	0	0	0	0	0	0	0	—	—	0	1.000
Clint Hurdle	rf	4	12	1	5	1	0	0	2	1	1	1	.417	.500	0	1.000
Pete LaCock	1b	1	0	0	0	0	0	0	0	0	0	0	—	—	0	1.000
Dennis Leonard	p	2	0	0	0	0	0	0	0	0	0	0	—	—	1	.000
Renie Martin	p	3	0	0	0	0	0	0	0	0	0	0	—	—	0	—
Hal McRae	dh	6	24	3	9	3	0	0	1	2	2	0	.375	.500	—	—
Amos Otis	cf	6	23	4	11	2	0	3	7	3	3	0	.478	.957	0	1.000
Marty Pattin	p	1	0	0	0	0	0	0	0	0	0	0	—	—	0	—
Darrell Porter	c-ph	5	14	1	2	0	0	0	0	3	4	0	.143	.143	0	1.000
Dan Quisenberry	p	6	0	0	0	0	0	0	0	0	0	0	—	—	0	1.000
Paul Splittorff	p	1	0	0	0	0	0	0	0	0	0	0	—	—	0	1.000
U. L. Washington	ss	6	22	1	6	0	0	0	2	0	6	0	.273	.273	1	.967
John Wathan	ph-rf-c	3	7	1	2	0	0	0	1	2	1	0	.286	.286	0	1.000
Frank White	2b	6	25	0	2	0	0	0	0	1	5	1	.080	.080	2	.943
Willie Wilson	lf	6	26	3	4	1	0	0	0	4	12	2	.154	.192	0	1.000
Totals		6	207	23	60	9	2	8	22	26	49	6	.290	.469	7	.970

Pitcher	G	GS	CG	IP	H	R	ER	BB	SO	W-L	Sv	ERA
Rich Gale	2	2	0	6⅓	11	4	3	4	4	0-1	0	4.26
Larry Gura	2	2	0	12⅓	8	4	3	3	4	0-0	0	2.19
Dennis Leonard	2	2	0	10⅔	15	9	8	2	5	1-1	0	6.75
Renie Martin	3	0	0	9⅔	11	3	3	3	2	0-0	0	2.79
Marty Pattin	1	0	0	1	0	0	0	0	2	0-0	0	0.00
Dan Quisenberry	6	0	0	10⅓	10	6	6	3	0	1-2	1	5.23
Paul Splittorff	1	0	0	1⅔	4	1	1	0	0	0-0	0	5.40
Totals	6	6	0	52	59	27	24	15	17	2-4	1	4.15

Series MVP: Mike Schmidt, Philadelphia Phillies. **Series Outstanding Pitcher:** Steve Carlton, Philadelphia Phillies. **Average Length of Game:** 2 hours, 58 minutes. **Total Attendance:** 324,516. **Average Attendance:** 54,086 (65,801 at Veterans Stadium; 42,371 at Royals Stadium). **Umpires:** Nick Bremigan (AL), Don Denkinger (AL), Bill Kunkel (AL), Paul Pryor (NL), Dutch Rennert (NL), Harry Wendelstedt (NL). **Winning Player's Share:** $34,693. **Losing Player's Share:** $32,212.

hitter Del Unser doubled down the right-field line to drive Schmidt home, and he later scored the second run of the inning on an infield single. After walking the bases full in the bottom of the ninth, McGraw got out of his own jam by striking out Jose Cardenal to end the game. The Phillies needed one more to clinch it, and they were heading home to Veterans Stadium for Game 6 with "Lefty" Carlton scheduled to take the hill. The Hall of Famer shut Kansas City out for seven innings, and Schmidt singled in two runs in the third as Philadelphia took a 4-1 lead into the last inning. The Royals loaded the bases against McGraw with one out in the ninth when Frank White popped a foul ball toward the Phillie dugout. Catcher Bob Boone and first baseman Pete Rose made chase, with Boone calling for it. The ball hit Boone's mitt and bounced out, but Rose was right there to snatch the ball before it hit the ground. McGraw then struck out Willie Wilson for the final out—and the Philadelphia Phillies had their first World Series title in franchise history, ending the longest drought in the Majors.

Left: A frustrated Willie Wilson has just struck out for the 12th time in the Series, setting a new record for futility.

Above: Despite his medical problems, Kansas City's third baseman George Brett contributed nine hits in the Series.

Right: Philadelphia reliever Tug McGraw came through with a clutch save in the deciding sixth game of the 1980 World Series.

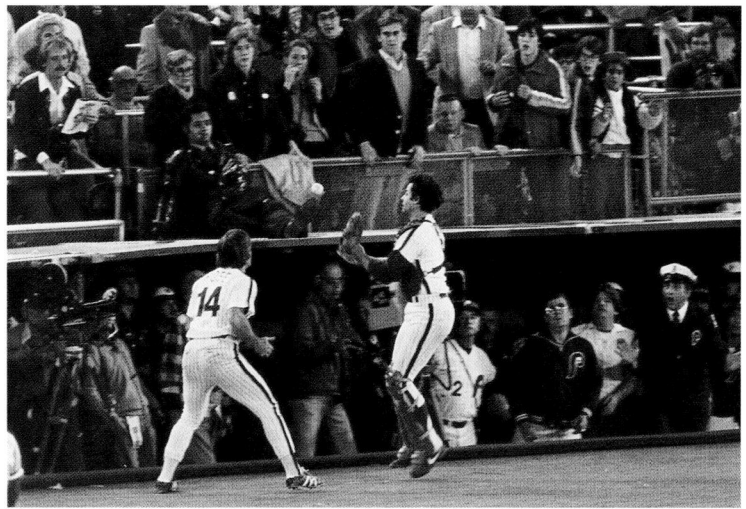

Above: With one out in the ninth inning of the final game, Bob Boone loses Frank White's foul pop, but Pete Rose is right there to make the save.

Kansas City's Willie Aikens became the only player to have two multi-homer games in one Series when he went deep twice in Game 1 (above) and again in Game 4 (right).

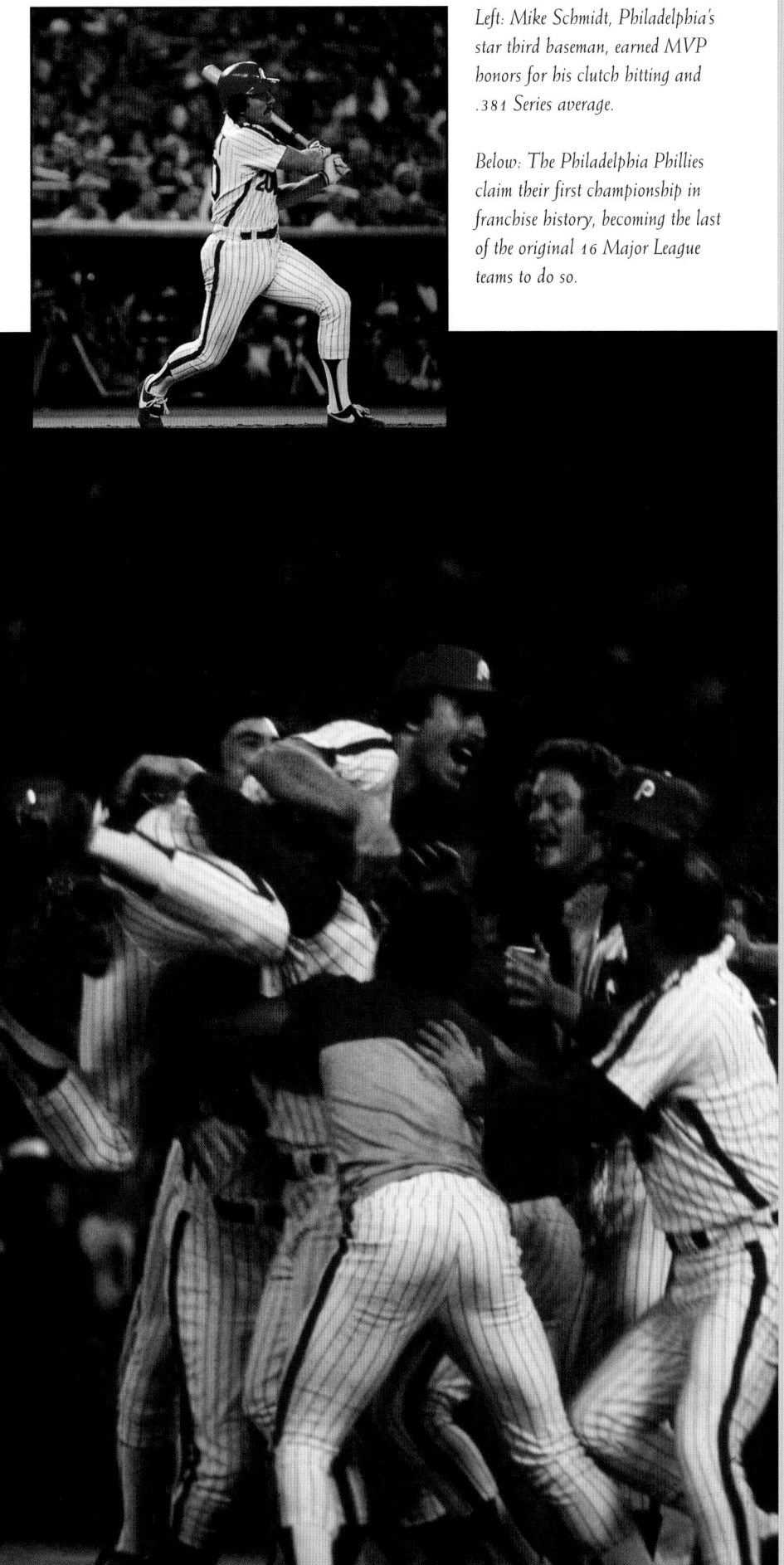

Left: Mike Schmidt, Philadelphia's star third baseman, earned MVP honors for his clutch hitting and .381 Series average.

Below: The Philadelphia Phillies claim their first championship in franchise history, becoming the last of the original 16 Major League teams to do so.

Game 1 Tuesday, October 14 at Veterans Stadium, Philadelphia

	1	2	3	4	5	6	7	8	9	R	H	E
Kansas City Royals	0	2	2	0	0	0	0	2	0	6	9	1
Philadelphia Phillies	0	0	5	1	1	0	0	0	x	7	11	0

Pitchers KC Dennis Leonard (L, 0-1), IP 3⅔, H 6, R 6, ER 6, BB 1, SO 3; Renie Martin, IP 4, H 5, R 1, ER 1, BB 1, SO 1; Dan Quisenberry, IP ⅓, H 0, R 0, ER 0, BB 0, SO 0
Phi Bob Walk (W, 1-0), IP 7, H 8, R 6, ER 6, BB 3, SO 3; Tug McGraw (Sv, 1), IP 2, H 1, R 0, ER 0, BB 0, SO 2

Top Performers at the Plate
KC Willie Aikens, 2 for 4, 2 R, 4 RBI, 2 HR; Amos Otis, 3 for 4, 1 R, 2 RBI
Phi Bob Boone, 3 for 4, 1 R, 2 RBI, 2 2B; Bake McBride, 3 for 4, 1 R, 3 RBI

2B-KC/Brett; Phi/Boone 2. **HR**-KC/Aikens 2, Otis; Phi/McBride. **SB**-KC/White; Phi/Bowa.
Time 3:01. **Attendance** 65,791.

Game 2 Wednesday, October 15 at Veterans Stadium, Philadelphia

	1	2	3	4	5	6	7	8	9	R	H	E
Kansas City Royals	0	0	0	0	0	1	3	0	0	4	11	0
Philadelphia Phillies	0	0	0	0	2	0	4	x		6	8	1

Pitchers KC Larry Gura, IP 6, H 4, R 2, ER 2, BB 2, SO 2; Dan Quisenberry (L, 0-1), IP 2, H 4, R 4, ER 4, BB 1, SO 0
Phi Steve Carlton (W, 1-0), IP 8, H 10, R 4, ER 3, BB 6, SO 10; Ron Reed (Sv, 1), IP 1, H 1, R 0, ER 0, BB 0, SO 2

Top Performers at the Plate
KC Hal McRae, 3 for 4, 1 R, 1 BB; Amos Otis, 2 for 5, 1 R, 2 RBI
Phi Keith Moreland, 2 for 4, 1 R, 1 RBI; Mike Schmidt, 2 for 4, 1 R, 1 RBI

2B-KC/Otis; Phi/Maddox, Schmidt, Unser. **SB**-KC/Chalk, Wilson. **Time** 3:01. **Attendance** 65,775.

Game 3 Friday, October 17 at Royals Stadium, Kansas City

	1	2	3	4	5	6	7	8	9	10	R	H	E
Philadelphia Phillies	0	1	0	0	1	0	0	1	0	0	3	14	0
Kansas City Royals	1	0	0	1	0	0	1	0	0	1	4	11	0

Pitchers Phi Dick Ruthven, IP 9, H 9, R 3, ER 3, BB 0, SO 7; Tug McGraw (L, 0-1), IP ⅔, H 2, R 1, ER 1, BB 2, SO 1
KC Rich Gale, IP 4⅓, H 7, R 2, ER 2, BB 3, SO 3; Renie Martin, IP 3⅓, H 5, R 1, ER 1, BB 1, SO 1; Dan Quisenberry (W, 1-1), IP 2⅓, H 2, R 0, ER 0, BB 2, SO 0

Top Performers at the Plate
Phi Larry Bowa, 3 for 5, 1 R; Lonnie Smith, 2 for 4, 1 RBI, 1 BB
KC Willie Aikens, 2 for 5, 1 R, 1 RBI; George Brett, 2 for 4, 1 R, 1 RBI, 1 BB

2B-Phi/Trillo; KC/Brett. **3B**-KC/Aikens. **HR**-Phi/Schmidt; KC/Brett, Otis. **SB**-Phi/Bowa; KC/Hurdle, Wilson. **Time** 3:19. **Attendance** 42,380.

Game 4 Saturday, October 18 at Royals Stadium, Kansas City

	1	2	3	4	5	6	7	8	9	R	H	E
Philadelphia Phillies	0	1	0	0	0	0	1	1	0	3	10	1
Kansas City Royals	4	1	0	0	0	0	0	0	x	5	10	2

Pitchers Phi Larry Christenson (L, 0-1), IP ⅓, H 5, R 4, ER 4, BB 0, SO 0; Dickie Noles, IP 4⅔, H 5, R 1, ER 1, BB 2, SO 6; Kevin Saucier, IP ⅔, H 0, R 0, ER 0, BB 2, SO 0; Warren Brusstar, IP 2⅓, H 0, R 0, ER 0, BB 1, SO 0
KC Dennis Leonard (W, 1-1), IP 7, H 9, R 3, ER 2, BB 1, SO 2; Dan Quisenberry (Sv, 1), IP 2, H 1, R 0, ER 0, BB 0, SO 0

Top Performers at the Plate
Phi Larry Bowa, 2 for 4, 1 RBI; Pete Rose, 2 for 4, 1 R
KC Willie Aikens, 2 for 3, 2 R, 3 RBI, 1 BB, 2 HR; Hal McRae, 2 for 4, 1 R, 2 2B

2B-Phi/McBride, Rose, Trillo; KC/Hurdle, McRae 2, Otis. **3B**-KC/Brett. **HR**-KC/Aikens 2. **SB**-Phi/Bowa. **Time** 2:37. **Attendance** 42,363.

Game 5 Sunday, October 19 at Royals Stadium, Kansas City

	1	2	3	4	5	6	7	8	9	R	H	E
Philadelphia Phillies	0	0	0	2	0	0	0	2		4	7	0
Kansas City Royals	0	0	0	0	1	2	0	0	0	3	12	2

Pitchers Phi Marty Bystrom, IP 5, H 10, R 3, ER 3, BB 1, SO 4; Ron Reed, IP 1, H 1, R 0, ER 0, BB 0, SO 0; Tug McGraw (W, 1-1), IP 3, H 1, R 0, ER 0, BB 4, SO 5
KC Larry Gura, IP 6⅓, H 4, R 2, ER 1, BB 1, SO 2; Dan Quisenberry (L, 1-2), IP 2⅔, H 3, R 2, ER 2, BB 0, SO 0

Top Performers at the Plate
Phi Mike Schmidt, 2 for 4, 2 R, 2 RBI; Del Unser, 1 for 1, 1 R, 1 RBI
KC Amos Otis, 2 for 3, 1 R, 1 RBI, 2 BB; U. L. Washington, 2 for 3, 1 R, 1 RBI, 1 SF

2B-Phi/Unser; KC/McRae, Wilson. **HR**-Phi/Schmidt; KC/Otis. **SB**-KC/Brett. **Time** 2:51.
Attendance 42,369.

Game 6 Tuesday, October 21 at Veterans Stadium, Philadelphia

	1	2	3	4	5	6	7	8	9	R	H	E
Kansas City Royals	0	0	0	0	0	0	0	1	0	1	7	2
Philadelphia Phillies	0	0	2	0	1	1	0	0	x	4	9	0

Pitchers KC Rich Gale (L, 0-1), IP 2, H 4, R 2, ER 1, BB 1, SO 1; Renie Martin, IP 2⅓, H 1, R 1, ER 1, BB 1, SO 0; Paul Splittorff, IP 1⅔, H 4, R 7, ER 1, BB 0, SO 0; Marty Pattin, IP 1, H 0, R 0, ER 0, BB 0, SO 2; Dan Quisenberry, IP 1, H 0, R 0, ER 0, BB 0, SO 0
Phi Steve Carlton (W, 2-0), IP 7, H 4, R 1, ER 1, BB 3, SO 7; Tug McGraw (Sv, 2), IP 2, H 3, R 0, ER 0, BB 2, SO 2

Top Performers at the Plate
KC George Brett, 2 for 4; John Wathan, 2 for 3, 1 R, 1 BB
Phi Pete Rose, 3 for 4; Mike Schmidt, 1 for 3, 2 RBI, 1 BB

2B-Phi/Bowa, Maddox, Smith. **Time** 3:00. **Attendance** 65,838.

Los Angeles Dodgers (4) vs. New York Yankees (2)

1981

After a two-month players' strike and a shortened season, the 1981 World Series featured two familiar adversaries. It was the 11th Yankee-Dodger match-up in the Fall Classic, and the third in five years. Many of the faces from the clubs' previous pairing were still around, with some important new additions. The Dodgers brought the young Dominican Pedro Guerrero into the starting lineup, and they got a marvelous rookie campaign from 20-year-old sensation Fernando Valenzuela. George Steinbrenner, meanwhile, laid out big bucks to bring veteran outfielder Dave Winfield to New York. (Big Dave did not produce his money's worth in October, going 1 for 22 in the Series). The Yanks also signed free-agent Bob Watson. Once the World Series got underway, it seemed as if 1981 might be another example of Yankee superiority over the Dodgers. Ron Guidry allowed just four hits to earn the win in the opener, with Watson supplying a three-run homer in the first and Graig Nettles making a diving catch of Steve Garvey's line drive to protect a 5-3 lead in the eighth. In the second game, ex-Dodger Tommy John blanked his former mates on three hits. It was the Dodgers' sixth straight loss to the Yankees in Series play, but Valenzuela came on and ended the streak with a complete-game win in Game 3, overcoming seven walks and two early homers by Watson and Rick Cerone. Ron Cey homered off rookie Dave Righetti with two on in the first, and the Dodgers got two runs on a Guerrero single and a Mike Scioscia grounder in the fifth inning to win 5-4. Both staffs got knocked around in Game 4, which ended in an 8-7 Dodger victory. Reggie Jackson, who sat out the first three games due to injury, came through with a 3 for 3 day with two walks and a solo homer, but his dropped fly ball in the sixth inning proved costly, as it allowed Davey Lopes to reach second base and ultimately score. Los Angeles claimed the Series advantage the following evening when Jerry Reuss out-dueled Guidry in Game 5. Back-to-back homers by Guerrero and Steve Yeager in the seventh inning gave Reuss a one-run edge. Tommy John had New York battling in a 1-1 tie in Game 6 when manager Bob Lemon pulled him for a pinch hitter with two outs in the fourth. The Yanks failed to score in the inning, and the Dodgers quickly took advantage of the Yankee bull pen, bringing in seven runs in the next two innings to claim an 8-1 lead. Guerrero scored two in the fifth with a triple and drove in two more with a bases-loaded single in the sixth. His solo homer in the eighth gave him five RBI on the day, and LA won its fourth straight game after losing the first two to defeat the Yankees for only the third time in 11 tries. It was a group effort, as Guerrero, Cey and Yeager shared MVP honors for the Series.

Above: With a .350 average and 6 RBI, Ron "The Penguin" Cey was one of three Dodger MVPs.

1981 WORLD SERIES COMPOSITE STATISTICS

LOS ANGELES DODGERS / Tommy Lasorda, Manager

Player	pos	G	AB	R	H	2B	3B	HR	RBI	BB	SO	SB	BA	SA	E	FPct
Dusty Baker	lf	6	24	3	4	0	0	0	1	1	6	0	.167	.167	0	1.000
Bobby Castillo	p	1	0	0	0	0	0	0	0	0	0	0	–	–	0	1.000
Ron Cey	3b	6	20	3	7	0	0	1	6	3	3	0	.350	.500	0	1.000
Terry Forster	p	2	0	0	0	0	0	0	0	0	0	0	–	–	0	1.000
Steve Garvey	1b	6	24	3	10	1	0	0	0	2	5	0	.417	.458	0	1.000
Dave Goltz	p	2	0	0	0	0	0	0	0	0	0	0	–	–	0	–
Pedro Guerrero	cf-rf	6	21	2	7	1	1	2	7	2	6	0	.333	.762	0	1.000
Burt Hooton	p	2	4	1	0	0	0	0	0	1	3	0	.000	.000	0	1.000
Steve Howe	p	3	2	0	0	0	0	0	0	0	2	0	.000	.000	1	.500
Jay Johnstone	ph	3	3	1	2	0	0	1	3	0	0	0	.667	1.667	–	–
Ken Landreaux	ph-cf-pr	5	6	1	1	1	0	0	0	2	1	0	.167	.333	0	1.000
Davey Lopes	2b	6	22	6	5	1	0	0	2	4	3	4	.227	.273	6	.867
Rick Monday	rf-ph	5	13	1	3	1	0	0	0	3	6	0	.231	.308	0	1.000
Tom Niedenfuer	p	2	0	0	0	0	0	0	0	0	0	0	–	–	0	–
Jerry Reuss	p	2	3	0	0	0	0	0	0	1	2	0	.000	.000	0	1.000
Bill Russell	ss	6	25	1	6	0	0	0	2	0	1	1	.240	.240	1	.968
Steve Sax	ph-pr-2b	2	1	0	0	0	0	0	0	0	0	0	.000	.000	0	–
Mike Scioscia	c-ph	3	4	1	1	0	0	0	0	0	1	0	.250	.250	0	1.000
Reggie Smith	ph	2	2	0	1	0	0	0	0	0	1	0	.500	.500	–	–
Dave Stewart	p	2	0	0	0	0	0	0	0	0	0	0	–	–	1	.000
Derrel Thomas	ph-ss-cf-3b	5	7	2	0	0	0	0	1	1	2	0	.000	.000	0	1.000
Fernando Valenzuela	p	1	3	0	0	0	0	0	0	1	0	0	.000	.000	0	1.000
Bob Welch	p	1	0	0	0	0	0	0	0	0	0	0	–	–	0	–
Steve Yeager	ph-c	6	14	2	4	1	0	2	4	0	2	0	.286	.786	0	1.000
Totals		6	198	27	51	6	1	6	26	20	44	6	.258	.389	9	.961

Pitcher	G	GS	CG	IP	H	R	ER	BB	SO	W-L	Sv	ERA
Bobby Castillo	1	0	0	1	0	1	1	5	0	0-0	0	9.00
Terry Forster	2	0	0	2	1	0	0	3	0	0-0	0	0.00
Dave Goltz	2	0	0	3⅓	4	2	2	1	2	0-0	0	5.40
Burt Hooton	2	2	0	11⅓	8	3	2	9	3	1-1	0	1.59
Steve Howe	3	0	0	7	7	3	3	1	4	1-0	1	3.86
Tom Niedenfuer	2	0	0	5	3	2	0	1	0	0-0	0	0.00
Jerry Reuss	2	2	1	11⅔	10	6	5	3	8	1-1	0	3.86
Dave Stewart	2	0	0	1⅔	1	0	0	2	1	0-0	0	0.00
Fernando Valenzuela	1	1	1	9	9	4	4	7	6	1-0	0	4.00
Bob Welch	1	1	0	0	3	2	2	1	0	0-0	0	–
Totals	6	6	2	52	46	22	19	33	24	4-2	1	3.29

NEW YORK YANKEES / Bob Lemon, Manager

Player	pos	G	AB	R	H	2B	3B	HR	RBI	BB	SO	SB	BA	SA	E	FPct
Bobby Brown	pr-rf-cf-ph	4	1	1	0	0	0	0	0	0	1	0	.000	.000	0	1.000
Rick Cerone	c	6	21	2	4	1	0	1	3	4	2	0	.190	.381	0	1.000
Ron Davis	p	4	0	0	0	0	0	0	0	0	0	0	–	–	0	–
Barry Foote	ph	1	1	0	0	0	0	0	0	0	1	0	.000	.000	–	–
George Frazier	p	3	2	0	0	0	0	0	0	0	0	0	.000	.000	0	–
Oscar Gamble	rf-lf-ph	3	6	1	2	0	0	0	1	1	0	0	.333	.333	0	1.000
Rich Gossage	p	3	1	0	0	0	0	0	0	0	1	0	.000	.000	0	–
Ron Guidry	p	2	5	0	0	0	0	0	0	0	3	0	.000	.000	0	–
Reggie Jackson	rf	3	12	3	4	1	0	1	1	2	3	0	.333	.667	1	.833
Tommy John	p	3	2	0	0	0	0	0	0	0	0	0	.000	.000	0	1.000
Dave LaRoche	p	1	0	0	0	0	0	0	0	0	0	0	–	–	0	–
Rudy May	p	3	1	0	0	0	0	0	0	0	0	0	.000	.000	0	1.000
Larry Milbourne	ss	6	20	2	5	2	0	0	0	3	4	0	.250	.350	2	.913
Jerry Mumphrey	cf	5	15	2	3	0	0	0	0	3	2	1	.200	.200	0	1.000
Bobby Murcer	ph	4	3	0	0	0	0	0	0	0	0	0	.000	.000	–	–
Graig Nettles	3b	3	10	1	4	1	0	0	3	0	1	0	.400	.500	1	.929
Lou Piniella	rf-ph-lf	6	16	2	7	1	0	0	3	0	1	1	.438	.500	0	1.000
Willie Randolph	2b	6	18	5	4	1	1	2	3	9	0	1	.222	.722	0	1.000
Rick Reuschel	p	2	2	0	0	0	0	0	0	0	0	0	.000	.000	0	–
Dave Righetti	p	1	1	0	0	0	0	0	0	0	1	0	.000	.000	0	–
Andre Robertson	pr	1	0	0	0	0	0	0	0	0	0	0	–	–	0	–
Aurelio Rodriguez	3b-pr	4	12	1	5	0	0	0	0	1	2	0	.417	.417	0	1.000
Bob Watson	1b	6	22	2	7	1	0	2	7	3	0	0	.318	.636	0	1.000
Dave Winfield	lf-cf	6	22	0	1	0	0	0	1	5	4	1	.045	.045	0	1.000
Totals		6	193	22	46	8	1	6	22	33	24	4	.238	.383	4	.981

Pitcher	G	GS	CG	IP	H	R	ER	BB	SO	W-L	Sv	ERA
Ron Davis	4	0	0	2⅓	4	8	6	5	4	0-0	0	23.14
George Frazier	3	0	0	3⅔	9	7	7	3	2	0-3	0	17.18
Rich "Goose" Gossage	3	0	0	5	2	0	0	2	5	0-0	2	0.00
Ron Guidry	2	2	0	14	8	3	3	4	15	1-1	0	1.93
Tommy John	3	2	0	13	11	1	1	0	8	1-0	0	0.69
Dave LaRoche	1	0	0	1	0	0	0	2	0	0-0	0	0.00
Rudy May	3	0	0	6⅓	5	2	2	1	5	0-0	0	2.84
Rick Reuschel	2	1	0	3⅔	7	3	2	3	2	0-0	0	4.91
Dave Righetti	1	1	0	2	5	3	3	2	1	0-0	0	13.50
Totals	6	6	0	51	51	27	24	20	44	2-4	0	4.24

Series MVP: Ron Cey, Pedro Guerrero, Steve Yeager, Los Angeles Dodgers. **Series Outstanding Pitcher:** Tommy John, New York Yankees. **Average Length of Game:** 2 hours, 51 minutes. **Total Attendance:** 338,081. **Average Attendance:** 56,347 (56,198 at Dodger Stadium; 56,496 at Yankee Stadium). **Umpires:** Larry Barnett (AL), Nick Colosi (NL), Terry Cooney (AL), Rich Garcia (AL), Doug Harvey (NL), Dick Stello (NL). **Winning Player's Share:** $38,120. **Losing Player's Share:** $28,845.

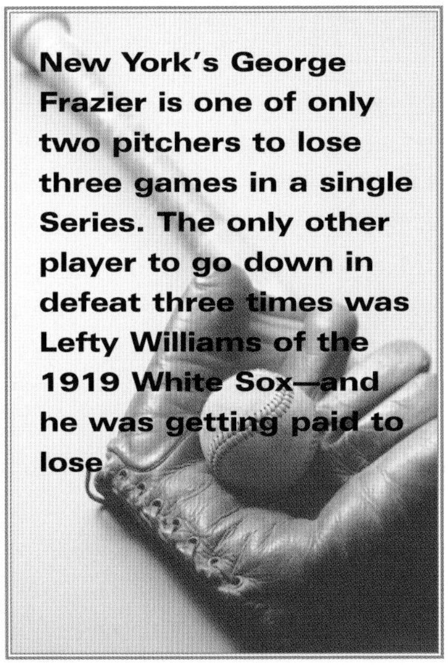

New York's George Frazier is one of only two pitchers to lose three games in a single Series. The only other player to go down in defeat three times was Lefty Williams of the 1919 White Sox—and he was getting paid to lose.

Above: Steve Yeager homered twice in the Series to earn his share of the MVP trophy, and the appreciation of his fellow Dodgers.

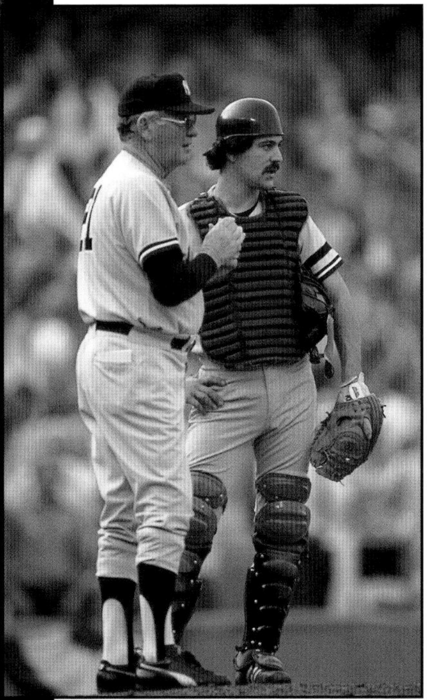

Below: Shown here with catcher Rick Cerone, Yankee manager Bob Lemon came on in midseason to lead New York to a pennant, but he was unable to get his team past the Dodgers in October.

Left: For only the third time in 11 match-ups with the Yankees, the Dodgers are victorious. Pitcher Steve Howe is flying high in the arms of catcher Steve Yeager after the Game 6 win in 1981.

Game 1 Tuesday, October 20 at Yankee Stadium, New York

	1	2	3	4	5	6	7	8	9	R	H	E
Los Angeles Dodgers	0	0	0	0	1	0	0	2	0	3	5	0
New York Yankees	3	0	1	1	0	0	0	0	x	5	6	0

Pitchers LA **Jerry Reuss** (L, 0-1), IP 2⅔, H 5, R 5, ER 4, BB 0, SO 2; **Bobby Castillo**, IP 1, H 0, R 0, ER 1, BB 5, SO 0; **Dave Goltz**, IP ⅓, H 0, R 0, ER 0, BB 0, SO 0; **Tom Niedenfuer**, IP 3, H 1, R 0, ER 0, BB 0, SO 0; **Dave Stewart**, IP 1, H 0, R 0, ER 0, BB 1, SO 0
NY **Ron Guidry** (W, 1-0), IP 7, H 4, R 1, ER 1, BB 2, SO 6; **Ron Davis**, IP 0, H 0, R 2, ER 2, BB 2, SO 0; **Rich "Goose" Gossage** (Sv, 1), IP 2, H 1, R 0, ER 0, BB 0, SO 2

Top Performers at the Plate
LA **Dusty Baker**, 1 for 2, 1 RBI, 1 BB, 1 SF; **Steve Yeager**, 1 for 3, 1 R, 1 RBI
NY **Jerry Mumphrey**, 2 for 3, 2 R, 1 BB; **Bob Watson**, 2 for 3, 1 R, 3 RBI, 1 BB

2B-NY/Piniella. **HR**-LA/Yeager; NY/Watson. **SB**-NY/Mumphrey, Piniella. **Time** 2:32. **Attendance** 56,470.

Game 2 Wednesday, October 21 at Yankee Stadium, New York

	1	2	3	4	5	6	7	8	9	R	H	E
Los Angeles Dodgers	0	0	0	0	0	0	0	0	0	0	4	2
New York Yankees	0	0	0	0	1	0	0	2	x	3	6	1

Pitchers LA **Burt Hooton** (L, 0-1), IP 6, H 3, R 1, ER 0, BB 4, SO 1; **Terry Forster**, IP 1, H 0, R 0, ER 0, BB 1, SO 0; **Steve Howe**, IP ⅓, H 2, R 2, ER 2, BB 0, SO 0; **Dave Stewart**, IP ⅔, H 1, R 0, ER 0, BB 1, SO 1
NY **Tommy John** (W, 1-0), IP 7, H 3, R 0, ER 0, BB 0, SO 4; **Rich "Goose" Gossage** (Sv, 2), IP 2, H 1, R 0, ER 0, BB 1, SO 3

Top Performers at the Plate
LA **Steve Garvey**, 2 for 3, 1 BB
NY **Graig Nettles**, 2 for 4, 1 R; **Bob Watson**, 2 for 4, 1 RBI

2B-NY/Milbourne. **Time** 2:29. **Attendance** 56,505.

Game 3 Friday, October 23 at Dodger Stadium, Los Angeles

	1	2	3	4	5	6	7	8	9	R	H	E
New York Yankees	0	2	2	0	0	0	0	0	0	4	9	0
Los Angeles Dodgers	3	0	0	0	2	0	0	0	x	5	11	1

Pitchers NY **Dave Righetti**, IP 2, H 5, R 3, ER 3, BB 2, SO 1; **George Frazier** (L, 0-1), IP 2, H 3, R 2, ER 2, BB 2, SO 1; **Rudy May**, IP 3, H 2, R 0, ER 0, BB 0, SO 2; **Ron Davis**, IP 1, H 1, R 0, ER 0, BB 0, SO 1
LA **Fernando Valenzuela** (W, 1-0), IP 9, H 9, R 4, ER 4, BB 7, SO 6

Top Performers at the Plate
NY **Rick Cerone**, 2 for 4, 2 R, 2 RBI; **Bob Watson**, 2 for 4, 1 R, 1 RBI
LA **Ron Cey**, 2 for 2, 2 R, 3 RBI, 2 BB; **Davey Lopes**, 2 for 4, 1 R, 1 SH

2B-NY/Cerone, Watson; LA/Guerrero, Lopes. **HR**-NY/Cerone, Watson; LA/Cey. **Time** 3:04. **Attendance** 56,236.

Game 4 Saturday, October 24 at Dodger Stadium, Los Angeles

	1	2	3	4	5	6	7	8	9	R	H	E
New York Yankees	2	1	1	0	0	2	0	1	0	7	13	1
Los Angeles Dodgers	0	0	2	0	1	3	2	0	x	8	14	2

Pitchers NY **Rick Reuschel**, IP 3, H 6, R 2, ER 2, BB 1, SO 2; **Rudy May**, IP 1⅓, H 2, R 1, ER 1, BB 0, SO 1; **Ron Davis**, IP 1, H 2, R 3, ER 2, BB 1, SO 2; **George Frazier** (L, 0-2), IP ⅔, H 2, R 2, ER 2, BB 1, SO 0; **Tommy John**, IP 2, H 2, R 0, ER 0, BB 0, SO 2
LA **Bob Welch**, IP 0, H 3, R 2, ER 2, BB 1, SO 0; **Dave Goltz**, IP 3, H 4, R 2, ER 2, BB 1, SO 2; **Terry Forster**, IP 1, H 1, R 0, ER 0, BB 2, SO 0; **Tom Niedenfuer**, IP 2, H 2, R 2, ER 0, BB 1, SO 0; **Steve Howe** (W, 1-0), IP 3, H 3, R 1, ER 1, BB 0, SO 1

Top Performers at the Plate
NY **Reggie Jackson**, 3 for 3, 2 R, 1 RBI, 2 BB; **Willie Randolph**, 2 for 5, 3 R, 1 RBI, 1 BB
LA **Steve Garvey**, 3 for 5, 1 R; **Davey Lopes**, 2 for 5, 2 R, 2 RBI, 2 SB

2B-NY/Milbourne; LA/Garvey, Landreaux, Monday. **3B**-NY/Randolph. **HR**-NY/Jackson, Randolph; LA/Johnstone. **SB**-NY/Winfield; LA/Lopes 2. **Time** 3:32. **Attendance** 56,242.

Game 5 Sunday, October 25 at Dodger Stadium, Los Angeles

	1	2	3	4	5	6	7	8	9	R	H	E
New York Yankees	0	1	0	0	0	0	0	0	0	1	5	0
Los Angeles Dodgers	0	0	0	0	0	0	2	0	x	2	4	3

Pitchers NY **Ron Guidry** (L, 1-1), IP 7, H 4, R 2, ER 2, BB 2, SO 9; **Rich "Goose" Gossage**, IP 1, H 0, R 0, ER 0, BB 1, SO 0
LA **Jerry Reuss** (W, 1-1), IP 9, H 5, R 1, ER 1, BB 3, SO 6

Top Performers at the Plate
NY **Lou Piniella**, 2 for 4, 1 RBI
LA **Pedro Guerrero**, 1 for 3, 1 R, 1 RBI; **Steve Yeager**, 2 for 3, 1 R, 1 RBI

2B-NY/Jackson; LA/Yeager. **HR**-LA/Guerrero, Yeager. **SB**-LA/Landreaux, Lopes. **Time** 2:19. **Attendance** 56,115.

Game 6 Wednesday, October 28 at Yankee Stadium, New York

	1	2	3	4	5	6	7	8	9	R	H	E
Los Angeles Dodger	0	0	0	1	3	4	0	1	0	9	13	1
New York Yankees	0	0	1	0	0	1	0	0	0	2	7	2

Pitchers LA **Burt Hooton** (W, 1-1), IP 5⅓, H 5, R 2, ER 2, BB 5, SO 2; **Steve Howe** (Sv, 1), IP 3⅔, H 2, R 0, ER 0, BB 1, SO 3
NY **Tommy John**, IP 4, H 6, R 1, ER 1, BB 0, SO 2; **George Frazier** (L, 0-3), IP 1, H 4, R 3, ER 3, BB 0, SO 1; **Ron Davis**, IP ⅓, H 1, R 3, ER 2, BB 2, SO 1; **Rick Reuschel**, IP ⅔, H 1, R 1, ER 0, BB 2, SO 0; **Rudy May**, IP 2, H 1, R 1, ER 1, BB 1, SO 2; **Dave LaRoche**, IP 1, H 0, R 0, ER 0, BB 0, SO 2

Top Performers at the Plate
LA **Ron Cey**, 2 for 3, 1 R, 1 RBI; **Pedro Guerrero**, 3 for 5, 1 R, 5 RBI
NY **Graig Nettles**, 2 for 3; **Willie Randolph**, 2 for 3, 1 R, 1 RBI, 2 BB

2B-NY/Nettles, Randolph. **3B**-LA/Guerrero. **HR**-LA/Guerrero; NY/Randolph. **SB**-LA/Lopes, Russell; NY/Randolph. **Time** 3:09. **Attendance** 56,513.

St. Louis Cardinals (4) vs. Milwaukee Brewers (3)

The 1982 World Series was a study in contrasts. The Milwaukee Brewers muscled their way to the American League pennant with a league-leading 216 home runs, led by Gorman Thomas's 39 and Ben Oglivie's 34. The entire Cardinal team didn't match that duo's 73 dingers (they hit a league-worst 67 homers), but manager Whitey Herzog built a successful group around speed and defense to bring St. Louis to its first Series in 14 years. Harvey Kuenn's Brewers lived up to their nickname—"Harvey's Wallbangers"—with an awesome offensive display in the opener. While starter Mike Caldwell threw a three-hitter, the Brew Crew hammered out 10 runs on 17 hits. Leadoff man Paul Molitor collected 5 hits in the game, and Robin Yount followed with 4 of his own. The Cardinals came back in Game 2, making up a 4-2 deficit on Darrell Porter's two-run double in the sixth. Having lost ace reliever Rollie Fingers to injury before the Series, Kuenn turned to Pete Ladd with one out in the eighth. Ladd proceeded to walk in the game-winning run on 4 straight balls with the bases loaded. Kuenn stuck with starter Pete Vuckovich for eight-plus innings in Game 3, but the Cy Young winner surrendered 2 home runs to Willie McGee in the loss. McGee, who knocked only 4 homers all year, drove in 4 runs with his two blasts, and he contributed some nifty fielding by robbing Molitor and Thomas of extra-base hits. Joaquin Andujar held Milwaukee to 3 hits through six innings, but had to leave the game after being struck in the shin by a line drive. Bruce Sutter got the save, despite yielding a two-run homer to Cecil Cooper; it was the only hit allowed by the reliever. The Cardinals carried a four-run lead into the seventh inning of Game 4, when an error by pitcher Dave LaPoint spurred a six-run Brewer offensive. Milwaukee faced four different pitchers in the seventh, and Yount and Cooper each drove in 2 runs with bases-loaded singles. Caldwell overcame 14 Cardinal hits in Game 5 to earn his second victory, and Yount had his second four-hit game of the Series, capping it off with a solo shot in the seventh. Back home at Busch Stadium, with their backs against the wall, the Cardinals erupted for 12 runs in Game 6. A two-hour rain delay interrupted their six-run sixth inning, but Keith Hernandez hit a two-run single after the skies cleared to jump-start the rally. Andujar returned to the hill in Game 7 and won the clincher for St. Louis, with Sutter pitching shutout relief. Darrell Porter, who was working his way back from drug and alcohol addiction, hit an RBI single in the eighth inning of the final game to cap off a banner postseason. The win gave the Cardinals their ninth Series title—the most in the National League and second only to the Yankees in all of baseball.

Above: Catcher Darrell Porter discusses strategy with manager Whitey Herzog during the 1982 Series. The Series marked a courageous comeback for the troubled catcher.

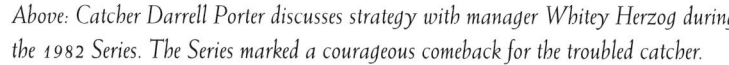

1982 WORLD SERIES COMPOSITE STATISTICS

ST. LOUIS CARDINALS/Whitey Herzog, Manager

Player	pos	G	AB	R	H	2B	3B	HR	RBI	BB	SO	SB	BA	SA	E	FPct
Joaquin Andujar	p	2	0	0	0	0	0	0	0	0	0	0	—	—	1	.750
Doug Bair	p	3	0	0	0	0	0	0	0	0	0	0	—	—	0	—
Steve Braun	ph-dh	2	2	0	1	0	0	0	2	1	0	0	.500	.500	—	—
Glenn Brummer	c	1	0	0	0	0	0	0	0	0	0	0	—	—	0	—
Bob Forsch	p	2	0	0	0	0	0	0	0	0	0	0	—	—	1	.500
David Green	cf-ph-dh-lf-pr	7	10	3	2	1	1	0	0	1	3	0	.200	.500	0	1.000
George Hendrick	rf	7	28	5	9	0	0	0	5	2	2	0	.321	.321	0	1.000
Keith Hernandez	1b	7	27	4	7	2	0	1	8	4	2	0	.259	.444	2	.972
Tom Herr	2b	7	25	2	4	2	0	0	5	3	3	0	.160	.240	1	.968
Dane Iorg	dh	5	17	4	9	4	1	0	1	0	0	0	.529	.882	—	—
Jim Kaat	p	4	0	0	0	0	0	0	0	0	0	0	—	—	0	—
Jeff Lahti	p	2	0	0	0	0	0	0	0	0	0	0	—	—	0	1.000
Dave LaPoint	p	2	0	0	0	0	0	0	0	0	0	0	—	—	1	.667
Willie McGee	cf	6	25	6	6	0	0	2	5	1	3	2	.240	.480	0	1.000
Ken Oberkfell	3b	7	24	4	7	1	0	0	1	2	1	2	.292	.333	1	.960
Darrell Porter	c	7	28	1	8	2	0	1	5	1	4	0	.286	.464	0	1.000
Mike Ramsey	3b-pr	3	1	1	0	0	0	0	0	0	1	0	.000	.000	0	—
Lonnie Smith	lf-dh	7	28	6	9	4	1	0	1	1	5	2	.321	.536	0	1.000
Ozzie Smith	ss	7	24	3	5	0	0	0	1	3	0	1	.208	.208	0	1.000
John Stuper	p	2	0	0	0	0	0	0	0	0	0	0	—	—	0	1.000
Bruce Sutter	p	4	0	0	0	0	0	0	0	0	0	0	—	—	0	1.000
Gene Tenace	dh-ph	5	6	0	0	0	0	0	0	1	2	0	.000	.000	—	—
Totals		7	245	39	67	16	3	4	34	20	26	7	.273	.472	7	.973

Pitcher	G	GS	CG	IP	H	R	ER	BB	SO	W-L	Sv	ERA
Joaquin Andujar	2	2	0	13⅓	10	3	2	1	4	2-0	0	1.35
Doug Bair	3	0	0	2	2	2	2	2	3	0-1	0	9.00
Bob Forsch	2	2	0	12⅔	18	10	7	3	4	0-2	0	4.97
Jim Kaat	4	0	0	2⅓	4	1	1	2	2	0-0	0	3.86
Jeff Lahti	2	0	0	1⅔	4	2	2	1	1	0-0	0	10.80
Dave LaPoint	2	1	0	8⅓	10	6	3	2	3	0-0	0	3.24
John Stuper	2	2	1	13	10	5	5	5	5	1-0	0	3.46
Bruce Sutter	4	0	0	7⅔	6	4	4	3	6	1-0	2	4.70
Totals	7	7	1	61	64	33	26	19	28	4-3	2	3.84

MILWAUKEE BREWERS/Harvey Kuenn, Manager

Player	pos	G	AB	R	H	2B	3B	HR	RBI	BB	SO	SB	BA	SA	E	FPct
Dwight Bernard	p	1	0	0	0	0	0	0	0	0	0	0	—	—	0	—
Mike Caldwell	p	3	0	0	0	0	0	0	0	0	0	0	—	—	0	1.000
Cecil Cooper	1b	7	28	3	8	1	0	1	6	1	1	0	.286	.429	1	.988
Marshall Edwards	pr-cf	1	0	0	0	0	0	0	0	0	0	0	—	—	0	—
Jim Gantner	2b	7	24	5	8	4	1	0	4	1	1	0	.333	.583	5	.894
Moose Haas	p	2	0	0	0	0	0	0	0	0	0	0	—	—	0	1.000
Roy Howell	dh	4	11	1	0	0	0	0	0	0	3	0	.000	.000	—	—
Pete Ladd	p	1	0	0	0	0	0	0	0	0	0	0	—	—	0	—
Bob McClure	p	5	0	0	0	0	0	0	0	0	0	0	—	—	0	—
Doc Medich	p	1	0	0	0	0	0	0	0	0	0	0	—	—	0	—
Paul Molitor	3b	7	31	5	11	0	0	0	3	2	4	1	.355	.355	0	1.000
Don Money	ph-dh	5	13	4	3	1	0	0	1	2	3	0	.231	.308	—	—
Charlie Moore	rf	7	26	3	9	3	0	0	2	1	0	0	.346	.462	0	1.000
Ben Oglivie	lf	7	27	4	6	0	1	1	1	2	4	0	.222	.407	1	.929
Ted Simmons	c	7	23	2	4	0	0	2	3	5	3	0	.174	.435	1	.968
Jim Slaton	p	2	0	0	0	0	0	0	0	0	0	0	—	—	0	—
Don Sutton	p	2	0	0	0	0	0	0	0	0	0	0	—	—	0	1.000
Gorman Thomas	cf	7	26	0	3	0	0	0	3	2	7	0	.115	.115	0	1.000
Pete Vuckovich	p	2	0	0	0	0	0	0	0	0	0	0	—	—	0	1.000
Ned Yost	c	1	0	0	0	0	0	0	0	1	0	0	—	—	0	1.000
Robin Yount	ss	7	29	6	12	3	0	1	6	2	4	1	.414	.621	3	.929
Totals		7	238	33	64	12	2	5	29	19	28	1	.269	.399	11	.960

Pitcher	G	GS	CG	IP	H	R	ER	BB	SO	W-L	Sv	ERA
Dwight Bernard	1	0	0	1	0	0	0	0	1	0-0	0	0.00
Mike Caldwell	3	2	1	17⅔	19	4	4	3	6	2-0	0	2.04
Moose Haas	2	1	0	7⅓	8	7	6	3	4	0-0	0	7.36
Pete Ladd	1	0	0	⅔	1	0	0	2	0	0-0	0	0.00
Bob McClure	5	0	0	4⅓	5	2	2	3	5	0-2	2	4.15
Doc Medich	1	0	0	2	5	4	4	1	0	0-0	0	18.00
Jim Slaton	2	0	0	2⅔	1	0	0	2	1	1-0	0	0.00
Don Sutton	2	2	0	10⅓	12	11	9	1	5	0-1	0	7.84
Pete Vuckovich	2	2	0	14	16	9	7	5	4	0-1	0	4.50
Totals	7	7	1	60	67	39	32	20	26	3-4	2	4.80

Series MVP: Darrell Porter, St. Louis Cardinals. **Series Outstanding Pitcher:** Joaquin Andujar, St. Louis Cardinals. **Average Length of Game:** 2 horus, 48 minutes. **Total Attendance:** 384,570. **Average Attendance:** 54,939 (53,723 at Busch Stadium; 56,559 at County Stadium). **Umpires:** Satch Davidson (NL), Jim Evans (AL), Bill Haller (AL), John Kibler (NL), Dave Phillips (AL), Lee Weyer (NL). **Winning Player's Share:** $43,280. **Losing Player's Share:** $31,935.

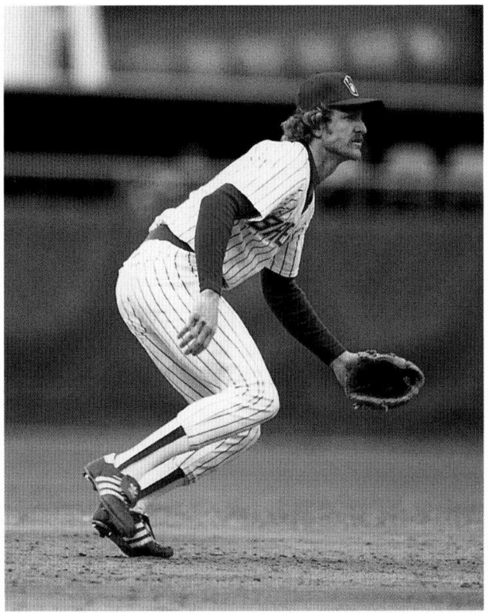

Above: *Hard-hitting shortstop Robin Yount twice got four hits in a game during the '82 Series.*

Below: *Willie McGee was clutch in the field and at the plate in Game 3. His two home runs in the game equaled half his season output.*

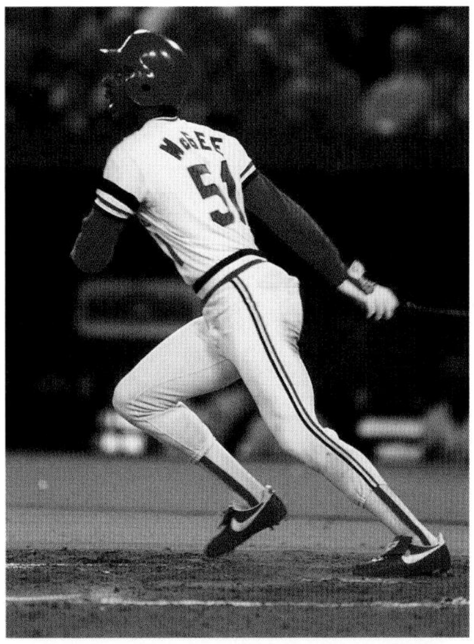

Robin Yount's 4 for 4 performance in Game 5 made him the first player to have two four-hit outings in Series play—and he did it in the same year, having gone 4 for 6 in Game 1.

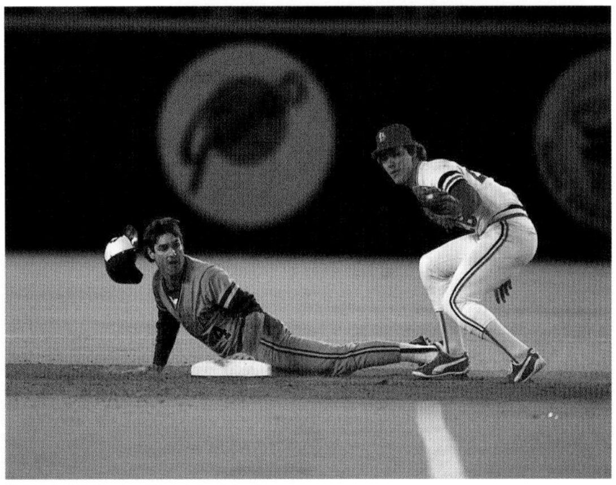

Above: *Paul Molitor collected five hits in Game 1 of 1982, helping to pace the Brewers to a 10-0 romp.*

Left: *Joaquin Andujar has to be carried off the field after Ted Simmons lined a single off his leg in the seventh inning of Game 3. Andujar was back to win Game 7 less than a week later.*

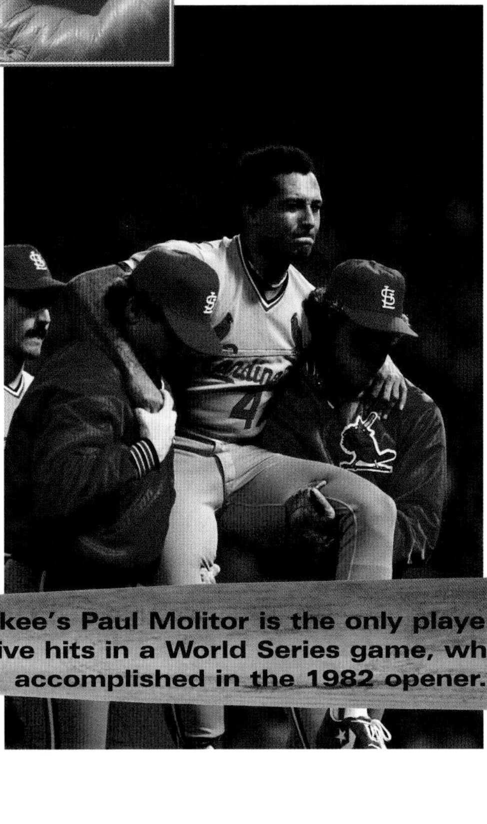

Milwaukee's Paul Molitor is the only player ever to get five hits in a World Series game, which he accomplished in the 1982 opener.

Game 1 Tuesday, October 12 at Busch Stadium, St. Louis

	1	2	3	4	5	6	7	8	9	R	H	E
Milwaukee Brewers	2	0	0	1	1	2	0	0	4	10	17	0
St. Louis Cardinals	0	0	0	0	0	0	0	0	0	0	3	1

Pitchers Mil **Mike Caldwell** (W, 1-0), IP 9, H 3, R 0, ER 0, BB 1, SO 3
StL **Bob Forsch** (L, 0-1), IP 5⅔, H 10, R 6, ER 4, BB 1, SO 1; **Jim Kaat**, IP 1⅓, H 1, R 0, ER 0, BB 1, SO 1; **Dave LaPoint**, IP 1⅔, H 3, R 2, ER 2, BB 1, SO 0; **Jeff Lahti**, IP ⅓, H 3, R 2, ER 2, BB 0, SO 1

Top Performers at the Plate
Mil **Paul Molitor**, 5 for 6, 1 R, 2 RBI; **Robin Yount**, 4 for 6, 1 R, 2 RBI
StL **Darrell Porter**, 2 for 3

2B-Mil/Moore, Yount; StL/Porter. **3B**-Mil/Gantner. **HR**-Mil/Simmons. **Time** 2:30. **Attendance** 53,723.

Game 2 Wednesday, October 13 at Busch Stadium, St. Louis

	1	2	3	4	5	6	7	8	9	R	H	E
Milwaukee Brewers	0	1	2	0	1	0	0	0	0	4	10	1
St. Louis Cardinals	0	0	2	0	0	2	0	1	x	5	8	0

Pitchers Mil **Don Sutton**, IP 6, H 5, R 4, ER 4, BB 1, SO 3; **Bob McClure** (L, 0-1), IP 1⅓, H 2, R 1, ER 1, BB 2, SO 2; **Pete Ladd**, IP ⅔, H 1, R 0, ER 0, BB 2, SO 0
StL **John Stuper**, IP 4, H 6, R 4, ER 4, BB 3, SO 3; **Jim Kaat**, IP ⅔, H 1, R 0, ER 0, BB 0, SO 0; **Doug Bair**, IP 2, H 1, R 0, ER 0, BB 0, SO 3; **Bruce Sutter** (W, 1-0), IP 2⅓, H 2, R 0, ER 0, BB 1, SO 1

Top Performers at the Plate
Mil **Cecil Cooper**, 3 for 5, 1 RBI; **Ted Simmons**, 1 for 3, 1 R, 1 RBI, 1 BB
StL **Ken Oberkfell**, 2 for 3, 1 R, 1 RBI; **Darrell Porter**, 2 for 4, 2 RBI

2B-Mil/Cooper, Moore, Yount; StL/Herr, Porter. **HR**-Mil/Simmons. **SB**-Mil/Molitor; StL/McGee, Oberkfell, O. Smith. **Time** 2:54. **Attendance** 53,723.

Game 3 Friday, October 15 at County Stadium, Milwaukee

	1	2	3	4	5	6	7	8	9	R	H	E
St. Louis Cardinals	0	0	0	0	3	0	2	0	1	6	6	1
Milwaukee Brewers	0	0	0	0	0	0	0	2	0	2	5	3

Pitchers StL **Joaquin Andujar** (W, 1-0), IP 6⅓, H 3, R 0, ER 0, BB 1, SO 3; **Jim Kaat**, IP ⅓, H 1, R 0, ER 0, BB 0, SO 1; **Doug Bair**, IP 0, H 0, R 0, ER 0, BB 1, SO 0; **Bruce Sutter** (Sv, 1), IP 2⅓, H 1, R 2, ER 2, BB 1, SO 1
Mil **Pete Vuckovich** (L, 0-1), IP 8⅔, H 6, R 6, ER 4, BB 3, SO 1; **Bob McClure**, IP ⅓, H 0, R 0, ER 0, BB 0, SO 0

Top Performers at the Plate
StL **Willie McGee**, 2 for 3, 2 R, 4 RBI, 2 HR; **Lonnie Smith**, 2 for 4, 2 R
Mil **Cecil Cooper**, 1 for 4, 1 R, 2 RBI; **Jim Gantner**, 2 for 3

2B-StL/Iorg, L. Smith; Mil/Gantner. **3B**-StL/L. Smith. **HR**-StL/McGee 2; Mil/Cooper. **Time** 2:53. **Attendance** 56,556.

Game 4 Saturday, October 16 at County Stadium, Milwaukee

	1	2	3	4	5	6	7	8	9	R	H	E
St. Louis Cardinals	1	3	0	0	0	1	0	0	0	5	8	1
Milwaukee Brewers	0	0	0	0	1	0	6	0	x	7	10	2

Pitchers StL **Dave LaPoint**, IP 6⅔, H 7, R 4, ER 1, BB 1, SO 3; **Doug Bair** (L, 0-1), IP 0, H 1, R 2, ER 2, BB 1, SO 0; **Jim Kaat**, IP 0, H 1, R 1, ER 1, BB 1, SO 0; **Jeff Lahti**, IP 1⅓, H 1, R 0, ER 0, BB 1, SO 0
Mil **Moose Haas**, IP 5⅓, H 7, R 5, ER 4, BB 2, SO 3; **Jim Slaton** (W, 1-0), IP 2, H 1, R 0, ER 0, BB 2, SO 1; **Bob McClure** (Sv, 1), IP 1⅔, H 0, R 0, ER 0, BB 0, SO 2

Top Performers at the Plate
StL **Dane Iorg**, 2 for 4, 1 RBI; **Ken Oberkfell**, 1 for 2, 2 R, 2 BB
Mil **Don Money**, 2 for 4, 2 R; **RobinYount**, 2 for 4, 1 R, 2 RBI

2B-StL/Iorg, Oberkfell, L. Smith; Mil/Gantner, Money. **3B**-Mil/Oglivie. **SB**-StL/McGee, Oberkfell. **Time** 3:04. **Attendance** 56,560.

Game 5 Sunday, October 17 at County Stadium, Milwaukee

	1	2	3	4	5	6	7	8	9	R	H	E
St. Louis Cardinals	0	0	1	0	0	0	1	0	2	4	15	2
Milwaukee Brewers	1	0	1	0	1	0	1	2	x	6	11	1

Pitchers StL **Bob Forsch** (L, 0-2), IP 7, H 8, R 4, ER 3, BB 2, SO 3; **Bruce Sutter**, IP 1, H 3, R 2, ER 2, BB 1, SO 2
Mil **Mike Caldwell** (W, 2-0), IP 8⅓, H 14, R 4, ER 4, BB 2, SO 3; **Bob McClure** (Sv, 2), IP ⅔, H 1, R 0, ER 0, BB 0, SO 1

Top Performers at the Plate
StL **George Hendrick**, 3 for 5, 2 RBI; **Keith Hernandez**, 3 for 4, 1 R, 2 RBI, 1 BB, 2 2B
Mil **Charlie Moore**, 2 for 4, 1 R, 1 RBI; **Robin Yount**, 4 for 4, 2 R, 1 RBI

2B-StL/Green, Hernandez 2; Mil/Moore, Yount. **3B**-StL/Green. **HR**-Mil/Yount. **SB**-StL/L. Smith. **Time** 3:02. **Attendance** 56,562.

Game 6 Tuesday, October 19 at Busch Stadium, St. Louis

	1	2	3	4	5	6	7	8	9	R	H	E
Milwaukee Brewers	0	0	0	0	0	0	0	0	1	1	4	4
St. Louis Cardinals	0	2	0	3	2	6	0	0	x	13	12	1

Pitchers Mil **Don Sutton** (L, 0-1), IP 4⅓, H 7, R 7, ER 5, BB 0, SO 2; **Jim Slaton**, IP ⅔, H 0, R 0, ER 0, BB 0, SO 0; **Doc Medich**, IP 2, H 5, R 6, ER 4, BB 1, SO 0; **Dwight Bernard**, IP 1, H 0, R 0, ER 0, BB 0, SO 1
StL **John Stuper** (W, 1-0), IP 9, H 4, R 1, ER 1, BB 2, SO 2

Top Performers at the Plate
Mil **Jim Gantner**, 1 for 3, 1 R
StL **Keith Hernandez**, 2 for 5, 2 R, 4 RBI; **Dane Iorg**, 3 for 4, 3 R, 2 2B

2B-Mil/Gantner; StL/Herr, Iorg 2. **3B**-StL/Iorg. **HR**-StL/Hernandez, Porter. **SB**-StL/L. Smith. **Time** 2:21. **Attendance** 53,723.

Game 7 Wednesday, October 20 at Busch Stadium, St. Louis

	1	2	3	4	5	6	7	8	9	R	H	E
Milwaukee Brewers	0	0	0	0	1	2	0	0	0	3	7	0
St. Louis Cardinals	0	0	0	1	0	3	0	2	x	6	15	1

Pitchers Mil **Pete Vuckovich**, IP 5⅓, H 10, R 3, ER 3, BB 2, SO 3; **Bob McClure** (L, 0-2), IP ⅓, H 2, R 1, ER 1, BB 1, SO 0; **Moose Haas**, IP 2, H 1, R 2, ER 2, BB 1, SO 1; **Mike Caldwell**, IP ⅓, H 2, R 0, ER 0, BB 0, SO 0
StL **Joaquin Andujar** (W, 2-0), IP 7, H 7, R 3, ER 2, BB 0, SO 1; **Bruce Sutter** (Sv, 2), IP 2, H 0, R 0, ER 0, BB 0, SO 2

Top Performers at the Plate
Mil **Jim Gantner**, 1 for 3, 1 R; **Paul Molitor**, 2 for 4, 1 R
StL **Keith Hernandez**, 2 for 3, 1 R, 2 RBI, 2 BB; **Lonnie Smith**, 3 for 5, 2 R, 1 RBI, 2 2B

2B-Mil/Gantner; StL/L. Smith 2. **HR**-Mil/Oglivie. **Time** 2:50. **Attendance** 53,723.

Baltimore Orioles (4) vs. Philadelphia Phillies (1)

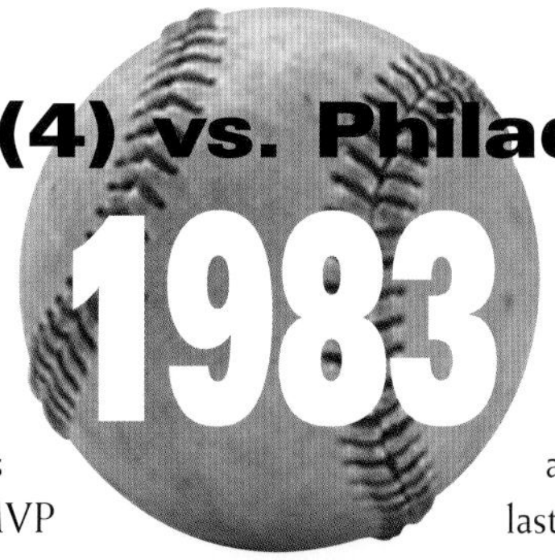

The Baltimore Orioles participated in four World Series during Earl Weaver's 15-year managerial reign, but came away with only one championship. In 1983, the first year of the post-Weaver era, new manager Joe Altobelli led the team to another Fall Classic, and brought Baltimore its first title since 1970. First baseman Eddie Murray and MVP shortstop Cal Ripken Jr. brought power and consistency to a lineup of mostly platoon players. The Philadelphia Phillies reached the postseason with an experienced squad consisting of former Big Red Machine cogs Pete Rose, Joe Morgan and Tony Perez—each one over 40—and Phillie mainstays Mike Schmidt and Steve Carlton. Ten-year-veteran John Denny was a Cy Young winner with Philadelphia in 1983, and he bested Baltimore's 18-game-winner Scott McGregor in Game 1 of the Series. Solo homers by Jim Dwyer and Joe Morgan forged a 1-1 tie until Garry Maddox launched McGregor's first pitch of the eighth inning into the left-field seats for the win. Rookie pitcher Mike Boddicker threw a complete-game three-hitter for Baltimore in Game 2, and his sacrifice fly in the fifth gave his team a two-run edge. Philadelphia manager Paul Owens created a stir in Game 3 by benching the slumping Rose in favor of Perez, an affront that Rose did not take kindly to. (Perez contributed a single in the second inning.) Gary Matthews and Morgan staked the 38-year-old Carlton a 2-0 lead on a pair of solo home runs, but a sixth-inning blast by Dan Ford and a two-out rally in the

seventh put the Phils in the hole. Benny Ayala followed Rick Dempsey's double with a game-tying RBI single in the seventh, and an error by shortstop Ivan DeJesus allowed Ayala to come around for the go-ahead run. Altobelli used a trio of pitchers in relief to keep the Phillies scoreless in the last six innings. Back in the starting lineup for Game 4, Rose stroked a single and scored a run in the fourth and hit an RBI double in the fifth to put Philadelphia up 3-2. Denny walked pinch hitter Ken Singleton with the bases loaded in the sixth to bring the Orioles even in the game, and reliever Willie Hernandez promptly yielded an RBI sac fly to John Shelby; left fielder Matthews prevented more serious damage with a leaping catch of Shelby's drive at the wall. Rich Dauer drove in an insurance run with a seventh-inning single, his third RBI on the day, as the Orioles mounted a three-games-to-one advantage. Baltimore got its second complete-game showing of the Series when McGregor shut the Phillies out on five hits in Game 5. Eddie Murray, who had driven in no runs in a 2 for 16 struggle through the first four games, came through with two homers and three RBIs, while eighth-place hitter Dempsey continued his superb Series with a double and a solo homer, giving him a .385 average and the Series MVP.

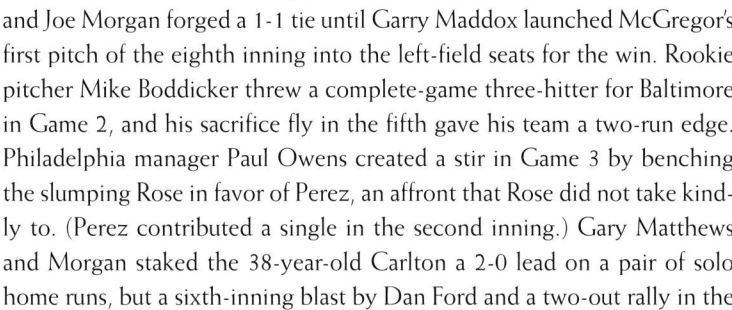

Above: The 1983 regular-season MVP, Cal Ripken Jr., pivots to turn a double play in the eighth inning of Game 2.

1983 WORLD SERIES COMPOSITE STATISTICS

BALTIMORE ORIOLES/Joe Altobelli, Manager

Player	pos	G	AB	R	H	2B	3B	HR	RBI	BB	SO	SB	BA	SA	E	FPct
Benny Ayala	ph	1	1	1	1	0	0	0	1	0	0	0	1.000	1.000	–	–
Mike Boddicker	p	1	3	0	0	0	0	0	1	0	1	0	.000	.000	0	1.000
Al Bumbry	cf	4	11	0	1	1	0	0	1	0	1	0	.091	.182	0	1.000
Todd Cruz	3b	5	16	1	2	0	0	0	0	1	3	0	.125	.125	2	.905
Rich Dauer	2b-3b	5	19	2	4	1	0	0	3	0	3	0	.211	.263	0	1.000
Storm Davis	p	1	2	0	0	0	0	0	0	0	2	0	.000	.000	0	1.000
Rick Dempsey	c	5	13	3	5	4	0	1	2	2	2	0	.385	.923	0	1.000
Jim Dwyer	rf	2	8	3	3	1	0	1	1	0	0	0	.375	.875	0	1.000
Mike Flanagan	p	1	1	0	0	0	0	0	0	0	1	0	.000	.000	0	–
Dan Ford	ph-rf	5	12	1	2	0	0	1	1	1	5	0	.167	.417	0	1.000
Tito Landrum	pr-lf-rf	3	0	0	0	0	0	0	0	0	0	1	–	–	0	1.000
John Lowenstein	lf	4	13	2	5	1	0	1	1	0	3	0	.385	.692	1	.800
Tippy Martinez	p	3	0	0	0	0	0	0	0	0	0	0	–	–	0	–
Scott McGregor	p	2	5	0	0	0	0	0	0	0	0	0	.000	.000	0	–
Eddie Murray	1b	5	20	2	5	0	0	2	3	1	4	0	.250	.550	1	.979
Joe Nolan	ph-c	2	2	0	0	0	0	0	0	1	0	0	.000	.000	0	1.000
Jim Palmer	p	1	0	0	0	0	0	0	0	0	0	0	–	–	0	–
Cal Ripken Jr.	ss	5	18	2	3	0	0	0	1	3	4	0	.167	.167	0	1.000
Gary Roenicke	ph-lf	3	7	0	0	0	0	0	0	0	2	0	.000	.000	0	1.000
Lenn Sakata	pr-2b	1	1	0	0	0	0	0	0	0	0	0	.000	.000	0	1.000
John Shelby	ph-cf	5	9	1	4	0	0	0	1	0	4	0	.444	.444	0	1.000
Ken Singleton	ph	2	1	0	0	0	0	0	1	1	1	0	.000	.000	–	–
Sammy Stewart	p	3	2	0	0	0	0	0	0	0	1	0	.000	.000	0	–
Totals		5	164	18	35	8	0	6	17	10	37	1	.213	.372	4	.979

Pitcher	G	GS	CG	IP	H	R	ER	BB	SO	W-L	Sv	ERA
Mike Boddicker	1	1	1	9	3	1	0	6	1-0	0	0.00
Storm Davis	1	1	0	5	6	3	3	1	3	1-0	0	5.40
Mike Flanagan	1	1	0	4	6	2	2	1	1	0-0	0	4.50
Tippy Martinez	3	0	0	3	3	1	1	0	0	0-0	2	3.00
Scott McGregor	2	2	1	17	9	2	2	2	12	1-1	0	1.06
Jim Palmer	1	0	0	2	2	0	0	1	1	1-0	0	0.00
Sammy Stewart	3	0	0	5	2	0	0	2	6	0-0	0	0.00
Totals	5	5	2	45	31	9	8	7	29	4-1	2	1.60

PHILADELPHIA PHILLIES/Paul Owens, Manager

Player	pos	G	AB	R	H	2B	3B	HR	RBI	BB	SO	SB	BA	SA	E	FPct
Larry Andersen	p	2	0	0	0	0	0	0	0	0	0	0	–	–	0	1.000
Marty Bystrom	p	1	0	0	0	0	0	0	0	0	0	0	–	–	0	1.000
Steve Carlton	p	1	3	0	0	0	0	0	0	0	1	0	.000	.000	0	–
Ivan DeJesus	ss	5	16	0	2	0	0	0	0	1	2	0	.125	.125	1	.950
John Denny	p	2	5	1	1	0	0	0	1	0	1	0	.200	.200	0	1.000
Bob Dernier	pr	1	0	1	0	0	0	0	0	0	0	0	–	–	–	–
Bo Diaz	c	5	15	1	5	1	0	0	0	1	2	0	.333	.400	1	.974
Greg Gross	cf	2	6	0	0	0	0	0	0	0	0	0	.000	.000	0	1.000
Von Hayes	ph-rf	4	3	0	0	0	0	0	0	0	1	0	.000	.000	0	1.000
Willie Hernandez	p	3	0	0	0	0	0	0	0	0	0	0	–	–	0	1.000
Al Holland	p	2	0	0	0	0	0	0	0	0	0	0	–	–	0	–
Charles Hudson	p	2	2	0	0	0	0	0	0	0	1	0	.000	.000	0	–
Joe Lefebvre	rf-ph	3	5	0	1	1	0	0	2	0	1	0	.200	.400	0	1.000
Sixto Lezcano	rf-ph	4	8	0	1	0	0	0	0	0	2	0	.125	.125	0	1.000
Garry Maddox	cf-ph	4	12	1	3	1	0	1	1	0	2	0	.250	.583	0	1.000
Gary Matthews	lf	5	16	1	4	0	1	1	2	2	2	0	.250	.438	0	1.000
Joe Morgan	2b	5	19	3	5	0	1	2	2	2	3	1	.263	.684	0	1.000
Tony Perez	ph-1b	4	10	0	2	0	0	0	0	0	2	0	.200	.200	0	1.000
Ron Reed	p	3	0	0	0	0	0	0	0	0	0	0	–	–	0	–
Pete Rose	1b-ph-rf	5	16	1	5	1	0	0	1	1	3	0	.313	.375	0	1.000
Juan Samuel	pr-ph	3	1	0	0	0	0	0	0	0	0	0	.000	.000	–	–
Mike Schmidt	3b	5	20	0	1	0	0	0	0	0	6	0	.050	.050	1	.917
Ossie Virgil	c-ph	3	2	0	1	0	0	0	1	0	0	0	.500	.500	0	1.000
Totals		5	159	9	31	4	1	4	9	7	29	1	.195	.308	3	.983

Pitcher	G	GS	CG	IP	H	R	ER	BB	SO	W-L	Sv	ERA
Larry Andersen	2	0	0	4	4	1	1	0	1	0-0	0	2.25
Marty Bystrom	1	0	0	1	0	0	0	0	1	0-0	0	0.00
Steve Carlton	1	1	0	6⅔	5	3	2	3	7	0-1	0	2.70
John Denny	2	2	0	13	12	5	5	3	9	1-1	0	3.46
Willie Hernandez	3	0	0	4	0	0	0	1	4	0-0	0	0.00
Al Holland	2	0	0	3⅔	1	0	0	0	5	0-0	1	0.00
Charles Hudson	2	2	0	8⅓	9	8	8	1	6	0-2	0	8.64
Ron Reed	3	0	0	3⅓	4	1	1	2	4	0-0	0	2.70
Totals	5	5	0	44	35	18	17	10	37	1-4	1	3.48

Series MVP: Rick Dempsey, Baltimore Orioles. **Series Outstanding Pitcher:** Mike Boddicker, Baltimore Orioles. **Average Length of Game:** 2 hours, 31 minutes. **Total Attendance:** 304,139. **Average Attendance:** 60,828 (52,168 at Memorial Stadium; 66,601 at Veterans Stadium). **Umpires:** Al Clark (AL), Steve Palermo (AL), Frank Pulli (NL), Dutch Rennert (NL), Marty Springstead (AL), Ed Vargo (NL). **Winning Player's Share:** $65,488. **Losing Player's Share:** $43,280.

Above: The young Mike Boddicker was practically untouchable in his three-hit shutout in Game 2.

Below: Forty-year-old Joe Morgan watches as he ties Game 1 with a homer—making him the oldest player to hit a World Series four-bagger. He hit another one three days later.

Above: Pete Rose did not appreciate being benched during the third game of the World Series.

Right: Rick Dempsey, the surprise star for Baltimore in the 1983 Series, receives a congratulatory pat from coach Cal Ripken Sr. as he rounds third.

Game 1   Tuesday, October 11 at Memorial Stadium, Baltimore

	1	2	3	4	5	6	7	8	9		R	H	E
Philadelphia Phillies	0	0	0	0	0	1	0	1	0		2	5	0
Baltimore Orioles	1	0	0	0	0	0	0	0	0		1	5	1

Pitchers   Phi   John Denny (W, 1-0), IP 7⅔, H 5, R 1, ER 1, BB 0, SO 5; Al Holland (Sv, 1), IP 1⅓, H 0, R 0, ER 0, BB 0, SO 1
      Bal   Scott McGregor (L, 0-1), IP 8, H 4, R 2, ER 2, BB 0, SO 6; Sammy Stewart, IP 2⅔, H 1, R 0, ER 0, BB 0, SO 1; Tippy Martinez, IP ⅓, H 0, R 0, ER 0, BB 0, SO 0

Top Performers at the Plate
      Phi   Garry Maddox, 1 for 3, 1 R, 1 RBI; Joe Morgan, 2 for 4, 1 R, 1 RBI
      Bal   Jim Dwyer, 1 for 3, 1 R, 1 RBI

2B-Bal/Bumbry. **HR**-Phi/Maddox, Morgan; Bal/Dwyer. **Time** 2:22. **Attendance** 52,204.

Game 2   Wednesday, October 12 at Memorial Stadium, Baltimore

	1	2	3	4	5	6	7	8	9		R	H	E
Philadelphia Phillies	0	0	0	1	0	0	0	0	0		1	3	0
Baltimore Orioles	0	0	0	0	3	0	1	0	x		4	9	1

Pitchers   Phi   Charles Hudson (L, 0-1), IP 4⅓, H 5, R 3, ER 3, BB 0, SO 3; Willie Hernandez, IP ⅔, H 0, R 0, ER 0, BB 1, SO 1; Larry Andersen, IP 2, H 3, R 1, ER 1, BB 0, SO 1; Ron Reed, IP 1, H 1, R 0, ER 0, BB 1, SO 1
      Bal   Mike Boddicker (W, 1-0), IP 9, H 3, R 1, ER 0, BB 0, SO 6

Top Performers at the Plate
      Bal   Rick Dempsey, 1 for 3, 1 RBI, 1 BB; John Lowenstein, 3 for 4, 1 R, 1 RBI

2B-Bal/Dempsey, Lowenstein. **HR**-Bal/Lowenstein. **SB**-Phi/Morgan; Bal/Landrum. **Time** 2:27. **Attendance** 52,132.

Game 3   Friday, October 14 at Veterans Stadium, Philadelphia

	1	2	3	4	5	6	7	8		R	H	E
Baltimore Orioles	0	0	0	0	0	1	2	0		3	6	1
Philadelphia Phillies	0	1	1	0	0	0	0	0		2	8	2

Pitchers   Bal   Mike Flanagan, IP 4, H 6, R 2, ER 2, BB 1, SO 1; Jim Palmer (W, 1-0), IP 2, H 2, R 0, ER 0, BB 1, SO 1; Sammy Stewart, IP 2, H 0, R 0, ER 0, BB 1, SO 3; Tippy Martinez (Sv, 1), IP 1, H 0, R 0, ER 0, BB 0, SO 0
      Phi   Steve Carlton (L, 0-1), IP 6⅔, H 5, R 3, ER 2, BB 3, SO 7; Al Holland, IP 2⅓, H 1, R 0, ER 0, BB 0, SO 4

Top Performers at the Plate
      Bal   Rick Dempsey, 2 for 4, 1 R, 2 2B; Dan Ford, 1 for 3, 1 R, 1 RBI, 1 BB
      Phi   Ivan DeJesus, 2 for 3, 1 BB; Joe Morgan, 1 for 3, 1 R, 1 RBI, 1 BB

2B-Bal/Dempsey 2. **HR**-Bal/Ford; Phi/Matthews, Morgan. **Time** 2:35. **Attendance** 65,792.

Game 4   Saturday, October 15 at Veterans Stadium, Philadelphia

	1	2	3	4	5	6	7	8		R	H	E
Baltimore Orioles	0	0	0	2	0	2	1	0		5	10	1
Philadelphia Phillies	0	0	0	1	2	0	0	1		4	10	0

Pitchers   Bal   Storm Davis (W, 1-0), IP 5, H 6, R 3, ER 3, BB 1, SO 3; Sammy Stewart, IP 2⅓, H 1, R 0, ER 0, BB 1, SO 2; Tippy Martinez (Sv, 2), IP 1⅔, H 3, R 1, ER 1, BB 0, SO 0
      Phi   John Denny (L, 1-1), IP 5⅓, H 7, R 4, ER 4, BB 3, SO 4; Willie Hernandez, IP ⅓, H 0, R 0, ER 0, BB 0, SO 0; Ron Reed, IP 1⅓, H 2, R 1, ER 1, BB 1, SO 3; Larry Andersen, IP 2, H 1, R 0, ER 0, BB 0, SO 0

Top Performers at the Plate
      Bal   Rich Dauer, 3 for 4, 1 R, 3 RBI; Jim Dwyer, 2 for 5, 2 R
      Phi   Bo Diaz, 2 for 4, 1 R; Pete Rose, 2 for 3, 1 R, 1 RBI, 1 BB

2B-Bal/Dauer, Dwyer; Phi/Diaz, Lefebvre, Rose. **Time** 2:50. **Attendance** 66,947.

Game 5   Sunday, October 16 at Veterans Stadium, Philadelphia

	1	2	3	4	5	6	7	8	9		R	H	E
Baltimore Orioles	0	1	1	2	1	0	0	0	0		5	5	0
Philadelphia Phillies	0	0	0	0	0	0	0	0	0		0	5	1

Pitchers   Bal   Scott McGregor (W, 1-1), IP 9, H 5, R 0, ER 0, BB 2, SO 6
      Phi   Charles Hudson (L, 0-2), IP 4, H 4, R 5, ER 5, BB 1, SO 3; Marty Bystrom, IP 1, H 0, R 0, ER 0, BB 0, SO 1; Willie Hernandez, IP 3, H 0, R 0, ER 0, BB 0, SO 3; Ron Reed, IP 1, H 1, R 0, ER 0, BB 0, SO 0

Top Performers at the Plate
      Bal   Rick Dempsey, 2 for 3, 2 R, 1 RBI; Eddie Murray, 3 for 4, 2 R, 3 RBI, 2 HR
      Phi   Garry Maddox, 2 for 4; Pete Rose, 2 for 4

2B-Bal/Dempsey; Phi/Maddox. **3B**-Phi/Morgan. **HR**-Bal/Dempsey, Murray 2. **Time** 2:21. **Attendance** 67,064.

At age 40, Joe Morgan became the oldest player to notch a World Series home run.

249

Detroit Tigers (4) vs. San Diego Padres (1)

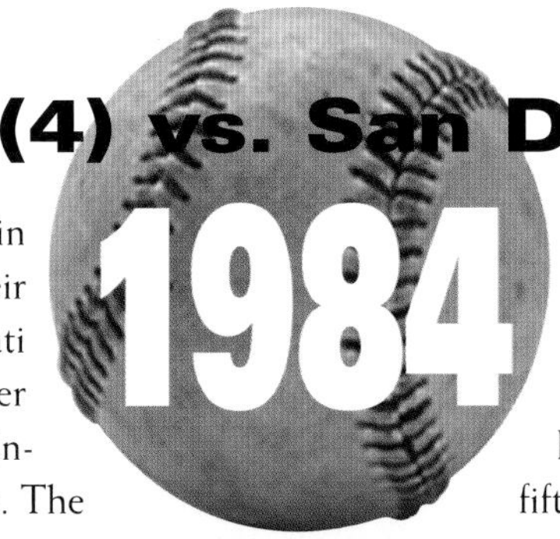

Two veteran managers with traditions of winning met in the World Series in 1984 for the second time in their careers, both with different teams. Former Cincinnati manager Sparky Anderson now skippered a Detroit Tiger team that ran away with the Eastern Division title, winning 35 of their first 40 games en route to 104 victories. The Tigers had superb defense up the middle, and Lance Parrish, Chet Lemon and Kirk Gibson were all 20-home-run hitters on the year. Anderson's starting trio of Jack Morris, Dan Petry and Milt Wilcox combined to win 54 games, and reliever Willie Hernandez claimed both the Cy Young award and the league MVP in 1984. Over in the National League, Dick Williams led the San Diego Padres to their first pennant with a combination of championship-tested veterans (Steve Garvey, Graig Nettles, Goose Gossage) and the pure hitting of Tony Gwynn. Most experts foresaw an easy win for Detroit, and sure enough, the Tigers snatched the opener behind Morris's complete game. After giving up a two-run double in the first inning, Morris shut San Diego out the rest of the way, including striking out the side in the sixth with two men on base. The Tigers started off Game 2 with three runs early on, but San Diego's Andy Hawkins and Craig Lefferts pitched scoreless ball for eight-plus innings in relief. The Padre hitters battled back against Petry, scattering two runs before Kurt Bevacqua capped the victory with a three-run homer. Marty Castillo got the Tigers going in Game 3 with a two-run blast in the second inning, and Alan Trammell's double drove in another. Then, the Padre pitching did itself in. Greg Booker walked in a run with the bases loaded, and the very next inning, he walked the bases full before Greg Harris came on and hit Gibson with a pitch to force in the fifth run of the game. Morris took care of Game 4, yielding five hits in his second complete-game performance. Trammell knocked a pair of two-run blasts to account for all the scoring for Detroit. In Game 5, the Tigers chased starter Mark Thurmond from the mound before the first inning was over. Gibson led the way with an upper-deck homer with a man on, and Lemon added an RBI single. San Diego tied the game in the fourth, but Gibson regained the lead for Detroit by hustling home from third base on Rusty Kuntz's short fly ball in the fifth inning. Bevacqua's solo shot in the eighth cut the score to 4-3, but Gibson stepped up big again in the bottom of the inning and pounded another ball into Tiger Stadium's upper deck for a three-run homer. Detroit got consistent clutch production from their star shortstop, Alan Trammell, who batted .450 for the Series and drove in six runs. With the win, Sparky Anderson became the first manager to lead a champion in both leagues, and Detroit had its fourth World Series title.

Above: Jack Morris fires one home during his Game 4 victory in Detroit.

1984 WORLD SERIES COMPOSITE STATISTICS

DETROIT TIGERS/Sparky Anderson, Manager

Player	pos	G	AB	R	H	2B	3B	HR	RBI	BB	SO	SB	BA	SA	E	FPct
Doug Bair	p	1	0	0	0	0	0	0	0	0	0	0	–	–	0	–
Dave Bergman	pr-1b	5	5	0	0	0	0	0	0	0	1	0	.000	.000	0	1.000
Tom Brookens	ph-3b	3	3	0	0	0	0	0	0	0	1	0	.000	.000	0	1.000
Marty Castillo	3b	3	9	2	3	0	0	1	2	2	1	0	.333	.667	0	1.000
Darrell Evans	1b-3b	5	15	1	1	0	0	0	1	4	4	0	.067	.067	0	1.000
Barbaro Garbey	dh-ph	4	12	0	0	0	0	0	0	0	2	0	.000	.000	–	–
Kirk Gibson	rf	5	18	4	6	0	0	2	7	4	4	3	.333	.667	2	.750
John Grubb	ph-dh	4	3	0	1	0	0	0	0	0	0	0	.333	.333	–	–
Willie Hernandez	p	3	0	0	0	0	0	0	0	0	0	0	–	–	0	1.000
Larry Herndon	lf-ph	5	15	1	5	0	0	1	3	3	2	0	.333	.533	0	1.000
Howard Johnson	ph	1	1	0	0	0	0	0	0	0	0	0	.000	.000	–	–
Ruppert Jones	lf	2	3	0	0	0	0	0	0	0	1	0	.000	.000	0	1.000
Rusty Kuntz	ph	2	1	0	0	0	0	0	1	0	1	0	.000	.000	–	–
Chet Lemon	dh	5	17	1	5	0	0	0	1	2	2	2	.294	.294	0	1.000
Aurelio Lopez	p	2	0	0	0	0	0	0	0	0	0	0	–	–	0	–
Jack Morris	p	2	0	0	0	0	0	0	0	0	0	0	–	–	0	1.000
Lance Parrish	c	5	18	3	5	1	0	1	2	3	2	1	.278	.500	1	.971
Dan Petry	p	2	0	0	0	0	0	0	0	0	0	0	–	–	0	1.000
Bill Scherrer	p	3	0	0	0	0	0	0	0	0	0	0	–	–	0	1.000
Alan Trammell	ss	5	20	5	9	1	0	2	6	2	2	1	.450	.800	1	.944
Lou Whitaker	2b	5	18	6	5	2	0	0	0	4	4	0	.278	.389	0	1.000
Milt Wilcox	p	1	0	0	0	0	0	0	0	0	0	0	–	–	0	1.000
Totals		**5**	**158**	**23**	**40**	**4**	**0**	**7**	**23**	**24**	**27**	**7**	**.253**	**.411**	**4**	**.979**

Pitcher	G	GS	CG	IP	H	R	ER	BB	SO	W-L	Sv	ERA
Doug Bair	1	0	0	⅔	0	0	0	0	1	0-0	0	0.00
Willie Hernandez	3	0	0	5⅓	4	1	1	0	0	0-0	2	1.69
Aurelio Lopez	2	0	0	3	1	0	0	1	4	1-0	0	0.00
Jack Morris	2	2	2	18	13	4	4	3	13	2-0	0	2.00
Dan Petry	2	2	0	8	14	8	8	5	4	0-1	0	9.00
Bill Scherrer	3	0	0	3	5	1	1	0	0	0-0	0	3.00
Milt Wilcox	1	1	0	6	7	1	1	2	4	1-0	0	1.50
Totals	**5**	**5**	**2**	**44**	**44**	**15**	**15**	**11**	**26**	**4-1**	**2**	**3.07**

SAN DIEGO PADRES/Dick Williams, Manager

Player	pos	G	AB	R	H	2B	3B	HR	RBI	BB	SO	SB	BA	SA	E	FPct
Kurt Bevacqua	dh	5	17	4	7	2	0	2	4	1	2	0	.412	.882	–	–
Bruce Bochy	ph	1	1	0	1	0	0	0	0	0	0	0	1.000	1.000	–	–
Greg Booker	p	1	0	0	0	0	0	0	0	0	0	0	–	–	0	1.000
Bobby Brown	cf-lf	5	15	1	1	0	0	0	2	0	4	0	.067	.067	0	1.000
Dave Dravecky	p	2	0	0	0	0	0	0	0	0	0	0	–	–	0	–
Tim Flannery	ph-2b	1	1	0	1	0	0	0	0	0	0	0	1.000	1.000	0	1.000
Steve Garvey	1b	5	20	2	4	2	0	0	2	0	2	0	.200	.300	0	1.000
Rich "Goose" Gossage	p	2	0	0	0	0	0	0	0	0	0	0	–	–	0	1.000
Tony Gwynn	rf	5	19	1	5	0	0	0	0	3	2	1	.263	.263	1	.929
Greg Harris	p	1	0	0	0	0	0	0	0	0	0	0	–	–	0	–
Andy Hawkins	p	3	0	0	0	0	0	0	0	0	0	0	–	–	0	1.000
Terry Kennedy	c	5	19	2	4	1	0	1	3	1	1	0	.211	.421	0	1.000
Craig Lefferts	p	3	0	0	0	0	0	0	0	0	0	0	–	–	0	–
Tim Lollar	p	1	0	0	0	0	0	0	0	0	0	0	–	–	0	–
Carmelo Martinez	lf	5	17	0	3	0	0	0	0	1	9	0	.176	.176	1	.875
Graig Nettles	3b	5	12	2	3	0	0	0	2	5	0	0	.250	.250	0	1.000
Ron Roenicke	lf-pr	2	0	0	0	0	0	0	0	0	0	0	–	–	0	–
Luis Salazar	pr-3b-cf-ph	4	3	0	1	0	0	0	0	0	0	0	.333	.333	0	1.000
Eric Show	p	1	0	0	0	0	0	0	0	0	0	0	–	–	0	–
Champ Summers	ph	1	1	0	0	0	0	0	0	0	1	0	.000	.000	–	–
Garry Templeton	ss	5	19	1	6	1	0	0	0	0	3	0	.316	.368	0	1.000
Mark Thurmond	p	2	0	0	0	0	0	0	0	0	0	0	–	–	0	1.000
Ed Whitson	p	1	0	0	0	0	0	0	0	0	0	0	–	–	0	–
Alan Wiggins	2b	5	22	2	8	1	0	0	1	0	2	1	.364	.409	2	.905
Totals		**5**	**166**	**15**	**44**	**7**	**0**	**3**	**14**	**11**	**26**	**2**	**.265**	**.361**	**4**	**.976**

Pitcher	G	GS	CG	IP	H	R	ER	BB	SO	W-L	Sv	ERA
Greg Booker	1	0	0	1	0	1	1	4	0	0-0	0	9.00
Dave Dravecky	2	0	0	4⅔	3	0	0	1	5	0-0	0	0.00
Rich "Goose" Gossage	2	0	0	2⅔	3	4	4	1	2	0-0	0	13.50
Greg Harris	1	0	0	5⅓	3	0	0	3	5	0-0	0	0.00
Andy Hawkins	3	0	0	12	4	1	1	6	4	1-1	0	0.75
Craig Lefferts	3	0	0	6	2	0	0	1	7	0-0	1	0.00
Tim Lollar	1	1	0	1⅔	4	4	4	4	0	0-1	0	21.60
Eric Show	1	1	0	2⅔	4	4	3	1	2	0-1	0	10.13
Mark Thurmond	2	2	0	5⅓	12	6	6	3	2	0-1	0	10.13
Ed Whitson	1	1	0	⅔	5	3	3	0	0	0-0	0	40.50
Totals	**5**	**5**	**0**	**42**	**40**	**23**	**22**	**24**	**27**	**1-4**	**1**	**4.71**

Series MVP: Alan Trammell, Detroit Tigers. **Series Outstanding Pitcher:** Jack Morris, Detroit Tigers. **Average Length of Game:** 2 hours, 54 minutes. **Total Attendance:** 271,820. **Average Attendance:** 54,364 (52,000 at Tiger Stadium; 57,910 at Jack Murphy Stadium). **Umpires:** Larry Barnett (AL), Bruce Froemming (NL), Rich Garcia (AL), Doug Harvey (NL), Mike Reilly (AL), Paul Runge (NL). **Winning Player's Share:** $51,381. **Losing Player's Share:** $42,426.

Above: Kirk Gibson gives a high-five to Marty Castillo after driving Castillo and Lou Whitaker (1) home with a three-run shot in the eighth inning of Game 5.

Above: Detroit's leading hitter in the Series was shortstop Alan Trammell, who batted a commanding .450 with a double and two homers.

Below: Reliever Willie Hernandez is hoisted in the air by catcher Lance Parrish after the Tigers defeated the Padres to become world champions.

Above: Larry Herndon's two-run homer in the fifth inning of Game 1 gave the Tigers a come-from-behind 3-2 victory.

Although Sparky Anderson edged out Dick Williams to become the first manager to win a World Series in both leagues, Williams had the distinction of being only the second man to bring three different teams to the Fall Classic. He also led the 1967 Boston Red Sox and the 1972-73 Oakland A's.

No Padre starter lasted more than five innings in a game, and in two of the games, the starting pitcher didn't make it out of the first inning before being replaced by a reliever.

Game 1   Tuesday, October 9 at Jack Murphy Stadium, San Diego

	1	2	3	4	5	6	7	8	9	R	H	E
Detroit Tigers	1	0	0	0	2	0	0	0	0	3	8	0
San Diego Padres	2	0	0	0	0	0	0	0	0	2	8	1

Pitchers   Det   Jack Morris (W, 1-0), IP 9, H 8, R 2, ER 2, BB 3, SO 9
SD   Mark Thurmond (L, 0-1), IP 5, H 7, R 3, ER 3, BB 3, SO 2; Andy Hawkins, IP 2⅔, H 1, R 0, ER 0, BB 3, SO 0; Dave Dravecky, IP 1⅓, H 0, R 0, ER 0, BB 0, SO 1

Top Performers at the Plate
Det   Larry Herndon, 2 for 3, 1 R, 2 RBI, 1 BB; Lance Parrish, 2 for 3, 1 R, 1 BB
SD   Terry Kennedy, 2 for 4, 2 RBI; Graig Nettles, 2 for 2, 1 R, 1 BB

2B-Det/Parrish, Whitaker; SD/Bevacqua, Kennedy. **HR**-Det/Herndon. **SB**-Det/Trammell; SD/Gwynn. **Time** 3:18. **Attendance** 57,908.

Game 2   Wednesday, October 10 at Jack Murphy Stadium, San Diego

	1	2	3	4	5	6	7	8	9	R	H	E
Detroit Tigers	3	0	0	0	0	0	0	0	0	3	7	3
San Diego Padres	1	0	0	1	3	0	0	0	x	5	11	0

Pitchers   Det   Dan Petry (L, 0-1), IP 4⅓, H 8, R 5, ER 5, BB 3, SO 2; Aurelio Lopez, IP ⅔, H 1, R 0, ER 0, BB 1, SO 0; Bill Scherrer, IP 1⅓, H 2, R 0, ER 0, BB 0, SO 0; Doug Bair, IP ⅔, H 0, R 0, ER 0, BB 0, SO 1; Willie Hernandez, IP 1, H 0, R 0, ER 0, BB 0, SO 0
SD   Ed Whitson, IP ⅔, H 5, R 3, ER 3, BB 0, SO 0; Andy Hawkins (W, 1-0), IP 5⅓, H 1, R 0, ER 0, BB 0, SO 3; Craig Lefferts (Sv, 1), IP 3, H 1, R 0, ER 0, BB 0, SO 5

Top Performers at the Plate
Det   Kirk Gibson, 2 for 4, 1 R, 1 RBI; Alan Trammell, 2 for 4, 1 RBI
SD   Kurt Bevacqua, 3 for 4, 2 R, 3 RBI; Alan Wiggins, 3 for 5, 1 R

HR-SD/Bevacqua. **SB**-Det/Gibson. **Time** 2:44. **Attendance** 57,911.

Game 3   Friday, October 12 at Tiger Stadium, Detroit

	1	2	3	4	5	6	7	8	9	R	H	E
San Diego Padres	0	0	1	0	0	0	1	0	0	2	10	0
Detroit Tigers	0	4	1	0	0	0	0	x		5	7	0

Pitchers   SD   Tim Lollar (L, 0-1), IP 1⅔, H 4, R 4, ER 4, BB 4, SO 0; Greg Booker, IP 1, H 0, R 1, ER 1, BB 4, SO 0; Greg Harris, IP 5⅓, H 3, R 0, ER 0, BB 3, SO 5
Det   Milt Wilcox (W, 1-0), IP 6, H 7, R 1, ER 1, BB 2, SO 4; Bill Scherrer, IP ⅔, H 2, R 1, ER 1, BB 0, SO 0; Willie Hernandez (Sv, 1), IP 2⅓, H 1, R 0, ER 0, BB 0, SO 0

Top Performers at the Plate
SD   Tony Gwynn, 2 for 5, 1 R; Alan Wiggins, 2 for 5, 1 R
Det   Chet Lemon, 2 for 5, 1 R; Alan Trammell, 2 for 3, 1 R, 1 RBI, 2 BB

2B-SD/Garvey, Wiggins; Det/Trammell. **HR**-Det/Castillo. **SB**-Det/Gibson. **Time** 3:11. **Attendance** 51,970.

Game 4   Saturday, October 13 at Tiger Stadium, Detroit

	1	2	3	4	5	6	7	8	9	R	H	E
San Diego Padres	0	1	0	0	0	0	0	1		2	5	2
Detroit Tigers	2	0	2	0	0	0	0	x		4	7	0

Pitchers   SD   Eric Show (L, 0-1), IP 2⅔, H 4, R 4, ER 3, BB 1, SO 2; Dave Dravecky, IP 3⅓, H 3, R 0, ER 0, BB 1, SO 4; Craig Lefferts, IP 1, H 0, R 0, ER 0, BB 0, SO 0; Rich "Goose" Gossage, IP 1, H 0, R 0, ER 0, BB 0, SO 0
Det   Jack Morris (W, 2-0), IP 9, H 5, R 2, ER 2, BB 0, SO 4

Top Performers at the Plate
Det   Alan Trammell, 3 for 4, 2 R, 4 RBI, 2 HR; Lou Whitaker, 2 for 4, 2 R

2B-SD/Bevacqua, Garvey; Det/Whitaker. **HR**-SD/Kennedy; Det/Trammell 2. **SB**-Det/Gibson, Lemon. **Time** 2:20. **Attendance** 52,130.

Game 5   Sunday, October 14 at Tiger Stadium, Detroit

	1	2	3	4	5	6	7	8	9	R	H	E
San Diego Padres	0	0	1	2	0	0	0	1	0	4	10	1
Detroit Tigers	3	0	0	0	1	0	1	3	x	8	11	1

Pitchers   SD   Mark Thurmond, IP ⅓, H 5, R 3, ER 3, BB 0, SO 0; Andy Hawkins (L, 1-1), IP 4, H 2, R 1, ER 1, BB 3, SO 1; Craig Lefferts, IP 2, H 1, R 0, ER 0, BB 1, SO 2; Rich "Goose" Gossage, IP 1⅔, H 3, R 4, ER 4, BB 1, SO 2
Det   Dan Petry, IP 3⅔, H 6, R 3, ER 3, BB 2, SO 2; Bill Scherrer, IP 1, H 1, R 0, ER 0, BB 0, SO 0; Aurelio Lopez (W, 1-0), IP 2⅓, H 0, R 0, ER 0, BB 0, SO 4; Willie Hernandez (Sv, 2), IP 2, H 3, R 1, ER 1, BB 0, SO 0

Top Performers at the Plate
SD   Kurt Bevacqua, 1 for 3, 2 R, 1 RBI, 1 BB; Alan Wiggins, 2 for 5, 1 RBI
Det   Kirk Gibson, 3 for 4, 3 R, 5 RBI, 1 BB; Lance Parrish, 2 for 5, 2 R, 1 RBI

2B-SD/Templeton. **HR**-SD/Bevacqua; Det/Gibson 2, Parrish. **SB**-SD/Wiggins; Det/Lemon, Parrish. **Time** 2:55. **Attendance** 51,901.

Kansas City Royals (4) vs. St. Louis Cardinals (3)

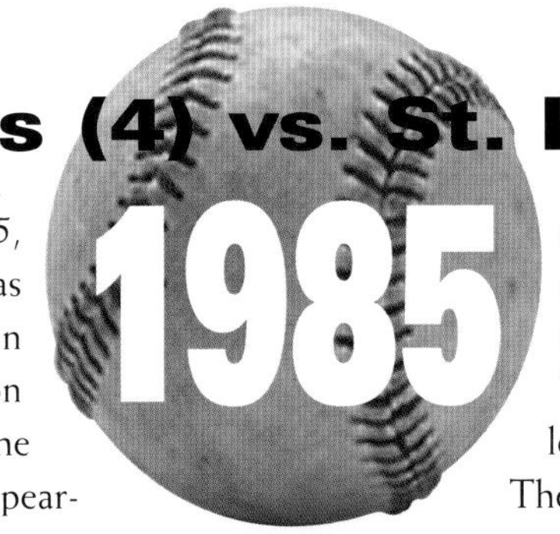

For years, New Yorkers had their Subway Series. In 1985, Missourians got their I-70 Series. St. Louis and Kansas City, located on opposite ends of Interstate 70 in Missouri, met in the Fall Classic with teams built on speed, defense and pitching. George Brett remained the cornerstone of a Royal team making its second Series appearance, and Ozzie Smith, Tommy Herr and Willie McGee were among the key leftovers from St. Louis's 1982 championship roster. Cardinal manager Whitey Herzog chose his left-handed 21-game-winner John Tudor (righty Joaquin Andujar also won 21 games) to start Game 1 in Kansas City against Dick Howser's number-one lefty, Danny Jackson. Tudor allowed one run in six and two-thirds innings to earn the win before giving way to reliever Todd Worrell. Back-to-back doubles by Brett and Frank White in the fourth inning of Game 2 gave the Royals a 2-0 lead that starter Charlie Leibrandt held into the ninth inning with a solid performance on the mound. McGee opened the top of the ninth with a double—only the third hit allowed by Leibrandt all game—but Leibrandt got the next two batters out without McGee

advancing. Then the bottom dropped out. Jack Clark singled home McGee. A double by Tito Landrum and an intentional walk to Cesar Cedeno loaded the bases, and Terry Pendleton cleared them with a double down the left-field line. Just like that, the Royals were down 4-2. They failed to score in the bottom of the inning, and Kansas City headed east on I-70 to Busch Stadium with two losses. In Game 3, 21-year-old Cy Young winner Bret Saberhagen came through with a six-hit, eight-strikeout outing for a 6-1 victory over Andujar. Former Cardinal Lonnie Smith knocked in the first two Royal runs on a fourth-inning double, and White drove in three with a homer and a double. Tudor's five-hit shutout in Game 4 halted Kansas City's momentum as the lefty struck out two in the eighth and retired the side in order in the ninth to put the Royals one loss away from elimination. Willie Wilson led an early assault against veteran Bob Forsch in Game 5 with a two-run

Above: Cesar Cedeno slides in safely on Terry Pendleton's bases-clearing double in the ninth inning of Game 2, giving St. Louis a 2-0 edge in the Series.

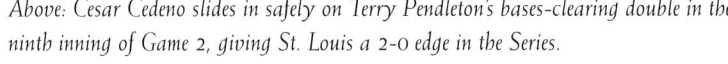

1985 WORLD SERIES COMPOSITE STATISTICS

KANSAS CITY ROYALS/Dick Howser, Manager

Player	pos	G	AB	R	H	2B	3B	HR	RBI	BB	SO	SB	BA	SA	E	FPct
Steve Balboni	1b	7	25	2	8	0	0	0	3	5	4	0	.320	.320	0	1.000
Joe Beckwith	p	1	0	0	0	0	0	0	0	0	0	0	—	—	0	—
Buddy Biancalana	ss	7	18	2	5	0	0	0	2	5	4	0	.278	.278	0	1.000
Bud Black	p	2	1	0	0	0	0	0	0	0	1	0	.000	.000	0	1.000
George Brett	3b	7	27	5	10	1	0	0	1	4	7	1	.370	.407	1	.967
Onix Concepcion	pr-ss	3	0	1	0	0	0	0	0	0	0	0	—	—	0	1.000
Dane Iorg	ph	2	2	0	1	0	0	0	2	0	0	0	.500	.500	—	—
Danny Jackson	p	2	6	0	0	0	0	0	0	0	5	0	.000	.000	1	.800
Lynn Jones	ph-lf	6	3	0	2	1	1	0	0	0	0	0	.667	1.667	0	1.000
Charlie Leibrandt	p	2	4	0	0	0	0	0	0	0	2	0	.000	.000	0	1.000
Hal McRae	ph	3	1	0	0	0	0	0	1	0	0	0	.000	.000	—	—
Darryl Motley	rf-ph	5	11	1	4	0	0	1	3	0	1	0	.364	.636	0	1.000
Jorge Orta	ph	3	3	0	1	0	0	0	0	0	0	0	.333	.333	—	—
Greg Pryor	3b	1	0	0	0	0	0	0	0	0	0	0	—	—	0	1.000
Dan Quisenberry	p	4	0	0	0	0	0	0	0	0	0	0	—	—	0	1.000
Bret Saberhagen	p	2	7	1	0	0	0	0	0	0	4	0	.000	.000	0	—
Pat Sheridan	ph-rf	5	18	0	4	2	0	0	1	0	7	0	.222	.333	0	1.000
Lonnie Smith	lf	7	27	4	9	3	0	0	4	3	8	2	.333	.444	0	1.000
Jim Sundberg	c	7	24	6	6	2	0	0	1	6	4	0	.250	.333	1	1.000
John Wathan	ph-pr	2	1	0	0	0	0	0	0	0	1	0	.000	.000	—	—
Frank White	2b	7	28	4	7	3	0	1	6	3	4	1	.250	.464	0	1.000
Willie Wilson	cf	7	30	2	11	0	1	0	3	1	4	2	.367	.433	0	1.000
Totals		**7**	**236**	**28**	**68**	**12**	**2**	**2**	**26**	**28**	**56**	**6**	**.288**	**.381**	**3**	**.989**

Pitcher	G	GS	CG	IP	H	R	ER	BB	SO	W-L	Sv	ERA
Joe Beckwith	1	0	0	2	1	0	0	3	0-0	0	0.00
Bud Black	2	1	0	5⅓	4	3	3	5	4	0-1	0	5.06
Danny Jackson	2	2	1	16	9	3	3	5	12	1-1	0	1.69
Charlie Leibrandt	2	2	0	16⅓	10	5	5	4	10	0-1	0	2.76
Dan Quisenberry	4	0	0	4⅓	5	1	1	3	3	1-0	0	2.08
Bret Saberhagen	2	2	2	18	11	1	1	1	10	2-0	0	0.50
Totals	**7**	**7**	**3**	**62**	**40**	**13**	**13**	**18**	**42**	**4-3**	**0**	**1.89**

ST. LOUIS CARDINALS/Whitey Herzog, Manager

Player	pos	G	AB	R	H	2B	3B	HR	RBI	BB	SO	SB	BA	SA	E	FPct
Joaquin Andujar	p	2	1	0	0	0	0	0	0	0	1	0	.000	.000	0	1.000
Steve Braun	ph	1	1	0	0	0	0	0	0	0	0	0	.000	.000	—	—
Bill Campbell	p	3	0	0	0	0	0	0	0	0	0	0	—	—	0	1.000
Cesar Cedeno	rf	5	15	1	2	1	0	0	1	2	2	0	.133	.200	0	1.000
Jack Clark	1b	7	25	1	6	2	0	0	4	3	9	0	.240	.320	0	1.000
Danny Cox	p	2	4	0	0	0	0	0	0	0	2	0	.000	.000	0	1.000
Ken Dayley	p	4	0	0	0	0	0	0	0	0	0	0	—	—	0	—
Ivan DeJesus	ph	1	1	0	0	0	0	0	0	0	0	0	.000	.000	—	—
Bob Forsch	p	2	0	0	0	0	0	0	0	0	0	0	—	—	0	—
Brian Harper	ph	4	4	0	1	0	0	0	1	0	1	0	.250	.250	—	—
Tom Herr	2b	7	26	2	4	2	0	0	2	2	2	0	.154	.231	0	1.000
Ricky Horton	p	3	1	0	0	0	0	0	0	0	1	0	.000	.000	0	1.000
Mike Jorgensen	lf-ph	2	3	0	0	0	0	0	0	0	0	0	.000	.000	—	—
Jeff Lahti	p	3	0	0	0	0	0	0	0	0	0	0	—	—	0	—
Tito Landrum	lf	7	25	3	9	2	0	1	1	0	2	0	.360	.560	0	1.000
Tom Lawless	pr	1	0	0	0	0	0	0	0	0	0	0	—	—	—	—
Willie McGee	cf	7	27	2	7	2	0	1	2	1	3	1	.259	.444	0	1.000
Tom Nieto	c	2	5	0	0	0	0	0	0	1	1	0	.000	.000	0	1.000
Terry Pendleton	3b	7	23	3	6	1	1	0	3	3	2	0	.261	.391	1	.952
Darrell Porter	c	5	15	0	2	0	0	0	0	2	5	0	.133	.133	0	1.000
Ozzie Smith	ss	7	23	1	2	0	0	0	0	4	0	1	.087	.087	1	.963
John Tudor	p	3	5	0	0	0	0	0	0	0	4	0	.000	.000	0	1.000
Andy Van Slyke	rf-ph-pr	6	11	0	1	0	0	0	0	0	5	0	.091	.091	0	1.000
Todd Worrell	p	3	1	0	0	0	0	0	0	0	1	0	.000	.000	0	1.000
Totals		**7**	**216**	**13**	**40**	**10**	**1**	**2**	**13**	**18**	**42**	**2**	**.185**	**.269**	**2**	**.992**

Pitcher	G	GS	CG	IP	H	R	ER	BB	SO	W-L	Sv	ERA
Joaquin Andujar	2	1	0	4	10	4	4	4	3	0-1	0	9.00
Bill Campbell	3	0	0	4	4	1	1	2	5	0-0	0	2.25
Danny Cox	2	2	0	14	14	2	2	4	13	0-0	0	1.29
Ken Dayley	4	0	0	6	1	0	0	3	5	1-0	0	0.00
Bob Forsch	2	1	0	3	6	4	4	1	3	0-1	0	12.00
Ricky Horton	3	0	0	4	4	3	3	5	5	0-0	0	6.75
Jeff Lahti	3	0	0	3⅔	10	6	5	0	2	0-0	1	12.27
John Tudor	3	3	1	18	15	6	6	7	14	2-1	0	3.00
Todd Worrell	3	0	0	4⅔	4	2	2	2	6	0-1	1	3.86
Totals	**7**	**7**	**1**	**61⅓**	**68**	**28**	**27**	**28**	**56**	**3-4**	**2**	**3.96**

Series MVP: Bret Saberhagen, Kansas City Royals. **Series Outstanding Pitcher:** Bret Saberhagen, Kansas City Royals. **Average Length of Game:** 2 hours, 45 minutes. **Total Attendance:** 327,494. **Average Attendance:** 46,785 (41,648 at Royals Stadium, 53,634 at Busch Stadium). **Umpires:** Don Denkinger (AL), Bob Engel (NL), Jim McKean (AL), Jim Quick (NL), John Shulock (AL), Bill Williams (NL). **Winning Player's Share:** $76,342. **Losing Player's Share:** $54,922.

triple in the second, and the Royals went on to coast to another 6-1 triumph. Danny Cox and Charlie Leibrandt dueled splendidly in Game 6 in a scoreless battle until Cardinal Brian Harper drove in the game's first run on a two-out pinch-single in the eighth inning. Todd Worrell came on to pitch the ninth for St. Louis, and the inning started off with a fierce controversy. The leadoff batter, pinch hitter Jorge Orta, bounced a grounder to Jack Clark at first base. Clark tossed the ball to Worrell covering the bag, and Orta appeared to be out in a close play. First base umpire Don Denkinger saw it differently, however, and called Orta safe. Herzog and the Cardinals objected vehemently, but Orta remained at first. Clark misplayed an easy foul pop from the next batter, Steve Balboni, and Balboni responded with a base hit. A bunt, a passed ball and an intentional walk later, and Kansas City had the bases jammed. Dane Iorg then won it with a two-run, pinch-hit single, sending the teams to Game 7. The final game was no contest. Saberhagen was dominant, walking none and giving up only five hits. The Royal hitters scored five runs off Tudor before the third inning was over, and then burst out with six more in the fifth. Tempers flared during the Royals' big inning, as both Herzog and Andujar were ejected for arguing with Denkinger. It was an ugly ending to a tense and dramatic Series, one in which the Kansas City Royals came back from losing the first two games at home, and three of the first four, to win their first World Series.

The Cardinals had to do without 1985 Rookie of the Year and stolen-base champ Vince Coleman in the Series. Coleman was sidelined with an injury resulting from a freak accident involving an automatic tarpaulin.

Above: Head over heels. Ozzie Smith does a flip as he takes the field for the opening of the 1985 World Series.

Above inset: Perennial Gold Glove winner Ozzie Smith turns two on George Brett's grounder in the sixth inning of Game 6.

Left: After shutting St. Louis out for 8 2/3 innings, Charlie Liebrandt lost Game 2 on a four-run barrage by the Cardinals in the ninth. Liebrandt was 0-4 in his World Series career.

Above: Joaquin Andujar has to be physically restrained by his teammates after getting thrown out for arguing with home plate umpire Don Denkinger in Game 7—the game following Denkinger's controversial call at first base.

Right: Manager Whitey Herzog also gives an earful to Denkinger during the final game.

Right: At just 21 years of age, Bret Saberhagen was dominant in 1985. He threw two complete-game victories in the Series, including the Game 7 clincher.

Below: George Brett and Bret Saberhagen rejoice in Kansas City's first championship.

Game 1 Saturday, October 19 at Royals Stadium, Kansas City

	1	2	3	4	5	6	7	8	9	R	H	E
St. Louis Cardinals	0	0	1	0	1	0	0	0	1	3	7	1
Kansas City Royals	0	1	0	0	0	0	0	0	0	1	8	0

Pitchers StL John Tudor (W, 1-0), IP 6⅔, H 7, R 1, ER 1, BB 2, SO 5; Todd Worrell (Sv, 1), IP 2⅓, H 1, R 0, ER 0, BB 1, SO 0
KC Danny Jackson (L, 0-1), IP 7, H 4, R 2, ER 2, BB 2, SO 7; Dan Quisenberry, IP 1⅔, H 3, R 1, ER 1, BB 0, SO 2; Bud Black, IP ⅓, H 0, R 0, ER 0, BB 2, SO 1

Top Performers at the Plate
StL Cesar Cedeno, 1 for 3, 1 RBI; Tito Landrum, 2 for 4, 1 R
KC Lonnie Smith, 1 for 3, 1 BB; Jim Sundberg, 1 for 3, 1 R, 1 BB

2B-StL/Cedeno, Clark, Landrum, McGee; KC/Sheridan, Sundberg. **3B**-KC/Jones. **SB**-StL/O. Smith. **Time** 2:48. **Attendance** 41,650.

Game 2 Sunday, October 20 at Royals Stadium, Kansas City

	1	2	3	4	5	6	7	8	9	R	H	E
St. Louis Cardinals	0	0	0	0	0	0	0	4		4	6	0
Kansas City Royals	0	0	0	2	0	0	0	0		2	9	0

Pitchers StL Danny Cox, IP 7, H 7, R 2, ER 2, BB 3, SO 5; Ken Dayley (W, 1-0), IP 1, H 1, R 0, ER 0, BB 0, SO 1; Jeff Lahti (Sv, 1), IP 1, H 1, R 0, ER 0, BB 0, SO 0
KC Charlie Leibrandt (L, 0-1), IP 8⅔, H 6, R 4, ER 4, BB 2, SO 6; Dan Quisenberry, IP ⅓, H 0, R 0, ER 0, BB 1, SO 0

Top Performers at the Plate
StL Jack Clark, 1 for 3, 1 R, 1 RBI, 1 BB; Terry Pendleton, 2 for 4, 3 RBI
KC Frank White, 3 for 3, 1 RBI, 1 BB, 2 2B; Willie Wilson, 2 for 4, 1 R

2B-StL/Landrum, McGee, Pendleton; KC/Brett, White 2. **SB**-KC/White, Wilson. **Time** 2:44. **Attendance** 41,656.

Game 3 Tuesday, October 22 at Busch Stadium, St. Louis

	1	2	3	4	5	6	7	8	9	R	H	E
Kansas City Royals	0	0	0	2	2	0	2	0	0	6	11	0
St. Louis Cardinals	0	0	0	0	1	0	0	0	0	1	6	0

Pitchers KC Bret Saberhagen (W, 1-0), IP 9, H 6, R 1, ER 1, BB 1, SO 8
StL Joaquin Andujar (L, 0-1), IP 4, H 9, R 4, ER 4, BB 3, SO 3; Bill Campbell, IP 1, H 0, R 0, ER 0, BB 1, SO 2; Ricky Horton, IP 2, H 2, R 2, ER 2, BB 1, SO 1; Ken Dayley, IP 2, H 0, R 0, ER 0, BB 2, SO 2

Top Performers at the Plate
KC George Brett, 2 for 2, 2 R, 3 BB; Frank White, 2 for 4, 2 R, 1 RBI, 1 BB
StL Jack Clark, 1 for 4, 1 RBI

2B-KC/L. Smith, White. **HR**-KC/White. **SB**-KC/Wilson; StL/McGee. **Time** 3:00. **Attendance** 53,634.

Game 4 Wednesday, October 23 at Busch Stadium, St. Louis

	1	2	3	4	5	6	7	8	9	R	H	E
Kansas City Royals	0	0	0	0	0	0	0	0	0	0	5	1
St. Louis Cardinals	0	1	1	0	1	0	0	x		3	6	0

Pitchers KC Bud Black (L, 0-1), IP 5, H 4, R 3, ER 3, BB 3, SO 3; Joe Beckwith, IP 2, H 1, R 0, ER 0, BB 0, SO 3; Dan Quisenberry, IP 1, H 1, R 0, ER 0, BB 2, SO 0
StL John Tudor (W, 2-0), IP 9, H 5, R 0, ER 0, BB 1, SO 8

Top Performers at the Plate
StL Tito Landrum, 1 for 4, 1 R, 1 RBI; Willie McGee, 2 for 3, 1 R, 1 RBI, 1 BB

2B-StL/Herr; KC/Jones. **3B**-StL/Pendleton. **HR**-StL/Landrum, McGee. **Time** 2:19. **Attendance** 53,634.

Game 5 Thursday, October 24 at Busch Stadium, St. Louis

	1	2	3	4	5	6	7	8	9	R	H	E
Kansas City Royals	1	3	0	0	0	0	0	1	1	6	11	2
St. Louis Cardinals	1	0	0	0	0	0	0	0	0	1	5	1

Pitchers KC Danny Jackson (W, 1-1), IP 9, H 5, R 1, ER 1, BB 3, SO 5
StL Bob Forsch (L, 0-1), IP 1⅔, H 5, R 4, ER 4, BB 1, SO 2; Ricky Horton, IP 2, H 1, R 0, ER 0, BB 3, SO 4; Bill Campbell, IP 1⅓, H 0, R 0, ER 0, BB 0, SO 2; Todd Worrell, IP 2, H 0, R 0, ER 0, BB 0, SO 6; Jeff Lahti, IP 2, H 5, R 2, ER 1, BB 0, SO 1

Top Performers at the Plate
KC Buddy Biancalana, 2 for 3, 1 R, 1 RBI, 1 BB; Willie Wilson, 2 for 5, 2 RBI
StL Jack Clark, 1 for 3, 1 RBI, 1 BB; Willie McGee, 2 for 4

2B-KC/Sheridan, Sundberg; StL/Clark, Herr. **3B**-KC/Wilson. **SB**-KC/L. Smith. **Time** 2:52. **Attendance** 53,634.

Game 6 Saturday, October 26 at Royals Stadium, Kansas City

	1	2	3	4	5	6	7	8	9	R	H	E
St. Louis Cardinals	0	0	0	0	0	0	1	0		1	5	0
Kansas City Royals	0	0	0	0	0	0	0	2		2	10	0

Pitchers StL Danny Cox, IP 7, H 7, R 0, ER 0, BB 1, SO 8; Ken Dayley, IP 1, H 0, R 0, ER 0, BB 1, SO 2; Todd Worrell (L, 0-1), IP ⅓, H 3, R 2, ER 2, BB 1, SO 0
KC Charlie Leibrandt, IP 7⅔, H 4, R 1, ER 1, BB 2, SO 4; Dan Quisenberry (W, 1-0), IP 1⅓, H 1, R 0, ER 0, BB 0, SO 1

Top Performers at the Plate
KC Steve Balboni, 2 for 3; Dane Iorg, 1 for 1, 2 RBI

2B-KC/L. Smith. **Time** 2:48. **Attendance** 41,628.

Game 7 Sunday, October 27 at Royals Stadium, Kansas City

	1	2	3	4	5	6	7	8	9	R	H	E
St. Louis Cardinals	0	0	0	0	0	0	0	0	0	0	5	0
Kansas City Royals	0	2	3	0	6	0	0	0	x	11	14	0

Pitchers StL John Tudor (L, 2-1), IP 2⅓, H 3, R 5, ER 5, BB 4, SO 1; Bill Campbell, IP 1⅔, H 4, R 1, ER 1, BB 1, SO 1; Jeff Lahti, IP ⅔, H 4, R 4, ER 4, BB 0, SO 1; Ricky Horton, IP 0, H 1, R 1, ER 1, BB 0, SO 0; Joaquin Andujar, IP 0, H 1, R 0, ER 0, BB 1, SO 0; Bob Forsch, IP 1⅓, H 1, R 0, ER 0, BB 0, SO 1; Ken Dayley, IP 2, H 0, R 0, ER 0, BB 0, SO 0
KC Bret Saberhagen (W, 2-0), IP 9, H 5, R 0, ER 0, BB 0, SO 2

Top Performers at the Plate
KC George Brett, 4 for 5, 2 R; Darryl Motley, 3 for 4, 1 R, 3 RBI

2B-KC/L. Smith. **HR**-KC/Motley. **SB**-KC/Brett, L. Smith. **Time** 2:46. **Attendance** 41,658.

255

"He Missed the Tag !"

Umpires and Great World Series Controversies

Though some players and managers might dispute it, umpires are human. They make mistakes just like anyone else on the playing field. The difference is that when an umpire makes a questionable decision, his name is forever associated with that one moment of imperfection. He can't redeem himself with an excellent call on another close play the way a player can make up for an error by hitting a home run later in the game. The names that stick out in people's minds are often those umpires who purportedly gave a team a bad break, not those who served diligently and reliably for years—though there are many more of the latter than the former.

Controversies, Miscalls and Other Shenanigans

While the action of the players on the field has the greatest impact on the outcome of a baseball game, a peripheral controversy or an umpire's decision can sometimes play heavily on the results. The following are some of the more notably contentious moments in World Series play. Eight of the controversies took place in games decided by a single run.

◆ **Doyle Credited with Winning Run Despite Missing Plate — Philadelphia Athletics vs. New York Giants, October 25, 1911**

It sounds like a Zen meditative question: If a player scores without touching home plate but nobody's there to argue, does the run count? That's what happened in 1911 when New York's Larry Doyle slid under the tag of catcher Jack Lapp in the last of the 10th inning of Game 5. The Philadelphia players walked off the field assuming the game-winning run had come in, even though umpire Bill Klem later admitted that Doyle missed the plate. With no appeal from the Athletics, Klem kept his mouth shut. The win kept the Giants alive for another day, but Philadelphia clinched the Series in Game 6.

◆ **Rice Disappears Over Fence with Ball; Batter Called Out — Pittsburgh Pirates vs. Washington Senators, October 10, 1925**

When, in the third game of the 1925 Series, Senator outfielder Sam Rice emerged from the Griffith Stadium bleachers, ball in glove, after tumbling over the fence chasing a fly ball, umpire Cy Rigler stuck up his thumb to signal an out. The Pirates were furious, believing that a Washington partisan had placed the ball in Rice's mitt. They appealed to Commissioner Kenesaw Mountain Landis in the ballpark, but the Judge refused to overrule an umpire's decision. Although the play had little impact on the final outcome (Washington won the game, but Pittsburgh won the Series), the controversy didn't go away. Up until his death (and in a sealed note opened after he passed away), Rice maintained that the catch was legit.

Above: Umpires and the commissioner of baseball have to intervene when Detroit fans get unruly during the 1934 Series.

Left: Cy Rigler was a veteran of 10 World Series.

◆ **Fans Shower Medwick with Trash, Insults — St. Louis Cardinals vs. Detroit Tigers, October 9, 1934**

The 1934 World Series was a hotly contested battle, and things boiled over in Game 7. Joe Medwick's controversial hard slide into Detroit third baseman Marv Owen led to a brief scuffle between the two, but umpire Bill Klem broke it up before any serious damage was done. Klem and his crew were powerless, however, when thousands of Detroit fans bombarded Medwick with garbage and debris the following inning. Commissioner Landis, stationed in his box seat, ordered Medwick to leave the game for his own safety and that of the rest of the players.

◆ **Former Tiger Moriarty Enrages Cubs — Detroit Tigers vs. Chicago Cubs, October 2–7, 1935**

Umpires are paid to be impartial, but the Chicago Cubs had doubts about George Moriarty in 1935. A former Detroit player and manager, Moriarty was continually harassed by Cub manager Charlie Grimm with charges of pro-Tiger bias, and the umpire often lashed back with less-than-polite rejoinders. In Game 3, Grimm apparently went too far in expressing his displeasure with a call at third base and was ejected from

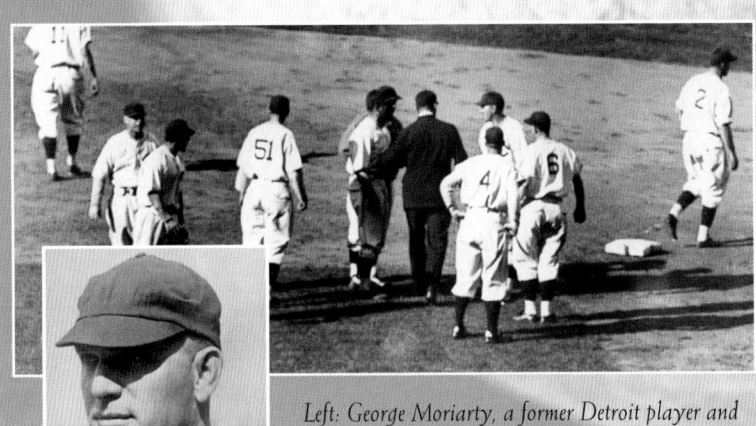

Left: George Moriarty, a former Detroit player and manager, was in the middle of a maelstrom when he umpired the 1935 World Series between the Tigers and the Chicago Cubs.

Above: Moriarty is surrounded by Cubs players protesting his call during Game 3 in 1935. The Cubs manager and several players ended up being ejected.

the game. Two innings later, Chicago subs Woody English and Tuck Stainback were both kicked out for riding Moriarty from the dugout. Moriarty, Grimm, English and Stainback all received $200 fines from the Commissioner after the Series.

◆ Missed Pick-off Call Leads to Braves' Victory — Cleveland Indians vs. Boston Braves, October 6, 1948

The opener of the 1948 Series featured a sensational pitchers' duel between Cleveland's Bob Feller and Boston's Johnny Sain—but it was an umpire's call that proved the difference. With runners on in the bottom of the eighth inning of the scoreless contest, Feller whirled around in a timed pick-off play and fired the ball to second base. Shortstop Lou Boudreau appeared to tag baserunner Phil Masi with room to spare, but Bill Stewart called him safe, and held firm despite Boudreau's objections. Masi went on to score the game's only run. Although the Braves took the opener with the help of the disputed play, Cleveland won the Series in six games.

◆ Orioles Squeak Out Victory with Phantom Tag — Baltimore Orioles vs. Cincinnati Reds, October 10, 1970

When Baltimore catcher Elrod Hendricks tagged Cincinnati's Bernie Carbo with his glove before Carbo touched home plate, umpire Ken Burkhart made the decisive call: Carbo was out. What Burkhart failed to notice—having been knocked down by Hendricks lunging at Carbo—and what photos later plainly revealed was that Hendricks held the ball in his bare hand while applying the tag with his empty mitt. At the time, Baltimore and Cincinnati were tied 3-3 in the 1970 Series opener, so when the Orioles took a one-run lead an inning later, the botched call at home plate proved to be the deciding play.

◆ Fisk and Armbrister Collide at Home Plate; No Interference Called — Cincinnati Reds vs. Boston Red Sox, October 14, 1975

The Cincinnati Reds were involved in another controversial collision at home plate in 1975, but this time they got the benefit of the call—or rather the non-call. With the Reds and Red Sox embroiled in a 5-5 tie in Game 3, a collision between Boston catcher Carlton Fisk and pinch hitter Ed Armbrister caused Fisk to make a wild throw. Fisk was livid, claiming that Armbrister should be called out for interfering while Fisk tried to field his bunt. Umpire Larry Barnett felt otherwise, asserting that the col-

lision was incidental. Cincinnati scored the game-winning run three batters later to take a one-game lead in the legendary 1975 World Series.

◆ Jackson's Hip Sets Up New York Triumph — New York Yankees vs. Los Angeles Dodgers, October 14, 1978

Reggie Jackson came to be known as "Mr. October" for his heroics with the bat; in 1978, however, it was his hip that got the attention. In Game 4, Dodger shortstop Bill Russell made a throw to first to complete a double play, but the ball hit Jackson, who was caught between first and second, and caromed into right field. It appeared to Los Angeles that Jackson stuck his hip out with the intention of interfering with the throw, but despite some 30 minutes of debate, the umpires maintained that it was unintentional. The play allowed a run to score, and the Yanks came from behind to win the game and tie the Series.

◆ Denkinger Miscall Causes St. Louis to Unravel — Kansas City Royals vs. St. Louis Cardinals, October 26, 1985

There's no instant-replay rule in baseball. No matter how many times a particular moment is played and replayed on televisions and jumbotrons, all that an umpire can refer to when making a judgment is his own two eyes (and sometimes those of his colleagues). When 17-year-veteran Don Denkinger called Jorge Orta safe at first base in Game 6 of the 1985 World Series, the St. Louis Cardinals would have loved to have been able to point to the TV screens, which clearly showed Orta out. Denkinger's ruling sparked a two-run game-winning rally for Kansas City, and St. Louis was unable to bounce back in Game 7.

◆ Hrbek Pulls Gant Off Bag in Suspicious Tag — Minnesota Twins vs. Atlanta Braves, October 20, 1991

Sometimes a play is not what it seems. From most angles, it looked like Atlanta's Ron Gant simply overran first base trying to get back to the bag. That's what umpire Drew Coble saw, and when Minnesota first baseman Kent Hrbek tagged Gant's leg with the ball, Coble called Gant out, ending the inning. What Coble would have seen had he been standing on the other side of the play was that it wasn't momentum but rather the strong arms of Hrbek that pulled Gant off the base. In a Series involving five one-run games, every baserunner was crucial, and the lost runner in inning three of Game 2 short-circuited a Braves rally.

Left: Umpire Ken Burkhart is caught in the middle while Baltimore catcher Ellie Hendricks attempts to tag out Cincinnati's Bernie Carbo during Game 1 of the 1970 Series.

Above: When Burkhart called Carbo out, Reds manager Sparky Anderson argued that Hendricks never tagged Carbo with the ball—as photos clearly reveal.

Men in Blue
Umpires in the World Series

Getting a chance to be in the Fall Classic is as much of an honor for an umpire as it is for a player. Experienced umps who have displayed sound judgment through the years are chosen to don the blue suits for the World Series. Since 1903, 161 different men have acted as arbiter in the Series.

Nobody—player, manager, umpire—appeared in more World Series than Bill Klem. Between 1908, his first Series, and 1940, his last, Klem umpired 104 games in 18 Series. He was in five straight from 1911 to 1915, an umpiring streak that will never be broken. (New rules regarding the rotation of umpires prohibit it.)

Hank O'Day and Tommy Connelly were the trailblazing umpires in the first World Series in 1903, and they contributed other notable firsts as well. O'Day had the honor of making the first postseason ejection when he tossed Tiger manager Hughie Jennings from the second game

of the 1907 Series for arguing a call at second base. Three years later, Connelly gave the first boot to a player in a Series game. Frank Chance acted as both manager and first baseman for the Chicago Cubs in 1910, and when Chance got in Connelly's face over a home-run ball that he thought should have been called foul, Connelly relieved him of both responsibilities.

Most World Series by an Umpire			
National League Umpires		**American League Umpires**	
Bill Klem	18	Bill Dinneen	8
Hank O'Day	10	Bill McGowan	8
Cy Rigler	10	Bill Summers	8
Al Barlick	7	Tommy Connolly	8
Babe Pinelli	6	Billy Evans	6
Ernie Quigley	6	Jim Honochick	6

Right: Bill Klem— about to make the out call on a play at second—umpired in 104 World Series games during his career, more than any other umpire.

Above: Hank O'Day was the umpire in the first Series in 1903, and in nine others during his 30-year career.

From 1903 to 1909, two umpires took the field for each World Series game, one behind the plate and one on the bases. Four umpires were employed starting in 1908, but only two were used at a time. The first time four umpires took the field at once was Game 3 in 1909 after a controversy on a fair-or-foul call led to the decision that more pairs of eyes were needed. The postseason umpiring crew was expanded to six in 1947.

Turning the Tables
Former World Series Players Who Later Umpired in the Series

Six World Series umpires also appeared in the Fall Classic as players. Bill Dinneen won three games as a pitcher for Boston in the first Series in 1903, and then umpired in eight contests between 1911 and 1932.

George Pipgras wore pinstripes in 1927, 1928 and 1932 with the New York Yankees, and he wore blue in the all-St. Louis Series in 1944. Ed Rommel, winner of championship rings with the Athletics in 1929–31, was on hand as an umpire in 1943 and 1947. One of the umps in the Giants' upset win over Cleveland in 1954 was Lon Warneke, a pitcher on two Cub pennant winners of the 1930s. Frank Secory went 1 for 5 as a pinch hitter with the 1945 Cubs before umpiring in four Series. Five-time Series ump George Moriarty was in blue in a contest involving his former team. A Tiger third baseman in 1909, Moriarty was selected to umpire in Detroit's duel with the Cubs in 1935—and not without controversy (see page 256). Ken Burkhart was a spot starter for the pennant-winning Cardinals in 1946 and Bill Kunkel was on the roster for the AL-champion Yankees in 1963, but the only action either of them saw in the World Series came many years later from the umpire's position, Burkhart on three occasions and Kunkel twice.

WORLD SERIES CLASSIC
1986

New York Mets (4) vs. Boston Red Sox (3)

Fred Merkle. Fred Snodgrass. Mickey Owen. Names that have carried down through baseball lore for the misplays that brought ignominious defeat to their teams. Perhaps no name stands out larger in this regard than that of Bill Buckner, whose 2,715 hits in 22 years as a Major League ballplayer are all forgotten in favor of the one that got away.

When the 1986 World Series opened on October 18, all signs pointed to a classic contest. The Boston Red Sox had batting leader Wade Boggs and league MVP/Cy Young winner Roger Clemens. The

club had come back from the brink of elimination in the ALCS to reach their ninth Fall Classic. The New York Mets won 108 games in 1986 behind veteran stars Gary Carter, Keith Hernandez and Ray Knight, young slugger Darryl Strawberry, and a deep pitching staff led by Dwight Gooden and Bob Ojeda. The Mets, too, were coming off a thrilling league championship series against Houston, concluding with a 16-inning finale.

Boston seemed to carry the momentum of their dramatic playoff

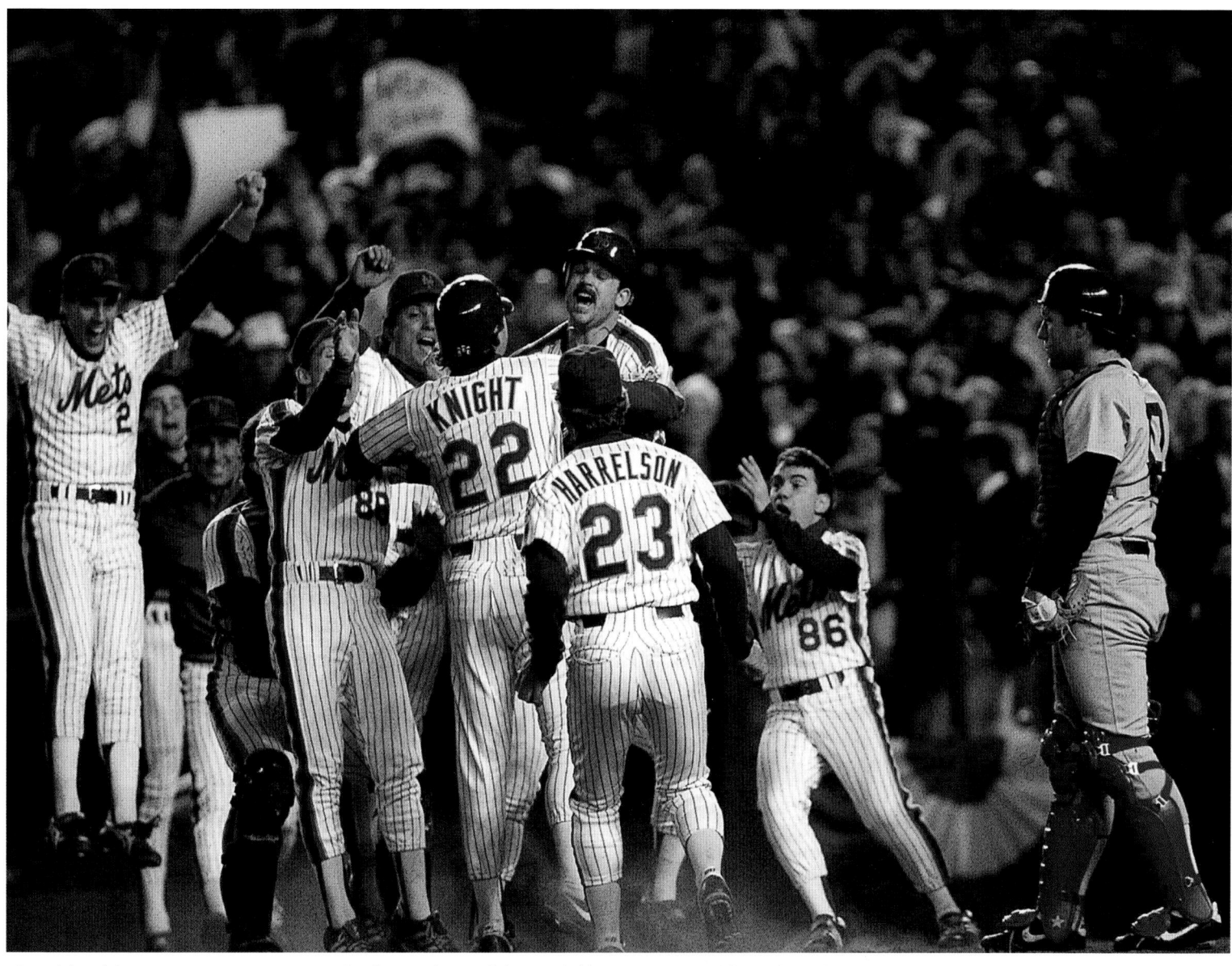

Above: The jubilant Mets converge on Ray Knight after Knight scored the improbable winning run on "The Buckner Play" in Game 6 of the 1986 Series.

Above: Lenny "Nails" Dykstra led off the third game of the Series with a home run down the right-field line, igniting a four-run first inning for New York.

Above: Boston took a one-game lead in the Series behind Bruce Hurst's shutout in Game 1.

Right: "Rocket" Roger Clemens was dominating during the regular season, but he finished the 1986 Series without a decision. Here he delivers a pitch in the first inning of Game 6.

success into the Series, winning the first two in New York. Starters Bruce Hurst and Ron Darling came out with masterful performances in the opener, Hurst allowing four hits to Darling's three before both were removed for pinch hitters. A seventh-inning error by Met second baseman Tim Teufel led to the game's only run, and Boston eked out a 1-0 triumph. Game 2 featured a match-up of baseball's top pitchers in Gooden and Clemens, but neither was in top form, and both were gone by the sixth inning. When it was all over, the Red Sox had 18 hits and a 9-3 victory. The Mets ruined Boston's homecoming in Game 3 with a 7-1 win behind former Red Sox Ojeda. Lenny Dykstra led the game off with a home run—the first of four hits on the day—and the Mets scored three more in the opening stanza. Darling brought New York even in the Series with a four-hitter in Game 4. Carter's two homers led the offensive charge, and Dykstra also went yard when his deep drive in the seventh deflected off Dwight Evans's glove and over the right-field fence. A complete-game win for Hurst in Game 5 put Boston one game away from Series victory. Dave Henderson, the goat-turned-hero from the ALCS, contributed a triple and a run in the second and an RBI double in the fifth.

The very first batter in Game 6 at Shea Stadium, Wade Boggs, singled and scored, and the Sox added another run in the second. New York came back with a two-run fifth inning, and each team scored one more to send a 3-3 tie into the 10th. With Rick Aguilera on in relief, Dave Henderson belted the second pitch of the inning into the left-field seats. A double by Boggs and a run-scoring single by Marty Barrett gave Boston a two-run bulge heading into the Mets' half of the 10th. Reliever Calvin Schiraldi got Wally Backman and Keith Hernandez to fly out for the first two outs. The Boston Red Sox were now one out away from a World Series championship, their first in 68 years. The next batter, Gary Carter, kept the game going with a single to left, and Kevin Mitchell followed with a pinch-hit single. Schiraldi got ahead of Ray Knight with no balls and two strikes, putting his team one strike away from the title. But Knight made contact on the next pitch and blooped a single to center, scoring Carter and sending Mitchell to third. Boston manager John McNamara had seen enough. He yanked Schiraldi and brought in Bob Stanley to face Mookie Wilson. Stanley worked the count to 2-2, but Wilson fouled off several of Stanley's offerings to stay alive. Stanley's seventh pitch of the sequence was wild at Wilson's feet, allowing Mitchell to score the game-tying run and Knight to advance to second. With the count now full, Wilson fouled off a couple more pitches before sending a grounder toward first base. First baseman Bill Buckner stooped down to field it, but the ball went between his legs and into right field. Knight dashed around third and leaped home with the dramatic game-winner.

Having let Game 6 slip away, the Red Sox got on top quickly in Game 7. Dwight Evans and Rich Gedman led off the second inning with back-to-back homers, and Boggs stroked an RBI single. Down 3-0, the Mets got it all back in the sixth on Hernandez's bases-loaded single and Carter's blooper to right, and then New York broke out with three more runs in the seventh. The Red Sox scored two in the eighth, but Jesse Orosco came on and got the Mets out of trouble by retiring the next three batters. New York extended the lead on Darryl Strawberry's homer and Orosco's RBI single. The Red Sox then went down in order in the ninth, with Orosco striking out Marty Barrett for the final out. Following their heartbreaking loss in Game 6, the Red Sox fell short in the decisive seventh game, and their string of October disappointments continued. For New York, the franchise's winningest season ended in a second World Series triumph.

Above: Boston second baseman
Marty Barrett established a new
record by stroking 13 hits in the
Series.

Left: Wade Boggs opens Game 6
with a leadoff single. He would come
around to score the game's first run.

Below: A Boston rally was cut short
when Jim Rice was thrown out at
the plate by Mookie Wilson on Rich
Gedman's seventh-inning single in
Game 6.

Game 1 Saturday, October 18 at Shea Stadium, New York

	1	2	3	4	5	6	7	8	9	R	H	E
Boston Red Sox	0	0	0	0	0	0	1	0	0	1	5	0
New York Mets	0	0	0	0	0	0	0	0	0	0	4	1

Pitchers Bos Bruce Hurst (W, 1-0), IP 8, H 4, R 0, ER 0, BB 4, SO 8; Calvin Schiraldi (Sv, 1), IP 1, H 0, R 0, ER 0, BB 1, SO 1
NY Ron Darling (L, 0-1), IP 7, H 3, R 1, ER 1, BB 3, SO 8; Roger McDowell, IP 2, H 2, R 0, ER 0, BB 2, SO 0

Top Performers at the Plate
Bos Dave Henderson, 2 for 4; Jim Rice, 1 for 2, 1 R, 2 BB
NY Tim Teufel, 2 for 3

SB–NY/Strawberry, Wilson. **Time** 2:59. **Attendance** 55,076.

Game 2 Sunday, October 19 at Shea Stadium, New York

	1	2	3	4	5	6	7	8	9	R	H	E
Boston Red Sox	0	0	3	1	2	0	2	0	1	9	18	0
New York Mets	0	0	2	0	1	0	0	0	0	3	8	1

Pitchers Bos Roger Clemens, IP 4⅓, H 5, R 3, ER 3, BB 4, SO 3; Steve Crawford (W, 1-0), IP 1⅔, H 1, R 0, ER 0, BB 0, SO 2; Bob Stanley (Sv, 1), IP 3, H 2, R 0, ER 0, BB 1, SO 3
NY Dwight Gooden (L, 0-1), IP 5, H 8, R 6, ER 5, BB 2, SO 6; Rick Aguilera, IP 1, H 5, R 2, ER 2, BB 1, SO 1; Jesse Orosco, IP 2, H 2, R 0, ER 0, BB 0, SO 3; Sid Fernandez, IP ⅓, H 3, R 1, ER 1, BB 0, SO 1; Doug Sisk, IP ⅔, H 0, R 0, ER 0, BB 1, SO 1

Top Performers at the Plate
Bos Dwight Evans, 2 for 4, 2 R, 2 RBI, 1 BB; Dave Henderon, 3 for 5, 2 R, 2 RBI
NY Wally Backman, 2 for 3, 1 R, 1 RBI, 2 BB; Rafael Santana, 2 for 4, 1 R

2B–Bos/Boggs 2. **HR**–Bos/Evans, Henderson. **Time** 3:36. **Attendance** 55,063.

Game 3 Tuesday, October 21 at Fenway Park, Boston

	1	2	3	4	5	6	7	8	9	R	H	E
New York Mets	4	0	0	0	0	0	2	1	0	7	13	0
Boston Red Sox	0	0	1	0	0	0	0	0	0	1	5	0

Pitchers NY Bob Ojeda (W, 1-0), IP 7, H 5, R 1, ER 1, BB 3, SO 6; Roger McDowell, IP 2, H 0, R 0, ER 0, BB 0, SO 0
Bos Dennis "Oil Can" Boyd (L, 0-1), IP 7, H 9, R 6, ER 6, BB 1, SO 3; Joe Sambito, IP 0, H 2, R 1, ER 1, BB 0, SO 0; Bob Stanley, IP 2, H 2, R 0, ER 0, BB 0, SO 1

Top Performers at the Plate
NY Gary Carter, 2 for 5, 1 R, 3 RBI; Lenny Dykstra, 4 for 5, 2 R, 1 RBI
Bos Marty Barrett, 2 for 4, 1 RBI; Dave Henderson, 1 for 2, 1 R, 1 BB

2B–NY/Carter, Knight; Bos/Baylor. **HR**–NY/Dykstra. **Time** 2:58. **Attendance** 33,595.

Game 4 Wednesday, October 22 at Fenway Park, Boston

	1	2	3	4	5	6	7	8	9	R	H	E
New York Mets	0	0	0	3	0	0	2	1	0	6	12	0
Boston Red Sox	0	0	0	0	0	0	2	0	0	2	7	1

Pitchers NY Ron Darling (W, 1-1), IP 7, H 4, R 0, ER 0, BB 6, SO 4; Roger McDowell, IP ⅔, H 3, R 2, ER 2, BB 1, SO 0; Jesse Orosco (Sv, 1), IP 1⅓, H 0, R 0, ER 0, BB 0, SO 1
Bos Al Nipper (L, 0-1), IP 6, H 7, R 3, ER 3, BB 1, SO 2; Steve Crawford, IP 2, H 4, R 3, ER 3, BB 0, SO 2; Bob Stanley, IP 1, H 1, R 0, ER 0, BB 0, SO 0

Top Performers at the Plate
NY Gary Carter, 3 for 4, 2 R, 3 RBI; Darryl Strawberry, 2 for 4, 1 R
Bos Dwight Evans, 1 for 3, 1 R, 1 RBI, 1 BB; Rich Gedman, 3 for 4

2B–NY/Carter, Strawberry; Bos/Barrett, Gedman, Rice. **HR**–NY/Carter 2, Dykstra.
SB–NY/Backman, Wilson 2. **Time** 3:22. **Attendance** 33,920.

Game 5 Thursday, October 23 at Fenway Park, Boston

	1	2	3	4	5	6	7	8	9	R	H	E
New York Mets	0	0	0	0	0	0	1	1		2	10	1
Boston Red Sox	0	1	1	0	2	0	0	x		4	12	0

Pitchers NY Dwight Gooden (L, 0-2), IP 4, H 9, R 4, ER 3, BB 2, SO 3; Sid Fernandez, IP 4, H 3, R 0, ER 0, BB 0, SO 5
Bos Bruce Hurst (W, 2-0), IP 9, H 10, R 2, ER 2, BB 1, SO 6

Top Performers at the Plate
NY Tim Teufel, 2 for 4, 1 R, 1 RBI; Mookie Wilson, 2 for 4, 1 R
Bos Dave Henderson, 2 for 4, 1 R, 1 RBI; Jim Rice, 2 for 3, 1 R, 1 BB

2B–NY/Teufel, Wilson; Bos/Barrett, Henderson. 3B–Bos/Henderson, Rice. **HR**–NY/Teufel.
Time 3:09. **Attendance** 34,010.

Game 6 Saturday, October 25 at Shea Stadium, New York

	1	2	3	4	5	6	7	8	9	10	R	H	E
Boston Red Sox	1	1	0	0	0	0	1	0	0	2	5	13	3
New York Mets	0	0	0	0	2	0	0	1	0	3	6	8	2

Pitchers Bos Roger Clemens, IP 7, H 4, R 2, ER 1, BB 2, SO 8; Calvin Schiraldi (L, 0-1), IP 2⅔, H 4, R 4, ER 3, BB 2, SO 1; Bob Stanley, IP 0, H 0, R 0, ER 0, BB 0, SO 0
NY Bob Ojeda, IP 6, H 8, R 2, ER 2, BB 2, SO 3; Roger McDowell, IP 1⅔, H 2, R 1, ER 0, BB 3, SO 1; Jesse Orosco, IP ⅓, H 0, R 0, ER 0, BB 0, SO 0; Rick Aguilera (W, 1-0), IP 2, H 3, R 2, ER 2, BB 0, SO 3

Top Performers at the Plate
Bos Marty Barrett, 3 for 4, 1 R, 2 RBI, 2 BB; Wade Boggs, 3 for 5, 2 R, 1 BB
NY Ray Knight, 2 for 4, 2 R, 2 RBI, 1 BB

2B–Bos/Boggs, Evans. **HR**–Bos/Henderson. SB–NY/Strawberry 2. **Time** 4:02. **Attendance** 55,078.

Game 7 Monday, October 27 at Shea Stadium, New York

	1	2	3	4	5	6	7	8	9	R	H	E
Boston Red Sox	0	3	0	0	0	0	0	2	0	5	9	0
New York Mets	0	0	0	0	0	3	3	2	x	8	10	0

Pitchers Bos Bruce Hurst, IP 6, H 4, R 3, ER 3, BB 1, SO 3; Calvin Schiraldi (L, 0-2), IP ⅓, H 3, R 3, ER 3, BB 0, SO 0; Joe Sambito, IP ⅓, H 0, R 0, ER 0, BB 2, SO 0; Bob Stanley, IP ⅓, H 0, R 0, ER 0, BB 0, SO 0; Al Nipper, IP ⅓, H 3, R 2, ER 2, BB 1, SO 0; Steve Crawford, IP ⅔, H 0, R 0, ER 0, BB 0, SO 0
NY Ron Darling, IP 3⅔, H 6, R 3, ER 3, BB 1, SO 0; Sid Fernandez, IP 2⅓, H 0, R 0, ER 0, BB 1, SO 4; Roger McDowell (W, 1-0), IP 1, H 3, R 2, ER 2, BB 0, SO 1; Jesse Orosco (Sv, 2), IP 2, H 0, R 0, ER 0, BB 0, SO 2

Top Performers at the Plate
Bos Bill Buckner, 2 for 4, 1 R; Dwight Evans, 2 for 4, 1 R, 3 RBI
NY Keith Hernandez, 1 for 4, 3 RBI; Ray Knight, 3 for 4, 2 R, 1 RBI

2B–Bos/Evans. **HR**–Bos/Evans, Gedman; NY/Knight, Strawberry. **Time** 3:11. **Attendance** 55,032.

Boston's Steve Crawford became the second man to win more games in the World Series (1) than in the regular season. Crawford finished 0-2 in 40 games with the Red Sox in 1986.

1986 WORLD SERIES COMPOSITE STATISTICS

NEW YORK METS/Davey Johnson, Manager

Player	pos	G	AB	R	H	2B	3B	HR	RBI	BB	SO	SB	BA	SA	E	FPct
Rick Aguilera	p	2	0	0	0	0	0	0	0	0	0	0	—	—	0	—
Wally Backman	pr-2b	6	18	4	6	0	0	0	1	3	2	1	.333	.333	0	1.000
Gary Carter	c	7	29	4	8	2	0	2	9	0	4	0	.276	.552	0	1.000
Ron Darling	p	3	3	0	0	0	0	0	0	1	0	0	.000	.000	0	1.000
Lenny Dykstra	cf-ph	7	27	4	8	0	0	2	3	2	7	0	.296	.519	0	1.000
Kevin Elster	ss	1	1	0	0	0	0	0	0	0	0	0	.000	.000	1	.857
Sid Fernandez	p	3	0	0	0	0	0	0	0	0	0	0	—	—	0	—
Dwight Gooden	p	2	2	1	1	0	0	0	0	0	0	0	.500	.500	0	1.000
Danny Heep	ph-lf-dh	5	11	0	1	0	0	0	2	1	1	0	.091	.091	0	1.000
Keith Hernandez	1b	7	26	1	6	0	0	0	4	5	1	0	.231	.231	1	.981
Howard Johnson	3b-ph-ss	2	5	0	0	0	0	0	0	0	2	0	.000	.000	0	1.000
Ray Knight	3b	6	23	4	9	1	0	1	5	2	2	0	.391	.565	1	.917
Lee Mazzilli	ph-rf	4	5	2	2	0	0	0	0	0	0	0	.400	.400	0	1.000
Roger McDowell	p	5	0	0	0	0	0	0	0	0	0	0	—	—	0	1.000
Kevin Mitchell	ph-lf-dh	5	8	1	2	0	0	0	0	0	3	0	.250	.250	0	1.000
Bob Ojeda	p	2	2	0	0	0	0	0	0	1	0	0	.000	.000	0	1.000
Jesse Orosco	p	4	1	0	1	0	0	0	1	0	0	0	1.000	1.000	0	—
Rafael Santana	ss	7	20	3	5	0	0	0	2	2	5	0	.250	.250	1	.966
Doug Sisk	p	1	0	0	0	0	0	0	0	0	0	0	—	—	0	—
Darryl Strawberry	rf	7	24	4	5	1	0	1	1	4	6	3	.208	.375	0	1.000
Tim Teufel	2b	3	9	1	4	1	0	1	1	1	2	0	.444	.889	1	.857
Mookie Wilson	lf-cf	7	26	3	7	1	0	0	1	1	6	3	.269	.308	0	1.000
Totals		**7**	**240**	**32**	**65**	**6**	**0**	**7**	**29**	**21**	**43**	**7**	**.271**	**.383**	**6**	**.981**

Pitcher	G	GS	CG	IP	H	R	ER	BB	SO	W-L	Sv	ERA
Rick Aguilera	1	0	0	3	8	4	4	1	4	1-0	0	12.00
Ron Darling	3	3	0	17⅔	13	4	3	10	12	1-1	0	1.53
Sid Fernandez	3	0	0	6⅔	6	1	1	1	10	0-0	0	1.35
Dwight Gooden	2	2	0	9	17	10	8	4	9	0-2	0	8.00
Roger McDowell	5	0	0	7⅓	10	5	4	6	2	1-0	0	4.91
Bobby Ojeda	2	2	0	13	13	3	3	5	9	1-0	0	2.08
Jesse Orosco	4	0	0	5⅔	2	0	0	6	6	0-0	2	0.00
Doug Sisk	1	0	0	⅔	0	0	0	1	1	0-0	0	0.00
Totals	**7**	**7**	**0**	**63**	**69**	**27**	**23**	**28**	**53**	**4-3**	**2**	**3.29**

BOSTON RED SOX/John McNamara, Manager

Player	pos	G	AB	R	H	2B	3B	HR	RBI	BB	SO	SB	BA	SA	E	FPct
Tony Armas	ph	1	1	0	0	0	0	0	0	0	1	0	.000	.000	—	—
Marty Barrett	2b	7	30	1	13	2	0	0	4	5	2	0	.433	.500	0	1.000
Don Baylor	dh-ph	4	11	1	2	1	0	0	1	1	3	0	.182	.273	—	—
Wade Boggs	3b	7	31	3	9	3	0	0	3	4	2	0	.290	.387	0	1.000
Dennis "Oil Can" Boyd	p	1	0	0	0	0	0	0	0	0	0	0	—	—	0	1.000
Bill Buckner	1b	7	32	2	6	0	0	0	1	0	3	0	.188	.188	1	.984
Roger Clemens	p	2	4	1	0	0	0	0	0	0	1	0	.000	.000	0	1.000
Steve Crawford	p	3	1	0	0	0	0	0	0	0	0	0	.000	.000	0	—
Dwight Evans	rf	7	26	4	8	2	0	2	9	4	3	0	.308	.615	1	.944
Rich Gedman	c	7	30	1	6	1	0	1	1	0	10	0	.200	.333	2	.961
Mike Greenwell	ph	4	3	0	0	0	0	0	0	0	1	2	0	.000	.000	—	—
Dave Henderson	cf	7	25	6	10	1	1	2	5	2	6	0	.400	.760	0	1.000
Bruce Hurst	p	3	3	0	0	0	0	0	0	0	3	0	.000	.000	0	1.000
Al Nipper	p	2	0	0	0	0	0	0	0	0	0	0	—	—	0	1.000
Spike Owen	ss	7	20	2	6	0	0	0	2	5	6	0	.300	.300	0	1.000
Jim Rice	lf	7	27	6	9	1	1	0	6	9	0	.333	.444	0	1.000
Ed Romero	pr-ss	3	1	0	0	0	0	0	0	0	0	0	.000	.000	1	1.000
Joe Sambito	p	2	0	0	0	0	0	0	0	0	0	0	—	—	0	—
Calvin Schiraldi	p	3	1	0	0	0	0	0	0	0	1	0	.000	.000	0	1.000
Bob Stanley	p	5	1	0	0	0	0	0	0	0	1	0	.000	.000	0	1.000
Dave Stapleton	1b-pr	3	1	0	0	0	0	0	0	0	0	0	.000	.000	0	1.000
Totals		**7**	**248**	**27**	**69**	**11**	**2**	**5**	**26**	**28**	**53**	**0**	**.278**	**.399**	**4**	**.985**

Pitcher	G	GS	CG	IP	H	R	ER	BB	SO	W-L	Sv	ERA
Dennis "Oil Can" Boyd	1	1	0	7	9	6	6	1	3	0-1	0	7.71
Roger Clemens	2	2	0	11⅓	9	5	4	6	11	0-0	0	3.18
Steve Crawford	3	0	0	4⅓	5	3	3	0	4	1-0	0	6.23
Bruce Hurst	3	3	1	23	18	5	5	6	17	2-0	0	1.96
Al Nipper	2	1	0	6⅓	10	5	5	2	2	0-1	0	7.11
Joe Sambito	2	0	0	⅓	2	1	1	2	0	0-0	0	27.00
Calvin Schiraldi	3	0	0	4	7	7	6	3	2	0-2	1	13.50
Bob Stanley	5	0	0	6⅓	5	0	0	1	4	0-0	1	0.00
Totals	**7**	**7**	**1**	**62⅔**	**65**	**32**	**30**	**21**	**43**	**3-4**	**2**	**4.31**

Series MVP: Ray Knight, New York Mets. **Series Outstanding Pitcher:** Jesse Orosco, New York Mets. **Average Length of Game:** 3 hours, 20 minutes. **Total Attendance:** 321,774. **Average Attendance:** 45,968 (55,062 at Shea Stadium; 33,842 at Fenway Park). **Umpires:** Joe Brinkman (AL), Jim Evans (AL), Dale Ford (AL), John Kibler (NL), Ed Montague (NL), Harry Wendelstedt (NL). **Winning Player's Share:** $86,254. **Losing Player's Share:** $74,986.

Left: Game 6 started off as something to remember when Michael Sergio parachuted onto the Shea Stadium field during the first inning of the classic game.

Right: Mookie Wilson is swept off his feet trying to avoid a wild pitch from Bob Stanley in the last inning of Game 6. The wild pitch allowed the tying run to score, and Wilson followed it with a game-winning single.

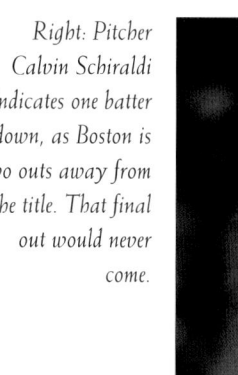

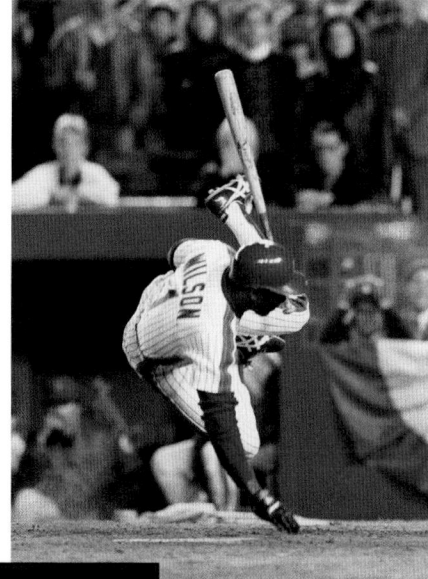

Right: Pitcher Calvin Schiraldi indicates one batter down, as Boston is two outs away from the title. That final out would never come.

Left: Ray Knight applauds as he reaches third on Mookie Wilson's single and Dwight Evans' error in the fifth inning of Game 6. He would score the tying run one batter later.

Left: Mookie Wilson lunges back past first baseman Bill Buckner on a pick-off play in Game 4. The two would be reunited in much more dramatic circumstances in Game 6.

Minnesota Twins (4) vs. St. Louis Cardinals (3)

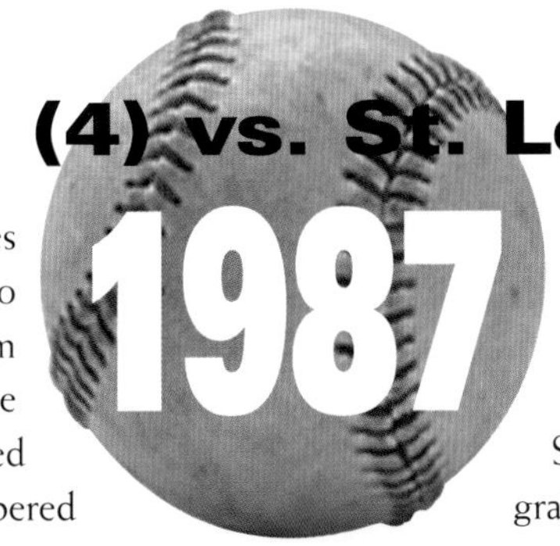

1987

Home-field advantage in the World Series alternates between the American and National Leagues from year to year; in even-numbered years, the National League team gets to host four games in the seven-game series, while the American League team has the advantage in odd-numbered years. Fortunately for Minnesota, 1987 was an odd-numbered year. Tom Kelly's Twins reached the postseason by virtue of a league-best 56-25 record at home during the regular season, and despite losing 52 of 81 games away from the Metrodome. Although their overall record of 85-77 would have placed them fifth in the AL's Eastern Division, they topped the second-place Royals by two games in the West and then defeated the Tigers in the league championship series, winning two of three in Detroit. The Twins boasted three sluggers with more than 30 homers, and a fourth, Kirby Puckett, who hit 28 and also led the league with 207 hits. The NL-champion St. Louis Cardinals were short on power (they hit fewer home runs than any other team in 1987), but they once again got to the Series with fleet feet, steady gloves and strong pitching arms.

On October 17, 1987, the World Series was played indoors for the first time in history. Frank Viola and the Twins hosted the Cardinals in the thunderously loud Metrodome, and they blasted their way to a 10-1 rout. Dan Gladden's grand-slam homer capped a seven-run fourth

inning. The home success continued in Game 2, as another high-scoring fourth inning paced Minnesota to an 8-4 victory. Veteran Bert Blyleven got the win pitching seven innings and striking out eight. Game 3 at Busch Stadium was a much quieter affair, with the Cardinals grabbing a 3-1 win behind John Tudor's four-hitter. In the seventh inning, Vince Coleman drove in 2 with a ground-rule double, stole third base and scored on Ozzie Smith's single. St. Louis exploded for a big fourth inning in Game 4, while three pitchers combined to hold Minnesota to 2 runs. Tom Lawless, who had only 2 hits in 1987 and one home run since entering the league in 1982, got the Cardinals going with a three-run blast in the fourth. Whitey Herzog's club employed their trademark style to win the following day, stealing 5 bases in Game 5 and scoring 2 runs with infield singles (and a Minnesota error) in the sixth. St. Louis's clean sweep at home put the team one win away from clinching the Series, but there would be no more games at cavernous Busch Stadium. The teams returned to the Metrodome for Game 6, and true to form, the Twins ran up 15 hits and 11 runs. They overcame a 5-2 Cardinal advan-

Above: Kirby Puckett notched ten hits in the Series and reached base five times in Game 6.

1987 WORLD SERIES COMPOSITE STATISTICS

MINNESOTA TWINS/Tom Kelly, Manager

Player	pos	G	AB	R	H	2B	3B	HR	RBI	BB	SO	SB	BA	SA	E	FPct
Keith Atherton	p	2	0	0	0	0	0	0	0	0	0	0	—	—	0	—
Don Baylor	dh-ph	5	13	3	5	0	0	1	3	1	1	0	.385	.615	—	—
Juan Berenguer	p	3	0	0	0	0	0	0	0	0	0	0	—	—	0	—
Bert Blyleven	p	2	1	0	0	0	0	0	0	0	1	0	.000	.000	0	1.000
Tom Brunansky	rf	7	25	5	5	0	0	0	2	4	4	1	.200	.200	0	1.000
Randy Bush	dh-ph	4	6	1	1	1	0	0	2	0	1	0	.167	.333	—	—
Sal Butera	c	1	0	0	0	0	0	0	0	0	0	0	—	—	0	—
Mark Davidson	rf-ph	2	1	0	0	0	0	0	0	0	0	0	.000	.000	0	—
George Frazier	p	1	0	0	0	0	0	0	0	0	0	0	—	—	0	1.000
Gary Gaetti	3b	7	27	4	7	2	1	1	4	2	5	2	.259	.519	0	1.000
Greg Gagne	ss	7	30	5	6	1	0	1	3	1	6	0	.200	.333	2	.929
Dan Gladden	lf	7	31	3	9	2	1	1	7	3	4	2	.290	.516	0	1.000
Kent Hrbek	1b	7	24	4	5	0	0	1	6	5	3	0	.208	.333	0	1.000
Gene Larkin	1b-ph	5	3	1	0	0	0	0	0	1	0	0	.000	.000	0	1.000
Tim Laudner	c	7	22	4	7	1	0	1	4	5	4	0	.318	.500	0	1.000
Steve Lombardozzi	2b	6	17	3	7	1	0	1	4	2	2	0	.412	.647	0	1.000
Al Newman	pr-2b-ph	4	5	0	1	0	0	0	0	1	1	0	.200	.200	0	1.000
Joe Niekro	p	1	0	0	0	0	0	0	0	0	0	0	—	—	0	1.000
Kirby Puckett	cf	7	28	5	10	1	1	0	3	2	1	1	.357	.464	1	.941
Jeff Reardon	p	4	0	0	0	0	0	0	0	0	0	0	—	—	0	—
Dan Schatzeder	p	3	0	0	0	0	0	0	0	0	0	0	—	—	0	—
Roy Smalley	ph	4	2	0	1	1	0	0	0	2	0	0	.500	1.000	—	—
Les Straker	p	2	2	0	0	0	0	0	0	0	2	0	.000	.000	0	1.000
Frank Viola	p	3	1	0	0	0	0	0	0	0	1	0	.000	.000	0	1.000
Totals		**7**	**238**	**38**	**64**	**10**	**3**	**7**	**38**	**29**	**36**	**6**	**.269**	**.424**	**3**	**.988**

Pitcher	G	GS	CG	IP	H	R	ER	BB	SO	W-L	Sv	ERA
Keith Atherton	2	0	0	1⅓	0	1	1	1	0	0-0	0	6.75
Juan Berenguer	3	0	0	4⅓	10	5	5	0	1	0-1	0	10.38
Bert Blyleven	2	2	0	13	13	5	4	2	12	1-1	0	2.77
George Frazier	1	0	0	2	1	0	0	0	2	0-0	0	0.00
Joe Niekro	1	0	0	2	1	0	0	1	1	0-0	0	0.00
Jeff Reardon	4	0	0	4⅔	5	0	0	0	3	0-0	1	0.00
Dan Schatzeder	3	0	0	4⅓	4	3	3	3	3	1-0	0	6.23
Les Straker	2	2	0	9	9	4	4	3	6	0-0	0	4.00
Frank Viola	3	3	0	19⅓	17	8	8	3	16	2-1	0	3.72
Totals	**7**	**7**	**0**	**60**	**60**	**28**	**25**	**13**	**44**	**4-3**	**1**	**3.75**

ST. LOUIS CARDINALS/Whitey Herzog, Manager

Player	pos	G	AB	R	H	2B	3B	HR	RBI	BB	SO	SB	BA	SA	E	FPct
Vince Coleman	lf	7	28	5	4	2	0	0	2	2	10	6	.143	.214	0	1.000
Danny Cox	p	3	2	0	0	0	0	0	0	0	1	0	.000	.000	0	1.000
Ken Dayley	p	4	1	0	0	0	0	0	0	0	1	0	.000	.000	0	—
Dan Driessen	1b	4	13	3	3	2	0	0	1	1	1	0	.231	.385	0	1.000
Curt Ford	rf-ph	5	13	1	4	0	0	0	2	1	1	0	.308	.308	0	1.000
Bob Forsch	p	3	2	0	0	0	0	0	0	0	0	0	.000	.000	0	1.000
Tom Herr	2b	7	28	2	7	0	0	1	1	2	2	0	.250	.357	0	1.000
Ricky Horton	p	2	0	0	0	0	0	0	0	0	0	0	—	—	0	1.000
Lance Johnson	pr	1	0	0	0	0	0	0	0	0	0	1	—	—	—	—
Steve Lake	c	3	3	0	1	0	0	0	1	0	0	0	.333	.333	0	1.000
Tom Lawless	3b	3	10	1	1	0	0	1	3	0	4	0	.100	.400	1	.900
Jim Lindeman	1b-ph-rf	6	15	3	5	1	0	0	2	0	3	0	.333	.400	3	.909
Joe Magrane	p	2	0	0	0	0	0	0	0	0	0	0	—	—	0	1.000
Greg Mathews	p	1	1	0	0	0	0	0	0	0	0	0	.000	.000	0	1.000
Willie McGee	cf	7	27	2	10	2	0	0	4	0	9	0	.370	.444	1	.957
John Morris	rf	1	2	0	0	0	0	0	0	0	0	0	.000	.000	0	1.000
Jose Oquendo	rf-3b	7	24	2	6	0	0	0	2	1	4	0	.250	.250	0	1.000
Tom Pagnozzi	dh-ph	2	4	0	1	0	0	0	0	0	0	0	.250	.250	—	—
Tony Pena	c-dh	7	22	2	9	1	0	0	4	3	2	1	.409	.455	1	.971
Terry Pendleton	dh-ph	3	7	2	3	0	0	0	1	1	2	0	.429	.429	—	—
Ozzie Smith	ss	7	28	3	6	0	0	0	2	2	3	2	.214	.214	0	1.000
John Tudor	p	2	2	0	0	0	0	0	0	0	2	0	.000	.000	0	1.000
Lee Tunnell	p	2	0	0	0	0	0	0	0	0	0	0	—	—	0	1.000
Todd Worrell	p	4	0	0	0	0	0	0	0	0	0	0	—	—	0	1.000
Totals		**7**	**232**	**26**	**60**	**8**	**0**	**2**	**25**	**13**	**44**	**12**	**.259**	**.319**	**6**	**.976**

Pitcher	G	GS	CG	IP	H	R	ER	BB	SO	W-L	Sv	ERA
Danny Cox	3	2	0	11⅔	13	10	10	8	9	1-2	0	7.71
Ken Dayley	4	0	0	4⅔	2	1	1	0	3	0-0	1	1.93
Bob Forsch	3	0	0	6⅓	8	7	7	5	3	1-0	0	9.95
Ricky Horton	2	0	0	3	5	2	2	0	1	0-0	0	6.00
Joe Magrane	2	2	0	7⅓	9	7	7	5	5	0-1	0	8.59
Greg Mathews	1	1	0	3⅔	2	1	1	2	3	0-0	0	2.45
John Tudor	2	2	0	11	15	7	7	3	8	1-1	0	5.73
Lee Tunnel	2	0	0	4⅓	4	2	1	2	1	0-0	0	2.08
Todd Worrell	4	0	0	7	6	1	1	4	3	0-0	2	1.29
Totals	**7**	**7**	**0**	**59**	**64**	**38**	**37**	**29**	**36**	**3-4**	**3**	**5.64**

Series MVP: Frank Viola, Minnesota Twins. **Series Outstanding Pitcher:** Frank Viola, Minnesota Twins. **Average Length of Game:** 3 hours, 1 minute. **Total Attendance:** 387,138. **Average Attendance:** 55,305 (55,274 at the Metrodome; 55,347 at Busch Stadium).
Umpires: Ken Kaiser (AL), Greg Kosc (AL), John McSherry (NL), Dave Phillips (AL), Terry Tata (NL), Lee Weyer (NL). **Winning Player's Share:** $85,581. **Losing Player's Share:** $56,053.

With an 85-77 regular-season record, the Minnesota Twins had the lowest winning percentage (.525) of any team to win a World Series.

tage by scoring 4 runs in the bottom of the fifth, with Don Baylor knocking a two-run homer. An inning later, Minnesota loaded the bases, and with two out, Herzog brought in Ken Dayley to pitch to Kent Hrbek. On Dayley's first pitch, Hrbek delivered Minnesota's second grand-slam of the Series. Kirby Puckett crossed the plate in all four innings in which the team scored, and he had 4 hits and one walk in five plate appearances. The deciding game featured no big innings, but the Twins snatched a 3-2 lead in the sixth when Greg Gagne beat out a hard grounder down the third-base line with the bases loaded, scoring Tom Brunansky from third. After Minnesota extended the score to 4-2 on Gladden's double in the eighth, Jeff Reardon retired the side in the ninth in relief of Frank Viola, who hurled another strong game for Minnesota to earn his second victory and Series MVP honors. For the first time in a World Series, all games were won by the home teams—and with that, along with some clutch hitting and gutsy pitching, the Minnesota Twins had their first championship title.

Above: The World Series moves indoors. The loud Metrodome crowd helped carry the Twins to a world championship.

Above inset: Series MVP Frank Viola put Minnesota on top with his opening-game victory and then closed out the Series with a win in Game 7.

Above: St. Louis' speedy Vince Coleman was a terror on the base paths, stealing six bases during the Series.

Background: The Twins made full use of home-field advantage in the Series to catapult them to the city's first title.

Inset, left. Dan Gladden blasts a bases-loaded home run during the Twins' 10-1 rout in Game 1. It was the first World Series grand slam in 17 years.

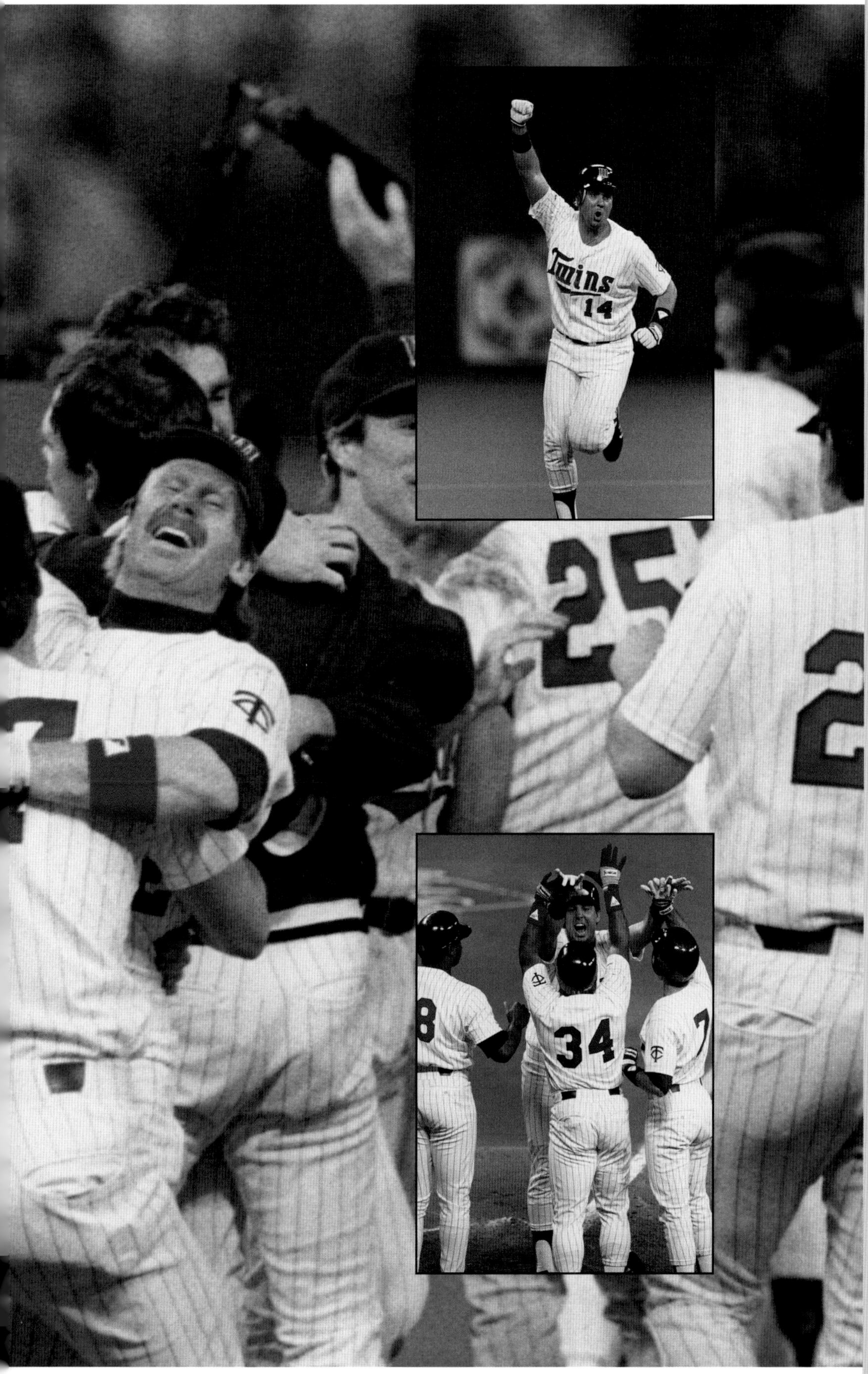

Inset, top: Kent Hrbek is pumped after his Game 6 grand slam put the Twins up 10-5 in the sixth inning. It was the Twins' second grand slam of the Series.

Inset, bottom: The beneficiaries of Hrbek's clout—Don Baylor (8), Kirby Puckett (34) and Greg Gagne (7)—congratulate him as he reaches the plate.

Game 1 Saturday, October 17 at the Metrodome, Minneapolis

	1	2	3	4	5	6	7	8	9	R	H	E
St. Louis Cardinals	0	1	0	0	0	0	0	0	0	1	5	1
Minnesota Twins	0	0	0	7	2	0	1	0	x	10	11	0

Pitchers StL **Joe Magrane** (L, 0-1), IP 3, H 4, R 5, ER 5, BB 4, SO 1; **Bob Forsch**, IP 3, H 4, R 4, ER 4, BB 2, SO 0; **Ricky Horton**, IP 2, H 3, R 1, ER 1, BB 0, SO 1
Min **Frank Viola** (W, 1-0), IP 8, H 5, R 1, ER 1, BB 0, SO 5; **Keith Atherton**, IP 1, H 0, R 0, ER 0, BB 0, SO 0

Top Performers at the Plate
StL **Jim Lindeman**, 2 for 4, 1 R; **Willie McGee**, 2 for 3
Min **Dan Gladden**, 2 for 4, 1 R, 5 RBI, 1 BB; **Steve Lombardozzi**, 2 for 3, 2 R, 2 RBI, 1 BB

2B-StL/Lindeman; Min/Gaetti, Gladden. **HR**-Min/Gladden, Lombardozzi. **SB**-Min/Gladden.
Time 2:39. **Attendance** 55,171.

Game 2 Sunday, October 18 at the Metrodome, Minneapolis

	1	2	3	4	5	6	7	8	9	R	H	E
St. Louis Cardinals	0	0	0	0	1	0	1	2	0	4	9	0
Minnesota Twins	0	1	0	6	0	1	0	0	x	8	10	0

Pitchers StL **Danny Cox** (L, 0-1), IP 3⅔, H 6, R 7, ER 7, BB 2, SO 3; **Lee Tunnell**, IP 2⅓, H 3, R 1, ER 1, BB 1, SO 1; **Ken Dayley**, IP 1⅓, H 0, R 0, ER 0, BB 0, SO 1; **Todd Worrell**, IP ⅔, H 1, R 0, ER 0, BB 1, SO 0
Min **Bert Blyleven** (W, 1-0), IP 7, H 6, R 2, ER 2, BB 1, SO 8; **Juan Berenguer**, IP 1, H 3, R 2, ER 2, BB 0, SO 0; **Jeff Reardon**, IP 1, H 0, R 0, ER 0, BB 0, SO 0

Top Performers at the Plate
StL **Curt Ford**, 2 for 3, 1 R, 1 BB; **Tony Pena**, 1 for 4, 2 RBI
Min **Gary Gaetti**, 2 for 3, 2 R, 1 RBI, 1 BB; **Tim Laudner**, 2 for 3, 2 R, 3 RBI, 1 BB

2B-StL/Driessen; Min/Bush, Gagne, Smalley. **HR**-Min/Gaetti, Laudner. **SB**-StL/Coleman.
Time 2:42. **Attendance** 55,257.

Game 3 Tuesday, October 20 at Busch Stadium, St. Louis

	1	2	3	4	5	6	7	8	9	R	H	E
Minnesota Twins	0	0	0	0	0	1	0	0	0	1	5	1
St. Louis Cardinals	0	0	0	0	0	0	3	0	x	3	9	1

Pitchers Min **Les Straker**, IP 6, H 4, R 0, ER 0, BB 2, SO 4; **Juan Berenguer** (L, 0-1), IP ⅓, H 4, R 3, ER 3, BB 0, SO 0; **Dan Schatzeder**, IP 1⅔, H 1, R 0, ER 0, BB 0, SO 1
StL **John Tudor** (W, 1-0), IP 7, H 4, R 1, ER 1, BB 2, SO 7; **Todd Worrell** (Sv, 1), IP 2, H 1, R 0, ER 0, BB 0, SO 1

Top Performers at the Plate
Min **Tim Laudner**, 2 for 3; **Kirby Puckett**, 1 for 3, 1 BB
StL **Vince Coleman**, 1 for 4, 1 R, 2 RBI, 2 SB; **Ozzie Smith**, 2 for 4, 1 RBI

2B-Min/Laudner; StL/Coleman, McGee. **3B**-Min/Puckett. **SB**-StL/Coleman 2. **Time** 2:45.
Attendance 55,347.

Game 4 Wednesday, October 21 at Busch Stadium, St. Louis

	1	2	3	4	5	6	7	6	9	R	H	E
Minnesota Twins	0	0	1	0	1	0	0	0	0	2	7	1
St. Louis Cardinals	0	0	1	6	0	0	0	0	x	7	10	1

Pitchers Min **Frank Viola** (L, 1-1), IP 3⅓, H 6, R 5, ER 5, BB 3, SO 4; **Dan Schatzeder**, IP ⅔, H 2, R 2, ER 2, BB 1, SO 1; **Joe Niekro**, IP 2, H 1, R 0, ER 0, BB 1, SO 1; **George Frazier**, IP 2, H 1, R 0, ER 0, BB 0, SO 2
StL **Greg Mathews**, IP 3⅔, H 2, R 1, ER 1, BB 2, SO 3; **Bob Forsch** (W, 1-0), IP 2⅔, H 4, R 1, ER 1, BB 1, SO 3; **Ken Dayley** (Sv, 1), IP 2⅔, H 1, R 0, ER 0, BB 0, SO 2

Top Performers at the Plate
Min **Al Newman**, 1 for 3, 1 BB; **Kirby Puckett**, 1 for 4, 1 RBI, 1 HBP
StL **Tom Herr**, 2 for 3, 1 R, 2 BB; **Jim Lindeman**, 2 for 4, 1 R, 2 RBI, 1 HBP

2B-StL/Coleman, McGee. **HR**-Min/Gagne; StL/Lawless. **SB**-Min/Brunansky, Gaetti; StL/Coleman.
Time 3:11. **Attendance** 55,347.

Game 5 Thursday, October 22 at Busch Stadium, St. Louis

	1	2	3	4	5	8	7	8	9	R	H	E
Minnesota Twins	0	0	0	0	0	0	0	2	0	2	6	1
St. Louis Cardinals	0	0	0	0	0	3	1	0	x	4	10	0

Pitchers Min **Bert Blyleven** (L, 1-1), IP 6, H 7, R 3, ER 2, BB 1, SO 4; **Keith Atherton**, IP ⅓, H 0, R 1, ER 1, BB 1, SO 0; **Jeff Reardon**, IP 1⅔, H 3, R 0, ER 0, BB 0, SO 3
StL **Danny Cox** (W, 1-1), IP 7⅓, H 5, R 2, ER 2, BB 3, SO 6; **Ken Dayley**, IP ⅓, H 0, R 0, ER 0, BB 0, SO 0; **Todd Worrell** (Sv, 2), IP 1⅓, H 1, R 0, ER 0, BB 2, SO 0

Top Performers at the Plate
Min **Gary Gaetti**, 1 for 4, 2 RBI; **Dan Gladden**, 1 for 3, 1 R, 2 BB
StL **Vince Coleman**, 1 for 3, 2 R, 1 BB, 2 SB; **Ozzie Smith**, 2 for 4, 1 R, 1 RBI

3B-Min/Gaetti. **SB**-Min/Gladden; StL/Coleman 2, Johnson, Smith 2. **Time** 3:21. **Attendance** 55,347.

Game 6 Saturday, October 24 at the Metrodome, Minneapolis

	1	2	3	4	5	6	7	8	9	R	H	E
St. Louis Cardinals	1	1	0	2	1	0	0	0	0	5	11	2
Minnesota Twins	2	0	0	0	4	4	0	1	x	11	15	0

Pitchers StL **John Tudor** (L, 1-1), IP 4, H 11, R 6, ER 6, BB 1, SO 1; **Ricky Horton**, IP 1, H 2, R 1, ER 1, BB 0, SO 0; **Bob Forsch**, IP ⅔, H 0, R 2, ER 2, BB 2, SO 0; **Ken Dayley**, IP ⅓, H 1, R 1, ER 1, BB 0, SO 0; **Lee Tunnell**, IP 2, H 1, R 1, ER 0, BB 1, SO 0
Min **Les Straker**, IP 3, H 5, R 4, ER 4, BB 1, SO 2; **Dan Schatzeder** (W, 1-0), IP 2, H 1, R 1, ER 1, BB 2, SO 1; **Juan Berenguer**, IP 3, H 3, R 0, ER 0, BB 0, SO 1; **Jeff Reardon**, IP 1, H 2, R 0, ER 0, BB 0, SO 0

Top Performers at the Plate
StL **Tom Herr**, 3 for 5, 1 R, 1 RBI; **Terry Pendleton**, 2 for 3, 1 R, 1 RBI, 1 BB, 2 SB
Min **Don Baylor**, 2 for 3, 2 R, 3 RBI, 1 BB; **Kirby Puckett**, 4 for 4, 4 R, 1 RBI, 1 BB

2B-StL/Driessen; Min/Gaetti, Lombardozzi. **3B**-Min/Gladden. **HR**-StL/Herr; Min/Baylor, Hrbek.
SB-StL/Pendleton 2; Min/Puckett. **Time** 3:22. **Attendance** 55,293.

Game 7 Sunday, October 25 at the Metrodome, Minneapolis

	1	2	3	4	5	6	7	8	9	R	H	E
St. Louis Cardinals	0	2	0	0	0	0	0	0	0	2	6	1
Minnesota Twins	0	1	0	0	1	1	0	1	x	4	10	0

Pitchers StL **Joe Magrane**, IP 4⅓, H 5, R 2, ER 2, BB 1, SO 4; **Danny Cox** (L, 1-2), IP ⅔, H 2, R 1, ER 1, BB 3, SO 0; **Todd Worrell**, IP 3, H 3, R 1, ER 1, BB 1, SO 2
Min **Frank Viola** (W, 2-1), IP 8, H 6, R 2, ER 2, BB 0, SO 7; **Jeff Reardon** (Sv, 1), IP 1, H 0, R 0, ER 0, BB 0, SO 0

Top Performers at the Plate
StL **Steve Lake**, 1 for 3, 1 RBI; **Tony Pena**, 2 for 3, 1 RBI
Min **Tom Brunansky**, 1 for 3, 2 R, 1 BB; **Greg Gagne**, 2 for 5, 1 R, 1 RBI

2B-StL/Pena; Min/Gladden, Puckett. **SB**-StL/Pena; Min/Gaetti. **Time** 3:04. **Attendance** 55,376.

Los Angeles Dodgers (4) vs. Oakland Athletics (1)

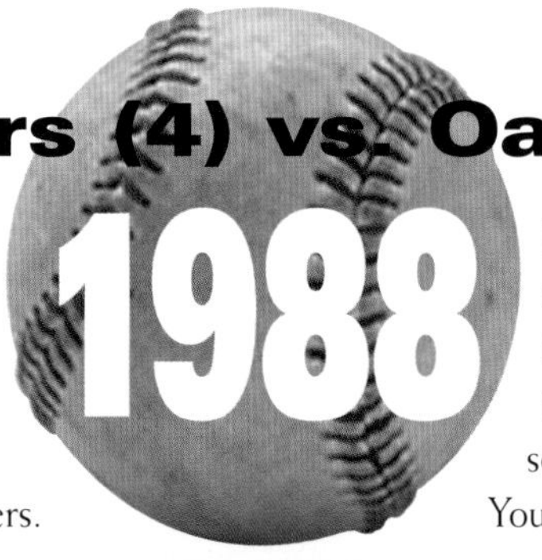

With 104 wins and a potent lineup, the Oakland Athletics appeared almost invincible in 1988. Jose Canseco produced MVP numbers during the season, and he and Bash Brother Mark McGwire walloped 74 homers. After sweeping Boston in the league championship series, Tony La Russa's A's headed south to face the Los Angeles Dodgers. The Dodgers, who defeated a heavily favored Met team in the NLCS, were racked with injuries. Most notably, their top hitter and emotional leader, Kirk Gibson, was hobbling on a bad leg and was questionable to play at all in the Series. Ace pitcher Orel Hershiser was unavailable after the final game of the NLCS, so Tommy Lasorda started Tim Belcher in Game 1 against Oakland's intimidating 21-game winner, Dave Stewart. Belcher got out of a bases-loaded jam in the first, and his team grabbed the lead in the bottom of the inning on Mickey Hatcher's two-run homer. The A's loaded the bases again in the second, and after Belcher struck out Dave Henderson for out number two, Canseco bashed one over the centerfield fence for a grand slam. The Dodger relievers shut Oakland out after that point, and the offense got them within a run. Heading into their last at-bats in the ninth, the Dodgers had to face Dennis Eckersley, the league's leading reliever, who had pitched scoreless ball throughout the ALCS. Eck got the first two out before walking pinch hitter Mike Davis to bring up the pitcher's spot in the order. Lasorda called the gimpy Gibson out of the clubhouse to

bat for Alejandro Pena. Gibson worked the count full, and then, wincing in pain, sent a fastball into the right-field bleachers. Gibson limped around the bases, pumping his arm in jubilation. It was the only action he would see in the Series, but it was enough to inspire his team. Cy Young winner Hershiser took over in Game 2, getting as many hits at the plate himself (3) as he gave up to the Oakland batters. The A's got some heroism of their own to win Game 3, as McGwire broke a 1-1 tie in the bottom of the ninth with a solo blast off reliever Jay Howell. The teams were battling in a tight 4-3 contest in Game 4 when Howell again faced off with McGwire in a climactic moment. The A's filled the bases in the seventh, but Howell avenged his Game 3 loss by getting McGwire to pop up for the third out of the inning. Hershiser closed Oakland out the next day, striking out nine, including two in the last inning, and surrendering just 4 hits for a 5-2 triumph. With Hershiser leading the way, the Dodger staff held the Bash Brothers to 2 hits in 36 times at bat (both were home runs), and the team to a .177 average for the Series. LA had pulled off a great upset, and Kirk Gibson provided an electrifying World Series moment.

Above: In heroic fashion, Kirk Gibson came off the bench to win the opening game of the 1988 World Series with a thrilling home run.

1988 WORLD SERIES COMPOSITE STATISTICS

LOS ANGELES DODGERS/Tommy Lasorda, Manager

Player	pos	G	AB	R	H	2B	3B	HR	RBI	BB	SO	SB	BA	SA	E	FPct
Dave Anderson	ph-dh	1	1	0	0	0	0	0	0	0	1	0	.000	.000	–	–
Tim Belcher	p	2	0	0	0	0	0	0	0	0	0	0	–	–	0	–
Mike Davis	ph-dh-rf	4	7	3	1	0	0	2	2	4	0	2	.143	.571	0	–
Rick Dempsey	c	2	5	0	1	1	0	0	1	1	2	0	.200	.400	0	1.000
Kirk Gibson	ph	1	1	1	1	0	0	1	2	0	0	0	1.000	4.000	–	–
Jose Gonzalez	ph-rf-lf	4	2	0	0	0	0	0	0	0	2	0	.000	.000	0	1.000
Alfredo Griffin	ss	5	16	2	3	0	0	0	0	2	4	0	.188	.188	1	.950
Jeff Hamilton	3b	5	19	1	2	0	0	0	1	4	0	.105	.105	1	.889
Mickey Hatcher	lf-rf	5	19	5	7	1	0	2	5	1	3	0	.368	.737	0	1.000
Danny Heep	ph-lf-dh	3	8	0	2	1	0	0	0	0	2	0	.250	.375	0	–
Orel Hershiser	p	2	3	1	3	2	0	0	1	0	0	0	1.000	1.667	0	1.000
Brian Holton	p	1	0	0	0	0	0	0	0	0	0	0	–	–	0	1.000
Jay Howell	p	2	0	0	0	0	0	0	0	0	0	0	–	–	0	–
Tim Leary	p	2	0	0	0	0	0	0	0	0	0	0	–	–	0	1.000
Mike Marshall	rf	5	13	2	3	0	1	1	3	0	5	0	.231	.615	0	1.000
Alejandro Pena	p	2	0	0	0	0	0	0	0	0	0	0	–	–	0	–
Steve Sax	2b	5	20	3	6	0	0	0	0	1	1	1	.300	.300	0	1.000
Mike Scioscia	c	4	14	0	3	0	0	0	1	0	2	0	.214	.214	1	.966
John Shelby	cf	5	18	0	4	1	0	0	1	2	7	1	.222	.278	0	1.000
Franklin Stubbs	1b	5	17	3	5	2	0	0	2	1	3	0	.294	.412	0	1.000
John Tudor	p	1	0	0	0	0	0	0	0	0	0	0	–	–	0	–
Tracy Woodson	ph-1b	4	4	0	0	0	0	0	1	0	0	0	.000	.000	0	1.000
Totals		5	167	21	41	8	1	6	19	13	36	4	.246	.395	3	.983

Pitcher	G	GS	CG	IP	H	R	ER	BB	SO	W-L	Sv	ERA
Tim Belcher	2	2	0	8⅔	10	7	6	6	10	1-0	1	6.23
Orel Hershiser	2	2	2	18	7	2	2	6	17	2-0	0	1.00
Brian Holton	1	0	0	2	0	0	1	1	0	0-0	0	0.00
Jay Howell	2	0	0	2⅔	3	1	1	1	2	0-1	1	3.38
Tim Leary	2	0	0	6⅔	6	1	1	2	4	0-0	0	1.35
Alejandro Pena	2	0	0	5	2	0	0	1	7	1-0	0	0.00
John Tudor	1	1	0	1⅓	0	0	0	0	1	0-0	0	0.00
Totals	5	5	2	44⅓	28	11	10	17	41	4-1	1	2.03

OAKLAND ATHLETICS/Tony La Russa, Manager

Player	pos	G	AB	R	H	2B	3B	HR	RBI	BB	SO	SB	BA	SA	E	FPct
Don Baylor	ph	1	1	0	0	0	0	0	0	0	1	0	.000	.000	–	–
Todd Burns	p	1	0	0	0	0	0	0	0	0	0	0	–	–	0	–
Greg Cadaret	p	3	0	0	0	0	0	0	0	0	0	0	–	–	0	–
Jose Canseco	rf	5	19	1	1	0	0	1	5	2	5	1	.053	.211	0	1.000
Storm Davis	p	2	1	0	0	0	0	0	0	1	0	0	.000	.000	0	1.000
Dennis Eckersley	p	2	0	0	0	0	0	0	0	0	0	0	–	–	0	–
Mike Gallego	pr-2b	1	0	0	0	0	0	0	0	0	0	0	–	–	0	–
Ron Hassey	c-ph	5	8	0	2	0	0	0	1	3	3	0	.250	.250	0	1.000
Dave Henderson	cf	5	20	1	6	2	0	0	1	2	7	0	.300	.400	0	1.000
Rick Honeycutt	p	3	0	0	0	0	0	0	0	0	0	0	–	–	0	–
Glenn Hubbard	2b	4	12	2	3	0	0	0	0	1	2	1	.250	.250	1	.923
Stan Javier	pr-lf	3	4	0	2	0	0	0	2	0	1	0	.500	.500	0	1.000
Carney Lansford	3b	5	18	2	3	0	0	0	1	2	2	0	.167	.167	0	1.000
Mark McGwire	1b	5	17	1	1	0	0	1	1	3	4	0	.059	.235	0	1.000
Gene Nelson	p	3	0	0	0	0	0	0	0	0	0	0	–	–	0	1.000
Dave Parker	lf-dh	4	15	0	3	0	0	0	0	2	4	0	.200	.200	0	1.000
Tony Phillips	lf-2b	2	4	1	1	0	0	0	0	1	2	0	.250	.250	0	1.000
Eric Plunk	p	2	0	0	0	0	0	0	0	0	0	0	–	–	0	–
Luis Polonia	ph-lf	3	9	1	1	0	0	0	0	0	2	0	.111	.111	0	1.000
Terry Steinbach	c-dh	3	11	0	4	1	0	0	2	0	2	0	.364	.455	0	1.000
Dave Stewart	p	2	3	1	0	0	0	0	0	1	3	0	.000	.000	0	1.000
Walt Weiss	ss	5	16	1	1	0	0	0	0	0	2	1	.063	.063	1	.941
Bob Welch	p	1	0	0	0	0	0	0	0	0	0	0	–	–	0	1.000
Curt Young	p	1	0	0	0	0	0	0	0	0	0	0	–	–	0	1.000
Totals		5	158	11	28	3	0	2	11	17	41	3	.177	.234	2	.989

Pitcher	G	GS	CG	IP	H	R	ER	BB	SO	W-L	Sv	ERA
Todd Burns	1	0	0	⅓	0	0	0	0	0	0-0	0	0.00
Greg Cadaret	3	0	0	2	2	0	0	0	3	0-0	0	0.00
Storm Davis	2	2	0	8	14	10	10	1	7	0-2	0	11.25
Dennis Eckersley	2	0	0	1⅔	2	2	2	1	2	0-1	0	10.80
Rick Honeycutt	3	0	0	3⅓	0	0	0	0	5	1-0	0	0.00
Gene Nelson	3	0	0	6⅓	4	1	1	3	3	0-0	0	1.42
Eric Plunk	2	0	0	1⅔	0	0	0	3	0	0-0	0	0.00
Dave Stewart	2	2	0	14⅓	12	7	5	5	5	0-1	0	3.14
Bob Welch	1	1	0	5	6	1	1	3	8	0-0	0	1.80
Curt Young	1	0	0	1	1	0	0	0	0	0-0	0	0.00
Totals	5	5	0	43⅔	41	21	19	13	36	1-4	0	3.92

Series MVP: Orel Hershiser, Los Angeles Dodgers. **Series Outstanding Pitcher:** Orel Hershiser, Los Angeles Dodgers. **Average Length of Game:** 2 hours, 58 minutes. **Total Attendance:** 259,984. **Average Attendance:** 51,997 (56,071 at Dodger Stadium; 49,317 at Oakland-Alameda County Coliseum). **Umpires:** Derryl Cousins (AL), Jerry Crawford (NL), Bruce Froemming (NL), Doug Harvey (NL), Larry McCoy (AL), Durwood Merrill (AL). **Winning Player's Share:** $108,665. **Losing Player's Share:** $86,223.

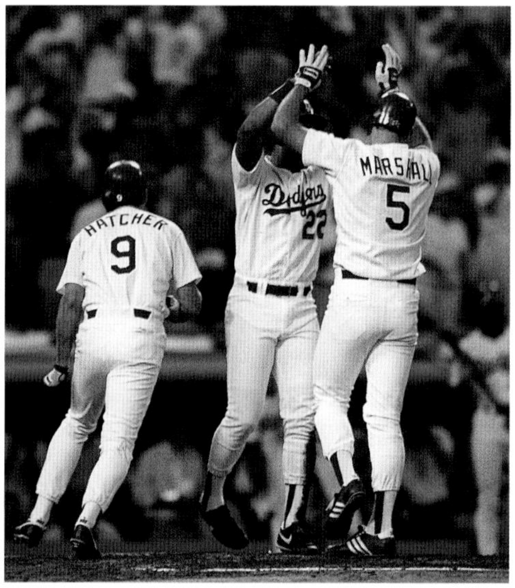

Above: The three-run homer by Mike Marshall in the third inning of Game 2 gave Los Angeles a comfortable 5-0 edge.

Kirk Gibson's dramatic Game 1 homer marked the first time that a team came from behind to win a Series game with a home run. (All other game-winning home runs up till then had broken a tie score.)

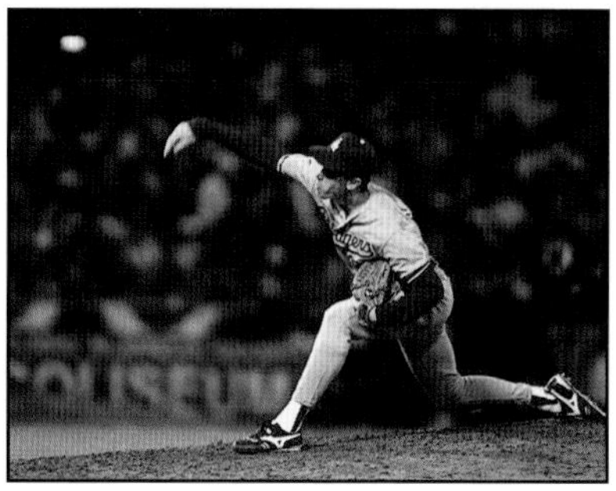

Above: Orel Hershiser was dominant in his two starts, allowing only 2 runs and 7 hits in 18 innings.

Left: The Dodgers exult in their upset victory over the A's in 1988.

Below: Jose Canseco had only one hit in the five games, but it was a doozy—a grand slam in his first World Series at-bat.

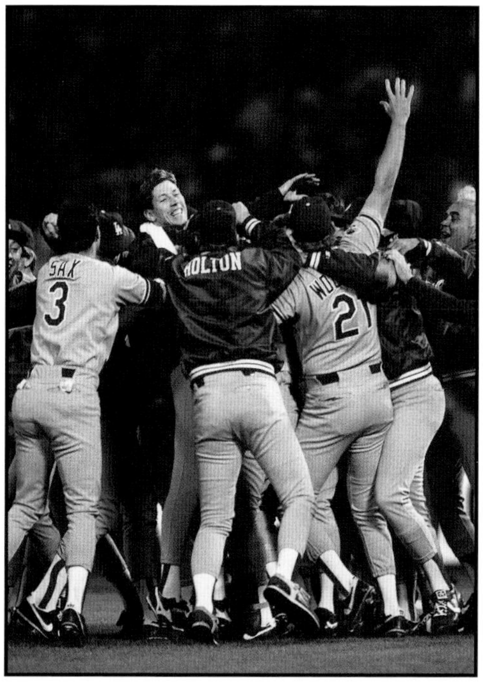

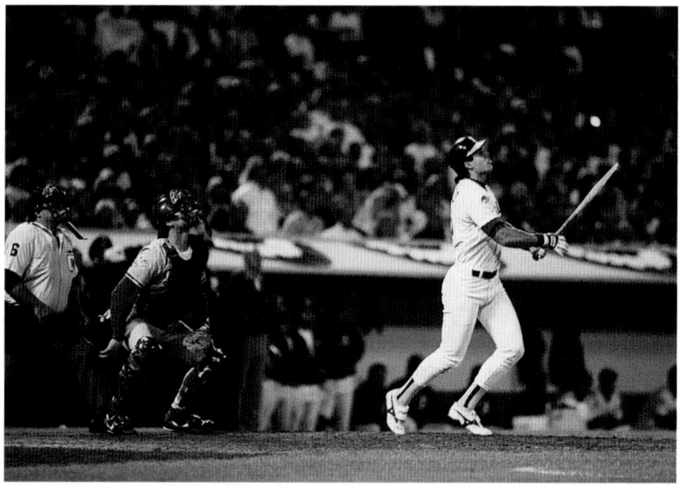

Game 1 Saturday, October 15 at Dodger Stadium, Los Angeles

	1	2	3	4	5	8	7	8	9	R	H	E
Oakland Athletics	0	4	0	0	0	0	0	0	0	4	7	0
Los Angeles Dodgers	2	0	0	0	0	1	0	0	2	5	7	0

Pitchers Oak **Dave Stewart**, IP 8, H 6, R 3, ER 3, BB 2, SO 5; **Dennis Eckersley** (L, 0-1), IP ⅔, H 1, R 2, ER 2, BB 1, SO 1
LA **Tim Belcher**, IP 2, H 3, R 4, ER 4, BB 4, SO 3; **Tim Leary**, IP 3, H 3, R 0, ER 0, BB 1, SO 3; **Brian Holton**, IP 2, H 0, R 0, ER 0, BB 1, SO 0; **Alejandro Pena** (W, 1-0), IP 2, H 1, R 0, ER 0, BB 0, SO 3

Top Performers at the Plate
Oak **Jose Canseco**, 1 for 4, 1 R, 4 RBI, 1 HBP; **Glenn Hubbard**, 2 for 4, 1 R
LA **Kirk Gibson**, 1 for 1, 1 R, 2 RBI; **Mickey Hatcher**, 1 for 3, 1 R, 2 RBI, 1 BB

2B-Oak/Henderson. **HR**-Oak/Canseco; LA/Gibson, Hatcher. **SB**-Oak/Canseco; LA/M. Davis, Sax. **Time** 3:04. **Attendance** 55,983.

Game 2 Sunday, October 16 at Dodger Stadium, Los Angeles

	1	2	3	4	5	6	7	8	9	R	H	E
Oakland Athletics	0	0	0	0	0	0	0	0	0	0	3	0
Los Angeles Dodgers	0	0	5	1	0	0	0	0	x	6	10	1

Pitchers Oak **Storm Davis** (L, 0-1), IP 3⅓, H 8, R 6, ER 6, BB 0, SO 2; **Gene Nelson**, IP 1⅔, H 1, R 0, ER 0, BB 1, SO 1; **Matt Young**, IP 1, H 1, R 0, ER 0, BB 0, SO 0; **Eric Plunk**, IP 1, H 0, R 0, ER 0, BB 0, SO 3; **Rick Honeycutt**, IP 1, H 0, R 0, ER 0, BB 0, SO 2
LA **Orel Hershiser** (W, 1-0), IP 9, H 3, R 0, ER 0, BB 2, SO 8

Top Performers at the Plate
Oak **Dave Parker**, 3 for 4
LA **Orel Hershiser**, 3 for 3, 1 R, 1 RBI, 2 2B; **Mike Marshall**, 2 for 4, 1 R, 3 RBI

2B-LA/Hershiser 2. **3B**-LA/Marshall. **HR**-LA/Marshall. **SB**-Oak/Weiss. **Time** 2:30. **Attendance** 56,051.

Game 3 Tuesday, October 18 at Oakland-Alameda County Coliseum, Oakland

	1	2	3	4	5	6	7	8	9	R	H	E
Los Angeles Dodgers	0	0	0	0	1	0	0	0	0	1	8	1
Oakland Athletics	0	0	1	0	0	0	0	0	1	2	5	0

Pitchers LA **John Tudor**, IP 1⅓, H 0, R 0, ER 0, BB 0, SO 1; **Tim Leary**, IP 3⅔, H 3, R 1, ER 1, BB 1, SO 1; **Alejandro Pena**, IP 3, H 1, R 0, ER 0, BB 1, SO 4; **Jay Howell** (L, 0-1), IP ⅓, H 1, R 1, ER 1, BB 0, SO 0
Oak **Bob Welch**, IP 5, H 6, R 1, ER 1, BB 3, SO 8; **Greg Cadaret**, IP ⅓, H 0, R 0, ER 0, BB 0, SO 0; **Gene Nelson**, IP 1⅔, H 2, R 0, ER 0, BB 0, SO 1; **Rick Honeycutt** (W, 1-0), IP 2, H 0, R 0, ER 0, BB 0, SO 3

Top Performers at the Plate
LA **Jeff Hamilton**, 1 for 3, 1 R, 1 BB; **John Shelby**, 2 for 3
Oak **Ron Hassey**, 1 for 1, 1 RBI, 2 BB; **Terry Steinbach**, 2 for 3

2B-LA/Hatcher, Heep, Stubbs; Oak/Steinbach. **HR**-Oak/McGwire. **SB**-LA/Shelby; Oak/Hubbard. **Time** 3:21. **Attendance** 49,316.

Game 4 Wednesday, October 19 at Oakland-Alameda County Coliseum, Oakland

	1	2	3	4	5	6	7	8	9	R	H	E
Los Angeles Dodgers	2	0	1	0	0	0	1	0	0	4	8	1
Oakland Athletics	1	0	0	0	0	1	1	0	0	3	9	2

Pitchers LA **Tim Belcher** (W, 1-0), IP 6⅔, H 7, R 3, ER 2, BB 2, SO 7; **Jay Howell** (Sv, 1), IP 2⅓, H 2, R 0, ER 0, BB 1, SO 2
Oak **Dave Stewart** (L, 0-1), IP 6⅓, H 6, R 4, ER 2, BB 3, SO 0; **Greg Cadaret**, IP 1⅔, H 1, R 0, ER 0, BB 0, SO 3; **Dennis Eckersley**, IP 1, H 1, R 0, ER 0, BB 0, SO 1

Top Performers at the Plate
LA **Alfredo Griffin**, 1 for 3, 1 R, 1 BB; **Franklin Stubbs**, 1 for 3, 1 R
Oak **Dave Henderson**, 4 for 5, 1 R, 1 RBI

2B-LA/Shelby, Stubbs; Oak/Henderson. **SB**-LA/M. Davis. **Time** 3:05. **Attendance** 49,317.

Game 5 Thursday, October 20 at Oakland-Alameda County Coliseum, Oakland

	1	2	3	4	5	6	7	8	9	R	H	E
Los Angeles Dodgers	2	0	0	2	0	1	0	0	0	5	8	0
Oakland Athletics	0	0	1	0	0	0	0	1	0	2	4	0

Pitchers LA **Orel Hershiser** (W, 2-0), IP 9, H 4, R 2, ER 2, BB 4, SO 9
Oak **Storm Davis** (L, 0-2), IP 4⅔, H 6, R 4, ER 4, BB 1, SO 5; **Greg Cadaret**, IP 0, H 1, R 0, ER 0, BB 0, SO 0; **Gene Nelson**, IP 3, H 1, R 1, ER 1, BB 2, SO 1; **Rick Honeycutt**, IP ⅓, H 0, R 0, ER 0, BB 0, SO 0; **Eric Plunk**, IP ⅔, H 0, R 0, ER 0, BB 0, SO 0; **Todd Burns**, IP ⅓, H 0, R 0, ER 0, BB 0, SO 0

Top Performers at the Plate
LA **Mike Davis**, 1 for 2, 2 R, 2 RBI, 2 BB; **Mickey Hatcher**, 2 for 4, 2 R, 2 RBI
Oak **Stan Javier**, 1 for 3, 2 RBI, 1 SF; **Carney Lansford**, 2 for 4, 1 R

2B-LA/Dempsey. **HR**-LA/M. Davis, Hatcher. **Time** 2:51. **Attendance** 49,317.

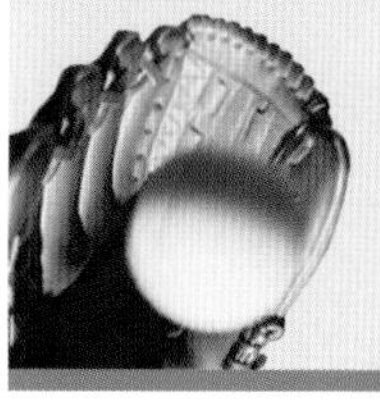

Jose Canseco came through big in his first World Series at-bat by hitting the 15th grand slam in Series history. His was only the second slam by a player on the losing side of a game.

Oakland Athletics (4) vs. San Francisco Giants (0)

The Bay Series of 1989 was an easy four-game sweep for the Oakland A's. They scored first in every game and did not trail at any point during the Series. They set or tied team records for triples, home runs and extra-base hits for a four-game bout. Jose Canseco redeemed his subpar outing of the previous year by batting .357 and scoring 5 runs. Rickey Henderson, a midseason acquisition, contributed a blistering .474 average and stole 3 bases. Dave Stewart and Mike Moore each started two games for Tony La Russa and each secured two victories, with Stewart named Series MVP for his efforts. The A's cruised to 5-0 and 5-1 wins in the first two games at home. Stewart went the distance with a five-hitter to shut out the San Francisco Giants in the opener, and Terry Steinbach hit a three-run homer in the fourth inning of Game 2 to put the contest out of reach. The San Francisco bats awakened for the next two games, delivering 19 hits and 13 runs on their home turf. Unfortunately for Roger Craig's club, Oakland collected 26 hits and 22 runs in those same two games. They smashed 5 homers in Game 3, including 2 by Dave Henderson, and produced four runs in the eighth inning on 5 singles and an error. Rickey Henderson led off Game 4 with a home run, and he tripled and scored in the sixth. San Francisco got a two-run homer from Kevin Mitchell, and in the seventh inning, a walk, single, double, triple and a two-run blast by Greg Litton brought in 4 more runs, but not enough in the 9-6 loss. That's the story of how the

1989

Oakland Athletics won the 1989 championship—but it doesn't begin to tell the story of the 1989 World Series. For the first time in more than 30 years, the Fall Classic was held in one metropolitan area. Although it's a short trip across the Bay Bridge from Oakland to San Francisco, the teams rested for a "travel day" between Games 2 and 3. At a few minutes after five o'clock on October 17, just as the fans and players were settling in for the start of the third game, a massive earthquake measuring 7.1 on the Richter scale rocked the Bay Area. Though the quake came and went quickly, the 62,000-seat Candlestick Park shook to the core and the stadium's power went out. Commissioner Fay Vincent immediately called off the game. Though no one in the ballpark was hurt, news quickly arrived of major destruction around the region. Billions of dollars' worth of damage affected millions of Bay Area residents, and dozens lost their lives. Vincent met with officials of the two cities, and they announced that play would resume after a 10-day hiatus. Oakland's domination continued when the Series resumed on October 27, but after the devastating earthquake, things weren't the same in the Bay Area, and the 1989 Series will always be remembered for the dramatic events that surrounded the game.

Above: Oakland's Carney Lansford batted a Series-best .438 in 1989.

1989 WORLD SERIES COMPOSITE STATISTICS

OAKLAND ATHLETICS/Tony La Russa, Manager

Player	pos	G	AB	R	H	2B	3B	HR	RBI	BB	SO	SB	BA	SA	E	FPct
Lance Blankenship	ph-2b	1	2	1	1	0	0	0	0	0	0	0	.500	.500	0	1.000
Todd Burns	p	2	0	0	0	0	0	0	0	0	0	0	—	—	0	—
Jose Canseco	rf	4	14	5	5	0	0	1	3	4	3	1	.357	.571	0	1.000
Dennis Eckersley	p	2	0	0	0	0	0	0	0	0	0	0	—	—	0	1.000
Mike Gallego	2b-ph-3b	2	1	0	0	0	0	0	0	0	0	0	.000	.000	0	—
Dave Henderson	cf	4	13	6	4	2	0	2	4	4	3	0	.308	.923	0	1.000
Rickey Henderson	lf	4	19	4	9	1	2	1	3	2	2	3	.474	.895	0	1.000
Rick Honeycutt	p	3	0	0	0	0	0	0	0	0	0	0	—	—	0	—
Stan Javier	rf	1	0	0	0	0	0	0	0	0	0	0	—	—	0	—
Carney Lansford	3b	4	16	5	7	1	0	1	4	3	1	0	.438	.688	0	1.000
Mark McGwire	1b	4	17	0	5	1	0	0	1	1	3	0	.294	.353	0	1.000
Mike Moore	p	2	3	1	1	1	0	0	2	0	1	0	.333	.667	0	1.000
Gene Nelson	p	2	0	0	0	0	0	0	0	0	0	0	—	—	0	—
Dave Parker	dh-ph	3	9	2	2	1	0	1	2	0	2	0	.222	.667	—	—
Ken Phelps	ph	1	1	0	0	0	0	0	0	0	0	0	.000	.000	—	—
Tony Phillips	2b-3b-lf	4	17	2	4	1	0	1	3	0	3	0	.235	.471	0	1.000
Terry Steinbach	c	4	16	3	4	0	0	1	7	2	1	0	.250	.563	0	1.000
Dave Stewart	p	2	3	0	0	0	0	0	0	0	1	0	.000	.000	1	.750
Walt Weiss	ss	4	15	3	2	0	0	1	1	2	2	0	.133	.333	0	1.000
Totals		**4**	**146**	**32**	**44**	**8**	**3**	**9**	**30**	**18**	**22**	**4**	**.301**	**.582**	**1**	**.993**

Pitcher	G	GS	CG	IP	H	R	ER	BB	SO	W-L	Sv	ERA
Todd Burns	2	0	0	1⅔	1	0	0	1	0	0-0	0	0.00
Dennis Eckersley	2	0	0	1⅔	0	0	0	0	0	0-0	1	0.00
Rick Honeycutt	3	0	0	2⅔	4	2	2	0	2	0-0	0	6.75
Mike Moore	2	2	0	13	9	3	3	3	10	2-0	0	2.08
Gene Nelson	2	0	0	1	4	6	6	2	1	0-0	0	54.00
Dave Stewart	2	2	1	16	10	3	3	2	14	2-0	0	1.69
Totals	**4**	**4**	**1**	**36**	**28**	**14**	**14**	**8**	**27**	**4-0**	**1**	**3.50**

SAN FRANCISCO GIANTS/Roger Craig, Manager

Player	pos	G	AB	R	H	2B	3B	HR	RBI	BB	SO	SB	BA	SA	E	FPct
Bill Bathe	ph	2	2	1	1	0	0	1	3	0	0	0	.500	2.000	—	—
Steve Bedrosian	p	2	0	0	0	0	0	0	0	0	0	0	—	—	0	—
Jeff Brantley	p	3	0	0	0	0	0	0	0	0	0	0	—	—	0	1.000
Brett Butler	cf	4	14	1	4	1	0	0	1	2	1	2	.286	.357	0	1.000
Will Clark	1b	4	16	2	4	1	0	0	1	3	0	0	.250	.313	0	1.000
Kelly Downs	p	3	0	0	0	0	0	0	0	0	0	0	—	—	0	—
Scott Garrelts	p	2	1	0	0	0	0	0	0	0	1	0	.000	.000	0	1.000
Atlee Hammaker	p	2	0	0	0	0	0	0	0	0	0	0	—	—	0	1.000
Terry Kennedy	c	4	12	1	2	0	0	0	2	1	3	0	.167	.167	1	.960
Mike LaCoss	p	2	1	0	0	0	0	0	0	0	0	0	.000	.000	0	1.000
Craig Lefferts	p	3	0	0	0	0	0	0	0	0	0	0	—	—	1	.500
Greg Litton	ph-2b-3b	2	6	1	3	1	0	1	3	0	0	0	.500	1.167	0	1.000
Candy Maldonado	rf-ph	4	11	1	1	0	1	0	0	0	4	0	.091	.273	0	1.000
Kirt Manwaring	c	1	1	1	1	1	0	0	0	0	0	0	1.000	2.000	0	—
Kevin Mitchell	lf	4	17	2	5	0	0	1	2	0	3	0	.294	.471	1	.909
Donell Nixon	ph-cf-rf	2	5	1	1	0	0	0	0	0	1	0	.200	.200	0	1.000
Ken Oberkfell	ph-3b	4	6	1	2	0	0	0	0	3	0	0	.333	.333	1	.833
Rick Reuschel	p	1	0	0	0	0	0	0	0	0	0	0	—	—	0	—
Ernie Riles	dh-ph	4	8	0	0	0	0	0	0	0	1	0	.000	.000	—	—
Don Robinson	p	1	0	0	0	0	0	0	0	0	0	0	—	—	0	—
Pat Sheridan	rf	1	2	0	0	0	0	0	0	0	0	0	.000	.000	0	—
Robby Thompson	2b-ph	4	11	0	1	0	0	0	0	2	4	0	.091	.091	0	1.000
Jose Uribe	ss	3	5	1	1	0	0	0	0	0	0	0	.200	.200	0	1.000
Matt Williams	3b-ss	4	16	1	2	0	0	1	1	0	6	0	.125	.313	0	1.000
Totals		**4**	**134**	**14**	**28**	**4**	**1**	**4**	**14**	**8**	**27**	**2**	**.209**	**.343**	**4**	**.973**

Pitcher	G	GS	CG	IP	H	R	ER	BB	SO	W-L	Sv	ERA
Steve Bedrosian	2	0	0	2⅔	0	0	0	2	2	0-0	0	0.00
Jeff Brantley	3	0	0	4⅓	5	2	2	3	1	0-0	0	4.15
Kelly Downs	3	0	0	4⅔	3	4	4	2	4	0-0	0	7.71
Scott Garrelts	2	2	0	7⅓	13	9	8	1	8	0-2	0	9.82
Atlee Hammaker	2	0	0	2⅓	8	4	4	0	2	0-0	0	15.43
Mike LaCoss	2	0	0	4⅓	4	3	3	3	2	0-0	0	6.23
Craig Lefferts	3	0	0	2⅔	2	1	1	2	1	0-0	0	3.38
Rick Reuschel	1	1	0	4	5	5	5	4	2	0-1	0	11.25
Don Robinson	1	1	0	1⅔	4	4	4	1	0	0-1	0	21.60
Totals	**4**	**4**	**0**	**34**	**44**	**32**	**31**	**18**	**22**	**0-4**	**0**	**8.21**

Series MVP: Dave Stewart, Oakland Athletics. **Series Outstanding Pitcher:** Dave Stewart, Oakland Athletics. **Average Length of Game:** 3 hours, 2 minutes. **Total Attendance:** 222,843. **Average Attendance:** 55,711 (49,387 at Oakland-Alameda County Coliseum; 62,036 at Candlestick Park). **Umpires:** Al Clark (AL), Rich Garcia (AL), Eric Gregg (NL), Dutch Rennert (NL), Paul Runge (NL), Vic Voltaggio (AL). **Winning Player's Share:** $114,252. **Losing Player's Share:** $53,529.

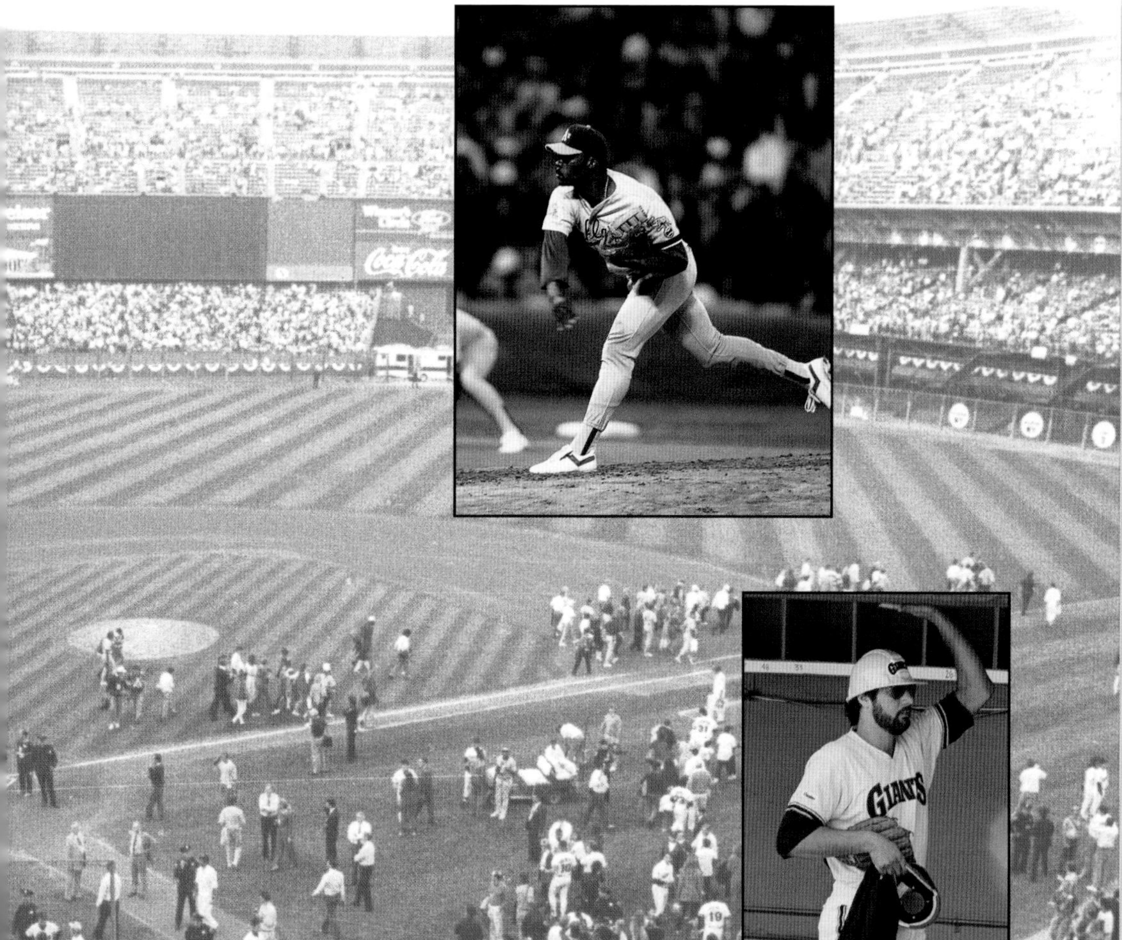

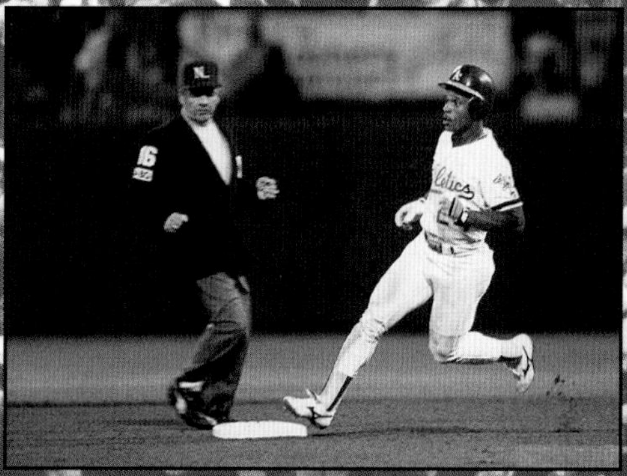

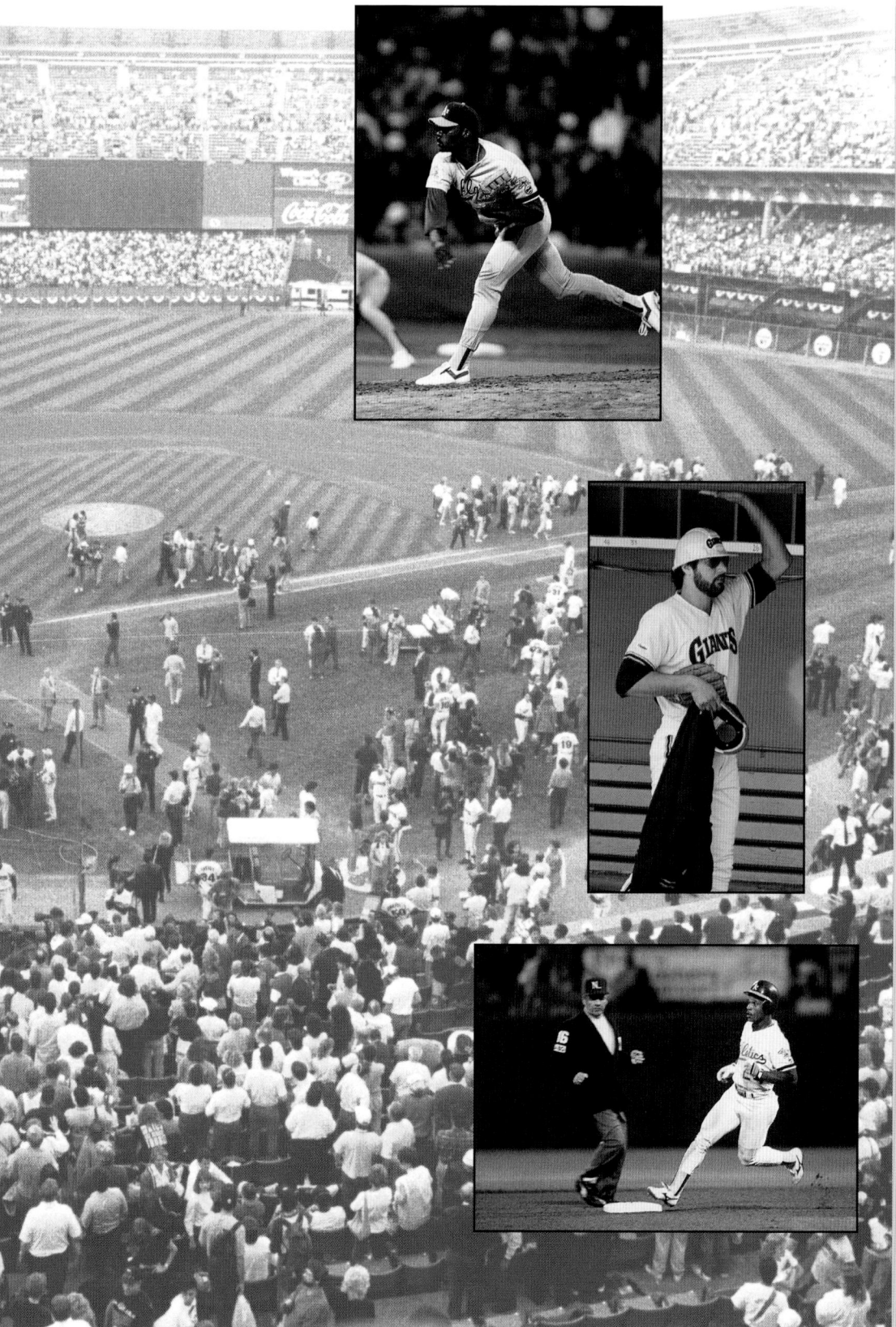

Game 1 Saturday, October 14 at Oakland-Alameda County Coliseum, Oakland

	1	2	3	4	5	6	7	8	9	R	H	E
San Francisco Giants	0	0	0	0	0	0	0	0	0	0	5	1
Oakland Athletics	0	3	1	1	0	0	0	0	x	5	11	1

Pitchers SF **Scott Garrelts** (L, 0-1), IP 4, H 7, R 5, ER 4, BB 1, SO 5; **Atlee Hammaker**, IP 1⅔, H 3, R 0, ER 0, BB 0, SO 2; **Jeff Brantley**, IP 1⅓, H 1, R 0, ER 0, BB 1, SO 0; **Mike LaCoss**, IP 1, H 0, R 0, ER 0, BB 0, SO 1
Oak **Dave Stewart** (W, 1-0), IP 9, H 5, R 0, ER 0, BB 1, SO 6

Top Performers at the Plate
SF **Will Clark**, 2 for 4; **Kevin Mitchell**, 2 for 4
Oak **Mark McGwire**, 3 for 4; **Tony Phillips**, 2 for 4, 1 R, 1 RBI

2B-SF/Clark. **HR**-Oak/Parker, Weiss. **Time** 2:45. **Attendance** 49,385.

Game 2 Sunday, October 15 at Oakland-Alameda County Coliseum, Oakland

	1	2	3	4	5	6	7	8	9	R	H	E
San Francisco Giants	0	0	1	0	0	0	0	0	0	1	4	0
Oakland Athletics	1	0	0	4	0	0	0	0	x	5	7	0

Pitchers SF **Rick Reuschel** (L, 0-1), IP 4, H 5, R 5, ER 5, BB 4, SO 2; **Kelly Downs**, IP 2, H 1, R 0, ER 0, BB 0, SO 2; **Craig Lefferts**, IP 1, H 1, R 0, ER 0, BB 1, SO 1; **Steve Bedrosian**, IP 1, H 0, R 0, ER 0, BB 0, SO 2
Oak **Mike Moore** (W, 1-0), IP 7, H 4, R 1, ER 1, BB 2, SO 7; **Rick Honeycutt**, IP 1⅓, H 0, R 0, ER 0, BB 0, SO 1; **Dennis Eckersley**, IP ⅔, H 0, R 0, ER 0, BB 0, SO 0

Top Performers at the Plate
SF **Brett Butler**, 1 for 2, 2 BB, 2 SB
Oak **Rickey Henderon**, 3 for 3, 1 R, 1 BB; **Terry Steinbach**, 1 for 4, 1 R, 3 RBI

2B-Oak/Lansford, McGwire, Parker. **3B**-Oak/R. Henderson. **HR**-Oak/Steinbach. **SB**-SF/Butler 2; Oak/R. Henderson. **Time** 2:47. **Attendance** 49,388.

Game 3 Friday, October 27 at Candlestick Park, San Francisco

	1	2	3	4	5	6	7	8	9	R	H	E
Oakland Athletics	2	0	0	2	4	1	0	4	0	13	14	0
San Francisco Giants	0	1	0	2	0	0	0	0	4	7	10	3

Pitchers Oak **Dave Stewart** (W, 2-0), IP 7, H 5, R 3, ER 3, BB 1, SO 8; **Rick Honeycutt**, IP 1, H 1, R 0, ER 0, BB 0, SO 1; **Gene Nelson**, IP ⅔, H 3, R 4, ER 4, BB 1, SO 1; **Todd Burns**, IP ⅓, H 1, R 0, ER 0, BB 1, SO 0
LA **Scott Garrelts** (L, 0-2), IP 3⅓, H 6, R 4, ER 4, BB 0, SO 3; **Kelly Downs**, IP 1, H 2, R 4, ER 4, BB 2, SO 1; **Jeff Brantley**, IP 2⅔, H 1, R 1, ER 1, BB 2, SO 1; **Atlee Hammaker**, IP ⅔, H 5, R 4, ER 4, BB 0, SO 0; **Craig Lefferts**, IP 1⅓, H 0, R 0, ER 0, BB 0, SO 0

Top Performers at the Plate
Oak **Jose Canseco**, 3 for 5, 3 R, 3 RBI; **Dave Henderson**, 3 for 4, 2 R, 4 RBI, 2 HR, 1 HBP
SF **Bill Bathe**, 1 for 1, 1 R, 3 RBI; **Greg Litton**, 2 for 2, 1 R

2B-Oak/D. Henderson, R. Henderson; SF/Litton, Manwaring. **HR**-Oak/Canseco, D. Henderson 2, Lansford, Phillips; SF/Bathe, Williams. **SB**-Oak/R. Henderson 2. **Time** 3:30. **Attendance** 62,038.

Game 4 Saturday, October 28 at Candlestick Park, San Francisco

	1	2	3	4	5	6	7	8	9	R	H	E
Oakland Athletics	1	3	0	0	3	1	0	1	0	9	12	0
San Francisco Giants	0	0	0	0	0	2	4	0	0	6	9	0

Pitchers Oak **Mike Moore** (W, 2-0), IP 6, H 5, R 2, ER 2, BB 1, SO 3; **Gene Nelson**, IP ⅓, H 1, R 2, ER 2, BB 1, SO 0; **Rick Honeycutt**, IP ⅓, H 3, R 2, ER 2, BB 0, SO 0; **Todd Burns**, IP 1⅓, H 0, R 0, ER 0, BB 0, SO 0; **Dennis Eckersley** (Sv, 1), IP 1, H 0, R 0, ER 0, BB 0, SO 0
SF **Don Robinson** (L, 0-1), IP 1⅔, H 4, R 4, ER 4, BB 1, SO 0; **Mike LaCoss**, IP 3⅓, H 4, R 3, ER 3, BB 3, SO 1; **Jeff Brantley**, IP ⅓, H 3, R 1, ER 1, BB 0, SO 0; **Kelly Downs**, IP 1⅔, H 0, R 0, ER 0, BB 0, SO 1; **Craig Lefferts**, IP ⅓, H 1, R 1, ER 1, BB 1, SO 0; **Steve Bedrosian**, IP 1⅔, H 0, R 0, ER 0, BB 2, SO 0

Top Performers at the Plate
Oak **Rickey Henderson**, 3 for 6, 2 R, 2 RBI; **Terry Steinbach**, 1 for 4, 1 R, 3 RBI, 1 BB
SF **Brett Butler**, 3 for 5, 1 R, 1 RBI; **Kevin Mitchell**, 1 for 4, 1 R, 2 RBI

2B-Oak/D. Henderson, Moore, Phillips; SF/Butler. **3B**-Oak/R. Henderson, Steinbach; SF/Maldonado. **HR**-Oak/R. Henderson; SF/Litton, Mitchell. **SB**-Oak/Canseco. **Time** 3:07. **Attendance** 62,032.

The A's and Giants broke the single-game Series record for home runs in Game 3 with 7, as the A's hit a single-team record 5 and the Giants contributed 2. The combined 13 homers over the four games set the 2-team record for a Series of that length, as did the 4 triples and 29 extra-base hits.

Background: An earthquake shook San Francisco's Candlestick Park before Game 3 of the 1989 World Series, but fortunately no one there was hurt.

Insets from, top: Dave Stewart struck out 14 and walked only 2 in his two victories, good enough for Series MVP. With a hard hat for protection, pitcher Steve Bedrosian helps to support the Candlestick Park dugout during a Giants' practice two days after the earthquake. The newly acquired Rickey Henderson came through big for Oakland in the Series, stealing three bases and notching a slugging percentage just below .900.

Cincinnati Reds (4) vs. Oakland Athletics (0)

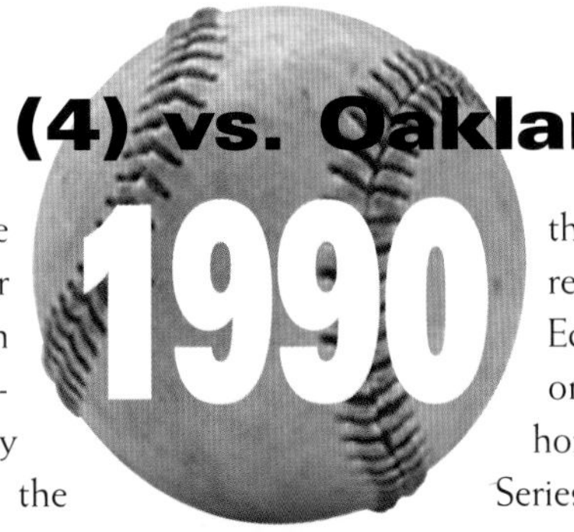

The Oakland A's were the dominant team of the late 1980s and early 1990s. Following in the footsteps of their precursors from 1929–31 and 1972–74, the club won three consecutive pennants, culminating in a 103-win season in 1990. That year, they had the league MVP (Ricky Henderson) and Cy Young winner (Bob Welch), and the powerful duo of Canseco and McGwire slugged 76 homers. After splitting their previous two trips to the World Series, Tony La Russa's A's hoped to win a second title by defeating the Cincinnati Reds in 1990. In their first season under manager Lou Piniella, the Reds led their division from start to finish and defeated a strong Pittsburgh Pirate team in the NLCS. Still, they were considered a long shot against the Oakland juggernaut. In the opener, the Reds sent a message, shutting the A's out 7-0. Eric Davis started it off with a two-run homer in the first inning against the imposing Dave Stewart. Meanwhile, Cincinnati starter Jose Rijo coasted through seven innings, and relievers Rob Dibble and Randy Myers, known as the "Nasty Boys," closed Oakland out for the last two innings. After falling behind 2-1 in the first inning of Game 2, the A's reclaimed the lead with three runs in the third. The Reds closed the gap to one in the fourth, and Billy Hatcher opened the eighth inning with a triple—his seventh hit in seven at-bats in two games—and scored the tying run on an infield grounder. Rickey Henderson robbed Todd Benzinger of a game-winning homer in the bottom of the ninth, but it was just a temporary reprieve. Facing Oakland's commanding reliever Dennis Eckersley in the 10th, the Reds put two men on base with one out when catcher Joe Oliver ripped a single to drive home the winning run. Oakland's hopes for a dramatic Series comeback became even slimmer following Cincinnati's seven-run barrage in the third inning of Game 3. Chris Sabo, who hit a solo shot in the second, belted a two-run clout in the big inning. Dibble and Myers again came through with shutout relief work to make the 8-3 margin stand. Game 4 saw Oakland hold a 1-0 lead through seven innings, as Stewart exerted control from the mound. In the eighth, Cincinnati scrapped together two runs to snatch the lead. Barry Larkin's single started it off, and a bunt base hit, an error by Stewart, an RBI groundout by Glenn Braggs and a sacrifice fly by Hal Morris was all it took. After giving up the first-inning run, Jose Rijo allowed no more Oakland hits, and he retired 20 batters in a row before giving way to Myers with one out in the ninth. Myers nailed the last two batters of the game, and the Reds accomplished the unthinkable: they not only beat a heavily favored Oakland team, they swept 'em in four straight.

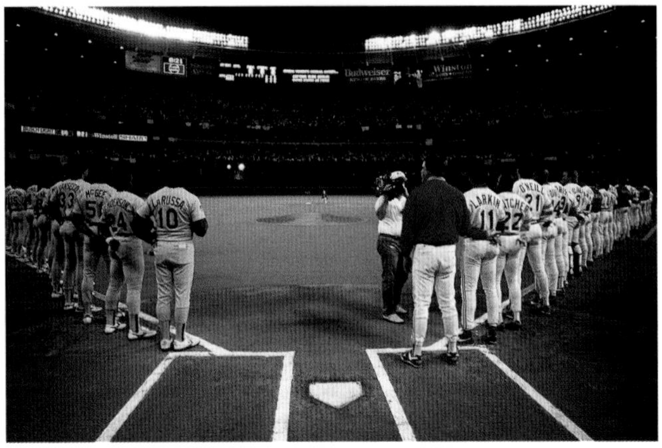

Above: The A's and Reds line up before the start of the 1990 Series at Cincinnati's Riverfront Stadium.

1990 WORLD SERIES COMPOSITE STATISTICS

CINCINNATI REDS/Lou Piniella, Manager

Player	pos	G	AB	R	H	2B	3B	HR	RBI	BB	SO	SB	BA	SA	E	FPct
Jack Armstrong	p	1	0	0	0	0	0	0	0	0	0	0	–	–	0	–
Billy Bates	ph	1	1	1	1	0	0	0	0	0	0	0	1.000	1.000	–	–
Todd Benzinger	ph-1b	4	11	1	2	0	0	0	0	0	0	0	.182	.182	0	1.000
Glenn Braggs	ph-lf	2	4	0	0	0	0	0	2	1	0	0	.000	.000	0	–
Tom Browning	p	1	0	0	0	0	0	0	0	0	0	0	–	–	0	–
Norm Charlton	p	1	0	0	0	0	0	0	0	0	0	0	–	–	0	–
Eric Davis	lf	4	14	3	4	0	0	1	5	0	0	0	.286	.500	fl	1.000
Rob Dibble	p	3	0	0	0	0	0	0	0	0	0	0	–	–	0	–
Mariano Duncan	2b	4	14	1	2	0	0	0	1	2	2	1	.143	.143	0	1.000
Billy Hatcher	cf	4	12	6	9	4	1	0	2	2	0	0	.750	1.250	0	1.000
Danny Jackson	p	1	1	0	0	0	0	0	0	0	1	0	.000	.000	1	.500
Barry Larkin	ss	4	17	3	6	1	1	0	1	2	0	0	.353	.529	0	1.000
Hal Morris	1b-dh	4	14	0	1	0	0	0	2	1	1	0	.071	.071	0	1.000
Randy Myers	p	3	0	0	0	0	0	0	0	0	0	0	–	–	0	–
Ron Oester	ph	1	1	0	1	0	0	0	1	0	0	0	1.000	1.000	–	–
Joe Oliver	c	4	18	2	6	3	0	0	2	0	1	0	.333	.500	3	.903
Paul O'Neill	rf	4	12	2	1	0	0	0	1	5	2	1	.083	.083	0	1.000
Jose Rijo	p	2	3	0	1	0	0	0	0	0	0	0	.333	.333	0	1.000
Chris Sabo	3b	4	16	2	9	1	0	2	5	2	2	0	.563	1.000	0	1.000
Scott Scudder	p	1	0	0	0	0	0	0	0	0	0	0	–	–	0	–
Herm Winningham	ph-cf	2	4	1	2	0	0	0	0	0	0	0	.500	.500	0	1.000
Totals		**4**	**142**	**22**	**45**	**9**	**2**	**3**	**22**	**15**	**9**	**2**	**.317**	**.472**	**4**	**.975**

Pitcher	G	GS	CG	IP	H	R	ER	BB	SO	W-L	Sv	ERA
Jack Armstrong	1	0	0	3	1	0	0	0	3	0-0	0	0.00
Tom Browning	1	1	0	6	6	3	3	2	2	1-0	0	4.50
Norm Charlton	1	0	0	1	1	0	0	0	0	0-0	0	0.00
Rob Dibble	3	0	0	4⅔	3	0	0	1	4	1-0	0	0.00
Danny Jackson	1	1	0	2⅔	6	4	3	2	0	0-0	0	10.13
Randy Myers	3	0	0	3	2	0	0	0	3	0-0	1	0.00
Jose Rijo	2	2	0	15⅓	9	1	1	5	14	2-0	0	0.59
Scott Scudder	1	0	0	1⅓	0	0	0	2	2	0-0	0	0.00
Totals	**4**	**4**	**0**	**37**	**28**	**8**	**7**	**12**	**28**	**4-0**	**1**	**1.70**

OAKLAND ATHLETICS/Tony La Russa, Manager

Player	pos	G	AB	R	H	2B	3B	HR	RBI	BB	SO	SB	BA	SA	E	FPct
Harold Baines	ph-dh	3	7	1	1	0	0	1	2	1	2	0	.143	.571	–	–
Lance Blankenship	ph	1	1	0	0	0	0	0	0	0	1	0	.000	.000	–	–
Mike Bordick	pr-ss	3	0	0	0	0	0	0	0	0	0	0	–	–	0	1.000
Todd Burns	p	2	0	0	0	0	0	0	0	0	0	0	–	–	0	–
Jose Canseco	rf-dh-ph	4	12	1	1	0	0	1	2	2	3	0	.083	.333	0	1.000
Dennis Eckersley	p	2	0	0	0	0	0	0	0	0	0	0	–	–	0	–
Mike Gallego	ss	4	11	0	1	0	0	0	1	1	3	1	.091	.091	1	.944
Ron Hassey	ph-c	3	6	0	2	0	0	0	1	0	0	0	.333	.333	1	.667
Dave Henderson	ph-cf	4	13	2	3	1	0	0	0	1	3	0	.231	.308	0	1.000
Rickey Henderson	lf	4	15	2	5	2	0	1	1	3	4	3	.333	.667	0	1.000
Rick Honeycutt	p	1	0	0	0	0	0	0	0	0	0	0	–	–	–	–
Doug Jennings	ph	1	1	0	1	0	0	0	0	0	0	0	1.000	1.000	–	–
Joe Klink	p	1	0	0	0	0	0	0	0	0	0	0	–	–	0	–
Carney Lansford	3b	4	15	0	4	0	0	0	1	1	0	1	.267	.267	0	1.000
Willie McGee	cf-ph-rf	4	10	1	2	1	0	0	0	0	2	1	.200	.300	0	1.000
Mark McGwire	1b	4	14	1	3	0	0	0	0	2	4	0	.214	.214	2	.956
Mike Moore	p	1	0	0	0	0	0	0	0	0	0	0	–	–	0	–
Gene Nelson	p	2	0	0	0	0	0	0	0	0	0	0	–	–	0	–
Jamie Quirk	c	1	3	0	0	0	0	0	0	0	2	0	.000	.000	0	1.000
Willie Randolph	2b	4	15	0	4	0	0	0	0	1	0	1	.267	.267	0	1.000
Scott Sanderson	p	2	0	0	0	0	0	0	0	0	0	0	–	–	0	–
Terry Steinbach	c	3	8	0	1	0	0	0	0	0	1	0	.125	.125	0	1.000
Dave Stewart	p	2	1	0	0	0	0	0	0	0	1	0	.000	.000	1	.750
Bob Welch	p	1	3	0	0	0	0	0	0	0	2	0	.000	.000	0	1.000
Curt Young	p	1	0	0	0	0	0	0	0	0	0	0	–	–	0	–
Totals		**4**	**135**	**8**	**28**	**4**	**0**	**3**	**8**	**12**	**28**	**7**	**.207**	**.304**	**5**	**.968**

Pitcher	G	GS	CG	IP	H	R	ER	BB	SO	W-L	Sv	ERA
Todd Burns	2	0	0	1⅔	5	3	3	2	0	0-0	0	16.20
Dennis Eckersley	2	0	0	1⅓	3	1	1	0	1	0-1	0	6.75
Rick Honeycutt	1	0	0	1⅔	2	0	0	1	0	0-0	0	0.00
Joe Klink	1	0	0	0,0	0	0	0	1	0	0-0	0	–
Mike Moore	1	1	0	2⅔	8	6	2	0	1	0-1	0	6.75
Gene Nelson	2	0	0	5	3	0	0	2	0	0-0	0	0.00
Scott Sanderson	2	0	0	1⅔	4	2	2	1	0	0-0	0	10.80
Dave Stewart	2	2	1	13	10	6	5	6	5	0-2	0	3.46
Bob Welch	1	1	0	7⅓	9	4	4	2	2	0-0	0	4.91
Curt Young	1	0	0	1	1	0	0	0	0	0-0	0	0.00
Totals	**4**	**4**	**1**	**35⅓**	**45**	**22**	**15**	**15**	**9**	**0-4**	**0**	**4.33**

Series MVP: Jose Rijo, Cincinnati Reds. **Series Outstanding Pitcher:** Jose Rijo, Cincinnati Reds. **Average Length of Game:** 3 hours. **Total Attendance:** 208,544. **Average Attendance:** 52,136 (55,831 at Riverfront Stadium; 48,441 at Oakland-Alameda County Coliseum). **Umpires:** Larry Barnett (AL), Bruce Froemming (NL), Ted Hendry (AL), Randy Marsh (NL), Frank Pulli (NL), Jim Quick (NL), Rocky Roe (AL). **Winning Player's Share:** $112,534. **Losing Player's Share:** $86,961.

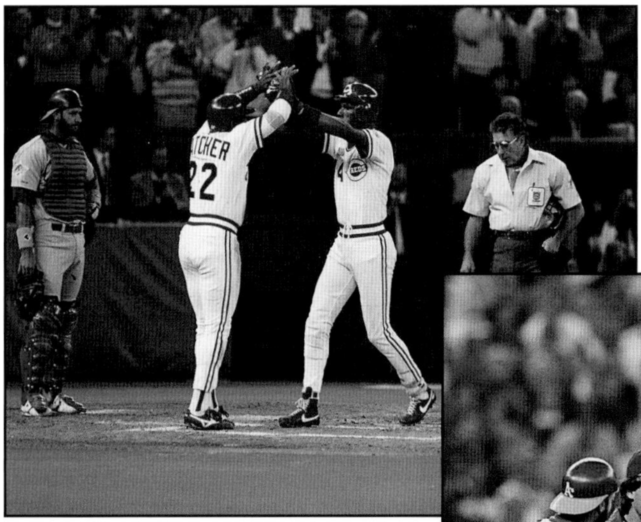

Left: Eric Davis got the Reds off to a good start with his first-inning homer in Game 1, driving in Billy Hatcher for a 2-0 lead.

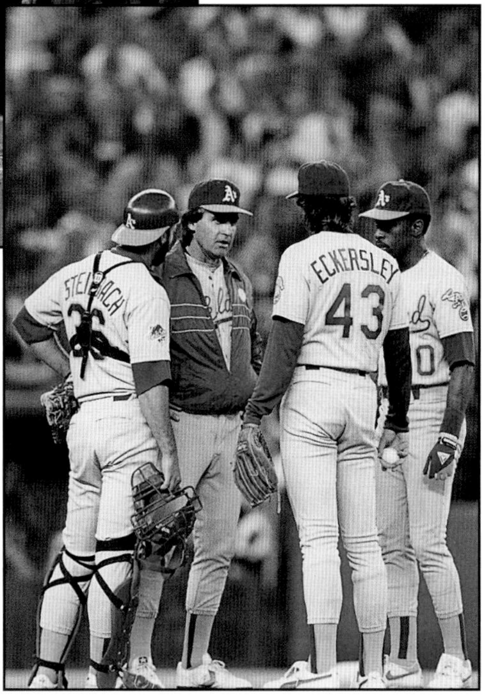

Right: Manager Tony La Russa confers with his ace reliever Dennis Eckersley, along with infielder Willie Randolph and catcher Terry Steinbach.

Below: Cincinnati fans were all pumped up for a four-game sweep over the favored Oakland A's.

Game 1 Tuesday, October 16 at Riverfront Stadium, Cincinnati

	1	2	3	4	5	6	7	8	9	R	H	E
Oakland Athletics	0	0	0	0	0	0	0	0	0	0	9	1
Cincinnati Reds	2	0	2	0	3	0	0	0	x	7	10	0

Pitchers Oak **Dave Stewart** (L, 0-1), IP 4, H 3, R 4, ER 3, BB 4, SO 3; **Todd Burns**, IP ⅔, H 4, R 3, ER 3, BB 1, SO 0; **Gene Nelson**, IP 1⅓, H 2, R 0, ER 0, BB 1, SO 0; **Scott Sanderson**, IP 1, H 1, R 0, ER 0, BB 0, SO 0; **Dennis Eckersley**, IP 1, H 0, R 0, ER 0, BB 0, SO 1

Cin **Jose Rijo** (W, 1-0), IP 7, H 7, R 0, ER 0, BB 2, SO 5; **Rob Dibble**, IP 1, H 1, R 0, ER 0, BB 1, SO 0; **Randy Myers**, IP 1, H 1, R 0, ER 0, BB 0, SO 2

Top Performers at the Plate

Oak **Rickey Henderson**, 3 for 5, 2 2B; **Carney Lansford**, 2 for 4

Cin **Eric Davis**, 2 for 4, 2 R, 3 RBI; **Billy Hatcher**, 3 for 3, 3 R, 1 RBI, 1 BB, 2 2B

2B-Oak/R. Henderson 2; Cin/Hatcher 2. **HR**-Cin/Davis. **SB**-Oak/Lansford, McGee. **Time** 2:38. **Attendance** 55,830.

Game 2 Wednesday, October 17 at Riverfront Stadium, Cincinnati

	1	2	3	4	5	6	7	8	9	10	R	H	E
Oakland Athletics	1	0	3	0	0	0	0	0	0	0	4	10	2
Cincinnati Reds	2	0	0	1	0	0	0	1	0	1	5	14	2

Pitchers Oak **Bob Welch**, IP 7⅓, H 9, R 4, ER 4, BB 2, SO 2; **Rick Honeycutt**, IP 1⅔, H 2, R 0, ER 0, BB 1, SO 0; **Dennis Eckersley** (L, 0-1), IP ⅓, H 3, R 1, ER 1, BB 0, SO 0;

Cin **Danny Jackson**, IP 2⅔, H 6, R 4, ER 3, BB 2, SO 0; **Scott Scudder**, IP 1⅓, H 0, R 0, ER 0, BB 2, SO 2; **Jack Armstrong**, IP 3, H 1, R 0, ER 0, BB 0, SO 3; **Norm Charlton**, IP 1, H 1, R 0, ER 0, BB 0, SO 0; **Rob Dibble** (W, 1-0), IP 2, H 2, R 0, ER 0, BB 0, SO 2

Top Performers at the Plate

Oak **Ron Hassey**, 2 for 4, 1 RBI, 1 SF; **Mark McGwire**, 2 for 4, 1 R, 1 BB

Cin **Billy Hatcher**, 4 for 4, 2 R, 1 RBI, 1 BB; **Joe Oliver**, 2 for 5, 1 R, 1 RBI

2B-Cin/Hatcher 2, Larkin, Oliver. **3B**-Cin/Hatcher. **HR**-Oak/Canseco. **SB**-Oak/R. Henderson. **Time** 3:31. **Attendance** 55,832.

Game 3 Friday, October 19 at Oakland-Alameda County Coliseum, Oakland

	1	2	3	4	5	6	7	8	9	R	H	E
Cincinnati Reds	0	1	7	0	0	0	0	0	0	8	14	1
Oakland Athletics	0	2	1	0	0	0	0	0	0	3	7	1

Pitchers Cin **Tom Browning** (W, 1-0), IP 6, H 6, R 3, ER 3, BB 2, SO 2; **Rob Dibble**, IP 1⅔, H 0, R 0, ER 0, BB 0, SO 2; **Randy Myers**, IP 1⅓, H 1, R 0, ER 0, BB 0, SO 1

Oak **Mike Moore** (L, 0-1), IP 2⅔, H 6, R 6, ER 2, BB 0, SO 1; **Scott Sanderson**, IP ⅔, H 3, R 2, ER 2, BB 1, SO 0; **Joe Klink**, IP 0, H 0, R 0, ER 0, BB 1, SO 0; **Gene Nelson**, IP 3⅔, H 1, R 0, ER 0, BB 1, SO 0; **Todd Burns**, IP 1, H 1, R 0, ER 0, BB 1, SO 0; **Curt Young**, IP 1, H 1, R 0, ER 0, BB 0, SO 0

Top Performers at the Plate

Cin **Eric Davis**, 2 for 5, 1 R, 1 RBI; **Chris Sabo**, 2 for 4, 2 R 3 RBI, 1 BB, 2 HR

Oak **Rickey Henderson**, 1 for 3, 1 R, 1 RBI, 1 BB; **Willie Randolph**, 3 for 4

2B-Cin/Oliver; Oak/D. Henderson. **3B**-Cin/Larkin. **HR**-Cin/Sabo 2; Oak/Baines, R. Henderson. **SB**-Cin/Duncan, O'Neill; Oak/R. Henderson, Randolph. **Time** 3:01. **Attendance** 48,269.

Game 4 Saturday, October 20 at Oakland-Alameda County Coliseum, Oakland

	1	2	3	4	5	6	7	8	9	R	H	E
Cincinnati Reds	0	0	0	0	0	0	0	2	0	2	7	1
Oakland Athletics	1	0	0	0	0	0	0	0	0	1	2	1

Pitchers Cin **Jose Rijo** (W, 2-0), IP 8⅓, H 2, R 1, ER 1, BB 3, SO 9; **Randy Myers** (Sv, 1), IP ⅔, H 0, R 0, ER 0, BB 0, SO 0

Oak **Dave Stewart** (L, 0-2), IP 9, H 7, R 2, ER 1, BB 2, SO 2

Top Performers at the Plate

Cin **Chris Sabo**, 3 for 4; **Herm Winningham**, 2 for 3, 1 R

2B-Cin/Oliver, Sabo; Oak/McGee. **SB**-Oak/Gallego, R. Henderson. **Time** 2:48. **Attendance** 48,613.

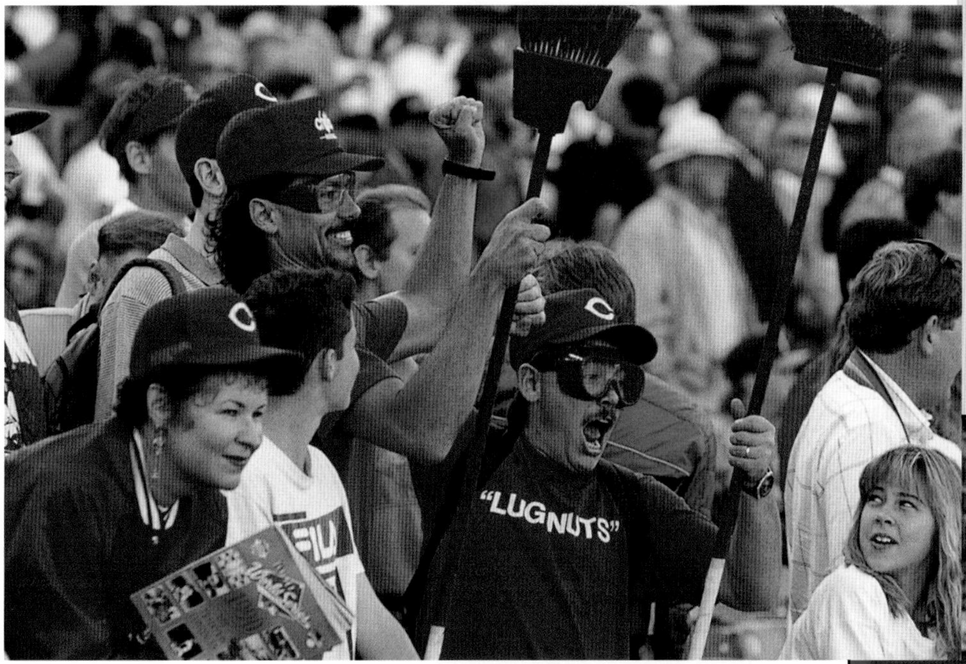

Cincinnati's Billy Hatcher set a World Series record with his .750 average over the four games.

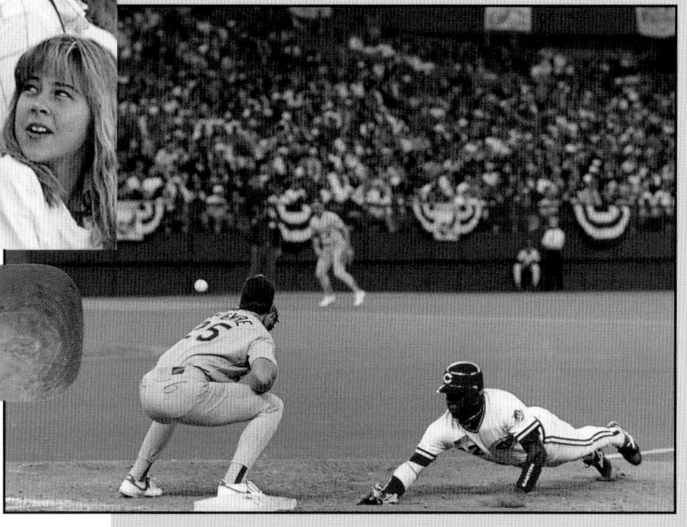

Right: Billy Hatcher, seen here diving back to first base, hit safely in his first seven at-bats and hit for a record .750 average in the Series

WORLD SERIES CLASSIC 1991

Minnesota Twins (4) vs. Atlanta Braves (3)

The Minnesota Twins finished the 1990 season with a 74-88 record, good enough for last place in the American League West. That year the Atlanta Braves finished 65-97, worst in their division, as well. Both teams made adjustments in the off-season, then turned their fortunes around in unprecedented fashion. Prior to 1991, no team in history had rebounded from a last-place finish to win a pennant the next season. In 1991, both the Twins and the Braves accomplished the feat, squaring off in an all "worst-to-first" World Series. The result was one of the best October showdowns baseball has ever seen.

The opener at the Metrodome was not exactly a sign of things to come, being one of only two games decided by more than one run. Minnesota-native Jack Morris held Atlanta to 5 hits in seven innings, and Greg Gagne and Kent Hrbek stroked home runs in the 5-2 win. Chili Davis gave the Twins an early lead in Game 2 with a two-run blast against Atlanta's 20-game winner, Tom Glavine. The Braves eventually tied the game, but a questionable play in the third inning prevented them from possibly taking the lead. With a runner on base, Ron Gant singled to left and took a big turn around first base. Seeing Gant off the bag, pitcher Kevin Tapani relayed the ball to Hrbek at first. Gant beat the throw back to the base, but his momentum appeared to carry him off the bag again, and Hrbek tagged him as he tumbled to the dirt. Gant argued that Hrbek had pulled him off first base, but umpire Drew Coble didn't see it and called Gant out. With the score still tied at two, Twins rookie Scott Leius stroked the first pitch of the eighth inning into the left-field seats for the game-winner. In Atlanta for Game 3, Minnesota's 20-game winner, Scott Erickson, was knocked for 4 runs in five innings, but home runs by Kirby Puckett and Davis brought Minnesota even 4-4. Second baseman Mark Lemke became Atlanta's hero of the day by driving in David Justice with a two-out single in the bottom of the 12th. The fourth game was also decided in the last at-bat, and once again, Lemke came through with the big play, tripling with one out and the game tied in the ninth. Lemke tagged up on Jerry Willard's fly to right, barely eluding catcher Brian Harper's tag in a close play at the plate. Game 5 was an ugly one for Minnesota. The Braves banged out 14 runs, with David Justice driving in 5 and veteran Lonnie Smith homering for the third straight game.

The Braves were up three games to two, but the Twins were hopeful. They were heading back to Minneapolis, and the home team had been victorious in every game thus far. Kirby Puckett started things off in Game 6 with an RBI triple and a run in the bottom of the first, and he gave his team another boost with a leaping, run-saving catch on Gant's drive to the wall in the third. The Braves tied the game on Terry Pendleton's fifth-inning homer, but Puckett regained the lead with an RBI sacrifice fly in the bottom of the inning. In the seventh, Lemke cele-

Above: Jack Morris' Game 7 performance was one of the best in postseason history. He also won the Series opener with a five-hitter.

brated his ninth hit of the Series by scoring Atlanta's third run, once again evening the score. With the game still tied in the last of the 11th, Puckett found himself in another key situation for his team. Leading off the inning, Kirby responded by driving a ball over the left-center-field fence. The Metrodome exploded in euphoria as Puckett sent the Series to a seventh game. Jack Morris was ready to go in Game 7, matching up against the young John Smoltz. When Lonnie Smith stepped to the plate as the game's first batter, he turned and shook hands with Minnesota catcher Brian Harper. The gesture represented what was obvious to all: 1991 was shaping up to be a truly classic World Series. The two pitchers were masterful in the finale, and the eighth inning provided particular drama in the scoreless contest. Smith led off with a single, and Pendleton drove a liner toward the gap in left-center, seemingly good enough to score Smith. But Smith lost sight of the ball and hesitated as he rounded second; Minnesota infielders Greg Gagne and Chuck Knoblauch confused him further by staging a decoy play at second base. As a result, Smith advanced only to third and Pendleton to second. Still, Atlanta had two runners in scoring position and nobody out, with the heart of the order coming up. Gant grounded out to first, and then Morris walked Justice intentionally to load the bases. The next batter, Sid Bream, grounded to Hrbek at first base, who threw to Harper for the force at home, and Harper returned the throw for a 3-2-3 double play, ending the threat without a run. Morris stayed on the hill for Minnesota, and he retired Atlanta easily in the ninth and tenth. Dan Gladden opened the bottom of the 10th with a double and then advanced to third on Knoblauch's sacrifice. Reliever Alejandro Pena walked Puckett and Hrbek intentionally, bringing up pinch hitter Gene Larkin. Larkin looped Pena's first pitch over the heads of the drawn-in outfield, and Gladden danced home with the winning run. In a marvelous performance, Jack Morris went the distance in the third extra-inning contest of the Series.

Above:The heart and soul of the Minnesota Twins, Kirby Puckett delivered a clutch game-winning home run in Game 6 to extend the memorable 1991 World Series to a seventh game.

Above: A collision at home plate sends Braves catcher Greg Olson tumbling, but he held on to nab Dan Gladden in Game 1.

Left: Pitcher Tom Glavine went the distance in Game 2, allowing just one earned run, but he lost a close one against Minnesota's Kevin Tapani.

Right: Leius' teammates swarm around him after he broke a 2-2 tie in Game 2 with a leadoff homer in the eighth. The lead stuck, giving Minnesota a two-games-to-one advantage.

Above: Scott Leius had less than 200 at-bats during the 1991 regular season—none as significant as his final at-bat in Game 2 of the World Series.

Above: Kirby Puckett broke a 3-3 deadlock in the 11th inning of Game 6 with a leadoff shot into the Metrodome seats.

Above inset: Terry Pendleton makes the play to nail Dan Gladden at third base, and then fires to first to try to complete the double play.

Game 1   Saturday, October 19 at the Metrodome, Minneapolis

	1	2	3	4	5	6	7	8	9		R	H	E
Atlanta Braves	0	0	0	0	0	1	0	1	0		2	6	1
Minnesota Twins	0	0	1	0	3	1	0	0	x		5	9	1

Pitchers   Atl   Charlie Leibrandt (L, 0-1), IP 4, H 7, R 4, ER 4, BB 1, SO 3; Jim Clancy, IP 2, H 1, R 1, ER 1, BB 2, SO 0; Mark Wohlers, IP 1, H 1, R 0, ER 0, BB 1, SO 1; Mike Stanton, IP 1, H 0, R 0, ER 0, BB 0, SO 2
Min   Jack Morris (W, 1-0), IP 7, H 5, R 2, ER 2, BB 4, SO 3; Mark Guthrie, IP ⅔, H 0, R 0, ER 0, BB 1, SO 0; Rick Aguilera (Sv, 1), IP 1⅓, H 1, R 0, ER 0, BB 0, SO 0

Top Performers at the Plate
Atl   Ron Gant, 3 for 4, 2 RBI; Jeff Treadway, 1 for 3, 1 R, 1 BB
Min   Greg Gagne, 1 for 3, 1 R, 3 RBI; Chuck Knoblauch, 3 for 3, 1 RBI, 1 BB, 2 SB

2B-Min/Harper, Hrbek. **HR**-Min/Gagne, Hrbek. **SB**-Min/Gladden, Knoblauch 2. **Time** 3:00. **Attendance** 55,108.

Game 2   Sunday, October 20 at the Metrodome, Minneapolis

	1	2	3	4	5	6	7	8	9		R	H	E
Atlanta Braves	0	1	0	0	1	0	0	0	0		2	8	1
Minnesota Twins	2	0	0	0	0	0	0	1	x		3	4	1

Pitchers   Atl   Tom Glavine (L, 0-1), IP 8, H 4, R 3, ER 1, BB 3, SO 6
Min   Kevin Tapani (W, 1-0), IP 8, H 7, R 2, ER 2, BB 0, SO 3; Rick Aguilera (Sv, 2), IP 1, H 1, R 0, ER 0, BB 0, SO 3

Top Performers at the Plate
Atl   Rafael Belliard, 1 for 2, 1 RBI, 1 SF; Terry Pendleton, 2 for 4
Min   Chili Davis, 1 for 3, 1 R, 2 RBI; Scott Leius, 1 for 3, 1 R, 1 RBI

2B-Atl/Bream, Olson. **HR**-Min/Davis, Leius. **Time** 2:37. **Attendance** 55,145.

Game 3   Tuesday, October 22 at Atlanta-Fulton County Stadium, Atlanta

	1	2	3	4	5	6	7	8	9	10	11	12	R	H	E
Minnesota Twins	1	0	0	0	0	0	1	2	0	0	0	0	4	10	1
Atlanta Braves	0	1	0	1	2	0	0	0	0	0	0	1	5	8	2

Pitchers   Min   Scott Erickson, IP 4⅔, H 5, R 4, ER 3, BB 2, SO 3; David West, IP 0, H 0, R 0, ER 0, BB 2, SO 0; Terry Leach, IP ⅓, H 0, R 0, ER 0, BB 0, SO 1; Steve Bedrosian, IP 2, H 0, R 0, ER 0, BB 0, SO 1; Carl Willis, IP 2, H 0, R 0, ER 0, BB 2, SO 0; Mark Guthrie, IP 2, H 1, R 0, ER 0, BB 1, SO 1; Rick Aguilera (L, 0-1), IP ⅔, H 2, R 1, ER 1, BB 1, SO 0
Atl   Steve Avery, IP 7, H 4, R 3, ER 2, BB 0, SO 5; Alejandro Pena, IP 2, H 4, R 1, ER 1, BB 0, SO 4; Mike Stanton, IP 2, H 1, R 0, ER 0, BB 1, SO 3; Mark Wohlers, IP ⅓, H 1, R 0, ER 0, BB 0, SO 0; Kent Mercker, IP ⅓, H 0, R 0, ER 0, BB 0, SO 1; Jim Clancy (W, 1-0), IP ⅓, H 0, R 0, ER 0, BB 1, SO 0

Top Performers at the Plate
Min   Chili Davis, 1 for 1, 1 R, 2 RBI; Dan Gladden, 3 for 6, 1 R
Atl   David Justice, 2 for 6, 2 R, 1 RBI; Greg Olson, 1 for 3, 1 R, 1 RBI, 3 BB

2B-Atl/Bream, Olson. **3B**-Min/Gladden. **HR**-Min/Davis, Puckett; Atl/Justice, Smith. **SB**-Atl/Knoblauch, Justice. **Time** 4:04. **Attendance** 50,878.

Game 4   Wednesday, October 23 at Atlanta-Fulton County Stadium, Atlanta

	1	2	3	4	5	6	7	8	9		R	H	E
Minnesota Twins	0	1	0	0	0	1	0	0			2	7	0
Atlanta Braves	0	0	1	0	0	0	1	0	1		3	8	0

Pitchers   Min   Jack Morris, IP 6, H 6, R 1, ER 1, BB 3, SO 4; Carl Willis, IP 1⅓, H 1, R 1, ER 1, BB 0, SO 1; Mark Guthrie (L, 0-1), IP 1, H 1, R 1, ER 1, BB 1, SO 1; Steve Bedrosian, IP ⅓, H 0, R 0, ER 0, BB 0, SO 0
Atl   John Smoltz, IP 7, H 7, R 2, ER 2, BB 0, SO 7; Mark Wohlers, IP ⅓, H 0, R 0, ER 0, BB 1, SO 0; Mike Stanton (W, 1-0), IP 1⅔, H 0, R 0, ER 0, BB 0, SO 1

Top Performers at the Plate
Min   Brian Harper, 2 for 4, 1 R; Mike Pagliarulo, 3 for 3, 1 R, 2 RBI
Atl   Mark Lemke, 3 for 4, 1 R; Lonnie Smith, 2 for 4, 1 R, 1 RBI

2B-Min/Harper, Knoblauch; Atl/Lemke, Pendleton. **3B**-Atl/Lemke. **HR**-Min/Pagliarulo; Atl/Pendleton, Smith. **SB**-Min/Knoblauch; Atl/Gant, Smith. **Time** 2:57. **Attendance** 50,878.

Game 5   Thursday, October 24 at Atlanta-Fulton County Stadium, Atlanta

	1	2	3	4	5	6	7	8	9		R	H	E
Minnesota Twins	0	0	0	0	3	0	1	1			5	7	1
Atlanta Braves	0	0	0	4	1	0	6	3	x		14	17	1

Pitchers   Min   Kevin Tapani (L, 1-1), IP 4, H 6, R 4, ER 4, BB 2, SO 4; Terry Leach, IP 2, H 2, R 1, ER 1, BB 0, SO 1; David West, IP 0, H 2, R 4, ER 4, BB 2, SO 0; Steve Bedrosian, IP 1, H 3, R 2, ER 2, BB 0, SO 1; Carl Willis, IP 1, H 4, R 3, ER 3, BB 0, SO 0
Atl   Tom Glavine (W, 1-1), IP 5⅓, H 4, R 3, ER 3, BB 4, SO 2; Kent Mercker, IP ⅔, H 0, R 0, ER 0, BB 0, SO 0; Jim Clancy, IP 2, H 2, R 1, ER 1, BB 1, SO 2; Randy St. Claire, IP 1, H 1, R 1, ER 1, BB 0, SO 0

Top Performers at the Plate
Min   Chili Davis, 1 for 3, 2 R, 1 BB; Chuck Knoblauch, 1 for 3, 1 R, 1 BB
Atl   Ron Gant, 3 for 4, 3 R, 1 RBI, 1 BB; David Justice, 2 for 5, 2 R, 5 RBI

2B-Min/Gagne; Atl/Belliard, Pendleton. **3B**-Min/Gladden, Newman; Atl/Gant, Lemke 2. **HR**-Atl/Hunter, Justice, Smith. **SB**-Atl/Justice, Olson. **SH**-Min/Puckett. **Time** 2:59. **Attendance** 50,878.

Game 6   Saturday, October 26 at the Metrodome, Minneapolis

	1	2	3	4	5	6	7	8	9	10	11	R	H	E
Atlanta Braves	0	0	0	2	0	1	0	0	0	0	0	3	9	1
Minnesota Twins	2	0	0	0	1	0	0	0	0	0	1	4	9	0

Pitchers   Atl   Steve Avery, IP 6, H 6, R 3, ER 3, BB 1, SO 3; Mike Stanton, IP 2, H 2, R 0, ER 0, BB 0, SO 1; Alejandro Pena, IP 2, H 0, R 0, ER 0, BB 0, SO 2; Charlie Leibrandt (L, 0-2), IP 0, H 1, R 1, ER 1, BB 0, SO 0
Min   Scott Erickson, IP 6, H 5, R 3, ER 3, BB 2, SO 2; Mark Guthrie, IP ⅓, H 1, R 0, ER 0, BB 1, SO 0; Carl Willis, IP 2⅔, H 1, R 0, ER 0, BB 0, SO 1; Rick Aguilera (W, 1-1), IP 2, H 2, R 0, ER 0, BB 0, SO 0

Top Performers at the Plate
Atl   Mark Lemke, 2 for 4, 1 R; Terry Pendleton, 4 for 5, 1 R, 2 RBI
Min   Shane Mack, 2 for 4, 1 RBI; Kirby Puckett, 3 for 4, 2 R, 3 RBI, 1 SF

2B-Min/Mack. **3B**-Min/Puckett. **HR**-Atl/Pendleton; Min/Puckett. **SB**-Min/Gladden, Puckett. **Time** 3:36. **Attendance** 55,155.

Game 7   Sunday, October 27 at the Metrodome, Minneapolis

	1	2	3	4	5	6	7	8	9	10	R	H	E
Atlanta Braves	0	0	0	0	0	0	0	0	0	0	0	7	0
Minnesota Twins	0	0	0	0	0	0	0	0	0	1	1	10	0

Pitchers   Atl   John Smoltz, IP 7⅓, H 6, R 0, ER 0, BB 1, SO 4; Mike Stanton, IP ⅔, H 2, R 0, ER 0, BB 1, SO 0; Alejandro Pena (L, 0-1), IP 1⅓, H 2, R 1, ER 1, BB 3, SO 1
Min   Jack Morris (W, 2-0), IP 10, H 7, R 0, ER 0, BB 2, SO 8

Top Performers at the Plate
Atl   Lonnie Smith, 2 for 4, 1 BB
Min   Dan Gladden, 3 for 5, 1 R, 2 2B; Gene Larkin, 1 for 1, 1 RBI

2B-Atl/Hunter, Pendleton; Min/Gladden 2. **Time** 3:23. **Attendance** 55,118.

1991 WORLD SERIES COMPOSITE STATISTICS

MINNESOTA TWINS/Tom Kelly, Manager

Player	pos	G	AB	R	H	2B	3B	HR	RBI	BB	SO	SB	BA	SA	E	FPct
Rick Aguilera	p-ph	4	1	0	0	0	0	0	0	0	0	0	.000	.000	0	—
Steve Bedrosian	p	3	0	0	0	0	0	0	0	0	0	0	—	—	0	1.000
Jarvis Brown	rf-ph-cf-pr	3	2	0	0	0	0	0	0	0	0	0	.000	.000	0	—
Randy Bush	ph-rf	3	4	0	1	0	0	0	0	0	1	0	.250	.250	0	—
Chili Davis	dh-ph-rf	6	18	4	4	0	0	2	4	2	3	0	.222	.556	0	1.000
Scott Erickson	p	2	1	0	0	0	0	0	0	0	1	0	.000	.000	0	1.000
Greg Gagne	ss	7	24	1	4	1	0	1	3	0	7	0	.167	.333	0	1.000
Dan Gladden	lf	7	30	5	7	2	2	0	3	4	2	2	.233	.433	1	.963
Mark Guthrie	p	4	0	0	0	0	0	0	0	0	0	0	—	—	0	1.000
Brian Harper	c-ph	7	21	2	8	2	0	0	1	2	2	0	.381	.476	1	.974
Kent Hrbek	1b	7	26	2	3	1	0	1	2	2	6	0	.115	.269	0	1.000
Chuck Knoblauch	2b	7	26	3	8	1	0	0	2	4	2	4	.308	.346	1	.967
Gene Larkin	ph	4	4	0	2	0	0	0	1	0	0	0	.500	.500	0	—
Terry Leach	p	2	0	0	0	0	0	0	0	0	0	0	—	—	0	—
Scott Leius	3b-ph-ss	7	14	2	5	0	0	1	2	1	2	0	.357	.571	1	.929
Shane Mack	rf	6	23	0	3	1	0	0	1	0	7	0	.130	.174	0	1.000
Jack Morris	p	3	2	0	0	0	0	0	0	0	1	0	.000	.000	0	1.000
Al Newman	ph-3b-2b-pr-ss	4	2	0	1	0	1	0	1	0	0	0	.500	1.500	0	—
Junior Ortiz	c	3	5	0	1	0	0	0	1	0	1	0	.200	.200	0	1.000
Mike Pagliarulo	ph-3b	6	11	1	3	0	0	1	2	1	2	0	.273	.545	0	1.000
Kirby Puckett	cf	7	24	4	6	0	1	2	4	5	7	1	.250	.583	0	1.000
Paul Sorrento	1b	3	2	0	0	0	0	0	0	1	2	0	.000	.000	0	1.000
Kevin Tapani	p	2	1	0	0	0	0	0	0	0	0	0	.000	.000	0	1.000
David West	p	2	0	0	0	0	0	0	0	0	0	0	—	—	0	—
Carl Willis	p	4	0	0	0	0	0	0	0	0	0	0	—	—	0	1.000
Totals		**7**	**241**	**24**	**56**	**8**	**4**	**8**	**24**	**21**	**48**	**7**	**.232**	**.398**	**4**	**.986**

Pitcher	G	GS	CG	IP	H	R	ER	BB	SO	W-L	Sv	ERA
Rick Aguilera	4	0	0	5	6	1	1	1	3	1-1	2	1.80
Steve Bedrosian	3	0	0	3⅓	3	2	2	0	2	0-0	0	5.40
Scott Erickson	2	2	0	10⅔	10	7	6	4	5	0-0	0	5.06
Mark Guthrie	4	0	0	4	3	1	1	4	3	0-1	0	2.25
Terry Leach	2	0	0	2⅓	2	1	1	0	2	0-0	0	3.86
Jack Morris	3	3	1	23	18	3	3	9	15	2-0	0	1.17
Kevin Tapani	2	2	0	12	13	6	6	2	7	1-1	0	4.50
David West	2	0	0	0	2	4	4	4	0	0-0	0	—
Carl Willis	4	0	0	7	6	4	4	2	2	0-0	0	5.14
Totals	**7**	**7**	**1**	**67⅓**	**63**	**29**	**28**	**26**	**39**	**4-3**	**2**	**3.74**

ATLANTA BRAVES/Bobby Cox, Manager

Player	pos	G	AB	R	H	2B	3B	HR	RBI	BB	SO	SB	BA	SA	E	FPct
Steve Avery	p	2	3	0	0	0	0	0	0	0	2	0	.000	.000	0	1.000
Rafael Belliard	ss	7	16	0	6	1	0	0	4	1	2	0	.375	.438	0	1.000
Jeff Blauser	ph-ss	5	6	0	1	0	0	0	0	1	1	0	.167	.167	0	1.000
Sid Bream	1b	7	24	0	3	2	0	0	3	4	0	.125	.208	0	1.000
Francisco Cabrera	ph-c	3	1	0	0	0	0	0	0	0	0	0	.000	.000	0	—
Jim Clancy	p	3	1	0	0	0	0	0	0	0	1	0	.000	.000	0	—
Ron Gant	cf	7	30	3	8	0	1	0	4	2	3	1	.267	.333	0	1.000
Tom Glavine	p	2	2	0	0	0	0	0	0	0	0	0	.000	.000	0	1.000
Tommy Gregg	ph	4	3	0	0	0	0	0	0	0	2	0	.000	.000	—	—
Brian Hunter	lf-ph-1b	7	21	2	4	1	0	1	3	0	2	0	.190	.381	1	.875
David Justice	rf	7	27	5	7	0	0	2	6	5	5	2	.259	.481	1	.957
Charlie Leibrandt	p	2	0	0	0	0	0	0	0	0	0	0	—	—	0	1.000
Mark Lemke	2b	6	24	4	10	1	3	0	4	2	4	0	.417	.708	1	.971
Kent Mercker	p	2	0	0	0	0	0	0	0	0	0	0	—	—	0	—
Keith Mitchell	lf-pr	7	2	0	0	0	0	0	0	0	0	0	.000	.000	0	—
Greg Olson	c	7	27	3	6	2	0	0	1	5	4	1	.222	.296	0	1.000
Alejandro Pena	p	3	0	0	0	0	0	0	0	0	0	0	—	—	0	—
Terry Pendleton	3b	7	30	6	11	3	0	2	3	3	1	0	.367	.667	2	.920
Lonnie Smith	dh-lf	7	26	5	6	0	0	3	3	3	4	1	.231	.577	0	1.000
John Smoltz	p	2	2	0	0	0	0	0	0	0	1	0	.000	.000	0	1.000
Randy St. Claire	p	1	0	0	0	0	0	0	0	0	0	0	—	—	0	—
Mike Stanton	p	5	0	0	0	0	0	0	0	0	0	0	—	—	0	—
Jeff Treadway	2b-ph	3	4	1	1	0	0	0	0	1	2	0	.250	.250	1	.800
Jerry Willard	ph	1	0	0	0	0	0	0	1	1	0	0	—	—	0	—
Mark Wohlers	p	3	0	0	0	0	0	0	0	0	0	0	—	—	0	—
Totals		**7**	**249**	**29**	**63**	**10**	**4**	**8**	**29**	**26**	**39**	**5**	**.253**	**.422**	**6**	**.979**

Pitcher	G	GS	CG	IP	H	R	ER	BB	SO	W-L	Sv	ERA
Steve Avery	2	2	0	13	10	6	5	1	8	0-0	0	3.46
Jim Clancy	3	0	0	4⅓	3	2	2	4	2	1-0	0	4.15
Tom Glavine	2	2	0	13⅓	8	6	4	7	8	1-1	0	2.70
Charlie Leibrandt	2	1	0	4	8	5	5	1	3	0-2	0	11.25
Kent Mercker	2	0	0	1	0	0	0	0	1	0-0	0	0.00
Alejandro Pena	3	0	0	5⅓	6	2	2	3	7	0-1	0	3.38
John Smoltz	2	2	0	14⅓	13	2	2	1	11	0-0	0	1.26
Randy St. Claire	1	0	0	1	1	1	1	0	0	0-0	0	9.00
Mike Stanton	5	0	0	7⅓	5	0	0	2	7	1-0	0	0.00
Mark Wohlers	3	0	0	1⅔	2	0	0	2	1	0-0	0	0.00
Totals	**7**	**7**	**1**	**65⅓**	**56**	**24**	**21**	**21**	**48**	**3-4**	**0**	**2.89**

Series MVP: Jack Morris, Minnesota Twins. **Series Outstanding Pitcher:** Jack Morris, Minnesota Twins. **Average Length of Game:** 3 hours, 14 minutes. **Total Attendance:** 373,160. **Average Attendance:** 53,309 (55,132 at the Metrodome; 50,878 at Atlanta-Fulton County Stadium). **Umpires:** Drew Coble (AL), Don Denkinger (AL), Ed Montague (NL), Rick Reed (AL), Terry Tata (NL), Harry Wendelstedt (NL). **Winning Player's Share:** $119,580. **Losing Player's Share:** $73,323.

Below, right: One of the greatest World Series of all time comes to an end, as Gene Larkin bloops a single off Alejandro Pena to send in the winning run in Game 7 of the 1991 Fall Classic.

Right: On his way home with the Series-winning run, Dan Gladden jumps for joy after Larkin's hit drops safely.

Left: In a close play at the plate, Mark Lemke squeezes by catcher Brian Harper to score the game-winning run in the ninth inning of Game 4 in Atlanta.

Below: This spectacular leaping catch by Kirby Puckett on Ron Gant's third-inning drive was a turning point in Game 6.

Toronto Blue Jays (4) vs. Atlanta Braves (2)

1992

Canada got a taste of World Series baseball in 1992, when the Toronto Blue Jays made it to their first Fall Classic, and the Atlanta Braves were back for the second straight year. Tom Glavine, coming off another 20-win season, started Game 1 opposite Toronto's new acquisition, Jack Morris. The 37-year-old Morris threw shutout ball for five innings until Damon Berryhill's three-run homer put Atlanta up 3-1. Glavine surrendered a solo homer to Joe Carter in the fourth, and then held the Jays to one single the rest of the way. Toronto snatched a 5-4 win from Atlanta in the top of the ninth inning of Game 2 when pinch hitter Ed Sprague homered off Jeff Reardon with a man on base. In Game 3, the first Series game played outside the United States, the Blue Jays pulled out another dramatic last-inning win as Candy Maldonado broke a 2-2 tie with a bases-loaded single in the bottom of the ninth. The third game had other excitement as well. In the top of the fourth, the Braves had Terry Pendleton on first and Deion Sanders on second, with nobody out, when David Justice sent a fly ball to deep center field. Toronto's Devon White made a leaping, backhanded grab against the wall to rob Justice. Pendleton was called out for passing Sanders on the base paths, and the Blue Jays nearly made it a triple play when Kelly Gruber dove at Sanders's feet to tag him before he got back to the bag. The umpire didn't see the tag, however, and Sanders was ruled safe. Gruber came through with a game-tying home run in the eighth, setting up Maldonado's last-inning heroics. Toronto took a three-games-to-one lead behind Jimmy Key's five-hitter in Game 4, and the Braves handed Morris his second loss in Game 5. Lonnie Smith put the game out of reach in the fifth inning with a grand slam.

David Cone paced the Jays to a 2-1 lead in Game 6 before leaving the mound in the seventh inning. Otis Nixon evened the score in the bottom of the ninth with a two-out, two-strike single to push the game into extra innings. In the top of the 11th, Toronto put men on first and second with one out and Dave Winfield up at the plate. With his first extra-base hit in 42 career World Series at-bats, Winfield drilled a double to send in both runners and give Toronto a 4-2 lead. Atlanta cut the lead to one in the bottom of the inning, but reliever Mike Timlin got the Jays out of a jam by throwing the speedy Nixon out at first base after Nixon tried to bunt his way on. The play ended the fourth one-run game of the Series, and Jimmy Key claimed his second win by pitching an inning and a third in relief. For the first time, baseball's championship trophy went over the border.

Above: Dave Winfield overcame his "Mr. May" label with this clutch RBI double in Game 6 that put the Blue Jays up by two runs in the 11th inning.

1992 WORLD SERIES COMPOSITE STATISTICS

TORONTO BLUE JAYS/Cito Gaston, Manager

Player	pos	G	AB	R	H	2B	3B	HR	RBI	BB	SO	SB	BA	SA	E	FPct
Roberto Alomar	2b	6	24	3	5	1	0	0	0	3	3	3	.208	.250	0	1.000
Derek Bell	ph	2	1	1	0	0	0	0	0	1	0	0	.000	.000	–	–
Pat Borders	c	6	20	2	9	3	0	1	3	2	1	0	.450	.750	1	.981
Joe Carter	1b-lf-rf	6	22	2	6	2	0	2	3	3	2	1	.273	.636	0	1.000
David Cone	p	2	4	0	2	0	0	0	1	1	0	0	.500	.500	0	–
Mark Eichhorn	p	1	0	0	0	0	0	0	0	0	0	0	–	–	0	–
Alfredo Griffin	ss	2	0	0	0	0	0	0	0	0	0	0	–	–	1	.500
Kelly Gruber	3b	6	19	2	2	0	0	1	1	2	5	1	.105	.263	1	.909
Juan Guzman	p	1	0	0	0	0	0	0	0	0	0	0	–	–	0	1.000
Tom Henke	p	3	0	0	0	0	0	0	0	0	0	0	–	–	0	1.000
Jimmy Key	p	2	1	0	0	0	0	0	0	0	0	0	.000	.000	0	1.000
Manuel Lee	ss	6	19	1	2	0	0	0	0	1	2	0	.105	.105	1	.960
Candy Maldonado	lf-ph	6	19	1	3	0	0	1	2	2	5	0	.158	.316	0	1.000
Jack Morris	p	2	2	0	0	0	0	0	0	0	2	0	.000	.000	0	1.000
John Olerud	1b	4	13	2	4	0	0	0	0	4	0	0	.308	.308	0	1.000
Ed Sprague	ph-1b	3	2	1	1	0	0	1	2	1	0	0	.500	2.000	0	–
Todd Stottlemyre	p	4	0	0	0	0	0	0	0	0	0	0	–	–	0	–
Pat Tabler	ph	2	2	0	0	0	0	0	0	0	0	0	.000	.000	–	–
Mike Timlin	p	2	0	0	0	0	0	0	0	0	0	0	–	–	0	1.000
Duane Ward	p	4	0	0	0	0	0	0	0	0	0	0	–	–	0	–
David Wells	p	4	0	0	0	0	0	0	0	0	0	0	–	–	0	–
Devon White	cf	6	26	2	6	1	0	0	2	0	6	1	.231	.269	0	1.000
Dave Winfield	rf-dh	6	22	0	5	1	0	0	3	2	3	0	.227	.273	0	1.000
Totals		6	196	17	45	8	0	6	17	18	33	6	.230	.362	4	.982

Pitcher	G	GS	CG	IP	H	R	ER	BB	SO	W-L	Sv	ERA
David Cone	2	2	0	10⅓	9	5	4	8	8	0-0	0	3.48
Mark Eichhorn	1	0	0	1	0	0	0	0	1	0-0	0	0.00
Juan Guzman	1	1	0	8	8	2	1	1	7	0-0	0	1.13
Tom Henke	3	0	0	3⅓	2	1	1	2	1	0-0	2	2.70
Jimmy Key	2	1	0	9	6	2	1	0	6	2-0	0	1.00
Jack Morris	2	2	0	10⅔	13	10	10	6	12	0-2	0	8.44
Todd Stottlemyre	4	0	0	3⅔	4	0	0	4	0	0-0	0	0.00
Mike Timlin	2	0	0	1⅓	0	0	0	0	0	0-0	1	0.00
Duane Ward	4	0	0	3⅓	1	0	0	1	6	2-0	0	0.00
David Wells	4	0	0	4⅓	1	0	0	2	3	0-0	0	0.00
Totals	6	6	0	55	44	20	17	20	48	4-2	3	2.78

ATLANTA BRAVES/Bobby Cox, Manager

Player	pos	G	AB	R	H	2B	3B	HR	RBI	BB	SO	SB	BA	SA	E	FPct
Steve Avery	p	2	1	0	0	0	0	0	0	0	1	0	.000	.000	0	1.000
Rafael Belliard	ss-2b	4	0	0	0	0	0	0	0	0	0	0	–	–	0	1.000
Damon Berryhill	c	6	22	1	2	0	0	1	3	1	11	0	.091	.227	0	1.000
Jeff Blauser	ss	6	24	2	6	0	0	0	0	1	9	2	.250	.250	0	1.000
Sid Bream	1b	5	15	1	3	0	0	0	4	0	0	0	.200	.200	1	.977
Francisco Cabrera	ph	1	1	0	0	0	0	0	0	0	0	0	.000	.000	–	–
Ron Gant	lf-ph	4	8	2	1	1	0	0	0	1	2	2	.125	.250	0	1.000
Tom Glavine	p	2	2	0	0	0	0	0	0	1	0	0	.000	.000	0	1.000
Brian Hunter	ph-1b-pr	4	5	0	1	0	0	0	0	2	1	0	.200	.200	0	1.000
David Justice	rf	6	19	4	3	0	0	1	3	6	5	1	.158	.316	0	.938
Charlie Leibrandt	p	1	0	0	0	0	0	0	0	0	0	0	–	–	0	1.000
Mark Lemke	2b	6	19	0	4	0	0	0	2	1	3	0	.211	.211	0	1.000
Otis Nixon	cf	6	27	3	8	1	0	0	1	1	3	5	.296	.333	0	1.000
Terry Pendleton	3b	6	25	2	6	2	0	0	2	1	5	0	.240	.320	0	1.000
Jeff Reardon	p	2	0	0	0	0	0	0	0	0	0	0	–	–	0	–
Deion Sanders	lf	4	15	4	8	2	0	0	1	2	1	5	.533	.667	0	1.000
Lonnie Smith	ph-dh	5	12	1	2	0	0	1	5	1	4	0	.167	.417	–	–
Pete Smith	p	1	1	0	0	0	0	0	0	0	0	0	.000	.000	0	–
John Smoltz	p-pr	3	3	0	0	0	0	0	0	0	2	0	.000	.000	0	1.000
Mike Stanton	p	4	0	0	0	0	0	0	0	0	0	0	–	–	0	–
Jeff Treadway	ph	1	1	0	0	0	0	0	0	0	0	0	.000	.000	–	–
Mark Wohlers	p	2	0	0	0	0	0	0	0	0	0	0	–	–	0	–
Totals		6	200	20	44	6	0	3	19	20	48	15	.220	.295	2	.991

Pitcher	G	GS	CG	IP	H	R	ER	BB	SO	W-L	Sv	ERA
Steve Avery	2	2	0	12	11	5	5	3	11	0-1	0	3.75
Tom Glavine	2	2	2	17	10	3	3	4	8	1-1	0	1.59
Charlie Leibrandt	1	0	0	2	3	2	2	2	0	0-1	0	9.00
Jeff Reardon	2	0	0	1⅓	5	2	2	1	1	0-1	0	13.50
Pete Smith	1	0	0	3	3	0	0	0	0	0-0	0	0.00
John Smoltz	2	2	0	13⅓	13	5	4	7	12	1-0	0	2.70
Mike Stanton	4	0	0	5	3	0	0	2	1	0-0	1	0.00
Mark Wohlers	2	0	0	⅔	0	0	0	1	1	0-0	0	0.00
Totals	6	6	2	54⅓	45	17	16	18	33	2-4	1	2.65

Series MVP: Pat Borders, Toronto Blue Jays. **Series Outstanding Pitcher:** Jimmy Key, Toronto Blue Jays. **Average Length of Game:** 3 hours, 5 minutes. **Total Attendance:** 311,460. **Average Attendance:** 51,910 (52,057 at Skydome; 51,763 at Atlanta-Fulton County Stadium). **Umpires:** Jerry Crawford (NL), Bob Davidson (NL), Dan Morrison (AL), Mike Reilly (AL), John Shulock (AL), Joe West (NL). **Winning Player's Share:** $114,962. **Losing Player's Share:** $84,259.

Right: The Fall Classic heads north of the border. Canadian Mounties stand at attention with the playing of the national anthems before the start of the 1992 Series.

Below: Joe Carter's fourth-inning home run provided Toronto's only run in Game 1, but the team came back to win four of the next five to win the Series.

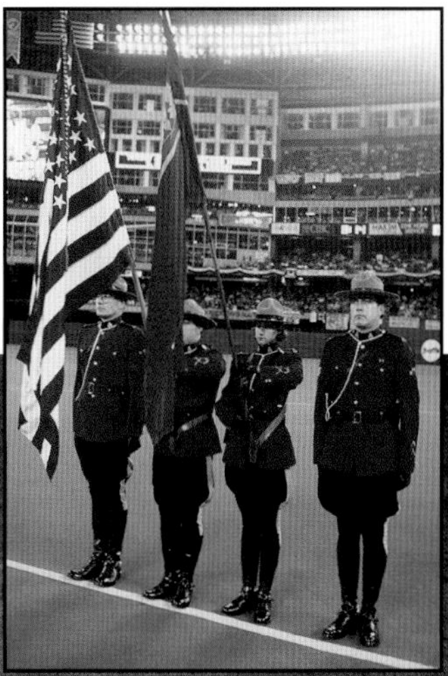

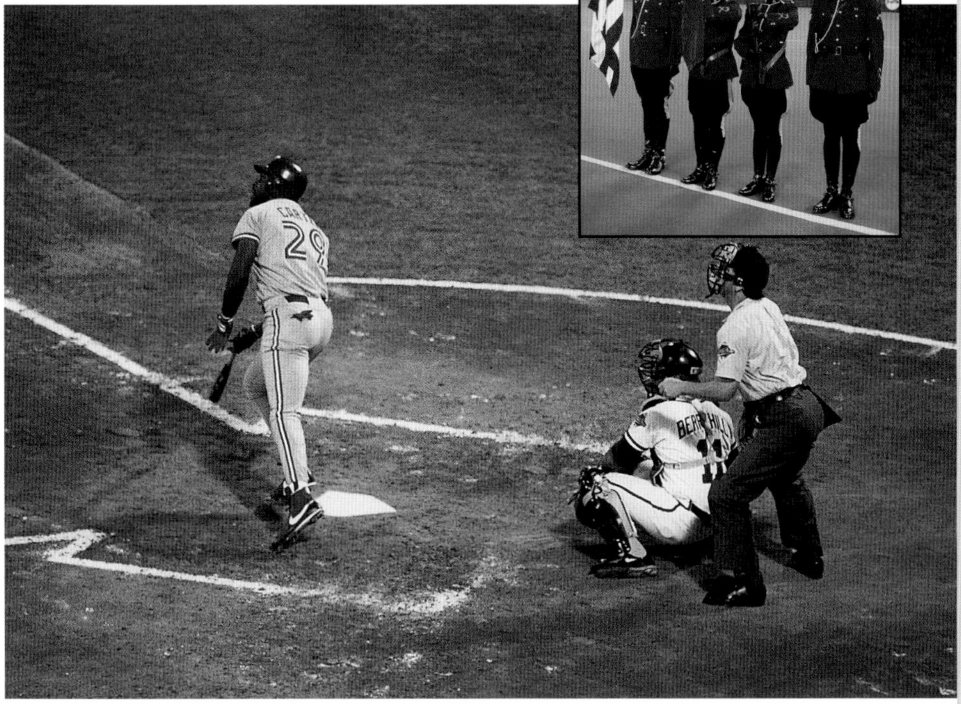

Below: Ed Sprague's two-run homer in the ninth inning of Game 2 puts Toronto ahead 5-4 in the game and ties the Series.

Jack Morris is the only pitcher to start the opening game of a World Series for three different teams. He won Game 1 of the 1984 Series with the Detroit Tigers and led the Minnesota Twins to victory in 1991. The 1992 Game 1 with Toronto is the only one he lost.

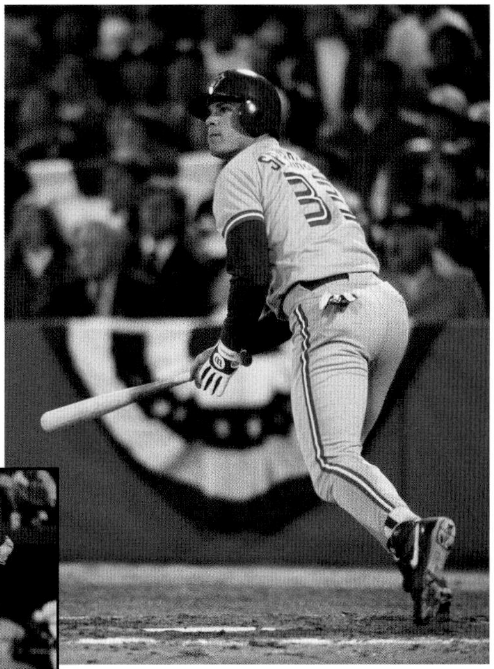

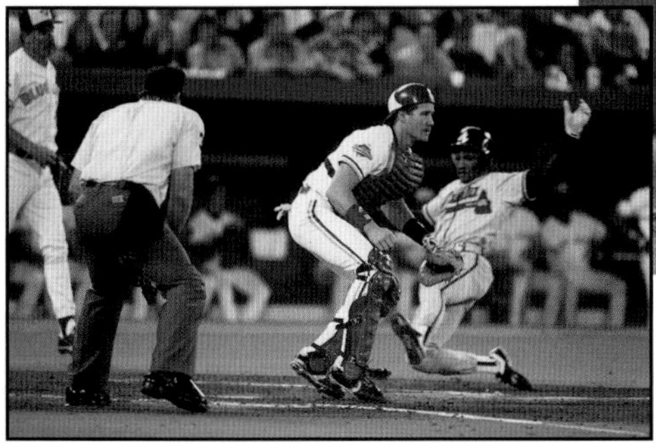

Left: Otis Nixon slides in with one of his two runs in Game 5 at SkyDome as catcher Pat Borders awaits the throw.

Game 1 Saturday, October 17 at Atlanta-Fulton County Stadium, Atlanta

	1	2	3	4	5	6	7	8	9	R	H	E
Toronto Blue Jays	0	0	0	1	0	0	0	0	0	1	4	0
Atlanta Braves	0	0	0	0	0	3	0	0	x	3	4	0

Pitchers Tor **Jack Morris** (L, 0-1), IP 6, H 4, R 3, ER 3, BB 5, SO 7; **Todd Stottlemyre**, IP 1, H 0, R 0, ER 0, BB 0, SO 2; **David Wells**, IP 1, H 0, R 0, ER 0, BB 1, SO 1
Atl **Tom Glavine** (W, 1-0), IP 9, H 4, R 1, ER 1, BB 0, SO 6

Top Performers at the Plate
Tor **Pat Borders**, 2 for 3
Atl **Damon Berryhill**, 1 for 4, 1 R, 3 RBI; **David Justice**, 0-for2, 1 R, 2 BB

HR-Tor/Carter; Atl/Berryhill. **SB**-Atl/Gant, Nixon. **Time** 2:37. **Attendance** 51,763.

Game 2 Sunday, October 18 at Atlanta-Fulton County Stadium, Atlanta

	1	2	3	4	5	6	7	8	9	R	H	E
Toronto Blue Jays	0	0	0	0	2	0	0	1	2	5	9	2
Atlanta Braves	0	1	0	1	2	0	0	0	0	4	5	1

Pitchers Tor **David Cone**, IP 4⅓, H 5, R 4, ER 3, BB 5, SO 2; **David Wells**, IP 1⅔, H 0, R 0, ER 0, BB 1, SO 2; **Todd Stottlemyre**, IP 1, H 0, R 0, ER 0, BB 0, SO 0; **Duane Ward** (W, 1-0), IP 1, H 0, R 0, ER 0, BB 0, SO 2; **Tom Henke** (Sv, 1), IP 1, H 0, R 0, ER 0, BB 1, SO 0
Atl **John Smoltz**, IP 7⅓, H 8, R 3, ER 2, BB 3, SO 8; **Mike Stanton**, IP ⅓, H 0, R 0, ER 0, BB 0, SO 0; **Jeff Reardon** (L, 0-1), IP 1⅓, H 1, R 2, ER 2, BB 1, SO 1

Top Performers at the Plate
Tor **David Cone**, 2 for 2, 1 RBI; **Ed Sprague**, 1 for 1, 1 R, 2 RBI
Atl **David Justice**, 1 for 3, 1 R, 1 RBI, 1 BB; **Deion Sanders**, 1 for 3, 1 R, 2 BB, 2 SB

2B-Tor/Alomar, Borders. **HR**-Tor/Sprague. **SB**-Atl/Blauser, Gant, Justice, Sanders 2. **Time** 3:30. **Attendance** 51,763.

Game 3 Tuesday, October 20 at Skydome, Toronto

	1	2	3	4	5	6	7	8	9	R	H	E
Atlanta Braves	0	0	0	0	0	1	0	1	0	2	9	0
Toronto Blue Jays	0	0	0	1	0	0	0	1	1	3	6	1

Pitchers Atl **Steve Avery** (L, 0-1), IP 8, H 5, R 3, ER 3, BB 1, SO 9; **Mark Wohlers**, IP ⅓, H 0, R 0, ER 0, BB 1, SO 0; **Mike Stanton**, IP 0, H 0, R 0, ER 0, BB 1, SO 0; **Jeff Reardon**, IP 0, H 1, R 0, ER 0, BB 0, SO 0
Tor **Juan Guzman**, IP 8, H 8, R 2, ER 1, BB 1, SO 7; **Duane Ward** (W, 2-0), IP 1, H 1, R 0, ER 0, BB 0, SO 2

Top Performers at the Plate
Atl **David Justice**, 1 for 3, 1 RBI, 1 BB; **Deion Sanders**, 3 for 4, 1 R
Tor **Joe Carter**, 1 for 3, 1 R, 1 RBI, 1 BB; **Kelly Gruber**, 1 for 2, 1 R, 1 RBI, 1 BB

2B-Atl/Sanders. **HR**-Tor/Carter, Gruber. **SB**-Atl/Nixon, Sanders; Tor/Alomar, Gruber. **Time** 2:49. **Attendance** 51,813.

Game 4 Wednesday, October 21 at Skydome, Toronto

	1	2	3	4	5	6	7	8	9	R	H	E
Atlanta Braves	0	0	0	0	0	0	0	1	0	1	5	0
Toronto Blue Jays	0	0	1	0	0	0	1	0	x	2	6	0

Pitchers Atl **Tom Glavine** (L, 1-1), IP 8, H 6, R 2, ER 2, BB 4, SO 2
Tor **Jimmy Key** (W, 1-0), IP 7⅔, H 5, R 1, ER 1, BB 0, SO 6; **Duane Ward**, IP ⅓, H 0, R 0, ER 0, BB 0, SO 1; **Tom Henke** (Sv, 2), IP 1, H 0, R 0, ER 0, BB 0, SO 1

Top Performers at the Plate
Atl **Ron Gant**, 1 for 3, 1 R; **Otis Nixon**, 2 for 4
Tor **Pat Borders**, 1 for 3, 1 R, 1 RBI; **Devon White**, 3 for 4, 1 RBI

2B-Atl/Gant; Tor/White. **HR**-Tor/Borders. **SB**-Atl/Blauser, Nixon; Tor/Alomar. **Time** 2:21. **Attendance** 52,090.

Game 5 Thursday, October 22 at Skydome, Toronto

	1	2	3	4	5	6	7	8	9	R	H	E
Atlanta Braves	1	0	0	1	5	0	0	0	0	7	13	0
Toronto Blue Jays	0	1	0	1	0	0	0	0	0	2	6	0

Pitchers Atl **John Smoltz** (W, 1-0), IP 6, H 5, R 2, ER 2, BB 4, SO 4; **Mike Stanton** (Sv, 1), IP 3, H 1, R 0, ER 0, BB 0, SO 1
Tor **Jack Morris** (L, 0-2), IP 4⅔, H 9, R 7, ER 7, BB 1, SO 5; **David Wells**, IP 1⅓, H 1, R 0, ER 0, BB 0, SO 0; **Mike Timlin**, IP 1, H 0, R 0, ER 0, BB 0, SO 0; **Mark Eichhorn**, IP 1, H 0, R 0, ER 0, BB 0, SO 1; **Todd Stottlemyre**, IP 1, H 3, R 0, ER 0, BB 0, SO 1

Top Performers at the Plate
Atl **David Justice**, 1 for 3, 2 R, 1 RBI, 1 BB; **Otis Nixon**, 3 for 5, 2 R, 2 SB
Tor **Pat Borders**, 2 for 4, 2 RBI; **John Olerud**, 2 for 3, 2 R

2B-Atl/Nixon, Pendleton 2; Tor/Borders. **HR**-Atl/Justice, Smith. **SB**-Atl/Nixon 2. **Time** 3:05. **Attendance** 52,268.

Game 6 Saturday, October 24 at Atlanta-Fulton County Stadium, Atlanta

	1	2	3	4	5	6	7	8	9	10	11	R	H	E
Toronto Blue Jays	1	0	0	1	0	0	0	0	0	0	2	4	14	1
Atlanta Braves	0	0	1	0	0	0	0	0	1	0	1	3	8	1

Pitchers Tor **David Cone**, IP 6, H 4, R 1, ER 1, BB 3, SO 6; **Todd Stottlemyre**, IP ⅔, H 1, R 0, ER 0, BB 0, SO 1; **David Wells**, IP ⅓, H 0, R 0, ER 0, BB 0, SO 0; **Duane Ward**, IP 1, H 0, R 0, ER 0, BB 1, SO 1; **Tom Henke**, IP 1⅓, H 2, R 1, ER 1, BB 1, SO 0; **Jimmy Key** (W, 2-0), IP 1⅓, H 1, R 1, ER 0, BB 0, SO 0; **Mike Timlin** (Sv, 1), IP ⅓, H 0, R 0, ER 0, BB 0, SO 0
Atl **Steve Avery**, IP 4, H 6, R 2, ER 2, BB 2, SO 2; **Pete Smith**, IP 3, H 3, R 0, ER 0, BB 0, SO 0; **Mike Stanton**, IP 1⅔, H 2, R 0, ER 0, BB 1, SO 0; **Mark Wohlers**, IP ⅓, H 0, R 0, ER 0, BB 0, SO 0; **Charlie Leibrandt** (L, 0-1), IP 2, H 3, R 2, ER 2, BB 0, SO 0

Top Performers at the Plate
Tor **Roberto Alomar**, 3 for 6, 1 R; **Devon White**, 2 for 5, 2 R, 1 HBP
Atl **Jeff Blauser**, 3 for 5, 2 R; **Deion Sanders**, 2 for 3, 1 R, 2 SB

2B-Tor/Borders, Carter 2, Winfield; Atl/Sanders. **HR**-Tor/Maldonado. **SB**-Tor/Alomar, White; Atl/Sanders 2. **Time** 4:07. **Attendance** 51,763.

Toronto Blue Jays (4) vs. Philadelphia Phillies (2)

The Toronto Blue Jays repeated as American League champs in 1993, with several new faces playing key roles: Paul Molitor brought a .332 average in his first year in Toronto, and all-stars Rickey Henderson and Dave Stewart came over from Oakland. On the other side of the diamond, the Philadelphia Phillies put together their best season in 16 years with a gritty bunch that included Lenny Dykstra, John Kruk and Darren Daulton. The Jays and Phils were knotted in a 4-4 tie after five innings of Game 1 until Toronto's John Olerud broke the deadlock with a home run in the bottom of the sixth. Toronto put the game out of reach with a three-run seventh, Roberto Alomar's double supplying two of the runs. Philadelphia jumped out to a 5-0 lead in Game 2 and held on for a 6-4 win. Jim Eisenreich drove in three runs with a third-inning homer, and Dykstra drilled a solo shot in the seventh. Forced to do without the designated hitter in Game 3 in Philadelphia, Toronto manager Cito Gaston benched Olerud, the American League batting champion, and put his usual DH, Paul Molitor, in at first base. Molitor made the move worthwhile, chipping in a two-run triple in the first and one-run homer in the third. Toronto's 13-hit, 10-run barrage in the third game was only a hint of things to come. Game 4 started with the Blue Jays bringing three runs across in the top of the first. Philadelphia retaliated with its own two-out rally in the bottom of the inning to go ahead 4-3; Milt Thompson's bases-loaded triple drove in three. Dykstra extended the lead to 6-3 in the second with his first of two home runs. Toronto kept coming, and each side had seven runs after four innings. Building on a five-run inning, the Phillies staked a 14-9 lead after seven. Toronto scored two and had the bases loaded in the eighth when Mitch "Wild Thing" Williams, Philadelphia's top reliever, entered the game. He struck out Ed Sprague for the second out of the inning, but Henderson sent two runners in with a single, and Devon White tripled home two more to give Toronto a 15-14 edge. Remarkably, no more runs crossed the plate for either side, and the Blue Jays came out triumphant in the highest-scoring game in World Series history. Curt Schilling turned things around dramatically in Game 5, shutting Toronto out on five hits to keep the Phillies alive. In Game 6, Molitor's hot bat produced a first-inning RBI triple and a solo homer in the fifth to help the Blue Jays grab a four-run lead. Dave Stewart limited the Phillies to one run through six, but in the top of the seventh,

Left: In one of baseball's most dramatic moments, Joe Carter connects for a three-run homer to give the Blue Jays the title in the sixth game of the 1993 Series.

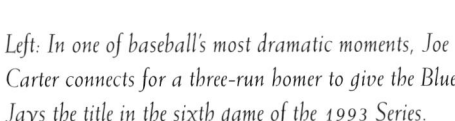

1993 WORLD SERIES COMPOSITE STATISTICS

TORONTO BLUE JAYS/Cito Gaston, Manager

Player	pos	G	AB	R	H	2B	3B	HR	RBI	BB	SO	SB	BA	SA	E	FPct
Roberto Alomar	2b	6	25	5	12	2	1	0	6	2	3	4	.480	.640	2	.938
Pat Borders	c	6	23	2	7	0	0	1	2	1	0	0	.304	.304	1	.981
Rob Butler	ph	2	2	1	1	0	0	0	0	0	0	0	.500	.500	–	–
Willie Canate	pr	1	0	0	0	0	0	0	0	0	0	0	–	–	–	–
Joe Carter	rf	6	25	6	7	1	0	2	8	0	4	0	.280	.560	2	.867
Tony Castillo	p	2	1	0	0	0	0	0	0	0	1	0	.000	.000	0	–
Danny Cox	p	3	1	0	0	0	0	0	0	0	0	0	.000	.000	0	1.000
Mark Eichhorn	p	1	0	0	0	0	0	0	0	0	0	0	–	–	0	–
Tony Fernandez	ss	6	21	2	7	1	0	0	9	3	3	0	.333	.381	0	1.000
Alfredo Griffin	pr-3b	3	0	0	0	0	0	0	0	0	0	0	–	–	0	–
Juan Guzman	p	2	2	0	0	0	0	0	0	0	1	0	.000	.000	0	1.000
Rickey Henderson	lf	6	22	6	5	2	0	0	2	5	2	1	.227	.318	0	1.000
Pat Hentgen	p	1	3	0	0	0	0	0	0	0	1	0	.000	.000	–	–
Randy Knorr	c	1	0	0	0	0	0	0	0	0	0	0	–	–	0	1.000
Al Leiter	p	3	1	0	1	1	0	0	0	0	0	0	1.000	2.000	0	–
Paul Molitor	dh-1b-3b	6	24	10	12	2	2	2	8	3	0	1	.500	1.000	0	1.000
John Olerud	1b	5	17	5	4	1	0	1	2	4	1	0	.235	.471	0	1.000
Ed Sprague	3b-ph-1b	5	15	0	1	0	0	0	2	1	6	0	.067	.067	2	.867
Dave Stewart	p	2	0	0	0	0	0	0	0	0	0	0	–	–	0	1.000
Todd Stottlemyre	p	1	0	0	0	0	0	0	0	1	0	0	–	–	0	–
Mike Timlin	p	2	0	0	0	0	0	0	0	0	0	0	–	–	0	–
Duane Ward	p	4	0	0	0	0	0	0	0	0	0	0	–	–	0	–
Devon White	cf	6	24	8	7	3	2	1	7	4	7	1	.292	.708	0	1.000
Totals		**6**	**206**	**45**	**64**	**13**	**5**	**6**	**45**	**25**	**30**	**7**	**.311**	**.510**	**7**	**.967**

Pitcher	G	GS	CG	IP	H	R	ER	BB	SO	W-L	Sv	ERA
Tony Castillo	2	0	0	3⅓	6	3	3	3	1	1-0	0	8.10
Danny Cox	3	0	0	3⅓	6	3	3	5	6	0-0	0	8.10
Mark Eichhorn	1	0	0	⅓	1	0	0	1	0	0-0	0	0.00
Juan Guzman	2	2	0	12	10	6	5	8	12	0-1	0	3.75
Pat Hentgen	1	1	0	6	5	1	1	3	6	1-0	0	1.50
Al Leiter	3	0	0	7	12	6	6	2	5	1-0	0	7.71
Dave Stewart	2	2	0	12	10	9	9	8	8	0-1	0	6.75
Todd Stottlemyre	1	1	0	2	3	6	6	4	1	0-0	0	27.00
Mike Timlin	2	0	0	2⅓	2	0	0	4	0	0-0	0	0.00
Duane Ward	4	0	0	4⅔	3	2	1	0	7	1-0	2	1.93
Totals	**6**	**6**	**0**	**53**	**58**	**36**	**34**	**34**	**50**	**4-2**	**2**	**5.77**

PHILADELPHIA PHILLIES/Jim Fregosi, Manager

Player	pos	G	AB	R	H	2B	3B	HR	RBI	BB	SO	SB	BA	SA	E	FPct
Larry Andersen	p	4	0	0	0	0	0	0	0	0	0	0	–	–	0	–
Kim Batiste	3b	3	0	0	0	0	0	0	0	0	0	0	–	–	0	1.000
Wes Chamberlain	ph	2	2	0	0	0	0	0	0	0	1	0	.000	.000	–	–
Darren Daulton	c	6	23	4	5	2	0	1	4	4	5	0	.217	.435	0	1.000
Mariano Duncan	2b-dh	6	29	5	10	0	1	0	2	1	7	3	.345	.414	1	.966
Lenny Dykstra	cf	6	23	9	8	1	0	4	8	7	4	4	.348	.913	0	1.000
Jim Eisenreich	rf	6	26	3	6	0	0	1	7	2	4	0	.231	.346	0	1.000
Tommy Greene	p	1	1	1	1	0	0	0	0	0	0	0	1.000	1.000	0	–
Dave Hollins	3b	6	23	5	6	1	0	0	2	6	5	0	.261	.304	0	1.000
Pete Incaviglia	ph-lf	4	8	0	1	0	0	0	1	0	4	0	.125	.125	0	1.000
Danny Jackson	p	1	1	0	0	0	0	0	0	0	1	0	.000	.000	0	–
Ricky Jordan	dh-ph	3	10	0	2	0	0	0	0	0	2	0	.200	.200	–	–
John Kruk	1b	6	23	4	8	1	0	0	4	7	7	0	.348	.391	0	1.000
Roger Mason	p	4	1	0	0	0	0	0	0	0	0	0	.000	.000	0	–
Mickey Morandini	ph-2b	3	5	1	1	0	0	0	0	1	2	0	.200	.200	0	1.000
Terry Mulholland	p	2	0	0	0	0	0	0	0	0	0	0	–	–	0	1.000
Ben Rivera	p	1	0	0	0	0	0	0	0	0	0	0	–	–	0	–
Curt Schilling	p	2	2	0	1	0	0	0	0	0	1	0	.500	.500	0	1.000
Kevin Stocker	ss	6	19	1	4	1	0	0	1	5	5	0	.211	.263	0	1.000
Bobby Thigpen	p	2	0	0	0	0	0	0	0	0	0	0	–	–	0	1.000
Milt Thompson	lf-pr	6	16	3	5	1	1	1	6	1	2	0	.313	.688	1	.909
David West	p	3	0	0	0	0	0	0	0	0	0	0	–	–	0	–
Mitch Williams	p	3	0	0	0	0	0	0	0	0	0	0	–	–	0	1.000
Totals		**6**	**212**	**36**	**58**	**7**	**2**	**7**	**35**	**34**	**50**	**7**	**.274**	**.425**	**2**	**.991**

Pitcher	G	GS	CG	IP	H	R	ER	BB	SO	W-L	Sv	ERA
Larry Andersen	4	0	0	3⅔	5	5	5	3	3	0-0	0	12.27
Tommy Greene	1	1	0	2⅓	7	7	7	4	1	0-0	0	27.00
Danny Jackson	1	1	0	5	6	4	4	1	1	0-1	0	7.20
Roger Mason	4	0	0	7⅔	4	1	1	1	7	0-0	0	1.17
Terry Mulholland	2	2	0	10⅔	14	8	8	3	5	1-0	0	6.75
Ben Rivera	1	0	0	1⅓	4	4	4	2	2	0-0	0	27.00
Curt Schilling	2	2	1	15⅓	13	7	6	5	9	1-1	0	3.52
Bobby Thigpen	2	0	0	2⅔	1	0	0	1	0	0-0	0	0.00
David West	3	0	0	1	1	3	3	1	0	0-0	0	27.00
Mitch Williams	3	0	0	2⅔	5	6	6	4	1	0-2	1	20.25
Totals	**6**	**6**	**1**	**52⅓**	**64**	**45**	**44**	**25**	**30**	**2-4**	**1**	**7.57**

Series MVP: Paul Molitor, Toronto Blue Jays. **Series Outstanding Pitcher:** Duane Ward, Toronto Blue Jays. **Average Length of Game:** 3 hours, 29 minutes. **Total Attendance:** 344,394. **Average Attendance:** 57,399 (52,089 at Skydome; 62,709 at Veterans Stadium).
Umpires: Dana DeMuth (NL), Mark Johnson (AL), Tim McClelland (AL), Dave Phillips (AL), Paul Runge (NL), Charlie Williams (NL). **Winning Player's Share:** $127,920. **Losing Player's Share:** $91,222.

Right: Paul Molitor added to his impressive October resume by batting .500 and scoring 10 runs in 1993.

Below: The Phillies and Blue Jays paired up in an action-packed Series in 1993.

Left: Pitcher Todd Stottlemyre is about to be tagged out by Dave Hollins at third base in the second inning of Game 4.

Right: With his second homer of Game 4, Lenny Dykstra helps Philadelphia extend its lead to five runs in the fifth inning—a lead they would ultimately lose.

In addition to being the highest-scoring game in World Series history, Game 4 in 1993 is also the longest nine-inning game in postseason play.

Game 1 Saturday, October 16 at Skydome, Toronto

	1	2	3	4	5	6	7	8	9	R	H	E
Philadelphia Phillies	2	0	1	0	1	0	0	0	1	5	11	1
Toronto Blue Jays	0	2	1	0	1	1	3	0	x	8	10	3

Pitchers Phi **Curt Schilling** (L, 0-1), IP $6\frac{1}{3}$, H 8, R 7, ER 6, BB 2, SO 3; **David West**, IP 0, H 2, R 1, ER 1, BB 0, SO 0; **Larry Andersen**, IP $\frac{2}{3}$, H 0, R 0, ER 0, BB 1, SO 1; **Roger Mason**, IP 1, H 0, R 0, ER 0, BB 0, SO 1
Tor **Juan Guzman**, IP 5, H 5, R 4, ER 4, BB 4, SO 6; **Al Leiter** (W, 1-0), IP $2\frac{2}{3}$, H 4, R 0, ER 0, BB 1, SO 2; **Duane Ward** (Sv, 1), IP $1\frac{1}{3}$, H 2, R 1, ER 0, BB 0, SO 3

Top Performers at the Plate
Phi **Mariano Duncan**, 3 for 5, 2 R; **John Kruk**, 3 for 4, 2 R, 2 RBI, 1 BB
Tor **John Olerud**, 2 for 3, 2 R, 1 RBI, 1 BB; **Devon White**, 2 for 4, 3 R, 2 RBI

2B-Tor/Alomar, White. **3B**-Phi/Duncan. **HR**-Tor/Olerud, White. **SB**-Phi/Duncan, Dykstra; Tor/Alomar. **Time** 3:27. **Attendance** 52,011.

Game 2 Sunday, October 17 at Skydome, Toronto

	1	2	3	4	5	6	7	8	9	R	H	E
Philadelphia Phillies	0	0	5	0	0	0	1	0	0	6	12	0
Toronto Blue Jays	0	0	0	2	0	1	0	1	0	4	8	0

Pitchers Phi **Terry Mulholland** (W, 1-0), IP $5\frac{2}{3}$, H 7, R 3, ER 3, BB 2, SO 4; **Roger Mason**, IP $1\frac{2}{3}$, H 1, R 1, ER 1, BB 0, SO 2; **Mitch Williams** (Sv, 1), IP $1\frac{2}{3}$, H 0, R 0, ER 0, BB 2, SO 0
Tor **Dave Stewart** (L, 0-1), IP 6, H 6, R 5, ER 5, BB 4, SO 6; **Tony Castillo**, IP 1, H 3, R 1, ER 1, BB 0, SO 0; **Mark Eichhorn**, IP $\frac{1}{3}$, H 1, R 0, ER 0, BB 1, SO 0; **Mike Timlin**, IP $1\frac{2}{3}$, H 2, R 0, ER 0, BB 0, SO 2

Top Performers at the Plate
Phi **Lenny Dykstra**, 2 for 4, 2 R, 1 RBI, 1 BB; **Jim Eisenreich**, 1 for 4, 1 R, 3 RBI, 1 BB
Tor **Tony Fernandez**, 2 for 3, 1 RBI, 1 BB; **Paul Molitor**, 2 for 3, 2 R, 1 BB

2B-Tor/Fernandez, Molitor, White. **HR**-Phi/Dykstra, Eisenreich; Tor/Carter. **SB**-Tor/Alomar, Molitor. **Time** 3:35. **Attendance** 52,062.

Game 3 Tuesday, October 19 at Veterans Stadium, Philadelphia

	1	2	3	4	5	6	7	8	9	R	H	E
Toronto Blue Jays	3	0	1	0	0	1	3	0	2	10	13	1
Philadelphia Phillies	0	0	0	0	0	1	1	0	1	3	9	0

Pitchers Tor **Pat Hentgen** (W, 1-0), IP 6, H 5, R 1, ER 1, BB 3, SO 6; **Danny Cox**, IP 2, H 3, R 1, ER 1, BB 2, SO 2; **Duane Ward**, IP 1, H 1, R 1, ER 1, BB 0, SO 2
Phi **Danny Jackson** (L, 0-1), IP 5, H 6, R 4, ER 4, BB 1, SO 1; **Ben Rivera**, IP $1\frac{1}{3}$, H 4, R 4, ER 4, BB 2, SO 3; **Bobby Thigpen**, IP $1\frac{2}{3}$, H 0, R 0, ER 0, BB 1, SO 0; **Larry Andersen**, IP 1, H 3, R 2, ER 2, BB 0, SO 0

Top Performers at the Plate
Tor **Roberto Alomar**, 4 for 5, 2 R, 2 RBI, 2 SB; **Paul Molitor**, 3 for 4, 3 R, 3 RBI, 1 BB
Phi **John Kruk**, 2 for 3, 1 R, 2 BB; **Milt Thompson**, 2 for 2, 2 R, 1 RBI

2B-Tor/Henderson; Phi/Kruk. **3B**-Tor/Alomar, Molitor, White. **HR**-Tor/Molitor; Phi/Thompson. **SB**-Tor/Alomar 2. **Time** 3:16. **Attendance** 62,689.

Game 4 Wednesday, October 20 at Veterans Stadium, Philadelphia

	1	2	3	4	5	6	7	8	9	R	H	E
Toronto Blue Jays	3	0	4	0	0	2	0	6	0	15	18	0
Philadelphia Phillies	4	2	0	1	5	1	1	0	0	14	14	0

Pitchers Tor **Todd Stottlemyre**, IP 2, H 3, R 6, ER 6, BB 4, SO 1; **Al Leiter**, IP $2\frac{2}{3}$, H 8, R 6, ER 6, BB 0, SO 1; **Tony Castillo** (W, 1-0), IP $2\frac{1}{3}$, H 3, R 2, ER 2, BB 3, SO 1; **Mike Timlin**, IP $\frac{2}{3}$, H 0, R 0, ER 0, BB 0, SO 2; **Duane Ward** (Sv, 2), IP $1\frac{1}{3}$, H 0, R 0, ER 0, BB 0, SO 2
Phi **Tommy Greene**, IP $2\frac{1}{3}$, H 7, R 7, ER 7, BB 4, SO 1; **Roger Mason**, IP $2\frac{2}{3}$, H 2, R 0, ER 0, BB 1, SO 2; **David West**, IP 1, H 3, R 2, ER 2, BB 0, SO 0; **Larry Andersen**, IP $1\frac{1}{3}$, H 2, R 3, ER 3, BB 1, SO 2; **Mitch Williams** (L, 0-1), IP $\frac{2}{3}$, H 3, R 3, ER 3, BB 1, SO 1; **Bobby Thigpen**, IP 1, H 1, R 0, ER 0, BB 0, SO 0

Top Performers at the Plate
Tor **Tony Fernandez**, 3 for 6, 2 R, 5 RBI; **Devon White**, 3 for 5, 2 R, 4 RBI, 1 BB
Phi **Lenny Dykstra**, 4 for 5, 4 R, 4 RBI, 1 BB, 2 HR; **Milt Thompson**, 3 for 5, 1 R, 5 RBI

2B-Tor/Carter, Henderson, Leiter, Molitor, White; Phi/Dykstra, Hollins, Thompson. **3B**-Tor/White; Phi/Thompson. **HR**-Phi/Daulton, Dykstra 2. **SB**-Tor/Henderson, White; Phi/Duncan, Dykstra. **Time** 4:14. **Attendance** 62,731.

Game 5 Thursday, October 21 at Veterans Stadium, Philadelphia

	1	2	3	4	5	6	7	8	9	R	H	E
Toronto Blue Jays	0	0	0	0	0	0	0	0	0	0	5	1
Philadelphia Phillies	1	1	0	0	0	0	0	0	x	2	5	1

Pitchers Tor **Juan Guzman** (L, 0-1), IP 7, H 5, R 2, ER 1, BB 4, SO 6; **Danny Cox**, IP 1, H 0, R 0, ER 0, BB 2, SO 3
Phi **Curt Schilling** (W, 1-1), IP 9, H 5, R 0, ER 0, BB 3, SO 6

Top Performers at the Plate
Tor **Pat Borders**, 2 for 3
Phi **John Kruk**, 1 for 3, 1 RBI, 1 BB; **Kevin Stocker**, 1 for 2, 1 RBI, 1 BB

2B-Phi/Daulton, Stocker. **SB**-Phi/Dykstra. **Time** 2:53. **Attendance** 62,706.

Game 6 Saturday, October 23 at Skydome, Toronto

	1	2	3	4	5	6	7	8	9	R	H	E
Philadelphia Phillies	0	0	0	1	0	0	5	0	0	6	7	0
Toronto Blue Jays	3	0	0	1	1	0	0	0	3	8	10	2

Pitchers Phi **Terry Mulholland**, IP 5, H 7, R 5, ER 5, BB 1, SO 1; **Roger Mason**, IP $2\frac{1}{3}$, H 1, R 0, ER 0, BB 0, SO 2; **David West**, IP 0, H 0, R 0, ER 0, BB 1, SO 0; **Larry Andersen**, IP $\frac{2}{3}$, H 0, R 0, ER 0, BB 1, SO 0; **Mitch Williams** (L, 0-2), IP $\frac{1}{3}$, H 2, R 3, ER 3, BB 1, SO 0
Tor **Dave Stewart**, IP 6, H 4, R 4, ER 4, BB 4, SO 2; **Danny Cox**, IP $\frac{1}{3}$, H 3, R 2, ER 2, BB 1, SO 1; **Al Leiter**, IP $1\frac{2}{3}$, H 0, R 0, ER 0, BB 1, SO 2; **Duane Ward** (W, 1-0), IP 1, H 0, R 0, ER 0, BB 0, SO 0

Top Performers at the Plate
Phi **Lenny Dykstra**, 1 for 3, 1 R, 3 RBI, 2 BB; **Jim Eisenreich**, 2 for 5, 1 RBI
Tor **Joe Carter**, 1 for 4, 1 R, 4 RBI, 1 SF; **Paul Molitor**, 3 for 5, 3 R, 2 RBI

2B-Phi/Daulton; Tor/Alomar, Olerud. **3B**-Tor/Molitor. **HR**-Phi/Dykstra; Tor/Carter, Molitor. **SB**-Phi/Duncan, Dykstra. **Time** 3:27. **Attendance** 52,195.

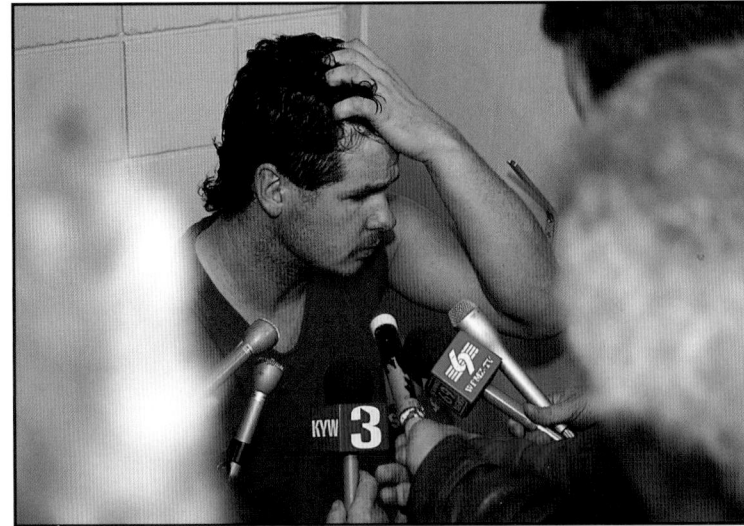

Above: As Darren Daulton slides in to try to break up the play, Roberto Alomar makes an acrobatic throw to turn a double play.

Below: Devon White caps off a wild inning in a wild game by driving in two runs with a triple in the eighth inning of Game 4. The hit gave the Blue Jays a 15-14 edge.

The agony (above) and the ecstasy (right). While Joe Carter could run glee-fully around the bases after hitting his game- and Series-winning home run in Game 6, pitcher Mitch Williams has to respond to questions about the pitch that got away.

Dykstra led his team to a gutty comeback. He connected for his fourth homer of the Series, a three-run bomb, to come within a run, and Dave Hollins's RBI single and Pete Incaviglia's pinch-hit sacrifice fly put the Phillies in the lead. The one-run margin held into the ninth, and manager Jim Fregosi went to his regular-season relief ace to close the door. The Wild Thing walked the first batter he faced and gave up a one-out single to Molitor to put the winning run on base, with Joe Carter representing the go-ahead run at the plate. Williams pitched to a 2-2 count, then Carter launched Williams's next offering over the left-field fence. Carter and the rest of Toronto leaped for joy with the come-from-behind Series-winning blast. Toronto had its second straight world championship, the first back-to-back winner since the 1977–78 Yankees, and the clinching sixth game of the 1993 Series would measure up with 1960's Game 7 and 1975's Game 6 as an all-time-great postseason moment.

In the Clutch
Dramatic Series Endings

The World Series is all about drama. After a grueling regular season and playoffs, the two teams left standing have seven games to determine who wins it all—and sometimes it comes down to one play, one instant of greatness when it matters most. This book is filled with stories of such dramatic moments, and when the play comes in the final game, it takes on even greater magnitude. The clutch plays described here helped teams wrap up the all-important clinching game of the Series.

Series Won in the Last At-Bat

Nine World Series have been won in the bottom of the last inning of the final game, and five were in a winner-take-all Game 7. (Actually, one of those was a Game 8 necessitated by a tie game earlier in the Series.)

◆ **Gardner's 10th-Inning Sac Fly Ends Series — Larry Gardner, Boston Red Sox, October 16, 1912**

Game 8, 10th inning, 2-2 tie, 1 out, runners on second and third. After falling behind by a run in the top of the 10th inning, Boston closed the door on the New York Giants with Larry Gardner's run-scoring fly ball in the deciding game of 1912. Given new life following two Giant misplays earlier in the inning, the Red Sox won baseball's first extra-inning Series clincher.

◆ **Bad Hop in 12th Gives Washington Title — Earl McNeely, Washington Senators, October 10, 1924**

Game 7, 12th inning, 3-3 tie, 1 out, runners on first and second. Both sides went scoreless for three and a half innings before Washington's Earl McNeely hit a bouncing single over the head of New York third baseman Fred Lindstrom, breaking a tie score in the final game of the 1924 Series. The 12th-inning hit ended the longest Game 7 in history.

◆ **Miller Doubles Off Scoreboard to Drive in Series-Winner — Bing Miller, Philadelphia Athletics, October 14, 1929**

Game 5, 9th inning, 2-2 tie, 2 outs, runners on first and second. Chicago's Pat Malone carried a 2-0 lead into the ninth, but Philadelphia's Mule Haas tied it with a one-out homer in the bottom of the inning. Four batters and one out later, a long double by Bing Miller sent in the go-ahead run. The three-run ninth inning sealed the five-game Series victory for Philadelphia.

◆ **Detroit Takes Game 6 Clincher on Goslin's RBI Single — Goose Goslin, Detroit Tigers, October 7, 1935**

Game 6, 9th inning, 3-3 tie, 2 outs, runner on second. Goose Goslin's two-out single in the last of the ninth inning wrapped up a six-game victory for Detroit in the 1935 Series. In the top half of the inning, Chicago had failed to capitalize on a leadoff triple by Stan Hack when pitcher Tommy Bridges retired the next three batters with a strikeout, an infield grounder and a fly ball.

◆ **Martin's 12th Series Hit Topples Dodgers — Billy Martin, New York Yankees, October 5, 1953**

Game 6, 9th inning, 3-3 tie, 1 out, runners on first and second. The Yankees' fifth straight World Series championship wasn't secured until the last batter of 1953. The Brooklyn Dodgers were looking to send the Series to a deciding seventh game when they brought in two runs in the top of the ninth, but Billy Martin ended that threat when his single up the middle sent in the winning run for New York.

◆ **Mazeroski Wins Series for Pittsburgh in Dramatic Fashion — Bill Mazeroski, Pittsburgh Pirates, October 13, 1960**

Game 7, 9th inning, 9-9 tie, no outs, bases empty. Bill Mazeroski personified "clutch" with his Game 7, ninth-inning homer in 1960. The Yankees had tied the see-saw final game by scoring two in the top of the inning after the Pirates scored five in the eighth. Pittsburgh's second baseman hit only 11 homers all season long, but he led off the bottom of the ninth with the historic round-tripper.

Above: Ending a truly classic Fall Classic, Gene Larkin delivered a clutch 10th-inning single in Game 7 of 1991.

Above left: Joe Carter celebrates his Series-winning 1993 blast.

Above: The improbable champions of 1997, the Florida Marlins defeated the Indians in the seventh game on Edgar Renteria's single in the 11th inning.

More Late-Game Heroics

Beyond the relatively few "walk-off" hits that have won a World Series in the bottom of the last inning, many other key hits, gutsy baserunning moves or clutch pitches late in the final game made the difference between winning and losing.

◆ **Classic Series Ends With Pinch-Hit Single in 10th — Gene Larkin, Minnesota Twins, October 27, 1991**

Game 7, 10th inning, 0-0 tie, 1 out, bases loaded. For nine and a half innings, neither side could score in the seventh game of the 1991 Series. Minnesota's Jack Morris got himself out of a tight spot in the eighth and shut Atlanta out in ten innings. Finally, the Twins broke the scoreless tie in the bottom of the 10th when Gene Larkin's bases-loaded, pinch-single ended the fifth one-run game of the Series.

◆ **Carter's Blast Gives Toronto Come-From-Behind Victory — Joe Carter, Toronto Blue Jays, October 23, 1993**

Game 6, 9th inning, Toronto trailing 6-5, 1 out, runners on first and third. Toronto had a one-game edge over the Phillies in the 1993 Series, but the Jays were trailing by a run in Game 6 when Joe Carter stepped to the plate in the last of the ninth. His game-winning three-run blast marked the only time a team came from behind to win the Series with a homer.

◆ **Cleveland Loses Series in 11th Inning — Edgar Renteria, Florida Marlins, October 26, 1997**

Game 7, 11th inning, 2-2 tie, 2 outs, bases loaded. Marlin Edgar Renteria crushed the hearts and hopes of Cleveland when his two-out, bases-loaded single in the bottom of the 11th inning ended the final game of the 1997 Series. Florida had extended the game into extra innings on Craig Counsell's clutch RBI sacrifice fly in the ninth after the team was held to two hits in the first eight innings.

Right: The heroes of St. Louis' dramatic 1942 victory head to the dugout after downing the Yankees. Whitey Kurowski (center) contributed a clutch homer in the top of the ninth of the final game, and Johnny Beazley (left of Kurowski) pitched out of a jam in the bottom of the inning.

Boston Comes Back in Fifth Game to Clinch Series — Duffy Lewis, Harry Hooper and Rube Foster, Boston Red Sox, October 13, 1915**

Although Boston held a three-games-to-one edge, the Phillies hoped to extend the 1915 Series to a sixth game when they took a 4-2 lead in Game 5. Such hopes hit a setback when Duffy Lewis hit a game-tying two-run homer in the eighth, and then were dashed further when Harry Hooper hit his second round-tripper of the day to give the Sox a 5-4 lead in the top of the ninth. Boston starter Rube Foster worked a perfect ninth inning to make Hooper's shot hold up as the Series winner.

◆ **Giants Sneak By Yankees 1-0 in Series Final — Johnny Rawlings and George Kelly, New York Giants, October 13, 1921**

After the New York Giants scored a run in the first inning in the final game of the 1921 Series, pitchers Art Nehf and Waite Hoyt put zeroes up on the scoreboard the rest of the way. In the last of the ninth, the Yanks got a runner on base with one out. Second baseman Johnny Rawlings's lunging stop of Frank Baker's hard grounder started a 4-3-5 double play that secured the Series' final out. George Kelly's throw to Frankie Frisch at third nabbed Aaron Ward to complete the play.

◆ **Peckinpaugh Error Opens Door for Series-Winning Hit — Kiki Cuyler and Red Oldham, Pittsburgh Pirates, October 15, 1925**

The Pittsburgh Pirates came back from a three-games-to-one deficit in the 1925 Series to force Washington to a seventh game, but when they fell behind in the top of the eighth inning of that game, it seemed as if it might all be for naught. Suddenly, given new life by Roger Peckinpaugh's costly errors, Kiki Cuyler knocked his 11th hit of the Series to drive in the winning runs with a two-out double. Red Oldham, making his first and only postseason appearance, then came on and got the Senators 1-2-3 in the ninth, including two strikeouts.

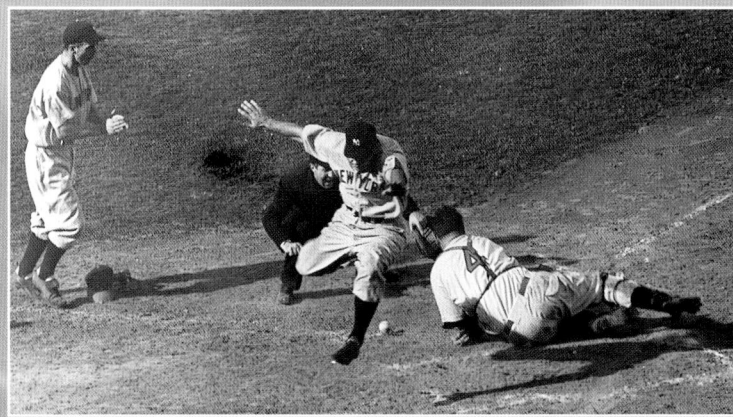

Above: Charlie Keller bounds past home after running into catcher Ernie Lombardi and giving Lombardi a "snooze" in 1939.

◆ **Giants Win Series in Extra Session in Fifth Game — Mel Ott and Dolf Luque, New York Giants, October 7, 1933**

Mel Ott's two-out home run in the top of the 10th inning of Game 5 put the Giants ahead 4-3 and three outs away from winning it all. Veteran Dolf Luque, coming off three-plus scoreless innings in relief, retired the first two batters in the last of the 10th before the Senators put two runners on base. Luque then struck out .322-hitter Joe Kuhel on three pitches to end the Series.

◆ **"Lombardi's Snooze" Gives Yanks Sweep — Joe DiMaggio and Johnny Murphy, New York Yankees, October 8, 1939**

The Yankees employed some aggressive baserunning to win their fourth straight Series in 1939. New York took a two-run lead in the fourth game when Charlie Keller scored from first on Joe DiMaggio's one-out single in the 10th inning; Joltin' Joe added one more for good measure by hustling around the bases after Cincinnati catcher Ernie Lombardi was knocked down by Keller at the plate. The Reds sent the potential tying run up to bat three times in the bottom of the inning, but pitcher Johnny Murphy nailed all three to end the game.

◆ **Kurowski Homer Wins It for Cards — Whitey Kurowski and Johnny Beazley, St. Louis Cardinals, October 5, 1942**

Nobody had beaten a Yankee team in the World Series since 1926, but the St. Louis Cardinals used a ninth-inning home run by Whitey Kurowski to send New York to defeat in the fifth game of the 1942 Series. The first two Yankee batters in the bottom of the ninth reached base, but starter Johnny Beazley picked a runner off second and induced two infield outs to get out of the jam without damage, clinching the title.

◆ **Slaughter's Mad Dash — Enos Slaughter and Harry Brecheen, St. Louis Cardinals, October 15, 1946**

Conventional baseball wisdom says that runners advance from first to third on a single, but a hustling Enos Slaughter stretched an extra base out

of Harry Walker's hit in the bottom of the eighth inning to give St. Louis a one-run lead in the final game of the 1946 Series. Pitcher Harry Brecheen put the first two Red Sox on base in the bottom of the inning but retired the next three in order to give St. Louis a victory.

◆ **Slugger Mathews Ends Series With Defense — Eddie Mathews, Milwaukee Braves, October 10, 1957**

In 1957, for the third year in a row, the New York Yankees fought to a winner-take-all seventh game in the World Series. They fell behind 5-0 in the deciding contest against Milwaukee. Down to their last gasps, the Yanks loaded the bases in the bottom of the ninth. When Bill Skowron threatened to close the gap with a hard grounder down the line, Eddie Mathews made a great stop at third, depriving New York of a chance at another championship.

◆ **Richardson Spears McCovey's Liner for Final Out — Bobby Richardson, New York Yankees, October 16, 1962**

It was the last Series win for the Yankees for 15 years, and it nearly didn't happen. With New York holding a slim one-run lead in Game 7 of the 1962 Series, San Francisco's Willie Mays stroked a two-out double with a runner on, but right fielder Roger Maris made a good play to hold the lead runner at third. With the go-ahead run in scoring position, Willie McCovey stepped to the plate and hit a scorching line drive. Yankee second baseman Bobby Richardson reached up and yanked the ball, and San Francisco's last hope, out of the air.

◆ **Morgan's Ninth-Inning Single Wins 1975 Series — Joe Morgan and Will McEnaney, Cincinnati Reds, October 22, 1975**

Most people think of Carlton Fisk's Game 6 homer when they think of the thrilling seven-game battle between Cincinnati and Boston in 1975, but Joe Morgan's clutch hit the following evening did more than win a game—it won the Series. The teams were tied going into the last inning of Game 7, and the Reds had two outs when Morgan drove home the game-winner with a single to center. Reliever Will McEnaney retired two pinch hitters and Hall of Famer Carl Yastrzemski in the bottom of the inning to close out the Series.

◆ **"Mr. May" Brings Title North of the Border — Dave Winfield and Mike Timlin, Toronto Blue Jays, October 24, 1992**

Dave Winfield had a reputation for coming up short at crunch time in October, but he more than made up for it with his clutch double in the top of the 11th inning in Game 6 of the 1992 World Series. Winfield delivered the key hit with one out and two men on base to put Toronto up 4-2, and Mike Timlin came on in relief to retire Otis Nixon on a bunt attempt to preserve the win.

Left: Eddie Mathews (center) celebrates with pitcher Lew Burdette (right) and catcher Del Crandell after Mathews snared Bill Skowron's hard grounder to end the 1957 Series.

Atlanta Braves (4) vs. Cleveland Indians (2)

After two difficult losses in 1991 and 1992, the Atlanta Braves returned to the World Series in 1995 with a team built around dominating pitching, featuring past, present and future Cy Young winners in Tom Glavine, Greg Maddux and John Smoltz. Over in the American League, the Cleveland Indians won 100 games to capture their first pennant in 41 years. In contrast to the Braves, the Indians powered through the season with a potent offense, boasting five players with more than 20 homers, led by Albert Belle's 50. Pitching was the name of the game in the Series opener. Veteran hurler Orel Hershiser held the Braves to three runs on 3 hits; Maddux did even better, allowing only three Indians to reach base (two on singles and one on an error) and throwing just 95 pitches in the 3-2 win. Glavine gave up 3 hits in Game 2 before giving way to a pinch hitter in the sixth inning. Javy Lopez's two-run homer earlier in the inning broke a 2-2 tie and put Atlanta ahead to stay. Moving to Cleveland for Game 3, the two teams exploded for 12 hits apiece. The Indians came back from a 6-5 deficit in the bottom of the eighth to send the game into extra innings. Eddie Murray won it with an RBI single in the 11th inning, giving Cleveland its first Series victory since the sixth game of the 1948 Series over the Boston Braves. The Indians fell behind three games to one the following evening when Atlanta's number four starter, Steve Avery, held them to three hits in six innings. The Braves broke out with a three-run seventh to

secure the 5-2 final, with David Justice knocking in two on a two-out single. Belle and Jim Thome drove in two runs each in Game 5 to give Hershiser the win in a rematch with Maddux. Thome's homer in the eighth inning proved to be the game-winner, as Atlanta's Ryan Klesko, homering for the third straight game, cut the score to 5-4 with a two-run blast in the ninth, but reliever Jose Mesa got out of the inning without further damage. Game 6 was a scoreless affair for five and a half innings, with starters Glavine and 40-year-old Dennis Martinez dueling it out from the mound. Justice, who had been under fire for criticizing Atlanta's fans for their lack of enthusiasm, brought the home crowd to its feet with a solo homer off Jim Poole in the bottom of the sixth for the game's only run. Glavine held on to preserve the first World Series one-hitter in nearly 30 years, with Mark Wohlers closing it out with a perfect ninth inning. The win gave the city of Atlanta its first championship in any major sport, and it made the Braves the only franchise to win a title in three different cities: Boston (1914), Milwaukee (1957) and Atlanta (1995).

Above: Tom Glavine pitched a one-hit shutout in the sixth game of the Series to clinch a championship for the Braves.

1995 WORLD SERIES COMPOSITE STATISTICS

ATLANTA BRAVES/Bobby Cox, Manager

Player	pos	G	AB	R	H	2B	3B	HR	RBI	BB	SO	SB	BA	SA	E	FPct
Steve Avery	p	1	0	0	0	0	0	0	0	0	0	0	—	—	0	—
Rafael Belliard	ss	6	16	0	0	0	0	0	1	0	4	0	.000	.000	2	.875
Pedro Borbon	p	1	0	0	0	0	0	0	0	0	0	0	—	—	0	—
Brad Clontz	p	2	0	0	0	0	0	0	0	0	0	0	—	—	0	—
Mike Devereaux	ph-lf-dh-rf	5	4	0	1	0	0	0	1	2	1	0	.250	.250	1	1.000
Tom Glavine	p	2	4	0	0	0	0	0	0	0	1	0	.000	.000	0	1.000
Marquis Grissom	cf	6	25	3	9	1	0	0	1	1	3	3	.360	.400	0	1.000
Chipper Jones	3b	6	21	3	6	3	0	0	1	4	3	0	.286	.429	1	.947
David Justice	rf	6	20	3	5	1	0	1	5	5	5	0	.250	.450	0	1.000
Ryan Klesko	lf-dh	6	16	4	5	0	0	3	4	3	4	0	.313	.875	0	1.000
Mark Lemke	2b	6	22	1	6	0	0	0	0	3	2	0	.273	.273	1	.971
Javy Lopez	c-ph	6	17	1	3	2	0	1	3	1	1	0	.176	.471	0	1.000
Greg Maddux	p	2	3	0	0	0	0	0	0	0	1	0	.000	.000	0	1.000
Fred McGriff	1b	6	23	5	6	2	0	2	3	3	7	1	.261	.609	1	.986
Greg McMichael	p	3	0	0	0	0	0	0	0	0	0	0	—	—	0	1.000
Kent Mercker	p	1	0	0	0	0	0	0	0	0	0	0	—	—	0	—
Mike Mordecai	ss-ph-dh	3	3	0	1	0	0	0	0	0	1	0	.333	.333	0	1.000
Charlie O'Brien	c	2	3	0	0	0	0	0	0	1	0	0	.000	.000	0	1.000
Alejandro Pena	p	2	0	0	0	0	0	0	0	0	0	0	—	—	0	—
Luis Polonia	ph-lf	6	14	3	4	1	0	1	4	1	3	1	.286	.571	0	1.000
Dwight Smith	ph	3	2	0	1	0	0	0	0	1	0	0	.500	.500	0	—
John Smoltz	p	1	0	0	0	0	0	0	0	0	0	0	—	—	0	—
Mark Wohlers	p	4	0	0	0	0	0	0	0	0	0	0	—	—	0	—
Totals		**6**	**193**	**23**	**47**	**10**	**0**	**8**	**23**	**25**	**34**	**5**	**.244**	**.420**	**6**	**.975**

Pitcher	G	GS	CG	IP	H	R	ER	BB	SO	W-L	Sv	ERA
Steve Avery	1	1	0	6	3	1	1	5	3	1-0	0	1.50
Pedro Borbon	1	0	0	1	0	0	0	2	0	0-0	1	0.00
Brad Clontz	2	0	0	3⅓	2	1	1	0	2	0-0	0	2.70
Tom Glavine	2	2	0	14	4	2	2	6	11	2-0	0	1.29
Greg Maddux	2	2	1	16	9	6	4	3	8	1-1	0	2.25
Greg McMichael	3	0	0	3⅓	3	2	1	2	2	0-0	0	2.70
Kent Mercker	1	0	0	2	1	1	1	2	2	0-0	0	4.50
Alejandro Pena	2	0	0	1	3	1	1	2	0	0-1	0	9.00
John Smoltz	1	1	0	2⅓	6	4	4	2	4	0-0	0	15.43
Mark Wohlers	4	0	0	5	4	1	1	3	3	0-0	2	1.80
Totals	**6**	**6**	**1**	**54**	**35**	**19**	**16**	**25**	**37**	**4-2**	**3**	**2.67**

CLEVELAND INDIANS/Mike Hargrove, Manager

Player	pos	G	AB	R	H	2B	3B	HR	RBI	BB	SO	SB	BA	SA	E	FPct
Sandy Alomar Jr.	c	5	15	0	3	2	0	0	1	0	2	0	.200	.333	0	1.000
Ruben Amaro	ph-rf	2	2	0	0	0	0	0	0	0	1	0	.000	.000	0	—
Paul Assenmacher	p	4	0	0	0	0	0	0	0	0	0	0	—	—	0	—
Carlos Baerga	2b	6	26	1	5	2	0	0	4	1	1	0	.192	.269	1	.975
Albert Belle	lf	6	17	4	4	0	0	2	4	7	5	0	.235	.588	1	.909
Alan Embree	p	4	0	0	0	0	0	0	0	0	0	0	—	—	0	1.000
Alvaro Espinoza	pr-3b	2	2	1	1	0	0	0	0	0	0	0	.500	.500	0	1.000
Orel Hershiser	p	2	2	0	0	0	0	0	0	0	0	0	.000	.000	1	.889
Ken Hill	p	2	0	0	0	0	0	0	0	0	0	0	—	—	0	1.000
Wayne Kirby	ph-pr-rf	3	1	0	0	0	0	0	0	0	1	0	.000	.000	0	1.000
Kenny Lofton	cf	6	25	6	5	1	0	0	0	3	1	6	.200	.240	0	1.000
Dennis Martinez	p	2	3	0	0	0	0	0	0	0	1	0	.000	.000	1	.750
Jose Mesa	p	2	0	0	0	0	0	0	0	0	0	0	—	—	0	—
Eddie Murray	1b-dh	6	19	1	2	0	0	1	3	5	4	0	.105	.263	0	1.000
Charles Nagy	p	1	0	0	0	0	0	0	0	0	0	0	—	—	0	1.000
Tony Pena	c	2	6	0	1	0	0	0	0	0	0	0	.167	.167	0	1.000
Herbert Perry	1b	3	5	0	0	0	0	0	0	0	2	0	.000	.000	0	1.000
Jim Poole	p	2	1	0	0	0	0	0	0	0	0	0	.000	.000	0	—
Manny Ramirez	rf	6	18	2	4	0	0	1	2	4	5	1	.222	.389	0	1.000
Paul Sorrento	1b-ph	6	11	0	2	1	0	0	0	0	4	0	.182	.273	1	.955
Julian Tavarez	p	5	0	0	0	0	0	0	0	0	0	0	—	—	0	1.000
Jim Thome	3b-ph	6	19	4	4	1	0	1	2	2	5	0	.211	.421	0	.889
Omar Vizquel	ss	6	23	3	4	0	1	0	1	3	5	1	.174	.261	0	1.000
Totals		**6**	**195**	**19**	**35**	**7**	**1**	**5**	**17**	**25**	**37**	**8**	**.179**	**.303**	**6**	**.975**

Pitcher	G	GS	CG	IP	H	R	ER	BB	SO	W-L	Sv	ERA
Paul Assenmacher	4	0	0	1⅓	1	2	1	3	3	0-0	0	6.75
Alan Embree	4	0	0	3⅓	2	1	1	2	2	0-0	0	2.70
Orel Hershiser	2	2	0	14	8	5	4	4	13	1-1	0	2.57
Ken Hill	2	1	0	6⅓	7	3	3	4	1	0-1	0	4.26
Dennis Martinez	2	2	0	10⅓	12	4	4	8	5	0-1	0	3.48
Jose Mesa	2	0	0	4	5	2	2	1	4	1-0	1	4.50
Charles Nagy	1	1	0	7	8	5	5	1	4	0-0	0	6.43
Jim Poole	2	0	0	2⅓	1	1	1	0	1	0-1	0	3.86
Julian Tavarez	5	0	0	4⅓	3	0	0	2	1	0-0	0	0.00
Totals	**6**	**6**	**0**	**53**	**47**	**23**	**21**	**25**	**34**	**2-4**	**1**	**3.57**

Series MVP: Tom Glavine, Atlanta Braves. **Series Outstanding Pitcher:** Tom Glavine, Atlanta Braves. **Average Length of Game:** 3 hours, 9 minutes. **Total Attendance:** 286,385. **Average Attendance:** 47,731 (51,876 at Atlanta-Fulton County Stadium; 43,586 at Jacobs Field).
Umpires: Joe Brinkman (AL), Bruce Froemming (NL), John Hirschbeck (AL), Jim McKean (AL), Frank Pulli (NL), Harry Wendelstedt (NL). **Winning Player's Share:** $206,635. **Losing Player's Share:** $121,946.

Left: Fred McGriff connects on an Orel Hershiser pitch and sends it into the seats to tie Game 1 at 1-1 in the second.

Below: A horizontal Carlos Baerga throws to first to complete a double play in the second inning of Game 6.

Below: The city of Atlanta hosted its third World Series of the decade in 1995, with Cleveland making its first appearance in more than forty years.

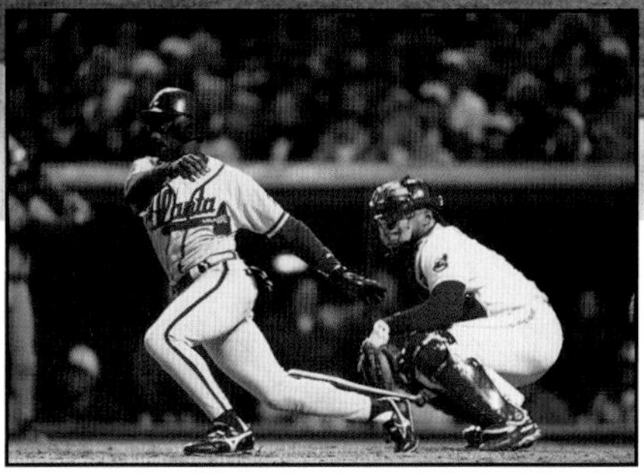

Above: Marquis Grissom batted .360 in 1995, contributing to his .390 career World Series average.

Right: Eddie Murray takes exception to an inside pitch from Greg Maddux in Game 5 and has to be restrained by umpire Frank Pulli and Atlanta catcher Charlie O'Brien.

Game 1 Saturday, October 21 at Atlanta-Fulton County Stadium, Atlanta

	1	2	3	4	5	6	7	8	9	R	H	E
Cleveland Indians	1	0	0	0	0	0	0	0	1	2	2	0
Atlanta Braves	0	1	0	0	0	0	2	0	x	3	3	2

Pitchers Cle Orel Hershiser (L, 0-1), IP 6, H 3, R 3, ER 3, BB 3, SO 7; Paul Assenmacher, IP 0, H 0, R 0, ER 0, BB 1, SO 0; Julian Tavarez, IP 1⅓, H 0, R 0, ER 0, BB 1, SO 0; Alan Embree, IP ⅔, H 0, R 0, ER 0, BB 0, SO 2
   Atl Greg Maddux (W, 1-0), IP 9, H 2, R 2, ER 0, BB 0, SO 4

Top Performers at the Plate
   Cle Kenny Lofton, 1 for 4, 2 R, 2 SB
   Atl Fred McGriff, 1 for 3, 2 R, 1 RBI, 1 BB

HR-Atl/McGriff. **SB**-Cle/Lofton 2. **Time** 2:37. **Attendance** 51,876.

Game 2 Sunday, October 22 at Atlanta-Fulton County Stadium, Atlanta

	1	2	3	4	5	6	7	8	9	R	H	E
Cleveland Indians	0	2	0	0	0	0	1	0	0	3	6	2
Atlanta Braves	0	0	2	0	0	2	0	0	x	4	8	2

Pitchers Cle Dennis Martinez (L, 0-1), IP 5⅔, H 8, R 4, ER 4, BB 3, SO 3; Alan Embree, IP ⅓, H 0, R 0, ER 0, BB 0, SO 0; Jim Poole, IP 1, H 0, R 0, ER 0, BB 0, SO 0; Julian Tavarez, IP 1, H 0, R 0, ER 0, BB 0, SO 0
   Atl Tom Glavine (W, 1-0), IP 6, H 3, R 2, ER 2, BB 3, SO 3; Greg McMichael, IP ⅔, H 1, R 1, ER 0, BB 1, SO 1; Alejandro Pena, IP 1, H 1, R 0, ER 0, BB 1, SO 0; Mark Wohlers (Sv, 1), IP 1⅓, H 1, R 0, ER 0, BB 0, SO 1

Top Performers at the Plate
   Cle Albert Belle, 1 for 3, 1 R, 1 BB; Eddie Murray, 1 for 3, 1 R, 1 RBI, 1 BB
   Atl Javier Lopez, 1 for 3, 1 R, 2 RBI, 1 HBP; David Justice, 2 for 3, 1 R, 1 RBI, 1 BB

2B-Atl/Jones. **HR**-Cle/Murray; Atl/Lopez. **SB**-Cle/Lofton 2, Vizquel. **Time** 3:17. **Attendance** 51,877.

Game 3 Tuesday, October 24 at Jacobs Field, Cleveland

	1	2	3	4	5	6	7	8	9	10	11	R	H	E
Atlanta Braves	1	0	0	0	0	1	1	3	0	0	0	6	12	1
Cleveland Indians	2	0	2	0	0	0	1	1	0	0	1	7	12	2

Pitchers Atl John Smoltz, IP 2⅓, H 6, R 4, ER 4, BB 2, SO 4; Brad Clontz, IP 2⅓, H 1, R 0, ER 0, BB 0, SO 1; Kent Mercker, IP 2, H 1, R 1, ER 1, BB 2, SO 2; Greg McMichael, IP ⅔, H 1, R 1, ER 1, BB 1, SO 1; Mark Wohlers, IP 2⅔, H 1, R 0, ER 0, BB 3, SO 2; Alejandro Pena (L, 0-1), IP 0, H 2, R 1, ER 1, BB 1, SO 0
   Cle Charles Nagy, IP 7, H 8, R 5, ER 5, BB 1, SO 4; Paul Assenmacher, IP ⅓, H 0, R 1, ER 1, BB 1, SO 0; Julian Tavarez, IP ⅔, H 1, R 0, ER 0, BB 0, SO 0; Jose Mesa (W, 1-0), IP 3, H 3, R 0, ER 0, BB 1, SO 3

Top Performers at the Plate
   Atl Ryan Klesko, 2 for 3, 1 R, 1 RBI; Fred McGriff, 3 for 5, 1 R, 2 RBI
   Cle Carlos Baerga, 3 for 6, 3 RBI; Kenny Lofton, 3 for 3, 3 R, 3 BB

2B-Atl/Grissom, Jones; Cle/Alomar Jr., Baerga, Lofton. **3B**-Cle/Vizquel. **HR**-Atl/Klesko, McGriff. **SB**-Atl/McGriff, Polonia; Cle/Lofton, Ramirez. **Time** 4:09. **Attendance** 43,584.

Game 4 Wednesday, October 25 at Jacobs Field, Cleveland

	1	2	3	4	5	6	7	8	9	R	H	E
Atlanta Braves	0	0	0	0	0	1	3	0	1	5	11	1
Cleveland Indians	0	0	0	0	1	0	0	1	0	2	6	0

Pitchers Atl Steve Avery (W, 1-0), IP 6, H 3, R 1, ER 1, BB 5, SO 3; Greg McMichael, IP 2, H 1, R 0, ER 0, BB 0, SO 0; Mark Wohlers, IP 0, H 2, R 1, ER 1, BB 0, SO 0; Pedro Borbon (Sv, 1), IP 1, H 0, R 0, ER 0, BB 0, SO 2
   Cle Ken Hill (L, 0-1), IP 6⅓, H 6, R 3, ER 3, BB 4, SO 1; Paul Assenmacher, IP ⅔, H 1, R 1, ER 0, BB 1, SO 2; Julian Tavarez, IP ⅔, H 2, R 0, ER 0, BB 1, SO 1; Alan Embree, IP 1⅓, H 2, R 1, ER 1, BB 0, SO 0

Top Performers at the Plate
   Atl Marquis Grissom, 3 for 4, 1 R, 1 BB, 2 SB; Luis Polonia, 2 for 4, 1 R, 1 RBI
   Cle Albert Belle, 1 for 3, 1 R, 1 RBI, 1 BB; Manny Ramirez, 1 for 3, 1 R, 1 RBI, 1 BB

2B-Atl/Lopez 2, McGriff, Polonia; Cle/Sorrento, Thome. **HR**-Atl/Klesko; Cle/Belle, Ramirez. **SB**-Atl/Grissom 2. **Time** 3:14. **Attendance** 43,578.

Game 5 Thursday, October 26 at Jacobs Field, Cleveland

	1	2	3	4	5	6	7	8	9	R	H	E
Atlanta Braves	0	0	0	1	1	0	0	0	2	4	7	0
Cleveland Indians	2	0	0	0	0	2	0	1	x	5	8	1

Pitchers Atl Greg Maddux (L, 1-1), IP 7, H 7, R 4, ER 4, BB 3, SO 4; Brad Clontz, IP 1, H 1, R 1, ER 1, BB 0, SO 1
   Cle Orel Hershiser (W, 1-1), IP 8, H 5, R 2, ER 1, BB 1, SO 6; Jose Mesa (Sv, 1), IP 1, H 2, R 2, ER 2, BB 0, SO 1

Top Performers at the Plate
   Atl Ryan Klesko, 2 for 4, 2 R, 2 RBI
   Cle Albert Belle, 1 for 3, 2 R, 2 RBI, 1 BB; Jim Thome, 2 for 4, 1 R, 2 RBI

2B-Atl/Jones, McGriff; Cle/Alomar Jr., Baerga. **HR**-Atl/Polonia, Klesko; Cle/Belle, Thome. **Time** 2:33. **Attendance** 43,595.

Game 6 Saturday, October 28 at Atlanta-Fulton County Stadium, Atlanta

	1	2	3	4	5	6	7	8	9	R	H	E
Cleveland Indians	0	0	0	0	0	0	0	0	0	0	1	1
Atlanta Braves	0	0	0	0	0	1	0	0	x	1	6	0

Pitchers Cle Dennis Martinez, IP 4⅔, H 4, R 0, ER 0, BB 5, SO 2; Jim Poole (L, 0-1), IP 1⅓, H 1, R 1, ER 1, BB 0, SO 1; Ken Hill, IP 0, H 1, R 0, ER 0, BB 0, SO 0; Alan Embree, IP 1, H 0, R 0, ER 0, BB 2, SO 0; Julian Tavarez, IP ⅔, H 0, R 0, ER 0, BB 0, SO 0; Paul Assenmacher, IP ⅓, H 0, R 0, ER 0, BB 0, SO 1
   Atl Tom Glavine (W, 2-0), IP 8, H 1, R 0, ER 0, BB 3, SO 8; Mark Wohlers (Sv, 2), IP 1, H 0, R 0, ER 0, BB 0, SO 0

Top Performers at the Plate
   Atl Chipper Jones, 2 for 3, 1 BB; David Justice, 2 for 2, 1 R, 1 RBI, 1 BB

2B-Atl/Justice. **HR**-Atl/Justice. **SB**-Cle/Lofton; Atl/Grissom. **Time** 3:02. **Attendance** 51,875.

New York Yankees (4) vs. Atlanta Braves (2)

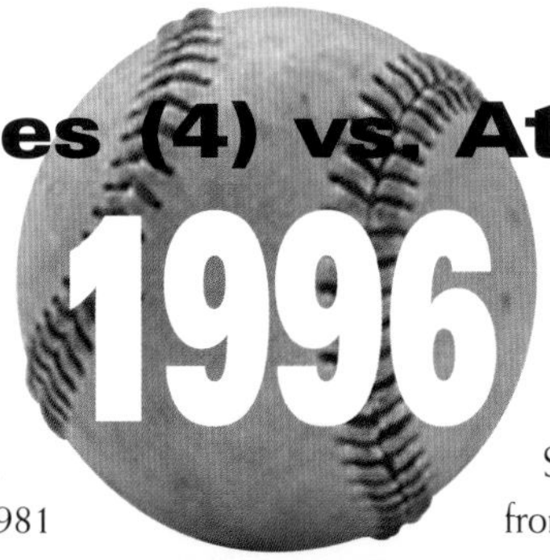

One familiar face (or, more to the point, familiar uniform) was back in the Fall Classic in 1996, along with a formerly-familiar-but-long-absent one. Bobby Cox's Atlanta Braves earned their fourth appearance since 1991, once again with pitching as their primary weapon. The New York Yankees, under new manager Joe Torre, won their first pennant since 1981 to play in their first Series in 15 years. After the first two games, the 1996 Yankees seemed a far cry from their pinstripe predecessors that had collected 22 championships since 1923. The Braves blasted Andy Pettitte and three Yankee relievers for 12 runs in the opener, while John Smoltz and three Atlanta relievers held New York to one run on 4 hits. The 19-year-old Andruw Jones drove in 5 runs in the game and made history by joining Gene Tenace as the only players to hit home runs in their first two World Series at-bats. Greg Maddux and closer Mark Wohlers combined to shut New York out in Game 2, and with the Yanks outscored 16-1 in the first two games, things looked bleak as the scene shifted to Atlanta for Game 3. David Cone got New York on the right track in the third game by pitching shutout ball for five innings. A two-run homer by Bernie Williams in the eighth, along with Luis Sojo's RBI single, provided the insurance runs they needed for the 5-2 win. New York stormed back from trailing 6-0 in Game 4, scoring 3 runs in the sixth before Jim Leyritz smashed a three-run homer off Wohlers in the

top of the eighth to tie the game. The Yankees then scored two in the 10th to even the Series; Steve Avery walked Wade Boggs with the bases loaded to bring in the go-ahead run. The Bronx Bombers continued to roll and took the Series lead in Game 5, though there wasn't much bombing from either side. Lefty starters Pettitte and Smoltz yielded 5 and 4 hits, respectively, and Pettitte redeemed his disastrous Game 1 performance by coming out on top in the 1-0 contest. The lone run came in the fourth when Marquis Grissom dropped Charlie Hayes's fly ball, and Cecil Fielder drove Hayes in with a double. Paul O'Neill ended the game with an over-the-shoulder catch of Luis Polonia's drive with the tying run on third and two men out in the last of the ninth. Back at the Stadium for Game 6, New York clinched the Series with another one-run triumph. A double by O'Neill, a triple by Joe Girardi, and singles by Derek Jeter and Bernie Williams put the Yanks up 3-0 in the third inning. After Jimmy Key and three relievers held Atlanta to a run through eight innings, closer John Wetteland came on and earned an unprecedented fourth save in the Series. After a long 18-year drought, the New York Yankees were once again at the top of the baseball world.

Above: Baseball returned to the Bronx in October for the first time in 15 years, and the Yankees added another championship flag to the Stadium.

1996 WORLD SERIES COMPOSITE STATISTICS

NEW YORK YANKEES/Joe Torre, Manager

Player	pos	G	AB	R	H	2B	3B	HR	RBI	BB	SO	SB	BA	SA	E	FPct
Mike Aldrete	rf-ph	2	1	0	0	0	0	0	0	0	0	0	.000	.000	0	—
Brian Boehringer	p	2	0	0	0	0	0	0	0	0	0	0	—	—	0	—
Wade Boggs	3b-ph	4	11	0	3	1	0	0	2	1	0	0	.273	.364	0	—
David Cone	p	1	2	0	0	0	0	0	0	0	1	0	.000	.000	0	1.000
Mariano Duncan	2b	6	19	1	1	0	0	0	0	0	4	1	.053	.053	2	.920
Cecil Fielder	dh-1b	6	23	1	9	2	0	0	2	2	2	0	.391	.478	0	1.000
Andy Fox	2b-pr-3b	4	0	1	0	0	0	0	0	0	0	0	—	—	0	1.000
Joe Girardi	c	4	10	1	2	0	1	0	1	1	2	0	.200	.400	0	1.000
Charlie Hayes	ph-3b-1b	5	16	2	3	0	0	0	1	1	5	0	.188	.188	0	1.000
Derek Jeter	ss	6	20	5	5	0	0	0	1	4	6	1	.250	.250	2	.947
Jimmy Key	p	2	0	0	0	0	0	0	0	0	0	0	—	—	0	1.000
Jim Leyritz	c-ph	4	8	1	3	0	0	1	3	3	2	1	.375	.750	0	1.000
Graeme Lloyd	p	4	1	0	0	0	0	0	0	0	0	0	.000	.000	0	—
Tino Martinez	1b-ph	6	11	0	1	0	0	0	0	2	5	0	.091	.091	0	1.000
Jeff Nelson	p	3	0	0	0	0	0	0	0	0	0	0	—	—	0	1.000
Paul O'Neill	rf-ph	5	12	1	2	2	0	0	3	2	0	0	.167	.333	0	1.000
Andy Pettitte	p	2	4	0	0	0	0	0	0	0	1	0	.000	.000	0	1.000
Tim Raines	lf	4	14	2	3	0	0	0	2	1	0	0	.214	.214	1	.833
Mariano Rivera	p	4	1	0	0	0	0	0	0	0	0	0	.000	.000	0	1.000
Kenny Rogers	p	1	1	0	1	0	0	0	0	0	0	0	1.000	1.000	0	—
Luis Sojo	ph-2b	5	5	0	3	1	0	0	1	0	0	0	.600	.800	0	1.000
Darryl Strawberry	lf-rf	5	16	0	3	0	0	0	1	4	6	0	.188	.188	0	1.000
Dave Weathers	p	3	0	0	0	0	0	0	0	0	0	0	—	—	0	—
John Wetteland	p	5	0	0	0	0	0	0	0	0	0	0	—	—	0	—
Bernie Williams	cf	6	24	3	4	0	0	2	4	3	6	1	.167	.292	0	1.000
Totals		**6**	**199**	**18**	**43**	**6**	**1**	**2**	**16**	**26**	**43**	**4**	**.216**	**.286**	**5**	**.979**

Pitcher	G	GS	CG	IP	H	R	ER	BB	SO	W-L	Sv	ERA
Brian Boehringer	2	0	0	5	5	5	3	0	5	0-0	0	5.40
David Cone	1	1	0	6	4	1	1	4	3	1-0	0	1.50
Jimmy Key	2	2	0	11⅓	15	5	5	5	1	1-1	0	3.97
Graeme Lloyd	4	0	0	2⅔	0	0	0	4	4	0-0	0	0.00
Jeff Nelson	3	0	0	4⅓	1	0	0	1	5	0-0	0	0.00
Andy Pettitte	2	2	0	10⅔	11	7	7	4	5	1-1	0	5.91
Mariano Rivera	4	0	0	5⅔	4	1	1	3	4	0-0	0	1.59
Kenny Rogers	1	1	0	2	5	5	5	2	0	0-0	0	22.50
Dave Weathers	3	0	0	3	2	1	1	3	3	0-0	0	3.00
John Wetteland	5	0	0	4⅓	4	1	1	1	6	0-0	4	2.08
Totals	**6**	**6**	**0**	**55**	**51**	**26**	**24**	**23**	**36**	**4-2**	**4**	**3.93**

ATLANTA BRAVES/Bobby Cox, Manager

Player	pos	G	AB	R	H	2B	3B	HR	RBI	BB	SO	SB	BA	SA	E	FPct
Steve Avery	p	1	0	0	0	0	0	0	0	0	0	0	—	—	0	—
Rafael Belliard	ss-pr	4	0	0	0	0	0	0	0	0	0	0	—	—	0	1.000
Mike Bielecki	p	2	1	0	0	0	0	0	0	0	1	0	.000	.000	0	1.000
Jeff Blauser	ss	6	18	2	3	1	0	0	1	1	4	0	.167	.222	1	.960
Brad Clontz	p	3	0	0	0	0	0	0	0	0	0	0	—	—	0	—
Jermaine Dye	rf	5	17	0	2	0	0	0	1	1	1	0	.118	.118	1	.938
Tom Glavine	p	1	1	1	0	0	0	0	0	1	1	0	.000	.000	0	1.000
Marquis Grissom	cf	6	27	4	12	2	1	0	5	1	2	1	.444	.593	1	.875
Andruw Jones	lf-rf	6	20	4	8	1	0	2	6	3	6	1	.400	.750	0	1.000
Chipper Jones	3b-ss	6	21	3	6	3	0	0	3	4	2	1	.286	.429	0	1.000
Ryan Klesko	dh-lf-1b-ph	5	10	2	1	0	0	0	1	2	4	0	.100	.100	0	.500
Mark Lemke	2b	6	26	2	6	1	0	0	2	0	3	0	.231	.269	0	1.000
Javy Lopez	c	6	21	3	4	0	0	0	1	3	4	0	.190	.190	0	1.000
Greg Maddux	p	2	0	0	0	0	0	0	0	0	0	0	—	—	0	1.000
Fred McGriff	1b	6	20	4	6	0	0	2	6	5	4	0	.300	.600	0	1.000
Greg McMichael	p	2	0	0	0	0	0	0	0	0	0	0	—	—	0	—
Mike Mordecai	ph	1	1	0	0	0	0	0	0	0	0	0	.000	.000	—	—
Denny Neagle	p	2	1	0	0	0	0	0	0	1	0	0	.000	.000	0	1.000
Terry Pendleton	dh-ph-3b	4	9	1	2	1	0	0	1	1	0	0	.222	.333	0	1.000
Eddie Perez	c	2	1	0	0	0	0	0	0	0	0	0	.000	.000	0	1.000
Luis Polonia	ph	6	5	0	0	0	0	0	0	1	2	0	.000	.000	—	—
John Smoltz	p	2	2	0	1	0	0	0	0	0	0	0	.500	.500	0	1.000
Terrell Wade	p	2	0	0	0	0	0	0	0	0	0	0	—	—	0	—
Mark Wohlers	p	4	0	0	0	0	0	0	0	0	0	0	—	—	0	1.000
Totals		**6**	**201**	**26**	**51**	**9**	**1**	**4**	**26**	**23**	**36**	**3**	**.254**	**.368**	**4**	**.983**

Pitcher	G	GS	CG	IP	H	R	ER	BB	SO	W-L	Sv	ERA
Steve Avery	1	0	0	⅔	1	2	1	3	0	0-1	0	13.50
Mike Bielecki	2	0	0	3	0	0	0	3	6	0-0	0	0.00
Brad Clontz	3	0	0	1⅔	1	0	0	1	2	0-0	0	0.00
Tom Glavine	1	1	0	7	4	2	1	3	8	0-1	0	1.29
Greg Maddux	2	2	0	15⅔	14	3	3	1	5	1-1	0	1.72
Greg McMichael	2	0	0	1	5	3	3	0	1	0-0	0	27.00
Denny Neagle	2	1	0	6	5	3	2	4	3	0-0	0	3.00
John Smoltz	2	2	0	14	6	2	1	8	14	1-1	0	0.64
Terrell Wade	2	0	0	⅔	0	0	0	1	0	0-0	0	0.00
Mark Wohlers	4	0	0	4⅓	7	3	3	2	4	0-0	0	6.23
Totals	**6**	**6**	**0**	**54**	**43**	**18**	**14**	**26**	**43**	**2-4**	**0**	**2.33**

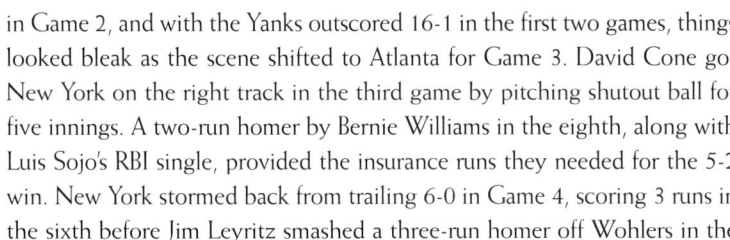

Series MVP: John Wetteland, New York Yankees. **Series Outstanding Pitcher:** John Wetteland, New York Yankees. **Average Length of Game:** 3 hours, 12 minutes. **Total Attendance:** 324,685. **Average Attendance:** 54,114 (56,360 at Yankee Stadium; 51,868 at Atlanta-Fulton County Stadium). **Umpires:** Gerry Davis (NL), Jim Evans (AL), Steve Ripley (NL), Terry Tata (NL), Tim Welke (AL), Larry Young (AL). **Winning Player's Share:** $216,870. **Losing Player's Share:** $143,678.

Above: In Game 6, Derek Jeter nails Marquis Grisson attempting to steal second after Grissom collected one of his 12 hits in the Series.

At nineteen-and-a-half years old, Atlanta's Andruw Jones became the youngest player ever to hit a World Series home run when he went long in the second (and third) inning of the 1996 Series opener.

Center right: Greg Maddux put the Braves up two-nil with his scoreless outing in Game 2.

Below: A game-tying three-run homer by Jim Leyritz in the eighth inning kept New York in Game 4. They ended up winning it in the tenth.

Right: The Yankees are champions once again. Charlie Hayes snares Mark Lemke's foul ball to end the sixth game of the 1996 Series.

Game 1 Sunday, October 20 at Yankee Stadium, New York

	1	2	3	4	5	6	7	8	9	R	H	E
Atlanta Braves	0	2	6	0	1	3	0	0	0	12	13	0
New York Yankees	0	0	0	0	1	0	0	0	0	1	4	1

Pitchers Atl **John Smoltz** (W, 1-0), IP 6, H 2, R 1, ER 1, BB 5, SO 4; **Greg McMichael**, IP 1, H 2, R 0, ER 0, BB 0, SO 1; **Denny Neagle**, IP 1, H 0, R 0, ER 0, BB 0, SO 0; **Terrell Wade**, IP ⅔, H 0, R 0, ER 0, BB 0, SO 0; **Brad Clontz**, IP ⅓, H 0, R 0, ER 0, BB 0, SO 0

NY **Andy Pettitte** (L, 0-1), IP 2⅓, H 6, R 7, ER 7, BB 1, SO 1; **Brian Boehringer**, IP 3, H 5, R 5, ER 3, BB 0, SO 2; **Dave Weathers**, IP 1⅔, H 1, R 0, ER 0, BB 0, SO 0; **Jeff Nelson**, IP 1, H 1, R 0, ER 0, BB 0, SO 1; **John Wetteland**, IP 1, H 0, R 0, ER 0, BB 0, SO 2

Top Performers at the Plate

Atl **Andruw Jones**, 3 for 4, 3 R, 5 RBI, 2 HR; **Fred McGriff**, 2 for 5, 2 R, 2 RBI

2B-NY/Boggs. **HR**-Atl/A. Jones 2, McGriff. **SB**-Atl/C. Jones. **Time** 3:02. **Attendance** 56,365.

Game 2 Monday, October 21 at Yankee Stadium, New York

	1	2	3	4	5	6	7	8	9	R	H	E
Atlanta Braves	1	0	1	0	1	1	0	0	0	4	10	0
New York Yankees	0	0	0	0	0	0	0	0	0	0	7	1

Pitchers Atl **Greg Maddux** (W, 1-0), IP 8, H 6, R 0, ER 0, BB 0, SO 2; **Mark Wohlers**, IP 1, H 1, R 0, ER 0, BB 0, SO 3

NY **Jimmy Key** (L, 0-1), IP 6, H 10, R 4, ER 4, BB 2, SO 0; **Graeme Lloyd**, IP ⅔, H 0, R 0, ER 0, BB 0, SO 2; **Jeff Nelson**, IP 1⅓, H 0, R 0, ER 0, BB 0, SO 2; **Mariano Rivera**, IP 1, H 0, R 0, ER 0, BB 0, SO 1

Top Performers at the Plate

Atl **Mark Lemke**, 2 for 4, 2 R, 1 SH; **Fred McGriff**, 2 for 3, 3 RBI, 1 SF

NY **Cecil Fielder**, 2 for 4; **Tim Raines**, 2 for 4

2B-Atl/Grissom, C. Jones, Lemke, Pendleton; NY/O'Neill. **Time** 2:44. **Attendance** 56,340.

Game 3 Tuesday, October 22 at Atlanta-Fulton County Stadium, Atlanta

	1	2	3	4	5	6	7	8	9	R	H	E
New York Yankees	1	0	0	1	0	0	0	3	0	5	8	1
Atlanta Braves	0	0	0	0	0	1	0	1	0	2	6	1

Pitchers NY **David Cone** (W, 1-0), IP 6, H 4, R 1, ER 1, BB 4, SO 3; **Mariano Rivera**, IP 1⅓, H 2, R 1, ER 1, BB 1, SO 1; **Graeme Lloyd**, IP ⅔, H 0, R 0, ER 0, BB 0, SO 1; **John Wetteland** (Sv, 1), IP 1, H 0, R 0, ER 0, BB 0, SO 2

Atl **Tom Glavine** (L, 0-1), IP 7, H 4, R 2, ER 1, BB 3, SO 8; **Greg McMichael**, IP 0, H 3, R 3, ER 3, BB 0, SO 0; **Brad Clontz**, IP 1, H 1, R 0, ER 0, BB 1, SO 1; **Mike Bielecki**, IP 1, H 0, R 0, ER 0, BB 2, SO 2

Top Performers at the Plate

NY **Derek Jeter**, 1 for 3, 1 R, 1 BB, 1 SH; **Bernie Williams**, 2 for 5, 2 R, 3 RBI

Atl **Marquis Grissom**, 3 for 4, 1 R

2B-NY/Fielder. **3B**-Atl/Grissom. **HR**-NY/Williams. **Time** 3:22. **Attendance** 51,843.

Game 4 Wednesday, October 23 at Atlanta-Fulton County Stadium, Atlanta

	1	2	3	4	5	6	7	8	9	10	R	H	E
New York Yankees	0	0	0	0	0	3	0	3	0	2	8	12	0
Atlanta Braves	0	4	1	0	1	0	0	0	0	0	6	9	2

Pitchers NY **Kenny Rogers**, IP 2, H 5, R 5, ER 5, BB 2, SO 0; **Brian Boehringer**, IP 2, H 0, R 0, ER 0, BB 0, SO 3; **Dave Weathers**, IP 1, H 1, R 1, ER 1, BB 2, SO 2; **Jeff Nelson**, IP 2, H 0, R 0, ER 0, BB 1, SO 2; **Mariano Rivera**, IP 1⅓, H 2, R 0, ER 0, BB 1, SO 1; **Graeme Lloyd** (W, 1-0), IP 1, H 0, R 0, ER 0, BB 0, SO 1; **John Wetteland** (Sv, 2), IP ⅔, H 1, R 0, ER 0, BB 0, SO 0

Atl **Denny Neagle**, IP 5, H 5, R 3, ER 2, BB 4, SO 3; **Terrell Wade**, IP 0, H 0, R 0, ER 0, BB 1, SO 0; **Mike Bielecki**, IP 2, H 0, R 0, ER 0, BB 1, SO 4; **Mark Wohlers**, IP 2, H 6, R 3, ER 3, BB 0, SO 1; **Steve Avery** (L, 0-1), IP ⅔, H 1, R 2, ER 1, BB 3, SO 0; **Brad Clontz**, IP ⅓, H 0, R 0, ER 0, BB 0, SO 1

Top Performers at the Plate

NY **Charlie Hayes**, 3 for 5, 1 R, 1 RBI, 1 BB; **Jim Leyritz**, 1 for 2, 1 R, 3 RBI

Atl **Andruw Jones**, 3 for 4, 1 R, 1 RBI, 1 BB; **Fred McGriff**, 2 for 3, 1 R, 1 RBI, 2 BB

2B-Atl/Grissom, A. Jones. **HR**-Atl/McGriff; NY/Leyritz. **Time** 4:17. **Attendance** 51,881.

Game 5 Thursday, October 24 at Atlanta-Fulton County Stadium, Atlanta

	1	2	3	4	5	6	7	8	9	R	H	E
New York Yankees	0	0	0	1	0	0	0	0	0	1	4	1
Atlanta Braves	0	0	0	0	0	0	0	0	0	0	5	1

Pitchers NY **Andy Pettitte** (W, 1-1), IP 8⅓, H 5, R 0, ER 0, BB 3, SO 4; **John Wetteland** (Sv, 3), IP ⅔, H 0, R 0, ER 0, BB 1, SO 0

Atl **John Smoltz** (L, 1-1), IP 8, H 4, R 1, ER 0, BB 3, SO 10; **Mark Wohlers**, IP 1, H 0, R 0, ER 0, BB 2, SO 0

Top Performers at the Plate

NY **Cecil Fielder**, 3 for 4, 1 RBI

Atl **Marquis Grissom**, 2 for 3, 1 BB

2B-NY/Fielder; Atl/C. Jones. **SB**-NY/Duncan, Leyritz; Atl/Grissom, A. Jones. **Time** 2:54. **Attendance** 51,881.

Game 6 Saturday, October 26 at Yankee Stadium, New York

	1	2	3	4	5	6	7	8	9	R	H	E
Atlanta Braves	0	0	0	1	0	0	0	0	1	2	8	0
New York Yankees	0	0	3	0	0	0	0	0	x	3	8	1

Pitchers Atl **Greg Maddux** (L, 1-1), IP 7⅔, H 8, R 3, ER 3, BB 1, SO 3; **Mark Wohlers**, IP ⅓, H 0, R 0, ER 0, BB 0, SO 0

NY **Jimmy Key** (W, 1-1), IP 5⅓, H 5, R 1, ER 1, BB 3, SO 1; **Dave Weathers**, IP ⅓, H 0, R 0, ER 0, BB 1, SO 1; **Graeme Lloyd**, IP ⅓, H 0, R 0, ER 0, BB 0, SO 0; **Mariano Rivera**, IP 2, H 0, R 0, ER 0, BB 1, SO 1; **John Wetteland** (Sv, 4), IP 1, H 3, R 1, ER 1, BB 0, SO 2

Top Performers at the Plate

Atl **Marquis Grissom**, 2 for 5, 1 RBI; **Ryan Klesko**, 1 for 2, 1 R

NY **Joe Girardi**, 2 for 3, 1 R, 1 RBI; **Bernie Williams**, 2 for 4, 1 RBI

2B-Atl/Blauser, C. Jones; NY/O'Neill, Sojo. **3B**-NY/Girardi. **SB**-NY/Jeter, Williams. **Time** 2:53. **Attendance** 56,375.

Florida Marlins (4) vs. Cleveland Indians (3)

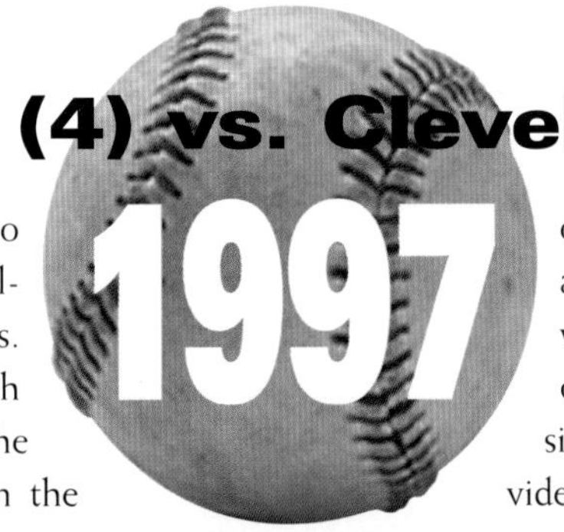

The four-year-old expansion Florida Marlins jumped into the playoffs in 1997, thanks in no small part to $89 million shelled out by owner Wayne Huizenga in salaries. The Marlins finished with a 92-70 record—good enough for a wild-card spot in the postseason. After sweeping the Giants in the divisional series, Florida upset Atlanta in the NLCS to become the first wild-card team to reach the World Series. The Cleveland Indians got past the defending-champion Yankees in the first round of the playoffs on their way to a second Fall Classic in three years. Florida's 22-year-old Cuban rookie Livan Hernandez won the opener over veteran Orel Hershiser. Moises Alou's three-run homer in the fourth was followed by a solo blast by Charles Johnson to put Florida ahead 5-1 before closing it out 7-4. Chad Ogea got Cleveland on track in Game 2 by shutting the Marlins out for six innings. The Indian offense broke the game open in the fifth and sixth innings against starter Kevin Brown. Despite a 30-degree temperature drop from sunny Miami to chilly Cleveland, the two teams combined for 26 hits in Game 3, with the Marlins coming out on top 14-11. A leaping catch by Gary Sheffield in the seventh inning denied Jim Thome a home run and preserved a 7-7 tie, and then Florida broke that tie in the top of the ninth when three errors and a wild pitch by the Indians contributed to a seven-run onslaught. Snow flurries and a record-low 38-degree temperature greeted the Game 4 starters, but Cleveland's 21-year-old Jaret Wright was red hot. The Indians struck early against Florida's rookie, Tony Saunders, and went on to win 10-3. In Game 5, Alou hit his second three-run homer off Hershiser to bring Florida back from a 4-2 deficit in the sixth. Alou's run scored and RBI in the eighth and ninth provided the necessary insurance runs for the 8-7 final. The Series flipped back to a 3-3 tie when Ogea earned his second win in a 4-1 victory over Brown. Ogea, in his third Major League plate appearance, drove in two runs with a single in the second, and then doubled and scored in the fifth. Wright offered up another stellar outing in the crucial seventh game, holding the Marlins to one hit in six shutout innings until Bobby Bonilla led off the seventh with a homer. Florida's Al Leiter, meanwhile, gave up two runs on Tony Fernandez's third-inning single. The Marlins tied the game in the last of the ninth on Craig Counsell's RBI sacrifice fly against closer Jose Mesa. Bonilla opened the bottom of the eleventh with a single and advanced to third when Counsell's grounder went through the legs of second baseman Fernandez. With the bases loaded, Edgar Renteria delivered a two-out single to score Counsell from third for the Series-winning run—making the Florida Marlins the youngest expansion team to win a championship.

Above: The expansion Marlins claimed a title in only their fourth year as a franchise, thanks to Edgar Renteria's clutch Game 7 single.

1997 WORLD SERIES COMPOSITE STATISTICS

FLORIDA MARLINS/Jim Leyland, Manager

Player	pos	G	AB	R	H	2B	3B	HR	RBI	BB	SO	SB	BA	SA	E	FPct
Kurt Abbott	ph-dh	3	3	0	0	0	0	0	0	0	1	0	.000	.000	–	–
Antonio Alfonseca	p	3	0	0	0	0	0	0	0	0	0	0	–	–	0	1.000
Moises Alou	lf	7	28	6	9	2	0	3	9	3	6	1	.321	.714	0	1.000
Alex Arias	ph-pr-3b	2	1	1	0	0	0	0	0	0	0	0	.000	.000	0	–
Bobby Bonilla	3b	7	29	5	6	1	0	1	3	3	5	0	.207	.345	2	.920
Kevin Brown	p	2	3	0	0	0	0	0	0	0	1	0	.000	.000	0	1.000
John Cangelosi	ph	3	3	0	1	0	0	0	0	0	2	0	.333	.333	–	–
Jeff Conine	1b-ph	6	13	1	3	0	0	0	2	0	0	0	.231	.231	0	1.000
Dennis Cook	p	3	0	0	0	0	0	0	0	0	0	0	–	–	0	–
Craig Counsell	2b	7	22	4	4	1	0	0	2	6	5	1	.182	.227	1	.971
Darren Daulton	1b-ph-dh	7	18	7	7	2	0	1	2	3	0	1	.389	.667	0	1.000
Jim Eisenreich	ph-dh-1b	5	8	1	4	0	0	1	3	3	1	0	.500	.875	0	1.000
Cliff Floyd	ph-dh	4	2	1	0	0	0	0	0	1	1	0	.000	.000	–	–
Felix Heredia	p	4	0	0	0	0	0	0	0	0	0	0	–	–	0	1.000
Livan Hernandez	p	2	2	0	0	0	0	0	0	0	0	0	.000	.000	1	.800
Charles Johnson	c	7	28	4	10	0	0	1	3	1	6	0	.357	.464	0	1.000
Al Leiter	p	2	0	0	0	0	0	0	0	2	0	0	–	–	1	.500
Robb Nen	p	4	0	0	0	0	0	0	0	0	0	0	–	–	0	–
Jay Powell	p	4	0	0	0	0	0	0	0	0	0	0	–	–	0	1.000
Edgar Renteria	ss	7	31	3	9	2	0	0	3	3	5	0	.290	.355	1	.974
Tony Saunders	p	1	0	0	0	0	0	0	0	0	0	0	–	–	1	.500
Gary Sheffield	rf	7	24	4	7	1	0	1	5	8	5	0	.292	.458	1	.941
Ed Vosberg	p	2	0	0	0	0	0	0	0	0	0	0	–	–	0	1.000
Devon White	cf	7	33	0	8	3	1	0	2	3	10	1	.242	.394	0	1.000
Greg Zaun	ph-pr-c	2	2	0	0	0	0	0	0	0	0	0	.000	.000	0	1.000
Totals		**7**	**250**	**37**	**68**	**12**	**1**	**8**	**34**	**36**	**48**	**4**	**.272**	**.424**	**8**	**.972**

Pitcher	G	GS	CG	IP	H	R	ER	BB	SO	W-L	Sv	ERA
Antonio Alfonseca	3	0	0	6⅓	6	0	0	1	5	0-0	0	0.00
Kevin Brown	2	2	0	11	15	10	10	5	6	0-2	0	8.18
Dennis Cook	3	0	0	3⅔	1	0	0	1	5	1-0	0	0.00
Felix Heredia	4	0	0	5⅓	2	0	0	1	5	0-0	0	0.00
Livan Hernandez	2	2	0	13⅔	15	9	8	10	7	2-0	0	5.27
Al Leiter	2	2	0	10⅔	10	9	6	10	10	0-0	0	5.06
Robb Nen	4	0	0	4⅔	8	5	4	2	7	0-0	2	7.71
Jay Powell	4	0	0	3⅔	5	3	3	4	2	1-0	0	7.36
Tony Saunders	1	1	0	2	7	6	6	3	2	0-1	0	27.00
Ed Vosberg	2	0	0	3	3	2	2	3	2	0-0	0	6.00
Totals	**7**	**7**	**0**	**64**	**72**	**44**	**39**	**40**	**51**	**4-3**	**2**	**5.48**

CLEVELAND INDIANS/Mike Hargrove, Manager

Player	pos	G	AB	R	H	2B	3B	HR	RBI	BB	SO	SB	BA	SA	E	FPct
Sandy Alomar Jr.	c	7	30	5	11	1	0	2	10	2	3	0	.367	.600	0	1.000
Brian Anderson	p	3	0	0	0	0	0	0	0	0	0	0	–	–	0	1.000
Paul Assenmacher	p	5	0	0	0	0	0	0	0	0	0	0	–	–	0	–
Jeff Branson	ph	1	1	0	0	0	0	0	0	0	1	0	.000	.000	–	–
Tony Fernandez	ph-2b	5	17	1	8	1	0	0	4	0	1	0	.471	.529	2	.920
Brian Giles	ph-lf	5	4	1	2	1	0	0	2	4	1	0	.500	.750	0	1.000
Marquis Grissom	cf	7	25	5	9	1	0	0	2	4	4	0	.360	.400	1	.950
Orel Hershiser	p	2	2	0	0	0	0	0	0	0	1	0	.000	.000	0	1.000
Mike Jackson	p	4	2	0	0	0	0	0	0	0	1	0	.000	.000	0	1.000
Jeff Juden	p	2	0	0	0	0	0	0	0	0	0	0	–	–	0	–
David Justice	lf-dh	7	27	4	5	0	0	0	4	6	8	0	.185	.185	0	1.000
Jose Mesa	p	5	0	0	0	0	0	0	0	0	0	0	–	–	0	1.000
Alvin Morman	p	2	0	0	0	0	0	0	0	0	0	0	–	–	0	–
Charles Nagy	p	2	0	0	0	0	0	0	0	0	0	0	–	–	0	1.000
Chad Ogea	p	2	4	1	2	1	0	0	2	0	1	0	.500	.750	0	1.000
Eric Plunk	p	3	0	0	0	0	0	0	0	0	0	0	–	–	0	–
Manny Ramirez	rf	7	26	3	4	0	0	2	6	6	5	0	.154	.385	1	.944
Bip Roberts	2b-lf	6	22	3	6	4	0	0	4	3	5	0	.273	.455	0	1.000
Kevin Seitzer	ph	1	1	0	0	0	0	0	0	0	0	0	.000	.000	–	–
Jim Thome	1b	7	28	8	8	0	1	2	4	5	7	0	.286	.571	1	.984
Omar Vizquel	ss	7	30	5	7	2	0	0	1	3	5	5	.233	.300	0	1.000
Matt Williams	3b	7	26	8	10	1	0	1	3	7	6	0	.385	.538	0	1.000
Jaret Wright	p	2	2	0	0	0	0	0	0	0	2	0	.000	.000	0	1.000
Totals		**7**	**247**	**44**	**72**	**12**	**1**	**7**	**42**	**40**	**51**	**5**	**.291**	**.433**	**5**	**.981**

Pitcher	G	GS	CG	IP	H	R	ER	BB	SO	W-L	Sv	ERA
Brian Anderson	3	0	0	3⅔	2	1	1	0	2	0-0	1	2.45
Paul Assenmacher	5	0	0	4	5	0	0	0	6	0-0	0	0.00
Orel Hershiser	2	2	0	10	15	13	13	6	5	0-2	0	11.70
Mike Jackson	4	0	0	4⅔	5	1	1	3	4	0-0	0	1.93
Jeff Juden	2	0	0	2	2	1	1	2	0	0-0	0	4.50
Jose Mesa	5	0	0	5	10	3	3	1	5	0-0	1	5.40
Alvin Morman	2	0	0	⅓	0	2	0	2	1	0-0	0	0.00
Charles Nagy	2	1	0	7	8	6	5	5	5	0-1	0	6.43
Chad Ogea	2	2	0	11⅔	11	2	2	3	5	2-0	0	1.54
Eric Plunk	3	0	0	3	3	4	3	4	3	0-1	0	9.00
Jaret Wright	2	2	0	12⅓	7	4	4	10	12	1-0	0	2.92
Totals	**7**	**7**	**0**	**63⅔**	**68**	**37**	**33**	**36**	**48**	**3-4**	**2**	**4.66**

Series MVP: Livan Hernandez, Florida Marlins. **Series Outstanding Pitcher:** Livan Hernandez, Florida Marlins. **Average Length of Game:** 3 hours, 25 minutes. **Total Attendance:** 403,617. **Average Attendance:** 57,660 (67,243 at Pro Player Stadium; 44,882 at Jacobs Field).
Umpires: Dale Ford (AL), Ken Kaiser (AL), Greg Kosc (AL), Randy Marsh (NL), Ed Montague (NL), Joe West (NL). **Winning Player's Share:** $188,468. **Losing Player's Share:** $113,226.

Left: This Game 4 action shows Matt Williams sliding in safely with a run for Cleveland in the first inning. Catcher Charles Johnson dives to make the tag a few seconds late.

Inset below: Gary Sheffield makes a sliding catch to retire Jim Thome in the fourth inning of Game 7.

Above: Cuban émigré Livan Hernandez won Series MVP after winning two games for Florida.

Inset above: Sandy Alomar Jr. drove in 10 runs for Cleveland in the Series while batting .367.

Left: Florida's Craig Counsell vaults home with the Series-winning run on Edgar Renteria's 11th-inning single in the final game.

Game 1 Saturday, October 18 at Pro Player Stadium, Miami

	1	2	3	4	5	6	7	8	9	R	H	E
Cleveland Indians	1	0	0	0	1	1	0	1	0	4	11	0
Florida Marlins	0	0	1	4	2	0	0	0	x	7	7	1

Pitchers Cle **Orel Hershiser** (L, 0-1), IP 4⅓, H 6, R 7, ER 7, BB 4, SO 2; **Jeff Juden**, IP ⅔, H 0, R 0, ER 0, BB 2, SO 0; **Eric Plunk**, IP 2, H 1, R 0, ER 0, BB 1, SO 1; **Paul Assenmacher**, IP 1, H 0, R 0, ER 0, BB 0, SO 2
Fla **Livan Hernandez** (W, 1-0), IP 5⅔, H 8, R 3, ER 3, BB 2, SO 5; **Dennis Cook**, IP 1⅔, H 0, R 0, ER 0, BB 1, SO 2; **Jay Powell**, IP ⅔, H 1, R 1, ER 1, BB 2, SO 1; **Robb Nen** (Sv, 1), IP 1, H 2, R 0, ER 0, BB 0, SO 2

Top Performers at the Plate
Cle **Marquis Grissom**, 2 for 3, 1 R, 1 BB; **Bip Roberts**, 2 for 4, 1 R, 1 BB, 2 2B
Fla **Moises Alou**, 1 for 3, 1 R, 3 RBI, 1 BB; **Bobby Bonilla**, 2 for 3, 2 R, 1 BB

2B-Cle/Grissom, Roberts 2; Fla/Counsell, Giles. **HR**-Cle/Ramirez, Thome; Fla/Alou, Johnson. **Time** 3:19. **Attendance** 67,245.

Game 2 Sunday, October 19 at Pro Player Stadium, Miami

	1	2	3	4	5	6	7	8	9	R	H	E
Cleveland Indians	1	0	0	0	3	2	0	0	0	6	14	0
Florida Marlins	1	0	0	0	0	0	0	0	0	1	8	0

Pitchers Cle **Chad Ogea** (W, 1-0), IP 6⅔, H 7, R 1, ER 1, BB 1, SO 4; **Mike Jackson**, IP 1⅓, H 1, R 0, ER 0, BB 0, SO 1; **Jose Mesa**, IP 1, H 0, R 0, ER 0, BB 1, SO 1
Fla **Kevin Brown** (L, 0-1), IP 6, H 10, R 6, ER 6, BB 2, SO 4; **Felix Heredia**, IP 1, H 1, R 0, ER 0, BB 0, SO 1; **Antonio Alfonseca**, IP 2, H 3, R 0, ER 0, BB 0, SO 0

Top Performers at the Plate
Cle **Sandy Alomar** Jr., 2 for 4, 2 R, 2 RBI; **Marquis Grissom**, 3 for 4, 1 R, 1 RBI
Fla **Moises Alou**, 2 for 4, 2 2B; **Edgar Renteria**, 2 for 4, 1 R

2B-Cle/Vizquel; Fla/Alou 2, Fernandez, Renteria, White. **HR**-Cle/Alomar Jr. **Time** 2:48. **Attendance** 67,025.

Game 3 Tuesday, October 21 at Jacobs Field, Cleveland

	1	2	3	4	5	6	7	8	9	R	H	E
Florida Marlins	1	0	1	1	0	2	2	0	7	14	16	3
Cleveland Indians	2	0	0	3	2	0	0	0	4	11	10	3

Pitchers Fla **Al Leiter**, IP 4⅔, H 6, R 7, ER 4, BB 6, SO 3; **Felix Heredia**, IP 2⅓, H 0, R 0, ER 0, BB 1, SO 0; **Dennis Cook** (W, 1-0), IP 1, H 1, R 0, ER 0, BB 0, SO 1; **Robb Nen**, IP 1, H 3, R 4, ER 4, BB 2, SO 1
Cle **Charles Nagy**, IP 6, H 6, R 5, ER 5, BB 4, SO 5; **Brian Anderson**, IP ⅓, H 1, R 1, ER 1, BB 0, SO 0; **Mike Jackson**, IP ⅔, H 2, R 1, ER 1, BB 1, SO 0; **Paul Assenmacher**, IP ⅔, H 3, R 0, ER 0, BB 0, SO 1; **Eric Plunk** (L, 0-1), IP ⅔, H 2, R 4, ER 3, BB 2, SO 1; **Alvin Morman**, IP ⅓, H 0, R 2, ER 0, BB 1, SO 1; **Jose Mesa**, IP ⅓, H 2, R 1, ER 1, BB 0, SO 0

Top Performers at the Plate
Fla **Darren Daulton**, 2 for 4, 3 R, 1 RBI, 2 BB; **Gary Sheffield**, 3 for 5, 2 R, 5 RBI, 1 BB
Cle **Marquis Grissom**, 2 for 3, 2 R, 1 RBI, 2 BB; **Jim Thome**, 2 for 4, 3 R, 2 RBI, 1 BB

2B-Fla/Sheffield; Cle/Roberts. **HR**-Fla/Daulton, Eisenreich, Sheffield; Cle/Thome. **Time** 4:12. **Attendance** 44,880.

Game 4 Wednesday, October 22 at Jacobs Field, Cleveland

	1	2	3	4	5	6	7	8	9	R	H	E
Florida Marlins	0	0	0	1	0	2	0	0	0	3	6	2
Cleveland Indians	3	0	3	0	0	1	1	2	x	10	15	0

Pitchers Fla **Tony Saunders** (L, 0-1), IP 2, H 7, R 6, ER 6, BB 3, SO 2; **Antonio Alfonseca**, IP 3, H 3, R 0, ER 0, BB 0, SO 4; **Ed Vosberg**, IP 2, H 3, R 2, ER 2, BB 2, SO 1; **Jay Powell**, IP 1, H 2, R 2, ER 2, BB 1, SO 0
Cle **Jaret Wright** (W, 1-0), IP 6, H 5, R 3, ER 3, BB 5, SO 5; **Brian Anderson** (Sv, 1), IP 3, H 1, R 0, ER 0, BB 0, SO 2

Top Performers at the Plate
Fla **Moises Alou**, 1 for 3, 1 R, 2 RBI, 1 BB; **Darren Daulton**, 2 for 3, 2 R, 1 BB
Cle **Sandy Alomar** Jr., 3 for 5, 3 RBI; **Matt Williams**, 3 for 3, 3 R, 2 RBI, 2 BB

2B-Fla/Daulton; Cle/Alomar Jr., Roberts. **HR**-Fla/Alou; Cle/Ramirez, Williams. **SB**-Fla/Counsell; Cle/Vizquel. **Time** 3:15. **Attendance** 44,877.

Game 5 Thursday, October 23 at Jacobs Field, Cleveland

	1	2	3	4	5	6	7	8	9	R	H	E
Florida Marlins	0	2	0	0	0	4	0	1	1	8	15	2
Cleveland Indians	0	1	3	0	0	0	0	0	3	7	9	0

Pitchers Fla **Livan Hernandez** (W, 2-0), IP 8, H 7, R 6, ER 5, BB 8, SO 2; **Robb Nen** (Sv, 2), IP 1, H 2, R 1, ER 0, BB 0, SO 1
Cle **Orel Hershiser** (L, 0-2), IP 5⅔, H 9, R 6, ER 6, BB 2, SO 3; **Alvin Morman**, IP 0, H 0, R 0, ER 0, BB 1, SO 0; **Eric Plunk**, IP ⅓, H 0, R 0, ER 0, BB 1, SO 1; **Jeff Juden**, IP 1⅓, H 2, R 1, ER 1, BB 0, SO 0; **Paul Assenmacher**, IP ⅔, H 1, R 0, ER 0, BB 0, SO 1; **Jose Mesa**, IP 1, H 3, R 1, ER 1, BB 0, SO 1

Top Performers at the Plate
Fla **Moises Alou**, 3 for 5, 2 R, 4 RBI; **Charles Johnson**, 3 for 5, 1 R, 2 RBI
Cle **Sandy Alomar** Jr., 2 for 5, 1 R, 4 RBI; **Jim Thome**, 2 for 4, 2 R, 1 RBI, 1 BB

2B-Fla/Bonilla, Daulton, White 2. **3B**-Cle/Thome. **HR**-Fla/Alou; Cle/Alomar Jr. **SB**-Fla/Alou, Daulton. **Time** 3:39. **Attendance** 44,888.

Game 6 Saturday, October 25 at Pro Player Stadium, Miami

	1	2	3	4	5	6	7	8	9	R	H	E
Cleveland Indians	0	2	1	0	1	0	0	0	0	4	7	0
Florida Marlins	0	0	0	0	1	0	0	0	0	1	8	0

Pitchers Cle **Chad Ogea** (W, 2-0), IP 5, H 4, R 1, ER 1, BB 2, SO 1; **Mike Jackson**, IP 2, H 2, R 0, ER 0, BB 2, SO 2; **Paul Assenmacher**, IP 1, H 1, R 0, ER 0, BB 0, SO 1; **Jose Mesa** (Sv, 1), IP 1, H 1, R 0, ER 0, BB 0, SO 1
Fla **Kevin Brown** (L, 0-2), IP 5, H 5, R 4, ER 4, BB 3, SO 2; **Felix Heredia**, IP 2, H 0, R 0, ER 0, BB 0, SO 4; **Jay Powell**, IP 1, H 2, R 0, ER 0, BB 0, SO 1; **Ed Vosberg**, IP 1, H 0, R 0, ER 0, BB 1, SO 1

Top Performers at the Plate
Cle **Chad Ogea**, 2 for 2, 1 R, 2 RBI; **Matt Williams**, 2 for 4, 1 R
Fla **Moises Alou**, 1 for 3, 1 R, 1 BB; **Devon White**, 3 for 5

2B-Cle/Ogea, Vizquel, Williams. **3B**-Fla/White. **SB**-Cle/Vizquel 2; Fla/White. **Time** 3:15. **Attendance** 67,498.

Game 7 Sunday, October 26 at Pro Player Stadium, Miami

	1	2	3	4	5	6	7	8	9	10	11	R	H	E
Cleveland Indians	0	0	2	0	0	0	0	0	0	0	0	2	6	2
Florida Marlins	0	0	0	0	0	0	1	0	1	0	1	3	8	0

Pitchers Cle **Jaret Wright**, IP 6⅓, H 2, R 1, ER 1, BB 5, SO 7; **Paul Assenmacher**, IP ⅔, H 0, R 0, ER 0, BB 0, SO 1; **Mike Jackson**, IP ⅔, H 0, R 0, ER 0, BB 0, SO 1; **Brian Anderson**, IP ⅓, H 0, R 0, ER 0, BB 0, SO 0; **Jose Mesa**, IP 1⅔, H 4, R 1, ER 1, BB 0, SO 2; **Charles Nagy** (L, 0-1), IP 1, H 2, R 1, ER 0, BB 1, SO 0
Fla **Al Leiter**, IP 6, H 4, R 2, ER 2, BB 4, SO 7; **Dennis Cook**, IP 1, H 0, R 0, ER 0, BB 0, SO 2; **Antonio Alfonseca**, IP 1⅓, H 0, R 0, ER 0, BB 1, SO 1; **Felix Heredia**, IP 0, H 1, R 0, ER 0, BB 0, SO 0; **Robb Nen**, IP 1⅔, H 1, R 0, ER 0, BB 0, SO 3; **Jay Powell** (W, 1-0), IP 1, H 0, R 0, ER 0, BB 1, SO 0

Top Performers at the Plate
Cle **Tony Fernandez**, 2 for 5, 2 RBI
Fla **Bobby Bonilla**, 2 for 5, 1 R, 1 RBI; **Edgar Renteria**, 3 for 5, 1 RBI, 1 BB

2B-Fla/Renteria. **HR**-Fla/Bonilla. **SB**-Cle/Vizquel 2. **Time** 4:10. **Attendance** 67,204.

New York Yankees (4) vs. San Diego Padres (0)

Following the formula that won them three straight pennants in the 1970s, the New York Yankees made several key free-agent acquisitions in 1998 to return to the top of the American League. Owner George Steinbrenner and general manager Brian Cashman brought all-star second baseman Chuck Knoblauch over from Minnesota, third baseman Scott Brosius from Oakland, and veteran slugger Chili Davis from Kansas City. Cuban-defector Orlando "El Duque" Hernandez and Japanese-import Hideki Irabu joined a talent-laden pitching staff, and the two combined to win 25 games in 49 starts. The result was 114 victories for New York in 1998—the highest total in American League history and the most since the Cubs won 116 in 1906. The team that earned the right to play this formidable club in the Series was the San Diego Padres, who won 98 games during the season and defeated the two top teams in the National League (Atlanta and Houston) in the playoffs for their second Fall Classic in franchise history. In Game 1, Greg Vaughn stroked two home runs and Tony Gwynn added another to give the Padres a three-run lead after five innings. Donne Wall relieved starter Kevin Brown with two men on base in the seventh inning, and Knoblauch took him deep, tying the game. The Yanks loaded the bases later in the same inning, and Tino Martinez emptied them with a grand slam off 37-year-old lefty Mark Langston. Before they knew it, San Diego's 5-2 lead morphed into a 9-6 loss. The Padres squandered a scoring opportunity in the first inning of Game 2 when Paul O'Neill ran down Wally Joyner's drive with two runners on base. New York proceeded to score seven times on Andy Ashby in the first three innings, and Jorge Posada tacked on two more with a homer in the fifth. El Duque held the Padres to one run through seven innings for his first World Series win. At home in San Diego, the Padres had a 3-0 lead in Game 3 until Brosius's seventh-inning homer, along with an unearned run, put New York within one. San Diego's relief ace Trevor Hoffman, who collected a league-record 53 saves in 1998, entered Game 3 in the eighth inning to pitch to Brosius with two runners on base. Brosius came through with his second home run to give the Yanks the lead. The Padres scored one more in the eighth, but New York's ace reliever Mariano Rivera closed the door. Andy Pettitte kept San Diego scoreless for seven and a third innings in Game 4, and Jeff Nelson and Rivera upheld the shutout in relief to clinch the sweep. Brosius finished the Series with a .471 average to go along with his pair of home runs, earning him MVP honors. But his wasn't the only productive bat, and New York finished with a .309 team average. The four-game sweep gave the Yankees an astounding 125 wins on the year.

Above: "El Duque" Orlando Hernandez shows his distinctive delivery during a Game 2 win in New York.

1998 WORLD SERIES COMPOSITE STATISTICS

NEW YORK YANKEES/Joe Torre, Manager

Player	pos	G	AB	R	H	2B	3B	HR	RBI	BB	SO	SB	BA	SA
Scott Brosius	3b	4	17	3	8	0	0	2	6	0	4	0	.471	.824
Homer Bush	dh	1	0	0	0	0	0	0	0	0	0	0	–	–
David Cone	p	1	2	0	1	0	0	0	0	0	0	0	.500	.500
Chili Davis	dh	3	7	3	2	0	0	0	2	3	2	0	.286	.286
Joe Girardi	c	2	6	0	0	0	0	0	0	0	2	0	.000	.000
Orlando Hernandez	p	1	0	0	0	0	0	0	0	0	0	0	.000	.000
Derek Jeter	ss	4	17	4	6	0	0	0	1	3	3	0	.353	.353
Chuck Knoblauch	2b	4	16	3	6	0	0	1	3	3	2	1	.375	.563
Ricky Ledee	lf	4	10	1	6	3	0	0	4	2	1	0	.600	.900
Graeme Lloyd	p	1	0	0	0	0	0	0	0	0	0	0	–	–
Tino Martinez	1b	4	13	4	5	0	0	1	4	4	2	0	.385	.615
Ramiro Mendoza	p	1	1	0	0	0	0	0	0	0	0	0	.000	.000
Jeff Nelson	p	3	0	0	0	0	0	0	0	0	0	0	–	–
Paul O'Neill	rf	4	19	3	4	1	0	0	0	1	2	0	.211	.263
Andy Pettitte	p	1	2	0	0	0	0	0	0	0	2	0	.000	.000
Jorge Posada	c	3	9	2	3	0	0	1	2	2	2	0	.333	.667
Mariano Rivera	p	3	1	0	0	0	0	0	0	0	0	0	.000	.000
Shane Spencer	lf	1	3	1	1	1	0	0	0	0	2	0	.333	.667
Mike Stanton	p	0	0	0	0	0	0	0	0	0	0	0	–	–
David Wells	p	1	0	0	0	0	0	0	0	0	0	0	–	–
Bernie Williams	cf	4	16	2	1	0	0	1	3	2	5	0	.063	.250
Totals		**4**	**139**	**26**	**43**	**5**	**0**	**6**	**25**	**20**	**29**	**1**	**.309**	**.475**

Pitcher	G	GS	CG	IP	H	R	ER	BB	SO	W-L	Sv	ERA
David Cone	1	1	0	6	2	3	2	3	4	0-0	0	3.00
Orlando Hernandez	1	1	0	7	6	1	1	3	7	1-0	0	1.29
Graeme Lloyd	1	0	0	⅓	0	0	0	0	0	0-0	0	0.00
Ramiro Mendoza	1	0	0	1	2	1	1	0	1	1-0	0	9.00
Jeff Nelson	3	0	0	2⅓	2	1	0	1	4	0-0	0	0.00
Andy Pettitte	1	1	0	7⅓	5	0	0	3	4	1-0	0	0.00
Mariano Rivera	3	0	0	4⅓	5	0	0	0	4	0-0	3	0.00
Mike Stanton	1	0	0	⅔	3	2	2	0	1	0-0	0	27.00
David Wells	1	1	0	7	7	5	5	2	4	1-0	0	6.43
Totals	**4**	**4**	**0**	**36**	**32**	**13**	**11**	**12**	**29**	**4-0**	**3**	**2.75**

SAN DIEGO PADRES/Bruce Bochy, Manager

Player	pos	G	AB	R	H	2B	3B	HR	RBI	BB	SO	SB	BA	SA
Andy Ashby	p	1	0	0	0	0	0	0	0	0	0	0	–	–
Brian Boehringer	p	2	0	0	0	0	0	0	0	0	0	0	–	–
Kevin Brown	p	1	2	0	1	0	0	0	0	0	0	0	.500	.500
Ken Caminiti	3b	4	14	1	2	1	0	0	1	2	7	0	.143	.214
Steve Finley	cf	3	12	0	1	1	0	0	0	0	2	1	.083	.167
Chris Gomez	ss	4	11	2	4	0	1	0	0	1	1	0	.364	.545
Tony Gwynn	rf	4	16	2	8	0	0	1	3	1	0	0	.500	.688
Joey Hamilton	p	1	0	0	0	0	0	0	0	0	0	0	–	–
Carlos Hernandez	c	4	10	0	2	0	0	0	0	0	3	0	.200	.200
Sterling Hitchcock	p	1	2	1	1	0	0	0	0	0	0	0	.500	.500
Trevor Hoffman	p	1	0	0	0	0	0	0	0	0	0	0	–	–
Wally Joyner	1b	3	8	0	0	0	0	0	0	3	1	0	.000	.000
Mark Langston	p	1	0	0	0	0	0	0	0	0	0	0	–	–
Jim Leyritz	c-1b	4	10	0	0	0	0	0	0	1	4	0	.000	.000
Dan Miceli	p	1	0	0	0	0	0	0	0	0	0	0	–	–
Greg Myers	c	2	4	0	0	0	0	0	0	0	2	0	.000	.000
Randy Myers	p	2	0	0	0	0	0	0	0	0	0	0	–	–
Ruben Rivera	lf-cf	3	5	1	4	2	0	0	1	0	0	0	.800	1.200
Andy Sheets	ss	2	2	0	0	0	0	0	0	0	1	0	.000	.000
Mark Sweeney	ph	3	3	0	2	0	0	0	1	0	0	0	.667	.667
John Vander Wal	lf	4	5	0	2	1	0	0	0	0	2	0	.400	.600
Greg Vaughn	dh-lf	4	15	3	2	0	0	2	4	1	2	0	.133	.533
Quilvio Veras	2b	4	15	3	3	2	0	0	1	3	4	0	.200	.333
Donnie Wall	p	2	0	0	0	0	0	0	0	0	0	0	–	–
Totals		**4**	**134**	**13**	**32**	**7**	**1**	**3**	**11**	**12**	**29**	**1**	**.239**	**.373**

Pitcher	G	GS	CG	IP	H	R	ER	BB	SO	W-L	Sv	ERA
Andy Ashby	1	1	0	2⅔	10	7	4	1	1	0-1	0	13.50
Brian Boehringer	2	0	0	2	4	2	2	2	3	0-0	0	9.00
Kevin Brown	2	2	0	14⅓	14	7	7	6	13	0-1	0	4.40
Joey Hamilton	1	0	0	1	0	0	0	1	1	0-0	0	0.00
Sterling Hitchcock	1	1	0	6	7	2	1	1	7	0-0	0	1.50
Trevor Hoffman	1	0	0	2	2	2	2	1	0	0-1	0	9.00
Mark Langston	1	0	0	⅔	1	3	3	2	0	0-0	0	40.50
Dan Miceli	2	0	0	1⅔	2	0	0	2	1	0-0	0	0.00
Randy Myers	3	0	0	1	0	1	1	1	2	0-0	0	9.00
Donne Wall	2	0	0	2⅔	3	2	2	3	1	0-1	0	6.75
Totals	**4**	**4**	**0**	**34**	**43**	**26**	**22**	**20**	**29**	**0-4**	**0**	**5.82**

Series MVP: Scott Brosius, New York Yankees. **Series Outstanding Pitcher:** Mariano Rivera, New York Yankees. **Average Length of Game:** 3 hours, 18 minutes. **Total Attendance:** 243,498. **Average Attendance:** 60,875 (56,702 at Yankee Stadium; 65,047 at Qualcomm Stadium). **Umpires:** Jerry Crawford (NL), Dana DeMuth (NL), Rich Garcia (AL), Mark Hirschbeck (NL), Dale Scott (AL), Tim Tschida (AL).

Right: Greg Vaughn did his part by knocking two homers and driving in three runs in the opener, but his Padres still lost, 9-6.

Below: Tino Martinez breaks open Game 1 with a grand-slam home run in the seventh inning.

New York's four-game sweep in 1998 started a streak of 14 consecutive World Series games without a loss for the Yankees.

Game 1 Saturday, October 17 at Yankee Stadium, New York

	1	2	3	4	5	6	7	8	9	R	H	E
San Diego Padres	0	0	2	0	3	0	0	1	0	6	8	1
New York Yankees	0	2	0	0	0	0	7	0	x	9	9	1

Pitchers SD Kevin Brown, IP $6\frac{1}{3}$, H 6, R 4, ER 4, BB 3, SO 5; Donne Wall (L, 0-1), IP 0, H 2, R 2, ER 2, BB 0, SO 0; Mark Langston, IP $\frac{2}{3}$, H 1, R 3, ER 3, BB 2, SO 0; Brian Boehringer, IP $\frac{1}{3}$, H 0, R 0, ER 0, BB 1, SO 1; Randy Myers, IP $\frac{2}{3}$, H 0, R 0, ER 0, BB 0, SO 2

NY David Wells (W, 1-0), IP 7, H 7, R 5, ER 5, BB 2, SO 4; Jeff Nelson, IP $\frac{2}{3}$, H 1, R 1, ER 0, BB 1, SO 1; Mariano Rivera (Sv, 1), IP $1\frac{1}{3}$, H 0, R 0, ER 0, BB 0, SO 2

Top Performers at the Plate

SD Tony Gwynn, 3 for 4, 1 R, 2 RBI; Greg Vaughn, 2 for 4, 3 R, 3 RBI, 2 HR

NY Chuck Knoblauch, 2 for 4, 1 R, 3 RBI, 1 HBP; Tino Martinez, 1 for 3, 2 R, 4 RBI, 1 BB

2B-SD/Finley; NY/Ledee. **HR**-SD/Gwynn, Vaughn 2; NY/Knoblauch, Martinez. **Time** 3:29. **Attendance** 56,712.

Game 2 Sunday, October 18 at Yankee Stadium, New York

	1	2	3	4	5	6	7	8	9	R	H	E
San Diego Padres	0	0	0	0	1	0	0	2	0	3	10	1
New York Yankees	3	3	1	0	2	0	0	0	x	9	16	0

Pitchers SD Andy Ashby (L, 0-1), IP $2\frac{2}{3}$, H 10, R 7, ER 4, BB 1, SO 1; Brian Boehringer, IP $1\frac{2}{3}$, H 4, R 2, ER 2, BB 1, SO 2; Donne Wall, IP $2\frac{2}{3}$, H 1, R 0, ER 0, BB 3, SO 1; Dan Miceli, IP 1, H 1, R 0, ER 0, BB 2, SO 1

NY Orlando Hernandez (W, 1-0), IP 7, H 6, R 1, ER 1, BB 3, SO 7; Mike Stanton, IP $\frac{2}{3}$, H 3, R 2, ER 2, BB 0, SO 1; Jeff Nelson, IP $1\frac{1}{3}$, H 1, R 0, ER 0, BB 0, SO 2

Top Performers at the Plate

SD Chris Gomez, 2 for 3, 1 R; John Vander Wal, 2 for 3

NY Scott Brosius, 3 for 5, 1 R, 1 RBI; Chuck Knoblauch, 2 for 3, 2 R, 2 BB

2B-SD/Caminiti, R. Rivera, Vander Wal, Veras; NY/Ledee. **3B**-SD/Gomez. **HR**-NY/Posada, Williams. **SB**-NY/Knoblauch. **Time** 3:31. **Attendance** 56,692.

Game 3 Tuesday, October 20 at Qualcomm Stadium, San Diego

	1	2	3	4	5	6	7	8	9	R	H	E
New York Yankees	0	0	0	0	0	0	2	3	0	5	9	1
San Diego Padres	0	0	0	0	0	3	0	1	0	4	7	1

Pitchers NY David Cone, IP 6, H 2, R 3, ER 2, BB 3, SO 4; Graeme Lloyd, IP $\frac{1}{3}$, H 0, R 0, ER 0, BB 0, SO 0; Ramiro Mendoza (W, 1-0), IP 1, H 2, R 1, ER 1, BB 0, SO 1; Mariano Rivera (Sv, 2), IP $1\frac{2}{3}$, H 3, R 0, ER 0, BB 0, SO 2

SD Sterling Hitchcock, IP 6, H 7, R 2, ER 1, BB 1, SO 7; Joey Hamilton, IP 1, H 0, R 0, ER 0, BB 1, SO 1; Randy Myers, IP 0, H 0, R 1, ER 1, BB 1, SO 0; Trevor Hoffman (L, 0-1), IP 2, H 2, R 2, ER 2, BB 1, SO 0

Top Performers at the Plate

NY Scott Brosius, 3 for 4, 2 R, 4 RBI; Shane Spencer, 1 for 3, 1 R

SD Tony Gwynn, 2 for 4, 1 R, 1 RBI; Quilvio Veras, 1 for 3, 2 R, 1 BB

2B-NY/Spencer; SD/Veras. **HR**-NY/Brosius 2. **SB**-SD/Finley. **Time** 3:14. **Attendance** 64,667.

Game 4 Wednesday, October 21 at Qualcomm Stadium, San Diego

	1	2	3	4	5	6	7	8	9	R	H	E
New York Yankees	0	0	0	0	0	1	0	2	0	3	9	0
San Diego Padres	0	0	0	0	0	0	0	0	0	0	7	0

Pitchers NY Andy Pettitte (W, 1-0), IP $7\frac{1}{3}$, H 5, R 0, ER 0, BB 3, SO 4; Jeff Nelson, IP $\frac{1}{3}$, H 0, R 0, ER 0, BB 0, SO 1; Mariano Rivera (Sv, 3), IP $1\frac{1}{3}$, H 2, R 0, ER 0, BB 0, SO 0

SD Kevin Brown (L, 0-1), IP 8, H 8, R 3, ER 3, BB 3, SO 8; Dan Miceli, IP $\frac{2}{3}$, H 1, R 0, ER 0, BB 0, SO 0; Randy Myers, IP $\frac{1}{3}$, H 0, R 0, ER 0, BB 0, SO 0

Top Performers at the Plate

NY Derek Jeter, 2 for 4, 2 R, 1 BB; Ricky Ledee, 2 for 3, 1 RBI, 1 SF

SD Tony Gwynn, 2 for 4; Ruben Rivera, 3 for 4

2B-NY/Ledee, O'Neill; SD/R. Rivera. **Time** 2:58. **Attendance** 65,427.

Left: Series MVP Scott Brosius drives one into the San Diego night against Sterling Hitchcock during Game 3.

Right: Paul O'Neill's leaping catch at the wall ended a San Diego threat in the first inning of Game 2. The Yanks responded with three runs in each of the next two innings.

New York Yankees (4) vs. Atlanta Braves (0)

The 1999 World Series was billed as a contest to crown the "Team of the Decade." The Atlanta Braves were entering their fifth Fall Classic of the 1990s—the most by a National League team in one decade since the 1950s Dodgers—and the New York Yankees were aiming to win their third in four years. The Yanks didn't stand pat after the 1998 championship, bringing five-time Cy Young winner Roger Clemens over from Toronto. While the big question heading into the Series was who would emerge as team of the 1990s, when it was over, there was no question about the dominant team of October 1999. With a four-game spanking, the Yankees became the first team since the 1938–39 Yankees to win back-to-back sweeps. It started with Orlando Hernandez's awesome performance in Game 1. El Duque held the Braves to just one hit (a Chipper Jones home run) and struck out ten in seven innings. Greg Maddux yielded only three singles in seven shutout innings until New York rallied for four runs in the eighth. Two errors by defensive-replacement Brian Hunter at first base led to three runs, and Atlanta's fiery closer John Rocker walked in a fourth. In Game 2, David Cone kept the Braves hitless through four innings and scoreless through seven. Although Atlanta ultimately got on the board with two runs in the ninth, the Yankee hitters had established a 7-0 lead at that point. Atlanta's young 18-game-winner Kevin Millwood was knocked for five runs, beginning with a three-run first inning that featured three straight singles to start the game. Limited to three runs and seven hits in the first two games, the Braves exploded for ten hits and five runs in Game 3 against starter Andy Pettitte. New York slowly chipped away at the lead, and Chuck Knoblauch's two-run homer in the eighth tied it up. Three relievers shut Atlanta out for the last six innings, and Chad Curtis delivered his second homer of the game in the bottom of the 10th to give New York a 6-5 victory. A fielding misplay led to three Yankee runs in Game 4. In the third inning, Tino Martinez hit a grounder to first with the bases loaded, but the ball hit off Ryan Klesko's arm for a two-run single. The Braves managed only five singles in the game, as Roger Clemens earned his first World Series win; Mariano Rivera pitched a perfect inning and a third to claim his fifth career World Series save. Overcoming several off-field distractions during the season—including manager Joe Torre's cancer diagnosis, Darryl Strawberry's cocaine arrest, and the loss of three players' fathers—New York won its 25th world championship. The Braves, meanwhile, joined rare company as one of only two teams to lose four Series in one decade (the other being the 1910–19 New York Giants).

Above: Derek Jeter's errorless fielding and .353 batting helped lead New York to a second-straight title.

1999 WORLD SERIES COMPOSITE STATISTICS

NEW YORK YANKEES/Joe Torre, Manager

Player	pos	G	AB	R	H	2B	3B	HR	RBI	BB	SO	SB	BA	SA	E	FPct
Scott Brosius	3b	4	16	2	6	1	0	0	1	0	5	0	.375	.438	0	1.000
Roger Clemens	p	1	0	0	0	0	0	0	0	0	0	0	—	—	0	1.000
David Cone	p	1	4	0	0	0	0	0	0	0	0	0	.000	.000	1	.500
Chad Curtis	pr-lf-ph	3	6	3	2	0	0	2	2	0	0	0	.333	1.333	0	1.000
Chili Davis	dh	1	4	0	0	0	0	0	0	0	2	0	.000	.000	—	—
Joe Girardi	c	2	7	1	2	0	0	0	0	1	0	0	.286	.286	0	1.000
Jason Grimsley	p	1	0	0	0	0	0	0	0	0	0	0	—	—	0	—
Orlando Hernandez	p	1	1	0	0	0	0	0	0	0	0	0	.000	.000	0	1.000
Derek Jeter	ss	4	17	4	6	1	0	0	1	1	3	3	.353	.412	0	1.000
Chuck Knoblauch	2b	4	16	5	5	1	0	1	3	1	3	1	.313	.563	0	1.000
Ricky Ledee	lf	3	10	0	2	1	0	0	1	1	4	0	.200	.300	0	1.000
Jim Leyritz	ph-dh	2	1	1	1	0	0	1	2	1	0	0	1.000	4.000	—	—
Tino Martinez	1b	4	15	3	4	0	0	1	5	2	4	0	.267	.467	0	1.000
Ramiro Mendoza	p	1	1	0	0	0	0	0	0	0	0	0	.000	.000	0	1.000
Jeff Nelson	p	4	0	0	0	0	0	0	0	0	0	0	—	—	0	1.000
Paul O'Neill	rf	4	15	0	3	0	0	0	4	2	2	0	.200	.200	0	1.000
Andy Pettitte	p	1	0	0	0	0	0	0	0	0	0	0	—	—	0	1.000
Jorge Posada	c	2	8	0	2	1	0	0	1	0	3	0	.250	.375	0	1.000
Mariano Rivera	p	3	0	0	0	0	0	0	0	0	0	0	—	—	0	1.000
Luis Sojo	2b	1	0	0	0	0	0	0	0	0	0	0	—	—	0	1.000
Mike Stanton	p	1	0	0	0	0	0	0	0	0	0	0	—	—	0	—
Darryl Strawberry	ph-dh	2	3	0	1	0	0	0	1	2	0	0	.333	.333	—	—
Bernie Williams	cf	4	13	2	3	0	0	0	4	2	1	1	.231	.231	0	1.000
Totals		**4**	**137**	**21**	**37**	**5**	**0**	**5**	**20**	**13**	**31**	**5**	**.270**	**.416**	**1**	**.994**

Pitcher	G	GS	CG	IP	H	R	ER	BB	SO	W-L	Sv	ERA
Roger Clemens	1	1	0	7⅔	4	1	1	2	4	1-0	0	1.17
David Cone	1	1	0	7	1	0	0	5	4	1-0	0	0.00
Jason Grimsley	1	0	0	2⅓	2	0	0	2	0	0-0	0	0.00
Orlando Hernandez	1	1	0	7	1	1	1	2	10	1-0	0	1.29
Ramiro Mendoza	1	0	0	1⅔	3	2	2	1	0	0-0	0	10.80
Jeff Nelson	4	0	0	2⅔	2	0	0	1	3	0-0	0	0.00
Andy Pettitte	1	1	0	3⅔	10	5	5	1	1	0	0	12.27
Mariano Rivera	3	0	0	4⅔	3	0	0	1	3	1-0	2	0.00
Mike Stanton	1	0	0	⅓	0	0	0	0	1	0-0	0	0.00
Totals	**4**	**4**	**0**	**37**	**26**	**9**	**9**	**15**	**26**	**4-0**	**2**	**2.19**

ATLANTA BRAVES/Bobby Cox, Manager

Player	pos	G	AB	R	H	2B	3B	HR	RBI	BB	SO	SB	BA	SA	E	FPct
Howard Battle	ph	1	0	0	0	0	0	0	0	0	0	0	—	—	—	—
Bret Boone	2b-ph	4	13	1	7	4	0	0	3	1	3	0	.538	.846	0	1.000
Jorge Fabregas	ph	1	1	0	0	0	0	0	0	0	1	0	.000	.000	—	—
Tom Glavine	p	1	0	0	0	0	0	0	0	0	0	0	—	—	0	1.000
Ozzie Guillen	ph-ss-dh	3	5	0	0	0	0	0	0	0	1	0	.000	.000	1	.875
Jose Hernandez	ss-dh	2	5	0	1	1	0	0	2	0	2	1	.200	.400	0	.846
Brian Hunter	1b	2	4	0	1	0	0	0	0	0	1	0	.250	.250	2	.846
Andruw Jones	cf	4	13	1	1	0	0	0	0	1	3	0	.077	.077	0	1.000
Chipper Jones	3b	4	13	2	3	0	0	1	2	4	2	0	.231	.462	0	1.000
Brian Jordan	rf	4	13	1	1	0	0	0	1	4	2	0	.077	.077	1	.889
Ryan Klesko	1b-ph	4	12	0	2	0	0	0	0	1	1	0	.167	.167	0	1.000
Keith Lockhart	ph-2b-dh	4	7	1	1	0	0	0	0	2	0	0	.143	.143	0	1.000
Greg Maddux	p	1	2	0	0	0	0	0	0	0	2	0	.000	.000	0	1.000
Kevin McGlinchy	p	1	0	0	0	0	0	0	0	0	0	0	—	—	0	—
Kevin Millwood	p	1	0	0	0	0	0	0	0	0	0	0	—	—	0	—
Terry Mulholland	p	2	0	0	0	0	0	0	0	1	0	0	—	—	0	1.000
Greg Myers	ph-c	2	6	0	2	0	0	0	1	1	0	0	.333	.333	0	1.000
Otis Nixon	cf-pr	2	2	0	1	0	0	0	0	0	0	0	.500	.500	0	—
Eddie Perez	c	3	8	0	1	0	0	0	0	1	3	0	.125	.125	0	1.000
Mike Remlinger	p	2	0	0	0	0	0	0	0	0	0	0	—	—	0	—
John Rocker	p	2	0	0	0	0	0	0	0	0	0	0	—	—	0	—
John Smoltz	p	1	0	0	0	0	0	0	0	0	0	0	—	—	0	—
Russ Springer	p	2	0	0	0	0	0	0	0	0	0	0	—	—	0	1.000
Walt Weiss	ss	3	9	1	2	0	0	0	0	1	1	0	.222	.222	0	1.000
Gerald Williams	lf	4	17	2	3	0	1	0	0	0	4	0	.176	.294	0	1.000
Totals		**4**	**130**	**9**	**26**	**5**	**1**	**1**	**9**	**15**	**26**	**1**	**.200**	**.277**	**4**	**.971**

Pitcher	G	GS	CG	IP	H	R	ER	BB	SO	W-L	Sv	ERA
Tom Glavine	1	1	0	7	7	5	4	0	3	0-0	0	5.14
Greg Maddux	1	1	0	7	5	4	2	3	5	0-1	0	2.57
Kevin McGlinchy	1	0	0	2	2	0	0	1	2	0-0	0	0.00
Kevin Millwood	1	1	0	2	8	5	4	2	2	0-1	0	18.00
Terry Mulholland	2	0	0	3⅔	5	3	3	1	3	0-0	0	7.36
Mike Remlinger	2	0	0	1	1	1	1	1	0	0-1	0	9.00
John Rocker	2	0	0	3	2	0	0	2	4	0-0	0	0.00
John Smoltz	1	1	0	7	6	3	3	3	11	0-1	0	3.86
Russ Springer	2	0	0	2⅓	1	0	0	0	1	0-0	0	0.00
Totals	**4**	**4**	**0**	**35**	**37**	**21**	**17**	**13**	**31**	**0-4**	**0**	**4.37**

Series MVP: Mariano Rivera, New York Yankees. **Series Outstanding Pitcher:** Mariano Rivera, New York Yankees. **Average Length of Game:** 3 hours, 6 minutes. **Total Attendance:** 216,114. **Average Attendance:** 54,029 (56,773 at Yankee Stadium; 51,284 at Turner Field).
Umpires: Derryl Cousins (AL), Gerry Davis (NL), Jim Joyce (AL), Randy Marsh (NL), Steve Rippley (NL), Rocky Roe (AL).

Right: Chad Curtis is the unexpected hero when his 10th-inning homer gave New York a Game 3 victory. It was Curtis' second clout of the game.

Below: Orlando Hernandez improved his career World Series record to 2-0 with a one-hit, ten-strikeout victory in Game 1.

Game 3 of 1999 was the 200th World Series game for the New York Yankee franchise.

Inset: Atlanta outfielder Brian Jordan makes a play on Knoblauch's deep fly in Game 3, but the ball popped out of his glove and over the wall for a two-run, game-tying home run.

Right: A dejected Kevin Millwood leaves the mound in Game 2 after yielding eight hits and five runs in two innings.

Above: Propelling a Yankee rally in the eighth inning of Game 1, Chuck Knoblauch lays down a bunt with two runners on. An error by Brian Hunter left the bases loaded, and New York went on to score four runs.

Game 1 Saturday, October 23 at Turner Field, Atlanta

	1	2	3	4	5	6	7	8	9	R	H	E
New York Yankees	0	0	0	0	0	0	0	4	0	4	6	0
Atlanta Braves	0	0	0	1	0	0	0	0	0	1	2	2

Pitchers NY Orlando Hernandez (W, 1-0), IP 7, H 1, R 1, ER 1, BB 2, SO 10;; Jeff Nelson, IP ⅓, H 0, R 0, ER 0, BB 1, SO 1; Mike Stanton, IP ⅓, H 0, R 0, ER 0, BB 0, SO 1; Mariano Rivera (Sv, 1), IP 1⅓, H 1, R 0, ER 0, BB 1, SO 1
Atl Greg Maddux (L, 0-1), IP 7, H 5, R 4, ER 2, BB 3, SO 5; John Rocker, IP 1, H 1, R 0, ER 0, BB 2, SO 3; Mike Remlinger, IP 1, H 0, R 0, ER 0, BB 1, SO 0

Top Performers at the Plate
NY Scott Brosius, 3 for 4, 1 R; Derek Jeter, 2 for 4, 1 R, 1 RBI, 1 BB
Atl Chipper Jones, 1 for 2, 1 R, 1 RBI, 1 BB

HR-Atl/C. Jones. **SB**-NY/Jeter, B. Williams. **Time** 2:57. **Attendance** 51,342.

Game 2 Sunday, October 24 at Turner Field, Atlanta

	1	2	3	4	5	6	7	8	9	R	H	E
New York Yankees	3	0	2	1	1	0	0	0		7	14	1
Atlanta Braves	0	0	0	0	0	0	2	0		2	5	1

Pitchers NY David Cone (W, 1-0), IP 7, H 1, R 0, ER 0, BB 5, SO 4; Ramiro Mendoza, IP 1⅔, H 3, R 2, ER 2, BB 1, SO 0; Jeff Nelson, IP ⅓, H 1, R 0, ER 0, BB 0, SO 0
Atl Kevin Millwood (L, 0-1), IP 2, H 8, R 5, ER 4, BB 2, SO 2; Terry Mulholland, IP 3, H 3, R 2, ER 2, BB 1, SO 3; Russ Springer, IP 2, H 1, R 0, ER 0, BB 0, SO 1; Kevin McGlinchy, IP 2, H 2, R 0, ER 0, BB 1, SO 2

Top Performers at the Plate
NY Tino Martinez, 2 for 5, 2 R, 2 RBI; Bernie Williams, 3 for 4, 1 R, 1 BB
Atl Chipper Jones, 1 for 3, 1 R, 1 BB; Greg Myers, 2 for 3, 1 RBI, 1 BB

2B-NY/Brosius, Jeter, Ledee; Atl/Boone. **SB**-NY/Knoblauch. **Time** 3:14. **Attendance** 51,226.

Game 3 Tuesday, October 26 at Yankee Stadium, New York

	1	2	3	4	5	6	7	8	9	10	R	H	E
Atlanta Braves	1	0	3	1	0	0	0	0	0	0	5	14	1
New York Yankees	1	0	0	0	1	0	1	2	0	1	6	9	0

Pitchers Atl Tom Glavine, IP 7, H 7, R 5, ER 4, BB 0, SO 3; John Rocker, IP 2, H 1, R 0, ER 0, BB 0, SO 1; Mike Remlinger (L, 0-1), IP 0, H 1, R 1, ER 1, BB 0, SO 0
NY Andy Pettitte, IP 3⅔, H 10, R 5, ER 5, BB 1, SO 1; Jason Grimsley, IP 2⅓, H 2, R 0, ER 0, BB 2, SO 0; Jeff Nelson, IP 2, H 0, R 0, ER 0, BB 0, SO 2; Mariano Rivera (W, 1-0), IP 2, H 2, R 0, ER 0, BB 0, SO 2

Top Performers at the Plate
Atl Bret Boone, 4 for 5, 1 R, 1 RBI, 3 2B; Gerald Williams, 2 for 5, 2 R
NY Chad Curtis, 2 for 4, 2 R, 2 RBI, 2 HR; Chuck Knoblauch, 2 for 4, 2 R, 2 RBI

2B-Atl/Boone 3, J. Hernandez; NY/Knoblauch. **3B**-Atl/G. Williams. **HR**-NY/Curtis 2, Knoblauch, Martinez. **SB**-Atl/J. Hernandez. **Time** 3:16. **Attendance** 56,794.

Game 4 Wednesday, October 27 at Yankee Stadium, New York

	1	2	3	4	5	6	7	8	9	R	H	E
Atlanta Braves	0	0	0	0	0	0	1	0		1	5	0
New York Yankees	0	0	3	0	0	0	1	x		4	8	0

Pitchers Atl John Smoltz (L, 0-1), IP 7, H 6, R 3, ER 3, BB 3, SO 11; Terry Mulholland, IP ⅔, H 2, R 1, ER 1, BB 0, SO 0; Russ Springer, IP ⅓, H 0, R 0, ER 0, BB 0, SO 0
NY Roger Clemens (W, 1-0), IP 7⅔, H 4, R 1, ER 1, BB 2, SO 4; Jeff Nelson, IP 0, H 1, R 0, ER 0, BB 0, SO 0; Mariano Rivera (Sv, 2), IP 1⅓, H 0, R 0, ER 0, BB 0, SO 0

Top Performers at the Plate
Atl Bret Boone, 1 for 3, 1 RBI, 1 BB; Walt Weiss, 1 for 3, 1 R
NY Tino Martinez, 1 for 3, 2 RBI, 1 BB; Jorge Posada, 2 for 4, 1 RBI

2B-NY/Posada. **HR**-NY/Leyritz. **SB**-NY/Jeter 2. **Time** 2:58. **Attendance** 56,752.

Every player in Atlanta's starting lineup in Game 3 had at least one base hit by the fourth inning.

New York Yankees (4) vs. New York Mets (1)

The New York Yankees continued to roll in the new millennium with the franchise's 37th World Series appearance. Across town in Queens, the Mets won their fourth pennant—and New Yorkers were treated to the first Subway Series in 44 years. Game 1 was a classic. Lefty starters Al Leiter and Andy Pettitte hurled dueling shutouts until David Justice hit a two-run double in the sixth to put the Yankees on top. The Mets had squandered an opportunity in the top of the inning after a baserunning gaffe. With two outs and Timo Perez on first base, Todd Zeile hit a deep drive that hit the very top of the wall in left. Perez, thinking it was a home run, initially jogged around the bases before he realized the ball was still in play. Although he picked up speed around third and into home, Perez was thrown out at the plate, ending the inning. The Mets rebounded and took the lead in the seventh, but the Yanks later tied the score against reliever Armando Benitez. Benitez gave up a walk and two singles in the ninth before Chuck Knoblauch drove in a run with a sacrifice fly. The Yankee relievers Mariano Rivera and Mike Stanton did their part, striking out six Mets and not allowing a baserunner in three extra innings. Jose Vizcaino, who delivered a key hit in the Yankees' ninth-inning rally, came to the plate with two outs and the bases loaded in the 12th and collected the game-winner with an RBI single, ending the longest game (by time) in Series history. With all the pre-Series media attention focused on Roger Clemens's beaning of Mike Piazza in a July 9th interleague game, it was no surprise that a bizarre incident involving those two players was the top story of the 2000 Series. Facing Clemens in the first inning of Game 2, Piazza shattered his bat fouling off a fastball. The severed end of the bat bounced toward the mound, and Clemens picked it up and inexplicably hurled it toward the sidelines. The bat crossed Piazza's path as he jogged toward first, much to the chagrin of Piazza and the Mets. The benches cleared, but the situation diffused without major incident, as Clemens insisted that he had no intention of hitting Piazza. Although his throw of a shattered piece of wood made the headlines, Clemens's throwing of the baseball was phenomenal. He gave up only two singles in the game, struck out nine, and allowed no runs. The Mets managed to score five against the Yankee bull pen in the ninth, but left fielder Clay Bellinger robbed Zeile of a homer to preserve the 6-5 final. Piazza's two-run homer in the inning ended Rivera's streak of consecutive shutout

2000 WORLD SERIES COMPOSITE STATISTICS

NEW YORK YANKEES/Joe Torre, Manager

Player	pos	G	AB	R	H	2B	3B	HR	RBI	BB	SO	SB	BA	SA	E	FPct
Clay Bellinger	pr-lf	4	0	0	0	0	0	0	0	0	0	0	—	—	0	1.000
Scott Brosius	3b	5	13	2	4	0	0	1	3	2	2	0	.308	.538	0	1.000
Jose Canseco	ph	1	1	0	0	0	0	0	0	0	1	0	.000	.000	—	—
Roger Clemens	p	1	0	0	0	0	0	0	0	0	0	0	—	—	1	.667
David Cone	p	1	0	0	0	0	0	0	0	0	0	0	—	—	0	—
Orlando Hernandez	p	1	2	0	0	0	0	0	0	0	2	0	.000	.000	0	—
Glenallen Hill	ph-lf	3	3	0	0	0	0	0	0	0	0	0	.000	.000	0	—
Derek Jeter	ss	5	22	6	9	2	1	2	2	3	8	0	.409	.837	0	1.000
David Justice	lf	5	19	1	3	2	0	0	3	3	2	0	.158	.263	0	1.000
Chuck Knoblauch	dh-ph	4	10	1	1	0	0	0	1	2	1	0	.100	.100	—	—
Tino Martinez	1b	5	22	3	8	1	0	0	2	1	4	0	.364	.409	0	1.000
Denny Neagle	p	1	2	0	0	0	0	0	0	0	1	0	.000	.000	0	—
Jeff Nelson	p	3	0	0	0	0	0	0	0	0	0	0	—	—	0	1.000
Paul O'Neill	rf	5	19	2	9	2	2	0	2	3	4	0	.474	.789	0	1.000
Andy Pettitte	p	2	3	0	0	0	0	0	0	0	0	1	.000	.000	0	.500
Luis Polonia	ph	2	2	0	1	0	0	0	0	0	0	0	.500	.500	—	—
Jorge Posada	c	5	18	2	4	1	0	0	1	5	4	0	.222	.278	0	1.000
Mariano Rivera	p	4	1	0	0	0	0	0	0	0	0	0	.000	.000	0	1.000
Luis Sojo	3b-2b	4	7	0	2	0	0	0	2	1	0	1	.286	.286	0	1.000
Mike Stanton	p	4	0	0	0	0	0	0	0	0	0	0	—	—	0	1.000
Jose Vizcaino	2b	4	17	0	4	0	0	0	1	0	5	0	.235	.235	0	1.000
Bernie Williams	cf	5	18	2	2	0	0	1	1	5	5	0	.111	.278	0	1.000
Totals		5	179	19	47	8	3	4	18	25	40	1	.263	.397	2	.989

Pitcher	G	GS	CG	IP	H	R	ER	BB	SO	W-L	Sv	ERA
Roger Clemens	1	1	0	8	2	0	0	0	9	1-0	0	0.00
David Cone	1	0	0	⅓	0	0	0	0	0	0-0	0	0.00
Orlando Hernandez	1	1	0	7⅓	9	4	4	3	12	0-1	0	4.91
Denny Neagle	1	1	0	4⅔	4	2	2	2	3	0-0	0	3.86
Jeff Nelson	3	0	0	2⅔	5	3	3	1	1	1-0	0	10.13
Andy Pettitte	2	2	0	13⅔	16	5	3	4	9	0-0	0	1.98
Mariano Rivera	4	0	0	6	4	2	2	1	7	0-0	2	3.00
Mike Stanton	4	0	0	4⅓	0	0	0	0	7	2-0	0	0.00
Totals	5	5	0	47	40	16	14	11	48	4-1	2	2.68

NEW YORK METS/Bobby Valentine, Manager

Player	pos	G	AB	R	H	2B	3B	HR	RBI	BB	SO	SB	BA	SA	E	FPct
Kurt Abbott	ss-ph	5	8	0	2	1	0	0	1	3	0	0	.250	.375	0	1.000
Benny Agbayani	lf	5	18	2	5	2	0	0	2	3	6	0	.278	.389	0	1.000
Edgardo Alfonzo	2b	5	21	1	3	0	0	0	1	1	5	0	.143	.143	0	1.000
Armando Benitez	p	3	0	0	0	0	0	0	0	0	0	0	—	—	0	—
Mike Bordick	ss	4	8	0	1	0	0	0	0	0	3	0	.125	.125	0	.917
Dennis Cook	p	3	0	0	0	0	0	0	0	0	0	0	—	—	0	—
John Franco	p	4	0	0	0	0	0	0	0	0	0	0	—	—	0	1.000
Matt Franco	1b	1	1	0	0	0	0	0	0	1	0	0	.000	.000	0	1.000
Darryl Hamilton	ph	4	3	0	0	0	0	0	0	2	0	0	.000	.000	—	—
Lenny Harris	dh-ph	3	4	1	0	0	0	0	0	1	1	0	.000	.000	—	—
Bobby J. Jones	p	1	2	0	0	0	0	0	0	1	0	0	.000	.000	0	1.000
Al Leiter	p	2	2	0	0	0	0	0	0	0	0	0	.000	.000	0	1.000
Joe McEwing	lf-pr	4	1	1	0	0	0	0	0	0	0	0	.000	.000	0	1.000
Jay Payton	cf	5	21	3	7	0	0	1	3	0	5	0	.333	.476	2	.895
Timo Perez	rf	5	16	1	2	0	0	0	0	1	4	0	.125	.125	1	.900
Mike Piazza	dh-c	5	22	3	6	2	0	2	4	4	4	0	.273	.636	0	1.000
Todd Pratt	c	1	2	0	0	0	0	0	0	0	2	0	.000	.000	0	1.000
Rick Reed	p	1	1	0	1	0	0	0	0	0	0	0	1.000	1.000	0	1.000
Glendon Rusch	p	3	0	0	0	0	0	0	0	0	0	0	—	—	0	—
Bubba Trammell	ph-rf	4	5	1	2	0	0	0	3	1	1	0	.400	.400	1	.750
Robin Ventura	3b	5	20	1	3	1	0	1	1	5	0	0	.150	.350	0	1.000
Turk Wendell	p	2	0	0	0	0	0	0	0	0	0	0	—	—	0	—
Todd Zeile	1b	5	20	1	8	2	0	0	1	1	5	0	.400	.500	0	1.000
Totals		5	175	16	40	8	0	4	15	11	48	0	.229	.343	5	.974

Pitcher	G	GS	CG	IP	H	R	ER	BB	SO	W-L	Sv	ERA
Armando Benitez	3	0	0	3	3	1	1	2	2	0-0	1	3.00
Dennis Cook	3	0	0	⅔	1	0	0	3	1	0-0	0	0.00
John Franco	4	0	0	3⅓	3	0	0	1	1	1-0	0	0.00
Mike Hampton	1	1	0	6	8	4	4	5	4	0-1	0	6.00
Bobby J. Jones	1	1	0	5	4	3	3	3	9	0-1	0	5.40
Al Leiter	2	2	0	15⅔	12	6	5	6	16	0-1	0	2.87
Rick Reed	1	1	0	6	6	2	2	1	8	0-0	0	3.00
Glendon Rusch	3	0	0	4	6	1	1	2	2	0-0	0	2.25
Turk Wendell	2	0	0	1⅔	3	1	1	2	2	0-1	0	5.40
Rick White	1	0	0	1⅓	1	1	1	1	1	0-0	0	6.75
Totals	5	5	0	46⅔	47	19	18	25	40	1-4	1	3.47

Series MVP: Derek Jeter, New York Yankees. **Series Outstanding Pitcher:** Roger Clemens, New York Yankees. **Average Length of Game:** 3 hours, 46 minutes. **Total Attendance:** 277,853. **Average Attendance:** 55,571 (55,986 at Yankee Stadium; 55,294 at Shea Stadium).
Umpires: Jerry Crawford (NL), Jeff Kellogg (AL), Tim McClelland (AL), Ed Montague (NL), Charlie Reliford (NL), Tim Welke (AL).

ALLIANCE
Strategic Business Services, LP

LAST

TIME !!

Recognize
Anyone ??

6990 Portwest Drive • Suite 170 • Houston, Texas 77024
• Phone 1-866-886-3400 • 713-627-3400 • Fax 713-627-0342
www.alliancesbs.cc

The Mets had an opportunity to take the lead in Game 1 when Todd Zeile (left) drove one to the top of the wall in left field during the sixth inning. Baserunner Timo Perez, thinking Zeile's shot was a home run, failed to hustle around the bases and was thrown out at the plate (below).

Piazza's bat shatters (above, left) as he makes contact with Clemens' pitch. The ball rolls foul while the broken end of the bat rolls toward the mound. Clemens (above, right) then fields the barrel of the broken bat and fires it in front of Piazza running up the first-base line.

Left: The umpire gets between Piazza and Clemens as the Mets catcher approaches with some choice words for the Yankee pitcher.

| Game 1 | Saturday, October 21 at Yankee Stadium, New York |

	1	2	3	4	5	6	7	8	9	10	11	12	R	H	E
New York Mets	0	0	0	0	0	3	0	0	0	0	0	0	3	10	0
New York Yankees	0	0	0	0	0	2	0	0	1	0	0	1	4	12	0

Pitchers NYM Al Leiter, IP 7, H 5, R 2, ER 2, BB 3, SO 7; John Franco, IP 1, H 1, R 0, ER 0, BB 0, SO 0; Armando Benitez, IP 1, H 2, R 1, ER 1, BB 1, SO 1; Dennis Cook, IP 0, H 0, R 0, ER 0, BB 2, SO 0; Glendon Rusch, IP 1⅔, H 1, R 0, ER 0, BB 2, SO 0; Turk Wendell (L, 0-1), IP 1, H 3, R 1, ER 1, BB 1, SO 0
NYY Andy Pettitte, IP 6⅔, H 8, R 3, ER 3, BB 1, SO 4; Jeff Nelson, IP 1⅓, H 1, R 0, ER 0, BB 0, SO 0; Mariano Rivera, IP 2, H 1, R 0, ER 0, BB 0, SO 3; Mike Stanton (W, 1-0), IP 2, H 0, R 0, ER 0, BB 0, SO 3

Top Performers at the Plate
NYM Benny Agbayani, 2 for 4, 1 R; Bubba Trammell, 1 for 1, 2 RBI
NYY David Justice, 1 for 4, 2 RBI, 1 BB; Jose Vizcaino, 4 for 6, 1 RBI

2B-NYM/Abbott, Agbayani, Zeile; NYY/Justice, Posada. **Time** 4:51. **Attendance** 55,913.

| Game 2 | Sunday, October 22 at Yankee Stadium, New York |

	1	2	3	4	5	6	7	8	9	R	H	E
New York Mets	0	0	0	0	0	0	0	0	5	5	7	3
New York Yankees	2	1	0	0	1	0	1	1	x	6	12	1

Pitchers NYM Mike Hampton (L, 1-0), IP 6, H 8, R 4, ER 4, BB 5, SO 4; Glendon Rusch, IP 1⅓, H 2, R 1, ER 1, BB 0, SO 0; Rick White, IP 1⅓, H 1, R 1, ER 1, BB 1, SO 1; Dennis Cook, IP ⅓, H 1, R 0, ER 0, BB 0, SO 0
NYY Roger Clemens (W, 1-0), IP 8, H 2, R 0, ER 0, BB 0, SO 9; Jeff Nelson, IP 0, H 3, R 3, ER 3, BB 0, SO 0; Mariano Rivera, IP 1, H 2, R 2, ER 2, BB 0, SO 1

Top Performers at the Plate
NYM Jay Payton, 1 for 4, 1 R, 3 RBI; Todd Zeile, 2 for 4
NYY Tino Martinez, 3 for 5, 1 R, 2 RBI; Jorge Posada, 2 for 3, 1 R, 1 RBI, 2 BB

2B-NYY/Jeter 2, Martinez, O'Neill. **HR**-NYM/Payton, Piazza; NYY/Brosius. **Time** 3:30. **Attendance** 56,059.

| Game 3 | Tuesday, October 24 at Shea Stadium, New York |

	1	2	3	4	5	6	7	8	9	R	H	E
New York Yankees	0	0	1	0	0	0	0	0	0	2	8	0
New York Mets	0	1	0	0	0	1	0	2	x	4	9	0

Pitchers NYY Orlando Hernandez (L, 0-1), IP 7⅓, H 9, R 4, ER 4, BB 3, SO 12; Mike Stanton, IP ⅔, H 0, R 0, ER 0, BB 0, SO 1
NYM Rick Reed, IP 6, H 6, R 2, ER 2, BB 1, SO 8; Turk Wendell, IP ⅔, H 0, R 0, ER 0, BB 1, SO 2; Dennis Cook, IP ⅓, H 0, R 0, ER 0, BB 1, SO 1; John Franco (W, 1-0), IP 1, H 1, R 0, ER 0, BB 0, SO 0; Armando Benitez (Sv, 1), IP 1, H 1, R 0, ER 0, BB 0, SO 1

Top Performers at the Plate
NYY Derek Jeter, 2 for 4, 1 R, 1 BB; Paul O'Neill, 3 for 4, 1 RBI
NYM Robin Ventura, 2 for 3, 1 R, 1 RBI, 1 BB; Todd Zeile, 2 for 4, 1 R, 1 RBI

2B-NYY/Justice, O'Neill; NYM/Agbayani, Piazza, Ventura, Zeile. **3B**-NYY/O'Neill. **HR**-NYM/Ventura. **Time** 3:39. **Attendance** 55,299.

| Game 4 | Wednesday, October 25 at Shea Stadium, New York |

	1	2	3	4	5	6	7	8	9	R	H	E
New York Yankees	1	1	1	0	0	0	0	0	0	3	8	0
New York Mets	0	0	2	0	0	0	0	0	0	2	6	1

Pitchers NYY Denny Neagle, IP 4⅔, H 4, R 2, ER 2, BB 2, SO 3; David Cone, IP ⅓, H 0, R 0, ER 0, BB 0, SO 0; Jeff Nelson (W, 1-0), IP 1⅓, H 1, R 0, ER 0, BB 1, SO 1; Mike Stanton, IP ⅔, H 0, R 0, ER 0, BB 0, SO 2; Mariano Rivera (Sv, 1), IP 2, H 1, R 0, ER 0, BB 0, SO 2
NYM Bobby J. Jones (L, 0-1), IP 5, H 4, R 3, ER 3, BB 3, SO 3; Glendon Rusch, IP 2, H 3, R 0, ER 0, BB 0, SO 2; John Franco, IP 1, H 1, R 0, ER 0, BB 0, SO 1; Armando Benitez, IP 1, H 0, R 0, ER 0, BB 1, SO 0

Top Performers at the Plate
NYY Derek Jeter, 2 for 5, 2 R, 1 RBI; Paul O'Neill, 2 for 4, 1 R
NYM Timo Perez, 1 for 3, 1 R; Mike Piazza, 1 for 4, 1 R, 2 RBI

3B-NYY/O'Neill, Jeter. **HR**-NYY/Jeter; NYM/Piazza. **SB**-NYM/Sojo. **Time** 3:20. **Attendance** 55,290.

| Game 5 | Thursday, October 26 at Shea Stadium, New York |

	1	2	3	4	5	6	7	8	9	R	H	E
New York Yankees	0	1	0	0	0	1	0	0	2	4	7	1
New York Mets	0	2	0	0	0	0	0	0	0	2	8	1

Pitchers NYY Andy Pettitte, IP 7, H 8, R 2, ER 0, BB 3, SO 5; Mike Stanton (W, 2-0), IP 1, H 0, R 0, ER 0, BB 0, SO 1; Mariano Rivera (Sv, 2), IP 1, H 0, R 0, ER 0, BB 1, SO 1
NYM Al Leiter (L, 0-1), IP 8⅔, H 7, R 4, ER 3, BB 3, SO 9; John Franco, IP ⅓, H 0, R 0, ER 0, BB 0, SO 0

Top Performers at the Plate
NYY Jorge Posada, 1 for 3, 1 R, 1 BB; Bernie Williams, 2 for 3, 1 R, 1 RBI, 1 BB
NYM Jay Payton, 2 for 4, 1 R; Bubba Trammell, 1 for 3, 1 R, 1 BB

2B-NYM/Piazza. **HR**-NYY/Jeter, Williams. **Time** 3:32. **Attendance** 55,292.

Left: The number 7 train whizzes by Shea Stadium in Queens.

Left: Luis Sojo's single past Al Leiter in the ninth inning of Game 5 drove in two runs for the Yankees and clinched the Subway Series for the team from the Bronx.

innings at 14 ⅓. In Game 3 at Shea Stadium, the Mets ended the Yankees' streak of 14 consecutive Series games won, and they handed Orlando Hernandez his first loss in eight postseason starts. Despite 12 K's by El Duque, the Mets pulled out the victory when Benny Agbayani doubled in a run in the eighth, snapping a 2-2 tie. Derek Jeter homered on the first pitch of Game 4, and the Yanks produced three runs on three hits by the third inning. In the bottom of the third, Piazza hit his second two-run homer of the Series to cut the lead to one, but Denny Neagle and the bull pen shut the Mets out the rest of the way. The Yanks wrapped up the title a day later. Bernie Williams got his first hit of the Series in the second inning—a solo home run—and Jeter's solo blast in the sixth knotted the game at two. Luis Sojo provided the clincher in the top of the ninth with a two-out, two-run single. Rivera pitched a scoreless ninth inning to notch his record seventh career save. With the win, the Yankees became the first team since the 1972–74 Oakland A's to capture three straight World Series, placing them among the all-time baseball dynasties.

Above: Somewhere in the middle of this pile is Jose Vizcaino, who has just won the first game of the Series with his 12th-inning single.

All-Time World Series Dynasties

The 1998–2000 New York Yankees were one of only four teams ever to win more than two World Series in a row. Casey Stengel's Yanks won a record five straight from 1949 to 1953, and the Bronx Bombers of 1936–39 took four in a row under Joe McCarthy. The only team not in Yankee pinstripes to claim three consecutive championships was the Oakland A's of the early 1970s. So, how does the most recent Yankee dynasty stack up against the others?

◆ Back-to-back sweeps in 1998 and 1999 and a five-game triumph over the Mets in 2000 gave the Yanks twelve wins and one loss over three years, for a .923 winning percentage.

◆ The 1936–39 team put together consecutive sweeps for their last two titles. Their 16-3 record over the four years earned them a .842 winning percentage.

◆ No team won more World Series games over a five-year span than the Yanks of 1949–53; the franchise went 20-8 (.714) in capturing an unmatched five titles in a row.

◆ The Oakland A's needed seven games to knock off the Reds and Mets in 1972 and 1973 before taking the Dodgers in five the following year. Their 12-7 record stacks up as a .632 winning percentage. The A's are also the only one of the four dynasties to be outscored by their opposition in their Series appearances.

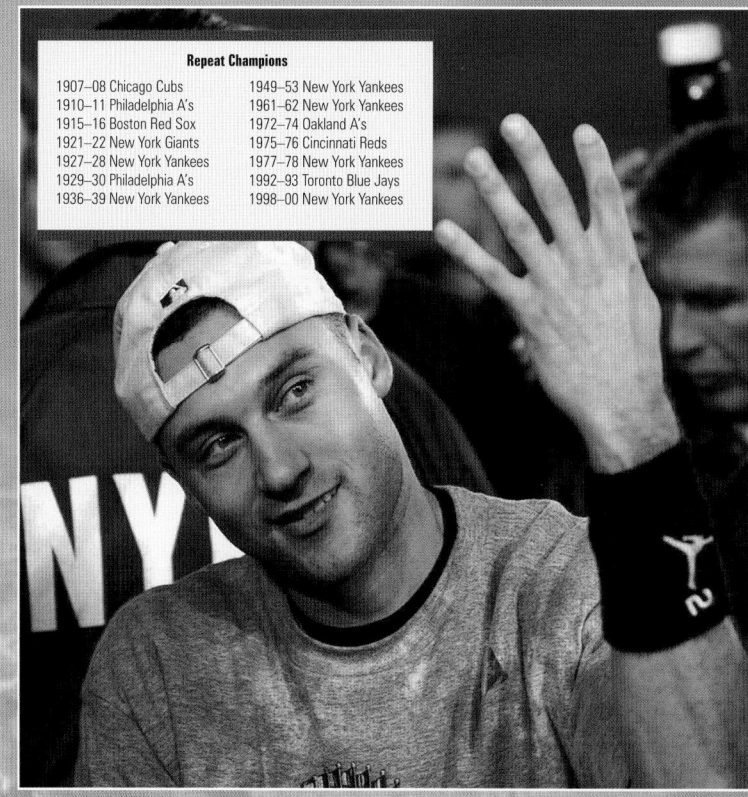

Above: After the conclusion of the 2000 Series, Yankee shortstop Derek Jeter lets it be known that his Yanks have won four world championships under Joe Torre.

Looking beyond the uninterrupted stretch of Series triumphs, these clubs were successful to an almost mind-boggling extent. In addition to their four straight wins, McCarthy's Yankees of the 1930s and 1940s also won it all in 1932, 1941 and 1943, giving them seven championships in twelve years. After their incredible "five-peat" ending in 1953, the Yanks were participants in nine of ten Fall Classics between 1955 and 1964, winning four. The A's took five consecutive Western Division titles from 1971 to 1975, only to fall to the Orioles and Red Sox in the 1971 and 1975 ALCS, respectively. Adding in their 1996 win over the Braves, the latest incarnation of the Bronx Bombers won a record 14 consecutive World Series games, amounting to four titles under Joe Torre in five years.

Although comparing teams from different eras is always a dubious proposition, we list here for comparison's sake the records and statistics during the historic runs of these four teams.

Above: Oakland owner Charlie O. Finley enjoys title number one, with Allan Lewis (left) and Sal Bando (right), in 1972. The A's would go on to win two more to become the only non-Yankee team to win three straight titles.

Team	Season Record	World Series Record	Series Average	Opponent Series Average	Series ERA	Opponent Series ERA	Series Run Total
1936–39 Yankees	409-201 (.670)	16-3 (.842)	.263	.234	2.32	5.39	113-52
1949–53 Yankees	487-280 (.635)	20-8 (.714)	.238	.237	2.65	4.01	120-84
1972–74 A's	277-202 (.578)	12-7 (632)[1]	.211	.232	2.51	2.34	53-56
1998–00 Yankees	299-186 (.616)	12-1 (.923)[2]	.279	.223	2.55	4.44	66-38

1) Including the league championship series, the A's were 21-12 (.636) in the postseason.
2) Including the league divisional and championship series, the Yankees were 33-8 (.805) in the postseason.

Mr. Octobers
All-Time Great World Series Performances

The Ten Greatest Single-Series Performances

1. "Mr. October" Homers Three Times in Final Game — Reggie Jackson, New York Yankees, 1977

Reggie Jackson's onslaught in the sixth game of the 1977 Series not only put him in rare company as one of only two players to homer three times in one game, it also established single-series records for home runs (5), runs scored (10) and total bases (25). The fact that the three home runs came on the first pitch of consecutive at-bats, each against a different pitcher, places the feat fully in the realm of the incredible.

Above: Scoring after his first home run of the 1932 Series, Lou Gehrig would go on to hit two more homers and score eight more runs.

Above: Reggie Jackson defined the label "Mr. October" with his performance in the 1977 World Series, culminating in his three-homer display in Game 6.

Player	G	AB	R	H	2B	3B	HR	RBI	BB	SO	SB	BA	SA
Lou Brock, Cardinals, 1967	7	29	8	12	2	1	1	3	2	3	7	.414	.655
Lou Gehrig, Yankees, 1928	4	11	5	6	1	0	4	9	6	0	0	.545	1.727
Lou Gehrig, Yankees, 1932	4	17	9	9	1	0	3	8	2	1	0	.529	1.118
Billy Hatcher, Reds, 1990	4	12	6	9	4	1	0	2	2	0	0	.750	1.250
Reggie Jackson, Yankees, 1977	6	20	10	9	1	0	5	8	3	4	0	.450	1.250
Pepper Martin, Cardinals, 1931	7	24	5	12	4	0	1	5	2	3	5	.500	.792
Paul Molitor, Blue Jays, 1993	6	24	10	12	2	2	2	8	3	0	1	.500	1.000
Bobby Richardson, Yankees, 1960	7	30	8	11	2	2	1	12	1	1	0	.367	.667
Brooks Robinson, Orioles, 1970	5	21	5	9	2	0	2	6	0	2	0	.429	.810
Babe Ruth, Yankees, 1928	4	16	9	10	3	0	3	4	1	2	0	.625	1.375

* Boldface indicates individual records for Series of that length.

2. Ruth Crushes Cardinals in Four-Game Sweep — Babe Ruth, New York Yankees, 1928

Babe Ruth went 3 for 4 in the first game of the 1928 Series, 2 for 3 in the second, 2 for 4 in the third, and 3 for 5 in the fourth. All 3 hits in Game 4 were home runs. Nobody else has collected 10 hits in a four-game series; his .625 average is the second highest ever. Ruth scored twice in each of the first three games and three times in the final game, giving him a record 9 runs for the Series.

3. Gehrig, Too, Crushes Cardinals in Four-Game Sweep — Lou Gehrig, New York Yankees, 1928

Babe Ruth's three-homer display in the final game may be the lasting memory of 1928, but Lou Gehrig's performance over the four games was no less impressive. He not only out-homered Ruth in the four games, he also drove in a record nine runs. His 1.727 slugging average has never been topped in a Series of any length. So fearful were the Cardinals of Gehrig's bat, they walked him in five consecutive plate appearances in the last two games.

4. Gehrig Crushes Cubs in Four-Game Sweep — Lou Gehrig, New York Yankees, 1932

In the 1932 Series against Chicago, Lou Gehrig picked up where he left off in 1928. He homered in the first game and scored three times, went 3 for 4 in Game 2, homered twice in Game 3, and went 2 for 4 with three RBI in the clincher. Although teammate Ruth again stole the show (his famous "Called Shot" came in the fifth inning of Game 3), Gehrig finished the four-game series with nine hits and a .529 average to go with his nine runs and eight RBI.

5. Robinson Silences Cincinnati with Bat and Glove — Brooks Robinson, Baltimore Orioles, 1970

Brooks Robinson's .429 average is testament enough to his success in the 1970 World Series. He hit the game-winning homer in Game 1, scored the eventual winning run in Game 2, and put Baltimore ahead in Game 3 with a first-inning double; he also went 4 for 4 in a losing effort in Game 4. But more than the runs he delivered with his bat, it was the runs that Robinson prevented in the field that repeatedly saved the day for the Orioles.

6. Molitor Bats .500 in Series Win — Paul Molitor, Toronto Blue Jays, 1993

Although Joe Carter's dramatic home run clinched the 1993 Series for Toronto, Paul Molitor's consistent production throughout the six games made it possible. He had two three-hit games, including a 3 for 5 outing in the final contest, and he scored three times each in Games 3 and 6. His 10 runs tied Reggie Jackson's record, as did his 6 extra-base hits. Molitor is one of only four players to get 12 hits in a six-game series, and one of three to bat .500 in a Series of that length.

7. Pepper Martin Spices Cardinal Victory — Pepper Martin, St. Louis Cardinals, 1931

The wonder of St. Louis's upset win in 1931, Pepper Martin went 3 for 4 in the opening-game loss and then came back to score the only 2 runs of Game 2. He scored another pair of runs in the third game, and drove in 4 of 5 Cardinal runs in Game 5. Although he went 0 for 6 in the last two games, Martin still finished with 12 hits and a .500 average. He also stole 5 bases in 6 tries against Philadelphia's Hall of Fame catcher, Mickey Cochrane.

8. Richardson Drives in 12 in Series Loss — Bobby Richardson, New York Yankees, 1960

Bobby Richardson notched 11 hits in 1960 and set or tied seven-game-series records with 12 runs batted in and 8 runs scored. He smacked a grand-slam in the first inning of Game 3 and tripled two times in Game 6. He twice started comeback rallies with leadoff singles in the all-important seventh game, scoring both times. All this earned Richardson MVP honors in the 1960 Series. The one problem? His team lost.

9. Brock Runs Ragged Against Boston — Lou Brock, St. Louis Cardinals, 1967

Some might argue that 1968 was Lou Brock's best Series; his batting average was 50 points higher and his slugging more than 200 points higher than in 1967. But his team lost in 1968, while the Cards were world champs in 1967. In addition, Brock stole seven bases in 1967 and was never caught. (He stole seven in 1968 but was nabbed three times.)

Above: Brooks Robinson's fielding attracted the most attention in 1970, but his nine hits and six RBI were equally effective in defeating the Reds.

Brock went 4 for 4 in the Series opener, and scored at least one run in five games. (He went hitless only in Jim Lonborg's one-hitter and three-hitter.)

10. Hatcher Bats Scorching .750 — Billy Hatcher, Cincinnati Reds, 1990

Billy Hatcher's .750 average against the formidable Oakland A's in 1990 is the highest ever for a single Series (with at least 10 at-bats). After walking his first time up, Hatcher hit safely in his next seven at-bats, including four doubles and a triple, for a record streak of seven consecutive hits. Hatcher was knocked out of Game 4 when he was hit by a pitch in the first inning, but he still led the Series with six runs and a 1.250 slugging average.

Above: Lou Brock ran all over the Red Sox in the 1967 Series, stealing a record 7 bases and collecting 12 hits.

Players Hitting Over .500 in One Series

As the old adage goes, hitting a baseball must be one of the hardest challenges in any sport because to succeed a mere three times out of ten is considered good or even great. (By contrast, a basketball player who makes three shots out of ten likely won't last long.) To succeed at the plate five times out of ten, even over a short period, is nothing short of brilliant. Twenty-five Major Leaguers have batted over .500 in a World Series (10 at-bats, minimum).

Player	G	AB	H	R	RBI	BB	BA	SA
Billy Hatcher, Cincinnati Reds, 1990	4	12	9	6	2	2	.750	1.250
Babe Ruth, New York Yankees, 1928	4	16	10*	9	4	1	.625	1.375
Ricky Ledee, New York Yankees, 1998	4	10	6	1	4	2	.600	.900
Chris Sabo, Cincinnati Reds, 1990	4	16	9*	2	5	2	.563	1.000
Hank Gowdy, Boston Braves, 1914	4	11	6	3	3	5	.545	1.273
Lou Gehrig, New York Yankees, 1928	4	11	6*	5	9	6	.545	1.727
Bret Boone, Atlanta Braves, 1999	4	13	7*	1	3	1	.538	.846
Johnny Bench, Cincinnati Reds, 1976	4	15	8*	4	6	0	.533	1.133
Deion Sanders, Atlanta Braves, 1992	4†	15	8	4	1	2	.533	.667
Lou Gehrig, New York Yankees, 1932	4	17	9*	9	8	2	.529	1.118
Thurman Munson, New York Yankees, 1976	4	17	9*	2	2	0	.529	.529
Dane Iorg, St. Louis Cardinals, 1982	5†	17	9	4	1	0	.529	.882
Larry McLean, New York Giants, 1913	5	12	6	0	2	0	.500	.500
Dave Robertson, New York Giants, 1917	6	22	11*	3	1	0	.500	.636
Mark Koenig, New York Yankees, 1927	4	18	9*	5	2	0	.500	.611
Pepper Martin, St. Louis Cardinals, 1931	7	24	12	5	5	2	.500	.792
Joe Marty, Chicago Cubs, 1938	3†	12	6	1	5	0	.500	.833
Joe Gordon, New York Yankees, 1941	5	14	7*	2	5	7	.500	.929
Johnny Lindell, New York Yankees, 1947	6†	18	9	3	7	5	.500	.778
Bobby Brown, New York Yankees, 1949	4†	12	6	4	5	2	.500	.917
Billy Martin, New York Yankees, 1953	6	24	12*	5	8	1	.500	.958
Vic Wertz, Cleveland Indians, 1954	4	16	8*	2	3	2	.500	.938
Phil Garner, Pittsburgh Pirates, 1979	7	24	12*	4	5	3	.500	.667
Paul Molitor, Toronto Blue Jays, 1993	6	24	12*	10	8	5	.500	1.000
Tony Gwynn, San Diego Padres, 1998	4	16	8*	2	3	1	.500	.688

† indicates player did not appear in all games of the Series
* indicates player hit safely in all games of the Series

The All-Time All-Star World Series Team

Not surprisingly, the All-Time World Series team is stacked with Yankees. Ruth and Gehrig put up impressive numbers year after year with the Bronx Bombers in the 1920s and 1930s, while Berra, Ford and Martin were regular October players during the Yankee dynasty of the 1950s and 1960s. From the more recent era, Jeter and Rivera won Series MVP honors in

New York's last two championship runs. The man who defined the term "Mr. October," Reggie Jackson, was with the Yanks for their back-to-back titles in 1977–78, but he first hit the October stage with Oakland earlier in the decade. Paul Molitor appeared in only two Fall Classics, one with the Brewers and later with Toronto, but his .418 average and 15 runs in 13 games earn him a place among the greats. The only entrants from the National League, Brock and Gibson, were teammates on three Cardinal pennant-winners in the 1960s.

1B - Lou Gehrig, New York Yankees, 1926–28, 1932, 1936–39

All-time leader in Series on-base percentage at .477 (50 or more at bats). Third all-time in runs batted in and slugging average; fourth in runs scored, total bases and extra-base hits; tied for fifth in home runs; fifth in bases on balls. Among the top ten in hits, doubles and triples. Established four-game-series records for triples in 1927, home runs, RBI and slugging in 1928, and runs in 1932. Twice batted over .500 (1928 and 1932). Won six titles in seven trips with the Yankees. (See also "Ten Greatest Single-Series Performances," previous page.)

2B - Billy Martin, New York Yankees, 1951–53, 1955–56

First among second basemen in triples, home runs, RBI and slugging average. Played in 23 consecutive games without committing an error, a post-season record for second basemen. Batted .500 in 1953 while collecting 12 base hits, including the Series-winning hit in Game 7. Hit 2 triples in 1953, tying the record for a six-game series. Martin's running catch in the seventh game in 1952 helped preserve the win for New York.

SS - Derek Jeter, New York Yankees, 1996, 1998–2000

Career .342 Series average is highest among shortstops. Scored 19 runs in 19 games. Knocked 5 extra-base hits in 2000, tying the record for a five-game series. Tied the record for a four-game series with 3 stolen bases in 1999. Fielded 13 consecutive errorless games from 1998 to 2000. Won four titles in five years with the Yankees. Awarded 2000 World Series MVP.

3B - Paul Molitor, Milwaukee Brewers, 1982; Toronto Blue Jays, 1993

Only player ever to get 5 hits in one World Series game, accomplished in Game 1 of 1982. Tied for first with highest all-time batting average (.418). Second in on-base percentage (.475), and among the top ten in slugging. Matched six-game-series records with 12 hits, 10 runs, 2 triples and 6 extra-base hits in 1993. Scored 15 runs and drove in 11 in 13 career games. Awarded 1993 World Series MVP.

OF - Reggie Jackson, Oakland Athletics, 1973–74; New York Yankees, 1977–78, 1981

Only player ever to win Series MVP awards with two teams: 1973 A's and 1977 Yankees. Has the highest career slugging average. Tied for fifth all-time in home runs. Among the top ten in runs, runs batted in, doubles and strikeouts. Holds the record for most home runs (5) and runs scored (10) in a Series of any length, and shares the record for most homers (3) and runs (4) in a game. Has top marks in total bases and slugging for a six-game series. (See also "Ten Greatest Single-Series Performances," previous page.)

OF - Babe Ruth, Boston Red Sox, 1915–16, 1918; New York Yankees, 1921–23, 1926–28, 1932

Twice hit three home runs in one game; hit two homers in a game two other times. Batted over .300 in a record six Series. Second all-time in home runs, slugging average and bases on balls; tied for second in extra-base hits; third in runs scored and total bases; fourth in runs batted in; tied for fourth in Series played. Set records for hits, total bases, runs and home runs in a four-game series in 1928. Walked a record 11 times in the 1926 Series. Reached base 5 times in a game twice in 1926. Stole 2 bases in one inning in 1921. (Also, pitched longest Series win in 1916; has the third lowest ERA among pitchers with more than 25 innings; and pitched 29 2/3 consecutive scoreless innings in 1916 and 1918.)

OF - Lou Brock, St. Louis Cardinals, 1964, 1967–68

Tied for first all-time in stolen bases; third all-time in batting average. Batted over .400 in consecutive Series (1967–68). Holds single-series record for stolen bases (7), accomplished in 1967 and again in 1968. Shares single-series record for hits, with 13 in 1968. Shares record for runs scored (8) in a seven-game series. Twice stole three bases in a game. Stole 11 consecutive bases without being caught, from the opening game of the 1967 Series to Game 3 in 1968.

C - Yogi Berra, New York Yankees, 1947, 1949–53, 1955–58, 1960–63

Played in more World Series than anybody: 14 series and 75 games. Won a record 10 Series with the Yankees. First all-time in at-bats, hits and singles; tied for first in doubles; second in runs, RBI and total bases; tied for second in extra-base hits; third in home runs and bases on balls. Hit safely in 12 different Series, scored at least one run in 12 Series, drove in at least one run in 11 Series, and homered in 9 different Series—all records. Played 30 consecutive games at catcher without committing an error. Recorded the most assists, putouts and double plays among catchers.

RHP - Bob Gibson, St. Louis Cardinals, 1964, 1967–68

Second all-time in strikeouts; tied for second in wins; first in strikeouts per nine innings; third in complete games; tied for fourth in shutouts. Holds single-game and single-series strikeout records; struck out ten or more in a game five different times. Won seven straight games without a loss from 1964 to 1967. Pitched eight consecutive complete games. Won Series opener two years in a row (1967–68); twice won a decisive Game 7 (1964 and 1967).

LHP - Whitey Ford, New York Yankees, 1950, 1953, 1955–58, 1960–64

First all-time in games pitched, starts, innings, strikeouts, wins and losses; tied for second in shutouts; fifth in complete games. Pitched a record 33 ²/₃ consecutive scoreless innings, 1960 through 1962. Started eight Series openers, more than any other pitcher, finishing with 4-3 record.

RP - Mariano Rivera, New York Yankees, 1996, 1998–2000

First all-time in saves; tied for third in games relieved. Saved three out of four games in 1998 and two out of five in 2000. Pitched 14 ¹/₃ consecutive scoreless innings from 1998 to 2000. Saved seven games and won one in 10 appearances as a closer. Awarded 2000 World Series MVP.

The All-Star Reserves

With only 11 spots on the All-Time World Series team, many outstanding performers are left out in the cold. Here are a few of the more notable also-rans.

Frank "Home Run" Baker earned his nickname with two round-trippers in 1911. He compiled a .363 average in six Series playing for the Athletics and Yankees, twice collecting nine hits in a five-game series. Baker made more putouts in the field than any other third baseman.

Eddie Collins played in six World Series in the 1910s, four with the Athletics and two with the White Sox, and batted over .400 in three of them. He stole a record 14 bases (since tied by Lou Brock). No second baseman scored more runs than Collins (20).

Frankie Frisch was in eight Series with the Giants and Cardinals, appearing in more games than anybody not on the New York Yankees. He also shares the all-time record for doubles (10) and leads all second basemen in assists, putouts, total chances and double plays.

Though he batted only .257 in 65 games, Mickey Mantle hit more home runs than any other player (18). He also ranks first in runs scored, runs batted in, extra-base hits, total bases and bases on balls (and strikeouts), and is second to Yogi Berra in games, at-bats and hits. Mantle hit a home run in nine different Series.

Following up on his outstanding 1931 Series (.500, 5 R, 5 RBI, 5 SB), Pepper Martin batted .355 for St. Louis in 1934, giving him a career average of .418, matching Paul Molitor for the highest ever. His eight runs scored in 1934 shares the record for a seven-game series.

Thurman Munson's best performance came in a 1976 loss when he hit .529, but in each of the next two years he batted .320, giving him a career mark of .373—highest among catchers and fifth-best overall. He drove in 12 runs and scored 11 in 16 games.

Pee Wee Reese played for the Dodgers in all seven Subway Series against the Yankees in the 1940s and 1950s. He is tops among shortstops in hits, runs batted in and bases on balls, and he batted over .300 three times, including .345 in 1952.

Al Simmons hit over .300 and homered twice in each of three consecutive Series with the Athletics in 1929–31. He shares the five-game record for runs scored (6 in 1929), and led all players in 1930 with a .364 average and .727 slugging average.

Only six people have hit four home runs in one series, and Duke Snider did it twice (1952 and 1955). He's fourth on the home-run list, and has the most RBIs among National Leaguers (seventh overall). Discounting his disappointing performances in 1949 and 1959, Snider batted .324 in his four middle Series appearances.

Above, top to bottom: Frank "Home Run" Baker, Frankie Frisch, Mickey Mantle and Duke Snider.

Fielders		Yrs	G	AB	R	H	2B	3B	HR	RBI	BB	SO	SB	BA	SA
1B	Lou Gehrig	7	34	119	30	43	8	3	10	35	26	17	0	.361	.731
2B	Billy Martin	5	28	99	15	33	2	3	5	19	5	15	1	.333	.566
SS	Derek Jeter	4	19	76	19	26	3	1	2	5	11	20	4	.342	.487
3B	Paul Molitor	2	13	55	15	23	2	2	2	11	5	4	2	.418	.636
OF	Reggie Jackson	5	27	98	21	35	7	1	10	24	15	24	1	.357	.755
OF	Babe Ruth	10	41	129	37	42	5	2	15	33	33	30	4	.326	.744
OF	Lou Brock	3	21	87	16	34	7	2	4	13	5	10	14	.391	.655
C	Yogi Berra	14	75	259	41	71	10	0	12	39	32	17	0	.274	.452

Pitchers		Yrs	G	CG	Sho	IP	H	BB	SO	W-L	Sv	ERA
RHP	Bob Gibson	3	9	8	2	81	55	17	92	7-2	0	1.89
LHP	Whitey Ford	11	22	7	3	146	132	34	94	10-8	0	2.71
RP	Mariano Rivera	4	14	0	0	20²/₃	16	5	18	1-0	7	1.31

Series Played
1.	Yogi Berra	14
2.	Mickey Mantle	12
3.	Whitey Ford	11
4.	Joe DiMaggio	10
	Elston Howard	10
	Babe Ruth	10

Games Played
1.	Yogi Berra	75 (14 series)
2.	Mickey Mantle	65 (12 series)
3.	Elston Howard	54 (10 series)
4.	Hank Bauer	53 (9 series)
	Gil McDougald	53 (8 series)
	Most by a Non-Yankee: Frankie Frisch	50 (8 series) — 8th overall

At-Bats
1.	Yogi Berra	259 (14 series, 75 games)
2.	Mickey Mantle	230 (12 series, 65 games)
3.	Joe DiMaggio	199 (10 series, 51 games)
4.	Frankie Frisch	197 (8 series, 50 games)
5.	Gil McDougald	190 (8 series, 53 games)

Batting Average (minimum 50 at-bats)
1.	Pepper Martin	.418 (23-for-55; 3 series, 15 games)
	Paul Molitor	.418 (23-for-55; 2 series, 13 games)
3.	Lou Brock	.391 (34-for-87; 3 series, 21 games)
4.	Marquis Grissom	.390 (30-for-77; 3 series, 19 games)
5.	Thurman Munson	.373 (25-for-67; 3 series, 16 games)

Hits
1.	Yogi Berra	71 (14 series, 75 games)
2.	Mickey Mantle	59 (12 series, 65 games)
3.	Frankie Frisch	58 (8 series, 50 games)
4.	Joe DiMaggio	54 (10 series, 51 games)
5.	Hank Bauer	46 (9 series, 53 games)
	Pee Wee Reese	46 (7 series, 44 games)

Singles
1.	Yogi Berra	49 (14 series, 75 games)
2.	Frankie Frisch	45 (8 series, 50 games)
3.	Joe DiMaggio	40 (10 series, 51 games)
	Phil Rizzuto	40 (9 series, 52 games)
5.	Pee Wee Reese	39 (7 series, 44 games)

Doubles
1.	Yogi Berra	10 (14 series, 75 games)
	Frankie Frisch	10 (8 series, 50 games)
3.	Jack Barry	9 (5 series 25 games)
	Pete Fox	9 (3 series, 14 games)
	Carl Furillo	9 (7 series, 40 games)

Triples
1.	Billy Johnson	4 (4 series, 18 games)
	Tommy Leach	4 (2 series, 15 games)
	Tris Speaker	4 (3 series, 20 games)
4.	Held by 14 players	3

Home Runs
1.	Mickey Mantle	18 (12 series, 65 games)
2.	Babe Ruth	15 (10 series, 41 games)
3.	Yogi Berra	12 (14 series, 75 games)
4.	Duke Snider	11 (6 series, 36 games)
5.	Lou Gehrig	10 (7 series, 34 games)
	Reggie Jackson	10 (5 series, 27 games)

Extra-Base Hits
1.	Mickey Mantle	26 (12 series, 65 games)
2.	Yogi Berra	22 (14 series, 75 games)
	Babe Ruth	22 (10 series, 41 games)
4.	Lou Gehrig	21 (7 series, 34 games)
5.	Duke Snider	19 (6 series, 36 games)

Total Bases
1.	Mickey Mantle	123 (12 series, 65 games)
2.	Yogi Berra	117 (14 series, 75 games)
3.	Babe Ruth	96 (10 series, 41 games)
4.	Lou Gehrig	87 (7 series, 34 games)
5.	Joe DiMaggio	84 (10 series, 51 games)

Slugging Average
1.	Reggie Jackson	.755 (5 series, 27 games)
2.	Babe Ruth	.744 (10 series, 41 games)
3.	Lou Gehrig	.731 (7 series, 34 games)
4.	Lenny Dykstra	.700 (2 series, 13 games)
5.	Al Simmons	.658 (4 series, 19 games)

Runs
1.	Mickey Mantle	42 (12 series, 65 games)
2.	Yogi Berra	41 (14 series, 75 games)
3.	Babe Ruth	37 (10 series, 41 games)
4.	Lou Gehrig	30 (7 series, 34 games)
5.	Joe DiMaggio	27 (10 series, 51 games)
	Most by a Non-Yankee: Jackie Robinson	22 (6 series, 38 games) — 9th overall

Runs Batted In
1.	Mickey Mantle	40 (12 series, 65 games)
2.	Yogi Berra	39 (14 series, 75 games)
3.	Lou Gehrig	35 (7 series, 34 games)
4.	Babe Ruth	33 (10 series, 41 games)
5.	Joe DiMaggio	30 (10 series, 51 games)
	Most by a Non-Yankee: Duke Snider	26 (6 series, 36 games) — 7th overall

Stolen Bases
1.	Lou Brock	14 (3 series, 21 games)
	Eddie Collins	14 (6 series, 34 games)
3.	Frank Chance	10 (4 series, 20 games)
	Davey Lopes	10 (4 series, 23 games)
	Phil Rizzuto	10 (9 series, 52 games)

Bases On Balls
1.	Mickey Mantle	43 (12 series, 65 games)
2.	Babe Ruth	33 (10 series, 41 games)
3.	Yogi Berra	32 (14 series, 75 games)
4.	Phil Rizzuto	30 (9 series, 52 games)
5.	Lou Gehrig	26 (7 series, 34 games)
	Most by a Non-Yankee: Mickey Cochrane	25 (5 series, 31 games) — 6th overall

Hit By Pitch
1.	Yogi Berra	3 (14 series, 75 games)
	Bert Campaneris	3 (3 series, 19 games)
	Max Carey	3 (1 series, 7 games)
	Frank Chance	3 (4 series, 20 games)
	Elston Howard	3 (10 series, 54 games)
	Reggie Jackson	3 (5 series, 27 games)
	Frank Robinson	3 (5 series, 26 games)
	Fred Snodgrass	3 (3 series, 16 games)
	Honus Wagner	3 (2 series, 15 games)

Strikeouts
1.	Mickey Mantle	54 (12 series, 65 games)
2.	Elston Howard	37 (10 series, 54 games)
3.	Duke Snider	33 (6 series, 36 games)
4.	Babe Ruth	30 (10 series, 41 games)
5.	Gil McDougald	29 (8 series, 53 games)

Other Career Batting Leaders
Consecutive-Game Hitting Streak	Hank Bauer	17 games (1956–58)
Stealing Home	Bob Meusel	2 (6 series, 34 games)
Caught Stealing	Frank Schulte	9 (4 series, 21 games)
Sacrifice Hits	Eddie Collins	8 (6 series, 34 games)
Sacrifice Flies	Joe Carter	4 (2 series, 12 games)
Grounding into Double Plays	Joe DiMaggio	7 (10 series, 51 games)
Pinch-Hit Appearances	Johnny Blanchard	10 (4 series)
	Luis Polonia	10 (3 series)
Pinch Hits	Johnny Blanchard	3 (4 series, 10 games)
	Ken Boswell	3 (1 series, 3 games)
	Bobby Brown	3 (4 series, 7 games)
	Bob Cerv	3 (3 series, 3 games)
	Carl Furillo	3 (3 series, 7 games)
	Gonzalo Marquez	3 (1 series, 5 games)
	Johnny Mize	3 (5 series, 8 games)
	Ken O'Dea	3 (5 series, 8 games)
	Dusty Rhodes	3 (1 series, 3 games)
	Carl Warwick	3 (1 series, 5 games)
Pinch-Hit Home Runs	Bernie Carbo	2
	Chuck Essegian	2

Games Pitched

1.	Whitey Ford	22 (11 series)
2.	Rollie Fingers	16 (3 series)
3.	Allie Reynolds	15 (6 series)
	Mike Stanton	15 (5 series)
	Bob Turley	15 (5 series)

Games Started

1.	Whitey Ford	22 (11 series)
2.	Waite Hoyt	11 (7 series)
	Christy Mathewson	11 (4 series)
4.	Charles "Chief" Bender	10 (5 series)
	Red Ruffing	10 (7 series)

Games Relieved

1.	Rollie Fingers	16 (3 series)
2.	Mike Stanton	15 (5 series)
3.	Clay Carroll	14 (3 series)
	Mariano Rivera	14 (4 series)
5.	Jeff Nelson	13 (4 series)
	Mark Wohlers	13 (4 series)

Complete Games

1.	Christy Mathewson	10 (4 series, 11 games)
2.	Charles "Chief" Bender	9 (5 series, 10 games)
3.	Bob Gibson	8 (3 series, 9 games)
	Red Ruffing	8 (7 series, 10 games)
5.	Whitey Ford	7 (11 series, 22 games)

Games Won

1.	Whitey Ford	10 (11 series, 22 games)
2.	Bob Gibson	7 (3 series, 9 games)
	Allie Reynolds	7 (6 series, 15 games)
	Red Ruffing	7 (7 series, 10 games)
5.	Charles "Chief" Bender	6 (5 series, 10 games)
	Lefty Gomez	6 (5 series, 7 games)
	Waite Hoyt	6 (7 series, 12 games)

Games Lost

1.	Whitey Ford	8 (11 series, 22 games)
2.	Joe Bush	5 (5 series, 9 games)
	Rube Marquard	5 (5 series, 11 games)
	Christy Mathewson	5 (4 series, 11 games)
	Eddie Plank	5 (4 series, 7 games)
	Schoolboy Rowe	5 (3 series, 8 games)

Saves

1.	Mariano Rivera	7 (4 series, 14 games)
2.	Rollie Fingers	6 (3 series, 16 games)
3.	Johnny Murphy	4 (6 series, 8 games)
	Allie Reynolds	4 (6 series, 15 games)
	John Wetteland	4 (1 series, 5 games)

Inning Pitched

1.	Whitey Ford	146 (11 series, 22 games)
2.	Christy Mathewson	101⅔ (4 series, 11 games)
3.	Red Ruffing	85⅔ (7 series, 10 games)
4.	Charles "Chief" Bender	85 (5 series, 10 games)
5.	Waite Hoyt	83⅔ (7 series, 12 games)

Strikeouts

1.	Whitey Ford	94 (11 series, 22 games)
2.	Bob Gibson	92 (3 series, 9 games)

Strikeouts (continued)

3.	Allie Reynolds	62 (6 series, 15 games)
4.	Sandy Koufax	61 (4 series, 8 games)
	Red Ruffing	61 (7 series, 10 games)

Bases on Balls Allowed

1.	Whitey Ford	34 (11 series, 22 games)
2.	Art Nehf	32 (5 series, 12 games)
	Allie Reynolds	32 (6 series, 15 games)
4.	Jim Palmer	31 (6 series, 9 games)
5.	Bob Turley	29 (5 series, 15 games)

Earned Run Average (minimum 25 innings)

1.	Jack Billingham	0.36 (3 series, 7 games, 25⅓ innings)
2.	Harry Brecheen	0.83 (3 series, 7 games, 32⅔ innings)
3.	Babe Ruth	0.87 (2 series, 3 games, 31 innings)
4.	Sherry Smith	0.89 (2 series, 3 games, 30⅓ innings)
5.	Sandy Koufax	0.95 (4 series, 8 games, 57 innings)

Shutouts

1.	Christy Mathewson	4 (4 series, 11 games)
2.	Mordecai "Three Finger" Brown	3 (4 series, 9 games)
	Whitey Ford	3 (11 series, 22 games)
4.	Lew Burdette	2 (2 series, 6 games)
	Dill Dinneen	2 (1 series, 4 games)
	Bob Gibson	2 (3 series, 9 games)
	Bill Hallahan	2 (4 series, 7 games)
	Sandy Koufax	2 (4 series, 8 games)
	Art Nehf	2 (5 series, 12 games)
	Allie Reynolds	2 (6 series, 15 games)

Runs Allowed

1.	Whitey Ford	51 (11 series, 22 games)
2.	Red Ruffing	32 (7 series, 10 games)
	Don Sutton	32 (4 series, 8 games)
4.	Charles "Chief" Bender	28 (5 series, 10 games)
	Carl Erskine	28 (5 series, 11 games)
	Burleigh Grimes	28 (4 series, 9 games)
	Waite Hoyt	28 (7 series, 12 games)
	Rube Marquard	28 (5 series, 11 games)

Hits Allowed

1.	Whitey Ford	132 (11 series, 22 games)
2.	Waite Hoyt	81 (7 series, 12 games)
3.	Christy Mathewson	76 (4 series, 11 games)
4.	Red Ruffing	74 (7 series, 10 games)
5.	Charles "Chief" Bender	64 (5 series, 10 games)

Home Runs Allowed

1.	Jim "Catfish" Hunter	9 (6 series, 12 games)
2.	Don Drysdale	8 (5 series, 7 games)
	Whitey Ford	8 (11 series, 22 games)
	Tom Glavine	8 (5 series, 8 games)
	Burleigh Grimes	8 (4 series, 9 games)
	Don Newcombe	8 (3 series, 5 games)
	Gary Nolan	8 (4 series, 7 games)
	Allie Reynolds	8 (6 series, 15 games)
	Charlie Root	8 (4 series, 6 games)

Other Career Pitching Leaders

Hit Batsmen	Bill Donovan	4 (3 series, 6 games)
	Eddie Plank	4 (4 series, 7 games)
Wild Pitches	Hal Schumacher	5 (3 series, 5 games)
Balks	Dave Stewart	2 (5 series, 10 games)

Most Series with One Team	14 — Yogi Berra, NY Yankees	
Most Series on Winning Team	10 — Yogi Berra, NY Yankees	
Most Series on Losing Team	6 — Elston Howard, NY Yankees and Boston AL	
	6 — Pee Wee Reese, Brooklyn	
Most Series with Different Teams	4 — Lonnie Smith (1980 Phillies, 1982 Cardinals, 1985 Royals, 1991–92 Braves)	
Most Series Won with Different Teams	3 — Joe Bush (1913 Athletics, 1918 Red Sox, 1923 Yankees); Stuffy McInnis (1911/1913 Athletics, 1918 Red Sox, 1925 Pirates); Wally Schang (1913/1930 Athletics, 1918 Red Sox, 1923 Yankees); Lonnie Smith (1980 Phillies, 1982 Cardinals, 1985 Royals)	
Most Years Between First and Last Series	22 — Willie Mays (1951–73)	
Most Years in Majors Before First Series	21 — Joe Niekro	
Youngest Player to Appear in the World Series	Non-pitcher: Fred Lindstrom, NY Giants, October 4, 1924 (Game 1)	18 years, 10 months, 13 days
	Pitcher: Ken Brett, Boston AL, October 8, 1967 (Game 4)	19 years, 20 days
Oldest Player to Appear in the World Series	Non-pitcher: Pete Rose, Philadelphia NL, October 16, 1983 (Game 5)	42 years, 6 months, 2 days
	Pitcher: Jack Quinn, Philadelphia AL, October 4, 1930 (Game 3)	46 years, 3 months, 29 days
Youngest Series MVP	Bret Saberhagen, Kansas City Royals, 1985	21 years, 6 months
Youngest Player to Hit a Home Run	Andruw Jones, Atlanta, October 20, 1996 (Game 1)	19 years, 5 months, 27 days
Oldest Player to Hit a Home Run	Joe Morgan, Philadelphia NL, October 14, 1983 (Game 3)	40 years, 25 days
Youngest Pitcher to Start, Win and Complete a Game	Bullet Joe Bush, Philadelphia AL, October 8, 1913 (Game 3)	20 years, 10 months, 12 days
Oldest Pitcher to Start a Game	Jack Quinn, Philadelphia AL, October 12, 1929 (Game 4)	45 years, 3 months, 7 days
Oldest Pitcher to Win a Game	Dolf Luque, NY Giants, October 7, 1933 (Game 5)	43 years, 2 months, 3 days
Oldest to Pitch a Complete Game	Grover Alexander, St. Louis NL, October 9, 1926 (Game 6)	39 years, 7 months, 13 days
Youngest to Pitch a Shutout	Jim Palmer, Baltimore, October 6, 1966 (Game 2)	20 years, 11 months, 21 days
Oldest to Pitch a Shutout	Walter Johnson, Washington, October 11, 1925 (Game 4)	37 years, 11 months, 5 days

4-Game Series	5-Game Series	6-Game Series	7-Game Series	8-Game Series
At-Bats				
19 — Mark Koenig, NY Yankees, 1928; Rickey Henderson, Oakland, 1989; Paul O'Neill, NY Yankees, 1998	23 — Hal Janvrin, Boston AL, 1916; Joe Moore, NY Giants, 1937; Bobby Richardson, NY Yankees, 1961	29 — Mariano Duncan, Philadelphia NL, 1993	33 — Bucky Harris, Washington, 1924; Sam Rice, Washington, 1925; Omar Moreno, Pittsburgh, 1979; Devon White, Florida, 1997	36 — Jimmy Collins, Boston AL, 1903
Batting Average				
.750 — Billy Hatcher, Cincinnati, 1990 (9-for-12)	.500 — Larry McLean, NY Giants, 1913 (6-for-12); Joe Gordon, NY Yankees, 1941 (7-for-14)	.500 — Dave Robertson, NY Giants, 1917 (11-for-22); Billy Martin, NY Yankees, 1953 (12-for-24); Paul Molitor, Toronto, 1993 (12-for-24)	.500 — Pepper Martin, St. Louis NL, 1931 (12-for-24); Johnny Lindell, NY Yankees, 1947 (9-for-18); Phil Garner, Pittsburgh, 1979 — .500 (12-for-24)	.400 — Buck Herzog, NY Giants, 1912 (12-for-30)
Hits				
10 — Babe Ruth, NY Yankees, 1928	9 — Frank Baker, Philadelphia AL, 1910; Eddie Collins, Philadelphia AL, 1910; Frank Baker, Philadelphia AL, 1913; Heinie Groh, NY Giants, 1922; Joe Moore, NY Giants, 1937; Bobby Richardson, NY Yankees, 1961; Paul Blair, Baltimore, 1970; Brooks Robinson, Baltimore, 1970; Alan Trammel, Detroit, 1984; Derek Jeter, NY Yankees, 2000	12 — Billy Martin, NY Yankees, 1953; Roberto Alomar, Toronto, 1993; Paul Molitor, Toronto, 1993; Marquis Grissom, Atlanta, 1996	13 — Bobby Richardson, NY Yankees, 1964; Lou Brock, St. Louis NL, 1968; Marty Barrett, Boston AL, 1986	12 — Buck Herzog, NY Giants, 1912; Joe Jackson, Chicago AL, 1919
Most Games with a Hit				
4 — Held by many players First: Johnny Evers and Butch Schmidt, Boston NL, 1914 Most recent: Bret Boone, Atlanta; Derek Jeter, NY Yankees, 1999	5 — Held by many players First: Wildfire Schulte, Chicago NL, 1907 Most recent: Derek Jeter, NY Yankees; Jay Payton and Mike Piazza, NY Mets, 2000	6 — Held by many players First: Dave Robertson, NY Giants, 1917 Most recent: Marquis Grissom, Atlanta, 1996	7 — Held by many players First: Bucky Harris, Washington; George Kelly, NY Giants, 1924 Most recent: Dan Gladden, Minnesota, 1987	7 — Held by many players First: Chick Stahl, Boston AL, 1903
Singles				
9 — Thurman Munson, NY Yankees, 1976	8 — Frank Chance, Chicago NL, 1908; Frank Baker, Philadelphia AL, 1913; Heinie Groh, NY Giants, 1922; Joe Moore, NY Giants, 1937; Bobby Richardson, NY Yankees, 1961; Paul Blair, Baltimore, 1970; Steve Garvey, Los Angeles, 1974	10 — Red Rolfe, NY Yankees, 1936; Monte Irvin, NY Giants, 1951	12 — Sam Rice, Washington, 1925	9 — Jimmy Sebring, Pittsburgh, 1903; Chief Meyers, NY Giants, 1912
Doubles				
4 — Billy Hatcher, Cincinnati, 1990	4 — Eddie Collins, Philadelphia AL, 1910; Rick Dempsey, Baltimore, 1983	5 — Chick Hafey, St. Louis NL, 1930	6 — Pete Fox, Detroit, 1934	4 — Buck Herzog, NY Giants, 1912; Red Murray, NY Giants, 1912; Buck Weaver, Chicago AL, 1919; George Burns, NY Giants, 1921
Triples				
2 — Lou Gehrig, NY Yankees, 1927; Tommy Davis, Los Angeles, 1963; Rickey Henderson, Oakland, 1989	2 — Eddie Collins, Philadelphia AL, 1913; Bobby Brown, NY Yankees, 1949	2 — George Rohe, Chicago AL, 1906; Billy Martin, NY Yankees, 1953; Paul Molitor, Toronto, 1993; Devon White, Toronto, 1993	3 — Billy Johnson, NY Yankees, 1947; Mark Lemke, Atlanta, 1991	4 — Tommy Leach, Pittsburgh, 1903
Home Runs				
4 — Lou Gehrig, NY Yankees, 1928	3 — Donn Clendenon, NY Mets, 1969	5 — Reggie Jackson, NY Yankees, 1977	4 — Babe Ruth, NY Yankees, 1926; Duke Snider, Brooklyn, 1952; Duke Snider, Brooklyn, 1955; Hank Bauer, NY Yankees, 1958; Gene Tenace, Oakland, 1972	2 — Patsy Dougherty, Boston AL, 1903
Extra-Base Hits				
6 — Babe Ruth, NY Yankees, 1928	5 — Rick Dempsey, Baltimore, 1983; Derek Jeter, NY Yankees, 2000	6 — Reggie Jackson, NY Yankees, 1977; Paul Molitor, Toronto, 1993; Devon White, Toronto, 1993	7 — Willie Stargell, Pittsburgh, 1979	5 — Buck Herzog, NY Giants, 1912; Red Murray, NY Giants, 1912; Buck Weaver, Chicago AL, 1919; George Burns, NY Giants, 1921
Total Bases				
22 — Babe Ruth, NY Yankees, 1928	19 — Derek Jeter, NY Yankees, 2000	25 — Reggie Jackson, NY Yankees, 1977	25 — Willie Stargell, Pittsburgh, 1979	18 — Buck Herzog, NY Giants, 1912; Joe Jackson, Chicago AL, 1919
Slugging Average				
1.727 — Lou Gehrig, NY Yankees, 1928	.929 — Joe Gordon, NY Yankees, 1941	1.250 — Reggie Jackson, NY Yankees, 1977	.913 — Gene Tenace, Oakland, 1972	.600 — Buck Herzog, NY Giants, 1912
Runs				
9 — Babe Ruth, NY Yankees, 1928; Lou Gehrig, NY Yankees, 1932	6 — Frank Baker, Philadelphia AL, 1910; Dan Murphy, Philadelphia AL, 1910; Harry Hooper, Boston AL, 1916; Al Simmons, Philadelphia AL, 1929; Lee May, Cincinnati, 1970; Boog Powell, Baltimore, 1970; Lou Whitaker, Detroit, 1984; Derek Jeter, NY Yankees, 2000	10 — Reggie Jackson, NY Yankees, 1977; Paul Molitor, Toronto, 1993	8 — Tommy Leach, Pittsburgh, 1909; Pepper Martin, St. Louis NL, 1934; Billy Johnson, NY Yankees, 1947; Mickey Mantle, NY Yankees, 1960; Bobby Richardson, NY Yankees, 1960; Mickey Mantle, NY Yankees, 1964; Lou Brock, St. Louis NL, 1967; Jim Thome, Cleveland, 1997; Matt Williams, Cleveland, 1997	8 — Freddy Parent, Boston AL, 1903
Runs Batted In				
9 — Lou Gehrig, NY Yankees, 1928	9 — Dan Murphy, Philadelphia AL, 1910	10 — Ted Kluszewski, Chicago AL, 1959	12 — Bobby Richardson, NY Yankees, 1960	8 — Pat Duncan, Cincinnati, 1919
Bases On Balls				
7 — Hank Thompson, NY Giants, 1954	7 — Jimmy Sheckard, Chicago NL, 1910; Mickey Cochrane, Philadelphia AL, 1929; Joe Gordon, NY Yankees, 1941	9 — Willie Randolph, NY Yankees, 1981	11 — Babe Ruth, NY Yankees, 1926; Gene Tenace, Oakland, 1973	7 — Josh Devore, NY Giants, 1912; Ross Youngs, NY Giants, 1921
Strikeouts				
7 — Bob Meusel, NY Yankees, 1927; Ken Caminiti, San Diego, 1998	9 — Carmelo Martinez, San Diego, 1984	12 — Willie Wilson, Kansas City, 1980	11 — Eddie Mathews, Milwaukee NL, 1958; Wayne Garrett, NY Mets, 1973	10 — George Kelly, NY Giants, 1921
Sacrifice Hits				
3 — Wes Westrum, NY Giants, 1954	4 — Duffy Lewis, Boston AL, 1916	3 — Jimmy Sheckard, Chicago NL, 1906; Harry Steinfeldt, Chicago NL, 1906; Joe Tinker, Chicago NL, 1906; Jack Barry, Philadelphia AL, 1911; Bill Lee, Chicago NL, 1935	5 — Fred Clarke, Pittsburgh, 1909	5 — Jake Daubert, Cincinnati, 1919
Stolen Bases				
3 — Rickey Henderson, Oakland, 1989; Rickey Henderson, Oakland, 1990; Derek Jeter, NY Yankees, 1999	6 — Jimmy Slagle, Chicago NL, 1907	6 — Kenny Lofton, Cleveland, 1995	7 — Lou Brock, St. Louis NL, 1967; Lou Brock, St. Louis NL, 1968	4 — Josh Devore, NY Giants, 1912
Caught Stealing				
2 — Luis Aparacio, Baltimore, 1966; George Foster, Cincinnati, 1976	5 — Frank Schulte, Chicago NL, 1910	3 — Josh Devore, NY Giants, 1911	3 — Lou Brock, St. Louis NL, 1968	4 — Greasy Neale, Cincinnati, 1919

Hit By Pitch	3 — Max Carey, Pittsburgh, 1925 (7-game series)	
Sacrifice Flies	3 — Joe Carter, Toronto, 1993 (6-game series)	
Grounding into Double Plays	5 — Irv Noren, NY Yankees, 1955 (7-game series)	
Pinch-Hit Appearances	6 — Luis Polonia, Atlanta, 1996 (6-game series)	
Pinch Hits	3 — Bobby Brown, NY Yankees, 1947 (7-game series)	
	3 — Dusty Rhodes, NY Giants, 1954 (4-game series)	
	3 — Carl Warwick, St. Louis NL, 1964 (7-game series)	
	3 — Gonzalo Marquez, Oakland, 1972 (7-game series)	
	3 — Ken Boswell, NY Mets, 1973 (7-game series)	

Pinch-Hit RBI	6 — Dusty Rhodes, NY Giants, 1954 (4-game series)
Pinch-Hit Home Runs	2 — Chuck Essegian, Los Angeles, 1959 (6-game series)
	2 — Bernie Carbo, Boston AL, 1975 (7-game series)
Pinch-Hit Bases on Balls	3 — Bennie Tate, Washington, 1924 (7-game series)
Pinch-Hit Strikeouts	3 — Gabby Hartnett, Chicago NL, 1929 (7-game series)
	3 — Rollie Hemsley, Chicago NL, 1932 (4-game series)
	3 — Otto Velez, NY Yankees, 1976 (4-game series)
	3 — Luis Polonia, Atlanta, 1996 (6-game series)

4-Game Series	5-Game Series	6-Game Series	7-Game Series	8-Game Series
Games Pitched				
4 — Jeff Nelson, NY Yankees, 1999	5 — Mike Marshall, Los Angeles, 1974	6 — Dan Quisenberry, Kansas City, 1980	7 — Darold Knowles, Oakland, 1973	5 — Deacon Phillippe, Pittsburgh, 1903
Games Started				
2 — Held by many players First: Dick Rudolph, Boston NL, 1914 Most recent: Kevin Brown, San Diego, 1998	3 — Christy Mathewson, NY Giants, 1905; Jack Coombs, Philadelphia AL, 1910	3 — Held by many players First: Mordecai "Three Finger" Brown, Chicago NL, 1906 Most recent: Early Wynn, Chicago AL, 1959	3 — Held by many players First: Babe Adams, Pittsburgh; George Mullin, Detroit, 1909 Most recent: Jack Morris, Minnesota, 1991	5 — Deacon Phillippe, Pittsburgh, 1903
Games Relieved				
4 — Jeff Nelson, NY Yankees, 1999	5 — Mike Marshall, Los Angeles, 1974	6 — Dan Quisenberry, Kansas City, 1980	7 — Darold Knowles, Oakland, 1973	3 — Jesse Barnes, NY Giants, 1921
Complete Games				
2 — Dick Rudolph, Boston NL, 1914; Waite Hoyt, NY Yankees, 1928; Red Ruffing, NY Yankees, 1938; Sandy Koufax, Los Angeles, 1963	3 — Christy Mathewson, NY Giants, 1905; Jack Coombs, Philadelphia AL, 1910	3 — Charles "Chief" Bender, Philadelphia AL, 1911; James "Hippo" Vaughn, Chicago NL, 1918	3 — Babe Adams, Pittsburgh 1909; George Mullin, Detroit, 1909; Stan Coveleski, Cleveland, 1920; Walter Johnson, Washington, 1925; Bobo Newsom, Detroit, 1940; Lew Burdette, Milwaukee NL, 1957; Bob Gibson, St. Louis NL, 1967; Bob Gibson, St. Louis NL, 1968; Mickey Lolich, Detroit, 1968	5 — Deacon Phillippe, Pittsburgh, 1903
Games Won				
2 — Bill James, Boston NL, 1914; Dick Rudolph, Boston NL, 1914; Waite Hoyt, NY Yankees, 1928; Red Ruffing, NY Yankees, 1938; Sandy Koufax, Los Angeles, 1963; Mike Moore, Oakland, 1989; Dave Stewart, Oakland, 1989; Jose Rijo, Cincinnati, 1990	3 — Christy Mathewson, NY Giants, 1905; Jack Coombs, Philadelphia AL, 1910	3 — Red Faber, Chicago AL, 1917	3 — Babe Adams, Pittsburgh, 1909; Stan Coveleski, Cleveland, 1920; Harry Brecheen, St. Louis NL, 1946; Lew Burdette, Milwaukee NL, 1957; Bob Gibson, St. Louis NL, 1967; Mickey Lolich, Detroit, 1968	3 — Bill Dinneen, Boston AL, 1903; Deacon Phillippe, Pittsburgh, 1903; Smokey Joe Wood, Boston AL, 1912
Games Lost				
2 — Held by many players First: Willie Sherdel, St. Louis NL, 1928 Most recent: Dave Stewart, Oakland, 1990	2 — Held by many players First: Eddie Plank, Philadelphia AL, 1905 Most recent: Storm Davis, Oakland, 1988	3 — George Frazier, NY Yankees, 1981	2 — Held by many players First: Ed Summers, Detroit, 1909 Most recent: Orel Hershiser, Cleveland, 1997	3 — Lefty Williams, Chicago AL, 1919
Saves				
3 — Mariano Rivera, NY Yankees, 1998	2 — Rollie Fingers, Oakland, 1972; Willie Hernandez, Detroit, 1984; Tippy Martinez, Baltimore, 1983; Mariano Rivera, NY Yankees, 2000	4 — John Wetteland, NY Yankees, 1996	3 — Roy Face, Pittsburgh, 1960; Kent Tekulve, Pittsburgh, 1979	
Innings Pitched				
18 — Dick Rudolph, Boston NL, 1914; Waite Hoyt, NY Yankees, 1928; Red Ruffing, NY Yankees, 1938; Sandy Koufax, Los Angeles, 1963	27 — Christy Mathewson, NY Giants, 1905; Jack Coombs, Philadelphia AL, 1910	27 — Christy Mathewson, NY Giants, 1911; Red Faber, Chicago AL, 1917; James "Hippo" Vaughn, Chicago NL, 1918	32 — George Mullin, Detroit, 1909	44 — Deacon Phillippe, Pittsburgh, 1903
Strikeouts				
23 — Sandy Koufax, Los Angeles, 1963	18 — Christy Mathewson, NY Giants, 1905	20 — Charles "Chief" Bender, Philadelphia AL, 1911	35 — Bob Gibson, St. Louis NL, 1968	28 — Bill Dinneen, Boston AL, 1903
Bases on Balls Allowed				
8 — Bob Lemon, Cleveland, 1954	14 — Jack Coombs, Philadelphia AL, 1910	11 — Lefty Tyler, Chicago NL, 1918; Lefty Gomez, NY Yankees, 1936; Allie Reynolds, NY Yankees, 1951	11 — Walter Johnson, Washington, 1924; Bill Bevens, NY Yankees, 1947	13 — Art Nehf, NY Yankees, 1921
Earned Run Average (most innings with 0.00 ERA)				
0.00 (11 IP) — Bill James, Boston NL, 1914	0.00 (27 IP) — Christy Mathewson, NY Giants, 1905	0.00 (14 IP) — Rube Benton, NY Giants, 1917	0.00 (18 IP) — Whitey Ford, NY Yankees, 1960	0.00 (27 IP) — Waite Hoyt, NY Yankees, 1921
Shutouts				
1 — Held by many players First: Bill James, Boston NL, 1914	3 — Christy Mathewson, NY Giants, 1905	1 — Held by many players First: Ed Walsh, Chicago AL; Three Finger Brown, Chicago NL, 1906	2 — Lew Burdette, Milwaukee NL, 1957; Whitey Ford, NY Yankees, 1960; Sandy Koufax, Los Angeles, 1965	2 — Bill Dinneen, Boston AL, 1903
Runs Allowed				
11 — Grover Alexander, St. Louis NL, 1928; Bob Lemon, Cleveland, 1954	16 — Mordecai "Three Finger" Brown, Chicago NL, 1910	10 — Slim Sallee, NY Giants, 1917; Red Ruffing, NY Yankees, 1936; Don Gullett, NY Yankees, 1976; Don Sutton, Los Angeles, 1978; Jack Morris, Toronto, 1992	17 — Lew Burdette, Milwaukee NL, 1958	19 — Deacon Phillippe, Pittsburgh, 1903
Hits Allowed				
17 — Red Ruffing, NY Yankees, 1938	23 — Mordecai "Three Finger" Brown, Chicago NL, 1910; Jack Coombs, Philadelphia AL, 1910	25 — Christy Mathewson, NY Giants, 1911	30 — Walter Johnson, Washington, 1924	38 — Deacon Phillippe, Pittsburgh, 1903
Home Runs Allowed				
4 — Willie Sherdel, St. Louis NL, 1928; Charlie Root, Chicago NL, 1932; Junior Thompson, Cincinnati, 1939; Scott Garrelts, San Francisco, 1989	4 — Gary Nolan, Cincinnati, 1970	4 — Allie Reynolds, NY Yankees, 1953	5 — Lew Burdette, Milwaukee NL, 1958; Dick Hughes, St. Louis NL, 1967	2 — Babe Adams, Pittsburgh, 1909; Harry Harper, NY Yankees, 1921
Hit Batsmen				
2 — Jakie May, Chicago NL, 1932	3 — Bill Donovan, Detroit, 1907	2 — Jack Pfiester, Chicago NL, 1906; Red Faber, Chicago AL, 1917; Carl Erskine, Los Angeles, 1953	3 — Bruce Kison, Pittsburgh, 1971	2 — Hugh Bedient, Boston AL, 1912; Jimmy Ring, Cincinnati, 1919
Wild Pitches				
2 — Held by many players First: Johnny Miljus, Pittsburgh, 1927	2 — Held by many players First: Jeff Pfeffer, Brooklyn, 1916	2 — Held by many players First: Rube Marquard, NY Giants, 1911	3 — John Stuper, St. Louis NL, 1982	3 — Jeff Tesreau, NY Giants, 1912

Game	Inning

At-Bats
7 — Don Hahn, NY Mets, October 14, 1973 (Game 2, 12 innings)
6 — Nine-Inning Game: Held by many players
First: Patsy Dougherty, Boston AL, October 7, 1903 (Game 5)
Most recent: Roberto Alomar and Joe Carter, Toronto; Mariano Duncan, Philadelphia NL, October 20, 1993 (Game 4)

2 — Held by many players
First: Chick Stahl, Boston AL, October 7, 1903 (6th inning, Game 5)
Most recent: Scott Brosius, NY Yankees, October 23, 1999 (8th inning, Game 1)

Hits
5 — Paul Molitor, Milwaukee AL, October 12, 1982 (Game 1)

2 — Held by 17 players
First: Ross Youngs, NY Giants, October 7, 1921 (7th inning, Game 3)
Most recent: Gary Gaetti, Minnesota, October 17, 1987 (4th inning, Game 1)

Singles
5 — Paul Molitor, Milwaukee AL, October 12, 1982 (Game 1)

2 — Jimmie Foxx, Philadelphia AL, October 12, 1929 (7th inning, Game 4); Jo-Jo Moore, NY Giants, October 4, 1933 (6th inning, Game 2); Joe DiMaggio, NY Yankees, October 6, 1936 (9th inning, Game 6); Hank Leiber, NY Giants, October 9, 1937 (2nd inning, Game 4); Bob Cerv, NY Yankees, October 8, 1960 (1st inning, Game 3); Norm Cash, Detroit, October 9, 1968 (3rd inning, Game 6); Al Kaline, Detroit, October 9, 1968 (3rd inning, Game 6); Merv Rettenmund, Baltimore, October 11, 1971 (5th inning, Game 2)

Doubles
4 — Frank Isbell, Chicago AL, October 13, 1906 (Game 5)

1 — Held by many players
First: Chick Stahl, Boston AL, October 2, 1903 (1st inning, Game 2)

Triples
2 — Tommy Leach, Pittsburgh, October 1, 1903 (Game 1); Patsy Dougherty, Boston AL, October 7, 1903 (Game 5); Dutch Ruether, Cincinnati, October 1, 1919 (Game 1); Bobby Richardson, NY Yankees, October 12, 1960 (Game 6); Tommy Davis, Los Angeles, October 3, 1963 (Game 2); Mark Lemke, Atlanta, October 24, 1991 (Game 5)

1 — Held by many players
First: Tommy Leach, Pittsburgh, October 1, 1903 (1st inning, Game 1)

Home Runs
3 — Babe Ruth, NY Yankees, October 6, 1926 (Game 4); Babe Ruth, NY Yankees, October 9, 1928 (Game 4); Reggie Jackson, NY Yankees, October 18, 1977 (Game 6)

1 — Held by many players
First: Jimmy Sebring, Pittsburgh, October 1, 1903 (7th inning, Game 1)

Extra-Base Hits
4 — Frank Isbell, Chicago AL, October 13, 1906 (Game 5; 4 2B)

2 — Ross Youngs, NY Giants, October 7, 1921 (7th inning, Game 3; 2B & 3B)

Total Bases
12 (3 HR) — Babe Ruth, NY Yankees, October 6, 1926 (Game 4); Babe Ruth, NY Yankees, October 9, 1928 (Game 4); Reggie Jackson, NY Yankees, October 18, 1977 (Game 6)

5 — Ross Youngs, NY Giants, October 7, 1921 (7th inning, Game 3; 2B & 3B); Al Simmons, Philadelphia AL, October 12, 1929 (7th inning, Game 4; 1B & HR)

Runs
4 — Babe Ruth, NY Yankees, October 6, 1926 (Game 4); Earle Combs, NY Yankees, October 2, 1932 (Game 4); Frank Crosetti, NY Yankees, October 2, 1936 (Game 2); Enos Slaughter, St. Louis NL, October 10, 1946 (Game 4); Reggie Jackson, NY Yankees, October 18, 1977 (Game 6); Kirby Puckett, Minnesota, October 24, 1987 (Game 6); Carney Lansford, Oakland, October 27, 1989 (Game 3); Lenny Dykstra, Philadelphia NL, October 20, 1993 (Game 4)

2 — Frankie Frisch, NY Giants, October 7, 1921 (7th inning, Game 3); Jimmie Foxx, Philadelphia AL, October 12, 1929 (7th inning, Game 4); Al Simmons, Philadelphia AL, October 12, 1929 (7th inning, Game 4); Al Kaline, Detroit, October 9, 1968 (3rd inning, Game 6); Dick McAuliffe, Detroit, October 9, 1968 (3rd inning, Game 6); Mickey Stanley, Detroit, October 9, 1968 (3rd inning, Game 6)

Runs Batted In
6 — Bobby Richardson, NY Yankees, October 8, 1960 (Game 3)

4 — Held by 17 players
First: Elmer Smith, Cleveland, October 10, 1920 (1st inning, Game 5)
Most recent: Tino Martinez, NY Yankees, October 17, 1998 (7th inning, Game 1)

Stolen Bases
3 — Honus Wagner, Pittsburgh, October 11, 1909 (Game 3); Willie Davis, Los Angeles, October 11, 1965 (Game 5); Lou Brock, St. Louis NL, October 12, 1967 (Game 7); Lou Brock, St. Louis NL, October 5, 1968 (Game 3)

2 — George Browne, NY Giants, October 12, 1905 (9th inning, Game 3); Jimmy Slagle, Chicago NL, October 8, 1907 (10th inning, Game 1); Ty Cobb, Detroit, October 12, 1908 (9th inning, Game 3); Eddie Collins, Chicago AL, October 7, 1917 (6th inning, Game 2); Babe Ruth, NY Yankees, October 6, 1921 (5th inning, Game 2); Lou Brock, St. Louis NL, October 12, 1967 (5th inning, Game 7); Davey Lopes, Los Angeles, October 15, 1974 (1st inning, Game 3); Kenny Lofton, Cleveland, October 21, 1995 (1st inning, Game 1); Omar Vizquel, Cleveland, October 26, 1997 (5th inning, Game 7)

Caught Stealing
2 — Frank Schulte, Chicago NL, October 17, 1910 (Game 1); Frank Schulte, Chicago NL, October 23, 1910 (Game 5); Fred Luderus, Philadelphia NL, October 8, 1915 (Game 1); Jimmy Johnston, Brooklyn, October 9, 1916 (Game 2); Mickey Livingston, Chicago NL, October 3, 1945 (Game 1); Billy Martin, NY Yankees, September 28, 1955 (Game 1)

1 — Held by many players
First: Tommy Leach, Pittsburgh, October 1, 1903 (8th inning, Game 1)

Bases On Balls
4 — Fred Clarke, Pittsburgh, October 16, 1909 (Game 7); Dick Hoblitzel, Boston AL, October 9, 1916 (Game 2, 14 innings); Ross Youngs, NY Giants, October 10, 1924 (Game 7, 12 innings); Babe Ruth, NY Yankees, October 10, 1926 (Game 7); Jackie Robinson, Brooklyn, October 5, 1952 (Game 5, 11 innings); Doug DeCinces, Baltimore, October 13, 1979 (Game 4)

2 — Lefty Gomez, NY Yankees, October 6, 1937 (6th inning, Game 1); Dick McAuliffe, Detroit, October 9, 1968 (3rd inning, Game 6)

Hit By Pitch
2 — Max Carey, Pittsburgh, October 7, 1925 (Game 1); Yogi Berra, NY Yankees, October 2, 1953 (Game 3); Frank Robinson, Cincinnati, October 8, 1961 (Game 4); Todd Pratt, NY Mets, October 21, 2000 (Game 1)

1 — Held by many players
First: Hobe Ferris, Boston AL, October 1, 1903 (7th inning, Game 1)

Strikeouts
5 — George Pipgras, NY Yankees, October 1, 1932 (Game 3)

2 — Edgar Renteria, Florida, October 23, 1997 (6th inning, Game 5)

Grounding into Double Plays
3 — Willie Mays, NY Giants, October 8, 1951 (Game 4)

1 — Held by many players
First: Lou Criger, Boston AL, October 2, 1903 (5th inning, Game 2)

Sacrifice Hits
3 — Joe Tinker, Chicago NL, October 12, 1906 (Game 4); Wes Westrum, NY Giants, October 2, 1954 (Game 4)

1 — Held by many players

Sacrifice Flies
2 — Wes Westrum, NY Giants, October 2, 1954 (Game 4); Manny Ramirez, Cleveland, October 25, 1997 (Game 6)

1 — Held by many players

Game	Inning
Strikeouts	
17 — Bob Gibson, St. Louis NL, October 2, 1968 (Game 1)	4 — Orval Overall, Chicago NL, October 14, 1908 (1st inning, Game 5)
Strikeouts, by a Relief Pitcher	
11 — Moe Drabowsky, Baltimore, October 5, 1966 (Game 1)	3 — Held by many players
Consecutive Strikeouts	
6 — Hod Eller, Cincinnati, October 6, 1919 (Game 5); Moe Drabowsky, Baltimore, October 5, 1966 (Game 1); Todd Worrell, St. Louis NL, October 24, 1985 (Game 5)	3 — Held by many players
Bases on Balls Allowed	
10 — Bill Bevens, NY Yankees, October 3, 1947 (Game 4)	4 — Bill Donovan, Detroit, October 16, 1909 (2nd inning, Game 7); Art Reinhart, St. Louis NL, October 6, 1926 (5th inning, Game 4); Guy Bush, Chicago NL, September 28, 1932 (6th inning, Game 1); Don Gullett, Cincinnati, October 22, 1975 (3rd inning, Game 7); Tom Glavine, Atlanta, October 24, 1991 (6th inning, Game 5); Todd Stottlemyre, Toronto, October 20, 1993 (1st inning, Game 4); Al Leiter, Florida, October 21, 1997 (4th inning, Game 3)
Runs Allowed	
10 — Bill Kennedy, Pittsburgh, October 7, 1903 (Game 5)	7 — Hooks Wiltse, NY Giants, October 26, 1911 (7th inning, Game 6); Carl Hubbell, NY Giants, October 6, 1937 (6th inning, Game 1)
Earned Runs Allowed	
7 — Danny Cox, St. Louis NL, October 18, 1987 (Game 2); Jack Morris, Toronto, October 22, 1992 (Game 5); Andy Pettitte, NY Yankees, October 20, 1996 (Game 1); Orel Hershiser, Cleveland, October 18, 1997 (Game 1)	6 — Hooks Wiltse, NY Giants, October 26, 1911 (7th inning, Game 6); Danny Cox, St. Louis NL, October 18, 1987 (4th inning, Game 2)
Hits Allowed	
15 — Walter Johnson, Washington, October 15, 1925 (Game 7)	7 — Smokey Joe Wood, Boston AL, October 15, 1912 (1st inning, Game 7)
Home Runs Allowed	
4 — Charlie Root, Chicago NL, October 1, 1932 (Game 3); Junior Thompson, Cincinnati, October 7, 1939 (Game 3); Dick Hughes, St. Louis NL, October 11, 1967 (Game 6)	3 — Dick Hughes, St. Louis NL, October 11, 1967 (4th inning, Game 6)
Hit Batsmen	
3 — Bruce Kison, Pittsburgh, October 13, 1971 (Game 4)	2 — Ed Willett, Detroit, October 11, 1909 (2nd inning, Game 3); Wayne Granger, St. Louis NL, October 9, 1968 (8th inning, Game 6)
Wild Pitches	
2 — Held by 13 players First: Jeff Tesreau, NY Giants, October 15, 1912 (Game 7) Most recent: John Smoltz, Atlanta, October 18, 1992 (Game 2)	2 — Vic Aldridge, Pittsburgh, October 15, 1925 (1st inning, Game 7); Bob Shawkey, NY Yankees, October 5, 1922 (5th inning, Game 2); Johnny Miljus, Pittsburgh, October 8, 1927 (9th inning, Game 7); Tex Carleton, Chicago NL, October 9, 1938 (8th inning, Game 4); Doc Medich, Milwaukee AL, October 19, 1982 (6th inning, Game 6)

GAME LENGTH AND ATTENDANCE RECORDS

Longest Average Game Length

4-Game Series	NY Yankees vs. San Diego, 1996	3:14
5-Game Series	NY Yankees vs. NY Mets, 2000	3:46
6-Game Series	Toronto vs. Philadelphia NL, 1993	3:29
7-Game Series	Florida vs. Cleveland, 1997	3:30
8-Game Series	Boston AL vs. NY Giants, 1912	2:14

Shortest Average Game Length

4-Game Series	NY Yankees vs. Cincinnati, 1939	1:46
5-Game Series	Chicago NL vs. Detroit, 1908	1:46
6-Game Series	Philadelphia AL vs. St. Louis NL, 1930	1:49
7-Game Series	Cleveland vs. Brooklyn, 1920	1:48
8-Game Series	Boston AL vs. Pittsburgh, 1903	1:48

Longest Nine-Inning Day Game 3:48 — Baltimore vs. Pittsburgh, October 13, 1979 (Game 4)

Longest Nine-Inning Night Game 4:14 — Toronto vs. Philadelphia NL, October 20, 1993 (Game 4)

Longest Extra-Inning Game 4:51 — NY Yankees vs. NY Mets, October 21, 2000 (12 innings, Game 1)

Shortest Game 1:25 — Chicago NL vs. Detroit, October 14, 1908 (Game 5)

Longest Game by Innings 14 innings — Brooklyn vs. Boston AL, October 9, 1916 (Game 2)

Most Extra-Inning Games 3 — Minnesota vs. Atlanta, 1991 (7-game series)

Largest Attendance

4-Game Series	NY Giants vs. Cleveland, 1954	251,507 (avg. 62,877)
5-Game Series	Baltimore vs. Philadelphia NL, 1983	304,139 (avg. 60,828)
6-Game Series	Los Angeles vs. Chicago AL, 1959	420,784 (avg. 70,131)
7-Game Series	Florida vs. Cleveland, 1997	403,617 (avg. 57,660)
8-Game Series	NY Giants vs. NY Yankees, 1921	269,976 (avg. 33,747)

Smallest Attendance

4-Game Series	Boston NL vs. Philadelphia AL, 1914	111,009 (avg. 27,752)
5-Game Series	Chicago NL vs. Detroit, 1908	62,232 (avg. 12,446)
6-Game Series	Chicago AL vs. Chicago NL, 1906	99,845 (avg. 16,641)
7-Game Series	Pittsburgh vs. Detroit, 1909	145,295 (avg. 20,756)
8-Game Series	Boston AL vs. Pittsburgh, 1903	100,429 (avg. 12,554)

Largest Attendance, Single Game
Chicago AL vs. Los Angeles, at Los Angeles Memorial Coliseum, October 6, 1959 (Game 5) — 92,706

Smallest Attendance, Single Game
Chicago NL vs. Detroit, at Bennett Park, Detroit, October 14, 1908 (Game 5) — 6,210

	4-Game Series	5-Game Series	6-Game Series	7-Game Series	8-Game Series
Most At-Bats, One Team	146 — Chicago NL, 1932; Oakland, 1989	179 — NY Yankees, 2000	222 — NY Yankees, 1978	269 — NY Yankees, 1960	282 — Boston AL, 1903
Most At-Bats, Both Teams	290 — NY Yankees (144) vs. Chicago NL (146), 1932	354 — NY Yankees (179) vs. NY Mets (175), 2000	421 — NY Yankees (222) vs. Los Angeles (199), 1978	512 — St. Louis NL (262) vs. Detroit (250), 1934	552 — Boston AL (282) vs. Pittsburgh (270), 1903
Highest Batting Average, One Team	.317 — Cincinnati, 1990	.316 — Philadelphia AL, 1910	.311 — Toronto, 1993	.338 — NY Yankees, 1960	.270 — NY Giants, 1912
Highest Batting Average, Both Teams	.283 — NY Yankees (.313) vs. Chicago NL (.253), 1932	.272 — Philadelphia AL (.316) vs. Chicago NL (.222), 1910	.292 — Philadelphia NL (.294) vs. Kansas City (.290), 1980; Toronto (.311) vs. Philadelphia NL (.274), 1993	.300 — Pittsburgh (.256) vs. NY Yankees (.338), 1960	.245 — Boston AL (.220) vs. NY Giants (.270), 1912
Lowest Batting Average, One Team	.142 — Los Angeles, 1966	.146 — Baltimore, 1969	.175 — NY Giants, 1911	.185 — St. Louis NL, 1985	.207 — NY Yankees, 1921
Lowest Batting Average, Both Teams	.171 — Baltimore (.200) vs. Los Angeles (.142), 1966	.184 — NY Mets (.220) vs. Baltimore (.146), 1969	.197 — Chicago AL (.198) vs. Chicago NL (.196), 1906	.209 — Oakland (.209) vs. Cincinnati (.209), 1972	.239 — Cincinnati (.255) vs. Chicago AL (.224), 1919
Most Hits, One Team	45 — NY Yankees, 1932; Cincinnati, 1990	56 — Philadelphia AL, 1910	68 — NY Yankees, 1978	91 — NY Yankees, 1960	74 — NY Giants, 1912
Most Hits, Both Teams	82 — NY Yankees (45) vs. Chicago NL (37), 1932	91 — Philadelphia AL (56) vs. Chicago NL (35), 1910	122 — Toronto (64) vs. Philadelphia NL (58), 1993	151 — Pittsburgh (60) vs. NY Yankees (91), 1960	135 — Boston AL (71) and Pittsburgh (64), 1903
Fewest Hits, One Team	17 — Los Angeles, 1966	23 — Baltimore, 1969	32 — Boston AL, 1918	40 — St. Louis NL, 1985	50 — NY Yankees, 1921
Fewest Hits, Both Teams	41 — Baltimore (24) vs. Los Angeles (17), 1966	56 — NY Giants (31) vs. Philadelphia AL (25), 1905	69 — Boston AL (32) vs. Chicago NL (37), 1918	92 — Oakland (46) vs. Cincinnati (46), 1972	121 — NY Giants (71) vs. NY Yankees (50), 1921
Most Singles, One Team	32 — NY Yankees, 1998	46 — NY Giants, 1922	57 — NY Yankees, 1978	64 — NY Yankees, 1960	55 — NY Giants, 1912
Most Singles, Both Teams	55 — NY Yankees (31) vs. Chicago NL (24), 1932	70 — NY Giants (39) vs. Washington (31), 1933	95 — NY Yankees (57) vs. Los Angeles (38), 1978	109 — Pittsburgh (45) vs. NY Yankees (64), 1960	96 — Boston AL (49) and Pittsburgh (47), 1903
Most Doubles, One Team	9 — Philadelphia AL, 1914; Cincinnati, 1990	19 — Philadelphia AL, 1910	15 — Philadelphia AL, 1911	19 — St. Louis NL, 1946	14 — Boston AL, 1912; NY Giants, 1912
Most Doubles, Both Teams	15 — Boston NL (6) vs. Philadelphia AL (9), 1914	30 — Philadelphia AL (19) vs. Chicago NL (11), 1910	26 — Philadelphia AL (15) vs. NY Giants (11), 1911	29 — Pittsburgh (13) vs. Detroit (16), 1909	28 — Boston AL (14) vs. NY Giants (14), 1912
Most Triples, One Team	3 — Cincinnati, 1976; Oakland, 1989	6 — Boston AL, 1916	5 — Toronto, 1993	5 — St. Louis NL, 1934; NY Yankees, 1947	16 — Boston AL, 1903
Most Triples, Both Teams	4 — Cincinnati (3) vs. NY Yankees (1), 1976; Oakland (3) vs. San Francisco (1), 1989	11 — Boston AL (6) vs. Brooklyn (5), 1916	7 — NY Yankees (4) vs. NY Giants (3); Toronto (5) vs. Philadelphia NL (2), 1993	8 — Minnesota (4) vs. Atlanta (4), 1991	25 — Boston AL (16) vs. Pittsburgh (9), 1903
Most Home Runs, One Team	9 — NY Yankees, 1928; Oakland, 1989	10 — Baltimore, 1970	9 — NY Yankees, 1953; Los Angeles, 1977	12 — NY Yankees, 1956	2 — Boston AL, 1903; NY Giants, 1921; NY Yankees, 1921
Most Home Runs, Both Teams	13 — Oakland (9) vs. San Francisco (4), 1989	15 — Baltimore (10) vs. Cincinnati (5), 1970	17 — NY Yankees (9) vs. Brooklyn (8), 1953; NY Yankees (8) vs. Los Angeles (9), 1977	17 — Brooklyn (9) vs. NY Yankees (8), 1955	4 — NY Giants (2) vs. NY Yankees (2), 1921
Fewest Home Runs, One Team	0 — Philadelphia AL, 1914; Pittsburgh, 1927; Cincinnati, 1939; Philadelphia NL, 1950	0 — NY Giants, 1905; Philadelphia AL, 1905; Chicago NL, 1907; Detroit, 1907; Detroit, 1908; Chicago NL, 1910	0 — Chicago AL, 1906; Chicago NL, 1906; NY Giants, 1911; Boston AL, 1918; Chicago NL, 1918	0 — Brooklyn, 1920	0 — Cincinnati, 1919
Fewest Home Runs, Both Teams	1 — Boston NL (1) vs. Philadelphia AL (0), 1914	0 — NY Giants (0) vs. Philadelphia AL (0), 1905; Chicago NL (0) vs. Detroit (0), 1907	0 — Chicago AL (0) vs. Chicago NL (0), 1906; Boston AL (0) vs. Chicago NL (0), 1918	2 — Cleveland (2) vs. Brooklyn (0), 1920	1 — Cincinnati (0) vs. Chicago AL (1), 1919
Teams With At Least One Home Run in Each Game	NY Yankees, 1928; Oakland, 1989	Baltimore, 1970	NY Yankees, 1936; Atlanta, 1995	Washington, 1925; NY Yankees, 1952	None
Most Extra-Base Hits, One Team	20 — Oakland, 1989	21 — Philadelphia AL, 1910	24 — Toronto, 1993	27 — NY Yankees, 1960	22 — Boston AL, 1903
Most Extra-Base Hits, Both Teams	29 — Oakland (20) vs. San Francisco (9), 1989	33 — Philadelphia AL (21) vs. Chicago NL (12), 1910	41 — NY Yankees (19) vs. Brooklyn (22), 1953	42 — Pittsburgh (15) vs. NY Yankees (27), 1960; St. Louis NL (23) vs. Milwaukee AL (19), 1982; Minnesota (20) vs. Atlanta (22), 1991	40 — Boston AL (21) vs. NY Giants (19), 1912
Most Total Bases, One Team	85 — Oakland, 1989	87 — Baltimore, 1970	105 — Toronto, 1993	142 — NY Yankees, 1960	113 — Boston AL, 1903
Most Total Bases, Both Teams	133 — NY Yankees (75) vs. Chicago NL (58), 1932	145 — Baltimore (87) vs. Cincinnati (58), 1970	200 — NY Yankees (97) vs. Los Angeles (103), 1953	225 — Pittsburgh (83) vs. NY Yankees (142), 1960	205 — Boston AL (113) vs. Pittsburgh (92), 1903
Highest Slugging Average, One Team	.582 — Oakland, 1989	.509 — Baltimore, 1970	.510 — Toronto, 1993	.528 — NY Yankees, 1960	.401 — Boston AL, 1903
Highest Slugging Average, Both Teams	.468 — Oakland (.582) vs. San Francisco (.343), 1989	.433 — Baltimore (.509) vs. Cincinnati (.354), 1970	.467 — Toronto (.510) vs. Philadelphia NL (.425), 1993	.447 — Pittsburgh (.355) vs. NY Yankees (.528), 1960	.344 — Boston AL (.326) vs. NY Giants (.361), 1912

4-Game Series	5-Game Series	6-Game Series	7-Game Series	8-Game Series
Most Runs, One Team				
37 — NY Yankees, 1932	35 — Philadelphia AL, 1910	45 — Toronto, 1993	55 — NY Yankees, 1960	39 — Boston AL, 1903
Most Runs, Both Teams				
56 — NY Yankees (37) vs. Chicago NL (19), 1932	53 — Baltimore (33) vs. Cincinnati (20), 1970	81 — Toronto (45) vs. Philadelphia NL (36), 1993	82 — Pittsburgh (27) vs. NY Yankees (55), 1960	63 — Boston AL (39) vs. Pittsburgh (24), 1903
Fewest Runs, One Team				
2 — Los Angeles, 1966	3 — Philadelphia AL, 1905	9 — Boston AL, 1918	8 — Brooklyn, 1920	20 — Chicago AL, 1919
Fewest Runs, Both Teams				
15 — Baltimore (13) vs. Los Angeles (2), 1966	18 — NY Giants (15) vs. Philadelphia AL (3), 1905	19 — Boston AL (9) vs. Chicago NL (10), 1918	29 — Cleveland (21) vs. Brooklyn (8), 1920	51 — NY Giants (29) vs. NY Yankees (22), 1921
Most Runs Batted In, One Team				
36 — NY Yankees, 1932	32 — Baltimore, 1970	45 — Toronto, 1993	54 — NY Yankees, 1960	34 — Boston AL, 1903
Most Runs Batted In, Both Teams				
52 — NY Yankees (36) vs. Chicago NL (16), 1932	52 — Baltimore (32) vs. Cincinnati (20), 1970	80 — Toronto (45) vs. Philadelphia NL (35), 1993	80 — Pittsburgh (26) vs. NY Yankees (54), 1960	56 — Boston AL (34) vs. Pittsburgh (22), 1903
Most Stolen Bases, One Team				
9 — Boston NL, 1914	16 — Chicago NL, 1907	15 — Atlanta, 1992	18 — Pittsburgh, 1909	12 — NY Giants, 1912
Most Stolen Bases, Both Teams				
11 — Boston NL (9) vs. Philadelphia AL (2), 1914	22 — Chicago NL (16) vs. Detroit (6), 1907	20 — Toronto (5) vs. Atlanta (15), 1992	24 — Pittsburgh (18) vs. Detroit (6), 1909	18 — Boston AL (6) vs. NY Giants (12), 1912
Fewest Stolen Bases, One Team				
0 — 7 times First: Pittsburgh, 1927 Most recent: Baltimore, 1966	0 — 7 times First: Philadelphia AL, 1929 Most recent: NY Mets, 2000	0 — Philadelphia AL, 1930; NY Giants, 1936; St. Louis AL, 1944; St. Louis NL, 1944; NY Yankees, 1951	0 — 8 times First: Philadelphia AL, 1931 Most recent: Boston AL, 1986	5 — Boston AL, 1903; Chicago AL, 1919
Fewest Stolen Bases, Both Teams				
1 — NY Yankees (0) vs. Cincinnati (1), 1939; NY Giants (1) vs. Cleveland (0), 1954; Baltimore (0) vs. Los Angeles (1), 1966	1 — 6 times First: Philadelphia AL (0) vs. Chicago NL (1), 1929 Most recent: NY Yankees (1) vs. NY Mets (0), 2000	0 — St. Louis NL (0) vs. St. Louis AL (0), 1944	1 — Cincinnati (1) vs. Detroit (0), 1940	12 — Cincinnati (7) vs. Chicago AL (5), 1919
Most Times Caught Stealing, One Team				
5 — Boston NL, 1914; Cincinnati, 1976	8 — Chicago NL, 1910	13 — NY Giants, 1911	7 — Cleveland, 1920; Washington, 1925; St. Louis NL, 1968	11 — NY Giants, 1912
Most Times Caught Stealing, Both Teams				
7 — Cincinnati (5) vs. NY Yankees (2), 1976	15 — Philadelphia AL (7) vs. Chicago NL (8), 1907	19 — Philadelphia AL (6) vs. NY Giants (13), 1911	11 — Pittsburgh (6) vs. Detroit (5), 1909	16 — Boston AL (5) vs. NY Giants (11)
Most Bases On Balls, One Team				
23 — NY Yankees, 1932	25 — NY Yankees, 2000	34 — Philadelphia NL, 1993	40 — Cleveland, 1997	27 — NY Yankees, 1921
Most Bases On Balls, Both Teams				
34 — NY Yankees (23) vs. Chicago NL (11), 1932	37 — NY Yankees (23) vs. Brooklyn (14), 1941	59 — Toronto (25) vs. Philadelphia NL (34), 1993	76 — Florida (36) vs. Cleveland (40), 1997	49 — NY Giants (22) vs. NY Yankees (27), 1921
Fewest Bases on Balls, One Team				
4 — Pittsburgh, 1927	5 — Philadelphia AL, 1905	4 — Philadelphia AL, 1911	9 — St. Louis NL, 1931	14 — Boston AL, 1903; Pittsburgh, 1903
Fewest Bases on Balls, Both Teams				
15 — NY Yankees (9) vs. Cincinnati (6), 1939	15 — Philadelphia AL (7) vs. NY Giants (8), 1913	17 — Chicago AL (11) vs. NY Giants (6), 1917	30 — Pittsburgh (12) vs. NY Yankees (18), 1960	28 — Boston AL (14) vs. Pittsburgh (14), 1903

MISCELLANEOUS SINGLE-SERIES TEAM BATTING RECORDS

Most Grand Slam Home Runs, One Team	2 — NY Yankees, 1956; Minnesota, 1987
Most Grand Slam Home Runs, Both Teams	2 — NY Yankees (2) vs. Brooklyn (0), 1956; St. Louis NL (1) vs. NY Yankees (1), 1964; Minnesota (2) vs. St. Louis NL (0), 1987
Most Times Hit by Pitch, One Team	6 — Pittsburgh, 1909
Most Times Hit by Pitch, Both Teams	10 — Pittsburgh (6) vs. Detroit (4), 1909
Most Sacrifice Hits, One Team	14 — Chicago NL, 1906
Most Sacrifice Hits, Both Teams	22 — St. Louis NL (12) vs. NY Yankees (10), 1926
Most Pinch Hitters Used, One Team	23 — Baltimore, 1979
Most Pinch Hitters Used, Both Teams	37 — Minnesota (21) vs. Atlanta (16), 1991
Most Pinch Hits, One Team	6 — NY Yankees, 1947; NY Yankees, 1960; Oakland, 1972; Baltimore, 1979
Most Pinch Hits, Both Teams	11 — NY Yankees (6) vs. Brooklyn (5), 1947
Lowest Batting Average by Series Winner	.186 — Boston AL, 1918
Highest Batting Average by Series Loser	.338 — NY Yankees, 1960
Fewest Runs by Series Winner	9 — Boston AL, 1918
Most Runs by Series Loser	55 — NY Yankees, 1960
Fewest Hits by Series Winner	24 — Baltimore, 1966
Most Hits by Series Loser	91 — NY Yankees, 1960

MISCELLANEOUS SINGLE-SERIES TEAM PITCHING RECORDS

Most Wild Pitches, One Team	5 — Pittsburgh, 1960
Most Wild Pitches, Both Teams	8 — NY Yankees (4) vs. Brooklyn (4), 1944
Most Balks, One Team	2 — Cleveland, 1948; Minnesota, 1987
Most Balks, Both Teams	2 — Cleveland (2) vs. Boston NL (0), 1948; Minnesota (2) vs. St. Louis NL (0), 1987; Los Angeles (1) vs. Oakland (1), 1988

MISCELLANEOUS SINGLE-SERIES TEAM FIELDING RECORDS

Most Passed Balls, One Team	3 — Chicago NL, 1906; Pittsburgh, 1960; NY Yankees, 1964
Most Passed Balls, Both Teams	4 — Chicago AL (1) vs. Chicago NL (3), 1906; NY Yankees (2) vs. Brooklyn (2), 1947

4-Game Series	5-Game Series	6-Game Series	7-Game Series	8-Game Series
Lowest ERA, One Team				
0.50 — Baltimore, 1966	0.00 — NY Giants, 1905	1.04 — Chicago NL, 1918	0.89 — Cleveland, 1920	1.63 — Cincinnati, 1919
Lowest ERA, Both Teams				
1.49 — NY Yankees (0.73) vs. Philadelphia NL (2.27), 1950	0.72 — NY Giants (0.00) vs. Philadelphia AL (1.47), 1905	1.37 — Boston NL (1.70) vs. Chicago NL (1.04), 1918	1.65 — Cleveland (0.89) vs. Brooklyn (2.44), 1920	2.26 — Boston AL (2.80) vs. NY Giants (1.71), 1912
Highest ERA, One Team				
9.26 — Chicago NL, 1932	6.70 — Cincinnati, 1970	7.57 — Philadelphia NL, 1993	7.11 — Pittsburgh, 1960	3.55 — Chicago AL, 1919
Highest ERA, Both Teams				
6.17 — NY Yankees (3.25) vs. Chicago NL (9.26), 1932	5.01 — Baltimore (3.40) vs. Cincinnati (6.70), 1970	6.66 — Toronto (5.77) vs. Philadelphia NL (7.57), 1993	5.34 — NY Yankees (3.54) vs. Pittsburgh (7.11), 1960	2.81 — NY Giants (2.54) vs. NY Yankees (3.09), 1921
Most Complete Games, One Team				
4 — NY Yankees, 1928	5 — Philadelphia AL, 1905; Philadelphia AL, 1910; Philadelphia AL, 1913; Boston AL, 1915	5 — Philadelphia AL, 1911; Boston AL, 1918; Detroit, 1935	5 — Cleveland, 1920; NY Yankees, 1956	7 — Boston AL, 1903
Most Complete Games, Both Teams				
5 — Boston NL (3) vs. Philadelphia AL (2), 1914	9 — NY Giants (4) vs. Philadelphia AL (5), 1905; Boston AL (5) vs. Philadelphia NL (4), 1915	9 — Boston AL (5) vs. Chicago NL (4), 1918	8 — 6 times First: Pittsburgh (4) vs. Detroit (4), 1909 Most recent: NY Yankees (5) vs. Brooklyn (3), 1956	13 — Boston AL (7) vs. Pittsburgh (6), 1903
Most Shutouts, One Team				
3 — Baltimore, 1966	4 — NY Giants, 1905	2 — NY Giants, 1917; Chicago AL, 1959	3 — Los Angeles, 1965	2 — Boston AL, 1903; Cincinnati, 1919; NY Yankees, 1921
Most Shutouts, Both Teams				
3 — Baltimore (3) vs. Los Angeles (0), 1966	5 — NY Giants (4) vs. Philadelphia AL (1), 1905	2 — 6 times First: NY Giants (2) vs. Chicago AL (0), 1917 Most recent: NY Yankees (1) vs. Atlanta (1), 1996	3 — Cleveland (2) vs. Brooklyn (1), 1920; NY Yankees (2) vs. Brooklyn (1), 1956; NY Yankees (2) vs. Milwaukee NL (1), 1958; Los Angeles (3) vs. Minnesota (0), 1965	3 — Cincinnati (2) vs. Chicago AL (1), 1919; NY Giants (1) vs. NY Yankees (2), 1921
Most One-Run Games Won, One Team				
3 — NY Yankees, 1950	4 — Boston AL, 1915	4 — Boston AL, 1918; Toronto, 1992	4 — Oakland, 1972	3 — Boston AL, 1912
Most One-Run Games Won, Both Teams				
3 — NY Yankees (3) vs. Philadelphia NL (0), 1950	4 — Boston AL (4) vs. Philadelphia NL (0), 1915; Oakland (3) vs. Los Angeles (1), 1974	5 — Atlanta (3) vs. Cleveland (2), 1995	6 — Oakland (4) vs. Cincinnati (2), 1972	4 — Boston AL (3) vs. NY Giants (1), 1912
Most Strikeouts, One Team				
37 — Los Angeles, 1963	50 — Philadelphia Athletics, 1929	50 — Toronto, 1993	62 — Los Angeles, 1973	45 — Boston AL, 1903
Most Strikeouts, Both Teams				
62 — Los Angeles (37) vs. NY Yankees (25), 1963	88 — NY Yankees (40) vs. NY Mets (48), 2000	92 — St. Louis NL (49) vs. St. Louis AL (43), 1944	99 — Detroit (40) vs. St. Louis NL (59), 1968; Florida (48) vs. Cleveland (51), 1997	82 — NY Giants (44) vs. NY Yankees (38), 1921
Fewest Strikeouts, One Team				
7 — NY Yankees, 1927	15 — NY Yankees, 1922	14 — Boston AL, 1918	20 — Cleveland, 1920	22 — Chicago, 1919
Fewest Strikeouts, Both Teams				
32 — NY Yankees (7) vs. Pittsburgh (25), 1927; Cincinnati (16) vs. NY Yankees (16), 1976	35 — Philadelphia AL (19) vs. NY Giants (16), 1913; NY Giants (20) vs. NY Yankees (15), 1922	35 — Boston AL (14) vs. Chicago NL (21), 1918	41 — Cleveland (20) vs. Brooklyn (21), 1920	52 — Cincinnati (30) vs. Chicago AL (22), 1919

4-Game Series	5-Game Series	6-Game Series	7-Game Series	8-Game Series
Highest Fielding Percentage, One Team				
1.000 — Baltimore, 1960	1.000 — NY Yankees, 1937	.996 — Boston AL, 1918; St. Louis NL, 1944; Los Angeles, 1977	.993 — Cincinnati, 1975	.984 — NY Giants, 1921
Highest Fielding Percentage, Both Teams				
.986 — Los Angeles (.979) vs. NY Yankees (.993), 1963	.986 — Los Angeles (.983) vs. Oakland (.989), 1988	.991 — NY Yankees (.987) vs. Los Angeles (.996), 1977	.990 — St. Louis NL (.992) vs. Kansas City (.989), 1985	.983 — NY Giants (.984) vs. NY Yankees (.981), 1921
Lowest Fielding Percentage, One Team				
.949 — NY Yankees, 1932	.942 — Brooklyn, 1916	.938 — NY Giants, 1911	.938 — Detroit, 1909	.942 — Pittsburgh, 1903
Lowest Fielding Percentage, Both Teams				
.954 — NY Yankees (.949) vs. Chicago NL (.959), 1932	.946 — Philadelphia AL (.947) vs. Chicago NL (.945), 1910	.947 — Philadelphia AL (.956) vs. NY Giants (.938), 1911	.945 — Pittsburgh (.951) vs. Detroit (.938), 1909	.950 — Boston AL (.957) vs. Pittsburgh (.942), 1903
Most Errors, One Team				
8 — NY Yankees, 1932	13 — Brooklyn, 1916	16 — NY Giants, 1911	18 — Detroit, 1909	19 — Pittsburgh, 1903
Most Errors, Both Teams				
14 — NY Yankees (8) vs. Chicago NL (6), 1932	23 — Philadelphia AL (11) vs. Chicago NL (12), 1910	27 — Philadelphia AL (11) vs. NY Giants (16), 1911	32 — Pittsburgh (14) vs. Detroit (18), 1909	33 — Boston AL (14) vs. Pittsburgh (19), 1903
Fewest Errors, One Team				
0 — Baltimore, 1966	0 — NY Yankees, 1937	1 — Boston AL, 1918; St. Louis NL, 1944; NY Yankees, 1953; Los Angeles, 1977	2 — Philadelphia AL, 1931; NY Yankees, 1955; Brooklyn, 1956; St. Louis NL, 1968; Cincinnati, 1975; St. Louis NL, 1985	5 — NY Giants, 1921
Fewest Errors, Both Teams				
4 — Los Angeles (3) vs. NY Yankees (1), 1963	5 — Los Angeles (3) vs. Oakland (2), 1988	4 — NY Yankees (3) vs. Los Angeles (1), 1977	5 — Kansas City (3) vs. St. Louis NL (2), 1985	11 — NY Giants (5) vs. NY Yankees (6), 1921
Most Double Plays, One Team				
7 — Chicago NL, 1932; NY Yankees, 1963	7 — NY Yankees, 1922; NY Yankees, 1941; Cincinnati, 1961	10 — NY Yankees, 1951	12 — Brooklyn, 1955	9 — Chicago AL, 1919
Most Double Plays, Both Teams				
10 — Cincinnati (4) vs. NY Yankees (6), 1976	12 — NY Yankees (7) vs. Brooklyn (5), 1941	16 — Philadelphia NL (8) vs. Kansas City Royals (8), 1980	19 — Brooklyn (12) vs. NY Yankees (7), 1955	16 — Cincinnati (7) vs. Chicago AL (9), 1919

Game	Inning
Most At-Bats, One Team	
54 — NY Mets, October 14, 1973 (12 innings; Game 2)	13 — Philadelphia AL, October 12, 1929 (7th inning, Game 4)
Nine-Inning Game	
45 — NY Yankees, October 2, 1932 (Game 4); NY Yankees, October 6, 1936 (Game 6); NY Yankees, October 6, 1960 (Game 2)	
Most At-Bats, Both Teams	
101 — NY Mets (54) vs. Oakland (47), October 14, 1973 (12 innings; Game 2)	17 — Philadelphia AL (13) vs. Chicago NL (4), October 12, 1929 (7th inning, Game 4)
Nine-Inning Game	
85 — Toronto Blue Jays (44) vs. Philadelphia NL (41), October 20, 1993 (Game 4)	
Most Hits, One Team	
20 — NY Giants, October 7, 1921 (Game 3); St. Louis NL, October 10, 1946 (Game 4)	10 — Philadelphia AL, October 12, 1929 (7th inning, Game 4)
Most Hits, Both Teams	
32 — NY Yankees (19) vs. Pittsburgh (13), October 6, 1960 (Game 2); Toronto (18) vs. Philadelphia NL (14), October 20, 1993 (Game 4)	12 — Philadelphia AL (10) vs. Chicago NL (2), October 12, 1929 (7th inning, Game 4)
Fewest Hits, One Team	
0 — Brooklyn, October 8, 1956 (Game 5)	0 — Held by many teams
Fewest Hits, Both Teams	
5 — NY Yankees (3) vs. NY Giants (2), October 6, 1921 (Game 2); NY Yankees (5) vs. Brooklyn (0), October 8, 1956 (Game 5); Atlanta Braves (3) vs. Cleveland Indians (2), October 21, 1995 (Game 1)	0 — Held by many teams
Most Singles, One Team	
16 — NY Yankees, October 15, 1978 (Game 5)	7 — Philadelphia AL, October 12, 1929 (7th inning, Game 4); NY Giants, October 4, 1933 (6th inning, Game 2); Brooklyn, October 8, 1949 (6th inning, Game 4)
Most Singles, Both Teams	
24 — NY Yankees (16) vs. Los Angeles (8), October 15, 1978 (Game 5)	8 — Philadelphia AL (7) vs. Chicago NL (1), October 12, 1929 (7th inning, Game 4); NY Giants (7) vs. Washington (1), October 4, 1933 (6th inning, Game 2); Brooklyn (7) vs. NY Yankees (1), October 8, 1949 (6th inning, Game 4)
Most Doubles, One Team	
8 — Chicago AL, October 13, 1906 (Game 5); Pittsburgh, October 15, 1925 (Game 7)	3 — 11 times
	First: Chicago AL, October 13, 1906 (4th inning, Game 5)
	Most recent: St. Louis NL, October 20, 1985 (9th inning, Game 2)
Most Doubles, Both Teams	
11 — Chicago AL (8) vs. Chicago NL (3), October 13, 1906 (Game 5)	4 — Philadelphia AL (3) vs. Chicago NL (1), October 18, 1910 (7th inning, Game 2); Brooklyn (3) vs. NY Yankees (1), October 5, 1947 (3rd inning, Game 6)
Most Triples, One Team	
5 — Boston AL, October 7, 1903 (Game 5); Boston AL, October 10, 1903 (Game 7)	2 — 9 times
	First: Boston AL, October 1, 1903 (7th inning, Game 1)
	Most recent: Detroit, October 7, 1968 (4th inning, Game 5)
Most Triples, Both Teams	
7 — Boston AL (5) vs. Pittsburgh (2), October 10, 1903 (Game 7)	3 — Boston AL (2) vs. Pittsburgh (1), October 10, 1903 (4th inning, Game 7)
Most Home Runs, One Team	
5 — NY Yankees, October 9, 1928 (Game 4); Oakland, October 27, 1989 (Game 3)	3 — Boston AL, October 11, 1967 (4th inning, Game 6)
Most Home Runs, Both Teams	
7 — Oakland (5) vs. San Francisco (2), October 27, 1989 (Game 3)	3 — NY Giants (2) vs. NY Yankees (1), October 11, 1921 (2nd inning, Game 6); Boston AL (3) vs. St. Louis NL (0), October 11, 1967 (4th inning, Game 6)
Most Extra Bases, One Team	
9 — Pittsburgh, October 15, 1925 (Game 7)	4 — Chicago White Sox, October 1, 1959 (3rd inning, Game 1); New York Yankees, October 9, 1961 (1st inning, Game 5); Kansas City Royals, October 18, 1980 (1st inning, Game 4)
Most Total Bases, One Team	
34 — Atlanta, October 24, 1991 (Game 5)	17 — Philadelphia AL, October 12, 1929 (7th inning, Game 4)
Most Total Bases, Both Teams	
47 — NY Yankees (27) vs. Brooklyn (20), October 4, 1953 (Game 5)	21 — Philadelphia AL (17) vs. Chicago NL (4), October 12, 1929 (7th inning, Game 4)
Most Runs, One Team	
18 — NY Yankees, October 2, 1936 (Game 2)	10 — Philadelphia AL, October 12, 1929 (7th inning, Game 4); Detroit, October 9, 1968 (3rd inning, Game 6)
Most Runs, Both Teams	
29 — Toronto (15) vs. Philadelphia NL (14), October 20, 1993 (Game 4)	11 — Philadelphia AL (10) vs. Chicago NL (1), October 12, 1929 (7th inning, Game 4); Brooklyn (6) vs. NY Yankees (5), October 5, 1956 (2nd inning, Game 2)
Most RBI, One Team	
18 — NY Yankees, October 2, 1936 (Game 2)	10 — Philadelphia AL, October 12, 1929 (7th inning, Game 4); Detroit, October 9, 1968 (3rd inning, Game 6)
Most RBI, Both Teams	
29 — Toronto (15) vs. Philadelphia NL (14), October 20, 1993 (Game 4)	11 — Philadelphia AL (10) vs. Chicago NL (1), October 12, 1929 (7th inning, Game 4); Brooklyn (6) vs. NY Yankees (5), October 5, 1956 (2nd inning, Game 2)

Game	Inning

Most Stolen Bases, One Team

7 — Chicago NL, October 8, 1907 (12 innings; Game 1)
Nine-Inning Game
5 — NY Giants, October 12, 1905 (Game 3); Chicago NL, October 10, 1906 (Game 2); Chicago NL, October 9, 1907 (Game 2); St. Louis NL, October 22, 1987 (Game 5); Atlanta, October 18, 1992 (Game 2)

3 — Pittsburgh, October 1, 1903 (1st inning, Game 1); NY Giants, October 12, 1905 (9th inning, Game 3); Chicago NL, October 8, 1907 (10th inning, Game 1); Chicago NL, October 11, 1908 (8th inning, Game 2); NY Giants, October 14, 1912 (1st inning, Game 6)

Most Stolen Bases, Both Teams

11 — Chicago NL (7) vs. Detroit (4), October 8, 1907 (12 innings; Game 1)
Nine-Inning Game
6 — NY Giants (5) vs. Philadelphia AL (1), October 12, 1905 (Game 3); Pittsburgh (4) vs. Detroit (2), October 13, 1909 (Game 5); NY Giants (3) vs. Philadelphia AL (3), October 9, 1913 (Game 3); St. Louis NL (5) vs. Minnesota (1), October 22, 1987 (Game 5)

4 — NY Giants (3) vs. Boston AL (1), October 14, 1912 (1st inning, Game 6)

Most Times Caught Stealing, One Team

5 — NY Giants, October 17, 1911 (11 innings; Game 3)

Most Times Caught Stealing, Both Teams

6 — NY Giants (5) vs. Philadelphia AL (1), October 17, 1911 (11 innings; Game 3)

Most Bases on Balls, One Team

11 — Brooklyn, October 5, 1956 (Game 2); NY Yankees, October 5, 1957 (Game 3); Detroit, October 12, 1984 (Game 3)

5 — NY Yankees, October 6, 1926 (5th inning, Game 4)

Most Bases on Balls, Both Teams

19 — NY Yankees (11) vs. Milwaukee NL (8), October 5, 1957 (game 3)

6 — NY Yankees (3) vs. NY Giants (3), October 7, 1921 (3rd inning, Game 3); NY Yankees (5) vs. St. Louis NL (1), October 6, 1926 (5th inning, Game 4)

Most Times Hit by Pitch, One Team

3 — Detroit, October 9, 1968 (Game 6); Baltimore, October 13, 1971 (Game 4)

2 — Pittsburgh, October 11, 1909 (2nd inning, Game 3); Detroit, October 9, 1968 (8th inning, Game 6); Pittsburgh, October 17, 1979 (9th inning, Game 7)

Most Times Hit by Pitch, Both Teams

3 — 7 times
First: Philadelphia NL (2) vs. Boston AL (1), October 13, 1915 (Game 5)
Most recent: Minnesota (2) vs. St. Louis NL (1), October 21, 1987 (Game 4)

2 — Held by many teams

Most Sacrifice Hits, One Team

5 — Chicago NL, October 12, 1906 (Game 4); Chicago NL, October 10, 1908 (Game 1); Pittsburgh, October 16, 1909 (Game 7); NY Giants, October 2, 1954 (Game 4)

3 — Brooklyn, October 4, 1955 (6th inning, Game 7)

Most Sacrifice Hits, Both Teams

7 — Chicago NL (5) vs. Detroit (2), October 10, 1908 (Game 1)

Most Pinch Hitters Used, One Team

8 — Minnesota, October 22, 1991 (12 innings; Game 3)
Nine-Inning Game
6 — Los Angeles, October 6, 1959 (Game 5)

4 — NY Mets, October 13, 1973 (9th inning, Game 1); Baltimore, October 15, 1983 (6th inning, Game 4); Minnesota, October 22, 1987 (9th inning, Game 5); Atlanta, October 23, 1999 (8th inning, Game 1)

Most Pinch Hitters Used, Both Teams

12 — Minnesota (8) vs. Atlanta (4), October 22, 1991 (12 innings; Game 3)
Nine-Inning Game
8 — Baltimore (4) vs. Philadelphia NL (4), October 15, 1983 (Game 4)

Most Pinch Hits, One Team

3 — Oakland, October 19, 1972 (Game 4); Baltimore, October 13, 1979 (Game 4); San Diego, October 18, 1998 (Game 2)

3 — Oakland, October 19, 1972 (9th inning, Game 4); San Diego, October 18, 1998 (8th inning, Game 2)

Most Strikeouts, One Team (pitching team)

17 — St. Louis NL, October 2, 1968 (Game 1)

4 — Chicago NL, October 14, 1908 (1st inning, Game 5)

Most Strikeouts, Both Teams

25 — Los Angeles (15) vs. NY Yankees (10), October 2, 1963 (Game 1); NY Mets (15) vs. Oakland (10), October 14, 1973 (12 innings; Game 2); NY Yankees (13) vs. NY Mets (12), October 24, 2000 (Game 3)

6 — Oakland (3) vs. Cincinnati (3), October 18, 1972 (5th inning, Game 3); St. Louis NL (3) vs. Kansas City Royals (3), October 24, 1985 (7th inning, Game 5); NY Yankees (3) vs. NY Mets (3), October 24, 2000 (second inning, Game 3)

Most Runs by Losing Team	14 — Philadelphia, October 20, 1993 (Game 4)
Fewest Runs by Winning Team	1 — Accomplished 23 times; First: NY Giants, October 13, 1905 (Game 4); Most Recent: NY Yankees, October 24, 1996 (Game 5)
Largest Shutout Victory	12-0 — NY Yankees vs. Pittsburgh, October 12, 1960 (Game 6)
Most Hits by Losing Team	17 — Pittsburgh, October 13, 1979 (Game 4)
Fewest Hits by Winning Team	1 — Brooklyn, October 3, 1947 (Game 4)
Longest Game Without a Stolen Base	14 innings — Boston AL vs. Brooklyn, October 9, 1916 (Game 2)
Longest Game Without a Base on Balls	12 innings — St. Louis NL, October 4, 1934 (Game 2)
Fewest Strikeouts in a Game, Both Teams	0 — Pittsburgh (0) vs. NY Yankees (0), October 13, 1960 (Game 7)
Most Errors, One Team	6 — Chicago AL, October 13, 1906 (Game 5); Pittsburgh, October 12, 1909 (Game 4); Chicago AL, October 13, 1917 (Game 5); Los Angeles, October 6, 1966 (Game 2)
Most Errors, Both Teams	9 — Chicago AL (6) vs. NY Giants (3), October 13, 1917 (Game 5)
Longest Errorless Game, One Team	12 innings — Detroit, October 4, 1934 (Game 2); NY Yankees, October 11, 1977 (Game 1)
Longest Errorless Game, Both Teams	12 innings — NY Yankees vs. Los Angeles, October 11, 1977 (Game 1)
Most Double Plays, One Team	4 — 7 times; First: Philadelphia AL, October 9, 1914 (Game 1); Most recent: Philadelphia NL, October 15, 1980 (Game 2)
Most Double Plays, Both Teams	6 — Brooklyn (3) vs. NY Yankees (3), September 29, 1955 (Game 2); Philadelphia NL (4) vs. Kansas City (2), October 15, 1980 (Game 2)

Everyone knows that the New York Yankees have been to the Fall Classic more than any other franchise (37 Series and 206 games), but who's next on the list? The Dodgers have appeared in 18 Series, 9 in Brooklyn and 9 in Los Angeles, and the other former New York team that moved West, the Giants, have played in 16, the last two while in San Francisco. The St. Louis Cardinals have been in one fewer Series than the Giants, but they've participated in 96 games, third behind the Yankees and Dodgers. The World Series records of every Major League franchise are listed here.

AMERICAN LEAGUE

	Series Tot.	W	L	Pct.	Games Tot.	W	L	Pct.	
Baltimore Orioles	6	3	3	.500	33	19	14	.576	
Boston Red Sox	9	5	4	.556	60	33	26	.559	(1 tie)
Chicago White Sox	4	2	2	.500	26	13	13	.500	
Cleveland Indians	5	2	3	.400	30	14	16	.467	
Detroit Tigers	9	4	5	.444	56	26	29	.473	(1 tie)
Kansas City Royals	2	1	1	.500	13	6	7	.462	
Milwaukee Brewers	1	0	1	.000	7	3	4	.429	
Minnesota Twins	3	2	1	.667	21	11	10	.524	
New York Yankees	37	26	11	.703	206	125	80	.610	(1 tie)
Oakland A's	6	4	2	.667	32	17	15	.531	
Philadelphia A's	8	5	3	.625	43	24	19	.558	
A's, combined	14	9	5	.643	75	41	34	.547	
St. Louis Browns	1	0	1	.000	6	2	4	.333	
Toronto Blue Jays	2	2	0	1.000	12	8	4	.667	
Washington Senators	3	1	2	.333	19	8	11	.421	
AL Totals	**96**	**57**	**39**	**.594**	**564**	**309**	**252**	**.551**	

AMERICAN LEAGUE

	4-Game Series	5-Game Series	6-Game Series	7-Game Series	8-Game Series
Baltimore Orioles	1-0	2-0	–	0-2	–
Boston Red Sox	–	2-0	1-0	0-4	2-0
Chicago White Sox	–	–	2-1	–	0-1
Cleveland Indians	0-1	–	1-1	1-1	–
Detroit Tigers	–	1-2	1-0	2-3	–
Kansas City Royals	–	–	0-1	1-0	–
Milwaukee Brewers	–	–	–	0-1	–
Minnesota Twins	–	–	–	2-1	–
New York Yankees	8-2	6-2	7-1	5-5	0-1
Oakland A's	1-1	1-1	–	2-0	–
Philadelphia A's	0-1	3-1	2-0	0-1	–
A's, combined	1-2	4-2	2-0	2-1	–
St. Louis Browns	–	–	0-1	–	–
Toronto Blue Jays	–	–	2-0	–	–
Washington Senators	–	0-1	–	1-1	–
AL Totals	**10-5**	**15-8**	**16-5**	**14-19**	**2-2**

NATIONAL LEAGUE

	Series Tot.	W	L	Pct.	Games Tot.	W	L	Pct.	
Atlanta Braves	5	1	4	.200	29	11	18	.379	
Boston Braves	2	1	1	.500	10	6	4	.600	
Milwaukee Braves	2	1	1	.500	14	7	7	.500	
Braves combined	9	3	6	.333	53	24	29	.453	
Brooklyn Dodgers	9	1	8	.111	56	20	36	.357	
Los Angeles Dodgers	9	5	4	.556	49	25	24	.510	
Dodgers combined	18	6	12	.333	105	45	60	.429	
Chicago Cubs	10	2	8	.200	53	19	33	.365	(1 tie)
Cincinnati Reds	9	5	4	.556	51	26	25	.510	
Florida Marlins	1	1	0	1.000	7	4	3	.571	
New York Giants	14	5	9	.357	82	39	41	.488	(2 ties)
San Francisco Giants	2	0	2	.000	11	3	8	.273	
Giants combined	16	5	11	.313	93	42	49	.462	(2 ties)
New York Mets	4	2	2	.500	24	12	12	.500	
Philadelphia Phillies	5	1	4	.200	26	8	18	.308	
Pittsburgh Pirates	7	5	2	.714	47	23	24	.489	
St. Louis Cardinals	15	9	6	.600	96	48	48	.500	
San Diego Padres	2	0	2	.000	9	1	8	.111	
NL Totals	**96**	**39**	**57**	**.406**	**564**	**252**	**309**	**.449**	

NATIONAL LEAGUE

	4-Game Series	5-Game Series	6-Game Series	7-Game Series	8-Game Series
Atlanta Braves	0-1	–	1-2	0-1	–
Boston Braves	1-0	–	0-1	–	–
Milwaukee Braves	–	–	–	1-1	–
Braves combined	1-1	–	1-3	1-2	–
Brooklyn Dodgers	–	0-3	0-1	1-4	–
Los Angeles Dodgers	1-1	1-1	2-2	1-0	–
Dodgers combined	1-1	1-4	2-3	2-4	–
Chicago Cubs	0-2	2-2	0-3	0-1	–
Cincinnati Reds	2-1	0-2	–	2-1	1-0
Florida Marlins	–	–	–	1-0	–
New York Giants	1-0	3-2	0-5	0-1	1-1
San Francisco Giants	0-1	–	–	0-1	–
Giants combined	1-1	3-2	0-5	0-2	1-1
New York Mets	–	1-1	–	1-1	–
Philadelphia Phillies	0-1	0-2	1-1	–	–
Pittsburgh Pirates	0-1	–	–	5-0	0-1
St. Louis Cardinals	0-1	1-1	1-1	7-3	–
San Diego Padres	0-1	0-1	–	–	–
NL Totals	**5-10**	**8-15**	**5-16**	**19-14**	**2-2**

The Anaheim Angels, Arizona Diamondbacks, Colorado Rockies, Houston Astros, Montreal Expos, Seattle Mariners, Tampa Bay Devil Rays and Texas Rangers are the only teams never to have made it to baseball's Fall Classic.

The Yankees and Dodgers have gone head-to-head a record 11 times (1941, 1947, 1949, 1952, 1953, 1955, 1956, 1963, 1977, 1978, 1981). The Yanks and their other former cross-town rivals, the New York Giants, hold the record for the most consecutive series played between the same two teams: 3 (1921–23).

Acknowledgments

I would like to thank Black Dog & Leventhal for giving me the opportunity to write about baseball's greatest annual event, and to everyone there who helped this book come to be, especially my editor, Michael Driscoll. Jorge Jaramillo of the AP Photo Department provided invaluable assistance bringing together most of the images that appear in these pages, offering a wealth of photographic selections from which to choose. Finally, thanks to Jenny, for reading over sections of the manuscript, offering fact-checking assistance on the statistics, and providing helpful suggestions and much-needed support along the way.

Index

2001- Arizona Dimondbacks (4)
NY YANKEES (3)

2002 Anheim Angels (4)
S.F. GIANTS (3)

2003- Florida Marlins (4)
N.Y. YANKEES (2)

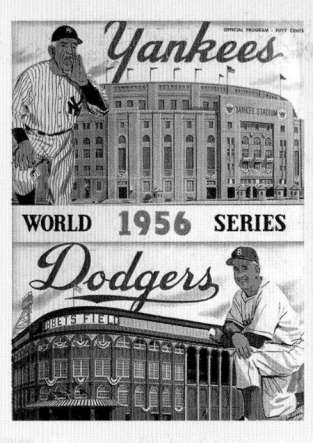

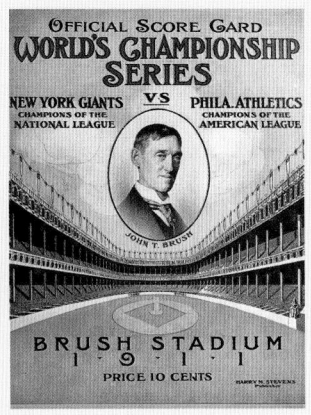

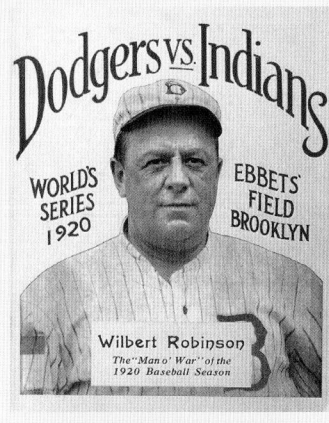

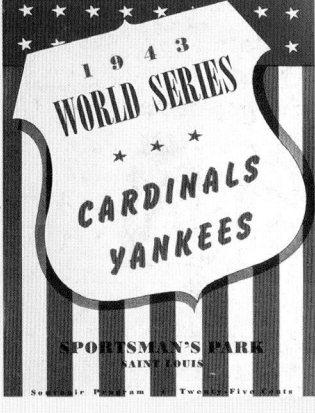

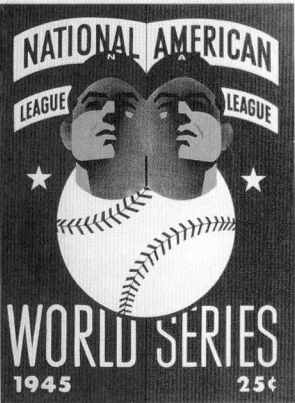

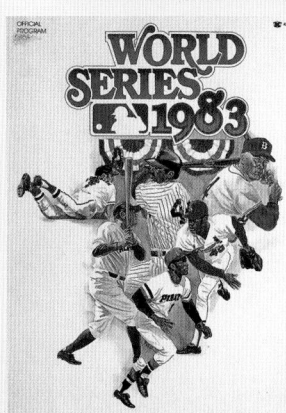

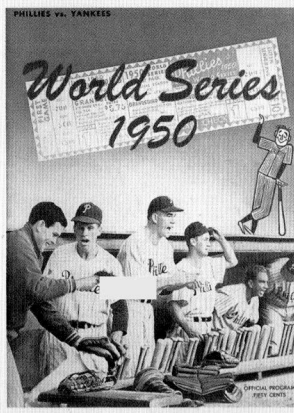

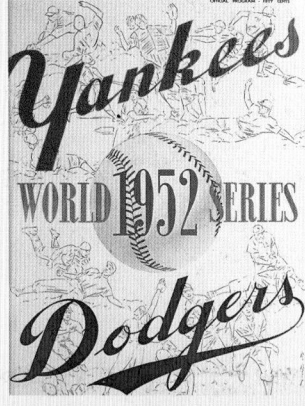